The History of American Ranks and Rank Insignia

By Steven A. Bingaman

The History of American Ranks and Rank Insignia

Forward

This book began as a project to help my sanity during a family illness. As time went on it turned out that the amount of information available, online and from other sources, was staggering.

My goal was to compile the complete history of the ranks and rank insignia used by the american uniformed services, and I hope I have succeeded. Having read may reference books on uniforms and insignia, I have tried to avoid some of the irritating problems with these books. First I have tried not to fudge around information I could not find. Even in the internet age you can never find every tidbit of information you need and when something was unclear and the answer was not found I simply admitted it and laid out what I could find. Hopefully these gaps can be filled in at some point. The other problem with some books written in the 1950s and 1960s it that they assume that the reader served in World War II and was thoroughly familiar with the military at that time. This book was written between 2010 and 2012 and the information is current at that time, with the full understanding that time will move on and things will change.

This book contains seven parts, one for each service, each with three chapters. The first chapter for each service gives a history of that service and it's organization and rank structure. The second lays out how rank was displayed, first in general then individual methods are explained in detail. The third chapter is an alphabetical list of every rank the service has used with a full history of each rank and each rank's insignia. The third chapters, and the detail sections of the second, are designed as a reference guide where things can be looked up, which make some of the text repetitive. For many ranks in the third chapters the names those who held the rank are listed. This is intended to give impression of how small the services once were and give the ranks a personal touch.

Information does not get online by itself and credit must be given to some of the people who put it there. First I have to thank Herbert "Sarge" Booker, who has a passion for placing information on uniforms and insignia on the internet. Second credit must be given to Justin Broderick who has put up several sites on navy insignia, sadly all down now. Mr. Broderick is a brilliant graphic artist and has uncanny talent for presenting complicated information clearly and simply.

Steve Bingaman
June 2012

The History of American Ranks and Rank Insignia

Table of Contents

Introduction

The History of American Ranks and Rank Insignia

There are two questions that usually come up when discussing the ranks and insignia of the american military:

1. Why does silver outrank gold?
2. Why does a Lieutenant General outrank a Major General when a Major outranks a Lieutenant?

Detailed answers are complicated and rooted deep in history, but in short the answers are:

1. Most of the badges on rank are silver so they would be visible on a gold epaulet.
2. Lieutenant General had the same roots as Lieutenant Colonel, as the fill-in leader for the General or the Colonel. The original third officer in line, in the seventieth century English army that is, was called a Sergeant Major or Sergeant Major General. The "sergeant" was eventually dropped.

Uniformed Services

The United States maintains seven uniformed services. The army, the navy, the marine corps, the air force, the coast guard, the commissioned corps of the public health service and the commissioned corps of the national oceanographic and atmospheric administration. By law the army, navy, marines, air force and coast guard are the nation's armed forces while the health service and the NOAA corps are not.

This legal structure come from The Career Compensation Act of October 12, 1949 (1). All of the services existed in one form or another before that, but the 1949 law created the overall structure that is still in use at this writing.

Prior to 1949 all of the services' structure was handled by individual legislation.

Types of Rank

The United States uses three types of ranks: Commissioned Officers, Warrant Officers and Enlisted Personnel.

Commissioned Officers, usually referred to simply as "Officers", are appointed by the President and confirmed by the Senate. They hold a commission that allows them to act in the name of the government.

Warrant Officers are specialists in their field and remain so thru out their career, while officers are more supervisors in charge of and organization in general (1). All but the lowest grade of warrant officers also hold commissions. At this writing there is a movement to grant commissions to all warrant officers.

Enlisted Personnel are the lower ranks who do most of the work, and have no authority to act for the government. Enlisted Personnel in the navy and the coast guard are referred to as holding a rate not a rank (2). This should not be confused with their rating, meaning their job specialty. For example a Boatswain's Mate Second Class holds a rating of Boatswain's Mate and a rate of Petty Officer Second Class.

Pay Grades

In the early days of the nation, the ranks of the military and how much they were paid was laid out in law directly. As time went on, the authority to set the pay of a specific rank rating was granted to the individual services.

The idea of grades, but not quite pay grades yet, began in the navy on January 8, 1885 (1). The enlisted rates and ratings were organized into six grades, pay was by rating but the seed was planted. A seventh grade was added on April 1, 1893 (2).

By the late nineteenth century the enlisted ranks of the army had grown considerably. The National Defense Act of June 3, 1916 (3) made the organization of the army more complex and created even more ranks, then World War I pushed the system over the edge. With well over 100 enlisted ranks, all tied to specific branches, simply supplying insignia became a problem in a large war time army, let alone trying to keep track of what ranks existed as new branches were added to deal with the needs of modern warfare such as tanks and airplanes.

A solution to the problem became law on June 4, 1920 (4). The law allowed the President to create ranks in seven grades setting the pay of each grade and the percentage of the enlisted force allowed in each. The grades were numbered with grade one being the highest and grade seven the lowest. From this time forward, army enlisted ranks were no longer tied to branches, the same ranks would be used in the infantry as in the corps of engineers or any other branch.

The navy, marine corps and coast guard joined the seven pay grades on June 10, 1922 (5). After this time basic pay was no longer tied to rating but to pay grade.

Equivalency among officer ranks of the army and the navy had been established as far back as November 15, 1776 (6), and was clearly laid out in law on July 16, 1862 (7).

The officer equivalencies and seven enlisted pay grades along with two grades of warrant officer, carried the services thru World War II but post war reorganization lead to changes A new system was created by The Career Compensation Act of October 12, 1949 (8). All ranks were placed in pay grades and basic pay was determined by the grade and the time in service. The new grades would carry a letter and a number with the higher rank now having higher numbers. For officers the grades began with an "O" with the O-1 grade being the lowest and the senior ranks being grouped in the O-8 grade. Warrant ranks began with a "W" and four of them were created numbered W-1 to W-4. The seven enlisted grades continued but were renamed with grade one becoming grade E-7 and grade seven E-1.

The act was amended on May 20, 1958 (9) to add O-9 and O-10 grades to give the senior officer ranks grades of their own and E-8 and E-9 grades to create more enlisted ranks. A W-5 warrant officer grade was added on December 5, 1991 (10).

Part 1.

Army

Chapter 1. Army Organization

The Continental Army

The United States Army celebrates June 14, 1775 as it's birth date. On that day the Continental Congress voted to raise six companies of riflemen (1). This was the beginning of the "Continental Army", The "Continental" meaning it was to serve (and be paid for by) all of the colonies.

The rank structure used was largely taken from the British Army as most soldiers came from the colonial militia units already in existence.

By September of 1783 the war had wound down and a peace treaty was being negotiated. The enlistment's of most of the army were about to expire and George Washington ordered all but 600 troops to be discharged (2). The Continental Congress ratified this decision on October 18th (3). Washington himself left the army on December 23rd (4).

The remaining army consisted of Washington's replacement Major General Henry Knox, the inspector General Major General Baron De Stueben, his aide Major William North (who replaced him as inspector on April 15, 1784), the Quartermaster General Colonel Timothy Pickering, the Paymaster General John Pierce and the Commissary of Military Stores Samuel Hodgden. The remaining artillery units were merged into a single 100 man corps under Major Sebastian Badman and the other 500 men made up an infantry regiment under Colonel Henry Jackson (5).

The Continental Army officially ceased to exist on June 2, 1784 when Congress ordered the discharge of all but 25 Privates at Fort Pitt and 55 at West Point with "a proportionate number officers" (7).

Knox and most of his army were discharged on June 20, 1784 (7).

It appears the only line officer left in the army was Captain and Brevet Major John Doughty who would command the 80 men that would technically make up an artillery battery. North, Pickering and Pierce would continue in their offices and Lieutenant William Price was made Deputy Commissary of Ordnance and Military Stores. The "Chief Medical Officer of the Army", meaning the only medical officer in the army, was Surgeon's Mate William Cogswell (8).

The "Federal Army"

We shall use the term "Federal Army" differentiate between the Continental Army and the United States Army as it has existed since 1784, which has had an entirely different organization.

On June 3, 1784 (1), the day after the Continental Army was abolished, the Continental Congress voted to raise a single regiment of infantry and another battery of artillery. The new army was organized and up and running on August 12th, making Doughty and his 80 Privates the entire army for only 53 days.

The rest is history, the army would grow or shrink as needed, leading to the army we know today.

Subdivisions of ranks

The History of American Ranks and Rank Insignia

In the army, the lower three grades of officers are referred to a "Company Grade Officers" as they would normally be the officers of a company. The next three grades are known as "Field Grade Officers" and the rest who are generals are known as..."General Officers" (1).

In the early days, commissioned ranks below Captain were referred to a "Subalterns".

Non Commissioned Officers are enlisted personnel with supervisory responsibilities. Corporals and above are regarded as non commissioned officers.

Brevet ranks

A Brevet was a higher rank granted to an officer, that was over and above the number of officers authorized by law to hold that rank. Brevets were often given if an officer needed higher rank or authority for a particular assignment and would end when that assignment was over. Brevets were also common as awards for gallantry and service, particularly in wartime. The practice ended when medals were created to honor distinguished service in the early twentieth century(1).

Staff Ranks

The army of the late eighteenth and early nineteenth centuries had very small staff departments. The titles used by staff officers would very greatly. Some positions came with a regular rank and others, such as the Commissary General of Purchases, simply had the title of the position, some officers were also detailed from regiments and held ranks in those branches. Most of these strange titles had disappeared by the Mexican War.

Medical Ranks

Until April 23, 1908 (1), medical officers held rank titles that were different from the title used by other officers. Surgeon was the basic rank of an army doctor with other titles such as Surgeon's Mate, Assistant Surgeon, Deputy Surgeon General or Medical Purveyor used over the years. Medical officer's ranks were made equivalent to regular ranks on June 30, 1834 (2), and from that point forward they wore the same insignia as other officers of their equivalent rank.

Senior Enlisted Advisors

Senior Enlisted Advisors are the top enlisted soldier in a unit who serve as a link between the commanding officer and common soldier.

The concept is not entirely new. The Regimental Sergeant Major and the Company First Sergeant filled this roll, but by the late 1960s the system became more formalized.

The modern ranks of First Sergeant (E-8) and Command Sergeant Major (E-9) are held by Senior Enlisted Advisors while they hold such a position. Those in the same pay grades who are not senior enlisted advisors are Master Sergeants (E-8) and Sergeants Major (E-9). The Sergeant Major of the Army is the senior enlisted advisor to the Army Chief of Staff and the law allows a senior enlisted advisor to the Chairman of the Joint Chiefs if one is desired.

At the platoon level the senior enlisted advisor is a Sergeant First Class holding the position of platoon sergeant.

All this forms what the army calls the "NCO Support Channel".

Law

The History of American Ranks and Rank Insignia

Prior to 1920 the rank structure of the army was set by law. Congress would pass a law laying out the organization of the army in detail, specifying the number of units (regiments, companies and so forth), what ranks would make up those units and how many people would hold those ranks. For example, the peace establishment act of March 16, 1802 stated "each regiment of infantry shall consist of one colonel, one lieutenant-colonel, one major, one adjutant, one sergeant-major, two teachers of music, and ten companies; each company to consist of one captain, one first and one second lieutenant, one ensign, four sergeants, four corporals, four musicians, and sixty-four privates." (1).

This process began of June 14, 1775 (2), when the Continental Congress voted to raise companies of riflemen. It continued over the next 145 years with the army growing to meet an emergency and shirking again the that emergency was over.

By the early twentieth century advancing technology had made warfare more complex and the army's organization became more complex as a result. The 1802 peace establishment act had called for an army consisting of two infantry regiments, one artillery regiment, a corps of engineers consisting of seven officers and ten cadets, one general, one paymaster, three military agents, two surgeons and 25 surgeons mates, making a total force of 3287 men (3). By the time of the National Defense Act of June 3, 1916 (4) the army included the regular army, volunteers, reservists, and the National Guard. There were numerous staff departments and regiments contained specialized companies to handle things such as supply or administrative duties.

The army regulations contained an article titled Rank and Command which listed the officer and noncommissioned officer ranks in order of precedence and numbering them. The numbers of the grades were not permanently tied to a particular rank and when new ranks were added the numbers would slip up or down.

If we look at the regulations of 1861, numbers 1 thru 9 run from Lieutenant General to Second Lieutenant, 10 is Cadet, 11 is Sergeant Major, 12 is Regimental Quartermaster Sergeants, 13 is Ordnance Sergeants and Hospital Stewards, 14 is First Sergeants, 15 is Sergeants and 16 is for Corporals (5).

This was simple compared to the 1917 regulations published after the National Defense Act. (6). 1 thru 9 were Lieutenant General thru Second Lieutenant, 10 was Aviators in the Signal Corps. and 11 was Cadets. Then things get complicated.

Grade 12 (a):
Regimental Sergeant Major
Sergeant Major Senior Grade of the Coast Artillery Corps.
Grade 12 (b):
Quartermaster Sergeant Senior Grade of the Quartermaster Corps.
Master Hospital Sergeant of the Medical Department
Master Engineer Senior Grade of the Corps. of Engineers
Master Electrician of the Coast Artillery Corps.
Master Signal Electrician of the Signal Corps.
Band Leader
Grade 12 (c):
Hospital Sergeant of the Medical Department
Master Engineer Junior Grade of the Corps. of Engineers
Engineer of the Coast Artillery Corps.
Grade 13:
Ordnance Sergeant
Quartermaster Sergeant of the Quartermaster Corps.
Regimental Supply Sergeant
Grade 14:
Battalion Sergeant Major
Squadron Sergeant Major
Sergeant Major Junior Grade of the Coast Artillery Corps.

Battalion Supply Sergeant of the Corps. of Engineers
Grade 15 (a):
First Sergeant
Grade 15 (b):
Sergeant First Class of the Medical Department
Sergeant First Class of the Quartermaster Corps.
Sergeant First Class of the Corps. of Engineers
Sergeant First Class of the Signal Corps.
Electrician Sergeant First Class of the Coast Artillery Corps.
Electrician Sergeant, Artillery Detachment U. S. Military Academy
Assistant Engineer of the Coast Artillery Corps.
Grade 15 (c):
Master Gunner of the Coast Artillery Corps.
Master Gunner, Artillery Detachment U . S. Military Academy
Band Sergeant of the U. S. Military Academy Band
Assistant Leader of the U. S. Military Academy Band
Assistant Band Leader
Sergeant Bugler
Electrician Sergeant Second Class of the Coast Artillery Corps.
Electrician Sergeant Second Class, Artillery Detachment U. S. Military Academy
Radio Sergeant of the Coast Artillery Corps.
Grade 16:
Color Sergeant
Grade 17:
Sergeant
Company Supply Sergeant
Mess Sergeant
Stable Sergeant
Fireman of the Coast Artillery Corps.
Grade 18:
Corporal

More ranks and more branches were added during World War I, and that pushed this system over the edge. As a result on June 4, 1920 (7) the National Defense Act was amended, adding the following: "On and after July 1, 1920, the grades of enlisted men shall be such as the President may from time to time direct, with monthly base pay at the rate of $74 for the first grade, $53 for the second grade, $45 for the third grade, $45 for the fourth grade, $37 for the fifth grade, $35 for the sixth grade, and $30 for the seventh grade. Of the total authorized number of enlisted men, those in the first grade shall not exceed 0.6 per centum, those in the second grade 1 .8 per centum, those in the third grade 2 per centum, those in the fourth grade 9.5 per centum, those in the fifth grade 9.5 per centum, those in the sixth grade 25 per centum. "

From this point forward, enlisted ranks were not created by congress but assigned to pay grades by the army in the name of the President. This also ended the practice of having a separate rank structure for each branch, for enlisted men rank and branch no longer related.

The enlisted grade reorganization of 1920

The June 1920 law created seven pay grades for enlisted ranks. The army responded to this law with General Order 36 on June 19, 1920 (1) that converted the numerous old ranks into ranks in the seven pay grades. Most of the ranks were abolished, some such as Sergeant Major dating back to the beginning. The rank of Master Sergeant was created for the first grade. The rank of Technical Sergeant for the second which it would share with the rank of First Sergeant that was retained. The rank of Staff Sergeant was created for the third grade and Sergeant, Corporal,

Private First Class and Private were retained for the fourth, fifth, sixth and seventh grades. Men in the sixth and seventh grades could be rated as specialists first thru sixth class making twelve specialist ranks in all.

This system served the army thru World War II with the only changes coming in 1942 when First Sergeants were moved to the first grade and the specialists in grades six and seven were replaced with technicians in grades three, four and five (2).

In 1948, with the war over, there was a reorganization of the enlisted grades. A second grade of Private was added in grade six causing Private First Class to move to grade five, Corporal to grade four and Sergeant to grade three. To make room the rank of Staff Sergeant was abolished. Technical Sergeants became Sergeants First Class in grade two and Master Sergeants and First Sergeants remained in grade one. Technicians were eliminated (3).

Pay Grades

The Career Compensation Act of October 12, 1949 (1) reorganized all military ranks into pay grades. The grades would carry a letter and a number. Officer's grades would start with an "O", warrant officer's with a "W" and Enlisted with an "E". Unlike the 1920 system, one would be the lowest rank with the numbers increasing for higher ranks.

Eight officer grades were created with Second Lieutenants being O-1 and Brigadier General being O-7. All higher generals would share the O-8 grade.

There were four warrant grades, with Warrant Officers Junior Grade taking the W-1 grade and Chief Warrant Officers being spread over grades W-2, W-3 and W-4.

The seven enlisted grades from 1920 became grades E-1 to E-7, the lower grade of Private being E-1 and Master and First Sergeants being E-7.

In 1954 congress changed the warrant ranks to Warrant Officer 1 in the W-1 grade, Chief Warrant Officer 2 in the W-2 grade, Chief Warrant Officer 3 in the W-3 grade and Chief Warrant Officer 4 in the W-4 grade (2).

1954 also saw the creation of specialist ranks. Specialists Third Class were in grade E-4, second class in E-5 and first class in E-6. E-7s were Master Specialists (3).

The Career Compensation Act was amended on May 20, 1958 (4) to create the grades of O-9, O-10, E-8 and E-9.

Major Generals now had O-8 to themselves while Lieutenant Generals moved to O-9 and full Generals to O-10.

The rank of Sergeant Major was revived for E-9. Staff Sergeant was also revived and placed in E-6 with Sergeant First Class moving to E-7 and First and Master Sergeant to E-8. The specialist ranks were changed to the simple, and boring, titles of Specialist 4, Specialist 5 ect.

In 1965 the army considered creating the rank of Senior Master Sergeant in the E-9 grade for those who were not senior enlisted advisors (5). This didn't happen but the idea remained, and in 1968 the E-9 grade was split into Sergeant Major for senior enlisted advisors and Staff Sergeant Major for others. This was changed in 1971 to Command Sergeant Major for senior enlisted advisors and Sergeant Major for others.

The ranks of Specialist 8 and Specialist 9 were never used and were formally eliminated in 1965 (6). The smaller post-Vietnam army had no use for noncommissioned officers without leadership training and the other specialist grades were phased out. Specialist 7 in 1978 and Specialists 5 and 6 in 1985. Specialist 4, who were not noncommissioned officers, remained as simply Specialists in the E-4 grade.

The W-5 grade was created in 1991 (7), and with it the rank of Chief Warrant Officer 5. The army had used the title of Master Warrant Officer in the W-4 grade since 1988 for those eligible for W-5 when the grade was created.

The Army Register, Historical Register and Tables of Organization

The army register is a list of the officers of the army, usually, but not always, published each year. It usually includes other information on the army's organization at the time it was published and is therefore an invaluable resource on how the army was organized at any particular time.

On December 13, 1815 the Senate passed a resolution stating "That the Secretary of War and the Secretary of the Navy be requested to furnish annually, on the first of January, each member of the Senate with a copy of the register of the officers of the army and navy of the United States" (1). The House of Representatives followed with resolutions on February 1, 1830 and August 30, 1842.

From the 1830s until 1917 the register included a table of organization. This was a spreadsheet showing all the army's ranks and how many people held each rank in each of the branches and staff departments. This is the ultimate "horses mouth" source for what ranks existed in any given year.

In 1903 Francis Heitman published the Historical Register and Dictionary of the United States Army. It was a complete analysis of the army's organization from September 29, 1789 to March 2, 1903. It included lists of the heads of the various staff departments, commanders and field grade officers of regiments and most importantly, an alphabetical list of every officer showing each promotion, reduction or change of assignment.

Chapter 2.
Army Rank Insignia

The first system of rank distinctions used by the Continental Army came about exactly a month after its creation. Tired of having his generals stopped by sentries, George Washington issued an order on July 14, 1775 stating:

"There being something awkward, as well as improper, in the General Officers being stopped at the outposts; asked for passes by the Sentries, and obliged often to send for the Officer of the Guard (who it sometimes happens is as much unacquainted with the Persons of the Generals, as the Private Men) before they can pass in or out: It is recommended to both Officers and Men to make themselves acquainted with the persons of all the Officers in General Command, and in the mean time to prevent mistakes: The General Officers and their Aids-de-Camp, will be distinguished in the following manner.

The Commander in Chief by a light blue Ribband, wore across his breast, between his Coat and Waistcoat.

The Majors and Brigadiers General, by a Pink Ribband wore in the like manner.

The Aids-de-Camp by a green ribband." (1)

On July 23rd he created a system for other ranks by ordering:

"As the Continental Army have unfortunately no Uniforms, and consequently many inconveniences must arise, from not being able always to distinguish the Commissioned Officers, from the non Commissioned, and the Non Commissioned from the private; it is desired that some Badges of Distinction may be immediately provided, for Instance, the Field Officers may have red or pink colored Cockades in their Hats: the Captains yellow or buff: and the Subalterns green. They are to furnish themselves accordingly. The Serjeants may be distinguished by an Epaulette, or stripe of red Cloth, sewed upon the right shoulder; the Corporals by one of green." (2).

The final touch came the next day, when Major Generals were ordered to wear purple instead of pink ribbands (3).

This system was simple and easy to create from materials at hand. A ribbon or piece of cloth could be worn over the shoulder by generals, tied in a bow and sewed on the hat of other officers or added to the right shoulder of sergeants and corporals.

This system lasted until mid 1780, when European allies had provided the army with better uniforms. A new system of epaulets worn on various shoulders and for generals with stars was adopted. It was similar to the system used by the French army at the time (4). It also included "button color" as a distinction of branch that would have direct effect on the future of the army's rank insignia.

In 1812 dragoons officers adopted uniforms that included "wings", a decorative shoulder covering that precluded the use of epaulets (5). There is no information on how dragoons in the War of 1812 showed their rank other than a system of stripes and bars on their horse cloth.

Wings began to appear on other uniforms by 1815. General Winfield Scott proposed that chevrons be used as rank insignia by soldiers wearing wings. It is possible that this occurred by there is no direct evidence to prove it (6).

The History of American Ranks and Rank Insignia

On March 27, 1821, the army issued a general order establishing a system of chevrons for company and field grade officers (7). New uniform regulations issued in July allowed field grade officers to keep their epaulets. The 1780 epaulet system was also kept for company grade officers in the Corps of Engineers. All others now wore wings, company grade and all noncommissioned officers show their rank by a single button colored chevron worn in various places on the sleeve (8). This system was ended in 1829 or 1830 (9). The army may have returned to the old epaulets system, at least for officers, but there is no information available.

In May of 1829, officers were given a frock coat for wear in the field. Rank on this coat was shown by an eagle, gilt for all branches, on the same side of the collar, or both, as the epaulet (10). By July, the eagles were replaced by shoulder straps.

New uniform regulations in 1832 called for epaulets to be worn on both shoulders of the dress tail coats, by all ranks. The only exception was medical and pay officers. Rank was determined by the design of the epaulet, particularly the size of the bullion (11). Line branches also had loops of lace on the cuff that varied by rank (12). Apparently the shoulder straps on the frock coats continued under the old system (13). The enlisted fatigue jacket carried no distinction of rank at all.

The next year a regiment of dragoons was added to the army. While the insignia worn by officers conformed to that of other branches, the enlisted coats carried a simple pointed cuff and metal scales on the shoulders. Rank was shown by chevrons for Sergeants and Corporals and aiguillette for senior noncommissioned officers (14).

Sometime around 1834, shoulder straps were modified to carry badges of rank in a rectangle of lace (15), and in 1839 special epaulet shaped shoulder straps were prescribed for dragoons (16).

In 1847, during the Mexican War, chevrons were added to the enlisted fatigue jackets (17), they have been used as the enlisted rank distinction ever since.

After the Mexican war ended the army tried to simplify its uniforms. New regulations in 1851 did away with the button color concept used since 1780. In its place came "facing color", using colored cloth as a distinction of branch. The dress tail coats and enlisted fatigue jackets were abolished and the frock coat was the only uniform for all members of the army. All officers now wore a gold epaulet on both shoulders with the badges of rank from the shoulder straps on them in silver in most cases. Shoulder straps were worn when epaulets were not. Overcoats gained a sleeve knot made of black cords to show rank. Enlisted men wore chevrons on the frock coat and the overcoat (18).

In 1860 light artillery officers were given a short jacket to wear in the field. Instead of shoulder straps, gold knots were worn with the badges of rank in silver (19).

During the Civil War it was found that officers distinctive uniforms were getting them killed. Rifled weapons that could be fired accurately from long range had become common on the battlefield. This began a battle, that has not ended to this day, between distinctions of rank that are easy to identify but not obvious enough to get the wearer shot by a sniper.

The solution at the time was to allow officers to wear the badges of rank from the shoulder straps directly on the shoulder (20). They were also allowed to wear enlisted overcoats. No ornaments were required but it is possible that some officers wore the badge of rank in a circle on the cuff (21).

The Civil War left the army with warehouses full of uniforms. It should not have had to purchase any new ones for decades and this would have precluded any change in style. It didn't quite work out that way. The problem was one that has always existed, crooked defense contractors. Companies had saved, and pocketed, money by making uniforms out of inferior cloth and producing them smaller that the sizes that they claimed to be therefore reducing the amount of material used (22).

The History of American Ranks and Rank Insignia

With stocks of larger sizes dwindling and complaints from the army rising, new uniforms were introduced in 1872. Epaulets were abolished for all but generals, being replaced with shoulder knots. Shoulder straps continued to be worn whenever epaulets or shoulder knots were not and the regulations specifically stated that officers were not allowed to remove the shoulder straps to avoid snipers (23). The overcoat sleeve knots continued as they had been since 1851. The regulations contain the statement "On the frontier and campaign, officers may wear the soldier's overcoat, with insignia of rank on the sleeve." (24). It is not clear if this meant the sleeve knots or the badge of rank. Enlisted men continued to wear chevrons. Instead of being made of cloth tape, chevrons were now cut from a single piece of cloth and the individual bars were formed by lines of stitching. This was the birth of "piping color". The Corps of Engineers used red as a facing color but to distinguish them from the artillery, white instead of black stitching was used on the chevrons (25).

The next major change in rank insignia came in May of 1898 when the army introduced a khaki uniform to be worn in the field. Officers rank was shown by facing colored shoulder loops. Generals and full Colonels wore the badge of rank centered on the loop while other officers wore them at the outer end with an eagle in the center. Enlisted men wore chevrons on a khaki background (26).

The warm climates that the Spanish American War was fought in lead to fighting in shirtsleeves. In July of 1898 the Secretary of War ruled that officers could wear badges of rank of the shirt collar and enlisted men could wear chevrons on the sleeve (27).

In 1900 rank insignia was added to the officers white coat, that had been worn without insignia since 1895. A white version of the colored shoulder loops from the khaki coat was used (28).

1902 saw a complete revamp of the army's uniforms. Officers were now had a full dress frock coat, a dress coat, a white coat, olive drab and khaki field coats, a mess jacket and an evening tail coat. On the full dress, mess and evening coats rank was shown on the cuff, generals with their stars above a line of oak leaf and acorn embroidery and other officers with gold cords knots following the 1851 overcoat pattern. Epaulets and shoulder knots were worn on all three coats, but as decoration. Shoulder straps were used on the dress coat and the white and field coats had plain cloth shoulder loops with the badges of rank on them. Badges of rank were still worn on shirt collars. The new olive drab overcoats still carried the sleeve knots in black cord but generals now wore stars between two black stripes (29).

Enlisted men had a blue dress coat, a white coat and olive drab and khaki field coats. Facing colored chevrons on a background that matched the coat were prescribed for each coat plus the olive drab chevrons were worn on shirt sleeves overcoats. The 1902 chevrons were much smaller than those previously used (30).

Between 1902 and the U.S. entry into Wold War I in 1917 there were only minor changes in rank insignia.

The facing color chevrons were restricted to the blue coat in 1904. On the rest of the coats chevron of a light olive color were used (31).

1912 saw the creation of a white mess jacket with white cord sleeve knots and generals wearing stars above a plain cuff (32).

1912 also saw the return of badges of rank to the epaulets and shoulder knots (33).

In 1917 the use of all dress, mess and evening uniforms was suspended (34). This meant that epaulets, shoulder knots, shoulder straps and sleeve knots, except for the overcoat, were no longer in use.

Officers added badges of rank to the garrison cap adopted during the war (35). Use of this cap ended, temporarily, with the war.

After the end of the war the suspended uniforms were not brought back right away. The white mess jacket returned in 1921 (36) and the blue uniforms in 1929 (37). The badges of rank were not initially worn on the shoulder ornaments of the white jacket (38), but did return with the other uniforms (39).

Cloth shoulder loops with badges of rank were added to the overcoats in 1926 (40). This brought an end to the black sleeve knots used since 1851. Loops were also added to officers shirts and badges of rank moved from the collar to the shoulder.

In 1938 the 1902 full dress frock coat and the dress sack coat, that had began as a field coat in 1892, were consolidated into a blue point lapel dress coat with shoulder straps. At the same time the badges of rank were removed from the shoulder knots still used on the mess and evening uniforms. The knots would now be worn by generals as well, this was the end of the long history of U.S. Army epaulets (42).

In 1942 the rank insignia was moved back to the shirt collar (43) and returned to the garrison cap (44). The use of dress uniforms was not suspended until April of 1943 (45).

The rank insignia situation during World War II saw officers wearing badges of rank of the shoulder loops of outer garments and on the right shirt collar when no outer garment was worn. The badges were also worn on garrison caps and other field caps introduced during the war. Enlisted chevrons were worn on the upper sleeve of most shirts and coats.

Dress uniforms returned around 1947 or 1948. The only real change from 1938 was the sleeve knots on the evening tail coat were now made of a single piece of lace with the badges of rank underneath. Generals returned to the old style in 1950 (46). This system was also used on a midnight blue evening uniform created for women in 1959 (47). This outfit included a cape that carried shoulder straps.

The Vietnam War brought back the old sniper problem. In response the army created subdued insignia in 1965 (48). Black or brown badges of rank and black on olive chevrons were introduced. The chevrons were moved to the collar in 1968 (49).

The women's midnight blue evening uniform was replaced by white and black mess jackets in 1969. Rank was shown on navy style hard shoulder boards (50).

The 1851 style sleeve knots were eliminated from the men's mess jackets in 1975 (51). It was replaced with a simple two strand knot with the badges of rank underneath.

In 1979 shoulder marks were introduced to replace collar insignia on shirts (52).

1986 saw new female mess jackets with sleeve knots instead of shoulder boards (53). The old mess uniforms stayed on until 2003 (54).

Also in 1986 the army introduced a parka made of water proof material called Gore-tex. This parka had a tab in the center of the chest for wearing rank insignia (55). Initially rank was pined or sewn to the tab but could lead to punctures in the parka itself and leaks. This lead to the creation of slip on cloth loops with the insignia embroidered on them similar to the shoulder marks around 2001 (56). Goretex had since become a term used for rank worn on the chest.

New combat uniforms were introduced in 2005, known as "The Army Combat Uniform". The uniforms are collar less to make the wear of body armor easier. Gortex style rank is worn on the chest of both the ACU jacket and the body armor itself (57).

Epaulets

The History of American Ranks and Rank Insignia

The term epaulet comes from epaulet, the French for shoulder (1). It is often used in the modern world for any shoulder decoration, but here it refers to a specific type of decoration. An epaulet in this context is a strap on the shoulder with fringe at the end called bullion. Above the bullion is a stiffening called a crescent. The area inside the crescent is called the frog and the area from the top of the crescent to the button by the collar is called the strap.

The first use of epaulets by the U.S. Army was in 1775 when Sergeants were ordered to wear a red one on the right shoulder and Corporals a green one (2). This lasted until 1780 when epaulets became the primary rank distinction used. The epaulets of 1780 were in button color. Generals wore an epaulet on each shoulder with stars to indicate rank, in silver for contrast. Field grade officers wore a plain epaulet on each shoulder while Captains wore one on the right and Subalterns one on the left. Sergeants wore an epaulet on both shoulders with Corporals wearing one on the right. Gunners, Bombardiers, Farriers and Saddlers were also to wear epaulets but wear and how many is not known (3).

Early epaulets were usually straight with the crescent and bullion at the far end, but in the early nineteenth century the frog began to grow. Pictures from the era (4) show the crescent now forming an oval frog with the bullion going all the way around. The larger epaulet was more difficult to keep in place. This led to a piece of matching lace being placed over the strap to help secure the epaulet (5).

The 1780 system was used until 1832 when all members of the army fro general to private were to wear an epaulet on both shoulders of their dress coat (6). The only exception to this was medical and pay officers and even this was rectified in 1840 for medical (7) and 1841 for pay (8).

The 1832 style officers epaulets terminated in a large metal crescent. Rank was determined by the size of the epaulet bullion, 1/2 inch by 3 1/2 inches for field grade officers, 1/4 by 2 1/2 for Captains and Lieutenants 1/8 by 2 1/2 inches. No bullion size was specified for generals but stars continued to be worn. Full colonels wore a spread eagle in contrasting color, silver on gold or gold on silver, on the strap. Lieutenant Colonel's epaulets were plain while for Majors the lace making up the strap and the inside of the frog was in contrasting color, gold for silver infantry epaulets and silver for the rest. A regimental number was worn in contrasting color inside the frog, staff officers left the frog empty(9).

Senior noncommissioned officers wore cloth epaulets with metallic, 1/2 inch wide bullion. Sergeants wore all cloth epaulets with 1/4 inch wide bullion and corporals 1/8 inch wide. Privates and various specialists wore 1/8 inch wide bullion half as long as a Corporals. In 1835 or so senior NCOs changed to metallic epaulets with 1/8 inch wide cloth bullion (10).

When dragoons returned to the army in 1833 the officers wore gold epaulets, but all enlisted men wore metal shoulder scales (11).

Staff departments began to show insignia on epaulets in 1839 when the Corps. of Topographical Engineers added a shield and the letters T.E. in the crescent (12). The regular engineers followed in February of 1840 by adding a castle in the crescent (13) and in October medical officers were given a wreath with the letters M.S. in it (14). In 1841 officers of the pay department were given a wreath with the letter P.D. (15).

When button color was abolished in 1851 all officers epaulets became gold. The basic design of the epaulets was not changed. Generals now were required to wear the same bullion as field grade officers. Badges of rank were now worn on the strap in silver. Colonels continued to wear the eagle, Lieutenant Colonels added an oak leaf, Captains wore two bars and First Lieutenants wore one bar. Majors and Second Lieutenants wore no badge on there epaulets, the size of the bullion showing their rank. Regimental numbers were now embroidered in gold on a circle of facing colored cloth with a silver border. Staff department badges remained as they had been with the addition of a bursting bomb for the Ordnance Department (16).

Enlisted men of the infantry, heavy artillery, engineers and ordnance, wore facing colored cloth epaulets with 1/2 inch bullion for senior NCOs, 1/4 inch for Sergeants and smaller for corporals and below. All others wore metal shoulder scales (17). In 1854 the metal scales were prescribed for all branches. Those entitled to 1/2 inch bullion had two rows of rivets running down the scales, those entitled to 1/4 inch bullion did not. The lower ranks used a smaller scale of stamped brass (18).

In 1872 epaulets were replaced by shoulder knots for all but generals (19).

In the 1890s Brigadier Generals who were the head of staff departments added the insignia of their department between the star and button (20).

The new uniforms of 1902 used the epaulets as a shoulder ornament for generals not a distinction of rank. They bore only the eagle from the Great Seal of the United States in the crescent (21). When the Generals Staff Corps. was created the following year, it's members replaced the eagle with the insignia of that corps (22).

The general's stars were returned to the epaulets in 1912 (23).

The use of epaulets was suspended in 1917 (24), and they did not return until 1929 (25). They continued until the dress uniforms were redesigned in 1937 or 1938 (26).

Button Color

Button color is the term we shall use to describe the system of uniform trimmings used form 1780 to 1851, which had an affect on the distinctions of rank.

The system began with a general order issued by George Washington on October 2, 1779 (1). The order prescribed "white" buttons, probably tin or pewter, for the infantry and dragoons and "yellow" buttons, probably brass, for the artillery.

Epaulets were worn in the corresponding color. White cloth for infantry and yellow cloth for artillery. Officers substituted silver for white and gold for yellow. Dragoon officers wore silver epaulets while enlisted men wore blue (2). Generals and staff officers used gold.

The system continued after the war into the tiny federal army. Exactly what color was used by dragoons in the early days is not clear. There is no information available on the button color used by dragoons form 1792 to 1799, but there is some evidence on gold/yellow being used on the green uniforms worn from 1799 to 1801 (3). Silver/white was used when dragoons returned in 1808 (4) and gold/yellow was used when they returned again in 1833 (5).

From the War of 1812 thru the Mexican War, uniforms included a great deal of lace. This was the most common use of button color. Chevrons in button color were worn by company grade and noncommissioned officers from 1821 to 1829 (6).

The most direct effect of button color on rank insignia was on the shoulder straps introduced in the early 1830s. Lieutenant Colonels and Majors would wear an oak leaf at each end of the strap as a badge of rank. The Lieutenant Colonels leafs would match the button colored border, silver for infantry or gold for others. The majors leafs would be of the opposite color of the border, gold for infantry and silver for others (7).

Button color was abolished by the uniform regulations of 1851. The new uniforms carried very little lace and all epaulets and shoulder strap borders were to be gold. Cloth "facing colors" were used as branch distinction (8).

The 1813 General Staff Uniform

Many staff officers in the War of 1812 wore the 1813 general staff uniform. It consisted of a dark blue tail coat that closed to the neck with 10 buttons. The collar was standing with one blind button hole and button. The button hole was embroidered for the Commissary General of Ordnance, the Adjutant General, the Inspector General, the

Quartermaster General and the Commissary General of Purchases. The cuffs were in a point down V shape, with four vertical buttons, the bottom one on the cuff. The tails were lined in blue. White or blue pantaloons, according to season, and a black cocked hat were also worn.

Hospital staff wore the same uniform in black, with "pocket flaps, and buttons placed across the cuff, four to each" and all buttons were to be covered in black cloth.

Shoulder Straps

Shoulder straps began as the extra pieces of lace used to hold the epaulets in place. In July of 1829 officers were allowed to wear a piece of button colored lace on the shoulder(s) of the undress frock coat. The straps were four inches by 1/2 inch and worn on both shoulders by field grade officers, the right shoulder by Captains and the left shoulder by Lieutenants (1), same as the epaulets. It is not clear if generals were allowed the frock coat.

Exactly when this system was changed has been lost to history. All rank began wearing epaulets on both shoulders in 1832. The lace system on the frock coats may or may not have continued. It was not until 1835 that regulations describe a new system for shoulder straps (2).

Under the new system shoulder straps were formed from a rectangle of button colored lace 3 1/2 inches long and 1 inch wide. The lace was 1/4 inch wide for generals and 1/8 inch for others. The background inside the rectangle was dark blue to match the coat. Generals wore stars, three for the Major General Commanding and two for Major Generals, inside the rectangle in silver with the border cut out around them. Full Colonels wore an eagle in the center of the strap, in the opposite color of the border, gold or silver, in other words the same color it would be on the epaulet. Lieutenant Colonels wore an oak leaf at each end of the rectangle in the same color as the border and Majors wore leafs in the opposite color. Captains wore two strips of lace, the same width and color as the border, at each end and First Lieutenants wore one strip. Second Lieutenants wore an empty frame.

The 1835 regulations don't mention Brigadier Generals (3). Legally the army of 1835 contained one Major General, Alexander Maccomb and two Brigadier Generals, Edmond Gaines and Winfield Scott, plus the Quartermaster General Thomas Jesup whose position carried the rank of Brigadier General. Gaines, Scott and Jesup all carried brevets as Major Generals. Brevets as Brigadier Generals were held by the Commissary General of Subsistence George Gibson, the chief engineer, Charles Graitiot, the paymaster Nathan Towson. The Colonels commanding several regiments were also brevet Brigadier Generals. Hugh Brady of the Second infantry, Henry Arkinson of the Sixth Infantry, William Armistead of the Third infantry, Duncan Clinch of the Fourth infantry, Matthew Arbuckle of the Seventh infantry, John Fenwick of the Fourth artillery, George Brooke of the Fifth Infantry and Abraham Eustis of the First artillery. Lieutenant Colonel Roger Jones of the Fourth artillery was also a brevet Brigadier General (4).

A uniform belonging to Brady's predecessor as commander of the Second infantry, Colonel and Brevet Brigadier General Henry Leavenworth, has shoulder straps containing the single star of a Brigadier General and silver oak leafs at each end (5). Leavenworth died on July 21, 1834 (6). This would seam to indicate that the straps were in use before 1835 and were used by Brigadier Generals.

The odd design with one star and oak leafs also appears on a drawing attached to an order creating shoulder straps in the Marine Corps (7). Along with the odd brigadier design, the drawing also shows the designs for Major General and "General Commander in Chief". The Marine Corps officers of 1835 consisted of one Colonel Commandant, one Lieutenant Colonel, four Majors, 13 Captains, 20 First Lieutenants and 20 Second Lieutenants (8). This drawing seams to have been intended for the army.

Regulations of 1836 call for Brigadier Generals straps to carry one star and no leafs (9).

The straps were no longer intended to be worn over the epaulets, but photographic evidence shows that they were used that way into the Civil War (10).

The History of American Ranks and Rank Insignia

In 1839 dragoon officers were given shoulder straps of a different design. The regulations describe them as: "Formed like the strap of the epaulette, and made of blue cloth, edged with gold lace like an epaulette; solid gilt crescent, with the number of regiment embroidered within. The strap of the colonel to have on it a silver embroidered eagle; that of the lieutenant colonel two gold leaves at the points, where the crescent joins it; that of the major two silver leaves; that of the captain two gold bars; that of the first lieutenant one bar; that of the second lieutenant plain." (11).

When the army's uniforms were simplified in 1851 the special dragoon straps were abolished. At the same time all borders for all ranks of all branches were changed to 1/4 inch wide gold embroidery, forming a rectangle 1 3/8 by 4 inches. The general's stars were sized to fit inside, so the lace no longer had to be cut away. The stars, the Colonel's eagle and the Lieutenant Colonel's Leafs were rendered in silver. The Major's leafs and the bars for Captains and Lieutenants were rendered in gold even though the bars were silver on the epaulets. The bars were widened to 1/4 inch to match the border. Staff officers continued to wear the dark blue background but regimental officers wore a background in facing color (12).

The bars for Captains and Lieutenants were changed to silver in 1872 leaving the Major's leafs the only gold device used in the shoulder straps (13).

Beginning in 1902 the use of shoulder straps declined. No longer worn in the field, they were restricted to the dress coat. The basic design was not changed but some staff branches began wearing facing colored backgrounds. For branches with piping colors they were added as a border inside the gold embroidery (14).

In 1912 the size of the border was increased to 3/8 inch with a 1/16 inch gold border inside and outside. This made the overall strap 1 5/8 inches wide(15). If a branch had a piping color, it replaced the inside gold border.

Regulations of 1915 enlarged the straps to 1 7/8 inches wide but the 1917 regulations returned them to 1 5/8 inches (16).

World War I saw the suspension of the dress coat and therefore shoulder straps. They did not return until 1929 (17).

New dress blue coats in 1938 carried shoulder straps. Instead of an empty frame Second Lieutenants now wore a gold bar at each end (18).

Wear of the dress coat was suspended again from 1943 to 1947 (19) and when they returned Warrant Officers were allowed straps with their rank bars at each end (20).

Shoulder straps were added to the dress blue coats of female officers in 1960. They were of the same basic design as the male straps but were only 3 1/2 inches long (21).

In addition to the basic ranks, shoulder straps were worn by Medical Cadets and Chaplains.

During the Civil War Medical Cadets wore a shoulder strap consisting of a green cloth rectangle, 3 3/4 inches long and 1 1/2 inches wide, with a strip of 1/2 inch gold lace, 3 inches long, centered in it (22).

Chaplains wore standard rectangular straps with a black background and a silver shepherds crook from 1880 to 1888. A similar strap with a cross was instituted in 1898 and lasted until Chaplains were given actual rank insignia in 1914 (23).

Badges of rank

Badges of rank is the term we shall use to refer to the stars, eagles, leafs and bars used to denote officers rank.

The History of American Ranks and Rank Insignia

They began in 1780 with the stars worn by generals on epaulets (1). Full Colonels gained an eagle as a badge of rank on their epaulets in 1832 (2). Lieutenant Colonels and Majors began wearing leafs on shoulder straps in the early 1830s. At the same time Captains and First Lieutenants used extra strips of lace that became bars (3). Second Lieutenants were not given a bar as a badge of rank until 1917.

Chaplains used a cross for a badge of rank form 1902 until 1926, except for 1914 to 1918 when they were allowed to wear the badges of their equivalent rank (4). After 1926 Chaplains once again wore rank insignia (5).

Field Clerks wore crossed quills, first on a disk in 1917, then in combination with the insignia of the Adjutant General's Department or the Quartermaster Corps, until they were abolished in 1926 (5).

Warrant Officers began in the Coast Artillery in January of 1920 and wore the insignia of that branch with a sea mine underneath until November. At that point Warrant Officers had been appointed in other branches and all were to were to wear U.S. letters as insignia. In March of 1921 Warrant Officers were given an eagle in a wreath, known as the "eagle rising" insignia (6). When Warrant Officers were split into multiple ranks in 1941, bars with enameled designs came into use (7). The system of the enameled designs was changed in 1954 and again in 1972.

The generals' stars have always been silver because they were originally worn on a gold epaulet. Colonel's eagles originally contrasted the epaulet. Infantry Colonels wore a gold eagle on their silver epaulets while others wore silver eagles on gold epaulets. The same colors were used on the shoulder straps. Lieutenant Colonel's leafs and the bars for Captains and Lieutenants, matched the shoulder strap border while Major's leafs were the opposite.

When button color was abolished in 1851, Badges of rank were worn on epaulets by all ranks but Majors and Second Lieutenants, in silver. On the shoulder straps, the stars, eagle and Lieutenant Colonel's leafs were silver and the Major's leafs and the bars for Captains and First Lieutenants were gold (8) until 1872 when they were changed to silver on both the shoulder straps and shoulder knots (9). By the time a badge of rank was developed for Second Lieutenants, the idea a silver leaf representing a Lieutenant Colonel and a gold leaf representing a Major was 66 years old and it seamed reasonable to extend the system to lieutenants.

The first time badges of rank were used alone, not on epaulets or in shoulder straps, was during the Civil War. General order 286, dated November 22, 1864 allowed "The marks of rank prescribed to be worn on the shoulder-straps will be worn on the shoulder in place of the strap." This did not continue after the war (10).

As early as 1879 it was recommended that badges of rank be worn on the collar on the undress coats, replacing the shoulder strap. This did not happen, at least partially because the Confederate Army has used collar insignia (11). The confederate system, one to three horizontal bars for Captains and lieutenants, one to three stars for Majors and Colonels and generals wearing three stars in a wreath, also effected the design of the Second Lieutenants insignia. The original proposal was to go to three bars for Captains, two for First Lieutenants and one for Second Lieutenants, but this seemed to close to the confederate insignia and the gold bar was chosen instead (12).

The next use of badges of rank, without an epaulet, shoulder strap or shoulder knot, was in 1898. New khaki field uniforms showed rank on shoulder loops of facing colored cloth (13). The regulations don't specify how the generals stars were worn. Colonels appear to have worn their eagles long ways down the center of the strap with the feet towards the front (14). Other officers wore their insignia "about one-third distant from the shoulder seam to the collar; and midway between the insignia of grade and the collar will be worn, on the strap, the coat of arms of the United States, 1 1/4 inches high, according to design." (15). Generals and Colonels wore the coat of arms on the collar.

The same system was applied to white summer coats in 1901. The only difference was the shoulder loops were to be white instead of facing color (16).

1898 also saw the badges of rank added to both shirt collars when the shirt was worn without a coat (17).

The History of American Ranks and Rank Insignia

New field uniforms introduced in 1902 had shoulder loops of the same cloth as the coat. The regulations simply say that insignia of rank, including a cross for chaplains, was to be worn on the loops "near the sleeve seam"(18).

The 1912 regulations were more specific. General's stars were spread evenly down the loop with one point towards the collar. Colonel's eagles were worn with the hear toward the collar and the feet towards the shoulder, 5/8 inches from the seam. The beak was worn to the front, requiring the insignia to be made in pairs. Leafs were worn 5/8 inches from the seam, with the stem towards the seam and bars were worn in the same place parallel to the seam. The chaplains cross was worn the bottom towards the seam (20). On the shirt collars stars were worn point up, eagles head up, leafs stem down and bars and crosses parallel to the edge. Second Lieutenants were to wear their insignia of branch on the shirt collar (21).

In 1916 shirt collar insignia got complicated (22). Generals would wear U.S. letters on both collars in front of their stars. Generals entitled to branch insignia would replace the left U.S. letters. Other officers would wear the U.S. letters on the right collar with the badge of rank behind and branch insignia alone on the left side. As a consequence, Second Lieutenants wore just the letters on the right collar (23). The letters were removed in 1918, by which time Second Lieutenants were using the gold bar (24).

Officers wore badges of rank on the left side of the garrison caps worn during World War I (25).

Shoulder loops were added to officer's shirts in 1924, and the badges of rank were moved to them, worn in the same manner as the coat. U.S. letters returned to fill the space on the right collar (26).

Sleeve knots were replaced on overcoats with shoulder loops and badges of rank in 1926 (27).

The badges moved back to the right shirt collar (28) and to the garrison cap (29) in 1942.

Field Clerks and then Warrant Officers wore their badges of rank as branch insignia. They essentially wore officer's uniforms without a badge of rank and with the Field Clerk or Warrant Officers branch insignia (30). When Warrant officers were split into two grades in 1942 they gained bars as a badge of rank worn the same as other officers. The bars were gold with rounded ends and covered in brown enamel. Chief Warrant Officers had a gold stripe running long ways down the center of the bar, while Warrant Officers Junior Grade and a gold stripe running across the bar (31). Flight Officers wore the junior grade insignia with blue instead of brown enamel (32).

In 1954 new insignia was prescribed for the now four grades of Warrant Officer. A "unified system" common to all armed forces was developed using the same pattern for each equivalent rank. The enameled portions would very by branch of service, brown for the army, dark blue for the Navy and Coast Guard, scarlet red for the Marine Corps, and sky blue for the Air Force. The new bars were rectangular, silver for the top two grades and gold for the other two. The enameled portion for W-1 and W-3 would be in two rectangles, showing only one stripe of gold or silver. For W-2 and W-4 there would be three enameled portions showing two sections of gold or silver (33).

During the Vietnam War, "subdued" insignia was developed to make insignia less visible to snipers. Silver badges of rank, generals, colonels, Captains and First Lieutenants, became black. Gold badges, Majors and Second Lieutenants, became brown. For warrant officers, silver became black and gold became olive drab. The brown portions remained brown.

In 1972 the army designed new badges of rank for warrant officers. The new bars were silver for all grades with one black block in the center for W-1, two blocks spaced evenly for W-2, three blocks gathered in the center for W-3 and four blocks covering the entire bar for W-4. Designs were also created for the proposed ranks of W-5, a black stripe running long ways, and W-6, two black stripes running long ways (34). Subdued insignia was olive and black (35). When Master Warrant Officers were created in 1988, in anticipation of a new W-5 grade, they wore four block with open centers (36). This insignia carried over when the W-5 grade was created in 1991 and was worn until 2004, when it was replaced by the original 1972 design.

Badges of rank were worn on the right shirt collar of dress uniforms until the creation of shoulder marks in 1979 (37). Subdued badges were worn on the right collar of field uniforms until 2005 when they were moved to the center of the chest (38). The last vestige of right collar badges of rank is on special medical uniforms.

Use on the shoulder loops of most coats has continued as has the use on most types of headgear except dress caps that use the national eagle.

Chevrons

A chevron is two lines meeting at an angle. A simple design to create with lace or tape, they had been used as rank insignia for noncommissioned officers by the British Army since 1803 (1). In this context we need to stretch the definition of "chevron" include all the cloth badges worn (mostly) on the upper sleeve to show rank. There is a popular novel that claims chevrons denote something else, but we wont go there.

The first use in the U.S. Army was, possibly, during the War of 1812 when wings replaced epaulets on the shoulders of light infantrymen. Chevrons may have been used to show rank, but there is no clear evidence to prove it (2).

The first clear evidence of chevrons was from a general order dated March 27, 1821. It called for line officers to wear button colored chevrons: three on each arm for Colonels, Two for Lieutenant Colonels and one for Majors. Captains were to have one on the right arm and both grades of lieutenant, one on the left (3).

It is not known if these chevrons were ever worn. New uniform regulations in July allowed field grade officers to keep their epaulets. Captain wore one chevron, point up, on each upper sleeve and lieutenants above each cuff. Sergeant Majors and Quartermaster Sergeants wore a cloth chevron on both upper sleeves while Sergeants and Senior Musicians wore them above both cuffs and Corporals above the right cuff only. Officers assigned as adjutants wore an arc of lace joining the ends of the chevrons (4). The chevron were in button color, gold for artillery officers with yellow for enlisted men, and silver for infantry officers with white for enlisted men (5). The regulations prescribe uniforms for a regiment of riflemen with gold chevrons for officers and black for enlisted men (6), but the regiment was eliminated in by legislation of March 2nd (7).

In 1825 the enlisted chevrons were changed to a chevron and an arc like the adjutants for Senior NCOs, one on each upper sleeve for Sergeants and one above each cuff for Corporals. This system was abolished in 1829 or 1830 (8).

Chevrons returned in 1832 but not as rank insignia. Soldiers wore a point up chevron on their dress coat sleeves for each five years of service (9).

The following year, a dragoon regiment was added to the army. Enlisted dragoons were to wear metal scales instead of epaulets on their shoulders and needed another way to distinguish rank. Point down chevrons were chosen, three for Sergeants and two for Corporals. Senior NCOs were distinguished by sashes and aiguillettes (10).

By 1847 the army as fighting the Mexican War. Fatigue jackets were being worn in the field instead of dress tail coats, and required a distinction of rank. Point up chevrons were added to the upper sleeves in all branches. A Sergeant Major would wear three chevrons and three arcs, a Quartermaster Sergeant three chevrons and three straight bars, a First Sergeant three chevron and a lozenge, a Sergeant three chevrons and a Corporal two chevrons (11). The chevrons were to be "of lace corresponding to their uniform". This meant white for infantry and yellow for dragoons. It may have meant yellow for artillery (12), but there was plenty of red on artillery uniforms and so the chevrons may have been red (13). Engineers and mounted riflemen wore yellow (14) and Voltigeurs appear to have worn white (15). The point down rank chevrons for dragoons and the point up service chevrons were continued leaving the potential for a great deal of confusion.

Things were simplified in 1851 when facing colored, downward pointing, chevrons became the main rank distinction for noncommissioned officers. The same basic designs from 1847 were carried over with Ordnance

Sergeants now wearing three chevrons and a star. Service was now shown by hash marks worn above the cuff. The chevrons were formed from 1/2 inch tape. Worsted cloth for Sergeants and Corporals and silk for higher ranks (16).

Late in 1851 an insignia was added for Hospital Steward. Instead of lines meeting at an angle, the insignia was one wide hash mark with a caduceus on it. At the same time crossed hatchets were authorized for soldiers serving as pioneers (17). These were the first of many "chevrons" that did not include an actual chevron.

In 1872 the army began using a new style chevrons. Credit for the idea goes to Francis S. Johnston of Philadelphia, who was granted patent no. 135124 on January 21, 1873.

Johnston's idea was to manufacture chevrons out of cloth, cut in to the overall shape and then add line of stitching to create individual chevrons, arc or bars. Designs inside the angle of the chevrons, such as the star for Ordnance Sergeants had the base piece of facing colored cloth include a cured topped section above where the lines of stitching would outline the chevrons, with the design cut out. A piece of dark blue cloth was applied to the back of the facing colored cloth to fill in the hole, and a second piece of blue cloth was added, covering the cured topped section with a larger design cut out. This created outline look that was previously crated with lace. A large number of chevron pieces could be cut out of a single bolt of cloth, reducing the overall cost of manufacturing (18).

The Corps of Engineers used white stitching instead of the black used by other branches (19). This created the idea that branches could have a second or "piping" color.

Chevrons on overcoats were moved to the cuff in 1883 (20).

A new design for chevrons on the dress coat was instituted in 1885. Chevrons were made of gold lace on a facing colored background (21), with engineers adding a line of white stitching around the lace (22). Non chevron chevrons, such as the Pioneer insignia were always rendered in facing color never in gold.

The Spanish War in 1898 saw soldiers fighting in shirt sleeves. Like the fatigue jackets during the Mexican War, a distinction of rank was needed (23). Chevrons were authorized on the shirts in July of 1898 (24), but at 9 inches wide they didn't fit on a shirt sleeve. Smaller chevrons were improvised until official sanction came in 1900 (25).

The last innovation of the nineteenth century was chevrons worn on khaki uniforms. They were identical to the cloth chevrons except the blue inserts were khaki (26).

When the army's uniforms were overhauled in 1902 it was decided to use the smaller shirt size chevrons, about 3 inches wide, on all coats, and to wear them with the point up instead of down (27).

The 1902 regulations gave enlisted men a dress blue coat, a white coat, an olive drab field coat and a khaki field coat. Chevrons were also worn on the olive drab overcoat and olive drab shirts. The chevrons would be in facing color, outlined in piping color if needed, on a blue, khaki, white or olive background to match the garment they were worn on. The coast artillery were given brown fatigue coats with tan or brown chevrons on a rust colored background.

The army of 1902 included 37 enlisted ranks spread over 10 branches plus 942 men that were unattached (28). All but five of the ranks wore chevrons. All those ranks and various facing colors times four different backgrounds was more than the army's supply system could handle. There was also a problem of the facing colored dye running when the coats were washed (29). This lead to a change in 1904 that left facing colored chevrons on the dress coat only. The rest used chevrons of light olive drab on olive, white or khaki backgrounds (30). The white coat was restricted to medical personnel in 1907, but was used in the summer by recruiting parties from 1908 to 1914 (31). The khaki coat was eliminated in 1912 (32).

The chevrons on the overcoat were moved from the cuff to the upper sleeve in 1904 (34).

The artillery brown uniform was replaced with one of blue denim in 1908. Khaki backed chevrons were used until 1910 when chevrons with the design formed from lines of red chain stitching on a denim background were introduced (35).

The chain stitched chevron concept would expand to cooks and bakers in the Quartermaster Corps in 1913 and members of the aviation section of the Signal Corps in 1914. The cooks and bakers uniforms were white, so the chevrons were formed with buff, the Quartermaster Corps facing color, on a white background. Aviation personnel wore the denim work uniform with chevrons formed from two lines of chain stitching, one orange, the signal facing color, and one white, the signal piping color (36). Chain stitch chevrons were replaced by standard olive on olive chevrons in April of 1918 to simplify the army's supply problems during World War I (37).

The white medical coat had it's chevrons changed to olive on olive at the same time. The dress uniforms had been suspended in 1917, leaving the olive on olive chevrons the only ones in use (38).

During World War I, chevrons were restricted to the right arm only. Thus cutting the supply burden in half. This was unpopular with the troops in the field (39).

One reason for the burden was the shear volume of enlisted ranks. The 1916 table of organization shows 51 enlisted ranks spread over 12 branches (40), and new branches added during the war aggravated the situation.

The use on non chevron chevrons had increased to the point that most senior NCOs in staff branches were wearing the branch insignia a wreath under a star.

After the war the army instituted a few changes to simplified the chevron situation. A common insignia for Privates First Class in all branches was adopted, and new, more colorful insignia was designed for senior NCOs in staff branches. The new insignia, approved in January of 1920, included facing colored badges in green wreaths, some under white stars. A few even showed a Navy Petty Officer's eagle (41).

Many of these were never worn. In June of 1920 the enlisted ranks were restructured into seven pay grades.

The new chevrons were olive on dark blue (42). Khaki uniforms returned in 1929 (43), and khaki on blue chevrons were eventually prescribed. When is not quite clear, but they were in use by 1936 (44).

The 1902 dress uniforms were revived in 1929 (45), and facing colored chevrons, outlined in piping color, on a blue background were worn (46). The uniform was modernized in 1936 or 1937, but the chevrons were not changed (47). This uniform in one of the most rare in army history. It was an optional uniform, not issued to every soldier, and was seldom worn by anyone. Regulations of the era tend not to describe enlisted uniforms, leaving very little documentation. The last irony is that the uniform was not suspended until mid 1943 (48), meaning it existed while millions of soldiers served in World War II, who probably were not aware of it. It is not clear if the uniform was revived when the officer's dress blues were in 1947, or even if anyone in the army remembered it existed.

In 1944 beige on beige chevrons were prescribed for a female off duty dress (49).

The chevrons were reduced to two inches wide in 1948. The new chevrons replaced the olive on blue, khaki on blue and beige on beige designs. Now gold chevrons on a blue background would be worn by those in combat positions, while blue on gold chevron were worn by noncombatants (50).

These chevrons were not deemed satisfactory and the 3 inch olive on blue chevrons were returned in 1951 (51). Women continued to wear the smaller design. Gold on white chevrons were introduced in 1951 for a new feamle white uniform and gold on taupe chevrons were introduced in 1952 for wear on the female taupe uniform (52).

In the mid 1950s the army began another overhaul of its uniforms. The army's 'indenity" class A uniform would be dark green with tan worn in the summer. There would also be optional dress blue and dress white uniforms.

Women were given a green cord blouse and skirt uniform. Olive drab fatigues would be worn in the field. Chevrons would be gold on a blue background for the blue uniform, a white background for the white uniform and dark green for all others, including fatigues (53).

The first of the new chevrons issued was for the new for specialists ranks in 1955. These were 2 inches wide until 1958 when a male version was created that was 3 inches wide. Other ranks received the new chevrons in 1957 (54).

The Vietnam War proved it was a bad idea to wear gold chevrons on a field uniform. Soldiers began darkening their chevrons to avoid being killed by snipers. In 1966 the army authorized black on olive chevrons to be worn on fatigue uniforms (55).

The climate in Vietnam often led to sleeve being rolled up, covering the chevrons. In 1967 black metal pin on chevrons were introduced, to be worn on the collar (56).

The utility of pin on chevrons soon became apparent. They could be worn in various places, such as overcoats and jackets, without sewing, that was time consuming and put holes in waterproof material.

In 1971 the black metal chevrons were authorized on outerwear, with a white plastic background for visibility. This lead to gold pin on insignia in 1975 (57).

By the 1980s small, black chevrons embroidered on an olive background became more common on the collars of field uniforms. An exact date has proved elusive, but the option is listed on page 106 of the 1992 uniform regulations. It probably began about the time that camouflage battle dress uniforms replaced fatigues in the early 1980s.

The gold pin on chevrons were worn on the cuff of enlisted dinner jackets from 1981 (58) to 1992, when regular gold on blue or white chevrons moved to the upper sleeve (59).

In 1980, the tan shirts worn under the green class A uniform were replaced with a light green shirt (60). Initially, gold pin-on chevrons were worn on the collar, but in 1981 shoulder marks were prescribed for Corporals and above (61). Specialists and below continued to wear gold pins on the collar, even when the green coat was worn.

The concept of large male chevrons and small female chevrons was changed to just large and small chevrons in 1996 (62). Either gender could wear either size at their discretion.

In 2008 the army announced the end of the white and green uniforms (63). The white mess jacket, and the gold on white chevrons to go with it, was continued. The new class A "Army Service Uniform", uses gold on blue chevrons on the blue coat and shoulder marks/collar pins on the white shirt.

Facing and Piping color

Facing color is the term we shall use to describe the colors used in shoulder straps and chevrons, among other places, to show branch. This is often referred to as "branch color", modern regulations use the term "first named color of the basic branch".

Piping color is the term we shall use for the secondary color. What the army now calls "the second named color of the basic branch".

Facing color began as a standard branch distinction in 1851 (1), but there were colors used by branches in various ways before that.

Eighteenth century uniform coats usually had the lapels buttoned back, a small lay down collar, the cuffs turned up and the skirt folded back, to show the color of the lining. This was used as a regimental distinction, not necessarily a distinction of branch. Coats were referred to using the overall color of the coat, "faced with" the color of the lining. For example generals and staff officers in the Continental Army wore coats that were "blue faced with buff" (2). Sometimes the skirt fold backs would be a different color. In this case the term was "faced with and lined with" For example Continental Army Engineering officers, as of 1780, wore blue faced with buff and lined with red (3).

In 1779 a standard facing system was attempted. Infantry regiments from New Hampshire, Massachusetts, Connecticut and Rhode Island, wore blue .aced with white. New York and New Jersey regiments wore blue faced with buff. Pennsylvania, Maryland, Delaware and Virginia were prescribed scarlet, but red was used. North Carolina, South Carolina and Georgia used blue faced with blue, with the button holes trimmed in white lace. All artillery units were to wear blue faced with red with yellow trimmings. Dragoons wore blue faced with white. Shortages kept the system from being fully implemented (4).

In 1783, as the war wound down, all infantry and dragoon facings were changed to red (5). With some exceptions, blue faced with red would be the look of the army until 1813 when plain blue uniforms were introduced as a cost cutting measure (6).

The 1832 uniform regulations prescribed colored plumes on the hats of officers of the staff departments, along with buff patches on the collar (7).

When facing color became official in 1851 it was worn by enlisted men on the collar, cuffs, trouser stripes, chevrons, and on the uniform cap, both as a colored band and as a pompom. The front of musicians coats were covered in facing color. Enlisted men of the Corps of Engineers and Ordnance Department wore piping instead of solid colors. Officers wore facing color behind the regimental number in the epaulet frog, as the background of the shoulder straps, as trouser stripes and on the pompom only on the cap. Staff officers had two color pompoms. While enlisted men of staff departments had facing colors, officers had plain dark blue backgrounds on the shoulder straps and a buff welt on the trousers (8).

The caps with pompoms were replaced in 1858 (9), and at the same time the buff welt became gold (10).

Piping color began in 1872 when the stitching on the engineer's chevrons was to be white instead of black and both red and white trimming was used on the uniform.

Staff officers in some departments began wearing facing and piping color in 1902 (11).

Colors were worn on the edge of the officer's garrison cap curtain in World War I. This lead to staff departments adding a piping color (12).

Garrison caps were the main use of colors on uniforms in World War II. This time for enlisted personnel (13).

ACQUISITION CORPS.
The Acquisition Corps was created on January 8, 2008, for enlisted men with Military Occupational Specialty code 51C.

No colors have been assigned, but the regimental insignia is in the army's colors of black and gold (31a).

ADJUTANT GENERAL'S CORPS
The Adjutant General's Department became the Adjutant General's Corps on June 28, 1950 (14), and inherited the blue and red colors (15).

ADJUTANT GENERAL'S DEPARTMENT
The Adjutant General's Department was created on March 13, 1813 (16). The name was changed on April 28, 1904 to The Military Secretary's Department (17), and changed back on March 2, 1907 (18). It became the Adjutant General's Corps on June 28, 1950.

Yellow hat plumes were worn from 1832 to 1839 and white from 1839 to 1851. The 1851 pompom was white in the upper third and the lower two-thirds buff (18a).

The dark blue of the staff departments was used, even after others instituted a piping color. Red was finally added as a piping color in 1936 (19).

AIR CORPS
The Air Service became the Air Corps on July 2, 1926 (20). Technically it remained a branch until the Air Force was created on July 26, 1947 (21). In reality it was part of the "Army Air Forces", a subdivision of the War Department, created by Executive order 9082 on February 28, 1942.

Ultramarine blue and golden yellow were inherited from Air Service (22).

AIR SERVICE
Originally part of the Signal Corps, the Air Service became a branch by executive order on May 24, 1918 (23). This was confirmed in law on June 4, 1920 (24). The name was changed to Air Corps on July 2, 1926 (25).

Green and black were the colors form 1918 to 1920 (26), when ultramarine blue and golden yellow were prescribed (27).

ARMOR
Armor officially became a branch of the army on June 28, 1950, replacing, and continuing the history of the cavalry (28).

Green and white may have been used until cavalry yellow was officially adopted on October 26, 1951 (29)

ARMORED FORCES
Not officially a branch but functioning as one, the Armored Forces existed from July 15, 1940 (30) until the creation of the Armor branch on June 28, 1950 (31).

The colors were green and white (32).

ARMY INTELLIGENCE
The Military Intelligence Reserve Corps became Army Intelligence, United States Army Reserve in 1959, and was merged with Army Security to form the Military Intelligence branch in 1963 (33).

It inherited golden yellow and pansy as colors (34).

ARMY SECURITY
The Army Security branch existed from 1950 until being merged with the intelligence branch in 1963 (35).

It used the branch immaterial colors of teal and white (36).

ARTILLERY
The artillery has been organized in any number of ways over the years. There were various artillery units in the Continental Army, a company remaining after the war to guard stores and three more added thereafter to form a The Battalion of Artillery on April 30, 1790 (37). On May 9, 1794 the Corps of Artillerists and Engineers was formed (38) and a separate Regiment of Artillerists and Engineers was formed on April 27, 1798 (39). They were combined into the Regiment of Artillerists on March 16, 1802 (40). A Separate Regiment of Light Artillery was raised on April 12, 1808 (41). Two more regiments were added on January 11, 1812 (42) and all but the light regiment were merged into the Corps of Artillery on March 30, 1814 (43). On March 2, 1821 the artillery was organized into

regiments, each with a company of light artillery (44). In 1901 the artillery was reorganized back into a Corps of Artillery consisting of two parts, the coast artillery and the field artillery both under a Colonel with the title of Chief of Artillery (45). On January 25, 1907 the field and coast artillery were made separate branches known as the Coast Artillery Corps and the Field Artillery with the chief being in charge of the Coast Artillery Corps only (46). The two branches were merged to form the Artillery Branch on June 28, 1950 (47), only to be separated again on June 20, 1968 into the Field Artillery and the Air Defense Artillery (48).

The red or scarlet facings of the continental army artillery was revived in 1832 with red piping, lining and other red accents on the artillery uniform (49), and scarlet became the artillery facing color in 1851. The chief of Artillery Wallace Randolph was made a Brigadier General on February 27, 1903 (50). He kept the scarlet background in his shoulder straps (51).

AVIATION

On April 12, 1983, 36 years after the Air Force became a separate service, the army Aviation branch was created (52).

The ultramarine blue and golden yellow of the Air Crop was revived (53).

BRANCH IMMATERIAL

Unassigned to Branch enlisted personnel became Branch Immaterial in 1976. Since only Command Sergeant Majors were left as Branch Immaterial the term was dropped in 1992.

The Branch Immaterial colors were teal and white (54).

BUREAU OF INSULAR AFFAIRS

The Bureau of Insular Affairs became a permanent part of the army on July 1, 1920 (55). It's duties were transferred to the Interior Department on May 9, 1939 (56).

The dark blue staff color was used (57).

BUREAU OF MILITARY JUSTICE

The Bureau of Military Justice was created on June 20, 1864 (58). It was combined with the Corps of Judge Advocates to form the Judge Advocate General's Department on July 5, 1884 (59).

The dark blue of the staff departments was used.

CAVALRY

The first regiments to be called "cavalry" were added to the army on March 3, 1855 (60). The cavalry was "continued" as the Armor branch on June 28, 1950 (61).

Yellow was chosen as a facing color (62) even though it was already used by enlisted men in the Corps of Engineers.

CHAPLAIN

Chaplains were given black uniforms in 1861 (63), and shoulder straps carried a black background starting in 1880 (64).

CHEMICAL CORPS

The Chemical Warfare Service became the Chemical Corps on August 2, 1946 (65), and inherited its cobalt blue and golden yellow colors (66).

CHEMICAL WARFARE SERVICE

The Gas Service was renamed the Chemical Warfare Service on June 28, 1918 (67), both were part of the American Expeditionary Force in France. Congress made it an official branch of the army on June 4, 1920 (68).

It's colors were cobalt blue and golden yellow (69).

CIVIL AFFAIRS

The Civil Affairs branch was created in 1955 (70).

It's colors are purple and white (71).

CORPS. OF ENGINEERS

A Corps of Engineers existed in the Continental Army (72). The engineers were part of the artillery from May 9, 1794 (73) to March 16, 1802 (74), When the Corps was created. Enlisted men were added to the Corps on February 28, 1803 (75) and eliminated again on March 2, 1821 (76), only to return again on May 15, 1846 (77).

Black was used on engineer uniforms from at least 1803 (78).

In 1851 the officer's pompom was a third black and two-thirds buff, while the shoulder strap backgrounds were the standard staff dark blue. Enlisted engineers used yellow as a facing color (79).

The colors on the enlisted uniforms were changed to scarlet and white in 1872, but officers continued to use dark blue (80).

Officer's finally adopted the scarlet and white in 1902 (81).

CORPS. OF INTERPRETERS

The Corps of Interpreters existed during World War I. It was folded into the Military Intelligence Reserve Corps in 1920 (82).

It's colors were green and white (83).

CORPS. OF JUDGE ADVOCATES

Judge advocates are listed as being in a Corps of Judge Advocates in the army registers of 1883 (84) and 1884 (85). The corps was merged with the Bureau of Military Justice to form the Judge Advocate General's Department on July 5, 1884 (86).

The blue staff color was used (87).

CORPS. TOPOGRAPHICAL OF ENGINEERS

The Corps of Topographical Engineers was created on July 5, 1838 (88). Enlisted men were added on August 6, 1861(89). It was merged with the Corps of Engineers on March 3, 1863 (90).

Black was used on pre 1851 uniforms (91)(92) and the same black and buff pompoms were used on the 1851 cap (93). Otherwise staff dark blue was used. There is no direct information on colors used by enlisted men. They may have worn the same yellow as the Corps of Engineers.

DETACHED ENLISTED MAN'S LIST

The Detached Enlisted Men's List was created in 1920, for men not assigned to a branch, such as Service School Detachments (94). The name was changed to Unassigned to Branch in 1953.

The color used was green, inherited from the Service School Detachments (95).

DRAGOONS
Dragoons existed in the Continental Army, and from March 5, 1792 (96) to May 17, 1800 (97), April 16, 1808 (98) to March 3, 1815 (99) and from March 2, 1833 until being combined with the cavalry on August 3, 1861 (100).

In 1779 dragoon uniforms were to be blue faced with white (101), changing to blue faced with red in 1782 (102). In 1799, dragoons were given uniforms of green faced with black, which were not actually authorized, but worn anyway (103). From 1808 (104) to 1815 (105) were plain blue. Yellow facings were used on the 1833 to 1851 uniforms (106) and the facing color chosen in 1851 was orange (107).

FINANCE CORPS
The Finance Department became the Finance Corps on June 28, 1950 (108).

Silver gray and golden yellow was continued as the colors (109).

FINANCE DEPARTMENT
The Finance Department was separated from the Quartermaster Corps on June 4, 1920 (110).

The colors were silver gray and golden yellow (111)

GAS SERVICE
The Gas Service was created in the American Expediency Force on September 3, 1917. The name was changed to Chemical Warfare Service on June 28, 1918 (112).

It is not clear if colors were used.

INDIAN SCOUTS
Indian scouts were officially added to the army's strength on June 28, 1866 (113). They continued until 1947 (114).

Special uniforms were prescribed in 1890 with white piped with red (115). It is not clear if white and red continued past 1902. The 1902 regulations state "The uniform for enlisted scouts will, in general, be the same as service uniform for enlisted men of the corresponding arm of service"(116).

INFANTRY
Light blue was chosen for the infantry in 1851, Dark blue was used as stripes for light blue trousers (117). Dark blue was also used on overcoat chevrons beginning in 1876 (118).

Infantry facings changed to white in 1884, but the overcoat chevrons remained dark blue until 1900. Light blue was used on the 1898 khaki uniforms, but this was changed to white in 1899 (119). It is difficult to say when the infantry changed back to light blue. It was some time between 1907 (120) and 1913 (121).

INSPECTOR GENERAL'S DEPARTMENT
The Inspector General's Department was created on March 3, 1813 (122).

A yellow plume was worn on the hat in 1832, same as the Adjutant General's Department (123). They gained their own green plume in 1839 (124). The 1851 pompom was upper two-thirds scarlet and lower two-thirds buff. Otherwise plain, staff dark blue was used until 1918 (125), when white was added as a piping color. In 1936, the white piping color was swapped for the light blue of the Judge Advocate General's Department (126).

INTELLIGENCE AND SECURITY
The Intelligence and Security Branch was established on July 1, 1962, and was remanned Military Intelligence on July 1, 1967.

The colors were Oriental blue and silver gray (126a).

INTELLIGENCE POLICE CORP
The Intelligence Police Corp was created in the American Expediency Force on during World War I, and was folded in to the Military Intelligence Reserve Corps in 1920 (127).

Green and white were used as colors (128).

JUDGE ADVOCATE GENERAL'S CORP
The Judge Advocate General's Department became the Judge Advocate General's Corps on June 24, 1948 (129).

Dark blue and light blue was continued as the colors (130).

JUDGE ADVOCATE GENERAL'S DEPARTMENT
The Corps of Judge Advocate and the Bureau of Military Justice were merged into the Judge Advocate General's Department on July 5, 1884 (131). It became the Judge Advocate General's Corps on June 24, 1948 (132).

Plain staff dark blue was used until 1918, when the colors became dark blue and light blue (133). The light blue was traded to the Inspector General's Department in 1936 for white (134).

LOGISTICS
The Logistics branch was created on January 1, 2008 (135).

It's colors are soldier red and bronze (136).

MEDICAL DEPARTMENT
The Medical Department was created on March 3, 1813 (137). Enlisted Hospital stewards were authorized on August 16, 1856 (138), and a full enlisted establishment, known at the time as the Hospital Corps, was added on March 1, 1887 (139).

Black uniforms were prescribed for medical officers in 1813 and this became blue with black collars and cuffs from 1821 to 1851 (140). The upper third of the otherwise buff pompom of 1851 was emerald green, as was the sash, otherwise standard staff dark blue was used (141).

The Hospital Stewards had emerald green insignia, but the trimming on their uniforms was crimson and their hat cords were buff and green mixed (142).

In 1872 Hospital Steward uniforms were trimmed in emerald green, while medical officers used staff dark blue (143). White was added to the emerald green as a piping color in 1887 (144).

Maroon became the officer's facing color in 1902 (145), while enlisted men used maroon and white (146). Officers added the white piping color on October 14, 1921 (147).

MILITARY INTELLIGENCE
Security and Intelligence became Military Intelligence on July 1, 1967.

The oriental blue and silver gray was continued (148).

MILITARY INTELLIGENCE RESERVE CORPS
The World War I Corps of Interpreters and Intelligence Police moved on to become the Military Intelligence Reserve Corps in 1920 (149).

The colors were golden yellow and purple (150).

MILITARY POLICE

Military police units grew out of the World War I Provost Marshal's Department. They became the Military Police Corps on September 26, 1941 (151).

Yellow and green were the colors from 1922 until 1950 when they were reversed to green and yellow (152).

MILITARY SECRETARY'S OFFICE

The Adjutant General's Department was changed on April 28, 1904 to The Military Secretary's Department (153), and changed back on March 2, 1907 (154).

Staff dark blue was used.

MILITIA BUREAU

The Militia Bureau was created from an office in the War Department by the National Defense Act of 1916 (155). It became the National Guard Bureau in 1933 (156)

Dark blue was used as a facing color with a red piping color added in 1921 (157).

MOTOR TRANSPORT CORPS

The Motor Transport Corps existed in the American Expeditionary Force during World War I (157a).

The color was purple (157b)

MOUNTED RIFLES

A regiment of Mounted Riflemen was added to the army on May 19, 1846 (158). They were merged into the Calvary on August 3, 1861 (159).

In 1846, mounted riflemen were to wear the undress uniforms of dragoons, which had yellow trimmings, and trouser strips of black with yellow piping (160).

Green became the facing color in 1851 (161).

NATIONAL GUARD BUREAU

The Militia Bureau became the National Guard Bureau on June 15, 1933 (162).

The red piping was not carried over and dark blue has been used ever since (163).

ORDNANCE CORPS

The Ordnance Department became the Ordnance Corps on June 28, 1950 (164), and inherited the crimson and golden yellow colors (165).

ORDNANCE DEPARTMENT

The Ordnance Department was first created on May 14, 1812 (166) and merged into the artillery on March 2, 1821 (167). It returned on April 5, 1832 (168) and became the Ordnance Corps on June 28, 1950 (169).

The 1839 uniform regulations describe officers wearing the same coats as the artillery, without the red piping, a cocked hat with a red artillery plume and a dark blue trouser stripe. Ordnance Sergeants wore an artillery Sergeant Major's uniform with dark blue trouser stripes. Enlisted Men of Ordnance wore an artillery privates uniform with red epaulets (170).

In 1851, crimson was chosen for the upper third of officers pompoms, with the rest buff, and crimson was used on enlisted uniforms. Beyond the pompoms, officers wore staff dark blue (171).

New colors of black and scarlet were introduced in 1902, for both officers and enlisted men. This became crimson and golden yellow in 1921 (172).

PAY DEPARTMENT
As a department, the Pay Departments dates from July 6, 1812 (173). It was merged into the Quartermaster Corps on August 12, 1912 (174).

Staff dark blue was used thru out the department's history (175). The only exception was the 1851 pompoms that were dark olive and buff (176).

PROVOST MARSHAL
Green and white were worn by officers on provost marshal duty during World War I (177).

PSYCHOLOGICAL OPERATIONS
The Psychological Operations branch was born on October 16, 2006. However enlisted men had worn insignia of this branch since 1990.

The colors are bottle green and silver gray (178).

PUBLIC AFFAIRS
Public affairs enlisted men were given special insignia in 1989.

Unassigned to branch teal and yellow are used when colors are needed (179)

PURCHASING DEPARTMENT
The Purchasing Department was created on April 24, 1816 (180) and abolished on August 23, 1842 (181), therefore predating the use of facing colors.

QUARTERMASTER CORP
On August 12, 1912 the Subsistence, Quartermaster and Pay Departments were merged into the Quartermaster Corps (182).

The buff of the Quartermaster's Department was carried over (183). It was even used by generals on shoulder straps (184) and the cuffs of dress uniforms (185).

QUARTERMASTER'S DEPARTMENT
The Quartermaster's Department was created on March 28, 1812 (186). Enlisted men were first added in 1884 (187). On August 12, 1912, it was merged with the Subsistence and Pay Departments to form the Quartermaster Corps (188).

Light blue was used on the 1832 plumes(189) and the upper third of the 1851 pompoms (190). Except for the pompoms. staff dark blue was used by officers. Buff was chosen with enlisted men were added in 1884 (191).

RANGERS
In the modern context Rangers are infantry, the 75th Regiment to be precise. However in the past there were separate organizations of rangers. From January 2, 1812 (192) to March 3, 1815 (193) companies of rangers, separate from regiments were authorized. A Battalion of Mounted Rangers was created on June 15, 1832 (194) and was converted to the First Dragoons on March 2, 1833 (195).

All this predates the use of facing colors.

RECORD AND PENSION OFFICE

The Record and Pension office existed from May 9, 1892 (196) to April 28, 1904 when it was combined with the Military Secretary's Department and the name was changed back to Adjutant General's Department (197).

Staff dark blue was used.

REGIMENT OF VOLTIGEURS AND FOOT RIFLEMEN

The Regiment of Voltigeurs and Foot Riflemen was created on February 11, 1847 (198), and eliminated on July 19, 1849 (199), predating the use of facing colors.

RIFLEMEN

Riflemen existed from March 3, 1799 (200) to May 14, 1800 (201), April 12, 1808 (202) to March 2, 1821 (203) and from March 4, 1843 (204) until April 4, 1844 (205) the 2nd Dragoons was a rifle regiment.

All of this predates facing colors, but green uniforms faced with black was used by riflemen.

SEA FENCIBLES

Also predating facing colors were the Sea Fencibles that existed from July 26, 1813 (206) to February 27, 1815 (207).

SERVICE SCHOOL DETACHMENTS

On March 3, 1909 (208), Congress allowed enlisted men to be assigned to schools run by various branches. Green was used as a facing color for these men (209). Branch specific ranks such as Hospital Sergeants or Master Signal Electricians also existed in the schools for their branch. As a result green versions of those chevrons existed. The Detached Enlisted Men's List absorbed the service school detachments in 1920 (210).

SIGNAL CORP.

The Signal Corps was born on March 3, 1863 (211) and included both officer's and enlisted men. A law of July 28, 1866 (212) limited the permanent Signal Corps to one officer, but allowed six officers and 100 enlisted men to be detailed from the Corps of Engineers. A regular enlisted force was added on June 20, 1878 (213).

During the Civil War signal officers wore staff dark blue (214), while enlisted men used yellow (215). The 1872 uniform regulations call for enlisted men to wear cavalry uniforms with orange facings (216). This must refer to the men detailed from the engineers. Black with white piping was used from 1891, or there abouts, to 1902 (217). From that point on Orange and white were used by both officers and enlisted men (218).

SPECIAL FORCES

Special Forces became a branch of the army on April 9, 1987.

Jungle green is its color (219).

STAFF SPECIALIST

Officers who were unassigned to branch became Staff Specialists after World War II.

The green color from the service schools and the Detached Enlisted Men's List was inherited (220).

SUBSISTENCE DEPARTMENT

The Subsistence Department dates from April 14, 1818 (221). Enlisted men were added on March 3, 1873 (222). It was merged with the Quartermaster's Department and the Pay Department to form the Quartermaster Corps on August 12, 1912 (223).

From 1832 to 1851 plumes with the top half light blue and the bottom half white were worn (224). In 1851 staff dark blue was worn with the pompom light blue and buff (225). When enlisted men were added the facings were gray (226).

TANK DESTROYER FORCES
Tank Destroyer Forces existed during World War II.

The colors were golden orange and black (227).

TANK CORPS
A Tank Corps was part of the American Expeditionary Force during World War I, and a separate Tank Corps was in the "National Army' raised for the emergency. They were merged in August of 1919 and abolished on June 4, 1920 (228).

The color was gray (229).

TRANSPORTATION CORPS
The Transportation Corps was born on July 31, 1942.

Its colors are brick red and golden yellow (230)

UNASSIGNED TO BRANCH
The Detached Enlisted Men's List became Unassigned to Branch in 1953, then Branch Immaterial in 1976.

The colors were teal blue and yellow (231).

U.S. MILITARY ACADEMY STAFF
On June 20, 1890 (232), an artillery detachment assigned to the academy was transferred to the Quartermaster's Department. They did not wear buff facing until 1900 (233). In 1909 they became a Service School Detachment, wearing green and white in lieu of the green worn by other detachments (234).

By the early twentieth century, professors wore staff dark blue (235), but in 1936 (236) they were given scarlet and silver gray (237).

WARRANT OFFICERS
From 1938 (238) to 2004 (239) Warrant Officers wore brown facings. After 2004 they wore the facings of the branch they serve in.

WOMEN'S ARMY CORPS.
The Women's Army Corps was created on July 1, 1943 (240), and abolished on October 20, 1978 (241).

Moss green and old gold were the colors (241).

Cuff Insignia

Usually associated with the navy, cuff insignia has a long history in the army.

The 1832 uniform regulations used buttons on a cuff flap, and button holes outlined in lace, that varied by rank. Four for field grades officers and senior NCOs, three for Captains and Sergeants and two for Lieutenants and other enlisted men. The lace was button colored, silver for infantry officers, white for enlisted infantry, gold piped in scarlet for artillery officers and yellow piped in scarlet for enlisted artillery. The system was also used by the Ordnance Department, with officers wearing gold without the scarlet piping and enlisted men the same as the artillery (1). Generals had buff cuffs (2), while officers of staff departments, including medical, had plain blue (3).

The Corps of Topographical Engineers and their cuffs embroidered in gold oak leafs and acorns (4). The regular Corps of Engineers' cuff design is not clear.

When dragoons were added in 1833, officers had yellow cuffs with the flap over them. On the flap was gold buttons outlined in lace, just as the infantry and artillery. Enlisted dragoons had a simple pointed cuff in yellow. (5)

In 1839, generals were allowed to use blue cuffs with gold oak leaf and acorn embroidery as an option (6). Also in 1839, topographical engineers began wearing "galloons of gold lace". These were 1/2 inch wide gold stripes, running diagonally above the cuff, four for filed grade officers, three for Captains, two for First Lieutenants, one for Second Lieutenants and none for those who had just graduated from the academy (7).

Medical and Pay officers were given gold laurel branch and vine embroidery on the cuffs in 1840 or 1841 (8) (9).

At some point between 1839 (10), when the regulations stated "cuffs, according to design in Engineer department;", and 1847 (11), the Corps of Engineers gained black velvet cuffs, with a black flap and buttons according to rank. Instead of lace, gold palm and laurel embroidery was in front of each button (12). The new enlisted engineers had a black cuff and flap, with button holes outlined in yellow tape, three for sergeants and two for others (13).

All of this was eliminated by the new uniform regulations of 1851, but at the same time a new system to show rank was added to the cuffs of officer's overcoats. On each cuff of the dark blue overcoat was a knot formed from 1/8 inch black cord. Both of the cord ends were at, or near the end of the cuff and formed two horizontal loops and one vertical loop, leaving a squashed pyramid shape underneath. Second Lieutenant's coats were without cords and First Lieutenants used a single cord. From there more cords were added, following the same outline, making the overall knot, thicker and thicker. Captains used two cords, Majors three, Lieutenant Colonels four and Colonels five. Generals, regardless of rank, wore five cords in a large, elaborate double knot (14). This system was used, unchanged until 1902.

During the Civil War, officers were allowed to wear light blue enlisted overcoats in the field (15). An order, issued in 1864, stated that "no ornaments will be required on the overcoat..." (16), but officers may have worn badges of rank on a round, facing colored background, outlined in gold (17). Regulations after the war, continued to allow enlisted overcoats in the field with "insignia of rank on the sleeve" (18).

In 1902 the system was expanded to the full dress frock coat, evening tail coat and mess jacket. The new olive drab overcoats carried the same knots as in 1851, except the general's double knot was replaced with two strips of black braid. The lower one was 1 1/4 inches wide and 2 1/2 inches from the button of the sleeve. The upper was 1/2 inch wide and 1 1/2 inches above the lower one. Between them the appropriate number of stars were worn in bronze. Other officers added bronze branch insignia in the squashed pyramid area under the knot (19). On the dress coats and jackets, generals wore a cuff of blue-black velvet with a line of gold oak leaf embroidery about 1 inch from the top. Above the cuff the stars were worn in silver. Other officers wore a strip of 1/2 inch gold lace, 2 1/2 inches from the end of the sleeve and the 1851 style knots, made of gold cord, rising from there. Full color insignia of branch was worn in the squashed pyramid area (20).

There were several changes in 1912. On the overcoat, the branch insignia was removed and the general's stars were changed to silver (21). A white mess jacket was added using knots of white cord, sitting a a strip of white lace. Generals wore their stars above a four inch wide, plan white cuff (22).

Wear of the full dress frock coat, evening tail coat, and blue and white mess jackets was suspended in 1917 (23), leaving the only knots in use on the overcoat.

Second Lieutenants were given a single cord knot in brown in 1917 (24).

In January of 1920, Warrant Officers in the Mine Planter Service of the Coast Artillery were given brown sleeve stripes as insignia. Masters and Chief Engineers of mine planting boats wore four stripes, First Mates and Assistant

Engineers wore three and Second Mates wore two. Masters and Mates wore a brown fouled anchor embroidered on an olive drab disc, above the stripes, while engineers used a three bladed propellor (25).

In 1921 the white mess jacket and the 1902 dress white coat returned (26). Officer's white sleeve knots were as before. Warrant Officers of the Mine Planter's Service wore white stripes and white anchors or propellors on both. Other Warrant Officers wore four white stripes without a badge above (27). A large "eagle rising" insignia embroidered in yellow was added to the overcoat cuffs of Warrant Officers, and Field Clerks wore their badges of rank in the same manner (28).

After 75 years of use, sleeve knots were removed from overcoats in 1926. The generals stripes would continue as decoration, but the stars were moved to shoulder loops. It appears that mine planter stripes and the "eagle rising" insignia remained on the cuff, but this is not clear (29).

Gold sleeve knots returned with the full dress frock coat, evening tail coat, and blue mess jackets in 1929 (30).

In the mid 1930s rethought its dress uniforms, both blue and white. This culminated in Army Regulation 600-38, dated August 17, 1938 (31). The frock coat was discarded in favor of modern sack coats, in both blue and white, and rank was no longer shown on the sleeve. The tail coat and blue mess jacket continued to have the sleeve insignia as they had since 1902, except for the lace forming the base of the knots. It was now 3/4 inch wide with the top and bottom quarters in gold and the middle quarter in facing color. The same braid was used as decoration on the new blue dress coats. The white mess jacket was not changed. Warrant officers were not allowed the tail coat or the blue mess jacket. The cuffs of their blue dress coats were plain, the white dress coat used the same 1/2 inch white braid used by all other ranks and the white mess jacket was "To be without knot or braid. Warrant officers' insignia to be worn on the sleeve, 4 inches from the edge of the sleeve."

These uniforms were suspended for World War II. When the evening/mess uniforms returned in 1948 the sleeve knots on the evening tail coat only were changed to a single cord knot made of 1/4 inch gold lace, sitting on a thick piece of lace, only the width of the knot (actually slightly narrower). Warrant Officers had a 1/4 inch base with two gaps in it. Badges of rank were worn inside the "squashed pyramid" area. The blue and white mess jackets continued as they had been with Warrant Officers wearing their badge of rank alone on the cuff. General's traditional cuffs were restored to the tail coat in 1950 (32).

In 1952, female officers were given a midnight blue evening dress uniform that carried the sleeve knots from the male tail coats. This uniform was eliminated in 1969 (33).

In 1975 the tail coat was eliminated and the knots on both mess jackets was simplified. On the blue jacket, a single strand of 1/4 inch lace formed the knot in the basic 1851 shape, resting on the gold, facing color, gold lace, with badges of rank worn in the "squashed pyramid" area. Warrant officer used the same knots as other officers. The white jacket was the same with white lace on a base of white lace (34). Jackets with the old design could be worn until they wore out. By the 2002 uniform regulations this was clarified, stating that the jacket must have been purchased before August 11, 1975 (35).

Female officers began wearing the sleeve knots in 1986 (36).

Shoulder Knots

In 1860 (1), gold knots were prescribed, instead of shoulder straps, on the shoulders of a jacket worn by officers of the light artillery. They were formed from four cords for field grade officers and three cords for company grade. The outer end terminated in three loops and scarlet cloth showed thru the holes of each turn. Silver badges of rank were worn over the three loops, with Majors and Second Lieutenants using plain knots (2). It is not clear if these knots continued after the Civil War, but they did not continue after the 1872 uniform change.

The History of American Ranks and Rank Insignia

In 1872 shoulder knots replaced epaulets for all but generals. They were made of two gold cords, loosely woven and showing facing colored cloth in the gaps. They terminated in a large, oval pad of facing color cloth surrounded by three lines of gold cord (3). In the center of the pad, line officers wore, in silver, a regimental number and staff officers wore old english letters, SS for the signal officer, PD for the Pay Department, OD for the Ordnance Department even though they had worn a bursting bomb on epaulets, MD for the Medical Department, AD for the Adjutant General's Department, QD for the Quartermaster's Department, SD for the Subsistence Department, JA for Judge Advocates, ID for the Inspector General's Department and EC for the Corps. of Engineers who had worn a castle on epaulets (5). Badges of rank, including a gold leaf for Majors, were worn on either side of the number or letters, except for Colonels, whose eagle was below (6).

The engineers and the Ordinance Department were not happy about giving up their insignia, so the castle (7) and the bomb (8) were restored almost immediately. At the same time, the Adjutant General's Department adopted a shield (9), meaning that the letters OD, EC and AD were probably never worn. It is also possible that the signal officer wore an insignia other than the SS letters (10). The rest of the staff departments replaced the letters with insignia in 1890 (11).

In 1873, Colonels in the Adjutant General's Department moved the shield to the knot (12). This was followed by other departments when granted insignia.

These knots were abolished in 1902 (13), and replaced on full dress frock coats and various evening wear, by plain, tightly woven gold knots that purely decorative. Badges of rank were added in 1912 (14).

With the exception of a 1917 to 1921 suspension for World War I, the knots with badges of rank were used until 1938 (15). There was a plan in the mid 1930s to continue the knots on the new dress coats, making them "full dress" (16), but in the end shoulder straps were used.

After 1938, plain knots were used on evening wear, and with the exception of World War II, have been ever since.

Shoulder Boards

Shoulder boards are a removable, stiff, shoulder decoration, usually rectangular with a point towards the collar. They have been used by the navy since 1899, but they do have a history in the army.

It appears that a version of shoulder boards were considered, in 1937, as a replacement for shoulder straps, but nothing came of it (1).

From 1969 (2) to 2003 (3) female officers, other than generals who wore the male generals cuffs, wore shoulder boards on black and white mess jackets. They were 4 11/16 inches long and 2 inches wide, covered in facing color. Two, 3/8 inch gold stripes ran long ways down the board 1/16 inches from each edge. A line of piping color was run inside each gold stripe if needed. Badges of rank were embroidered 5/8 inches from the end of the board (4).

Shoulder Marks

Shoulder marks, also known as soft shoulder boards, are a relatively new concept. They consist of a cloth tube that can be pulled over the shoulder loops of a shirt or sweater. The idea is an insignia that can be easily removed without having to worry about placement and doesn't create bulk if worn under a uniform coat. This allowed a class "A" (coat and tie) uniform to be converted to a class "B" (shirtsleeve) uniform but simply removing the coat.

Officers were prescribed shoulder marks in 1980 (1). They were dark green with a gold stripe near the outer end and badges of rank embroidered above the stripe.

In 1981 enlisted personnel, Corporal and above, were authorized shoulder marks made of black with gold chevrons (2).

Officers green marks were changed to black in 1991 (3).

Chapter 3.
Army Ranks

Acting Hospital Steward

In 1887 congress created a Hospital Corps that was an enlisted component of the Medical Department(1). This act created the rank of Acting Hospital Steward in order to be promoted to Hospital Steward at east a year had to be spent as Acting Hospital Steward (2).

Acting Hospital Stewards were given three chevrons of green cloth with black stitching, with a red cross inside the chevrons. Dress chevrons were of gold lace on a green background but the cross was still red. The dress chevrons were used until the Hospital Corps stopped wearing dress uniforms in 1896(3). In addition to the chevrons Acting Hospital Stewards wore a red cross on the collars of their dress uniforms until 1896 (4).

In 1901 the chevrons were changed to green with white stitching with a green maltese cross outlined in white (5).

The 1902 uniform change brought three now point up maroon chevrons outlined in white with a maroon caduceus also outlined in white (6).

On March 2, 1903 congress changed Acting Hospital Stewards to Sergeants of the Hospital Corps(7).

Additional Second Lieutenant

An Additional Second Lieutenant is a Second Lieutenant serving over and above the authorized strength.

The rank was used in the Artillery and Cavalry from 1878 to 1879 and the Artillery, Cavalry and Infantry from 1897 to 1898. It was also used in the Corps of Engineers in 1872, 1882 and from 1891 to 1898.

They wore the same insignia as other Second Lieutenants.

Apothecary

Apothecary is an old term for pharmacist. The Continental Army used the title, John Cutting, Andrew Craigie and John Crane were listed (1).

Apothecary General

The Title Apothecary General was used by the Continental Army. Josiah Root and a Doctor Giles are listed (1).

The next use of the title was in legislation on March 2, 1799 in a law creating an army medical establishment in preparations for war with France. It stated "An apothecary-general, and one or more deputies, who shall be charged with the safekeeping and delivery of all medicines, instruments, dressings and other articles for the use of the hospital and army."(2) The war never came and the position was never filled.

The title was revived when the army was expanded for the War of 1812. On March 3, 1813 Congress created an Apothecary General (3), and Francis Le Barron was appointed to the post.

1813 regulations for General Staff uniforms prescribe black coats with black covered buttons and a gold star on the collar for all medical officers. How long this uniform lasted is not known(4).

Le Barron served as Apothecary General until June 1,1821 the post having been abolished with an act reorganizing the army on March 2nd of that year (5).

Armorer

An Armorer is a repairer of weapons. The Continental Dragoons used the rank of Armorer in 1777. They appear to have been eliminated in a reorganization in 1778(1).

Artificer

The rank of Artificer is one of the oldest in the army. Because it had no insignia until 1899 it is not remembered very well.

The rank started as an artillery equivalent of an armorer, a repairer of cannons. The Continental Army had whole artillery artificer regiments. The rank was used by the artillery from 1792 until 1907, the Corps of Engineers from 1808 to 1820 and from 1861 to 1863, and the Infantry form 1866 to 1916. Some Artificers were assigned to the Army Service School Detachment from 1909 to 1916.

The National Defense Act of 1916 changed the title to Mechanic(1).

Artificers wore privates uniforms with no rank insignia until 1899 when the army authorized them to wear crossed hammers (2).

Assistant Apothecary (General)

William Johnnot is listed as an Assistant Apothecary General in the Continental Army (1).

On March 30, 1813 congress allowed the president to appoint as many Assistant Apothecaries as necessary (2). Six were appointed Christopher Backus, Richard Brownell, Thomas Cave, James Catbush, David Low and Joseph West. Five other officers were names Acting Apothecary (3). By the following year only Backus and Catbush remained. Backus resigned on November 15, 1819 and Catbush was promoted to Post Surgeon on May 16, 1820. They were replaced by Charles Foster and Robert MaCalla who served until June 1, 1821. The rank was eliminated by the act of March 2, 1821.

Assistant Apothecaries wore the general staff medical uniform in 1814, after that is unclear.

The title Assistant Apothecary General seems to have been used interchangeably even though the legal title was Assistant Apothecary.

Assistant Band Leader

The rank of Assistant Band Leader was created by the national defense act of 1916, replacing Principal Musicians, In the infantry, cavalry, artillery and corps of engineers(1). Three chevrons over a bugle was the insignia until December of 1917 when three chevrons and two arcs with a lyre in the middle was ordered, this had been the chevrons of the assistant leader of the west point band since 1904 (2). This lasted until May of 1918 when the insignia became a lyre in a wreath.

When the enlisted ranks were reorganized on July 1, 1920 the west point assistant became a Master Sergeant and the others Staff Sergeants (3).

Assistant Commissary (of Issues) (Purchases)

Both Assistant Commissaries of Issues and Purchases existed in the Continental Army.

After 1813 the titles of Assistant Commissary, Assistant Commissary of Issues and Assistant Commissary of Purchases appear to be the same position.

On March 3, 1813 a congress created the title of Assistant Commissary with six officers assigned(1) Mattew Irwin, Maurice Prevost, Robert Irvine, George Wadsworth, James Heron and Robinson Moore (2). Irwin and Wadsworth were discharged on June 15, 1815. The army register for January 1, 1816 shows their positions filled by Edwin Starke and William Carson (3), Starke is listed in the army register as a Storekeeper and Carson is not listed at all(4). An act of April 24, 1816 allowed six Assistant Commissaries of Issue in the Purchasing Department (5). The register for august 1816 shows Carson replaced with an Eli Clemson(6). Not listed is Jonas Simonds who served from March 29th to July 14th. Clemson resigned on December 1, 1819 and was replaced by Peter Fayssoux.

The act of March 2, 1821 allowed 50 Assistant Commissary of Subsistence but these were to be taken from the subalterns of line regiments (7).

Fayssoux was made a Storekeeper in the Quartermaster's Dept. on May 17th. All the others, including Edwin Starke were discharged on June 1st.

The army register lists only Clemson and Fayssoux as Assistant Commissaries of Issues, the others except for Starke are listed as Assistant Commissaries of Purchases(8)

Assistant Commissaries would have worn the 1813 general staff uniform, a single breasted coat with ten buttons with holes worked in blue twist and a standing collar with a button and blue twist hole. (9)

Assistant Deputy Apothecary

John Carne was the Assistant Deputy Apothecary of the Southern Department from September 20, 1781 until the end of the revolution (1).

Assistant Deputy Director of Hospitals

Jonathan Arnold is listed as Assistant Deputy Director of Hospitals in the eastern Department from January 7, 1777 to May 9, 1777 (1).

Assistant Deputy Paymaster General

The Position of Assistant Deputy Paymaster General was created by congress on July 6, 1812(1), to be filled by officers taken from line regiments. It was not until May 17, 1815 that it was decided that two of these officers, Captain Ambrose Whitlock of the first infantry and First Lieutenant Joseph Bell of the second Infantry, were to be provisionally retained as a permanent staff officers(2). The Position was eliminated on April 24, 1816.

Calling this a rank is generous, Whitlock and Bell probably thought of themselves as holding the ranks of Captain and Lieutenant respectively.

Assistant Director of Hospitals
Daniel Whiple is listed as Assistant Director of Hospitals in 1777 (1).

Assistant District Paymaster

Congress created Assistant District Paymasters on April 18, 1814 (1). They were to have the pay and emoluments of a Captain.

All were discharged on June 15, 1815 at the end of the war of 1812 (2).

Assistant Engineer

The national defense act of 1916 created the rank of Assistant Engineer in the Coast Artillery Corps(1). The insignia was a mechanical governor in a wreath (2).

When the enlisted ranks were reorganized on July 1, 1920 Assistant Engineers became Technical Sergeants (3).

Assistant Medical Purveyor

Congress reorganized the Medical Department on July 28, 1866. Four Assistant Medical Purveyors were to have the equivalent rank of Lieutenant Colonel(1).

Appointments dated July 28, 1866 were Eugene Abadie, Charles McDougall, Robert Murray and Charles Sutherland. Abadie left on March 4, 1867 and was Replaced by Jedadiah Baxter. McDougall retired in 1869 and was not immediately replaced. Baxter was promoted in 1872 leaving only two Assistant Medical Purveyors both of whom were promoted in 1876. To replace them Charles Laub and Charles McCormick were appointed on June 26, 1876. Laub died on December 2nd and was replaced with George Cooper. Ebenezer Swift was appointed on December 31, 1876 and McCormick died on April 28, 1877. Cooper died on April 13, 1881 and was replaced by Thomas McParlin. Swift retired on October 8, 1883 and was replaced by John Moore. McParlin was promoted on September 16, 1885 and was replaced by Bernard Irwin. Moore was made Surgeon General on November 18, 1886 and Joseph Baily became an Assistant Medical Purveyor. Irwin was promoted on August 28, 1890 and along came Blencowe Fryer who retired on February 24, 1891 and was replaced with Charles Greenleaf. Baliy (we are almost to the end of this) was promoted on March 9, 1892 and was replaced with William Wolverton (2).

On July 27, 1892 congress made all equivalent Lieutenant Colonels of the Medical Department into Assistant Surgeon Generals (3).

Assistant Medical Purveyors wore standard staff Lieutenant Colonel's shoulder straps, dark blue background, silver oak leaf at each end.

From 1866 to 1872, epaulets with 1/2 inch wide bullion, a silver oak leaf on the strap and the silver letters M.S. in a gold wreath in the frog were worn. These were replaced in 1872 with shoulder knots with a dark blue background and silver oak leafs on the pad with the letters M.D. between them (4).

Assistant Purveyor

There is an Issac Ledyard listed as an Assistant Purveyor in 1780 (1).

Assistant Steward, Mine Planter Service

Upon the creation of the Mine Planter Service on July 9, 1918, each mine planter was to have one Assistant Steward (1).

Insignia of a red crescent on a blue background was prescribed in January of 1919 (2).

The enlisted grade reorganization of July 1920 made Assistant Stewards into Specialists Fifth Class (3)

Assistant Surgeon

The rank of Assistant Surgeon was created on March 2, 1821 from the ranks of Post Surgeon and Regimental Surgeon's Mate (1), 45 were authorized(2).

On June 28, 1832 congress passed a law authorizing 10 more. Here is the full text of the bill:

An Act to increase the number of surgeons and assistant surgeons in the army of the United States.

Be it enacted by the Senate and House of Representatives of the United States of America, in Congress assembled, That the President be, and he is hereby, authorized, by and with the advice and consent of the Senate, to appoint four additional surgeons and ten additional surgeon's mates, in the army of the United States.
APPROVED, June 28, 1832.(3)

The heading refers to Assistant Surgeons but the text calls them Surgeon's Mates, the army register continued to use Assistant Surgeon(4).

On June 30, 1834 congress gave medical officers equivalent rank (5). Assistant Surgeons over five years service would have "the pay and emoluments" of a Captain and under five years as a First Lieutenant.

When the army was increased for the Mexican war an Assistant Surgeon was added to each dragoon and infantry regiment (5). For the first time since 1821 these officers were listed as part of line branches and not the Medical Department. This only lasted until the end of the war. The same law finally gave medical officers official rank. It stated "the rank of the officers of the Medical Department of the Army shall be arranged upon the same basis which at present determines the amount of their pay and emoluments:".

At the end of the civil war, a bill was passed on July 28, 1866 to set the army's post war size (6). This bill required only three years service for Assistant Surgeons to be promoted to Captain. This was moved back to five years by an act of February 2, 1901 (7).

On April 23, 1908 the concept of separate rank titles for medical officers was abolished(8).
Assistant Surgeons over three years service became Captains and under became First Lieutenants.

The 1821 uniform regulations call for medical officers to were a blue coat with black collar and cuffs.

In 1832 Assistant Surgeons were distinguished by having no ornament on the black collar (9).

Gold epaulets were allowed in 1840 (10) with the silver letters M.S. in a gold wreath within the frog and 1/4 inch wide bullion for those equivalent of captains and 1/8 inch wide for those equivalent of lieutenants. Gold edged shoulder straps were worn, with gold bars, one for equivalent lieutenants and two for captains, at each end.

The 1851 uniform regulations added silver bars to the epaulet straps. The shoulder straps would be the standard staff straps with dark blue backgrounds. One or two black cords made the sleeve knots worn on the overcoats.

When shoulder knots replaced epaulets in 1872 the background was still dark blue with the bars in silver on both the knot pads and the shoulder straps. The knot pads carried the letters M.D. between the bars until 1890, a gold shield until 1896 and a gold Maltese cross until they were abolished in 1902 (11).

The appropriate number of silver bars was worn on the dark blue shoulder loops of the 1898 khaki coat.

In 1902 shoulder strap backgrounds became maroon and gold corded sleeve knots were used on the full dress coat with a caduceus underneath. A bronze caduceus was also worn under the knots on the overcoat.

Assistant Surgeon General

The History of American Ranks and Rank Insignia

On April 14, 1818 Congress created the position of Assistant Surgeon General (1). Two were authorized, James Bronaugh and Tobias Watkins (2). The rank was abolished on March 2, 1821(3) and they were both discharged on June 1st.

They may have worn the black general staff medical uniform (3).

An act of April 16, 1862 called for one Assistant Surgeon General with the equivalent rank of colonel (4) and Robert Wood was appointed.

Wood was demoted to Surgeon on October 31, 1865 and replaced with Charles Crane on July 28, 1866. Crane was made Surgeon General on July 3, 1882 and the position remained vacant until July 2, 1884 when Glover Perin was appointed. Perin Retired on November 17, 1887 and was replaced with Charles Page (5).

On July 27, 1892 a new law gave all of the equivalent Colonels in the Medical Department the title of Assistant Surgeon General (6). They officially became Colonels on April 23, 1908 (7).

From 1862 to 1902 they wore the standard staff colonels shoulder straps with a silver eagle on a dark blue background. In 1902 the background became maroon.

The epaulets would have had a silver eagle on the strap and the Silver letter M.S. in a gold wreath in the frog and 1/2 inch wide bullion. These would be replaced in 1872 with shoulder knots with a dark blue background and a silver eagle at the bottom of the pad and the letters M.D. above them. The letters were replaced with a gold shield in 1890 and the shield with a gold maltese cross in 1896. The cross moved from the pad to the knot in 1899 (8).

The silver eagle was worn long ways in the center of the dark blue shoulder loops of the 1898 khaki coat (9).

Five black loop sleeve knots were worn on the overcoat form 1862 to 1908 with a bronze caduceus after 1902, and in gold with a gold caduceus form 1902 to 1908.

Aviator

The national defense act of 1916 allowed qualified pilots to be enlisted as aviators in the Signal Corps, they were to have rank equal to a Master Signal Electrician (1).

The proscribed insignia was white wings with crossed propellers between them on a blue background (2).

The rank is in the pay table in the army register of 1920 page 1104, but is not on the register of 1921 page 1404.
Band Corporal

Band Corporals were added to the infantry, cavalry coast and field artillery and the corps of engineers (1).

They initially wore two chevrons (2). A lyre was added under the chevrons in December of 1917 (3).

Band Corporals were made regular Corporals in the reorganization of July 1, 1920 (4).

Band Leader

Band Leader was another creation of the national defense act of 1916. Assigned to the infantry, cavalry coast and field artillery and the corps of engineers (1).

Band Leaders were given the three chevrons and two arcs with a bugle between that had been used by Chief Musicians (2). This was changed in December of 1917 to three chevrons and three arcs with a lyre between (3). This only lasted until May of 1918 when it was changed to a lyre in a wreath under a star (4).

Band Leaders were made Warrant Officers by act of June 4, 1920 (5).
Band Sergeant

Band Sergeants were also added to the infantry, cavalry coast and field artillery and the corps of engineers (1).

They initially wore three chevrons (2). A lyre was added under the chevrons in December of 1917 (3).

Band Sergeants were made regular Sergeants in the reorganization of July 1, 1920 (4).

Battalion Commissary Sergeant

Congress expanded the army for the army for the civil war on July 29, 1861 (1). The new regiments of infantry and cavalry added to the army were divided into battalions with an extensive headquarters staff including a Commissary Sergeant.

The cavalry was reorganized by an act of July 17, 1862 (2) and battalions were eliminated.

When congress set the peacetime size of the army on July 28, 1866 (3), Battalion Commissary Sergeants were not included.

No insignia was ever prescribed, but the use of the term sergeant would make three chevrons a possibility.

Battalion Hospital Steward

Hospital Stewards were added to the infantry and cavalry at the battalion level on July 29, 1861 (1).

Battalions, and their Hospital Stewards with them disappeared in the cavalry on July 17.1862 (2) and the infantry on July 28, 1866 (3).

Battalion Quartermaster Sergeant

Quartermaster Sergeants were also added to battalions of the infantry and cavalry on July 29, 1861 (1).

Cavalry battalions were eliminated on July 17, 1862 (2) and infantry battalions on July 28, 1866 (3).

The same legislation created a battalion of engineers which included a Quartermaster Sergeant.

The Artillery reorganization of January 25,1907(4) added Quartermaster Sergeants to battalions of field artillery.

They all continued until the act of 1916 changed the title to Battalion Supply Sergeant (5).

The infantry and cavalry Battalion Quartermaster Sergeants during the civil war may have worn the three chevrons and three bars of other Quartermaster Sergeants.

The engineer Quartermaster Sergeants wore the three chevrons and three bars from 1866 to 1901 when it was changed to three chevrons and two bars (6). The artillery also used three chevrons and two bars after 1907.

Battalion Saddler Sergeant

Battalion Saddler Sergeants existed in cavalry battalions from July 29, 1861(1) to July 17, 1862 (2).

They may have worn three chevrons.

Battalion Sergeant Major

A Battalion Sergeant Major is the senior noncommissioned officer in a battalion. They were first used in the battalions created during the civil war. In the infantry from July 29, 1861(1) to July 28, 1866 (2) and the cavalry from July 29, 1861 to July 17, 1862 (3).

They may have worn the same three chevrons and three arcs as other Sergeant Majors.

After the civil war only the Corps of Engineers had a battalion(4) and its Sergeant Major wore the same three chevrons and three arcs (5).

Battalions were added to the infantry on April 26, 1898 (6), but he law didn't provide for a battalion organization until March 2, 1899 (6a) and three chevrons and two arcs were prescribed for all Battalions Sergeant Majors(7).

Battalions and therefore Battalions Sergeant Majors, were added to the field artillery on January 25, 1907 (8).

They were abolished with the reorganization of July 1, 1920 (9) and became Staff Sergeants.

Battalion Supply Sergeant

The National Defense act of 1916 (1) changed the title of Battalion Quartermaster Sergeant to Battalion Supply Sergeant. Used only in the Corps of Engineers, they continued to wear three chevrons and two bar (2).

They were made Staff Sergeants on July 1, 1920 (3).

Battalion Veterinary Sergeant

Battalion Veterinary Sergeants existed in cavalry battalions from July 29, 1861(1) to July 17, 1862 (2).

They may have worn three chevrons.

Battery Quartermaster Sergeant

Artillery Batteries were given Quartermaster Sergeants on April 26, 1898 (1). They wore three chevrons and one bar (2).

They Continued until 1916 when the title was changed to Battery Supply Sergeant (3).

Battery Supply Sergeant

In 1916 Quartermaster Sergeants became Supply Sergeants(1).

They initially continued to wear the three chevrons and one bar, but a few months later they were ordered to wear the three chevrons of a regular Sergeant (2). The Three chevron and one bar insignia continued to be manufactured and it is possible this order was ignored (3).

The one bar insignia officially returned in May of 1918 (4).

The Reorganization of July 1, 1920 made them regular sergeants with three chevrons (5).

Blacksmith

When the army was expanded for the possible war with France on March 3, 1799, regiments of Dragoons were added that Included Blacksmiths (1).

On May 14, 1800, a law was passed to discharge most of the force setup in 1799. It stated "Provided always, that nothing in this act contained shall be construed to authorize any reduction of the first four regiments of infantry, the two regiments of artillerists and engineers, the two troops of light dragoons, or of the general and other staff, authorized by the several laws for the establishing and organizing of the aforesaid corps" (2). This would seem to indicate that the organization of the two troops of dragoons retained would continue unchanged including Blacksmiths. However they are not listed on the table of organization in the army register relative to that law (3).

The next act organizing the army on April 12, 1808 (4) did not include Blacksmiths.

Blacksmiths returned with the act of June 26, 1812 (5).

On March 3, 1815 congress set the peace establishment of the army that abolished all mounted troops (6), and Blacksmiths with them.

Blacksmiths wore privates uniforms with no insignia.

Boatswain

On July 26, 1813 congress created a Corps of Sea Fencibles as a defense for ports and harbors (1). Boatswain is a naval title for someone in charge of lines, cables, boats. Ect. Each fenicible company was allowed one Boatswain, probably to operate barges and such.

The law creating the fencibles was repealed on February 27, 1815 (2).

A plate from The Company of Military Historians (3) shows an officer in an infantry uniform leading men in sailor type dress.

Bombardier

Bombardier was an artillery rank. It is listed in a law setting the pay of the army form July 29, 1775 (1). It is mentioned by the Continental Congress a late a February of 1780 (2).

One company of artillery commanded by John Doughty, was retained after the end of the revolution, and was briefly the entire United States Army. It may have continued the title of Bombardier.

On April 12, 1785 the Congress set the pay of the army (3) and Bombardiers were not listed.

As of March 1779 Bombardiers were to wear epaulets. Where and how many is not known (4).

Brevet Second Lieutenant

A Brevet Second Lieutenant is a Second Lieutenant serving over and above the authorized strength.

The rank was used in the Artillery in 1863 and the Corps of Engineers, Corps of Topographical Engineers and Regiment of Mounted Rifles from 1855 to 1860. It. Returned in the Corps of Engineers From 1870 to 1871.

They wore the same insignia as other Second Lieutenants.

The History of American Ranks and Rank Insignia

Brigadier General

The term Brigadier General comes from the commander of a brigade hence brigadier.

Brigadier Generals existed in the american army from the beginning.

On July 14, 1775 George Washington ordered Brigadier Generals to wear a pink ribbon across the breast between the coat and waistcoat (1).

This lasted until June 18, 1780 when they were ordered to wear a gold epaulette with one silver star on both shoulders (2).

After the end of the revolution the tiny U.S. Army had no need of generals. On July 31, 1787 the army's senior officer, Lieutenant Colonel Josiah Harmar, was given a brevet to Brigadier General (3). Congress was concerned that Harmar needed sufficient authority when his regulars were combined with state militia troops. A brevet is a temporary promotion granting an officer higher rank but not the pay that goes with it. Brevets were common in the early years of the army to reward officers for service without having to pay them for an actual promotion. In this case however congress was more concerned about creating a vacancy in Harmar's position as Lieutenant Colonel Commandant of the First American Regiment (4). It is not know if Harmar wore stars on his epaulettes. Harmar retired on January 1, 1792.

On March 3, 1791 congress authorized the president to appoint a Brigadier General if thought one was necessary (5). James WIlkinson was made Brigadier General and senior officer in the army on March 5th.

Another law was passed on March 28, 1792 allowing the president to appoint four Brigadier Generals if he thought they were needed (6). This lead to the appointment of John Brooks on April 11th and Rufus Putnam on May 4th. Putnam resigned on February 14, 1793 and was replaced with Thomas Posey. Posey resigned on February 28, 1794 and was not replaced. Brooks was discharged on November 1, 1796 leaving Wilkinson as the only Brigadier General.

With war with France Looming, congress on July 16, 1798 (7) added three Brigadier Generals in addition to the four slots already allowed, three of which were vacant. This lead to the appointment on July 19th of William Washington, Ebenezer Huntlngton, Anthony White, William Davie, John Sevier and William North who would serve as Adjutant General (8).

The threat of war passed, and on May 14, 1800 (9) Congress called for officers to be discharged. Washington, Huntington, White, Davie, Sevier and North were all discharged on June 15th. Wilkinson resumed his position as the Army's only General.

On April 12, 1808 two more Brigadier Generals were authorized (10). Peter Gansevoort and Wade Hampton took office on February 14, 1809.

Expansion of the army for the War of 1812 Brought as many as 18 Brigadier Generals in the regular establishment. Many officers were also given brevets during the war, this can complicate tracing the history of officers holding a certain rank.

On March 3, 1815 congress set the army's peacetime size (11). Four Brigadier Generals were allowed, Alexander Macomb, Edmond Gaines, Eleazer Ripley and Winfield Scott. Also holding the rank of Brigadier General was the Adjutant and Inspector Daniel Parker and the Quartermaster General Robert Swartwount. Swartwount left the army on June 5, 1815.

The office of Quartermaster General was split between two Colonels on April 24, 1816 (12), and consolidated back into one Brigadier General on April 14, 1818 (13). Thomas Jesup was appointed on May 8th.

Ripley Resigned on February 1. 1820 and was replaced with Henry Atkinson.

On March 2, 1821 Congress Reduced the army to two Brigadier Generals plus the Quartermaster General (14). The office of Adjutant and Inspector was abolished and Parker was made Paymaster General an office that did not carry a rank. The new position of Adjutant General with the rank of Colonel was given to Atkinson. Macomb was made Chief Engineer with rank of Colonel. Scott and Gains were retained as was Jesup (15).

In 1829 the army added a frock coat for use by officers in the field (16). Rank was originally shown by collar eagles (17) then later by shoulder straps made from a strip of lace (18). Both of these systems showed which side the epaulets would be worn on the dress coat. This system didn't quite fit generals whose rank was shown by stars on the epaulets. It is possible that generals wore their epaulets on the frock coats or even didn't wear the frock coats at all.

The 1832 uniform regulations continued the silver star on the epaulets. Regulations didn't specify a size of generals bullion until 1851 when 1/2 inch was required, but epaulets form the 1832 to 1851 era appear to have used that size (18a).

A system of rectangular shoulder straps with badges of rank in them was created about 1834 (19). The exact date of the creation of this system is not known and the early straps for Brigadier Generals are particularly problematic. There is a portrait of Colonel Henry Leavenworth who held a brevet to Brigadier General, showing him wearing shoulder straps with a star in the middle and silver oak leafs at each end (20). The uniform Leavenworth was wearing in the portrait still exists and still has the odd shoulder straps on it. There is also a set of drawings that are an attachment to a general order creating shoulder straps in the Marine Corps. The Drawing shows shoulder straps for the army's not the marine's rank structure and Leavenworth's odd shoulder straps are shown (21). The first army documentation of shoulder straps came in the General Regulations for the Army for 1835 which does not list insignia for Brigadier Generals at all (22). This may be because Scott, Gaines and Jesup all held brevets as Major Generals and were wearing two stars at the time. Regulations of 1836 did show insignia for Brigadier Generals including shoulder straps with a 1/4 inch border, one star in the center and no oak leafs (23). The border on the general's straps, including Leavenworth's, were cut in an arc around the star.

Winfield Scott was promoted on June 25, 1841 and his place was taken by John Wool (24).

With the coming of the war with Mexico congress, on June 18, 1846 (25), added two more Brigadier Generals, David Twiggs and Stephen Kearny were appointed on June 30th (26). On June 26th congress ordered the volunteers called up for the war organized into divisions and brigades and allowed the appointment of however many generals that were needed to command them (27).

On March 3, 1847 congress added three more regular Brigadier Generals (28), future president Franklin Pierce, George Cadwalader and Enos Hopping although Hopping and Cadwalader are listed in the register as being Brigadier Generals of Volunteers (29). Hopping died on September 1, 1847.

At the end of the war the number of Brigadier Generals was reduced to two plus Thomas Jesup the Quartermaster General (30). Pierce resigned on March 2, 1848 Cadawalder was discharged on July 20th and Kearny died on October 31st, Leaving Twiggs and Wool.

The 1851 uniform regulations didn't change the insignia for Brigadier Generals very much. The epaulets still had 1/2 inch wide bullion and a silver star centered on the strap between the button and the top of the crescent. The shoulder straps had a gold 1/4 inch wide border, a dark blue background and a silver star in the center. The border was no longer cut around the star, it was sized to fit inside the strap. Sleeve knots made of 1/8 inch black silk braid were added overcoats, all generals regardless of rank wore five braids in an elaborate double knot (31).

An act of March 3, 1855 added a third Brigadier General (32). Persifor Smith was appointed to fill the slot on December 30, 1856 and held it until he died on May 17, 1858. He was Replaced with William Harney. Jesup died on June 10, 1860 and was replaced as Quartermaster General by Joseph Johnston (32).

During the civil war officers were allowed to wear the badges from the shoulder straps directly on the shoulder to make them less of at target for snipers. They were also allowed to wear enlisted overcoats with a round gold edged device with the badge of rank inside, on the sleeve (33).

After the civil war congress allowed 10 regular Brigadier Generals plus the heads of most of the staff departments making 19 in all as of 1866(34).

As the staff departments gained insignia of their own, these badges found their way on to the chiefs epaulets. In 1895 badges were added to the epaulets of the heads of the Quartermaster's Department and the Subsistence Department, the Pay Department in 1896, the Corps of Engineers, the Judge Advocate General's Department, the Ordnance Department and the Records and Pensions Office in 1899 and the Signal Corps in 1900 (35).

In 1898 the army added a khaki field uniform. Rank was shown on shoulder loops with a Brigadier General wearing a silver star in the center of the dark blue loop (36).

In July of 1898 officers were allowed to wear badges of rank on shirt collars (37). Also in 1901 badges of rank were worn on the shoulder loops of the white coat (37a).

In 1902 the army did a complete overhaul of its uniforms. The various uniforms had different ways of distinguishing rank. on the full dress, evening and mess coats rank was shown on the sleeve, a four inch wide blue-black velvet cuff was worn with a band of gold oak leaf and acorn embroidery and inch from the top above all this the silver star was worn, Brigadier Generals from staff departments wore the department's insignia between the cuff and the star. Epaulets were now decorative only they carried an american eagle in the frog but no badge of rank. On the dress coat shoulder straps were worn in the same pattern they had been since 1851. On the white coat and the olive drab and khaki service coats badges of rank were worn on the shoulder loops, in the case of Brigadier Generals the silver star was worn in the center of the loop. Badges of rank were still allowed on shirt collars. On the overcoat a band of black mohair braid and inch and a quarter wide was placed two and a half inches above the end of the now olive drab sleeve, the star this time in bronze was placed a quarter of an inch above that and a second band of braid an inch wide was placed a quarter of an inch above that (38).

1912 brought the return of the star to the epaulets (39). Also in 1912 the star on the overcoat became silver (40) and the border on the shoulder straps was increased to 3/8 of an inch (41). 1912 also brought a white dinner jacket. The star was worn above the plain white four inch cuff (42).

When the U.S. entered World War I in 1917 the use of all uniforms requiring epaulets, shoulder straps or cuff insignia, except overcoats, was suspended (43). They would not return until 1929 (44). New dress uniforms were introduced in 1937 (45), these used shoulder straps only and the use of epaulets by the army came to an end.

The stars were moved to shoulder loops on the overcoat in 1926. (45a)

Use of dress uniforms was suspended again in April of 1943 and lasted until September of 1946 (46). The only change was on the cuff of the blue evening jacket. The star would be worn under a gold trefoil knot and above a band of lace connecting the ends of the knot. This would only last until 1950 when the cuffs reverted to their 1902 pattern (47).

The Career Compensation Act of October 12, 1949 (48) put Brigadier Generals into pay grade O-7.

Subdued insignia was introduced in 1965 in Vietnam and in 1966 for the rest of the army to make insignia less conspicuous on field uniforms (49). Silver rank insignia, including generals stars, were to be rendered in black.

The History of American Ranks and Rank Insignia

Bugler

The first mention of buglers in the regular army was on March 30, 1814 (1) in an act consolidating the two regiments of dragoons into one. Each troop of dragoons was to have two trumpeters or buglers. While the law says "trumpeters or buglers" the table of organization lists them as musicians (2). Dragoons were eliminated on March 3, 1815 (3).

As far as is known Buglers wore Privates uniforms.

Dragoons and Buglers with them returned to the army on March 2, 1833 (4). Except for their dress coat being red instead of blue they dress the same as privates (5).

On August 23, 1842 congress changed the second regiment of dragoons to a regiment of riflemen (6) but changed their minds on April 2, 1844 (7) and made them dragoons again. During that time the regiment presumably kept its same organization. A regiment of mounted riflemen including buglers was added on May 19, 1846 (8).

New uniform regulations in 1851 had buglers still a standard blue privates uniform with the front of the coat covered in facing color cloth, orange for dragoons and green for riflemen (9). This lasted until 1854 when the facing was changed to an outline of lace in the same shape with lace running across from each button in a herringbone pattern (10).

In 1855 congress added two regiments of cavalry (11). They were given yellow facings (12).

On August 3, 1861 congress changed the title of the dragoon and mounted rifle regiments to cavalry (13) and orange and green facings became yellow.

A reorganization in 1863 used the term Trumpeters instead of Buglers (14), although a bill giving a pay increase to the army did refer to buglers in 1864 (15). Trumpeter is used on the tables of organization for the rest of the 19th century.

The National Defense act of 1916 (16) revived the title of bugler in the cavalry, coast artillery, corps of engineers, field artillery and infantry. In December of 1917 the army prescribed a hunting horn type bugle as insignia (17).

When the enlisted grade were combined on July 1, 1920 (18), Buglers were made Specialists Sixth Class.

Bugler First Class

Bugler First Class was added to the army in July of 1918 (1). The insignia was a hunting horn type bugle with a line under it. (2)

When the enlisted grade were combined on July 1, 1920 (3), Buglers First Class were made Specialists Sixth Class.

Captain

The title Captain comes from the Latin caput meaning head, this led to the term capitaneus or head man (1). In the middle ages captains commanded companies of soldiers. The company was the basic unit when an army was formed, higher ranks were created when more the one company was fielded together.

By the 18th century companies were a sub division of regiments and the title of Captain was still used by their commander. Even in the early 21st century commanding companies is the job of a Captain.

The History of American Ranks and Rank Insignia

On July 23, 1775 George Washington ordered that Captains would be distinguished by a buff or yellow cockade on their hats (2). This would have been a ribbon tied in a bow and attached to the front of the hat. An order August 20, 1776 called for captain's cockades to be buff or white (3).

In 1780 epaulets were ordered to show both rank and branch. This was the beginning of a system we will call button color. This refers to the color of buttons, trimmings, lace and most important here epaulets. Infantry officers had silver trimmings, epaulets, ect. while artillery and staff officers had gold, Dragoons never quite fit into the system but in 1780 they had silver epaulets. Under the button color system enlisted men in the infantry used white artillery yellow and dragoon blue (4).

Captains were ordered to wear a button colored epaulet on the right shoulder (5). This would remain the insignia for captains until 1821.

Horses are expensive, so the army contained no dragoons from the end of the revolution until 1792 when one squadron was raised (6). It is not clear what button color was used. Dragoons were abolished again in 1801 (7) only to return in 1808 (8).

The dragoon officers uniforms of 1808 were trimmed in silver but wings were worn on both shoulders by all officers precluding the use of epaulets (9). If rank was shown on an officer's uniform the method has been lost to history. Rank was shown on the horse, however. A Captain's saddle cloth had a silver border and three bars in the lower corners (10). Dragoons were eliminated again in 1815 (11).

On March 27, 1821 the army issued a general order calling for infantry and artillery officers to wear chevrons as badges of rank (12). Captains were to wear a gold (for artillery) or silver (for infantry) chevron on the right upper sleeve. New uniform regulations in July changed this to both sleeves. Neither of these orders affected the six Captains in the Corps of Engineers or the four in the Corps of Topographical Engineers who still wore a gold epaulet on the right side. For the record, there were 40 Captains in the artillery and 70 in the infantry in 1821 making a total of 120 Captains (13). Chevrons were worn until 1829 or 30 (14).

What was used on the dress coats from 1830 to 1832 is not clear but the button colored epaulet on the right shoulder is possible.

In 1829 the army added a frock coat for use by officers in the field (15). Rank was originally shown by collar eagles, Captains wore a gold eagle, regardless of branch on the right side (16). This was replaced by a button colored shoulder strap made from a strip of lace on the right shoulder a few months later (17).

New uniform regulations in 1832 had epaulets worn on both shoulders, rank was now distinguished by the size of the bullion (18). Captains had "bullion smaller than a Majors", the 1839 regulations call for bullion 1/4 inch wide. 1832 also saw the rank by buttons on the cuff, for captains three outlined in button colored lace.

When rectangular shoulder straps were created Captains were given straps with a 1/8 inch button colored border and two matching strips of lace at each end (19). This was the beginning of a captains two bars.

The 1851 uniform regulations saw the end of buttons color. Bars on the shoulder straps were widened to 1/4 inch and all branches now used gold. Silver bars were added to the strap of the epaulet and a sleeve knot made of two cords was added to the overcoat (20).

When epaulets were abolished in 1872, Captains were ordered to wear two sets of two silver bars on the shoulder knot pad. At the same time the bars on the shoulder straps were changed to silver (21).

The 1851 overcoat sleeve knots were used in gold on the full dress and mess coats in 1902 (22).

Medal pin on bars began to be used on shirt collars in 1898 (23). Most photographs show the bars connected at the ends (24). The uniform specifications of 1913 and 1917 simply say "Two silver bars, each 1/4 inch wide and 1 inch long. Bars to be 1/4 inch apart".

In 1912 the width of the shoulder strap edging was increased to 3/8 inch and the captains bars in the strap were to be the same distance apart (25).

New dress uniforms of 1938 had the captains shoulder strap bars "...each 1/4 inch in width and 5/8 inch in length, parallel to ends of strap, 3/16 inch apart and 3/16 inch from the inside border." (26), there also appear to have pieces of wire added to simulate the connectors on the pin on insignia (27).

The bars were widened to 3/8 of an inch in 1941, and the connector was moved slightly away from each end(28).

The Career Compensation Act of October 12, 1949 (29) put Captains into pay grade O-3.

When subdued insignia was introduced in 1965 the bars were to be black (30).

The 2005 uniform regulations describe the insignia as "Captain. The non-subdued grade insignia is two silver-colored bars, each 3⁄8 inch in width and 1 inch in length, with a smooth surface. The bars are spaced 1⁄4 inch apart and are worn lengthwise on shirt collars, parallel to the shoulder seam on shoulder loops. The subdued grade insignia is the same as above, except the color is black" (31).

Captain Lieutenant

Captain Lieutenant was a rank in the continental army used by the senior Lieutenant in a company whose commander is also the regimental commander (1).

As a subaltern a Captain Lieutenant would have worn a green Cockade from 1775 to 1780, then a button colored epaulet on the left shoulder (2).

Chaplain

Members of the clergy have been with military units for centuries. The Continental Army had many Chaplains.

In June of 1784 congress called for the army to have one Chaplain (1), however there is no evidence of any appointment.

On March 3, 1791 congress reorganized the army and once again there was to be one Chaplain (2), John Hurt took the office the next day (3). Hurt resigned on April 30, 1794 and was replaced with David Jones on May 13th.

When the army was expanded for the possible war with France four Chaplains were to be allowed (4), Israel Evans, Andrew Hunter and William Hill were considered for the other three of these posts (David Jones being the fourth) but they were never confirmed by the Senate (5). Jones continued at the army's Chaplain until June 15, 1800.

On April 12, 1808 congress established that "That there shall be appointed to each brigade one chaplain, who shall be entitled to the same pay and emoluments as a major in the infantry,"(6). The table of organization for 1808 shows three chaplains (7). Samuel Carrick appears to have been the only Chaplain in service at the time.

When the army was expanded in January of 1812 the same text was used in the law (8) and the table of organization calls for eight (9). This repeated itself in January of 1813 (10) with the table calling for 16 (11), and again in April of 1816 (12). The only Chaplain authorized in the law of April 14, 1818 was at West Point (13), and he was not carried on the table of organization.

The army register shows David Jones returning to the army on April 2, 1813 alongside Peter Van Pelt who was appointed the same day. May 20th saw the appointment of Robert Elliott, James Wilmer and Joseph Hughes Who Resigned on August 5th. Aaron Booge was appointed on June 16th and Stephen Lindsley on June 29th. Adam Empie was made the West Point Chaplain on August 9th and Thomas Hersey was made a Chaplain on August 20th. Wilmer died on April 14, 1814. Soloman Aiken was appointed on September 16th and John Brannon and Carter Tarrant on December 10th. On June 15, 1815 Van Pelt, Booge, Lindsley, Hersey, Aiken and Brannon were discharged. Tarrant died on February 17, 1816. William Maccalla and Cave Jones were made Chaplains on April 29, 1816 and Aaron Booge returned to the army on May 16th. Empie resigned as West Point Chaplain on April 30, 1817 and was replaced by Cave Jones. Elliott, Maccalla, and Booge were discharged on April 14, 1818 and Cave Jones Resigned on the 18th. There is no record of when David Jones left the army. Thomas Picton replaced Cave Jones at West Point on July 22nd (14).

From 1818 until the civil war no Chaplains appear on the Tables of Organization. Chaplains did continue to exist. Picton and his successors Charles Mcllvaine, Thomas Warner, Jasper Adams, William Sprole and John French continued at West Point. In 1838 congress decreed “That it shall be lawful for the officers composing the council of administration at any post, from time, to time employ such person as they may think proper to officiate as chaplain who shall also perform the duties of schoolmaster at such post” (15). Only 20 Chaplains were allowed (16).

In February of 1847 congress allowed Chaplains in brigades then fighting the war with Mexico (17). The only name in the army register that was appointed under this legislation is John McCarty who served from April 11, 1847 to July 6, 1848 (18).

Ten more post were allowed Chaplains in March of 1849 (19).

On July 22, 1861 congress allowed Chaplains to be appointed to each regiment (20), they were to have pay and allowances of a Captain. On May 20, 1862 Chaplains were allowed at hospitals (21), They were listed on the tables as Hospital Chaplains.

Uniforms for Chaplains were slow in coming. In 1820 the West Point Chaplain was allowed the uniform of the general staff without an eagle on the hat. This was only allowed until the next year when civilian clothes were one again prescribed. In 1832 Corps of Engineers buttons and a round hat with a black cockade and gold eagle were allowed, and in 1839 an engineers forage cap and frock coat was allowed for the West Point Chaplain (22).

In 1861 Chaplains were prescribed a black frock coat with one row of nine black covered buttons, black trousers and a black felt hat or plain army forage cap. On occasions of ceremony a plain chapeau de bras could be worn. In 1864 herringbone lace was added around the buttons and the forage cap gained a staff officers cap device (23). Their status as equivalent Captains led some Chaplains to wear shoulder straps with two bars, however this was against regulations (24).

After the civil war the 30 Chaplains allowed at posts were carried on the tables as “Post Chaplains”. In addition congress allowed “one chaplain may be appointed by the President, by and with the advice and consent of the Senate, for each regiment of colored troops, whose duty shall include the instruction of the enlisted men in the common English branches of education” (25).

Chaplains were given shoulder straps in 1880. They were the standard size with a black background and a silver shepherds crook in the center. Use of these shoulder straps was stopped in 1888 (26). Shoulder straps returned in 1898, this time with a silver cross in the center instead of the crook (27).

The herringbone lace was removed from the frock coat sometime between 1872 and 1875 (28).

The 1897 uniform regulations state “CHAPLAIN - Plain black frock coat, with standing collar; one row of nine black buttons on the breast, or, if desired, a plain double-breasted frock coat of black cloth, falling collar; with two rows of black silk buttons on the breast, seven in each row, placed at equal distances. For "undress", either the black frock or a plain black sack coat of cloth or serge, falling collar, single-breasted, one row of five black buttons in front, the skirt to extend from one-third to three-fourths the distance from hip-joint to the bend of the knee. Provided, that when a particular coat or vestment is required by the church to which the chaplain belongs, he may wear such coat or vestment while conducting religious services."(29)

The 1902 regulations kept the black frock coat as a full dress uniform. Chaplains would wear the other uniforms of regular officers with the Chaplain's shoulder straps on the dress coat and a silver cross on the shoulder loops of the white and service coats and on shirt collars. Chaplains assigned to the regiments wore the branch insignia with a small cross underneath. Bronze insignia was worn on field uniforms after 1907 (30).

On April 24, 1904 congress allowed the promotion of Chaplains over ten years service to equivalent Major, and newly appointed Chaplains would start as equivalent First Lieutenants (31).

In 1914 Chaplains were allowed to wear regular rank insignia. The cross became branch insignia and was worn in silver on all uniforms (32). This only lasted until 1918. General Pershing believed that rank got in the way of the relationship between Chaplains and soldiers (33). Chaplains were to wear the branch insignia on the shoulder loops instead of rank insignia.

Jewish Chaplains received insignia in August of 1918. Tablets of law with numbers one to ten under a star of David was prescribed (34).

On June 4, 1920 a new law stated "Chaplains shall hereafter have rank, pay, and allowances according to length of active commissioned service in the Army, or, since April 6, 1917, in the National Guard while in active service under a call by the President, as follows:Less than five years, first lieutenant; five to fourteen years, captain; fourteen to twenty years, major; over twenty years, lieutenant colonel. One chaplain, of rank not below that of major may be appointed by the President, by and with the advice and consent of the Senate, to be chief of chaplains. He shall serve as such for four years, and shall have the rank, pay and allowances of colonel while so serving." (35). At this point Chaplain was no longer a rank unto itself.

Chaplains regained their rank insignia in 1926 (36). Their unique position was shown by the branch insignia. In 1979 new green class B shirt and pants combination uniforms were created. They were to be without branch insignia. Chaplains however were to wear the branch insignia above the left breast pocket (37).

In 1990 Buddhist Chaplains were given branch insignia of a dharma cakra and in 1992 Muslim Chaplains of a crescent (38).

New field uniforms without branch insignia came along in 2005. Once again Chaplains were to wear the branch insignia above the left breast pocket (39).

Chauffeur

The rank of Chauffeur was created in the Signal Corps on July 24, 1917, it was to be equal to a Sergeant (1). The book chevrons by Colonel William K. Emerson shows the insignia of a twelve spoked wheel with a tire above a bar. In the text it says that the insignia was created in May of 1918 for general application (2). The law only allowed Chauffeurs in the Signal Corps and only Signal Corps Chauffeurs are shown on the pay chart in the 1920 army register (3). However it is quite possible that in the chaotic organization of enlisted ranks in World War I Chauffeurs were used by other branches.

When the ranks were reorganized on July 1, 1920 Chauffeurs became Specialists fifth class (4).

Chauffeur First Class

The rank of Chauffeur First Class was also created in the Signal Corps on July 24, 1917, it was to be equal to a Sergeant First Class(1). The book chevrons by Colonel William K. Emerson shows the insignia of a twelve spoked wheel with a tire above an arc. In the text it says that the insignia was created in May of 1918 for general application (2). The law only allowed Chauffeurs First Class in the Signal Corps and only Signal Corps Chauffeurs First Class are shown on the pay chart in the 1920 army register (3). However it is quite possible that in the chaotic organization of enlisted ranks in World War I Chauffeurs First Class were used by other branches.

When the ranks were reorganized on July 1, 1920 Chauffeurs First Class, like Chauffeurs, became Specialists fifth class (4).

Chief Bugler

Chief Buglers were senior musicians in mounted regiments. The rank was created when dragoons returned in 1833 (1) and lasted until a reorganization of 1862 (2) when the title became Chief Trumpeter.

From 1833 to 1851 they wore red dress uniforms with yellow sashes and a yellow aiguilette on the left shoulder (3). In 1851 they wore regular blue uniforms with the breast covered in facing color and a red sash (4). The facing became a herringbone pattern in 1854 (5).

Chief Hospital Physician

Chief Hospital Physician was a title in the Continental Army, created in September of 1780 (1).

The law called for three, James Craik, Charles McKnight and Malachi Treat Were Appointed on October 6, 1780. Craik was made Chief Physician on March 3, 1781 and does not appear to have been replaced (2).

The title was abolished in January of 1782 (3).

Chief Mechanic

Chief Mechanic was a rank in the field artillery. It was created in 1907 (1) and lasted until the grade reorganization on 1920 when it was placed in Specialist Fourth Class (2).

Chief Mechanics wore crossed hammers in a wreath until May of 1918 when it was changed to crossed hammers over a bar (3).

Chief Medical Purveyor

On July 28, 1866 congress set the organization of the medical department to include one Chief Medical Purveyor who was to be equivalent of a Lieutenant Colonel (1).

The appointment went to Richard Satterlee who held it until he retired on February 22, 1869. The position remained vacant until March 12, 1872 when Jedediah Baxter was appointed (2).

The Chief Medical Purveyor wore standard staff Lieutenant Colonel's shoulder straps, dark blue background, silver oak leaf at each end.

From 1866 to 1872, epaulets with 1/2 inch wide bullion, a silver oak leaf on the strap and the silver letters M.S. in a gold wreath in the frog were worn. These were replaced in 1872 with shoulder knots with a dark blue background and silver oak leafs on the pad with the letters M.D. between them (3).

On June 23, 1874 congress moved the Chief Medical Purveyor up to full Colonel (4) and Baxter was duly promoted. A silver eagle replaced the oak leafs on the shoulder straps and knots.

Baxter served until August 16, 1890. He was replaced on August 28th by Edward Vollum who retired on September, 11, 1891 and was replaced by Charles Alexander (5).

On July 27, 1892 congress made all equivalent Colonels in the medical department Assistant Surgeon Generals (6).

Chief Musician

The first use of the title Chief Musician was when the army was enlarged for the possible war with France in 1799 (1).

The law adding dragoons to the army on March 2, 1833 (2) calls for a Chief Musician, but the tables of organization for 1834 (3) and 1837 (4) refer to them as Principal Musicians.

From 1847 until 1865 the term "Principal or Chief Musician" was used on the tables of organization.

A new law in 1869 stated "That there shall be enlisted in each regiment a chief musician, who shall be instructor of music," (5).

No insignia was prescribed until 1899 but they probably wore musicians dress coats with the herringbone pattern on the breast.

In April of 1899 Chief Musicians were ordered to wear three chevrons and two arcs with a bugle between (6).

The National Defense act of 1916 changed the title to Band Leader (7).

Chief Physician

William Shippen was Chief Physician of the flying camp from July 15. 1775 to December 1, 1776.

James Brown was Chief Physician and Surgeon, Southern Dept. form March 22, 1780 to June 1, 1782.

Peter Fayssoux was Chief Physician and Hospital Surgeon of the Southern Dept. form March 15, 1781 to the end of the war.

Chief Physician and Hospital Surgeon

Chief Physician and Hospital Surgeon was a title in the continental army held by William Burnet from March 1, 1781 to the end of the war (1).

Chief Physician and Surgeon of the Army

Chief Physician and Surgeon of the Army was a title in the continental army held by John Cochran from October 6, 1780 to January 7, 1781 and James Craik from march 3, 1781 to December 23, 1783 (1)

Chief Trumpeter

Chief Trumpeters replaced Chief Buglers in Calvary regiments in 1862 (1).

They wore musicians uniforms with the herringbone pattern and a red sash. The sashes were eliminated in 1872 (2).

In 1873 Chief Trumpeters were given three chevrons and one arch with a bugle between (3).

Chief Trumpeters were added to the artillery in 1899.

The rank was abolished by the National Defense Act of 1916 (4)

Chief Warrant Officer

Congress created the rank of Chief Warrant Officer on August 21, 1941 (1), splitting the rank of Warrant Officer into two grades, Chief Warrant Officer and Warrant Officer Junior Grade. Warrant Officers in the Mine Planter Service holding the titles of Master and Chief Engineer were classified as Chief Warrant Officers and continued to wear four stripes and an anchor or propellor on their sleeves.

The regulations described the insignia as "One gold bar 3/8 inch in width and 1 inch in length, with rounded ends, having a brown enameled top and a longitudinal center of gold 1/8 inch in width." (2). When dress uniforms returned after the war, this insignia was worn on shoulder straps with a brown background(3), under a sleeve knot with the base a broken line on the evening tailcoat and by itself on the blue a white mess jackets (4).

The Career Compensation Act of October 12, 1949 (5) placed Chief Warrant Officers in pay grades W-2, W-3 and W-4 (6). All three grades using the same insignia.

The Mine Planter Service was abolished along with the Coast Artillery Corps in 1951 (7)

On May 29, 1954 congress passed the "Warrant Officer Act of 1954" (8). This act created three separate ranks of Chief Warrant Officers in the three pay grades, adding the grade number to the title of each.

Chief Warrant Officer 2

Chief Warrant Officer 2 was created by the "Warrant Officer Act of 1954" (1) in pay grade W-2.

Design of the insignia was coordinated with the Navy, Marine Corps and Coast Guard to create a unified system. The insignia authorized in 1956 was a gold bar with a brown square in the center and a brown rectangle at each end (2).

When subdued insignia was introduced in 1965 (3), the gold parts were rendered in olive drab and the brown remained brown (4).

The army abandoned the unified system in 1972 and the insignia was changed.

The 2005 uniform regulations describe the insignia as "Chief warrant officer 2 (CW2). The non-subdued grade insignia is a silver-colored bar, 3⁄8 inch in width and 1 1⁄8 inches in length, with two black enamel squares. The bar is worn lengthwise on shirt collars, parallel to the shoulder seam on shoulder loops. The subdued grade insignia is the same as above, except that the color is olive-drab with black squares." (5) The squares are spaced apart from the center.

Chief Warrant Officer 3

Chief Warrant Officer 3 was also created by the "Warrant Officer Act of 1954" (1) in pay grade W-3.

Design of the insignia was coordinated with the Navy, Marine Corps and Coast Guard to create a unified system. The insignia authorized in 1956 was a silver bar with two brown rectangles, showing a square of silver in the middle (2).

When subdued insignia was introduced in 1965 (3), the silver parts were rendered in black and the brown remained brown (4).

The army abandoned the unified system in 1972 and the insignia was changed.

The 2005 uniform regulations describe the insignia as "Chief warrant officer 3 (CW3). The non-subdued grade insignia is a silver-colored bar, 3⁄8 inch in width and 1 1⁄8 inches in length, with three black enamel squares. The bar is worn lengthwise on shirt collars, parallel to the shoulder seam on shoulder loops. The subdued grade insignia is the same as above, except that the color is olive-drab with black squares." (5). The squares are tight together with the space at the ends of the bar.

Chief Warrant Officer 4

Chief Warrant Officer 4 was also created by the "Warrant Officer Act of 1954" (1) in pay grade W-4.

Design of the insignia was coordinated with the Navy, Marine Corps and Coast Guard to create a unified system. The insignia authorized in 1956 was a silver bar with a brown square in the center and a brown rectangle at each end (2).

When subdued insignia was introduced in 1965 (3), the silver parts were rendered in black and the brown remained brown (4).

The army abandoned the unified system in 1972 and the insignia was changed.

The 2005 uniform regulations describe the insignia as "Chief warrant officer 4 (CW4). The non-subdued grade insignia is a silver-colored bar, 3⁄8 inch in width and 1 1⁄8 inches in length, with four black enamel squares. The bar is worn lengthwise on shirt collars, parallel to the shoulder seam on shoulder loops. The subdued grade insignia is the same as above, except that the color is olive-drab with black squares." (5). The squares are tight together showing almost no silver.

Chief Warrant Officer 5

In the early 1970s Congress considered creating pay grades W-5 and W-6. In anticipation the army designed insignia of silver bars, with a thin black line running long ways for W-5 and Covered in black showing a thin silver line for W-6 (1). The bill didn't pass and the matter was dropped.

In 1991 congress did finally create the W-5 grade only (2). The army had created the rank of Master Warrant Officer in the W-4 pay grade in 1988 and these became Chief Warrant Officers 5 when the rank was created (3). The Master Warrant Officer's insignia was continued. The 2002 regulations described it as "Chief warrant officer 5 (CW5). The non-subdued grade insignia is a silver-colored bar, 3⁄8 inch in width and 1 1⁄8 inches in length, with four silver squares outlined with a 1/16–inch wide black border. The bar is worn lengthwise on shirt collars, parallel to the shoulder seam on shoulder loops. The subdued grade insignia is the same as above, except that the color is olive-drab with the squares outlined in black"(4). This insignia is best described as the same at the W-4 insignia but with silver centers in the squares.

In 2004 the army changed the insignia to the original 1970s design (6). Described in the 2005 regulations "Chief warrant officer 5 (CW5). The non-subdued grade insignia is a silver-colored bar, 3⁄8 inch in width and 1 1⁄8 inches in length, with a black line in the center of the bar." (7).

The same order also changed some long standing uniform distinctions of warrant offices of all grades. Warrant officers had worn an eagle with a wreath superimposed, usually called the "eagle rising insignia", as a cap badge and as branch insignia since 1921, (8) and brown facings had been used since 1938 (9). Now all warrant officers were to wear the branch insignia and facings of their assigned branch.

The History of American Ranks and Rank Insignia

Clothier General

Clothier General was a title in the Continental Army. James Mease was appointed on April 4, 1777. He was replaced by Peter Wikoff on June 24, 1779, who was replaced on July 15th by Persifor Frazer who was replaced on July 24th by James Wilkinson. Wilkinson was replaced on April 17, 1781 by John Moyan (1).

Colonel

During the sixtieth century, the spanish Army was organized into columns or in Spanish colunelas each made up of multiple companies. The commander was called capo d colunela, head of the column. The French and later the British copied the column idea and eventually developed into regiments with a Colonel in charge (1). Colonels are sometime referred to a "full Colonels" to differentiate them from Lieutenant Colonels.

On July 23 1775 George Washington ordered field grade officers to wear red or pink cockades, this lasted until June 18, 1780 when the insignia became a button colored epaulet on each shoulder (2).

The U.S. Army had no full Colonels from the end of the revolution until 1802.

On March 8, 1802 congress allowed a Colonel to command each of the army's three regiments (3). On April 1st James Hamtramck and Thomas Butler were appointed to command the two infantry regiments and Henry Burbeck to command the regiment of artillery (4). They continued to wear the two button colored epaulets.

Field officers Horse cloths had two strips of silver lace (4a).

On March 27, 1821 a general order called for the army's then four artillery Colonels and seven infantry Colonels to wear three button colored chevrons on each arm (5). The Colonels in staff departments consisting of the Commissary General George Gibson, The Inspector Generals John Wool and James Gadsden and the Chief Engineer Alexander Macomb, were to continue to wear the two gold epaulets. New uniforms regulations in July had all Colonels wearing the two epaulets. The chevrons were probably never worn

The new frock coat in May of 1829 was to have Colonels wearing a gilt eagle on both collars (6), this became a strip of button colored lace as a shoulder strap on each side in July (7).

In 1832 Colonels were ordered to wear epaulets with bullion 1/2 inch wide with an american eagle on the strap. An american eagle comes from the Great Seal of the United States it has a shield over its breast with vertical stripes and a solid portion called a chief at the top. It holds the olive branch of peace in the right talon and arrows of war in the left. The eagles on the epaulets were to be in the contrasting color of the strap, gold on silver or silver on gold. The same regulations gave field grade officers four lace outlined buttons on the cuff of the dress coat, worn until 1851 (8).

When rectangular shoulder straps were created, Colonels had an 1/8 inch button colored border and an eagle in the opposite color in the center with its wings spread to fill the space. The eagle was to be two inches between the tips of the wings (9).

New uniforms in 1851 standardized the shoulder strap borders to 1/4 inch for all ranks ended the concept of button color. All epaulets and shoulder strap borders were now gold and all eagles silver. The 1851 regulations also brought a five cord sleeve knot on the overcoat cuff (10).

Shoulder knots replaced epaulets in 1872 and colonels wore the eagle in the center of the pad (11). The regimental number or the staff department letters were worn above the eagle (12).

In 1890, Colonels in the Inspector General's Dept. (13) and the Judge Advocate General's Dept. (14) began wearing the insignia of those departments on the knot portion above the pad. This was expanded to the Quartermaster's (15) and Subsistence (16) Departments in 1895, the Pay Dept. in 1896 (17) and the Adjutant General's (18) and Ordinance (19) Departments in 1899.

When the new khaki field uniform was created in 1898, full Colonels wore the eagle running long ways in the center of the shoulder loop (20).

Silver eagles were added to shirt collars in 1901 (21) and the five cord knot was worn in gold on the dress and evening uniforms of 1902 (22). The 1902 regulations also changed how the eagles were worn on shoulder loops. They now were worn at the end of the loop with the talons towards the shoulder and the head towards the collar (23).

In 1926 the eagles were to be made in pairs so the head always faced the front. The eagles were redesigned in 1951 and the head now always faced the olive branch resulting in the arrows and the olive branch being on different sides on each shoulder (24).

The Career Compensation Act of October 12, 1949 placed Colonels in pay grade O-6 (25).

The subdued eagles introduced in 1965 were black.

The 2005 uniform regulations describe the insignia as "Colonel. The non-subdued grade insignia is a silver-colored spread eagle, in a shiny finish, 3⁄4 inch high, with 11⁄2 inches between the tips of the wings. The head of the eagle faces to the wearer's right, or to the front. The subdued grade insignia is the same as above, except the color is black." (26)

Color Sergeant

The concept of a Color Sergeant or rather Colour Sergeant to use the British spelling, began as a Sergeant responsible for protecting the officer carrying a regimental flag in the British army (1). Eventually they came to carry the flag themselves.

In the U.S. Army There was no rank of Color Sergeant until 1883, or technically not even then.

On March 12, 1883 the Delos Sacket the Inspector General, suggested to Robert Lincoln the Secretary of War that the Sergeants that carried the regimental colors be allowed to wear a star above their chevrons. Lincoln liked the idea, but the star over the chevrons was already worn by Ordnance Sergeants. A sphere (a circle with an open center) was chosen instead (2).

The insignia is described in the 1889 equipment specifications as "Regimental and Battalion Color Sergeant. - Three bars and a sphere one-fourth (1/4) of an inch wide, and one-fourth (1/4) of an inch in outside diameter, and placed one and three-fourths (13/4) inches above inner angle of chevron." (3). The "Regimental" referred to the Color Sergeants in the infantry, cavalry and artillery regiments, "Battalion" referred to the Battalion of Engineers.

All this having been said, congress had not created the rank by law and it did not appear in any tables of organization.

Congress finally recognized Color Sergeants on February 2, 1901(4). That same year, a star replaced the sphere as originally intended (5).

When the enlisted grades were reorganized in July of 1920, all Color Sergeants became Staff Sergeants (6)

Command Sergeant Major

The History of American Ranks and Rank Insignia

A Command Sergeant Major is the senior enlisted advisor to a battalion or higher commander, and ranks in pay grade E-9. The title was created on July 12, 1967 (1).

The insignia, authorized in 1968, is three chevrons and three arcs with a star in a wreath between (2).

In June of 1976 command Sergeant Majors were directed to stop wearing branch insignia and wearing what was then called "Branch Immaterial" insignia showing the Coat of Arms of the United States (3).

The 2005 uniform regulation describe the insignia as "Command sergeant major: three chevrons above three arcs, with a five-pointed star within a wreath between the chevrons and arcs" (4).

Commissary General of Issues

The position of Commissary General of Issues was created in the Continental Army on June 10, 1777 (1). It was held by Charles Stewart from June 18, 1777 to July of 1782 (2).

On July 10, 1781 congress replaced army commissaries with an officer in the Treasury Department (3).

Commissary General of Purchases

The Continental Congress reorganized the army supply system on June 10, 1777 (1). This law replaced the Commissary General of Stores and Purchases with a Commissary General of Issues and a Commissary General of Purchases.

Joseph Trumbull who had been the Commissary General of Stores and Purchases, assumed the title of Commissary General of Purchases on June 18, 1777. Trumbull resigned on August 2nd and was replaced by William Buchanan on August 5th. Buchanan resigned on March 23, 1778 and was replaced on April 9th by Jeremiah Wadsworth. Wadsworth resigned on January 1, 1780 and was replaced by Ephraim Baline (2).

On July 10, 1781 congress replaced army commissaries with an officer in the Treasury Department (3).

The Commissary General of Purchases returned in the War of 1812, On March 28, 1812 (4) and on March 3, 1813 he was made head of the Purchasing Department (5).

Callender Irvine held the post from August 8, 1812 until his death on October 9, 1841. His replacement James Tyson took over on October 11th (6) and served until congress abolished the position on April 22, 1842 (7).

A law organizing the army on March 2, 1821(8) uses the title "Commissary of Purchases" without the "General". The usage in the army registers after that is inconsistent. The Law Abolishing the position actually says "the office of Commissary General of Purchases, sometimes called Commissary of Purchases" (9), so there appears to have been no intended change in Irvine's title.

The Commissary General of Purchases was to wear the 1813 general staff uniform with the button holes on the collar embroidered in gold. Under the 1821 regulations, Irvine was not to wear a uniform. The 1832 regulations allowed a blue double breasted coat with ten buttons in each row, a standing collar with two gold embroidered button holes and buff lining on the tails. A black cocked hat with a black cockade under a gilt eagle was also worn without the feathers that distinguished other staff officers. In 1839 this was changed to plain blue coat and a round hat with cockade. (10)

Commissary of Hides

The History of American Ranks and Rank Insignia

On June 20, 1777 the Continental Congress decreed "Resolved, That a suitable person be appointed commissary, to receive all raw hides belonging to the United States, and that he be authorized to exchange the same for tanned leather, or men's shoes, at the customary rates of exchange, and have the leather so obtained, worked into shoes, and deliver them to the clothier general, or his order, taking duplicate receipts; one of which he shall transmit to the Board of Treasury:" (1)

Peter Philips was chosen for the position (2) but he turned it down and George Ewing took the job (3). Ewing Resigned on April 20, 1779 (4). There is a mention of a Robert Lamb holding the positions in 1781 (5) but no record of his appointment.

Commissary of Military Stores

Ezekiel Cheevar was named Commissary of Military Stores on August 17, 1775. The register so the title was also held by Benjamin Flower, Samule French, Jonathan Gostelow and Samuel Hogon (1).

Commissary Sergeant

Commissary Sergeants had been authorized at the regimental, battalion and company levels during the civil war and at the regimental level from 1866 to 1870. In 1873 they were added to the noncommissioned staff of army posts.

On March 3, 1873 a new law stated "That the Secretary of War be and he is hereby, authorized and empowered to select from the sergeants of the line of the army who shall have faithfully served therein five years, three years of which in the grade of non-commissioned officer, as many commissary-sergeants as the service may require, not to exceed one for each military post or place of deposit of subsistence supplies, whose duty it shall be to receive and preserve the subsistence supplies at the posts, under the direction of the proper officers of the subsistence department, and under such regulations as shall be prescribed by the Secretary of War." (1). These men would answer to the subsistence department and not the commander of the post, giving the department better control of the record keeping at far flung forts. A similar concept had been used by the ordnance department since the 1830s and would be used by the quartermaster's department after 1884.

Commissary Sergeants were given gray as a facing color and three chevrons with a crescent as insignia. The points of the crescent were supposed to face forward but until 1885 the usually pointed up (2).

When the Commissary Sergeants we returned to regiments in 1898 (3), the term "Post Commissary Sergeant" began to be used for the Commissary Sergeants in the subsistence department (4).

Commissary Sergeant (Regimental)

Commissary Sergeants were placed in infantry regiments on July 22nd (1) and cavalry and artillery regiments on July 29, 1861 (2).

No insignia was prescribed but the title of "sergeant" would make three chevrons a possibility.

The rank was continued when the organization of the army was set at the end of the Civil War (3). Three chevrons and "an angular tie of three bars" which was essentially three more chevrons with less of an angle, pointing in the opposite direction, was prescribed as the insignia in the spring of 1867(4).

The rank was abolished on July 15, 1870 (5), only to return on March 2, 1899 (6).

This time the insignia was the three chevrons and three bars of a Quartermaster Sergeant with a crescent in the middle (7).

This insignia was used until the rank was abolished by, or at least not included in, the National Defense Act of 1916 (8).

Company Commissary Sergeant

Commissary Sergeants were added to companies of cavalry on July 17, 1862 (1).

No insignia was ever authorized, but they may have worn a sergeant's three chevrons.

When the size of the army was set at the end of the civil war, there were no more Company Commissary Sergeants (2).

Company Quartermaster Sergeant

The rank of Company Quartermaster Sergeant began to be used in the cavalry and artillery on July 29, 1861 (1).

No insignia was authorized but there is photographic evidence that at least some wore three chevrons and one bar (2). This insignia was made official in 1866 (3) when Company Quartermaster Sergeants were also added to infantry regiments (4).

Promotions to Company Quartermaster Sergeant ceased in 1873 (5).

The rank returned in the infantry on April 26, 1898 (6), and the three chevrons and one bar was revived (7). It was added to engineer companies on February 2, 1901(8).

The title was changed to Supply Sergeant by the National Defense Act of 1916 (9).

Company Supply Sergeant

In 1916 Quartermaster Sergeants became Supply Sergeants(1).

They initially continued to wear the three chevrons and one bar, but a few months later they were ordered to wear the three chevrons of a regular Sergeant (2). The Three chevron and one bar insignia continued to be manufactured and it is possible this order was ignored (3).

The one bar insignia officially returned in May of 1918 (4).

The Reorganization of July 1, 1920 made them regular sergeants with three chevrons (5).

Cook

Cook became an official rank of the army on July 7, 1898. The law stated that they would be equal to a Corporal (1).

The insignia chosen wash a cooks cap, essentially a rectangle with an oval on top of it (2).

Initially Cooks were authorized in infantry, cavalry, artillery and the Signal Corps Companies. In 1901 they were added to the Corps of Engineers in 1901 (3). A law in 1908 setting the pay of the army (4) mentions "Acting Cooks" in the Hospital Corps, and Acting Cooks of the Hospital Corps appear on the tables of organization until 1916. The reorganization that created the Quartermaster Corps on August 24, 1912 added cooks there as well (5).

Cooks were also included to the Mine Planter service on July 9, 1918 (6).

The enlisted grade reorganization of July 1, 1920 made cooks into Specialists fourth class (7).

Cornet

A cornet was a small flag carried by mounted soldiers in the 16th and 17th century. When a third officer was added to cavalry companies or troops he was to carry this flag and his title became Cornet (1). The equivalent flag and rank in the infantry was called an Ensign.

Cornets existed in the dragoons of the Continental Army. Classified as subalterns they would have worn the green cockade from July 1775 to June 1780 and then a silver epaulet on the left shoulder (2).

After the war Cornets would come and go as dragoon units were formed and abolished. The first time was on March 3, 1792 (3). Four were authorized and appointed on March 14th, Leonard Covington, Tarleton Fleming, James Taylor and Solomon Van Rensselaer (4).

They continued to wear the epaulet on the left but is unclear whether it was silver or gold.

The law in 1799 that expanded the army for a possible war with France stated "And be it further enacted, That every ensign and every cornet in the regiments heretofore appointed shall be denominated hereafter second lieutenants." (5).

The army register listing for each of the Cornets on active duty at the time show them going from Cornet to Second Lieutenant on March 3rd or 4th 1799 (6).

The threat from France passed and congress reduced the army on May 14, 1800 (7). This law allowed only two troops of dragoons. The table of organization in the historical register shows the army containing two Cornets, one in each troop (8). It appears, however that there were three men in that position but they were using the title of Second Lieutenant.

Archibald Lee was appointed to fill one of the positions created in 1799. In the Executive Journal of the Senate the nomination on April 1, 1800 was worded "I nominate the following list of officers in the Army of the United States:
Cavalry
Archibald Lee, Virginia, second Lieutenant, vice Grimes, deceased...." (8).

This would seem to indicate that Second Lieutenant was the title in use, not Cornet.

Lee was promoted on June 1, 1801. The other two, William Rodgers and Charles Tutt, were discharged on June 1, 1802 (9).

When the army was reorganized on March 16, 1802 (10) dragoons were eliminated. They returned in 1808 (11) with each troop having both a Second Lieutenant and a Cornet.

In 1808 a blue horse cloth with a single line of silver lace and one silver bar in the corner was prescribed to Cornets (12).

Dragoons were eliminated again in 1815 (13) and this brought an end to the rank of Cornet.

Corporal

The term Corporal comes from the Italian for leader of a squadra or square, Capo De'squadra. The title was changed in the 16th century to Caporale meaning leader of a small body of soldiers (1).

The rank of Corporal has existed continuously in the U.S. Army from the beginning. In 1775 Corporals were ordered to wear a green epaulet or at least a strip of green cloth on the right shoulder (2). In 1779 this was changed to a button colored, white for infantry, yellow for artillery and blue for dragoons, on the right shoulder.

This remained the insignia for Corporals until 1821 when a button colored chevron on the right upper sleeve was ordered (3). This was changed to a chevron above each cuff in 1825 and these were worn until 1830 (4). What happened between 1830 and 1832 is not clear.

In 1832 Corporals were given two button colored laced button holes on the cuff and button colored cloth epaulette on each shoulder with 1/8 inch wide by 2 1/2 inch long bullion (5).

When Dragoons returned to the army in 1833 (6), They were to wear coats with a simple pointed cuff and metal shoulder scales (7). Rank for corporals was indicated by two yellow chevrons, point down, on both upper sleeves (8). Two chevrons has been the insignia for a Corporal ever since.

The enlisted grade reorganization in 1920 Corporal was combined with the ranks of Band Corporal and Corporal Bugler in grade 5 (9).

With the reorganization after The Career Compensation Act of October 12, 1949 (10) Corporals were placed in pay grade E-4.

The 2005 uniform regulations describe the insignia as "Corporals: two chevrons" (11).

Corporal Bugler

The rank of Corporal Bugler existed form July 9, 1918 (1) until the enlisted grade reorganization of July 1, 1920 (2), when they became regular Corporals.

The insignia was two chevrons over a bugle (3).

Deck hand, Mine Planter Service

Upon the creation of the Mine Planter Service on July 9, 1918, each mine planter was to have four Deck hands (1).

Insignia of a red sea mine on a blue background was prescribed in January of 1919 and worn until late 1919 when it was replaced with one arc (2).

The enlisted grade reorganization of July 1920 made Deck hands into Specialists Fifth Class (3)

Deputy Commissary General of Issues

Deputy Commissary General of Issues was a staff position in the Continental Army. It was Created on June 10, 1777 (1) and lasted until it function was moved to the treasury on June 28, 1780 (2). The register shows the position being held by Elisha Avery, William Green Mumford, John Garardeau, Robert White, Bethuel Washburn, James Gray and Robert Hoops. There is also a Ebenezer Winship listed as a Deputy Commissary of Issues without the General (3).

Deputy Commissary General of Military Stores

The register shows the title of Deputy Commissary General of Military Stores being held by Cornelius Sweers, David Mason, Samuel Hodgdon, John Collins, George Everson and Alex Henderson (1).

Deputy Commissary (of Purchases)

A law of March 28, 1812 allowed "as many deputy commissaries, as, in the opinion of the President of the United States, the public service may require," (1).

John McKinney was appointed on April 25th and Thomas Buford, John Plummer, and John Landgon on June 25th. Amasa Stetson was added on June 22nd, Elisha Tracy on July 6th and John Platt and Samuel Russell on September 18th. James Calhoun took office on June 29, 1813 and Robert Jennings on July 19th. 1814 brought William Foster on April 15th to replace Buford who left the army on April 12th, and Darby Noon on July 15th (2).

When the army was reduced in 1816 (3) all but two, McKinney and Noon, were discharged on June 15th.

The Purchasing Department was further reduced on March 2, 1821 (4) and the position of Deputy Commissary was Abolished. McKinney and Noon left the army on June 1st.

Deputy Commissaries would have worn the 1813 General Staff uniform (5).

Deputy Commissary General of Purchases

The title of Deputy Commissary General of Purchases existed from June 10, 1777 (1) until the commissary functions were transferred to the treasury on July 10, 1781 (2).

The title was held by Jeremiah Wadswotrh, Jacob Cuyler, William Buchanan and James Roe (3).

Deputy Director General of Hospitals

The Title of Deputy Director General of Hospitals was created in the Continental Army on April 7, 1777 (1).

It was held by Jonathan Potts and Issac Foster (2).

The title was not included in a reorganization of September 30, 1780 (3).

Deputy Paymaster General

The title of Deputy Paymaster General was used in the Continental Army. Holding it were Benjamin Harrision, Jr., Ebenezer Hancock, Richard Dallam, John Pierce and Benjamin Stelle (1).

On July 6, 1812 congress allowed the president to appoint a line officer as a Deputy Paymaster General (2). Major Washington Lee of the Sixteenth Infantry was appointed on April 23, 1813. Lee was a Major in the infantry and not a staff officer holding a staff title. He was made a Lieutenant Colonel in the Eleventh Infantry on June 9, 1814 (3) but retained his position as Deputy Paymaster General. His commission with the Eleventh infantry expired, along with that regiment on June 15, 1815 but he was provisionally retained as Deputy Paymaster General until April 29, 1816. He probably still considered himself a Lieutenant Colonel and may have continued to wear the two silver epaulets.

Lee's "provisional retention" was part of a decision of May 17, 1815 to retain two Deputy Paymaster Generals under the authority of the president (4)(5). The second was Ambrose Whitlock, a former District Paymaster. Whitlock had held a commission as a Captain in the First Infantry until June 30, 1814 and probably continued to wear his silver epaulet on the right shoulder.

On April 24, 1816 congress passed a law setting the size of the Pay Department that did not include a Deputy Paymaster General (6). Whitlock left the army that day.

Deputy Surgeon General

On July 27, 1892 congress made all equivalent Lieutenant Colonels in the Medical Department into Deputy Surgeons General (1). This combined the ranks of Assistant Medical Purveyor and Surgeons that ranked a Lieutenant Colonels.

They were to wear standard staff shoulder straps with a dark blue background and silver oak leafs at each end. Shoulder knots also had a dark blue background and silver oak leafs on each side of the pad with a gold shield between until 1896 when it became a gold maltese cross (2). The overcoat cuffs contained the Lieutenant Colonel's four cord knot which were used a the dress coat knot after 1902 (3).

Medical officers received regular rank on April 23, 1908 (4) Making them simply Lieutenant Colonels.

Director General (and Chief Physician)

The position of the senior medical officer in the Continental Army was fraught with confusion and politics. On July 27, 1775 (1) congress created the position of Director General and Chief Physician. Benjamin Church was appointed to fill the position (2).

Church immediately found himself in conflict with the regimental surgeons over whether they should treat wounded soldiers themselves or send them to central hospitals that were cheaper to run. His authority was further undermined by the appointment of Samuel Stringer as Director General and Chief Physician of the Northern Department. Was Stringer Church's equal or subordinate? Nobody knew and congress refused to clarify the situation (3).

In September of 1775 Church was found to have corresponded with the British in July. He was dismissed from the army and jailed (4).

John Morgan was chosen to replace Church on October 17, 1775 (5).

Morgan found himself in the same predicament as Church, in regard to Stringer and the regimental surgeons. Things got worse on July 15, 1776 when William Shippen was named Chief Physician of the flying camp of militia raised to defend New York. Shippen was well connected and Morgan thought he was out to replace him. In October congress put Shippen in charge of all the hospitals on the New Jersey side of the Hudson. A department that was struggling with two heads now had three (6).

On January 9, 1777 congress abruptly fired both Morgan and Stringer (7).

A new organization for the Hospital Department was passed on April 7, 1777 (8). It was to have one Director General, the Chief Physician part was not used this time, and Shippen was appointed on April 11th (9).

Shippen resigned on January 3, 1781 and was replaced by John Cochran who served to the end of the war (10).

District Paymaster

District Paymasters were created on May 16, 1812 (1). Some of them were to be line officers taken from their regiments an others were to be just District Paymasters. On the army list those taken from the line are listed by their line rank and the others are listed under "Citizens" (2).

On March 30, 1814 a new law stated that District Paymasters would not be taken from the line (3).

There are several officers who remained District Paymasters after March 30, 1814 with their line commissions ending.

Before March 30, 1814, on June 30, 1813 to be precise, Captain Neheimah Freeman of the Artillery "relinquished his line commission"(4). Likewise Artillery First Lieutenant Satterlee Clark remained a District Paymaster after the closing date of his commission on December 31, 1813 (5).

Remaining as District Paymasters after the law required them not to be taken from the line were First Lieutenant Jacob Albright of the First Infantry on May 2, 1814 (6), First Lieutenant James Wilde of the Eighth Infantry on June 12th (7) and Captain Henry Phillips (8) of the Sixth Infantry, Captain Ambrose Whitlock (9) of the First Infantry, Captain Alpha Kingsley (10) of the First Infantry, Captain John Pemberton (11) of the Second Infantry and Captain Walter Sheldon (12) of the Eleventh Infantry on June 30, 1814.

District Paymasters were eliminated when congress set the peace establishment at the end of the War of 1812 on March 3, 1815 (13). All of them were discharged on June 15, 1815 except Whitlock who was retained as a Deputy Paymaster General. In fact all of the District paymasters whether they had held line commissions or not were still on active duty on June 15, 1815 except a "Citizen" named Samuel Huntington who had resigned on May 31st, Phililps who resigned on March 22nd and Wilde who was killed in a duel on January 16th.

In addition to Huntington the "citizen" District Paymasters were Samuel Eakin, Thompson Douglass, Joseph Watson, Samuel Phelps, Jesse Hunt, Joseph Boyd, Robert Gardner, George Perkins, John Bates Cooper, William Rathbone, Archibald Sneed, Junius Sneed, Peter Gordon Voorhies, John Linton and Joseph Coleman (14).

On April 24, 1816 a new law called for regimental and battalion of artillery paymasters to perform the duties of District paymasters (15).

There is no information on uniforms to cover all this. The line officers could have worn their regular uniforms even after they became only District Paymasters.

Dragoon

On March 5, 1792 congress added dragoons to the army. the law stated there would be "four troops, each of which shall consist of-one captain, one lieutenant, one cornet, four sergeants, four corporals, one farrier, one saddler, one trumpeter, and sixty-nine dragoons;" (1). The use "dragoons" instead of private was probably an error but the law is the law.

This would remain the case, whether anybody in the army realized it or not, until a law of May 20, 1796 stated "the company of dragoons shall consist of one captain, two lieutenants, one cornet, four sergeants, four corporals, one farrier, one saddler, one trumpeter, and fifty-two privates;" (2).

This is the only use of a term other than Private by the U.S. Army. In the British army "Private Soldiers" as the category is called, have many different titles. Trooper is the term for a British mounted Private (3).

Driver

A law passed on May 16, 1812 stated "That in addition to the non-commissioned officers and privates allowed to the regiment of light artillery, each company shall be entitled to twelve drivers of artillery, who shall be enlisted for five years, unless sooner discharged, and receive the same pay, rations and clothing, as the privates of the army" (1).

They lasted until a reorganization on March 30, 1814 (2).

Drum Major

Drum Majors were used in the Continental Army starting on July 16, 1776 (1).

The first use of Drum Majors in the federal army was in a law crating new infantry regiments on July 29, 1861 (2). Each of the new regiments was allowed one Drum Major or Band Leader.

There was no specific insignia prescribed but they should have worn a musicians coat with the herringbone pattern and a red sash.

When the size of the army was set at the end of the Civil War (3) this rank or ranks was not included.

Regimental bands were added to infantry, cavalry and artillery regiments on March 2, 1899 (4) and each was allowed a Drum Major.

The insignia was three chevrons and crossed batons (5).

A band, and a Drum Major with it was added to the Corps of Engineers on February 2, 1901 (6).

The National Defense Act of 1916 (7) Stated that the First Sergeant of the headquarters company would act as Drum Major. These men added the crossed batons under the First Sergeants lozenge (8).

Electrician Sergeant

Electrician Sergeants came out of an effort to improve coastal defenses after the Spanish American War (1). The law of March 2, 1899 stated "In addition to the enlisted men specified there shall be one electrician sergeant to each post garrisoned by coast artillery having electrical appliances, who shall have the pay and allowances of an ordnance sergeant."(2).

The insignia was three chevrons and a group of five lightning bolts (3). In full color the chevrons were red and the lightning bolts white. How this worked on the pre 1902 gold lace chevron is not clear.

On January 25, 1907 the rank was split into first and second class electrician sergeants (4).

Electrician Sergeant First Class

The rank of Electrician Sergeant was split into classes on January 25, 1907 (1).

Initially the were to wear three chevrons and one arc with the bolts between (2). In January 1908 they were given three chevrons over a group of lightning bolts over a bar in a wreath. In full color the chevrons were red, bolts white, the bar red and the wreath yellow (3).

This was changed in May of 1918 when the bolts and bar were placed inside three chevrons and one arc. Color chevrons were not in use at the time but in 1920 there was a plan to render the bolts in white. The rank was abolished before this could happen (4).

With the enlisted grade reorganization of July 1, 1920, Electrician Sergeants First Class became Technical Sergeants (5).

Electrician Sergeant Second Class

When Electrician Sergeants were split into classes on January 25, 1907 (1), those of the second class were to continue to wear the three chevrons and group of lightning bolts as before (2).

In 1908 the were given three chevrons and the bolts in a wreath, in other words the same and first class without the bar. The chevron were red, the bolts white and the wreath yellow.(3)

In May of 1918 the received three chevrons and one arc with the bolts between. Once again the same as first class without the bar and the same as the original insignia for first class (4).

With the enlisted grade reorganization of July 1, 1920, Electrician Sergeants Second Class became Staff Sergeants (5).

Engineer

Engineers were added to the Coast Artillery on January 25, 1907 (1).

The insignia was a mechanical governor in a wreath under a star. In full color the governor was red, the star white and the wreath yellow (2).

This was one of the insignias that the army tried to add some color back into in early 1920, The governor was to be red, the star white and the wreath green (3).

With the enlisted grade reorganization of July 1, 1920, Engineers became Master Sergeants (4).

Enlisted Men of (for) Ordnance

Enlisted men of or for Ordnance was a term used for the enlisted men in the ordnance Department other than Ordnance Sergeants.

When the Ordnance Department was created on May 14, 1812 the law stated "And be it further enacted, That the commissary general be authorized, from time to time, to employ as many wheelwrights, carriage makers, blacksmiths and laborers, as the public service may in his judgment require." (1). It is not clear at this point if these men were to be soldiers or civilian employees of the army.

This was clarified in a law passed on March 30, 1814 that said "And be it further enacted, That the commissary general of ordnance may employ in his department, besides blacksmiths and wheelwrights, other mechanics, such as the public, service may require, who shall, together with the said blacksmiths and wheelwrights, be mustered under the general denomination of artificers; and such artificers, being hereafter, or having been heretofore enlisted to serve for the term of five years, or during the war, shall be entitled to the same annual allowance of clothing as is or may be provided for the soldiers of the army.
And be it further enacted, That the laborers who may be hereafter enlisted to serve in the ordnance department, for the term of five years, or during the war, shall be entitled to a bounty of twenty-five dollars in money, and the same annual allowance of clothing as is or may be provided for the soldiers of the army." (2). This would seam to indicate that the various craftsmen were in the army with the rank of Artificer. The laborers were also clearly in the army but their rank was not clear.

A new law reorganized the Ordnance Department on February 8, 1815. It laid our the pay for each specialty, $30 for master armorers, master carriage makers and master blacksmiths, $16 for regular armorers, carriage makers and blacksmiths, $13 for artificers and $9 for laborers (3).

On March 2, 1821 the Ordnance Department was merged into the artillery (4). This law limited the number of enlisted men in the Ordnance Department to 56. Since the law abolished the department these men would be in the artillery. An order from the Adjutant General distributing the army's personnel into the new organization calls for 56 "Enlisted men for ordnance duties". They were to be in addition to the army's authorized enlisted strength of 5586 making a total of 5642 (5).

The History of American Ranks and Rank Insignia

There is no information available on uniforms before 1821. The 1821 and 1825 uniform regulations called for artillery uniforms (6).

When the Ordnance Department returned in 1832 the law allowed "as many enlisted men as the public service may required, not exceeding two hundred fifty."(7).

The 1839 uniform regulations called for artillery uniforms with red epaulets (8).

The new uniforms of 1851 were the same as Privates of other branches with crimson as the facing color (9).

On July 5, 1862 congress distributed them in to regular ranks, the master workmen became Sergeants, regular workmen became Corporals, artificers became Privates First Class and laborers became Privates Second Class (10).

The terms "Enlisted Men for Ordnance" and Enlisted Men of Ordnance" were never official titles created by congress. The "for" was changed to "of" in 1838 (11).

Ensign

Ensigns are usually associated with the navy, but in fact it was originally an army rank.

In the 16th century a third officer was added to companies who was to carry the company flag and his title became Ensign (1). The equivalent flag and rank in the cavalry was called an Cornet.

Ensigns existed in the Continental Army. Classified as subalterns they would have worn the green cockade from July 1775 to June 1780 and then a silver epaulet on the left shoulder (2).

When the Federal army was formed in June of 1784 (3) the rank of Ensign continued.

They continued to wear the silver epaulet on the left shoulder.

The law in 1799 that expanded the army for a possible war with France stated "And be it further enacted, That every ensign and every cornet in the regiments heretofore appointed shall be denominated hereafter second lieutenants." (4).

When the army was reorganized on March 16, 1802 (5) each company of infantry was to have both a Second Lieutenant and a Ensign.

When the army was reorganized again at the end of the war of 1812 (6), Ensigns were abolished.

Ensigns of Riflemen also existed from 1792 to 1795 and form 1808 to 1814. The button color for riflemen from 1792 to 1795 was silver (7) and gold from 1808 to 1814 (8).

Farrier

A Farrier is a blacksmith that shoes horses. As a rank title it was used in the Continental Army as a part of dragoon regiments from the beginning.

They probably wore privates uniforms until 1779 when they were to wear one blue epaulet, which side the epaulet was to be worn on is not known but on the left would make sense (1).

When dragoons returned to the army in 1792 (2), so did Farrier. They lasted until the dragoons were abolished again in 1802 (3). There is no evidence of any special insignia used during this period.

The same goes for when dragoons returned in 1808 (4) and lasted until 1815 (5).

From the time dragoons came back again in 1833 until 1910 the army used the rank of "Farrier and Blacksmith"

On March 23, 1910 (6) Farrier without the blacksmith part was made a rank of the army again. The insignia was a horse's head (7).

The National Defense Act of 1916 eliminated Farriers in the cavalry but added them to the Medical Department (8). The horse's head insignia continued to be authorized until 1918 but was probably worn by medical Farrier until 1920 (9).

Medical Farriers are on the pay table in the 1920 army register (10) but not in the list of ranks from the 1920 enlisted grade reorganization (11). What rank Farriers were given is not known.

Farrier and Blacksmith

Farrier and Blacksmith was the title of those responsible for shoeing horses from March 2, 1833 (1) until March 23, 1910 (2) when "Farrier and Blacksmith" became the two ranks of Farrier and Horseshoer.

They wore privates uniforms until 1874 when an insignia of a horseshoe was prescribed (3). This was worn until 1908 when it became a horse's head (4).

Field Clerk

Field Clerks were created on August 29, 1916 (1) but their roots run a lot deeper.

On July 5, 1838 the Pay Department was allowed to hire civilians if no soldiers were available, to serve as "Paymaster's Clerks" (2). When the Pay Department was merged into the Quartermaster Corps in 1912 they became known a "Pay Clerks" (3). Pay Clerks were made into Second Lieutenants of the Quartermaster Corps on June 3, 1916 (3a).

On July 29, 1886 (4)"General Service Clerks" were added to the enlisted men of the army for clerical work at army headquarters and various other headquarters around country. This lasted until an appropriations bill of August 6, 1894 (5) funded clerks at the various headquarters and at the same time repealed the law creating the "General Service Clerks". Apparently these clerks were to be civilian employees of the army.

The August 1916 law changed the clerks at the various headquarters to "Army Field Clerks" and clerks in the Quartermaster Corps to "Field Clerks, Quartermaster Corps" and made them "subject to the rules and articles of war.", making them military personnel not civilians.

Subject to the rules and articles of war or not their position in the military hierarchy was a little murky. They were not saluted by enlisted men but were, in way officers (6).

When Field Clerks were sent off to the trenches of World War I they had to be placed in uniform. In July 1917 the were ordered to wear uniforms with no rank insignia and enlisted style branch and U.S. insignia on discs, the branch insignia showing crossed quill pens (7).

The Field Clerks objected to the enlisted style insignia, so in December of 1917 they were given officer's uniforms without sleeve braid and officer's style outline U.S. and Branch insignia. The branch insignia was now crossed quill pens over the insignia for the Adjutant General's Department for Army Field Clerks and the Quartermaster Corps for Field Clerks, Quartermaster Corps (8).

A new law of June 4, 1920 (9) stopped appointment of Field Clerks.

The insignia was altered for those remaining, in 1924. The quill pens were now to be superimposed over the center of the Adjutant General or Quartermaster insignia (10).

All remaining Field Clerks officially became Warrant Officers on April 27, 1926 (11).

Fife Major

The title of Fife Major was used in the Continental Army. It was created on July 16, 1776 (1), and continued to the end of the war. The title was never used in the federal army.

Fireman

Firemen were part of the Coast Artillery Corps created on January 25, 1907 (1).

The initial insignia was shovel crossed with a poker in a ring. In full color the shovel and poker were red and the ring gold. Apparently this insignia was never issued. In 1908 one chevron and one arc with a mechanical governor between was prescribed, in full color the chevron and arc were red and the governor gold (2).

In 1914 the insignia was changed to three chevrons over the governor. This was worn until 1917 when it became the governor over an arc. This insignia was one of the ones that color was added to in 1920 with both the governor and the arc rendered in red (3).

Firemen were also part of the Mine Planter Service when it was created on July 9, 1918 (4). They were to wear three chevrons with a three bladed propellor, all in red on a blue background, as of January 1919 (5).

The enlisted grade reorganization of July 1920 made Firemen into Specialists Third Class (6).

First Lieutenant

The term lieutenant comes from the French for "placeholder" (1). It can be thought of a someone who hold a place or is a tenant instead of or in lieu of. A tenant in lieu of is a lieutenant.

As medieval captains became involved in court politics, they needed someone to fill in for them while they were away, and the rank of Lieutenant was born (2).

The "First" in First Lieutenant was originally used to denote the ranking of the Lieutenants in a company first being the most senior. Use of the terms in the Continental Army is a little hard to pin down. The term "First Lieutenant" was certainly used, but whether it was considered a rank or a position for those holding the rank of "Lieutenant" is not clear.

Lieutenant, without a modifier, was used in the Federal Army from its inception in 1784 (3) until 1799 (4) when First Lieutenant came into permanent use.

As subalterns they were to wear the green cockade from July 1775 to June 1780 and then a button colored epaulet on the left shoulder (5).

The 1808 to 1814 horse cloths for dragoons had a single line of silver lace and two silver bars in the corner (6).

In March of 1821 a general order prescribed a button colored chevron, silver for infantry gold for artillery, on the left upper sleeve (7). This was changed in July to a chevron above each cuff (8). In both cases the six, first lieutenants in the Corps of Engineers continued to wear a gold epaulet on the left shoulder. These were used until 1829 or 1830 (9).

What was used on the dress coats from 1830 to 1832 is not clear, but the button colored epaulet on the left shoulder is possible.

New uniform regulations in 1832 had epaulets worn on both shoulders, rank was now distinguished by the size of the bullion (10). Lieutenants regardless of rank had "same as for a Captain, except the bullion is smaller", the 1839 regulations call for bullion 1/4 inch wide. 1832 also saw the rank by buttons on the cuff, for Lieutenants two outlined in button colored lace.

When rectangular shoulder straps were created First Lieutenants were given straps with a 1/8 inch button colored border and a matching strip of lace at each end (11).

The 1851 uniform regulations saw the end of buttons color. Bars on the shoulder straps were widened to 1/4 inch and all branches now used gold. Silver bars were added to the strap of the epaulet and a sleeve knot made of one cord was added to the overcoat (12).

When epaulets were abolished in 1872, First Lieutenants were ordered to wear a silver bar on each side of the shoulder knot pad. At the same time the bars on the shoulder straps were changed to silver (13).

The 1851 overcoat sleeve knots were used in gold on the full dress and mess coats in 1902 (14).

Medal pin on bars began to be used on shirt collars in 1898 (15). The uniform specifications of 1913 and 1917 simply say "One silver bar,1/4 inch wide and 1 inch long".

New dress uniforms of 1938 had the First Lieutenants shoulder strap bars "... 1/4 inch in width and 5/8 inch in length, parallel to ends of strap, and 3/16 inch from the inside border." (16).

The bars were widened to 3/8 of an inch in 1941(17).

The Career Compensation Act of October 12, 1949 (18) put First Lieutenants into pay grade O-2.

When subdued insignia was introduced in 1965 the bars were to be black (19).

The 2005 uniform regulations describe the insignia as "First lieutenant. The non-subdued grade insignia is one silver-colored bar, 3⁄8 inch in width and 1 inch in length, with a smooth surface. The bar is worn lengthwise on shirt collars, parallel to the shoulder seam on shoulder loops. The subdued grade insignia is the same as above, except the color is black" (20).

First Sergeant

A First Sergeant is the senior enlisted advisor to the commander of a company. The rank does not appear on the tables of organization until 1861 but its history is a lot longer than that.

In 1778 the Prussian officer Frederick De Steuben, sometimes known as Von Steuben, was appointed to help train the Continental Army. He published a manual laying out the drill for the army as well as duties for officers and noncommissioned officers and First Sergeant was among them (1)

First Sergeants came from the Prussian tradition of the Feldwebel, a rank deriving its name from the German Feld Weybel or "Field Woman". Felwebels were known as the "mother of the company" (2).

The title of First Sergeant was used by the senior sergeant of a company form at least 1778 but it was not legally a separate rank from Sergeant. Its exact use is therefore hard to trace.

The 1832 uniform regulations allowed "first sergeants of companies" to wear a sergeants uniform with a red sash (3). When dragoons were added to the army the next year their First Sergeants were given yellow sashes (4).

The first mention of First Sergeants in legislation came on July 5, 1838 (5). The law set the pay of "each first sergeant of a company" at $16 per month while other sergeants made $13. This did not make them a separate rank from Sergeant, but it was a start. In 1838 there were 320 sergeants in the infantry, 160 in the artillery and 80 in the dragoons making a total of 560, not including the 44 Ordnance Sergeants that were listed on the sergeant line on the table of organization (6). The army had 70 infantry companies, 36 artillery batteries and 20 troops of dragoons. The senior Sergeant of each being a First Sergeant would mean that of the 560 sergeants 126 of them were first sergeants.

When chevrons were added to fatigue jackets in 1847, First Sergeants were given three chevrons with a lozenge (a diamond with an open center) in the angle (7).

First Sergeant finally became a separate rank of July 22, 1861 (8) when they were listed separately from sergeants.

In the book Chevrons by William K. Emerson there is a color photograph an insignia for First Sergeant of the Corps of Engineers (9) from the post 1872 era. It is made of red cloth with the chevrons outlined with white stitching and the lozenge white. In the text of the book (10), it is stated the first sergeants were in the infantry, cavalry, artillery and the Corps of Engineers. However the army registers from that time show that there were no first sergeants in the engineers (11). It is quite possible that the senior sergeants of the engineer companies wore the lozenge on their chevrons but they were not first sergeants. First sergeants were added to the engineers on April 26, 1898 (12).

First Sergeants survived the enlisted grade reorganization of 1920, they would share grade two with Technical Sergeants (13). The insignia was the Technical Sergeants three chevron and two arcs with the lozenge in between (14).

In September of 1942 First Sergeant was moved up to grade one and given a third arc (15).

The Career Compensation Act of October 12, 1949 converted grade one into grade E-7 (16) where First Sergeants remained until two new grades were created in 1958 (17) and they were moved up to grade E-8.

The 2005 uniform regulations descried the insignia as "First sergeant: three chevrons above three arcs, with a pierced lozenge between the chevrons and arcs" (18).

Flight Officer

On July 8, 1942 congress created the rank of Flight Officer in the Army Air Force (1). It was equal to a Warrant Officer Junior Grade.

The insignia was described as " one gold bar 3/8 inch in width and 1 inch in length, with rounded ends, having a blue enameled top and a latitudinal center of gold 1/8 inch in width." (2).

No "closing date" could be found for the rank of flight officers. It would have ceased to be a rank of the army when the air force became a separate service in 1947 (3), but no information is available on whether use of the rank stopped before that.

Garrison Surgeon

On March 16, 1802, congress allowed for "two surgeons; twenty-five surgeons' mates, to be attached to garrisons or posts, and not to corps." (1).

Appointed were John Carmichael and David Davis. However in the historical register they are listed as "Post Surgeons" (2), the army list shows them as just "surgeons" (3).

Carmichael resigned on June 27, 1804 and was replaced on October 9th by Oliver Spencer. Davis resigned on January 27, 1804 and was replaced with Francis Le Barren on December 12th. Both Spencer and Le Barren are listed as Garrison Surgeons in both the historical register (4) and the army list (5).

La Barren was promoted to Apothecary General on June 11, 1813 leaving only Spencer listed a a Garrison Surgeon on the 1813 army list (6). The 1814 list adds a Foster Swift appointed on February 18, 1814 (7). The historical register shows Swift was made a Garrison Surgeon's Mate on that date (8), this may be in error.

Spencer resigned on June 20, 1814 and was replaced on James McCulloh on July 17th.

Garrison Surgeons were not part of the army's organization after the War of 1812 laid out in a law of March 3, 1815 (9) but both Swift and McCulloh were provisionally retained (10).

A law dated April 24, 1816 (11) reorganizing the army's staff allowed for "as many post surgeons as the service may require". With this Garrison Surgeons became Post Surgeons. Swift stayed on as a Post Surgeon and McCulloh was discharged.

There is no evidence of medical uniforms before 1813 when they were to wear a black version of the general staff uniform with cuff flaps and cloth covered buttons (12).

Garrison Surgeon's Mate

The table of organization in the historical register for 1792 shows six "Garrison Surgeon's Mates" (1). The only legislation that might have created this position was on March 3, 1791 (2) that allowed the president to appoint more Surgeon's Mates if he deemed them necessary. The law was repealed in 1795 (3).

Garrison Surgeon's Mates returned on March 16, 1802 (4) when 25 of them that were attached to garrisons or posts were allowed.

They lasted until April 24, 1816 when they became "Post Surgeons" (5).

There is no evidence of medical uniforms before 1813 when they were to wear a black version of the general staff uniform with cuff flaps and cloth covered buttons (6).

General

The term "general" comes from the Latin Generalis meaning the whole of something. A medieval Captain General would be officer in charge of a whole army. The "Captain" part was dropped by the English army by the 18th century and the rank became just General, sometimes called "full" general (1).

George Washington, Ulysses S. Grant, William Tecumseh Sherman, and Philip Sheridan all held rank that were arguably equal to Full General, but in each case other titles were used.

The first time "General" was used as a rank title by itself was on October 6, 1917 when a a law was passed that was to "authorize the President, in accordance with the provisions of said Act and for the period of the existing emergency only, to appoint as generals the Chief of Staff and the commander of the United States forces in France;" (2).

The Chief of Staff was Tasker Bliss and the commander in France was John Pershing. Bliss was relieved as Chief of Staff by Payton March on May 19, 1918 (3).

Initially two stars with the "Coat of arms of the United States" between them was the insignia (4) but this was changed to four stars (5).

After the war, Pershing was made General of the Armies on September 15, 1919 (6) and March reverted to Major General on June 30, 1920 (7).

On February 23, 1929 (8) a new law made the Army Chief of Staff a temporary Full General during his time in office. The current Chief Charles Summerall was duly promoted. He was replaced on November 21, 1930 by Douglas MacArthur, who was in turn replaced on October 2, 1935 by Marlin Craig, who gave way to George Marshall on September 1, 1939 (9).

With the coming of World War II, Craig and MacArthur were recalled to duty. The register shows them as retired officers on active duty (10). Dwight Eisenhower was made a Full General on February 11, 1943 when he was given command of the African Theater of Operations (11). Henry Arnold, the head of the Army Air Force was made a Full General on March 19, 1943. Next was Joseph Stilwell on August 1, 1944 (12).

As the war continued more Full Generals were appointed, Walter Krueger on March 5, 1945, Brehon Somervell on March 6th, Joseph McNarney on March 7th, Jacob Devers on March 8th, George Kenney on March 9th, Mark Clark on March 10th, Carl Spaatz on March 11th, Omar Bradley on March 12th, Thomas Handy on March 13th, George Patton on April 14th, Courtney Hodges on April 15th and Jonathan Wainwright on September 5th (13).

Craig died on July 25, 1945 (14) as did Patton on December 21st (15) and Stilwell (16) on October 12, 1946.

Marshall (17), Eisenhower (18), MacArthur (19), and Arnold (20) were Promoted to General of the Army in December of 1944 as was Bradley in 1950 (21).

Kenny, Spaatz and McNarney left the Army when the Air Force became a separate service.

The rest retired, Somervell on April 30, 1946 (22), Kruger on July 20, 1946 (23), Wainwright on August 31, 1947 (24), Hodges on January 31, 1949 (25), Devers on September 30, 1949 (26), Clark on October 31, 1953 (27) and Handy on March 31, 1954 (28).

The Officer Personnel Act of August 7, 1947 (29) stopped any permanent appointments to Full General but allowed certain positions to "carry the rank of general". Officers appointed to these positions would become Full Generals while they held the office and revert to their permanent grade when their tenure was over. They were, however allowed to retire with their higher rank.

The Career Compensation Act of October 12, 1949 (30) placed the rank of General in pay grade O-8 which it shared with Lieutenant General and Major General. This lasted until May 20, 1958 when a new law (31) created pay grade O-10 for Full Generals.

When subdued insignia was introduced in 1965 the four Stars were to be black (32).

The 2005 uniform regulations describe the insignia for Full Generals as "General. The non-subdued grade insignia has four silver-colored, five-pointed stars, each 1 inch in diameter. Medium silver-colored stars, 3⁄4 inch in diameter, and miniature silver-colored stars, 5⁄8 inch in diameter, also are authorized. The subdued grade insignia is the same as above, except the color is black"(33).

General and Commander in Chief

The History of American Ranks and Rank Insignia

First in war, first in peace and first in generals was George Washington. He became "General and Commander in chief" in 1775 (1). He wore a blue sash across his chest as a badge of rank (2). There is no record of a prescribed insignia for Washington himself after 1780 when other generals were to wear gold epaulets with silver stars. Contemporary portraits do however, show him wearing three stars (3).

Washington's rank during the revolution has been a subject of confusion and controversy. The term "General and Commander in chief" could be considered a separate rank not equivalent to any modern rank. Congress's intention at the time was simply to make him the guy in charge of the army. The three stars and the fact that the next lowest rank was Major General have led many to believe Washington was a Lieutenant General. This was reinforced when Washington was made a Lieutenant General in 1798 to command the army in the possible war with France. The evidence that Washington was equal to a Full General?

1. he is listed as such in Heitmans historical register (4).
2. There is correspondence between Washington and congress asking them to create a rank of Lieutenant General that would be subordinate to him (5)(6).

Washington returned his commission on December 23, 1783 (7).

General of the Armies of the United States

On March 3, 1799, as preparations were being made for war with France a new law stated "And be it further enacted, That a commander of the army of the United States shall be appointed and commissioned by the style of " General of the Armies of the United States," and the present office and title of Lieutenant-General shall thereafter be abolished."(1). The Lieutenant General to be promoted was George Washington. The appointment However, was never made and Washington remained a Lieutenant General until he died on December 14th (2). The plural proboably refered to the various parts of the military establishment, the standing army, newly rasied troops, state militia, ect., that he was to command.

In 1866 congress revived the rank of "General of the Army of the United States" (3). The use of the word "revive" would seem to indicate congress thought it was bringing back the 1799 rank but the usage is singular, "Army" not Armies" so this is usually considered a different title.

General of the Armies was seen again in 1919 when congress passed this law:

"Be it enacted by the Senate and House of Representatives of the United States of America in Congress assembled, That the office of General of the Armies of the United States is hereby revived, and the President is hereby authorized, in his discretion and by and with the advice and consent of the Senate, to appoint to said office a general officer of the Army who, on foreign soil and during the recent war, has been especially distinguished in the higher command of military forces of the United States; and the officer appointed under the foregoing authorization shall have the pay prescribed by section 24 of the Act of Congress approved July 15,1870, and such allowances the President shall deem appropriate; and any provision of existing law that would enable any other officer of the Army to take rank and precedence over said officer is hereby repealed: Provided, That no more than one appointment to office shall be made under the terms of this Act."(4)

The "especially distinguished" officer was John Pershing who became General of the Armies on September 3rd (5).

No insignia was ever officially adopted. There is a painting (6) of Pershing wearing four stars but in Gold but this may be just the artists interpretation of Pershing's uniform.

Pershing retired on September 13, 1924 (7) and became General of the Armies on the retired list until his death on July 15, 1948.

The History of American Ranks and Rank Insignia

When the "five star" rank of General of the Army was created in 1944, the law contained a section that said "Nothing in this Act shall affect the provisions of the Act of September 3, 1919 (41 Stat . 283; 10 U. S. C. 671a), or any other law relating to the office of General of the Armies of the United States." (8). Pershing was to remain senior the five star generals, but did this make Pershing a six star general? There were diplomatic implications. The five star rank was meant to be equal the European rank of Field Marshall and if Pershing held six star rank he would be senior to the highest ranking officers in allied armies (9). An elderly retired officer would probably not have been a threat to the Field Marshals, but the ranks existence could have led to serving officers being promoted. As a result Pershing was never called a six star general.

During the bicentennial celebration in 1976 congress revisited George Washington's rank. The media at the time reported that he was to be made a five star general but this was in error. The law, passed on October 11, 1976 stated "Resolved by the Senate and House of Representatives of the United States of America in Congress assembled, That (a) for purposes of subsection (b) of this section only, the grade of General of the Armies of the United States is established, such grade to have rank and precedence over all other grades of the Army, past or present.(b) The President is authorized and requested to appoint George Washington posthumously to the grade of General of the Armies of the United States, such appointment to take effect on July 4, 1976." (10).

General of the Army

During World War II the U.S. forces worked closely with the British military. The highest British rank was Field Marshal ranking just above Full General. Except for Pershing the U.S. had no such rank. This bothered President Roosevelt who tried to get higher ranks created but ran into opposition from the Army Chief of Staff George Marshall and Secretary of State Henry Stimson. Marshall believed that higher ranking generals would be disrespectful to Pershing and that such ranks be used as a reward for service after the war. Stimson believed that american generals would appear not to have earned their ranks (1).

In September of 1944 Sir Bernard Montgomery was promoted to Field Marshal. Montgomery was Army Group commander under General Dwight Eisenhower's command. Differences in rank among senior staff officers was one thing but now it was effecting commanders in the field (2).

Congress created the rank of General of the Army on December 14, 1944 (3).

Appointed were Marshall the Chief of Staff, the theater commanders Eisenhower and Douglas MacArthur and the chief of the Army Air Forces Henry Arnold (4).

Why use General of the Army and not Field Marshal? There is a story that George Marshall did not want to be known as Marshal Marshall but this is probably a newspaper columnist with a sense of humor (5). In american usage, Marshal is usually a law enforcement title and it could have been seen as inappropriate to use it in the military (6).

The insignia was five silver stars joined at the points to form a pentagon. When worn on shoulder loops they were worn at the sleeve end with "the arms of the United States" in gold with a red white and blue enameled shield centered between the top star and the button.

Arnold retired on June 30, 1946 (7) and left the Army's retired list when the Air Force became a separate service.

Marshall retired on February 28, 1947 (8) and became Secretary of State.

On June 28, 1948 congress passed a law allowing the President to return the generals of the army to active duty (9), essentially allowing them to keep their ranks for life. Marshall resigned as Secretary of State on January 7, 1949 (11) and had his rank in the army returned to him on March 1st (12). In 1950 he was named Secretary of Defense. This required special legislation for him to hold a civilian cabinet post while still an active duty army officer, which was passed on September 18, 1950 (12). He served as Secretary of Defense until September of 1951 and remained a General of the Army until his death on October 16, 1959 (13).

Omar Bradley was promoted to General of the Army on September 20, 1950 (14).

Eisenhower resigned to run for President on July 15, 1952 (15). He had his rank restored to him by special legislation on March 22, 1961 (16), and held it until his death on March 28, 1969 (17).

MacArthur held his rank until he died on April 5, 1964 (18).

This left Bradley, who was the last "five star" general. He died on April 8, 1981 (19).

When dress uniforms returned after World War II, the generals of the army were allowed to design there own shoulder straps (20). Eisenhower came up with some very attractive straps with the coat of arms in the center and the stars in an arc with the middle star above the coat of arms (21). The 1979 uniform regulations call for Bradley's shoulder straps to just be the regular insignia in miniature in the center of the strap (22).

General of the Army of the United States

After 1783 the U.S. Army was not big enough to require any high ranking generals, even during the Civil War. After the war however, the top generals were promoted as a reward for service, but this would cause more controversy and confusion about the title.

On July 25, 1866 congress created the rank of "General of the Army of the United States" (1) and conferred it on Ulysses S. Grant. Grant was ordered to wear four stars on his epaulets and shoulder straps by General Order 75 on September 5th (2).

Grant left the army to become President on March 4, 1869 and was replaced by William Tecumseh Sherman (3).

The July 1872 Uniform regulations continued the four stars. The largest an inch and a half wide was worn in the crescent of the epaulet with the other three getting smaller, an inch and a quarter, an inch and an eighth and an inch, as they went up the strap. The stars on the shoulder straps were all the same size (4). This was changed in November to two stars with the "arms of the United States" in gold between them (5).

An appropriations bill on July 15, 1870 (6) decreed that the rank would cease to exist if it became vacant. Sherman retired on February 8, 1884 (7). His replacement as the Army's senior officer was Lieutenant General Philip Sheridan, who remain a Lieutenant General for the next four years. On June 1, 1888 (8) congress combined the ranks of General of the Army and Lieutenant General allowing Sheridan to hold the higher rank until his death on August 5th.

The controversy has come from the title "General of the Army" which was used as the next rank above Full General during World War II. Were Grant, Sherman and Sheridan equal to General of the Army or Full General? There is no clear answer to this, but like Washington there is some evidence that they were full Generals:

1. The law setting the size of the army after the Civil War says "there shall be one general" (9) there is no "of the Army" in the law.
2. The 1870 law abolishing the rank does not use "of the Army" either.

Gunner

Gunner was a rank in the Continental Army artillery. No insignia was mentioned until 1780 (1) when they were to wear a yellow epaulet. There is no information on which side the epaulet was to be worn on, but the left would make sense.

Gunner was also a rank in the Sea Fencibles raised in 1813 (2).

Horseshoer

The rank of Horseshoer was born on March 23, 1910 (1) when one of the two Farrier and Blacksmiths in each cavalry troop was re-designated a Horseshoer and the other a Farrier. One of the Mechanics in each battery of artillery was also made a Horseshoer.

They continued the Farrier and Blacksmith insignia of a horseshoe (2).

The National Defense Act of 1916 (3) added Horseshoes to the infantry, signal corps, corps of engineers and medical department.

The 1920 enlisted grade reorganization converted Horseshoers to Specialists Fourth Class (4).

Hospital Chaplain

On May 20, 1862 a new law said "That the President of the United States is hereby authorized to appoint, if be shall deem it necessary, a chaplain for each permanent hospital, whose pay, with that of chaplains of hospitals heretofore appointed by him, shall be the same as that of regimental chaplains in the volunteer force; and who shall be subject to such rules in relation to leave of absence from duty as are prescribed for commissioned officers of the army."(1)

They would have worn the 1861 Chaplains uniform of a black frock coat with one row of nine black covered buttons, black trousers and a black felt hat or plain army forage cap or on occasions of ceremony a plain chapeau de bras. (2)

The rank was combined with other Chaplains on April 9, 1864 (3).

Hospital Physician and Surgeon

On September 30, 1780 the continental congress reorganized the army's medical personnel (1). This law called for "fifteen hospital physicians, who shall also be a surgeon".

The title existed until the end of the war.

Hospital Sergeant

Hospital Sergeants were created in the Medical Department by The National Defense Act of 1916 (1).

The insignia was three chevrons and two arcs with a caduceus in the middle until May of 1918 when it became a caduceus in a wreath. When color was added to some of the drab insignias in 1920 the wreath became green and the caduceus maroon (2).

With the enlisted grade reorganization of 1920 they became Technical Sergeants (3)

Hospital Steward

Stewards were employed in hospitals from the beginning and were first mentioned in law as far back as 1799 (1) but they were not soldiers carried on the tables of organization until April 15, 1856 when a law was passed that said "That the Secretary of War be, and he is hereby, authorized to appoint, from the enlisted men of the army, or to cause to be enlisted, as many competent hospital stewards as the service may require, not to exceed one for each military post. The said hospital stewards to be mustered and paid on hospital muster rolls, as noncommissioned staff officers, with the rank, pay, and emoluments of a sergeant of ordnance, and to be permanently attached to the medical and hospital department, under such regulations as shall be prescribed by the Secretary of War."(2).

They were to wear an Ordnance Sergeants coat right down to the crimson piping with instead of the chevrons a 1 3/4 inch wide green hash mark with 1/8 inch yellow stripes 1/8 inch from each side and and yellow caduceus in the center (3).

A general order in 1857 changed the color from green to buff (a light beige color), but by the 1861 uniform regulations the color was again green. It is possible that the order was never implemented (4).

The 1872 regulations gave them coats with green piping replacing the crimson of the Ordnance Department (5).

When gold dress chevrons were introduced in 1884 the caduceus and stripes were rendered in gold instead of yellow (6).

New chevrons were introduced in August of 1887. They consisted of three chevrons and one arc with a red geneva cross in between. The cloth undress version was made of green cloth with the chevrons outlined in black stitching, while the gold dress version was made of gold lace on a green ground. The geneva cross was red on both versions (7).

The gold chevrons were eliminated in 1896 when medical personnel were no longer allowed dress uniforms (8).

The remaining cloth chevrons were changed in February of 1901 to green with white stitching with the cross now in Maltese style, in green and outlined in white (9).

The new uniform regulations of 1902 continued the three chevron and one arc in the new point up style, now there was a caduceus in the middle. All, including the caduceus, in maroon piped in white (10).

This was short lived however as the Hospital Corps, as the enlisted portion of the Medial Department was known, was reorganized in 1903 and Hospital Stewards became Sergeants First Class of the Hospital Corps (11).

Hospital Steward (Regimental)

Hospital Stewards were placed in infantry regiments on July 22nd (1) and cavalry and artillery regiments on July 29, 1861 (2).

They probably wore the same insignia as the Hospital Stewards in the Medical Department, a 1 3/4 inch wide green hash mark with 1/8 inch yellow stripes 1/8 inch from each side and and yellow caduceus in the center (3), but this is not certain.

The rank was continued when the organization of the army was set at the end of the Civil War (3). Three chevrons and an oval with a caduceus embroidered on it in dark blue, was prescribed as the insignia in the spring of 1867(4).

The rank was abolished on July 15, 1870 (5).

Hospital Surgeon

Hospital Surgeon seams to have been a title used by surgeons at Continental Army hospitals prior to September of 1780 (1). There is however, no indication that this was an official title created by congress.

Hospital Surgeons in the federal army were first mentioned in a law of March 2, 1799 (2), in a plan for army medical services during the coming war with France. The war never came and the plan was never implemented.

We next see Hospital Surgeons on April 12, 1808 (3) when a new law allowed "such number of hospital surgeons and surgeon's mates as the service may require but not exceeding five surgeons and fifteen mates". Apparently the service only required one. His name was John Moncure Daniel and he took office on July 7, 1809 (4).

When the army was expanded for the War of 1812, a law on January 11, 1812 (5) allowed as many Hospital Surgeons as may be required with no limit.

During the war Appointments were made to James Mann on April 9, 1812, Josiah Foster and Garret Pendergrast on April 25th, David Kerr who is listed in the historical register as a Hospital Surgeon's Mate named David Key, on April 30th, William Wilson on May 25th, Samuel Akerly and John Gough on July 6th, William Ross on March 18, 1813, Walter Wheaton on March 28th, Samuel Shaw on April 6th, Hozea Blood on May 5th, William McCaw on May 20th, George Proctor on June 11th, Thomas Akin and Benjamin Waterhouse on June 29th, John Martin on July 2nd, Ezekiel Bull on August 9th, William Thomas on February 18, 1814, Henry Huntt on March 17th, Adams Hays and Tobais Watkins on March 30th, James Bronaugh on May 15th, Joseph Lovell on June 30th, James Mease on September 2 and William Mercer on November 2nd (6).

Foster Died on December 22, 1812 and Daniel on October 8, 1813. Gough Resigned on June 30, 1813 and Pendergrast on November 30, 1814. McCaw was dismissed on March 22, 1814 and Wilson took a post as a regimental surgeon on April 15th.

With the war over the army was reduced to having five Hospital Surgeons on March 3, 1815 (7). All were discharged on June 15, 1815 except Bronaugh, Walkins, Waterhouse, Lovell and Kerr (the 1815 register (8) shows an Arnold Elzey who the historical register has as a Garrison Surgeon's Mate (9), instead of Watkins. Shaw was reappointed on September 13, 1815 and the January 1816 register show him, Kerr, Waterhouse, Bronaugh and Lovell, with Watkins is listed as provisionally retained and Elzey back to being a Garrison Mate (10).

Egbert Bell was appointed as a Hospital Surgeon on April 29, 1816 and James Mann was reappointed on May 3rd.

Hospital Surgeons were abolished by a law of April 14, 1818 (11).

Lovell was made Surgeon General, Watkins and Bronaugh were made Assistant Surgeons General, Mann, Kerr, Shaw and Waterhouse were made Post Surgeons and Bell was made regimental surgeon of the 8th infantry (12).

There is no evidence of medical uniforms before 1813 when they were to wear a black version of the general staff uniform with cuff flaps and cloth covered buttons (13).

Hospital Surgeon's Mate

The law of March 2, 1799 that set the medical establishment for the possible war with France called for "A suitable number of hospital mates" (1), but it as never implemented.

On April 12, 1808 (2) a new law allowed "such number of hospital surgeons and surgeon's mates as the service may require but not exceeding five surgeons and fifteen mates". 15 were authorized but only one was appointed, William Thomas on July 7, 1809 (3).

When the army was expanded for the War of 1812, a law on January 11, 1812 (4) put no limit on the number of Hospital Surgeon's Mates, but it was returned to 15 at the end of the war (5). This was raised to 16 with eight in each of the Army's two divisions on April 24, 1816 (6).

Hospital Surgeon's Mates were abolished on April 14, 1818 (7), and were converted into Post Surgeons (8).

There is no evidence of medical uniforms before 1813 when they were to wear a black version of the general staff uniform with cuff flaps and cloth covered buttons (9).

Indian Scouts

On July 28, 1866 congress allowed "the President is hereby authorized to enlist and employ in the Territories and Indian country a force of Indians, not to exceed one thousand, to act as scouts, who shall receive the pay and allowances of cavalry soldiers,"(1). There is no indication in the law about them holding any rank other that Indian Scout, and they are shown in the enlisted total column on the 1868 table of organization but not in any of the rank columns(2).

An appropriations bill of July 22, 1876 (3) set aside "For the pay proper of three hundred privates employed as Indian scouts forty six thousand eight hundred dollars.", this would seam to indicate that scouts were in fact Privates.

Scouts were moved to the Privates column on the table of organization in the 1881 register (4), and split into Sergeants, Corporals and Privates in 1885 (5).

Judge Advocate

Judge Advocates are the army's lawyers. The first Judge Advocate was William Tudor, appointed July 29, 1775 (1). He was just the "judge advocate" until August 10, 1776 when he was given the rank of Lieutenant Colonel.

Tudor was replaced by John Lawrence on April 10, 1777 (2). It is not clear whether Lawrence held a regular rank or not. Lawrence resigned in June of 1782 (3) and his successors in the Continental army appear to have held regular ranks.

A law of March 3, 1797(4) allowed one Judge Advocate, but he was to be taken from the line officers. Captain Campbell Smith of the Fourth Infantry held the office(5) until it was abolished on March 16, 1802 (6).

Judge Advocates returned on January 11, 1812 (7) when they were given the "pay and emoluments as a major in the infantry" but apparently not the rank.

The first appointment was Thomas Gale on September 26, 1812 (who resigned on December 16, 1814). He was followed by Evert Bancker on March 18, 1813, Robert Tillotson on April 12th (who resigned on October 4th), John Wills on May 7th, James Dent on July 19th, Stephen Lush on October 5th, Rider Winder on July 9, 1814, Henry Wheaton on August 6th, Leonard Parker on September 16th and Samuel Wilcocks on December 19th (8).

When the War of 1812 ended the army was reduced and Bancker, Wills, Winder, Parker, Lush and Wilcocks were discharged on June 15th, 1815. Leaving only Dent and Wheaton.

More Judge Advocates were added by a law of April 24, 1816 (9). Thomas Hanson and William Winston were appointed on April 29th and Rider Winder was reappointed on May 3rd. Wheaton was discharged on May 9, 1816 and John Leib and Samuel Storrow were appointed on July 9th. The Senate did not confirm Lieb's appointment and he left the army on January 15, 1817 (10).

A new law on April 14, 1818 (11) reduced the number of Judge Advocates to two. Hanson and Winston were discharged on April 14th and Winder Resigned on July 23rd. Stokely Hays was appointed on September 10th.

A reorganization of the army on March 2, 1821 (12) did not include Judge Advocates and Storrow and Hays were discharged on June 1st.

In 1820, and 1820 only were allowed to wear the general staff uniform without and eagle on the cockade on the hat. Other than that they wore civilian clothes (13).

Lance Acting Hospital Steward

Similar to Lance Corporals, Lance Acting Hospital Stewards were Privates of the Hospital Corps who were "getting a try out" as an Acting Hospital Steward. They were given three months to show they were able to perform at the higher rank. As such, Lance Acting Hospital Steward was not a rank created by law but by a general order in November 1901 (1).

The insignia was one green chevron outlined in white, under a green Maltese cross also outlined in white (2).

One chevron and a caduceus was briefly used from 1902 to 1903 (3).

In 1903 the title was changed to Lance Corporal of the Hospital Corps (4).

Lance Corporal

Congress never created a rank of Lance Corporal and it never appears on any table of organization.

The army created Lance Corporals in May of 1891 as a method of testing the leadership capacity of soldiers for possible promotion to Corporal (1).

One chevron was worn as an insignia (2). Lance Corporals were added to the Signal Corps, in 1898 and they wore the crossed flags and torch of the Signal Corps, in the angle of their chevron (3). When Lance Acting Hospital Steward became Lance Corporals in 1903 they wore one chevron and a caduceus (4). The clothing specifications of 1905 through 1908 also show Lance Corporals of the Ordnance Department wearing a bursting bomb with the one chevron (5).

The National Defense Act of 1916 (1) expanded the use of privates first class and ended the need for lance corporals. Only the West Point Band used the rank from 1916 until 1920 (7).

Leader of the Band

A law of July 29, 1861 (1) called for the new infantry regiments raised for the Civil War to have "one drum-major, or leader of the band". They were to have the emoluments of Second Lieutenants.

On July 17, 1862 (2) the regimental bands were eliminated and replaced with brigade bands, whose leaders would receive the emoluments of a Quartermaster Sergeant.

The 1863 table of organization lists them a Drum Majors (3). Brigade bands were not part of the post war organization (4).

There is no information on insignia for Leaders of the Band. They may have worn the same uniforms as other senior musicians.

Lieutenant

The term lieutenant comes from the French for "placeholder" (1). It can be thought of a someone who hold a place or is a tenant instead of or in lieu of. A tenant in lieu of, is a lieutenant.

As medieval captains became involved in court politics, they needed someone to fill in for them while they were away, and the rank of Lieutenant was born (2).

Lieutenant, without a "first", "second" or "third" was the official title of the rank between Ensign/Cornet and Captain until 1799. However "first", "second" or "third" was often used to denote the officer's position in their company.

As subalterns they were to wear the green cockade from July 1775 to June 1780 and then a button colored epaulet on the left shoulder (3).

In 1799 Ensigns and Cornets became Second Lieutenants and this made Lieutenants, First Lieutenants (4).

Lieutenant Colonel

Like Captains, sixteenth century Colonels often left there columns or regiments to attend to business at royal courts (1). While they were gone a lieutenant was needed to take their place, and Lieutenant Colonels were born.

Lieutenant Colonels existed in the Continental Army from the beginning. Being "field grade" officers along with Majors and Full Colonels they were to wear a red cockade from July 23, 1775 until June 18, 1780, then a button colored epaulet on each shoulder (2).

When the federal army was founded, Lieutenant Colonel was it's highest rank. It's commander was Josiah Harmar who took office on August 12, 1784. Harmar was given a brevet as a Brigadier General on July 31, 1787 to give him authority over the state militia troops under his command (3) but he still was Lieutenant Colonel Commandant of the army's only infantry regiment. He was given a brevet and not promoted so not to created a vacancy in that office. Whether Harmar wore silver or gold epaulets is not known. Harmar resigned on January 1, 1792 (4).

A second regiment and therefore a second Lieutenant Colonel was added on March 3, 1791 (5). The new officer was James Wilkinson (6).

On March 5, 1792 the army was divided into four sub legions each command by a Brigadier General one of which was Wilkinson. The structure included no Lieutenant Colonels until February of 1793 (7) when a one was added to each sub legion. They were John Hamtramek, David Strong, John Clark and Henry Gaither. Clark was replaced by Thomas Butler on July 1, 1794 (8).

The artillery and engineers were combined on May 9, 1794 (9), and a Lieutenant Colonel was added to command them. Stephen Rochefontaine was appointed on February 26, 1795 (10).

As the army grew more and more Lieutenant Colonels were added. After 1802 regiments were commanded by Full Colonels and Lieutenant Colonels became second in command (11).

In 1812 the dragoon Lieutenant Colonels, Electrus Backus and Archibald MacNiell, had two strips of silver lace on their horse cloths (12).

In March of 1821 Lieutenant Colonels were ordered to wear two buttons colored chevrons on each upper sleeve (13), but new regulations in July continued the two epaulets, the seven in the infantry wearing silver and the four in the artillery and the one engineer, Charles Gratiot, wearing gold.

The new frock coat in May of 1829 was to have field officers wearing a gilt eagle on both collars (14), this became a strip of button colored lace as a shoulder strap on each side in July (15).

New uniforms of 1832 had Field Officers wearing four buttons on the cuff of the dress coats outlined in button colored lace. Lieutenant Colonels were to have button colored epaulets with 1/2 inch wide bullion (16).

When rectangular shoulder straps were created around 1834, Lieutenant Colonels had an 1/8 inch button colored border and oak leafs at each end in the same color as the border (17).

The 1851 uniform regulations made all epaulets and shoulder strap borders gold. For Lieutenant Colonels a silver oak leaf was worn on the epaulet strap and at each end of the shoulder strap. A sleeve knot of four black cords was worn on the overcoat (18).

The silver oak leaf has been the badge of rank for Lieutenant Colonels ever since. Worn on either side of the shoulder knot pad that replaced epaulets in 1872, at the sleeve end of the shoulder loops on the 1898 khaki coat, and on shoulder loops, collars ect. thereafter.

Black oak leafs have been worn a subdued insignia since 1965 (19).

The four loop knot was used on the dress and mess uniforms of the early twentieth century.

The Career Compensation Act of October 12, 1949 placed Lieutenant Colonels in pay grade O-5 (20).

The 2005 uniform regulations describe the insignia as "Lieutenant colonel. The non-subdued grade insignia is a silver-colored oak leaf, in a satin finish with an irregular surface, 1 1⁄8 inches high and 1 inch wide. The leaf is worn with the stem facing the outside shoulder seam. The subdued grade insignia is the same as above, except the color is black" (21).

Lieutenant General

Captains had their Lieutenants, Colonels had their Lieutenant Colonels, and Generals had their Lieutenant Generals to fill in for them or assist them in command (1).

George Washington argued for the creation of the rank of Lieutenant General in the Continental Army (2)(3), but nothing came of it.

Washington himself would become the first american Lieutenant General in 1798 when he was placed in command of troops raised for a possible war with France. The law stated "a commander of the army which may be raised by virtue of this act, and who being commissioned as lieutenant-general may be authorized to command the armies of the United States" (4).

On March 3, 1799 congress moved to change Washington's title stating "That a commander of the army of the United States shall be appointed and commissioned by the style of " General of the Armies of the United States," and the present office and title of Lieutenant-General shall thereafter be abolished."(5), however the threat of war passed and Washington died on December 14th (6) still a Lieutenant General.

It is not known if Washington ever wore a uniform during this period, or if any insignia was intended for this rank.

The rank of Lieutenant General was next used in February of 1855 when Winfield Scott was given a brevet backdated to March 29, 1847 to honor his service in the Mexican War (7).

Scott had been entitled to three stars on his epaulets and shoulder straps since he became commander of the army in 1841 (8). His predecessor, Alexander Macomb, had changed the insignia to three stars in 1834 (9).

Scott served until he retired on November 1, 1861 (10).

In 1864, President Lincoln wanted to appoint Ulysses S. Grant to command the army. There would have been problems with the other Major Generals who were higher in seniority or had better political connections that Grant, if he had just been made Major General Commanding the Army. In response to this problem, congress passed a law stating "Be it enacted by the Senate ad House of Representatives of the United States of America in Congress assembled, That the grade of lieutenant-general be and the same is hereby revived in the army of the United States;

and the President is hereby authorized, whenever he shall deem it expedient, to appoint, by and with the advice and consent of the senate, a lieutenant-general, to be selected from among those officers in the military service of the United States, not below the grade of major-general, most distinguished for courage, skill, and ability, who, being commissioned as lieutenant general, may be authorized, under the direction, and during the pleasure of the President, to command the armies of the United states." (11).

When the size of the army was set after the Civil War (12), the army was allowed one Full General or General of the Army as it was called, and one Lieutenant General. Grant was given his fourth star on July 25, 1866 and William Tecumseh Sherman was made Lieutenant General. Sherman was promoted on March 4, 1869 and Philip Sheridan became Lieutenant General (13).

The insignia used by Scott, Grant, Sherman and Sheridan went unchanged throughout the period. The 1851 uniform regulations called for epaulets of "gold with solid crescent; device, three silver embroidered stars, one, and one half inches in diameter, one, and one fourth inches in diameter, and one, and one eighth inches in diameter, placed on the strap in a row, longitudinally, and equidistant, the largest star in the center of the crescent, the smallest at the top; dead and bright gold bullion one half inch in diameter and three and one half inches long." Shoulder straps were described as "dark blue cloth, one and three-eighth inches wide by four inches and; bordered with and embroidery of gold one fourth of an inch wide; three silver embroidered stars of five rays, one star on the centre of the strap, and one on each side equidistant between the centre and the outer edge of the strap; the centre star to be the largest." Overcoat sleeve knots were described for generals of all ranks were described at "of five braids, double knot."(14).

On July 15, 1870 a new law stated "That the offices of general and lieutenant-general of the army shall continue until a vacancy shall occur in the same, and no longer; and when such vacancy shall occur in either of said offices, immediately thereupon all laws and parts of laws creating said office shall become inoperative, and shall, by virtue of this act, from thenceforward be held to be repealed."(15). This meant that when Sherman retired, which happened on February 4, 1884, Sheridan would take command of the army as a Lieutenant General and Sheridan's successor would be a Major General.

Special legislation was passed on June 1, 1888 (16) to merge the ranks of General of the Army of the United States and Lieutenant General. The purpose of this was to allow Sheridan, who was seriously ill, to be promoted without changing the 1870 law. Sheridan held the combined rank until his death two months later, on August 5th (17).

Sheridan was replaced by Major General John Schofield. Congress made Schofield a Lieutenant General on February 5, 1895 by stating "Resolved by the Senate and House of Representatives of the United States of America in Congress assembled, That the grade of lieutenant-general be, and the same is hereby, revived in the Army of the United States, in order that when, in the opinion of the President and Senate, it shall be deemed proper to acknowledge distinguished services of a major general of the Army, the grade of lieutenant-general may be specially, conferred: Provided, however, That when the said grade of lieutenant general shall have once been filled and become vacant, this joint resolution shall thereafter expire and be of no effect."(18) This allowed Schofield to be promoted but did nothing to create a permanent rank. Schofield held his rank until his retirement on September 29th.(19)

Part of an appropriations bill of June 6, 1900 stated "That the senior major-general of the line commanding the Army shall have the, rank, pay, and allowances of a lieutenant-general, " (20). This promoted Schofield's successor Nelson Miles. In 1901 (21) Lieutenant General was made a permanent rank of the army, allowing one.

Miles retired on August 8, 1903 and the senior Major General was the Adjutant General Henry Corbin but he June 1900 required a "major-general of the line". As head of a staff department Corbin was ineligible so the next and final commanding general was Samuel Young (22).

On February 14, 1903 (23), to take affect in August, the position of commanding general was abolished and replaced with a Chief of Staff. Young was immediately appointed to this position which he held until he retired on January 9,

1904. He was replaced by Adna Chaffee who served until February 1, 1906. The next senior general was John Bates who was due to retire in April. Bates took the office for those few months (24).

With the office of commanding general no longer existing there was no barrier to making Corbin Lieutenant General and Chief of Staff, except in his opinion, age. Corbin was 64 and due to retire in September. He was made the army's one allowed Lieutenant General on April 15, 1906 but turned down the position of Chief of Staff, which was given to Major General Franklin Bell (25). The position could have gone to Arthur MacArthur who was next in line and did become Lieutenant General when Corbin retired, but MacArthur had had many fights with the Secretary of War William Howard Taft while MacArthur was military governor of the Philippines (26). This left MacArthur as the highest ranking officer in the army but having to answer to Bell.

The rank was abolished upon MacArthur's retirement by a law of March 2, 1907 (27). On June 2, 1909 MacArthur's became a Lieutenant General on the retired list and the rank ceased to exist.

The insignia remained the same until 1902. After that, shoulder straps remained the same but other insignia was to be "such as they may prescribe" (28). Assuming they were similar to other generals, three stars were worn on collars and shoulder loops and above a line of oak leaf and acorn embroidery on full dress and mess coats. Overcoat cuffs had two lines of black braid, the lower one was 1/14 inches wide and the upper 1/2 inches wide with the three stars in bronze between them (29).

During World War I, on October 6, 1918 to be precise, congress allowed for the period of the existing emergency only, to appoint as generals the Chief of Staff and the commander of the United States forces in France; and as lieutenant general each commander of an army or army corps" (30). Hunter Liggett and Robert Bullard were appointed on October 16th (31). The war ended on November 11th and Liggett and Bullard reverted to Major Generals on June 30, 1920.

The rank of Lieutenant General returned for good on August 5, 1939 with a law stating "Be it enacted by the Senate and House of Representatives of the United States of America in Congress assembled That the major generals of the Regular Army specifically assigned by the Secretary of War to command the four armies of the United States Army shall have the rank and title of lieutenant general while so serving:" (32). From this point forward the Lieutenant Generals were appointed to various positions that called for them.

The Career Compensation Act of October 12, 1949 (33) placed the rank of Lieutenant General in pay grade O-8 which it shared with Full General and Major General. This lasted until May 20, 1958 when a new law (34) created pay grade O-9 for Lieutenant Generals.

When subdued insignia was introduced in 1965 the three Stars were to be black (35).

The 2005 uniform regulations describe the insignia for Lieutenant Generals as "Lieutenant general. The non-subdued grade insignia has three silver-colored, five-pointed stars, each 1 inch in diameter. Medium silver-colored stars, 3⁄4 inch in diameter and miniature silver-colored stars, 5⁄8 inch in diameter, also are authorized. The subdued grade insignia is the same as above, except the color is black"(36).

Major

In the seventieth century English army of Oliver Cromwell each regiment had a sergeant who was third in command and was in charge of administrative matters. He was known as a great sergeant or sergeant major (1). Despite being called sergeant, it was a higher rank than Captain or Lieutenant. It is assumed that this is the reason the "sergeant" part dropped away and the title became just "major" (2).

Majors have always existed in the american army. Classified as "field grade" officers along with both grades of Colonel, they were to wear a red cockade from July 23, 1775 until June 18, 1780, then a button colored epaulet on each shoulder (3).

Major was the army's highest rank from June 20th to August 12, 1784 when the entire army was an artillery company commanded by Brevet Major John Doughty (4).

In 1812 the dragoon Majors had two strips of silver lace on their horse cloths (5).

In March of 1821 Majors were ordered to wear one buttons colored chevron on each upper sleeve (6), but new regulations in July continued the two epaulets, the seven in the infantry wearing silver and the four in the artillery and the two engineers and six topographical engineers, wearing gold.

The new frock coat in May of 1829 was to have field officers wearing a gilt eagle on both collars (7), this became a strip of button colored lace as a shoulder strap on each side in July (8).

New uniforms of 1832 had Field Officers wearing four buttons on the cuff of the dress coats outlined in button colored lace. Majors were to have epaulets with 1/2 inch wide bullion, The bullion, border and crescent were to be of button color, silver for infantry and gold for others, while the lace making the strap was to be of the other color (9). Under this system an infantry major would have an epaulet with silver bullion, crescent and border with the lace inside the border and crescent being gold. An artillery major would have the opposite.

This carried over when rectangular shoulder straps were created. The 1/8 inch border was of button color while the oak leafs at each end were in the opposite color, gold border, silver leafs and silver border, gold leafs (10).

When new uniforms arrived in 1851 and "button color" was abolished, Majors were to wear gold leafs on their shoulder straps and three cords on their overcoat sleeve knots. Their epaulets had no device on the strap. The only difference between the epaulet of a Major and a Second Lieutenant was the 1/2 inch wide bullion worn by majors versus the 1/8 inch worn by lieutenants (11).

When epaulets were replaced by shoulder knots in 1872, a gold leaf was worn on each side of the pad and the lack of a device was restricted to Second Lieutenants (12).

The gold oak leaf has been the badge of rank for Majors ever since. Worn at the sleeve end of the shoulder loops on the 1898 khaki coat, and on shoulder loops, collars ect. thereafter.

Brown oak leafs have been worn a subdued insignia since 1965 (13).

The three loop knot was used on the dress and mess uniforms of the early twentieth century.

The Career Compensation Act of October 12, 1949 placed Majors in pay grade O-4 (14).

The 2005 uniform regulations describe the insignia as "Major. The non-subdued grade insignia is a gold-colored oak leaf, in a satin finish with an irregular surface, 1 1⁄8 inches high and 1 inch wide. The leaf is worn with the stem facing the outside shoulder seam. The subdued grade insignia is the same as above, except the color is brown" (15).

Major General

While seventieth century English regiments had a Sergeant Major as third ranking officer handling administrative duties, the entire army had a Sergeant Major General (1). The "sergeant" part was dropped over time and the rank became Major General ranking just below Lieutenant General. This is why a Lieutenant General outranks a Major General but a Major outranks a Lieutenant.

Twenty-nine officers held the rank of Major General at various times in the Continental Army. On July 14, 1775 they were ordered to wear a pink ribbon across the breast between the coat and waistcoat, the same as Brigadier Generals. Later that month the color for Major Generals was changed to purple (2). The ribbons were replaced on

June 18, 1780 with a gold epaulet on each shoulder with two silver stars on each (3). The last of the Continental Army Major Generals was Henry Knox who was the army's senior officer from when George Washington returned his commission on December 23, 1783 until June 20, 1784 (4).

The army was expanded on March 3, 1791 (5), and a Major General was placed in command. His name was Arthur St. Clair, and he was appointed on March 4th. St. Clair had been a Major General in the Continental Army from February 19, 1777 until November 3, 1783 (6).

St. Clair resigned on March 5, 1792 and was replaced by Anthony Wayne. Wayne commanded the army as a Major General until his death of December 15, 1796 (7).

On March 3, 1797 (8), congress eliminated Major Generals from the army, but this would only last until May 28, 1798 (9), when preparations began for a possible war with France. Under this law a Major Generals was to be appointed to serve an Inspector General, and on July 16, 1798 (11) two more Major Generals were added. Alexander Hamilton took office as Inspector General on July 19th, as did Charles Pinkney (12), Henry Knox turned down the other position (13). Provisional appointments were also made to Henry Lee and Edward Hand (14) but the emergency passed and they never held the rank.

The Quartermaster General was "to be entitled to the rank, pay, emoluments, and privileges of a major-general", under a law of on March 3, 1799 (15). The serving Quartermaster General, John Wilkins, apparently was made a Major General (16), but in the historical register he is just listed as quartermaster general (17) and there is note saying the appointment to Major general was never made (18).

Hamilton took command of the army when George Washington died on December 14, 1799.

On May 14, 1800 (19) an act was passed to discharge the officers appointed for the war that never came. Hamilton and Pinckey left the army on June 15th. On March 16, 1802 (20) congress set the size of the peace time army. Its one and only general would be a Brigadier, so the rank of Major General ceased to exist again. The law also did away with the office of Quartermaster General. Wilkins, a Major General or not, left the army on June 1st (21).

Major Generals next appeared during the War of 1812. Two were allowed on January 11, 1812 (22), The first was Henry Dearborn who became a Major General and took command of the army on January 27th (23). The other was Thomas Pinckney who took office on March 27th (24). Six more were added on February 24, 1813 (25), and James Wilkinson, Wade Hampton, Morgan Lewis and future President William Henry Harrison became Major Generals on March 2nd (26). The other two slots were filled on January 24, 1814 by George Izard and Jacob Brown. Hampton resigned on March 16, 1814 (27) and Harrison on May 31st (28). Another future President, Andrew Jackson became a Major General on May 1st (29).

The postwar organization, passed on March 3, 1815 (30), allowed for two Major Generals. Brown (who would command the army) and Jackson were chosen, and the rest were discharged on June 15th.

Four officers were given brevets to Major General in 1814 as a reward for there service in the war, Edmund Gaines on August 14th, Alexander Macomb on September 11th and Eleazer Ripley and on Winfield Scott July 25th. The Quartermaster General Thomas Jesup was given a brevet on May 8, 1828.

The army was reduced to one Major General on March 2, 1821 (31), and Jackson left the army on June 1st (32).

Brown died on February 24, 1828 (33), and was replaced by Alexander Macomb on May 29th (34).

It is not known if Macomb wore the 1829 frock coat or how his rank was shown on it.

In 1834 Macomb ordered that the Major General commanding the army would wear three stars (35). Why would the Major General commanding need to be set apart from other Major Generals in an army with only one Major

General? The answer may lie in the brevets held by the two Brigadier Generals, Winfield Scott and Edmond Gaines. They may have been wearing two stars and Macomb need three to establish his authority.

This almost coincides with the introduction of rectangular shoulder straps. An illustration attached to a general order creating shoulder straps in the Marine Corps in 1835, shows straps of both two stars for Major General and three for General Commander in Chief (36). Since the highest rank in the Marine Corps in 1835 was Colonel, this drawing had to be made for the army.

According to the 1839 uniform regulations the insignia for the Major General Commanding the Army was "Epaulettes gold, with solid crescent; device, three silver embroidered stars, one 11/2 inch in diameter, one 1 1/4 inch, and one 1 1/8 inch, placed on the strap, in a row longitudinally, and equidistant; the largest star in the centre of the crescent, the smallest at the top; dead and bright gold bullion.", and for shoulder straps "strap of blue cloth, one inch in breadth, and not less than three and a half inches nor more than four inches in length; bordered with an embroidery of gold a quarter of an inch wide; three silver embroidered stars of five rays, one star on the centre of the strap, and one on each side, equidistant between the centre and outer edge of the strap. The centre star to be the largest; where these stars would come in contact with the embroidery of the strap, there must be described an arc of a circle, (having the centre of the star for its centre, and the radius of the star for its radius,) taking out a sufficient quantity of the embroider to admit them.". For other Major Generals the insignia was "Epaulettes the same, excepting that there shall be two stars on the straps, instead of three.", and shoulder straps "the same as the Major General commanding the army, except that there will be two stars instead of three; the centre of each star to be one inch from the outer edge of the gold embroidery on the ends of the strap; both stars of the same size." (37).

Macomb died on June 25, 1841, and was replaced by Scott (38).

More Major Generals were added to serve under Scott when war broke out with Mexico. On June 16, 1846 (39) a second Major General was added. He was future President Zachary Taylor who took office on June 29th (40). On June 26th (41) congress authorized the President to appoint officers to command the volunteer forces assembled for the war. Two Major Generals of Volunteers were appointed, William Butler on June 29th and Robert Patterson on July 6th (42). Two more regular Major Generals were added on March 3, 1847 (43). They were Gideon Pillow appointed April 13th and John Quitman appointed the next day (44).

After the war the army was reduced to just one Major General, Scott, by a law of July 19, 1848 (45). Taylor resigned to become President on January 31, 1849 (46), Butler was discharged on August 15, 1848 (47) and Patterson (48), Pillow (49) and Quitman (50) on July 20th.

Brevets for the Mexican War were given to David Twiggs on September 23, 1846, Stephen Kearny on December 6, 1846, John Wool on February 23, 1847, James Shields on April 18, 1847, Riley Bennet and Persifor Smith on August 20, 1847. George Cadwalader on September 13, 1847, Joseph Lane on October 9, 1847 and Hugh Brady, George Brooke, George Gibson and Roger Jones on May 30, 1848 (51). Twiggs, Wool and Smith all served a Brigadier Generals between the Mexican War and The Civil War and may have worn two stars.

The 1851 uniform regulation didn't change the insignia for Major Generals all that much. The center star on Scott's shoulder straps was now to fit inside the strap and the border no longer needed to be cut away, and the five cord double sleeve knot was added to the overcoat (52).

Scott retired on November 1, 1861 and was replaced as Major General Commanding with George McClellan, who served until March 11, 1862. The office was vacant until Henry Halleck was appointed on July 23rd. Halleck was superseded when Grant was made a Lieutenant General on March 2, 1864 (53). As for other Major Generals, the Civil War brought them, regular, brevet or volunteers, by the barrel full.

The insignia did not change from the 1851 regulations until 1902, with the exception of the two stars worn on the dark blue shoulder loops of the 1898 khaki coat (54).

The 1902 regulations put the two stars above the cuffs of the full dress and mess/evening coats, on the shoulder straps, unchanged from 1851, on the dress coat, on the shoulder loops of field coats, on shirt collars and in bronze between two lines of black braid on the overcoat cuff (55).

The two stars, wherever they need to be worn, have been the insignia ever since.

The Career Compensation Act of October 12, 1949 (56) placed the rank of Major General in pay grade O-8 which it shared with Full General and Lieutenant General. This lasted until May 20, 1958 when a new law (57) gave Major Generals the grade all to themselves.

When subdued insignia was introduced in 1965 the two Stars were to be black (58).

The 2005 uniform regulations describe the insignia for Major Generals as "Major general. The non-subdued grade insignia has two silver-colored, five-pointed stars, each 1 inch in diameter. Medium silver-colored stars, 3⁄4 inch in diameter, and miniature silver-colored stars, 5⁄8 inch in diameter, also are authorized. The subdued grade insignia is the same as above, except the color is black"(59).

Master Chemical Sergeant

The rank of Master Chemical Sergeant or Master Chemist, existed from February to May of 1918 and wore the insignia of the Chemical Warfare Service in a wreath (1).

This rank was never created by law, and that along with the nature of the rank organization of World War I, makes it hard to trace and verify.

Master Electrician

The rank of Master Electrician was created in the coast artillery on March 2, 1903 (1).

The insignia was three chevrons and one arc that was not attached to the chevrons, with five lightning bolts between. In full color the chevrons and arc were red and the bolts white (2).

In 1907 this was changed to the lightning bolts in a wreath. In full color the bolts were silver and the wreath gold (3).

A star was added above the bolts in 1908 the color version had red bolts, a yellow wreath and a white star. Then color was returned to chevron in 1920, the bolts and stars were white and the wreath green (4).

In the 1920 enlisted grade reorganization Master Electricians were made Master Sergeants (5).

Master Electricians also were used in the Quartermaster Corps. They were added on August 24, 1912 (6) and wore the insignia of the Quartermaster Corps in a wreath under the lightning bolts. In full color the bolts were buff, the wreath yellow and the insignia yellow and white (7).

They were changed to quartermaster sergeants senior grade on June 2, 1916 (8).

Master Engineer Junior Grade

The rank Master Engineer Junior Grade was created in the Corps of Engineers, by the National Defense Act of June 3, 1916 (1). They wore the insignia of the Corps of Engineers in a wreath. In full color the wreath was yellow and the insignia red outlined in white (2).

Master Engineer Junior Grade was also used in the Transportation Corps in 1919 and 1920 with the winged wheel of that corps replacing the castle of the engineers (3).

In January of 1920 the army intended to change the insignia for both branches to a red wheel in a green wreath, all under a white navy petty officer's eagle (4). However the enlisted grade reorganization in July made this unnecessary as master engineers junior grade became Technical Sergeants (5).

Master Engineer Senior Grade

The rank Master Engineer Senior Grade was also created in the Corps of Engineers, by the National Defense Act of June 3, 1916 (1). They wore the insignia of the Corps of Engineers in a wreath under a star. In full color the wreath was yellow, the insignia red outlined in white and the star white (2).

Master Engineer Senior Grade was also used in the Transportation Corps and Tanks Corps. in 1919 and 1920 with the winged wheel for transportation or a tank replacing the castle of the engineers (3).

In January of 1920 the army intended to change the insignia for all three branches to a red wheel in a green wreath, all under a white navy petty officer's eagle, all under a white star (4). However the enlisted grade reorganization in July made this unnecessary as master engineers senior grade became Master Sergeants (5).

Master Gunner

On January 25, 1907 the rank of Master Gunner was added to the coast artillery (1). The insignia was an artillery shell in a wreath under a star. In full color the shell was red the wreath yellow and the star white (2).

When color was added to chevrons in 1920 the wreath was green, the shell red and the star white (3).

The enlisted grade reorganization of July of 1920 made the senior 50% of Master Gunners into Master Sergeants and the rest into Staff Sergeants (4).

Master Hospital Sergeant

Master Hospital Sergeants were created in the Medical Department by The National Defense Act of 1916 (1).

The insignia was a caduceus in a wreath under a star. When color was added to some of the drab insignias in 1920 the wreath became green, the star white and the caduceus maroon (2).

With the enlisted grade reorganization of 1920 they became Master Sergeants (3).

Master of the Sword

A Master of the Sword was added to each troop of light dragoons on June 26, 1812 (1).
The law stated “the pay and emolument of a master of the sword shall be the same as those of a riding master”.

They would have been abolished, along with the dragoons, on March 3, 1815 (2).

They Probably wore the uniform of a Private of dragoons.

Master Sergeant

The rank of Master Sergeant was created in the enlisted grade reorganization of 1920 from the grades of Regimental Sergeant Major. Sergeant Major Senior Grade, Quartermaster Sergeant Senior Grade, Master Hospital Sergeant, Master Engineer Senior Grade, Master electrician, Master Signal Electrician, Engineer, Regimental Supply

Sergeant, the senior 25% of Ordnance Sergeants, the senior 50% of Master Gunners and the Band Sergeants and Assistant Band Leader of the West Point band (1).

Placed in grade one, it was the army's highest enlisted rank.

The insignia was, and still is, three chevrons and three arcs (2).

The Career Compensation Act of October 12, 1949 converted grade one into grade E-7 (3) where Master Sergeants remained until two new grades were created in 1958 (4) and they were moved up to grade E-8.

The 2005 uniform regulations descried the insignia as "Master sergeant: three chevrons above three arcs" (5).

Master Signal Electrician

An appropriations bill of April 28, 1904 (1) created the rank of Master Signal Electrician in the Signal Corps. The insignia was the same three chevron and one arc with lighting bolts as a Master Electrician except in full color the chevrons were orange piped in white (2).

The insignia was changed in 1909 to signal flags in a wreath under lightning bolts and a torch was added to the flags in 1918 (3).

When the air service separated form the signals in 1918 the rank went with it. The crossed wings and propeller replacing the signal insignia (4)

With the enlisted grade reorganization of 1920 they became Master Sergeants (5).

Master Specialist

Master Specialist was the original title for the specialist rank in the E-7 pay grade. Created in 1954 it lasted until 1958 when it became Specialist 7 (1).

The insignia was the eagle device from the great seal under three arcs (2).

Master Wagoner

A law of August 3, 1861 stated "there shall be added to the quartermaster's department as many master wagoners, with the rank, pay, and allowances of sergeants of cavalry, and as many wagoners, with the pay and allowances of corporals of cavalry, as the military service, in the judgment of the President, may render necessary."(1).

From then until at least 1878 there is a column on the tables of organization for Master Wagoners with a footnote stating there is to be as many as necessary. A table for 1879 is not available and they are not on the 1880 table (2). There never was a law eliminating them but they must have stopped between 1878 and 1880.

There is no information on uniforms or insignia for Master Wagoners.

Master Warrant Officer

In 1988 the creation of the W-5 pay grade was pending. In anticipation the army designated the most senior Chief Warrant Officer 4s as Master Warrant Officers (1).

The insignia was a silver bar with four black squares with silver centers. The subdued version was olive drab and black (2). This insignia was chosen instead of the W-5 insignia design in the 1970s of a silver bar with a black stripe down the center, so it would like the army was jumping the gun on the creation of the W-5 rank before congress acted (3).

When congress did act, appointments of Master Warrant Officers stopped and those serving were to continue until being promoted or discharged. It was decided that the same insignia would continue for W-5s to save the cost of a change and avoid the confusion of having six warrant insignias (4).

Mechanic

Mechanics were added to the heavy artillery on March 2, 1899 (1).

The insignia was the same as Artificers, crossed hammers (2).

The field artillery had Artificers instead of Mechanics so there are references to "Mechanics and Artificers" in the artillery, but they are two different ranks with the same insignia. The heavy artillery became the coast artillery in 1901 (3), but the law continued the organizations as the had stood, so the use of both ranks continued. Mechanics replaced Artificers in the Field Artillery in 1907 (4).

The National Defense Act of 1916 (5) made the Artificers in the infantry into Mechanics and added them to the cavalry and the Medical Department.

The enlisted grade reorganization of 1920 made the into Specialists Fifth Class (6).

Medical Cadet

The Civil War brought a need for trained medical personnel. With that in mind, on August 3, 1861 congress passed a law saying "That there be added to the medical staff of the army a corps of medical cadets, whose duty it shall be to act as dressers in the general hospitals and as ambulance attendants in the field, under the direction and control of the medical officers alone They shall have the same rank and pay as the military cadets at West Point Their number shall be regulated by the exigencies of service, at no time to exceed fifty. It shall be composed of young men of liberal education, students of medicine, between the ages of eighteen and twenty-three, who have been reading medicine, for two years, and have attended at least one coarse of lectures in a medical college. They shall enlist for one year, and be subject to the rules and articles of war. On the fifteenth day of the last month of their service, the near approach of their discharge shall be reported to the surgeon general, in order, if desired, that they may be relieved by another detail of applicants." (1).

Medical Cadets wore officer's undress uniforms with a special shoulder strap. The strap was rectangle of green cloth 3 3/4 inches by 1 1/4 inches with a strip of gold lace 1/2 inch wide and 3 inches long in the center (2).

Medical Cadets did not continue after the end of the war.

Medical Inspector

Medical Inspectors were added to the Medical Department on April 16, 1862 (1) to monitor the sanitary conditions at army medical facilities. They were to rank with Lieutenant Colonels.

Appointed on June 11th were Charles Keeeney, John Cuyler, Richard Cooledge, Edward Vollum and George Lyman. William Mussey and George Allen were appointed on June 14th and Lewis Humphreys on June 30th (2).

On December 27, 1862 (3) more inspectors were added and their duties were expanded to recommending soldiers in hospitals to be discharged or returned to their units.

The new appointments went to Joseph Barnes, Frank Hamilton, George Johnson, Augustus Hamlin and Peter Pineo on February 9, 1863. John Summers was appointed on February 27th, Norton Townshend on March 11th ad George Stipp on March 12th (4).

Barnes was promoted to Medical Inspector General on April 10, 1863 and was replaced with John Wilson. Hamilton resigned on August 29, 1863 and was replaced with John LeConte. Summers left the army on October 31, 1863, Mussey resigned on January 1, 1864 as did Johnson on October 1, 1865. Edward Kittoe was made a Medical Inspector General on March 30, 1864.

As equivalent Lieutenant Colonels they were to wear epaulets with 1/2 inch wide bullion, a silver oak leaf on the strap and the silver letters M.S. in a gold wreath in the frog. Their shoulder straps would be the standard straps for staff Lieutenant Colonels, a dark blue background and a silver oak leaf at each end.

The Medical Inspectors were all mustered out on October 31, 1862 except Lyman who stayed until November 20th (5).

Medical Inspector General

A Medical Inspector General was also added to the Medical Department on April 16, 1862 (1) to supervise the Medical Inspectors. They were to rank with full Colonels.

As equivalent Colonels they were to wear epaulets with 1/2 inch wide bullion, a silver eagle leaf on the strap and the silver letters M.S. in a gold wreath in the frog. Their shoulder straps would be the standard straps for staff Colonels, a dark blue background and a silver eagle in the center.

Originally the office went to Thomas Perley on July 1, 1862. He resigned on August 10, 1863 and was replaced with Joseph Barnes. Barnes was promoted to Surgeon General on April 22, 1864 and the office wasn't filled until December 1st when Madison Mills was Appointed. Mills was mustered out with the rest of the Medical Inspectors on October 31, 1865 (2).

Medical Storekeeper

On May 20, 1862 congress passed a law stating "That the Secretary of War be authorized to add to the medical department of the army medical storekeepers, not exceeding six in number, who shall have the pay and emoluments of military storekeepers in the quartermaster's department, who shall be skilled apothecaries or druggists, who shall give, the bond and security required by existing laws for military storekeepers in the quartermaster's department, and who shall be stationed at such points as the necessities of the army may require: Provided, That the Act, how long provisions of this act shall remain in force only during the continuance of the present rebellion ." (1)

Appointed on August 13th were Robert Creamer, Henry Rittenhouse, Hennell Stevens, Victor Zoeller, Henry Johnson, and George Wright. Zoeller resigned on April 6, 1863 and William Giles was appointed on June 20th only to resign himself on September 10th. Rittenhouse resigned on February 13, 1865, Wright on January 1, 1866 and Stevens on March 14th. Creamer was mustered out on December 9, 1865, Leaving only Johnson (2).

The Quartermaster Department's Storekeepers wore a plain blue frock coat and trousers with a round black hat. The medical storekeepers may have worn this uniform as well (3).

When the size of the army was set at the end of the Civil War, there were to be five Medical Storekeepers. They were to have "the same compensation as is now provided by law". The original law made them the same as storekeepers in the Quartermaster's Department and this law made those storekeepers "have the rank, pay and emoluments of captains of infantry"(4).

As of July 28, 1866, Henry Johnson was still serving and George Wright returned that day. Added were Andrew Cherbonnier and George Beall, also that day. The fifth slot was filled on August 3, 1867 by Florence O'Donnoghue (5).

The 1872 uniform regulations describe a coat for storekeepers as "For all Storekeepers: A single-breasted coat, as lately worn by Captains of the staff, with staff shoulder-straps to indicate rank. This coat shall be worn on all dress 'occasions, such as reviews, inspections, dress parades, guards, and court-martials." (6).

Medical Storekeepers were abolished on June 26, 1876 (7), but the law allowed those in service to be eliminated by attrition, and attrition took awhile. Wright had died on May 19, 1872 and O'Donnoghue died on June 29, 1882. Cherbonnier retired on October 12, 1890, Johnson on March 24, 1891 and Beall on February 25, 1894. Meaning it took 18 years for the rank to cease to exist after it was abolished (8).

Mess Sergeant

Mess Sergeants were created by the National Defense Act of 1916 (1).

They were to wear the three chevrons until mid 1918 when a cook's cap was added under the three chevrons (2).

With the enlisted grade reorganization of 1920 they became Sergeants (3)

Military Agent

Three Military Agents were added to the army's staff March 16, 1802 (1).

The appointments of April 29, 1802 were Abraham Abrahams, Peter Gansevoort and William Linnard. Gansevoort was made a Brigadier General on February 15, 1809 and Abrahams resigned on May 31st. Andrew McCulloh was made a Military Agent on May 3rd but died on December 23rd. It appears only Linnard stayed in the army until Military Agents were abolished (2).

This Happened on March 28, 1812 (3), when the Quartermaster's Department was established and their duties were taken up by Deputy Quartermasters. Linnard was made a Deputy on April 3, 1812.

There is no evidence of them wearing uniforms.

Military Storekeeper

Military Storekeeper could be called the rank that wouldn't go away. It was first created in the Purchasing Department on March 3, 1813 (1). However there are references to storekeepers at arsenals as early as 1810 (1a) (1b). When the Purchasing Department was abolished in 1842 (2) they were moved to the Quartermaster's Department and apparently those at arsenals to the Ordnance Department. Some of the storekeepers at arsenals also acted as paymasters (2a).

They had no uniform until 1839 (3) when they were to wear a plain blue coat with general staff buttons, plain blue or white trousers, a round hat with a black cockade and yellow eagle, the sword and belt of the Pay Department, The undress uniform substituted the standard forage cap and a single breasted frock coat without shoulder straps (4).

The 1851 regulations call for a plain blue frock coat, round black hat and plain white or blue pantaloons (5).

The 1872 uniform regulations describe a coat for storekeepers as "For all Storekeepers: A single-breasted coat, as lately worn by Captains of the staff, with staff shoulder-straps to indicate rank. This coat shall be worn on all dress 'occasions, such as reviews, inspections, dress parades, guards, and court-martials." (6).

On July 28, 1866 (7) they were given the equivalent rank of Captain. The same law made Military Storekeepers in the Ordnance Department into Ordnance Storekeepers.

On March 3, 1875 a new law said "That no more appointments shall be made in the grade of military storekeepers in the Quartermaster's Department, and this grade shall cease to exist as soon as the same becomes vacant by death, resignation, or otherwise of the present incumbents." (8).

The 1875 army register show nine storekeepers, Ruben Potter, Charles Alligood, John Rodgers, John Liver, Gustavus Hull, Hamilton Lieber, Verplanck Van Antwerp, Addison Barrett and William Martin (9). Potter Retired on June 30, 1882 (10), Alligood died on March 31, 1890 (11), Rodgers retired on January 13, 1894 (12), Hull retired on April 18, 1891 (13), Lieber Retired on December 13, 1875 (14), Van Antwerp died on December 2, 1875 (15), Martin retired on March 20, 1885 (16), Livers retired on June 20, 1882 (17), and Barret died on September 22, 1896 (18) 21 years after the rank was abolished.

The army was without a Storekeeper for 621 days. On July 1, 1898 congress authorized the appointment of a Storekeeper (19) and Charles Loeffler took office on July 5th, serving until he retired on January 12, 1901 (20). Loeffler probably wore the uniform of a Captain in the Quartermaster's Department.

Was this the end of Military Storekeepers? No, it wasn't. On August 29, 1916 an appropriations bill revved the rank and gave it by name to Charles Daly (21). The "present military storekeeper" was made an equivalent Major on June 4, 1920 (22), a rank he held until he died on November 13, 1926 (23).

.

Motor Sergeant

The rank of Motor Sergeant wearing three chevrons over a twelve spoke wheel with tire, is shown in the book Chevrons by William K. Emerson as being used for general application along with the Chauffeur grades (1). From 1783 to 1813 this put most Musicians in red faced with blue (2).

There is no law creating Motor Sergeants, but when dealing with ranks from World War I it is difficult to be precise.

Musician

Musician is a rank with a very long history. Musicians were used to communicate commands on the battlefield and keep time when marching. In the dragoons or cavalry the terms "bugler" or "trumpeter" were usually used in place of Musician.

Traditionally musicians would wear the reverse colors of their regiment (1). If a regiment wore blue uniforms with green facings (lapels, collar, ect.) the musicians would wear green uniforms with blue facings.

In 1813 the red facings of the infantry and artillery were removed as a cost cutting measure. The coats for musicians were to be of all red (3). Musicians in rifle regiments who had been wearing buff faced with green since 1810 and continued to do so (4), and musicians in the engineers wore red faced with black (5).

The red dress uniforms were worn until 1851. The 1832-1851 version had two loops of button colored lace on the cuff (6).

The 1851 uniforms regulations prescribed Private's uniforms with the breast covered in facing colored cloth (7). This was changed in 1854 with a herringbone pattern with tape outlining the basic shape of the old facing and more tape going across from each button (8). From 1872 to 1902 musicians dress coats hand tape coming out from each button, coming to a point and going back to the button (9).

Beginning in 1885 the musicians of bands added a lyre to the eagle on their dress helmets (10).

In 1902 musicians wore the same uniforms as other enlisted men, with band musicians replacing the branch insignia with a lyre and regimental number or lyre and castle in the case of engineers (11).

The National Defense Act of 1916 divided the rank of Musician into classes (12).

Musician First Class

The National Defense Act of 1916 divided the rank of Musician into classes, creating the rank of Musician First Class (1).

No insignia was prescribed until January of 1920 when a yellow lyre was to be worn on the upper sleeve like other enlisted rank insignia (2).

The insignia was never used as the enlisted grade reorganization of July 1920 eliminated the rank. Musicians First Class of the West Point Band became Specialists First Class, and the rest Specialist Third Class (3).

Musician Second Class

The National Defense Act of 1916 divided the rank of Musician into classes, creating the rank of Musician Second Class (1).

No insignia was prescribed until January of 1920 when a yellow lyre was to be worn on the upper sleeve like other enlisted rank insignia (2).

The insignia was never used as the enlisted grade reorganization of July 1920 eliminated the rank. Musicians Second Class of the West Point Band became Specialists Third Class, and the rest Specialist Fourth Class (3).

Musician Third Class

The National Defense Act of 1916 divided the rank of Musician into classes, creating the rank of Musician Third Class (1).

No insignia was prescribed until January of 1920 when a yellow lyre was to be worn on the upper sleeve like other enlisted rank insignia (2).

The insignia was never used as the enlisted grade reorganization of July 1920 eliminated the rank. Musicians Third Class of the West Point Band became Specialists Fourth Class, and the rest Specialist Fifth Class (3).

Oiler

Oilers were part of the Mine Planter Service at it's inception in 1918 (1).

The insignia prescribed in January of 1919 was three chevrons and a connected arc with a three bladed propeller in the middle (2). The chevrons, arc and propeller, were all red on a blue background.

In 1920 it was replaced with the same insignia as an Assistant Engineer, a mechanical governor in a wreath (3).

The enlisted grade reorganization on July 1920 made Oilers into Specialist Second Class (4)

Ordnance Sergeant

A new law on April 5, 1832 stated "That the Secretary of War be authorized to select from the sergeants of the line of the army, who shall have faithfully served eight years in the service, four years of which in the grade of noncommissioned officer, as many ordnance sergeants as the service may require, not to exceed one for each military post; whose duty it shall be to receive and preserve the 'ordnance, arms, ammunition, and other military stores, at the post under the direction of the commanding officer of the same, and under such regulations as shall be prescribed by the Secretary of War, and who shall receive for their services five dollars per month, in addition to their pay in the line."(1). The intent here was to give older sergeants a chance at a desk job (2) and allow the Ordnance Department to keep tack of equipment without having to rely on the individual regimental quartermasters.

Ordnance Sergeants were to wear the uniform of a Sergeant Major of Artillery without an aiguillette and the trouser stripe in blue (3). This would have meant they would wear plan gold epaulets with 1/8 inch bullion made of yellow cord.

When chevrons were added to fatigue jackets in 1847 one were prescribed for Ordnance Sergeants. It is possible that as staff at army posts Ordnance Sergeants didn't wear fatigue jackets.

The 1851 uniform regulations called for three chevrons and a star, all in crimson, the facing color of the Ordnance Department (4). When gold lace dress chevrons were introduced in 1884 the star was rendered in gold (5). The star was replaced with a crimson/gold busting bomb in 1901 (6).

In 1902 the insignia was changed to three chevrons and one arc that was not attached to the chevron, with the bursting bomb in the middle. In fill color the chevrons and arc were black, the new ordnance facing color, piped with red and the bomb was black with a red flame (7).

In September of 1917 the arc was replaced with a straight bar which was worn until May of 1918 when the insignia became a busting bomb in a wreath (8). When color was added to some insignias in 1920 the wreath was green the bomb black with the flame in two shades of red (9).

The 1920 enlisted grade reorganization made the top 25% of Ordnance Sergeants in to Master Sergeants and the rest into Technical Sergeants (10).

Ordnance Storekeeper

Military Storekeepers in the Ordnance Department were changed to Ordnance Storekeepers on July 28, 1866 (1). The law made the storekeeper at the Springfield armory an equivalent Major and all others equivalent Captains.

Appointed were James Abeel, William Wiley, Henry Brigham, Eusebius Jones, Thomas Deane, Benjamin Gilbreath, Frederick White, Edward Ingersoll who was the Major in Springfield, William Shoemaker, Ephraim Ellsworth, William Adams, Daniel Young, William Rexford, Alergnon Morgan and Michael Grealish (2).

They would have worn the plain blue frock coat, round black hat and plain white or blue pantaloons of other Storekeepers.

The 1872 uniform regulations describe a coat for storekeepers as "For all Storekeepers: A single-breasted coat, as lately worn by Captains of the staff, with staff shoulder-straps to indicate rank. This coat shall be worn on all dress 'occasions, such as reviews, inspections, dress parades, guards, and court-martials." (3).

Wiley left the army on October 1, 1870, Brigham died on November 15, 1870 and Jones on December 3, 1871. Abeel retired on February 22, 1869 and Deane, Gilbreth, White, Ingersoll, Shoemaker and Ellsworth retired on June 30, 1882 (4).

A law of May 1, 1882 (5) allowed the appointments of another Ordnance Storekeeper, and Valentine McNally took office on May 5th. There doesn't appear to be a law that stopped appointments before this, but none of the vacancies were filled as they came up.

Adams Retired on July 14, 1883, Young on December 11, 1888 and Morgan on June 9, 1894. Grealish died on May 1, 1897. Rexford was promoted to equivalent Major on December 6, 1889 six years after Ingersoll had retired. Rexford himself retired on November 3, 1898(6).

McNally was made an equivalent Major on June 6, 1896. A law of June 30, 1902 (7) allowed McNally to retire as a Lieutenant Colonel.

Paymaster

The was responsible for paying the troops. He was usually "taken from them line", meaning a regimental officer assigned to this duty, but Paymaster was used as a title for a time.

A pay table from May of 1778 (1) shows paymasters were to be taken from the line and paid $20 in addition to their regular salary. This would seam to indicate that Continental Army paymaster held regular ranks.
The federal army used officers taken from the line until the appointment of District Paymasters for the War of 1812. After the war the law once again stated "the brigade quartermasters, the adjutants, regimental quartermasters, and paymasters, from subalterns of the line." (3).

On April 24, 1816 (4), a Paymaster was added to each battalion in the Corps of Artillery. They could either taken from the subalterns of the line or citizens. The citizens would not have another rank so they would be simply Paymasters. Both the battalion and regimental paymasters were to have the "pay and emoluments of a major".

If we examine the army register dated August 1816 (5) (it shows dates of rank in 1817, so the date is not correct) we find listed under Battalion Paymaster in the artillery are Satterlee Clark, Joseph Woodruff, David Gwynn, David Townsend and Leory Opie all appointed on April 29, 1816, Cary Nicholas appointed on February 17, 1817, Simeon Knight on May 16th and Richard Platt on November 21st. The Regiment of Light Artillery had an officer of the line serving as its paymaster, First Lieutenant John Gates Jr. The duties for the engineers were handled by Second Lieutenant Thomas Leslie. The paymaster for the First Infantry was taken from the line in the form of First Lieutenant John Tarrant, but the Second Infantry's paymaster Jacob Albright was listed under "Paymaster". The Third Infantry had First Lieutenant Asher Phillips in the post. The Fourth Infantry appears to have been without a paymaster, the Fifth had First Lieutenant Benjamin Larned and the Sixth, First Lieutenant Alphonso Wetmore. The Seventh Infantry had John Hogan listed as just a "Paymaster", and the Eighth had First Lieutenant Stoughton Gantt.

Richard Platt was made a battalion paymaster of Artillery on November 21, 1817 (6). Daniel Randall became a just "Paymaster" in the First Infantry on July 21, 1818 (7). Thomas Broom became a just "Paymaster" in the Fourth Infantry on February 13, 1818 (8). John Hall was named Paymaster of the new rifle regiment on April 18, 1818 (9). Broom and Hogan Traded regiments on June 10, 1818. Opie died on October 30, 1819 (10) and was replaced with Charles Smith on November 24th (11). The January 1820 register (12) shows Thomas Wright, who was listed as a Captain of the line of the 8th Infantry in previous registers, now listed a a just "Paymaster". The historical register shows his commission as a Captain ending on January 1, 1819 (13). Knight resigned on November 20, 1820 (14) and Platt on November 24th (15), Abraham Massias was appointed as a replacement on December 20th (16) and Captain Daniel Burch of the Seventh Infantry was taken from the line on July 24th (17). In the January 1821 register (18), Phillips is no longer listed as a First Lieutenant but just as a Paymaster. Hall's appointment was recalled on August 7, 1820 (19), and he was replaced with Captain Thomas Biddle (20).

This brings us to the reorganization of the army on March 2, 1821 (21). The Corps of Artillery was broken up into regiments and as a result battalion paymasters were no longer needed. There was also no provision for regimental paymasters in either the infantry or the artillery. Instead there would be 14 Paymasters assigned to the Pay Department having "the pay and emoluments of regimental paymasters".

The 14 slots went to Wright, Phillips, Wetmore, Larned, Clark, Woodruff, Gwynn, Townsend, Albright, Tallmadge, Randall, Smith, Biddle and Massias, with their appointments backdated to when they first became paymasters (22). Three more slots were added in 1836 (23).

The one Paymaster not in the Pay Department after 1821 was the Paymaster for the Corps of Engineers, First Lieutenant and Brevet Captain Thomas Leslie. This was remedied by law on July 5, 1838 (24), and Leslie became a Paymaster in the Pay Department.

Paymasters officially became Majors on March 3, 1847 (25) when a new law stated "That the officers of the Pay Department shall have rank corresponding with the rank to which their pay and allowances are assimilated:".

It is not known if the Paymasters without other ranks wore uniforms prior to 1820, but it is doubtful. In 1820 they wore the generals staff uniform but by 1821 they were back in civilian clothes (26). In 1825 they were allowed the standard army uniform with the wings worn by Captains and Lieutenants (27). It is interesting that even though they were paid as Majors, they were to wear the wings of junior officers.

The 1832 uniform regulations gave Paymasters a double breasted coat with ten gold buttons in each row. The standing collar and the cuffs were blue to match the coat. On each side of the collar was a single blind button hole, outlined in gold lace, with a gold button (28).

In 1841 the collar and cuffs were outlined in a vine of laurel leaves and a a laurel branch. A Major's two colored epaulets were to be worn with the letters "P.D." in the frog in gold, inside a gold wreath (29). Shoulder straps with a gold border and a silver oak leaf at each end would be worn on the undress frock coat.

Paymaster General/ Paymaster of the Army

The man in overall charge of paying the army is the Paymaster General.

The office in the Continental Army was created on June 16, 1775 (1) and James Warren was appointed on July 27th (2). Warren Resigned on April 19, 1776 and was replaced by William Palfrey. Palfey was given the rank of Lieutenant Colonel on July 9, 1776 (3). Palfrey was named Council to France on November 4, 1780, Unfortunately the ship he took to France was lost at sea in December (4). Palfrey's replacement as Paymaster General was John Pierce, appointed on January 17, 1781 (5). The register does not indicate that Pierce held a regular rank.

Pierce served to the end of the war and continued in office until his death on August 1, 1788 as both the Paymaster General and a Commissioner for settling accounts of the army. The Continental Congress combined the two offices in March of 1787 (6). After Piece died, another commissioner named Joseph Howell looked after the army's pay.

As a Lieutenant Colonel, Plafrey would have been entitled to red cockade on his hat until 1780 then a gold epaulet on each shoulder. There is no information on uniforms for Warren or Pierce, it is doubtful if any were worn.

On May 8, 1792 congress passed a law that said "That there be a paymaster to reside near the headquarters of the troops of the United States."(7). Caleb Swan was appointed (8).

A law created a Paymaster General on May 30, 1796 (9), again on March 3, 1797 (10), and on May 28, 1798 (11), and March 3, 1799 (12), but no action was ever taken. Swan remained in office whatever it was called. The Peace Establishment Act of March 16, 1802 (13) allowed one Paymaster of the Army. Once again this was Swan, until he resigned on June 30,1808 (14) and was replaced with Robert Brent (15).

Brent's title was finally changed to Paymaster General on April 24, 1816 (16), which he held until he resigned on August 28, 1819 (17) and was replaced with Nathan Towson (18). Towson had been a Captain in the light artillery regiment and held a brevet as a Lieutenant Colonel dated July 5, 1814. He was nominated to be the Full Colonel commanding the Second Artillery on June 1, 1821 and Daniel Parker was made Paymaster General in his place. Parker had been a brevet Brigadier General as the army's Adjutant and Inspector (19). The Senate did not confirm Towson as commander of the Second Artillery, and he resumed his post as Paymaster General on May 8, 1822 (20), and Parker left the army.

There is no law making the Paymaster General equivalent to a Colonel, even in pay. Unlike regular Paymasters who were paid as Majors from 1816, the same law just gives the Paymaster General a salary of $2500.00 (21). A reorganization on March 2, 1821 (22) just calls for one Paymaster General "with present compensation". On July 5, 1838 (23) a law said "That hereafter the officers of the pay and medical departments of the army shall receive the pay and emoluments of officers of cavalry of the same grades respectively". Then finally on March 3, 1847 (24) "That the officers of the Pay Department shall have rank corresponding with the rank to which their pay and allowances are assimilated:". This made the Paymaster General a Colonel.

It may have been because of Towson's brevet and his aborted appointment as a Colonel, it was simply assumed the Paymaster General was equal to a Colonel.

It is not known if Swan or Brent wore uniforms. Towson and Parker may have worn uniforms of their old ranks, but this to is not known.

In 1820 Towson was to have worn the General Staff uniform (25) and he may have worn a field officers epaulets due to his brevet. However in 1821 Paymasters were to be without uniforms (26), it is unknown if this applied to Towson. In 1825 was to wear a regular army uniform with the wings of a junior officer (27).

The 1832 uniform regulations gave Towson a double breasted coat with ten gold buttons in each row. The standing collar and the cuffs were blue to match the coat. On each side of the collar were two blind button holes, outlined in gold lace, with gold buttons (28).

In 1841 the collar and cuffs were outlined in a vine of laurel leaves and a a laurel branch. A Colonels gold epaulets were to be worn with a silver eagle on the strap and the letters "P.D." in the frog in silver, inside a gold wreath (29). Shoulder straps with a gold border and a silver eagle in the middle would be worn on the undress frock coat.

Physician and Surgeon General

A Physician and Surgeon General was added in each of the Continental Army's three departments on April 7, 1777 (1). Appointed on April 11th were John Bartlett in the Northern Department, John Cochran in the Middle Department and William Burnett in the Eastern Department (2). Cochran and Burnett served until October 6, 1780 and Bartlett until January 1, 1781 (3).

On March 3, 1813 (4) the title was revived for the War of 1812. James Tilton took office on June 11th and served until June 15, 1815 (5).

1813 regulations for General Staff uniforms prescribe black coats with black covered buttons and a gold star on the collar for all medical officers. How long this uniform lasted is not known(6).

Physician General

On May 28, 1798 (1), in preparation for the possible war with France, Congress authorized the appointment of a Physician General with the pay of a Lieutenant Colonel. James Craik, the former head of the Continental Army's Hospital Department was appointed on July 19th (2). The historical register shows the appointment in 1789 (3), but this is probably a transposition error.

The threat of war passed and Craik was discharged on June 15, 1800 (4).

Physician General of Hospitals

Physician General of Hospitals was a title of the Continental Army's Hospital Department Created on April 7, 1777 (1). Appointed were Malchi Treat, Ammi Cutler and Walter Jones (2). Jones resigned on July 1, 1777 and was replaced by Benjamin Rush. Rush resigned on July 21, 1780 and was replaced by William Brown. Treat left the army on August 1, 1777, Cutler resigned on March 9, 1778 and Brown on July 21, 1780 (3).

Pioneer

Pioneer was never a rank of the Army. It never appeared on any table of organization. However it is included here because the insignia of crossed hatchets was usually listed with the enlisted rank insignia in uniform regulations.

Pioneers were responsible for clearing the path in front of a marching army, such as building roads or fixing bridges (1).

The crossed hatchets were worn from 1851 (2) until 1899 (3). If a pioneer was a corporal, the hatchets were worn in the angle of the chevrons.

Platoon Sergeant

A platoon sergeant is the senior noncommissioned officer in a platoon. It is one of the most important positions in the army because the platoon sergeant had a great deal more experience in leadership than the Lieutenant commanding the platoon.

Platoon Sergeant is a position not a rank, but it appears to have been a rank at one time. The position is held by Sergeants First Class, but there are some references (1) (2) (3) (4) of a rank of Platoon Sergeant sharing the E-7 pay grade and the three chevrons and two arcs. The system would have been similar to the situation in the E-8 grade, those who are a senior noncommissioned officer in a company are First Sergeants, those who are not are Master Sergeants.

It apparently began in 1958 (5) but when it ended is difficult to say. It was probably in the early 1980s but the best reference it the 1992 uniform regulations (6) that just show Sergeant First Class in E-7.

Post Chaplain

When the army was reorganized at the end of the Civil War (1), 30 Post Chaplains were assigned to various army posts around the country.

They would have worn the Chaplains uniform established in 1864 a black frock coat with one row of nine black covered buttons with black herringbone lace around them, black trousers and a black felt hat or army forage cap with staff officers insignia. On occasions of ceremony a plain chapeau de bras could be worn (2)

Chaplains were given shoulder straps in 1880. They were the standard size with a black background and a silver shepherds crook in the center. Use of these shoulder straps was stopped in 1888 (3). Shoulder straps returned in 1898, this time with a silver cross in the center instead of the crook (4).

The herringbone lace was removed from the frock coat sometime between 1872 and 1875 (5).

The 1897 uniform regulations state “CHAPLAIN - Plain black frock coat, with standing collar; one row of nine black buttons on the breast, or, if desired, a plain double-breasted frock coat of black cloth, falling collar; with two rows of black silk buttons on the breast, seven in each row, placed at equal distances. For "undress", either the black frock or a plain black sack coat of cloth or serge, falling collar, single-breasted, one row of five black buttons in front, the skirt to extend from one-third to three-fourths the distance from hip-joint to the bend of the knee. Provided, that when a particular coat or vestment is required by the church to which the chaplain belongs, he may wear such coat or vestment while conducting religious services.”(6)

A reorganization of the army on February 2, 1901 (7) stated "That the office of post chaplain is abolished, and the officers now holding commissions as chaplains, or who may hereafter be appointed chaplains, shall be, assigned to regiments or to the corps of artillery".

Post Commissary Sergeant

On March 3, 1873 a new law stated "That the Secretary of War be and he is hereby, authorized and empowered to select from the sergeants of the line of the army who shall have faithfully served therein five years, three years of which in the grade of non-commissioned officer, as many commissary-sergeants as the service may require, not to exceed one for each military post or place of deposit of subsistence supplies, whose duty it shall be to receive and preserve the subsistence supplies at the posts, under the direction of the proper officers of the subsistence department, and under such regulations as shall be prescribed by the Secretary of War." (1). These men would answer to the subsistence department and not the commander of the post, giving the department better control of the record keeping at far flung forts. A similar concept had been used by the ordnance department since the 1830s and would be used by the quartermaster's department after 1884.

These men, however were known a Commissary Sergeants. The "Post" was added in 1898 when Commissary Sergeants were added to line branches (2).

The continued to wear the three chevrons and a crescent (3) until the merger of the Subsistence Department, The Quartermaster's Department and The Pay Department to form the Quartermaster Corps in 1912 (4). That law stated "The noncommissioned officers now known as post quartermaster sergeants and post commissary sergeants shall hereafter be known as quartermaster sergeants;".

Post Quartermaster Sergeant

Following in the footsteps of the Ordnance Department in 1832 and the Subsistence Department in 1873, the Quartermaster's Department was given Post Quartermaster Sergeants by a law of July 5, 1884 (1) that said "That the Secretary of War is authorized to appoint, on the recommendation of the Quartermaster as many post quartermaster sergeants, not to exceed eighty as lie may deem necessary for the interests of the service, said sergeants to be selected by examination from the most competent enlisted men of the Army who have served at least four years, and whose character and education shall fit them to take charge of public property and to act as clerks and assistants to post and other quartermasters. Said post quartermaster sergeants shall, so far as practicable, perform the duties of store keepers and clerks, in lieu of citizen employees. The post quartermaster sergeants shall be subject to the rules and articles of war and shall receive for their services the same pay and allowances as ordnance sergeants .".

They were to wear three chevrons with a crossed key and quill in the angle, all in buff (2). On the gold lace dress chevrons the chevrons were gold lace on a buff background and the key and quill were embroidered in gold (3).

In 1902 Post Quartermaster Sergeants were to wear three chevrons with the insignia of the Quartermaster's Department (4).

The Quartermaster's Department was merged with the Pay and Subsistence Departments in 1912 (5), and Post Quartermaster Sergeants became Quartermaster Sergeants of the Quartermaster Corps.

Post Surgeon

On April 24, 1816, the Medical Department was given "as many post surgeons as the service may require, not exceeding twelve to each division, who shall receive the same pay and emoluments as hospital surgeon's mates,"(1). This law replaced the previous title of Garrison Surgeon with Post Surgeon. This only affected the one Garrison Surgeon left in the army Foster Swift (2).

The rank lasted until March 2, 1821 when it was combined with Regimental Surgeon's Mate, and became the rank of Assistant Surgeon (3).

There is no evidence of medical uniforms before 1813 when they were to wear a black version of the general staff uniform with cuff flaps and cloth covered buttons (4).

Principal Musician

Principal Musicians replaced Teachers of Music in 1808 (1) as the senior musicians in a regiment. They existed in the infantry continuously from 1808 until 1916 and in other branches for a great deal of that time. They were finally eliminated by The National Defense Act of 1916 (2), when they became Assistant Band Leaders (3).

As musicians the would have worn red uniforms in the early days. In 1821 they were to wear a button colored, white for infantry or yellow for artillery, above each cuff (4). Beginning in 1832 they wore the uniform of a Sergeant Major of their branch expect the dress coat would be red (5). This became a blue Sergeant Major style uniform with the breast covered in facing color cloth in 1851 (6) and a herringbone pattern of lace after 1854 (7).

Finally in 1872 Principal Musicians were given three chevrons and a bugle (8), which they wore until the rank was abolished in 1916.

Principal Teamster

On March 3, 1847 a new law said "That to each regiment of dragoons, artillery, and mounted riflemen, in the regular army, there shall be added one principal teamster, with the rank and compensation of quartermaster-sergeant"(1).

There is no evidence of uniforms for Principal Teamsters.

The rank was not part of the army after the end of the Mexican War (2).

Private

Private is the army's lowest rank and always has been. The term comes from the Latin for someone without office (1). It's use as a military rank comes from the sixteenth century when men would sign "private contracts" to serve in armies (2).

As the lowest rank, Privates wore plain uniforms with no insignia. From 1832 to 1851 they wore dress uniforms with two laced button holes on the cuff and cloth epaulets with very short bullion (3).

Privates of the Signal Corps wore crossed signal flags during the Civil War (4), and the crossed flags and a torch of the Signal Corps from 1903 to 1911 (5).

The 1920 enlisted grade reorganization (6) placed Privates in grade seven.

The Career Compensation Act of October 12, 1949 converted grade seven into grade E-1 (7) but the army placed ranks of Private in both the E-1 and E-2 grades (8). For clarity the ranks are referred to as Private E-1 and Private E-2. It is possible that the E-1 rank was initially called Recruit, but the evidence on this is far from clear and it may have just been a colloquialism.

In 1965 the army came up with a plan to eliminate Private E-2 by moving Private First Class down to E-2 and reviving the old title of Lance Corporal for E-3. This plan went far enough that there are rank charts and even encyclopedias that show the ranks this way, but the plan was never put into effect. The only result of this idea was to give Privates E-2 an insignia of one chevron in 1968 (9).

The 2005 uniform regulations describe the insignia as "Private (E-2): one chevron" and "Private (E-1): no insignia" (10).

Private First Class

The rank Private First Class was born on May 15, 1846 (1) when enlisted men were added to the Corps of Engineers. The law called for "thirty-nine privates of the first class, or artificers". The rank also existed the Corps of Topographical Engineers when enlisted men were added on August 6, 1861 (2). This lasted until the two corps were merged on March 3, 1863 (3).

On July 5, 1862 the enlisted men of the Ordnance Department were given regular ranks and "those now designated as artificers shall be designated and mustered as privates of the first class" (4).

The Signal Corps was organized on March 3, 1863 (5) with enlisted men "who shall receive the pay of similar grades of engineer soldiers". This may, or may not have placed Privates First Class in the Signal Corps.

There was nothing to distinguish Privates of the First Class from other Privates. In fact they there was no separate column on the tables of organization until 1866 (6). That chart shows 320 in the Corps of Engineers and 287 in the Ordnance Department, the Signal Corps was not carried as an organization on after the Civil War but the law of July 28, 1866 (7) allowed engineer soldiers to be detailed for signal service.

The 1872 uniform regulations contain a curious paragraph calling for "Enlisted men of the Signal Service" to wear cavalry style uniforms with orange as a facing color (8). Since the only men in the signal service were detached from the Corps of Engineers, it seams odd that they would have their own uniforms. The regulations call for Privates of the first class to wear crossed signal flags on both upper sleeves.

A permanent enlisted presence in the Signal Service was created in 1878 (9), but Privates First Class Don't appear on the tables of organization until 1885 (10) and disappear again in 1889 (11). All enlisted men but Sergeants were eliminated from the Signal Corps on October 1, 1890 (12). Privates First Class were specifically added to the Signal Corps on April 26, 1898 (13) as a temporary measure for the war with Spain. This structure was made permanent on March 2, 1899 (14). The insignia of the Signal Corps was worn on the upper sleeve by Privates First Class after 1898 (15).

In 1902 Privates First Class in the Corps of Engineers (16) and the Ordnance Department (17) began wearing the insignia of those branches on the upper sleeve as rank insignia. What happened in the Signal Corps is a mystery. References from the era (18) (19) show the Signal Corps insignia worn by Privates, they don't say Privates First Class. It is possible the insignia was worn by both ranks (21). The 1912 regulations have the insignia worn by Privates First Class (22).

Privates First Class were added to the Hospital Corp. (the enlisted portion of the Medical Department) on March 2, 1903 (23) replacing the rank of Private of the Hospital Corps, and wore the caduceus of the Medical Department (24).
When the Quartermaster Corps was created in 1912 (25), it included Privates First Class who wore the branch insignia (26).

The National Defense Act of 1916 (27) put Privates First Class in most branches, replacing Lance Corporals. All wore their branch insignia embroidered on the upper sleeve (28).

This made it harder for the army to be rid of the branch specific insignia that was complicating it's supply system in World War I. While a Sergeant of the Quartermaster Corp. could be identified just as easily by his three chevrons whether or not they had the branch insignia under them, Privates First Class could not. Special insignia had to be manufactured for each new branch added to the army. This led to the creation of an employ wreath insignia for men serving at general headquarters (29).

Finally in September of 1919 the army approved a common insignia for all Privates First Class, an arc (30).

It is doubtful many arcs were actually worn, because of the enlisted grade reorganization in July of 1920 (31). This placed Privates First Class in grade six, they were to wear one chevron (32).

With the reorganization after The Career Compensation Act of October 12, 1949 (33), Privates First Class were placed in pay grade E-3 (34).

In 1965 there was a plan to move Private First Class and it's one chevron down to E-2 and revive the title of Lance Corporal in E-3 with one chevron and one arc (35). This never happened but in 1968 the insignia for Private First Class was changed to one chevron and one arc (36).

The 2005 uniform regulations describe the insignia as "Private first class: one chevron above one arc" (37).

Private of the Hospital Corps.

On March 1, 1887 congress created organized the enlisted men in the Medical Department into the Hospital Corps. Sections five and six of that law stated "SEC 5. That the Secretary of War is empowered to enlist, or cause to be enlisted, as many privates of the Hospital Corps as the service may require, and to limit or fix the number, and make such regulations For their government as may be necessary; and any enlisted man in the, Army shall be eligible for transfer to the Hospital Corps as a private. They shall perform duty as wardmasters, cooks, nurses, and attendants in hospitals, and as stretcher-bearers, litter-bearers, and ambulance attendants in the field, and such other duties as may by proper authority be required of them.
SEC. 6. That the pay of privates of the Hospital Corps shall be thirteen dollars per month, with the increase on account of length of service as is now or may hereafter be allowed by law to other enlisted men; they shall be entitled to the same allowances as a corporal of the arm of service with which on duty." (1).

In February of 1901 they were given the insignia of a green maltese cross outlined in white (2). This was changed to a maroon caduceus outlined in white in 1902 (3).

The Hospital Corps was given a more conventional rank structure on March 2, 1903 (4). The law made all Privates of the Hospital Corps into Privates First Class.

Private Second Class

The history of the rank of Private Second Class mirrors that of Private First Class.

The rank was first used in the Corps of Engineers starting on May 15, 1846 (1) and was used continuously until the National Defense Act of 1916 (2) gave the engineers regular Privates.

It was used in the Corps of Topographical Engineers from August 6, 1861 (3) until the two corps were merged on March 3, 1863 (4).

It became part of the Ordnance Department when laborers became "Privates of the Second Class" on July 5, 1862 (5). The National Defense Act of 1916 left the organization of the Ordnance Department unchanged and Private Second Class is shown on the pay chart in the 1920 army register (6). It was eliminated by the enlisted grade reorganization of 1920, presumably becoming Privates in grade seven.

The use of the rank in the Signal Corps is more complicated. It may have been used starting on March 3, 1863 (7) when signal soldiers were given similar rank to engineer soldiers. After the Civil War there were to enlisted men officially belonging to the Signal Corps, but men were detailed from the Corps of Engineers. The 1872 uniform regulations (8) call for signal service Privates Second Class to wear crossed signal flags on the left sleeve. Enlisted men were returned to the Signal Corps in 1878 (9) and once again they were to have similar ranks to the engineers. This might have created first and second class privates but it also might not have. They are not separated on the tables of organization until 1885 (10), but combined back into the regular Privates column in 1889 (11). From 1890 (12) to 1898 there were no privates of any kind in the Signal Corps. On April 29, 1898 (13) Privates of both classes were returned temporally for the war with Spain and they were made permanent on March 2, 1899 (14). An appropriations bill on June 30, 1902 (15) stated "That hereafter second-class privates of the Signal Corps shall be designated as privates, with the same pay and allowances as now allowed by law to second-class privates"

Purveyor

On March 2, 1799 the a medical establishment for the army was setup for the possible war with France. It was to include "A purveyor, who shall be charged with providing medicines, stores, and whatsoever else may be necessary in relation to the said practice or service." (1).

The position was never filled.

Quarter Gunner

On July 26, 1813 congress created a Corps of Sea Fencibles as a defense for ports and harbors (1). Each fenicible company was allowed six Quarter Gunners.

The law creating the fencibles was repealed on February 27, 1815 (2).

A plate from The Company of Military Historians (3) shows an officer in an infantry uniform leading men in sailor type dress.

Quartermaster (General)

A law of March 3, 1791 (1) allowed the appointment of a Quartermaster to be in charge of the army's supplies. He was to be allowed the pay of a Lieutenant Colonel.

The appointment went to Samuel Hodgdon on March 4th (2).

On April 19, 1792 Hodgdon was replaced by James O'Hara who was appointed "Quartermaster General" (3), even though no such position existed in law. A law setting O'Hara's pay on March 3, 1795 (4) does refer to the position as "Quartermaster General".

O'Hara resigned on May 1, 1796 (5).

Twenty-nine days later on May 30th, congress passed a law calling for "one Quartermaster-General" (6). Appointed was John Wilkins (7). The Quartermaster General was given "the rank, pay and emoluments of a lieutenant-colonel" on May 28, 1798 (8), and was moved up to Major General on March 3, 1799 (9).

It is not clear if Wilkins ever held the rank of Lieutenant Colonel or Major General. He is listed in the historical register just Quartermaster General (10).

The office was replaced with Military Agents on March 16, 1802 (11), and Wilkins was discharged on June 1st (12).

It is possible that Hodgdon, O'Hara and Wilkins wore the two gold epaulets of a Lieutenant Colonel and Wilkins wore the two silver stars of a Major General.

Quartermaster Sergeant (Regimental)

A Quartermaster Sergeant was an assistant to the regimental quartermaster. The rank was created in the Continental Army on July 16, 1776 (1), and used to the end of the war.

As far as is known they wore the same insignia, a red epaulet on the right shoulder until 1780 then a button colored epaulet on both shoulders, as other sergeants.

The first mention in law of Quartermaster Sergeants in the federal army was on March 5, 1792 (2). This law didn't add them to the structure of regiments but just set their pay, so it is possible that sergeants were serving as quartermaster sergeants before that.

Quartermaster Sergeants were not part of the organization of the army set in 1802 (3) but returned in 1808 (4).

The first insignia that is known to definitively identify a Quartermaster Sergeant was created in July of 1821 when they, and Sergeant Majors, were ordered to wear a single button colored cloth chevron on both upper sleeves (5). An arc was added in 1825 (5a).

In 1832 they were to wear the same uniform as a Sergeant Major, four laced button holes on the cuff and cloth button colored epaulets with 1/2 inch wide bullion and an aiguillette on the left side (6), and a red sash. Instead of the white for infantry or red for artillery hackle (tall feather) on the cap worn by Sergeant Majors, Quartermaster Sergeants wore a hackle of light blue for both branches (7).

The epaulets were changed to officer's metallic button color with 1/8 inch wide cloth bullion around 1835 (8).

When dragoons were added to they army in 1833, the enlisted uniforms had a simple pointed cuff, metal shoulder scales and a white horsehair plume on the cap. Quartermaster Sergeants and Sergeant Majors were distinguished by aiguillettes and yellow sashes (9).

When chevrons were added to fatigue jackets in 1847, Quartermaster Sergeants were to wear three chevrons and three straight bars (10).

This remained the insignia (11) until The National Defense Act of 1916 changed the title to Regimental Supply Sergeant (12).

Quartermaster Sergeant (Quartermaster Corps)

When the Quartermaster's, Subsistence and Pay Departments were merged into the Quartermaster Corps in 1912 (1), Post Quartermaster Sergeants and Post Commissary Sergeants became Quartermaster Sergeants of the Quartermaster Corps.

They were to wear the three chevrons over the insignia of the corps, continuing the insignia worn by Post Quartermaster Sergeants since 1902 (2).

In 1913 the insignia was changed placing a wreath around the corps insignia (3). In full color the chevrons were buff and the insignia was in it's normal colors. When the wreath was added it was yellow.

In May of 1918 the chevrons were eliminated and just the insignia in a wreath was worn (4). In 1920 a new insignia was designed with a white Navy Petty Officers eagle over a sword crossed with a key in buff in a green wreath (5).

The new insignia was never implemented because in July of 1920 the enlisted grade reorganization made Quartermaster Sergeants into Technical Sergeants (6).

Quartermaster Sergeant Senior Grade

The rank of Quartermaster Sergeant Senior Grade was created in the Quartermaster Corps by The National Defense Act of 1916 replacing Master Electricians (1).

They were to wear the insignia of the corps in a wreath under a star. In full color the insignia was in it's normal colors, the wreath yellow and the star white (2).

The rank was also used in the Motor Transport Corps after 1918 (3).

In 1920 a new insignia was designed with a white Navy Petty Officers eagle over a sword crossed with a key for the in buff, for the Quartermaster Corps, or a red wheel for the Motor Transport Corps, all in a green wreath (4).

The new insignia was never implemented because in July of 1920 the enlisted grade reorganization made Quartermaster Sergeants Senior Grade into Master Sergeants (5).

Radio Sergeant

Radio Sergeant was another rank created by The National Defense Act of 1916 (1). It existed only in the Coast Artillery Corps.

Initially Radio Sergeants wore three chevrons and a group of five bolts of lightning (2) but the following year an arc was added under the bolts (3). The arc was removed in May of 1918 (4).

The enlisted grade reorganization of 1920 made Radio Sergeants into Staff Sergeants (5).

Regimental Supply Sergeant

The National Defense Act of 1916 (1) changed Regimental Quartermaster Sergeants into Regimental Supply Sergeants.

The insignia of three chevrons and three bars was continued (2).

The enlisted grade reorganization of 1920 made them Master Sergeants (3).

Riding Master

Riding Masters were part of the dragoons of the Continental Army (1)(2). They were to provide instruction in horsemanship.

They were also added to the dragoons of the federal army in 1808 (3) and lasted until the end of the War of 1812.

The law placed them on a par with Blacksmiths and Farriers (4). This may have meant that they wore the same Privates uniforms of those ranks.

Saddler

Dragoon regiments in the Continental Army had Saddlers (1). After 1779 they were to wear a blue epaulet on one shoulder (2), which shoulder is not known.

When dragoons returned in 1792 (3) saddlers returned with them, and lasted until dragoons disappeared again in 1802 (4). They came back again with dragoons in 1808 (5), and went away again in 1815 (6). There is no evidence that Saddlers wore anything more than a standard privates uniform.

Saddlers were not seen again until the Civil War. On July 29, 1861 (7) they were added to cavalry regiments. The rank was continued after the war.

It wasn't until 1899 that insignia was prescribed for Saddlers, an outline of a saddler's knife (8). This insignia lasted until 1920 (9).

The National Defense Act of 1916 expanded the use of Saddlers into most branches (10).

The enlisted grade reorganization of 1920 made Saddlers into Specialists Fifth Class (11).

Saddler Sergeant

Saddler Sergeants were added to Cavalry Regiments on July 29, 1861 (1). No insignia was ordered but three chevron is always possible when the word "sergeant" is used.

The rank was continued after the Civil War and in 1873 was allowed to wear three chevron and a saddlers knife (2).

Saddler Sergeants disappeared when they were left out of a reorganization of March 2, 1899 (3).

Second Lieutenant

The term lieutenant comes from the French for "placeholder" (1). It can be thought of a someone who hold a place or is a tenant instead of or in lieu of. A tenant in lieu of is a lieutenant.

As medieval captains became involved in court politics, they needed someone to fill in for them while they were away, and the rank of Lieutenant was born (2).

The "Second" in Second Lieutenant was originally used to denote the ranking of the Lieutenants in a company. Use of the terms in the Continental Army is a little hard to pin down. The term "Second Lieutenant" was certainly used, but whether it was considered a rank or a position for those holding the rank of "Lieutenant" is not clear.

Lieutenant, without a modifier, was used in the Federal Army from its inception in 1784 (3) until 1799 (4) when Second Lieutenants formally replaced Cornets and Ensigns. Even when Cornets and Ensigns returned in 1802, Second Lieutenants remained (5).

As subalterns they were to wear the green cockade from July 1775 to June 1780 and then a button colored epaulet on the left shoulder (6).

The 1808 to 1814 horse cloths for dragoons had a single line of silver lace and a silver bar in the corner (7).

In March of 1821 a general order prescribed a button colored chevron, silver for infantry gold for artillery, on the left upper sleeve (8). This was changed in July to a chevron above each cuff (9). In both cases the six Second Lieutenants in the Corps of Engineers continued to wear a gold epaulet on the left shoulder. These were used until 1829 or 1830 (10).

What was used on the dress coats from 1830 to 1832 is not clear but the button colored epaulet on the left shoulder is possible.

New uniform regulations in 1832 had epaulets worn on both shoulders, rank was now distinguished by the size of the bullion (11). Lieutenants regardless of rank had "same as for a Captain, except the bullion is smaller", the 1839 regulations call for bullion 1/4 inch wide. 1832 also saw the rank by buttons on the cuff, for Lieutenants two outlined in button colored lace.

When rectangular shoulder straps were created it gave Second Lieutenants their first insignia, except for the horse cloths, distinctive from First Lieutenants. The shoulder straps would be empty with no badge of rank at all (12).

The 1851 uniform regulations continued the lack of insignia. The epaulets were gold with 1/8 inch wide bullion but no badge of rank on the strap, the shoulder straps were still empty and the overcoat cuffs were plain (13).

When epaulets were abolished in 1872, those for Second Lieutenants had the regimental number or staff corps device on the pad by itself (14).

The same goes for the 1898 khaki coat shoulder loops. The eagle was in the center but there was no badge at the end (15).

The new uniforms of 1902 had them wearing no sleeve knot, the branch insignia was worn alone above the cuff stripe. The new field uniforms had no badge of rank on the shoulder loops or the shirt collar (16).

In 1912 Second Lieutenants were ordered to wear branch insignia on shirt collars to make up for their lack of a badge of rank. Branch insignia replaced officers badges of rank on left shirt collar, and U.S. letter joined the badges on the right on December 30, 1916. Under this system Second Lieutenants wore only the letters on the right (17).

The lack of a badge of rank may have worked in the relatively small peacetime army, but when World War I started it became a problem. In December of 1917 Second Lieutenants were given a single gold bar (18). They were even given an overcoat sleeve knot of one loop in brown instead of black (19).

When shoulder straps returned to use in 1929, they were still empty. The gold bar was finally added in 1937 (20).

The bars were widened to 3/8 of an inch in 1941(21).

The Career Compensation Act of October 12, 1949 (22) put Second Lieutenants into pay grade O-1.

When subdued insignia was introduced in 1965 the bars were to be brown (23).

The 2005 uniform regulations describe the insignia as "Second lieutenant. The non-subdued grade insignia is one gold-colored bar, 3⁄8 inch in width and 1 inch in length, with a smooth surface. The bar is worn lengthwise on shirt collars, parallel to the shoulder seam on shoulder loops. The subdued grade insignia is the same as above, except the color is brown" (24).

Senior Enlisted Advisor to the Chairman

On October 1, 2005 the Chairman of the Joint Chiefs of Staff, Marine General Peter Pace, Appointed Command Sergeant Major William Gainey to be his senior enlisted advisor. While the individual service chiefs had had senior enlisted advisors for years, including the Sergeant Major of the Army, this was the first time the chairman had one (1).

The position was placed in the same pay grade (E-9), and given the same pay as the senior enlisted advisors of the various services (2).

The army decided not to create a new rank insignia for Gainey (3) and he continued to wear the insignia of a Command Sergeant Major. His branch insignia was replaced with the blue and white insignia of the chairman (4).

In 2007 Pace was replaced by Navy Admiral Michael Mullen who did not believe the position was necessary. When Gainey retired on April 25, 2008, no replacement was appointed (5).

Mullen's replacement, Army General Martin Dempsey, Appointed Marine Sergeant Major Bryan Battaglia to the post on October 1, 2011 (6).

Senior Musician

Senior Musicians were first mentioned on April 30, 1790 (1) when the law stated that the senior musician in a battalion would be paid five dollars instead of the three for a regular musician.

The first mention as a separate rank is on May 20, 1796 (2) when two were allowed for each regiment.

The title "Chief Musician" is used by the law of March 3, 1799 (3). Senior Musician was used once after that on January 11, 1812 (4) but the lack of use of the title in other legislation concerning the organization of the army during the War of 1812 but the actual use of the title in doubt.

They probably wore red, musicians uniforms.

Sergeant

The basic rank of Sergeant (spelled Serjeant in some early references) has existed in the U.S. Army from the beginning.

It's root stretch to the middle ages when the servants, or serviens in Latin, of knights would fight alongside their master to take charge of a group of peasants called to fight (1).

Continental Army Sergeants wore a red epaulet on the right shoulder from 1775 to 1779 then a button colored epaulet on each shoulder (2).

The two epaulets were used until 1821 when a button colored chevron above each cuff was prescribed. They were moved to the upper sleeve in 1825 (3).

The chevrons were eliminated in 1830 (4) and what happened for the next two years is unclear.

In 1832 Sergeants were to wear epaulets with 1/4 inch wide bullion and three laced button holes on the cuff (5). When dragoons were added to the army in 1833 they wore metal shoulder scales and pointed cuffs. Rank was shown by three chevrons on the upper sleeve (6).

When chevrons were added to the fatigue jackets of all branches in 1847, three were ordered for Sergeants (7). Three chevron would denote a Sergeant for the next 100 years.

The 1920 enlisted grade reorganization placed Sergeants in grade four, absorbing the ranks of Band Sergeant, Stable Sergeant, Mess Sergeant and Company Supply Sergeant (8).

Sergeants were moved to grade three in 1948 (9) which became grade E-5 under The Career Compensation Act of October 12, 1949 (10). The change in grade also ended a 114 year streak of the same insignia. They were now to wear three chevrons and one arc. The traditional three chevrons were restored in 1958 (11).

The 2005 uniform regulation describe the insignia as "Sergeant: three chevrons" (12).

Sergeant Bugler

The rank of Sergeant Bugler existed form July 9, 1918 (1) until the enlisted grade reorganization of July 1, 1920 (2), when they became regular Sergeants.

The insignia was three chevrons over a bugle (3).

Sergeant First Class

On October 1, 1890 a law was passed that said "That the enlisted force of the Signal Corps of the Army shall hereafter consist of fifty sergeants, of which ten shall be of the first class, with pay of hospital stewards." (1). The Sergeants who were "of the first class" were to wear three chevrons on one arc with the insignia of the Signal Corps in the middle (2).

The rank existed only in the Signal Corps until March 2, 1903 (3) when the Hospital Corps (the enlisted part of the Medical Department) was given a regular rank structure, and Hospital Stewards became Sergeants First Class of the Hospital Corps. They continued to wear the three chevrons and one arc with a caduceus that had been used by Hospital Stewards (4).

The next branch to use Sergeants First Class was the Quartermaster Corps. 600 were authorized upon the corps creation on August 24, 1912 (5). They wore three chevrons and one straight bar with the insignia of the corps between (6).

The National Defense Act of 1916 (7) added them to the Corps of Engineers, and once again three chevrons, one arc and the branch insignia were used (8).

There is a reference to Sergeants First Class in the Ordnance Department wearing three chevrons and the branch insignia in a wreath (9). However there is no law creating the rank in the Ordnance Department and it doesn't appear on the pay charts in the army registers of 1918 (10) or 1920 (11).

Sergeant First Class was used by many of the branches created during World War I. Initially the three chevrons, one arc and the branch insignia was used but this taxed the supply system. In May of 1918 all Sergeants First Class were ordered to wear three chevrons and one arc without any branch distinction (12). This order was largely ignored.

The enlisted grade reorganization of 1920 made all Sergeants First Class into Staff Sergeants (13).

When in 1948, the grades were reorganized in anticipation of The Career Compensation Act of October 12, 1949 (14), the title of Sergeant First Class was revived and placed into what was grade two, and would be made by the act into grade E-6. This replaced the old grade two title of Technical Sergeant (15).

In 1958 the rank was moved up to grade E-7 (16).

The 2005 uniform regulation describe the insignia as "Sergeant first class: three chevrons above two arcs" (17).

Sergeant Major

The rank of Sergeant Major has its roots in the seventeenth century English Army of Oliver Cromwell. Cromwell insisted on careful record keeping to keep a handle on his army's administrative and supply issues. To do this a Sergeant in each company was put in charge of the paperwork, but at the regimental level a great sergeant or sergeant major was appointed as the third ranking officer in the regiment. For the whole army a sergeant major general was appointed. These two positions became the ranks of Major and Major General (1).

Exactly when title was revived as a senior noncommissioned officer is not clear. There is a reference in the papers of George Washington dated August 30, 1756 when he was a Colonel of colonial militia (2).

Sergeant Majors were first recognized by american law on July 16, 1776 (3) and was apparently used until the end of the war. There is no clear evidence of Sergeant Majors of the Continental Army having any insignia different from other sergeants. There is some evidence of unit specific distinctions such as extra borders on the epaulets or red sashes (4).

The first mention of Sergeant Majors in the federal army was in 1792 when they were given the pay of seven dollars (5). There is no law placing a Sergeant Major into the structure of the army until May 20, 1796 (6), but the 1792 law may indicate that Sergeants were being given the position of Sergeant Major before 1796.

In 1821 The army's 11 Sergeant Majors were finally given insignia separate from other Sergeants, or at least the first we have definite proof of. It was a cloth button colored chevron on both upper sleeves (7). This lasted until 1825 when an arc was added to the chevron (8).

The chevrons were worn until 1829 or 1830 (9) and rank was distinguished after that is not clear.

New uniform regulations in 1832 gave Sergeant Majors four laced button holes on the cuff and cloth epaulets with 1/2 inch wide bullion with a aiguillette on the left side, and a red sash. The epaulets were changed to officer's metallic button color with 1/8 inch wide cloth bullion around 1835 (10).

When dragoons were added to they army in 1833, the enlisted uniforms had a simple pointed cuff, metal shoulder scales and a white horsehair plume on the cap. Sergeant Majors were distinguished by aiguillettes and yellow sashes (11).

Three chevrons and three arcs, sometimes described as an arc or an arc of three bars, but always meaning three arcs, were added to the fatigue jacket in 1847 (12). This would remain the insignia for a Sergeant Major for the next 73 years.

With the addition of Battalion Sergeant Majors to the infantry and cavalry on March 2, 1899 (13), and the abolition of artillery regiments on February 2, 1901 (14), the remaining Sergeant Majors who were the senior enlisted men in a regiment were often referred to as "Regimental Sergeant Majors".

The rank was abolished with the enlisted grade reorganization of July 1920, when all Regimental Sergeant Majors became Master Sergeants (15).

When the E-9 pay grade was created on May 20, 1958 (16) the rank was revived, now wearing three chevrons and three arcs with a star in the middle (17).

The title was changed to Staff Sergeant Major in 1968 only to be changed back in 1971 (18).

The 2005 uniform regulation describe the insignia as "Sergeant major: three chevrons above three arcs, with a five-pointed star between the chevrons and arcs" (19).

Sergeant Major, Junior Grade

On February 2, 1901(1) the artillery was reorganized. It was split into two branches, the Field Artillery who moved with the army and the Coast Artillery Corps who manned fixed fortifications. Together they formed the Artillery Corps. Regimental and battalion organizations were abolished and only batteries, for the field artillery, or companies for the coast artillery, remained. The corps was allowed "twenty-seven sergeants-major with the rank, pay and allowances of battalion sergeants-major of infantry".

They were to wear the Battalion Sergeant Major's insignia of three chevrons and two arcs (2).

The Artillery Corps only lasted until January 25, 1907 (3). The Coast Artillery Corps kept the same organization with now 42 "sergeants-major with the rank, pay and allowances of battalion sergeants-major of infantry". The

Field Artillery was organized back into regiments and battalions, each having regimental or battalion Sergeant Majors.

The actual title "Sergeant Major, Junior Grade" was not used in law until The National Defense Act of 1916 (4). However, the pay chart in the 1909 army register (5) uses "Junior Sergeant Major" and the table of organization (6) "Sergeant Major, Junior Grade".

With the enlisted grade reorganization of July 1920, Sergeants Major, Junior Grade became Staff Sergeants (7).

Sergeant Major of the Army

The Sergeant Major of the Army is the senior enlisted advisor to the Army Chief of Staff.

The position was created in 1966 and William Woolridge was the first to hold it (1).

The insignia was the same three chevrons and three arcs with a star worn by other Sergeant majors, Woolridge's branch insignia was replaced with the red and white insignia of the Army Chief of Staff (2).

When the rank of Command Sergeant Major in 1968 was created for senior enlisted advisors in the E-9 pay grade, the insignia for the Sergeant Major of the Army became three chevrons, three arcs and a star in a wreath (3).

Woolridge served until August of 1968 and was replaced by George Dunaway on September 1st. Dunaway retired in September of 1970 and was replaced by Silas Copeland on October 1st. Leon Van Autreve succeeded Copeland on July 1, 1973 and he was in turn succeeded by William Bainbridge on July 1, 1975 (4).

Bainbridge's insignia was changed in 1979 to three chevrons, three arcs and two stars (5).

William Connelly replaced Bainbridge on July 2, 1979 and was replaced by Glen Morrell on July 1, 1983. Julius Gates stepped in on July 1, 1987 and was succeeded by Richard Kidd on July 2, 1991 (6).

The insignia was changed again in 1994, adding the Coat of Arms of the United States between the stars (7).

The new insignia was worn by Gene McKinney starting on July 1, 1995 and then by Robert Hall starting on October 21, 1997. Jack Tilley held the office from June 23, 2000 until January 15, 2004 and was replaced by Kenneth Preston, who at this writing in the fall of 2010 is still the Sergeant Major of the Army (8).

The 2005 uniform regulations describe the insignia as "The Sergeant Major of the Army: three chevrons above three arcs, with the eagle from the Great Seal of the United States centered between two five-pointed stars centered horizontally between the chevrons and arcs" (9).

Sergeant Major, Senior Grade

On February 2, 1901(1) the artillery was reorganized. It was split into two branches, the Field Artillery who moved with the army and the Coast Artillery Corps who manned fixed fortifications. Together they formed the Artillery Corps. Regimental and battalion organizations were abolished and only batteries, for the field artillery, or companies for the coast artillery, remained. The corps was allowed "twenty-one sergeants-major with the rank, pay and allowances of regimental sergeants-major of infantry".

They were to wear the Regimental Sergeant Major's insignia of three chevrons and three arcs (2).

The Artillery Corps only lasted until January 25, 1907 (3). The Coast Artillery Corps kept the same organization, still with 21 "sergeants-major with the rank, pay and allowances of regimental sergeants-major of infantry". The

Field Artillery was organized back into regiments and battalions, each having regimental or battalion Sergeant Majors.

The actual title "Sergeant Major, Senior Grade" was not used in law until The National Defense Act of 1916 (4). However, the pay chart in the 1909 army register (5) uses "Senior Sergeant Major" and the table of organization (6) "Sergeant Major, Senior Grade".

With the enlisted grade reorganization of July 1920, Sergeants Major, Senior Grade became Master Sergeants (7).

Specialist Grades 1920-1942

The history of specialists ranks stretches back thorough all the Farriers, Musicians, Mechanics, Ect. that the army had in the years before 1920.

The enlisted grade reorganization under the law of June 4, 1920 (1) converted all such ranks into specialists in grades six and seven. Six classes of specialists were in each grade making twelve in total. As for the proper title for these ranks, the pay chart in the 1921 army register (2) refers to Privates and Privates First Class "with the rating of specialist first class" or second class and so on.

The initial men to hold these ranks were converted from the various existing ranks, assigning them to a class of specialist. How they were split between Private and Private First Class is not clear. Musicians First Class from the west point band were made into Specialists First Class. Oilers from the Mine Planter Service became Specialists Second Class. Stewards from the Mine Planter Service, Firemen from the Coast Artillery and the Mine Planter Service, Musicians First Class that were not from the west point band and Musicians Second Class that were, became Specialists Third Class. Chief Mechanics, Horseshoers, Cooks, Musicians Second Class not from the west point band, Musicians Third Class from the west point band and Sergeants who had duty as bakers, blacksmiths, clerks, harness makers, laundry workers, storekeepers, warehousemen, wheelwrights, checkers, painters, plumbers, carpenters, horseshoers and chauffeurs, became Specialists Fourth Class. Chauffeurs and Chauffeurs First Class from the Signal Corps, Musicians Third Class not from the west point band, Saddlers, Assistant Stewards and Deck Hands from the Mine Planter Service, Mechanics, Wagoners and Corporals ho had duty as bakers, blacksmiths, clerks. harness makers, laundry workers, storekeepers, warehousemen, wheelwrights, checkers, painters, plumbers, carpenters, horseshoers and chauffeurs, became Specialists Fifth Class and Buglers and Buglers First Class became Specialists Sixth Class (3).

Theses ranks lasted until 1942. The Pay Readjustment Act of June 16, 1942 (4) did not include the extra pay for specialists ratings. Instead the army created Technician ranks in grades three, four and five (5).

Specialist

Specialist, without a class or pay grade in the title has been a rank of the army since 1985 (1). It is a continuation of the rank of Specialist 4, referring to the specialist rank in the E-4 pay grade. The "4" was dropped when specialist ranks were eliminated from all other grades (2).

The insignia of the Great Seal of the United States on a chevron and arc shaped background was also continued.

The rank shares the E-4 pay grade with Corporals. The main difference being that Corporals are noncommissioned officers with leadership training, while Specialists are not.

The 2005 uniform regulations describe the insignia as:
"Non-subdued, sew-on grade insignia for specialist.
(1) Large insignia. The large embroidered, sew-on grade insignia is goldenlite in color, shaped like an inverted chevron at the bottom, with an eagle device in the center. The insignia has a background of Army green, blue, or white cloth, 27⁄8 inches wide, which provides a 1⁄8-inch edging around the entire insignia.

(2) Small insignia. The small embroidered, sew-on grade insignia is goldenlite, shaped like an inverted chevron at the bottom, with an eagle device in the center. The insignia has a background of Army green, blue, or white cloth, 21⁄2 inches wide, which provides a 1⁄8-inch edging around the entire insignia".

Specialist 4

The E-4 rank of Specialist Third Class was changed to Specialist 4 in June of 1958 (1) when the addition of the E-8 and E-9 pay grades required a change in the specialist rank titles and just adding the pay grade number was simpler (2).

The insignia of the Great Seal of the United States on a chevron and arc shaped background was continued from Specialist Third Class, but made slightly wider for male personnel (3).

With the abolition of all other grades of specialist, the title was shortened to simply "Specialist" in 1985 (4).

Specialist 5

The E-5 rank of Specialist Second Class was changed to Specialist 5 in June of 1958 (1) when the addition of the E-8 and E-9 pay grades required a change in the specialist rank titles and just adding the pay grade number was simpler (2).

The insignia of the Great Seal of the United States beneath an arc was continued from Specialist Second Class, but made slightly wider for male personnel (3).

The rank was abolished in 1985 (4).

Specialist 6

The E-6 rank of Specialist First Class was changed to Specialist 6 in June of 1958 (1) when the addition of the E-8 and E-9 pay grades required a change in the specialist rank titles and just adding the pay grade number was simpler (2).

The insignia of the Great Seal of the United States beneath two arcs was continued from Specialist First Class, but made slightly wider for male personnel (3).

The rank was abolished in 1985 (4).

Specialist 7

The E-7 rank of Master Specialist was changed to Specialist 7 in June of 1958 (1) when the addition of the E-8 and E-9 pay grades required a change in the specialist rank titles. Because Master Specialist was already in use, it was either come up with something that sounded higher, or change the system entirely. In the end they just used the title Specialist with the grade number (2).

The insignia of the Great Seal of the United States beneath three arcs was continued from Master Specialist, but made slightly wider for male personnel (3).

The rank was abolished in 1978 (4).

Specialist 8

The rank of Specialist 8 was created along with the E-8 pay grade in 1958 (1).

The prescribed insignia was the Great Seal of the United States beneath three arcs and above one down pointing chevron (2).

No appointments were ever made and it was discontinued in 1965, never having been used (3).

Specialist 9

The rank of Specialist 9 was created along with the E-9 pay grade in 1958 (1).

The prescribed insignia was the Great Seal of the United States beneath three arcs and above two down pointing chevrons (2).

No appointments were ever made and it was discontinued in 1965, never having been used (3).

Specialist First Class

Specialist First Class was the original title for the specialist rank in the E-6 pay grade. Created in 1954 it lasted until 1958 when it became Specialist 6 (1).

The insignia was the eagle device from the great seal under two arcs (2).

Specialist Second Class

Specialist Second Class was the original title for the specialist rank in the E-5 pay grade. Created in 1954 it lasted until 1958 when it became Specialist 5 (1).

The insignia was the eagle device from the great seal under an arc (2).

Specialist Third Class

Specialist Third Class was the original title for the specialist rank in the E-4 pay grade. Created in 1954 it lasted until 1958 when it became Specialist 4 (1).

The insignia was the eagle device from the great seal under on a chevron and arc shaped background (2).

Squadron Sergeant Major

Squadron is the name for battalions in the cavalry just as troop is the name for company.

Squadron Sergeant Majors were added on March 2, 1899 (1). They wore the same three chevrson and two arcs as Battalion Sergeant Majors (2).

With the enlisted grade reorganization of July 1920, Squadron Sergeant Majors became Staff Sergeants (3).

Squadron Supply Sergeant

Cavalry squadrons gained Supply Sergeants in 1918. They wore three chevrons and two straight bars (1).

With the enlisted grade reorganization of July 1920, Squadron Supply Sergeants became Staff Sergeants (2).

Stable Sergeant

Stable Sergeants were added to batteries of field artillery on March 2, 1899 (1). They wore three chevrons until 1901, then three chevrons and the outline of a horses head (2).

The National Defense Act of 1916 (3) added Stable Sergeants to engineer companies, both regimental and mounted, headquarters, supply and machine gun companies in the infantry, and to most formation of cavalry and field artillery.

The 1917 uniform regulations called for them to were the same three chevrons as other sergeants, but use of the horse's head continued anyway until it was made official again in 1918 (4).

With the enlisted grade reorganization of July 1920, Stable Sergeants became Sergeants (7).

Staff Sergeant

The rank of Staff Sergeant was created in grade three, by the enlisted grade reorganization of 1920 form the ranks of Squadron or Battalion Sergeant Major, Squadron or Battalion Supply Sergeant, Sergeant Major Junior Grade, Sergeant First Class, the junior 50% of Master Gunners, Assistant Band Leader except from the west point band, Sergeant Bugler, Electrician Sergeant, Radio Sergeant, Color Sergeant and Sergeant of Field Music form the west point band (1).

The insignia was three chevrons and one arc (2).

The rank continued until the reorganization of 1948. With the addition of a second rank of Private to the seven pay grades, a rank would have to be eliminated and Staff Sergeant was chosen and the three chevrons and one arc became the insignia for Sergeants (3).

It returned in 1958 when the E-8 and E-9 pay grades were created (4). Master Sergeant and First Sergeant were moved up to E-8 and Sergeant First Class was moved up to E-7, leaving an opening at E-6. The rank of Staff Sergeant was revived to fill that opening and it's three chevron and one arc insignia was returned to it, with Sergeants returning to their traditional three chevrons (5).

The 2005 uniform regulations describe the insignia as “Staff sergeant: three chevrons above one arc” (6).

Staff Sergeant Major

Staff Sergeant Major was the title for those in the E-9 pay grade who were not senior noncommissioned officers of a unit from 1968 to 1971. They wore three chevrons and three arcs with as star between (1).

The idea was first floated in 1965 when the army considered the creation of the rank of Chief Master Sergeant but nothing came of it at the time (2).

The title was changed to simply Sergeant Major in 1971 (3).

Steward, Mine Planter Service

Upon the creation of the Mine Planter Service on July 9, 1918, each mine planter was to have one Steward (1).

Insignia of three chevrons and one arc with a red crescent between, on a blue background was prescribed in January of 1919. This was changed to A red crescent in a red ring in 1920 (2).

The enlisted grade reorganization of July 1920 made Assistant Stewards into Specialists Third Class (3)

Supply Sergeant

The National Defense Act of 1916 (1) changed the title of Company/Troop/Battery Quartermaster Sergeant to Supply Sergeant.

The original insignia for Company Quartermaster Sergeants was three chevrons and one straight bar (2), but with the 1917 uniform specifications call for the same three chevrons worn by sergeants (3).

The bar was reauthorized in May of 1918 but was probably worn all along (4).

With the enlisted grade reorganization of July 1920, Supply Sergeants became Sergeants (5).

Surgeon

Surgeon was the basic rank of an army doctor.

In the Continental Army Surgeons were part of individual regiments. Doctors serving at hospitals were called Hospital Physicians and Surgeons (1). The battle over whether the Surgeons of regiments answered to the army's hospital department or the regimental commanders was a major controversy of the time (2).

At the end of the war John Hart remained on duty to serve the army's medical needs until August 12, 1784 (3). He was replaced by John McDowell who served as the army's only doctor until July 24, 1788 (4). The position had been officially created by congress on June 3, 1784 (5). McDowell's replacement was Richard Allison (6).

When a Second regiment of infantry was added on March 3, 1791 (7), Allison became the Surgeon of the First Infantry and John Elliot was made Surgeon of the Second (8).

The army was enlarged again on March 5, 1792 (9), and was organized into the "Legion of the United States", comprised of four sub-legions. There was to be an overall surgeon for the legion and a Surgeon for each sub-legion (10). Allison was Surgeon of the Legion and Elliot was joined by John Scott, Nathan Hayward and John Carmicheal as Surgeons of the sub-legions. Hayward resigned on May 31, 1796 and was replaced by Joseph Phillips (11).

The artillery was coveted to a Corps of Artillerists and Engineers on May 9, 1794 (12). The called for only a Surgeon's Mate in the corps, but Charles Brown was appointed, and confirmed by the Senate as a Surgeon on May 31st (13).

The Legion was replaced by four regular infantry regiments on November 1, 1796 (14) under a law of May 30, 1796 (15). Allison was discharged, Elliot, Scott, Carmicheal and Phillips became Surgeons of the four regiments and Brown remained with the artillery and engineers. Scott resigned on January 1, 1797 and was replaced by George Gillaspie on March 3rd. He in turn, transferred to the navy on March 13, 1798 and was replaced by William McCoskry on April 30th (16).

A second regiments was added to the Artillerists and Engineers on April 27, 1798 (17) and once again the Surgeon's Mate called for by the law was appointed as a Surgeon, his name was James Scanlan (18).

The expansion of the army for the possible war with France in 1798 and 1799 added may more regiments to the army, at least on paper, and each was to have a Surgeon. The historical register shows appointments to Roger Curtler, Francis Peyton, Edward Conrad, Robert Geddes, William Hurst, John Chetwood, Samuel Finley, Joseph Towbridge, Charles Blake and Oliver Mann, all of whom had left the army by June 15, 1800 (19).

When the peacetime size of the army was set on March 16, 1802 (20) there were two regiments of infantry and one of artillery, regimental surgeons were abolished and replaced with two Garrison Surgeons. McCoskry had resigned on February 1st and Phillips, Brown, Elliot and Scanlan were discharged on June 1st. Carmichael took one of the Garrison Surgeon posts (21).

On April 12, 1808 (22) the army was expanded by adding five more infantry regiments, a rifle regiment, a light artillery regiment and a regiment of light dragoons. Each of these was to have a Surgeon but the two, old infantry and one artillery regiments did not. Taking office on December 12, 1808 were: Dennis Claude in the light artillery, Lewis Dunham in the light dragoons, Josiah Foster in the Fourth Infantry, William Upshaw in the Fifth Infantry, Isaac Davis in the Sixth Infantry and Alfred Thruston in the Seventh Infantry. The Third Infantry didn't get it's Surgeon until August 8, 1809 in the form of Richard Shubrick. Claude resigned on October 1, 1810 and was replaced by James Stewart on February 8, 1811 (23).

During the war of 1812, most regiments had surgeons.

It was also during the War of 1812 the first confirmed uniforms for medical officers (24). A black version of the general staff uniform with cuff flaps and cloth covered buttons was ordered in 1813, but the order reefers to "hospital staff", and this may mean that this uniform was not worn by regimental surgeons.

When the war was over the army was restructured by a law of March 3, 1815 (25). The law called for the regiment of light artillery to be organized as it had been in 1808, which included a Surgeon and the rest of the artillery to continue as a corps that had been set up during the war (26), without Surgeons. The law also allowed for infantry and rifle regiments that did include a Surgeon. The army could create as many as they needed without exceeding a total strength of 10,000 men. On May 17, 1815 a general order (27) set the army at eight regiments of infantry and one rifle regiment.

Lewis Dunham had transferred to the Light Artillery Regiment on May 12, 1814 and remained that regiment's Surgeon, Louis Near, who had been the Surgeon of the Fourth Rifle Regiment during the war was retained as Surgeon of the Rifle Regiment. Edward Scull was moved from the Eighth Infantry to the First Infantry. Franklin Bache got the slot in the Second Infantry, moving from the Thirty-Second Infantry. Adam Goodlet moved from the Seventh to the Third Infantry. Marcus Buck of the Twentieth Infantry became Surgeon of the Fourth Infantry. Sylvester Day moved from the Fourth to the Fifth Infantry. Thomas Mower of the Ninth Infantry took over in the Sixth. Thomas Lawson became Surgeon of the Seventh Infantry transferring from the Sixth and Phineas Woodbury, who had been Surgeon of the Twenty-fifth Infantry during the war became Surgeon of the Eighth (28).

Turn over was heavy for these ten positions. Dunham resigned on September 21, 1819 (29) and was not replaced until January 28, 1820 (30) by Josiah Everett . Bache resigned on July 1, 1816 and was replaced by Walter Wheaton on September 4th. Goodlet resigned on October 1, 1817 and was replaced by William Madison October 5th. Buck resigned on September 4, 1816 and Moses Elliott took over the Surgeon of the Fourth Infantry on October 31, 1817. Day became a Post Surgeon on April 18, 1818 and was replaced by Edward Purcell on July 21st. Woodbury died in February 1818 and Edbert Bell stepped in on April 18th. He served until he was made a Post Surgeon on January 28, 1820 and Joseph Russell took over as Surgeon of the Eighth Infantry (31).

Near was discharged on June 15, 1815 (32) and William Thomas was appointed on September 13th and resigned on November 15, 1816 (33). Edwin Wyatt or Wiatt took office on February 17, 1817 and resigned on April 16, 1818 (34). The historical register shows Perry Maloan being Surgeon of the Rifle Regiment from August 10, 1818 until resigning on October 31, 1820 (35). It also shows John Gale a being the Surgeon of the Rifle Regiment from April 18, 1818 until June 1, 1821 (36). The army register dated May 1818 (37) shows Gale as the rifle Surgeon, as does the registers from January 1, 1819 (38), 1820 (39) and 1821 (40).

The army was reorganized again on March 2, 1821(41). Under this law, Surgeons were not included in the structure of regiments. Instead it called for "the medical department shall consist of one surgeon general, eight surgeons, with the compensation of regimental surgeons, and forty-five assistant surgeons, with the compensation of post surgeons." Under this law: Lawson, Mower, Harney, Wheaton, Madsion, Elliott, Gale and Everett, became the eight Surgeons in the Medical Department with their appointments dating from their original appointments a regimental surgeons (42). Madison was killed on May 14th (43) and Prucell took his place on June 1st (44), and Russell took one the Assistant Surgeon positions (45).

The 1821 uniform regulations call for medical officers to wear a blue coat with black collar and cuffs.

In 1832 Surgeons were distinguished by having one gold embroidered button hole on the black collar (46).

The Surgeon's status was clarified on June 30, 1834 (47) when they were given "the pay and emoluments of a major". Starting in 1840 they were allowed to wear the Major's two color epaulets. The 1/2 inch wide bullion, the crescent and the border were gold and the strap was silver. The gold letters M.S. in a gold wreath were worn inside the frog. Gold edged shoulder straps were worn with a silver oak leaf at each end(48).

On February 11, 1847 (49) the army was enlarged for the war with Mexico. This law gave Surgeons actual rank saying "the rank of the officers of the Medical Department of the Army shall be arranged upon the same basis which at present determines the amount of their pay and emoluments:". The law also added Surgeons to the various regiments it created. The historical register shows surgeons were appointed to the Tenth, Eleventh, and Fifteenth Infantry along with the Third Dragoons and the Regiment of Voltigeurs and Foot Riflemen, all of whom were out of the army by late simmer of 1848 (50).

Whether the regimental surgeons wore medical uniforms or the uniforms of their regiments is not known. Since the law gave rank to "officers of the Medical Department" they may not have held the equivalent rank of Major.

With the new uniform regulations of 1851, Surgeons would wear the plain gold epaulets of a Major with the M.S. letters in silver in a gold wreath, in the frog, and a staff Major's shoulder straps with a gold leaf at each end and a dark blue background (51).

When shoulder knots replaced epaulets in 1872, Surgeons wore them with a dark blue background and gold oak leafs at each side of the pad with the letters M.D. between (52).

A Law of June 26, 1876 (53), expanded the rank of Surgeon beyond equivalent Major to include equivalent Lieutenant Colonels and equivalent Colonels. Silver oak leafs replaced the gold for equivalent Lieutenant Colonels and a silver eagle was worn in the center of the shoulder strap and below the M.D. on the shoulder knot pad. In 1890 the letters were replaced with a gold shield (54).

Surgeons with the equivalent ranks of Colonel and Lieutenant Colonel were eliminated on July 27, 1892 (55), when all equivalent Colonels in the Medical Department became Assistant Surgeon Generals and the equivalent Lieutenant Colonels, Deputy Surgeon Generals.

A maltese cross replaced the shield on the shoulder knots in 1896 (56) and the gold leaf was worn on the dark blue shoulder loops of the 1898 khaki coat (57).

In 1902 shoulder strap backgrounds became maroon and gold corded sleeve knots were used on the full dress coat with a caduceus underneath. A bronze caduceus was also worn under the knots on the overcoat (58).

The history of the rank of Surgeon ended on April 23, 1908 (59), when medical ranks were abolished and all Surgeons became Majors.

Surgeon General

The rank of Surgeon General was created on April 14, 1818 (1), and Hospital Surgeon Joseph Lovell was promoted to fill the position four days later (2).

In 1818 medical officers may have still been wearing a black version of the general staff uniform with cuff flaps and cloth covered buttons prescribed in 1813 (3). In 1821 they were to wear a blue coat with black collar and cuffs, and in 1832 the Surgeon General was distinguished by two gold embroidered button holes on the collar (4).

Lovell died on October 17, 1836 (5), and was replaced by Thomas Lawson on November 30th (6).

Even though there was never a law making the Surgeon General an equivalent Colonel, Lawson was allowed to wear a Colonels epaulets and shoulder straps starting in 1840 (7). The epaulets were gold with a silver eagle on the strap and silver letters M.S. in a gold wreath in the frog, with 1/2 inch wide bullion. The shoulder straps had gold edges with a silver eagle in the center. Lawson was given a brevet as a Brigadier General on May 30, 1848 (8) and it is possible that he replaced the eagle with a star.

Lawson continued as Surgeon General until his death on May 15, 1861. His replacement was Clement Finley, who served, as an equivalent Colonel, until he retired on April 14, 1862 (9).

The day after Finely retired a law was passed stating "That the surgeon general to be appointed under this act shall have the rank, pay and emoluments of a brigadier general."(10). William Hammond was appointed to the position on April 25, 1862 (11).

Hammond instituted may reforms in the Medical Department, and that made him unpopular, most importantly with the Secretary of War Edwin Stanton. On September 3, 1863, Stanton ordered Hammond to turn his office over to Joseph Barnes and go and inspect the sanitary conditions of the Department of the South. Hammond demanded to be returned to his office or have any charges against him aired in a court marshal. Unfortunately, the court marshal found him guilty of trumped up charges of irregularities concerning the purchase of medical supplies and he was dismissed from the Army on August 18, 1864 (12).

Barnes was officially made Surgeon General on August 22, 1864 and served until he died on April 5, 1883 (13). Charles Crane took the office on July 3rd but died on October 10th (14). Next up was Robert Murray, who took office on November 23rd and retired on August 6, 1886 (15). Then came John Moore on November 18, 1886, retiring on August 16, 1890 (16). Jedediah Baxter took office on August 16th and died on December 4th (17). On December 23rd Charles Sutherland became Surgeon General serving until his retirement on May 29, 1893 (18). The next day George Sternberg took office (19).

In 1896 Sternberg was to add a silver Maltese cross above the star on his epaulets (20) (21).

Sternberg retired on June 8, 1902 (22) and was replaced by William Forwood, who himself retired on September 7th (23), and was replaced by Robert O'Rielly (24).

Medical officers ceased to have separate rank titles on April 23, 1908 (25) and O'Reilly became a Brigadier General.

Surgeon's Mate

Surgeon's Mates were created in the Continental Army on July 27, 1775 (1).

A Surgeon's Mate named William Cogswell remained on duty after the Continental army was dissolved, serving until August 12, 1785 (2).

For the most part Surgeon's Mates were part of the organization of regiments, however on May 20, 1796 some extras were allowed to be deployed as needed (3).

On March 16, 1802 (4), Surgeon's Mates were replaced by 25 Garrison Surgeon's Mates that were "to be attached to garrisons or post and not to corps.".

Surgeon's Mates returned to regimental organizations on April 12, 1808, and would remain until all medical staff was removed from regiments and consolidated in the Medical Department on March 2, 1821 (5). Surgeon's Mates were combined with Post Surgeons to create the rank of Assistant Surgeon.

There is no evidence of medical uniforms before 1813 when they were to wear a black version of the general staff uniform with cuff flaps and cloth covered buttons (6).

Teacher of Drawing

A Teacher of Drawing was added to the Corps of Engineers on February 28, 1803 (1), "whose compensation shall not exceed the pay and emolument of a captain in the line of the army".

When the Military Academy at West Point was set up on April 29, 1812 (2), the Teacher of Drawing was made part of the faculty.

Teacher of Music

Teacher of Music was the title of the senior musicians in infantry regiments under the law of March 16, 1802 (1). They were added to the artillery regiment on February 28, 1803 (2). With the army reorganization of April 12, 1808 (3) the title was "Principal Musician".

Teachers of Music appeared once more on April 29, 1812 (4) in the Corps of Engineers. There is no further mention in law and enlisted engineers were eliminated form the army on March 2, 1821 (5).

They all probably wore red, musicians uniforms.

Teacher of The French Language

A Teacher of the French Language was also added to the Corps of Engineers on February 28, 1803 (1), "whose compensation shall not exceed the pay and emolument of a captain in the line of the army".

When the Military Academy at West Point was set up on April 29, 1812 (2), the Teacher of French Language was made part of the faculty.

Teamster

A teamster was someone who drove a wagon pulled by a team of animals, such as oxen or horses (1). This job evolved into truck drivers, and the truck drivers union is still called "The Teamsters".

On March 3, 1847 (2) a new law added two Teamsters to each regiment of dragoons, artillery, and mounted riflemen. They were to have the "compensation of artificers".

There is no evidence of uniforms for Teamsters.

The rank was not part of the army after the end of the Mexican War (3).

Technical Sergeant

The rank of Technical Sergeant was created in grade two by the enlisted grade reorganization of July 1920, from the ranks of Hospital Sergeant, Master Engineer Junior Grade, the junior 75% of Ordnance Sergeants, Electrician Sergeant First Class, Assistant Engineer, Quartermaster Sergeant and Electrician Sergeants from the Artillery School and West Point (1).

They were to wear three chevron and two arcs (2).

The rank lasted until 1948 when the title became Sergeant First Class (3)

Technician Grade 3

Under the Pay Readjustment act of June 16, 1942 (1), the specialists in grade six and seven were replaced with Technicians in grades three, four and five (2).

Technicians in grade three were to wear the Staff Sergeants three chevrons and one arc with a "T" in the middle (3).

Technician grades were eliminated on August 1, 1948 (4).

Technician Grade 4

Under the Pay Readjustment act of June 16, 1942 (1), the specialists in grade six and seven were replaced with Technicians in grades three, four and five (2).

Technicians in grade four were to wear the Sergeants three chevrons above a "T" (3).

Technician grades were eliminated on August 1, 1948 (4).

Technician Grade 5

Under the Pay Readjustment act of June 16, 1942 (1), the specialists in grade six and seven were replaced with Technicians in grades three, four and five (2).

Technicians in grade five were to wear the Corporals two chevrons above a "T" (3).

Technician grades were eliminated on August 1, 1948 (4).

Third Lieutenant

While the ranks of First and Second Lieutenant have existed since 1799, there was once a rank of Third Lieutenant.

On January 20, 1813 a new law (1) stated "That there be appointed, in manner aforesaid, one third lieutenant to each troop or company, in the army of the United States, who, if of cavalry or light dragoons, shall receive the monthly pay of thirty dollars, and of other corps, twenty-three dollars, and be allowed the same forage, rations, and other emoluments, as second lieutenants of the same corps to which they belong."

As subalterns they would have worn a button colored epaulet on the left shoulder. How the insignia on dragoon horse cloths was handled is not known.

Third Lieutenants were part of the Corps of Sea Fencibles created on July 26, 1813 (2), the companies of Rangers created on August 2nd (3) and in the Ordnance Department from February 8, 1815 (4).

When the size of the army was set at the end of the War of 1812 (5), there were no more Third Lieutenants in regiments. The Ordnance Department had been created under a separate law and was preserved with its current organization (6). This was confirmed in law on April 24, 1816 (7).

The rank of Third Lieutenant ended when the Ordnance Department was merged into the artillery on March 2, 1821 (8).

The January 1, 1821 army register shows nine Third Lieutenants in the Ordnance Department (9), Joseph Buckely, Charles Thomas, James Dawson, Thomas Sudler, William Bell, William DeHart, Francis Barbarin, Daniel Tompkins and William Buchanan. Buckely became a Second Lieutenant in the Sixth Infantry, Thomas in the Fourth Artillery, Dawson in the Seventh Infantry, Sudler, Barbarin and Bell in the Third Artillery and DeHart, Tomkins and Buchanan in the Second Artillery (10).

Third Lieutenants made a brief return on June 15, 1832 when a battalion of Mounted Rangers was formed as the army's only mounted troops (11). This battalion became the First Dragoons the following year, without Third Lieutenants.

Troop Quartermaster Sergeant

Quartermaster Sergeants were added to troops of cavalry on April 26, 1898 (1), the three chevrons and one bar previously used by company Quartermaster Sergeants was revived (2).

The title was changed to Supply Sergeant by the National Defense Act of 1916 (3).

Trumpeter

Trumpeter was the title of musicians in a mounted regiments.

It was used in the Continental Army (1) and was revived when dragoons were added to the federal army on March 5,1792 (2). When the army was enlarged for the possible war with France, a law of March 3, 1799 (3) used "musician" instead of "trumpeter".

Trumpeters were seen again in dragoon regiments on January 11, 1812 (4), and a law of March 30, 1814 (5) calls for "trumpeters or buglers".

Trumpeters were eliminated along with the dragoon regiments on March 3, 1815 (6).

They returned for the Civil War on March 3, 1863 (7) and lasted until The National Defense act of 1916 (8) changed the title to bugler.

Trumpeters in the Continental Army wore the reverse colors of their regiment (9) and there is no clear evidence of dragoon musicians uniforms in the early federal army, but they probably continued to wear reverse colors.

Civil War era Trumpeters wore a herringbone pattern with tape outlining basic shape of the jacket and more tape going across from each button (10).

From 1872 to 1902 musicians dress coats hand tape coming out from each button, coming to a point and going back to the button (11).

After that they wore standard enlisted uniforms with no rank insignia.

Veterinary Surgeon

Veterinary Surgeons were added to cavalry regiments on March 3, 1863 (1) in a law stating "and each regiment shall have one veterinary surgeon, with the rank of a regimental sergeant major,". The army had hired Veterinary Surgeons for years to look after horses but this was the first time they were an official part of the army, but by the 1870s they were once again considered civilian employees (2).

They were placed back in uniform in 1901, wearing an officers uniform with silver branch insignia (cavalry or artillery) and a a silver eagle with the letters U.S. in silver on the field uniform shoulder loop (3).

In 1902 they were ordered to wear the uniforms (except full dress) of a Second Lieutenant with no insignia except the cavalry or artillery branch insignia on the collar, with a winged foot of a horse with shoe underneath. In full color the branch insignia was gold and the winged foot silver and on filed uniforms the device was all bronze (4).

The National Defense Act of 1916 made them into officers of the Medical Department (5).

Wagoner

Wagoner became a rank of the army on July 22, 1861 (1) and remained until the enlisted grade reorganization of July 1920, when they became Specialists Fifth Class (2).

They wore Private's uniforms until 1910 when they were authorized to wear a wagon wheel as insignia (3).

Warrant Officer

On July 9, 1818 (1) an appropriations bill was passed that said "That hereafter there shall be in the Coast Artillery Corps of the Regular Army a service to be known as the Army Mine Planter Service, which shall consists for each mine planter in the service of the united states, of one master, one first mate, one second mate, one chief engineer and one assistant engineer, who shall be warrant officers appointed by and holding their offices at the discretion of the Secretary of War". They were to wear the branch insignia of the Coast Artillery Corps with a sea mine underneath (2)

They were joined on June 4, 1920 (3) by 1120 more Warrant Officers under a law that said "In addition to those authorized for the Army Mine Planter Service, there shall be not more than one thousand one hundred and twenty warrant officers, including band leaders, who shall hereafter be warrant officers. Appointments shall be made by the Secretary of War from among noncommissioned officers who have had at least ten years' enlisted service; enlisted men who served as officers of the Army at some time between April 6, 1917, and November 11, 1918, and whose total service in the Army, enlisted and commissioned, amounts to five years; persons serving or who have served as Army field clerks or field clerks, Quartermaster Corps; and, in the case of those who are to be assigned to duty as band leaders, from among persons who served as Army band leaders at some time between April 6, 1917, and November 11, 1918, or enlisted men possessing suitable qualifications. Hereafter no appointments as Army field clerks or field clerks, Quartermaster Corps, shall be made."

The Warrant officers in the Mine Planter Service were given sleeve stripes as rank insignia on January 17, 1920. Masters and Chief Engineers wore four stripes, First Mates and Assistant Engineers three stripes and Second Mates two stripes. Above the stripes was disk with an anchor for Masters and Mates or a three bladed propeller for engineers (4).

All Warrant officers were to wear just the U.S. Letter on their collars after November of 1920 and until the Warrant Officer's branch insignia was created in March of 1921. It was an eagle in a wreath with its wings sticking out above the wreath. This became known as the "eagle rising" insignia. Officer's uniforms with no rank insignia and the "eagle rising" as branch and cap insignia, and the sleeve insignia for the Mine Planter Service, denoted Warrant Officers thru the 20s and 30s. On white uniforms, four white stripes were worn on the sleeve by Warrant Officers not in the Mine Planter Service (5).

The white stripes were not continued outside the Mine Planter Service after 1938 (5a)

On October 15, 1940 the two stripe position of Second Assistant Engineer was added to the mine planter Warrant Officers (6).

Warrant Officers were split into the ranks of Chief Warrant Officer and Warrant Officer Junior Grade on August 21, 1921 (7). In the Mine Planter Service, Masters and Chief Engineers became Chief Warrant Officers and the rest became Warrant Officers Junior Grade.

Warrant Officer 1

Warrant Officer 1 was created by the "Warrant Officer Act of 1954" (1) in pay grade W-1.

Design of the insignia was coordinated with the Navy, Marine Corps and Coast Guard to create a unified system. The insignia authorized in 1956 was a gold bar with a brown rectangle at each end (2).

When subdued insignia was introduced in 1965 (3), the gold parts were rendered in olive drab and the brown remained brown (4).

The army abandoned the unified system in 1972 and the insignia was changed.

The 2005 uniform regulations describe the insignia as "Warrant officer 1 (WO1). The non-subdued grade insignia is a silver-colored bar, 3⁄8 inch in width and 1 1⁄8 inches in length, with one black enamel square. The bar is worn lengthwise on shirt collars, parallel to the shoulder seam on shoulder loops. The subdued grade insignia is the same as above, except that the color is olive-drab with one black square." (5)

Warrant Officer Junior Grade

Congress created the rank of Warrant Officer Junior Grade on August 21, 1941 (1), splitting the rank of Warrant Officer into two grades, Chief Warrant Officer and Warrant Officer Junior Grade. Warrant Officers in the Mine Planter Service holding the titles of First Mates, Second Mates, Assistant Engineers and Second Assistant Engineers were classified as Warrant Officers Junior Grade and continued to wear the same sleeve stripes, three for First Mates and Assistant Engineers and two for Second Mates and Second Assistant Engineers (2).

The regulations described the insignia for the others as "One gold bar 3/8 inch in width and 1 inch in length, with rounded ends, having a brown enameled top and a latitudinal center of gold 1/8 inch in width." (3). When dress uniforms returned after the war, this insignia was worn on shoulder straps with a brown background(4), under a sleeve knot with the base a broken line on the evening tailcoat and by itself on the blue a white mess jackets (5).

The Career Compensation Act of October 12, 1949 (6) placed Warrant Officers Junior Grade in pay grade W-1 (7).

The Mine Planter Service was abolished along with the Coast Artillery Corps in 1951 (8)

On May 29, 1954 congress passed the "Warrant Officer Act of 1954" (9). This act created Warrant Officer Junior Grade into Warrant Officer 1.

Part 2.
Navy

Chapter 1. Navy Organization

The Continental Navy

The american naval force during the revolutionary war was called the Continental Navy. It was born on October 13, 1775 (1). Congress authorized the sale of the Continental Navy's last ship on June 3, 1785 (2), and the navy ceased to exist. Unlike the Continental Army there was no residual force left, the new United States was without a navy.

The "Federal Navy"

Trouble with pirates in North Africa showed the need for a navy. On March 27, 1794 (1) Congress authorized the construction and manning of six ships. The law specifically stated that the new ships were for the purpose of fighting "Algerine corsairs", and if a treaty could be achieved with Regency of Algiers, construction would stop. Such a treaty was negotiated and ratified by the Senate on March 2, 1796 (2).

It was decided that construction would continue on three of the ships, and Congress passed a law to that effect on April 20, 1796 (3). Congress provided for the manning of the three ships with a law of July 1, 1797 (4). The threat of war with France caused Congress to approve the money to finish the other three ships on July 16, 1798 (5) and the United States Navy was born. For clarity, we shall use the term "federal navy" to refer to the navy after 1794.

Subdivisions of ranks

The highest ranks in the navy, Admiral, Vice Admiral and Rear Admiral (both) are known as "Flag Officers" as any ship they are on displays a flag to show they are there (1).

The next three ranks, Captain, Commander and Lieutenant Commander are referred to as "Mid-Grade Officers" and the next three, Lieutenant, Lieutenant Junior Grade and Ensign are "Junior Officers" (2).

The navy contains both "line" and "staff" officers. Staff officers belong to a staff department, such as the medical or supply. Line officers are further divided into "Unrestricted Line Officers", "Restricted Line Officers" and "Limited Duty Officers". Unrestricted Line Officers are eligible to command ships while Restricted Line Officers have duties such as engineers or aviators that don't lead to commanding a vessel at sea (3). Limited Duty Officers are former enlisted personnel whose technical skills were needed in the officers ranks (4).

The proper term for navy enlisted rank is "rate" (5).

The highest rates of enlisted personnel, Master Chief Petty Officer, Senior Chief Petty Officer and Chief Petty Officer can be referred to a "Chiefs". The middle three rates, Petty Officers first, second and third class are known as "Petty Officers". The bottom three rates are known as "Non rated Sailors".

Ratings

While "rate" is the level of seniority, "rating" is the job specialty a sailor holds. Warships are, and always have been, the most technology advanced devices in the world, and the people who operate them require technical skills. Qualification in those skills earns them a "rating". Chiefs and Petty Officers all hold ratings and are equivalent to army noncommissioned officers. Non rated Sailors are in training for ratings. Many do earn ratings before promotion to Petty Officer, they are called "Strikers" (1).

In 1969, Charles A. Malin did a review of the history of enlisted titles, ratings and non rated, for the navy (2).

Civil or Staff Ranks, Assimilated Ranks and Relative Ranks

In the beginning staff officers held different ranks from line officers. Over the years, how these ranks related to line rank became an issue.

In the Continental Navy (1), and the early days of the federal navy, (2) these were the medical staff, Surgeons and Surgeon's Mates, and Chaplains. Pursers, who had been warrant officers, became commissioned staff officers in 1812 (3). In 1835 a law setting the navy's pay added, or at least clarified the position of, Passed Assistant Surgeons, Professors of Mathematics, Secretaries and Clerks (4).

The regulations governing the navy, issued in 1841, allowed "civil officers", as they were referred to, "assimilated rank". This was an attempt to create an equivalence between line ranks and staff ranks. Ranking with Lieutenants were Surgeons, Pursers, Chaplains and Secretaries. Ranking with Masters were Passed Assistant Surgeons. Ranking with Passed Midshipmen were Assistant Surgeons and Professors of Mathematics. Clerks ranked with Midshipmen (5).

This system was not satisfactory. It ranked commissioned staff officers with warranted line officers, such as Assistant Surgeons with Passed Midshipmen. It also placed Secretaries, who's status was unclear, with Lieutenants (6).

The next staff ranks were to be created were for engineering officers in 1842 (6). There is no evidence of them being given assimilated rank.

The next attempt was on August 31, 1846, during the Mexican War when "relative rank" was created. A General Order from the Secretary of the Navy George Bancroft made Surgeons of the Fleet (the senior medical officer in a fleet) and Surgeons over 12 years service into relative Commanders and Surgeons under 12 years service into relative Lieutenants. Passed Assistant Surgeons ranked "next after" Lieutenants placing them above but slightly equal to Masters and Assistant Surgeons were "next after" Masters placing them above but slightly equal to Passed Midshipmen (7). Bancroft's successor, John Young Mason, gave Pursers relative rank on May 27, 1847. Again over 12 years were Commanders and under were Lieutenants (8).

However was this Legal? Did the navy have the power to grant commissioned ranks on its own? The answer was no. On August 5, 1854, with the war long over, Congress passed a law stating that the two general orders had the power of law (9). Relative rank was now a concept recognized in law.

Engineering officers were given relative rank with a general order of January 13, 1859 (10), that was made into a law on March 3rd (11). Chief Engineers over 12 years service were relative Commanders and those under relative Lieutenants. First Assistant Engineers were next after Lieutenants, Second Assistants next after Masters and Third Assistants with, not next after, Midshipmen.

All this left Chaplains, Professors, Secretaries and Clerks without relative rank.

Then came the Civil War. On July 16, 1862 (12) line officer's ranks were expanded, giving staff officers more ranks to be relative to. Nothing was done until March 13, 1863 when the Secretary of the Navy Gideon Wells completely restructured the relative rank equivalents. Wells gave relative rank to Chaplains, Professors, Secretaries and Clerks, as well as Naval Constructors who had been civilian employees of the navy for many years. The Chiefs of the Bureaus of Medicine and Surgery, Provisions and Clothing, Steam Engineering and Construction and Repair were relative Commodores. Fleet Surgeons and the new concept of Fleet Paymasters and Fleet Engineers, along with Surgeons, Paymasters (as Pursers were called after 1861) and Chief Engineers over 15 years service and Naval Constructors over 20 years service were all relative Captains. Surgeons, Paymasters and Chief Engineers over five years service and Naval Constructors, Chaplains and Professors of Mathematics over 12 years service were relative Commanders. Surgeons, Paymasters and Chief Engineers under five years service and Naval Constructors,

Chaplains and Professors of Mathematics under 12 years service were relative Lieutenant Commanders. Passed Assistant Engineers and Secretaries were relative Lieutenants. Assistant Surgeons, Paymasters and Naval Constructors and First Assistant Engineers were relative Masters. Second Assistant Engineers were relative Ensigns and Third Assistant Engineers and Clerks were relative Midshipmen (13).

Just as had happened during the Mexican War, this was done by the navy, not done in law. It was only a matter of time after the war ended that this would come up. It finally came on March 29, 1869, when Attorney General Ebenezer Hoar issued a ruling that the navy had exceeded its authority. All relative ranks were returned to where they were in 1859 (14).

An appropriations bill, passed by Congress on March 3, 1871 (14) created a new system of relative rank. Staff ranks could be spread over more than one relative rank based on seniority. For example Surgeons could be relative Lieutenant Commanders or relative Lieutenants. The law created the ranks of Medical Director and Pay Director, who were relative Captains and Medical Inspector and Pay Inspector who were relative Commanders. Paymasters, like Surgeons, were relative Lieutenant Commanders or Lieutenants. Passed Assistant Surgeons and the new rank of Passed Assistant Paymasters were relative Lieutenants or relative Masters. Assistant Surgeons and Paymasters were relative Masters or Ensigns. Chief Engineers could be relative Captains, Commanders or Lieutenant Commanders, while First Assistants were relative Lieutenants or Masters and Second Assistants, relative Masters or Ensigns. Third Assistant Engineers were abolished. Like Chief Engineers, Naval Constructors were relative Captains, Commanders or Lieutenant Commanders and Assistants were relative Lieutenants or Masters. Chaplains were spread from Lieutenant to Captain and Secretaries were relative Lieutenants. Finally the bureau chiefs became Surgeon General, Paymaster General, Engineer-in-Chief and Chief Constructor.

Professors of Mathematics were not included in the 1871 law. There relative rank was set by a law of May 31, 1872 (15) that spread them from Lieutenant to Captain.

The 1871 law had allowed relative rank for Civil Engineers, but no action was taken until February 24, 1881, when they were spread from Lieutenant to Captain.

The concept of relative rank came to an end on March 3, 1899 (17) when a new law stated "That all sections of the Revised Statutes which, in defining the rank of officers or positions in the Navy, contain the words "the relative rank of" are hereby amended so as to read "the rank of," but officers whose rank is so defined shall not be entitled, in virtue of their rank to command in the line or in other staff corps. Neither shall this Act be construed as changing the titles of officers in the staff corps of the Navy." Relative rank was now just rank, staff officers now held the same ranks as line officers, but the titles didn't change. A Paymaster with the relative rank of Lieutenant Commander was now a Paymaster with the rank of Lieutenant Commander.

In November of 1918 the navy ordered the end of the use of the staff titles (18). A Paymaster with the relative rank of Lieutenant Commander would now be referred to as a Lieutenant Commander of the Pay Corps, but legally he was still a Paymaster with the rank of Lieutenant Commander and was so listed in the navy register.

Staff ranks came to an end on August 7, 1947 (19) with a law that stated "The grades above that of commissioned warrant officer in the line of the Navy established under permanent provisions of existing law or of titles I through IV of this Act are hereby similarly established in each of the staff corps of the Regular Navy and the Naval Reserve in lieu of existing grades above that of commissioned warrant officer in each staff corps. Each staff officer on the active list of the Navy or Naval Reserve serving in a grade above that of commissioned warrant officer on the date of this Act shall be regarded as having been appointed to either or both the permanent or temporary grade established by this section in his corps corresponding to the permanent or temporary rank, or both, then held by him under the conditions of his existing appointment. Nothing in this section shall operate to establish in any staff corps a grade higher than the highest rank now provided for that corps under permanent provisions of law."

Pay Grades

The History of American Ranks and Rank Insignia

The navy divided it's enlisted rates and ratings into six grades on January 8, 1885 (1). Calling them pay grades is not entirely accurate at that point because different ratings had different rates of pay, but what would become pay grades began here.

The six grades were: Petty Officer First, Second and Third Class and Seaman First, Second and Third Class. Each grade had ratings in three different classes, a Seaman Class, a Special Class and an Artificer Class. There was also a Messman class that was not in the six grades. A law of May 18, 1920 refers to the "seaman" grades as "nonrated men" (2). A Chief Petty Officer grade was added on April 1, 1893.

On June 4, 1920, Congress gave the Secretary of the Navy the authority "to establish such grades and ratings as may be necessary for the proper administration of the enlisted personnel of the Navy and Marine Corps." (3). Secretary Denby proceeded to reorganize the enlisted ratings with letters of March 24th (4) and May 2nd (5), 1921. The May letter placed every rating, even messmen, in the seven pay grades.

A new law of June 10, 1922 (6) made the seven grades into true "pay grades". The pay of enlisted sailors was now tied to which grade the rate or rating was in. The grades were now numbered one to seven, with one being the highest and seven the lowest.

This system served the navy until The Career Compensation Act of October 12, 1949 (7) reorganized all military ranks into pay grades. The grades would carry a letter and a number. Officer's grades would start with an "O", warrant officer's with a "W" and Enlisted with an "E". Unlike the 1922 system, one would be the lowest rank with the numbers increasing for higher ranks.

Eight officer grades were created with Ensigns being O-1 and Commodores being O-7. All higher admirals would share the O-8 grade.

There were four warrant grades, with Warrant Officers taking the W-1 grade and Chief Warrant Officers being spread over grades W-2, W-3 and W-4.

The seven enlisted grades became grades E-1 to E-7.

In 1954 congress changed the warrant ranks to Warrant Officer 1 in the W-1 grade, Chief Warrant Officer 2 in the W-2 grade, Chief Warrant Officer 3 in the W-3 grade and Chief Warrant Officer 4 in the W-4 grade (8).

The Career Compensation Act was amended on May 20, 1958 (9) to create the grades of O-9, O-10, E-8 and E-9.

Rear Admirals now had O-8 to themselves while Vice Admirals moved to O-9 and full Admirals to O-10.

The rate of Senior Chief Petty Officer was added in the E-8 grade and Master Chief Petty Officer in the E-9 grade.

The W-5 grade was created in 1991 (10), but the navy didn't create the rank of Chief Warrant Officer 5 until 2004 (11).

Chapter 2.
Navy Rank and Rate Insignia

It is hard to determine what qualified as a distinction of rank in the early navy. Regulations described officers uniforms in detail for each rank, and their rank was shown by the design of the uniform. Style of cuffs, placement and number of buttons and placement of lace, among other thing, served as a distinction of officer's rank. Enlisted sailors were not mentioned at all. Officer's uniforms were usually centered around a tail coat worn in full dress with an undress coat that was identical but without as much decoration. A some point the undress coat became a frock coat instead of a tail coat. When this happened is not clear. It could have been as early as 1830 when the regulations describe it as "made according to the prevailing fashion of citizens of the time". The first definite use of the undress frock coat is in 1852 when the uniform regulations included illustrations showing the frock coat. When they eventually came, enlisted uniforms consisted of white or blue jumpers worn over matching bell bottoms, and a blue jacket.

Line officers began to wear epaulets in 1797 (1), and shoulder straps were added, for use when epaulets were not, in 1830 (2).

The first evidence of enlisted uniforms comes from a message from the President to Congress from 1833 (3) that informed Congress of the navy's rules and regulations. It shows the first use of a petty officer's badge on the upper sleeve.

Medical officers began to use a system of cuff stripes in 1835, which had it's roots in a strip of lace worn by Assistant Surgeons since 1832 (4).

Having been given relative rank, staff officers began wearing epaulets and shoulder straps in 1847 (5).

The 1852 uniform regulations (6) set out a system of gold cuff stripes (or buttons), epaulets and shoulder straps for most ranks. There were still some ranks, such as Chaplains or Professors of Mathematics, that were distinguished by the design of their uniforms, but the navy was well on it's way to a recognizable rank system.

Further progress was made on August 23, 1856, when Surgeons and Pursers were ordered to wear the uniforms of their relative rank with appropriate epaulets and shoulder straps. This was extended, in most details, to engineering officers on February 8, 1861 (7).

In June of 1862, rated Master's Mates, who were petty officers, were ordered to wear a double breasted jacket instead of the standard enlisted jumper (8).

On July 31st, the insignia was changed to reflect the reorganization of the navy's rank structure and it equivalency to the rank structure of the army. Cuff stripes had to be modified to show more ranks, and line officers began to wear army badges of rank on their epaulets and shoulder straps. Staff officers changed the cuff stripes along with their relative rank, but their epaulets and shoulder straps were unaffected. Use of the dress tail coat was suspended for the balance of the Civil War (9).

It was the uniform regulations of January 28, 1864 that set out a common system of rank distinctions for line and staff officers. The plain wartime uniform for all officers and most warrant officers, was to be a double breasted frock coat with two rows of nine buttons. The only differences between ranks was that Midshipmen, Third Assistant Engineers and Clerks wore smaller buttons than other ranks and warranted Masters Mates wore a single breasted coat. Rank was shown by cuff lace and shoulder straps. Line officers wore a star above the stripes and an anchor in the center of the straps, and staff officers did not wear the star and replaced the anchor with a corps device. Shoulder straps for warrant officers were of a strip of gold lace. Epaulets were not worn for the rest of the war. The army style badges of rank were worn on the collar of the overcoat, and the jackets for rated Master's Mates were expanded to other ratings (10).

In 1865 a service dress sack coat was added for officers. It could carry cuff stripes and shoulder straps, but badges of rank could be worn on the collar instead (11).

The first postwar uniform regulations were issued on December 1, 1866. The full dress tail coat returned and epaulets along with it, and the service sack coat was now only to carry collar insignia (12). The biggest changes were for enlisted sailors. The petty officer's device was now worn on the jackets by those rating so allowed, and specialty marks were added, in various places on the uniform, to show a sailor's rating. All enlisted sailors gained cuff and collar stripes on the jumper to show rate and non rated sailors were given watch marks to show what side of a ship they were assigned to (13).

On March 11, 1869 a general order replaced the cuff stripes for admirals on the tail coat with lines of oak leaf and acorn embroidery, and eliminated epaulets and shoulder straps for officers and warrant officers under the rank of Lieutenant. For Master, Ensigns, gradated Midshipmen and equivalent staff officers, shoulder knots were now worn. The shoulder straps for warrant officers were replaced with collar insignia. Staff officers were ordered to wear colored cloth between their cuff stripes or piping if they only had one stripe. The stripes were removed form the collars of non rated sailors (14). Masters would have their epaulets and shoulder straps retuned to them on October 3, 1871 (15).

Later in 1869 the collar stripes on the enlisted jumpers would be eliminated (16).

In July of 1873 the lines of oak leaf and acorn embroidery were eliminated for Rear Admirals. The lines for other admirals would be eliminated along with those ranks (17).

The jackets for jacketed petty officers were changed to the 1865 officer's sack coat on August 12, 1874 (18).

In 1877 a new sack coat was introduced. It was a more military looking coat, outlined in black mohair braid, including the standing collar. Badges of rank were worn on the collar and black cuff stripes were worn without the line star or colored cloth. Officers and Clerks began wearing this coat in July of 1878, warrant officers in October and Mates in June of 1880 (19). It is not clear if petty officers ever wore this coat.

Ensigns regained shoulder straps on June 21, 1881 (20), and epaulets with the uniform regulations of 1883 (21). The 1883 regulations also added a white sack coat, identical to the blue service coat, including white cuff stripes, but with no collar insignia (22). Black stripes were worn on overcoats, instead of collar insignia at this point (23). It is possible that this began when the 1877 service coat was created, but 1883 is the first regulations that show them.

The petty officer's device and specialty marks were combined onto rating badges in 1886, with only Petty Officers First Class, then after 1894 Chief Petty Officers, wearing the now double breasted sack coat. Watch marks were changed to show a different color (red) for Firemen making part of the system of rate insignia (24).

The cuff stripes were changed on the service coats in 1897. On the blue coat the stripes were now gold with the line star or colored cloth. The stripes were removed from the white coat and shoulder straps were authorized to show rank (25).

In 1898 a red cross was added to the upper sleeve of non rated Hospital Apprentices. This was the beginning of some non rated rates being shown by what became known as "distinguishing marks" (26).

Shoulder straps were not satisfactory, in 1899 shoulder boards were created for use on the white service coat, the overcoat and after 1902 a white dinner jacket (27).

We should pause here to take a look at how complicated the uniform situation had become. In the 1905 uniform regulations officers had 10 different uniform combinations. Special Full Dress used the tail coat with cuff stripes and epaulets, Full Dress and Dress used the frock coat with cuff stripes and epaulets, Undress A and Undress B used the frock coat with cuff stripes and shoulder straps, Service Dress used the 1877 blue service coat with cuff stripes and collar insignia, White Service Dress used the white service coat, which had been modified in 1902 to remove the mohair braid and add buttons and patch pockets, shoulder boards were used to shoe rank, Evening Dress A used an evening tail coat with epaulets and cuff stripes, Evening Dress B and Uniform C with the evening coat with cuff stripes but no epaulets, Mess Dress used the white dinner jacket with shoulder boards (28).

In 1912, watch marks became branch marks. They no longer showed what side a ship that a sailor was assigned to, but what branch they were in (29).

New uniform regulations were issued on January 25, 1913 with many changes, mostly on officers' shoulders. Shoulder straps were no longer authorized, it is possible that they were eliminated before this, but this is not certain. Also eliminated were shoulder boards. On the white service coat and the mess jacket, metal badges of rank were worn on white cloth shoulder loops. The shoulders of the overcoat were plain (30).

Shoulder boards returned on June 24th, 150 days later (31). It is doubtful that the shoulder loops were widely worn.

In 1917, khaki and green uniforms were authorized for officers assigned to aviation duties. The uniform coats were identical in design to the 1902 white service coat right down to the shoulder boards (32).

World War I also saw the suspension of the frock and tail coats, and with them epaulets (33).

On November 16, 1918, the system of colored cloth around cuff stripes was ended and replaced with corps devices, worn in the same manner as the line star (34).

The 1877 blue service coat was replaced with a double breasted, rolling collar version on March 17, 1919. This coat did not carry collar insignia. (35).

The navy formally abolished epaulets on June 24, 1919 (36), only to bring them back on April 25, 1921 (37).

In 1922 it was announced that the full dress tail coat and the aviation uniforms were to be abolished (38). This was reflected in the 1922 uniform regulations which contained no less than 19 officer's uniform combinations, but only three methods of showing rank, epaulets, cuff stripes and shoulder boards (39).

Aviation uniforms returned in 1925. The new coats, in both green and khaki, were single breasted with rolling collars. Rank was shown by black cuff stripes with a black line star or corps device (40).

The khaki uniform was extended to submarine officers in 1931. Because the coat was often removed in the heat of a submarine, pin on badges of rank were added to the shirt collar (41).

The khaki uniform was extended to all officers and chief petty officers in 1941. The black cuff stripes were replaced with shoulder boards (42).

The stage was set for the uniforms of World War II. The frock coat and epaulets were suspended and never returned (43). Otherwise, officers entered the war in the 1919 blue service coat with gold cuff stripes, the 1902 white service uniform with shoulder boards and the 1941 khaki working uniform with shoulder boards on the coat and badges of rank on the shirt collar. Aviation officers and could wear the 1925 green working uniform with black cuff stripes and badges of rank of the shirt collar (44). Chief Petty Officers wore the 1886 blue and white uniforms and the 1941 khaki uniform with rating badges. Chiefs in aviation ratings could wear the green uniform (45). Officer's stewards and cooks were allowed the chief's blue and white uniforms but not the khaki or green (46). Other enlisted men wore the dress blue jumper with rating badges or cuff stripes and branch marks or a blue or white undress jumper without cuffs, therefore without stripes. The white dress jumper with cuffs was suspend in late 1941, and like the frock coat and epaulets, never returned. All ranks could wear dungarees consisting of a chambray shirt over denim bellbottoms, but they were more often worn by enlisted men of all rates (47). Dungarees were not considered a proper military uniform a the beginning of the war, therefore no rating badges were worn on the shirt sleeve.

Relative rank for female nurses in 1942 lead to proper naval uniforms. They were ordered to wear a blue double breasted uniform coat with gold or yellow cuff stripes and a white single breasted coat with shoulder boards and badges of rank on the shirt collar (48).

Also in 1942, other women, who were not nurses, were prescribed single breasted blue coats. Officers wore cuff stripes of reserve blue. Female chiefs and petty officers wore rating badges, but non rated women had no insignia (49). White coats with navy blue cuff stripes and badges of rank of the shirt collar were added in early 1943 (50).

In mid-1943 it was decided to replace the 1941 khaki working uniform with a gray version. It was identical in design with gray and black shoulder boards (51). This uniform was hated by the navy at large, who clung to their khaki uniforms as long as they could.

In September of 1944 non rated women were given hash marks on the upper sleeve to show rate (52).

In 1947 the black cuff stripes were removed from the overcoats, and the gray uniform was eliminated to be replaced with the 1941 khaki uniform (53).

In April of 1948 the hash marks used by non rated women since 1944 became group rate marks used by all non rated sailors, replacing branch marks and cuff stripes (54).

In October of 1948 the uniforms for women were combined. There were no longer separate uniforms for nurses and other women. The single breasted coats were chosen with reserve blue cuff stripes on the blue and now white cuff stripes on the white, replacing the shoulder boards that had been worn by nurses and navy blue stripes by other women. The reserve blue stripes were changed to gold in 1951 (55).

Rating badges were added to the dungarees in 1956 (56).

1959 saw the creation of badges of rank for Chief Petty Officers (57), and 1960 saw the cuff stripes on women's white coats were changed from white to gold (58).

Pin on badges of rank were added for petty officers in 1969 for wear on caps (59), they were eventually expanded for wear on collars and on outerwear.

Shoulder marks were added in 1979 for use on the white shirt when worn under the 1919 blue service coat (60). They were expanded to Chief Petty Officers in 1999 (61).

In 2008, petty officers and non rated sailors were given the Navy Service Uniform. Rate was shown by badges of rank on the collar. This precipitated the creation of badges of rank for non rated sailors (62).

Black cuff stripes passed into history at the end of 2010, when the 1925 green uniform was abolished (63).

Epaulets

The term epaulet comes from epaulet, the French for shoulder (1). It is often used in the modern world for any shoulder decoration, but here it refers to a specific type of decoration. An epaulet in this context is a strap on the shoulder with fringe at the end called bullion. Above the bullion is a stiffening called a crescent. The area inside the crescent is called the frog and the area from the top of the crescent to the button by the collar is called the strap.

They were first used by the navy in 1797. The system was simple, two plain gold epaulets for Captains and one on the right shoulder for Lieutenants (2).

It is possible that epaulets were worn by Masters Commandant during the time that rank first existed form 1799 to 1801. It would make sense for them to wear an epaulet on the right and Lieutenants moving theirs to the left, but this is just speculation.

The 1802 uniform regulations call for Captains to were two epaulets, with those serving as a "Commodore" adding a silver star, Lieutenants in command of vessels one on the right shoulder and other Lieutenants one on the left shoulder (3).

The 1813 uniform regulations are the same with both the now returned Masters Commandant and Lieutenants in command wear their epaulet on the right (4).

With the 1820 regulations, Captains added silver crossed anchors in the frog if they had been a Captain for more than five years. Those under five years wore one anchor, and any Captain serving as a "Commodore" wore a silver star on the strap. Masters Commandant now wore two plain epaulets, Lieutenants in command or First Lieutenants of line battleships one on the right and other Lieutenants one on the left (5).

The 1830 uniform regulations gave all Captains a silver eagle and anchor device in the frog, with "Commodores" and the navy's senior officer the star on the strap. Masters Commandant wore two plain epaulets and all Lieutenants one on the right (6).

The 1841 regulations used the same system, but gave a more detained description as to what the epaulets would look like. They stated "The epaulettes shall be made of gilt gold bullion, and the bullion is to be half an inch in diameter and three inches long; straps to be plain and have an edging and crescent." (7). The crescent was made of gold embroidery.

On June 1, 1845 and ordered changed the epaulets system. All officers would now wear two epaulets. "Commodores" with the star and eagle and anchor device, Captains with just the eagle and anchor device, Commanders with a silver anchor and Lieutenants plain (8).

At some point, the date is not clear, rank began to be shown by the size of the bullion. It could have been with the 1845 order or it could have been when staff officers were given epaulets in 1847. The bullion for Lieutenants was 3/8 inch wide and three inches long, Commodores wore bullion that was 1/2 inch wide and three inches long and Captains, at least as of the 1852 uniform regulations, used 5/8 by 3 1/2 bullion.

Pursers and medical officers were given epaulets to reflect their relative rank on May 27, 1847. Instead of the embroidered crescents used by line officers, crescents of flat gold lace was used. Pursers and Surgeons over 12 years service wore the 1/2 inch wide bullion of a Commander and those under 12 years service the 3/8 bullion of a Lieutenant. Passed Assistant and Assistant Surgeons wore 1/4 inch wide bullion. Medical officers placed the letters M.D. in an old english font in the frog and Pursers wore the letters P.D.. Surgeons of the Fleet added a silver rosette above the letters (9).

The uniform regulations of March 8, 1852 called for "Commodores" to wear two silver stars on the strap and a modified eagle and anchor device in the frog. Captains wore only one star. Commanders wore silver crossed anchors in the frog, Lieutenants one silver anchor and Masters' epaulets were plain. Bullion size was as before with Masters wearing the bullion of Lieutenants. Medical and Purser epaulets were not changed and Chief Engineers were given an epaulet with the strap portion in silver with a gold E on the frog and 3/8 inch wide bullion (10).

On September 24th the letters, and probably the rosette, were removed from the Medical and Purser epaulets, leaving them plain gold. (11). Engineers lost their E on February 8, 1861 (12). It is possible that Chief Engineers over 12 years service began wearing 1/2 inch bullion at this point, but this is not clear.

The insignia for naval line officers was modified on July 31, 1862 to show the reorganization of the rank structure and equivalence with the army from a law of July 16th. The new rank of Rear Admiral now wore the eagle and anchor device in the frog and the two stars of a Major General on the strap, the same as had been worn by "Commodores" before. The now official rank of Commodore wore the old epaulets of a Captain, eagle and anchor and the one star of a Brigadier General. Captains were reduced to just the eagle and anchor as a naval equivalent of a Colonel's eagle. Commanders wore the silver oak leaf of a Lieutenant Colonel at either side of the frog with a silver horizontal anchor between them. The new rank of Lieutenant Commander wore the gold oak leafs of a Major, with the anchor between, unlike army Majors gold leafs were worn on the gold epaulet. Lieutenants wore the two gold bars of an army Captain with the silver anchor running vertically between them. Army Captains wore silver on the epaulets and gold on the shoulder straps at the time, but navy Lieutenants used gold only. Masters wore the same with only the one bar of a First Lieutenant. Ensigns wore only the anchor, showing the lack of insignia of a Second Lieutenant. Bullion sizes are not clear and staff officers epaulets were not changed (13).

The uniform regulations of 1864 (14) did not include epaulets as part of it's plain and simple wartime uniforms.

Epaulets returned in 1866. Full Admirals wore four silver stars in the frog with gold anchors under the outer two. Vice Admirals wore three stars with a gold anchor under the middle one. Rear Admirals wore two stars with a silver anchor between. Commodores wore one star in the center of the frog with silver anchors on either side. Captains now used a more Colonel like silver eagle between two silver anchors. Other line officers wore the army style badges of rank from 1862 with the anchor in the middle. Staff officers wore the same epaulets as line officers of the same relative rank, right down to the embroidered crescent, with the corps device replacing the anchors, or no device in the case of medical officers (15).

On March 11, 1869 Masters, Ensigns and equivalent staff officers were ordered to wear shoulder knots instead of epaulets (16). A regulation circular of October 3, 1871, mostly concerning stateroom assignments, restored epaulets for Masters and equivalent (17).

At some point the bars for Lieutenants and Masters were changed to silver. The exact date is not known, but they are gold in the 1876 uniform regulations (18) and silver in the 1883 uniform regulations (19). The change may have happened with the creation of the 1877 service coat, but this is not clear.

The 1883 regulations also restored the epaulets for Ensigns and gave medical officers a corps device (20).

When the rank of Admiral of the Navy was created in 1899, he was given the epaulets of a full Admiral, with the four stars and the two anchors (21).

The 1913 uniform regulations redesigned the epaulets for senior officers. The Admiral of the Navy wore three silver stars in the frog with a gold anchor under the middle one and one silver star with a gold anchor under it on the strap. Full Admirals wore the same without the anchor in the frog. Vice Admirals, Rear Admirals, retired Commodores, Captains, Commanders and Lieutenant Commanders wore a single badge of rank in the center of their frog and a line anchor or corps device on the strap. Junior officers' epaulets remained the same (22).

The use of epaulets was stopped for World War I (23) and the navy officially abolished them on June 24, 1919 (24), only to bring them back on April 25, 1921 (25).

The epaulets described in the 1922 uniform regulations expand the 1913 epaulet style to all ranks, with a single badge of rank in the frog, including a gold bar for Ensigns. The anchor was worn on the strap by all officers with staff officers wearing the corps device superimposed on top of it (26).

The use of Epaulets was suspended for World War II and the suspension was never lifted, making epaulets pass into history (27).

Shoulder Straps

Shoulder straps were created in 1830 for use when epaulets were not worn. The first shoulder straps were simple strips of gold lace, worn on both shoulders by Captains and Masters Commandant and on the right by Lieutenants (1).

The system was expanded by the 1841 uniform regulations. Captains now wore a blue strap 2 1/2 inches long and 1/2 inch wide, outlined in gold embroidery. "Commodores" added a silver star in the center of the strap. Commanders wore a strip of gold lace 2 1/2 inches long and 1/2 inch wide on both shoulders and Lieutenants one on the right (2).

In 1845 a silver eagle and anchor device was added to the straps of Captains (3). The same order gave Lieutenants an epaulet on each shoulder, so it would make sense that the straps for Commanders became the empty blue frame and Lieutenants gold strips on both shoulders, but it is not clear that this is what happened.

On May 27, 1847, Pursers and Medical officers were given shoulder straps. Surgeons of the Fleet wore 1/4 inch wide gold border around the blue center with the silver letters M.D. in the middle and a silver rosette at each end. Surgeons over 12 years service wore the same with gold acorns replacing the rosettes. Surgeons under 12 years service were without end devices. Passed Assistant Surgeons had a smaller, 1/8 inch wide, border with a gold bar at each end and the M.D. letter in the middle. Assistant Surgeons omitted the bars. Pursers wore the same straps as Surgeon with P.D replacing M.D. and an oak leaf replacing the acorn for those over 12 years service (4).

The March 8, 1852 uniform regulations prescribed straps for line officers that were 1 3/8 inches wide and four inches long with a 1/4 inch wide gold boarder around a blue center. "Commodores" wore a silver eagle and anchor device in the center with a silver star at each end, other Captains omitted the stars. Commanders wore silver crossed anchors in the center, Lieutenants a single anchor and Masters an empty frame. Passed Midshipmen wore a strip of gold lace 1/2 inch wide and four inches long. The straps for Pursers and medical officers were not changed from 1847 and Chief Engineers were given a strap with a 1/4 inch border and a silver E in the center (5).

On September 24th the M.D. on the medical straps was replaced with an olive sprig and the P.D. with an oak sprig (6).

On February 8, 1861, the Chief Engineers E was replaced with crossed oak branches and those over 12 years service added an acorn at each end (7).

The insignia for naval line officers was modified on July 31, 1862 to show the reorganization of the rank structure and equivalence with the army from a law of July 16th. Rear Admirals wore two silver stars with a silver anchor between and Commodore the anchor at one end and a single star at the other. Captains continued to wear the eagle and anchor device in the center. Other officers wore the anchor in the center and the army style badges of rank, silver oak leafs for Commanders, gold for Lieutenant Commanders, two gold bars for Lieutenants, one for Masters and nothing for Ensigns, at each end (8).

Shoulder straps became standardized with the regulations of January 28, 1864. All Straps for commissioned officers were 1 1/2 inches wide and 4 1/4 inches long including the 1/4 inch border. Line officers wore a slightly modified anchor in the center of the strap and staff officers wore a corps device, except medical officers who wore nothing. The army style badges of rank, with staff officers wearing the badges of their relative rank, were worn at each end except for Commodores and equivalent who wore their star superimposed over the anchor or device that was rendered in gold instead of silver, and Captains and equivalent who wore the anchor or device in the talons of the eagle. Boatswains were given a strip of gold lace 3/4 inch wide and four inches long with a silver letter B in the center. Carpenters wore the same with a C. Gunners and Sailmakers wore the same straps without letters (9).

Straps were prescribed for the Vice Admiral on January 14, 1865. He was to wear three silver stars with a gold anchor under the middle one (10).

The 1866 uniform regulations added straps for the full Admiral, with four stars with gold anchors under the end ones. The anchors and corps devices for Commodore and Captains and their equivalent staff officers were now worn on either side the stars or eagle (11).

Mates were given plain gold lace straps, same as Gunners and Sailmakers, on September 3, 1867 and Clerks were given straps with a silver C in the center of the gold lace, the same as Carpenters (12).

A general order of March 11, 1869 (13) restricted the use of shoulder straps the Lieutenants and above. Masters and Ensigns were given shoulder knots and warrant officers collar insignia. Masters had their straps returned to them on October 3, 1871 (14), and Ensigns on June 21, 1881 (15).

At some point the bars for Lieutenants and Masters were changed to silver. The exact date is not known, but they are gold in the 1876 uniform regulations (16) and silver in the 1883 uniform regulations (17). The change may have happened with the creation of the 1877 service coat, but this is not clear.

From 1881 to 1883 civil engineering officers wore straps with a light blue background (18). This is the only time that the navy used any background color that navy blue.

The 1883 uniform regulations show dark blue backgrounds for all, a corps device for medical officers and straps for the new rank of Ensign Junior Grade consisting to an unfolded anchor in the center and no end devices (19).

When the rank of Admiral of the Navy was created in 1899, he was given the straps of a full Admiral, with the four stars and the two anchors (20).

In the book The Uniforms of the United States Navy by Captain James C. Tily it is stated that shoulder straps were abolished when they weren't included in the 1905 uniform regulations (21). This is not correct, straps are prescribed for not only officers but chief warrant officers (22). When chief warrant officers began wearing straps is not clear, it may have been when the ranks were created in 1898, or at some point after that. The straps showed the specialty device in silver in the center, and those who had retired with the rank of Lieutenant Junior Grade could add a silver bar at each end. It is possible that Captain Tiily was reading an updated copy of the regulations where straps were removed. It is also possible that straps were abolished with the next uniform regulations in 1913, or at sometime in between.

Shoulder Knots

Shoulder knots, referred to in regulations as "shoulder loops", were created on March 11, 1869 (1) for use by Masters, Ensigns, equivalent staff officers and graduated Midshipmen.

The entire text describing them regulations is: "gold-embroidered shoulder loops as per patterns; Staff-Officers omitting the anchor." (2). All we have to go on is an illustration from the 1869 uniform regulations (3) (4) that shows the knots for Masters to be of two gold cords with an oval shaped pad over the shoulder. Blue cloth shows thru the cords and in the pad. A third cord surrounds the pad which contains a vertical gold fouled anchor between two silver bars, staff officers would be without the anchor. The knots for ensigns were the same without the third cord around the pad and a horizontal gold anchor with a silver bar superimposed on top of it, staff officers would have worn the bar by itself. The straps for Midshipmen were oval shaped knots made of two cords with two sets of perpendicular loops and a silver anchor in the opening near the outer end.

Masters only wore the knots until October 3, 1871 (5), Ensigns until 1883 (6) and Midshipmen until they were no longer part of the navy's regular rank structure.

Shoulder Boards

Shoulder boards, known as shoulder marks into the 1960s, were born in 1899 for use on the white service coat and overcoat. They consisted of a rectangle of stiffened, dark blue cloth with one pointed end containing a button. The Admiral of the Navy wore a strip of two inch wide gold lace running long ways with a line of four silver stars with gold anchors under the top and bottom ones. Rear Admirals wore two stars with a line anchor or corps device between them. For other officers the stripes were the same as worn on the cuff, four 1/2 inch stripes for Captains, three for Commanders, Two with a 1/4 inch stripe between for Lieutenant Commanders, two 1/2 inch stripes for Lieutenants, one under a 1/2 inch stripe for Lieutenants Junior Grade and one 1/2 inch stripe for Ensigns. Line officers wore the line star above the stripes and staff officers wore colored cloth between the stripes, or as piping for Ensigns. The colors were maroon for medical officers, white for supply officers, dark violet for constructors and light blue for civil engineers. It is possible that staff admirals wore the colors on the sides of the gold lace (1), but this is not in the 1905 uniform regulations (2).

Another feature of the 1905 regulations is shoulder boards for chief warrant officers. They showed one 1/2 inch stripe with a 1/2 inch blue break in the middle. The line star was worn above the stripe by Chief Boatswains and Chief Gunners (3). It is not clear when chief warrant officers began wearing shoulder boards, it may have been when the ranks were created in 1899 or at some later point.

In 1902 shoulder boards were placed on a new white mess jacket. Chaplains were granted boards at the same time with stripes of black mohair braid (4).

Warrant officers gained shoulder boards in 1908, with no stripes, and the specialty device in gold worn at the outer end. Gold specialty devices, were also placed above the stripes of chief warrant officers (5).

Shoulder boards were abolished by the uniform regulations of January 25, 1913, and replaced with white cloth shoulder loops with badges of rank, on the white service coat and white mess jacket, the shoulders of the overcoat were left plain (6). They returned on June 24th (7) and it is doubtful that the loops were ever worn. The 1913 regulations included insignia for full Admirals, four stars with a gold anchor under the top one when boards returned, and Vice Admirals, Three stars with a silver anchor above them, and two new colors, orange for dental officers and crimson for medical reserve officers (8).

Shoulder boards were worn the green and khaki aviation uniforms worn during World War I (9).

Chaplains were allowed gold stripes with black cloth on June 26, 1918 (10).

The colored cloth for staff officers was eliminated on November 16, 1918 and replaced with corps devices, on an anchor, above the stripes (11).

In 1919 the shoulder boards for chief warrant officers and warrant officers were changed to an unbroken 1/2 inch stripe, for chief warrants, and a 1/4 inch stripe for warrants, both under the specialty devices. Mates continued to wear just the specialty device (12).

The 1922 uniform regulations changed the boards for admirals. The anchor was worn at the top with the stars below, in a diamond for full Admirals, a triangle for Vice Admirals and one above the other for Rear Admirals. The corps device was superimposed on the anchor for staff admirals. The anchor was not worn by other staff officers, the corps device was worn alone above the stripes. The stripes for chief warrant officers and warrant officers regained the blue break (13).

Shoulder boards were added to the khaki uniform when it was expanded to the entire navy in 1941 (22).

Female nurses began wearing shoulder boards, without corps devices, in 1942 (23). Other female officers did not wear boards.

When the gray uniform was created in 1943, it was to use special gray shoulder boards (24). They were made of gray cloth with a rounded ends and no button. They were more of a trapezoidal shape, with the sides at a slight angle. Admirals wore black stars, anchors and corps devices, and other officers wore black stripes with black line stars or corps devices (25). On August 11, 1943, full color boards were permitted on the gray uniform (26). This option was revoked on March 7, 1944 (27).

Nurses added a corps device above their stripes on June 30, 1944 (28).

Shoulder boards for Fleet Admirals were authorized on January 31, 1945, consisted of five stars in a pentagon below the anchor (29).

The full color boards were allowed on the gray uniform again on March 15, 1946 (30). In 1947 the gray uniform was abolished and with it the gray shoulder boards (31).

Nursers lost their shoulder boards when their uniforms were combined with other female officers on October 21, 1948 (32).

Sometime between 1947 (33) and 1956 (34), shoulder boards were placed on the male white shirt, when worn without a coat, as the tropical uniform.

In 1954 the shoulder boards for warrant officers had to be modified to show four ranks instead of two. W-4s continued to wear the 1/2 inch stripe with one 1/2 inch blue break. W-3s were given two breaks and W-2s three breaks. W-1s wore 1/4 inch stripe with three breaks (35).

Female officers began wearing shoulder boards on the summer white shirts and overcoats on June 1, 1986 (36).

In 2004 boards were prescribed for Chief Warrant Officers 5, with one 1/2 inch stripe, one blue break and an 1/8 inch blue line running down the center of the stripe (37).

The modern term, used in uniform regulation is hard shoulder boards, as opposed to soft shoulder boards or “shoulder marks”.

Shoulder Marks

What we will call shoulder marks are referred to by the navy as soft shoulder boards. This refers to a scaled down version of the shoulder boards that are applied to an open ended tube of cloth that can be slipped over a cloth shoulder loop of a shirt or sweater.

They are described as: “3. SOFT SHOULDER BOARDS. Combination insignia in dictating the wearer's grade and corps are 3/4 the size of the men's hard shoulder boards. Soft shoulder boards are worn on white epauletted shirts when worn with Service Dress Blue, and on the Navy black V-neck sweater.” (1).

They began in 1979 (2) for use by officers on the white shirt worn under the 1919 blue coat. Allowing rank to be showed when the coat was removed, and on the summer white shirts for female officers (3).

On June 1, 1986 female officers switched to hard shoulder boards on the summer white shirts (4).

In 1999, Chief Petty Officers were given shoulder marks consisting of a black background with their badge of rank embroidered at the outer end (5)

The History of American Ranks and Rank Insignia

Badges of Rank

Badges of rank is the term we shall use for the stars, eagles, leafs and bars used by officers and warrant officers, and the, mostly, pin on insignia used by enlisted personnel. We will use "badge of rank" for enlisted insignia, even though "badge of rate" would be correct.

Badges began in 1802 with the stars worn on the epaulets by "Commodores" (1). This was expanded with the addition of crossed anchors on the epaulets of Captains over five years service and a single anchor for Captains under five years service, in 1820 (2), which was then replaced by an eagle and anchor device for all Captains in 1830 (3).

The "Commodores'" stars were placed on shoulder straps in 1841 (4), and the Captains eagle and anchor device in 1845 (5). Commanders were given a single anchor on the epaulets but not the shoulder straps until 1848 (6).

In 1847 staff officers were given shoulder straps with what could be classified as badges of rank. Surgeons of the Fleet wore a silver rosette on both the epaulets and shoulder straps, while Surgeons over 12 years service wore an acorn at the ends of the shoulder straps, and Pursers over 12 years service an oak leaf. Passed Assistant Surgeons had a bar at the ends of the straps (7).

The 1852 uniform regulations placed two stars and an eagle and anchor device on the epaulets and shoulder straps of "Commodores", one star and the eagle on the epaulets of Captains, only the eagle was worn on the shoulder straps, crossed anchors on both the epaulets and shoulders straps of Commanders and a single anchor fro Lieutenants (8).

Chief Engineers over 12 years service, probably, received an acorn at the ends of their shoulder straps in 1861 (9).

The insignia for naval line officers was modified on July 31, 1862 to show the reorganization of the rank structure and equivalence with the army from a law of July 16th. The new rank of Rear Admiral now wore the two stars of a Major General, Commodores the one star of a Brigadier General, Captains continued the silver eagle and anchor as a naval equivalent of a Colonel's eagle.

Commanders wore the silver oak leaf of a Lieutenant Colonel, Lieutenant Commander wore the gold oak leafs of a Major, unlike army Majors gold leafs were worn on the gold epaulet. Lieutenants wore the two gold bars of an army Captain, army Captains wore silver on the epaulets and gold on the shoulder straps at the time, but navy Lieutenants used gold only. Masters wore the same with only the one bar of a First Lieutenant. Ensigns had no badge of rank, showing the lack of insignia of a Second Lieutenant (10).

Badges of rank came into their own with the uniform regulations of 1864. Staff officers wore the same army style badges as line officers of their relative. Most importantly the regulations placed the badges alone on the collar of the overcoat, stating "On each end of the collar of the overcoat shall be the following devices: For a rear admiral, two silver stars; commodore, one silver star; captain, a silver eagle; commander, a silver leaf; lieutenant commander, a gold leaf; lieutenant, two silver bars; master, one silver bar; ensign, a small gold cord on the front edge of the collar. Staff officers of corresponding assimilated rank are to wear the same designations. Stars, eagle and bars to be parallel to the ends of the collar. The overcoats of all other officers than those above mentioned are to have no devices..." (11). This was first use of badges of rank without epaulets or shoulder straps. The bars for Lieutenants and Masters are listed as silver not gold. This begins a period of when the use of gold or silver is not clear, and direct source material is scarce.

Insignia of three silver stars was prescribed for the Vice Admiral on January 14, 1865 (12).

The same concept was used on collar of the service sack coat created in 1865, with Ensigns and equivalent wearing the line anchor or corps device instead of the gold cord (13). It is not clear if the overcoat collars were changed to match.

The 1866 uniform regulations continued the collar insignia with the addition of a line anchor or corps device. The full Admiral was prescribed four stars with line anchors under the outer ones and the anchor was placed under the middle star for the Vice Admiral (14).

On March 11, 1869 (15), collar insignia replaced shoulder straps for warrant officers, consisting of gold stars for Boatswains and Gunners and gold diamonds for Carpenters and Sailmakers. The insignia was placed on the collar of the frock coat but not the sack coat (16). The same order prescribed shoulder knots for Masters and Ensigns. The best information we have about the knots has Masters wearing two silver bars and Ensigns one. It was a serious break with precedent for Ensigns to wear a bar, but that is the information we have (17)(18).

In 1877 a new service coat with a standing, black mohair collar was introduced. The badges of rank, but not the line anchor or corps device, were worn on the collar. The bars for Lieutenants and Masters were silver not gold. Warrant officers were allowed the coat the following year with the star or diamond on the collar. This now included a star for Mates and a Diamond for Paymaster's Clerks (19).

The use of silver for the bars may, or may not have extended to the bars on the epaulets and shoulder straps at this point. The exact time of the change is far from clear. The 1876 uniform regulations call for gold, even on the sack coat collar (20), but does not describe Ensigns' shoulder knots in detail (Masters stopped wearing them in 1871). The next uniform regulations in 1883 call for silver (21), and the bars have remained silver ever since. Shoulder knots were eliminated by these regulations.

The 1883 regulations placed line anchors and corps devices, (even for medical officers, since 1864 medical officers had been noted by the lack of a device) on the collar of the 1877 service coat For the Admiral the anchor was under the outer star. This left Ensigns and equivalent with just the anchor or device on the collar. The short lived rank of Ensign Junior Grade wore an unfouled anchor. The various warrant ranks gained specialty devices to replace the gold stars and diamonds. Boatswains wore crossed anchors, Gunners a bursting bomb, Carpenters a chevron representing a Carpenter's square, Sailmakers continued to wear the diamond, Mates wore a pair of binoculars and Paymaster's Clerks an oak sprig The devices were silver for warrant officers over 20 years service and gold for those under 20 years service (22).

During the Spanish-American War, the temporary rank of Warrant Machinist wore a gold four bladed propellor (23).

In 1899 the new rank of Admiral of the Navy was given four stars on the collar, with anchors under both end stars. The new chief warrant ranks inherited the silver specialty device from warrant officers over 20 years service (24), other warrant officers wore gold. This included Pharmacists who wore a Geneva cross, and the now permanent rank of Machinist who wore a cross of oak branches until 1900 when a three bladed propellor was prescribed (25).

The January 1913 uniform regulations prescribed metal badges of rank on white cloth shoulder to replace shoulder boards. The Admiral of the Navy was to wear four stars in a cross with anchors under the top and bottom ones. Full Admirals wore the four stars in a cross with an anchor under the top one and Vice Admirals wore the cross with an anchor replacing the to star. Other officers wore the anchor or corps device in the middle of the loop and the badge of rank at the outer end, and warrant officers wore the specialty device. The device for Pharmacists was changed to a caduceus (26)(27). This was rescinded in June, and shoulder boards returned (28).

The use of badges of rank declined after 1913. Shoulder straps were abolished in, or sometime before, 1913, epaulets were suspended in 1917 (29) and the 1877 service coat was abolished in 1919 (30). This left only the stars on admirals shoulder boards.

A decision was made to restore epaulets in 1921 (31) and the 1922 uniform regulations include them with, for the first time, a gold bar for Ensigns (32).

When the aviation khaki uniform was expanded to submarine officers in 1931, badges of rank were placed on the shirt collar. This allowed rank to be shown when the coat was removed, which was common in the heat of a submarine (33). Line officers wore the badges on both collars and staff officers on the right with the corps device on the left. Chief warrant officers wore silver specialty devices on both collars and other warrant officers gold specialty devices (34). These now included a globe for Electricians and lighting bolts for Radio Electricians (35). This opened the floodgates, and from then on badges were worn on by officers on shirt collars, garrison cap curtains, working caps, and various outerwear.

During World War II several new warrant ranks, and therefore insignia, were created. Torpedomen wore a torpedo, Areographers wore a winged circle with a six feather arrow passing vertically through the circle, Ship's Clerks wore crossed quills and Photographers wore a billows camera (36).

A standard badge of rank was created for chief warrant officers and warrant officers in 1952, consisting of a gold bar with a 1/8 inch wide blue stripe running across it the short way for chief warrant officers and a 1/16 inch wide stripe for warrant officers (37).

In 1954 new insignia was prescribed for the now four grades of Warrant Officer. A "unified system" common to all armed forces was developed using the same pattern for each equivalent rank. The enameled portions would very by branch of service, brown for the army, dark blue for the Navy and Coast Guard, scarlet red for the Marine Corps, and sky blue for the Air Force. The new bars were rectangular, silver for the top two grades and gold for the other two. The enameled portion for W-1 and W-3 would be in two rectangles, showing only one stripe of gold or silver. For W-2 and W-4 there would be three enameled portions showing two sections of gold or silver (38).

In 1959 Chief Petty Officers were given badges of rank consisting of a gold fouled anchor and the silver letter U.S.N.. The insignia was the same for all three ranks of chief petty officer (39). This changed in 1961 when a silver star was added to the top of the anchor for senior chiefs and two stars for master chiefs (40). The Master Chief Petty Officer of the Navy may have worn three stars as early as 1967.

Next up to get badges of rank were petty officers in 1969 (41). A silver eagle with the three silver chevrons was prescribed for Petty Officers First Class, two chevrons for second class and one for third class. Those allowed gold chevrons on their rating badges could wear gold instead of silver chevrons on the badge of rank (42).

Two, for E-2s, or Three, for E-3s, silver hash marks were prescribed for non rated sailors for wear on the shirt collar of the navy service uniform in 2008 (43).

Cuff Stripes (and buttons)

The most commonly known distinction of rank for naval officers is gold stripes worn around the cuffs. Since early uniform regulation varied rank by the decoration and design of the uniform, it is hard to say when distinctions of rank on the cuff began.

The Continental Navy's uniform regulations stated that Captains would wear "slash cuffs" meaning a flap like a pocket flap running vertically over the cuff, and Lieutenants and Midshipmen had "round cuffs" meaning a simple turn back, probably with buttons running across the top (1).

The federal navy's first uniform regulations called for Captains to wear round cuffs with four buttons, Lieutenants, Surgeons, Surgeon's Mates and Sailing Masters slash cuffs with three buttons on the flap and Pursers and Midshipmen plain cuffs (2).

The 1802 uniform regulations have Captains wearing four buttons with gold button holes and a strip of gold lace across the top of the cuff on the dress coat and the same without the gold button holes and lace on the undress coat. Lieutenants wore three buttons with "button-holes laced with such lace as id directed for the captain's;". Since the Captain's button holes were worked in gold thread, it is hard to tell what this meant. It is possible that the holes were outlined in lace instead to thread. This is backed up by the fact the undress coat is described as "The same as the full dress, excepting the lace.", thread is not mentioned. Midshipmen wore a slash sleeve on the dress coat and the cuff of the undress jacket were not mentioned. Surgeons wore three buttons with gold frogs and Surgeon's Mates three buttons with gold worked holes. Sailing Masters wore a slash and Pursers a cuff that opened with three buttons (3).

The 1813 regulations gave Captains and Masters Commandant four buttons with plain holes and gold lace on top in full dress and the same without the lace in undress. Lieutenants wore the same with three buttons. Midshipmen wore no buttons on the cuff. Hospital Surgeons wore three buttons under two rows of 1/4 inch lace on the full dress coat and the same without the lace on the undress coat. Surgeons wore three buttons and Surgeon's Mates and Sailing Masters two. Pursers continued to have a cuff that opened with three buttons. The cuffs of Boatswains, Gunners, Carpenters and Sailmakers were not mentioned. (4).

In 1820 Captains, Masters Commandant, Lieutenants Commandant, First Lieutenants of line Battle Ships and Lieutenants were ordered to wear four buttons with laced button holes under a strip of lace in full dress and the same without the lace in undress. Midshipmen continued to wear not buttons on the cuff. Hospital Surgeons continued to have three buttons with the two strips of lace on the full dress coat and the same without the lace on the undress coat. Surgeons wore three buttons on both coats. Surgeon's Mates wore two buttons but Sailing Masters not wore three. Pursers continued to have a cuff that opened with three buttons. Master's Mates wore three buttons and the cuffs of Boatswains, Gunners, Carpenters and Sailmakers were not mentioned (5).

Things changed in 1830. Captains' full dress cuffs now opened with two buttons with holes "worked with twist", four buttons were worn across the cuffs that were covered in gold oak leaf and acorn embroidery. The undress cuffs had simply four buttons. Masters Commandant wore same with three buttons and Lieutenants, Passed Midshipmen, Midshipmen and Masters the same without the embroidery. Surgeons and Pursers wore the cuffs of a Master Commandant in full dress and cuffs with three buttons and a strip of gold lace in undress. Assistant Surgeon wore the same as the Surgeons without the embroidery on the full dress coat or the lace on the undress coat. Boatswains, Gunners, Carpenters and Sailmakers wore a slash cuff with three buttons. Chaplains wore three buttons covered in black cloth. The cuffs for Schoolmasters and Clerk were not Mentioned (6).

Assistant Surgeons were given a strip of gold lace on the undress coat in 1832 and Surgeons added a second strip in 1834 (7).

Under the 1841 uniform regulations Captains wore four buttons on the cuffs and Commanders, Lieutenants, Passed Midshipmen, Midshipmen, Masters, Second Masters, Surgeons, Passed Assistant Surgeons, Assistant Surgeons, Pursers and Chaplains three. Secretaries, Professors of Mathematics and Clerks wore none and Boatswains, Gunners, Carpenters and Sailmakers wore a slash cuff with three buttons. The only gold lace was worn on both coats by medical officers. Surgeons had three strips of 1 1 /2 inch wide lace on the dress coat, one strip above the buttons and two below. The undress coat had the same with 1/4 inch lace. Passed Assistant Surgeons wore the same without the lowest strip of lace and Assistant Surgeons wore only the top strip (8).

In 1847, the lace and the buttons were removed from cuffs of medical officers. Surgeon were given three sprigs of live oak in gold and Passed Assistant Surgeons and Assistant Surgeons' cuffs were plain (9).

The next uniform regulations, in 1852, saw the true birth of a system of cuff stripes to indicate rank. The traditional four buttons of a Captain were now worn as small, vertical, closure buttons. In the spaces between them were three strips of 3/4 inch wide lace with another strip running vertically form the bottom stripe to the end of the sleeve. Commanders wore the same with only three buttons and two strips of lace and Lieutenants wore three buttons and only one strip of lace. Both Commanders and Lieutenants wore the vertical strip. Masters had the three closure buttons and three medium sized buttons around the cuff. Passed Midshipmen and Midshipmen wore the three closure buttons alone. Boatswains, Gunners, Carpenters and Sailmakers wore only two closure buttons and the three medium buttons around the cuff. Surgeons wore the three closure buttons and the three oak sprig from 1847 on the dress tail coat and three closure buttons and three large buttons around the cuffs on the undress frock coat. Passed

Assistant Surgeons wore the three closure buttons and three medium sized buttons around the cuffs of the tail coat and three closure buttons three large buttons around the cuffs of the frock coat. Assistant Surgeons wore just the three closure buttons on the tail coat and three closure buttons and three large buttons around the cuffs of the frock coat. Pursers wore the three closure buttons on the tail coat with a line of oak leaf and acorn embroidery between the top two buttons and three closure buttons and three large buttons around the cuffs of the frock coat. Chief Engineers wore the three closure buttons and three large buttons around the cuffs of both coats. First Assistant Engineers used medium buttons and second third assistants wore only the three closure buttons. Chaplains, Secretaries, Professors of Mathematics and Clerks wore only the three closure buttons on both coats (10).

Surgeons and Pursers were given cuff stripes, on both coats, on August 23, 1856. Those over 12 years service wore the two stripes of a Commander and those under the one strip of a Lieutenant (11). The same system was applied to Chief Engineers on February 8, 1861 (12).

On February 25th, a gold five pointed star was placed above the cuff stripes of Lieutenants who were ship's executive officers (13).

On July 31, 1862 the cuff stripes system was altered to reflect the new rank structure. All buttons, both closure and decorative, were removed, along with the vertical stripe, and the 3/4 inch lace was joined by strips of 1/4 inch lace to sow more ranks. Rear Admirals wore three 3/4 inch stripes alternating with three 1/4 inch stripes, the top stripe was 1/4 inch and the bottom 3/4. Commodores wore three 3/4 inch stripes with two 1/4 inch stripes between them, or the same as a Rear Admiral without the top stripe. Captains continued to wear three 3/4 inch stripes. Commanders and Surgeons, Paymasters and Chief Engineers over 12 years service now had two 3/4 inch stripes with a 1/4 inch stripes between them. Lieutenant Commanders inherited the two 3/4 inch stripes. Lieutenants and Surgeons, Paymasters and Chief Engineers under 12 years service wore one 3/4 inch stripe under one 1/4 inch stripe. Masters, Passed Assistant Surgeons and First Assistant Engineers wore just the 3/4 inch stripe. Ensigns, Assistant Surgeons, Assistant Paymasters and Second Assistant Engineers wore just a 1/4 inch stripe. Plain cuffs were worn by Midshipmen, Third Assistant Engineers, Boatswains, Gunners, Carpenters, Sailmakers, Masters Mates, Chaplains, Secretaries, Professors of Mathematics and Clerks (14).

Yet another system of cuff stripes, the third since the start of the Civilv War, was ordered on May 23, 1863 (15) and is reflected in the uniform regulations of January 28, 1864 (16). All line officers and warrant officers now wore the gold star above the stripes or by itself if no stripe were authorized. The stripes themselves were of 1/4 inch lace 1/4 inch apart with 1/2 inch spaces in some places to make the many stripes of senior officers easier to read. The extra space created groups of three stripes and a combination of groups of three and single stripes was worn by higher ranks. Rear Admirals wore eight stripes in two groups of three with a single stripe between and one above, all under the line star. Commodores wore seven stripes in two groups of three with a single stripe between, all under the line star. The Chiefs of the Bureaus of Medicine and Surgery, Provisions and Clothing, Steam Engineering and Construction and Repair wore the same without the star. Captains wore six stripes in two groups of three under the line star and Fleet Surgeons, Fleet Paymasters, Fleet Engineers, Surgeons, Paymasters and Chef Engineers over 15 years service and Naval Constructors over 20 years service wore the same without the star. Commanders wore five stripes in one group of three with single stripes above and below, under the line star. Surgeons, Paymasters and Chief Engineers over five years service and Naval Constructors, Chaplains and Professors of Mathematics over 12 years service wore the same without the star. Lieutenant Commanders wore four stripe with one group of three and a single stripe above, under the line star. Surgeons, Paymasters and Chief Engineers under five years service and Naval Constructors, Chaplains and Professors of Mathematics under 12 years service wore the same without the star. Lieutenants wore three stripes under the star and Passed Assistant Surgeons and Secretaries wore the same without the star. Masters wore two stripes under the star and Assistant Surgeons, Assistant Paymasters, First Assistant Engineers and Assistant Naval Constructors the same without the star. Ensigns wore one stripe under the star and Second Assistant Engineers wore the same without the star. Midshipmen, Boatswains, Gunners and Master's Mates wore the star alone in the same position as Ensigns. Third Assistant Engineers, Clerks, Carpenters and Sailmakers wore plain cuffs.

On January 14, 1865 stripes were prescribed for the Vice Admiral. Nine stripes would have been ridiculous, so one, two inch wide stripe under two 1/4 inch wide stripes were worn under the line star. The stripes for Rear Admirals were changed to one two inch stripe under one 1/4 inch stripe under a line star (17).

Cuff stripes could be worn on the 1865 service coat, but usually were not. However, line officer did wear the line star on the cuffs (18).

The 1866 uniform regulations prescribed cuff stripes for the full Admiral of two two inch stripes with one one inch stripe between them under a special star showing the U.S.S. Hartford, Admiral Farragut's flagship at the battle of Mobile Bay. The Vice Admiral now wore one two inch stripe under two one inch stripes under a regular line star. Rear Admirals wore only one one inch stripe and Commodores and equivalent, just the two inch stripe. Other ranks wore the same 1/4 inch stripes from 1864. Stripes were now defiantly not worn on the service coat, but the star was (19).

1866 also saw the creation of cuff stripes for enlisted men. Petty officers, Seamen and Firemen First Class wore three 1/8 inch white stripes on the blue cuffs of both the blue and white jumpers. Ordinary Seamen and Firemen Second Class wore two stripes and Landsmen Coal Heavers and Boys, one (20).

The next cuff stripe system was created by a general order on March 11, 1869. The cuffs on the full dress tail coat of the Admiral showed four closure buttons with three lines of gold and white oak leaf and acorn embroidery with a small line running vertically from the bottom line to the end of the sleeve, in the style of the 1852 stripes, all under the special star. On his undress coat, the Admiral wore one two inch stripe under three 1/2 inch stripes under the special star. The Vice Admiral wore only two rows on embroidery on the full dress coat and one two inch stripe under two 1/2 inch stripes on his undress coat, both under a regular line star. Rear Admirals wore only one line of embroidery on the full dress coat and one two inch stripe under one 1/2 inch stripe on the undress coat, both under a line star. Commodores and equivalent continued to wear one two inch stripe on both coats. For other officers the system returned to 1862 with 1/2 inch stripes replacing 3/4 inch stripes. Captains and equivalent wore three 1/2 inch stripes, Commanders and equivalent two with a 1/4 inch stripe between them, Lieutenant Commanders and equivalent wore two 1/2 inch stripes, Lieutenants and equivalent one under a 1/4 inch stripe, Masters and equivalent one 1/2 inch stripe and Ensigns and equivalent one 1/4 inch stripe. Graduated Midshipmen were allowed one 1/8 inch stripe. Line officers wore the line star above the stripe, and staff officers added colored cloth in between the stripes, or as piping if there was only one stripe. Medical officers wore cobalt blue cloth, paymasters white cloth and engineers red cloth (21). Other staff officers had lost their relative rank at the time.

On May 27th, 77 days later, Captains were increased to four 1/2 inch stripes and Commanders to three (22).

The July 14, 1869 uniform regulations changed the enlisted stripes. Petty officers were now allowed four stripes and all stripes were now 1/2 inch wide (23). Possibly then, but by the 1876 uniform regulations (24) the stripes on the blue cuffs of the white jumper were changed to blue or dungaree tape.

When David Dixon Porter replaced David Farragut as Admiral in 1870, he wore the regular line star (25).

With their relative rank restored, naval constructors were ordered to wear dark violet cloth on March 21, 1872, and Professors of Mathematics were ordered to wear olive green cloth on May 31st (26).

Rear Admirals lost their special embroidered cuffs on their full dress coats on July 31, 1873. They now wore the same stripes on both coats (27).

On August 12, 1874, Lieutenant Commanders and equivalent had their cuff stripes changed to two 1/2 inch stripes with one 1/4 inch stripes between them, and Lieutenants and equivalent two 1/2 inch stripes (28).

The new service coat of 1877 carried cuff stripes of black mohair braid, with no line star or colored cloth. When warrant officers were authorized the coat in 1878, Boatswains and Gunners were ordered to wear the gold line star on the cuffs (29).

Overcoats gained the black stripes at some point. It may have been in 1877 when the service coat was created, but it was by 1883 (30)

On August 10, 1881, the stripes for Masters and equivalent were changed to one 1/2 inch stripes under one 1/4 inch stripe and the stripe for Ensigns and equivalent was increased to 1/2 inch. On August 24th, civil engineers were ordered to wear light blue cloth between their stripes (31).

The 1883 uniform regulations called for a 1/4 inch stripe for the short lived rank of Ensign Junior Grade and a 1/2 inch stripe with 1/4 inch long blue breaks every two inches for Naval Cadets (32). All officers were given a white service coat with white mohair braid as cuff stripes (33).

It is not clear how broken stripes were translated to the black and white stripes. It is possible that they wore a solid stripe, a broken stripe or no stripe at all.

The 1886 uniform regulations changed the enlisted stripes to 3/16 inch wide, white tape on both jumpers. They now reflected the pay grades created in 1885, petty officers and the Seaman First Class grade wore three stripes, the Seaman Second Class grade wore two and the Seaman Third Class grade one (34).

On June 12, 1897, gold stripes, with line stars and colored cloth, replaced the black stripes on the 1877 blue service coat. The stripes on the 1883 white coat were removed and rank was shown by shoulder straps (35). The black stripes continued on the overcoat.

Under the July 1, 1897 uniform regulations, the stripe for Naval Cadets is unbroken (36).

On December 23, 1897, Chaplains were allowed to wear stripes of their relative rank in black mohair (37).

In 1899 the rank of Admiral of the Navy was given the old stripes of a full Admiral, two two inch stripes with a one inch stripes between them, under a line star. At the same time the broken stripes, 1/2 inch wide this time, was revived for chief warrant officers (38). Once again it is not clear how this was supposed to work on the overcoat.

The 1905 uniform regulations describe the enlisted stripes as being "joined by tape", meaning the cuffs with two or three stripes had vertical tape at the ends of the stripes forming a box (39).

The 1913 uniform regulation added two new colors, crimson for medical reserve officers and orange for dental officers (40).

During World War I, aviation officers were allowed a green overcoat with brown cuff stripes (41)

Chaplains were granted gold stripes, with black cloth, on June 26, 1918. Hopefully not many Chaplains spent money on new stripes. On November 16th colored cloth was abolished as a distinction for staff officers, and replaced by gold corps devices worn above the stripes in the same manner as the line star (42).

In 1919 warrant officers were given a 1/4 inch unbroken stripe and chief warrant officers a 1/2 inch unbroken stripe now worn under the specialty device in gold (43).

The 1922 uniform regulations prescribed broken stripes for warrant officers (44).

The new aviation green and khaki uniforms of 1925 showed rank by black cuff stripes with for the first time, black lines stars or corps devices (45). This brings back the question of had broken stripes were handled. This time we have a clue from a 1943 uniform catalog that shows a picture of a solid stripe with a caption describing it as being for warrant officers (46).

The black stripes worked well on the green uniform but on the khaki uniform the stripes shrank when the coat was washed. When the khaki uniform was expanded to the entire navy in 1941, the stripes were replaced with shoulder boards (47).

In 1942 female nurses were given blue uniforms with yellow or gold cuff stripes, without corps devices (48). Other female officers were given light or reserve blue stripes on blue uniforms (49) and navy blue stripes on white uniforms (50), both without corps devices.

Female officers added corps devices above the stripes in late 1943. The devices were in the same color as the stripes, gold, reserve blue or navy blue (51).

Proof that the black stripes for warrant officers were previously unbroken comes from May 15, 1944, when they were ordered to wear green breaks (52).

Nurses added gold corps devices on June 30, 1944 (53), and female line officers gained a line star on September 15, 1944 (54).

The new rank of Fleet Admiral was given on two inch stripes under three 1/2 inch stripes on January 31, 1945 (55).

The black stripes on the overcoat were removed in 1947 (56).

The use of cuff stripes to show the rate of enlisted sailors ended in 1948 (57), and were replaced with group rate marks. The blue jumpers of all rates now carried three stripes, which were purely decorative.

Female uniforms were combined in 1948. Both nurses and other officers wore the same uniform with reserve blue stripes on blue uniforms and white stripes on white uniforms (58). The reserve blue stripes were changed to gold in 1951 (59).

The stripes for warrant officers were changed in 1954 to reflect four ranks instead of two. W-4s wore a 1/2 inch stripe with one blue break, W-3 had two breaks, two inches apart and W-2s three breaks, two inches apart. W-1s wore a 1/4 inch stripe with three breaks (60).

In 1960 the stripes for female officers on the white coat were changed from white to gold (61).

In 2004 cuff stripes were prescribed for Chief Warrant Officers 5, with one 1/2 inch stripe, one blue break and an 1/8 inch blue line running down the center of the stripe (62).

The black stripes on the green aviation uniform were abolished, along with that uniform in December of 2010 (63).

Petty Officer’s Device

The first known enlisted insignia was an anchor worn by petty officers. Navy regulations of 1833 prescribe the anchor to be worn the right sleeve by Boatswain's Mates, Gunner's Mates, Carpenter's Mates, Masters at Arms, Ship's Stewards, and Ship's Cooks, and on the left by Quartermasters, Quarter Gunners, Captains of Forecastles, Captains of Tops, Armorers, Coopers, Ship's Corporals, and Captains of the Hold (1). The anchors were to be in white on blue uniforms and blue on white uniforms. This idea of white/blue insignia had been used on enlisted uniforms ever since.

The 1841 uniform regulations added an eagle with it's wings down on top of the anchor, in the pattern used on the navy uniform button. The ratings listed are the same with addition of Captains of Afterguard wearing the device on the left (2).

The 1852 uniform regulations placed a star above the device. Boatswain's Mates, Gunner's Mates, Carpenter's Mates, Sailmaker's Mates, Ship's Steward, and Ship's Cooks wore the device on the right sleeve and "All other petty officers, except officers stewards and yoemen" on the left sleeve (3).

The text in the 1864 regulations was identical to the 1852 regulations, except Ship's Stewards were no longer listed (4), the rating was abolished in 1864 (5), and Yoemen were no longer listed as not wearing the device.

In 1866 the design of the device was changed when the wings of the eagle to be out horizontally. The star was only worn by ratings that were considered of the line. Those line ratings wore the device on the right and staff ratings wore the device on the left without the star. The device was joined by various specialty marks worn in various places on the uniform to indicate different ratings (6).

The petty officer's device was replaced by rating badges in 1886 (7).

Rating Badges

The 1886 uniform regulations (1) replaced the petty officer's device with rating badges that reflected the division of ratings into three grades in 1885 (2).

The new rating badges combined the eagles and specialty marks already in use with chevrons to create a single device that would show both rate, as in level of seniority, and rating, as in job specialty.

First class petty officers wore three chevrons, point down, with a diamond in the angle, the same as an army First Sergeant, except for Masters at Arms who wore the three chevrons and three arcs of an army Sergeant Major. Second class petty officers wore three chevrons, same as an army Sergeant and third class the two of an army Corporal. The chevrons were made of scarlet cloth with the chevrons and arcs created with dark stitching. Petty officers with three or more consecutive good conduct badges could wear chevrons and arcs of gold lace. The specialty marks were placed in the angle of the chevrons, with the diamond forming a background for those of the first class. The eagle, with it's wings outstretched and head facing it's left wing, was the same as had been used on the petty officer's device since 1866. It was worn above the specialty mark or the diamond, and the eagle for Masters at Arms was superimposed over the arcs. Both the eagle and specialty mark were white on blue uniforms and blue on white uniforms. The rating badge was worn on the right sleeve for men of the starboard watch and left for men of the port watch (3). It is doubtful that the gold lace was worn on the white uniforms, regulations are unclear, but washing the uniform would have been difficult with the valuable lace attached and removing it every time the uniform was washed impractical (4).

When the rate of Chief Petty Officer was created in 1894, it was given the Master at Arms, Sergeant Major style rating badge, Master at arms was one of the ratings moved up to chief (5).

The design of the rating badges was changed in 1894. The eagle now had it's wings pointing up. Chief Petty Officers were reduced to three chevrons and one arc, Petty Officers First Class to three chevrons with no diamond, Petty Officers Second Class to two chevrons and Petty Officers third Class to one. The chevrons were now had space between them (6), probably to make them easier to read from a distance. This design has been used ever since. There have been slight changes to the eagle over the years, but basic design of rating badges in the second decade of the 21st century is the design of 1894.

The 1913 uniform regulations changed the color of the chevrons on white uniforms from scarlet to blue, making the badge all blue. The eagle and specialty mark were to made in silver for those entitled to gold chevrons. Rating of the seaman branch wore the badge on the right and others on the left, replacing the system of right for starboard watch and left for port (7).

The silver eagles and specialty marks were expanded to all Chief Petty Officers in 1929 (8).

In 1941 the eagles for ratings of the seaman branch had their heads reversed to face right, making all eagles face the wearers front (9).

Chiefs had been allowed green and khaki aviation uniforms in 1931, but it is not clear what colors were used on the rating badges. The 1941 uniform regulations, published just after the khaki uniform was expanded to the entire navy, shows in illustration what appears to be an all blue on khaki background rating badge on the khaki coat (10). The green coat is not illustrated and the text is of no help. The Naval Officer's Uniform Plan, a catalog of uniforms approved by the navy in 1943, shows the green uniform with what appears to be a full color badge on a blue background (11), but sells full color badges on green backgrounds (12). Finally in 1944 the navy ordered that all rating badges, other than on the blue coats, were to be all blue on a background matching the coat, including the gray uniform introduced in 1943 (13). This included reserve blue and gray uniforms worn by female petty officers (14).

1948 saw the end of rating badges on the right sleeve. From then on all ratings wore the badge on the left sleeve with the eagle facing forward (15).

The following year the badges on the khaki coats for chiefs were changed to a silver eagle and specialty mark and blue chevrons and arc (16).

Rating badges were added to khaki shirts of chiefs sometime in late 1950 (17), they appear to have been all blue (18). They were eliminated in 1952 (19).

In 1956 rating badges were added to dungaree shirts. The were all blue on a chambray background with no rating badge (20).

When the rates of Senior Chief Petty Officer and Master Chief Petty Officer were added in 1958, stars, the same color as the eagle, were added above the badge, one for senior chiefs and two for master chiefs (21).

The position of Master Chief Petty Officer of the Navy was created in 1967. On the suggestion of Ima Black, the wife of the first holder of the office, three stars were placed above the rating badge (22). The stars were changed to gold and a fourth gold star replaced the specialty mark in 1971 (23).

The white and khaki uniforms for chiefs were eliminated in 1973 and the all blue on white and silver and blue on khaki rating badges with them.

1975 also saw the creation of blue and white dinner jackets for chiefs. Regular full color rating badges were worn on the blue jacket and badges with silver eagles and specialty marks and blue chevrons and arc (or gold if entitled) were worn on the white jacket. The 1975 regulations actually call for red chevrons, but this was a printing error (25).

Female light blue uniforms were eliminated in 1978, eliminating the need for rating badges with a light blue background (26).

The all blue on green for aviation uniforms and the all blue on chambray for dungarees were eliminated with those uniforms in 2010 (27).

Group Rate Marks

The roots of group rate marks date back to 1944 when a method was developed to show the rate of non rated women who didn't wear jumpers with cuff stripes. The solution was two or three hash marks on the upper sleeve to represent the two or three cuff stripes, no mark represented one stripe (1).

On April 2, 1948 these hash marks, now known as group rate marks, replaced the cuff stripes and branch marks as the insignia of the lowest three grades. Seamen, Hospitalmen, Dentalmen and Stewardsmen wore three white/blue hash marks, Firemen wore three red hash marks and Airmen three green hash marks. Seamen Apprentice, Hospitalmen Apprentice, Dentalmen Apprentice and Steweardmen Apprentice wore two white/blue hash marks. Firemen Apprentice wore two red hash marks and Airmen Apprentice two green hash marks. Seamen Recruit and Stewardsmen Recruit wore one white/blue hash mark. Hospitalmen and Hospital Apprentices added a white/blue caduceus above the marks, Dentalmen and Dentalmen Apprentice added a caduceus and a letter D. Stewardsmen, Stewardsmen Apprentice and Stewardsmen Recruit added a crescent. All group rate marks were worn on the upper left sleeve (2).

Some additions were made to the system on June 15, 1948. A construction group was added using light blue hash marks, three for Constructionmen, two for Constructionmen Apprentices and one for Constructionmen Recruits. Also added were Firemen Recruits with one red hash mark, Airmen Recruits with one green hash mark, Hospitalmen Recruits with one white/blue hash mark under a caduceus and Dentalmen Recruits with one white/blue hash mark under a caduceus and a letter D (3).

The one hash mark for the various recruits was abolished in 1975, Hospitalmen Recruits and Dentalmen Recruits now wore the specialty marks by themselves and other recruits were without insignia (4).

Watch Marks and Branch Marks

Watch marks were created in the 1866 uniform regulations to show what watch a non rated sailor was assigned to, they had nothing to do with his rate. The marks were white/blue horizontal bars 1 1/4 inches long and 1/4 inch wide, worn one inch below the shoulder seam. The first watch wore one bar and the second two. Men of the starboard watch wore the bars on the right and port watch on the left (1).

The 1886 uniform regulations changed the marks to a strip of 3/8 inch tape covering the shoulder seam. It was in red for Firemen and Coal Heavers and white/blue for all others except Messmen and bandsmen, who didn't wear regular uniforms (2). Therefore to recognize a Firemen First Class over a Seaman First Class, for example, it was necessary to look at the color of the watch mark as well as the number of cuff stripes.

By the 1905 uniform regulations Mess Attendants were wearing regular jumpers but with no watch mark (3).

Watch marks were changed to branch marks on October 25, 1912. Men of the seaman branch wore a white/blue mark on the right and men of the engine room force of the artificer branch a red mark on the left. The commissary and messmen branches, along with Hospital Apprentices, Shipwrights Musician and Buglers, wore no branch mark (4).

Branch marks were abolished altogether on April 2, 1948, and replaced with the colors of the group rate marks (5).

Distinguishing Marks

Distinguishing marks, know as simply marks until 1905 were a catchall term for miscellaneous enlisted insignia. Most were qualification badges, but some were used to show rates of non petty officers (1).

Hospital Apprentices were ordered to wear red crosses on the upper sleeve in 1898 (2).

The 1913 uniform regulations (3) list several distinguishing marks that were added October 12, 1912 (4). They were a bugle for Buglers, crossed axes for Shipwrights, a crescent for steward and cooks and a lyre for musicians.

The axes were eliminated, along with Shipwrights, in 1921 (5).

Beginning in the mid 1920s, non rated sailors who earned a rating could wear the specialty mark of that rating on the lower sleeve (6).

The use of distinguishing marks to show rate ended with the creation of group rate marks. Non rated sailors with a rating were now allowed the specialty mark above the group rate mark (7).

Chapter 3.
Navy Ranks and Rates

Able Seaman

Able Seaman is a contraction of Able-bodied Seaman, a title used on merchant ships for a sailor who is fully qualified. It is also used as a rate in the British Royal Navy (1).

Able Seaman may, or may not, have been a title used by non rated sailors in the U. S Navy. The 1969 survey of enlisted titles has it existing form 1798 to 1864 (2). However laws governing the early navy are inconstant on the usage of "Able Seaman" and just "Seaman".

A pay table for the Continental Navy, passed by the Continental Congress on November 28, 1775 (3), does list Able Seaman. The laws creating the federal navy in 1794 (4) and 1797 (5) add to the confusion. Both law state that ships with 44 guns should have 150 Seaman and ships with 36 guns should have 130 Able Seaman. A later section of both laws setting the pay of the navy refers to Seaman not Able Seaman. It is doubtful that seamen on a larger ship were of a different rate than those on a smaller one.

Later laws refer to Able Seaman on April 21, 1806 (6), March 3, 1807 (7), January 31, 1809 (8), January 2, 1813 (9), March 3, 1823 (10), June 17, 1844 (11), and even as late as August 6, 1861 (12).

Most pay tables refer to just "Seamen" (13) (14) (15).

Best guess, the titles were used interchangeably, the "able" being used to make a clear distinction with the next rate down, Ordinary Seaman, such as "full admiral" is used to clearly identify officers with the rank of Admiral.

Admiral

The title "admiral" comes from the Arabic Amir-al-Bahr or leader of the sea. The Romans used the term Sarraccenorum Admirati which led to the Latin Admiralius and was then corrupted to the Anglo Admyrall (1).

In the English tradition the "Lord High Admiral" was a titled noblemen and the title became associated with royalty. As a result it, many people in the new United States believed title "Admiral" had no place in a navy of democracy. To be fair the U.S. Navy was not big enough to require any admirals before the Civil War.

It wasn't until after the Civil War that the rank of Admiral, or for clarity "Full Admiral" was created. The law of July 25, 1866 (2), setting the size of the navy after the war allowed one Admiral. The appointment went to David Farragut the next day (3).

Farragut was to wear cuff lace with two, two inch stripes with one, one inch stripe between them. Above the stripes was a two inch wide gold, five pointed star with a silver representation of the steam frigate Hartford on it. On his service coat collar, overcoat collar, shoulder straps and epaulet frog were worn four silver stars in a line with a gold fouled anchor under the outer stars (4).

In 1869 the cuff lace on Farragut's undress frock coat was changed to one two inch stripe under three 1/2 inch stripes and the Hartford star. His full dress tail coat carried three lines of gold oak leaf and acorn embroidery with a small vertical piece of embroidery running from the bottom line to the cuff edge. The Hartford star was worn above the lines of embroidery (5).

Farragut died on August 14, 1870 (6). His foster brother David Dixon Porter became the Admiral the next day (7).

Porter's insignia was the same, except he wore the normal star of a line officers above his cuff decorations (8).

A law of January 24, 1873 stated "That vacancies occurring in the grades of admiral and vice-admiral, in the navy of the United States, shall not be filled by promotion, or in any other manner whatever; and when the offices of said grades shall become vacant, the grade itself, shall cease to exist."(9) .

On his new 1878 service coat, Porter was to wear four silver stars alone on each side of the standing collar and sleeve stripes in the same pattern as the frock coat, but in black and without the star (10). It is possible, but not certain, that the same sleeve stripes were added to the overcoat at this point.

In 1883 a gold anchor was added under the outermost star on the service coat collar, and white stripes were added to the white service coat sleeves (11).

Porter died on February 13, 1891 (12), and under the 1873 law the rank died with him.

There is some evidence that Admiral of the Navy George Dewey was made a full Admiral in 1899, then retroactively promoted to Admiral of the Navy in 1903, but this is not clear.

On March 3, 1915 a new law revived the rank of Admiral. It stated "That hereafter the commander in chief of the United States Atlantic Fleet, the commander in chief of the United States Pacific Fleet, and the commander in chief of the Asiatic Fleet, respectively, shall each, after being designated as such commander in chief by the President, and from the date of assuming command of such fleet until his relinquishment of such command, have the rank of and pay of an admiral;" (13). The same law created the office of Chief of Naval Operations as the navy's administrative head, but that officer was to be a Rear Admiral. It wasn't until August 29, 1916 (14), that the "CNO" became a full admiral. The rank has existed for various senior officers of the navy ever since.

The insignia for the new admirals was similar to Porter's. The sleeve stripes were the same design, one two inch and three 1/2 inch (15). The same design was used on all blue uniform coats except the black stripes and no line star was still worn on the overcoat (16). The service coat collar still carried four silver stars with a gold anchor under the outermost one as it had since 1883 (17). Epaulets now carried three silver stars in an arc inside the frog and the fourth superimposed on a gold anchor on the strap (18). Shoulder straps were no longer in use and cloth shoulder loops with four silver stars and a gold anchor under the top star were worn on white coats until June of 1913, when they were replaced by shoulder boards. The boards for full admirals had a two inch wide strip of gold lace running long ways down the board, showing only 1/4 inch blue borer on each side. Four silver stars ran in a line down the lace with a gold anchor under the one closest to the button (19).

With the elimination of the standing collar service coat in 1919, the corresponding collar insignia came to an end (20).

The design of the shoulder boards changed in 1922. A now silver anchor was worn near the button and the four stars were arranged in a diamond beneath them (21).

Four silver stars became the badge of rank when pin-on badges were created in 1931 (22).

The black stripes were removed from the khaki coat in 1941 (22a) and the overcoat in 1947 (23).

The Career Compensation Act of October 12, 1949 (23a) placed the rank of Admiral in pay grade O-8 which it shared with Vice Admiral and Rear Admiral (Upper Half). This lasted until May 20, 1958 when a new law (23b) created pay grade O-10 for full Admirals.

The April 2010 uniform regulations descried the insignia for full Admirals as:

Sleeve Stripes - "ADMIRAL. Wear one 2 inch stripe with three 1/2 inch stripes above it." (24).

Shoulder Boards - "The surface is covered with gold lace showing a 1/8 inch blue cloth margin on each of the long sides. A silver embroidered fouled anchor is placed with its center line along the shoulder board's longer dimension and the crown pointing toward the squared end of the board. The unfouled arm of the stock points to the front of the wearer (right and left). Designation of grade consists of silver embroidered five-pointed star(s), placed between the crown of the anchor and the squared end of the shoulder board."(the number of stars is shown as four in illustration) (25).

Metal Grade Insignia - "Flag Officer. Wear insignia lengthwise on the strap so that the single rays of each star point toward the collar. (the number of stars is shown as four in illustration).
Collar grade insignia replicates metal shoulder insignia except flag officers' miniature multiple stars which are connected as follows" (the number of stars is shown as four in illustration) (26).

Admiral of the Navy

On March 2, 1899 Congress passed a law stating "That the President is hereby authorized to appoint, by selection and promotion, an Admiral of the Navy, who shall not be placed upon the retired list except upon his own application; and whenever such office shall be vacated by death or otherwise the office shall cease to exist." (1). George Dewey received the appointment (2).

Was Dewey given a new rank of "Admiral of the Navy", or was he just promoted to full Admiral? The Naval History & Heritage Command website (3) claims he was made a full Admiral on March 8, 1899 and then retroactively made Admiral of the Navy on March 24, 1903 with his commission dating from March 2, 1899. This is backed up by the Navy Registers of 1900 (4), 1902 (5) and 1903 (6) who list Dewey as and Admiral.

On the other hand there is no law creating another rank for Dewey. Congress wasn't even in session on March 24, 1903.

The original 1899 law is of little help. The term "Admiral of the Navy" was used at times, even in legislation, to refer to the two previous full Admirals David Farragut and David Dixion Porter (7). The law itself was titled "CHAP. 378 - An Act Creating the office of Admiral of the Navy", but the reference in the margin says "Navy. Grade of Admiral revived".

Whether it happened in 1899 or 1903, Admiral of the Navy was a separate and higher rank than Admiral. This can be proved by the law that made the Chief of Naval Operations a full Admiral that stated "while so serving as such Chief of Naval Operations, shall have the rank and title of admiral, to take rank next after The Admiral of the Navy," (8).

Dewey was to wear the original sleeve lace for a full Admiral, two inch stripes with a one inch stripe between them (9). His service coat collar, shoulder boards, shoulder straps and epaulet frogs, had four silver stars with gold anchors under the outer two (10).

By the January 1913 regulations, shoulder straps and shoulder boards had been abolished. Badges of rank were to be worn on the cloth shoulder loops of white coats consisting of four silver stars arranged in a cross, with gold anchors under the top and bottom stars (11). Shoulder boards returned to replace the cloth shoulder loops in June (12).

Dewey died on January 16, 1917 (13).

Airman

The rate of Airman was created on April 2, 1948 from Seamen First Class that were assigned to aviation duties (1).

It continued the Seaman First Class position in pay grade five. Grade five became grade E-3 with The Career Compensation Act of October 12, 1949 (2).

It was given a group rate mark of three green hash marks (3).

In 2008 a pin on badge of rank consisting of three silver metal hash marks was introduced on the shirt collar of the navy service uniform (4).

Airman Apprentice

The rate of Airman Apprentice was created on April 2, 1948 from Seamen Second Class that were assigned to aviation duties (1).

It continued the Seaman Second Class position in pay grade six. Grade six became grade E-2 with The Career Compensation Act of October 12, 1949 (2).

It was given a group rate mark of two green hash marks (3).

In 2008 a pin on badge of rank consisting of two silver metal hash marks was introduced on the shirt collar of the navy service uniform (4).

Airman Recruit

Airman Recruit was added to the Aviation Group in late 1948, for use with special recruiting programs (1).

It was placed in grade seven until The Career Compensation Act of October 12, 1949 made grade seven into grade E-1 (2)

They were to wear one green hash mark (3) until 1975, when they would be without insignia (4).

Apprentice (First, Second and Third Class)

Apprentices were created by General Order (1) in 1883 (2). There is no actual proof, but the end of Boy First, Second and Third Class in 1884 (3) would seam to indicate Apprentice replaced Boy as the rate of trainee sailors in the navy's "Apprentice System".

Applicants, usually between 14 and 17 years old, had to be literate and of good character. There were three classes of Apprentice. For the first six months of training on land and a summer and a winter cruse on a training ship, they were rated as Apprentice Third Class. After this they were assigned to a regular ship and rated as Apprentice Second Class. After a year they became an Apprentice First Class (4). When enlisted sailors were divided into pay grades in 1885, all three grades were placed in "Seaman Third Class" (5) (6). At some point in the early 1890s, the exact date has proved elusive, the apprentice rates were placed in their corresponding grade of seaman, first, second or third class (7).

Boys would have worn one stripe on the cuffs of their jumpers and after 1883 Apprentices may have as well. Being in the Seaman Third Class grade they certainly would have worn the single stripe after 1886 (8). After they were spread into other grades, first class would have worn three stripes, second class two stripes and third class one stripe (9).

They were in the seaman branch and therefore would have worn white/blue watch marks but this is not certain.

The 1886 regulations did grant them a badge of their own. A knot was worn in white or blue as needed under the neck opening of the jumper or on coats, above the cuff on the same side as the rating badge. The knot was worn thoughout their naval career (10).

The apprentice system ended in 1904 and apprentices were folded into the non rated grades of the day. They continued to wear the knot, now called an Ex-Apprentice Mark. The last ex-apprentice was Harry Morris, who left the navy as a Chief Torpedoman in 1958 (11).

Apprentice Seaman

Apprentice Seaman was created in the Seaman Third Class pay grade in 1904 (1).

They wore one stripe on the cuff of the jumpers(2) and a white/blue watch mark (3), that was changed to a white/blue branch mark on the right side in 1912 (4).

The Seaman Third Class or Nonrated man third class pay grade officially became grade seven on June 10, 1922 (5).

The title was changed to Seaman Recruit in 1948 (6).

Aerographer

The warrant grade of Aerographer was created on July 28, 1942 (1). Aerographer had been a petty officer's rating since 1926 and that rating was changed to Aerographer's Mate (2).

The lace worn on the cuffs was 1/4 inch wide gold with 1/2 inch long blue breaks every 2 inches. The device of an Aeroprapher, a winged circle with a six feather arrow passing vertically through the circle, placed on the sleeve, arrow pointing down, was worn above the stripes. Shoulder boards showed the 1/4 inch lace with a single 1/2 inch break, under the device. The gold, winged circle and arrow device was also used as a badge of rank (3).

The aviation green coat was given a black stripe with green breaks in 1944 (4). It is possible that a solid stripe was worn previous to this (5).

The Career Compensation Act of October 12, 1949 (6) placed Areographers in pay grade W-1.

A standard, warrant officers badge of rank was introduced on July 1,1952 (7) consisting of a gold bar with a 1/16 inch blue break across the middle (8).

Aerographers became Warrant Officer 1, with the Warrant Officer Act of 1954 (9).

Assistant Civil Engineer

A law of March 3, 1903 (1) added "twelve assistant civil engineers, of whom six shall have the rank of lieutenant (junior grade) and six the rank of ensign:".

They would have worn the same stripes on the cuffs and the shoulder boards as line officers, a 1/2 inch under a 1/4 inch for the Lieutenants Junior Grade and a 1/2 inch for the Ensigns. Instead of the line star, the space between the stripes, or in the case of the equivalent Ensigns a border along the stripe, was of light blue cloth (2).

The shoulder straps and epaulet frogs would have had the silver letters C.E. in the center and a silver bar at each end for the equivalent Lieutenants junior grade. The C.E. would have also been worn the service coat collar, behind a silver bar for equivalent Lieutenants junior grade (3).

In 1905 the C.E. was replaced with two sets of two long skinny oak leafs, each pair meeting at a point covered with an acorn. Thus having the appearance of crossed dividers (4).

An appropriations bill passed on August 29, 1916 (5) allowed Assistant Civil Engineers up the rank of Lieutenant Commander.

A general order in 1918 decreed that staff officers would be addressed by their regular ranks instead of there staff titles (6).

At that time the colors in and around the sleeve and shoulder board stripes were abolished and corps device was placed above them and an anchor was added under the device on the service coat collar until the coat was abolished the next year (7).

Staff rank titles officially ended (if anyone remembered they existed by then) on August 7, 1947 (8).

Assistant Dental Surgeon

Assistant Dental Surgeons were added to the navy on September 22, 1912 (1) and had the rank of Lieutenant Junior Grade.

They would have worn the same insignia as a Lieutenant Junior Grade with orange between the stripes (2), a badge of rank of a silver bar (3) and a corps device of a gold oak leaf with silver acorns on either side of the stem (4).

A general order in 1918 decreed that staff officers would be addressed by their regular ranks instead of there staff titles (5).

At that time the colors in and around the sleeve and shoulder board stripes were abolished and corps device was placed above them and an anchor was added under the device on the service coat collar until the coat was abolished the next year (6).

Staff rank titles officially ended on August 7, 1947 (7).

Assistant Engineer

Second Assistant Engineers became Assistant engineers on February 24, 1874 (1). Second assistants had been given the relative ranks of Master or Ensign in 1871 (2).

The relative Masters were identified by a 1/2 inch sleeve stripe with red piping, a single gold bar at either end of the shoulder straps and epaulets frogs with a silver corps device, a cross of oak branches, between them and a gold bar and corps device on the service coat collar (3).

Relative Ensigns wore a 1/4 inch sleeve stripe, piped in red and the corps device alone on the collar. Instead of epaulets and shoulder straps, shoulder knots were worn (4). It is possible that a single silver bar was worn in the center of the shoulder knot pad (5).

On the new service coat of 1878, badges of rank but not the corps device was worn on the standup collar and black stripes without the colored piping was worn on the cuffs. As a result, relative Masters had a silver bar alone on the collar and Relative Ensigns' collar was blank (6). The bars on the epaulets and shoulder straps may have been changed to silver at the same time.

Relative Ensigns were allowed to wear shoulder straps again in 1881, with a silver corps device in the center only (7).

Also in 1881 the sleeve stripes were changed. Relative Ensigns now had one 1/2 inch stripe and Relative Masters one 1/2 inch stripe below one 1/4 inch stripe (8).

Relative Masters became relative Lieutenants Junior Grade on March 3, 1883 when the title of that grade was changed (9).

New uniform regulations in 1883 added the corps device to the collar of the service coat, by itself in the case of relative ensigns. If the bars were not silver on the epaulets and shoulder straps by then, they were now. The regulation also introduced at white service coat with white sleeve stripes and no collar insignia. Epaulets, with the corps device in the center of the frog, replaced shoulder knots for relative Ensigns (10).

In 1897, gold stripes with red distinctions replaced the black stripes on the blue service coat and shoulder straps were added to the white coat, eliminating the need for the sleeve stripes (11).

Engineering ranks were abolished on March 3, 1899 (12), and all engineering officers became line officers.

Assistant Naval Constructor

The rank of Assistant Naval Constructor was created by navy regulations, not by law, on March 13, 1863. It had the relative rank of Master (1). The one and only appointment went to Thomas Davidson on May 4th (2).

The 1864 uniform regulations gave Davidson two 1/4 inch Sleeve stripes, shoulder straps with a gold bar at each end and the silver corps device, two live oak sprigs and an acorn, in the center, and a gold bar on the overcoat collar (3). The bar was also worn on the collar of the service coat added in 1865 (4).

Davidson was joined by Thomas Webb on February 28, 1865 (5).

The 1866 uniform regulations, returned epaulets with the corps device between gold bars in the frog (6).

More appointments as Assistant Naval Constructors were made on May 17, 1866, Theodore Wilson, John Easby, George Much and Samuel Pook. Davidson was promoted to Naval Constructor on July 25th (7).

July 25th was also the day that Congress passed a law officially making Naval Constructors naval officers. However it did not mention relative rank (8).

Webb was promoted on July 17, 1868 (9).

On March 29, 1869 Attorney General Ebenezer Hoar issued a ruling that the navy had exceeded its authority in granting relative rank to certain staff officers during the Civil War (10). The 1866 law had made them naval officers but they did not hold rank.

Congress fixed this problem on March 3, 1871 with a law that stated “assistant naval constructors shall have the relative rank of lieutenant or master” (11).

On March 21st the navy prescribed that they would wear the uniforms of their relative ranks with the oak sprig device replacing the line anchor and dark violet cloth between the sleeve stripes (12).

A law of March 3, 1899 (13) ended relative rank and granted staff officers actual rank. The law was clear that it did not change the rank titles. Staff officers now had “the rank of...” instead of “the relative rank of...”.

An appropriations bill passed on August 29, 1916 (14) allowed Assistant Naval Constuctors to rank below Commander.

A general order in 1918 decreed that staff officers would be addressed by their regular ranks instead of there staff titles (15). The colors were removed from the stripes and the corps device added above them.

All construction officers were transferred to the line at their equivalent ranks on June 25, 1940 (16)

Assistant Paymaster

The rank of Assistant Paymaster was created on July 7, 1861 (1). The law gave them the same relative rank as Assistant Surgeons, "next after Masters", this probably meant with Passed Midshipmen until 1862 when the rank was changed to Ensign.

The were given plain gold epaulets with 1/4 inch wide bullion, a narrow shoulder strap (4 X 1 1/8 with a 3/16 border) that were without a device inside and plain cuffs (2).

In 1862 the a single 1/4 inch stripe was placed on the cuff for Ensigns and staff officers were to wear the stripes of their relative rank (3).

The reorganization of relative rank on March 13, 1863 made Assistant Paymasters relative Masters (4).

The 1864 uniform regulations called for two 1/4 inch cuff stripes (5), eliminated epaulets and called for full size shoulder straps with the paymaster's corps device, an oak sprig and leaf in silver, in the center and a gold bar at each end (6). The overcoat carried one gold bar. In other words the insignia of a Master without a star over the cuff stripes and the corps device replacing the line anchor on the shoulder straps.

Their status as relative masters was overruled by the Attorney General in March of 1869 and they returned to "next after Masters" or with Ensigns (7).

New uniform regulations in April of 1869 prescribed white piping around the now 1/4 inch sleeve stripe of an Ensign. The 1869 shoulder knots for staff officers were to be "as per patterns -- Staff Officers omitting the anchor". If the pictures are to be believed this left a single silver bar alone on the pad (8).

A law of March 3, 1871 (9) gave them relative rank of Masters or Ensigns.

The insignia remained the same as Masters (Lieutenants Junior Grade after 1883) or Ensigns with the corps device replacing the line anchor and white cloth in and around the stripes instead of the line star.

Staff rank ceased to be relative on March 3, 1899 (10).

The corps device was redesigned in 1905 (11).

A general order in 1918 decreed that staff officers would be addressed by their regular ranks instead of there staff titles (12).

At that time the colors in and around the sleeve and shoulder board stripes were abolished and corps device was placed above them and an anchor was added under the device on the service coat collar until the coat was abolished the next year (13).

Staff rank titles officially ended on August 7, 1947 (14).

Assistant Surgeon

Surgeon's Mates probably became Assistant Surgeons on May 24, 1828 (1). The law does not specifically change the title, but does mention examinations for appointments of Assistant Surgeons. The 1828 naval register (2) lists Surgeon's Mates, but the 1829 (3) register lists the same people as Assistant Surgeons.

Surgeon's Mates of 1828 were wearing dress uniforms with one button and laced button hole on the standing collar and two buttons on the cuff. The undress uniform had a rolling collar with two unlaced buttons (4)(5).

In 1830 the uniform was changed. The dress coat collar was outlined in gold oak leaf embroidery with the club of Esculapius (a caduceus without wings) underneath and three buttons on the cuffs. The undress coats had collars and three button cuffs of black velvet (6).

In 1832 the club of Esculapius was replaced with an oak branch and the black velvet was removed form the undress coat. A strip of gold lace was added across the top of the undress cuffs for Assistant Surgeons even though Surgeons' cuffs were plain(7).

The 1841 regulations called for a coat of a different design but with the same dress collar without the oak branch under the embroidery. The line of 14 inch gold lace was now worn above the three buttons on both the dress and undress coat (8).

Navy regulations of 1841 created equivalents between line and staff officers, placing Assistant Surgeons with Passed Midshipmen (9). This was followed by a General Order on August 31, 1846 placing them "next after Masters" (10). Congress made this official on August 5, 1854 (11) by declaring the General Order to be law.

With relative rank came epaulets and shoulder straps. The epaulets had 1/4 inch wide bullion and the old english letters M.D. in the frog. The crescent was of solid lace instead of being embroidered like line officers. The shoulder straps were the small size with 1/8 inch borders with the M.D. in the center. The line of embroidery on the dress collar was replaced with three live oak sprigs and the sleeve lace was eliminated (12).

The March 8, 1852 regulations replaced the undress coat with a frock coat with three buttons on the cuffs (13). In September the insignia for medical officers was changed. A gold sprig of olive replaced the M.D. on the shoulder straps and the letters were removed from the epaulets (14).

Use of the dress coat was suspended on July 31, 1862 and all buttons were removed from the cuffs of the frock coat. The cuffs now carried the 1/4 inch stripe of an Ensign (15).

The navy made Assistant Surgeons relative Masters on March 13, 1863 (16).

The 1864 uniform regulations called for two 1/4 inch cuff stripes, eliminated epaulets and called for full size shoulder straps with gold bar at each end and no device in the center (17). The overcoat carried one gold bar. In other words the insignia of a Master without a star over the cuff stripes and no corps device on the shoulder straps.

Their status as relative masters was overruled by the Attorney General in March of 1869 and they returned to "next after Masters" or with Ensigns (18).

New uniform regulations in April of 1869 prescribed cobalt blue piping around the now 1/4 inch sleeve stripe of an Ensign. The 1869 shoulder knots for staff officers were to be "as per patterns -- Staff Officers omitting the anchor". If the pictures are to be believed this left a single silver bar alone on the pad (19).

A law of March 3, 1871 (20) gave them relative rank of Masters or Ensigns.

The insignia remained the same as Masters or Ensigns with no corps device and cobalt blue cloth in and around the stripes instead of the line star.

In 1883 medical officers were given a corps device of a gold oak leaf with a silver acorn in the center of if and the color was changed to maroon (21).

Staff rank ceased to be relative on March 3, 1899 (22).

A medical reserve corps was formed on September 22, 1912 (23) and the 1913 uniform regulation prescribed a silver oak leaf with gold acorn for the corps device and crimson cloth in and around the stripes (24).

A general order in 1918 decreed that staff officers would be addressed by their regular ranks instead of there staff titles (25).

At that time the colors in and around the sleeve and shoulder board stripes were abolished and corps device was placed above them and an anchor was added under the device on the service coat collar until the coat was abolished the next year (26).

Staff rank titles officially ended on August 7, 1947 (27).

Attendant

Attendants were created in 1885 (1) as part of the messmen branch (2).

According to the 1886 uniform regulations they were to wear "Blue cloth or white jacket, Blue cloth or white trousers, blue cap or canvas hat, waistcoat (only with blue jacket), white shirt, and collar and cravat." (3).

The title was changed to Mess Attendant in 1893 (4).

Baker First Class

Bakers First Class were added in 1902 (1). They were originally part of the messmen branch and therefore wore blue or white coats and visored caps instead of the standard navy uniform.

In 1905 they were moved to the commissary branch and Bakers First Class were placed in the Seaman First Class pay grade and therefore authorized to wear the sailor's jumper uniform with three stripes on the cuff (2). It is not clear if they wore a white/blue watch mark. The regulations stated that watch marks were "To be worn on the overshirt and the dress and undress jumpers, except by petty officers and mess attendants."(3). When watch marks became branch marks in 1912, it was clear that Bakers did not wear them (4).

In 1908 Bakers First Class became a Petty Officer's rating in the special branch (5).

Baker Second Class

Bakers Second Class were added in 1902 (1). They were originally part of the messmen branch and therefore wore blue or white coats and visored caps instead of the standard navy uniform.

In 1905 the messmen branch became the commissary branch and Bakers Second Class were placed in the Seaman Second Class pay grade and therefore authorized to wear the sailor's jumper uniform with two stripes on the cuff (2). It is not clear if they wore a white/blue watch mark. The regulations stated that watch marks were "To be worn on the overshirt and the dress and undress jumpers, except by petty officers and mess attendants."(3). When watch marks became branch marks in 1912, it was clear that Bakers did not wear them (4).

In 1908 Bakers First Class became a Petty Officer's rating and bakers Second class moved up to the Seaman First Class pay grade in the special branch, and gained a third stripe on the cuff. A distinguishing mark of a white/blue crescent was added to the upper left sleeve (5).

In 1921 Bakers Second Class became a Petty Officer's rating (6).

Barber

Barbers were changed from Ship's Barbers in 1885 and lasted until 1893 (1).

They were placed in the Seaman First Class pay grade (2) and therefore wore three stripes on the cuffs and a white/blue watch mark (3).

Bayman

Baymen were non rated medics. They became a part of the navy with U.S. Navy Regulation Circular, No. 5. dated June 1, 1877.

There is no information on how many cuff stripes or other insignia Baymen wore before 1885. At that point they were placed in the Seaman Second Class pay grade (1) and therefore wore two stripes on the cuffs and a white/blue watch mark (2).

At some point between 1890 (3) and 1893 (4), they were moved down to the Seaman Third Class pay grade with one cuff stripe.

The title was changed to Hospital Apprentice in 1898 (5).

Boatswain

Boatswain, pronounced bow-sun, comes for the Saxon swein meaning boy or servant of a boat (1).

Boatswains were the warrant officers in charge of a ships deck operations.

They existed in the Continental Navy (2) and were listed among the warrant ranks in both the 1794 (3) and 1796 (4) laws creating the navy.

Uniforms were first prescribed by the 1814 uniform regulations (5). They called for "Short blue coats, with six buttons on the lappels; rolling cape, blue pantaloons, white vests, round hats, with cockade. No side-arms."

In 1830 a double breasted, dark blue dress coat with lapels buttoned back with eight buttons was prescribed. It had a standing collar with one button on it and slashed sleeves closed with three buttons. The undress rolling collar coatee had the same buttons as the dress coat except the one on the collar (6).

The only coat listed in the 1841 regulations was described as "To be of dark blue cloth, lined with the same, double breasted, seven navy buttons on each breast, slashed sleeves with three small navy buttons on each, two large navy buttons under each pocket flap, one on each hip, and one at the bottom of each skirt". Blue cloth caps were also called for (7). On April 5, 1849 a large button and a button hole worked in black twist was added to the coat collars. At the same time a 1 1/4 inch wide gold lace band was added around the cap (8).

The 1852 regulations list the warrant officers coats with the descriptions of the officers dress tail coats, but they may have been frock coats. This is by no means clear. They are described as "shall be of Navy blue cloth, lined with the same; rolling collar, double breasted, two rows of large Navy buttons on the breast, eight in each row; pointed pocket flaps, with three large buttons underneath each, showing one half their diameter; three medium size buttons around each cuff and two small ones in each opening; one button behind on each hip, one in the middle of each fold and one in each fold near the bottom of the skirt. On each side of the collar to have one loop of three-quarters wide gold lace to show one inch and a half wide, and four inches long, with a small size Navy button in the point of each loop." They were worn over blue or white pantaloons, according to season and blue caps with a gold anchor on the front (9).

A band of two 1/2 inch strips of gold lace 1/4 apart, showing blue in between, were added to the caps on February 17, 1853 (10).

The uniforms may have been simplified in 1862 with the removal of the cuff buttons and maybe the collar button and lace, but this is not clear (11).

New uniform regulations of 1864 (12) gave warrant officers the same frock coats and caps as officers. As line officers a star was worn alone above the cuff. Shoulder straps were added consisting of a strip of gold lace 3/4 inches wide by 4 inches long with an old english letter B in silver. Caps were plain except for an empty wreath.

On March 11, 1869 the shoulder straps were replaced with a gold star on the collar of the frock coat (13).

Use of the service dress sack coat by warrant officers is clear but it is authorized by the 1876 regulations with the star on the cuffs but not the collar (14).

They were authorized the new standing collar service coat in October 1878. The star was worn in gold on the cuff and silver on the collar (15).

In 1883 the stars on the collars of both the frock coat and the service coat were replaced with crossed anchors, in silver for those over 20 years service and gold for those under (16). Silver was reserved for Chief Boatswains in 1899.

Shoulder boards were authorized in 1908 with the crossed anchors near the outer end with a silver star on them. The star was added to the devices on the collars in 1913 (17).

It is possible, but not certain, that the crossed anchors (without the star) replaced the star on the cuffs in 1918. It was certainly there on the new service coats of 1919, now above a strip of 1/4 inch gold lace. Shoulder boards of 1919 also carried the 1/4 inch lace and crossed anchors (18).

The 1922 regulations added a 1/2 inch dark blue break every two inches on the cuff stripes and a single 1/2 inch break in the center of the shoulder board stripe (19).

Black sleeve stripes were used on khaki and green coats starting in 1925. The format used by warrant officers is not clear. It is possible that a solid stripe was used (20). The black stripes were removed from the khaki coat in 1941 (21) and stripes with green breaks were definitely prescribed for warrant officers in 1944 (22).

The gold crossed anchors became the Boatswain's pin on badge of rank in 1931.

The Career Compensation Act of October 12, 1949 (23) placed Boatswains in pay grade W-1.

A standard, warrant officers badge of rank was introduced on July 1,1952 (24) consisting of a gold bar with a 1/16 inch blue break across the middle (25).

Boatswain became Warrant Officer 1, with the Warrant Officer Act of 1954 (26).

Boy, Boy First Class, Boy Second Class and Boy Third Class

The history of the rate of Boy is somewhat clouded and mixed up with the rate of Apprentice.

Boys were young men, usually teenagers, who were training for positions in the navy.

There is a mention of Boys in the Continental Navy (1), but they are not on the pay table (2). Boys are specifically mentioned as a rate of the navy in the laws of 1794 (3) and 1796 (4) and are mentioned in various legislation thereafter such as in 1806(5), 1813(6) and 1823 (7).

On March 2, 1837 (8) a law was passed calling for boy to be enlisted from age 13 to 17. This was to create a formal training system and increase the overall pool of qualified sailors available to the navy and the merchant service (9). Apparently it was incorrectly believed that this was a back door to appointment as a Midshipman. When this didn't turn out to be the case, the training program began to peter out (10). Boy continued to be a rate of the navy.

Another attempt was made at a formal system in 1864 (11). This corresponds with the rate of Boy being split in to first, second and third classes (12) that year.

The rate of Boy continued in three classes until 1883 when it was reestablished as just Boy. The rates of Apprentice first, second and third class also were created in 1883 (13). It is possible that the three classes of boys became the three classes of apprentices in the formal training system and boy retuned to be the rate used outside the formal system.

Insignia was first prescribed in 1866. One stripe around the collar of the jumper and on stripe on the cuffs (14). The stripes on the collar were removed in 1869 (15).

As part of the seaman branch, boys would have worn a white/blue watch mark after 1886 (16).

Boys were eliminated in 1893 (17).

Bugler

A Bureau of Equipment and Recruiting circular dated November 15, 1871 allowed one bugler per ship.

There is no information on how many cuff stripes or other insignia Buglers wore before 1885. At that point they were placed in the Seaman First Class pay grade (1) and therefore wore three stripes on the cuffs and a white/blue watch mark (2).

At some point between 1890 (3) and 1895 (4), they were moved down to the Seaman Second Class pay grade with two cuff stripes.

The watch mark was eliminated in 1912 (5), and a distinguishing mark of a white/blue bugle was added to the left upper sleeve (6).

Buglers became Buglers Second Class in 1920 (7).

Bugler First Class

Buglers First Class were created in 1920 (1) in the Seaman First Class pay grade, which became grade five on June 10, 1922.

They were allowed three cuff stripes (2), no branch mark (3) and a distinguishing mark of a white/blue bugle on the left upper sleeve (4).

Buglers First Class were folded into the rate of Seaman in 1948 (5).

Bugler Second Class

Buglers Second Class were created from Buglers in 1920 (1) in the Seaman Second Class pay grade, which became grade six on June 10, 1922.

They were allowed two cuff stripes (2), no branch mark (3) and a distinguishing mark of a white/blue bugle on the left upper sleeve (4).

Buglers Second Class were folded into the rate of Seaman Apprentice in 1948 (5).

Cabin Cook

Cabin Cook was one of the rates that Officer's Cook was split into in 1864 (1).

Officer's cooks had been considered petty officers as of the 1841 regulations, but are not listed, as Officer's Cooks or any of the titles it was divided into, on the list of petty officer rates in the regulations of 1865 (3). Their status was clarified when the rates were organized in 1885. Stewards, Cooks (not Ship's Cooks) and Attendants were made into a special category that were not petty officers (4).

There is also no information on uniforms or insignia before 1886. At that time they were to wear single breasted sack coats of blue with black buttons or a similar white coat with white buttons, matching trousers and a blue visored cap or white canvas hat (5). The canvas hat was replaced with a white cap by 1897 (6), and the coats became double breasted between the 1897 and 1905 (7) regulations.

In 1912 a white/blue cresent was added as a distinguishing mark (8).

The 1922 uniform regulations prescribed a cap devices of the letters U.S.N. (9).

1922 also saw them moved to pay grade two, along side first class petty officers (10).

Cabin Cooks were changed to Officer's Cooks First Class in 1923 (11).

Cabin Steward

Cabin Steward was one of the rates that Officer's Steward was split into in 1864 (1).

Officer's Stewards had been considered petty officers as of the 1841 regulations, but are not listed, as Officer's Stewards or any of the titles it was divided into, on the list of petty officer rates in the regulations of 1865 (3). On the other hand, the 1864 uniform regulations call for the petty officers badge to be worn on the left sleeve by "All other petty officers, except officer's stewards," (4).

Their status was clarified when the rates were organized in 1885. Stewards, Cooks (not Ship's Cooks) and Attendants were made into a special category that were not petty officers (5).

The lack of a petty officers badge infers that they were wearing regular navy uniforms in 1864.

In 1886 they were to wear single breasted sack coats of blue with black buttons or a similar white coat with white buttons, matching trousers and a blue visored cap or white canvas hat (6). The canvas hat was replaced with a white cap by 1897 (7), and the coats became double breasted between the 1897 and 1905 (8) regulations.

In 1912 a white/blue crescent was added as a distinguishing mark (9).

The 1922 uniform regulations prescribed a cap devices of the letters U.S.N. (10).

1922 also saw them moved to pay grade two, along side first class petty officers (11).

Cabin Stewards were changed to Officer's Stewards First Class in 1923 (12).

Cadet Engineer

Cadet Engineer was the title of students a the Naval Academy studying to be engineers or constructors from July 4, 1864 (1) to August 5, 1882 (2) when they became Naval Cadets.

Cadet Midshipman

Cadet Midshipman was the title of students a the Naval Academy from July 15, 1870 (1) to August 5, 1882 (2) when they became Naval Cadets.

Captain

The title Captain comes from the Latin caput meaning head, this led to the term capitaneus or head man (1). In the middle ages captain was an army rank of an officer commanding companies of soldiers. It came to navies when those companies were placed on merchant ships in time of war. Captains were in charge of fighting while the ships Master was in charge of sailing (2). As permanent navies were created, the captain became the man in overall charge of a ship.

The first pay table, dated November 28, 1775 (3) refers to the Continental Navy's highest rank as "Captain or commander". It is not clear if the rank of Commander was used in the Continental Navy, but it is doubtful. There is no evidence of any appointments of commanders (4). A law of November 15, 1776 (5) setting the relative rank of army and navy officers does not mention Commanders. It places Captains of ships over 40 guns equal to full Colonels, from 20 to 40 guns with Lieutenant Colonels and under 20 guns with Majors.

The first uniforms prescribed were on September 5, 1776. The coats were blue faced with red with a stand up collar and slashed cuff. It was worn over blue britches and a red waistcoat with narrow lace (6).

The 1794 law (7) creating the federal navy called for one Captain for each of the six frigates. These were the new navy's first appointments to oversee construction of the ships. The appointments were made on June 4, 1794 to, in order of seniority, John Barry, Samuel Nicholson, Silas Talbot, Joshua Barney, Richard Dale and Thomas Truxtun (8). Because the navy had only one senior rank, the captain's relative rank to each other was considered very important. If higher ranks were ever created, the senior Captain would be first in line. In a vain attempt to avoid controversy, seniority was determined by their date of commission in the Continental Navy, with Truxtun, who had not served in the Continental Navy, last (9). Barney was unhappy at being fourth and refused the appointment. Instead he took an offer from the French Navy (10). His place was filled on July 18, 1794 by James Sever who would rank after Truxtun (11).

When work was stopped on three of the frigates the choice was made on how far along they were in construction, not on the seniority of their captains. As a result Barry, Nicholson and Truxtun remained, and Dale, Talbot and Sever were let go (12).

The first uniforms for the federal navy were prescribed on August 24, 1797 (13). Captains were to wear:
"FULL DRESSED COAT. Blue Cloth with long buff lappels, and a standing collar, and lining of buff--to be made and trimmed full with a gold epaulet on each shoulder. The cuffs buff, with four buttons to the pockets. Lappels to have nine buttons, and one to the standing collar. Buttons, yellow metal, and to have the foul anchor and American eagle on the same.

VEST AND BREECHES. Buff, with flaps and four buttons to the pockets of the vests, so as to correspond and be in uniform with the coat. Buttons the same kind as the coat, only proportionably smaller."

By 1798 war with France was looming. Work resumed on the other three frigates and other ships were converted for naval use. Dale, Sever and Talbot were reappointed on May 11, 1798. This left the question of seniority. Were Dale and Talbot to resume their previous positions above Truxtun? Talbot appealed directly to President Adams and was rewarded with his old rank. This angered Truxtun, who had proved to be one of the most capable officers in the navy. He did resign in protest but had a change of heart and returned to duty (14).

The U.S. Navy was now firmly established with Captain as it's highest rank.

The 1802 uniform regulations (15) described the uniform for a Captain as:
"THE COAT of blue cloth, with long lappels and lining of the same; a standing collar, and to be trimmed with gold lace, not exceeding one half inch in breadth, nor less than three eighths of an inch; in the following manner, to wit:--To commence from the upper part of the standing collar, and to descend round the lappels to the bottom of the coat; the upper part of the cuffs, round the pocket flaps and down the folds with one single lace; four buttons on the cuffs and on the pocket flap, nine on the lappels, and one on the standing collar; a gold epaulet on each shoulder; the buttons of yellow metal, with the foul anchor and American eagle, surrounded with fifteen stars; the button-holes to be worked with gold thread.

VEST AND BREECHES, white. The vest single breasted, with flaps and four buttons to the pockets, the buttons the same as the coat, only proportionably smaller.

THE UNDRESS--The same as the full dress, excepting the lace and the gold worked button- holes."

As with the 1797 regulations, rank was displayed by epaulets on both shoulders. The four buttons on the cuffs and the pockets were also unique to a Captain. These distinctions would continue thru the November 1813 regulations (16).

The 1820 regulations added a device to the straps of the epaulets (17). The Captains with over five years service were to wear silver crossed anchors.

As of 1820 those Captains were, Alexander Murray, John Rodgers, James Barron, William Brainbridge, Hugh Campbell, Stephen Decatur, Thomas Tingey, Charles Stewart, Issac Hull, Issac Chauncey, John Shaw, John Dent, David Porter, John Cassin, Samuel Evans, Jacob Jones, Charles Morris, Arthur Sinclair, Thomas Macdonough, Lewis Warraington, Joseph Branbridge, and William Crane.

Captains under five years service would wear a single anchor.

There names were, James Leonard, James Biddle, Charles Ridgley, Robert Spence, Daniel Patterson, Samuel Angus, Melancthon Woolsey, John, Creighton, Edward Trenchard, John Downes, John Henley and Jesse Elliott (18).

The devices were changed to "an eagle couched upon an anchor" for all Captains in the 1830 regulations. 1830 also saw the first use of shoulder straps, strips of gold lace were worn on both shoulders were worn when the epaulets were not (19).

The shoulder straps were changed in 1841 to a narrow rectangle of gold embroidery around a blue center (20). An eagle in silver was added in the center of the strap in 1845 (21).

The 1852 regulations saw the beginning of Captain's cuff stripes. The traditional four buttons now ran vertically. Between them were three strips of 3/4 inch gold lace with a short strip of lace running vertically from the bottom strip to the end of the sleeve. A modified silver eagle and anchor device was worn in the epaulet frog with a silver star at the end of the strap. Bullion was 5/8 inches wide. The same eagle and anchor device was worn in the center of the shoulder straps. The straps were now 4 inches long and 1 3/8 inches wide with a 1/4 inch border (22).

The insignia was altered on July 31, 1862. The buttons and the vertical strip of lace were removed from the cuffs and the star was removed from the strap of the epaulets (23).

On May 23, 1863 all line officers were ordered to wear a gold star above their cuff stripes. It is possible that the stripes were changed at the same time, but were certainly changed by the new uniform regulations of January 28, 1864 (24).

The new system used 1/4 inch wide stripes 1/4 inch apart. Because senior officers would require a large number of stripes, they were placed in groups of three with a 1/2 inch space instead of a 1/4 inch space between the groups. For Captains there were six stripes in two groups of three (25). The new regulations suspended the use of epaulets (26) and changed the device in the shoulder straps to a two inch wide silver eagle grasping a 1 1/8 inch long anchor in it's talons (27). The eagle, most likely with empty talons, was also worn on the collar of the overcoat (28).

In January of 1865 a new service dress coat was introduced. It could carry cuff stripes or shoulder straps, or the eagle, again probably with empty talons, could be worn on the collar (29).

With the Civil War over, new uniform regulations were issued on December 1, 1866. Epaulets returned with 1/2 inch bullion for Captains and the silver eagle in the center of the frog with a silver anchor on either side, the same arrangement was used in the shoulder straps. The eagle with an anchor behind it was also worn on the collar of the sack coat and over coat (30).

On March 11, 1869 (31) the cuff stripes for Captains were changed to three 1/2 inch stripes below the line star. This only lasted until May 27th when the stripes were increased to four (32). Four Stripes has denoted a Captain ever since.

The service dress coat was replaced in 1877. The eagle, but not the anchor, was worn on each side of the standing collar (33).

The 1883 uniform regulations returned the anchor behind the eagle on the service coat collar A white coat with white cuff stripes and no collar insignia was also authorized (34).

The white cuff stripes were replaced on the white coat with shoulder straps in 1897 (34a).

In 1899 the shoulder straps on the white coat were replaced with shoulder boards. The boards for Captains matched the cuffs, four stripes and a line star (35).

Shoulder straps make their last appearance in regulations in 1905 (36) and may have been abolished with the next regulations in 1913 or sometime in between.

The January 13, 1913 regulations did abolish shoulder boards, replacing them with a white cloth shoulder loop with a metal eagle and anchor (37). This was undone on June 24th and shoulder boards returned (38).

Epaulets were also changed in 1913. The eagle was now alone in the frog and a single anchor was worn on the strap (39).

The use of epaulets was suspended in 1917 (40).

The end of the use of staff titles in November 1918 led to equivalent staff captains wearing the corps device in place of the line star on the cuffs and superimposed on the anchor on the blue service coat collar and above the stripes on the shoulder boards. The collar insignia disappeared when the 1877 service coat was replaced in 1919 (41).

Use of epaulets resumed with the 1922 uniform regulations, the line anchor was now worn on the strap by all officers, with the corps device for staff officers superimposed over it (42).

The silver eagle began to be used as a pin on badge of rank in 1931 (43).

Use of epaulets was suspended for World War II and never unsuspended (44).

The Career Compensation Act of October 12, 1949 (45) placed the rank of Captain in pay grade O-6.

The April 2010 uniform regulations descried the insignia for Captains as:

Sleeve Stripes - "CAPTAIN. Wear four 1/2 inch stripes." (46).

Shoulder Boards - "Officers below Flag Grade. The surface is black cloth. Gold lace stripes, the same width, number, and spacing, specified for stripes on sleeves of the blue coat, designate rank. The first stripe starts 1/4 inch... from the widest end. Line and staff corps devices replicate sleeve insignia and are placed as far from the stripes as specified for devices on sleeves of blue coats." (47).

Metal Grade Insignia - "Captain. Wear with the top of eagle's head toward the collar, and head and olive branch pointing to the front (right and left). (the silver eagle is shown in illustration).
Collar grade insignia replicates metal shoulder insignia." (48).

Captain Commanding a Squadron

The lack of any ranks in the early navy above Captain lead to the officers in command of squadrons to be treated as holding a higher rank, even though they were still Captains and were listed as such in the Navy Register. Officers would revert to plain Captain when their tour as a squadron commander was over. They were usually referred to and addressed as "Commodore".

The first of these was the commander of the Continental Navy Esek Hopkins who was appointed on December 22, 1775 and relieved on January 2, 1778 (1). There is no evidence of Hopkins wearing a special uniform or badge of rank.

Beginning in 1802 (2), "Commodores" wore a Captain's uniform with silver star on the epaulets.

The 1820 regulation called for a silver eagle above the anchors a Captain's epaulets (3).

With the 1830 regulations they wore a 1 inch silver star above the Captain's eagle and anchor device and a plain strip of lace on each shoulder as a shoulder strap, same as Captains (4).

In 1841 new shoulder straps were prescribed. A blue rectangle 2 1/2 inches long and 1/2 inch wide outlined in 1/8 inch gold embroidery with a star in the center (5).

The 1852 regulations saw them continue to wear the uniform of a Captain, three stripes and all, with two stars above the eagle and anchor device on the epaulets and on either side of the device on the shoulder straps (6).

Congress gave them an official title on January 16, 1857 (7) when a law included a section stating "And be it further enacted, That captains in command of squadrons shall be denominated flag officers."

Carpenter

Carpenter was used as both a warrant rank and a non rated rate (1).

The Warrant version of Carpenters were in charge of a repairing a ships hull.

They existed in the Continental Navy (2) and were listed among the warrant ranks in both the 1794 (3) and 1796 (4) laws creating the navy.

Uniforms were first prescribed by the 1814 uniform regulations (5). They called for "Short blue coats, with six buttons on the lappels; rolling cape, blue pantaloons, white vests, round hats, with cockade. No side-arms."

In 1830 a double breasted, dark blue dress coat with lapels buttoned back with eight buttons was prescribed. It had a standing collar with one button on it and slashed sleeves closed with three buttons. The undress rolling collar coatee had the same buttons as the dress coat except the one on the collar (6).

The only coat listed in the 1841 regulations was described as "To be of dark blue cloth, lined with the same, double breasted, seven navy buttons on each breast, slashed sleeves with three small navy buttons on each, two large navy buttons under each pocket flap, one on each hip, and one at the bottom of each skirt". Blue cloth caps were also called for (7). On April 5, 1849 a large button and a button hole worked in black twist was added to the coat collars. At the same time a 1 1/4 inch wide gold lace band was added around the cap (8).

The 1852 regulations list the warrant officers coats with the descriptions of the officers dress tail coats, but they may have been frock coats. This is by no means clear. They are described as "shall be of Navy blue cloth, lined with the same; rolling collar, double breasted, two rows of large Navy buttons on the breast, eight in each row; pointed pocket flaps, with three large buttons underneath each, showing one half their diameter; three medium size buttons around each cuff and two small ones in each opening; one button behind on each hip, one in the middle of each fold and one in each fold near the bottom of the skirt. On each side of the collar to have one loop of three-quarters wide gold lace to show one inch and a half wide, and four inches long, with a small size Navy button in the point of each loop." They were worn over blue or white pantaloons, according to season and blue caps with a gold anchor on the front (9).

A band of two 1/2 inch strips of gold lace 1/4 apart, showing blue in between, were added to the caps on February 17, 1853 (10).

The uniforms may have been simplified in 1862 with the removal of the cuff buttons and maybe the collar button and lace, but this is not clear (11).

New uniform regulations of 1864 (12) gave warrant officers the same frock coats and caps as officers. Shoulder straps were added consisting of a strip of gold lace 3/4 inches wide by 4 inches long with an old english letter C in silver. Caps were plain except for an empty wreath.

On March 11, 1869 the shoulder straps were replaced with a gold diamond on the collar of the frock coat (13).

Use of the service dress sack coat by warrant officers is clear but it is authorized by the 1876 regulations but no insignia was mentioned (14).

They were authorized the new standing collar service coat in October 1878. The diamond was worn on the collar (15).

In 1883 the diamonds on the collars of both the frock coat and the service coat were replaced with a chevron representing a carpenter's square, in silver for those over 20 years service and gold for those under (16). Silver was reserved for Chief Carpenters in 1899.

Shoulder boards were authorized in 1908 with the chevron near the outer end (17).

It is possible, but not certain, that the chevron was worn on the cuffs in 1918. It was certainly there on the new service coats of 1919, now above a strip of 1/4 inch gold lace. Shoulder boards of 1919 also carried the 1/4 inch lace and crossed anchors (18).

The 1922 regulations added a 1/2 inch dark blue break every two inches on the cuff stripes and a single 1/2 inch break in the center of the shoulder board stripe (19).

Black sleeve stripes were used on khaki and green coats starting in 1925. The format used by warrant officers is not clear. It is possible that a solid stripe was used (20). The black stripes were removed from the khaki coat in 1941 (21) and stripes with green breaks were definitely prescribed for warrant officers in 1944 (22).

The gold chevron became the Carpenter's pin on badge of rank in 1931.

The Career Compensation Act of October 12, 1949 (22a) placed Areographers in pay grade W-1.

A standard, warrant officers badge of rank was introduced on July 1,1952 (23) consisting of a gold bar with a 1/16 inch blue break across the middle (24).

Carpenter became Warrant Officer 1, with the Warrant Officer Act of 1954 (25).

The non rated version was created in 1885 from the rate of Carpenter and Caulker (26).

It was in the Seaman First Class pay grade and therefore they would have worn three stripes on the cuffs of the jumpers and a white/blue watch mark (27).'

The rate was eliminated in 1893 (28).

Carpenter and Caulker

The rate of Carpenter and Caulker was created in 1864 and split in two seperate rates in 1885 (1).

There is no information on uniforms or insignia. When the rate was split in 1885, both Carpenters and Caulkers were in the Seaman First Class pay grade (2), so three stripes might have been worn before 1885.

Caulker

The rate of caulker was created in 1885 from the rate of Carpenter and Caulker (1).

It was in the Seaman First Class pay grade and therefore they would have worn three stripes on the cuffs of the jumpers and a white/blue watch mark (2).'

The rate was eliminated in 1893 (3).

Chaplain

Chaplains in the early navy were primarily responsible for training of midshipmen. They were also used a secretaries of squadron commanders. In their spare time they might conduct religious services or preside at a funeral (1).

Chaplains appear on the pay tables of the Continental Navy (2)(3), and appear in both the 1794 (4) and 1797 (5) laws creating the federal navy.

Chaplains did not wear uniforms until 1830. They were described as "Plain black coat, vest and pantaloons, the pantaloons to be worn over boots or shoes, or black breeches, silk stockings with shoes, coat to have three black covered buttons under the pocket flaps and on the cuffs." (6).

The 1841 regulations (7) allowed Chaplains to wear a navy blue coat like other officers. It had three buttons on the cuffs and pocket flaps and a rolling collar of black velvet.

The 1852 regulations added an undress frock coat of plain blue. It was single breasted with one row of nine buttons and plain cuffs with three small opening buttons (8).

On March 3, 1853, the uniform for Chaplains was changed to black. Both the dress coat and the undress frock coat were in black, with one row of nine buttons covered in black cloth (9).

The order of March 13, 1863 granting relative rank, made Chaplains over 12 years service relative Commanders and Chaplains under 12 years service relative Lieutenant Commanders (10).

The 1864 uniform regulations gave them the same uniforms as other officers with the sleeve stripes and shoulder straps appropriate for their relative rank and a corps device of a silver cross (11).

They continued to wear the uniform of their relative rank, which after 1866 would have included epaulets, with the silver cross as a corps device until the Attorney General ruled that their relative rank was not valid in March of 1869 (12). After that they wore plain blue uniforms, but not the full dress tail coat, without lace or insignia (13).

Congress restored relative rank of March 3, 1871 (14) with a law stating "four chaplains shall have the relative rank of captain, seven that of commander, and not more than seven that of lieutenant commander or lieutenant".

The 1876 uniform regulations contain a passage stating "Chaplains, when performing divine service, may wear either the vestments of the church to which they belong or the uniform proscribed in the regulations." (15). A silver cross is prescribed as a corps device (16), but that is the only mention of Chaplains in the regulations. Did this mean that Chaplains wore identical uniform as other officers? Unlike other staff officers, no color was prescribed between the cuff stripes, but the final sentence of the section on sleeve ornaments states "No other officers are entitled to wear the above-described ornaments." (17). This could mean that Chaplains wore gold stripes without colors, or it could mean they wore no stripes at all.

The 1883 regulations are equally unclear. They do not include the sentence about "No other officers are entitled to wear the above-described ornaments." This may mean that gold stripes were allowed, but it not clear. There is also a provision similar to the one in the 1876 regulations stating "In place of the prescribed uniform, chaplains may wear the single-breasted coat, waistcoat, and trousers commonly worn by clergymen, made of black or navy-blue cloth." (18). The use of the uniform by Chaplains was beginning to be discouraged.

The 1886 regulations are perfectly clear. "Chaplains shall wear the dress commonly worn by clergymen, consisting of a single-breasted coat, with standing collar, waistcoat, and trousers of black or dark navy-blue cloth, and black, low crowned soft felt hat." (19). The "shall" tells the whole story. Despite their status as naval officers up the relative rank of Captain, they were not to wear uniforms.

Chaplains dress was modified slightly in the 1897 regulations. They now said "Chaplains shall wear the dress commonly worn by clergymen, consisting of a single-breasted frock coat, with standing collar, waistcoat, and trousers, of black or dark navy-blue material, and a black hat. A navy cap with black buttons and strap, and without ornaments, may be worn." (20).

Uniforms were finally returned on December 23, 1898. They could wear the blue service coat of other officers with collar insignia according to rank and a silver cross as a corps device and cuff stripes of black mohair (21). It appears they could also wear the white coat with no insignia at all (22). A special frock coat was prescribed. It was single breasted with black buttons and carried cuff lace in black (23). It is possible that the cross was worn on the collar of the frock coat, it at least appears in the 1905 regulations (24).

On March 3, 1899 (25), staff officers stopped holding relative rank and started holding actual rank with staff titles.

Shoulder boards were permitted on white uniforms beginning in 1902. They had the proper number of stripes in black mohair (26).

A law of June 29, 1906 (27) made the entry level rank of Chaplains, Lieutenant Junior Grade.

In March of 1908 the buttons on the frock coat were changed to gold and in October they were permitted the same frock coat as other officers, (28). It is not clear if the cross was still worn on the collar.

The 1913 regulations returned Chaplains to the 1898 frock coat, black buttons, black cuff stripe, cross and all (29).

Finally on June 26, 1918, chaplains were allowed to wear gold stripes. Black cloth was worn between them until November when cloth inserts were abolished and the corps device was worn above them in gold. The corps device remained a cross for Christian Chaplains and the June 1918 order added a shepherd's crook for Jewish Chaplains (30).

The 1922 regulations allowed the same uniforms as other officers except full dress (31). The corps device for Jewish Chaplains was not included (32), but was revived for Jewish Chaplains in the Naval Reserve in 1932 (33).

The 1941 regulations prescribed a new device for Jewish Chaplains. The tables of law with a star of david on top of them (34).

A law of May 15, 1947 (35) made the Chief of Chaplains a Rear Admiral.

The navy commissioned it's first muslim chaplain. M. Malak Abd al Muta'ali Ibn Noel, in 1998 (36). The corps device for muslim chaplains is a crescent (37).

The first Buddhist Chaplain was Jeanette G. Shin, commissioned in 2004 (38). The corps device for Buddhist Chaplains is a dharma cakra (39).

Chief Areographer

The warrant grade of Chief Aerographer was created on July 28, 1942 (1).

The lace worn on the cuffs was 1/2 inch wide gold with 1/2 inch long blue breaks every 2 inches. The device of an Aeroprapher, a winged circle with a six feather arrow passing vertically through the circle, placed on the sleeve, arrow pointing down, was worn above the stripes. Shoulder boards showed the 1/2 inch lace with a single 1/2 inch break, under the device. The winged circle and arrow device, in silver, was also used as a badge of rank (2).

The aviation green coat was given a black stripe with green breaks in 1944 (3). It is possible that a solid stripe was worn previous to this (4).

The Career Compensation Act of October 12, 1949 (5) spread Chief Areographers across pay grades W-2, W-3 and W-4.

A standard, chief warrant officers badge of rank was introduced on July 1,1952 (6) consisting of a gold bar with a 1/8 inch blue break across the middle (7).

Chief Aerographers became Chief Warrant Officer 2, Chief Warrant Officer 3 and Chief Warrant Officer 4, with the Warrant Officer Act of 1954 (8).

Chief Boatswain

A law of March 3, 1899 (1) stated "That boatswains, gunners, carpenters, and sailmakers shall, after ten years from date of warrant be commissioned chief boatswains, chief gunners, chief carpenters, and chief sailmakers, to rank with but after ensign".

They were given cuff stripes if one 1/2 inch wide strip of gold lace with a 1/2 blue break every two inches, below a line star. The insignia on the coat collars was silver crossed anchors inherited from Boatswains over 20 years service (2). It is not clear how this worked with the black stripes on the overcoat. They may have worn an unbroken stripe or no stripe at all.

At some point between 1899 and 1905 (3) the crossed anchors were removed from the frock coat collar and placed in shoulder straps, and shoulder boards (4), with one 1/2 gold stripe with 1 1/2 inch blue break below a line star, were created.

In 1908 the silver crossed anchors with a small gold star replaced the line star on the shoulder boards (5).

In the January 1913 uniform regulations the silver crossed anchors with the small gold star was back on the collar of the frock coat (6). It was also worn on white cloth shoulder loops on the white service coat that replaced shoulder boards (7). It continued to be worn on the collar of the blue service coat and the broken stripe and line star were still used on the blue service coat and frock coat.

Shoulder boards returned to replace the cloth shoulder loops in June (8).

The crossed anchors (in gold and without the star) replaced the star on the cuffs in 1918. A year later the stripes were made plain gold without breaks. Shoulder boards of 1919 also carried the 1/2 inch lace and crossed anchors (9).

The 1922 regulations added a 1/2 inch dark blue break every two inches on the cuff stripes and a single 1/2 inch break in the center of the shoulder board stripe (10).

Black sleeve stripes were used on khaki and green coats starting in 1925. The format used by warrant officers is not clear. It is possible that a solid stripe was used (11). The black stripes were removed from the khaki coat in 1941 (12) and stripes with green breaks were definitely prescribed for warrant officers in 1944 (13).

The silver crossed anchors returned as the Chief Boatswain's pin on badge of rank in 1931.

The Career Compensation Act of October 12, 1949 (14) spread Chief Boatswains across pay grades W-2, W-3 and W-4.

A standard, chief warrant officers badge of rank was introduced on July 1,1952 (15) consisting of a gold bar with a 1/8 inch blue break across the middle (16).

Chief Boatswains became Chief Warrant Officer 2, Chief Warrant Officer 3 and Chief Warrant Officer 4, with the Warrant Officer Act of 1954 (17).

Chief Carpenter

A law of March 3, 1899 (1) stated "That boatswains, gunners, carpenters, and sailmakers shall, after ten years from date of warrant be commissioned chief boatswains, chief gunners, chief carpenters, and chief sailmakers, to rank with but after ensign"

They were given cuff stripes if one 1/2 inch wide strip of gold lace with a 1/2 blue break every two inches. The insignia on the coat collars was silver a chevron representing a carpenter's square inherited form Carpenters over 20 years service (2). It is not clear how this worked with the black stripes on the overcoat. They may have worn an unbroken stripe or no stripe at all.

At some point between 1899 and 1905 (3) the chevron was removed from the frock coat collar and placed in shoulder straps, and shoulder boards (4), with one 1/2 gold stripe with 1 1/2 inch blue break, were created.

In 1908 the silver chevron was placed above the stripe on the shoulder boards (5).

In the January 1913 uniform regulations the silver chevron was back on the collar of the frock coat (6). It was also worn on white cloth shoulder loops on the white service coat that replaced shoulder boards (7). It continued to be worn on the collar of the blue service coat and the broken stripe used on the blue service coat and frock coat.

Shoulder boards returned to replace the cloth shoulder loops in June (8).

The chevron (in gold) was placed above the stripe on the cuffs in 1918. A year later the stripes were made plain gold without breaks. Shoulder boards of 1919 also carried the 1/2 inch lace and chevron (9).

The 1922 regulations added a 1/2 inch dark blue break every two inches on the cuff stripes and a single 1/2 inch break in the center of the shoulder board stripe (10).

Black sleeve stripes were used on khaki and green coats starting in 1925. The format used by warrant officers is not clear. It is possible that a solid stripe was used (11). The black stripes were removed from the khaki coat in 1941 (12) and stripes with green breaks were definitely prescribed for warrant officers in 1944 (13).

The silver chevron returned as the Chief Carpenter's pin on badge of rank in 1931.

The Career Compensation Act of October 12, 1949 (14) spread Chief Carpenters across pay grades W-2, W-3 and W-4.

A standard, chief warrant officers badge of rank was introduced on July 1,1952 (15) consisting of a gold bar with a 1/8 inch blue break across the middle (16).

Chief Carpenters became Chief Warrant Officer 2, Chief Warrant Officer 3 and Chief Warrant Officer 4, with the Warrant Officer Act of 1954 (17).

Chief Constructor

On March 3, 1871 (1) the title of the Chief of the Bureau of Construction and Repair, Isiah Hanscom, was changed to Chief Constructor. He continued to have the relative rank of Commodore.

Hanscom wore the uniform of a Commodore with dark violet piping around his cuff stripe and a corps device of two oak leafs and an acorn in gold (2).

Hanscom retired on June 29, 1877 (3) and was replaced by John Easby on April 15, 1878 (4). Easby retired on December 13, 1881 (5) and was replaced by Theodore Wilson on March 3, 1882 (6). Wilson was granted a leave of absence on July 13, 1893 and was replaced by Philip Hichborn (7).

When the rank of Commodore, and relative ranks, were abolished on March 3, 1899 (8), the chiefs of bureaus were made into Rear Admirals with "the same pay and allowance as are now allowed a brigadier-general in the Army". In other words Rear Admiral lower half.

Francis Bowles took over from Hanscom on March 4, 1901 (9). Bowles resigned on October 31, 1903 (10) and was replaced by Washington Capps (11). Capps Is listed as having "special duty abroad" as of November 29, 1910, but was still a Chief Constructor with the rank of Rear Admiral. The actual Chief of Bureau was Richard Watt, appointed October 2nd who was also a Chief Constructor with the rank of Rear Admiral (12). David Taylor became the chief of the bureau on December 13, 1914 and Watt reverted to his permanent rank of Naval Constructor with the rank of Lieutenant Commander (13).

The use of staff titles ended in November of 1918 (14) and Capps and Taylor became more Rear Admiral and less Chief Constructor.

The position itself ended when construction officers were eliminated on June 25, 1940 (15).

Chief Electrician

Chief Electricians were created on March 4, 1925 (1) as a chief warrant rank.

The lace worn on the cuffs was 1/2 inch wide gold with 1/2 inch long blue breaks every 2 inches. The device of an electrician, a globe, as in picture of the earth with longitude and latitude lines, placed on the sleeve above the stripes. Shoulder boards showed the 1/2 inch lace with a single 1/2 inch break, under the device (2).

Black sleeve stripes were used on khaki and green coats starting in 1925. The format used by warrant officers is not clear. It is possible that a solid stripe was used (3). The black stripes were removed from the khaki coat in 1941 (4) and stripes with green breaks were definitely prescribed for warrant officers in 1944 (5).

The silver globe was used as the Chief Electrician's pin on badge of rank starting in 1931.

The Career Compensation Act of October 12, 1949 (6) spread Chief Electricians across pay grades W-2, W-3 and W-4.

A standard, chief warrant officers badge of rank was introduced on July 1,1952 (7) consisting of a gold bar with a 1/8 inch blue break across the middle (8).

Chief Electricians became Chief Warrant Officer 2, Chief Warrant Officer 3 and Chief Warrant Officer 4, with the Warrant Officer Act of 1954 (9).

Chief Engineer

Prior to 1842 the people who operated and repaired the engines of steam powered ships were civilian employes.

The first Chief Engineer was Charles Haswell of the steamship Fulton, hired on July 12, 1836 (1).

The Fulton's Captain, Matthew Perry, sought and received from the Secretary of the Navy permission the put his engineers in uniform. For Haswell, as Chief Engineer, he prescribed a blue, double breasted coat with a rolling collar of black velvet and a gold star on each collar (2).

Other Chief Engineers were soon hired, John Faron (who moved up from First Assistant) on January 13, 1840, Henry (or possibly Andrew) Hebard on February 6, 1841, and James Thompson on April 14, 1842 (3).

Chief Engineer became an official rank of the navy with a law of August 31, 1842 (4). The law stated that Chief Engineer would be "appointed by commission" and would share in prize money as if they were Lieutenants. It also allowed the Secretary of the Navy to prescribe a uniform for engineers. This was an odd detail for Congress to get involved with.

Despite the mention of them in law, there is no record of uniforms begin prescribed for engineers before the uniform regulations of 1852 (5), ten years after they became an official part of the navy. It is possible that the uniform from the Fulton was used for all that time, or it is equally possible that civilian clothes were worn. It is also possible that the order for engineer's uniforms has been lost.

Haswell, Faron, Hebard and Thompson all remained as now official naval officers, and William Williamson was added on October 20, 1842 (6).

Haswell was promoted to Engineer-in-Chief of the navy on October 3, 1844 and Thomspon resigned on July 3, 1845. Charles Moss was appointed on May 29, 1844 and William Sewell and William Wood on March 15, 1845. Hebard died on August 4, 1846 and Moss was dropped from the rolls on January 30th. Alexander Birkbeck was added on March 2, 1847 but resigned on December 23rd. May 14, 1847 saw the appointment of Daniel Martin and Henry Hunt. Jesse Gay. Benjamin Isherwood and Joshua Follansbie were added on October 31, 1848 and Samuel Archibald on March 11, 1851 (7).

Uniforms finally came on March 8, 1852. The dress tail coat was single breasted with one row of nine buttons, three large buttons on the cuff and a standing collar with a corps device of a silver anchor on a gold paddle wheel in an L shaped gold wreath. The undress frock coat was also single breasted and had three large buttons around the cuff. Epaulets were similar to an army major's with a silver strap with a gold border, crescent (of flat braid) and bullion (3/8 inch wide). A silver "E" was worn in the frog. Shoulder Straps were large size (4 inches by 1 1/2 inches) with a Silver "E" in the center (8).

George Sewell became a Chief Engineer on July 15, 1852. William Everett on August 30th, William Shock on September 16th and James King on November 12th. Daniel Martin became Engineer-in-Chief on October 18, 1853 and William Sewell resigned on November 10th. Michael Quinn was appointed on December 15th. June 27, 1855 saw the appointment of John Whipple and Theodore Zeller and June 26, 1856 welcomed Robert Long, Eldridge Lawton and Robert Danby. Samuel Archibald was promoted to Engineer-in-Chief on October 16, 1857. In 1858 Benjamin Garvin was appointed on May 11th and Allen Stimers and Henry Stewart on July 21st (9).

On January 13, 1859 the navy issued a general order granting relative rank to engineers. Chief Engineers over 12 years service, Williamson and Wood, became relative Commanders and those under 12 years service, Hunt, Gay, Isherwood, Follansbie, George Sewell, Everett, Shock, King, Quinn, Whipple, Zeller, Long, Lawton, Danby, Garvin, Stimers and Stewart, became relative Lieutenants. Congress confirmed this order in law on March 3rd (10).

Uniforms were changed to reflect the engineer's new status on February 8, 1861. The dress tail coats were now double breasted with the cuff lace according to relative rank. The collar device was removed and replaced with a 1/2 inch wide border of gold beaded lace. The "E" was removed from the epaulets and shoulder straps. The new corps device, four oak branches in a cross, was worn in the shoulder straps with an acorn, probably, added at each end for Chief Engineers over 12 years service (11). The frock coat, presumably, became double breasted with appropriate cuff lace as well.

That lace was altered slightly when the lace for line officers was changed in 1862 (12).

The March 13, 1863 realignment of relative rank made Chief Engineers over 15 years service relative Captains, those form 5 to 15 years service relative Commanders and those under 5 years service relative Lieutenant Commanders (13).

The 1864 uniform regulations (14) prescribed cuff lace according to rank without a line star and shoulder straps with the crossed oak branch device in the center, or in the talons of the eagle on the straps of relative Captains.

The 1866 regulations moved the device for relative Captains to either side of the eagle on shoulder straps and in the frogs of the restored epaulets (15). 1869 saw red used at the color between the cuff stripes (16).

On March 29, 1869 Attorney General Ebenezer Hoar issued a ruling that the navy had exceeded its authority in granting relative rank to certain staff officers during the Civil War (17). Chief Engineers reverted to relative Commanders for those over 12 years service and relative Lieutenants for those under.

Congress fixed this problem on March 3, 1871 (18) with a law that spread the now 56 (19) Chief Engineers over the ranks of Captain, Commander and Lieutenant Commander.

The rank was abolished on March 3, 1899 (20), when all engineering officers were converted to line officers.

Chief Gunner

A law of March 3, 1899 (1) stated "That boatswains, gunners, carpenters, and sailmakers shall, after ten years from date of warrant be commissioned chief boatswains, chief gunners, chief carpenters, and chief sailmakers, to rank with but after ensign"

They were given cuff stripes if one 1/2 inch wide strip of gold lace with a 1/2 blue break every two inches, below a line star. The insignia on the coat collars was a silver bursting bomb inherited from Gunners over 20 years service (2). It is not clear how this worked with the black stripes on the overcoat. They may have worn an unbroken stripe or no stripe at all.

At some point between 1899 and 1905 (3) the bursting bomb was removed from the frock coat collar and placed in shoulder straps, and shoulder boards (4), with one 1/2 gold stripe with 1 1/2 inch blue break below a line star, were created.

In 1908 the silver bursting bomb with a small gold star replaced the line star on the shoulder boards (5).

In the January 1913 uniform regulations the silver bursting bomb with the small gold star was back on the collar of the frock coat (6). It was also worn on white cloth shoulder loops on the white service coat that replaced shoulder boards (7). It continued to be worn on the collar of the blue service coat and the broken stripe and line star were still used on the blue service coat and frock coat.

Shoulder boards returned to replace the cloth shoulder loops in June (8).

The bursting bomb (in gold and without the star) replaced the star on the cuffs in 1918. A year later the stripes were made plain gold without breaks. Shoulder boards of 1919 also carried the 1/2 inch lace and bursting bomb (9).

The 1922 regulations added a 1/2 inch dark blue break every two inches on the cuff stripes and a single 1/2 inch break in the center of the shoulder board stripe (10).

Black sleeve stripes were used on khaki and green coats starting in 1925. The format used by warrant officers is not clear. It is possible that a solid stripe was used (11). The black stripes were removed from the khaki coat in 1941 (12) and stripes with green breaks were definitely prescribed for warrant officers in 1944 (13).

The silver bursting bomb returned as the Chief Gunner's pin on badge of rank in 1931.

The Career Compensation Act of October 12, 1949 (14) spread Chief Gunners across pay grades W-2, W-3 and W-4.

A standard, chief warrant officers badge of rank was introduced on July 1,1952 (15) consisting of a gold bar with a 1/8 inch blue break across the middle (16).

Chief Gunner became Chief Warrant Officer 2, Chief Warrant Officer 3 and Chief Warrant Officer 4, with the Warrant Officer Act of 1954 (17).

Chief Machinist

The warrant rank of Chief Machinist was created on March 3, 1909 (1).

They were given cuff stripes if one 1/2 inch wide strip of gold lace with a 1/2 blue break every two inches under a line star. The insignia on the coat collars, and above the shoulder board stripes was a three bladed propellor, silver on the collars and gold on the shoulder boards (2). It is not clear how this worked with the black stripes on the overcoat. They may have worn an unbroken stripe or no stripe at all.

In the January 1913 uniform regulations the silver three bladed propellor with the small gold star was back on the collar of the frock coat (3). It was also worn on white cloth shoulder loops on the white service coat that replaced shoulder boards (4). It continued to be worn on the collar of the blue service coat and the broken stripe and line star were still used on the blue service coat and frock coat.

Shoulder boards returned to replace the cloth shoulder loops in June (5).

The three bladed propellor (in gold and without the star) replaced the star on the cuffs in 1918. A year later the stripes were made plain gold without breaks. Shoulder boards of 1919 also carried the 1/2 inch lace and three bladed propellor (6).

The 1922 regulations added a 1/2 inch dark blue break every two inches on the cuff stripes and a single 1/2 inch break in the center of the shoulder board stripe (7).

Black sleeve stripes were used on khaki and green coats starting in 1925. The format used by warrant officers is not clear. It is possible that a solid stripe was used (8). The black stripes were removed from the khaki coat in 1941 (9) and stripes with green breaks were definitely prescribed for warrant officers in 1944 (10).

The silver three bladed propellor returned as the Chief Machinist's pin on badge of rank in 1931.

The Career Compensation Act of October 12, 1949 (11) spread Chief Machinists across pay grades W-2, W-3 and W-4.

A standard, chief warrant officers badge of rank was introduced on July 1,1952 (12) consisting of a gold bar with a 1/8 inch blue break across the middle (13).

Chief Machinist became Chief Warrant Officer 2, Chief Warrant Officer 3 and Chief Warrant Officer 4, with the Warrant Officer Act of 1954 (14).

Chief of Bureau of Construction and Repair

The Bureau of Construction and Repair began as the Bureau of Construction, Equipment and Repairs on August 31, 1842 (1). The name was changed on July 5, 1862 (2) with the equipment part moving to the Bureau of Equipment and Recruiting, Leaving the Bureau of Construction and Repair.

Both laws call for the chief of the bureau to be a "skillful Naval Constructor", but the early chief appear to have been line officers. The first was Captain David Conner serving from September 1, 1842 to March 1, 1843. He was replaced by Captain Beverly Kennon who served until he was killed in an accident on February 28, 1844. Next up was Captain Charles Morris who served from April 10, 1844 to May 31, 1847. He was replaced by Captain Charles Skinner who served until February 28, 1852. Next in line was Caption William Shubrick who was in office until June 30, 1853. Shubrick's replacement was not a naval officer but a Naval Constructor, who were civilian employees of the navy at the time. His name was Samuel Hartt. He held the office until another Naval Constructor, John Lenthall took over on November 17, 1853 (3).

On March 13, 1863 the Secretary of the Navy granted relative rank of Naval Constructors, making them naval officers for the first time. As the chief of the bureau, Lentahll was given the relative rank of Commodore (4).

Uniforms were prescribed by the 1864 regulations. Lenthall was to wear the uniform of a Commodore, seven cuff stripes, star and all, without a line star above the stripes and with the a corps device of al live oak sprig (5).

A law of July 25, 1866 (6) officially made Naval Constructors naval officers.

On March 29, 1869 the Attorney General overruled the relative ranks granted in 1863 (7). Despite the 1866 law Naval Constructors no longer held relative ranks.

Lenthall was replaced by Isiah Hanscom on January 23, 1871 (8), and on March 3rd Congress restored the relative rank of Commodore with a better title, Chief Constructor (9).

Chief of Bureau of Medicine and Surgery

On August 31, 1842 the Bureau of Medicine and Surgery was born, and one of the Navy's Surgeons was to be it's chief (1).

The first was Surgeon William Barton who headed the bureau until March 31, 1844, when Surgeon Thomas Harris took office (2).

As Surgeons, they would have worn the uniform of a Surgeon. When Surgeons were given relative rank in 1846 (3)(4), epaulets and shoulder straps soon followed. Harris would have been a relative Commander with 1/2 inch wide bullion on his epaulets, the letters "M.D." in the frog and a silver rosette on the strap. Shoulder straps carried the "M.D." in the center and silver rosettes at each end (5). The rosettes were actually prescribed for Surgeons of the Fleet. The 1852 Uniform Regulations (6) also allow them for the "Senior Surgeon of the Navy" which would have been Harris. It is fairly safe to assume that this was allowed all the way back to 1847.

A sprig of olive replaced the "M.D." and all insignia was removed from epaulets in September of 1852 (7). It is not clear if the rosettes were still worn on the shoulder straps. If they were not, Harris would have worn the acorn of a Surgeon over 12 years service on each end of his shoulder straps.

Harris was replaced by William Whelen on September 30, 1853 (8).

The reorganization of relative rank on March 13, 1863 made Whelen a relative Commodore (9), and the uniform regulations of 1864 gave him a Commodore's uniform with no corps device on his shoulder straps. His star was alone (10).

Whelen was replaced by Phineas Horwitz on June 12, 1865 (11).

Cobalt blue was the color placed in and around medical officers cuff stripes in 1869 (12).

When the Attorney General overruled the 1863 order on relative rank (13), Horwitz reverted to a relative Commander and his uniform would have reflected that with no corps device on the epaulets and shoulder straps and cobalt blue between the cuff stripes.

William Wood took over from Horwitz on July 1, 1869 (14).

When Congress restored the 1863 relative ranks on March 3, 1871 (15), they gave Wood the title of Surgeon General with relative rank of Commodore.

Chief of Bureau of Provisions and Clothing

On August 31, 1842 the Bureau of Provisions and Clothing was created (1).

It's first chief was a civilian named Charles Goldsborough who served until January 30, 1844 (2). Next was a line officer Captain William Shubrick who served until April 14, 1846. Next up was another civilian and future Navy Secretary Gideon Welles who was in office until July 8, 1849. After Welles, Purser William Sinclair became the chief of bureau (2).

Sinclair, as Purser over 12 years service (he had been one since 1814) would have been a relative Commander with 1/2 inch wide bullion on his epaulets and the letters "P.D." in the frog. Shoulder straps carried the "P.D." in the center and a single oak leaf at each end (3).

A sprig of oak replaced the "P.D." and all insignia was removed from epaulets in September of 1852 (4).

Horatio Bridge took over from Sinclair on October 1, 1854 (5).

On June 22, 1860 (6), Bridge's official rank was changed when navy Pursers became Paymasters.

The reorganization of relative rank on March 13, 1863 made Bridge a relative Commodore (7), and the uniform regulations of 1864 gave him a Commodore's uniform with the oak sprig as a corps device on his shoulder straps (8).

White was the color placed in and around medical officers cuff stripes in 1869 (9).

When the Attorney General overruled the 1863 order on relative rank (10), Bridge reverted to a relative Commander and his uniform would have reflected that with the corps device of an oak sprig on the epaulets and shoulder straps and white between the cuff stripes.

Edward Dunn took over from Bridge on July 1, 1869 (11).

When Congress restored the 1863 relative ranks on March 3, 1871 (12), they gave Dunn the title of Paymaster General with relative rank of Commodore.

Chief of Bureau of Steam Engineering

The Bureau of Steam Engineering was created on July 5, 1862 (1). It's chief was to be one of the Chief Engineers. There already was a post of Engineer in Chief being held at the time by Benjamin Isherwood, and Isherwood became the Chief of the Bureau (2).

Engineer-in-chief appears on the pay table in the January 1864 navy register (3) but not in the January 1865 register (4).

Whatever his title, Isherwood would have worn the uniform of a Chief Engineer over 12 years service with epaulets with a silver strap (5) and shoulder straps with crossed oak branches in the middle and an acorn at each end (6).

The reorganization of relative rank on March 13, 1863 made Isherwood a relative Commodore (7), and the uniform regulations of 1864 gave him a Commodore's uniform with the cross of oak branches as a corps device on his shoulder straps (8).

Red was the color placed in and around engineering officers cuff stripes in 1869 (9).

When the Attorney General overruled the 1863 order on relative rank (10), Isherwood reverted to a relative Commander and his uniform would have reflected that with the corps device of a cross of oak branches on the epaulets and shoulder straps and red between the cuff stripes.

James King took over from Isherwood on March 23, 1869 (11).

When Congress restored the 1863 relative ranks on March 3, 1871 (12), the title returned to Engineer In Chief with relative rank of Commodore.

Chief Pay Clerk

The warrant rank of Chief Pay Clerk was created on March 3, 1915 (1).

The were given cuff stripes if one 1/2 inch wide strip of gold lace with a 1/2 blue break every two inches. The insignia on the coat collars, and above the shoulder board stripes was a gold (not silver) oak sprig composed of three leafs and three acorns (2). It is not clear how this worked with the black stripes on the overcoat. They may have worn an unbroken stripe or no stripe at all.

The oak sprig was placed above the cuff stripes in 1918. A year later the stripes were made plain gold without breaks. Shoulder boards of 1919 also carried the 1/2 inch lace the oak sprig (3).

The 1922 regulations added a 1/2 inch dark blue break every two inches on the cuff stripes and a single 1/2 inch break in the center of the shoulder board stripe (4).

Black sleeve stripes were used on khaki and green coats starting in 1925. The format used by warrant officers is not clear. It is possible that a solid stripe was used (5). The black stripes were removed from the khaki coat in 1941 (6) and stripes with green breaks were definitely prescribed for warrant officers in 1944 (7).

The oak sprig, in silver this time, returned as the Chief Pay Clerk's pin on badge of rank in 1931.

The Career Compensation Act of October 12, 1949 (8) spread Chief Pay Clerks across pay grades W-2, W-3 and W-4.

A standard, chief warrant officers badge of rank was introduced on July 1,1952 (9) consisting of a gold bar with a 1/8 inch blue break across the middle (10).

Chief Pay Clerk became Chief Warrant Officer 2, Chief Warrant Officer 3 and Chief Warrant Officer 4, with the Warrant Officer Act of 1954 (11).

Chief Petty Officer

Chief Petty Officers or "Chiefs" as they are known are the lowest rate of senior noncommissioned officers. They are distinctive because they wear officer's style uniforms.

The rate was created on April 1, 1893 (1), but the roots run much deeper.

Various petty officers were placed in different uniform over the years. In the early navy Captain's Clerks were sometimes dressed in the uniform of a Midshipman (2). In 1862 petty officers rated as Master's Mate's, not to be confused with the warrant rank of Master's Mate, were placed in double breasted jackets and visored caps instead of the traditional jumper (3). More ratings were "jacketed" in 1864 (4) and in 1874 the jackets became a single breasted sack coat (5).

Pay tables from the Civil War era show ratings of Chief Boatswain's Mate, Chief Gunner's Mate, Chief Quartermaster, Boatswain's Mate in charge and Gunner's Mate in charge (6). Chief Boatswain's Mate's and Chief Gunner's Mates were assigned to larger vessels, Chief Quartermasters are listed as Signal Quartermasters in navy regulations and was in charge of signaling. "In charge" ratings were assigned to ships without a warranted Boatswain or Gunner. Eventually the "in charge" ratings fell away and the "chief" ratings were used when there was no warrant officer (7).

When the petty officer's ratings were divided into classes in 1885 (8) the "chief" ratings were in the first class, while the same ratings without "chief" were in the second class. All ratings of the first class were "jacketed", but one rating was elevated above them, Master at Arms. Instead of the first class rating badge of three chevrons and a diamond under the petty officer's eagle, they wore a badge of three chevrons and three arcs with the eagle resting on the middle arc (9).

When the rate of Chief Petty Officer was created in 1893, it encompassed the ratings of Chief Boatswain's Mate, Chief Gunner's Mate, Chief Quartermaster, Machinist, Chief Carpenter's Mate, Yoeman, Apothecary and Bandmaster (10). With the exception of Schoolmaster's and Ship Writer's, these were all of the first class ratings (11).

They inherited the double breasted blue and white coats prescribed for first class petty officers in 1886 (12) and the Master at Arms' rating badge. The badge had three point down chevrons and three arcs bade of red wool outlined in blue stitching. The eagle was white on blue uniforms and blue on white uniforms with it's wings out horizontally and head toward it's left wing. The specialty mark was worn in the center and over the lower arc. It was in the color of the eagle (13). The rating bade was worn on the upper right sleeve for starboard watch and left sleeve for the port watch. Chief Petty Officers with three consecutive good conduct badges could replace the red wool with gold lace (14). Shipboard Laundry services being what they were it is doubtful that the gold lace was worn on the white coat.

The design of the rating badge was changed in 1894. The wings of the eagle were now up, the chevrons now separate pieces with a gap between and there was now only one arc, touching the top chevron, leaving more room for the specialty mark (15). This basic design has been used ever since.

In 1897 a new cap device was prescribed, before this a large navy button was worn. The new device was a gold fouled anchor with the silver letters U.S.N. (16).

In 1913 the red chevrons on the white uniforms were changed to blue and the eagle and specialty mark on the blue uniforms when gold chevrons were authorized was made silver (17). They were made silver with the red chevrons in 1929 (18). Also in 1913 the rating badges began to be worn on the right sleeve for ratings in the seaman branch and the left for all others.

The Chief Petty Officer's pay grade became grade one on June 10, 1922 (19).

Chiefs were allowed green and khaki aviation uniforms in 1931, but it is not clear what colors were used on the rating badges. The 1941 uniform regulations, published just after the khaki uniform was expanded to the entire navy, shows in illustration what appears to be an all blue on khaki background rating badge on the khaki coat (20). The green coat is not illustrated and the text is of no help. The Naval Officer's Uniform Plan, a catalog of uniforms approved by the navy in 1943, shows the green uniform with what appears to be a full color badge on a blue background (21), but sells full color badges on green backgrounds (22). Finally in 1944 the navy ordered that all rating badges, other than on the blue coats, were to be all blue on a background matching the coat, including the gray uniform introduced in 1943 (23).

The blue coats used by chiefs became identical to those worn by officers in 1945 (24). The double breasted coats, in both blue and white, had two rows of five buttons when they were prescribed for first class petty officers in 1886 (25), but by the 1905 regulations (26) it was down to four in each row. Officers had begun wearing blue coats with three buttons in each row in 1919 and the 1945 order extended this to chiefs as well. The white coat continued to have four buttons in each row.

1948 saw the end of rating badges on the right sleeve. From then on all ratings wore the badge on the left sleeve with the eagle facing forward (27).

The following year the badges on the khaki coats were changed to a silver eagle and specialty mark and blue chevrons and arc (28).

The Career Compensation Act of October 12, 1949 made grade one into grade E-7 (29).

Rating badges were added to khaki shirts sometime in late 1950 (30), they appear to have been all blue (31). They were eliminated in 1952 (32).

In 1959 chiefs were given a pin on badge of rank. A smaller version of the fouled anchor and U.S.N cap device was added to the collar of the khaki shirt (33).

In 1970 a replacement was announced for the white coat. The new coat would be single breasted and have patch pockets, essentially a white version of the khaki and green coats. Optional wear was to have begun in May of 1971 and it would have become mandatory in May of 1973 (34). This never happened, In June of 1973 the navy announced sweeping changes in it's uniforms. For chiefs this meant the end of the white coat (worn since 1886) and the khaki coat (worn since 1931). Both became optional on July 1, 1973 and ended on July 1, 1975 (35).

1975 also saw the creation of blue and white dinner jackets for chiefs. Regular full color rating badges were worn on the blue jacket and badges with silver eagles and specialty marks and blue chevrons and arc (or gold if entitled) were worn on the white jacket. The 1975 regulations actually call for red chevrons, but this was a printing error (36).

White uniforms returned in 1979 in the same style as officers, standing collar for men and point lapel for women. The magazine article announcing them refers to a "sleeve rating badge" (37) but in fact badges of rank were placed on the collar.

Shoulder marks in black with the badge of rank embroidered on them were placed on white shirts worn under the blue coat in 1999. At the same time the use of the badge of rank on outerwear was expanded (38).

The aviation green uniform came to an end in December of 2010 (39), and the all blue rating badges on a green background passed into history. Ironically, the return of the 1931 khaki uniform began around the same time (40).

Chief Pharmacist

An appropriations bill passed on August 22, 1912 (1) stated "That pharmacists shall, after six years from date of warrant, be commissioned chief pharmacists after passing satisfactorily such examination as the Secretary of the Navy may prescribe, and shall, on promotion, have the rank, pay, and allowances of chief boatswains."

The January 1913 uniform regulations called for a silver caduceus on the collar of the frock coat (2). It was also worn on white cloth shoulder loops on the white service coat that replaced shoulder boards (3). It continued to be worn on the collar of the blue service coat and the broken stripe and line star were still used on the blue service coat and frock coat.

Shoulder boards returned to replace the cloth shoulder loops in June (4).

The caduceus (in gold) was placed above the cuffs in 1918. A year later the stripes were made plain gold without breaks. Shoulder boards of 1919 also carried the 1/2 inch lace and the caduceus (5).

The 1922 regulations added a 1/2 inch dark blue break every two inches on the cuff stripes and a single 1/2 inch break in the center of the shoulder board stripe (6).

Black sleeve stripes were used on khaki and green coats starting in 1925. The format used by warrant officers is not clear. It is possible that a solid stripe was used (7). The black stripes were removed from the khaki coat in 1941 (8) and stripes with green breaks were definitely prescribed for warrant officers in 1944 (9).

The silver caduceus returned as the Chief Pharmacists pin on badge of rank in 1931 (10).

Chief Pharmacists became Chief Warrant Officers, Hospital Corps on August 4, 1947 (11).

Chief Photographer

The warrant grade of Chief Photographer was created on July 28, 1942 (1).

The lace worn on the cuffs was 1/2 inch wide gold with 1/2 inch long blue breaks every 2 inches. The device of a Photographer, an old fashioned camera with the bellows extended, was worn above the stripes. Shoulder boards showed the 1/2 inch lace with a single 1/2 inch break, under the device. The camera device, in silver, was also used as a badge of rank (2).

The aviation green coat was given a black stripe with green breaks in 1944 (3). It is possible that a solid stripe was worn previous to this (4).

The Career Compensation Act of October 12, 1949 (5) spread Chief Photographers across pay grades W-2, W-3 and W-4.

A standard, chief warrant officers badge of rank was introduced on July 1,1952 (6) consisting of a gold bar with a 1/8 inch blue break across the middle (7).

Chief Photographers became Chief Warrant Officer 2, Chief Warrant Officer 3 and Chief Warrant Officer 4, with the Warrant Officer Act of 1954 (8).

Chief Radio Electrician

Chief Radio Electricians were created on March 4, 1925 (1) as a chief warrant rank.

The lace worn on the cuffs was 1/2 inch wide gold with 1/2 inch long blue breaks every 2 inches. The device of four lightning bolts, placed on the sleeve above the stripes. Shoulder boards showed the 1/2 inch lace with a single 1/2 inch break, under the device (2).

Black sleeve stripes were used on khaki and green coats starting in 1925. The format used by warrant officers is not clear. It is possible that a solid stripe was used (3). The black stripes were removed from the khaki coat in 1941 (4) and stripes with green breaks were definitely prescribed for warrant officers in 1944 (5).

Silver lightning bolts were used as the Chief Radio Electrician's pin on badge of rank starting in 1931.

The Career Compensation Act of October 12, 1949 (6) spread Chief Radio Electricians across pay grades W-2, W-3 and W-4.

A standard, chief warrant officers badge of rank was introduced on July 1,1952 (7) consisting of a gold bar with a 1/8 inch blue break across the middle (8).

Chief Radio Electricians became Chief Warrant Officer 2, Chief Warrant Officer 3 and Chief Warrant Officer 4, with the Warrant Officer Act of 1954 (9).

Chief Sail-Maker

A law of March 3, 1899 (1) stated "That boatswains, gunners, carpenters, and sailmakers shall, after ten years from date of warrant be commissioned chief boatswains, chief gunners, chief carpenters, and chief sailmakers, to rank with but after ensign"

The decline of sailing ships had caused appointments of Sailmakers to stop in 1888 (2) with the appointment of Michael Barr (3).

They were given cuff stripes if one 1/2 inch wide strip of gold lace with a 1/2 blue break every two inches. The insignia on the coat collars was a silver diamond inherited from Sailmakers over 20 years service (4). It is not clear how this worked with the black stripes on the overcoat. They may have worn an unbroken stripe or no stripe at all.

At some point between 1899 and 1905 (5) the diamond was removed from the frock coat collar and placed in shoulder straps, and shoulder boards (6), with one 1/2 gold stripe with 1 1/2 inch blue break, were created.

In 1908 the silver diamond was placed above the stripe on the shoulder boards (7).

In the January 1913 uniform regulations the silver diamond was back on the collar of the frock coat (6). It was also worn on white cloth shoulder loops on the white service coat that replaced shoulder boards (7). It continued to be worn on the collar of the blue service coat and the broken stripe used on the blue service coat and frock coat.

Shoulder boards returned to replace the cloth shoulder loops in June (8).

Barr was the last Chief Sailmaker left on the active list. He was given a temporary appointment as a Lieutenant on July 1, 1918 (9), which was made permanent on August 3, 1920 (10).

Chief Ship's Clerk

The warrant grade of Chief Ships' Clerk was created on July 28, 1942 (1).

The lace worn on the cuffs was 1/2 inch wide gold with 1/2 inch long blue breaks every 2 inches. The device of a Ship's Clerk, crossed quill pens, was worn above the stripes. Shoulder boards showed the 1/2 inch lace with a single 1/2 inch break, under the device. The crossed quill pens, device, in silver, was also used as a badge of rank (2).

The aviation green coat was given a black stripe with green breaks in 1944 (3). It is possible that a solid stripe was worn previous to this (4).

The Career Compensation Act of October 12, 1949 (5) spread Chief Ships Clerks across pay grades W-2, W-3 and W-4.

A standard, chief warrant officers badge of rank was introduced on July 1,1952 (6) consisting of a gold bar with a 1/8 inch blue break across the middle (7).

Chief Ship's Clerks became Chief Warrant Officer 2, Chief Warrant Officer 3 and Chief Warrant Officer 4, with the Warrant Officer Act of 1954 (8).

Chief Steward

The rate of Chief Steward was created in 1948 by combining the rates of Chief Steward and Chief Cook (1). They were not petty officers (2), but they did wear regular rating badges with a the eagle, three chevrons, an arc and a crescent as a specialty mark.

Stewards were reclassified as petty officers in late 1949 (3).

Chief Torpedoman

The warrant grade of Chief Torpedoman was created on July 28, 1942 (1).

The lace worn on the cuffs was 1/2 inch wide gold with 1/2 inch long blue breaks every 2 inches. The device of a Torpedoman, a torpedo, was worn above the stripes. Shoulder boards showed the 1/2 inch lace with a single 1/2 inch break, under the device. The torpedo, device, in silver, was also used as a badge of rank (2).

The aviation green coat was given a black stripe with green breaks in 1944 (3). It is possible that a solid stripe was worn previous to this (4).

The Career Compensation Act of October 12, 1949 (5) spread Chief Torpedomen across pay grades W-2, W-3 and W-4.

A standard, chief warrant officers badge of rank was introduced on July 1,1952 (6) consisting of a gold bar with a 1/8 inch blue break across the middle (7).

Chief Torpedomen became Chief Warrant Officer 2, Chief Warrant Officer 3 and Chief Warrant Officer 4, with the Warrant Officer Act of 1954 (8).

Chief Warrant Officer 2

Chief Warrant Officer 2 was created by the "Warrant Officer Act of 1954" (1) in pay grade W-2, from the various chief warrant grades.

New insignia was prescribed to be worn as of November 1st. The cuff stripes were to be 1/2 inch wide with three 1/2 inch blue breaks, two inches apart, under a specialty device. On the shoulder boards, the 1/2 inch stripe had breaks 1/2 inch apart (which resulted in three blue portions and two gold portions) under the specialty device. The pin on badge of rank conformed to the unified system shared with other services, a gold bar with a blue square in the center and a blue rectangle at each end (2).

These insignias are still in use (3).

Chief Warrant Officer 3

Chief Warrant Officer 3 was created by the "Warrant Officer Act of 1954" (1) in pay grade W-3, from the various chief warrant grades.

New insignia was prescribed to be worn as of November 1st. The cuff stripes were to be 1/2 inch wide with two 1/2 inch blue breaks, two inches apart, under a specialty device. On the shoulder boards, the 1/2 inch stripe had breaks 1/2 inch apart (which resulted in three gold portions and two blue portions) under the specialty device. The pin on badge of rank conformed to the unified system shared with other services, a silver bar with two blue rectangles, showing a square of silver in the middle (2).

These insignias are still in use (3).

Chief Warrant Officer 4

Chief Warrant Officer 4 was created by the "Warrant Officer Act of 1954" (1) in pay grade W-4, from the various chief warrant grades.

New insignia was prescribed to be worn as of November 1st. The cuff stripes were to be 1/2 inch wide with one 1/2 inch blue break, under a specialty device. On the shoulder boards, the 1/2 inch stripe one break under the specialty device. The pin on badge of rank conformed to the unified system shared with other services, a silver bar with a blue square in the center and a blue rectangle at each end (2).

These insignias are still in use (3).

Chief Warrant Officer 5

When the W-5 pay grade was created in 1991, the navy choose not to create a rank to fill it.

It wasn't until 2004 that Chief Warrant Officer 5 became a rank of the navy (2).

The insignia that was created was the same as Chief Warrant Officer 4 with a 1/8 inch wide blue stripe running long ways thru the middle to the cuff stripe and shoulder board stripe. The pin on badge of rank is a silver bar with a blue stripe running down the middle (3).

Chief Warrant Officer, Hospital Corps.

Chief Pharmacists became Chief Warrant Officer, Hospital Corps on August 4, 1947 (1) during an expansion of that corps (2).

The insignia of a Chief Pharmacists was continued consisting of a 1/2 inch cuff stripe with blue breaks under a gold caduceus, shoulder boards with one 1/2 inch stripe with one blue break under a gold caduceus and a silver caduceus as a badge of rank (3).

The Career Compensation Act of October 12, 1949 (4) spread medical warrant officers across pay grades W-2, W-3 and W-4.

A standard, chief warrant officers badge of rank was introduced on July 1,1952 (5) consisting of a gold bar with a 1/8 inch blue break across the middle (6).

They became Chief Warrant Officer 2, Chief Warrant Officer 3 and Chief Warrant Officer 4, with the Warrant Officer Act of 1954 (7).

Civil Engineer

Originally Civil Engineers were civilian employees. A law of March 2, 1867 (1) required them to appointed by the President and confirmed by the Senate like officers, but no rank was conferred.

The July 1868 Navy Register lists five Civil Engineers: B.F. Chandler, Charles Hastings, R.G. Packard, Franklin Stratton and W.M. Spear (2).

F.C. Prindle became a Civil Engineer on April 17, 1869 and Packard resigned on April 28th. Calvin Brown was appointed on May 13, 1869 and George Van Clelf was appointed on January 27, 1870 and dropped on March 2, 1871 (3). Norman Stratton was appointed on December 27, 1870 (4)

On March 3, 1871 (5) stated "that the President of the United States is hereby authorized, in his discretion, to determine and fix the relative rank of civil engineers". President Grant's discretion was to do nothing.

Even without relative rank the appointments continued. Spear died on July 26, 1873 and Peter Assserson was appointed on March 6, 1874. Mordecai Endicott came along on July 13, 1874, Brownell Granger the next day and Anecito Menocal the day after that. Prindle resigned on January 1, 1876 and Norman Stratton moved to the retired list on March 2nd. Grainger was removed on January 22, 1877 and U.S.G. White was appointed the same day. Franklin Stratton died on July 18, 1879 and H. Smith Craven was appointed on march 12th. Franklin C. Prindle was appointed on July 22, 1879. It is not clear if this is the same F.C. Prindle who was a civil engineer from 1869 to 1876 (6).

Finally on February 24, 1881 (7) Civil Engineers were granted relative rank. One (Asserson) was a relative Captain, Two (Endicott and Menocal) were relative Commanders, Three (White, Craven and Prindle) were Relative Lieutenant Commanders. Four new appointments were made with the relative rank of Lieutenant (T.C. McCollum, Chris Wolcott, Frank Maxson and Robert Peary) (8).

Uniforms were prescribed on August 24, 1881. Civil Engineers were to wear the uniform of their relative rank with old english letters "C.E." as a corps device. The cloth in around the cuff stripes was light blue. Breaking with the norm, the background of the shoulder straps was also to be light blue. This is the only instance when navy shoulder straps had anything other than a dark blue background (9). The backgrounds were dark blue with the 1883 uniform regulations (10).

Endicott became the Chief of the Bureau of Yards and Docks with the Relative rank of Commodore on April 4, 1898 (11).

Ranks stopped being relative with a law of March 3, 1899. The same law abolished the rank of Commodore and Endicott became a Rear Admiral (12).

A corps device of two sets of two long skinny oak leafs, each pair meeting at a point covered with an acorn, thus having the appearance of crossed dividers, was created in 1905 (13).

The use of staff titles ended in 1918 (14) and was formally abolished on August 7, 1947 (15).

Clerk

The origin of Clerk as a rank of the Navy is a bit of a mystery. Uniforms were first prescribed for Clerks in regulations of 1830 (1). There was a petty officer's rating of Captain's Clerk, that was created by the 1794 (2) and 1797 (3) laws creating the navy. It is possible that these are the clerks the uniforms were for. The navy also employed many civilian clerks on shore. It is the generic nature of the title that make tracing it difficult.

Whatever there origins the uniforms prescribed for Clerks in 1830 were "Coats of plain blue cloth, single-breasted, rolling collar, and made according to the prevailing fashion for the citizens of the time, with six Navy buttons on each breast, one on each hip, and one on the bottom of the skirts" (4). "according to the prevailing fashion of the day" may have meant a frock coat instead of the regular tail coat. Frock coats were popular by 1830 (5) and the army had adopted them the year before (6).

Captain's Clerk ended as a rating in 1835 (7). A law of March 3rd of that year (8) set the pay of naval officers. It listed Clerks of yards, Clerks to commandants of yards and Clerks to commanders of squadrons, fleets and vessels.

The Clerks are listed after Midshipmen and before Boatswains, Gunners, Carpenters and Sailmakers. However no law could be found making Clerks into officers and they do not appear in the Navy Register. Navy regulations from 1841 state that Clerks would have the "assimilated" rank of a Midshipman (9). This was the navy's first attempt at relating line and staff ranks and this is not the only oddity (10).

The 1841 uniform regulations prescribe at coat "To be of dark blue cloth, lined with the same, double breasted, rolling collar, seven navy buttons on each breast, one on each hip, and one at the bottom of the folds of each skirt." Blue or white trousers and plain blue caps were also prescribed (11).

Pursers were allowed Clerks by a law of August 26, 1842 (12).

The 1852 uniform regulations allow a dress tail coat and undress frock coat both single breasted with seven buttons on the dress coat and six on the frock coat. They were worn with blue or white trousers and a blue visored cap with an empty wreath on the front in gold (13).

Their status as relative Midshipmen was confirmed by the order of March 13, 1863 (14). This lead to the uniform regulations of 1864 prescribing the same double breasted frock coat as all other officers, with the smaller buttons worn by Midshipmen, and an empty cap wreath (15).

In 1867 shoulder straps were authorized. They were be a strip of gold lace with a silver letter "C" in the center, the same as worn by Carpenters. The straps were eliminated by the uniform regulations of 1869. At the same time a gold unfouled anchor was added to the cap in place of the wreath (16).

A law of May 4, 1878 eliminated Clerks for Admirals, commanders of squadrons and commanders of vessels as of July 1st (17). This left only clerks at navy yards and stations, and clerks to Paymasters, as Pursers were now known.

The uniform regulations beginning in 1883 reflect this. Warrant officers uniforms are prescribed with the insignia of the Pay Corps, an oak sprig, worn in gold on the collar (18). The insignia is prescribed for "Pay Clerks" while the descriptions of uniform combinations refer to "Clerks". This may or may not mean that Clerks at navy yards and stations wore the same uniforms without insignia. The best guess would be not, the regulations could be more specific, but there is no way to be sure. They were eliminated on March 3, 1909 (19), leaving just paymaster's clerks.

Finally on March 3, 1915 paymaster's clerks officially became warrant officers with the rank of Pay Clerk (20).

Coal Heaver

Coal Heaver was a non rated title for men who shoveled coal into boilers, usually known a stokers on railroads. It was created by law with the other engineering ranks and rates on August 31, 1842 (1).

They wore the same uniforms as other non rated sailors until stripes were prescribed in 1866. One stripe was worn around the collar and cuffs of the jumper (2). The stripe was removed from the collar in 1869 (3).

When the rates were organized into pay grades in 1885, Coal Heavers were placed in the Seaman Third Class grade (4).

The 1886 regulations added a red watch mark to the jumpers (5).

The title was changed to Coal Passer in 1893 (6).

Coal Passer

Coal Heavers became Coal Passers in 1893 (1), still in the Seaman Third Class pay grade (2).

They inherited the one stripe and red watch mark from Coal Heavers.

The watch mark became a red branch mark on the left side in 1912 (3).

The title was Fireman Third Class in 1917 (4).

Command Master Chief Petty Officer

The rate of Command Master Chief Petty Officer was born in 1977 as a senior enlisted advisor in smaller units(1).

Like other master chiefs it is in pay grade E-9.

The insignia, if not in begun 1977 by the 1981 uniform regulations, is the same as other master chiefs with a silver star replacing the specialty mark on the rating badge (2).

Commander

The rank of Commander originated in the British Royal Navy as Master and Commander. It was used for officers commanding ships that were small enough that the commanding officer also did duty as the Sailing Master, hence "master and commander". It was also used for commanders of ships to large for Lieutenants to command, but to small for a Captain (1). The title gave its name to a 1969 novel by Patrick O'Brian, which lead to a 2003 film starring Russell Crowe. The Royal Navy shortened the title of Commander in 1794 (2).

When such a rank was needed in the U.S. Navy, the title of Master Commandant was used until a law of March 3, 1877 stated "That from and after the passage of this act all " masters commandant" in the navy shall be taken to be and shall be called "commanders, "(3).

Commanders inherited the Master Commandant's uniform of 1830 that was the same a s Captains but with three buttons on the cuff and pockets. A plain gold epaulet was worn on both shoulders. When the epaulets was not worn, a strip of gold lace was worn on both shoulder as a shoulder strap (4).

The style of the uniform was changed in 1841, but none of the details such as the buttons, epaulets and shoulder straps (5).

In 1845 a silver anchor was added to the epaulets (6) It is possible that the shoulder straps became an empty rectangle of narrow gold embroidery with a blue center at this point, but this is not clear. The straps of that design with a gold anchor was placed in the center in 1848 (7).

The 1852 uniform regulations moved the three buttons on the cuff from horizontal to vertical and between them was two strips of 3/4 inch gold lace with another piece running perpendicular from the bottom strip to the end of the cuff. Epaulets had 1/2 inch wide bullion and sliver crossed anchors in the frog. Shoulder straps were now full sized, 1/4 inch border 4 by 1 3/8 inches, with the silver crossed anchors in the center (8).

On July 31, 1862, the buttons and the vertical strip of lace were removed from the cuffs and a third stripe, 1/4 inch wide, was placed between the to 3/4 inch stripes. The shoulder straps were changed to a silver oak leaf at each end and a silver anchor in the center. The same insignia was worn in the frog of the epaulets (9).

On May 23, 1863 all line officers were ordered to wear a gold star above their cuff stripes. It is possible that the stripes were changed at the same time, but were certainly changed by the new uniform regulations of January 28, 1864 (10).

The 1864 regulations prescribed five 1/4 inch stripes, the middle three 1/4 inch apart and a 1/2 inch space between them and the top and bottom stripes, making a group of three stripes in the center with single stripes above and below (11). Epaulets were suspended (12) and shoulder straps were unchanged except for a smaller anchor (13). A silver oak leaf was also worn on the collar of the overcoat (14).

In January of 1865 a new service dress coat was introduced. It could carry cuff stripes or shoulder straps, or the oak leaf could be worn on the collar (15).

With the Civil War over, new uniform regulations were issued on December 1, 1866. Epaulets returned and the silver oak leaf was worn at either end of the frog with a silver anchor in the middle, the same arrangement was used in the shoulder straps. The oak leaf with an anchor behind it was also worn on the collar of the sack coat and over coat (16).

On March 11, 1869 (17) the cuff stripes for Commanders were changed to two 1/2 inch stripes with one 1/4 inch stripe between them all below the line star. This only lasted until May 27th when the they were changed to three 1/2 inch stripes (18). Three Stripes has denoted a Commander ever since.

The service dress coat was replaced in 1877. The oak leaf, but not the anchor, was worn on each side of the standing collar (19).

The 1883 uniform regulations returned the anchor behind the oak leaf on the service coat collar (20).

In 1899 the shoulder straps on the white coat were replaced with shoulder boards. The boards for Commanders matched the cuffs, four stripes and a line star (21).

Shoulder straps make their last appearance in regulations in 1905 (22) and may have been abolished with the next regulations in 1913 or sometime in between.

The January 13, 1913 regulations did abolish shoulder boards, replacing them with a white cloth shoulder loop with a metal oak leaf and anchor (23). This was undone on June 24th and shoulder boards returned (24).

Epaulets were also changed in 1913. The oak leaf was now alone in the frog and a single anchor was worn on the strap (25).

The use of epaulets was suspended in 1917 (26).

The end of the use of staff titles in November 1918 led to equivalent staff Commanders wearing the corps device in place of the line star on the cuffs and superimposed on the anchor on the blue service coat collar and above the stripes on the shoulder boards. The collar insignia disappeared when the 1877 service coat was replaced in 1919 (27).

Use of epaulets resumed with the 1922 uniform regulations, the line anchor was now worn on the strap by all officers, with the corps device for staff officers superimposed over it (28).

The silver oak leaf began to be used as a pin on badge of rank in 1931 (29).

Use of epaulets was suspended for World War II and never unsuspended (30).

The Career Compensation Act of October 12, 1949 (31) placed the rank of Commander in pay grade O-5.

The April 2010 uniform regulations descried the insignia for Commanders as:

<u>Sleeve Stripes</u> - “Commander. Wear three 1/2 inch stripes.” (32).

The History of American Ranks and Rank Insignia

Shoulder Boards - "Officers below Flag Grade. The surface is black cloth. Gold lace stripes, the same width, number, and spacing, specified for stripes on sleeves of the blue coat, designate rank. The first stripe starts 1/4 inch... from the widest end. Line and staff corps devices replicate sleeve insignia and are placed as far from the stripes as specified for devices on sleeves of blue coats." (33).

Metal Grade Insignia -. (the silver oak leaf is shown in illustration).

Collar grade insignia replicates metal shoulder insignia (34)

The leafs worn by navy Commanders are quite different from those worn by army Lieutenant Colonels. The navy style leafs have more pointed pedals with veins embossed on them.

Commodore

Commodore has one of the strangest histories of any rank. Long before it was a rank it was a courtesy title used by the navy's senior captains. The Continental Navy's original commander Esek Hopkins, Captains Commanding Squadrons and Flag Officers were all addressed as "Commodore". The title comes from the Dutch rank of comendador. (1).

As a rank in the United States Navy it began on July 16, 1862 (2) when the navy's rank structure was overhauled at the beginning of the Civil War.

The insignia prescribed was cuff stripes of three 3/4 inch stripes alternating with two 1/4 inch stripes. The epaulets were the same as had been used by Captains since 1852, with an eagle device in the frog and a star on the strap (Captains now used just the eagle device). Shoulder straps held a silver star at one end and a silver anchor at the other (3).

On May 23, 1863 all line officers were ordered to wear a gold star above their cuff stripes. It is possible that the stripes were changed at the same time, but were certainly changed by the new uniform regulations of January 28, 1864 (4).

The 1864 regulations prescribed shoulder straps with a silver star directly on top of a gold anchor. There were seven cuff stripes, each 1/4 inch wide and 1/4 inch apart except the space between the 3rd and 4th rows and the 4th and 5th rows that was 1/2 inch, making two groups of three stripes with a single stripe between, all under a line star. The silver star was worn on the collar of the overcoat. Epaulets were not to be worn for the rest of the war (5).

The 1865 service coat could have the star on the collar (6).

The 1866 uniform regulations moved the anchor from under the star. A silver anchor was now worn on either side of the star on shoulder straps and the newly returned epaulets. The seven cuff stripes were traded in for one, two inches wide. The collar of the service coat carried the star with an anchor behind it (7).

The new service coats of 1877 carried only the star on the standing collar (8), until 1883 when the anchor returned (9).

The Naval Personnel Act of March 3, 1899 (10) listed the officers rank of the navy and how many men were allowed in each rank. It called for 18 Rear Admirals, 70 Captains, 112 Commanders, 170 Lieutenant Commanders, 300 Lieutenants, and 350 Lieutenants (Junior Grade) and Ensigns. Commodores are not mentioned but the junior nine Rear Admirals were to receive "the same pay and allowance as are now allowed a brigadier-general in the Army". This created the concept of a "Rear Admiral Lower Half". The reason for this appears to have been american Commodores were not being treated as flag officers by foreign navies (11). By making all 18 officers above the rank of Captain into admirals, they would all be treated with the respect they, and their egos, thought they deserved.

Did this law abolish the rank of Commodore or stop it's use? That would be an open question if Admiral Frederick Rodgers hadn't entered the neighborhood. In 1902 he sued the navy over a pay dispute. The case made it to the Supreme Court, and in their decision they ruled that the law had abolished the rank of Commodore (12).

The navy had no rank between Captain and Rear Admiral until April 9, 1943 (13). The navy had requested the rank be restored for use in intermediate size commands not large enough for an admiral but to big for a Captain. It was also better in joint operations with the army to have an officer equal to a Brigadier General (14). The appointments were only temporary and the rank expired at the end of the war.

For insignia the single two inch cuff stripe returned, along with the single silver star as a pin on badge of rank. Shoulder boards carried an anchor at the top with a star below it (15).

All of the temporary wartime Commodores were out of the navy by 1950 (16).

The rank returned one more time. On December 12, 1980 (17), an odd sounding rank of "Commodore Admiral" was added to the list of navy ranks in the O-7 pay grade between Captain and Rear Admiral. The title was changed to just Commodore on December 1, 1981 (18), and to Rear Admiral (lower half) on November 8, 1985 (19).

Whatever they were called, after 1981 the officers of this rank wore the one stripe/ one star insignia (20).

Commodore Admiral

Commodore Admiral was the title used in the O-7 pay grade from a law of December 12, 1980 (1) to a law of December 1, 1981 (2), when the title became Commodore.

The insignia was one two inch cuff stripe and one silver star on the shoulder boards and as a badge of rank (3).

Constructionman

The rate of Constructionman was created in 1948 from Firemen First Class that were assigned to construction duties (1). Originally non rated men in the construction group were to continue to be Firemen, but by August of 1948 it had been decided to create a rate of Constructionman (2)

It continued the Fireman First Class position in pay grade five. Grade five became grade E-3 with The Career Compensation Act of October 12, 1949 (3).

It was given a group rate mark of three light blue hash marks (4).

In 2008 a pin on badge of rank consisting of three silver metal hash marks was introduced on the shirt collar of the navy service uniform (5).

Constructionman Apprentice

The rate of Constructionman Apprentice was created in late 1948 from Firemen Second Class and Seamen Second Class that were assigned to construction duties (1). Originally non rated men in the construction group were to continue to be Firemen Apprentice, but by November of 1948 it had been decided to create a rate of Constructionman Apprentice (2)

It continued the Seaman and Fireman Second Class position in pay grade five. Grade five became grade E-3 with The Career Compensation Act of October 12, 1949 (3).

It was given a group rate mark of two light blue hash marks (4).

In 2008 a pin on badge of rank consisting of two silver metal hash marks was introduced on the shirt collar of the navy service uniform (5).

Constructionman Recruit

Constructionman Recruit was added to the Construction Group in late 1948, for use with special recruiting programs (1).

It was placed in grade seven until The Career Compensation Act of October 12, 1949 made grade seven into grade E-1 (2)

They were to wear one light blue hash mark (3) until 1975, when they would be without insignia (4).

Cook to Commander in Chief

Cook to Commander-in-Chief was one of the rates that Officer's Cook was split into in 1864 (1).

Officer's cooks had been considered petty officers as of the 1841 regulations, but are not listed, as Officer's Cooks or any of the titles it was divided into, on the list of petty officer rates in the regulations of 1865 (3). Their status was clarified when the rates were organized in 1885. Stewards, Cooks (not Ship's Cooks) and Attendants were made into a special category that were not petty officers (4).

There is also no information on uniforms or insignia before 1886. At that time they were to wear single breasted sack coats of blue with black buttons or a similar white coat with white buttons, matching trousers and a blue visored cap or white canvas hat (5). The canvas hat was replaced with a white cap by 1897 (6), and the coats became double breasted between the 1897 and 1905 (7) regulations.

In 1912 a white/blue crescent was added as a distinguishing mark (8).

Cooks to Commander-in-Chief were abolished in 1921 (9).

Cook to Navy yard Commandant

The Rate of Cook to Commandant of a Navy Yard was created in 1883 (1).

Like other steward and cooks they were not petty officers. Their status was clarified when the rates were organized in 1885. Stewards, Cooks (not Ship's Cooks) and Attendants were made into a special category that were not petty officers (2).

There is also no information on uniforms or insignia before 1886. At that time they were to wear single breasted sack coats of blue with black buttons or a similar white coat with white buttons, matching trousers and a blue visored cap or white canvas hat (3). The canvas hat was replaced with a white cap by 1897 (4), and the coats became double breasted between the 1897 and 1905 (5) regulations.

In 1912 a white/blue crescent was added as a distinguishing mark (6).

Cooks to Commandant of a Navy Yard were abolished in 1921 (7).

Dental Surgeon

Dental Surgeons were added to the navy on March 4, 1913 (1).

It appears that the only Dental Surgeon to hold the rank before the use of staff titles was stopped in November of 1918 was Richard Grady the dentist at the Naval Academy (2).

Grady was a Dental Surgeon with rank of Lieutenant (Junior Grade) with the March 4th law. (3), and was made a Lieutenant Commander on July 1, 1918 (4). He was probably a Lieutenant in between the dates have proved unavailable.

He was to have worn the uniform of his rank with orange cloth around the stripes (5) and a corps device of a gold oak leaf with silver acorns on either side of the stem (6).

Dentalman

The rate of Dentalman was created on April 2, 1948 from Hospital Apprentices First Class with dental like duties (1).

It continued the Hospital Apprentices First Class position in pay grade five. Grade five became grade E-3 with The Career Compensation Act of October 12, 1949 (2).

It was given a group rate mark of three white/blue hash marks under a caduceus with a "D" on it, the specialty mark of a petty officer rated as a Dental Technician (3).

In 2008 a pin on badge of rank consisting of three silver metal hash marks was introduced on the shirt collar of the navy service uniform (4).

The Dental Technician rating was merged with the rating of Hospital Corpsman in 2005 (5), but it appears non rated Dentalmen continued. It is still on the navy's web site listing the non rated titles (6), and is in the April 2011 uniform regulations.

Article 4222-3e of the April 2011 uniform regulations states "Hospitalman, Dentalman and Apprentices. Hospital men, dentalmen and apprentices wear white stripes and specialty marks on blue uniform and navy blue stripes and specialty marks on white uniforms." The specialty mark for a Dental Technician is still in the regulations as well with a note that it was disestablished (7).

Dentalman Apprentice

The rate of Dentalman Apprentice was created on April 2, 1948 from Hospital Apprentices Second Class with dental like duties (1).

It continued the Hospital Apprentices Second Class position in pay grade five. Grade five became grade E-3 with The Career Compensation Act of October 12, 1949 (2).

It was given a group rate mark of two white/blue hash marks under a caduceus with a "D" on it, the specialty mark of a petty officer rated as a Dental Technician (3).

In 2008 a pin on badge of rank consisting of two silver metal hash marks was introduced on the shirt collar of the navy service uniform (4).

The Dental Technician rating was merged with the rating of Hospital Corpsman in 2005 (5), but it appears non rated Dentalmen continued. It is still on the navy's web site listing the non rated titles (6), and is in the April 2011 uniform regulations.

Article 4222-3e of the April 2011 uniform regulations states "Hospitalman, Dentalman and Apprentices. Hospital men, dentalmen and apprentices wear white stripes and specialty marks on blue uniform and navy blue stripes and specialty marks on white uniforms." The specialty mark for a Dental Technician is still in the regulations as well with a note that it was disestablished (7).

Dentalman Recruit

Dentalman Recruit was added in late 1948, for use with special recruiting programs (1).

It was placed in grade seven until The Career Compensation Act of October 12, 1949 made grade seven into grade E-1 (2)

They were to wear one white/blue hash marks under a caduceus with a "D" on it, the specialty mark of a petty officer rated as a Dental Technician (3) until 1975, when they would wear only the caduceus and "D" (4).

The Dental Technician rating was merged with the rating of Hospital Corpsman in 2005 (4), but it appears non rated Dentalmen continued. It is still on the navy's web site listing the non rated titles (5), and is in the April 2011 uniform regulations.

Article 4222-3e of the April 2011 uniform regulations states "Hospitalman, Dentalman and Apprentices. Hospital men, dentalmen and apprentices wear white stripes and specialty marks on blue uniform and navy blue stripes and specialty marks on white uniforms." The specialty mark for a Dental Technician is still in the regulations as well with a note that it was disestablished (6).

Electrician

The warrant rank of Electrician were created on March 4, 1925 (1). Previously Gunners had been assigned to electrical duties. The petty officers rating of Electrician had been changed to Electrician's Mate in 1921 (2).

The lace worn on the cuffs was 1/4 inch wide gold with 1/2 inch long blue breaks every 2 inches. The device of an electrician, a globe, as in picture of the earth with longitude and latitude lines, placed on the sleeve above the stripes. Shoulder boards showed the 1/4 inch lace with a single 1/2 inch break, under the device (3).

Black sleeve stripes were used on khaki and green coats starting in 1925. The format used by warrant officers is not clear. It is possible that a solid stripe was used (4). The black stripes were removed from the khaki coat in 1941 (5) and stripes with green breaks were definitely prescribed for warrant officers in 1944 (6).

A gold globe was used as the Electrician's pin on badge of rank starting in 1931.

Why a globe to represent electricians? Legend has it the that when the petty officer's rating was created in 1898, the orders were sent to the manufactures for rating badges with a globe, as in light bulb, as the specialty mark. When they arrived with a actual globe, the design was liked so well it was decided to keep it (7).

The Career Compensation Act of October 12, 1949 (8) placed Electricians in pay grade W-1.

A standard, warrant officers badge of rank was introduced on July 1,1952 (9) consisting of a gold bar with a 1/16 inch blue break across the middle (10).

Electricians became Warrant Officer 1, with the Warrant Officer Act of 1954 (11).

Engineer-in-Chief

The position of Engineer-in-Chief was created on August 21,1842 along with the other engineering grades. The law stated "And be it further enacted, That the Secretary of the Navy shall appoint a skillful and scientific engineer in chief, who shall receive for his services the sum of three thousand dollars per annum, and shall perform such duties as the Secretary of the Navy shall require of him touching that branch of the service."(1).

The position went to Gilbert Thompson who was not "skillful and scientific". He was not even an engineer, he was a lawyer and politician. Thompson had come to the aid of the engineers on naval vessels to get the 1842 law passed to make them official naval officers after an an engineer had been appointed for his political connections not his engineering skills. Much to the surprise of the serving engineers, Thompson himself was then made Engineer-in-Chief through politics and not engineering (2).

In the spring of 1843 Thompson ordered some modifications to the steamer Missouri.
When they didn't work, the Missouri's Chief Engineer Charles Haswell was selected to take the fall for Thompson's incompetence. Haswell had been the navy's first steam engineer, supervising the construction and installation of the engines for the Fulton in 1836. Haswell was suspended from duty and went off to design engines for revenue cutters. By October of 1844 the navy had figured out that Thompson was incompetent and replaced him with Haswell on October 3rd (3).

Haswell was demoted back to Chief Engineer over a dispute on the design of the engines on the steamer San Jancinto and was replaced by Charles Stuart on December 1, 1850 (4). Stuart resigned on June 30, 1853 and was replaced by Chief Engineer Daniel Martin on October 18th (5). Martin was relieved on October 17, 1857 and replaced by Chief Engineer Samuel Archbold (6). After Archbold resigned on March 25, 1861 Chief Engineer Benjamin Isherwood took Office (7).

Isherwood became the Chief of the Bureau of Steam Engineering with Relative Rank of Commodore when it was created on July 5, 1862 (8), it is not clear whether this replaced the title of Engineer-in-Chief or not. Engineer-in-chief appears on the pay table in the January 1864 navy register (9) but not in the January 1865 register (9).

Thompson and Stuart appear to have been civilians but Haswell, Martin, Archbold and Isherwood were Chief Engineers and would have worn the uniform of that rank, such as it was.

Congress changed the title of the Chief of the Bureau of Steam Engineering back to Engineer-in-Chief on March 3, 1871 (11). This gave him the relative rank of Commodore.

Isherwood's successor James King was the first to hold this new position (12).

King would have worn the uniform of a Commodore with red piping the cuff stripe and crossed oak branches as a corps device (13).

King was replaced by William Wood on March 20, 1873, who served until March 3, 1877 (14). His replacement was William Shock who retired on June 15, 1883 (15). Charles Loring took over on January 18, 1884, and was replaced by George Melville on August 7, 1887 (16).

Both engineering ranks and commodores were abolished on March 3, 1899 (17), leaving Melville a Rear Admiral.

Ensign

Historically, an Ensign is the lowest ranking officer in an infantry regiment. It became a navy rank on July 16, 1862, ranking below Master (1). The rank hadn't been used by the army since 1814 (2) and there is no information as to why it was suddenly being used in the navy.

For insignia Ensigns were given one 1/4 inch wide cuff stripe and shoulder straps and epaulet frogs with an anchor alone (3). On the epaulets the anchor ran vertically.

The gold star of a line officer was added above the cuff stripe on May 23, 1863 (4).

The 1864 uniform regulations continued the 1/4 inch stripe and the shoulder strap with an anchor but no badge of rank at the ends. The overcoat collar carried "a small gold cord on the front edge" (5).

On the collar of the 1865 service coat the anchor was worn alone (6).

In 1866 epaulets returned with the anchor alone in the frog (7), probably horizontal this time.

A General Order of March 11, 1869 prohibited the use of epaulets and shoulder straps by officers below the rank of Lieutenant (8). As a replacement, shoulder knots were prescribed on April 27th (9). The order and subsequent regulations describe these knots as "per pattern", which is no help in figuring out what they looked like. There is, however an illustration in the 1869 regulations (10). It shows a twisted knot made of two gold cords, terminating in a large oval pad, of dark blue, over the shoulder. In the center of the pad is a gold anchor with a silver bar directly on top of it. The use of a bar goes against every system used by the navy up to that time, and for a considerable time after, but this is all the information we have.

The new service coat of 1877 did not use corps devices on the collar, leaving the collar for an Ensign blank (11).

In June of 1881 shoulder straps returned with the anchor in the center and nothing at either end, the shoulder knot now only replaced the epaulet. In August the cuff stripe was increased to 1/2 inch (12).

The 1883 uniform regulations replaced the shoulder knots with epaulets with the silver fouled anchor alone on the frog. Corps devices were also added to the blue service coat, allowing Ensigns to wear a silver anchor by itself (13).

The 1/2 inch stripe below the line star was used on the shoulder boards in 1899 (14) and the silver anchor by itself was used on the shoulder loops during the period from January to June of 1913 when shoulder boards had been abolished (15).

1913, probably, also saw the end of shoulder straps.

The use of epaulets was suspended in 1917 (16).

The end of the use of staff titles in November 1918 led to equivalent staff Ensigns wearing the corps device in place of the line star on the cuffs and superimposed on the anchor on the blue service coat collar and above the stripes on the shoulder boards. The collar insignia disappeared when the 1877 service coat was replaced in 1919 (17).

Use of epaulets resumed with the 1922 uniform regulations, the line anchor was now worn on the strap by all officers, with the corps device for staff officers superimposed over it and for the first time Ensigns wore a badge of rank in the frog, a gold bar (18).

The gold bar began to be used as a pin on badge of rank in 1931 (19).

Use of epaulets was suspended for World War II and never unsuspended (20).

The Career Compensation Act of October 12, 1949 (21) placed the rank of Ensign in pay grade O-1.

The April 2010 uniform regulations descried the insignia for full Admirals as:

Sleeve Stripes - "Ensign. Wear one 1/2 inch stripe." (22).

Shoulder Boards - "Officers below Flag Grade. The surface is black cloth. Gold lace stripes, the same width, number, and spacing, specified for stripes on sleeves of the blue coat, designate rank. The first stripe starts... (1/2 inch for ensigns) from the widest end. Line and staff corps devices replicate sleeve insignia and are placed as far from the stripes as specified for devices on sleeves of blue coats." (23).

Metal Grade Insignia -. (the gold bar is shown in illustration).

Collar grade insignia replicates metal shoulder insignia (24)

The bars worn by navy Ensigns are quite different from those worn by army Second Lieutenants. The navy style bars are flatter and have no beveled edge.

Ensign Junior Grade

On March 3, 1883 a law was passed that the navy would consist of "ninety-one midshipmen, the title of which grade is hereby changed to that of ensign, and the midshipman now on the list shall constitute a junior grade of, and be commissioned as, ensign having the same rank and pay as now provided by law for midshipmen, but promotions to and from said grade shall be under the same regulations and requirements as now provided by law for promotion to and from the grade of midshipmen,"(1).

From 1870 to 1882 the title of the officers in training at the Naval Academy had been "Cadet Midshipman" (2), and after 1882 "Naval Cadets" (3), Midshipman had been a post graduate title. Ensign Junior Grade was an attempt to give them something that sounded better.

They were to wear Ensign's uniforms with a 1/4 inch cuff stripe instead of 1/2 inch (4), and the corps device, that was worn alone because of an ensigns lack of a badge of rank, was to be an unfouled anchor instead of the fouled anchor used by all other line officers (5).

The rank lasted 481 days. On June 26, 1884 congress passed this law:

"Be it enacted by the Senate and House of Representatives of the United States of America in Congress assembled, That from and after the passage of this act all graduates of the Naval Academy who are assigned to the line of the Navy, on the successful completion of the six years course, shall be commissioned ensigns in the Navy.

SEC. 2. That the grade of junior ensign in the Navy is hereby abolished and the junior ensigns now on the list shall be commissioned ensigns in the Navy: Provided, That nothing in this act shall be so construed as to increase the number of officers in the Navy now allowed by law.

SEC. 3. That all acts and parts of acts inconsistent with the provisions of this act be and the same are hereby repealed." (6).

The "six years course" refers to four years at the academy and two years at sea.

Fireman

Fireman is the non rated title for engineering sailors. It was created by statute on August 31, 1842 (1), and was split into Fireman First Class and Fireman Second Class in 1847 (2).

Firemen would have worn the standard enlisted uniform. There were no special insignia for non rated sailors during that period.

Fireman First Class was changed back to Fireman on April 2, 1948 (3).

It continued the Fireman First Class position in pay grade five. Grade five became grade E-3 with The Career Compensation Act of October 12, 1949 (4).

It was given a group rate mark of three red hash marks (5).

In 2008 a pin on badge of rank consisting of three silver metal hash marks was introduced on the shirt collar of the navy service uniform (6).

Fireman Apprentice

Fireman Second Class became Fireman Apprentice on April 2, 1948 (1).

It continued the Fireman Second Class position in pay grade six. Grade Six became grade E-2 with The Career Compensation Act of October 12, 1949 (2).

It was given a group rate mark of two red hash marks (3).

In 2008 a pin on badge of rank consisting of two silver metal hash marks was introduced on the shirt collar of the navy service uniform (4).

Fireman First Class

Firemen were split into first and second classes in 1847 (1).

They wore the same uniform as all non rated sailors until 1866 when they were allowed three stripes on the cuffs, and unitl 1869 collars, of the jumpers. The 1866 regulations also allowed Firemen First Class to wear the staff petty officer's device, an eagle on an anchor, on the left sleeve (2).

When enlisted rates were split into pay grades in 1885, Firemen First Class was placed in the Seaman First Class grade (3).

With the 1886 uniform regulations they no longer wore the petty officer's device but added a red watch mark (4), which became a red branch mark on the left side in 1912 (5).

When enlisted rates were placed in numbered pay grades on June 10, 1922 (6), Firemen First Class were not placed in grade five with Seamen First Class but grade four with Petty Officers Third Class (7). The rate was moved down to grade five on January 1, 1944 (8).

Firemen First Class were converted into Firemen on April 2, 1948 (9).

Fireman Recruit

Fireman Recruit was added in late 1948, for use with special recruiting programs (1).

It was placed in grade seven until The Career Compensation Act of October 12, 1949 made grade seven into grade E-1 (2)

They were to wear one red hash mark (3) until 1975, when they would be without insignia (4).

Fireman Second Class

Firemen were split into first and second classes in 1847 (1).

They wore the same uniform as all non rated sailors until 1866 when they were allowed two stripes on the cuffs, and unitl 1869 collars, of the jumpers (2).

When enlisted rates were split into pay grades in 1885, Firemen Second Class was placed in the Seaman Second Class grade (3).

With the 1886 a red watch mark was added (4), which became a red branch mark on the left side in 1912 (5).

When enlisted rates were placed in numbered pay grades on June 10, 1922 (6), Firemen Second Class were not placed in grade six with Seamen Second Class but grade five with Seaman First Class (7). The rate was moved down to grade six on January 1, 1944 (8).

Firemen Second Class were converted into Fireman Apprentices on April 2, 1948 (9).

Fireman Third Class

Coal Passers became Firemen Third Class in 1917 (1) and maintained Coal Passers place in the Seaman Third Class pay grade (2).

The Coal Passers one stripe on the cuffs of the jumper and the red branch mark on the left side was continued.

When a law of June 10, 1922 (3) placed the navy's rates in numbered pay grades the Seaman Third Class grade became grade seven, but Firemen Third Class were placed in grade six, equal to Seamen Second Class (4). The rate was moved down to grade seven on January 1, 1944 (5).

Firemen Third Class were eliminated in 1948 (9).

First Assistant Engineer

Prior to 1842 the people who operated and repaired the engines of steam powered ships were civilian employes.

The first Engineers were appointed on steamship Fulton in 1836 (1).

The Fulton's Captain, Matthew Perry, sought and received from the Secretary of the Navy permission the put his engineers in uniform. For his First Assistant Engineers, Nelson Burt and John Faron, he prescribed a blue, double breasted coat with a rolling collar of black velvet and a silver star on each collar (2).

First Assistant Engineer became an official rank of the navy with a law of August 31, 1842 (3). The law stated that would share in prize money as if they were Lieutenants of Marines. It also allowed the Secretary of the Navy to prescribe a uniform for engineers. This was an odd detail for Congress to get involved with.

Despite the mention of them in law, there is no record of uniforms begin prescribed for engineers before the uniform regulations of 1852 (4), ten years after they became an official part of the navy. It is possible that the uniform from the Fulton was used for all that time, or it is equally possible that civilian clothes were worn. It is also possible that an order for engineer's uniforms has been lost.

Uniforms finally came on March 8, 1852. The dress tail coat was single breasted with one row of nine buttons, three large buttons on the cuff and a standing collar with a corps device of a silver anchor on a gold paddle wheel in an L shaped gold wreath. The undress frock coat was also single breasted and had three medium buttons around the cuff (5).

On January 1, 1853 they were allowed shoulder straps on the frock coat, but probably not the dress coat. They were made from a strip of gold lace 1/2 inch wide and four inches long, outlined in 1/8 inch wide beaded lace (6).

On January 13, 1859 the navy issued a general order granting relative rank to engineers, and First Assistants were to rank 'next after" Lieutenants, meaning with Masters (7). Congress confirmed this order in law on March 3rd (8).

Uniforms were changed to reflect the engineer's new status on February 8, 1861. The collar device was removed and replaced with a 1/2 inch wide border of gold beaded lace. (9). The frock coat, presumably, became double breasted as well.

Cuffs and the use of lace was altered slightly when the lace for line officers was changed in 1862 (10).

The March 13, 1863 realignment of relative rank confirmed First Assistant Engineers as relative Masters (11).

The 1864 uniform regulations prescribed cuff lace according to rank without a line star and shoulder straps with the crossed oak branch device in the center and the gold bars of a Master at each end (12).

The 1866 regulations restored epaulets with same devices in the frog as the shoulder straps (13).

1869 saw red used at the color between the cuff stripes and shoulder knots replacing epaulets and shoulder straps (14). The best information we have on the design of the shoulder knots for staff officers who were relative Masters is a gold bar on each side of the pad and no device in the center (15).

On March 29, 1869 Attorney General Ebenezer Hoar issued a ruling that the navy had exceeded its authority in granting relative rank to certain staff officers during the Civil War (16). First Assistant Engineers reverted to "next after" Lieutenants, which wasn't a big change in their case.

Congress fixed this problem on March 3, 1871 (17) with a law that spread the First Assistant Engineers over the ranks of Lieutenant and Master.

They were to wear the uniforms of those ranks with red cloth in and around the cuff stripes and crossed oak branches as a corps device. Those with the relative rank of Master continued to wear the shoulder knots until they were abolished on October 3, 1871 (18) and epaulets and shoulder straps with bars and crossed oak branches returned.

The rank was title was changed to Passed Assistant Engineer on February 24, 1874 (19).

Flag Officer

A law of January 16, 1857 stated "That captains in command of squadrons shall be denominated flag officers" (1).

This gave a semiofficial title to the navy's various "Commodores" but they were still listed as Captains in the Navy Register (2).

They wore the "Commodore's" insignia as prescribed in the 1852 regulations. Three strips of lace on the cuffs, two stars and eagle and anchor device on the epaulets and the eagle and anchor device between the stars on the shoulder straps (3).

It all ended when Commodore became and official rank of July 16, 1862 (4).

Fleet Admiral

The rank of Fleet Admiral was created on December 14, 1944 (1) to give american naval officers equal rank the British Royal Navy's Admirals of the Fleet (2).

The first appointment went to William Leahy the Chief of Staff to the Commander in Chief, a forerunner of the modern Chairman of the Joint Chiefs of Staff, on December 15th. Earnest King the Chief of Naval Operations was made a Fleet Admiral on December 17th and Chester Nimitz the commander of the Pacific Fleet on December 19th. A fourth appointment was made to William Halsey on December 21, 1945 (3).

The prescribed insignia was cuff stripes of one two inch under four 1/2 inch, all under a line star. Five silver stars joined by their inner points in the shape of a pentagon were worn on the shoulder boards and as a pin on badge of rank (3).

Each appointment was for life (6), however Halsey was moved to the retired list at his own request on March 1, 1947 (7).

King died on June 25, 1956 (8), Lehey on July 20, 1959 (9), Halsey on August 15, 1959 (10) and Nimitz on February 20, 1966 (11), at which point the rank ceased to exist.

It is however still in the navy's uniform regulations as of April of 2011 (12).

Fleet Engineer

Fleet Engineer was the senior engineering officer of a squadron of ships. It was first used, with the relative rank of Captain, with the reorganization of relative ranks on March 13, 1863 (1).

As a relative Captain, the 1864 uniform regulations gave them a Captain's uniform with crossed oak branches as a corps device and no line star. The branches were held in the talons of the eagle on the shoulder straps (2).

As of November 1, 1866 Fleet Engineer became a title held by the Chief Engineer in a squadron with the most seniority as an additional duty assignment (3).

A General Order of August 1, 1877 stated that Fleet Engineers would be appointed by the Navy Department from Chief Engineers with the relative rank of Commander (4).

Fleet/Force Master Chief Petty Officer

Senior enlisted advisors of fleets or forces were known as Master Chief Petty Officers of the Fleet/Force until 1977 when they became Fleet/Force Master Chief Petty Officers (1).

They wear the same insignia as other master chiefs except the two stars above the eagle of the rating badge are gold instead of silver. Another gold star replaces the specialty mark. After their tour is over, a former a Fleet/Force Master Chief wears the specialty mark of his earned rating in gold (2).

Fleet Paymaster

Fleet Paymaster was the senior supply officer of a squadron of ships. It was first used, with the relative rank of Captain, with the reorganization of relative ranks on March 13, 1863 (1).

As a relative Captain, the 1864 uniform regulations gave them a Captain's uniform with oak sprig as a corps device and no line star. The sprig was held in the talons of the eagle on the shoulder straps (2).

As of November 1, 1866 Fleet Paymaster became a title held by the Paymaster in a squadron with the most seniority as an additional duty assignment (3).

A General Order of August 1, 1877 stated that Fleet Paymasters would be appointed by the Navy Department from Pay Inspectors with the relative rank of Commander (4).

Fleet Surgeon

Fleet Surgeon was the senior medical officer of a squadron of ships. It replaced “Surgeon of the Fleet” which had been in use since 1828. It first appears in a law setting the navy’s pay, passed on June 1, 1860 (1).

They would have worn the uniform of a Surgeon.

Reorganization of relative ranks on March 13, 1863 made Fleet Surgeons relative Captains (2)

As a relative Captain, the 1864 uniform regulations gave them a Captain’s uniform with no corps device and no line star. The eagle on the shoulder straps had empty talons (3).

As of November 1, 1866 Fleet Surgeon became a title held by the Surgeon in a squadron with the most seniority as an additional duty assignment.

A General Order of August 1, 1877 stated that Fleet Surgeons would be appointed by the Navy Department from Medical Inspectors with the relative rank of Commander (4).

Gunner

Gunners were the warrant officers in charge of a ships weapons.

They existed in the Continental Navy (1) and were listed among the warrant ranks in both the 1794 (2) and 1796 (3) laws creating the navy.

Uniforms were first prescribed by the 1814 uniform regulations (4). They called for “Short blue coats, with six buttons on the lappels; rolling cape, blue pantaloons, white vests, round hats, with cockade. No side-arms.”

In 1830 a double breasted, dark blue dress coat with lapels buttoned back with eight buttons was prescribed. It had a standing collar with one button on it and slashed sleeves closed with three buttons. The undress rolling collar coatee had the same buttons as the dress coat except the one on the collar (5).

The only coat listed in the 1841 regulations was described as “To be of dark blue cloth, lined with the same, double breasted, seven navy buttons on each breast, slashed sleeves with three small navy buttons on each, two large navy buttons under each pocket flap, one on each hip, and one at the bottom of each skirt”. Blue cloth caps were also called for (6). On April 5, 1849 a large button and a button hole worked in black twist was added to the coat collars. At the same time a 1 1/4 inch wide gold lace band was added around the cap (7).

The 1852 regulations list the warrant officers coats with the descriptions of the officers dress tail coats, but they may have been frock coats. This is by no means clear. They are described as “shall be of Navy blue cloth, lined with the same; rolling collar, double breasted, two rows of large Navy buttons on the breast, eight in each row; pointed pocket flaps, with three large buttons underneath each, showing one half their diameter; three medium size buttons around each cuff and two small ones in each opening; one button behind on each hip, one in the middle of each fold and one in each fold near the bottom of the skirt. On each side of the collar to have one loop of three-quarters wide gold lace to show one inch and a half wide, and four inches long, with a small size Navy button in the point of each loop.” They were worn over blue or white pantaloons, according to season and blue caps with a gold anchor on the front (8).

A band of two 1/2 inch strips of gold lace 1/4 apart, showing blue in between, were added to the caps on February 17, 1853 (9).

The uniforms may have been simplified in 1862 with the removal of the cuff buttons and maybe the collar button and lace, but this is not clear (10).

New uniform regulations of 1864 (11) gave warrant officers the same frock coats and caps as officers. As line officers a star was worn alone above the cuff. Shoulder straps were added consisting of a strip of gold lace 3/4 inches wide by 4 inches long with an old english letter B in silver. Caps were plain except for an empty wreath.

On March 11, 1869 the shoulder straps were replaced with a gold star on the collar of the frock coat (12).

Use of the service dress sack coat by warrant officers is clear but it is authorized by the 1876 regulations with the star on the cuffs but not the collar (13).

They were authorized the new standing collar service coat in October 1878. The star was worn in gold on the cuff and silver on the collar (14).

In 1883 the stars on the collars of both the frock coat and the service coat were replaced with a bursting bomb, in silver for those over 20 years service and gold for those under (15). Silver was reserved for Chief Gunners in 1899.

Shoulder boards were authorized in 1908 with the bursting bomb near the outer end with a silver star on them. The star was added to the devices on the collars in 1913 (16).

It is possible, but not certain, that the bursting bomb (without the star) replaced the star on the cuffs in 1918. It was certainly there on the new service coats of 1919, now above a strip of 1/4 inch gold lace. Shoulder boards of 1919 also carried the 1/4 inch lace and bursting bomb (17).

The 1922 regulations added a 1/2 inch dark blue break every two inches on the cuff stripes and a single 1/2 inch break in the center of the shoulder board stripe (18).

Black sleeve stripes were used on khaki and green coats starting in 1925. The format used by warrant officers is not clear. It is possible that a solid stripe was used (19). The black stripes were removed from the khaki coat in 1941 (20) and stripes with green breaks were definitely prescribed for warrant officers in 1944 (21).

The gold bursting bomb became the Gunner's pin on badge of rank in 1931.

The Career Compensation Act of October 12, 1949 (22) placed Gunners in pay grade W-1.

A standard, warrant officers badge of rank was introduced on July 1,1952 (23) consisting of a gold bar with a 1/16 inch blue break across the middle (24).

Gunner became Warrant Officer 1, with the Warrant Officer Act of 1954 (25).

Hospital Apprentice First Class

Hospital Apprentice First Class was created as a petty officer's rating on June 17, 1898 (1). Despite the title "first class", it was placed in the Petty Officer Third Class pay grade and wore a third class rating badge with a red cross as a specialty mark (2).

When the rating of Pharmacist's Mate was created, by statute, in all four petty officer's grades on August 29, 1916 (3), Hospital Apprentices First Class moved down to the Seaman First Class grade, which became grade five on June 10, 1922 (4).

The wore the three stripes on the cuffs of a seaman first class, no branch mark, and a red cross on the left sleeve as a distinguishing mark (5).

In September of 1944, female Hospital Apprentices First Class were allowed to wear three white/blue hash marks on the upper left sleeve, with the red cross directly above (6).

On April 12, 1948, Hospital Apprentices First Class became Hospitalmen (7).

Hospital Apprentice Second Class

Hospital Apprentice Second Class was created by statute on June 17, 1898 (1). Despite the title "second class", it was placed in the Seaman First Class pay grade and wore three stripes on the cuff of the jumper, a white/blue watch mark and a red cross on the upper sleeve (2). The watch marks were abolished in 1912 (3)

When the rating of Pharmacist's Mate was created, by statute, in all four petty officer's grades on August 29, 1916 (4), Hospital Apprentices First Class moved down to the Seaman Second Class grade, which became grade six on June 10, 1922 (5).

The wore the two stripes on the cuffs of a seaman second class, no branch mark, and a red cross on the left sleeve as a distinguishing mark (6).

In September of 1944, female Hospital Apprentices Second Class were allowed to wear two white/blue hash marks on the upper left sleeve, with the red cross directly above (7).

On April 12, 1948, Hospital Apprentices First Class became Hospitalman Apprentices (8).

Hospital Surgeon

The 1813 uniform regulations have a section for "HOSPITAL SURGEONS, Or Naval Surgeons, acting as such, by order of the Secretary of the Navy." (1). There is also a similar section in the 1820 regulations (2).

There is no special listing for Hospital Surgeons in the Navy Registers of the era, so it appears that Hospital Surgeon was not a separate rank in the Navy as it was in the Army.

Nevertheless Surgeons assigned to hospitals were given fancier uniforms that Surgeons assigned to ships. The 1813 description is: "A Coat of blue cloth, with broad lappels, and lining of the same, nine navy buttons on the lappels; standing collar the same as the coat, three navy buttons below the pockets, and the same number of buttons on the cuffs; two rows of gold lace, not exceeding one quarter of an inch broad, around the upper edge of the cuffs, and around the collar; one laced button hole on each side of the collar, with a navy button. Pantaloons and Vest white, with navy buttons; plain cocked hat, half boots, and small sword. UNDRESS. The same as the full dress, excepting the lace on the cuffs, and instead of a standing collar, a rolling cape edged with gold cord." (3). The 1820 description uses slight differences in wording but describes the exact same uniform (4).

The next regulations in 1830 do not include a section for Hospital Surgeons (5), so this uniform stopped then or sometime in between.

Hospitalman

The rate of Hospitalman was created on April 2, 1948 from Hospital Apprentices First Class (1).

It continued the Hospital Apprentices First Class position in pay grade five. Grade five became grade E-3 with The Career Compensation Act of October 12, 1949 (2).

It was given a group rate mark of three white/blue hash marks under a caduceus (3).

In 2008 a pin on badge of rank consisting of three silver metal hash marks was introduced on the shirt collar of the navy service uniform (4).

Hospitalman Apprentice

The rate of Hospitalman Apprentice was created on April 2, 1948 from Hospital Apprentices Second Class (1).

It continued the Hospital Apprentices Second Class position in pay grade five. Grade five became grade E-3 with The Career Compensation Act of October 12, 1949 (2).

It was given a group rate mark of two white/blue hash marks under a caduceus (3).

In 2008 a pin on badge of rank consisting of two silver metal hash marks was introduced on the shirt collar of the navy service uniform (4).

Hospitalman Recruit

Hospitalman Recruit was added in late 1948, for use with special recruiting programs (1).

It was placed in grade seven until The Career Compensation Act of October 12, 1949 made grade seven into grade E-1 (2)

They were to wear one white/blue hash marks under a caduceus (3) until 1975, when they would wear only the caduceus (4).

Jack of the Dust

A Jack of the dust was in charge getting food stuffs out of storage. The term comes from the British Navy, a “jack” was a sailor who worked in a bakery who was usually covered in flour or “dust” (1).

The title was first used in the U.S. Navy in 1876 (2).

There is no Information on uniforms or insignia until Jacks of the Dust were placed in the Seaman First Class pay grade in 1885 (3).

The 1886 uniform regulations prescribed three stripes on the cuff of the jumper and a white/blue watch mark (4).

Jacks of the Dust were eliminated in 1893 (5).

Lamplighter

Ship’s Lamplighters became Lamplighters in 1885 (1), and they were placed in the Seaman First Class pay grade (2).

The 1886 uniform regulations prescribed three stripes on the cuff of the jumper and a white/blue watch mark (3).

Lamplighters were eliminated in 1893 (4).

Landsman

A Landsman is someone who is not an experienced sailor, hence "landsman" not "seaman".

It was a rate in the British Royal Navy in the 18th century (1) but the beginning of it's use in the american navy is clouded.

It does not appear as a rate on the pay tables of the Continental Navy (2)(3), but there are mentions, in 1781 (4) and 1784 (5), to "the balances now due to the officers, seamen, landsmen and marines, in the Sea Service".

Things are no different with the federal navy. The 1797 law setting the organization of the navy does not include Landsmen, but a law of June 30, 1798 (7) allows the President to vary the number of Landsmen on frigates.

It's first mention on a pay table is in the estimates submitted to congress by the Secretary of the Navy in his report of 1828 (8). It was certainly a rate of the navy by 1838 (9).

They wore standard enlisted uniforms until 1866 when they were given one stripe on the cuff (10), and until 1869 the collar (11), of the jumper.

In 1885 Landsmen were placed in the Seaman Third Class pay grade (12).

The 1886 uniform regulations continued the one stripe on the cuffs and added a white/blue watch mark (13).

Apprentice Seaman replaced Landsman in the seaman branch in 1904, but Landsmen were added to the artificer and special branches (14). Those in the artificer branch might have worn a red watch mark but the 1905 uniform regulations restrict red to Firemen and Coal Passers (15), so white/blue was probably continued.

Watch marks became branch marks in 1912 (16) and under the 1913 uniform regulations men of the artificer branch wore a red mark on the left shoulder (17). It is not clear if Landsmen in the special branch wore a branch mark.

The rate of Landsman was eliminated in 1921 (18).

Lieutenant

The term lieutenant comes from the French for "placeholder" (1). It can be thought of a someone who hold a place or is a tenant instead of or in lieu of. A tenant in lieu of is a lieutenant.

The title may have come to navies from the soldiers placed on merchant ships in the middle ages to create military vessels. It was added to the English Navy in 1580 (2) as a junior officers rank and has been used in navies ever since.

Lieutenants were part of the Continental Navy (3)(4), and wore blue coats faced in red with round cuffs, over blue britches and a red waistcoat. Unlike Captains there was no slash on the cuffs or gold lace on the waistcoat (5).

The rank of Lieutenant was listed in both the 1794 (6) and 1797 (7) laws creating the federal navy.

The 1797 uniform regulations prescribed a blue coat faced with buff, with a buff standing collar and a slash sleeve with three buttons. The coats lapels were only half length with three buttons below them on the right side and three button holes on the left. There was one button and button hole on the collar and a plain gold epaulet on the right shoulder (8).

In 1802, the new regulations called for an all blue coat with three buttons and laced button holes on the cuffs and pocket flaps and nine on each lapel. The epaulet was worn on the right shoulder if the Lieutenant in command of a ship, and on the left if he wasn't. An undress coat without the laced button holes was also authorized (9).

The History of American Ranks and Rank Insignia

The 1813 regulations provided for a strip of gold lace around the collar and above the cuffs, and added a button the collar. The undress coat of 1813 had a rolling collar and was without lace (10).

In 1820 Lieutenants were ordered to wear the same coats as Master Commandants, with were described as "Blue cloth, with broad lappels, and lining of the same, standing collar; trimmed with gold lace as follow: around the standing collar descending around the lappels to the bottom of the coat, the upper part of the cuffs, around the pocket flaps, and down the folds, with one single lace; four buttons on each of the cuffs, and four on each of the pocket flaps, nine on each of the lappels, and one on the standing collar.". It is unusual for Lieutenants to have four buttons on the cuffs and pockets, but that is what is says. The system of epaulets was continued. Lieutenants in command, referred to as "Lieutenants Commandant" wore a plain gold epaulet on the right shoulder. This honor was also extended to First Lieutenants (executive officers) of line battle ships. Other Lieutenants wore their epaulets on the left. Undress coats with rolling collars and no lace were continued (11).

The uniform of 1830 was double breasted with buttoned back lapels cut in a swell, with the coat closing with hooks down the front. Cuffs had three buttons and no other ornament. Collars were outlined in gold rope and covered in oak leaf and acorn embroidery in gold. The undress coat was "according to the prevailing fashion of citizens of the time", which may have meant a frock coat. Whatever it's design it double breasted with a rolling collar and buttons as the dress coat. Plain gold epaulets were worn on the right shoulder by all Lieutenants. When epaulets were not worn a shoulder strap made of 3/4 inch wide gold lace was worn on the right shoulder (12).

An epaulet or a shoulder strap on the right shoulder continued to denote a Lieutenant in the 1841 regulations (13).

On June 1, 1845 Lieutenants were allowed to wear an epaulet on both shoulders (14). This may have lead to a shoulder strap on both shoulders as well, but this is not clear.

In 1852 Lieutenants were given cuff stripes of one 3/4 inch wide stripe in gold, set between the lower two of the now vertical three cuff buttons. Another strip of 3/4 inch lace ran perpendicular to the cuff stripe down to the end of the cuff. Epaulets had 3/8 inch wide bullion and a silver fouled anchor in the frog. The same anchor was worn in the center of the shoulder strap that were now full size with a 1/4 inch border (15).

The restructuring of the navy's officer ranks in 1862 caused changes in insignia. The buttons were removed from the cuff along with the perpendicular stripe. The 3/4 inch stripe was now joined by a 1/4 inch stripe above it. Two gold bars were worn at each end of the shoulder straps and each side of the epaulet frog. The silver anchor of a line officer was worn in the horizontally center of the shoulder strap, and vertically in the center of the epaulet frog (16).

A star was added above the cuff stripes of line officers on May 23, 1863. The stripes may have been changed at that point, or they were changed with the uniform regulations of January 28, 1864 (17). The new stripes were three 1/4 inch stripes. The 1864 regulations also added the two gold bars to the collar of the overcoat. Epaulets were not worn but shoulder straps, with the two gold bars at each end and the silver anchor in the center, were (18).

The bars were also used on the collar of the service coat introduced in 1865 (19).

Epaulets returned in 1866 with the two gold bars and silver anchor, now horizontal, in the frog. The bar and anchor were also worn on the collar of the service coat (20).

The cuff stripes were changed on March 11, 1869 to one 1/2 inch under one 1/4 inch stripes under the line star (21).

The stripes were changed again on November 7, 1874 (22) to two 1/2 inch stripes under the line star and have remained so ever since.

On the new service coat of 1877, black cuff stripes without a line star and two silver, not gold, bars were worn alone on the collar (23). It is possible that the bars on the shoulder straps and epaulets were changed to silver at this point.

The bars were silver in the 1883 regulations and the silver line anchor joined them on the collar (24). The regulations created a white service coat with white cuff stripes and no collar insignia (25).

The white cuff stripes were replaced on the white coat with shoulder straps in 1897 (26).

In 1899 the shoulder straps on the white coat were replaced with shoulder boards. The boards for Lieutenants matched the cuffs, two stripes and a line star (27).

Shoulder straps make their last appearance in regulations in 1905 (28) and may have been abolished with the next regulations in 1913 or sometime in between.

The January 13, 1913 regulations did abolish shoulder boards, replacing them with a white cloth shoulder loop with a two silver bars and anchor (29). This was undone on June 24th and shoulder boards returned (30).

Epaulets were also changed in 1913. The anchor was once again vertical with the pairs of silver bars on either side (31).

The use of epaulets was suspended in 1917 (32).

The end of the use of staff titles in November 1918 led to equivalent staff lieutenants wearing the corps device in place of the line star on the cuffs and superimposed on the anchor on the blue service coat collar and above the stripes on the shoulder boards. The collar insignia disappeared when the 1877 service coat was replaced in 1919 (33).

Use of epaulets resumed with the 1922 uniform regulations, the line anchor was now worn on the strap by all officers, with the corps device for staff officers superimposed over it. The two silver bars were alone in the frog (34).

The two silver bars began to be used as a pin on badge of rank in 1931 (35).

Use of epaulets was suspended for World War II and never unsuspended (36).

The Career Compensation Act of October 12, 1949 (37) placed the rank of Lieutenant in pay grade O-3.

The April 2010 uniform regulations descried the insignia for Lieutenants as:

Sleeve Stripes - "Lieutenant. Wear two 1/2 inch stripes." (38).

Shoulder Boards - "Officers below Flag Grade. The surface is black cloth. Gold lace stripes, the same width, number, and spacing, specified for stripes on sleeves of the blue coat, designate rank. The first stripe starts 1/4 inch... from the widest end. Line and staff corps devices replicate sleeve insignia and are placed as far from the stripes as specified for devices on sleeves of blue coats." (39).

Metal Grade Insignia -. (the two silver bars are shown in illustration).

Collar grade insignia replicates metal shoulder insignia (40)

The bars worn by navy Lieutenants are quite different from those worn by army Captains. The navy style bars are longer, thinner and falter. The bars are connected at the end instead of part wary down as army bars are.

Lieutenant Commander

The History of American Ranks and Rank Insignia

The rank of Lieutenant Commander was created on July 16, 1862 (1).

Lieutenants who were in command of a vessel had been referred to as "Lieutenants Commandant" or "Lieutenant Commanding" (2).

Insignia was prescribed on July 31st. There were to be two 3/4 inch wide cuff stripes. The shoulder straps were to be to a gold oak leaf at each end and a silver anchor in the center. The same insignia was worn in the frog of the epaulets (3).

On May 23, 1863 all line officers were ordered to wear a gold star above their cuff stripes. It is possible that the stripes were changed at the same time, but were certainly changed by the new uniform regulations of January 28, 1864 (4).

The 1864 regulations prescribed four 1/4 inch stripes, the lower three 1/4 inch apart and a 1/2 inch space between them and the top stripe, making a group of three stripes in the center a single stripe above (5). Epaulets were suspended (6) and shoulder straps were unchanged except for a smaller anchor (7). A gold oak leaf was also worn on the collar of the overcoat (8).

In January of 1865 a new service dress coat was introduced. It could carry cuff stripes or shoulder straps, or the oak leaf could be worn on the collar (9).

With the Civil War over, new uniform regulations were issued on December 1, 1866. Epaulets returned and the gold oak leaf was worn at either end of the frog with a silver anchor in the middle, the same arrangement was used in the shoulder straps. The oak leaf with an anchor behind it was also worn on the collar of the sack coat and over coat (10).

On March 11, 1869 (11) the cuff stripes for Lieutenant Commanders were changed to two 1/2 inch stripes below the line star.

The stripes were changed again on November 7, 1874 (12) to two 1/2 inch stripes with one 1/4 inch stripe between them all under the line star and have remained so ever since.

The service dress coat was replaced in 1877. The oak leaf, but not the anchor, was worn on each side of the standing collar (13).

The 1883 uniform regulations returned the anchor behind the oak leaf on the service coat collar (14).

In 1899 the shoulder straps on the white coat were replaced with shoulder boards. The boards for Lieutenant Commanders matched the cuffs, three 1/2 inch stripes and one 1/4 inch stripe and a line star (15).

Shoulder straps make their last appearance in regulations in 1905 (16) and may have been abolished with the next regulations in 1913 or sometime in between.

The January 13, 1913 regulations did abolish shoulder boards, replacing them with a white cloth shoulder loop with a metal oak leaf and anchor (17). This was undone on June 24th and shoulder boards returned (18).

Epaulets were also changed in 1913. The oak leaf was now alone in the frog and a single anchor was worn on the strap (19).

The use of epaulets was suspended in 1917 (20).

The end of the use of staff titles in November 1918 led to equivalent staff Lieutenant Commanders wearing the corps device in place of the line star on the cuffs and superimposed on the anchor on the blue service coat collar and above the stripes on the shoulder boards. The collar insignia disappeared when the 1877 service coat was replaced in 1919 (21).

Use of epaulets resumed with the 1922 uniform regulations, the line anchor was now worn on the strap by all officers, with the corps device for staff officers superimposed over it (22).

The gold oak leaf began to be used as a pin on badge of rank in 1931 (23).

Use of epaulets was suspended for World War II and never unsuspended (24).

The Career Compensation Act of October 12, 1949 (25) placed the rank of Lieutenant Commander in pay grade O-4.

The April 2010 uniform regulations descried the insignia for Lieutenant Commanders as:

Sleeve Stripes - "Lieutenant Commander. Wear two 1/2 inch stripes with one 1/4 inch stripe in between" (26).

Shoulder Boards - "Officers below Flag Grade. The surface is black cloth. Gold lace stripes, the same width, number, and spacing, specified for stripes on sleeves of the blue coat, designate rank. The first stripe starts 1/4 inch... from the widest end. Line and staff corps devices replicate sleeve insignia and are placed as far from the stripes as specified for devices on sleeves of blue coats." (27).

Metal Grade Insignia -. (the gold oak leaf is shown in illustration).

Collar grade insignia replicates metal shoulder insignia (28)

The leafs worn by navy Lieutenant Commanders are quite different from those worn by army Majors. The navy style leafs have more pointed pedals with veins embossed on them.

Lieutenant Junior Grade

On March 3, 1883 a law stated that the navy would consist of "one hundred masters, the title of which grade is hereby changed to that of lieutenants, and the masters now on the list shall constitute a junior grade of, and be commissioned as, lieutenants, having the same rank and pay as now provided by law for masters," (1).

They inherited the Master's insignia. One 1/2 inch stripe under one 1/4 inch stripe under a line star and one silver bar, accompanying a line anchor, on the collar, shoulder straps and epaulet frogs (2).

In 1899 the shoulder straps on the white coat were replaced with shoulder boards. The boards for Lieutenants Junior Grade matched the cuffs, two stripes, one 1/2 inch and one 1/4 inch, and a line star (3).

Shoulder straps make their last appearance in regulations in 1905 (4) and may have been abolished with the next regulations in 1913 or sometime in between.

The January 13, 1913 regulations did abolish shoulder boards, replacing them with a white cloth shoulder loop with a silver bar and anchor (5). This was undone on June 24th and shoulder boards returned (6).

Epaulets were also changed in 1913. The anchor was once again vertical with a silver bar on either side (7).

The use of epaulets was suspended in 1917 (8).

The end of the use of staff titles in November 1918 led to equivalent staff lieutenants junior grade wearing the corps device in place of the line star on the cuffs and superimposed on the anchor on the blue service coat collar and above the stripes on the shoulder boards. The collar insignia disappeared when the 1877 service coat was replaced in 1919 (9).

Use of epaulets resumed with the 1922 uniform regulations, the line anchor was now worn on the strap by all officers, with the corps device for staff officers superimposed over it. The silver bar was alone in the frog (10).

The silver bar began to be used as a pin on badge of rank in 1931 (11).

Use of epaulets was suspended for World War II and never unsuspended (12).

The Career Compensation Act of October 12, 1949 (13) placed the rank of Lieutenant Junior Grade in pay grade O-2.

The April 2010 uniform regulations descried the insignia for Lieutenants Junior Grade as:

Sleeve Stripes - "Lieutenant. Wear one 1/2 inch stripe with one 1/4 inch stripe above it." (14).

Shoulder Boards - "Officers below Flag Grade. The surface is black cloth. Gold lace stripes, the same width, number, and spacing, specified for stripes on sleeves of the blue coat, designate rank. The first stripe starts 1/4 inch... from the widest end. Line and staff corps devices replicate sleeve insignia and are placed as far from the stripes as specified for devices on sleeves of blue coats." (15).

Metal Grade Insignia -. (the two silver bars are shown in illustration).

Collar grade insignia replicates metal shoulder insignia (16).

The bars worn by navy Lieutenants Junior Grade are quite different from those worn by army First Liuetenants. The navy style bars are longer, thinner and falter.

Machinist

The rank of Warrant Machinist was changed to Machinist on March 3, 1909 (1).

They were given insignia on the coat collars of a gold three bladed propellor, and a line star was worn alone on the cuffs (2).

In the January 1913 uniform regulations a small silver star was added to the gold three bladed propellor (3). It was also worn on white cloth shoulder loops on the white service coat (4). It continued to be worn on the collar of the blue service coat.

Shoulder boards were allowed to replace the cloth shoulder loops in June. The propellor with star was worn at the outer end (5).

The three bladed propellor (in gold and without the star) replaced the star on the cuffs in 1918. A year later a 1/4 inch gold cuff stripe was added under the propellor. Shoulder boards of 1919 also carried the 1/4 inch lace and three bladed propellor (6).

The 1922 regulations added a 1/2 inch dark blue break every two inches on the cuff stripes and a single 1/2 inch break in the center of the shoulder board stripe (7).

Black sleeve stripes were used on khaki and green coats starting in 1925. The format used by warrant officers is not clear. It is possible that a solid stripe was used (8). The black stripes were removed from the khaki coat in 1941 (9) and stripes with green breaks were definitely prescribed for warrant officers in 1944 (10).

The gold three bladed propellor returned as the Machinist's pin on badge of rank in 1931.

The Career Compensation Act of October 12, 1949 (11) placed Machinists in pay grade W-1.

A standard, chief warrant officers badge of rank was introduced on July 1,1952 (12) consisting of a gold bar with a 1/16 inch blue break across the middle (13).

Machinist became Warrant Officer 1 with the Warrant Officer Act of 1954 (14).

Machinist was also a petty officer's rating from 1866 to 1904 when it was changed to Machinist's Mate (15).

Master

Master is the original term for a commander of a merchant ship. In the middle ages ships would be taken to serve as warships with the addition of a company of soldiers commanded by a Captain. The Captain was in charge of the fighting and the Master the sailing. Eventually when ships became permanent parts of navies, the Captain was in permanent command and the Master was a warrant officer in charge of navigation, trim, sail and line condition and log books. In the U.S. Navy the original term used was Sailing Master (0), but just Master appears on Continental navy pay tables.

The Warrant rank of Sailing Master was changed to Master on March 3, 1837 (1).

The 1830 uniform regulations had placed them in a blue coat with one button and laced button hole on the collar (2). This was increased to two buttons and laced button holes, on the now rolling collar in 1841 (3).

An appropriations bill passed on August 10, 1846 (4) stated "Passed midshipmen performing the duties of master, under the authority of the Secretary of the Navy, to receive the compensation allowed to such higher grade, while actually so employed". Master was not a higher rank than Passed Midshipman. They were officers and Masters were warrant officers. By "performing the duties of master", Passed Midshipmen were taking another path to Lieutenant, serving as a master instead of waiting for an opening to occur above them.

There is no law creating a second category of Master, but the navy registers tell the story. The 1846 register lists 28 Masters after Midshipmen and before Master's Mates (5). The 1847 register list 25 Masters in the same position. This list is the same (6) except for the absence of George Marshall, John Freeman, who had resigned and Marmaduke Dove who had died (7). There is, however a second list of "Masters in the line of promotion" that was not there in 1846, ahead of Passed Midshipmen and after Chaplains (8). Six are listed, William Blanton, Benjamin Gantt, John Neville, Henry Wise, C. St. Geo. Noland and Edward Anderson. All but Neville had been listed as Passed Midshipmen in 1846 (9), it is not clear why Neville was not included, he had been a Passed Midshipman since July 8, 1839 (10). In the book The Uniforms of the United States Navy by Captain James Tily, it is stated that the second category of Masters began in the 1837 register (11), this is probably a misprint, it was in 1847.

The 1852 uniform regulations prescribed plain gold epaulets with 3/8 inch wide bullion, full size shoulder straps with no device in them and three medium buttons around the cuff (12).

Master ceased to be a warrant rank and officially became the commissioned rank between Lieutenant on Passed Midshipman on February 28, 1855 (13). A new law stated "That all vacancies occurring in the grade of masters shall be filled by the promotion of the senior passed midshipmen, to be entitled masters in the line of promotion, who when promoted shall receive the pay allowed by law to masters". 16 of the 17 Masters not in the line of promotion, listed in the 1855 navy register (14) were moved to the reserved list in the fall of 1855 (15). The other, Augustus Ford, had died.

In 1862 the insignia was changed to a 3/4 inch wide cuff stripe and shoulder straps and epaulet frogs with an anchor and a single gold bar on either side (16). On the epaulets the anchor ran vertically.

The gold star of a line officer was added above the cuff stripe on May 23, 1863 (17).

The 1864 uniform regulations prescribed two 1/4 inch stripes and the shoulder strap with an anchor in the middle and gold bars at the ends. The overcoat collar carried the gold bar on the collar (18).

On the collar of the 1865 service coat the bar and the anchor were worn (19).

In 1866 epaulets returned with the anchor and bars in the frog (20), probably horizontal this time.

A General Order of March 11, 1869 prohibited the use of epaulets and shoulder straps by officers below the rank of Lieutenant (21). As a replacement, shoulder knots were prescribed on April 27th (22). The order and subsequent regulations describe these knots as "per pattern", which is no help in figuring out what they looked like. There is, however an illustration in the 1869 regulations (23). It shows a twisted knot made of two gold cords, terminating in a large oval pad, of dark blue, over the shoulder, outlined in three cords. In the center of the pad is a gold anchor with silver bars on either side of it. At the same time the cuff stripes were changed to one 1/2 inch stripe under the line star.

The shoulder knots were abolished on October 3, 1871 (24) and epaulets and shoulder straps with the anchors and bars returned.

On the new service coat of 1877, black cuff stripes without a line star and a silver, not gold, bar were worn alone on the collar (25). It is possible that the bars on the shoulder straps and epaulets were changed to silver at this point.

In August of 1881 the cuff stripe was changed to 1/2 inch stripe under one 1/4 inch stripe under the line star (26).

The rank of Master was changed to Lieutenant Junior Grade on March 3, 1883 (27).

Master Chief Petty Officer

When the E-9 pay grade was created on May 20, 1958 (1), the rate of Master Chief Petty Officer was created to fill it (2).

The rating badge was a standard Chief Petty Officers badge, three chevrons and one arc under an eagle with a specialty mark under the arc, with two stars above the eagle (3). In full color the chevrons and arc were red, or gold if authorized, and the eagle, specialty mark and stars silver. Otherwise all blue was used.

In 1959 all three grades of chiefs were given a pin on badge of rank. A smaller version of the fouled anchor and U.S.N cap device was added to the collar of the khaki shirt (4). Two silver stars were added above the anchor stock for Master Chiefs in 1961 (5).

1975 also saw the creation of blue and white dinner jackets for chiefs. Regular full color rating badges were worn on the blue jacket and badges with silver eagles and specialty marks and blue chevrons and arc (or gold if entitled) were worn on the white jacket. The 1975 regulations actually call for red chevrons, but this was a printing error (6).

White uniforms returned in 1979 in the same style as officers, standing collar for men and point lapel for women. The magazine article announcing them refers to a "sleeve rating badge" (7) but in fact badges of rank were placed on the collar.

Shoulder marks in black with the badge of rank embroidered on them were placed on white shirts worn under the blue coat in 1999. At the same time the use of the badge of rank on outerwear was expanded (8).

The aviation green uniform came to an end in December of 2010 (9), and the all blue rating badges on a green background passed into history. Ironically, the return of the 1931 khaki uniform began around the same time (10).

Master Chief Petty Officer of the Command

The Master Chief Petty Officer of the Command program began in 1971 to give senior enlisted advisors to various commands (1).

They wore the insignia of a regular Master Chief with the stars above the eagle in gold instead of silver. Another gold star replaced the specialty mark (2).

The use of the title seam to peter out in the mid 1970s. The 1975 uniform regulations list only Master Chief Petty Officer of the Fleet/Force (3).

Master Chief Petty Officer of the Fleet/Force

A Master Chief Petty Officer of the Fleet or Force was the senior enlisted advisor of a fleet. The first appointment was made in the Pacific Fleet in 1971 (1).

They wore the insignia of a regular Master Chief with the stars above the eagle in gold instead of silver. Another gold star replaced the specialty mark. After a tour as a master chief of the fleet was over, they would retain the gold stars above the eagle and their specialty mark would be rendered in gold (2). The post tour marks were in the 1975 regulations but it is not clear they were used before that.

The title was changed to Fleet/Force Master Chief Petty Officer in 1977 (3).

Master Chief Petty Officer of the Navy

In 1966 the navy was trying to improve communication between the sailors in the fleet and the leadership in Washington. Other services had created senior enlisted advisors to the senior leadership to facilitate that communication, and the navy followed suit.

The first idea for a title was Leading Chief Petty Officer of the Navy (1). When the fist appointment was made on January 13, 1967 the title was Senior Enlisted Advisor of the Navy. That was changed to the better sounding Master Chief Petty Officer of the Navy on April 28th (2).

The official abbreviation is MCPON and the position is often referred to as the "mick-pon".

The first MCPON was Delbert Black who served until April 1, 1971 (3).

Credit for the new MCPON insignia goes to Black's wife Ima. She suggested that a third silver star be added above the standard master chief's rating badge (4). It is not clear, but he probably wore three stars on his pin on badge of rank as well. He certainly did after the three stars were added to his cap device in 1968. Black continued to wear his specialty mark as a Gunner's Mate.

John Whittet replaced Black on April 1, 1971 (5) and the Black's Gunner's Mate mark was replaced by Whittet's Aviation Machinist's Mate mark (6).

In July of 1971, it was announced that Whittet would replace his specialty mark with a gold star and the three stars above the eagle were changed to gold as well (7)(8).

Whittet was replaced by Robert Walker on September 25, 1975. Walker served until September 28, 1979 when Thomas Crow took the office. Crow left on October 1, 1982 and was replaced by Billy Sanders, who served until October 4, 1985. Next up was William Plackett who held the office until September 9, 1988, when Duane Bushey took over. Bushey was replaced by John Hagan on August 28, 1992. James Herdt replaced Hagan on March 27, 1998 and served until April 22, 2002. Terry Scott was then made MCPON and remained so until July 10, 2006. Joe Campa then held the office until December 13, 2008 when Richard West took over. At this writing in the spring of 2011, West is still in office (9).

After a tour as MCPON is over the specialty mark returns to replace the star. It, and the three stars above the eagle remain gold.

Master Commandant

The idea of an intermediate rank between Captain and Lieutenant that would both command ships and service as sailing master existed in the British Royal Navy of the mid 18th century as "Master and Commander" (1), shortened to just Commander in 1794 (2).

For the U.S. Navy the title used was Master Commandant.

As war with France loomed, a law was passed on February 25, 1799 (3) stated that ships under 18 guns would be commanded "by masters or lieutenants, according to the size of the vessel, to be regulated by the President of the United States". Notice that master was ahead of lieutenant. The next section lists the pay of various officers commanding ships. The actual term "Master Commandant" is used here. It is not only listed ahead of Lieutenant, it gives them more money.

According to the List of Officers of the Navy of the United States and the Marine Corps from 1775 to 1900 by Edward Callahan. Appointments were made to William Bainbridge on March 29th, 1799, David Jewett on April 6th, Timothy Newman on July 1st, William Cowper on July 12th, Hugh Campbell on July 27th and Richard Law on December 16th (4).

This does not quite match the records of Congress. According to the Senate's Executive Journal, Law was confirmed on December 13th (5) and the others on January 8, 1800, along with Cyrus Talbot who Callahan has taking office on the 15th (6).

There are two further appointments. Benjamin Hiller who the Senate Confirmed on December 11, 1800 (7), but Callahan has on February 8th, and John Spotswood in February of 1800 (the dates are close enough not to be concerned with).

Bainbridge was promoted to Captain on May 20, 1800 and Campbell on October 16th. Newman died on August 15th and Hillar does not appear in records again (8).

On March 3, 1801 a new law set the size of the navy (9). It called for six Captains and 36 Lieutenants but Master Commandant is not mentioned.

This effectively abolished the rank and Jewett, Cowper, Law and Spotswood were all discharged (10).

In 1804 President Jefferson made several recess appointments of Masters Commandant even though the rank did not legally exist (11).

On April 21, 1806 Congress amended the 1801 act and the navy was now legally allowed nine Master Commandant (12).

There is no information on uniforms before 1813 when they were ordered to wear the uniform of a Captain with an epaulet on the right shoulder only (13).

The 1820 uniform regulations called for "Coat. - Blue cloth, with broad lappels, and lining of the same, standing collar; trimmed with gold lace as follow: around the standing collar descending around the lappels to the bottom of the coat, the upper part of the cuffs, around the pocket flaps, and down the folds, with one single lace; four buttons on each of the cuffs, and four on each of the pocket flaps, nine on each of the lappels, and one on the standing collar. Two Plain gold epaulets. Pantaloons and Vest, white. Vest single breasted, nine buttons, four buttons under each of the pocket flaps; buttons same as those on the coat, but to be proportionably smaller. Undress - Same as full dress, excepting the lace and standing collar." (14). The main difference was the epaulets were now on both shoulder now that Captains had devices on theirs.

The 1830 regulations reduced the buttons on the pockets and cuffs to three and added shoulder straps of a strip of gold lace on each shoulder when epaulets were not worn (15).

The rank title was changed to Commander on March 3, 1837 (16).

Master's Mate

The rank or rate of Master's Mate walked the line between warrant officer and petty officer in the early years of the navy. Their exact status is far from clear.

Master's Mate was a petty officer's rating in the Continental Navy (0) and listed in both the 1794 (1) and 1797 (2) laws setting the organization of the federal navy.

A law of January 2, 1813 to increase the size of the navy for the War of 1812 listed Master's Mates as warrant officers instead of petty officers (3).

The early navy registers do list some Master's Mates, often with their dates of appointment missing. There are records of appointments as early as 1805 (4).

As far as the records can be analyzed the last of these Master's Mates, Thomas King, died in 1821 (5).

A law of March 3, 1835 (6) set the pay for various ranks and "Warranted Master's Mates" were listed between Passed Midshipmen and Midshipmen. The use of the word "Warranted" probably meant that Master's Mate was both a warrant rank and a petty officers rate. This is born out in a Navy Department circular of January 30, 1838 that shows the personnel requirements for various classed of ships. Master's Mates are listed twice, once as warrant officers and once as petty officers.

The 1969 compilation of enlisted titles by Charles Malin states that the petty officer version of Master's Mate existed form 1797 to 1813 and was reestablished in 1838 (7).

The navy regulations of 1841 lists "Master's Mate, if warranted as such" after Passed Midshipmen and before Boatswains in seniority (8). Article 39 also states that Warranted Master's Mates can only be promoted to Second Master (9).

Better record keeping shows us that appointments as Warranted Master's Mates resumed in 1839 with William Morse on July 1st. He was followed by John Palmer on July 1, 1840, Adam Young on September 19th, Thomas Crooker on March 3, 1841, G.G. Decker on February 16, 1842, William Burns on May 11th and Jonathan Ballard on June 14th. Decker was dismissed on July 6, 1842 just days before the appointment of Richard Robinson and James power on July 19th. 1843 saw John Dyes appointed on March 15th and James Polley, Charles Oliver and Edmund Olmsetad on May 3rd. Crooker was made a Gunner on May 14, 1844 and Polley a Boatswain on February 27, 1846. Oliver was made a Gunner on June 2, 1846 as was Ballard on November 23, 1847. Olmstead was promoted to

Second Master on March 2, 1849 and so were Morse and Burns the next day. Robinson deserted on December 6, 1850 and Palmer died on July 23, 1853. Power died on August 20, 1853 and Dyes on September 11, 1855. This left Young as the only one on the list. He resigned on March 22, 1858 (10).

There is no information on uniforms for Master's Mates of this era. The rank does not appear in the uniform regulations of 1841 or 1852.

When the Civil War began, the navy started to make appointments as "Acting Master's Mate" on it's own authority. Congress made this legal on July 24, 1861 (11).

Warranted Master's Mates were prescribed uniforms on June 18, 1862. The order prescribed single breasted frock coats with one row of nine buttons, a plain rolling collar and plain cuffs. A visored cap was worn with a band of two strips of 1/2 inch wide gold lace showing 1/2 inch of blue between them, under a cap device of a silver unfouled anchor. Rated Master's Mates were given uniforms that were different then other enlisted sailors, A double breasted blue jacket with two rows of six buttons and a plain visored cap with the silver anchor (12). The anchor was removed on July 31st (13).

A line star was added to the cuffs of Warranted Master's Mates on May 23, 1863 (14).

The 1864 uniform regulations refer to the two grades of Master's Mate by their salary, stating "For a master's mate receiving $40 per month, frock coat of navy blue cloth or flannel; rolling collar; single breasted, with nine navy buttons of medium size on the breast, one behind on each hip, one near the bottom on each fold, and none on the cuffs. They will also wear a gold star above the cuff, and the navy cap with simply the wreath." This was the warranted version. The rated version is referred to as receiving $25 per month, and along with other ratings allowed a jacket, was to wear " blue cloth or flannel jacket; rolling collar, double-breasted, with two rows of medium sized navy buttons on the breast, six in each row; and slashed sleeves, with four small sized navy buttons. They will also wear the navy cap without wreath or device." (15).

A law of March 3, 1865 (16) changed the title to "Mates". This apparently applied to both versions and the grades were merged to create a rank of Mate that was still somewhere between a warrant officer and a petty officer.

Mate

The rank of Mate was created on March 3, 1865 from Master's Mates (1). It continued the unusual status of almost a warrant officer but above a petty officer.

They continued the Master's Mates uniforms of a single breasted frock coat with one row of nine buttons, a gold star above the cuff and a visored cap with an empty wreath (2).

It is not clear if mates were allowed the 1865 service coat. It is prescribed for them in the regulations of 1876 with only the star on the cuffs for insignia (3).

The coats were changed to double breasted in 1867 and shoulder straps of a plain strip of gold lace were prescribed. The shoulder straps were removed again in 1869 (4).

In 1880 the service coat was replaced with the new design used by other officers since 1878. It was to have gold stars on the collar and cuff (5).

The 1883 uniform regulations prescribed a device of a pair of binoculars on the collar of the frock and service coats. They were in silver for Mates over 20 years service and gold for those under (6).

On August 1, 1894 a law was passed that allowed the 28 Mates on active duty at time to retire as warrant officers (7). Mates appointed after this law, no appointments were made until 1897 (8), were paid at a different rate as those appointed before (9).

On October 15, 1907 the Attorney General issued an opinion that Mates were both "officers of the navy and enlisted men" (10). As a result of this ruling, Mates were considered to be enlisted men and the category was removed from the navy register (11)(12). This makes tracking the usage of the rank, or rate actually, difficult.

Shoulder boards, carrying only the binoculars, were prescribed in 1908 (13).

The January 1913 uniform regulations abolished those boards and replaced them with white cloth shoulder loops with pin on binoculars (14). Otherwise the binoculars were worn on the collars of the blue coats as before. The shoulder boards returned in June (15).

The binoculars, now only in gold, moved to the cuff, in place of the star, in 1918 (16).

A law of June 10, 1922 placed Mates in Grade 1 with Chief Petty Officers (17), securing their place as enlisted men.

Both the 1922 (18) and 1941 (19) uniform regulations call for the binoculars to be worn "above the cuff line", which probably means no stripes were worn. The wording of both regulations makes the use of shoulder boards unclear, but since they were to duplicate the cuffs, binoculars alone on the boards is possible.

Mate makes it's last appearance on the pay table in the 1943 Navy Register (20). If the rate was in use at that time it was no longer.

Medical Director

The rank of Medical Director was created on March 3, 1871 (1) for medical officers with the relative rank of Captain.

They wore a Captain's uniform with cobalt blue cloth between the cuff stripes and no corps device (2).

In 1883 the cloth was changed to maroon and a corps device of a gold oak leaf with a silver acorn was added (3).

Staff rank ceased to be relative on March 3, 1899 (4).

A few Medical Directors were made Rear Admirals in 1916 (5).

A general order in 1918 decreed that staff officers would be addressed by their regular ranks instead of there staff titles (6).

At that time the colors in and around the sleeve and shoulder board stripes were abolished and corps device was placed above them and an anchor was added under the device on the service coat collar until the coat was abolished the next year (7).

Staff rank titles officially ended on August 7, 1947 (8).

Medical Inspector

The rank of Medical inspector was created on March 3, 1871 (1) for medical officers with the relative rank of Commander.

They wore a Commander's uniform with cobalt blue cloth between the cuff stripes and no corps device (2).

In 1883 the cloth was changed to maroon and a corps device of a gold oak leaf with a silver acorn was added (3).

Staff rank ceased to be relative on March 3, 1899 (4).

A general order in 1918 decreed that staff officers would be addressed by their regular ranks instead of there staff titles (5).

At that time the colors in and around the sleeve and shoulder board stripes were abolished and corps device was placed above them and an anchor was added under the device on the service coat collar until the coat was abolished the next year (6).

Staff rank titles officially ended on August 7, 1947 (7).

Mess Attendant

Attendants became Mess Attendants in 1893 (1).

They would have continued the Attendant's uniforms form 1886 of "Blue cloth or white jacket, Blue cloth or white trousers, blue cap or canvas hat, waistcoat (only with blue jacket), white shirt, and collar and cravat." (2).

The 1897 uniform regulations are basically the same with white caps replacing canvas hats (3).

Mess Attendants were split in to first, second and third classes in 1902 (4).

Mess Attendant First Class

Mess Attendants were split into classes in 1902 (1).

They wore the blue or white jackets and caps until the 1905 regulations prescribed regular enlisted uniforms, with one stripe on the cuff of the jumper for all classes (2), and no watch mark (3).

A white/blue crescent was added to the upper left sleeve in 1921 (4).

In 1922 the three classes were split across the lower three pay grades with first class in grade five (5). This gave them three stripes on the cuffs of the jumper.

Mess Attendants First Class became Steward's Mates First Class in 1943 (6).

Mess Attendant Second Class

Mess Attendants were split into classes in 1902 (1).

They wore the blue or white jackets and caps until the 1905 regulations prescribed regular enlisted uniforms, with one stripe on the cuff of the jumper for all classes (2), and no watch mark (3).

A white/blue crescent was added to the upper left sleeve in 1921 (4).

In 1922 the three classes were split across the lower three pay grades with second class in grade six (5). This gave them two stripes on the cuffs of the jumper.

Mess Attendants Second Class became Steward's Mates Second Class in 1943 (6).

Mess Attendant Third Class

Mess Attendants were split into classes in 1902 (1).

They wore the blue or white jackets and caps until the 1905 regulations prescribed regular enlisted uniforms, with one stripe on the cuff of the jumper for all classes (2), and no watch mark (3).

A white/blue crescent was added to the upper left sleeve in 1921 (4).

In 1922 the three classes were split across the lower three pay grades with third class in grade seven (5). They would have kept the single stripe on the cuffs.

Mess Attendants Third Class became Steward's Mates Third Class in 1943 (6).

Mess Management Specialist

The 1975 uniform regulations refer to non rated Mess Management Specialists wearing white/blue group rate marks under a specialty mark of crossed keys over a quill on an open ledger book (1).

It is not clear if this was a non rated title or not, or how long it may have existed.

Midshipman

A Midshipman is an officer in training. There are too many stories as to the origin of the title to be sure which is correct. One is that in the 16th or 17th century english navy the title was used as a rating for sailors who worked in the middle of a ship (1). Another is that as officers in training they were quartered in the middle of the ship instead of aft with the officers or forward with the crew (2). Yet another is that the title came from sailors who carried messages back and forth thru the middle of the ship (3).

Whatever the origin, by the late 18th century Midshipmen were trainee officers. They were also an integral part of the navy's rank structure, serving as junior officers in line to command ships.

American Midshipmen first appeared in the Continental Navy (4). In 1776 they were ordered to wear "Blue lapelled coast, a round cuff, faced with red, standup collar, with red at the button and button hole, blue britches, and red waistcoat" (5).

Midshipmen were listed with the warrant ranks in both the 1794 (6) and 1797 (7) laws creating the federal navy. Strangely it is also listed as a non rated rate in both laws. There is no information as to why this was.

Uniforms for Midshipmen were usually quite plain. The 1797 regulations call for "COAT. Plain frock coat of blue, lined and edged with buff, without lappels, a standing collar of buff, and plain buff cuffs, open underneath with three buttons. VEST AND BREECHES. Buff-- former to be made round and plain-- Buttons (for the suit) the same as before described." (8).

The section in the 1802 uniform regulations read "THE COAT of blue cloth, with the lining and lappels of the same; the lappels to be short, with six buttons; standing collar, with a diamond formed of gold lace on each side, not to exceed two inches square; a slash sleeve, with three small buttons; all the button-holes to be worked with gold thread. VEST AND BREECHES, white, the same as the lieutenants, except the buttons on the pockets of the vest. THE UNDRESS--A short coat without worked button-holes, a standing collar with a button and a slip of lace on each side. A MIDSHIPMAN, when he acts as a lieutenant, by order of the Secretary of the Navy, will assume the uniform of a lieutenant." (9).

Then in 1813 "The Coat of blue cloth, with lining and lappels of the same; the lappels to be short, with six buttons; standing collar, with a diamond formed of gold lace on each side, not exceeding two inches square; with no buttons on the cuffs or pockets. Pantaloons and Vest white, the same as the lieutenant's, except the buttons on the pockets of the vest." (10).

The 1820 regulations are basically the same as 1813 but included and undress "short coat, rolling cape (meaning collar), with a button on each side." (11).

1830 saw a blue coat with white lining and a standing collar with oak leaf and acorn embroidery around the edges and a gold fouled anchor under the embroidery. The coat had nine buttons on the right and matching holes on the left with three buttons on the cuffs and pockets. For undress there was "Round Jacket - cloth blue, and lining of the same: standing collar, with anchor inserted in white cloth: breast single; buttons arraigned as on the full dress coat, but small instead of large." (12).

In 1841 both dress coats and undress jackets had rolling collars with an anchor on them in gold on the coat and buff on the jacket (13).

In 1845 the navy created a Naval School in Annapolis Maryland, which became the United States Naval Academy in 1850 (14).

This left Midshipmen with two circumstances, studying at the academy and serving with the fleet. It was only a matter of time before some distinction would be made. As of the 1852 register (15) Midshipmen at the academy are referred to as "Acting Midshipmen".

In 1852 a dress tail coat with plain cuffs and a gold anchor on the collar and a plain undress frock coat with medium sized buttons were prescribed (16).

A law of July 16, 1862 (17) changed the navy's rank structure. It lists Midshipman as the ninth highest of nine ranks. It also states "That the 'students at the Naval Academy shall be styled midshipmen and until their final graduating examination, when, successful, they shall be commissioned ensigns, ranking according to merit." Those at the academy were no longer "acting"

On July 31st the dress tail coat was suspended and Midshipmen wore only the plain frock coat (18).

If the intention of the 1862 law was to make Midshipman the title of academy students, with them being made Ensigns when they reached the fleet, it didn't work. The 1863 navy register lists only nine non academy Midshipman whose test results had not come in yet (19). The problem was the older officers running the navy didn't want newly commissioned Ensigns fresh form the academy, they wanted Midshipmen learning at sea as they always had. They got around the law by delaying the final exam until after a year of sea service and once again there was a second category of Midshipmen (20).

On March 3, 1865 congress created a different pay rate for "midshipmen, after their final academic examination and until their promotion to the grade of, ensign" (21).

As line officers, they began wearing a line star by itself on the cuff on May 23, 1863 (22).

On July 4, 1864 (23), a title of "Cadet Engineer" was created for academy students who were studying to become engineers, civil engineers of naval constructors.

In 1865 Midshipmen at the academy were given a jacket with a standing collar with the traditional anchor (24).

Uniforms worn at the academy carry insignia relating to the Midshipman's position in the corps of that institution, which has no bearing on insignia used by the rest of the navy.

It is possible that graduated Midshipmen wore empty shoulder straps with the 1866 uniform regulations, with an anchor being added a few weeks later (25).

Midshipmen were allowed the full dress tail coat on March 11, 1869. It had a the traditional anchor on the collar and a 1/8 inch wide cuff stripe. Midshipmen at the academy added gold piping around the collar of the jacket (26).

1869 also saw shoulder straps being replaced with shoulder knots. Graduated Midshipmen were to wear oval shaped knots made of two cords with two sets of perpendicular loops and a silver anchor in the opening near the outer end (27).

On July 15, 1870 (28) Midshipmen at the academy were given the title of Cadet Midshipman, while those with the fleet remained simply Midshipmen.

The 1876 uniform regulations show the 1/8 inch stripe being worn the cuffs of both the tail and frock coats and a 1/8 inch gold edging on the front of the collar of the service coat (29). These may have been introduced previously (30).

On August 5, 1882 Cadet Midshipmen and Cadet Engineers were made into Naval Cadets (31). Those who were serving with the fleet remained Midshipmen until March 3, 1883 when they were made Ensigns Junior Grade (32).

The title was changed back on July 1, 1902 (33) but by this time they were no longer an integral part of the navy's rank structure.

Musician First Class

Musician First Class was a non rated title from 1838 (1) until musicians were made petty officers in 1944 (2).

They wore the standard enlisted uniform. When stripes were added in 1866, they must have worn them but there is no information as to how many.

In 1885 they were placed in the Seaman First Class pay grade (3) meaning three stripes on the cuff of the jumper and white/blue watch mark (4).

In 1912 a white/blue lyre was added to the upper sleeve (5) and the watch mark was eliminated and not replaced with a branch mark (6).

In 1922 or 1923 Musicians First Class were placed in grade four equal to third class petty officers (7).

The lyre became the specialty mark of rated musicians after 1944.

Musician Second Class

Musician Second Class was a non rated title from 1838 (1) until musicians were made petty officers in 1944 (2).

They wore the standard enlisted uniform. When stripes were added in 1866, they must have worn them but there is no information as to how many.

In 1885 they were placed in the Seaman Second Class pay grade (3) meaning two stripes on the cuff of the jumper and white/blue watch mark (4).

In 1912 a white/blue lyre was added to the upper sleeve (5) and the watch mark was eliminated and not replaced with a branch mark (6).

In 1922 or 1923 Musicians Second Class were placed in grade five equal to seamen first class (7).

The lyre became the specialty mark of rated musicians after 1944.

Naval Cadet

Midshipmen became Naval Cadets on August 5, 1882 (1). After a six year course, usually four at the academy and two as sea, they would be appointed to the "lower grades" of the navy. Naval Cadets were no longer an integral part of the navy's rank structure.

The 1883 uniform regulations called for Naval Cadets who had completed the four years at the academy were a shoulder knot on the frock coat as Midshipmen had since 1869 (2). It consisted of an oval shaped knot made of two cords with two sets of perpendicular loops and a silver anchor in the opening near the outer end (3). The frock coat also carried cuff stripes of 1/4 inch gold with 1/2 inch blue breaks every two inches, under a line star (4). The service coat carried a gold anchor on the collar (5). It is not clear if a 1/4 inch black stripe was worn.

The cuff stripe was made solid gold as of the 1897 regulations (6).

The title was changed back to Midshipman on July 1, 1902 (7).

Naval Constructor

Each of the six frigates commissioned in 1784 had a Naval Constructor assigned to oversee design and construction. Their names were Josiah Fox, George Claghorn, Forman Cheeseman, Joshua Humphreys, James Hackett and David Stodder (1). None were naval officers, only civilian employees of the navy.

There were usually a few Naval Constructors on staff before the Civil War. Known names are Josiah Barker, William Doughty, Samuel Humphreys, Francis Grice, Henry Eckford, Samuel Hart, John Floyd, Charles Brodie, John Lenthall, Samuel Pook, Benjamin Delano, Samuell Hartt, C.G. Selfridge, William Hanscom and Isiah Hanscom (2).

On March 13, 1863 (3) a the Secretary of the Navy, on his own authority, granted the status of naval officers and relative rank to Naval Constructors. Those over 20 years service, Francis Grice and Samuel Pook, ranked with Captains, those over 12 years service, just Benjamin Delano, ranked with Commanders and those under 12 years service, William Hanscom, Isaiah Hanscom, Henry Hoover, Melvin Simmons and Edward Hartt, with Lieutenant Commanders (4).

The 1864 uniform regulations prescribed the uniform of their relative rank with a gold oak sprig as a corps device (5).

A law of July 25, 1866 made Naval Constructors naval officers but did not mention the were entitled to relative rank (6)

Constructors relative rank was taken away in 1869, when the Attorney General ruled the navy had exceeded it's authority in 1863 (7). Congress restored it on March 3, 1871, with constructors spread over the ranks of Captain, Commander, Lieutenant Commander and Lieutenant (8). Judging from the navy registers, Lieutenant Commander was rarely used.

On March 21st the navy prescribed that they would wear the uniforms of their relative ranks with the oak sprig device replacing the line anchor and dark violet cloth between the sleeve stripes (9).

A law of March 3, 1899 (10) ended relative rank and granted staff officers actual rank. The law was clear that it did not change the rank titles. Staff officers now had "the rank of..." instead of "the relative rank of...".

An appropriations bill passed on August 29, 1916 (11) allowed Naval Constructors to rank below from Rear Admiral to Commander.

A general order in 1918 decreed that staff officers would be addressed by their regular ranks instead of there staff titles (12). The colors were removed from the stripes and the corps device added above them.

All construction officers were transferred to the line at their equivalent ranks on June 25, 1940 (13).

(Officers') Chief Cook

Officers' Chief Cooks were added in 1942 in grade one (1).

They wore CPO style uniforms with a blue/white distinguishing mark on the left upper sleeve consisting of a crescent and four horizontal bars (2).

The title was changed to just "Chief Cook" in 1944 and a regular Chief Petty Officers rating badge with the crescent for a specialty mark replaced the bars (3).

It was combined with Chief Stewards in 1948 to form the rate of Steward (4).

Despite their pay grade and rating badges, Stewards and Cooks were not petty officers, they were considered non rated (5).

Officer's Chief Steward

Officers' Chief Stewards were added in 1942 in grade one (1).

They wore CPO style uniforms with a blue/white distinguishing mark on the left upper sleeve consisting of a crescent and four horizontal bars (2).

The title was changed to just "Chief Steward" in 1944 and a regular Chief Petty Officers rating badge with the crescent for a specialty mark replaced the bars (3).

It was combined with Chief Cook in 1948 to form the rate of Chief Steward (4).

Despite their pay grade and rating badges, Stewards and Cooks were not petty officers, they were considered non rated (5).

Officers' Cook

Officers' Cook began as an enlisted title in 1838 and was split into Cook to Commander-in-Chief, Cabin Cook, Wardroom Cook, Steerage Cook and Warrant Officers cook in 1864 (1).

It is not clear if they were ever considered petty officers.

They wore the standard enlisted uniform.

(Officer's) Cook First Class

Cabin Cooks became Officers' Cooks First Class in 1924 and took their place in grade two (1).

They wore CPO style uniforms with a blue/white distinguishing mark on the left upper sleeve consisting of a crescent and three horizontal bars (2).

The title was changed to just "Cook First Class" in 1944 and a regular First Class Petty Officers rating badge with the crescent for a specialty mark replaced the bars (3).

It was combined with Steward First Class in 1948 to form the rate of Steward (4).

Despite their pay grade and rating badges, Stewards and Cooks were not petty officers, they were considered non rated (5).

(Officers') Cook Second Class

Wardroom Cooks and Steerage Cooks became Officers' Cooks Second Class in 1924 and took their place in grade three (1).

They wore CPO style uniforms with a blue/white distinguishing mark on the left upper sleeve consisting of a crescent and two horizontal bars (2).

The title was changed to just "Cook Second Class" in 1944 and a regular Second Class Petty Officers rating badge with the crescent for a specialty mark replaced the bars (3).

It was combined with Steward Second Class in 1948 to form the rate of Steward (4).

Despite their pay grade and rating badges, Stewards and Cooks were not petty officers, they were considered non rated (5).

(Officers') Cook Third Class

Warrant Officer's Cooks became Officers' Cooks Third Class in 1924 and took their place in grade four (1).

They wore CPO style uniforms with a blue/white distinguishing mark on the left upper sleeve consisting of a crescent and one horizontal bar (2).

The title was changed to just "Cook Third Class" in 1944 and a regular Third Class Petty Officers rating badge with the crescent for a specialty mark replaced the bars (3).

It was combined with Steward Third Class in 1948 to form the rate of Steward (4).

Despite their pay grade and rating badges, Stewards and Cooks were not petty officers, they were considered non rated (5).

(Officers') Steward First Class

Cabin Stewards became Officers' Stewards First Class in 1924 and took their place in grade two (1).

They wore CPO style uniforms with a blue/white distinguishing mark on the left upper sleeve consisting of a crescent and three horizontal bars (2).

The title was changed to just "Steward First Class" in 1944 and a regular First Class Petty Officers rating badge with the crescent for a specialty mark replaced the bars (3).

It was combined with Cook First Class in 1948 to form the rate of Steward (4).

Despite their pay grade and rating badges, Stewards and Cooks were not petty officers, they were considered non rated (5).

(Officers') Steward Second Class

Wardroom Stewards and Steerage Stewards became Officers' Stewards Second Class in 1924 and took their place in grade three (1).

They wore CPO style uniforms with a blue/white distinguishing mark on the left upper sleeve consisting of a crescent and two horizontal bars (2).

The title was changed to just "Steward Second Class" in 1944 and a regular Second Class Petty Officers rating badge with the crescent for a specialty mark replaced the bars (3).

It was combined with Cook Second Class in 1948 to form the rate of Steward (4).

Despite their pay grade and rating badges, Stewards and Cooks were not petty officers, they were considered non rated (5).

(Officers') Steward Third Class

Warrant Officer's Stewards became Officers' Stewards Third Class in 1924 and took their place in grade four (1).

They wore CPO style uniforms with a blue/white distinguishing mark on the left upper sleeve consisting of a crescent and one horizontal bar (2).

The title was changed to just "Steward Third Class" in 1944 and a regular Third Class Petty Officers rating badge with the crescent for a specialty mark replaced the bars (3).

It was combined with Cook Third Class in 1948 to form the rate of Steward (4).

Despite their pay grade and rating badges, Stewards and Cooks were not petty officers, they were considered non rated (5).

Ordinary Seaman

An Ordinary Seaman is just that, an ordinary seaman. Not a trainee like a Boy or lacking naval skills like a Landsman, but below a Seaman, or Able Seaman if that title was used. It was the midlevel rank among the non rated.

It was created by the 1794 (1) and 1797 (2) laws creating the federal navy.

They wore the same uniform as other enlisted men until 1866 when two stripes were prescribed around the cuffs and collar of the jumper (3). The collar stripes were removed in 1869 (4).

In 1885 Ordinary Seamen were placed in the Seaman Second Class pay grade (5).

A white/blue watch mark was added in 1886 (6), which became a white/blue branch mark on the right side in 1912 (7).

Ordinary Seamen became Seaman Second Class in 1917 (8).

Ordinary Seaman Second Class

The rate of Ordinary Seaman Second Class existed form 1876 to 1885 (1).

It is not known how many cuff stripes they wore.

Passed Assistant Dental Surgeon

Passed Assistant Dental Surgeons were added on July 1, 1918 (1), with the rank of Lieutenant Commander and later Lieutenant. Since the use of staff titles ended in November of 1918 (2), it is doubtful the rank was ever used as a direct title.

They would have worn the uniform of their ranks with a corps device of a gold oak leaf with silver acorns on either side of the stem (3).

Used as a title or not it was an official rank of the navy until staff ranks were eliminated on August 7, 1947 (4).

Passed Assistant Engineer

First Assistant Engineers became Passed Assistant Engineers on February 24, 1874 (1). They had the relative rank of Lieutenants or Masters.

They wore the uniform of their relative rank with red cloth around the stripes and a corps device of crossed oak branches (2).

Engineering officers were converted to line officers on March 3, 1899 (3).

Passed Assistant Paymaster

The rank of Passed Assistant Paymaster was created on May 3, 1866 (1). They originally held the relative rank of Lieutenant (2).

They wore a Lieutenant's uniform with an oak sprig and leaf as a corps device (3).

When the Attorney General reset the relative ranks on March 29, 1869 (4), Passed Assistant Paymasters were not mentioned. This was probably because the ranks were reset to they way they were in 1862 and Passed Assistant Paymasters didn't exist then. Congress had created the rank in law in 1866, but did not mention relative rank. The 1870 navy register lists them as ranking "next after Lieutenants" (5).

White cloth had been prescribed around the stripes of Paymasters on March 11, 1869 (6).

Congress gave them the relative rank of Lieutenant or Master on March 3, 1871 (7), and they continued to wear the uniform of their relative rank with the white cloth and the oak sprig and leaf as a corps device.

Staff rank ceased to be relative on March 3, 1899 (8).

The corps device was redesigned in 1905 (9).

Staff titles were no longer used after November of 1918 (10), and were officially abolished on August 7, 1947 (11).

Passed Assistant Surgeon

On March 3, 1835 a law setting the pay of the navy, stated that Assistant Surgeons "After being passed and stationed as above, one thousand one hundred and fifty dollars." (1). This created Passed Assistant Surgeon as a midlevel rank of medical officers.

They probably dressed as Assistant Surgeons at first. The 1841 uniform regulations call for a full dress coat with oak leaf and acorn embroidery around the collar and an undress coat with a plain rolling collar. Both coats had three buttons around the cuffs with a strip of gold lace above and below them (2).

Navy regulations of 1841 gave them "assimilated rank" of Master (3) and a General Order of August 31, 1846 gave them a similar position "next after Lieutenants" (4). Congress confirmed this on August 5, 1854 (4a).

With relative rank came epaulets and shoulder straps. The epaulets had 1/4 inch wide bullion and the old english letters M.D. in the frog. The crescent was of solid lace instead of being embroidered like line officers. The shoulder straps were the small size with 1/8 inch borders with the M.D. in the center and a silver bar at each end. The line of embroidery on the dress collar was replaced with three live oak sprigs and the sleeve lace was eliminated (5).

The March 8, 1852 regulations replaced the undress coat with a frock coat with three buttons on the cuffs (6). In September the insignia for medical officers was changed. A gold sprig of olive replaced the M.D. on the shoulder straps and the letters were removed from the epaulets (7).

Use of the dress coat was suspended on July 31, 1862 and all buttons were removed from the cuffs of the frock coat. The cuffs now carried the 3/4 inch stripe of a Master (8).

The navy made Passed Assistant Surgeons relative Lieutenants on March 13, 1863 (9).

The 1864 uniform regulations called for three 1/4 inch cuff stripes, eliminated epaulets and called for full size shoulder straps with two gold bars at each end and no device in the center (10). The overcoat carried two gold bars. In other words the insignia of a Lieutenant without a star over the cuff stripes and no corps device on the shoulder straps.

Epaulets returned in 1866 with two gold bars on either side of the frog (11).

Their status as relative masters was overruled by the Attorney General in March of 1869 and they returned to "next after lieutenants" or with Masters (12).

New uniform regulations in April of 1869 prescribed cobalt blue piping around the now 1/2 inch sleeve stripe of a Master. The 1869 shoulder knots for staff officers were to be "as per patterns -- Staff Officers omitting the anchor". If the pictures are to be believed this left two silver bars alone on the pad (13).

A law of March 3, 1871 (14) gave them relative rank of Lieutenants or Masters.

The insignia remained the same as Lieutenants or Masters with no corps device and cobalt blue cloth in and around the stripes instead of the line star.

In 1883 medical officers were given a corps device of a gold oak leaf with a silver acorn in the center of if and the color was changed to maroon (15).

Staff rank ceased to be relative on March 3, 1899 (16).

A medical reserve corps was formed on September 22, 1912 (17) and the 1913 uniform regulation prescribed a silver oak leaf with gold acorn for the corps device and crimson cloth in and around the stripes (18).

A general order in 1918 decreed that staff officers would be addressed by their regular ranks instead of there staff titles (19).

At that time the colors in and around the sleeve and shoulder board stripes were abolished and corps device was placed above them and an anchor was added under the device on the service coat collar until the coat was abolished the next year (20).

Staff rank titles officially ended on August 7, 1947 (21).

Passed Midshipman

The rank of Passed Midshipman first appears in the navy register of 1829 (1). Ten are listed, George Adams, John Calhoun, Thomas Craven, Andrew Foot, Alexander Gibson, N.C. Lawrence, Lawrence Pennington, Robert Robb, Edward Schermerhorn and Samuel Stockton. All of them have an appointment date of May 24, 1828.

On that date, Congress passed two naval appropriations bills (2), raised the pay of navy lieutenants (3) and reorganized the navy's medical department (4), but none of these laws mention creating a rank of Passed Midshipman.

The term refers to Midshipmen who have passed the exam to complete their training but are waiting for an opening to become a Lieutenant. It may have been used before 1828, but this was the first time a separate category was used in the register.

The first mention in law was on March 3, 1835 (5) when their pay rate was set.

The 1830 uniform regulations call for a dress coat with gold oak leaf and acorn embroidery around the collar with an anchor and a star underneath, and an undress coat without the embroidery on the collar and the anchor and star in white. Both coats had three buttons around the cuffs (6).

The anchor and star, but not the oak leaf embroidery, were continued in the 1841 uniform regulations, as were the three buttons on the cuff. The undress coat now had a rolling collar that included the anchor and star in gold (7).

In 1852 the dress coat had a strip of 1/2 inch lace around the front and top of the collar and no other decoration. Cuffs were plain. The undress coat had a plain collar and cuffs and a shoulder straps of a 1/2 inch strip of gold lace (8).

A law of February 28, 1855 (9) allowed all of the Passed Midshipmen on the active list to be promoted to Master. Another batch of 20 was appointed on June 20, 1856 with four more added on November 22nd (10), all of whom had moved on by 1859.

No further appointments were made and the law of July 16, 1862 reorganizing the navy's rank structure did not include Passed Midshipmen. The new rank of Ensign now took the place after Master (11).

Pay Clerk

Paymaster's Clerks became the warrant rank of Pay Clerk on March 3, 1915 (1).

The insignia on the coat collars, and shoulder boards was a gold oak sprig composed of three leafs and three acorns (2).

The oak sprig was placed on the cuffs in 1918. A year later a stripe 1/4 inch wide was added under it. Shoulder boards of 1919 also carried the 1/4 inch lace the oak sprig (3).

The 1922 regulations added a 1/2 inch dark blue break every two inches on the cuff stripes and a single 1/2 inch break in the center of the shoulder board stripe (4).

Black sleeve stripes were used on khaki and green coats starting in 1925. The format used by warrant officers is not clear. It is possible that a solid stripe was used (5). The black stripes were removed from the khaki coat in 1941 (6) and stripes with green breaks were definitely prescribed for warrant officers in 1944 (7).

The oak sprig, in gold, returned as the Pay Clerk's pin on badge of rank in 1931.

The Career Compensation Act of October 12, 1949 (8) placed Pay Clerks in pay grade W-1.

A standard, warrant officers badge of rank was introduced on July 1,1952 (9) consisting of a gold bar with a 1/16 inch blue break across the middle (10).

Pay Clerk became Warrant Officer 1, with the Warrant Officer Act of 1954 (11).

Pay Director

Pay Director was the title for supply officers with the relative rank of Captain. It was created on March 3, 1871 (1) and as with other staff titles, "relative rank of" became "rank of" on March 3, 1899 (2), it stopped being used in November of 1918 (3) and was eliminated on August 7, 1947 (4).

They wore the uniform of a Captain with a corps device of an oak sprig and, until 1918, white cloth around the cuff and shoulder stripes.

Pay Inspector

Pay Inspector was the title for supply officers with the relative rank of Commander. It was created on March 3, 1871 (1) and as with other staff titles, "relative rank of" became "rank of" on March 3, 1899 (2), it stopped being used in November of 1918 (3) and was eliminated on August 7, 1947 (4).

They wore the uniform of a Commander with a corps device of an oak sprig and, until 1918, white cloth around the cuff and shoulder stripes.

Paymaster General

The title of the Chief of the Bureau of Provisions and Clothing, Edward Dunn, was changed to Paymaster General on March 3, 1871 (1).

Dunn was still a relative Commodore and wore that uniform with an oak sprig as a corps device and white piping on his cuff stripe (2).

Dunn retired on January 22, 1873 (3) and was replaced by John Bradford on February 18th (4). Bradford retired on February 22, 1877. The next day James Watmough, who had been acting Paymaster General since March 1 of 1873 was appointed and he served until November 17th (5). Next was George Cutter, who served until August 30, 1881. Then came Joseph Smith form June 27, 1882 to January 29, 1886, James Fulton form November 17, 1886 to March 15, 1890 and Edwin Stewart was then appointed on May 16th (6).

When the rank of Commodore, and relative ranks, were abolished on March 3, 1899 (7), the chiefs of bureaus were made into Rear Admirals with "the same pay and allowance as are now allowed a brigadier-general in the Army". In other words Rear Admiral lower half.

Stewart was replaced by Albert Kenny on May 5, 1899 (8), who retired on January 19, 1903 (9), and was replaced by Henry Harris on July 1st (1). Harris retired on March 5, 1905 (11). His replacement was Eustace Rogers on February 16, 1906 (12). Rogers retired on June 30, 1910 (13) and was replaced with Thomas Cowle (14).

When staff titles stopped being used in November of 1918 (15) Cowle became a Rear Admiral more than a Paymaster General.

Staff titles were officially eliminated on August 7, 1947.

Paymaster

Pursers became Paymasters on June 22, 1860 (1). They inherited Pursers' relative rank, those over 12 years service ranked with Commanders and those under with Lieutenants (2).

Paymasters over 12 years service wore plain gold epaulets with 1/2 inch wide bullion, Shoulder straps with an oak sprig in the center and a leaf at each end (3), ant the two cuff stripes of a Commander.

Those under 12 years service had 3/8 inch bullion, no leafs on the shoulder straps and only one cuff stripe (4).

When the cuff stripes changed for line officers in 1862, equivalent staff officers changed as well, relative Commanders now wore two 3/4 inch stripes with at 1/4 inch stripe between them (5).

The navy, on it's own authority, realigned the relative ranks on March 13, 1863. Paymasters over 15 years service were relative Captains, Paymasters from five to 15 years service were Relative Commanders and Paymasters under five years service were relative Lieutenant Commanders (6).

The uniform regulations of 1864 prescribed the uniform of their relative rank with no line star on the cuffs and an oak sprig as a corps device (7).

When, in 1869, the Attorney General overruled the 1863 order on relative ranks, they returned to Commander for over 12 years and Lieutenant for under (8).

On March 11 1869 white coth was prescribed between the cuff stripes (9).

A law of March 3, 1871 gave Paymasters the relative rank of Lieutenant Commander or Lieutenant (10).

There was a slight redesign of the oak sprig in 1905 (11).

Staff officers ranks were no longer relative after March 3, 1899 (12). The staff titles were no longer used after November of 1918 (13) and abolished on August 7, 1947 (14).

Petty Officer (before 1885)

Petty Officers are the noncommissioned officers of the navy. The term derives from the French petite meaning small. In medieval English villages the assistants to senior officials became known as petite or petty officials. Sailors took this concept to sea with them calling the assistants to officers and warrant officers "Petty Officers" (1).

A Petty Officer is a specialist in a particular job, this is known as a "rating". Many ratings have come and gone over the years. One problem is determining which enlisted title was considered a petty officer at any specific time. Pay table prior to 1885 simply list all enlisted tittles with no indication as to which is a petty officer and which is non rated. Charles Malin did a review of all enlisted titles used by the navy in 1969. This is available on the web site of the Naval Historical Foundation (2) and is an invaluable resource for anyone researching the history of the navy's organization.

A pay table for the Continental Navy from November 28, 1775 listed petty officers of Boatswain's First Mate, Boatswain's Second Mate, Gunner's Mate, Carpenter's Mate, Cooper, Captain's or Commander's Clerk and Steward (3).

Another table, this one form November 15, 1776 shows only one grade of Boatswain's Mate, refers to Captain's Clerk instead of Captain's or Commander's Clerk and adds Armourer, Sailmaker's Mate, Yeoman, Quartermaster, Cook, Coxswain and Yeoman of Powder Room (that's where gunpowder was stored, not the lavatory) (4).

The laws of 1794 (5) and 1797 (6) laws that crated the federal navy called for ratings of Master's Mate, Captain's Clerk, Boatswain's Mate, Cockswain, Sailmaker's Mate, Gunner's Mate, Yeoman of the Gun Room, Quarter Gunner, Carpenter's Mate, Armourer, Steward, Cooper, Master-at-arms and Cook.

From there on rating came and went reflecting the needs of the navy.

The first known insignia for Petty Officers comes from 1833. A white/blue anchor worn on the right upper sleeve by some ratings and the left by others (7). Wearing the anchor on the right side were Boatswain's Mates, Gunner's Mates, Carpenter's Mates, Masters-at-arms, Stewards and Cooks. On the left side were Quartermasters, Quarter Gunners, Armorers and Coopers.

The 1841 uniform regulations (8) were the first to include enlisted uniforms. The badge for petty officers was modified to a white/blue eagle, with it's wings down, on an anchor. The regulations call for it to be worn on the right sleeve by Boatswain's Mates, Carpenter's Mates, Gunner's Mates, Masters-at-arms, Ship's Cooks and Ship's Stewards. Wearing the device on the left were Quarter Gunners, Quartermasters, Captains of Forecastle, Captains of Tops, Captain's of Holds, Armorers, Coopers, Ship's Corporals and Captains of Afterguard.

The 1852 uniform regulations stated "Boatswain's Mates, Gunner's Mates, Carpenter's Mates, Sailmaker's Mates, Ship's Steward, and Ship's Cook, will wear, embroidered in white silk, on the right sleeve of their blue jackets, above the elbow in front, an eagle and anchor, of not more than three inches in length, with a star of one inch in diameter, one inch above. The same device embroidered in blue, to be worn on the sleeves of their white frocks in summer. All other petty officers, except officers stewards, and yeomen, will wear the same device on their left sleeves." (9). The device was the same as 1841 except for the addition of the star.

On June 18, 1862 Master's Mate's were "jacketed". That is they were given different uniforms than other enlisted men that consisted of a double breasted jacket with two rows of six buttons and a blue cap with a silver anchor (10). It appears that the eagle and anchor was not worn. The anchor was removed from the caps on July 31st. (11).

In 1863 petty officer's ratings were divided in to line and staff, and a seniority of the various ratings was established (12).

The 1864 uniform regulations expanded the "jacketed" ratings to Yeomen Masters-at-arms, Surgeon's Stewards and Paymaster's Stewards. The petty officer's device was worn on the right by Boatswain's Mates, Gunner's Mates, Carpenter's mates, Sailmakers' Mates and Ship's Cooks. All others wore it on the left except Officer's Stewards (13).

The uniform regulations of December 1, 1866 altered the design of the petty officer's device. The wings of the eagle were now out horizontally. The star was now only worn by line ratings, who wore it on the right sleeve. Staff ratings wore the device on the left sleeve without the star (14). "jacketed" ratings did wear the device on the jacket (15).

Specialty marks were also introduced in 1866. They were worn on the forearm by some ratings and the collar by others. Some wore them on both sides and others on the side to indicate the side of the ship they were assigned to, right for starboard or left for port (16).

The last change in 1866 was the stripes worn around the cuffs and collars of jumpers. This was primarily a mark for non rated men but petty officers were ordered to wear three stripes, the same as Seamen (17). The stripes were removed from the collar (18), and the cuff stripes were increased to four for petty officers in 1869 (19).

The jacket for "jacketed" ratings was changed to a single breasted sack coat in 1874 (20).

A general order of January 8, 1885 spread the ratings across three classes (21). This created the rates of Petty Officer First Class, Petty Officer Second Class, and Petty Officer Third Class.

Petty Officer First Class

Chief Boatswain's Mates, Chief Quartermasters, Chief Gunner's Mates, Masters-at-Arms, Equipment Yeomen, Apothecaries, Paymaster's Yeomen, Engineer's Yeomen, Ship's Writers, Schoolmasters, Bandmasters and Machinists were designated Petty Officers First Class on January 8, 1885 (1).

The 1886 uniform regulations continue the concept of "jacketed" ratings by prescribing blue and white double breasted sack coats for First Class Petty Officers, instead of the jumpers worn by other rates (2).

1886 also saw the creation of the rating badge. For Petty Officers First Class, except Masters-at-Arms, it consisted of three chevrons with a diamond in the angle, the insignia of an army First Sergeant. The eagle in the 1866 style was worn above the chevrons and diamond and a specialty mark was worn over the diamond. Master-at-Arms, who were the senior petty officers on a ship, wore three chevrons and three arcs, the insignia of an army Sergeant Major, with the eagle resting on the lower arc. A specialty mark of a star was worn just below the eagle (3).

When the rate of Chief Petty Officer was created in 1893, they inherited the Master-at-Arms' Sergeant Major style rating badge (4), and the coat and cap style uniforms (5). Most of the ratings that were in the first class were moved up to chief, so this caused minimal problems (6).

The following year the rating badges were redesigned. The wings of the eagle were now pointing up, the diamond was eliminated and the three chevrons were moved further apart from each other (7). This basic style has been used ever since.

The petty officer first class pay grade became grade two on June 10, 1922 (8) and grade E-6 on October 12, 1949 (9).

Pin-on badges of rank were authorized in 1969 consisting of three silver chevrons and an eagle, no specialty mark was used (10).

Petty Officer Second Class

Boatswain's Mates, Quartermasters, Gunner's Mates, Coxswains to Commander in Chief, Ship's Corporals, Ship's Cooks, Chief Musicians, Boilermakers, Armorers, Carpenter's Mates, Blacksmiths, Sailmaker's Mates and Water Tenders were designated Petty Officers Second Class on January 8, 1885 (1).

The 1886 uniform regulations saw the creation of the rating badge. For Petty Officers Second Class it consisted of three chevrons, the insignia of an army Sergeant. The eagle in the 1866 style was worn above the chevrons and a specialty mark was worn under it. (2).

In 1894 the rating badges were redesigned. The wings of the eagle were now pointing up and the chevrons were reduced to two and spread further apart from each other (3). This basic style has been used ever since.

The petty officer second class pay grade became grade three on June 10, 1922 (4) and grade E-5 on October 12, 1949 (5).

Pin-on badges of rank were authorized in 1969 consisting of three silver chevrons and an eagle, no specialty mark was used (6).

Petty Officer Third Class

Captains of Forecastle, Captains of Main top, Captains of Fore Top, Captains of Mizzen top Captains of Afterguard, Coxswains, Quarter Gunners, Seaman Gunners, Captains of Hold, Printers, Painters and Oilers were designated Petty Officers Third Class on January 8, 1885 (1).

The 1886 uniform regulations saw the creation of the rating badge. For Petty Officers Third Class it consisted of two chevrons, the insignia of an army Corporal. The eagle in the 1866 style was worn above the chevrons and a specialty mark was worn under it. (2).

In 1894 the rating badges were redesigned. The wings of the eagle were now pointing up and the chevrons were reduced to one (3). This basic style has been used ever since.

The petty officer third class pay grade became grade four on June 10, 1922 (4) and grade E-4 on October 12, 1949 (5).

Pin-on badges of rank were authorized in 1969 consisting of three silver chevrons and an eagle, no specialty mark was used (6).

Pharmacist

The rank of Pharmacist was Created on June 17, 1898 (1).

They were given insignia on the coat collars of a gold cross (2).

In the January 1913 uniform regulations the cross was changed to a caduceus (3). It was also worn on white cloth shoulder loops on the white service coat (4). It continued to be worn on the collar of the blue service coat.

Shoulder boards were allowed to replace the cloth shoulder loops in June. The caduceus was worn at the outer end (5).

The caduceus moved to the cuffs in 1918. A year later a 1/4 inch gold cuff stripe was added under the caduceus. Shoulder boards of 1919 also carried the 1/4 inch lace and cross (6).

The 1922 regulations added a 1/2 inch dark blue break every two inches on the cuff stripes and a single 1/2 inch break in the center of the shoulder board stripe (7).

Black sleeve stripes were used on khaki and green coats starting in 1925. The format used by warrant officers is not clear. It is possible that a solid stripe was used (8). The black stripes were removed from the khaki coat in 1941 (9) and stripes with green breaks were definitely prescribed for warrant officers in 1944 (10).

The gold three bladed propellor returned as the Pharmacist's pin on badge of rank in 1931 (11).

Pharmacists became Warrant Officers, Hospital Corps on August 4, 1947 (12).

Photographer

The warrant grade of Photographer was created on July 28, 1942 (1).

The lace worn on the cuffs was 1/4 inch wide gold with 1/2 inch long blue breaks every 2 inches. The device of an Photographer, an old fashioned camera with the bellows extended, was worn above the stripes. Shoulder boards showed the 1/4 inch lace with a single 1/2 inch break, under the device. The camera device, in gold, was also used as a badge of rank (2).

The aviation green coat was given a black stripe with green breaks in 1944 (3). It is possible that a solid stripe was worn previous to this (4).

The Career Compensation Act of October 12, 1949 (5) placed Photographers across pay grade W-1.

A standard, warrant officers badge of rank was introduced on July 1,1952 (6) consisting of a gold bar with a 1/16 inch blue break across the middle (7).

Photographers became Warrant Officer with the Warrant Officer Act of 1954 (8).

Professor of Mathematics

Professors of Mathematics are first mentioned in a law of March 3, 1835 (1) setting the pay of various officers of the navy. They may have replaced Schoolmasters who appear to have been petty officers, but all this is far from clear.

The first known uniforms were prescribed in 1841. They were to wear the same uniform as Clerks. It was described as "To be of dark blue cloth, lined with the same, double breasted, rolling collar, seven navy buttons on each breast, one on each hip, and one at the bottom of the folds of each skirt." (2) Schoolmasters had worn the same uniform as Clerks in the 1830 uniform regulations (3), which raises the possibility that Professor of Mathematics replaced the rate of Schoolmaster.

A Law of August 31, 1842 stated" That professors of mathematics in the navy of the United States shall be entitled to live and mess with the lieutenants of sea going vessels, and shall receive such rations as lieutenants of the same ship or stations shall receive." (4).

They officially became naval officers on August 3, 1848 when a law stated "That the number of professors of mathematics in the navy shall not exceed twelve; that they shall be appointed and commissioned by the President of the United States; by and with the advice and consent of the Senate, and shall perform such duties as may be assigned them by order of the Secretary of the Navy, at the Naval School, the Observatory, and on board ships-of-war, instructing the midshipmen of the navy, or otherwise." (5).

The 1852 uniform regulations called for a single breasted dress tail coat with a plain rolling collar and an undress frock coat with same buttons and collar. A visored cap was worn with both coats with an empty gold wreath on the front (6).

On March 13, 1863 the navy granted Professors of Mathematics relative rank. Those over 12 years service were relative Commanders and those under relative Lieutenant Commanders (7).

The new status was reflected in the 1864 uniform regulations. They wore the uniform of their relative rank with no line star and a corps device of a gold disc with a silver letter "P" on it (8).

Relative rank was taken from Professors on April 1, 1869 when the Attorney General ruled that the navy exceeded it's authority in 1863 (9). Professors do not appear in the July 14, 1869 uniform regulations (10) and if they wore uniforms during this period, their design is not known.

Congress returned Professors relative rank on May 31, 1872 (11) spreading them over the ranks of Captain, Commander, Lieutenant Commander and Lieutenant.

Uniforms were prescribed on June 12th. Professors were to wear the uniform of their relative rank with olive green cloth around the stripes and a corps device of a silver oak leaf with a silver acorn (12).

The ranks ceased to be relative on March 3, 1899 (13).

Appointment of Professors of Mathematics were stopped by a law of August 29, 1916 (14).

The use of staff titles stopped in November of 1918 (15).

Theodore Woolsey Johnson, the last Professor on the active list, retired on July 1, 1936 (16).

Purser

A Purser was responsible for a ships supplies and finances. He was responsible for the ship's payroll, including any advances or deductions. He also kept track of the ship's inventory of supplies and saw that they were issued appropriately. He also ran the ship's store, selling items known as slops, clothing and such, to the crew. If the ship was in a port that didn't have an agent assigned by the Navy Department, the Purser might be responsible for handling the ship's expenses, if the captain didn't want to do this themselves. All of this required the Purser to be responsible for large sums of public money, in cash (1).

Pursers do not appear on the pay tables of the Continental Navy (2)(3), but are mentioned in legislation (4).

They are listed as warrant officers in the 1794 (5) and 1797 (6) laws creating the federal navy.

For uniforms the 1797 regulations say "COAT. Plain frock blue coat, with the proper naval buttons-- no lappels. VEST AND BREECHES. Buff and plain." (7). What this meant is up to interpretation. The term "frock coat" may mean that the coat was buttoned up instead of open as was usual at the time.

in 1802 the uniforms were described as " THE COAT of blue cloth, with standing collar, long lappels and lining of the same, with nine buttons on the lappels, cuffs open behind, with three buttons, two above and one below; the collar to be embroidered with gold, not exceeding three-fourths of an inch in breadth, with one button on each side, the folds to have each three buttons, and three buttons under each pocket, the buttons the same as worn by the other officers of the navy. VEST AND BREECHES, white--cocked hat." (8).

There were, in the early 1800s, charges that Pursers were overcharging sailors for slops and pocketing the difference (9). This, and other questions on the handling of public money, lead to a change in the Pursers status. As warrant officers their appointments were not subject to senate confirmation. A law of March 30, 1812 (10) made them commissioned officers, giving the Senate more control over who was handling the people's money.

The 1813 uniform regulations made very minor changes to the uniform coat. The lapels are decried as broad instead of long and the 3/4 inch embroidery was replaced with 1/2 inch gold lace. An undress coat with no lace and a rolling collar with one button on it, was also added (11).

The 1820 uniform was also the same except there was no button the undress collar (12).

The uniforms of 1830 had lines of gold oak leaf and acorn embroidery around the top of the cuffs and the front and top of the collar, of the dress coat. A cornucopia was embroidered on the collar under the oak leafs (13).

With the 1841 uniform regulations the embroidery was no longer worn around the cuffs and an extra strip replaced the cornucopia on the collar (14).

On May 27,1847 the navy issued an order giving pursers relative rank. Those over 12 years service were relative Commanders and those under relative Lieutenants (15). Congress made this legal on August 5, 1854 (16).

Epaulets and shoulder straps were authorized now that Pursers had relative rank. The epaulets had solid lace crescents instead of the embroidered crescents used by line officers. The bullion was 1/2 inch wide for those over 12 years service and 3/3 for those under. Old english letters "P.D." were worn in silver in the frog. The shoulder straps had 1/4 inch wide borders and the "P.D." in the center. The over 12s had an oak leaf at each end (17).

The March 8, 1852 uniform regulations didn't make any great changes to Purser's uniforms. The dress tail coat was double breasted with two rows on nine buttons down the front, three under the pockets and three vertical on the cuffs. The standing collar continued to have the line of oak leaf and acorn embroidery around the top and down the front of the V opening under the chin. The cuffs continued to have a similar line of embroidery. The undress frock coat had the same two rows of nine buttons down the front and three vertical buttons on the cuffs. The rolling collar was plain and the cuff carried three large buttons running perpendicular to the three small ones. Epaulets and shoulder straps were the same as they had been since 1847 (18).

Change came 200 days later on September 24th. The letters were removed from the epaulet frogs and shoulders straps. An oak sprig replaced them on the shoulder straps but the epaulets were left plain (19).

On August 23, 1856, Pursers were ordered to wear the uniforms of their relative rank, except for the Epaulets and shoulder straps. This put an end the lines of oak leaf and acorn embroidery. Cuff stripes were now worn on both coats, two for Pursers over 12 years service and one for Pursers under 12 years service (20).

The rank of Purser was changed to Paymaster on June 22, 1860 (21).

Radio Electrician

Radio Electricians were created on March 4, 1925 (1) as a warrant rank. Previously Gunners had been assigned to radio duties.

The lace worn on the cuffs was 1/4 inch wide gold with 1/2 inch long blue breaks every 2 inches. A device of four lightning bolts was placed on the sleeve above the stripes. Shoulder boards showed the 1/4 inch lace with a single 1/2 inch break, under the device (2).

Black sleeve stripes were used on khaki and green coats starting in 1925. The format used by warrant officers is not clear. It is possible that a solid stripe was used (3). The black stripes were removed from the khaki coat in 1941 (4) and stripes with green breaks were definitely prescribed for warrant officers in 1944 (5).

Gold lightning bolts was used as the Radio Electrician's pin on badge of rank starting in 1931.

The Career Compensation Act of October 12, 1949 (6) placed Radio Electricians in pay grade W-1.

A standard, warrant officers badge of rank was introduced on July 1,1952 (7) consisting of a gold bar with a 1/16 inch blue break across the middle (8).

Radio Electricians became Warrant Officer, with the Warrant Officer Act of 1954 (9).

The History of American Ranks and Rank Insignia

Rear Admiral/ Rear Admiral (upper half)

The title of Rear Admiral originated in the Sixteenth or Seventeenth Century. English fleets were organized into three lines with the admiral commanding the middle line, his deputy or vice admiral commanding the front line and the lowest ranking admiral commanding the rear line. As a result the most junior rank of admiral became Rear Admiral (1).

The rank was not used in the U.S. Navy until the rank structure was overhauled on June 16, 1862 (2).

They Inherited the insignia of a Flag Officer, Epaulets with and eagle and anchor device under two stars and shoulder straps with two stars with an anchor in between. The cuff lace was three 3/4 inch stripes alternating with three 1/4 inch stripes. The bottom stripe was 3/4 and the top 1/4 (3).

On May 23, 1863 all line officers were ordered to wear a gold star above their cuff stripes. It is possible that the stripes were changed at the same time, but were certainly changed by the new uniform regulations of January 28, 1864 (4).

The 1864 regulations changed the shoulder straps slightly, making he anchor smaller and parallel to the border. There were eight cuff stripes, each 1/4 inch wide and 1/4 inch apart except the space between the 3rd and 4th rows, the 4th and 5th rows and the 7th and 8th rows that was 1/2 inch, making two groups of three stripes with a single stripe between and one above, all under a line star. Two silver stars were worn on the collar of the overcoat. Epaulets were not to be worn for the rest of the war (5).

In January of 1865 the cuff lace was changed to one two inch stripe under one 1/4 inch stripe under a line star. At the same time a service coat was added that had the two stars on the collar (6).

The 1866 uniform regulations changed the cuff stripes of one two inch stripe under one 1/2 inch stripe under a line star. The two silver stars with an anchor between were worn on the shoulder straps, epaulet frogs and service coat collars (7).

In 1869 the stripes on the full dress coat were replaced with a single line of oak leaf and acorn embroidery (8). The stripes returned in 1873 (9).

The stars were worn alone on the 1877 service coat collar (10) until 1883 when the anchor was added behind the stars (11).

The phasing out of the senior ranks created during the Civil War and the abolishment of the rank of Commodore in 1899, made every officer in the navy above the rank of Captain, except Admiral of the Navy George Dewy, a Rear Admiral. The lower ranking half were still paid as Commodores, laying the foundation of two ranks of Rear Admiral.

When shoulder boards were created in 1899 they were covered in two inch wide gold lace and carried two silver stars with a silver anchor between (12).

Shoulder straps make their last appearance in regulations in 1905 (13) and may have been abolished with the next regulations in 1913 or sometime in between.

The January 13, 1913 regulations did abolish shoulder boards, replacing them with a white cloth shoulder loop with a metal stars and anchor worn in a line (14). This was undone on June 24th and shoulder boards returned (15).

Epaulets were also changed in 1913. The stars were now side by side in the frog with the anchor on the strap (16).

The use of epaulets was suspended in 1917 (17).

A law of October 6, 1917 (18) stated "That brigadier generals of the Army shall hereafter rank relatively with rear admirals of the lower half of the grade." The lower half of Rear Admirals continued to wear same two stars as the upper half. This was always a sore point with the Brigadier Generals (19).

The end of the use of staff titles in November 1918 led to equivalent staff admirals wearing the corps device in place of the line star on the cuffs and superimposed on the anchor on the blue service coat collar and between the stars on the shoulder boards. The collar insignia disappeared when the 1877 service coat was replaced in 1919 (20).

Use of epaulets resumed with the 1922 uniform regulations, the line anchor was now worn on the strap by all officers, with the corps device for staff officers superimposed over it. The shoulder boards now had the stars one above the other under the anchor (21).

The two silver stars began to be used as a pin on badge of rank in 1931 (22).

The Career Compensation Act of October 12, 1949 (23) placed the rank of Rear Admiral (upper half) in pay grade O-8 and Rear Admiral (lower half) in pay grade O-7. The law used "(upper half)" after the O-8 grade title, while a law of August 10, 1956 (24) used "entitled to pay of upper half" and lower half for that matter.

The 1956 law was amended on December 12, 1980 (25) to remove the "(upper half)". Presumably it mean to remove the "entitled to pay of" as well. The law also made Rear Admiral (lower half) into the separate rank of Commodore Admiral. The "(upper half)" is still sometimes used for clarity but the official title of the navy's O-8 rank is Rear Admiral.

The April 2010 uniform regulations descried the insignia for Rear Admirals as:

Sleeve Stripes - "REAR ADMIRAL. Wear one 2 inch stripe with one 1/2 inch stripes above it." (26).

Shoulder Boards - "The surface is covered with gold lace showing a 1/8 inch blue cloth margin on each of the long sides. A silver embroidered fouled anchor is placed with its center line along the shoulder board's longer dimension and the crown pointing toward the squared end of the board. The unfouled arm of the stock points to the front of the wearer (right and left). Designation of grade consists of silver embroidered five-pointed star(s), placed between the crown of the anchor and the squared end of the shoulder board."(the number of stars is shown as two in illustration) (27).

Metal Grade Insignia - "Flag Officer. Wear insignia lengthwise on the strap so that the single rays of each star point toward the collar. (the number of stars is shown as two in illustration).
Collar grade insignia replicates metal shoulder insignia except flag officers' miniature multiple stars which are connected as follows" (the number of stars is shown as two in illustration) (28).

Rear Admiral (lower half)

The concept of a Rear Admiral (lower half) dates from March 3, 1899 (1) when the rank of Commodore was abolished and all those on the active list were made Rear Admirals. To avoid having to pay them as Rear Admirals, the lower half of the active list would be paid the same as army Brigadier Generals. They were still Rear Admirals, despite their pay and this did not please the generals who were out ranked by their equivalent rank in the navy (2).

Congress made the lower half of Rear Admirals equivalent to Brigadier Generals on October 6, 1917 (3), but they were still allowed to wear the insignia of the upper half.

Finally on December 12, 1980 (4) a separate rank was created, equal to Brigadier Generals in the O-7 pay grade. The rank was called Commodore Admiral.

Now the admirals were unhappy. The title Commodore Admiral seamed clumsy and not in keeping with naval tradition (5).

The title was changed to Commodore on December 1, 1981 (6) and then to Rear Admiral (lower half) on November 8, 1985 (7).

The insignia, as described in the April 2010 uniform regulations is:

Sleeve Stripes - "REAR ADMIRAL (lower half). Wear one 2 inch stripe." (8).

Shoulder Boards - "The surface is covered with gold lace showing a 1/8 inch blue cloth margin on each of the long sides. A silver embroidered fouled anchor is placed with its center line along the shoulder board's longer dimension and the crown pointing toward the squared end of the board. The unfouled arm of the stock points to the front of the wearer (right and left). Designation of grade consists of silver embroidered five-pointed star(s), placed between the crown of the anchor and the squared end of the shoulder board."(the number of stars is shown as one in illustration) (9).

Metal Grade Insignia - "Flag Officer. Wear insignia lengthwise on the strap so that the single rays of each star point toward the collar. (the number of stars is shown as one in illustration).
Collar grade insignia replicates metal shoulder insignia except flag officers' miniature multiple stars which are connected as follows" (the number of stars is shown as one in illustration) (10).

Sailing Master

Master is the original term for a commander of a merchant ship. In the middle ages ships would be taken to serve as warships with the addition of a company of soldiers commanded by a Captain. The Captain was in charge of the fighting and the Master the sailing. Eventually when ships became permanent parts of navies, the Captain was in permanent command and the Master was a warrant officer in charge of navigation, trim, sail and line condition and log books. In the U.S. Navy the original term used was Sailing Master (1).

Sailing Master was listed in the 1794 (2) and 1797 (3) laws creating the federal navy. The actual usage of the rank was to allow experienced merchant seamen to come into the navy with some degree of authority. Sailing Masters were often placed in command of gunboats freeing up Lieutenants and Midshipmen for service on larger vessels (4).

Uniforms were generally plain. The 1797 uniform regulations prescribed "COAT. Long, blue, with facings and standing collar of the same, edged with buff-- nine buttons to the lappels, and one to the standing collar. Lining blue, or faced with the same as the coat-- Slash sleeves, with three buttons-- Pockets plain. VEST AND BREECHES. Plain buff vest-- and blue breeches. Buttons (for the suit) the same as for the officers." (5).

In 1802 they were to wear "THE COAT of blue cloth, with standing collar, long lappels and lining of the same, nine buttons on the lappels and one on the standing collar, with a slip of lace; slash sleeves with three buttons, and three buttons to the pockets. VEST AND BREECHES, white, and plain--cocked hat." (6).

On August 18, 1802, the Secretary of the Navy Robert smith issued a general order requiring examinations before promotion to Lieutenant. The order stated that the examinations could be tanked by both Midshipmen and Sailing Masters. Smith's intention was to allow experienced semen an entry into the navy's officer corps. Midshipmen saw this as someone else competing for limited positions and Smith's successor, Paul Hamilton, ended the program in 1809 (7).

In 1813 the prescribed uniform was "The Coat of blue cloth, with standing collar, broad lappels and lining of the same, with nine buttons on the lappels, cuffs open behind with three buttons, two above and one below; the collar to be laced round with gold lace, not exceeding one half of an inch in breadth, with one button on each side, the folds to have each three buttons, and three buttons under each pocket, the buttons the same as worn by the other officers of the navy. Pantaloons and Vest white; cocked hat, plain, half boots, and dirk." (8).

For the 1820 uniform regulations, Sailing Masters were to wear the similar "Coat. - Blue cloth, with standing collar, broad lappels and lining of the same, nine buttons on the lappels, one on the standing collar, three on each of the pocket flaps, and three on each of the cuffs. Pantaloons and Vest, white. Plain cocked hat, half boots, and cut and thrust swords, with yellow mounting." (9).

The 1830 uniform regulations called for the standard officer's uniform with a button and gold laced button hole on the collar of the dress coat (10).

Sailing Master was changed to Master on March 3, 1837 (11).

Sailmaker

Sailmakers were warrant officers in charge of a repairing a ships sails.

They existed in the Continental Navy (1) and were listed among the warrant ranks in both the 1794 (2) and 1796 (3) laws creating the navy.

Uniforms were first prescribed by the 1814 uniform regulations (4). They called for "Short blue coats, with six buttons on the lappels; rolling cape, blue pantaloons, white vests, round hats, with cockade. No side-arms."

In 1830 a double breasted, dark blue dress coat with lapels buttoned back with eight buttons was prescribed. It had a standing collar with one button on it and slashed sleeves closed with three buttons. The undress rolling collar coatee had the same buttons as the dress coat except the one on the collar (5).

The only coat listed in the 1841 regulations was described as "To be of dark blue cloth, lined with the same, double breasted, seven navy buttons on each breast, slashed sleeves with three small navy buttons on each, two large navy buttons under each pocket flap, one on each hip, and one at the bottom of each skirt". Blue cloth caps were also called for (6). On April 5, 1849 a large button and a button hole worked in black twist was added to the coat collars. At the same time a 1 1/4 inch wide gold lace band was added around the cap (7).

The 1852 regulations list the warrant officers coats with the descriptions of the officers dress tail coats, but they may have been frock coats. This is by no means clear. They are described as "shall be of Navy blue cloth, lined with the same; rolling collar, double breasted, two rows of large Navy buttons on the breast, eight in each row; pointed pocket flaps, with three large buttons underneath each, showing one half their diameter; three medium size buttons around each cuff and two small ones in each opening; one button behind on each hip, one in the middle of each fold and one in each fold near the bottom of the skirt. On each side of the collar to have one loop of three-quarters wide gold lace to show one inch and a half wide, and four inches long, with a small size Navy button in the point of each loop." They were worn over blue or white pantaloons, according to season and blue caps with a gold anchor on the front (8).

A band of two 1/2 inch strips of gold lace 1/4 apart, showing blue in between, were added to the caps on February 17, 1853 (9).

The uniforms may have been simplified in 1862 with the removal of the cuff buttons and maybe the collar button and lace, but this is not clear (10).

New uniform regulations of 1864 (11) gave warrant officers the same frock coats and caps as officers. Shoulder straps were added consisting of a strip of gold lace 3/4 inches wide by 4 inches long. Caps were plain except for an empty wreath.

On March 11, 1869 the shoulder straps were replaced with a gold diamond on the collar of the frock coat (12).

Use of the service dress sack coat by warrant officers is clear but it is authorized by the 1876 regulations but no insignia was mentioned (13).

They were authorized the new standing collar service coat in October 1878. The diamond was worn on the collar (14).

In 1883 the diamonds on the collars of both the frock coat and the service coat were rendered in silver for those over 20 years service and gold for those under (15).

The use of engines to move ships made sailmakers obsolete. The last appointment went to Michael Barr on May 4, 1888 (16). A law of March 3, 1899 (17) made Sailmakers into Chief Sailmakers after ten years service. All of the Sailmakers on the list, including Barr, qualified, and the rank of Sailmaker ceased to exist.

Schoolmaster

The status and usage of Schoolmasters is far from clear. Charles Malin's study of enlisted rank titles (1) shows them existing from 1802 to 1820, but it is possible some existed as early as the 1790s (2). They also appear in the annual report to Congress of the Secretary of the Navy as late as 1834 (3). A law setting the pay of the navy from March 3, 1835 (4) lists Professors of Mathematics for the first time, but does not mention Schoolmasters. It is possible that Professors of Mathematics replaced Schoolmasters in 1835, but this is not definite.

As to their status, they seam to have been petty officers, but like Captain's Clerks they held a nebulous position between petty officer and warrant officer (5).

Their only mention in uniform regulations is in 1830, where they were to wear the same uniform as Clerks: "Coats of plain blue cloth, single-breasted, rolling collar, and made according to the prevailing fashion for the citizens of the time, with six Navy buttons on each breast, one on each hip, and one on the bottom of the skirts" (6).

Schoolmaster returned as a petty officer's rating in 1864 and lasted until 1900 (7).

Seaman

Seaman is the basic title of a non rated sailor. It appears to have been used interchangeably with Able Seaman in the early days. A Continental Navy pay table from November 28, 1775 (1) used Able Seaman, but a table of November 15, 1776 (2) uses Seaman. The laws creating the federal navy in 1794 (3) and 1797 (4) add to the confusion. Both law state that ships with 44 guns should have 150 Seaman and ships with 36 guns should have 130 Able Seaman. A later section of both laws setting the pay of the navy refers to Seaman not Able Seaman. It is doubtful that seamen on a larger ship were of a different rate than those on a smaller one. The best guess is that "able" was used for clarity to differentiate between Semen and the lower rate of Ordinary Seaman.

Seamen wore standard enlisted uniforms. When stripes were added to the collar and cuffs of the jumper in 1866, they received three (5). The stripes were removed from the collar in 1869 (6).

Seamen were placed in the Seaman First Class pay grade on January 8, 1885 (7).

The 1886 uniform regulations (8) added a white/blue watch mark which became a white/blue branch mark on the right slide in 1912 (9).

Seaman became Seaman First Class in 1921 (10).

The rate of Seaman returned on April 2, 1948 by combining Seamen First Class and Bugler First Class (11).

It continued the Seaman First Class position in pay grade five. Grade five became grade E-3 with The Career Compensation Act of October 12, 1949 (12).

It was given a group rate mark of three white/blue hash marks (13).

In 2008 a pin on badge of rank consisting of three silver metal hash marks was introduced on the shirt collar of the navy service uniform (14).

Seaman Apprentice

Seaman Second Class and Bugler Second Class were combined into Seaman Apprentice on April 2, 1948 (1).

It continued the Seaman Second Class position in pay grade six. Grade Six became grade E-2 with The Career Compensation Act of October 12, 1949 (2).

It was given a group rate mark of two white/blue hash marks (3).

In 2008 a pin on badge of rank consisting of two silver metal hash marks was introduced on the shirt collar of the navy service uniform (4).

Seaman First Class

Seamen became the rate of Seamen First Class in 1921 (1). It continued Seaman's place in the seaman, or non rated, first class pay grade (2), which became grade five on June 10, 1922 (3).

It inherited the Seaman's insignia, three cuff stripes and a white/blue branch mark on the right side (4).

Female Seamen First Class were ordered to wear three white/blue hash marks on the left upper sleeve in 1944 (5).

Seaman First Class was combined with Bugler First Class, back into the rate of Seaman on April 2, 1948 (6).

Seaman Gunner

According to Charles Malin's study of enlisted titles Seaman Gunner began in 1869 (1), but it doesn't appear in the pay table in the navy register until 1871 (2).

They, apparently, were not petty officers. Seaman Gunner was not on the list of ratings in the 1876 navy regulations (3). However the appendix that makes up the 1876 uniform regulations calls for them to wear the petty officers badge in addition to a crossed cannons and star specialty mark on the lower sleeve (4), as they had, presumably, since 1869.

On June 28, 1881 the navy created a gunnery school whose graduates would receive Seaman Gunner's Certificates (5). With this Seaman Gunner became a qualification as well as a rate.

When the enlisted rates were divided into pay grades in 1885, Seaman Gunner was placed in the petty officer third class grade (6). At last they were petty officers, but not for long. On January 1, 1886 they were moved down to the Seaman First Class grade (7).

In the 1886 uniform regulations show as "Seaman Gunners Mark" of a white/blue bursting bomb, to be worn on the chevrons of the rating badge. It doesn't mention the mark begin worn by non rated men, which is what Seamen Gunners in the seamen first class grade would have been (8). Apparently the mark was worn by those with the certificate regardless of rate, but maybe not actual Seamen Gunners. Three stripes would have been worn on the cuff.

The 1897 regulations allowed the mark instead of a rating badge for non petty officers and allowed it's wear below the rating badge for petty officers (9).

The rate was eliminated in 1921 (10) but the mark continued for those who earned it.

Seaman Recruit

Apprentice Seaman became Seaman Recruit on April 2, 1948 (1).

It was placed in grade seven until The Career Compensation Act of October 12, 1949 made grade seven into grade E-1 (2)

They were to wear one white/blue hash mark (3) until 1975, when they would be without insignia (4).

Seaman Second Class

Ordinary Seamen became the rate of Seamen Second Class in 1917 (1). It continued Ordinary Seaman's place in the seaman, or non rated, second class pay grade (2), which became grade five on June 10, 1922 (3).

It inherited the Ordinary Seaman's insignia, two cuff stripes and a white/blue branch mark on the right side (4).

Female Seamen Second Class were ordered to wear two white/blue hash marks on the left upper sleeve in 1944 (5).

Seaman Second Class was combined with Bugler Second Class, into the rate of Seaman Apprentice on April 2, 1948 (6).

Second Assistant Engineer

Prior to 1842 the people who operated and repaired the engines of steam powered ships were civilian employes.

The first Engineers were appointed on steamship Fulton in 1836 (1).

The Fulton's Captain, Matthew Perry, sought and received from the Secretary of the Navy permission the put his engineers in uniform. For his Second Assistant Engineers he prescribed a blue, double breasted coat with a rolling collar of black velvet and a silver star on the right collar (2).

Second Assistant Engineer became an official rank of the navy with a law of August 31, 1842 (3). The law stated that would share in prize money as if they were Midshipmen. It also allowed the Secretary of the Navy to prescribe a uniform for engineers. This was an odd detail for Congress to get involved with.

Despite the mention of them in law, there is no record of uniforms begin prescribed for engineers before the uniform regulations of 1852 (4), ten years after they became an official part of the navy. It is possible that the uniform from the Fulton was used for all that time, or it is equally possible that civilian clothes were worn. It is possible that an order for engineer's uniforms has been lost.

Uniforms finally came on March 8, 1852. The dress tail coat was single breasted with one row of nine buttons and a standing collar with a corps device of a silver anchor on a gold paddle wheel in an L shaped gold wreath. The undress frock coat was also single breasted (5).

On January 1, 1853 they were allowed shoulder straps on the frock coat, but probably not the dress coat. They were plain blue, outlined in 1/8 inch wide beaded lace (6).

On January 13, 1859 the navy issued a general order granting relative rank to engineers, and Second Assistants were to rank 'next after" Masters, meaning with Midshipmen (7). Congress confirmed this order in law on March 3rd (8).

Uniforms were changed to reflect the engineer's new status on February 8, 1861. The collar device was removed and replaced with a 1/2 inch wide border of gold beaded lace. (9). The frock coat, presumably, became double breasted as well.

Cuffs and the use of lace was altered slightly when the lace for line officers was changed in 1862 (10).

The March 13, 1863 realignment of relative rank confirmed Second Assistant Engineers as relative Ensigns (11).

The 1864 uniform regulations prescribed cuff lace according to rank without a line star and shoulder straps with the crossed oak branch device in the center (12).

The 1866 regulations restored epaulets with same devices in the frog as the shoulder straps (13).

1869 saw red used at the color between the cuff stripes and shoulder knots replacing epaulets and shoulder straps (14). The best information we have on the design of the shoulder knots for staff officers who were relative Ensigns is a gold bar, alone in the center of the pad (15).

On March 29, 1869 Attorney General Ebenezer Hoar issued a ruling that the navy had exceeded its authority in granting relative rank to certain staff officers during the Civil War (16). Second Assistant Engineers reverted to "next after" Masters, which wasn't a big change in their case.

Congress fixed this problem on March 3, 1871 (17) with a law that spread the First Assistant Engineers over the ranks of Master and Ensign.

They were to wear the uniforms of those ranks with red cloth in and around the cuff stripes and crossed oak branches as a corps device. Those with the relative rank of Master continued to wear the shoulder knots until they were abolished on October 3, 1871 (18). The knots contented for relative ensigns.

The rank was title was changed to Assistant Engineer on February 24, 1874 (19).

Second Master

Second Masters first appear in a law setting the pay of the navy passed on March 3, 1835 (1).

Naval regulations of 1841 list the rank as a warrant officer, below Master and above Passed Midshipman (2).

1841 uniform regulations gave them uniforms with a single button and loop of gold lace on the collar, instead of the two loops worn by Masters (3).

All that having been said there is no evidence of any appointments to the rank of Second Master until March 2, 1849 when Edmund Olmstead was appointed (4). The next day William Burns (5) and William Morse(6) were appointed. Burns died on February 4, 1851, Olmstead was promoted to Master on September 1, 1851 and Morse Resigned on May 25, 1859.

Second Masters don't appear in the 1852 uniform regulations, so it is unknown how William Morse dressed from 1852 to 1859.

Secretary

Secretaries began as administrative assistants to commander of squadrons. They first appear in a law setting the pay of the navy passed on March 3, 1835. It listed them between Professors of Mathematics and Sailing Masters (1). It seams they had a similar status as Clerks, not officers listed in the navy register but not enlisted men. Navy regulations from 1841 state that Secretaries would have the "assimilated" rank of a Lieutenant (2).

The 1841 uniform regulations prescribed a double breasted coat with a plain rolling collar and plain cuffs (3).

In 1852 they were given a single breasted dress tail coat and undress frock coat, both with plain rolling collars and only three vertical closure buttons on the cuffs. They could wear a cocked hat in full dress or a blue cap with an empty wreath in undress (4).

In 1863 they were given the relative rank of Lieutenant (5) and with the 1864 uniform regulations they wore a Lieutenant's uniform with an old english letter "S" in silver for a corps device.

A law of May 16, 1866 allowed the Vice Admiral a Secretary "with the rank and sea pay and allowances of a lieutenant in the navy." (6). When the rank of Admiral was created on July 25th, he was also allowed a secretary who was a Lieutenant (7). These two officers were Lieutenants by law while the Secretaries to commanders of squadrons were Lieutenants by virtue of the general order of 1863 that was overturned by the Attorney General in 1869 (8).

What happened to Secretaries to commanders of squadrons is not known. There is no law granting them relative rank, just a law in 1870 setting their pay (9). The 1876 uniform regulations call for "Secretaries to Commanders of fleets and squadrons" to continue to use the "S" as a corps device (10), so they must have still been in uniform. There is no cloth color for Secretaries, but there is nothing saying the were allowed a line star.

The Admirals' Secretaries first appear in the navy register in 1870 (11). It shows that Admiral Farragut's Secretary, James Montgomery, was appointed on November 17, 1868 and Vice Admiral Porter's Secretary, James Alden, on July 26, 1866. When Admiral Farragut died on August 14, 1870, Montgomery probably left the navy. The 1871 registers shows Alden still the Secretary to Porter, now the full Admiral (12). Charles Poor was made Secretary to Vice Admiral Rowan on August 26, 1870 (13), with George Yardley taking over on April 1, 1873 (14).

A law of May 4, 1878 ended appointments as Secretaries to both Admirals and commanders of squadrons. Line officers would now be detailed to the duty (15).

R.W. Stevens replaced George Yardley as Rowan's Secretary on April 16, 1887 (16). Despite the 1878 law, Stevens is shown as entering the navy on April 16th. He was not a line officer. Admiral Rowan retired in 1889, but Stevens is still listed as his Secretary in the 1890 register, probably serving him in retirement (17). Rowan died in 1890 and Stevens is not in the 1891 register (18).

Admiral Porter died in 1891 and James Alden, or a listing for Secretaries with the rank of Lieutenant for that matter, are not in the 1892 register (19).

The letter "S" continued to be worn as a corps device in the 1883 (20) and 1886 (21) uniform regulations. No color was listed for use around the cuff stripes and it is quite possible they wore the line star but that is not certain.

Secretaries, or rather as Secretary with the rank of Lieutenant, returned in 1899. The 1900 register shows John Crawford to be the Secretary to Admiral of the Navy Dewey (22). Once again Crawford's date of rank and his date of entry into the navy are the same, October 7, 1899.

At least by the 1905 uniform regulations (23) Crawford wore a Lieutenant's uniform with the letter "S" as a corps device and no colored cloth, leaving the possibility of a line star.

Leonard Hoffman entered the navy, and became Dewey's Secretary on December 4, 1907 (24).

Dewey died in 1917 and Hoffman, and Secretaries in general, are not in the 1918 register (25).

Senior Flag Officer

On March 2, 1859, Congress passed this law:
"Resolved by the Senate and House of Representatives of the United States of America in Congress assembled, That the President of the United States, by and with the advice and consent of the Senate be, and he is hereby, authorized and empowered to confer on Captain Charles Stewart of the United States navy, in recognition of his distinguished and meritorious service, the commission of senior flag officer of the United States navy on the active service list." (1).

Unlike other Flag Officers, who were still listed as Captains in the navy register, Stewart was officially listed as Senior Flag Officer (2).

Presumably, he wore the uniform of a Flag Officer.

Stewart retired on December 21, 1861 and was made a Rear Admiral on the retired list on July 16, 1862 (3).

Senior Chief Petty Officer

When the E-8 pay grade was created on May 20, 1958 (1), the rate of Senior Chief Petty Officer was created to fill it (2).

The rating badge was a standard Chief Petty Officers badge, three chevrons and one arc under an eagle with a specialty mark under the arc, with one star above the eagle (3). In full color the chevrons and arc were red, or gold if authorized, and the eagle, specialty mark and stars silver. Otherwise all blue was used.

In 1959 all three grades of chiefs were given a pin on badge of rank. A smaller version of the fouled anchor and U.S.N cap device was added to the collar of the khaki shirt (4). One silver star was added above the anchor stock for Senior Chiefs in 1961 (5)

1975 also saw the creation of blue and white dinner jackets for chiefs. Regular full color rating badges were worn on the blue jacket and badges with silver eagles and specialty marks and blue chevrons and arc (or gold if entitled) were worn on the white jacket. The 1975 regulations actually call for red chevrons, but this was a printing error (6).

White uniforms returned in 1979 in the same style as officers, standing collar for men and point lapel for women. The magazine article announcing them refers to a "sleeve rating badge" (7) but in fact badges of rank were placed on the collar.

Shoulder marks in black with the badge of rank embroidered on them were placed on white shirts worn under the blue coat in 1999. At the same time the use of the badge of rank on outerwear was expanded (8).

The aviation green uniform came to an end in December of 2010 (9), and the all blue rating badges on a green background passed into history. Ironically, the return of the 1931 khaki uniform began around the same time (10).

Ships's Barber

Ship's Barbers began in 1870 and became Barbers in 1885 (1).

They don't appear to have been petty officers, and there is no information on their uniforms. Barbers were placed in the Seaman First Class pay grade in 1885 (2), so three stripes on the jumpers is a possibility.

Ship's Clerk

The warrant grade of Ships Clerk was created on July 28, 1942 (1).

The lace worn on the cuffs was 1/4 inch wide gold with 1/2 inch long blue breaks every 2 inches. The device of a Ships Clerk, crossed quill pens, was worn above the stripes. Shoulder boards showed the 1/4 inch lace with a single 1/2 inch break, under the device. The crossed quill pens, device, in gold, was also used as a badge of rank (2).

The aviation green coat was given a black stripe with green breaks in 1944 (3). It is possible that a solid stripe was worn previous to this (4).

The Career Compensation Act of October 12, 1949 (5) placed Ships Clerks in pay grade W-1.

A standard warrant officers badge of rank was introduced on July 1,1952 (6) consisting of a gold bar with a 1/16 inch blue break across the middle (7).

Ships Clerks became Warrant Officer 1 with the Warrant Officer Act of 1954 (8).

Ship's Cook (First, Second, Third and Fourth Class)

The petty officer's rating of Ship's Cook disappears form the pay tables in 1891 (1). The title returned on February 25, 1893 as a non rated title with four classes (2).

All four classes were placed in the messmen branch alongside officers' stewards and cooks and Mess Attendants (3), who did not wear regular navy uniforms.

Did Ship's Cooks wear regular uniforms? The 1897 uniform regulations prescribes the spacial uniforms for "stewards, and officers' cooks" and Mess Attendants, Ship's Cooks are not mentioned, so they must fall into what the regulations call "all other enlisted men". However, the regulations give us no information on how many stripes a Ship's Cook should wear (4).

Beginning with the 1905 pay table (5), Ship's Cooks were moved to a separate commissary branch. The 1905 uniform regulations do prescribe regular uniforms with three stripes for first and second class and two for third and fourth class (6). It is implied that a white/blue branch mark was worn (11). This could mean that they wore stewards uniforms before 1905 when they were part of the messmen branch, but there is no proof.

A white/blue crescent was added to the upper left sleeve in 1908 (12), and when watch marks became branch marks in 1912, they were not to wear one (13).

On the 1910 pay table (14) Ship's Cooks moved to the special branch with first class in the petty officer first class pay grade, second class in the petty officer second class pay grade, third class in the Seaman First Class pay grade and fourth class in the Seaman Second Class pay grade.

The 1913 uniform regulations call for first and second class to wear the appropriate rating badges with the crescent as the specialty mark and third and fourth class to wear crescent alone (15). As for stripes on the jumpers, Ship's Cooks first and second class are listed separately from petty officers, but were still allowed the three stripes. This may mean, despite the rating badges and pay grade, they were not considered petty officers. The third and fourth classes were to wear two stripes, despite third class being in the Seaman First Class grade (16).

On March 24, 1921 Ship's Cook Third Class was moved up to petty officer third class and those of the fourth class were made Seaman Second Class (17).

Ship's Lamplighter

Ship's Lamplighters came along in 1876 and became Lamplighters in 1885 (1).

They don't appear to have been petty officers, and there is no information on their uniforms. Lamplighters were placed in the Seaman First Class pay grade in 1885 (2), so three stripes on the jumpers is a possibility.

Ship's Tailor

Ship's Tailors began in 1869 and became Tailors in 1885 (1).

They don't appear to have been petty officers, and there is no information on their uniforms. Tailors were placed in the Seaman First Class pay grade in 1885 (2), so three stripes on the jumpers is a possibility.

Shipwright

The rate of Shipwright was added in 1893 (1) in the Seaman Second Class pay grade (2), allowing them two stripes on the cuff and a white blue watch mark (3).

They were moved up to the Seaman First Class grade in 1905 (4) and therefore were entitled to three stripes.

An order of October 25, 1912 prescribed white/blue crossed axes on the left upper sleeve (5) and no branch mark (6).

Shipwrights were made into Seamen First Class on March 24, 1921 (7).

Steerage Cook

Steerage Cook was one of the rates that Officer's Cook was split into in 1864 (1).

Officer's cooks had been considered petty officers as of the 1841 regulations, but are not listed, as Officer's Cooks or any of the titles it was divided into, on the list of petty officer rates in the regulations of 1865 (3). Their status was clarified when the rates were organized in 1885. Stewards, Cooks (not Ship's Cooks) and Attendants were made into a special category that were not petty officers (4).

There is also no information on uniforms or insignia before 1886. At that time they were to wear single breasted sack coats of blue with black buttons or a similar white coat with white buttons, matching trousers and a blue visored cap or white canvas hat (5). The canvas hat was replaced with a white cap by 1897 (6), and the coats became double breasted between the 1897 and 1905 (7) regulations.

In 1912 a white/blue crescent was added as a distinguishing mark (8).

The 1922 uniform regulations prescribed a cap devices of the letters U.S.N. (9).

1922 also saw them moved to pay grade three, along side second class petty officers (10).

Steerage Cooks were changed to Officer's Cooks Second Class in 1923 (11).

Steerage Steward

Steerage Steward was one of the rates that Officer's Steward was split into in 1864 (1).

Officer's Stewards had been considered petty officers as of the 1841 regulations, but are not listed, as Officer's Stewards or any of the titles it was divided into, on the list of petty officer rates in the regulations of 1865 (3). On the other hand, the 1864 uniform regulations call for the petty officers badge to be worn on the left sleeve by "All other petty officers, except officer's stewards," (4).

Their status was clarified when the rates were organized in 1885. Stewards, Cooks (not Ship's Cooks) and Attendants were made into a special category that were not petty officers (5).

The lack of a petty officers badge infers that they were wearing regular navy uniforms in 1864.

In 1886 they were to wear single breasted sack coats of blue with black buttons or a similar white coat with white buttons, matching trousers and a blue visored cap or white canvas hat (6). The canvas hat was replaced with a white cap by 1897 (7), and the coats became double breasted between the 1897 and 1905 (8) regulations.

In 1912 a white/blue crescent was added as a distinguishing mark (9).

The 1922 uniform regulations prescribed a cap devices of the letters U.S.N. (10).

1922 also saw them moved to pay grade three, along side second class petty officers (11).

Steerage Stewards were changed to Officer's Stewards Second Class in 1923 (12).

Steward First Class

The rate of Steward First Class was created in 1948 by combining the rates of Steward First Class and Cook First Class (1). They were not petty officers (2), but they did wear regular rating badges with a the eagle, three chevrons and a crescent as a specialty mark.

Stewards were reclassified as petty officers in late 1949 (3).

Steward Second Class

The rate of Steward Second Class was created in 1948 by combining the rates of Steward Second Class and Cook Second Class (1). They were not petty officers (2), but they did wear regular rating badges with a the eagle, two chevrons and a crescent as a specialty mark.

Stewards were reclassified as petty officers in late 1949 (3).

Steward Third Class

The rate of Steward Third Class was created in 1948 by combining the rates of Steward Third Class and Cook Third Class (1). They were not petty officers (2), but they did wear regular rating badges with a the eagle, one chevron and a crescent as a specialty mark.

Stewards were reclassified as petty officers in late 1949 (3).

Steward to Commander in Chief

Steward to Commander-in-Chief was one of the rates that Officer's Steward was split into in 1864 (1).

Officer's cooks had been considered petty officers as of the 1841 regulations, but are not listed, as Officer's Cooks or any of the titles it was divided into, on the list of petty officer rates in the regulations of 1865 (3). Their status was clarified when the rates were organized in 1885. Stewards, Cooks (not Ship's Cooks) and Attendants were made into a special category that were not petty officers (4).

The 1876 uniform regulations stated "Stewards to Commanders-in-Chiefs, of other Commanding Officers, and of wardroom messes, will wear blue cloth or flannel jackets, with rolling collar, to be double-breasted, with two rows of medium-size navy buttons, six in each row, and plain blue-cloth caps, with visors, and without covers. On special occasions they may be directed to wear citizens' clothes." (5).

In 1886 they were to wear single breasted sack coats of blue with black buttons or a similar white coat with white buttons, matching trousers and a blue visored cap or white canvas hat (6). The canvas hat was replaced with a white cap by 1897 (7), and the coats became double breasted again between the 1897 and 1905 (8) regulations.

In 1912 a white/blue crescent was added as a distinguishing mark (9).

Stewards to Commander-in-Chief were abolished in 1921 (10).

Steward to Navy yard Commandant

The Rate of Steward to Commandant of a Navy Yard was created in 1884 (1).

Like other steward and cooks they were not petty officers. Their status was clarified when the rates were organized in 1885. Stewards, Cooks (not Ship's Cooks) and Attendants were made into a special category that were not petty officers (2).

There is also no information on uniforms or insignia before 1886. At that time they were to wear single breasted sack coats of blue with black buttons or a similar white coat with white buttons, matching trousers and a blue visored cap or white canvas hat (3). The canvas hat was replaced with a white cap by 1897 (4), and the coats became double breasted between the 1897 and 1905 (5) regulations.

In 1912 a white/blue crescent was added as a distinguishing mark (6).

Stewards to Commandant of a Navy Yard were abolished in 1921 (7).

Steward's Mate First Class

Mess Attendants First Class became Steward's Mates First Class in 1943 (1). They continued Mess Attendants First Class' place in grade five (2).

The insignia continued to be three cuff stripes (3), a white/blue crescent on the left upper sleeve (4) and no branch mark (5).

Steward's Mate First Class became Stewardsman in 1948 (6).

Steward's Mate Second Class

Mess Attendants Second Class became Steward's Mates Second Class in 1943 (1). They continued Mess Attendants Second Class' place in grade six (2).

The insignia continued to be two cuff stripes (3), a white/blue crescent on the left upper sleeve (4) and no branch mark (5).

Steward's Mate Second Class became Stewardsman Apprentice in 1948 (6).

Steward's Mate Third Class

Mess Attendants Third Class became Steward's Mates Third Class in 1943 (1). They continued Mess Attendants Third Class' place in grade seven (2).

The insignia continued to be one cuff stripe (3), a white/blue crescent on the left upper sleeve (4) and no branch mark (5).

Steward's Mate Third Class became Stewardsman Recruit in 1948 (6).

Stewardsman

Steward's Mate First Class became Stewardsman on April 2, 1948 (1).

It continued the Steward's Mate First Class position in pay grade five. Grade five became grade E-3 with The Career Compensation Act of October 12, 1949 (2).

It was given a group rate mark of three white/blue hash marks under a crescent (3).

The petty officers' ratings of Steward and Commisaryman were merged into Mess Management Specialist in 1975 (4). The 1975 uniform regulations refer to non rated Mess Management Specialists wearing white/blue group rate marks under a specialty mark of crossed keys over a quill on an open ledger book (5). This would seam to indicate that Stewardsmen were abolished at that point.

Stewardsman Apprentice

Steward's Mate Second Class became Stewardsman Apprentice on April 2, 1948 (1).

It continued the Steward's Mate Second Class position in pay grade Six. Grade Six became grade E-2 with The Career Compensation Act of October 12, 1949 (2).

It was given a group rate mark of two white/blue hash marks under a crescent (3).

The petty officers' ratings of Steward and Commisaryman were merged into Mess Management Specialist in 1975 (4). The 1975 uniform regulations refer to non rated Mess Management Specialists wearing white/blue group rate marks under a specialty mark of crossed keys over a quill on an open ledger book (5). This would seam to indicate that Stewardsmen Apprentice were abolished at that point.

Stewardsman Recruit

Steward's Mate Third Class became Stewardsman Recruit on April 2, 1948 (1).

It continued the Steward's Mate Third Class position in pay grade Seven. Grade seven became grade E-1 with The Career Compensation Act of October 12, 1949 (2).

It was given a group rate mark of one white/blue hash mark under a crescent (3).

The petty officers' ratings of Steward and Commisaryman were merged into Mess Management Specialist in 1975 (4). The 1975 uniform regulations refer to non rated Mess Management Specialists wearing white/blue group rate marks under a specialty mark of crossed keys over a quill on an open ledger book (5). This would seam to indicate that Stewardsmen Recruits were abolished at that point.

Surgeon

Surgeon was the basic rank for a navy doctor. It existed in the Continental Navy (1) and was listed in the ranks created in the 1794 (2) and 1797 (3) laws. It would be used until the use of staff titles ended in 1918 (3) and be officially abolished with the other staff ranks on August 7, 1947 (5).

There is no record of Continental Navy Surgeons wearing uniforms.

The 1797 uniform regulations for the federal navy called for "COAT. Long, dark green, with black velvet lappels, and standing collar.--Lappels to have nine buttons, and one to the standing collar-- No linings, other than being faced with the same cloth as the coat. Slash sleeves, the cuff the same as the facings, with three buttons. Pocket flaps, plain. VEST AND BREECHES. The former, red, double breasted. The latter green, same as the coat. Buttons, the same as the officers." (6). A colorful outfit indeed.

Things became less colorful in 1802 when they were ordered to wear " THE COAT of blue cloth, with long lappels and lining of the same, nine navy buttons, and button-holes worked with gold thread; standing collar the same as the coat, with two navy buttons, and worked button-holes on each side; three navy buttons below the pockets, and three worked button-holes on the flaps--the same number of buttons on the cuffs, with worked button-holes. VEST AND BREECHES, white, and plain--cocked hat."(7).

The 1813 regulations stated "FULL DRESS. The Coat of blue cloth, with broad lappels and lining of the same, nine navy buttons on the lappels, standing collar the same as the coat, and two laced button-holes on each side of the collar, three navy buttons below the pockets, and the same number of navy buttons on the cuffs. Pantaloons and Vest white, with navy buttons; cocked hat, plain, half boots, and small sword. UNDRESS. The same as the full dress, excepting the laced button holes, and a rolling cape instead of a standing collar." (8).

The uniform in the 1820 regulations were pretty much identical (9).

In 1830 the uniform style changed to a fold back lapels cut in a swell with the coat closing with hooks and eyes. A line of gold oak leaf embroidery went around the top of the cuffs and the front and top of the collar. Under the collar embroidery was a gold club of Esculapius (a caduceus without wings). The undress coat was "according to the prevailing fashion for citizens for the time", with a rolling collar of black velvet and black velvet cuffs with a strip of gold lace above them. Three buttons were worn around the cuffs of both coats (10).

On January 20, 1832 the club of Esculapius was replaced with an oak branch and the black velvet and gold lace was removed from the undress coat. A button was placed on the undress collar (11).

On December 24, 1834 Surgeons were authorized two strips of gold lace on the undress cuffs (12)., probably one above the three buttons and one below.

The 1841 uniform regulations returned to a more conventional stye dress coat. The line of oak leafs and the oak branch on the collar were continued, but the oak leafs on the cuffs were removed. The button was removed from the collar of the undress coat. Both coats now had three strips of gold lace on the cuff, one above the buttons and two below (13)

The first stab at relative rank was in naval regulations of 1841 (14) that gave Surgeons "assimilated rank" of Lieutenant. This was followed, on August 31, 1846, with the relative rank of Commander being given to Surgeons over 12 years service and Lieutenant for those under 12 years service (15). Congress gave the order the weight of law on August 5, 1854 (16).

Epaulets and shoulder straps were authorized now that Surgeons had relative rank. The epaulets had solid lace crescents instead of the embroidered crescents used by line officers. The bullion was 1/2 inch wide for those over 12 years service and 3/4 for those under. Old english letters "M.D." were worn in silver in the frog. The shoulder straps had 1/4 inch wide borders and the "M.D." in the center. The over 12s had an acorn at each end (17).

With the March 8, 1852 uniform regulations the dress tail coat was double breasted with two rows on nine buttons down the front, three under the pockets and three vertical on the cuffs. The standing collar and the cuffs showed three sprigs of live oak. The undress frock coat had the same two rows of nine buttons down the front and three vertical buttons on the cuffs. The rolling collar was plain and the cuff carried three large buttons running perpendicular ot the three small ones. Epaulets and shoulder straps were the same as they had been since 1847 (18).

Change came 200 days later on September 24th. The letters were removed from the epaulet frogs and shoulders straps. An olive sprig replaced them on the shoulder straps but the epaulets were left plain (19).

On August 23, 1856, Surgeons were ordered to wear the uniforms of their relative rank, except for the Epaulets and shoulder straps. Cuff stripes were now worn on both coats, two for Surgeons over 12 years service and one for Surgeons under 12 years service (20).

The alteration of line officer's cuff stripes on July 31, 1862 also altered the stripes for equivalent staff officers. This meant that Surgeons over 12 years service wore two 3/4 inch stripes with a 1/4 inch stripe between them and Surgeons under 12 years service wore one 3/4 inch stripe under one 1/4 inch stripe (21).

The navy, on it's own authority, realigned the relative ranks on March 13, 1863. Surgeons over 15 years service were relative Captains, Surgeons from five to 15 years service were Relative Commanders and Surgeons under five years service were relative Lieutenant Commanders (22).

The uniform regulations of 1864 prescribed the uniform of their relative rank with no line star on the cuffs and and no corps device (23).

When, in 1869, the Attorney General overruled the 1863 order on relative ranks, they returned to Commander for over 12 years and Lieutenant for under (24).

On March 11, 1869 cobalt blue cloth was prescribed between the cuff stripes (25).

A law of March 3, 1871 gave Surgeons the relative rank of Lieutenant Commander or Lieutenant (26).

In 1883 the cloth between the cuff stripes was changed to maroon (27) and a corps device was finally authorized of a gold oak leaf with a silver acorn (28).

A medical reserve corps was formed on September 22, 1912 (29) and the 1913 uniform regulation prescribed a silver oak leaf with gold acorn for the corps device and crimson cloth in and around the stripes (30).

In 1918 the colors in and around the sleeve and shoulder board stripes were abolished and corps device was placed above them and an anchor was added under the device on the service coat collar until the coat was abolished the next year (31).

Surgeon General

The title of William Wood, the Chief of the Bureau of Medicine and Surgery, became Surgeon General on March 3, 1871, with relative rank of Commodore (1).

Wood would have worn a Commodore's uniform with no corps device and cobolt blue piping around the cuff stripe (2).

Wood retired on May 27, 1871 (3) and was replaced by Jonathan Foltz (4). Turnover was frequent for the Surgeron General. James Palmer replaced Foltz on June 10, 1872, Jospeh Beal took over on July 5, 1873, William Grier on February 2, 1877, J. Winthorop Taylor on October 21, 1878 then Philip Wales on January 26, 1880 (5).

In 1883 the cloth piping on the cuff stripes was changed to maroon (6) and a corps device was finally authorized of a gold oak leaf with a silver acorn (7).

More turnover followed. Wales gave way to Francis Gunnell on March 27, 1884. Gunnell was replaced by John Browne on April 2, 1888 and he was replaced by James Tryon on September 7, 1893. William Van Reypen became Surgeon General on October 22, 1897 (8).

When the rank of Commodore, and relative ranks, were abolished on March 3, 1899 (9), the chiefs of bureaus were made into Rear Admirals with "the same pay and allowance as are now allowed a brigadier-general in the Army". In other words Rear Admiral lower half.

Surgeon of the Fleet

On May 24, 1828 a new law stated "That the President of the United States may designate - and appoint to every fleet or squadron an experienced and intelligent surgeon, then in the naval service of the United States, to be denominated "Surgeon of the Fleet," who shall be surgeon of the flag ship, and who, in addition to his duties as such, shall examine and approve all requisitions for medical and hospital stores for the fleet, and inspect their quality; and who shall, in difficult cases, consult with the surgeons of the several ships, and make records of the character and treatment of diseases, to be transmitted to the Navy Department" (1).

They wore the uniform of a Surgeon. When medical officers were given epaulets and shoulder straps in 1846, Surgeons of the Fleet were to wear a silver rosette on the epaulet strap and at either end of the shoulder strap (2).

Most devices were removed form epaulets in 1852 (3) and it is not clear if this applied to the rosette. It is also not clear if the shoulder straps were changed.

A law of June 1, 1860 changed to title, or at least the usage, to Fleet Surgeon (4).

Surgeon's Mate

Surgeons Mate's were junior medical officers. The rank was first created in the Continental Navy (1), and is in both laws creating the federal navy (2) (3).

The first uniforms were prescribed in the 1797 uniform regulations (4). They consisted of a green coat faced with black with half length lapels with six buttons on them and three below them. This was worn over a red waistcoat and green breeches.

The 1802 uniform regulations stated "THE COAT of blue cloth, with long lappels and lining of the same, nine navy buttons, and button-holes worked with gold thread; standing collar the same as the coat, with two navy buttons, and worked button-holes on each side; three navy buttons below the pockets, and three worked button-holes on the flaps--the same number of buttons on the cuffs, with worked button-holes. VEST AND BREECHES, white, and plain--cocked hat." (5).

The uniforms from the 1813 uniform regulations were similar. They were described as "FULL DRESS. The Coat of blue cloth, with broad lappels, and lining of the same, nine navy buttons; standing collar, the same as the coat, with one navy button and laced button hole on each side; two navy buttons below the pockets, and the same number of buttons on the cuffs. Pantaloons and Vest white, cocked hat, plain, half boots, and dirk.
UNDRESS. Same as full dress, except rolling cape, with two buttons on each side without lace." (6).

The only difference in the 1820 uniform regulations was that there were no buttons on the collar of the undress coat (7).

Surgeon's Mates probably became Assistant Surgeons on May 24, 1828 (8). The law does not specifically change the title, but does mention examinations for appointments of Assistant Surgeons. The 1828 naval register (9) lists Surgeon's Mates, but the 1829 (10) register lists the same people as Assistant Surgeons.

Tailor

Ship's Tailors became Tailors in 1885 (1).

They were placed in the Seaman First Class pay grade in 1885 (2), so they would have worn three stripes on the cuffs of the jumpers.

Tailors were eliminated in 1893 (3).

Third Assistant Engineer

Prior to 1842 the people who operated and repaired the engines of steam powered ships were civilian employes.

The first Engineers were appointed on steamship Fulton in 1836 (1).

The Fulton's Captain, Matthew Perry, sought and received from the Secretary of the Navy permission the put his engineers in uniform. For his Third Assistant Engineers he prescribed a blue, double breasted coat with a rolling collar of black velvet and a silver star on the left collar (2).

Third Assistant Engineer became an official rank of the navy with a law of August 31, 1842 (3). The law stated that would share in prize money as if they were "forward officers", probably meaning warrant officers. It also allowed the Secretary of the Navy to prescribe a uniform for engineers. This was an odd detail for Congress to get involved with.

Despite the mention of them in law, there is no record of uniforms begin prescribed for engineers before the uniform regulations of 1852 (4), ten years after they became an official part of the navy. It is possible that the uniform from the Fulton was used for all that time, or it is equally possible that civilian clothes were worn. It is possible that an order for engineer's uniforms has been lost.

Uniforms finally came on March 8, 1852. The dress tail coat was single breasted with one row of nine buttons and a standing collar with a corps device of a silver anchor on a gold paddle wheel in an L shaped gold wreath. The undress frock coat was also single breasted (5).

On January 13, 1859 the navy issued a general order granting relative rank to engineers, and Third Assistants were to rank with Midshipmen (6). Congress confirmed this order in law on March 3rd (7).

Uniforms were changed to reflect the engineer's new status on February 8, 1861. The collar device was removed and replaced with a 1/2 inch wide border of gold beaded lace. (8). The frock coat, presumably, became double breasted as well.

Cuffs and the use of lace was altered slightly when the lace for line officers was changed in 1862 (9).

The March 13, 1863 realignment of relative rank confirmed Third Assistant Engineers as relative Midshipmen (10).

The 1864 uniform regulations prescribed a frock coat with smaller buttons that other ranks and no other decoration (11).

The 1866 regulations restored epaulets with same devices in the frog as the shoulder straps (12).

1869 saw the addition of a 1/8 inch cuff stripe with red used at the colored piping (13).

On March 29, 1869 Attorney General Ebenezer Hoar issued a ruling that the navy had exceeded its authority in granting relative rank to certain staff officers during the Civil War (14). Third Assistant Engineers remained relative Midshipmen.

The rank was eliminated on March 3, 1871 (15).

Torpedoman

The warrant grade of Torpedoman was created on July 28, 1942 (1).

The lace worn on the cuffs was 1/4 inch wide gold with 1/2 inch long blue breaks every 2 inches. The device of a Ships Clerk, a torpedo, was worn above the stripes. Shoulder boards showed the 1/4 inch lace with a single 1/2 inch break, under the device. The torpedo, device, in gold, was also used as a badge of rank (2).

The aviation green coat was given a black stripe with green breaks in 1944 (3). It is possible that a solid stripe was worn previous to this (4).

The Career Compensation Act of October 12, 1949 (5) placed Torpedomen in pay grade W-1.

A standard, warrant officers badge of rank was introduced on July 1,1952 (6) consisting of a gold bar with a 1/16 inch blue break across the middle (7).

Torpedomen became Warrant Officer 1 with the Warrant Officer Act of 1954 (8).

Vice Admiral

The rank of Vice Admiral was born on December 21, 1864 (1). One was authorized, and the appointment went to Rear Admiral David Farragut on December 31st (2).

Insignia was prescribed for Farragut on January 15, 1865. For cuff stripes he was to wear one 1 1/2 inch wide stripe under two 1/4 inch wide stripes, under a line star. Shoulder straps carried three silver stars with a gold anchor under the middle one. The stars were worn alone on the collar (3).

Farragut was promoted to full Admiral on July 25, 1866 and his foster brother David Dixon Porter became Vice Admiral (4).

When epaulets returned in 1866 the same three stars and an anchor from the shoulder straps was worn in the epaulet frog (5). The same arrangement was probably worn on the collar at this point, it certainly was by 1876 (6). The 1866 uniform regulations also prescribed cuff stripes of one two inch stripe under two one inch stripes under a line star.

The cuff stripes were changed on March 11, 1869. On the full dress tail coat, two strips of oak leaf and acorn embroidery were worn with a small vertical strip running form the bottom line to the end of the cuff. On the undress frock coat, one two inch wide stripe was worn under two 1/2 inch wide stripes. Line stars were worn on both coats (7).

Porter was promoted to full Admiral on August 15, 1870 and Stephen Rowan became Vice Admiral (8).

A law of January 24, 1873 stated "That vacancies occurring in the grades of admiral and vice-admiral, in the navy of the United States, shall not be filled by promotion, or in any other manner whatever; and when the offices of said grades shall become vacant, the grade itself, shall cease to exist."(9) .

On the new 1878 service coat, Rowan was to wear three silver stars alone on each side of the standing collar and sleeve stripes in the same pattern as the frock coat, but in black and without the star (10). It is possible, but not certain, that the same sleeve stripes were added to the overcoat at this point.

In 1883 a silver anchor was added under the behind stars on the service coat collar, and white stripes were added to the white service coat sleeves (11).

Rowan retired on February 26, 1889, and died on March 31, 1890 (12), and under the 1873 law the rank ceased to exist.

On March 3, 1915 a new law revived the rank of Vice Admiral for those second in command of fleets (13).

The insignia for the new Vice Admirals had been laid out in the January 1913 uniform regulations in anticipation. The sleeve stripes were the same design, one two inch and two 1/2 inch (15). The same design was used on all blue uniform coats except the black stripes and no line star was still worn on the overcoat (16). The service coat collar still carried three silver stars with a silver anchor under the outermost one as it had since 1883 (17). Epaulets now carried three silver stars in an arc inside the frog and an anchor on the strap (18). Shoulder straps were no longer in use. Cloth shoulder loops were worn on white coats with an anchor near the button and three silver stars in a triangle below it (18a).

The cloth loops were replaced with shoulder boards in June. The boards for Vice Admirals had a two inch wide strip of gold lace running long ways down the board, showing only 1/4 inch blue borer on each side. Three silver stars ran in a line down the lace with a silver anchor above them (19).

With the elimination of the standing collar service coat in 1919, the corresponding collar insignia came to an end (20).

The design of the shoulder boards changed in 1922. The anchor was worn near the button and the three stars were arranged in a triangle beneath them (21).

Three silver stars became the badge of rank when pin-on badges were created in 1931 (22).

The black stripes were removed from the khaki coat in 1941 (22a) and the overcoat in 1947 (23).

The Career Compensation Act of October 12, 1949 (23a) placed the rank of Vice Admiral in pay grade O-8 which it shared with Admiral and Rear Admiral (Upper Half). This lasted until May 20, 1958 when a new law (23b) created pay grade O-9 for full Vice Admirals.

The April 2010 uniform regulations descried the insignia for Vice Admirals as:

Sleeve Stripes - "ADMIRAL. Wear one 2 inch stripe with two 1/2 inch stripes above it." (24).

Shoulder Boards - "The surface is covered with gold lace showing a 1/8 inch blue cloth margin on each of the long sides. A silver embroidered fouled anchor is placed with its center line along the shoulder board's longer dimension and the crown pointing toward the squared end of the board. The unfouled arm of the stock points to the front of the wearer (right and left). Designation of grade consists of silver embroidered five-pointed star(s), placed between the crown of the anchor and the squared end of the shoulder board."(the number of stars is shown as three in illustration) (25).

Metal Grade Insignia - "Flag Officer. Wear insignia lengthwise on the strap so that the single rays of each star point toward the collar. (the number of stars is shown as three in illustration).
Collar grade insignia replicates metal shoulder insignia except flag officers' miniature multiple stars which are connected as follows" (the number of stars is shown as three in illustration) (26).

Wardroom Cook

Wardroom Cook was one of the rates that Officer's Cook was split into in 1864 (1).

Officer's cooks had been considered petty officers as of the 1841 regulations, but are not listed, as Officer's Cooks or any of the titles it was divided into, on the list of petty officer rates in the regulations of 1865 (3). Their status was clarified when the rates were organized in 1885. Stewards, Cooks (not Ship's Cooks) and Attendants were made into a special category that were not petty officers (4).

There is also no information on uniforms or insignia before 1886. At that time they were to wear single breasted sack coats of blue with black buttons or a similar white coat with white buttons, matching trousers and a blue visored cap or white canvas hat (5). The canvas hat was replaced with a white cap by 1897 (6), and the coats became double breasted between the 1897 and 1905 (7) regulations.

In 1912 a white/blue crescent was added as a distinguishing mark (8).

The 1922 uniform regulations prescribed a cap devices of the letters U.S.N. (9).

1922 also saw them moved to pay grade three, along side second class petty officers (10).

Wardroom Cooks were changed to Officer's Cooks Second Class in 1923 (11).

Wardroom Steward

Wardroom Steward was one of the rates that Officer's Steward was split into in 1864 (1).

Officer's Stewards had been considered petty officers as of the 1841 regulations, but are not listed, as Officer's Stewards or any of the titles it was divided into, on the list of petty officer rates in the regulations of 1865 (3). On the other hand, the 1864 uniform regulations call for the petty officers badge to be worn on the left sleeve by "All other petty officers, except officer's stewards," (4).

Their status was clarified when the rates were organized in 1885. Stewards, Cooks (not Ship's Cooks) and Attendants were made into a special category that were not petty officers (5).

The lack of a petty officers badge infers that they were wearing regular navy uniforms in 1864.

In 1886 they were to wear single breasted sack coats of blue with black buttons or a similar white coat with white buttons, matching trousers and a blue visored cap or white canvas hat (6). The canvas hat was replaced with a white cap by 1897 (7), and the coats became double breasted between the 1897 and 1905 (8) regulations.

In 1912 a white/blue crescent was added as a distinguishing mark (9).

The 1922 uniform regulations prescribed a cap devices of the letters U.S.N. (10).

1922 also saw them moved to pay grade three, along side second class petty officers (11).

Wardroom Stewards were changed to Officer's Stewards Second Class in 1923 (12).

Warrant Machinist

The warrant rank of Warrant Machinist started as a temporary rank used during the Spanish-American War. It was created by law on May 4, 1898 (1).

They were distinguished by a gold four bladed propellor on the collar (2).

A permanent rank was created on March 3, 1899 (3).

They wore the gold crossed oak branches of engineering officers until January 5, 1900, when they were given a gold three bladed propellor (4).

The title was shortened to Machinist on March 3, 1909 (5).

Warrant Officer 1

Warrant Officer 1 was created by the "Warrant Officer Act of 1954" (1) in pay grade W-1, from the various warrant grades.

New insignia was prescribed to be worn as of November 1st. The cuff stripes were to be 1/4 inch wide with three 1/2 inch blue breaks, two inches apart, under a specialty device. On the shoulder boards, the 1/4 inch stripe had breaks 1/2 inch apart (which resulted in three blue portions and two gold portions) under the specialty device. The pin on badge of rank conformed to the unified system shared with other services, a gold bar with two blue rectangles, showing a square of gold in the middle (2).

The creation of the rates of Master Chief and Senior Chief Petty Officer in 1958, made Warrant Officer 1 redundant. A chief who was made a warrant officer would take a pay cut. As a result the rank was eliminated in 1975 (3).

Warrant Officer's Cook

Warrant Officer's Cook was one of the rates that Officer's Cook was split into in 1864 (1).

Officer's cooks had been considered petty officers as of the 1841 regulations, but are not listed, as Officer's Cooks or any of the titles it was divided into, on the list of petty officer rates in the regulations of 1865 (3). Their status was clarified when the rates were organized in 1885. Stewards, Cooks (not Ship's Cooks) and Attendants were made into a special category that were not petty officers (4).

There is also no information on uniforms or insignia before 1886. At that time they were to wear single breasted sack coats of blue with black buttons or a similar white coat with white buttons, matching trousers and a blue visored cap or white canvas hat (5). The canvas hat was replaced with a white cap by 1897 (6), and the coats became double breasted between the 1897 and 1905 (7) regulations.

In 1912 a white/blue crescent was added as a distinguishing mark (8).

The 1922 uniform regulations prescribed a cap devices of the letters U.S.N. (9).

1922 also saw them moved to pay grade four, along side third class petty officers (10).

Warrant Officer's Cooks were changed to Officer's Cooks Third Class in 1923 (11).

Warrant Officer's Steward

Warrant Officer's Steward was one of the rates that Officer's Steward was split into in 1864 (1).

Officer's Stewards had been considered petty officers as of the 1841 regulations, but are not listed, as Officer's Stewards or any of the titles it was divided into, on the list of petty officer rates in the regulations of 1865 (3). On the other hand, the 1864 uniform regulations call for the petty officers badge to be worn on the left sleeve by "All other petty officers, except officers's stewads," (4).

Their status was clarified when the rates were organized in 1885. Stewards, Cooks (not Ship's Cooks) and Attendants were made into a special category that were not petty officers (5).

The lack of a petty officers badge infers that they were wearing regular navy uniforms in 1864.

In 1886 they were to wear single breasted sack coats of blue with black buttons or a similar white coat with white buttons, matching trousers and a blue visored cap or white canvas hat (6). The canvas hat was replaced with a white cap by 1897 (7), and the coats became double breasted between the 1897 and 1905 (8) regulations.

In 1912 a white/blue cresent was added as a distinguishing mark (9).

The 1922 uniform regulations prescribed a cap devices of the letters U.S.N. (10).

1922 also saw them moved to pay grade four, along side third class petty officers (11).

Warrant Officer's Stewards were changed to Officer's Stewards Third Class in 1923 (12).

Warrant Officer, Hospital Corps.

Pharmacists became Warrant Officers, Hospital Corps on August 4, 1947 (1) during an expansion of that corps (2).

The insignia of a Pharmacists was continued consisting of a 1/4 inch cuff stripe with blue breaks under a gold caduceus, shoulder boards with one 1/2 inch stripe with one blue break under a gold caduceus and a gold caduceus as a badge of rank (3).

The Career Compensation Act of October 12, 1949 (4) placed medical warrant officers in pay grade W-1.

A standard, warrant officers badge of rank was introduced on July 1,1952 (5) consisting of a gold bar with a 1/16 inch blue break across the middle (6).

They became Warrant Officer 1 with the Warrant Officer Act of 1954 (7).

Part 3.
Marine Corps

Chapter 1. Marine Corps Organization

The Continental Marines

Marines began as soldiers who served on naval ships to provide landing parties, boarding parties or any other need for armed men the ship may encounter. By the 16th century, european navies had found it for practical to have special soldiers to service on ships than it was to train sailors to fight as soldiers in addition to operating the ship (1).

The Continental Congress approved the enlistment of marines on November 10, 1775 (2). This is still celebrated as the Marine Corps' birthday.

The Continental Marines served honorably on the ships of the Continental navy throughout the Revolutionary War. By the end of the war, funding run out and the marines faded away (3).

The United States Marine Corps

Both the 1794 (5) and the 1797 laws creating the federal navy included marines in the ships' compliment. These men were organized into the United States Marine Corps by a law of July 11, 1798 (7).

Subdivisions of Rank

As in the army, the lower three grades of officers in the marine corps are referred to a "Company Grade Officers" as they would normally be the officers of a company. The next three grades are known as "Field Grade Officers" and the rest who are generals are known as..."General Officers" (1).

In the early days, commissioned ranks below Captain were referred to a "Subalterns".

Non Commissioned Officers are enlisted personnel with supervisory responsibilities. Corporals and above are regarded as non commissioned officers.

Marine Staff Ranks

The 1798 law that created the marine corps allowed for an Adjutant, Quartermaster and Paymaster if any part of the corps was serving on land (1). These positions were to be given to subaltern of the line, or in other words three of the corps lieutenants would get the jobs. In 1814 the staff positions were allowed to given to Captains (2), and the Adjutant became the Adjutant and Inspector in 1817 (3). An Assistant Quartermaster was added in 1834 (4).

On March 2, 1847 a new law stated "the staff of the marine corps be, and the same is hereby, separated from the line of said corps; the officers of the former to receive the same pay and emoluments they now' receive by law, and to hold the same assimilated rank, to wit: quartermasters, paymasters, and adjutants and inspectors, the rank of major, and assistant quartermasters the rank of captain." (5). As a result of this legislation, the corps four staff officers were now organized separately from the line officers. There ranks were: Adjutant and Inspector with the rank of Major, Paymaster with the rank of Major, Quartermaster with the rank of Major and Assistant Quartermaster with the rank of Captain, and that is how they are listed in the navy register (6).

A second Assistant Quartermaster with the rank of Captain was added in 1861 (7), and for the rest of the 19th century, almost, the marine corps staff remained five people.

A law of March 3, 1899 (8) doubled the size of the staff to 10. The Adjutant and Inspector, Paymaster and Quartermaster now held the rank of Colonel, two Assistant Quartermasters were now Majors and three more Assistant Quartermasters with the rank of Captain were added along with an Assistant Adjutant and Inspector with the rank of Major and an Assistant Paymaster with the rank of Major.

The staff was expanded again in 1903 (9) with the addition of one Assistant Adjutant and Inspector, with the rank of Lieutenant Colonel, two Assistant Adjutants and Inspectors with the rank of Major, one Assistant Quartermaster with the rank of Lieutenant Colonel, five Assistant Quartermasters with the rank of Captain, one Assistant Paymaster with the rank of Lieutenant Colonel and one Assistant Paymaster with the rank of Captain, making a total of 21. The Adjutant and Inspector and his four assistants were organized into the Adjutant and Inspector's Department, the Quartermaster and his 11 assistants were organized into the Quartermaster's Department and the Paymaster and his three assistants were organized into the Paymaster's Department (10).

The staff was expanded to 29 in 1908 (11) with the addition of one Assistant Adjutant and Inspector with the rank of Lieutenant Colonel, one Assistant Quartermaster with the rank of Lieutenant Colonel, one Assistant Quartermaster with the rank of Major, three Assistant Quartermaster with the rank of Captain, one Assistant Paymaster with the rank of Major and one Assistant Paymaster with the rank of Captain.

Permanent staff appointments ended in 1916 when a new law stated "No further permanent appointments shall be made in any grade in any staff department. Any vacancy hereafter occurring in the lower grade of any staff department shall be filled by the detail of an officer of the line for a period of four years unless sooner relieved; any vacancy hereafter occurring in the upper grade of any staff department shall be filled by the appointment of an officer with the rank of colonel holding a permanent appointment in the staff department in which the vacancy exists, or of some other officer holding a permanent appointment in such staff department in case there be no permanent staff officer with the rank of colonel in that department, or of a colonel of the line in case there be no officer holding a permanent appointment in such staff department. Such appointments shall be made by the President and be for a term of four years, and the officer so appointed shall be recommissioned in the grade to which appointed" (12). With this law the 29 staff officers on the list could remain, or not at there discretion, in there staff positions, but from then on vacancies would be filled by line officers of special assignment. Comparing the names of staff officers listed in the marine section of the 1916 navy register (13) to the list in the 1939 register (14) shows us that even after all that time, some of the names are the same.

Pay Grades

When the navy divided it's ratings into grades in 1885, not quite pay grades at this point, marine enlisted ranks were also listed in the order. The Sergeant Major and First Sergeants were equal to First Class Petty Officers, Sergeant were equal to Second Class Petty Officers, Corporals were equal to Third Class Petty Officers, Musicians were equal to the non rated titles in the Seaman First Class grade and Privates equaled the Seaman Second Class grade (1). The Quartermaster Sergeant does not appear in the order at all. This appears have been meant to settle shipboard seniority and had little to do with the organization of the marine corps.

On June 10, 1922 (2) the marine corps enlisted ranks were organized into the seven pay grades that the army had adopted in 1920. The grades were numbered one to seven with one being the highest and seven the lowest. In the first grade were Sergeants Major and Quartermaster Sergeants, in the second grade were the ranks of First Sergeant, Gunnery Sergeant and Drum Major, no ranks were assigned to the third grade, Sergeants were in the fourth grade, Corporals in the fifth grade, Privates First Class in the six grade and the seventh grade was shared by Privates, Drummers and Trumpeters (3).

The army had used the change to pay grades to simplify it's enlisted rank structure which had become so complicated it was unworkable. In the marine corps it had the opposite effect. The simple rank structure of 1922 began to grow, beginning with the creation of the rank of Staff Sergeant in 1923 to fill the third grade. After that the flood gates opened and more and more ranks were created covering a wide variety of technical specialties. To add to the confusion, the corps began to add extra titles in parentheses such as Staff Sergeant (Mess) or Master Technical

Sergeant (Clerical) (Line). By the 1937 uniform regulations insignia was assigned by pay grade not rank (4). This divided the upper grades into line or staff with line grades wearing arcs and staff grades wearing stright bars, which had been the case for most of the rank already (5).

Just as had happened to the army in World War I, grade expansion and reorganization in World War II left the corps with a rank structure that was incomprehensible. Plans to introduce the primitive computers of the time to keep track of personnel issues lead the corps to reorganize the enlisted ranks on December 1, 1946 into something the IBM machines, as the computers were then known, could understand (6). The new system was almost too simple, each grade would have one rank. In grade one the ranks of Sergeant Major, First Sergeant, Master Gunnery Sergeant, Master Technical Sergeant, Quartermaster Sergeant, Paymaster Sergeant, Master Cook and Master Steward were combined into the new rank of Master Sergeant. The rank of Technical Sergeant was kept in the second grade and into it was absorbed the ranks of Gunnery Sergeant, Drum Major, Supply Sergeant, Steward First Class and Cook First Class. The rank of Staff Sergeant in the third grade absorbed the ranks of Platoon Sergeant, Chief Cook, Steward Second Class and Cook Second Class. The rank of Sergeant in the fourth grade absorbed the ranks of Field Music Sergeant, Field Cook, Steward Third Class and Cook Third Class. The rank in the fifth grade was still Corporal which absorbed the ranks of Assistant Cook, Field Music Corporal and Stewards Assistant First Class. In the sixth grade the rank of Private First Class absorbed the ranks of Field Music First Class and Steward's Assistant Second Class. Finally in the seventh grade the rank of Private absorbed the ranks of Field Music and Steward's Assistant Third Class (7).

The Career Compensation Act of October 12, 1949 (8) reorganized all military ranks, not just enlisted, into pay grades. The grades would carry a letter and a number. Officer's grades would start with an "O", warrant officer's with a "W" and Enlisted with an "E". The numbering system was inverted and grades E-1, W-1 and O-1 were the lowest. Privates were now in grade E-1, Privates First Class in grade E-2, Corporals in Grade E-3, Sergeants in Grade E-4, Staff Sergeants in grade E-5, Technical Sergeants in Grade E-6 and Master Sergeants in Grade E-7. Warrant Officers were placed in grade W-1 and Commissioned Warrant Officers spread across grade W-2, W-3 and W-4. Second Lieutenants were placed in the O-1 grade, First Lieutenants in O-2, Captains in O-3, Majors in O-4, Lieutenant Colonels in O-5, Colonels in O-6 and Brigadier Generals in O-7. The O-8 grade was shared by the ranks of Major General, Lieutenant General and General.

In 1954 the ranks of Sergeant Major and First Sergeant were revived and placed in the E-7 pay grade (9).

Also in 1954 the Warrant Officer Act (10) replaced the two ranks in four pay grades with the ranks of Warrant Officer 1 in the W-1 grade, Chief Warrant Officer 2 in the W-2 grade, Chief Warrant Officer 3 in the W-3 grade and Chief Warrant Officer 4 in the W-4 grade.

The Career Compensation Act was amended on May 20, 1958 (11) to create the grades of O-9, O-10, E-8 and E-9. Major Generals now had O-8 to themselves while Lieutenant Generals moved to O-9 and full Generals to O-10. The old title of Lance Corporal was made an official rank and placed in the E-3 grade. Corporals were moved up to the E-4 grade, Sergeants to E-5 and Staff Sergeants to E-6. Technical Sergeants were abolished altogether and replaced with the old rank of Gunnery Sergeant in the E-7 grade. Master Sergeants and First Sergeants shared the E-8 grade and Sergeants Major shared the E-9 grade with the revived rank of Master Gunnery Sergeant (12). To smooth the transition to the new system, all marines remained in there original rank and grade until they were promoted. "Acting was placed in front of the rank title. For example an Acting Corporal was still in the E-3 grade. The "acting" title was dropped in 1960 and the transition was complete by 1963 (13).

The W-5 grade was created in 1991 (7), and with it the rank of Chief Warrant Officer 5.

Chapter 2.
Marine Corps Rank Insignia

The 1775 uniform regulations for the Continental Navy (1) call for marine officers to wear a silver epaulet on the right shoulder. That is all the information we have on rank distinctions for the Continental Marines. Uniforms at the time were green faced with white. Around 1779 the facings were changed to red (2).

The federal navy's first uniform regulations in 1797 prescribed blue uniforms faced with red for marines with Lieutenants wearing an epaulet (3).

After the establishment of the marine corps in 1798, noncommissioned officers began wearing silk epaulets (4).

The corps issued it's first uniform regulations of it's own in 1804. Officers were distinguished by epaulets and noncommissioned officers by shoulder knots (5).

Chevrons were prescribed for junior officers in 1820 (6).

In 1833 new green uniforms were authorized. Officer's rank was shown by a system of laced button holes on the cuff and by epaulets. Enlisted marines wore the same cuff decorations as the officers and cloth wings instead of epaulets, those for Sergeants included a fringe edge (7). Sergeants and Corporals were allowed to wear hash marks on the cuff of fatigue jackets (8). It is possible that the has marks were replaced by chevrons in 1836, but the 1841 regulations still show the hash marks (9).

Officers were allowed to wear shoulder straps, with badges of rank inside them, in 1835 (10).

The dye in the green uniforms faded too quickly and they were ordered to be replaced with blue uniforms in 1839, and finally were in 1841 (11). The 1841 uniform regulations continue the cuff decorations from 1833. All marines now wore epaulets on both shoulders. Officers wore shoulder straps when epaulets were not worn and Sergeants and Corporals had hash marks on the cuffs of the fatigue jacket (12).

New uniform regulations were issued in 1859, but they may not be exactly what is now considered as the 1859 regulations. The 1859 regulations were published in a catalog of the company Schuyler Hartly and Graham in 1864, along with uniform regulations for the army, navy and revenue marine. The catalog was republished by Dover Publications of Mineola New York in 1985. The rank structure that insignia was prescribed for comes from after the corps was expanded for the Civil War in 1861, not from 1859. It is possible that the text in the catalog was updated to 1864 and this is what has come to us through history. The regulations continue the cuff decorations from 1833. Epaulets now carried the badge of rank on the strap. Shoulder straps were replaced by shoulder knots with the badge of rank on the outer end. Officers also showed rank by black knots on the cuff of the overcoat. A system of chevrons was introduced to show enlisted ranks (13).

In 1875 the loops of lace and the overcoat knots were replaced with elaborate cuff decorations. The 1875 uniform regulations also separated the uniforms of the corps five staff officers from those of line officers. Line officers were allowed a full dress coat with epaulets and the new cuff decoration, an undress coat with shoulder knots and plain cuffs, blue and white fatigue jackets with the cuff decorations in black or white and a mess jacket that appears not to have any indication of rank. The black cuff decorations were worn on the overcoat. Staff officers wore the same full dress coat as line officers with shoulder knots instead of epaulets. The undress coat was similar to the line officers fatigue jacket with black shoulder knots, it is not clear how rank was shown. Enlisted marines wore chevrons on all coats (14).

In 1877 the staff officers uniforms were modified to a single coat with gold shoulder knots for full dress and black shoulder knots for undress (15). It is still not clear if the badge of rank was worn on the black knot. Line officers were given a jacket for "social dress" that carried the cuff decorations (16). The cuff decorations may have been added to the mess jacket at the same time.

The next uniform regulations were in 1892. The 1875 full dress coat for line officers was worn with epaulets for special full dress and shoulder knots for full dress. The 1875 undress coat was eliminated. Undress was now the designation of the blue fatigue jacket, which now showed badges of rank on the collar in addition to the black cuff decorations. The white fatigue jacket was now known as the summer undress coat. It carried white cuff decorations but no collar insignia. Full color cuff decorations were worn on the mess and social jackets and black decorations were still worn on the overcoat. Staff officers continued to wear the 1877 coat with gold shoulder knots for full dress and black for undress. Enlisted marines had a full dress coat, an undress coat of blue cloth and a summer undress coat made of lighter weight blue cloth, all with chevrons (17).

In 1894, black cuff decorations were added to the staff officers coats. The summer undress uniform for enlisted marines was replaced with an all white uniform (18). Chevrons were added to this coat, along with a change of cloth, in 1896 (19).

The 1900 uniform regulations prescribe badges of rank on the 1875 white undress coat and adds a new stye white coat without cuff decorations but with collar insignia. Badges of rank were also worn on the collar of a new khaki campaign coat. The social dress was now known as evening dress and shoulder knots were worn on both the evening and mess jackets. Staff officers now wore gold shoulder knots, of a different design that those worn by line officers, in both special full dress and full dress. They were authorized an undress coat the same as for line officers, except longer, and all other line uniforms. Enlisted marines wore gray chevrons on the khaki campaign coat and the white summer undress coat (20).

Under the 1904 uniform regulations the 1875 white coat had been fully replaced by the 1900 coat. Badges of rank were moved from the collar to the shoulder loops of the white and khaki coats and shoulder loops were added to the blue coat to accommodate the badges (21). Badges of rank were also placed on shirt collars when the coat was not worn (22). A white mess jacket was added with shoulder loops with badges of rank (23). The cuff decoration for staff officers was changed from black to gold (24). The khaki campaign uniform was now referred to a the field uniform (25)

In 1908 the officers blue undress was changed to the same design as the white and khaki coats, eliminating the cuff decoration. At the same time small chevrons were added to shirt sleeves (26).

The 1912 uniform regulations added a forest green winter field uniform of the same design as the khaki uniform, now known as the summer field uniform (27). The overcoat was changed from blue to forest green and the cuff decoration was now green. Shoulder loops with badges of rank were also worn on the overcoat (28). Enlisted marines now wore the smaller shirt sized chevrons on both field coats, on shirts and on the overcoat (29). The white coat and the blue full dress coat were eliminated, and the blue undress coat was renamed the dress coat (30).

Marines serving in Europe in World War I were required to wear olive drab army uniforms instead of the forest green marine uniforms. Officers wore badges of rank on the shoulder loops and enlisted marines wore marine style chevron on the upper sleeve (31).

The 1922 uniform regulations simplified the corps uniforms. Permanent staff appointments had been eliminated in 1916 and the 1922 uniform regulations eliminated any difference between line and staff uniforms (32). Officers had eight uniform combinations: dress, white dress, undress, white undress, evening dress, winter service and summer service. The 1908 style blue coat was worn with the dress and undress, The 1900 style white coat was worn with the white dress and white undress, the 1900 style khaki coat was worn with summer service, the 1912 green coat was worn with winter service and the blue mess jacket was worn with evening dress (33). Badges of rank were worn on the shoulder loops of the blue, white, khaki and green coats (34). The evening jacket still carried shoulder knots and cuff decorations (35). The overcoat carried only badges of rank on the shoulder loops, the green cuff decorations were eliminated (36). Badges of rank continued to be worn on shirt collars (37). Enlisted marines wore the blue coat in dress and undress, the khaki coat in summer service and the green coat in winter service (38). Small sized chevrons were worn on all coats and shirts (39).

By this time the presidents had been set. Officers wore badges of rank on the shoulder loops of coats and the collars of shirt, and enlisted marines wore chevrons on all upper sleeves. That is the basic system that is still in use.

The 1929 uniform regulations allowed the return of the full dress uniform for White House aides. This meant the return of the full dress frock coat with cuff decoration and shoulder knots (40). The 1937 regulations upgraded it to special full dress, replacing the shoulder knots with epaulets (41). Wear of this uniform probably stopped during World War II.

Shoulder knots and cuff decorations came to an end in 1952 when the evening jacket was changed to include embroidered badges of rank on shoulder loops and simplified system of three cuff designs (42).

In 1954 enlisted marines started wearing black metal or plastic chevrons on the collars of fatigues (43).

Marine officers resisted subdued insignia until 2002, when it was authorized for use at the discretion of the local commander (44).

Epaulets

The term epaulet comes from epaulet, the French for shoulder (1). It is often used in the modern world for any shoulder decoration, but here it refers to a specific type of decoration. An epaulet in this context is a strap on the shoulder with fringe at the end called bullion. Above the bullion is a stiffening called a crescent. The area inside the crescent is called the frog and the area from the top of the crescent to the button by the collar is called the strap.

Continental marine officers were ordered to wear a plain silver epaulet on the right shoulder in 1775 (2). That is all that is known about the use of epaulets in the Continental Marines.

The navy's 1797 uniform regulations preceded a plain gold epaulet for Lieutenants of Marines. It was worn on the right shoulder except when a ship had two marine Lieutenants the junior officer wore his on the left (3).

When the marine corps was established in 1798, Sergeants were ordered to were a yellow silk epaulet on each shoulder and Corporals one on the right (4). There is no information on epaulets for officers.

In 1804 the corps first uniform regulations prescribed a plain gold epaulet on each shoulder for the commandant, one on the right with a gold strap on the left for Captains, one on the right for First Lieutenants and one on the left for Second Lieutenants (5). The enlisted epaulets were replaced with shoulder knots (6).

Chevrons were prescribed to show the rank of Captains and Lieutenants in 1820 (7). It is not clear if epaulets continued to be worn, but if the army's example was followed, they were not.

Epaulets were prescribed for all officers on the new green uniforms in 1833 (8). It is not clear if the 1804 system was used at the time. It is also not clear if epaulets were worn by the Sergeant Major, Quartermaster Sergeant, Fife Major and Drum Major. Sergeants did have fringe on their shoulder wings.

When the uniforms were changed back to blue in 1839, all officers wore an epaulet on each shoulder. Rank was shown by the size of the bullion. Regulations describe the epaulets as "For Field Officers--gold, bright bullion, half an inch in diameter, three and a half inches long; plain strap, crescent solid. For Captains and Staff--same, except that the bullion be smaller, and but two and a half inches long. Lieutenants same as Captains, with smaller bullion.

All Officers to wear one epaulette on each shoulder." The senior noncommissioned officers wore the epaulets of a Lieutenants with "fringe of gold will be substituted for bullion;". Sergeants wore epaulets in the style of a Captain, but made of yellow cloth. Corporals, Privates and Musicians wore the Sergeant's epaulets with smaller bullion (10).

The new uniforms of 1859 included epaulets designed after the system adopted by the army in 1851. All officers wore a gold epaulet on each shoulder with a large oval frog and metal crescent. The bullion was 3 1/2 inches long an 1/2 inch wide for field grade officers, 2 1/2 inches long and 1/4 inch wide for Captains and 2 1/2 inches long and 1/8 inches wide for Lieutenants. A silver bugle with a silver letter M in the loop was worn in the crescent. Badges of rank were worn on the strap, a silver star for the Colonel Commandant, a silver eagle for the other Colonel, a silver oak leaf for Lieutenant Colonels, two silver bars for Captains and one for First Lieutenants. Majors and Second Lieutenants had plain straps. It must be remembered that in 1859 the only Colonel was the commandant, the other Colonel was added in 1861. Therefore the commandant may have worn the eagle until that time. Enlisted marines wore metal shoulder scales, but unlike the army all ranks wore the same pattern and they included bullion that made them look like epaulets. The bullion was made of yellow worsted cloth and were 3 1/2 inches long. The width varied by rank, 3/8 inch for senior NCOs, 1/4 inch for Sergeants and 1/8 inch for others (11).

The bugle was replaced as the marine emblem with the eagle globe and anchor in 1867 (12). It is not clear how fast the epaulets were changed, it may have been in 1869 or as late as the new uniform regulations in 1875.

Under the 1875 regulations, epaulets were worn by line officers only. The design was the same as in 1859 except the badges of rank were embroidered on a scarlet background, with Majors now wearing a gold oak leaf, and the eagle globe and anchor replacing the bugle (13). Enlisted marines continued to wear the scales (14).

The 1892 uniform regulations replaced the enlisted scales with shoulder knots (15).

The officers epaulets changed very little after that. The commandant would wear the appropriate number of stars on the strap as his rank went up or down. The 1904 uniform regulations prescribe 2 1/2 by 1/4 inch bullion for Lieutenants as well as Captains (16), and the 1912 regulations lengthened them to 3 1/4 inches (17). Second Lieutenants gained a gold bar as a badge of rank during World War I. It is not clear if it was were worn on epaulets.

The fancy 19th century style dress uniforms were abolished in 1922 and epaulets with them (18).

Epaulets were prescribed in the 1937 uniform regulations for White House aides wearing the special full dress uniform. They were identical in design to the 1912 regulations (19). Their use more that likely ended during World War II.

Shoulder Straps

The marine corps introduced shoulder straps, to be worn when epaulets were not, on February 17, 1835 (1). They were formed from a rectangle of 1/8 inch wide gold lace 4 inches long and 1 inch wide with a green center to match the uniform. Badges of rank were placed inside the rectangle. The Colonel Commandant wore a gold eagle in the center, Lieutenant Colonels wore a gold oak leaf at each end, Majors wore a silver leaf at each end, Captains wore "two oblong squares, three-eighths of an inch long and one-eighth of an inch wide", First Lieutenants had one oblong square and Second Lieutenants had an empty frame (2).

The background was changed to blue when the uniforms were changed in 1839 (3).

Shoulder straps were replaced with shoulder knots in 1859 (4).

Shoulder Knots

From 1804 to 1833 Sergeants wore a yellow shoulder knot on both shoulders and Corporals one on the right (1).

The knots returned in 1859 to replace officers shoulder straps. They were formed from four cords for field grade officers and three cords for company grade. The outer end terminated in three loops and scarlet cloth showed thru the holes of each turn. Silver badges of rank were worn over the three loops, with Majors and Second Lieutenants using plain knots (2).

In 1875 a scarlet outline was added around the badges of rank, allowing the gold leaf of a Major to be worn (3). Staff officers now wore knots of different design. 1/4 inch gold cord was braided into a dense rectangular knot with a slight flair at the outer end. Badges of rank on scarlet were worn at the outer end (4) (5). Black knots were worn on the undress coat. It is not clear if badges were worn.

The 1892 uniform regulations slightly shortened the knots for line officers and all ranks now wore knots of four cords (6). The full dress uniforms of enlisted marines carried a knot of scarlet cord, similar to the staff officers design, with at large oval of red cloth outlined in a metal crescent, at the out end. An eagle globe and anchor was worn in the center of the cloth (7).

The 1900 uniform regulations eliminate the black knots for staff officers. The badge of rank was moved to the middle of the knot and an eagle globe and anchor was added to the outer end. Line officers' knots were not changed (8).

The enlisted knots were eliminated in 1904 (9).

In 1912 the eagle globe and anchor on the staff knots was replaced with the insignia of the staff department (10).

By 1922 the only uniform left with shoulder knots was the evening dress. All officers were ordered to wear the staff style knots with an eagle globe and anchor at the outer end and the badge of rank in the center. Officers on staff duty added the department device above the badge of rank (11).

Knots were worn on the full dress uniform of White House aides under the 1929 uniform regulations (12), but by the 1937 regulations aides were wearing the special full dress uniform with epaulets (13).

The knots on the evening jackets were removed in 1952 (14) and marine shoulder knots came to an end.

Badges of rank

Badges of rank is the term we shall use to refer to the stars, eagles, leafs and bars used to denote officers rank.

The first use was in the shoulder straps in 1835. The Colonel Commandant wore a gold eagle, Lieutenant Colonels wore a gold oak leaf, Majors wore a silver oak leaf, Captains wore two gold bars, First Lieutenants wore one gold bar and Second Lieutenants were without a badge of rank (1)(2).

In 1859 the badges moved to epaulets and shoulder straps. All the badges were in silver for contrast with the gold epaulet strap and gold shoulder knot. Lieutenant Colonels wore the silver leaf and Majors were without a badge of rank. The Colonel Commandant wore a star and the other Colonel wore the eagle, at least after 1861 when there were two Colonels, and certainly from 1867 to 1876 when the commandant was a Brigadier General (3).

The badges were placed on a scarlet background in 1875, eliminating the contrast problem and allowing Majors to wear a gold leaf (4).

The 1892 uniform regulations placed the badges of rank, outlined in scarlet, on the collar of the blue undress coat. Both Colonels wore and eagle (5).

Under the 1900 uniform regulations the badges were worn on the collar of the blue coat, two styles of white coat and a khaki coat. The commandant had been raised to Brigadier General in 1899, so a star was one again worn (6).

The commandant wore two stars from 1902 to 1903, while he was a Major General.

In 1904 the uniform regulations prescribed cloth shoulder loops be added to the blue, white and khaki coats, and the badges, without the scarlet outline, were worn on them (7). The badges were also worn on the collars of shirts (8). The badges were also worn on the shoulder loops of a white mess jacket (9).

In 1908 the commandant's rank was raised again to Major General, and therefore he was allowed to wear two stars.

The 1912 regulations added a green coat with the badges on the shoulder loops (10) and a green overcoat with shoulder loops and badges (11).

Warrant ranks were created in 1916, and insignia was prescribed by the 1917 uniform regulations. Behind the eagle globe and anchor on the collar Marine Gunners wore a bursting bomb and Quartermaster Clerks wore a Marine Corps sword in miniature and a key crossed and surmounted by a wheel with rim set with 13 stars. The insignia was all bronze on the green and khaki coats, on shirt collars and on the shoulder loops of overcoats. On the blue and white coats it was silver with a blue rim on the wheel of the Quartermaster Clerk's insignia (12).

Second Lieutenants were finally given a badge of rank in 1918, a gold bar (14).

The 1922 uniform regulations kept the same insignia for Quartermaster Clerks in the Quartermaster's Department but those assigned to the Adjutant and Inspectors Department wore a gold Marine Corps sword crossed with gold fasces, surmounted by a silver wreath which encircles a gold shield of 13 bars, side points and base point of shield touching inside of wreath with the field above bars to containing one large star in center and 12 small stars, with a bronze insignia worn on green and khaki coats and shirt collars. Pay Clerks wore a sword crossed with a gold quill pen, surmounted by a silver oak leaf and three acorns, with bronze insignia worn as usual. On coats the various warrant insignia was moved from the collar to the shoulder loops. All officers now wore the badges of rank on the curtain of garrison caps (15).

When the ranks of Chief Marine Gunner, Chief Quartermaster Clerk and Chief Paymaster Clerk were added in 1926, they were given a badge of rank consisting of a gold bar with a 1/4 inch blue stripe running horizontally across it (16).

The Quartermaster Clerks insignia was changed to gold in 1937 (17).

In 1943 the chief warrant and warrant ranks were combined into the ranks of Commissioned Warrant Officer and Warrant Officer. The eventual insignia was a gold bar with a scarlet stripe across it, 1/8 inch wide for commissioned warrants and 1/16 for warrants. It is not clear if this insignia was adopted in 1943, but it was in use by 1950 (18).

The rank of the commandant was raised to Lieutenant General in 1942, allowing him three stars, and to General in 1944 allowing him four stars.

In 1954 new insignia was prescribed for the now four grades of Warrant Officer. A "unified system" common to all armed forces was developed using the same pattern for each equivalent rank. The enameled portions would very by branch of service, brown for the army, dark blue for the Navy and Coast Guard, scarlet red for the Marine Corps, and sky blue for the Air Force. The new bars were rectangular, silver for the top two grades and gold for the other two. The enameled portion for W-1 and W-3 would be in two rectangles, showing only one stripe of gold or silver. For W-2 and W-4 there would be three enameled portions showing two sections of gold or silver (19).

When the rank of Chief Warrant Officer 5 was created in 1991, it was given a badge of rank of a silver bar with a scarlet stripe running long ways down the middle (20).

The army had developed subdued insignia during the Vietnam War to address a centuries old problem of officers being killed by snipers who saw their insignia. In earlier conflicts officers had removed or hidden there insignia, and marine officers continued to do so until 2002, when local commanders were allowed to prescribe subdued badges of rank at their desertion. Silver badges were to be rendered in black and gold ones in brown. The scarlet on the warrant badges remained (21)

Cuff Decoration

Cuff decorations began on the green uniforms of 1833. Field grade officers wore four button holes outlined in gold lace, Captains wore three and Lieutenants two (1). Enlisted marines wore the same pattern with senior noncommissioned officers wearing four loops, Sergeants three and others two (2), probably in yellow binding instead of gold lace. This system continued thru the change to blue uniforms in 1839 (3) and the new uniforms of 1859 (4).

The 1859 uniform regulations (5) also added a system of knots on the cuffs of officer's overcoats that the army had been using since 1851. Rank was shown by black cords formed into a three loop knot. First Lieutenants wore one cord, Captains two, Majors three, Lieutenant Colonels four and the Colonel may have worn five. After 1861 when there was two Colonels, the Colonel Commandant wore five cords in a double knot, if he had done this since 1859 is no clear. Second Lieutenants wore a plain cuff.

A whole new system was introduced in for officers 1875 (6) (7). Field grade officers wore a large, point up, chevron of gold lace with loops of gold tracing braid running up both sides of the top of the chevron and forming a knot over the point. On the bottom side of the chevron loops of gold tracing braid follow the bottom edges meeting in series of long loops and a twist in the angle. Scarlet cloth showed thru the openings on the knot and around the tracing braid. Captains a strip of gold lace formed into a knot of five interlocking loops. Loops of gold tracing braid ran all around the outer edges of the knot and formed an elaborate pattern underneath. It is not clear if scarlet cloth was worn at this point. First Lieutenants wore the Captains decoration without the outline of tracing braid loops but with the underneath pattern and Second Lieutenants were without both. The decorations were worn on the full dress coat but not the undress coat. The same pattern, in black and without any scarlet backing, were worn on blue fatigue jackets and overcoats, and in white on white fatigue coats.

The 1875 regulations prescribed that the Brigadier General Commandant continue to wear the old uniforms. When a new commandant, who was a Colonel, took office in 1876 he appears, according to a photograph, to have worn the field officers cuff decoration with an extra set of loops of tracing braid above the point of the chevron (8). This was confirmed by the 1892 uniform regulations (9).

In 1877 staff officers were given uniforms without cuff decorations, however they still wore them on overcoats. Line officers gained a "social dress" with cuff decorations and they may have been added to the mess jackets at this point (10).

On July 18, 1894 the knot of tracing braid above the chevron of field officers was changed to "the shape of a single three-leaf clover". At the same time staff officers added black cuff decorations to their coats (11).

The 1900 uniform regulations gave a much better description of the decorations. Those for the commandant, who was once again a Brigadier General, were described as "gold lace placed upon red cloth. The chevron to be backed by gold tracing braid one-eighth of an inch wide in double overhand loops placed close together around the edge of the chevron, except at the top of the chevron where the design will be in the shape of a knot topped by a loop, and at the lower angle of the chevron, where the design will be in the shape of four loops. The red cloth to show one-eighth of an inch between the gold lace and the tracing braid, and to show fully between the parts of the design at the top and lower angle of the chevron.". The decoration for field officers was the same except for the three loop cover leaf. The decoration for Captains was described as "A Marine Corps knot of plain round gold cord, one-fourth of an inch wide, backed on both sides by gold tracing braid one-eighth of an inch wide placed close to the cord; the knot to be on red cloth, the cloth to show between the openings of the knot. The entire knot to be backed, except in the angle of the bottom of same, by double overhand loops of one-eighth inch gold tracing braid, made so as to abut. The cord and tracing braid will extend evenly around the sleeve. Full length of complete knot to be from nine to ten and one-half inches from the bottom of sleeve, according to length of arm of wearer; vertical height of knot inside of tracing braid from top to angle of bottom of center, to be from six to seven and one-half inches. The width of the knot inside of tracing braid at widest point to be from three and three-quarters to four and one-quarter inches. The diamond at center of the knot to be about one and one-eighth inches in height and seven-eighths of an inch wide. The point at which the cord crosses at the angle at the bottom of the knot to be from two and one-half to three inches from the bottom of the sleeve; distance of round cord from bottom of sleeve at side to be from one and three-quarters to two and one-quarter inches. The angle at the bottom of knot to be trimmed with design similar to that in the angle of the field officer's chevrons; the bottom of the design to be about one-eighth of an inch from bottom of cuff.". First Lieutenants continued to wear the Captains decoration without the overhand loops and Second Lieutenants the same without the design in the angle at the bottom. Staff officers now wore a gold decoration on dress coats but without the scarlet backing and the braid closer. As with line officers, black or white was used on all other coats (12).

The commandant was raised to Major General in 1902, and a photograph shows him wearing the 1900 cuff decoration (13). The commandant's rank went back to Brigadier General in 1903.

The 1904 uniform regulations prescribed a different design for each field rank. The commandant continued to wear the 1900 design. Colonels wore the same without the "extreme top loop over the point of the chevrons". Lieutenant Colonels wore the clover leaf above the chevrons and Majors were without a knot above the chevrons (14). The white coat of 1875 had been replaced with a coat without cuff decorations (15). A similar blue coat was adopted in 1908 (16).

1908 also saw the commandant move back up to Major General. A photograph shows a cuff decoration of two strips of gold lace with a line of oak leaf and acorn embroidery between them. It is possible that a cuff flap is also worn, but it is not clear (17).

The 1912 uniform regulations prescribed cuff decorations for the Major General Commandant on his full dress coat of a strip of gold lace over a line of oak leaf and acorn embroidery with a cuff flap with three buttons that was outlined in gold lace and covered in oak leaf and acorn embroidery (18). On his mess jacket cuffs, he wore a line of oak leaf and acorn embroidery crossed with another line (19). The blue overcoat was replaced with a green overcoat with darker green cuff decorations (20). The decoration on the mess jackets of line officers were now without the scarlet cloth backing, just the blue of the sleeve showed in the spaces (21).

With the rank of Brigadier General and the warrant ranks of Marine Gunner and Quartermaster Clerk in 1916, new cuff decorations had be devised. The 1917 uniform regulations show Brigadier Generals wearing a line of oak leaf and acorn embroidery under a strip of lace (22). Warrant officers were not allowed any uniforms with cuff decorations except the overcoat, where a simple green figure eight knot was prescribed (23). The Major General Commandant now wore a smaller version of the decoration on the full dress coat on his mess jacket (24).

The 1922 uniform regulations abolished the full dress coat and the decorations on the overcoat, leaving the decoration on the mess jacket only. All generals wore the old decoration for Brigadier Generals. Other officers wore the decorations of their rank without a scarlet backing (25). These decorations were also worn in the full dress coat of White house aides as prescribed by the 1929 (26) and 1937 (27) uniform regulations.

The full dress uniforms at the White House probably came to an end during World War II.

The mess/evening jackets were modified in 1952 to include three designs of cuff decoration (28), and the decoration as a distinction of rank came to an end.

Chevrons

The History of American Ranks and Rank Insignia

A chevron is two lines meeting at an angle. A simple design to create with lace or tape, they had been used as rank insignia for noncommissioned officers by the British Army since 1803 (1). In this context we need to stretch the definition of "chevron" include all the cloth badges worn (mostly) on the upper sleeve to show rank.

The first use of chevrons by the marine corps was in 1820 when Captains were ordered to wear three on the upper sleeve, First Lieutenants two and Second Lieutenants one, all in gold (2).

The system was altered slightly the next year when First Lieutenants were ordered to wear one chevron on both sleeves and Second Lieutenants one on the right. First Lieutenants that were filling a staff position wore two chevrons on each sleeve and Second Lieutenants in as staff position wore two on the right and one on the left (3).

The chevrons did not continue on the new green uniforms of 1833. That year Sergeants were ordered to wear two yellow hash marks above the cuff of the fatigue jackets and Corporals were ordered to wear one (4).

It is possible that the hash marks were altered in 1836 to two gold point up chevrons on the upper sleeve for senior noncommissioned officers, one for Sergeants and one above each cuff for Corporals (5). However the 1839 uniform regulations state "Sergeants--When in fatigue dress will be designated by wearing two plain stripes of worsted lace on each arm below the elbow, placed diagonally on the upper side of the arm from one seam to the other, the outer points inclining towards the elbow. Corporals--will wear one stripe on each arm in the manner designated for Sergeants." (6).

A proper system of chevrons to show noncommissioned rank was introduced by the 1859 uniform regulations. The insignia was made of yellow silk for senior NCOs and yellow worsted cloth for other, all on a scarlet background and pointing up. The Sergeant Major wore three chevrons and three arcs, the Quartermaster Sergeant wore three chevrons and three straight bars, the Drum Major wore three chevrons and three straight bars with a star in the middle, First Sergeants wore three chevrons with a lozenge or diamond in the angle, Sergeants wore three chevrons and Corporals two chevrons (7).

On July 25, 1896 white chevrons were added to the white fatigue coat that had been introduced in 1894 (8). The chevrons were to be white but it is not clear if a scarlet background was worn, but it is doubtful for reasons of colorfastness if nothing else.

When the rank of Gunnery Sergeant was created in 1898, they were ordered to wear three chevrons and three straight bars with a rifle crossed with a naval gun with an eagle globe and anchor superimposed, in between (9).

The 1900 uniform regulations prescribe that all ranks wear yellow silk chevrons with senior noncommissioned officers wearing gold lace on full dress coats. Chevrons on the white and khaki coats were to be of "gray linen braid" (10).

In 1904 the Gunnery Sergeants insignia was changed to three chevrons with crossed rifles and a bursting bomb in the angle (11).

In 1908 Quartermaster Sergeants assigned to the Paymaster's Department added a stack of coins crossed with a quill to the center of their chevrons. Drummer were ordered to wear crossed drumsticks and Trumpeters a trumpet (12).

1908 also saw the introduction of smaller chevrons made of olive drab on a khaki background to be worn on shirt sleeves (13).

Under the 1912 uniform regulations, the large (8 inches wide) chevrons were made of yellow silk on scarlet and worn on the blue coat. On the green field coat and overcoat, smaller (3 1/2 inches wide) chevrons of forest green on scarlet were worn. On the khaki field coat and shirts, small chevrons were made on a khaki background with the designs in a darker shade. Lance Corporals were allowed one chevron in the small size, even on the blue coat (14).

In 1918 the new rank of Private First Class was ordered to wear crossed rifles (15).

The 1922 uniform regulations reduced the dress chevrons to the small size (16), and the chevrons on khaki coats and shirts became green on khaki (17).

At this point marine chevrons become hard to track accurately. The organizing the enlisted ranks into pay grades in 1922 opened the flood gates of enlisted ranks, and many titles were added during the 20s and 30s. To add to the confusion neither the 1922 (18) or the 1929 (19) uniform regulations give a description of the chevrons. As on August of 1936 the insignia was, Sergeant Major three chevrons and three arcs, Quartermaster Sergeant three chevrons and three straight bars with a wheel in the center, Master Technical Sergeant three chevrons and three straight bars, Master Technical Sergeant (Mess) three chevrons and three straight bars with a crescent in the center, Paymaster Sergeant three chevrons and three straight bars with a stack of coins crossed with a quill in the center, Master Gunnery Sergeant three chevrons and three arcs with crossed rifle and a bursting bomb in the center, First Sergeant three chevrons and two arcs with a diamond in the center. Gunner Sergeant three chevrons and two arcs with crossed rifle and a bursting bomb in the center, Supply Sergeant three chevrons and two straight bars with a wheel in the center, Drum Major three chevrons and two straight bars with a baton in the center, Technical Sergeant three chevrons and two straight bars, Technical Sergeant (Mess) three chevrons and two straight bars with a crescent in the center, Staff Sergeant three chevrons and one arc, Staff Sergeant (Mess) three chevrons and one arc with crescent in the center, Platoon Sergeant three chevrons and one arc with a star in the center, Sergeant three chevrons, Drum Sergeant three chevrons over crossed drumsticks, Trumpet Sergeant three chevrons over a trumpet, Mess Sergeant and Chief Cook three chevrons over a crescent, Corporal two chevrons, Drum Corporal two chevrons over crossed drumsticks, Trumpet Corporal two chevrons over a trumpet, Mess Corporal and Field Cook two chevrons over a crescent, Private First Class one chevron, Drummer First Class one chevron over crossed drumsticks, Trumpeter First Class one chevron over a trumpet, Assistant Cook one chevron over a crescent, Drummer crossed drumsticks and Trumpeter a trumpet (20). There is a semblance of a system to be found here, six stripes, chevrons and arcs or bars, for grade one, five for grade two, four for grade three, three for grade four, two for grade five, one for grade six and none for grade seven. For the most part, arcs were worn by line ranks and bars by staff ranks, the exception being Staff Sergeant.

Under the 1937 uniform regulations, chevrons showed pay grade not rank. Three chevrons and three arcs were worn by ranks in the first grade (line) and three chevrons and three straight bars were worn by rank in the first grade (staff). Three chevrons and two arcs were worn by ranks in the second grade (line) and three chevrons and two straight bars were worn by rank in the second grade (staff). Three chevrons and one arc were worn by ranks in the third grade (line) and three chevrons and one straight bar were worn by rank in the third grade (staff). Three chevrons were worn by the fourth grade, two by the fifth and one by the sixth (21). This system remained in effect thru World War II and allowed the corps enlisted rank structure to become even more complex and confusing.

During World War II olive drab fatigues became the uniform worn in the field and chevrons were simply drawn on the sleeve in black ink. After the war stenciling kits became available to give the chevrons a more polished look (22)

In 1946 everything was simplified to one rank per grade with all ranks that were entitled to them wearing arcs, not bars.

In 1952 female marines were given green on white chevrons for wear on the summer service uniform (23).

In 1954 the stenciled chevrons were replaced with black metal or plastic chevrons worn on the collar (24).

Crossed rifles were added to most ranks in 1958. The old design was worn until promotion.

The full sized chevrons returned for use on the mess jackets of Senior NCOs. The exact date of when they returned has proved elusive, but the best guess would be in the early 1970s.

The green on white chevrons were abolished in 1979 (25).

Another changed that probably happened in the 70s was the wearing of the black collar chevrons on khaki shirts when wearing a green sweater.

In 1992 a blue sweater with gold metal chevrons on the shoulder loops was authorized for recruiting duty (26).

Chapter 3. Marine Corps Ranks

Adjutant and Inspector with rank of Colonel

The rank of the Adjutant and Inspector of the Marine Corps, George Reid, was increased from Major to Colonel on March 3, 1899 (1).

Reid wore the eagle of a Colonel on his shoulder knots (2), and the Colonel's cuff decoration of a large chevron outlined in tight loops of tracing braid, with tight loops of braid in the angle of the chevron and a long vertical and two short horizontal loops above the point (3).

Reid retired on December 14, 1904 and was replaced by Charles Lauchheimer (4).

The 1900 uniform regulations show the eagle also being worn on various collars (5).

The 1904 uniform regulations prescribe cuff decoration for Colonels as being the same as the Commandant but without the "extreme top loop over the point of the chevrons." (6). The decoration for the Commandant is described as having, over the chevron lace "in the shape of a knot, topped by a loop" (7).

The Commandant, George Elliott, was made a Major General in 1908 and pictures of him show a different decoration on the cuffs (8). This may have meant that Colonels were allowed to wear the top loop at that point. The illustrations in the 1912 uniform regulations (9) show the decoration for Colonels to have, above the chevron, two oval, horizontal loops below an oval vertical loop interlocked with two round loops and topped by a pointed loop. From this we can speculate that the 1904 decoration was this was this without the pointed loop and this decoration took over in 1908 or 1912.

The 1912 regulations also added the insignia of the Adjutant and Inspectors' Department, a sword crossed with a faces under a wreathed shied, to Lauchheimer's coat collars (10) and shoulder knots (11).

The National Defense Act of August 29, 1916 (12) ended the permanent staff appointments. Promotions in the staff department would be from within the officers on duty in 1916, but any new staff officers would be on temporary duty from the line. The act also made the Adjutant and Inspector a Brigadier General.

Adjutant and Inspector with rank of Major

On March 2, 1847, the marine corps a given a permanent Adjutant and Inspector, who held the rank of Major (1). Prior to 1847 the position of Adjutant and Inspector was, supposedly, held by an officer taken form the line. The position had replaced Adjutant on March 3, 1817 (2). In reality the Adjutant and Inspector was not taken from the line, but held by a permanent officer, Parke Howle, who had been the Adjutant and Inspector since 1822 (3).

Howle's uniform, as prescribed by the 1840 uniform Regulations (4) showed four laced button holes on the cuff and a gold epaulet on each shoulder with an aigullette attached to the right one. When epaulets were not worn, shoulder straps were with a silver oak leaf at each end.

Howle died on July 16, 1857 (5), and was replaced by Henry Tyler (6).

Under the 1859 uniform regulations (7), Tyler continued to wear the four loops on the cuffs. Epaulets had bullion that was 1/2 inch wide and 3 1/2 inches long with no device on the strap. Shoulder knots were worn when epaulets were not. Those for Majors were made of four cords and no device at the end. A sleeve knot made of three strips of black cord was worn on the overcoat.

Tyler was dismissed from the corps on June 21, 1861 (8), and was replaced by A.S. Nicholson (9).

In 1875, the corps' five staff officers were given uniforms of a different design from the line officers. The full dress coat was the same as line officers, but with shoulder knots, with an aigullette on the right, instead of epaulets. The knots now carried a gold oak leaf at the end. The line field officers gold cuff decoration was worn on the cuffs, consisting of a large chevron outlined in tight loops of tracing braid, with tight loops of braid in the angle of the chevron and a loose three loop knot above the point. Scarlet cloth showed in the spaces between the braid. The staff officer's undress coat was a modification of the line officers fatigue coat, it is not clear how rank was shown. A black version cuff decoration was on the overcoat (10).

In 1877 staff officers gained a coat that was used for both full dress and undress. The cuff decoration was not worn on this coat. Gold shoulder knots were worn for full dress and black for undress. The gold oak leaf was worn on the gold shoulder knot, but it is not clear if it was worn on the black knot (11).

Nicholson retired on May 1, 1894 (12), and was replaced by George Reid (13).

The cuff decoration, in black, was added to the cuffs of the coat on July 18, 1894 (14). At the same time the loops above the chevron were changed to be "be in the shape of a single three-leaf clover"

On March 3, 1899 (15), a new law raised the rank of the Adjutant and Inspector to Colonel.

Assistant Adjutant and Inspector with rank of Lieutenant Colonel

An Assistant Adjutant and Inspector with rank of Lieutenant Colonel was added on March 3, 1903 (1). The position went to Charles Lauchheimer (2).

Under the 1900 uniform regulations, Lauchheimer would have worn a silver oak leaf on his shoulder knots and on the collars of the undress and campaign coats. The field officers cuff decoration was worn on the cuffs, consisting of a large chevron outlined in tight loops of tracing braid, with tight loops of braid in the angle of the chevron and a long vertical and two short horizontal loops above the point, and four loops underneath. It was in gold on the dress coat, black on the blue undress coat and overcoat and white on the summer undress coat (3).

The cuff decoration for field officers became the specific decoration for Lieutenant Colonels in 1904 (4). The regulations also call for the oak leaf to be worn on the shoulder loops of coats instead of the collar (5).

Lauchheimer became the Adjutant and Inspector with rank of Colonel on December 14, 1904 and the Lieutenant Colonels post went to Henry Haines (6).

A second Assistant Adjutant and Inspector with rank of Lieutenant Colonel was added by Congress on May 13, 1908 (7), and the appointment went to Rufus Lane (8).

The 1912 regulations added the insignia of the Adjutant and Inspectors' Department, a sword crossed with a faces under a wreathed shied, to the coat collars (9) and shoulder knots (10).

The National Defense Act of August 29, 1916 (11) ended the permanent staff appointments. Promotions in the staff department would be from within the officers on duty in 1916, but any new staff officers would be on temporary duty from the line.

Assistant Adjutant and Inspector with rank of Major

An Assistant Adjutant and Inspector with rank of Major was added on March 3, 1899 (1). The position went to Charles Lauchheimer (2).

Lauchheimer would have worn the field officers cuff decoration was worn on the cuffs, consisting of a large chevron outlined in tight loops of tracing braid, with tight loops of braid in the angle of the chevron and a long vertical and two short horizontal loops above the point, and four loops underneath, all in black (3).

Under the 1900 uniform regulations, Lauchheimer would have worn a gold oak leaf on his shoulder knots and on the collars of the undress and campaign coats. The field officers cuff decoration was worn on the cuffs, consisting of a large chevron outlined in tight loops of tracing braid, with tight loops of braid in the angle of the chevron and a long vertical and two short horizontal loops above the point, and four loops underneath. It was in gold on the dress coat, black on the blue undress coat and overcoat and white on the summer undress coat (4).

Two more Assistant Adjutants and Inspectors with rank of Major were added on March 3, 1903 (5). Lauchheimer moved up to Lieutenant Colonel and the three new Majors were Henry Haines, Rufus Lane and Louis Magill (6).

In 1904 the cuff decoration for Majors was changed to just the chevron and the tracing braid with the loops underneath, no top knot (7). The regulations also call for the oak leaf to be worn on the shoulder loops of coats instead of the collar (8).

A third Assistant Adjutant and Inspector with rank of Major was added by Congress on May 13, 1908 (9), Lane moved up to Lieutenant Colonel and Albert McLemore and David Porter took the two open spots (10).

The 1912 regulations added the insignia of the Adjutant and Inspectors' Department, a sword crossed with a faces under a wreathed shied, to the coat collars (11) and shoulder knots (12).

The National Defense Act of August 29, 1916 (13) ended the permanent staff appointments. Promotions in the staff department would be from within the officers on duty in 1916, but any new staff officers would be on temporary duty from the line.

Assistant Baker

In early 1941 the rank of Assistant Cook (Baker) wash changed to Assistant Baker (1). Assistant Cooks (Baker) had been in grade six wearing one chevron (2).

The title was changed back to Assistant Cook (Baker) in 1943 (3).

Assistant Cook

The rank of Assistant Cook was created in grade six, in 1935 (1).

They wore one chevron with a crescent underneath (2) until 1937 when the crescent was removed (3).

The title was changed to Assistant Cook (Commissary) in 1943 (3).

Assistant Cook (Baker)

In 1940, bakers were separated from cooks and the, slightly, separate title of Assistant Cook (Baker) was born (1).

The rank shared grade six and one chevron with Assistant Cook (2).

The title was changed to Assistant Baker in early 1941, and back to Assistant Cook (Baker) in 1943 (3).

The 1943 change moved the rank up to grade five (4), entitling it to two chevrons (5).

When the enlisted grades were overhauled on December 1, 1946, Assistant Cooks (Baker) became Corporals (6).

Assistant Cook (Commissary)

Assistant Cooks became Assistant Cooks (Commissary) in 1943, and were moved up to the fifth grade (1), with two chevrons (2).

When the enlisted grades were overhauled on December 1, 1946, Assistant Cooks (Commissary) became Corporals (3).

Assistant Paymaster with rank of Captain

One Assistant Paymaster with the rank of Captain was added to the staff on March 3, 1903 (1). The appointment went to William Powell (2).

Under the 1900 uniform regulations, a Captain of staff would wear two silver bars as a badge of rank and cuff decoration of a large knot outlined in loops of tracing braid with four loops underneath (3).

A second Assistant Paymaster with the rank of Captain was added on May 13, 1908 (4). Powell moved up to Major and the two Captain slots went to Harold Reisinger and Davis Willis (5).

Reisnger became an Assistant Paymaster with the rank of Major in 1910 and Russell Putnam took the open Captain's position (6).

The 1912 regulations added the insignia of the Paymasters' Department, a sword crossed with a quill under an oak leaf and acorn, to the coat collars (7) and shoulder knots (8).

The National Defense Act of August 29, 1916 (9) ended the permanent staff appointments. Promotions in the staff department would be from within the officers on duty in 1916, but any new staff officers would be on temporary duty from the line.

Assistant Paymaster with rank of Lieutenant Colonel

One Assistant Paymaster with the rank of Lieutenant Colonel was added to the staff on March 3, 1903 (1). The appointment went to George Richards (2).

Under the 1900 uniform regulations, a Lieutenant Colonel of staff would wear a silver oak leaf as a badge of rank the field officers' cuff decoration of a large chevron outlined in tight loops of tracing braid, with tight loops of braid in the angle of the chevron and a long vertical and two short horizontal loops above the point, and four loops underneath (3).

The cuff decoration for field officers became the specific decoration for Lieutenant Colonels in 1904 (4).

Richards became the Paymaster with rank of Colonel in 1910, and William Dawson became Assistant Paymaster with rank of Lieutenant Colonel (5).

The 1912 regulations added the insignia of the Paymasters' Department, a sword crossed with a quill under an oak leaf and acorn, to the coat collars (6) and shoulder knots (7).

The National Defense Act of August 29, 1916 (8) ended the permanent staff appointments. Promotions in the staff department would be from within the officers on duty in 1916, but any new staff officers would be on temporary duty from the line.

Assistant Paymaster with rank of Major

An Assistant Paymaster with rank of Major was added on March 3, 1899 (1). The position went to George Richards (2).

Richards would have worn the field officers cuff decoration was worn on the cuffs, consisting of a large chevron outlined in tight loops of tracing braid, with tight loops of braid in the angle of the chevron and a long vertical and two short horizontal loops above the point, and four loops underneath, all in black (3).

Under the 1900 uniform regulations, Richards would have worn a gold oak leaf on his shoulder knots and on the collars of the undress and campaign coats. The field officers cuff decoration was worn on the cuffs, consisting of a large chevron outlined in tight loops of tracing braid, with tight loops of braid in the angle of the chevron and a long vertical and two short horizontal loops above the point, and four loops underneath. It was in gold on the dress coat, black on the blue undress coat and overcoat and white on the summer undress coat (4).

Richards moved up to Lieutenant Colonel in 1903 and the Major's slot went to William Dawson (5).

In 1904 the cuff decoration for Majors was changed to just the chevron and the tracing braid with the loops underneath, no top knot (6). The regulations also call for the oak leaf to be worn on the shoulder loops of coats instead of the collar (7).

A second Assistant Paymaster with rank of Major was added by Congress on May 13, 1908 (8), Dawson moved up to Lieutenant Colonel and William Powell (9) and Harold Reisinger (10) took the two open spots.

The 1912 regulations added the insignia of the Paymasters' Department, a sword crossed with a quill under an oak leaf and acorn, to the coat collars (11) and shoulder knots (12).

The National Defense Act of August 29, 1916 (13) ended the permanent staff appointments. Promotions in the staff department would be from within the officers on duty in 1916, but any new staff officers would be on temporary duty from the line.

Assistant Quartermaster with rank of Captain

On March 2, 1847, the marine corps a given a permanent Assistant Quartermaster, who held the rank of Captain (1). Prior to 1847 the position of Assistant Quartermaster was, supposedly, held by an officer taken form the line. The position had been created on June 30, 1834 (2). In reality the Assistant Quartermaster was not taken from the line, but held by a permanent officer, George Lindsey, who had been the Assistant Quartermaster since 1838 (3).

Lindsey's uniform, as prescribed by the 1840 uniform Regulations (4) showed three laced button holes on the cuff and a gold epaulet on each shoulder with an aigullette attached to the right one. When epaulets were not worn, shoulder straps were with two gold bars at each end.

Lindsey was made Quartermaster on July 19, 1855, and was replaced by Daniel Sutherland (5). Sutherland was made Quartermaster on September 28, 1857 and replaced by William Maddox (6).

Under the 1859 uniform regulations (7), Maddox continued to wear the three loops on the cuffs. Epaulets had bullion that was 1/4 inch wide and 2 1/2 inches long with two silver bars on the strap. Shoulder knots were worn when epaulets were not. Those for Captains were made of three cords and had two silver bars at the end. A sleeve knot made of two strips of black cord was worn on the overcoat.

A second Assistant Quartermaster with the rank of Captain was added on July 25, 1861 (8), in the person of James Wiley, who served until he retired on June 20, 1872 (9). Wiley's replacement was Horatio Lowry (10)

In 1875, the corps' five staff officers were given uniforms of a different design from the line officers. The full dress coat was the same as line officers, but with shoulder knots, with an aigullette on the right, instead of epaulets. The knots carried the two silver bars at the end. The line Captain's gold cuff decoration was worn on the cuffs, consisting of a large knot outlined in loops of tracing braid with four loops underneath. Scarlet cloth showed in the spaces between of the knot. The staff officer's undress coat was a modification of the line officers fatigue coat, it is not clear how rank was shown. A black version cuff decoration was on the overcoat (11).

In 1877 staff officers gained a coat that was used for both full dress and undress. The cuff decoration was not worn on this coat. Gold shoulder knots were worn for full dress and black for undress. The silver bars were worn on the gold shoulder knot, but it is not clear if they were worn on the black knot (12).

Maddox retired on January 1, 1880 (13), and was replaced by Woodbull Schenck (14).

Lowry was made Quartermaster on May 4, 1885 (15), and was replaced by Richard Collum (16)

The cuff decoration, in black, was added to the cuffs of the coat on July 18, 1894 (17).

Schenck retired on October 12, 1891 (18) and was replaced with Frank Denny (19).

Denny was made Quartermaster on June 20, 1897 (20) and was replaced with Thomas Prince (21).

Collum retired on June 26, 1897 (22) and was replaced with Charles McCawley (23).

A third Assistant Quartermaster with rank of Captain was added on March 3, 1899 (24). At the same time Prince (25) and McCawley (26) moved up to Major and the three new Assistant Quartermasters with rank of Captain were Cyrus Radford, Robert Faunt Le Roy and William Lemy (27).

Under the 1900 uniform regulations, a Captain of staff would wear two silver bars as a badge of rank and cuff decoration of a large knot outlined in loops of tracing braid with four loops underneath (28).

Faunt Le Roy retired on December 12, 1901 (29) and was replaced with Edwin Jonas (30).

Five more Assistant Quartermasters with rank of Captain were added on March 3, 1903 (31). Radford moved up to Major (32), and the six new officers were Henry Roosevelt, Norman Burton, Hugh Matthews, Rupert Dewey, Frank Schwable and Percy Archer (33).

Three more Assistant Quartermasters with rank of Captain were added on May 13, 1908 (34). Roosevelt moved up to Major, and the next four officers were Frank Halford, Seth Williams, Charles Sanderson and Walter Noa (35).

Lemy moved up to Major in 1909, and was replaced by Warren Banker (36).

Burton moved up to Major in 1911, and was replaced by Bennet Puryear (37).

The 1912 uniform regulations added the insignia of the Quartermasters' Department, a sword crossed with a key under a wheel with stars, to the coat collars (38) and shoulder knots (39).

The 1915 navy register shows Matthews as a Major and adds Captains named Bennet Puryear, Jeter Horton and Russell Davis (40).

The National Defense Act of August 29, 1916 (41) ended the permanent staff appointments. Promotions in the staff department would be from within the officers on duty in 1916, but any new staff officers would be on temporary duty from the line.

Assistant Quartermaster with rank of Lieutenant Colonel

One Assistant Quartermaster with the rank of Lieutenant Colonel was added to the staff on March 3, 1903 (1). The appointment Thomas Prince (2).

Under the 1900 uniform regulations, a Lieutenant Colonel of staff would wear a silver oak leaf as a badge of rank the field officers' cuff decoration of a large chevron outlined in tight loops of tracing braid, with tight loops of braid in the angle of the chevron and a long vertical and two short horizontal loops above the point, and four loops underneath (3).

The cuff decoration for field officers became the specific decoration for Lieutenant Colonels in 1904 (4).

A second Assistant Quartermaster with the rank of Lieutenant Colonel was added to the staff on May 13, 1908 (5), in the person of Charles McCawley (6).

Prince Retired on February 10, 1911 (7), and was replaced with Cyrus Radford (8).

The 1912 regulations added the insignia of the Quartermasters' Department, a sword crossed with a key under a wheel with stars, to the coat collars (9) and shoulder knots (10).

McCawley became Quartermaster in 1913 and was replaced with William Lemy (11).

The National Defense Act of August 29, 1916 (12) ended the permanent staff appointments. Promotions in the staff department would be from within the officers on duty in 1916, but any new staff officers would be on temporary duty from the line.

Assistant Quartermaster with rank of Major

Two Assistant Quartermaster with rank of Major was added on March 3, 1899 (1). The positions went to Thomas Prince and Charles McCawley (2).

They would have worn the field officers cuff decoration was worn on the cuffs, consisting of a large chevron outlined in tight loops of tracing braid, with tight loops of braid in the angle of the chevron and a long vertical and two short horizontal loops above the point, and four loops underneath, all in black (3).

Under the 1900 uniform regulations, they would have worn a gold oak leaf on his shoulder knots and on the collars of the undress and campaign coats. The field officers cuff decoration was worn on the cuffs, consisting of a large chevron outlined in tight loops of tracing braid, with tight loops of braid in the angle of the chevron and a long vertical and two short horizontal loops above the point, and four loops underneath. It was in gold on the dress coat, black on the blue undress coat and overcoat and white on the summer undress coat (4).

Prince moved up to Lieutenant Colonel in 1903 and the Major's slot went to Cyrus Radford (5).

In 1904 the cuff decoration for Majors was changed to just the chevron and the tracing braid with the loops underneath, no top knot (6). The regulations also call for the oak leaf to be worn on the shoulder loops of coats instead of the collar (7).

A second Assistant Quartermaster with rank of Major was added by Congress on May 13, 1908 (8), McCawley moved up to Lieutenant Colonel and Henry Roosevelt (9) and William Lemly took the two open spots.

Radford moved up to Lieutenant Colonel in 1911 and was replaced by Norman Burton (10).

The 1912 regulations added the insignia of the Quartermasters' Department, a sword crossed with a key under a wheel with stars, to the coat collars (11) and shoulder knots (12).

Lemly moved up to Lieutenant Colonel in 1913 and was replaced by Hugh Matthews (13).

The National Defense Act of August 29, 1916 (14) ended the permanent staff appointments. Promotions in the staff department would be from within the officers on duty in 1916, but any new staff officers would be on temporary duty from the line.

Brigadier General

The term Brigadier General comes from the commander of a brigade hence brigadier. It was many years before the corps was large enough to require an officer of that rank.

On January 27, 1837, the Colonel Commandant of the Marine Corps, Archibald Henderson, was made a brevet Brigadier General (1). This was a personal honor for service in Florida, not a regular rank in the Marine Corps (2). Army Brigadier Generals had been wearing a single silver star as a badge of rank since 1783, but it is not known if Henderson wore a star.

The 1859 uniform regulations (3) prescribe a star on the epaulets and shoulder knots Henderson's Successor John Harris, or maybe the didn't. What is usually regarded as the 1859 regulations was published in a catalog of military goods from the retailer Schuyler Hartly and Graham in 1864, along with regulations from the army, navy and revenue marine. However it must be questioned if this is the true text issued in 1859. The rank structure that the regulations prescribe uniforms for, comes from a law of July 25, 1861 (4), that increased the size of the corps for the Civil War. This law added a Colonel, who wore the traditional Colonel's eagle, in addition to Harris who wore the star. It is possible that the regulations published in the catalog were updated to 1864, and not as they stood in 1859. As a result it is possible that Harris did not wear the star until 1861.

The first official use of the rank of Brigadier General by the Marine Corps began on March 2, 1867 (5) when the rank of the Commandant, now Harris' successor Jacob Zeliin (6), was raised to Brigadier General.

The 1859 uniform regulations were still in effect and Zeilin would have worn a silver star on his epaulets and shoulder knots and four loops of lace on the cuffs and a double knot of five black cords on the overcoat cuffs (7).

An appropriations bill passed by Congress on June 6, 1874 (8) stated "That the office of commandant of the Marine Corps having the rank of a brigadier general of the Army shall continue until a vacancy shall occur in the same, and no longer; and when such vacancy shall occur in said office, immediately thereupon all laws and parts of laws creating said office shall become inoperative, and shall, by virtue of this act, from thenceforth be repealed: And provided further, That thereafter the commandant of the Marine Corps shall have the rank and pay of a colonel, shall be appointed by selection by the President from the officers of said corps.". Zeilin would continue as a Brigadier General, but the next Commandant would be a Colonel.

The 1875 uniform regulations specified that Zeilin's uniform would not change (9).

Zeilin retired on November 1, 1876 (10), and the rank of Brigadier General ceased to exist in the Marine Corp.

The rank returned on March 3, 1899 (11), when the rank of the Commandant, now Charles Haywood, was raised.

The 1900 uniform regulations call for Heywood to wear one silver star as a badge of rank and cuff decorations of a large chevron outlined in loops of tracing braid that formed into four loops under the chevron and an elaborate knot above the point (12).

Heywood was made a Major General by Congress on July 1, 1902 (13). The law specified that when the Commandant's position became vacant, it would revert to Brigadier General.

Heywood retired on October 3, 1903 (14) and the new Brigadier General Commandant was George Elliott (15).

The rank distinctions for Elliott in the 1904 uniform regulations (16) are identical to Heywood's distinctions in the 1900 regulations.

The rank of the Commandant was, permanently this time, raised to Major General on May 14, 1908 (17), and once again the rank of Brigadier General ceased to exist in the Marine Corps.

The National Defense Act of August 29, 1916 allowed the Marine Corps Brigadier Generals, and the rank has existed ever since (18).

The 1917 uniform regulations continued the one silver star (19) and prescribed cuff decorations of a strip of lace over a line of oak leaf and acorn embroidery (20).

Use of the cuff decoration was restricted to the mess jacket in 1922 (21) and even that was eliminated in 1952 (22).

The Career Compensation Act of October 12, 1949 (23) put Brigadier Generals into pay grade O-7.

The 2003 uniform regulations describe the insignia as "Brigadier General. One silver-colored star... Additionally, the 5/8-inch insignia is authorized for wear as long as the same size insignia is worn on both collars." (24).

Captain

The title Captain comes from the Latin caput meaning head, this led to the term capitaneus or head man (1). In the middle ages captains commanded companies of soldiers. The company was the basic unit when an army was formed, higher ranks were created when more the one company was fielded together.

By the 18th century companies were a sub division of regiments and the title of Captain was still used by their commander. Even in the early 21st century commanding companies is the job of a Captain.

The law creating the Continental Marines calls for "other officers as usual in other regiments" (2), and the rank of "Captain of Marines" appears on the pay tables of the Continental Navy (3). 36 officers were known to hold the rank of Captain in the Continental Marines, including the Continental Marine's senior officer Captain Samuel Nicholas, who was not made am Major until June 25, 1776 (4).

It is known that Continental Marine officers wore a silver epaulet on the right shoulder (5).

The two laws of 1794 (6) and 1797 (7) that created the federal navy did not include Captains of Marines, but the July 11, 1798 law creating the Marine Corps did, four in all. The appointments were issued on August 3rd to Daniel Carmick, Lemuel Clark, George Memminger and Franklin Wharton. Memminger died on August 31st and was replaced by James McKnight, who was killed in a duel on October 14, 1802. Clark resigned on November 30, 1801, and Wharton became Commandant on March 7, 1804, but the only appointment between 1798 and 1808 was to Anthony Gale on April 24, 1804 (8).

It is not clear how rank was shown before 1804, but at that time Captains were ordered to wear one gold epaulet on the right shoulder and a shoulder strap, meaning a strip of lace, on the left (9).

Carmick and Gale were joined by Robert Rankin on January 16, 1808 and John Hall on December 1, 1808, filling the four slots (10). Rankin resigned on January 1, 1809 and was replaced by Henry Caldwell on January 23rd (11). Three more Captains were appointed that day, Edward Hall, Michael Reynolds and James Thompson (12). They were confirmed by the Senate in March (13) and one of them was to replace Carmick who had been promoted, why the others were appointed is unknown. Edward Hall resigned on August 13, 1809 and was replaced with John Fenwick. Thompson resigned on January 12, 1810 and was not replaced. Fenwick resigned on April 1, 1811 and was replaced by Archibald Henderson. 1812 saw Williams killed in battle in August and the appointment of Richard Smith on March 13th and R.W. Wainwright on September 29th (14).

The Marine Corps was enlarged on April 16, 1814 to include 14 more Captains (15). This was reduced to nine on March 3, 1817 (16).

Chevrons were introduced as a distinction of rank in 1820. Captains were ordered to wear three chevrons of gold lace on both upper sleeves (17).

New uniforms in 1833 eliminated the chevrons. Rank was shown by gold epaulets again, it is not clear if this meant the 1804 system of one on the right and a strap on the left, and cuff decoration of three laced button holes (18).

When shoulder straps were introduced in 1835 (19), those for Captains were "to be embroidered at the ends with gold, (crosswise,) with two oblong squares, three-eighths of an inch long and one-eighth of an inch wide, each." (20), or in other words, they had two gold bars at the ends of the straps. In 1841 epaulets were prescribed for both shoulders with 2 1/2 inch long Bullion (20a).

In 1859 the two bars were changed to silver and placed on the epaulets and the shoulder knots that replaced the shoulder straps (21). Two silver bars have been the badge of rank for Captains ever since. The 1859 over coats had a cuff decoration of a three loop knot made of two black cords.

In 1875 the three laced button holes, and the two black cords, on the cuff were replaced with a cuff decoration of a large knot outlined in loops of tracing braid with four loops underneath (22). This pattern was worn on various cuffs by Captains until 1952 (23).

The Career Compensation Act of October 12, 1949 (24) put Captains into pay grade O-3.

The 2003 uniform regulations describe the insignia for Captains as "Captain. Two smooth silver-colored bars, without bevel, attached at each end by a holding bar. Shoulder insignia; each bar slightly curved, 1-1/8 inches long by 3/8-inch wide, and 3/8-inch apart. Collar insignia; flat, each bar 3/4-inch long by 1/4-inch wide and 1/4-inch apart." (25).

The bars worn by marine Captains are in flat, navy, style with the connector bars at the ends, instead of the beveled style with the connectors inset, worn by army Captains.

Chief Baker

In early 1941 the rank of Chief Cook (Baker) wash changed to Chief Baker (1). Chief Cooks (Baker) had been in grade fourth wearing three chevrons (2).

The title was changed back to Chief Cook (Baker) in 1943 (3).

Chief Cook

The rank of Chief Cook was created in grade four, in 1935 (1).

They wore three chevrons with a crescent underneath (2) until 1937 when the crescent was removed (3).

The title was changed to Chief Cook (Commissary) in 1943 (3).

Chief Cook (baker)

In 1940, bakers were separated from cooks and the, slightly, separate title of Chief Cook (Baker) was born (1).

The rank shared grade four and three chevrons with Chief Cook (2).

The title was changed to Chief Baker in early 1941, and back to Chief Cook (Baker) in 1943 (3).

The 1943 change moved the rank up to grade three staff (4), entitling it to three chevrons and one straight bar (5).

When the enlisted grades were overhauled on December 1, 1946, Chief Cooks (Baker) became Staff Sergeants (6).

Chief Cook (Commissary)

Chief Cooks became Chief Cooks (Commissary) in 1943, and were moved up to the third grade staff (1), with three chevrons and one straight bar (2).

When the enlisted grades were overhauled on December 1, 1946, Chief Cooks (Commissary) became Staff Sergeants (3).

Chief Marine Gunner

The warrant rank of Chief Marine Gunner was created on June 10, 1926 (1).

They wore a Badge of rank consisting of "One gold bar, Broken across the center with a blue-enamel stripe. To have narrow border, diagonally chased of beaded; gold and enamel within the border to be rounded, and the gold diagonally chased bar to lie flat, and have clasp pin or screw or clutch fastener. For Shoulder Straps and garrison caps, the bar was to be 1 1/16 inches long and 5/16 inch wide, blue-enamel stripe being 1/4 inch measuring with long axis of bar; for collar of cotton and flannel shirts, three-fourths of foregoing size." (2). The badge of rank was worn in addition to the bursting bomb of a Marine Gunner, worn on coat collars alongside the eagle globe and anchor.

The rank of Chief Marine Gunner was included in the new rank of Commissioned Warrant Officer on October 21, 1943 (3).

The concept of Marine Gunners, within the current warrant ranks, was revived in 1956, eliminated in 1959, revived again in 1964, eliminated again in 1974 and finally revived again in 1989 (4).

Chief Paymaster Clerk

The warrant rank of Chief Paymaster Clerk was created on June 10, 1926 (1).

They wore a Badge of rank consisting of "One gold bar, Broken across the center with a blue-enamel stripe. To have narrow border, diagonally chased of beaded; gold and enamel within the border to be rounded, and the gold diagonally chased bar to lie flat, and have clasp pin or screw or clutch fastener. For shoulder straps and garrison caps, the bar was to be 1 1/16 inches long and 5/16 inch wide, blue-enamel stripe being 1/4 inch measuring with long axis of bar; for collar of cotton and flannel shirts, three-fourths of foregoing size." (2). The badge of rank was worn in addition to the insignia of the paymaster's department, a sword crossed with a quill under an oak leaf and acorn, worn on coat collars alongside the eagle globe and anchor.

The rank of Chief Paymaster Clerk was included in the new rank of Commissioned Warrant Officer on October 21, 1943 (3).

Chief Quartermaster Clerk

The warrant rank of Chief Quartermaster Clerk was created on June 10, 1926 (1).

They wore a Badge of rank consisting of "One gold bar, Broken across the center with a blue-enamel stripe. To have narrow border, diagonally chased of beaded; gold and enamel within the border to be rounded, and the gold diagonally chased bar to lie flat, and have clasp pin or screw or clutch fastener. For shoulder straps and garrison caps, the bar was to be 1 1/16 inches long and 5/16 inch wide, blue-enamel stripe being 1/4 inch measuring with long axis of bar; for collar of cotton and flannel shirts, three-fourths of foregoing size." (2). The badge of rank was worn in addition to the insignia of the quartermaster's department, a sword crossed with a key under a wheel with stars, worn on coat collars alongside the eagle globe and anchor.

The rank of Chief Quartermaster Clerk was included in the new rank of Commissioned Warrant Officer on October 21, 1943 (3).

Chief Warrant Officer 2

Chief Warrant Officer 2 was created by the "Warrant Officer Act of 1954" (1) in pay grade W-2.

Design of the insignia was coordinated with the Navy, Marine Corps and Coast Guard to create a unified system. The insignia authorized around 1954 was a gold bar with a scarlet square in the center and a scarlet rectangle at each end (2).

The 2003 uniform regulations describe the insignia as "Chief Warrant Officer, CWO-2. One gold-colored bar of the same type as for a second lieutenant, with three scarlet enamel blocks arranged in the same manner as for a CWO-4." (3).

Chief Warrant Officer 3

Chief Warrant Officer 3 was created by the "Warrant Officer Act of 1954" (1) in pay grade W-3.

Design of the insignia was coordinated with the Navy, Marine Corps and Coast Guard to create a unified system. The insignia authorized around 1954 was a silver bar with two scarlet rectangles, showing a square of silver in the middle (2).

The 2003 uniform regulations describe the insignia as "Chief Warrant Officer, CWO-3. One silver-colored bar of the same type as for a CWO-4, with two scarlet enamel blocks superimposed. Shoulder insignia blocks are 3/8-inch wide and 1/4-inch apart. Collar insignia; blocks are 1/4-inch wide and 5/32-inch apart." (3).

Chief Warrant Officer 4

Chief Warrant Officer 4 was created by the "Warrant Officer Act of 1954" (1) in pay grade W-4.

Design of the insignia was coordinated with the Navy, Marine Corps and Coast Guard to create a unified system. The insignia authorized around 1954 was a silver bar with a scarlet square in the center and a scarlet rectangle at each end (2).

The 2003 uniform regulations describe the insignia as "Chief Warrant Officer, CWO-4. One silver-colored bar of the same type as for a first lieutenant, with three scarlet enamel blocks superimposed. Shoulder insignia; center enamel block is 1/4 inch wide, with 1/8 inch wide outer blocks, 1/4 inch from the edges of the center block. Collar insignia; center enamel block is 5/32 inch wide, with 3/32 inch wide outer blocks, 5/32 inch from the edges of the center block." (3).

Chief Warrant Officer 5

The W-5 pay grade was created in 1991 (1), and the marine corps created the rank of Chief Warrant Officer 5 to fill it.

The insignia, authorized on March 16, 1992 (2), was a silver bar with a scarlet stripe down the middle.

The 2003 uniform regulations describe the insignia as "Chief Warrant Officer, CWO-5. One silver-colored bar of the same type as for a first lieutenant, with one scarlet enamel stripe superimposed lengthwise. Shoulder insignia; center enamel stripe is 1/8-inch wide and 1- 1/8 inch long. Collar insignia; center enamel stripe is 1/8-inch wide and 3/4-inch long." (3).

Colonel

During the sixtieth century, the Spanish Army was organized into columns or in Spanish colunelas each made up of multiple companies. The commander was called capo d colunela, head of the column. The French and later the British copied the column idea and eventually developed into regiments with a Colonel in charge (1). Colonels are sometime referred to a "full Colonels" to differentiate them from Lieutenant Colonels.

The Marine Corps was not large enough to require a Colonel until June 30, 1834 (2), when the rank of the Commandant, Archibald Henderson at the time, was raised from Lieutenant Colonel.

The corps six field grade officers were, in 1834, distinguished by four laced button holes on the cuffs and plain gold epaulets on both shoulders with bullion 1/2 inch wide and 3 1/2 inches long (3)(4). It should be noted that Henderson was a Brevet Brigadier General, and it is not known if he wore any indication of that rank.

When shoulder straps were created in 1835, they were to show a gold, spread eagle in the center of the strap (4a).

Henderson died on January 6, 1859 and was replaced the next day by John Harris (5).

What we know as the 1859 uniform regulations (6) gave Harris, as Colonel Commandant, a silver star on his epaulets and shoulder knots, that were made of four cords, and other Colonels a silver eagle. Since Harris was the only Colonel in the corps, this raises some questions. The 1859 regulations were published in a catalog of the company Schuyler Hartly and Graham in 1864, along with uniform regulations for the army, navy and revenue marine. The catalog was republished by Dover Publications of Mineola New York in 1985. It is possible that the regulations in the catalog were updated to the rank structure of 1864, when there was a second Colonel. If this is true, Harris may have worn the eagle until the second Colonel was authorized on July 25, 1861 (7). The regulations, whatever their year of origin, continued the four laced button holes on the cuff and cuff knots of five black cords on the overcoat, in a three loop knot for Colonels and a double knot for the Commandant.

The second Colonel was part of a law that enlarged the corps for the Civil War. His name was William Dulany (8).

Harris died on May 12, 1864 and was replaced by Jacob Zeilin (9). Dulany retired on June 10th, and was replaced by William Suttleworth (10).

The rank of the Commandant, and by consequence the rank of Jacob Zeilin, was raised to Brigadier General on March 2, 1867 (11).

Shuttleworth retired on December 4, 1867, and was replaced by Matthew Kintzing (12).

The 1875 uniform regulations (13), continued the eagle on Kintzing's epaulets and shoulder knots and replaced the four laced button holes with a cuff decoration of a large chevron outlined in tight loops of tracing braid, with tight loops of braid in the angle of the chevron and a loose three loop knot above the point.

A law of June 6, 1874 (14), stated that the rank of the Commandant would drop back to Colonel when the position became vacant. Zeilin retired on November 1, 1876, and the new Colonel Commandant was Charles McCawley (15).

A photograph of McCawley (16) shows him wearing the eagle on his epaulets and the cuff decorations of a field grade officer with two extra, horizontal loops just above the point of the chevron.

Kintsing retired on March 15, 1879, and was replaced by James Jones, who died on April 17, 1880, and was replaced by Thomas Field. Field retired on August 17, 1889, and was replaced by Clement Hebb. McCawley retired on January 29, 1891, and was replaced by Charles Heywood. Hebb retired on July 10, 1892 and was replaced by James Forney (17).

New uniform regulations were issued on July 14th (18). They prescribe cuff decorations for Heywood to be "as now prescribed", and for other field grade officers "The same as for the Colonel Commandant, omitting the first pair of loops over the point of the chevrons.". This would seam to confirm the photograph of McCawley. The eagle was prescribed, on the epaulets, shoulder knots and as a badge of rank on collars, for both Heywood and Forney.

On July 18, 1894, the loose three loop knot on the cuff decoration was changed to be "in the shape of a single three-leaf clover" (19).

On August 10, 1898, President Mckinley promoted Robert Huntington to full Colonel for his service in the battle of Guantanamo Bay (20).

A new law of March 3, 1899 (21) raised the Commandant back to Brigadier General and allowed the Marine Corps a total of five Colonels. Forney and Huntington were joined by Percival Pope, Robert Meade and Charles WIlliams (22). Huntington retired on January 10, 1900 (23) and was replaced by Henry Cochrane (24). Williams died on January 30, 1900 (25), and was replaced by William Muse, who in turn retired on August 14th and was replaced by Francis Harrington (26). Mead retired on December 26, 1903 (27), and was replaced by Allan Kelton (28).

The number of Colonels was raised to six on March 3, 1903 (29), and Mancil Goodrell took the open position (30).

The 1904 uniform regulations called for the Colonel's cuff decoration to be the same as the Commandants, but without the "extreme top loop over the point of the chevrons." (31).

Forney retired on June 3, 1904 (32), and was replaced by Otway Berryman (33). Harriington retired on December 8, 1904 (34) and was replaced by Paul Murphy (35). Pope retired on February 28, 1905 (36) and was replaced by William Biddle (37). Cochrane retired on March 10, 1905 (38) and was replaced by Littleton Waller (39). Berryman retired on March 31, 1905 (40) and was replaced by Randolph Dickins (41). Goodrell retired on January 31, 1906 (42) and was replaced by Thomas Wood (43). Harry White was made a Colonel on June 16, 1916 (44), apparently not replacing anyone.

The number of Colonels was raised to seven on May 13, 1908 (45) and would grow from there.

The 1912 uniform regulations, show the cuff decoration had changed to having the loose knot and two side loops, above the chevron, that had previously been worn by the Commandant (46). The change may have occurred in 1908 when the rank of the Commandant was raised to Major General. A photograph of Commandant George Elliott (47), who left office in 1910, shows him wearing cuff decorations that are close, but not exact, to the deceptions prescribed to the Major General Commandant in the 1912 regulations. The 1912, or 1908, style cuff decoration was worn on various coats until 1952 (48).

The Career Compensation Act of October 12, 1949 placed Colonels in pay grade O-6 (49).

The 2003 uniform regulations describe the insignia for Colonels as "Colonel. A silver-colored spread eagle, made in pairs, right and left, talons of 1 foot grasping an olive branch, the other, a bundle of arrows. Shoulder insignia; slightly curved, with 1-1/2-inch wingspan. Collar insignia; flat, with 31/32-inch wingspan." (50).

Commissioned Warrant Officer

The rank of Commissioned Warrant Officer was created on October 21, 1943 (1) from the ranks of Chief Marine Gunner, Chief Paymaster Clerk and Chief Quartermaster Clerk.

A badge of rank was authorized consisting of a gold bar with a scarlet line across it (2). The navy would adopt a similar bar with a blue line 1/8 inch wide, in 1952 (3) and the marine scarlet line may have also been 1/8 inch wide. It is not clear when the corps introduced the bars. It may have been when the rank was created in 1943, or later, but certainly by 1950.

The Career Compensation Act of October 12, 1949 (4) spread Commissioned Warrant Officers across pay grades W-2, W-3 and W-4.

The rank became Chief Warrant Officer 2, Chief Warrant Officer 3 and Chief Warrant Officer 4, with the Warrant Officer Act of 1954 (5).

Cook First Class

Cooks First Class, or Officer's Cooks First Class, were created on February 26, 1944 in grade two staff (1), and was therefore entitled to three chevrons and two straight bars (2).

When the enlisted grades were overhauled on December 1, 1946, Cooks First Class became Technical Sergeants (3).

Cook Second Class

Cooks Second Class, or Officer's Cooks Second Class, were created on February 26, 1944 in grade three staff (1), and was therefore entitled to three chevrons and one straight bar (2).

When the enlisted grades were overhauled on December 1, 1946, Cooks Second Class became Staff Sergeants (3).

Cook Third Class

Cooks Third Class, or Officer's Cooks Third Class, were created on February 26, 1944 in grade four (1), and was therefore entitled to three chevrons (2).

When the enlisted grades were overhauled on December 1, 1946, Cooks Third Class became Sergeants (3).

Corporal

The term Corporal comes from the Italian for leader of a squadra or square, Capo De'squadra. The title was changed in the 16th century to Caporale meaning leader of a small body of soldiers (1).

Corporals appear on the pay tables of the Continental Navy (2), and both laws organizing the federal navy (3)(4), and finally the July 11, 1798 law (5) that created the marine corps allowed for 48 Corporals, and the rank has existed ever since.

It is not known if enlisted men of the Continental Marines wore any distinction of rank. The Corporals of 1798 were distinguished by a yellow epaulet on the left shoulder. This was replaced by a yellow shoulder knot in 1804 (6).

In 1833, Corporals were given uniforms with two button holes outlined in yellow tape on the cuff (7), and yellow fringe on the shoulder wings (8). Fatigue jackets carried one yellow hash mark above each cuff.

It is possible that the insignia on the fatigue jacket was changed in 1836 to one yellow chevron above each cuff (9), however the uniform regulations on 1839 (10) still prescribe the hash marks. The regulations also replaced the shoulder wings with epaulets that had bullion smaller than a Sergeants'.

The 1859 uniform regulations prescribed two chevrons (11), and marine Corporals have worn two chevrons ever since.

When marine enlisted ranks were organized into pay grades on June 10, 1922 (12), Corporals were placed in grade five (13), which became E-3 with the Career Compensation Act of October 12, 1949 (14). Corporals were moved up to the E-4 grade in 1958 (15).

Crossed rifles were added under the chevrons in 1959 (16).

An Illustration in the 2003 uniform regulations show the insignia for Corporals to be two Chevrons over crossed rifles (17).

Drum Corporal

The rank of Drum Corporal was created in 1934, in grade five (1).

The insignia was two chevrons over crossed drumsticks (2). The drumsticks are not included in the 1937 uniform regulations (3).

Drum Corporals became Field Music Corporals on November 13, 1937 (4).

Drum Major

The 1798 law that created the marine corps allowed the Commandant to appoint a Drum Major if any portion of the corps was to operate on shore (1), and an appointment was made by 1799 (2).

The ranks existence after 1799 is not clear. The 1817 law that set the size of the corps does not include a Drum Major (3), but the next law in 1833 does (4).

The first known uniforms come from the 1833 uniform regulations. The Drum Major wore a red coat with white trim. Four buttons holes, outlined in white tape were worn on the cuffs, and fringe was worn on the shoulder wings (5).

In 1839 the wings were replaced with gold epaulets with small gold fringe, and the white tape may have been changed to yellow (6).

In 1859, the Drum Major was ordered to wear three chevrons over three straight bars with a star between (7).

William Farr was known to be the Drum Major in 1799 (8). Farr was followed by Charles Ashworth in 1804, Venerando Pulizzi in 1816, John Powley in 1817. Pulizzi Returned to the position in 1824 and was replaced by John Cuvillier in 1827. Joseph Cuvillier, maybe a relative, took over in 1829 and was followed by Francis Schenig in 1835. Next up was Rapheal Triay who served form December 10, 1836 to May 22, 1843. Then came Antonio Pons, who served until May 1, 1844. After Pons came Joseph Lucchesi, who served until July 31, 1846, when Pons returned to the position, and held it until July 7, 1848. This time Pons was replaced by the returning Triay, who served until September 9, 1855 (9). John Roach was the Drum Major from 1855 to 1875, when he was replaced by Richard Johnson. Edward Hughes replaced Johnson in 1882, and he was followed by August Gaeckler in 1886, James Barton in 1895, Ruben Bradley in 1897, Reynold Nothbohm in 1908, James Culleton in 1909 and Hurshel Pyror in 1911 (10).

The 1912 uniform regulations show a cuff decoration for the Drum Major's full dress coat, consisting of a 1/2 inch gold braid tracing the point of the cuff and a second line of braid following above the first, then forming a knot of two horizontal loops and two vertical loops, one above the other (11) (12).

When marine enlisted ranks were organized into pay grades on June 10, 1922 (13), Drum Majors (the 1922 uniform regulations refers to "Drum Majors (Post Bands)" (14), so it may have applied to more people than Hurshel Pryor) were placed in grade two staff (15). Grade two staff would have entitled him (or them) to three chevrons and two straight bars. The star may have continued, but by 1936 the chevrons for a drum major contained a baton between the three chevrons and two bars (16). The 1937 uniform regulations removed all center devices, including the baton (17).

Hiram Forea replaced Pryor as Drum Major of the Marine Band in 1927, and he was replaced by Elmer Hansen in 1943 (18).

When the enlisted grades were overhauled on December 1, 1946, Drum Major(s) became Technical Sergeants (19). The position, however continued even though it was not a rank.

Drum Sergeant

The rank of Drum Sergeant was created in 1934, in grade four (1).

The insignia was three chevrons over crossed drumsticks (2). The drumsticks are not included in the 1937 uniform regulations (3).

Drum Sergeants became Field Music Sergeants on November 13, 1937 (4).

Drummer

Drummers existed in the Continental Marines (1)(2), were included in both the 1794 (3) and 1797 (4) law organizing the federal navy and were listed in the 1798 law creating the corps (5).

Drummers probably wore Private's uniforms in the early days. It was traditional that musicians would wear the opposite colors of the soldiers that they served with. The first uniforms for the Continental Marines were green faced with white, so musicians would have worn white faced with green, but there is no evidence that this was done.

In 1833 musicians were ordered to wear the same uniform as privates, but in scarlet (6). Even as late as the 1904 uniform regulations, the full dress for field musicians was a Private's uniform in scarlet (7).

Insignia was finally prescribed in 1908, when crossed drumsticks were added to the upper sleeve (8). The drumsticks were eliminated by the 1937 uniform regulations (9).

In November of 1937, Drummers were combined with Trumpeters to become Field Musics (10).

Drummer First Class

In 1931 Drummers were allowed to be promoted to Private First Class. It is not clear if they wore the one chevron. This became an accrual rank of Drummer First Class in 1934 (1).

Placed in grade six they wore one chevron with the crossed drumsticks underneath (2). The drumsticks are not included in the 1937 uniform regulations (3).

Drummers First Class became Field Musics First Class on November 13, 1937 (4).

Field Baker

In early 1941 the rank of Field Cook (Baker) wash changed to Field Baker (1). Field Cooks (Baker) had been in grade five wearing two chevrons (2).

The title was changed back to Field Cook (Baker) in 1943 (3).

Field Cook

The rank of Field Cook was created in grade five, in 1935 (1).

They wore two chevrons with a crescent underneath (2) until 1937 when the crescent was removed (3).

The title was changed to Field Cook (Commissary) in 1943 (3).

Field Cook (baker)

In 1940, bakers were separated from cooks and the, slightly, separate title of Field Cook (Baker) was born (1).

The rank shared grade five and two chevrons with Field Cook (2).

The title was changed to Field Baker in early 1941, and back to Field Cook (Baker) in 1943 (3).

The 1943 change moved the rank up to grade four (4), entitling it to three chevrons (5).

When the enlisted grades were overhauled on December 1, 1946, Field Cooks (Baker) became Sergeants (6).

Field Cook (Commissary)

Field Cooks became Field Cooks (Commissary) in 1943, and were moved up to the fourth grade (1), with three chevrons (2).

When the enlisted grades were overhauled on December 1, 1946, Field Cooks (Commissary) became Sergeants (3).

Field Music

The ranks of Drummer and Trumpeter were combined in for Field Musics in 1937 (1). They were in grade seven and wore no insignia.

When the enlisted grades were overhauled on December 1, 1946, Field Musics became Privates (2).

Field Music Corporal

The ranks of Drum Corporal and Trumpet Corporal were combined into Field Music Corporal in 1937 (1). They were in grade five and wore two chevrons (2).

When the enlisted grades were overhauled on December 1, 1946, Field Music Corporals became just Corporals (2).

Field Music First Class

The ranks of Drummer First Class and Trumpeter First Class were combined in to Field Music First Class in 1937 (1). They were in grade six and wore one chevron (2).

When the enlisted grades were overhauled on December 1, 1946, Field Music First Class became Privates First Class (2).

Field Music Sergeant

The ranks of Drum Sergeant and Trumpet Sergeant were combined into Field Music Sergeant in 1937 (1). They were in grade four and wore three chevrons (2).

When the enlisted grades were overhauled on December 1, 1946, Field Music Sergeants became just Sergeants (2).

Fifer

Fifers existed in the Continental Marines (1)(2), were included in both the 1794 (3) and 1797 (4) law organizing the federal navy and were listed in the 1798 law creating the corps (5).

Fifers probably wore Private's uniforms in the early days. It was traditional that musicians would wear the opposite colors of the soldiers that they served with. The first uniforms for the Continental Marines were green faced with white, so musicians would have worn white faced with green, but there is no evidence that this was done.

In 1833 musicians were ordered to wear the same uniform as privates, but in scarlet (6). Even as late as the 1904 uniform regulations, the full dress for field musicians was a Private's uniform in scarlet (7).

They stopped playing fifes and started playing trumpets in 1881 (8), but the rank title remained Fifer until 1899 when it became Trumpeter (9).

Fife Major

The 1798 law that created the marine corps allowed the Commandant to appoint a Fife Major if any portion of the corps was to operate on shore (1), and an appointment was made by 1799 (2).

The ranks existence after 1799 is not clear. The 1817 law that set the size of the corps does not include a Fife Major (3), but the next law in 1834 does (4).

The first known uniforms come from the 1833 uniform regulations. The Fife Major wore a red coat with white trim. Four buttons holes, outlined in white tape were worn on the cuffs, and fringe was worn on the shoulder wings (5).

In 1839 the wings were replaced with gold epaulets with small gold fringe, and the white tape may have been changed to yellow (6).

What we know as the 1859 uniform regulations lists a "Chief Musician" instead of a Fife Major (7). A law of July 25, 1861 (8) replaced the rank of Fife Major with "Principal Musician". The 1859 regulations were published in a catalog of the company Schuyler Hartly and Graham in 1864, along with uniform regulations for the army, navy and revenue marine. The catalog was republished by Dover Publications of Mineola New York in 1985. It is possible that the regulations in the catalog were updated to the rank structure of 1864, and "Chief" was used instead of "Principal" in error.

Antoine Duplessis was known to be the Fife Major in 1804 (8). After that the names are not known until 1812 when Venerando Pulizzi was made Fife Major, he served until he became Drum Major in 1816. The next known Fife Major was Antonio Pons who served form 1842 to 1846, and again form 1850 to 1854. The last known Fife Major was Francis Scala, who served either before Pons, after Pons or both (9).

First Lieutenant

It appears that the Continental Marines did not make a distinction between First and Second Lieutenants. The November 10, 1775 law (1) that created the marines just calls for "other officers as usual in other regiments", and the pay table for the Continental Navy from November 28th (2) only a rank of Lieutenant. Likewise, the 1794 (3) and 1797 (4) laws that organized the federal navy, allowed each ship an "Lieutenant of Marines". Finally the July 11, 1798 law (5) that crated the Marine Corps called for 16 First Lieutenants.

It should be noted that there are some appointments of First Lieutenant or Second Lieutenant the Continental Marines (5a). It is possible that this referred to seniority onboard ship.

Lieutenants of Marines were included in the navy's 1797 uniform regulations (6). They were to wear: "COAT. Long, blue, with long lappels of red; standing collar and lining red. The lappels to have nine buttons, and one to the standing collar. Three buttons to the pocket flaps, and three to a slash sleeve, with a red cuff. One gold epaulet on the right shoulder, for the senior lieutenant, where there are two lieutenants for the same ship, and one on the left shoulder for the second officer. Where there is only one lieutenant, he is also to wear the epaulet on the right shoulder. Trimmings plain. VEST AND BREECHES. The former, red with skirts and pocket flaps, but to have no buttons to the pockets.-- The latter blue-- Buttons for the suit, the same as the captains and lieutenants.".

It is not clear how long 1797 uniforms were worn. The first Marine Corps uniform regulations were issued in 1804 and they called for First Lieutenants to be distinguished by a gold epaulet on the right shoulder (7).

In 1821 First Lieutenants were ordered to wear two gold chevrons on both upper sleeves (8). This was changed in 1821 to one chevron for all First Lieutenants except for First Lieutenants of staff who continued to wear two. In 1821 "First Lieutenants of Staff" referred only to the Paymaster Robert Desha, the Quartermaster and the Adjutant and Inspector were Captains (9). In 1822 The extra chevron would have been worn by the new Paymaster, Joseph Kuhn and the new Adjutant and Inspector, Parke Howle (10), a new Quartermaster, Elijah Weed, came along in 1823 (11), and Kuhn moved up to Captain by 1824 (12).

New uniforms in 1833 showed rank by two laced button holes on the cuff and a gold epaulet (13). It is not clear if the epaulet was worn on the right as in 1804.

Shoulder straps were introduced in 1835 to show rank when epaulets were not worn. Those for a First Lieutenant had a 1/4 inch border and a gold "oblong square" at each end (14).

In 1841 epaulets were prescribed for both shoulders with small Bullion (14a).

In 1859 the gold "oblong square" became a silver bar and was placed on the epaulets and the shoulder knots that replaced the shoulder straps (15). One silver bar has been the badge of rank for First Lieutenants ever since. The 1859 overcoats had a cuff decoration of a three loop knot made of one black cord.

In 1875 the two laced button holes, and the one black cord, on the cuff were replaced with a cuff decoration of a large knot with four loops underneath (16). This pattern was worn on various cuffs by First Lieutenants until 1952 (17).

The Career Compensation Act of October 12, 1949 (18) put First Lieutenants into pay grade O-2.

The 2003 uniform regulations describe the insignia for First Lieutenants as "First Lieutenant. One silver-colored bar of the same type as for a captain" (19).

The bars worn by marine First Lieutenants are in flat, navy style, instead of the beveled style with the connectors inset, worn by army First Lieutenants.

First Sergeant

A law of March 2, 1833 (1) that increased the pay of the army and marine corps stated "the orderly sergeants of posts, and first sergeants of guards at sea, sixteen dollars each". This is the first mention of First Sergeants in law in the army or the marine corps, however the army may have been using them for decades. It is possible that the corps used First Sergeants for the senior NCO on a ship, but the is no evidence.

As of 1833 Orderly Sergeants, and therefore probably First Sergeants, wore the uniform of a Sergeant with the addition of a red sash (2). It is not clear if this applied to the two yellow hash marks that Sergeants wore on the cuff of the fatigue jacket.

In 1859 the insignia was changed to three chevrons with a diamond or lozenge in the angle (3).

In 1922 First Sergeants were placed in grade two (4), entitling them to three chevrons and two arcs with the lozenge between (5). The lozenge was removed in 1937 (6).

On February 10, 1943, First Sergeants were moved up the grade one (7), giving them third arc (8). By 1945 the lozenge had been restored (9).

When the enlisted ranks were reorganized on December 1, 1946, the rank of First Sergeant was abolished all First Sergeants became Master Sergeants (10).

The rank returned in 1954, in the E-7 pay grade (11). The same three chevrons and three arcs with a lozenge in-between was prescribed as the insignia (12).

First Sergeants were moved up the E-8 pay grade in 1958 (13).

An Illustration in the 2003 uniform regulations show the insignia for First Sergeants continues to be three Chevrons and three arcs with a lozenge in-between (14). Unlike army First Sergeants, the "lozenge" is more of a diamond with a solid center.

First Sergeant (Aviation)

The rank of First Sergeant (Aviation) existed form April of 1945 (1) to December of 1946, when it was included in Master Sergeant (2).

The insignia was three chevron and three arcs with a lozenge between (3).

General

The History of American Ranks and Rank Insignia

The term "general" comes from the Latin Generalis meaning the whole of something. A medieval Captain General would be officer in charge of a whole army. The "Captain" part was dropped by the english army by the 18th century and the rank became just General, sometimes called "full" general (1).

The rank of the Commandant of the Marine Corps, Alexander Vandegrift, was raised to full General on March 21, 1945 (2). Like full Generals in the army, Vandergrift wore four silver stars as a badge of rank (3).

The Commandant was the only full General position in the corps, but Lieutenant General Roy Geiger was posthumously promoted in 1947 (4), and 17 Lieutenant Generals were allowed to retire as full Generals from 1944 to 1959 (5).

The Career Compensation Act of October 12, 1949 (6) placed the rank of General in pay grade O-8 which it shared with Lieutenant General and Major General. This lasted until May 20, 1958 when a new law (7) created pay grade O-10 for full Generals.

The Assistant Commandant of the Marine Corps was made a full General on May 2, 1969 (8).

Within the corps structure, the Commandant and the Assistant Commandant are the only full Generals. Other Generals can be appointed to joint commands, such as a theater commander, that require an O-10 officer. The best example of this is General Peter Pace who was never Commandant of the Marine Corps, but made a full General on September 8, 2000 when he became Commander-in-Chief, United States Southern Command. He then moved up to be Vice Chairman of the Joint Chiefs of Staff on September 30, 2001, and became Chairman of the Joint Chiefs of Staff, the highest military position in the United States, on September 30, 2005. Pace retired on October 1, 2007 (9).

The 2003 uniform regulations describe the insignia of a full General as "General. Four silver-colored, five-pointed, pyramid-shaped stars. Shoulder stars are 1 inch in diameter and are either fastened together on a metal holding bar or placed individually with one point of each star in the same line; distance between the centers of adjacent stars will be 3/4 inch. Collar stars are 9/16 inch in diameter and will be fastened together on a metal holding bar in a straight line with one ray of each star pointing upward and at right angles to the holding bar." (10).

Gunnery Sergeant

Gunnery Sergeants, known as "gunnys", are the backbone of marine noncommissioned officers.

The rank was created on May 4, 1898 (1) as part of a temporary increase in the size of the corps for the Spanish-American War. It was made a permanent rank of March 3, 1899 (2).

Until 1904 the insignia was three chevrons and three straight bars with a rifle crossed with a naval gun with an eagle globe and anchor superimposed, in between. In 1904 it was changed to three chevrons with crossed rifles and a bursting bomb in the angle (3).

In 1922 Gunnery Sergeants were placed in grade two (4), entitling them to three chevrons and two arcs with the crossed rifles and bomb in between. Chevron styles from that era are not entirely clear but this was the insignia by 1929 (5). The center device was removed in 1937 (6).

When the enlisted ranks were reorganized on December 1, 1946, the rank of Gunnery Sergeant was abolished all Gunnery Sergeants became Technical Sergeants (7).

The rank returned, replacing Technical Sergeant, in 1958, in the E-7 pay grade (8), the were given three chevrons and two arcs with crossed rifles (9).

An Illustration in the 2003 uniform regulations show the insignia for Gunnery Sergeants continues to be three Chevrons and two arcs with crossed rifles in-between (10).

Lance Corporal

The original version of Lance Corporal was not a rank, but a temporary position given to Privates to do the duties of a Corporal. The idea goes at least as far back as the 1830s, and perhaps further (1).

Insignia was not prescribed until the 1912 uniform regulations. One chevron was to be worn on the right sleeve. Unlike the large dress uniform chevrons worn by other ranks, the dress chevron for Lance Corporals was only 3 1/2 inches wide (2).

The creation of the rank of Private First Class in 1917 limited the need for Lance Corporals. It is not clear when the idea ended. Insignia for Lance Corporals was prescribed by the 1929 uniform regulation, although it doesn't say what it looked like, but it was only worn on the right sleeve while the insignia for Privates First Class were worn on both sleeves (3). This would seam to indicate that both ranks shared the one chevron.

An actual rank of Lance Corporal was created in 1958, in the E-3 pay grade. The insignia was one chevron over crossed rifles (4).

An Illustration in the 2003 uniform regulations show the insignia for Lance Corporal s continues to be one Chevron with crossed rifles underneath (10).

Leader of the Band/ Principal Musician/ Chief Musician

The law that created the marine corps in 1798 (1) allowed for 32 “drums and fifes”. Most of these were assigned to ships, but some remained in Washington and became the Marine Band, with the Drum Major and Fife Major in charge. It wasn’t until the corps was expanded for the Civil War, on July 25, 1861 (2), that separate band musicians were allowed over an above the corps field musicians. The same law does not include the rank of Fife Major. Instead the title of “Principal Musician” is used. The 1859 uniform regulations, that were current at the time, refer to a “Chief Musician”, however they were published in a catalog of the company Schuyler Hartly and Graham in 1864, along with uniform regulations for the army, navy and revenue marine. The catalog was republished by Dover Publications of Mineola New York in 1985. It is possible that the regulations in the catalog were updated to the rank structure of 1864, and “Chief” was used instead of “Principal” in error, and it is that copy of the regulations that has survived. There is no other mention of the position in law until May 4, 1878 (3), when the appropriations bills for the pay of the corps began listing each rank, and its authorized strength, individually. The law called for one “Leader of the Band” and does not mention Principal or Chief Musicians.

Whatever his title, Francis Scala was the head of the band in 1861. He had been Fife Major since 1855, and continued in the position (4).

The 1859, or possibly 1864, uniform regulations call for Scala to wear the uniform of the Sergeant Major with the dress coat being scarlet piped with white instead of blue piped with scarlet, and no chevrons (5).

Scala was discharged on December 13, 1871 and replaced the next day by Henry Fries, who served until discharged on August 27, 1873. Next up was Louis Schendier, who became Leader of the Band on September 2, 1873, and served until October 1, 1880, when John Philip Sousa took over. Sousa served until July 30, 1892 when he was persuaded to form his own band. His replacement was Francesco Fanciulli who served until October 31, 1897. William H. Santlemann was next, taking office on March 3, 1898 (6).

There little direct source material on the uniforms of the band from this era. It is likely that they continued to wear a scarlet version of the Sergeant Major’s dress uniform. Under the 1892 uniform regulations the leader wore a scarlet coat with blue cuffs and a gold cuff decoration, along with epaulets similar to those for a Second Lieutenant (7). Pictures of Sousa show the cuff decoration was the two horizontal loops and two vertical loops worn by the Drum Major (8).

On March 3, 1899 the Leader of the Band was given "the pay and allowances of a first lieutenant" (9). This was reflected in the 1900 Uniform Regulations that gave the leader a scarlet full dress coat with a simple pointed cuff outlined in gold lace. Other coats carried the cuff decoration of a First Lieutenant. A silver lyre was worn as a badge of rank in the same manner as the First Lieutenant's bar (10). The 1904 regulations added the First Lieutenant's cuff decoration to the scarlet coat (11).

In 1916 the rank of the leader was raised to Captain (12), and the 1917 uniform regulations allowed Santlemann the uniform of a Captain with the lyre replacing the bars (13).

Santlemann gave up his post on May 1, 1927, and was replaced by Taylor Branson.

On June 7, 1935 (14), Congress made the Leader of the Band a full fledged Captain. The law referred to the "present leader", so it only applied to Branson.

The 1937 uniform regulations state that if the leader was "in a commissioned status", and Branson was due to the 1935 law, he could wear the bars of a Captain instead of the lyre (15).

Branson served until April 1, 1940. Two days later Santlemann's son William F. Santlemann became leader of the band (16). No law could be found that gave him "commissioned status", but there is a picture of him wearing bars (17). Santlemann the younger was promoted to Major in 1947 and Lieutenant Colonel in 1951, he retired on April 30, 1955 (18).

Despite Santlemann's rank, a law of October 12, 1949 stated "The band of the United States Marine Corps shall consist of one leader, who shall be paid the basic pay, the basic allowances, and such other allowances as are authorized by the Career Compensation Act of 1949 to be paid to commissioned officers in pay grade O-3" (19). O-3 being the pay grade of a Captain.

Santlemann's replacement, on May 1, 1955, was Albert Schoepper (20). It is not clear what rank he was given, but he was allowed to retire as a full Colonel.

The concept of Leader of the Band being a rank of the Marine Corps had ebbed away with the leader holding a regular rank. The official end came on July 24, 1956 (21), when a new law replaced the Leader with a Director, with a rank no higher than Lieutenant Colonel.

Lieutenant

The term lieutenant comes from the French for "placeholder" (1). It can be thought of a someone who hold a place or is a tenant instead of or in lieu of. A tenant in lieu of, is a lieutenant.

It appears the that Lieutenant or "Lieutenant of Marines" was the junior officers' rank in the Continental Marines. The law of November 10,1775 that created the marines simply says "other officers as usual in other regiments" (2). For an infantry regiment this would have meant junior officer ranks of Lieutenant and Ensign, but the pay table issued 18 days later lists only Lieutenants (3). When the first law organizing the federal navy was passed in 1794 (4), it gave each ship a "Lieutenant of Marines", and this was repeated in 1797 (5). The law that created the Marine Corps in 1798 (6), called for the ranks of First Lieutenant and Second Lieutenant.

Continental Marine officers wore a silver epaulet on the right shoulder (7).

The navy's 1797 uniform regulations stated that a Lieutenant of Marines would wear "COAT. Long, blue, with long lappels of red; standing collar and lining red. The lappels to have nine buttons, and one to the standing collar. Three buttons to the pocket flaps, and three to a slash sleeve, with a red cuff. One gold epaulet on the right shoulder, for the senior lieutenant, where there are two lieutenants for the same ship, and one on the left shoulder for the second officer. Where there is only one lieutenant, he is also to wear the epaulet on the right shoulder. Trimmings plain. VEST AND BREECHES. The former, red with skirts and pocket flaps, but to have no buttons to the pockets.-- The latter blue-- Buttons for the suit, the same as the captains and lieutenants." (8).

Lieutenant Colonel

Like Captains, sixteenth century Colonels often left there columns or regiments to attend to business at royal courts (0). While they were gone a lieutenant was needed to take their place, and Lieutenant Colonels were born.

The rank of the Commandant, William Burrows, was raised to Lieutenant Colonel on April 22, 1800 (1).

Officer's rank distinctions before 1804 are unknown. At that time a gold epaulet was worn on each shoulder (2). It is possible that Burrows wore two epaulets before 1804, as it was the insignia of field grade officers in the army.

Burrows resigned on March 6, 1804 and was replaced by Franklin Wharton the next day (3). Wharton died on September 1, 1818 and was replaced by Anthony Gale on March 3, 1819.

The delay was caused by infighting among the officer's in line for the position, namely Gale, Samuel Miller and Archibald Henderson. An old charge of misuse of pubic funds was brought up to keep Gale from becoming Commandant, but no proof was found and the promotion went ahead. This left Gale with enemies among his immediate subordinates. On top of this the Secretary of the Navy, Smith Thompson, began to overrule Gale on personnel issues. This lead Gale to demand to know where is authority began and ended. It all blew up on August 29, 1820 when Gale was arrested and charged with public drunkenness, conduct unbecoming an officer and signing a false certificate involving the use of an enlisted man as a personal servant. Gale's court marshal contains several irregularities. The most obvious being the dates of the drunkenness and the conduct unbecoming (involving prostitution) came after he was arrested for them. Another was that Samuel Miller was appointed to prosecute. Joseph Desha, the corps' Paymaster and son of the Congressman who had charged Gale with misuse of funds was a key witness in the case, and was also an extra member of the court, in civilian terms he was an alternate juror. Even Desh thought this was inappropriate but was overruled. In the end, Gale was convicted and dismissed from the corps on October 18, 1820 (4). Archibald Henderson was named as his replacement (5).

The new uniforms of 1833 continued the epaulets and added four laced button holes on the cuff (5a).

The rank of the Commandant was raised to full Colonel on June 30, 1834 (6), and Henderson moved up. The same law allowed to corps one Lieutenant Colonel, and R.D. Wainwright was appointed to fill the position (7).

In 1835 shoulder straps were added for wear when epaulets were not (8). Those for the Lieutenant Colonel showed a gold "flower" at each end (9).

Wainwright died on October 5, 1841 (10) and was replaced with Samuel Miller, yes that Samuel Miller (11). Miller died on December 9, 1855 and was replaced with John Harris (12). Harris was made Colonel Commandant on January 7, 1859 (13), and the Lieutenant Colonel's slot fell to James Edelin (14).

The 1859 uniform regulations gave Edelin a silver oak leaf as a badge of rank on his epaulets and shoulder knots. The four laced button holes were continued and the overcoat cuff gained a three loop knot of four black cords (15).

Eldein retired on November 16, 1861 (16). A law of July 25th had expanded the corps' Lieutenant Colonels to two (17). One officer, Ward Maston, was appointed to fill the new slot and another, John Reyonds, to replace Eldein (18). Marston retired on June 1, 1864 (19) and Reynolds died on November 2, 1865 (20). The two replacements were Matthew Kintsing (21) and James Jones (22). Kintzing was promoted on December 5, 1867 and was replaced by Charles G. McCawley (23).

The 1875 uniform regulations (24), continued the silver oak leafs on the epaulets and shoulder knots and replaced the four laced button holes with a cuff decoration of a large chevron outlined in loops of tracing braid, with loops of braid in the angle of the chevron and a loose three loop knot above the point. The oak leaf has continued to be the badge of rank for a Lieutenant Colonel.

McCawley was promoted on November 1, 1876 and was replaced by Thomas Field (25). Jones was promoted on March 16, 1879 and replaced by John Broome (26). Field was promoted on April 18, 1880 and was replaced by Clement Hebb (27). Broome retired on March 8, 1888 and was replaced by Charles Heywood (28). Hebb was promoted on August 18, 1889 and was replaced by George Collier (29), who retired on October 23, 1889 and was replaced by George Houston (30). Heywood was promoted on January 30, 1890 and replaced by James Forney (31). Houston retired on February 1, 1891 and was replaced by McLane Tillton (32). Forney was promoted on July 11, 1892 and was replaced by John Higbee (33).

In 1894 the knot above the cuff decoration was changed to “shape of a single three-leaf clover” (34).

McLane retired on February 1, 1897 and was replaced by Robert Huntington (35). Higbee retired on June 1, 1898 and was replaced by Percival Pope (36). Huntington was promoted on August 10, 1898 and was replaced by Robert Meade (37).

On March 3, 1899 the corps was expanded (38) to five Lieutenant Colonels. Both Pope and Mead were promoted to full Colonel and the five Lieutenant Colonels listed in the 1900 navy register (39) were Henry Cochrane, William Muse, Francis Harrington, Mancil Goodrell and George Elliott.

The cuff decoration with the clover leaf had been worn by all field grade officers. The 1904 regulations made that design particular to Lieutenant Colonels (40).

The Career Compensation Act of October 12, 1949 placed Lieutenant Colonels in pay grade O-5 (41).

The 2003 uniform regulations describe the insignia for Lieutenant Colonels as “Lieutenant Colonel. A seven-pointed, silver-colored oak leaf, raised and veined. Shoulder insignia; slightly curved, 1 inch from stem tip to center leaf tip. Collar insignia; flat, 23/32 inch from stem tip to center leaf tip.” (42).

Lieutenant General

A law of January 20, 1942 stated “That hereafter the office of "Major General Commandant of the Marine Corps" shall be known as "Commandant of the Marine Corps". The officer occupying that office shall be known by that title and shall, while so serving, have corresponding rank and shall receive the same pay and allowances as are now or may hereafter be prescribed by or in pursuance of law for Lieutenant General in the Army” (1). Previously the rank of the Commandant (all the way back to when it was Major) had been part of the title, now he was simply the Commandant and the rank was separate.

Thomas Holcomb, who had been Major General Commandant since 1936 was duly promoted (2) and was given a badge of rank of three stars (3).

The commander of the First Marine Amphibious Corps, Alexander Vandegrift, was made the first Lieutenant General who was not the Commandant on July 28, 1943 (4)(5).

The Career Compensation Act of October 12, 1949 (6) placed the rank of Lieutenant General in pay grade O-8 which it shared with Full General and Major General. This lasted until May 20, 1958 when a new law (7) created pay grade O-9 for Lieutenant Generals.

The 2003 uniform regulations describe the insignia for Lieutenant Generals as "Lieutenant General. Three silver-colored stars, of the same type and arranged in the same manner as for a general, except the distance between centers of adjacent shoulder stars will be 1 inch."(8).

Major

In the seventieth century English army of Oliver Cromwell each regiment had a sergeant who was third in command and was in charge of administrative matters. He was known as a great sergeant or sergeant major (0). Despite being called sergeant, it was a higher rank than Captain or Lieutenant. It is assumed that this is the reason the "sergeant" part dropped away and the title became just "major" (0a).

On June 25, 1776, Captain Samuel Nicholas, the founder of the Continental Marines, was promoted to Major (1). He was the only Continental Marine with a rank higher that Captain, and is considered the first Commandant of the Marine Corps, even though the term was never used in his time. Nicholas served as a Major until the end of the war.

The navy's 1775 uniform regulations prescribed a silver epaulet on the right shoulder for marine officers (2). It is possible that Nicholas wore two epaulets, as was the custom for army majors, But there is no evidence that he did.

When the United States Marine Corps was created on July 11, 1798 (3), it was allowed one Major as the Commandant. The job went to William Burrows (4).

Burrows remained Major Commandant until April 22, 1800, when the rank of the Commandant was raised to Lieutenant Colonel. The law specifically stated that this abolished the rank of Major (5).

It returned on March 3, 1809 (6). President Jefferson had decided that the marine garrison in New Orleans was to large to be commanded by a Captain (7). The new Major was Daniel Carmick (8).

The 1804 uniform regulations had prescribed two gold epaulets for the Lieutenant Colonel Commandant (9). It is possible that they were worn by Burrows, when he was a Major and Carmick as well, as this was the case with Lieutenant Colonels and Majors of the army.

A law of April 16, 1814 (10) that expanded the corps for the War of 1812 added a second Major. His name was John Hall (11).

Carmick was still in command in New Orleans when the British attacked in December of 1814, and was wounded in the battle (12).

When the war was over, Congress set the size of the corps for peacetime. The law of March 3, 1817 (13) did not include the rank of Major. Carmick had died from his wounds on November 16, 1816 (14), and Hall was Discharged on April 18, 1817 (15).

There was now no permanent rank of Major, but the 1814 law had allowed brevets to be given as awards for "gallant actions or meritorious conduct". As a result, many marine Captains could call themselves "Brevet Major".

Seventeen years would pass until June 30, 1834 (16), when the corps was expanded again to include four Majors. There names were William Freeman, John Gamble, Samuel Watson and Samuel Miller (17).

When shoulder straps were introduced in 1835, Majors wore a silver oak leaf at each end (18).

Gamble died on September 11, 1836 and was replaced by Charles Broom (19). Broom died on November 14, 1840 and was replaced by Levi Twiggs (20). Miller was promoted on October 6, 1841 and replaced by John Harris (21). Freeman died on March 11, 1843 and was apparently not replaced until March 12, 1845 by Thomas Linton (22). Twigs was killed in action on September 13, 1847 and replaced by James Edelin (23). Watson died on November

17, 1847 and was replaced by William Dulany (24). Linton died on February 17, 1853 and was replaced by Thomas English (25). Harris was promoted on December 9, 1855 and was replaced by Ward Marston (26). Edelin was promoted on January 7, 1859 and replaced by Benjamin Macomber (27).

The 1859 uniform regulations (28) prescribed the cuffs with four laced button holes of a field officer, along with epaulets with 1/2 inch wide bullion and shoulder knots of four cords, but with no badge of rank on either. The cuffs of the overcoat carried a three loop knot made of three cords.

Macomber died on May 29, 1861(29) and was replaced by John Reynolds (30). Marston, Dulany and Reynolds were promoted on July 26, 1861 and English retired on November 26th. This left all four slots open, the new Majors were Jacob Zelin, Addison Garland, Joshia Watson and Issac Doughty (31). They would all serve until 1864. Watson died on February 5th (32), Doughty retired on June 6th (33), Zelin became Commandant on June 10th (34) and Garland died on June 20th (35). The next four Majors appointed were Charles McCawley and Thomas Field on June 10th, George Graham on June 21st and John Broome on December 8th (36). McCawley was promoted on December 5, 1867 and replaced by David Cohen (37), who retired on October 12, 1869 and was replaced by James Lewis (38).

In 1875, new uniform regulations (39) replaced the four laced button holes on the cuff and the knot on the overcoat cuff with a cuff decoration of a large chevron outlined in loops of tracing braid, with loops of braid in the angle of the chevron and a loose three loop knot above the point. A gold oak leaf was added to the epaulets and shoulder straps (40), and a has been the badge of rank for marine Majors ever since.

1876 saw Graham's retirement on January 1st (41), Lewis's resignation on January 11th (42) and Field's promotion on November 1st (43). The new Majors for 1876 were Clement Hebb on January 22nd, and Philip Fendall and Charles Heywood on November 1st (44). Fendall retired on May 15, 1878 (45) and was replaced by Lucien Dawson. Broome was promoted on March 16, 1879 and replaced by George Butler (46). Hebb was promoted on April 18, 1880 and replaced by George Collier (47). Dawson resigned on December 20, 1880 and was replaced by George Houston (48). Buyler died on February 23, 1884 and was replaced by James Forney (49). Heywood was promoted on March 9, 1888 and replaced by Tilton McLane (50). Collier was promoted on August 18, 1889 and replaced by John Higbee (51). Houston was promoted on October 24, 1889 and replaced by Robert Huntington (52). Forney was promoted on January 30, 1891 and replaced by Henry Bartlett (53). McLane was promoted on February 28, 1891 and replaced by Percival Pope(54). Higbee was promoted on July 11, 1892 and replaced by William Brown (55), who retired on September 5th and was replaced by Robert Meade (56).

In 1894 the knot above the cuff decoration was changed to "shape of a single three-leaf clover" (57).

Huntington was promoted on February 2, 1897 and was replaced by Charles Williams (58). Bartlett retired on February 1, 1898 and was replaced by Henry Cochrane (59).

A law of March 3, 1898 (60) increased the corps Majors to ten.

The cuff decoration with the clover leaf had been worn by all field grade officers. The 1904 regulations made a design particular to Majors that was the same without a knot above the chevron (61).

The Career Compensation Act of October 12, 1949 placed Lieutenant Colonels in pay grade O-4 (62).

The 2003 uniform regulations describe the insignia for a Major as "Major. A gold-colored oak leaf of the same type as for a lieutenant colonel." (63).

Major General

While seventieth century English regiments had a Sergeant Major as third ranking officer handling administrative duties, the entire army had a Sergeant Major General (0). The "sergeant" part was dropped over time and the rank became Major General ranking just below Lieutenant General. This is why a Lieutenant General outranks a Major General but a Major outranks a Lieutenant.

On July 1, 1902, part of an appropriations bill stated "That from and after the date of the approval of this Act, the commandant of the Marine Corps shall have the rank, pay, and allowances of a major-general in the Army, and when a vacancy shall occur in the office of commandant of the corps, on the expiration of the service of the present incumbent, by retirement or otherwise, the commandant of the Marine Corps shall thereafter have the rank, pay, and allowances of a brigadier-general." (1). This raised the rank of the Commandant Charles Heywood to Major General, but made it clear that his Successor would be a Brigadier General.

A photograph of Heywood (2) shows him wearing two stars on his epaulets and the cuff decoration of a large chevron outlined in loops of tracing braid that formed into four loops under the chevron and an elaborate knot above the point, that had been prescribed for the Brigadier General Commandant by the 1900 uniform regulations (3).

Heywood retired on October 3, 1903 (4), and the rank of the new Commandant George Elliott reverted to Brigadier General.

The rank of the Commandant, and therefore George Elliott, was permanently raised to Major General on May 14, 1908 (4).

A photograph of Elliott (5) shows him wearing the cuff decoration of two strips of gold lace with a line of oak leaf and acorn embroidery between them. It is possible that a cuff flap is also worn, but it is not clear. The picture does not show Elliott's epaulets, but it is safe to assume he wore the two silver stars as a badge of rank.

Elliott retired on November 10, 1910 (6) and was replaced by William Biddle on February 3, 1911 (7).

The 1912 uniform regulations prescribed cuff decorations on the full dress coat of a strip of gold lace over a line of oak leaf and acorn embroidery with a cuff flap with three buttons that was outlined in gold lace and covered in oak leaf and acorn embroidery (8). On his mess jacket cuffs, Biddle was to wear a line of oak leaf and acorn embroidery crossed with another line (9). The two silver stars continued to be worn as a badge of rank (10), and on the epaulets (11) and shoulder knots (12).

Biddle retired on February 3, 1911 and was replaced by George Barnett (13).

The 1917 uniform regulations replaced the crossed embroidery on the mess jacket with a smaller version of the decoration on the full dress jacket (14).

On July 1, 1918, Congress passed a law that stated "The rank and title of Major General is hereby created in the Marine Corps, and the President is authorized to nominate, and, by and with the advice and consent of the Senate, to appoint one Major General, who Shall at all times be junior in rank to the Major General Commandant, and also one temporary Major General in the Marine Corps, who shall at all times be junior to the permanent Major General." (15). The permanent general was John Lajeune, and the temporary general was Littleton Waller (16).

Waller retired on March 27, 1920 (17) and LaJeune replaced Barnett as Commandant on July 1st (18). Barnett reverted to Brigadier General. A new Major General was appointed to the temporary position on March 28th. His name was Wendell Neville (19). Barnett was given the permanent Major General's slot on March 5, 1921 (20), and retired on December 9, 1923 (21). The 1924 navy register shows two Major Generals, Neville and Joseph Pendelton. Neither appears to be temporary and both commissions are dated December 10, 1923 (22). Pendelton retired on June 2, 1924 (23), and was replaced by Eli Cole (24). Cole died on July 4, 1929 and Lajeune retired on November 12th (24) and Neville became Commandant. The two new Major Generals were Smedley Butler and Logan Feland (25). Neville died on July 8, 1930 (26) and the Assistant Commandant, Brigadier General Benjamin Fuller was promoted to Major General Commandant, and Butler retired in protest on October 1, 1931 (28). Butler's slot as a Major General was given to John Myers (29). Feland retired on September 1, 1933 (30) and was replaced by John Russell (31). Fuller retired on March 1, 1934 and was replaced as Commandant by Russell. Myers retired on February 1, 1935 (32). The two new Major Generals were James Breckinridge and Charles Lyman (33). A fourth Major General, Louis Little, was appointed on July 27, 1935 (34). Russell retired on December 1, 1936 (35) and Thomas Holcomb became Commandant. Lyman retired on October 1, 1939 (36) and was replaced by William Upshur. Clayton Vogel was made a Major General on March 1, 1941 . Breckinridge retired on October 1, 1941 and was replaced by Holland Smith (37). This brings us to World War II and after when there were numerous Major Generals, all wearing two silver stars.

The Career Compensation Act of October 12, 1949 (38) placed the rank of Major General in pay grade O-8 which it shared with Full General and Lieutenant General. This lasted until May 20, 1958 when a new law (39) gave Major Generals the grade all to themselves.

The 2003 uniform regulations describe the insignia for a Major General as "Major General. Two silver-colored stars of the same type and arranged in the same manner as for a lieutenant general.) (40).

Marine Gunner

The warrant rank of Marine Gunner was created on August 29, 1916 (1), and was to be equal to warrant officers in the navy.

The 1917 uniform regulations require warrant officers to wear the undress and field uniforms of a Second Lieutenant. Behind the eagle globe and anchor on the collar, Marine Gunners wore a bursting bomb in silver on the white and blue undress coats and bronze on the green and khaki field coats, shoulder loops of the overcoat and shirt collars (2). Warrant officers did not wear the full dress and mess coats that require the cuff decoration, but a decoration was worn on the overcoat cuff. It is described as "The sleeve ornament for the overcoat shall consist of a strip of mohair braid 5/8 of an inch wide of the same color as the coat. The ends of the braid shall join at the back of the sleeve and passing around the sleeve 2 inches from bottom at seam and extending diagonally shall cross and form on front of sleeve an elongated figure "8"; the top point of top of loop shall be 10 1/4 inches from bottom of sleeve. The inside of lower loop of the figure "8" shall be 3 1/4 inches high by 1 3/4 inches wide; the upper loop, inside, to be 2 inches high by 1 1/4 inches wide." (3).

The 1922 uniform regulations eliminated the cuff decoration on the overcoat (4) and moved the bomb to the shoulder loops of all coats (5).

The rank of Marine Gunner was included in the new rank of Warrant Officer on October 21, 1943 (6).

The concept of Marine Gunners, within the current warrant ranks, was revived in 1956, eliminated in 1959, revived again in 1964, eliminated again in 1974 and finally revived again in 1989 (7).

Master Cook

The rank of Master Cook was created in 1944 in the first grade staff (1), and was therefore entitled to three chevrons and three straight bars (2).

When the enlisted grades were overhauled on December 1, 1946, Master Cooks became Master Sergeants (3).

Master Gunnery Sergeant

The rank of Master Gunnery Sergeant was created in 1935 in the first grade line (1).

The insignia was three chevron and three arcs with crossed rifles and bursting bomb in the center (2). The center device was removed in 1937 (3).

When the enlisted grades were overhauled on December 1, 1946, Master Gunnery Sergeants became Master Sergeants (4).

The rank returned in 1958 in the E-9 pay grade (5). The new insignia was three chevrons and four arcs with a bursting bomb in the center (6).

An Illustration in the 2003 uniform regulations show the insignia for Master Gunnery Sergeants continues to be three Chevrons and four arcs with a bomb in-between (7).

Master Sergeant

The rank of Master Sergeant was created in the first grade by the enlisted grade reorganization of December 1, 1946, from the ranks of Sergeant Major, First Sergeant, Master Gunnery Sergeant, Master Technical Sergeant, Quartermaster Sergeant, Paymaster Sergeant, Master Steward and Master Cook (1).

The insignia was three chevrons and three arcs (2).

The Career Compensation Act of October 12, 1949 (3) changed the first grade to the E-7 pay grade.

Master Sergeants were moved up the E-8 grade in 1958 (4), and crossed rifles were added between the chevrons and arcs (5).

An Illustration in the 2003 uniform regulations show the insignia for Master Sergeants continues to be three Chevrons and three arcs with crossed rifles in-between (6).

Master Steward

The rank of Master Steward was created in 1944 in the first grade staff (1), and was therefore entitled to three chevrons and three straight bars (2).

When the enlisted grades were overhauled on December 1, 1946, Master Stewards became Master Sergeants (3).

Master Technical Sergeant

Master Technical Sergeants came along in 1925 in the first grade staff (1).

The insignia was three chevrons and three straight bars (2).

When the enlisted grades were overhauled on December 1, 1946, Master Technical Sergeants became Master Sergeants (3).

Master Technical Sergeant (Baker)

In 1940, bakers were separated from cooks and the most senior had title of Master Technical Sergeant (Baker) (1).

The rank was in grade one staff with three chevrons and three straight bars, the same as other Master Technical Sergeants (2).

Despite the changes in the lower ranks of bakers, the rank remained until the enlisted grades were overhauled on December 1, 1946, when it became Master Sergeant (3).

Master Technical Sergeant (Clerical) line

The rank of Master Technical Sergeant (Clerical)line was created in grade one staff in 1943 for grade one NCOs with general clerical duties (1).

Like other Master Technical Sergeants, they wore three chevrons and three straight bars (2)

The rank lasted until the grade overhaul of December 1, 1946, when Master Technical Sergeant (Clerical)line became Master Sergeant (3).

Master Technical Sergeant (Clerical) (RW)

The rank of Master Technical Sergeant (Clerical)(RW) was created in grade one staff in 1943 for grade one NCOs on recruiting duty (1). The RW stood for recruiting warrant.

Like other Master Technical Sergeants, they wore three chevrons and three straight bars (2)

The rank lasted until the grade overhaul of December 1, 1946, when Master Technical Sergeant (Clerical)(RW) became Master Sergeant (3).

Master Technical Sergeant (Clerical) (SplW)

The rank of Master Technical Sergeant (Clerical)(SplW) was created in grade one staff in 1943 for grade one NCOs serving in staff offices (1). The SplW stood for special warrant.

Like other Master Technical Sergeants, they wore three chevrons and three straight bars (2)

The rank lasted until the grade overhaul of December 1, 1946, when Master Technical Sergeant (Clerical)(SplW) became Master Sergeant (3).

Master Technical Sergeant (Commissary)

Master Technical Sergeants (Mess) became Master Technical Sergeant (Commissary) in 1943 (1).

They continued to wear the three chevrons and three straight bars of grade one staff (2).

When the enlisted grades were overhauled on December 1, 1946, Master Technical Sergeants (Commissary) became Master Sergeants (3).

Master Technical Sergeant (Mess)

The rank of Master Technical Sergeant (Mess) was created in grade one in 1935, to provide a path of advancement for cooks (1).

The insignia was three chevrons and three straight bars with a crescent between (2), until the crescent was removed in 1937 (3).

Master Technical Sergeants (Mess) became Master Technical Sergeant (Commissary) in 1943 (4).

Mess Corporal

The rank of Mess Corporal was created in grade five, in 1935 (1).

They wore two chevrons with a crescent underneath (2) until 1937 when the crescent was removed (3).

The rank was included in Field Cook (Commissary) in 1943 (3).

Mess Sergeant

The rank of Mess Sergeant was created in grade four, in 1935 (1).

They wore three chevrons with a crescent underneath (2) until 1937 when the crescent was removed (3).

The rank was included in Chief Cook (Commissary) in 1943 (3).

Musician, Marine Band (Principal, First Class, Second Class and Third Class)

Officially the Marine Band was made up of field musicians stationed in the capitol from 1798 to 1861. In fact they were considered separate from the Drummers and Fifers in line units and on ships. It became official on July 25, 1861 (1), when the corps was authorized "thirty musicians for band".

At some point, when is not clear but it was before 1879 (2), the corps divided the musicians into first, second and third class. The division is not mentioned in law until March 3, 1899 (3), when all classes were given the allowances of Sergeants. Principal Musicians, also with the allowances of a Sergeant, were added on August 29, 1916 (4). This situation was in place as late as June of 1946 (5). On October 12, 1949 a law allowed the musicians to be "distributed in such grades and ranks as the Secretary of the Navy may determine necessary and appropriate" (6).

In the early days Musicians wore the uniform of a Private with the full dress coat in scarlet (7). By the 20th century, the full dress uniform was elaborate with fancy cords and shoulder knots (8).

A chevron for band musicians first appears in the 1917 uniform regulations (9). It consisted of a widely separated chevron and arc with a lyre between (10). When this insignia ended is not clear. It may have been when the enlisted grades were overhauled in 1946.

Orderly Sergeant

A law of March 2, 1833 (1) set the pay for "the orderly sergeants of posts, and first sergeants of guards at sea". It would seam from that law that the rank of Orderly Sergeant was used on land and First Sergeant on board ships. It is possible that the rank had been in use for years, with the Orderly Sergeant being the title of the senior Sergeant at a post. 1833 was the first time the position was recognized with higher pay.

The 1833 uniform regulations prescribe the uniform of a Sergeant with a red sash (2). It is not clear if this applied to the two yellow hash marks won on the cuffs of the fatigue jacket.

In 1859, Orderly Sergeants were given three chevrons with a diamond or lozenge in the angle (3).

The use of the title "Orderly Sergeant" ended in 1872 (3) and "First Sergeant" was used on both land and sea.

Pay Clerk or Paymaster's Clerk

The creation, legal status and even the title of the rank of Pay Clerk or Paymaster's Clerk falls in a gray area. They began as clerks in the office of the Assistant Paymaster, who were civilian employees, and listed under "Civil Force" in the laws appropriating money for the corps beginning in 1900 (1).

A part of the 1910 appropriations law stated that a clerk "shall hereafter be available where his services are required and who shall receive the same pay, allowances, and other benefits as are now or may hereafter be provided for paymasters' clerks of corresponding length of service in the United States Army" (2). Army Paymaster's Clerks in

1910 were civilians. The marine corps section of the 1911 appropriations law is the first to begin with "PAY, MARINE CORPS: For pay and allowances prescribed by law of officers on the active list, including clerks for assistant paymasters," (3). Did this mean that the clerks were now officers? The marine section of the 1912 navy register does not include clerks on the active list, but does include a "Paymaster's Clerk" on the retired list named John DeMeritt, who had retired on May 1, 1911 (4).

A law of May 22, 1917 allowed temporary wartime appointments of "clerks to assistant paymasters" (5), and a law of July 1, 1918 officially changed the title to "Pay Clerk" (6). The marine section of the 1918 navy register shows 19 of them, but uses the title "Paymaster's Clerk" (7), but the 1919 register uses the proper "Pay Clerks" (8).

The 1922 uniform regulations refer to "warrant officers and pay clerks", which would seam to indicate they were in a special category between enlisted marines and warrant officers. The regulations prescribe warrant officer's uniforms with the insignia of the pay department, a sword crossed with a gold quill pen, surmounted by a silver oak leaf and three acorns, as a badge of rank on shoulder loops and shirt collars. The badge was worn in bronze on the green and khaki coats and shirts (10). It is not clear when Pay Clerks started wearing uniforms. They do not appear in the 1917 uniform regulations, but they probably wore uniforms if they were serving overseas in World War I.

The legal status question was settled when Pay Clerk officially became a warrant rank of the marine corps on June 11, 1926 (11).

The rank of Pay Clerk was included in the new rank of Warrant Officer on October 21, 1943 (12).

Paymaster Sergeant

Quartermaster Sergeants, Paymaster's Department became Paymaster Sergeants in 1926 (1).

They remained in grade one and continued to wear three chevrons and three straight bars with a stack of coins crossed with at quill between (2). The center device was removed in 1937 (3).

Paymaster with rank of Colonel

The rank of the Paymaster of the Marine Corps, Green Clay Goodloe, was increased from Major to Colonel on March 3, 1899 (1).

Goodloe wore the eagle of a Colonel on his shoulder knots (2), and the Colonel's cuff decoration of a large chevron outlined in tight loops of tracing braid, with tight loops of braid in the angle of the chevron and a long vertical and two short horizontal loops above the point (3).

The 1900 uniform regulations show the eagle also being worn on various collars (4).

The 1904 uniform regulations prescribe cuff decoration for Colonels as being the same as the Commandant but without the "extreme top loop over the point of the chevrons." (5). The decoration for the Commandant is described as having, over the chevron lace "in the shape of a knot, topped by a loop" (6).

The Commandant, George Elliott, was made a Major General in 1908 and pictures of him show a different decoration on the cuffs (7). This may have meant that Colonels were allowed to wear the top loop at that point. The illustrations in the 1912 uniform regulations (8) show the decoration for Colonels to have, above the chevron, two oval, horizontal loops below an oval vertical loop interlocked with two round loops and topped by a pointed loop. From this we can speculate that the 1904 decoration was this was this without the pointed loop and this decoration took over in 1908 or 1912.

Goodloe retired on January 1, 1909, and was replaced by George Richards (9).

The 1912 regulations also added the insignia of the Paymaster's Department, a sword crossed with a gold quill pen, surmounted by a silver oak leaf and three acorns, to Richards coat collars (10) and shoulder knots (11).

The National Defense Act of August 29, 1916 (12) ended the permanent staff appointments. Promotions in the staff department would be from within the officers on duty in 1916, but any new staff officers would be on temporary duty from the line. The act also made the Paymaster a Brigadier General.

Paymaster with rank of Major

On March 2, 1847, the marine corps a given a permanent Paymaster, who held the rank of Major (1). Prior to 1847 the position of Paymaster was, supposedly, held by an officer taken form the line. In reality the Paymaster was not taken from the line, but held by a permanent officer, George Walker, who had been the Paymaster since October 7, 1836 (2).

Walker's uniform, as prescribed by the 1840 uniform Regulations (3) showed four laced button holes on the cuff and a gold epaulet on each shoulder with an aigullette attached to the right one. When epaulets were not worn, shoulder straps were with a silver oak leaf at each end.

Walker died on August 29, 1851 (4), and was replaced by William Russell (5).

Under the 1859 uniform regulations (6), Russell continued to wear the four loops on the cuffs. Epaulets had bullion that was 1/2 inch wide and 3 1/2 inches long with no device on the strap. Shoulder knots were worn when epaulets were not. Those for Majors were made of four cords and no device at the end. A sleeve knot made of three strips of black cord was worn on the overcoat.

Russell died on October 31, 1862 (7), and was replaced by John Cash (8).

In 1875, the corps' five staff officers were given uniforms of a different design from the line officers. The full dress coat was the same as line officers, but with shoulder knots, with an aigullette on the right, instead of epaulets. The knots now carried a gold oak leaf at the end. The line field officers gold cuff decoration was worn on the cuffs, consisting of a large chevron outlined in tight loops of tracing braid, with tight loops of braid in the angle of the chevron and a loose three loop knot above the point. Scarlet cloth showed in the spaces between the braid. The staff officer's undress coat was a modification of the line officers fatigue coat, it is not clear how rank was shown. A black version cuff decoration was on the overcoat (9).

Cash died on March 8, 1877 (10) and was replaced by Green Clay Goodloe (11)

In 1877 staff officers gained a coat that was used for both full dress and undress. The cuff decoration was not worn on this coat. Gold shoulder knots were worn for full dress and black for undress. The gold oak leaf was worn on the gold shoulder knot, but it is not clear if it was worn on the black knot (12).

The cuff decoration, in black, was added to the cuffs of the coat on July 18, 1894 (13). At the same time the loops above the chevron were changed to be "be in the shape of a single three-leaf clover"

On March 3, 1899 (14), a new law raised the rank of the Paymaster to Colonel.

Platoon Sergeant

The rank of Platoon Sergeant was created in 1935 in the third grade line (1).

The insignia was three chevron and one arc with a star in the center (2). The center device was removed in 1937 (3).

When the enlisted grades were overhauled on December 1, 1946, Platoon Sergeants became Staff Sergeants (4).

Private First Class

A law of July 1, 1918 stated "That not more than twentyfive per centum of the authorized number of privates in the Marine Corps shall have the rank of private, first class, which rank is hereby established in the Marine Corps." (1).

The first insignia was crossed rifles, worn on the upper sleeve like chevrons (2).

When marine enlisted ranks were organized into pay grades on June 10, 1922 (3), Privates First Class were placed in grade six (4).

The 1922 uniform regulations prescribe insignia for Privates First Class, but don't state what they looked like, but they do state that the rifle butts be downward (5), which would indicate that the crossed rifle insignia was still in use.

The 1929 regulations also don't describe the insignia, but prescribe the chevrons for a Lance Corporal be worn on the right sleeve and the chevrons for Privates First Class on both sleeves (6). This probably means that the one chevron of Lance Corporals was now worn by both ranks. This is confirmed by the 1937 regulations (7), and one chevron has been the insignia ever since.

The Career Compensation Act of October 12, 1949 (8) made grade six into pay grade E-2.

An Illustration in the 2003 uniform regulations show the insignia for Privates First Class to be one Chevron (9).

Quartermaster Clerk

The warrant rank of Quartermaster Clerk was created on August 29, 1916 (1), and was to be equal to warrant officers in the navy.

The 1917 uniform regulations require warrant officers to wear the undress and field uniforms of a Second Lieutenant. Behind the eagle globe and anchor on the collar, Quartermaster Clerks wore a Marine Corps sword in miniature and a key crossed and surmounted by a wheel with a rim set with 13 gold stars. The device was in silver with the wheel rim in blue, on the white and blue undress coats and bronze on the green and khaki field coats, shoulder loops of the overcoat and shirt collars (2). Warrant officers did not wear the full dress and mess coats that require the cuff decoration, but a decoration was worn on the overcoat cuff. It is described as "The sleeve ornament for the overcoat shall consist of a strip of mohair braid 5/8 of an inch wide of the same color as the coat. The ends of the braid shall join at the back of the sleeve and passing around the sleeve 2 inches from bottom at seam and extending diagonally shall cross and form on front of sleeve an elongated figure "8"; the top point of top of loop shall be 10 1/4 inches from bottom of sleeve. The inside of lower loop of the figure "8" shall be 3 1/4 inches high by 1 3/4 inches wide; the upper loop, inside, to be 2 inches high by 1 1/4 inches wide." (3).

The 1922 uniform regulations kept the same insignia for Quartermaster Clerks in the Quartermaster's Department but those assigned to the Adjutant and Inspectors Department wore a gold Marine Corps sword crossed with gold fasces, surmounted by a silver wreath which encircles a gold shield of 13 bars, side points and base point of shield touching inside of wreath with the field above bars to containing one large star in center and 12 small stars, with a bronze insignia worn on green and khaki coats and shirt collars. The insignia was moved from the collar to the shoulder loops (4), and the cuff decoration on the overcoat was eliminated (5).

The Quartermaster's Department insignia was changed from silver to gold in 1937 (6).

The rank of Quartermaster Clerk was included in the new rank of Warrant Officer on October 21, 1943 (7).

Quartermaster Sergeant

The History of American Ranks and Rank Insignia

The law of 1798 that created the marine corps, allowed for a Quartermaster Sergeant to be appointed if any part of the corps was to operate on land (1). On land or not the corps had a Quartermaster Sergeant by May of 1800 (2). It is not known if he wore a uniform different from other Sergeants.

The next law to enumerate the size of the marine corps was on March 3, 1817 when the size of the corps was set following the War of 1812. It does not mention a Quartermaster Sergeant, or Sergeants of any kind for that matter (3). It is possible that is was an oversight by Congress and there continued to be a Quartermaster Sergeant, but it was the law of the land.

On March 2, 1833, Congress set the pay for the enlisted men of the army and marine corps. The law list each rank individually and Quartermaster Sergeant is among them (4). This was the first time the corps was permanently allowed a Quartermaster Sergeant by law.

Under the 1833 uniform regulations, the Quartermaster Sergeant wore an officer's style uniform with cloth shoulder wings with fringe (5) and four laced button holes on the cuff (6). Sergeants wore two yellow hash marks on the cuff of the fatigue jacket (7), it is not clear if this applied to the Quartermaster Sergeant, or even if the Quartermaster Sergeant wore a fatigue jacket. It is possible that the Quartermaster Sergeant was ordered to wear two chevrons on the jacket in 1836 (8), but this is not in the 1839 regulations (9).

In 1859 the Quartermaster Sergeant was ordered to wear three chevrons and three straight bars (10).

A law of March 3, 1899 added 19 more Quartermaster Sergeants to the corps (11).

When marine enlisted ranks were organized into pay grades on June 10, 1922 (12), they were placed in grade one (13).

In 1925 a wheel was added between the chevrons and the bars (14). It remained until it was removed in 1937 (15).

When the enlisted grades were overhauled on December 1, 1946, Quartermaster Sergeants became Master Sergeants (16).

Quartermaster Sergeant, Adjutant and Inspector's Dept.

The 1929 uniform regulations prescribe separate insignia for Quartermaster Sergeants assigned to the Adjutant and Inspector's Department (1). It was three chevrons and three straight bars with a shield between (2). It is not clear when this insignia was first authorized. It may have been in 1925 when the rank of Master Technical Sergeant was created and took the three chevrons and three bars insignia and Quartermaster Sergeants in the Quartermaster's Department added a wheel. The shield was removed in 1937 (3).

This rank would have been abolished along with the Adjutant and Inspector's Department on May 25, 1943 (4).

Quartermaster Sergeant, Paymaster's Dept.

Quartermaster Sergeants were assigned to the Paymaster's Department on May 13, 1908 (1).

They were given the traditional three chevrons and three straight bars of a Quartermaster Sergeant, adding a stack of coins crossed with a quill, in the center (2).

The title of Quartermaster Sergeant, Paymaster's Department was changed to, and improved, to Paymaster Sergeant in 1926 (3).

Quartermaster with rank of Colonel

The rank of the Quartermaster of the Marine Corps, Frank Denny, was increased from Major to Colonel on March 3, 1899 (1).

Denny wore the eagle of a Colonel on his shoulder knots (2), and the Colonel's cuff decoration of a large chevron outlined in tight loops of tracing braid, with tight loops of braid in the angle of the chevron and a long vertical and two short horizontal loops above the point (3).

The 1900 uniform regulations show the eagle also being worn on various collars (4).

The 1904 uniform regulations prescribe cuff decoration for Colonels as being the same as the Commandant but without the "extreme top loop over the point of the chevrons." (5). The decoration for the Commandant is described as having, over the chevron lace "in the shape of a knot, topped by a loop" (6).

The Commandant, George Elliott, was made a Major General in 1908 and pictures of him show a different decoration on the cuffs (7). This may have meant that Colonels were allowed to wear the top loop at that point. The illustrations in the 1912 uniform regulations (8) show the decoration for Colonels to have, above the chevron, two oval, horizontal loops below an oval vertical loop interlocked with two round loops and topped by a pointed loop. From this we can speculate that the 1904 decoration was this was this without the pointed loop and this decoration took over in 1908 or 1912.

The 1912 regulations also added the insignia of the Quartermaster's Department, a Marine Corps gold sword in miniature and a gold key crossed and surmounted by a gold wheel with a blue enamel rim set with 13 gold stars, to Denny coat collars (9) and shoulder knots (10).

Denny retired on June 1, 1913 (11) and was replaced by Charles McCawley (12)

The National Defense Act of August 29, 1916 (13) ended the permanent staff appointments. Promotions in the staff department would be from within the officers on duty in 1916, but any new staff officers would be on temporary duty from the line. The act also made the Quartermaster a Brigadier General.

Quartermaster with rank of Major

On March 2, 1847, the marine corps a given a permanent Quartermaster, who held the rank of Major (1). Prior to 1847 the position of Quartermaster was, supposedly, held by an officer taken form the line. In reality the Quartermaster was not taken from the line, but held by a permanent officer, A.A Nicholson, who had been the Quartermaster since Marcy 14, 1838 (2).

Nicholson's uniform, as prescribed by the 1840 uniform Regulations (3) showed four laced button holes on the cuff and a gold epaulet on each shoulder with an aigullette attached to the right one. When epaulets were not worn, shoulder straps were with a silver oak leaf at each end.

Nicholson died on July 18, 1855 (4), and was replaced by George Lindsay (5), who died on September 27, 1857 and was replaced by Daniel Sutherland (6).

Under the 1859 uniform regulations (7), Sutherland continued to wear the four loops on the cuffs. Epaulets had bullion that was 1/2 inch wide and 3 1/2 inches long with no device on the strap. Shoulder knots were worn when epaulets were not. Those for Majors were made of four cords and no device at the end. A sleeve knot made of three strips of black cord was worn on the overcoat.

Sutherland was dismissed from the corps on July 23, 1860 (8), and was replaced by William Slack (9).

In 1875, the corps' five staff officers were given uniforms of a different design from the line officers. The full dress coat was the same as line officers, but with shoulder knots, with an aigullette on the right, instead of epaulets. The knots now carried a gold oak leaf at the end. The line field officers gold cuff decoration was worn on the cuffs, consisting of a large chevron outlined in tight loops of tracing braid, with tight loops of braid in the angle of the chevron and a loose three loop knot above the point. Scarlet cloth showed in the spaces between the braid. The staff officer's undress coat was a modification of the line officers fatigue coat, it is not clear how rank was shown. A black version cuff decoration was on the overcoat (10).

In 1877 staff officers gained a coat that was used for both full dress and undress. The cuff decoration was not worn on this coat. Gold shoulder knots were worn for full dress and black for undress. The gold oak leaf was worn on the gold shoulder knot, but it is not clear if it was worn on the black knot (11).

The cuff decoration, in black, was added to the cuffs of the coat on July 18, 1894 (12). At the same time the loops above the chevron were changed to be "be in the shape of a single three-leaf clover"

Slack retired on May 3, 1885 (13) and was replaced by Horatio Lowry (14). Lowry retired on June 19, 1897 and was replaced by Frank Denny (15).

On March 3, 1899 (16), a new law raised the rank of the Quartermaster to Colonel.

Second Leader of the Band

Salvator Petrola was the second in command of the Marine Band in the 1870s and 1880s. There was no official position, but it was Petrola who lead the band when it was between leaders, and was considered the second leader by John Philip Sousa. Petrola retired on October 9, 1891 (1).

An official position of Second Leader, with the allowances of a Sergeant Major, was created on March 3, 1899 (2), and the position went to Walter Smith (3).

The 1900 uniform regulations call for Smith to wear the three chevrons and three arcs of a Sergeant Major (4).

A cornet was added in the center of the chevrons sometime between 1904 (5) and 1912 (6).

Smith retired in 1921 and was replaced by Taylor Branson (7).

The 1922 uniform regulations replaced the cornet with a lyre (8).

Branson was made Leader of the Band on May 2, 1927 and replaced by Arthur Witcomb. Whitcomb served until 1935 when he was replaced by William F. Santelmann. Santelmann was made Leader of the Band on April 1, 1940 and was replaced by Henry Weber (9).

During World War II, Weber was apparently granted an officer's uniform with a lyre as a badge of rank (10)(11).

Dispute the uniform, a law of June 29, 1946 confirmed the Second Leader's status as having the allowances of a Sergeant Major (12).

The Career Compensation Act of October 12, 1949 (13) moved the Second Leader up to the W-3 pay grade, equal to a Commissioned Warrant Officer.

Weber died on February 4, 1951, and was replaced by Albert Schoepper (14).

The end of the rank of Second Leader came on July 24, 1956 (15), when a new law replaced the Second Leader with two Assistant Directors, who were to be officers no higher than Captain.

Second Lieutenant

The History of American Ranks and Rank Insignia

There were appointments in the Continental Marines to " First Lieutenant of Marines" and Second Lieutenant of Marines" (1). However the pay tables (2) show only a rank of "Lieutenant".

The rank of Second Lieutenant has definitely existed in the marine corps since the corps was created on July 11, 1798 (3), when 12 were authorized.

The first Marine Corps uniform regulations were issued in 1804 and they called for Second Lieutenants to be distinguished by a gold epaulet on the Left shoulder (4).

In 1821 Second Lieutenants were ordered to wear two gold chevrons above both cuffs (5). This was changed in 1821 to one chevron on the upper right sleeve for all Second Lieutenants except for Second Lieutenants of staff who continued to wear two on the right sleeve and one on the left. There is no record of a Second Lieutenant holding one the three staff positions during this period.

New uniforms in 1833 showed rank by two laced button holes on the cuff and a gold epaulet (6). It is not clear if the epaulet was worn on the left as in 1804.

Shoulder straps were introduced in 1835 to show rank when epaulets were not worn. Those for a Second Lieutenant had a 1/4 inch border with nothing inside (7).

In 1841 epaulets were prescribed for both shoulders with small Bullion (7a).

The 1859 uniform regulations prescribe epaulets with 1/8 inch wide bullion and shoulder knots made of three cords, with no badge of rank worn on either. Two loops of lace continued to be worn on the cuffs, but the overcoat cuffs were plain (8)

In 1875 the three laced button holes on the cuff were replaced with a cuff decoration of a large knot (9). This pattern was worn on various cuffs by Second Lieutenants until 1952 (10).

As the badges of rank began to be worn alone on uniforms, Second Lieutenants were distinguished by wearing officer's uniforms with no badge. During World War I the corps followed the army in granting a gold bar as a badge of rank for Second Lieutenants (11), which have been used ever since.

The Career Compensation Act of October 12, 1949 (12) put Second Lieutenants into pay grade O-1.

The 2003 uniform regulations describe the insignia for Second Lieutenants as "Second Lieutenant. One gold-colored bar of the same type as for a first lieutenant." (13).

Senior Enlisted Advisor to the Chairman

The position of Senior Enlisted Advisor to the Chairman of the Joint Chiefs of Staff was created on October 1, 2005. Like the chairman, the senior enlisted advisor could come from any service. Army Command Sergeant Major William Gainey held the office until April 25, 2008, Serving under marine General Peter Pace as Chairman. By the time Gainey retired in 2008, pace had been replaced by navy Admiral Michael Mullen, who believed the post was unnecessary, and therefore left it vacant (1).

It wasn't until Mullen was replaced by Army General Martin Dempsey on October 1, 2011 that the position was revived and a marine was chosen, in the person of Sergeant Major Bryan Battaglia (2).

Pay law the Senior Enlisted Advisor to the Chairman is in the E-9 pay grade (3).

In is official picture, Battaglia is wearing the insignia of a Sergeant Major (4).

The History of American Ranks and Rank Insignia

Sergeant

The roots of the rank of Sergeant stretch to the middle ages when the servants, or serviens in Latin, of knights would fight alongside their master to take charge of a group of peasants called to fight (1).

Marine Sergeants appear on the pay tables of the Continental Navy (2), the 1794 (3) and 1797 (4) laws creating the federal navy and in the July 11, 1798 (5) law creating the marine corps.

There is no information available on rank distinctions of noncommissioned officers in the Continental Marines. In 1798 Sergeants were ordered to wear a yellow epaulet on both shoulders. This was changed to yellow shoulder knots in 1804 (6).

The number of Sergeants in the early marine corps was very small. Fourty-eight were authorized in 1798 (7). Eight more were added in 1799 (8) taking the total to 56, where it remained until the corps was expanded in 1814 (9), giving it a whooping 117 Sergeants.

Then came "An Act to fix the peace establishment of the marine corps" on March 3, 1817 (10), that set the size of the corps after the War of 1812. This is the full text of the law:

Be it enacted by the Senate and House of Representatives of the United States of America, in Congress assembled, That the peace establishment of the marine corps shall consist of the following officers, noncommissioned officers, musicians and privates, viz.: one lieutenant colonel commandant, nine captains, twenty-four first lieutenants, sixteen second lieutenants, one adjutant and inspector, one paymaster and one quartermaster, to be taken from the said captains and lieutenants, seventy-three corporals, forty-two drums and fifes, and seven hundred and fifty privates.
Sec. 2. And be it further enacted, That the President of the United States cause the provisions of this act to be carried into effect on the first day of April next, or as soon thereafter as circumstances will admit, and cause any supernumerary officers to be discharged from the service of the United States; and to all persons so discharged, there shall be paid three months' additional pay.
Sec. 3. And be it further enacted, That the President of the United States may, in the recess of the Senate, appoint any of the officers authorized by this act, which appointments shall be submitted to the Senate at their next session, for their advice and consent.
APPROVED, March 3, 1817.

Sergeants are not mentioned at all. The next law organizing the marine corps was on June 30, 1834 (11). Did this mean that there were no marine Sergeants between 1817 and 1834? Probably not. A law of March 2, 1833 (12) that set the pay of the army and marine corps does mention Sergeants. This may mean that the rank of Sergeant was still in use despite the 1817 law.

The new uniforms of 1833 gave Sergeants three laced button holes on the cuff and fringe on the shoulder wings (13). Two yellow hash marks were worn above the cuffs of the fatigue jacket.

It is possible that the insignia on the fatigue jacket was changed in 1836 to one yellow chevron on each upper sleeve (13a), however the uniform regulations on 1839 (13b) still prescribe the hash marks.

New orders issued in 1839, and phased in over the next two years, describe the uniform coat for a Sergeant as "Sergeants--to be navy blue cloth, single-breasted, with one row of nine buttons; the skirt to extend within eight inches of the bend of the knee; to conform to the pattern of the Officers' coats in other respects, excepting that the cuff shall have three buttons and loops on the slash sleeve, like that designated for a Captain, the lace to be of yellow worsted. Yellow worsted epaulettes will be worn with worsted fringe, in imitation of bullion" (14).

The 1859 uniform regulations (15) continued the three button holes, which would last until 1875, and added three chevrons on the upper sleeve, which, except for the addition of crossed rifles in the angle in 1959 (16), have been worn ever since.

When marine enlisted ranks were organized into pay grades on June 10, 1922 (17), Sergeants were placed in grade four (18), which became E-4 with the Career Compensation Act of October 12, 1949 (19). Sergeants were moved up to the E-5 grade in 1958 (20).

An Illustration in the 2003 uniform regulations show the insignia for Sergeants to be three Chevrons over crossed rifles (21).

Sergeant Major

The law of 1798 that created the marine corps, allowed for a Sergeant Major to be appointed if any part of the corps was to operate on land (1). On land or not the corps had a Sergeant Major by January of 1801, by the name of Archibald Summers (2). It is not known if he wore a uniform different from other Sergeants.

The next law to enumerate the size of the marine corps was on March 3, 1817 when the size of the corps was set following the War of 1812. It does not mention a Sergeant Major, or Sergeants of any kind for that matter (3). It is possible that is was an oversight by Congress and there continued to be a Sergeant Major, but it was the law of the land.

On March 2, 1833, Congress set the pay for the enlisted men of the army and marine corps. The law list each rank individually and Sergeant Major is among them (4). This was the first time the corps was permanently allowed a Sergeant Major by law.

Under the 1833 uniform regulations, the Sergeant Major wore an officer's style uniform with cloth shoulder wings with fringe (5) and four laced button holes on the cuff (6). Sergeants wore two yellow hash marks on the cuff of the fatigue jacket (7), it is not clear if this applied to the Sergeant Major, or even if the Sergeant Major wore a fatigue jacket. It is possible that the Sergeant Major was ordered to wear two chevrons on the jacket in 1836 (8), but this is not in the 1839 regulations (9).

In 1859 the Sergeant Major was ordered to wear three chevrons and arcs (10).

On March 3, 1899 (11), the number of Sergeants Major was increased to five.

When marine enlisted ranks were organized into pay grades on June 10, 1922 (17), Sergeants Major were placed in grade one line (13).

The rank was abolished when the enlisted grades were overhauled on December 1, 1946, and Sergeants Major became Master Sergeants (14).

It returned in 1954, in the E-7 pay grade (15). The new insignia was the traditional three chevrons and three arcs, now with a star in the middle (16).

Sergeant Major was moved up the E-9 pay grade in 1958 (17), and a fourth arc was added to the insignia (18).

An Illustration in the 2003 uniform regulations show the insignia for Sergeants Major to be three Chevrons and four arcs with a star in the center (19).

Sergeant Major (Aviation)

The rank of Sergeant Major (Aviation) existed form April of 1945 (1) to December of 1946, when it was included in Master Sergeant (2).

The insignia was three chevron and three arcs (3).

Sergeant Major of the Marine Corps

The Sergeant Major of the Marine Corps is the senior enlisted advisor to the commandant and the senior enlisted person in the corps (1). Other services created a senior enlisted position in the late 1960s, but the marine corps set the president in 1957 when Wilber Bestwick was named Sergeant Major of the Marine Corps on May 23rd (2).

The concept of a single Sergeant Major for the whole corps goes back a lot further than 1957. Until 1899 the corps was only large enough to have one Sergeant Major.

Bestwick retired on September 1, 1959 and was replaced by Francis Rauber. Rauber retired on June 28, 1962 and was replaced by Thomas McHugh. McHugh was transferred to a post in Japan on July 16, 1965 and replaced by Herbert Sweet. Sweet was replaced by Joseph Dailey on August 1, 1973. Dailey retired on January 31, 1973 and was replaced by Clinton Puckett. Puckett retired on May 31, 1975 and was replaced by Henry Black. Black served until March 31, 1977 when John Massaro took over. Next up was Leland Crawford, who served from August 16, 1979 to June 27, 1983. Then came Robert Cleary who served until June 26, 1987, when David Sommers took over. Sommers was replaced by Harold Overstreet on June 28, 1991, who served until June 29, 1995 and was replaced by Lewis Lee. Alford McMichael replaced Lee on July 1, 1999, and was in turn replaced by John Estrada on June 26, 2003. Next was Carlton Kent who served from April 25, 2007 to June , 2011, when Michael Barrett took the office he holds as of this writing in December of 2011 (3).

Until 1970, the Sergeant Major of the Marine Corps wore the standard three chevrons and four arcs with a star between, of a Sergeant Major. In 1970 a new insignia was introduced with three chevrons and four arcs with an eagle globe and anchor and two stars (4), and this insignia is shown in an illustration in the 2003 uniform regulations (5).

Staff Sergeant

When marine enlisted ranks were organized into pay grades on June 20, 1922 (1), there was no rank in grade three (2). This was remedied in 1923 when the rank of Staff Sergeant was created (3), wearing three chevrons and one arc (4).

In 1926 Staff Sergeants were split into the ranks of Staff Sergeant (Clerical) and Staff Sergeant (Mechanical) (5).

Plain Staff Sergeants returned when the enlisted grades were overhauled on December 1, 1946, combining the various types of Staff Sergeant with the ranks of Platoon Sergeant, Chief Cook, Steward Second Class and Cook Second Class (6).

The three chevrons and one arc returned as the insignia (7).

The Career Compensation Act of October 12, 1949 (8) made grade three into grade E-5.

In 1958 Staff Sergeants were moved up to the E-6 grade (9), and crossed rifles were placed between the chevrons and the arc (10).

An Illustration in the 2003 uniform regulations show the insignia for Sergeants to be three Chevrons and one arc with crossed rifles (11).

Staff Sergeant (Clerical)

Staff Sergeants were divided into Staff Sergeant (Clerical) and Staff Sergeant (Mechanical) in 1926, grade three. Staff Sergeants (Clerical) were to serve as stenographers (1).

Both ranks continued to wear three chevrons and one arc (2).

In 1937 the arc was replaced with a straight bar, indicating a grade three staff rank (3).

Staff Sergeants (Clerical) were folded back into staff sergeants when the enlisted grades were overhauled on December 1, 1946 (4).

Staff Sergeant (Mechanical)

Staff Sergeants were divided into Staff Sergeant (Clerical) and Staff Sergeant (Mechanical) in 1926, grade three. Staff Sergeants (Mechanical) were to serve as carpenters, upholsterers and plumbers (1).

Both ranks continued to wear three chevrons and one arc (2).

In 1937 the arc was replaced with a straight bar, indicating a grade three staff rank (3).

Staff Sergeants (Mechanical) were folded back into staff sergeants when the enlisted grades were overhauled on December 1, 1946 (4).

Staff Sergeant (Baker)

In 1940, bakers were separated from cooks and the rank of Staff Sergeant (Baker) was born in grade (1).

The rank shared grade three staff and three chevrons and one straight bar with Staff Sergeant (Mess) (2).

The title was changed to Chief Baker in early 1941, and back to Chief Cook (Baker) in 1943 (3).

Staff Sergeants (Baker) became Cooks Second Class in February of 1944 (4).

Staff Sergeant (Commissary)

Staff Sergeants (Mess) became Staff Sergeants (Commissary) in January of 1943 (1). They continued to be in grade three staff, and continued to wear three chevrons and one straight bar (2).

When the enlisted grades were overhauled on December 1, 1946, they became simply Staff Sergeants (3).

Staff Sergeant (Mess)

In 1935 a career path was created for cooks. When they reached grade three, the title was Staff Sergeant (Mess) (1).

They wore the three chevrons and one arc of a Staff Sergeant with a crescent in the middle (2). In 1937 the crescent was removed and the arc became a straight bar (3).

Staff Sergeants (Mess) became Staff Sergeants (Commissary) in January of 1943 (4).

Steward First Class

Stewards First Class, or Officer's Stewards First Class, were created on February 26, 1944 in grade two staff (1), and was therefore entitled to three chevrons and two straight bars (2).

When the enlisted grades were overhauled on December 1, 1946, Stewards First Class became Technical Sergeants (3).

Steward Second Class

Stewards Second Class, or Officer's Stewards Second Class, were created on February 26, 1944 in grade three staff (1), and was therefore entitled to three chevrons and one straight bar (2).

When the enlisted grades were overhauled on December 1, 1946, Stewards Second Class became Staff Sergeants (3).

Steward Third Class

Stewards Third Class, or Officer's Stewards Third Class, were created on February 26, 1944 in grade four (1), and was therefore entitled to three chevrons (2).

When the enlisted grades were overhauled on December 1, 1946, Stewards Third Class became Sergeants (3).

Supply Sergeant

The rank of Supply Sergeant was created in 1925, in grade two staff (1).

The insignia was three chevrons and two straight bars with a wheel in the middle (2). The wheel was removed in 1937 (3).

When the enlisted grades were overhauled on December 1, 1946, Supply Sergeants became Technical Sergeants (4).

Technical Sergeant

Technical Sergeants came along in 1925 in the first grade staff (1).

The insignia was three chevrons and two straight bars (2).

When the enlisted grades were overhauled on December 1, 1946, Technical Sergeants absorbed the ranks of Gunnery Sergeant, Drum Major, Supply Sergeant, Steward First Class, Cook First Class and the other versions of Technical Sergeant (3).

The insignia was changed to three chevrons and two arcs (4).

The Career Compensation Act of October 12, 1949 (5) changed the second grade to the E-6 pay grade.

The rank of Technical Sergeant was replaced with the revived rank of Gunnery Sergeant in 1958 (6).

Technical Sergeant (Baker)

In 1940, bakers were separated from cooks and the second most senior had title of Technical Sergeant (Baker) (1).

The rank was in grade two staff with three chevrons and two straight bars, the same as other Technical Sergeants (2).

Despite the changes in the lower ranks of bakers, the rank remained until the enlisted grades were overhauled on December 1, 1946, when it became just Technical Sergeant (3).

Technical Sergeant (Clerical) line

The rank of Technical Sergeant (Clerical)line was created in grade two staff in 1943 for grade two NCOs with general clerical duties (1).

Like other Technical Sergeants, they wore three chevrons and two straight bars (2)

The rank lasted until the grade overhaul of December 1, 1946, when Technical Sergeant (Clerical) line became just Technical Sergeant (3).

Technical Sergeant (Clerical) (RW)

The rank of Technical Sergeant (Clerical)(RW) was created in grade two staff in 1943 for grade two NCOs on recruiting duty (1). The RW stood for recruiting warrant.

Like other Technical Sergeants, they wore three chevrons and two straight bars (2)

The rank lasted until the grade overhaul of December 1, 1946, when Technical Sergeant (Clerical)(RW) became just Technical Sergeant (3).

Technical Sergeant (Clerical) (SplW)

The rank of Technical Sergeant (Clerical)(SplW) was created in grade two staff in 1943 for grade two NCOs serving in staff offices (1). The SplW stood for special warrant.

Like other Technical Sergeants, they wore three chevrons and two straight bars (2)

The rank lasted until the grade overhaul of December 1, 1946, when Technical Sergeant (Clerical)(SplW) became just Technical Sergeant (3).

Technical Sergeant (Commissary)

Technical Sergeants (Mess) became Technical Sergeant (Commissary) in 1943 (1).

They continued to wear the three chevrons and two straight bars of grade two staff (2).

When the enlisted grades were overhauled on December 1, 1946, Technical Sergeants (Commissary) became just Technical Sergeants (3).

Technical Sergeant (Mess)

The rank of Technical Sergeant (Mess) was created in grade two in 1935, to provide a path of advancement for cooks (1).

The insignia was three chevrons and two straight bars with a crescent between (2), until the crescent was removed in 1937 (3).

Technical Sergeants (Mess) became Technical Sergeant (Commissary) in 1943 (4).

Trumpet Corporal

The rank of Trumpet Corporal was created in 1934, in grade five (1).

The insignia was two chevrons over a trumpet (2). The trumpet is not included in the 1937 uniform regulations (3).

Trumpet Corporals became Field Music Corporals on November 13, 1937 (4).

Trumpet Sergeant

The rank of Trumpet Sergeant was created in 1934, in grade four (1).

The insignia was three chevrons over a trumpet (2). The trumpet is not included in the 1937 uniform regulations (3).

Trumpet Sergeants became Field Music Sergeants on November 13, 1937 (4).

Trumpeter

Fifers replaced there fifes with trumpets on July 1, 1881 (1), but there title wasn't changed to Trumpeter until March 3, 1899 (2).

They continued to wear the uniform of a Private with the dress coat in scarlet (3).

Insignia was finally prescribed in 1908, when a trumpet were added to the upper sleeve (4). The trumpet was eliminated by the 1937 uniform regulations (5).

In November of 1937, Trumpeter were combined with Drummers to become Field Musics (6).

Trumpeter First Class

In 1931 Trumpeters were allowed to be promoted to Private First Class. It is not clear if they wore the one chevron. This became an accrual rank of Trumpeter First Class in 1934 (1).

Placed in grade six they wore one chevron with a trumpet underneath (2). The trumpet are not included in the 1937 uniform regulations (3).

Trumpeters First Class became Field Musics First Class on November 13, 1937 (4).

Warrant Officer

The rank of Warrant Officer was created on October 21, 1943 (1) from the ranks of Marine Gunner, Paymaster Clerk and Quartermaster Clerk.

A badge of rank was authorized consisting of a gold bar with a scarlet line across it (2). The navy would adopt a similar bar with a blue line 1/16 inch wide, in 1952 (3) and the marine scarlet line may have also been 1/16 inch wide. It is not clear when the corps introduced the bars. It may have been when the rank was created in 1943, or later, but certainly by 1950.

The Career Compensation Act of October 12, 1949 (4) placed Warrant Officers in pay grade W-1.

The rank became Warrant Officer 1, with the Warrant Officer Act of 1954 (5).

Warrant Officer 1

Warrant Officer 1 was created by the "Warrant Officer Act of 1954" (1) in pay grade W-1.

Design of the insignia was coordinated with the Navy, Marine Corps and Coast Guard to create a unified system. The insignia authorized around 1954 was a gold bar with two scarlet rectangles, showing a square of gold in the middle (2).

The 2003 uniform regulations describe the insignia as "Warrant Officer, WO-1. One gold-colored bar of the same type as for a CWO-2, with two scarlet enamel blocks arranged in the same manner as for a CWO-3." (3).

Part 4.
Air Force

Chapter 1. Air Force Organization

The worlds first military aviation unit was created in the French Army in 1794, to operate three balloons. Napoleon disbanded the unit in 1799 (1).

The first use of military balloons by the U.S. Army was during the Civil war when a Balloon Corps lead by Thaddeus Owe was created. Lowe and his corps were civilian contractors not military personnel, and therefore had trouble securing transportation for their equipment. Owe resigned on May 8, 1863 over a pay dispute, and the corps was disbanded by August (2).

In 1892 the army purchased a balloon from France, and assigned it operation to the Signal Corps. When this balloon wore out a copy was made and this balloon saw action in the Spanish War (3).

On August 1, 1907, four years after the Wright Brothers first flight, and Aeronautical Division was set up within the Signal Corps (4).

In 1908 the army purchased it's first airplane from the Wright Brothers (5).

On July 18, 1914 a new law stated "That there shall hereafter be, and there is hereby created, an aviation section, which shall be a part of the Signal Corps of the Army, and which shall be, and is hereby, charged with the duty of operating or supervising the operation of all military air craft, including balloons and aeroplanes, all appliances pertaining to said craft, and signaling apparatus of any kind when installed on said craft; also with the duty of training officers and enlisted men in matters pertaining to military aviation." (6). The Aviation section replaced the Aeronautical Division.

The Aeronautical Division was reorganized into the Division of Military Aeronautics on April 24, 1918 (7)

On May 20, 1918 Congress passed a law allowing the President to reorganize the government and the military as he saw fit, for the duration of World War I plus six months (8). With this authority, President Wilson transferred the Division of Military Aeronautics out of the Signal Corps. It remained an independent part of the army for the next four days. On May 24th it became the Army Air Service, a branch of the army equal to the infantry or the cavalry (9).

Wilson's authority to reorganize the government expired on July 11, 1919. On that date congress passed an apportions law that recognized the Air Service by funding it (10). The matter was settled by the National Defense Act of June 4, 1920 that listed the Air Service as a branch of the army (11).

The name was changed form "Air Service" to "Air Corps" on July 2, 1926 (12).

On June 20,1941 the army was divided into Air Forces, Ground Forces and Services of Supply, with the Air Corps making up the bulk of the personnel in the Army Air Forces (13).

Finally on July 26, 1947 the Army Air Forces became the United States Air Force, a separate military branch equal to the army or the navy (14).

Transfer of rank from the Army

The law that created the Air Force stated "All commissioned officers, warrant officers, and enlisted men, commissioned, holding warrants, or enlisted, in the Air Corps, United States Army, or the Army Air Forces, shall be transferred in branch to the United States Air Force. All other commissioned officers, warrant officers, and enlisted men, who are commissioned, hold warrants, or are enlisted, in any component of the Army of the United States and who are under the authority or command of the Commanding General, Army Air Forces, shall be continued under the authority or command of the Chief of Staff, United States Air Force, and under the jurisdiction of the Department of the Air Force. Personnel whose status is affected by this subsection shall retain their existing commissions, warrants or enlisted status in existing components of the armed forces unless otherwise altered or terminated in accordance with existing law; and they shall not be deemed to have been appointed to a new or different office or grade, or to have vacated their permanent or temporary appointments in an existing component of the armed forces, solely by virtue of any change in status under this subsection. No such change in status shall alter or prejudice the status of any individual so assigned, so as to deprive him of any right, benefit, or privilege to which he may be entitled under existing law." (1). In other words the personnel and rank structure of the army was transferred, without change, to the air force.

Pay Grades

The air force inherited the enlisted pay grades that the army had set up in 1920. Grade one contained Master Sergeant and First Sergeant, Grade two Technical Sergeant, Grade three Staff Sergeant and Technician Third Grade, grade four Sergeant and Technician Fourth Grade, grade five Corporal and Technician Fifth Grade, Grade six Private First Class and grade seven Private.

When it became a separate service, the air force choose to make First Sergeant a position for senior enlisted advisors rather than a rank (1). It is not clear, but apparently the technician grades were dropped all together.

The Career Compensation Act of October 12, 1949 (2) reorganized all military ranks into pay grades. The grades would carry a letter and a number. Officer's grades would start with an "O", warrant officer's with a "W" and Enlisted with an "E". Unlike the 1920 system, one would be the lowest rank with the numbers increasing for higher ranks.

Eight officer grades were created with Second Lieutenants being O-1 and Brigadier General being O-7. All higher generals would share the O-8 grade.

There were four warrant grades, with Warrant Officers Junior Grade taking the W-1 grade and Chief Warrant Officers being spread over grades W-2, W-3 and W-4.

The seven enlisted grades from 1920 became grades E-1 to E-7, the lower grade of Private being E-1 and Master Sergeants being E-7.

In 1952 the air force changed the names of the lower enlisted rank titles to more air force sounding titles. Privates became Basic Airmen, Privates First Class became Airmen Third Class, Corporals became Airmen Second Class and Sergeants became Airmen First Class (3).

In 1954 congress changed the warrant ranks to Warrant Officer 1 in the W-1 grade, Chief Warrant Officer 2 in the W-2 grade, Chief Warrant Officer 3 in the W-3 grade and Chief Warrant Officer 4 in the W-4 grade (4).

The Career Compensation Act was amended on May 20, 1958 (5) to create the grades of O-9, O-10, E-8 and E-9.

Major Generals now had O-8 to themselves while Lieutenant Generals moved to O-9 and full Generals to O-10.

For the E-8 grade the rank of Senior Master Sergeant was created, and for the E-9 grade the new rank was Chief Master Sergeant. With the creation of the new grades, the air force decided that the warrant officer ranks were no longer needed (6) and they were phased out by attrition.

On February 5, 1959 the rank of Basic Airman was changed, slightly, to Airman Basic (7).

The lower enlisted titles were changed again in 1967. Airman Third Class became Airman, Airman Second Class became Airman First Class and Airman First Class became Sergeant (8).

In 1976 the rank of Senior Airman was added to the E-4 grade that it would share with Sergeant. Sergeants were noncommissioned officers and Senior Airmen were not.

The rank of Sergeant was abolished in 1991.

In 1998 the rank of Command Chief Master Sergeant was created for senior enlisted advisors in large units (9).

Chapter 2.
Air Force Rank Insignia

When the air force separated from the army in 1947, army uniforms continued to be worn, with now long established methods of showing rank. Officers wore badges of rank on the shoulder loops of coats and on the collars of shirts, and enlisted personnel wore cloth chevrons on the upper sleeve.

New air force uniforms were authorized in 1949 and became mandatory on July 1, 1952 (1). The army style badges of rank continued to be worn by officers on shoulder loops, shirt collars and garrison caps, and the newly designed air force chevrons were worn on the upper sleeve by enlisted personnel (2). Male officers were allowed and evening dress uniform with rank showed by a gold cuff decoration (3).

Shoulder boards were introduced on a new mess dress uniform in 1958 (4), and they were expanded to informal/ceremonial uniforms in 1965 (5).

In 1974 small metal chevrons were authorized for wear on outerwear (6).

The evening dress with cuff decorations was replaced in the late 70s with a version with the shoulder boards. There was an attempt to return to the cuff decorations in the early 80s, but nothing came of it (7).

Shoulder marks were also introduced in the early 80s for wear on light blue shirts and sweaters (8).

In 1991 the Air Force Chief of Staff, General Merrill McPeak made a radical change to the air force's service dress uniform. The basic uniform coat used by the air force had been based on a design first used by the army on a dress white coat in 1937, a four button sack coat with a rolling collar, pointed lapels, two pleated patch pockets and two inside pockets all with scalloped flaps and cloth shoulder loops. McPeak's new coat was intended to be much plainer. It had only three buttons, the patch pockets were eliminated and with one flap less interior pocket, the lower pockets now had plain flaps with no buttons and the shoulder loops were eliminated. Insignia was reduced to a minimum. Because of the lack of shoulder loops, officers showed rank by silver cuff stripes (9). The uniform was unpopular with air force officers who found themselves being mistaken for airline pilots (10). When McPeak retired in 1994, his replacement General Ronald Fogleman abolished the cuff stripes and returned the shoulder loops with badges of rank (11).

Part of the change over to the new uniforms was the abolition of the ceremonial uniforms with shoulder boards (12).

In 2006 enlisted shoulder marks were abolished (13).

Badges of Rank

Badges of rank is the term we shall use to refer to the stars, eagles, leafs and bars used to denote officers rank.

The air force's badges of rank were taken, without change, from the army when the services separated. They were five silver stars for General of the Army or Air Force, four for Generals, three for Lieutenant Generals, two for Major Generals and one for Brigadier Generals. Colonels wore a silver eagle, Lieutenant Colonels a silver oak leaf, Majors a gold oak leaf, Captains two silver bars, First Lieutenants one silver bar, Second Lieutenants one gold bar, Chief Warrant Officers one gold bar with rounded ends covered in brown enamel with a gold stripe running down the middle and Warrant Officers Junior Grade one gold bar with rounded ends covered in brown enamel with a gold stripe running down the across (1).

They were worn on the shoulder loops of coats, the collars of shirts, garrison caps and on the cuff decoration of the evening dress coat (2).

In 1954 new insignia was prescribed for the now four grades of Warrant Officer. A "unified system" common to all armed forces was developed using the same pattern for each equivalent rank. The enameled portions would very by branch of service, brown for the army, dark blue for the Navy and Coast Guard, scarlet red for the Marine Corps, and sky blue for the Air Force. The new bars were rectangular, silver for the top two grades and gold for the other two. The enameled portion for W-1 and W-3 would be in two rectangles, showing only one stripe of gold or silver. For W-2 and W-4 there would be three enameled portions showing two sections of gold or silver (3).

The army had adopted subdued badges of rank during the Vietnam War, for use on field uniforms to make officers less conspicuous to snipers. The beginning of subdued insignia in the air force in unclear. The 1969-70 Air Officer's Guide does not mention the being worn on fatigue uniforms (4), and period photos show the badges embroidered in full color on a blue background (5). Subdued insignia is mentioned in the 1983 uniform regulations (6), with silver insignia being dark blue and gold brown.

Shoulder Broads

The air force introduced shoulder boards in 1958 for use on black and white mess jackets. They consisted of a stiffened cloth rectangle with a point at one end, covered in black cloth. Two strips of sliver lace ran long ways down the board, Boards for generals added a strip of wide silver lace under the other lace with the black showing only at the very edge. Generals wore the appropriate number of stars centered down the middle of the board and other officers wore the badge of rank between the strips of lace at the outer end (1).

Use was expanded in 1965 to a black informal uniform, which later became known as the black ceremonial uniform (2).

The 1983 uniform regulations prescribe a blue mess jacket and blue ceremonial uniform, and even added shoulder boards to a white ceremonial uniform(3). The old black and white uniforms were still listed but their days were numbered and they were soon gone (4).

The 1983 regulations are not clear on the color of the background of the shoulder board, but with the change from black to blue uniforms the background became blue (5).

The new blue and white ceremonial uniforms lasted until the changes instituted by General McPeak in the early 1990s. The white uniform could be worn until March 1, 1993 and the blue uniform until August 1, 1994 (6).

Shoulder boards are still worn on the blue mess jacket.

Cuff Decoration and Cuff Stripes

The first uniform specific to the air force was the evening dress uniform adopted in 1947 while army uniforms were still in use for other purposes. Rank was shown by a cuff decoration made of 1/4 inch gold lace formed in a house like shape with a diamond on top. Because of the point of the diamond shape this became known as the "spearhead". Above the bottom of the house like section another strip of lace was added the width of which varied by rank. Generals wore 2 inch wide lace, field grade officers 1 inch lace, company grade officers 1/2 inch and warrant officers wore no lace and the bottom lace of the house was broken twice. The point of the spearhead was 7 inches above the top of the extra lace, making the design for higher ranks taller. Badge of rank were placed in the center of the house like area (1) (2).

The gold lace was changed to a silver in 1959 (3).

The formal uniform was eliminated in 1977 (4). The spearhead is listed in he 1980 uniform regulations for use on the back mess jacket (5), but the 1983 regulations prescribe shoulder boards (6).

The next use of cuffs to show rank was in 1991 when the shoulder loops with badges of rank on the service dress coat were replaced with silver cuff stripes.

The system was the same as used by they navy, Generals wore one 2 inch stripe under three 1/2 inch stripes, Lieutenant Generals wore one 2 inch stripe under two 1/2 inch stripes, Major Generals wore one 2 inch stripe under one 1/2 inch stripes, Brigadier Generals wore only the 2 inch stripe, Colonels wore four 1/2 inch stripes, Lieutenant Colonels Three 1/2 inch stripes, Majors wore two 1/2 inch stripes with a 1/4 inch stripe between them, Captains wore two 1/2 inch stripes, First Lieutenants wore one 1/2 inch stripe under one 1/4 inch stripe and Second Lieutenants wore one 1/2 inch stripe. The 2 inch stripes for generals were decorated with silver clouds and lightning bolts (7).

The stripes were unpopular and were eliminated in 1994.

Shoulder Marks

Shoulder marks, also known as soft shoulder boards, are a relatively new concept. They consist of a cloth tube that can be pulled over the shoulder loops of a shirt or sweater. The idea is an insignia that can be easily removed without having to worry about placement and doesn't create bulk if worn under a uniform coat. This allowed a class “A” (coat and tie) uniform to be converted to a class “B” (shirtsleeve) uniform but simply removing the coat.

The senior enlisted grades, E-7, E-8 and E-9, began to wear shoulder marks on light blue shirts in 1982 (1). It is not clear if officers were allowed the marks at the same time. However he 1983 uniform regulations prescribe uniform combinations with both the shoulder marks on the light blue shirts and badges of rank on the collar (2). This would seam to indicate that the transition was fairly recent.

The 1983 uniform regulations show generals wearing a thin silver stripe and the top of the mark and a thicker one at he bottom with the stars centered between them. Majors and colonels wore only a thin stripe at the bottom with the badges of rank embroidered just above it. Captains and lieutenants wore only the badge of rank near the lower end. NCOs had their chevrons, including the first sergeant’s diamond, embroidered near the center of the mark (3).

The dates are not clear, but the marks for generals were changed in the early 1990s, to have a sliver stripe running long ways down each side (4). By 1995 the original design had returned (5).

The enlisted marks were removed from the shirts in 1996, but can still be worn on sweaters.

Chevrons

A chevron is two lines meeting at an angle. A simple design to create with lace or tape, they had been used as rank insignia for noncommissioned officers by the British Army since 1803 (1). In this context we need to stretch the definition of “chevron” include all the cloth badges worn (mostly) on the upper sleeve to show rank.

When the air force split off from the army it continued to wear army chevrons. The chevrons used by the army at the time were olive drab or khaki on a blue background. Master Sergeants wore three chevrons and three arcs, Technical Sergeants wore three chevrons and two arcs, Staff Sergeants wore three chevrons and one arc, Sergeants wore three chevrons, Corporals wore two chevrons, Privates First Class wore one chevron and Privates wore no insignia (2). The army’s ranks of First Sergeant and Technician apparently did not make the transition to the air force.

In 1948 various ideas for air force chevrons were circulated around Boling Air Force Base and a poll was taken. The winning design got 55% of the vote (3). The same number of chevrons and arcs were maintained but the chevrons now pointed down and the points were covered by a disc containing a star with another disc on it. The arcs were placed under the chevrons and went around the bottom of the disc. The chevrons, arcs and star were in a silver gray color on a dark blue background (4).

The disc is reminiscent of the roundels that were previously used on American aircraft. Roundels are the national insignia that identify military aircraft. They derive from cockades made from concentric circles of colored ribbon worn by soldiers in european armies beginning in the 18th century. During World War I French planes began to carry an insignia of painted circles of blue, white and red, from the inside out, replicating the French cockade. This soon spread to other countries and aircraft roundels were born. American planes carried a blue disc filled with a white star with a red disc or dot in the center. In 1918 this insignia was changed to white blue and red concentric circles, but the old insignia returned in 1941 (5). The red disc was removed in May of 1942 after it was discovered it could be mistaken for the red disc on Japanese aircraft (6). In March of 1942 a shoulder patch was adopted for the Army Air Force showing the white star with the red dot with wings coming out at an angle (7). The shape of the new chevrons reflected this insignia with the disc and star in the middle and the chevrons reflecting the wings.

In 1954 Master Sergeants with the duties of First Sergeants added a diamond in the angle above their chevrons (8).

When the ranks of Chief Master Sergeant and Senior Master Sergeant were created in 1958, it was decided to add point up chevrons, two for chief and one for senior, to the existing Master Sergeant's insignia (9). This left a blue field between the chevrons where the first sergeant's device could be permanently applied instead of a separate piece as it was for Master Sergeants.

In 1959 a white informal uniform was authorized for enlisted members of the air force. It carried white chevrons on a white background (10), which must have been hard to see.

The next uniform authorized was a black mess jacket in 1961. Its chevrons were of metallic aluminum on black. The aluminum on black chevrons were placed on the black informal uniform and replaced the white chevrons on the white uniform in 1969 (11).

After a period of experimenting with metal and plastic chevron, small metal pin on insignia was authorized for wear in 1974 (12). A silver background with blue enamel was used.

It is not clear when the air force began to wear subdued chevrons, but it was probably in the early 1970s. The chevrons were blue on green (13).

In 1976 it was decided to create a distinction between noncommissioned officers and other enlisted personnel. This was done by making the star the same color as the background on the insignia for the ranks of Airman, Airman First Class and Senior Airman (14). On the pin on insignia the star was omitted.

When desert uniforms were introduced in the 1980s, they included brown on beige chevrons (15).

In October of 1991, several changes to chevrons were announced. The top three grades would loose the third arc from the bottom of their insignia and add a point up chevrons on top. The lower grades would have the color restored to their stars. All dress chevrons would in bright silver instead of gray, eliminating the need for the aluminum on black chevrons (16).

In 2007 the field uniforms were replaced with the Airman Battle Uniform that carried midnight blue chevrons on a gray background (17).

Chapter 3.
Air Force Ranks

Airman

The rank of Airman Third Class became the rank of Airman on October 19, 1967. It continued it's position in the E-2 pay grade (1).

The insignia continued to be one chevron, point down with a disc covering the point with a star in the center and a smaller disc covering the center of the star (2).

From 1976 to 1991 color of the star matched the color of the background disc. (3).

An illustration in the 2011 uniform regulations shows the insignia for Airmen continues to be one chevron, point down with a disc covering the point with a star in the center and a smaller disc covering the center of the star (4).

Airman First Class

The grade E-4 rank of Sergeant became Airman First Class on April 24, 1952 (1).

The insignia continued to be three chevron, point down with a disc covering the points with a star in the center and a smaller disc covering the center of the star (2).

On October 19, 1967 the E-4 rank was changed back to Sergeant and the title of Airman First Class was moved down to the E-3 grade replacing Airman Second Class (3). This changed the insignia to two chevrons.

From 1976 to 1991 color of the star matched the color of the background disc. (3).

An illustration in the 2011 uniform regulations shows the insignia for Airmen First Class continues to be two chevron, point down with a disc covering the points with a star in the center and a smaller disc covering the center of the star (5).

Airman Second Class

The grade E-3 rank of Corporal became Airman Second Class on April 24, 1952 (1).

The insignia continued to be two chevron, point down with a disc covering the points with a star in the center and a smaller disc covering the center of the star (2).

Airmen Second Class became Airmen First Class on October 19, 1967 (3).

Airman Third Class

The grade E-2 rank of Private First Class became Airman Third Class on April 24, 1952 (1).

The insignia continued to be one chevron, point down with a disc covering the point with a star in the center and a smaller disc covering the center of the star (2).

Airmen Third Class became Airmen on October 19, 1967 (3).

Brigadier General

The term Brigadier General comes from the commander of a brigade hence brigadier.

The rank was inherited from the army along with it's badge of rank of one silver star that the army had used since 1780.

The Career Compensation Act of October 12, 1949 (1) put Brigadier Generals into pay grade O-7.

An illustration in the 2011 uniform regulations shows the insignia for Brigadier Generals continues to be one silver star (2).

Captain

The title Captain comes from the Latin caput meaning head, this led to the term capitaneus or head man (1). In the middle ages captains commanded companies of soldiers. The company was the basic unit when an army was formed, higher ranks were created when more the one company was fielded together.

The rank was inherited from the army along with it's badge of rank of two silver bars. The bars had been used by the army since around 1833, and were made silver in 1872.

The Career Compensation Act of October 12, 1949 (2) put Captains into pay grade O-3.

An illustration in the 2011 uniform regulations shows the insignia for Captains continues to be two silver bars (2).

Chief Master Sergeant

When the E-9 pay grade was created on May 20, 1958 (1), the air force created the rank of Chief Master Sergeant to fill it (2).

The new insignia was three chevrons, point down with a disc covering the points with a star in the center and a smaller disc covering the center of the star, three arcs followed the bottom of the chevrons and the disc and two more chevrons pointed up just above the point down chevrons (3).

In 1991 the insignia was changed to three point up chevrons and only two arcs below the point down chevrons and disc (4).

An illustration in the 2011 uniform regulations shows the insignia for Chief Master Sergeants continues to be three point up and three point down chevrons over two arcs with a disc covering the point of the point down chevron with a star in the center with a disc in the center of it (5).

Chief Master Sergeant of the Air Force

The Chief Master Sergeant of the Air Force is the senior enlisted advisor to the Air Force Chief of Staff.

The position was announced on October 24, 1966 (1) and filled on April 3, 1967 by Paul Airey (2).

Airiey's insignia was the same a for other Chief Master Sergeants, two point up chevrons, three point down chevrons three arcs with the disc and star, with the star on the disc smaller with a wreath around it (3).

Airey served until July 31, 1969 and was replaced by Donald Harlow. Harlow served until September 30, 1971 and was replaced by Richard Kisling. Kisling held the office until October 1, 1971 when Thomas Barns took over. Barns left on July 31, 1977 and was replaced by Robert Gaylor. James McCoy replaced Gaylor on August 1, 1979 and he was in turn replaced by Arthur Andrews on August 1, 1981. Andrews served until July 31, 1983 when he was replaced by Sam Parish who served until June 30, 1986. Next up was James Binnicker who had the job until July 31, 1990 when he was replaced by Gary Pfingston (4).

In 1991 Pfingston's insignia was changed to three point up and three point down chevrons over two arcs with the disc and the star in a wreath (5).

David Campanale replaced Pfingston on October 26, 1994. After him came Eric Benken on November 5, 1996. Fredrick Finch replaced Benken on November 5, 1996 and was himself replaced by Gerald Murray on July 1, 2002 (6).

Murray's insignia was changed in 2004 when the eagle of the Great Seal of the United States, flanked by two stars was placed in the space between the point up chevrons and the point down chevrons (7).

Rodney McKinley replaced Murray on June 1, 2006, and he was replaced by James Roy on July 1, 2009, who is, at this writing in early 2012, the current Chief Master Sergeant of the Air Force (8).

An illustration in the 2011 uniform regulations shows the insignia for the Chief Master Sergeant of the Air Force continues to be three point up and three point down chevrons over two arcs with a disc covering the point of the point down chevron with a star in the center with a disc in the center of it, surrounded by a wreath, and the great seal and two stars (9).

Chief Warrant Officer

The rank of Chief Warrant Officer was inherited from the army. Since 1941 the badge of rank had been "One gold bar 3/8 inch in width and 1 inch in length, with rounded ends, having a brown enameled top and a longitudinal center of gold 1/8 inch in width." (1).

The Career Compensation Act of October 12, 1949 (2) placed Chief Warrant Officers in pay grades W-2, W-3 and W-4 (3). All three grades using the same insignia.

On May 29, 1954 congress passed the "Warrant Officer Act of 1954" (4). This act created three separate ranks of Chief Warrant Officers in the three pay grades, adding the grade number to the title of each.

Chief Warrant Officer 2

Chief Warrant Officer 2 was created by the "Warrant Officer Act of 1954" (1) in pay grade W-2.

Design of the insignia was coordinated with the Navy, Marine Corps and Coast Guard to create a unified system. The insignia was a gold bar with a sky blue square in the center and a sky blue rectangle at each end (2).

Warrant officers counted against the air force's budget for commissioned officers. The more warrant officers there were, there was less money for officers. When the E-8 and E-9 enlisted pay grades were created in 1958, the air force decided to phase out warrant officers and replace them with the new enlisted grades that came out of a different budget item (3).

Chief Warrant Officer 3

Chief Warrant Officer 3 was also created by the "Warrant Officer Act of 1954" (1) in pay grade W-3.

Design of the insignia was coordinated with the Navy, Marine Corps and Coast Guard to create a unified system. The insignia was a silver bar with two sky blue rectangles, showing a square of silver in the middle (2).

Warrant officers counted against the air force's budget for commissioned officers. The more warrant officers there were, there was less money for officers. When the E-8 and E-9 enlisted pay grades were created in 1958, the air force decided to phase out warrant officers and replace them with the new enlisted grades that came out of a different budget item (3).

Chief Warrant Officer 4

Chief Warrant Officer 4 was also created by the "Warrant Officer Act of 1954" (1) in pay grade W-4.

Design of the insignia was coordinated with the Navy, Marine Corps and Coast Guard to create a unified system. The insignia was a silver bar with a sky blue square in the center and a sky blue rectangle at each end (2).

Warrant officers counted against the air force's budget for commissioned officers. The more warrant officers there were, there was less money for officers. When the E-8 and E-9 enlisted pay grades were created in 1958, the air force decided to phase out warrant officers and replace them with the new enlisted grades that came out of a different budget item (3).

The last warrant officer on active duty, James Long, retired in 1980. The last reservist was Bob Barrow who was given the rank of Chief Warrant Officer 5 when he retired in 1992 (4).

Colonel

During the sixtieth century, the Spanish Army was organized into columns or in Spanish colunelas each made up of multiple companies. The commander was called capo d colunela, head of the column. The French and later the British copied the column idea and eventually developed into regiments with a Colonel in charge (1). Colonels are sometime referred to a "full Colonels" to differentiate them from Lieutenant Colonels.

The rank was inherited from the army along with it's badge of rank of a silver eagle. The eagle had been used by the army since 1832, and were made silver in 1851.

The Career Compensation Act of October 12, 1949 (2) put Colonels into pay grade O-6.

An illustration in the 2011 uniform regulations shows the insignia for Colonels continues to be a silver eagle (2).

Command Chief Master Sergeant

The rank of Command Chief Master Sergeant was created in 1998 as a senior enlisted advisor in large units (1).

The insignia is three chevrons, point down with a disc covering the points with a star in the center and a smaller disc covering the center of the star, two arcs followed the bottom of the chevrons and the disc and three more chevrons pointed up just above the point down chevrons with a star in the space between the point up and point down chevrons (2).

Corporal

The term Corporal comes from the Italian for leader of a squadra or square, Capo De'squadra. The title was changed in the 16th century to Caporale meaning leader of a small body of soldiers (1).

Corporal was the army's grade five rank when the air force became a separate service.

The army's insignia of two point up chevrons was used until the air force style insignia was introduced in 1948. The new style retained the two chevrons but pointed them down and covered the point with a disc with a star in the center with a disc in the center of the star (2).

With the reorganization after The Career Compensation Act of October 12, 1949 (3) Corporals were placed in pay grade E-3.

Corporals became Airmen Second Class on April 24, 1952 (4).

First Lieutenant

The term lieutenant comes from the French for "placeholder" (1). It can be thought of a someone who hold a place or is a tenant instead of or in lieu of. A tenant in lieu of is a lieutenant.

As medieval captains became involved in court politics, they needed someone to fill in for them while they were away, and the rank of Lieutenant was born (2).

The "First" in First Lieutenant was originally used to denote the ranking of the Lieutenants in a company first being the most senior. Use of the terms in the Continental Army is a little hard to pin down. The term "First Lieutenant" was certainly used, but whether it was considered a rank or a position for those holding the rank of "Lieutenant" is not clear.

The rank was inherited from the army along with it's badge of rank of one silver bar. The bars had been used by the army since around 1833, and were made silver in 1872.

The Career Compensation Act of October 12, 1949 (3) put First Lieutenants into pay grade O-2.

An illustration in the 2011 uniform regulations shows the insignia for First Lieutenants continues to be one silver bar (4).

First Sergeant

A First Sergeant is the senior enlisted advisor of a unit.

The air force inherited the grade one rank of First Sergeant, but choose to make it a position held by Master Sergeants not a rank (1).

On September 22, 1954, Master Sergeants assigned as First Sergeants were ordered to wear a diamond above their chevrons (2).

When the ranks of Senior Master Sergeant, in the E-8 grade, and Chief Master Sergeant, in the E-9 grade, were created in 1958, First Sergeants were placed in those grades as well. They wore the diamond in the space between the point up and point down chevrons (3).

From that time on First Sergeants were referred to as First Sergeant E-7, First Sergeant E-8 and First Sergeant E-9.

E-7 First Sergeants wore the diamond as a separate piece until the Master Sergeants insignia was changed in 1991, when the addition of a point up chevron created the same space used by the upper ranks (4).

General

The term "general" comes from the Latin Generalis meaning the whole of something. A medieval Captain General would be officer in charge of a whole army. The "Captain" part was dropped by the english army by the 18th century and the rank became just General, sometimes called "full" general (1).

The rank was inherited from the army along with it's badge of rank of four silver stars. The stars had been used by the army continuously since 1919.

The Career Compensation Act of October 12, 1949 (2) placed the rank of General in pay grade O-8 which it shared with Lieutenant General and Major General. This lasted until May 20, 1958 when a new law (3) created pay grade O-10 for Full Generals.

An illustration in the 2011 uniform regulations shows the insignia for Generals continues to be four silver stars (4).

General of the Air Force

On May 7, 1949 a new law stated "Be it enacted by the Senate and House o f Representatives of the United States o f America in Congress assembled, That there is hereby established in the United States Air Force the grade of General of the Air Force. SEC. 2. The grade of any individual transferred in the grade of General of the Army from the Regular Army to the United States Air Force, pursuant to the National Security Act of 1947 (Act of July 26, 1947; 61 Stat . 695), is herewith redesignated "General of the Air Force". SEC. 3. Nothing herein shall be construed as appointing any individual to a new or different office or to alter or prejudice the status of any individual concerned so as to deprive him of any pay or allowances, rights, benefits, or privileges to which he may be entitled under existing law. Approved May 7, 1949." (1).

The only General of the Army in the air force was Henry Arnold, who had held the rank since December 14, 1944 (2), and had retired on June 30, 1946 (3).

On June 28, 1948 congress passed a law allowing the President to return the generals of the army to active duty (4), essentially allowing them to keep their ranks for life. This made Arnold an active General of the Army when the title was changed in 1949.

Arnold died 253 day later on January 15, 1950, and the rank died with him.

Arnold continued to wear five silver stars, joined in a pentagon as a badge of rank, with a gold eagle of the great seal added on the shoulder loops (5).

General of the Army

The rank of General of the Army had been created on December 14, 1944 (1) and the chief of the Army Air Force, Henry Arnold was one of the officers appointed (2).

He had retired on June 30, 1946 (3), but a law of June 28, 1948 had essentially made General of the Army a lifetime appointment on active duty (4).

The badge of rank was five silver stars, joined in a pentagon as a badge of rank, with a gold eagle of the great seal added on the shoulder loops.

Arnold's title was changed to General of the Air Force on May 7, 1949 (5).

Lieutenant Colonel

Like Captains, sixteenth century Colonels often left there columns or regiments to attend to business at royal courts (1). While they were gone a lieutenant was needed to take their place, and Lieutenant Colonels were born.

The rank was inherited from the army along with it's badge of rank of a silver oak leaf. The leaf had been used by the army since about 1833 and was made silver in 1851.

The Career Compensation Act of October 12, 1949 (2) placed the rank of Lieutenant Colonel in pay grade O-5.

An illustration in the 2011 uniform regulations shows the insignia for Lieutenant Colonels continues to be a silver oak leaf (3).

Lieutenant General

Captains had their Lieutenants, Colonels had their Lieutenant Colonels, and Generals had their Lieutenant Generals to fill in for them or assist them in command (1).

The rank was inherited from the army along with it's badge of rank of a three silver stars. The stars had been used by the army continuously since 1939.

The Career Compensation Act of October 12, 1949 (33) placed the rank of Lieutenant General in pay grade O-8 which it shared with Full General and Major General. This lasted until May 20, 1958 when a new law (34) created pay grade O-9 for Lieutenant Generals.

An illustration in the 2011 uniform regulations shows the insignia for Lieutenant Generals continues to be three silver stars (4).

Major

In the seventieth century English army of Oliver Cromwell each regiment had a sergeant who was third in command and was in charge of administrative matters. He was known as a great sergeant or sergeant major (1). Despite being called sergeant, it was a higher rank than Captain or Lieutenant. It is assumed that this is the reason the "sergeant" part dropped away and the title became just "major" (2).

The rank was inherited from the army along with it's badge of rank of a gold oak leaf. The leaf had been used by the army since about 1833 and was made gold in 1851.

The Career Compensation Act of October 12, 1949 (2) placed the rank of Major in pay grade O-4.

An illustration in the 2011 uniform regulations shows the insignia for Majors continues to be a gold oak leaf (3).

1.
Major General

While seventieth century English regiments had a Sergeant Major as third ranking officer handling administrative duties, the entire army had a Sergeant Major General (1). The "sergeant" part was dropped over time and the rank became Major General ranking just below Lieutenant General. This is why a Lieutenant General outranks a Major General but a Major outranks a Lieutenant.

The rank was inherited from the army along with it's badge of rank of a two silver stars. The stars had been used by the army since 1780.

The Career Compensation Act of October 12, 1949 (2) placed the rank of Major General in pay grade O-8 which it shared with Full General and Lieutenant General. This lasted until May 20, 1958 when a new law (3) gave Major Generals the grade all to themselves.

An illustration in the 2011 uniform regulations shows the insignia for Major Generals continues to be two silver stars (4).

Master Sergeant

The air force inherited the enlisted grade one rank of Master Sergeant from the army. The rank had existed in the army since 1920, wearing three chevrons and three arcs, point up.

When air force style insignia was introduced in 1948 the three chevrons were inverted and the point was covered with a disc with a star in the center with a disc in the center of the star. The three arcs were below the chevrons and followed the bottom of the chevrons and around the bottom of the disc (1).

The Career Compensation Act of October 12, 1949 converted grade one into grade E-7 (2). The army moved it's Master Sergeants up to the E-8 grade in 1958, but in the air force they remain in the E-7 grade.

In 1991 the arcs were reduced to two and a point up chevron was added above the point down chevrons (3).

An illustration in the 2011 uniform regulations shows the insignia for Master Sergeants of the Air Force continues to be one point up and three point down chevrons over two arcs with a disc covering the point of the point down chevron with a star in the center with a disc in the center of it (4).

Private

Private was the army's grade seven rank when the air force became a separate service.

Privates were distinguished by the lack of insignia (1).

With the reorganization after The Career Compensation Act of October 12, 1949 (2) Privates were placed in pay grade E-1.

Privates First Class became Basic Airmen on April 24, 1952 (3).

Private First Class

Private First Class was the army's grade six rank when the air force became a separate service.

The army's insignia of one point up chevron was used until the air force style insignia was introduced in 1948. The new style retained the chevron but pointed it down and covered the point with a disc with a star in the center with a disc in the center of the star (1).

With the reorganization after The Career Compensation Act of October 12, 1949 (2) Privates First Class were placed in pay grade E-2.

Privates First Class became Airmen Third Class on April 24, 1952 (3).

Second Lieutenant

The term lieutenant comes from the french for "placeholder" (1). It can be thought of a someone who hold a place or is a tenant instead of or in lieu of. A tenant in lieu of is a lieutenant.

As medieval captains became involved in court politics, they needed someone to fill in for them while they were away, and the rank of Lieutenant was born (2).

The "Second" in Second Lieutenant was originally used to denote the ranking of the Lieutenants in a company first being the most senior. Use of the terms in the Continental Army is a little hard to pin down. The term "Second

Lieutenant" was certainly used, but whether it was considered a rank or a position for those holding the rank of "Lieutenant" is not clear.

The rank was inherited from the army along with it's badge of rank of one gold bar. The bars had been used by the army since 1917.

The Career Compensation Act of October 12, 1949 (3) put Second Lieutenants into pay grade O-1.

An illustration in the 2011 uniform regulations shows the insignia for Second Lieutenants continues to be one gold bar (4).

Senior Airman

The rank of Senior Airman was created in 1976, in the E-4 grade which it shared with the rank of Sergeant (1). Sergeants were noncommissioned officers and Senior Airmen were not.

The insignia was three chevron, point down with a disc covering the points with a star in the center and a smaller disc covering the center of the star, and the star the same color as the disc (2).

In 1991 the star was changed to the color of the chevrons (3).

An illustration in the 2011 uniform regulations shows the insignia for Senior Airmen continues to be three chevron, point down with a disc covering the points with a star in the center and a smaller disc covering the center of the star (4).

Senior Master Sergeant

When the E-8 pay grade was created on May 20, 1958 (1), the air force created the rank of Senior Master Sergeant to fill it (2).

The new insignia was three chevrons, point down with a disc covering the points with a star in the center and a smaller disc covering the center of the star, three arcs followed the bottom of the chevrons and the disc and another chevron pointed up just above the point down chevrons (3).

In 1991 the insignia was changed to two point up chevrons and only two arcs below the point down chevrons and disc (4).

An illustration in the 2011 uniform regulations shows the insignia for Senior Master Sergeants continues to be two point up and three point down chevrons over two arcs with a disc covering the point of the point down chevron with a star in the center with a disc in the center of it (5).

Sergeant

The roots of the rank of Sergeant stretch to the middle ages when the servants, or serviens in Latin, of knights would fight alongside their master to take charge of a group of peasants called to fight (1).

Sergeant was the army's grade four rank when the air force became a separate service.

The army's insignia of three point up chevrons was used until the air force style insignia was introduced in 1948. The new style retained the three chevrons but pointed them down and covered the point with a disc with a star in the center with a disc in the center of the star (2).

With the reorganization after The Career Compensation Act of October 12, 1949 (3) Sergeants were placed in pay grade E-4 .

Sergeants became Airmen First Class on April 24, 1952 (4).

The rank of Sergeant returned, with the same pay grade and insignia, in 1967 and the title of Airman First Class was moved down to the E-3 grade.

Sergeants were abolished again in 1991 (5), and the last one James Garstecki left the air force in 1998 (6)

Staff Sergeant

The air force inherited the enlisted grade three rank of Staff Sergeant from the army. The rank had existed in the army since 1920, wearing three chevrons and one arc, point up.

When air force style insignia was introduced in 1948 the three chevrons were inverted and the point was covered with a disc with a star in the center with a disc in the center of the star. The arc was below the chevrons and followed the bottom of the chevrons and around the bottom of the disc (1).

The Career Compensation Act of October 12, 1949 converted grade three into grade E-5 (2).

An illustration in the 2011 uniform regulations shows the insignia for Staff Sergeants of the Air Force continues three point down chevrons over two arcs with a disc covering the point of the chevron with a star in the center with a disc in the center of it (3).

Technical Sergeant

The air force inherited the enlisted grade two rank of Technical Sergeant from the army. The rank had existed in the army since 1920, wearing three chevrons and two arcs, point up.

When air force style insignia was introduced in 1948 the three chevrons were inverted and the point was covered with a disc with a star in the center with a disc in the center of the star. The arcs were below the chevrons and followed the bottom of the chevrons and around the bottom of the disc (1).

The Career Compensation Act of October 12, 1949 converted grade two into grade E-6 (2).

An illustration in the 2011 uniform regulations shows the insignia for Technical Sergeants of the Air Force continues to be three point down chevrons over two arcs with a disc covering the point of the chevron with a star in the center with a disc in the center of it (3).

Warrant Officer 1

Warrant Officer 1 was created by the “Warrant Officer Act of 1954” (1) in pay grade W-1.

Design of the insignia was coordinated with the Navy, Marine Corps and Coast Guard to create a unified system. The insignia authorized in 1956 was a gold bar with a sky blue rectangle at each end (2).

Warrant officers counted against the air force’s budget for commissioned officers. The more warrant officers there were, there was less money for officers. When the E-8 and E-9 enlisted pay grades were created in 1958, the air force decided to phase out warrant officers and replace them with the new enlisted grades that came out of a different budget item (3).

Warrant Officer Junior Grade

The rank of Warrant Officer Junior Grade was inherited from the army. Since 1941 the badge of rank had been "One gold bar 3/8 inch in width and 1 inch in length, with rounded ends, having a brown enameled top and a latitudinal center of gold 1/8 inch in width." (1).

The Career Compensation Act of October 12, 1949 (2) placed Warrant Officers Junior Grade in pay grade W-1 (3).

On May 29, 1954 congress passed the "Warrant Officer Act of 1954" (9). This act created Warrant Officer Junior Grade into Warrant Officer 1.

Part 5.
Coast Guard

Chapter 1.
Coast Guard Organization

The United States Coast Guard was created on January 28, 1915 by the merger of two agencies, the Revenue Cutter Service and the Lifesaving Service (1). The Lighthouse Service was merged into the coast guard on July 1, 1939 (2) and the Bureau of Marine Inspection and Navigation was temporarily placed under the coast guard on February 28, 1942 (3), this was made permanent on July 16, 1946 (4).

The Revenue Cutter Service

On August 4, 1790, four years before the creation of the federal navy, Congress passed "An Act to provide more effectually for the collection of the duties imposed by law on goods, wares and merchandise imported into the United States, and on the tonnage of ships or vessels" (1). The law authorized the construction of ten "revenue cutters" to help ensure goods were not smuggled into the country to avoid the taxes.

The service was under the Treasury Department, answering to the Secretary of the Treasury. On March 2, 1799 a law (2) allowed the navy to take control of the cutters if they extra vessels were needed. As a result the revenue cutters participated in many naval actions during the 19th century.

Over the years the service was also referred to as the Revenue Marine, Revenue Marine Service or the Revenue Marine Cutter Service.

The Life Saving Service

On March 3, 1849 congress appropriated funds to create life saving stations to aid ships in distress (1). Ironically they were administered by the revenue cutter service.

The stations were staffed by volunteer boat crews who would be called in the case of an emergency. A poor response to a major storm in 1854 lead to the expansion of the stations and the appointment of permanent keepers (2).

Another poor response to a storm in 1871 lead to permanent boat crews and more stations (3).

On June 18, 1878 a separate Life Saving Service was set up in the Treasury Department (4).

The Lighthouse Service

Congress provided for the construction of lighthouses on August 7, 1789 (1). The operation of the houses was handled by local customs officials answering to the Secretary of the Treasury (2).

In 1852 The Lighthouse Board was established consisting of two naval officers, an officer of the army corps of engineers, an officer of the army corps of topographical engineers and two civilian scientists (3).

On June 17, 1910 control of lighthouses and other navigation aides and various support vessels was given to a new Lighthouse Board under the Department of Commerce and Labor (4). The operational section of the Lighthouse Board was the Lighthouse Service.

Bureau of Marine Inspection and Navigation

The History of American Ranks and Rank Insignia

The first law requiring inspections of passenger vessels was passed on July 7, 1838 (1). Inspectors were appointed by the local federal judge.

On August 30, 1852 congress passed comprehensive steamboat legislation that placed inspectors under the Treasury Department (2).

A Steamboat Inspection Service was created in the Treasury Department on February 28, 1871 (3), and was moved to the Department of Commerce and Labor when it was established on February 14, 1903 (4).

The Steamboat Inspection Service was merged with the Bureau of Navigation on June 30, 1932, to form the Bureau of Navigation and Steamboat Inspection (5).

Finally the name was changed on May 27, 1936 to Bureau of Marine Inspection and Navigation (6).

Types of Rank

The United States Coast Guard currently uses three types of ranks: Commissioned Officers, Warrant Officers and Enlisted Personnel.

Commissioned Officers, usually referred to simply as "Officers", are appointed by the President and confirmed by the Senate. They hold a commission that allows them to act in the name of the government.

Warrant Officers are specialists in their field and remain so thru out their career, while officers are more supervisors in charge of and organization in general. In the army, Warrant Officers in the lowest grade are given a warrant authorizing them to perform their duties. Upon promotion to the next grade they receive a commission the same as other officers. The navy however, stopped using the lowest grade in 1975 and navy warrant officers begin as commissioned officers (1).

Enlisted Personnel are the lower ranks who do most of the work, and have no authority to act for the government.

Rank Structure

The military structure of the coast guard descends directly from the revenue cutter service. The law that crated the coast guard states "all of said offices, respectively, corresponding to the present offices of the Revenue-Cutter Service, which are transferred to the Coast Guard, and all the present incumbents, officers and enlisted men, are also transferred to corresponding positions in the Coast Guard." (1). The law goes on to list how lifesaving personnel would be integrated into the coast guard ranks. When the lighthouse service was merged into the coat guard, the President was allowed to place them into the coast guard's rank structure "in grades appropriate to their qualifications, experience, and lengths of service" (2).

The cutter service's rank structure, especially enlisted ranks, is difficult to track. The law of August 4, 1790 that created the cutters stated that each one would have one Master, a First Mate, a Second Mate, a Third Mate, four Mariners and two Boys (3).

A law of March 2, 1799 refers to "captain or master" and "lieutenant or mate". It also refers to "noncommissioned officers, gunners and mariners" (4).

A pay table from 1799 lists the compliment of a 14 gun cutter a one Captain, one First Mate, one Second Mate, one Third Mate, one Boatswain, one Carpenter, one Gunner, one Cook, 30 Able Seamen, 10 Ordinary Seamen, 14 Marines and eight Boys. Ten gun cutters were staffed by one Captain, one First Mate, one Second Mate, one Third Mate, 15 Able Seamen, eight Marines and seven Boys (5). This leaves a number of unanswered questions. When did Masters become Captains? When will Mates become Lieutenants? Were Boatswains, Gunners, Carpenters and Cooks warrant officers? Also were Marines soldiers or sailors? There are no clear answers. Captain appears to have replaced Master by the War of 1812 (6), but Mate may have held on until the 1830s (7). A list of officers from 1832 includes men listed as "Warrant Officer", but there is no legal basis for warrant officers in the cutter service. A wild guess at the title of Marine is that it is a derivation of Mariner.

A law of July 2, 1836, setting the pay of revenue cutter officers uses Captain and first, second and third lieutenant (8). No mention is made of masters or mates.

An estimate of the payroll expense for 1843, lists the service as containing 20 Captains, 20 First Lieutenants, 20 Second Lieutenants, 20 Third Lieutenants, 45 Petty Officers, seven Pilots, 30 Stewards, 15 Cooks and 323 Seamen (9). The concept of warrant officers appears to have been replaced with petty officers.

Engineering officers were added to the service on March 3, 1845 (10).

On July 25, 1861 another law was passed setting the pay of officers and the number of officers and men per cutter. It stated "That the number of officers for each revenue vessel shall be one captain and three lieutenants, first, second, and third; and of a steam-vessel, one engineer, and one assistant engineer, and such number of petty officers and men as in the opinion of the Secretary of the Treasury may be required to make the vessels efficient for the duties required of them:" (11).

The Civil War placed the cutters under the direction of the navy. This brought up the inevitable question of the relative rank of revenue cutter officers with naval officers. The issue had been brought up in 1840 when revenue cutters had been assigned to the naval squadron the West Indies, but nothing had come of it (12). On February 4, 1863 a law was passed that stated "That the officers of the revenue cutter service, when serving in accordance with law, as part of the navy, shall be entitled to relative rank, as follows: Captains, with and next after lieutenants commanding in the navy; first lieutenants, with and next after lieutenants in the navy; second lieutenants, with and next after masters in line in the navy; third lieutenants, with and next after passed midshipmen in the navy:" (13). Congress had apparently forgotten it had changed the navy's rank structure a year earlier. Lieutenant commanding had been a title given to navy lieutenants who commanded their own vessels. The rank of Lieutenant Commander had been created to fill this need on July 16, 1862. The same law had created the rank of Ensign and placed in the place of Passed Midshipman (14).

The February 4th law also replaced the ranks of Engineer and Assistant Engineer with the ranks of Chief Engineer, who would have the pay and relative rank of a First Lieutenant, First Assistant Engineer, who would have the pay and relative rank of a Second Lieutenant and Second Assistant Engineer, who would have the pay and relative rank of a Third Lieutenant. The law stated "commissioned officers of the United States revenue cutter service shall be appointed by the President, by and with the advice and consent of the Senate.". Confirming once and for all their status as military officers.

Uniform regulations for the cutter service were published a catalog of the company Schuyler Hartly and Graham in 1864, along with uniform regulations for the army, navy and marine corps. The catalog was republished by Dover Publications of Mineola New York in 1985. The officer's rank structure shown it that of the February 4, 1863 law. Uniforms are also described for enlisted rates of Petty Officer, Seaman, Fireman, Coal Passer, Steward, Cook and Boy.

Beginning on June 10, 1872, the Revenue Cutter Service's rank and rate structure was listed in the law that appropriated the service's funding for the year. The law allowed pay for Captains, Lieutenants (meaning First, Second and Third Lieutenants), Engineers (meaning Chief, First Assistant and Second Assistant Engineers), "pilots employed" (probably meaning that harbor pilots were paid out the service's budget, but were not part of the rank structure), Petty Officers, Seamen, Cooks, Stewards, Boys, Coal Passers and Firemen (15).

The appropriations law of July 31, 1876 added cadets ranking below Third Lieutenant (16).

On July 31, 1894 a new law stated "That the Secretary of the Treasury shall detail a captain of the Revenue Cutter Service who shall be chief of the division of Revenue Cutter Service, and a chief engineer, who shall be engineer in chief of said Service, but no additional pay or emoluments shall be allowed on account of such detail" (17). This didn't create any new rank but it laid the foundation for the future. On May 28, 1896 the Engineer In Chief given the relative rank with Captains in the Revenue Cutter Service (18).

The title of Engineer in Chief was changed to Captain of Engineers by the June 4, 1897 appropriations law (19). The 1897 law also added the enlisted rates of Oiler and Bugler.

The appropriations law of July 1, 1898 added "one constructor in and for the Revenue-Cutter Service, who shall have the relative rank and pay of a first lieutenant" (20).

The next appropriations law, on March 3, 1899, changed the title of Coal Passer to Coal Heaver (21).

On April 12, 1902, Congress passed "An Act To promote the efficiency of the Revenue-Cutter Service.". The law laid out the rank structure for officers, confirming the changes that had been made by the various appropriations laws over the years by stating "That on And after the passage of this Act the commissioned officers of the Revenue-Cutter Service shall be as follows: Captains, first lieutenants, second lieutenants, third lieutenants, captain of engineers, chief engineers, first assistant engineers, second assistant' engineers, and constructor; and the captain of engineers, chief engineers, first assistant engineers, second assistant engineers shall have the rank of captain, first. second, and third lieutenants, respectively; and the constructor shall have the rank of first lieutenant". The law also laid out how the ranks related to the ranks in army and navy. Captains and Captains of Engineers were now equal to army Majors and navy Lieutenant Commanders. First Lieutenants, Chief Engineers and Constructors were equal to army Captains and navy Lieutenants. Second Lieutenants and First Assistant Engineers were equal to army First Lieutenants and navy Lieutenants Junior Grade, and Third Lieutenants and Second Assistant Engineers were equal to army Second Lieutenants and navy Ensigns (22).
On March 3, 1905 a law was passed allowing a surgeon named Samuel Call to be appointed to the cutter service (23). The 1903 (24), 1904 (25) and 1905 (26) appropriations laws had listed "surgeons and pilots employed", probably meaning the service was paying civilian doctors as well as harbor pilots. The appropriations law dated June 30, 1906 acknowledges the commissioned surgeon, Call, and two "contract surgeons" (27).

Congress changed the title of Captain of Engineers back to Engineer in Chief on February 26, 1906 (28).

A law of June 23, 1906 created the rank of Cadet Engineer (28a).

A law concerning punishments on revenue cutter was passed on May 26, 1906. It contained the sentence "That no commander of a vessel of the Revenue Cutter Service shall inflict upon any commissioned or warrant officer under his command any other punishment than private reprimand, suspension from duty, arrest, or confinement, and such suspension, arrest, or confinement shall not continue longer than ten days, unless a further period be necessary to bring the offender to trial;" (29). Warrant officers had not been mentioned in conjunction with the cutter service in a long time. The 1891 uniform regulations had listed Boatswains, Gunners and Carpenters, all warrant ranks in the navy, as petty officers (30), and warrant officers had not been mentioned in the appropriations laws. This changed with the appropriations law of June 30, 1906, where the term used was now "warrant and petty officers" (31). There is no law directly creating warrant ranks, but it seams warrant officers had retuned. The same law also added enlisted rates of Ship's Writer and Water tender.

A clear picture of the cutter service's rank structure is presented in a book on the organization of the federal government published in 1908 (31a). Commissioned line officers were listed as Captain, First Lieutenant, Second Lieutenant, Third Lieutenant and Cadet. Non line officers are listed as Engineer-in-Chief, Chief Engineer, Constructor, First Assistant Engineer, Second Assistant Engineer and Cadet Engineer. Warrant ranks are listed as Master's Mate, Boatswain, Gunner, Carpenter and Machinist. Petty officers were divided into two classes, the first class contained the ratings, in order of seniority, of Master at Arms, Electrician, Ship's Writer and Signal Quartermaster, the second class contained the ratings of Assistant Master at Arms, Quartermaster, First and Second

Oiler, Coxswain and Water tender. The non rated rates, again in order of seniority were Seaman, Fireman, Bugler, Ordinary Seaman, Coal Heaver, Cabin Steward, Wardroom Steward, Cook, Steerage Cook, Boy First Class and Bay Second Class.

The service's rank structure was given an overhaul by a law of April 16, 1908. The Captain designated as Chief of the Division of Revenue Cutter Service was given the rank of Captain Commandant that was equal to a navy Captain and an army Colonel. New rank of Senior Captain, equal to a navy Commander or Mary Lieutenant Colonel was created. The law also changed the titles of engineering officers. It is not clear but it seams that six "senior engineers" would hold the rank of Captains of Engineers, Chief Engineers became First Lieutenants of Engineers, First Assistant Engineers became Second Lieutenants of Engineers and Second Assistant Engineers became Third Lieutenants of Engineers (32).

The Commissioned Surgeon disappears from the appropriations laws starting on June 25, 1910 (33), and the two contract surgeons are not in the laws staring on August 24, 1912 (34). Other than that the service's ranks remain consistent thru it's final appropriations law on August 1, 1914 (35).

When the Revenue Cutter Service was combined with the Life Saving Service to form the Coast Guard on January 28, 1915, the cutter service's ranks and the life saving service employees had to be combined into the coat guard's rank structure. The cutter service's rank structure was continued by the law stating "That in the Coast Guard there shall be a captain commandant, senior captains, captains, first lieutenants, second lieutenants, third lieutenants, engineer in chief, captains of engineers, first lieutenants of engineers, second lieutenants of engineers, third lieutenants of engineers and constructors, cadet and cadet engineers, warrant officers, petty officers, and other enlisted men, all of said offices, respectively, corresponding to the present offices of the Revenue-Cutter Service, which are transferred to the Coast Guard, and all the present incumbents, officers and enlisted men, are also transferred to corresponding positions in the Coast Guard" (36). The life saving service had contained a General Superintendent, an Assistant General Superintendent, District Superintendents, Keepers who were in charge of the individual stations and Surfmen who operated the lifeboats and were numbered by seniority (37). The superintendents were given the new commissioned rank of District Superintendent with relative rank by seniority. The 1915 Coast Guard Register shows one District Superintendent with the rank of Captain, three with the rank of First Lieutenant, five with the rank of Second Lieutenant and five with the rank of Third Lieutenant (38). Keeper became a warrant rank of the Coast Guard and the surfmen were enlisted with number one surfmen being rated as petty officers. The 1915 register shows warrant ranks of Master's Mate, Keeper, Boatswain, Gunner, Machinist and Carpenter (38a)

On July 1, 1918 a new law stated "That the President be, and he is hereby, authorized during the period of the present war to promote temporarily, with the advice and consent o the Senate, the captain commandant of the Coast Guard to the rank of commodore in the Navy and brigadier general in the Army, and the engineer in chief of the Coast Guard to the rank of captain in the Navy and colonel in the Army," (39). The temporary ranks were continued after the war, with the Engineer in Chief becoming a relative Commander or Lieutenant Colonel at some point (40).

In 1920 an effort was made to bring the coast guard's rank structure in line with the navy's. First a law of May 18, 1920 stated that "the grades and ratings of warrant officers, chief petty officers, petty officers and other enlisted persons in the Coast Guard shall be the same as in the Navy, in so far as the duties of the Coast Guard may require, with the continuance, in the Coast Guard, of the grade of surfman," (41). The coast guard implemented the law with general order 43 of the same date. Warrant ranks were now to be Boatswain, Gunner, Machinist, Carpenter, Pharmacist, Pay Clerk, Acting Pay Clerk and Sailmaker. The ranks of Master's Mate and Keeper were combined into Boatswain. Enlisted rates were organized into the navy's seven grades plus a separate messman branch. This created the rates of Chief Petty Officer, Petty Officer First Class, Petty Officer Second Class and Petty Officer Third Class with the various ratings divided among them. The other three grades, known as seaman first class, seaman second class and seaman third class, continued the non rated rates (42).

With the enlisted rates and warrant ranks taken care of, Congress moved on to officer's ranks on June 5th. An appropriations law stated "Titles of commissioned officers of the Coast Guard are hereby changed as follows: Senior captain to Commander, captain to Lieutenant commander, first lieutenant to lieutenant, second lieutenant to lieutenant junior grade, third lieutenant to ensign, captain of engineers to lieutenant commander (engineering), first lieutenant of engineers to lieutenant (engineering), second lieutenant of engineers to lieutenant, junior grade (engineering), and third lieutenant of engineers to ensign (engineering)" (43).

A new law of June 10, 1922 (44) made the seven grades into true "pay grades". The pay of enlisted men was now tied to which grade there rate or rating was in. The grades were now numbered one to seven, with one being the highest and seven the lowest.

The ranks of Captain, Captain (Engineering) and Commander (Engineering) were added on January 13, 1923. The same law abolished the rank of Captain Commandant, who had been a Commodore since 1918, and replaced it with an office of commandant who's holder would have the rank of Rear Admiral (Lower Half) (45).

More changes were made to the coast guard's rank structure on July 2, 1926. The title of District Superintendent was changed to District Commander, and Chief Warrant Officers were added (46). This created the ranks of Chief Boatswain, Chief Gunner, Chief Machinist, Chief Carpenter and Chief Pay Clerk (47). The ranks of Lieutenant (Engineering), Lieutenant (Junior Grade) (Engineering), Ensign (Engineering) and Cadet Engineer were abolished, and all personnel in them were transferred to the equivalent line ranks.

When the lighthouse service was merged into the coast guard on August 5, 1939, the law allowed it's personnel to be given ranks, commissioned, warrant or enlisted, according to their ability and seniority (48). The very next law Congress passed abolished the ranks of Constructor and District Commander and placing them in to the equivalent line ranks (49).

During World War II the coast guard was under the control of the navy. There is a noted lack of laws expanding the guard to it's wartime size. This may be due to the guard being covered by the laws governing the size of the navy. The best picture of the wartime coast guard comes from the 1944 Coast Guard Register. It shows the commandant being promoted to Vice Admiral on March 10, 1942, a list of 16 Rear Admirals and four Commodores (50). The navy had revived the rank of Commodore on April 9, 1943 and the law includes the sentence "Personnel of the Coast Guard in relationship to the Coast Guard in the same manner and to the same extent as they apply to personnel of the Navy in relationship to the Navy." (51). The 1944 register no longer lists engineering officers as having a separate rank from line officers.

A law was passed on March 21, 1945 making the commandant a full Admiral (52). The law was to expire six months after the end of the war. On March 23, 1946 the rank was made permanent for the commandant that was serving in 1945 (he had retired by then), and his successor (53).

The post war commissioned rank structure was set by a law of July 23, 1947. The law stated "The commissioned officers shall be distributed in the ranks of rear admiral, captain, commander, lieutenant commander, lieutenant, lieutenant (junior grade), and ensign" (54). The rank of Commodore had been allowed to expire. In it's place the law calls for the coast guard to divide the rank of Rear Admiral in half as the navy had done since 1899, with the upper half being equal to an army Major General and the lower half equal to a Brigadier General. No mention is made of engineering ranks except for the Engineer in Chief who was to be a Rear Admiral (Upper Half).

In 1948 the navy overhauled the rates in the lower three pay grades. A list of rates and ratings of the coast guard (54a) shows that the rates of the coast guard were similar but not exactly the same. The rates of Seaman (grade 5), Seaman Apprentice (grade 6) and Seaman Recruit (grade 7) were the same as were three similar grades of firemen, hospitalmen and dentalmen, with hospitalmen and dentalmen being eliminated in 1982. The navy's three rates of stewardsmen are shown to have existed from a vague 1950s to 1970s and the navy's constuctionman rates are not listed at all. The real confusion comes from the rates of airman. The list is not clear but it appears that the rates of Airman, Airman Apprentice and Airman Recruit did not become part of the coast guard until 1975.

On August 4, 1949, Congress passed Title 14 that laid out the mission, duties and organization of the coast guard. The rank structure was enumerated in chapter three, section 41 that stated "In the Coast Guard there shall be a vice admiral, rear admirals, captains, commanders, lieutenant commanders, lieutenants, lieutenants (junior grade), ensigns, commissioned warrant officers, cadets, warrant officers, and enlisted men. Enlisted men shall be distributed in ratings established by the Secretary." Section 44 made the commandant a Vice Admiral (55).

The Career Compensation Act of October 12, 1949 completely reorganized the rank of all of the uniformed services. All ranks were organized into 19 pay grades. The seven enlisted grades became grades E (for enlisted) -1 to E-7 with E-1 being the lowest and E-7 the highest. Grades W (for warrant) -1 to W-4 were created for warrant ranks with warrant officers placed in W-1 and chief or commissioned warrant officers spread across W-2, W-3 and W-4. Officer pay grades began with an O. Ensigns were placed in O-1, Lieutenants (Junior Grade) in O-2, Lieutenants in O-3, Lieutenant Commanders in O-4, Commanders in O-5, Captains in O-6, Rear Admirals (Lower Half) in O-7 and Rear Admirals (Upper Half) and the Vice Admiral in O-8 (56).

In 1954 congress changed the warrant ranks to Warrant Officer 1 in the W-1 grade, Chief Warrant Officer 2 in the W-2 grade, Chief Warrant Officer 3 in the W-3 grade and Chief Warrant Officer 4 in the W-4 grade (57).

The Career Compensation Act was amended on May 20, 1958 (58) to create the grades of O-9, O-10, E-8 and E-9. Rear Admirals (Upper Half) now had O-8 to themselves while the Vice Admiral moved to O-9. The rate of Senior Chief Petty Officer was added in the E-8 grade and Master Chief Petty Officer in the E-9 grade.

The new grades created a problem for warrant officers. Master Chief Petty Officers who were eligible for promotion to Warrant Officer 1 began turning down the new rank because it involved a pay cut (59). A remedy was attempted in 1967 when all Warrant Officer 1s were given a temporary promotion to Chief Warrant Officer 2. This ended the use of the W-1 grade.

On May 14, 1960, the rank of the commandant was raised to full Admiral and the Assistant Commandant became a Vice Admiral (60)

The rank of Rear Admiral (Lower Half) was changed back to Commodore on October 30, 1984 (61), and changed back again on November 8, 1985 (62).

Chapter 2.
Coast Guard Rank and Rate Insignia

The information on rank distinctions in the early revenue cutter service and even the early coast guard is spotty and incomplete. Fortunately the coast guard has gone to a great deal of effort to assemble the information that is available and place it on their web site. This includes the tireless efforts of retired Chief Boatswain Dana Lewis who has assembled information on warrant and enlisted insignia that is an invaluable research tool.

The earliest information on uniforms of the cutter service comes from Captain N. L. Coste who remembered that in his youth, which he placed in 1819, that officers rank was determined by epaulets worn on various shoulders (1), which was the common system to show rank at the time.

The first known uniform regulations for the cutter service date from 1830. They prescribe blue uniforms with yellow piping and plain gold epaulets, plus an extra cuff button on the cuff for Captains, to show rank (2). Enlisted men are not mentioned, as was the case with navy regulations of the time.

Cuff stripes were introduced in 1833 (3).

The service's uniforms would be changed in 1834 due to an incident in Charleston South Carolina. A group of naval officers from the sloop Natchez attended a grand ball. A particularly dashing revenue cutter captain named William Howard appeared in his dress uniform and made a great impression, which probably means he drew the most attention of the ladies present. The jealous naval officers complained to Secretary of the Navy Levi Woodbury that the service's uniforms were to close the those of the navy. The cutter service was out of Woodbury's jurisdiction until later that year when he was made Secretary of the Treasury. He ordered the service to wear gray uniforms with black piping, however he allowed the officers to keep their epaulets, which had been the main complaint of the naval officers, but the cuffs were decorated by buttons not stripes (4). There is a version of the story that takes place in Boston with the naval officers coming from the frigate Potomac , but if claims to have happened in late 1834 and the uniform change happened on July 21st (5). It is always possible that Howard went to a ball in Boston as well.

Woodbury relented on January 15, 1836 and blue uniforms returned, now with black piping. Uniforms were now prescribed for warrant officers and enlisted men (6).

Shoulder straps were authorized in 1838, to be used when epaulets were not worn (7).

Engineering officers were given uniforms in 1845. They were the same as line officers, without epaulets and with a shield on the collar (8).

The shoulder straps were modified in 1853 to include badges of rank (9).

New uniforms were introduced in 1862. Officers wore a frock coat with gold cuff stripes or buttons for assistant engineers. Line officers wore a gold epaulet on each shoulder or shoulder straps when the epaulets were not worn. Engineering officers wore shoulder straps at all times. Petty officers wore a short jacket and other enlisted men a standard sailor's jumper (10).

Officer's rank distinctions were changed in 1864 to reflect the relative rank with the army and the navy that had been granted the previous year. Army style badges of rank were now worn on the shoulder straps to show the equivalency (11).

Shoulder straps were replaced with badges of rank on the collar in 1871, only to return in 1873 when the badges proved to be unpopular. 1871 also saw badges of rank placed on the epaulets. The badges of rank would return on the service sack coat collar in 1878 (12).

New uniform regulations were issued in 1891. By then the uniform situation had become much more complex. Officers had five different uniform combinations, full dress, social dress, dress, undress and service dress. The full dress uniform consisted of a tail coat, laced trousers and a cocked hat, rank was shown by epaulets and gold cuff stripes. The social dress was a white tie and tails type uniform with gold cuff stripes on the coat. The dress uniform used a frock coat, plain blue or white trousers and a cocked hat or pith helmet, rank was shown by epaulets and gold cuff stripes. The undress uniform consisted of the frock coat, plain blue or white trousers and a blue visored cap or the pith helmet, rank was shown by shoulder straps and gold cuff stripes. The service dress uniform consisted of a blue sack coat with a fly front and standing collar, all outlined in black mohair braid that also covered the collar. In summer a white coat with white braid was used. Both coats could be worn with plain blue or white trousers and the cap or helmet. Rank was shown by badges of rank on the collar of the blue coat, but not on the white coat, and black cuff stripes on the blue coat and white cuff stripes on the white coat, black stripes were also used on the overcoat. Petty officers in the ratings of Boatswain, Gunner, Carpenter and Master at arms wore a blue double breasted sack coat, plain blue trousers and a visored cap. A gold rating badge was worn on the right sleeve. Stewards and Cooks wore a single breasted coat with black buttons. Other enlisted men wore a blue jumper, bellbottoms and a flat cap. White cuff stripes were worn to show rate. A white jumper and bellbottoms could be worn over the blue uniform to serve as overalls. Petty officers wore a white rating badge on the blue jumper and a blue one on the white jumper (12a).

The 1900 regulations added the eagle worn by navy petty officers above all rating badges (13).

The next uniform regulations were in 1908. Epaulets were replaced with shoulder knots and shoulder boards, showing badges of rank, were prescribed for use on the white service coat and overcoat. The cuff stripes on the blue service coat were changed from black to gold, but the overcoat stripes remained black. Boatswains, Gunners and Carpenters, along with Master's Mates and Machinists were now classified as warrant officers. They wore the blue or white service uniforms. The blue coat had a wide black stripe on the cuffs and badges of rank on the collar, the white coat was plain. Masters at Arms were joined by Electricians, Ships Writers and Wheelmen as jacketed petty officers wearing a blue or white double breasted sack coat. Stewards and Cooks wore blue or white single breasted coats and other enlisted men wore blue or white jumpers. Rate was shown by rating badges on the right sleeve for men of the starboard watch and the left sleeve for men of the port watch. Non rated men wore cuff stripes and watch marks (14).

The next available information comes from World War I (15) (16), after the cutter service merged with the life saving service to form the coast guard. The shoulder marks had been changed to duplicate the cuff stripes instead of showing badges of rank, when this happened is not clear. The braid had been removed from the white service coat and it now closed exposed buttons, and warrant officers now wore badges of rank on the collar. Surfmen at life saving stations wore olive drab uniforms.

The guard's uniforms, at least for officers, changed dramatically after the war, but accurate dates of the changes are not averrable. The next uniform regulations available are dated June 24, 1930. It is known that green and khaki aviation uniforms were created in the 1920s, with shoulder boards worn on at least the green uniform (17).

The uniforms of 1930 are almost identical to those of the navy. Commissioned officers were allowed a full dress blue frock coat, a blue service coat, a white service coat, a blue evening coat and were allowed to wear the navy's white mess jacket. Epaulets were worn on the frock coat, having replaced the shoulder knot at some point between 1918 and 1930, the frock coat also carried gold cuff stripes. The new blue service coat was identical to one adopted by the navy in 1919, with two rows of buttons and a rolling collar. Rank was shown by gold cuff stripes and there was no insignia on the collar. Shoulder boards continued to be worn on the white service coat. The evening dress coat showed rank by gold cuff stripes and could be worn with epaulets. The navy used shoulder boards on it's white mess jacket. Aviation officers could also wear green and khaki uniforms with black cuff stripes and badges of rank pined to garrison caps and shirt collars. Overcoats continued to carry black cuff stripes and shoulder boards. Warrant officers wore only the frock coat, the blue and white service coats and the aviation uniforms. Rank was shown by cuff stripes on the blue coats, shoulder boards on the white coat and black cuff stripes on the aviation coats. Chief Petty Officers, Stewards and Cooks wore blue and white double breasted coats with rating badges. Chiefs also were allowed the aviation uniforms. Surfmen wore single breasted coats. Other enlisted men continued to wear blue and white jumpers with rating badges, cuff stripes and branch marks and working uniforms without insignia (18).

On June 18, 1941, the khaki uniform was prescribed as a working uniform for officers, warrant officers and chief petty officers. Instead of black cuff stripes, shoulder boards were worn on the coat by officers and warrant officers, and badges of rank were pinned to the shirt collar (19).

1941 saw the coast guard's uniforms becoming a modification of the navy's uniforms (20). From this we can infer that most of the navy's uniform changes also applied to the coast guard. Even as late as 1970 is was assumed that uniform changes by the navy would eventually be adopted by the coast guard (21). The first of these was the end of the frock coat and epaulets, the navy suspended them at the beginning of World War II and they never returned.

Female uniforms were authorized during World War II. If the coast guard followed the navy's pattern, and there is some photographic evidence that they did (22), officers wore cuff stripes of reserve blue on blue uniforms until they were changed to gold in 1951. Stripes on white coats were dark blue from 1942 to 1948, when they were changed to white. Rated enlisted women wore rating badges and hash marks were prescribed for non rated women (22a).

It is known that the guard adopted the navy's gray working uniform, with gray shoulder boards, in 1943 and abandoned it in 1947 (23).

The navy, and therefore probably the coast guard, removed the black stripes form the overcoat in 1947.

The navy's female hash marks lead to all non rated rates being shown by group rate marks in 1948. Presumably the coast guard followed this practice as well.

The coast guard authorized badges of rank for chief petty officers in 1959 (24).

The cuff stripes for female officers were changed from white to gold in 1960 (25).

In the early 1970s the coast guard and the navy went their separate ways as far a uniforms were concerned. The guard''s new uniforms were closer to the air force than the navy. The basic uniform for all ranks was a medium blue coat and pants/ skirt, worn over a light blue shirt. A light blue shirt and medium blue and pants/ skirt combination was worn in warmer weather and the working uniform was a dark blue shirt and pants. Officers retained the dress white uniforms and white and navy blue evening wear. Gone were enlisted jumpers and officers khakis (26).

The display of rank was, and still is, cuff stripes and shoulder boards for officers and warrant officers, rating badges for chiefs and petty officers and group rate marks for non rated personnel. Badges of rank are worn various uniforms by officers, warrant officers, chiefs and petty officers.

Epaulets

The term epaulet comes from epaulet, the French for shoulder (1). It is often used in the modern world for any shoulder decoration, but here it refers to a specific type of decoration. An epaulet in this context is a strap on the shoulder with fringe at the end called bullion. Above the bullion is a stiffening called a crescent. The area inside the crescent is called the frog and the area from the top of the crescent to the button by the collar is called the strap.

It is possible that epaulets were used to show officer's rank from the beginning of the revenue cutter service. The earliest evidence of epaulets comes from a recollection of Captain N. L. Coste who remembered that in his youth, which he placed in 1819, that officers rank was determined by epaulets worn on various shoulders (2). The system as it stood in 1830, which may have dated all the way back of 1790, was Captains wearing a plain gold epaulet on each shoulder, First Lieutenants one on the right, Second Lieutenants one on the left and Third Lieutenants no epaulets at all (3).

In 1844 a device was placed in the frog of the epaulets to help distinguish revenue officers from naval officers (4). The device was a fouled anchor across the top a the shield of the Treasury Department, which contained scales, a chevron with stars and a key (5).

All ranks began wearing an epaulet on each shoulder in 1853 (6).

The device in the frog was removed in 1862 and the epaulets were once again plain (7).

The 1871 uniform regulations placed an anchor and army style badges of rank in the frog. Captains wore a gold oak leaf, First Lieutenants two gold bars, Second Lieutenants one gold bar and Third Lieutenants no badge (8). It is not clear if epaulets were worn by engineering officers. If they did, a four bladed propellor was probably worn instead of the anchor with two bars for Chief Engineers, one for First Assistant Engineers and none for Second Assistants.

The 1891 uniform regulations prescribe epaulets for all officers, including engineers. They were described as "All commissioned officers shall wear two gold-bullion epaulets of the following dimensions: The strap to be 2 1/2 inches wide and 6 inches long; crescent nine sixteenths of an inch in broadest part; bullions 3 inches long and three eighths of an inch in diameter. When overcoats are worn, epaulets will be dispensed with.". A gold anchor with a silver american shield, with stars and stripes, was worn in the center of the frog by line officers, and the propellor by engineers, with the leafs and bars on either side (9).

It is not clear how long these epaulets were worn. By the 1908 uniform regulations they had been replaced by shoulder knots (10). The knots continued at least thru 1918 (11).

The next information we have, comes from the 1930 coast guard uniform regulations. Epaulets had returned to replace shoulder knots. Bullion was 3 1/2 inches long and 5/8 inches wide for a Rear Admiral or Commodore (meaning the Commandant), 3 inches long and 1/2 inch wide for Captains and Commanders and 3 inches long and 3/8 inches wide for junior officers. A single badge of rank was worn in the frog. Two silver stars for the Rear Admiral Commandant, one star would have been worn for a Commodore if there was one, a silver eagle for Captains, a silver oak leaf for Commanders, a gold oak leaf for Lieutenant Commanders, two silver bars for Lieutenants, one silver bar for Lieutenants (Junior Grade) and one gold bar for Ensigns. A silver anchor, without a shied, was worn on the strap (12).

If the coast guard followed the navy's pattern, use of the epaulets was suspended for World War II and they never returned.

Shoulder Straps

The cutter service began wearing shoulder straps in 1838. They began as a strip of gold lace worn over the epaulet to help keep it in place. When the epaulet was removed the strap itself showed rank. Captains would have worn a strap on both shoulders, First Lieutenants one the right and Second Lieutenants one on the left (1).

In 1853 shoulder straps became a gold rectangle with a blue center worn on both shoulders (2). Captains wore a gold treasury shield on an anchor in the center with a star above and below and two gold bars at each end of the strap. First Lieutenants wore only one bar at each end, Second Lieutenants wore the same without the stars and Third Lieutenants wore only the anchor and shield (3).

The straps were changed in 1862 (4). Captains now wore plain crossed anchors, First Lieutenants wore the treasury shield and anchor with two bars at each end, Second Lieutenants wore one bar, Third Lieutenants wore just the anchor and shield, Chief Engineers wore a gold paddle wheel on an anchor in the center of the strap, First Assistnat Engineers wore just the paddle wheel and Second Assistant Engineers wore an empty frame (5).

The 1864 uniform regulations altered the straps to reflect the revenue cutter officer's new relative rank with army and navy officers (6). Captains retained the crossed anchors in the center and added a gold oak leaf at each end. Lieutenants now wore an anchor covered with three stars in the center. First Lieutenants wore two gold bars at each end, Second Lieutenants one and Third Lieutenants none. Chief Engineers continued to wear the anchor and paddle wheel and added two gold bars at each end. First Assistant Engineers wore the paddle wheel with one gold bar at each end and Second Assistants continued to wear plain straps (7).

The straps were replaced with badges of rank on the collar in 1871. This proved unpopular and shoulder straps retuned in 1873 (8). The new straps saw the return of the treasury shield and anchor in the center for line officers and the use of a four bladed propellor for engineers. Badges of rank were worn at each end, or not in the case of Third Lieutenants and Second Assistant Engineers (9).

The 1891 uniform regulations describe shoulder straps as "For all commissioned officers, the shoulder strap shall be 4 1/2 inches long and 1 1/2 inches wide, including the border, which is to be a quarter of an inch wide embroidered in dead gold. The center to be of dark navy blue cloth, upon which are to be embroidered the corps and rank devices as follows: For Captains: At each end, a gold oak leaf 5/8 of an inch long, and in the center a gold embroidered foul anchor, 1 1/4 inches long, with a 5/8 inch shield embroidered in silver on the shank, and perpendicular to the crown of the anchor. For First Lieutenants: At each end, two gold bars 3/4 of an inch long and 1/4 of an inch wide; center same as for captains, For Second Lieutenants: Same as for first lieutenants, omitting one bar at each end of the frogs of the epaulets and of the shoulder straps. For Third Lieutenants: Same as for second lieutenants, omitting the bars. For Engineers: Same rank devices as are prescribed for line officers with whom they have relative rank, and substituting for the foul anchor and shield prescribed for line officers, a silver wheel, 7/8 of an inch in diameter, four bladed, with a gold embroidered boss.". The shield was an american shield with stars and stripes instead of the treasury shield (10).

This is the last were hear of shoulder straps. They are not included in the 1908 uniform regulations, and information in-between is scarce.

Shoulder Knots

The 1908 uniform Regulations prescribe shoulder knots instead of epaulets. It is not clear when wear of these knots began.

The knots are described as "For all commissioned officers, to be made of three strands of gold-wire cord 3/16 inch in diameter; to consist of a twisted strap of three loops terminating in an oval-shaped pad; to be about 5 3/4 inches long; the pad and two lower loops to be backed with plain gold-wire lace (no vellums); the knot to be slightly stiffened with a flexible backing, which will be covered with dark blue cloth. The corps and rank devices prescribed for the collar of the blue service coat, of reduced size, shall be embroidered on the gold lace in the center of the pad, the rank device toward the front, and for fastening to the coat the knot is to be provided with a strap about 1 inch wide of same material as the back covering, sewed about 3/4 inch from lower end, passing through cloth loops on coat, and secured at upper loop by small revenue-cutter service screw button; all as per pattern." (1). The badges of rank, or rank devices as they are referred to, in 1908 were a silver eagle for the Captain Commandant, a silver oak leaf for Senior Captains and the Engineer in Chief, a gold oak leaf for Captains and Captains of Engineers, two gold bars for First Lieutenants, Constructors and First Lieutenants of Engineers, one gold bar for Second Lieutenants and Second Lieutenants of Engineers and no insignia for Third Lieutenants on Third Lieutenants of Engineers. The corps device was a gold anchor with a silver american shield for line officers, crossed oak branches for engineers and a branch of oak leafs for constructors.

The next information we have comes from 1918. The coast guard was still using the knots, but they no longer showed rank, the pad showed only the corps device with the shield of the line for all officers (2).

It is not clear when use of the knots ended, however they are not in the 1930 uniform regulations.

Shoulder Boards

Shoulder boards are prescribed by the 1908 uniform regulations. The navy began using them in 1899 but when the cutter service began to use them is not clear.

They consisted of a rectangle of stiffened blue cloth with a point at one end and a button near the point. The corps device was worn just below the button and badges of rank were worn at the outer end. They were worn on white service coats and overcoats (1). The badges of rank, or rank devices as they are referred to, in 1908 were a silver eagle for the Captain Commandant, a silver oak leaf for Senior Captains and the Engineer in Chief, a gold oak leaf for Captains and Captains of Engineers, two gold bars for First Lieutenants, Constructors and First Lieutenants of Engineers, one gold bar for Second Lieutenants and Second Lieutenants of Engineers and no insignia for Third Lieutenants on Third Lieutenants of Engineers. The corps device was a gold anchor with a silver american shield for line officers, crossed oak branches for engineers and a branch of oak leafs for constructors.

Sometime between 1908 (2) and 1917 (3) the boards were changed to reflect the cuff stripes. The Captain Commandant wore four gold 1/2 inch stripes, Senior Captains three 1/2 inch stripes, Captains two 1/2 inch stripes with a 1/4 inch stripe between them, First Lieutenants wore two 1/2 inch stripes, Second lieutenants one 1/2 inch stripe under one 1/4 inch stripe and Third Lieutenants one 1/2 inch stripe. An american shield was worn above the top stripe. Engineering officers, constructors and district superintendents wore the stripes of their equivalent rank without the shield. Constructors wore light brown velvet cloth between the stripes and district superintendents light green, the colors were used as piping if there was only one stripe.

If the coast guard followed the navy's pattern, when the commandant was made a Commodore in 1918 he would have worn shoulder boards covered with a strip of gold lace running long ways down the middle of the board with a silver anchor, possibly with a silver shield, near the button and a silver star at the outer end. Two stars would have been worn by the commandant after he became a Rear Admiral in 1923. The 1930 uniform regulations prescribe an anchor without a shield (4). It is not clear when the shield returned the anchor, but it was there during World War II (5).

When the coast guard's officer ranks were made the same as the navy's in 1920, the stripes on the boards would have become, three 1/2 inch stripes for Commanders, two with a 1/4 inch between them for Lieutenant Commanders, two 1/2 stripes for Lieutenants, one under one 1/4 inch stripe for Lieutenants Junior Grade and one alone for Ensigns. Four 1/2 inch stripes would have been worn by Captains when the rank was added in 1923.

Green shoulder boards with black stripes and shields were worn on the green aviation uniform developed in the 1920s (5a), but were replaced by cuff stripes by 1930.

Warrant officers began wearing shoulder boards in the 1920s. Eventually chief warrant officers wore a 1/2 inch stripe with a blue break in the center and warrant officers wore a 1/4 inch stripe with the break. An american shield was worn above the stripes and a specialty mark above the shield (6). When this design began is not clear. Chief warrant officers were not authorized until 1926, and warrant officers stripes may have been unbroken in the early 20s (6a).

Shoulder boards were added to the aviation khaki uniform when it was expanded to the entire coast guard in 1941 (7).

When the guard adopted the navy's gray uniform in 1943, it was to use special gray shoulder boards (8). They were made of gray cloth with a rounded ends and no button. They were more of a trapezoidal shape, with the sides at a slight angle. Admirals wore black stars, anchor and shield, and other officers wore black stripes with a black shield (9). The uniform was eliminated in 1947 (10).

As the rank of the commandant rose and the number of other admirals increased, shoulder boards were prescribed for the ranks of Vice Admiral (three stars in a triangle) and Admiral (four stars in a diamond).

Shoulder boards were placed on the white shirts of male tropical uniforms in 1956 (11).

Also in 1956 the shoulder boards for warrant officers had to be modified to show four ranks instead of two. W-4s continued to wear the 1/2 inch stripe with one 1/2 inch blue break. W-3s were given two breaks and W-2s three breaks. W-1s wore 1/4 inch stripe with three breaks (12).

The change to the new uniforms in the 1970s caused the background color of the shoulder boards to become a lighter blue, otherwise the design remained the same (13).

Shoulder Marks

What we will call shoulder marks are now referred to by the coast guard as enhanced shoulder boards. This refers to a scaled down version of the shoulder boards that are applied to an open ended tube of cloth that can be slipped over a cloth shoulder loop of a shirt or sweater.

In 1991 the new air force style shirts with shoulder loops were introduced. Either "soft shoulder boards" or "enhanced shoulder boards'" were to be worn on the new shirts (1). It is not clear what the difference between the two was. It is possible that "enhanced" boards had a point at the end that covered the button of the shoulder loop.

By the 2003 uniform regulations, the term enhanced shoulder boards referred to the to only the tube type insignia (2).

Badges of Rank

Badges of rank is the term we shall use for the stars, eagles, leafs and bars used by officers and warrant officers, and the, mostly, pin on insignia used by enlisted personnel. We will use "badge of rank" for enlisted insignia, even though "badge of rate" would be correct.

The first use of badges of rank by the revenue cutter service was in 1845 when engineering officers were ordered to wear a treasury shield on the collar, gold for Chief Engineers and silver for assistants (1). It is not clear how long these badges were worn, but they were gone by 1862 (2).

Gold bars, Two for Captains and one for First and Second Lieutenants, were placed at the ends of shoulder straps in 1853 (3). This became two bars for First Lieutenants one for Second Lieutenants and none for Third Lieutenants in 1862. Captains were identified by crossed anchors in the center of the straps, Chief Engineers wore a gold paddle wheel on an anchor in the center of the strap and First Assistant Engineers wore just the paddle wheel (4).

The coming of relative rank with army and navy officers in 1863 lead to the equivalent badges of rank on the shoulder straps in 1864 (5). Captains wore a gold oak leaf, First Lieutenants and Chief Engineers two gold bars, Second Lieutenants one, First Assistant Engineers one bar and Third Lieutenants no bars (6).

Badges of rank moved from shoulder straps to collars in 1871 (7), the letters U.S.R.M. were arched over a fouled anchor for line officers or a propellor for engineers. Captains wore the gold oak leaf between the anchor and the letters, First Lieutenants wore the two gold bars running horizontally, Second Lieutenants one bar and Third Lieutenants no bars. Engineers wore the propellor in the arch of the letters with two gold bars for Chief Engineers and probably one bar for first assistants and none for second assistants (8). The badges were hated by officers and many refused to wear them, claiming they were to small to be seen from a distance. Their complaints were heeded and the badges were removed in 1873, and shoulder straps returned (9).

Badges were also placed in the frog of the epaulets in 1871.

Badges of rank were added to the collar of service dress sack coats in 1878 (10). The leafs and bars were worn behind a treasury shield or propellor (11).

The 1891 Uniform Regulations changed the treasury shield for line officers to a gold fouled anchor with a silver american shield superimposed on it. Engineers wore a silver propellor with a gold boss. The badge of rank was worn in front of the anchor or propellor (12).

The 1908 uniform regulations show badges of rank on shoulder knots, that had replaced epaulets, shoulder boards, that had replaced shoulder straps and on the collars f the service coats. New ranks had brought new badges, the Captain Commandant wore a silver eagle, Senior Captains and the Engineer in Chief a silver oak leaf and Constructors two gold bars. A corps device was worn behind the badges on the collar and shoulder knots and above on the shoulder boards, consisting of a gold fouled anchor with a silver american shield superimposed for line officers, crossed oak branches for engineers and a branch of oak leafs for constructors. Badges were also worn on the collar by warrant officers. Master's Mates wore crossed gold anchors and a silver american shield, Boatswains just the crossed anchors, Gunners a gold bursting bomb, Carpenters a gold chevron representing a carpenter's square and Machinists a gold three bladed propellor (13).

The next information we have comes from 1918. The badges were no longer worn on the shoulder knots or shoulder boards, and the anchor on the collar ah become silver with the shield or device in gold. The bars for lieutenants and equivalent were now silver. Keepers wore a badge of a lifesaver and crossed oars in gold on dress uniforms and bronze on green service uniforms (14).

When the commandant was made a Commodore in 1918, he wore a badge of rank of one silver star (15).

The standing collar service coat with badges on the collar was abolished after World War I (16).

By the 1930 uniform regulations epaulets with badges of rank had returned. They were worn alone in the frog. The commandant, now a Rear Admiral, wore two silver stars and Ensigns wore a gold bar. The badges were also placed on the shirt collars and garrison caps, with chief warrant officers and warrant officers wearing their specialty device, which now include an oak sprig for Pay Clerks, three lightning bolts for Radio Electricians, a globe for Electricians and a diamond for a Sailmaker. Chief warrant ranks wore silver badges and warrant ranks gold badges (17).

The khaki aviation uniform, and badges of rank on the shirt collars and caps, was expanded to the entire coast guard on June 18, 1841 (18).

As the rank of the commandant rose, Vice Admirals were ordered to wear three silver stars, Admirals four silver stars.

Between 1930 and the end of World War II, warrant badges were added consisting of a caduceus for Pharmacists, crossed quills for ship's clerks and a camera for photographers (19).

In the early 1950s, probably at the same time as the navy in 1952, the warrant officers were given a standard badge of rank consisting of a gold bar with a 1/8 inch wide blue stripe running across it the short way for chief warrant officers and a 1/16 inch wide stripe for warrant officers (20).

In 1954 new insignia was prescribed for the now four grades of Warrant Officer. A "unified system" common to all armed forces was developed using the same pattern for each equivalent rank. The enameled portions would very by branch of service, brown for the army, dark blue for the Navy and Coast Guard, scarlet red for the Marine Corps, and sky blue for the Air Force. The new bars were rectangular, silver for the top two grades and gold for the other two. The enameled portion for W-1 and W-3 would be in two rectangles, showing only one stripe of gold or silver. For W-2 and W-4 there would be three enameled portions showing two sections of gold or silver (21).

In 1959 Chief Petty Officers were given badges of rank consisting of a gold fouled anchor and the silver shield. The insignia was the same for all three ranks of chief petty officer. This changed in 1961 when a silver star was added to the top of the anchor for senior chiefs and two stars for master chiefs (22).

The navy granted petty officers badges of rank in 1969 of a silver eagle with the three silver chevrons was prescribed for Petty Officers First Class, two chevrons for second class and one for third class. It is probable that the coast guard wore these badges as well.

At some point, probably with the 1970s uniform change, the badges of rank for petty officers became gold chevrons under a silver shield (23).

Cuff Stripes (and buttons)

The navy had showed rank by buff buttons since 1797, and it is possible that the cutter service wore them as well. The first known evidence of cuff buttons comes from the 1830 uniform regulations. Captains were prescribed four buttons and First Lieutenants "the same omitting one button on the cuff", meaning three buttons. The sections for second and third lieutenants both contain the phrase "the same omitting one button on the cuff" as well (1). The problem is that it doesn't say what they are the same as. This might mean that the Second Lieutenant's cuffs had two buttons, one fewer than First Lieutenants, and Third Lieutenants wore one buttons, one fewer than Second Lieutenants. On the other hand it might of meant the same as a Captain, meaning all three grades of lieutenant wore three buttons.

In 1833 the buttons were replaced with gold stripes. Captains wore one 1 inch stripe, First Lieutenants one 1/2 inch Stripe, Second Lieutenants wore, oddly, two 1/2 inch stripes and Third Lieutenants three 1/4 inch stripes (2).

The buttons returned the next year when the service was forced into gray uniforms. Once again Captains wore four buttons, now with a strip of black braid above them. Three buttons were worn by all three grade of lieutenant, First and Second Lieutenants wore the black braid, Third Lieutenants did not. The system continued after blue uniforms returned in 1836 (3).

When engineering officers were added in 1845, Chief Engineers wore the uniform of a First Lieutenants (three buttons and black stripe) and Assistant Engineers wore the uniform of a Third Lieutenant (three buttons and no stripe) (4).

The button system of 1834 lasted until 1862 when Captains were ordered to wear two 1/2 inch gold stripes and all lieutenants and Chief Engineers one, assistant Engineers wore three buttons (5).

The system was changed again in 1864. Captains were given four 1/2 inch stripes with an extra gap between the top one and the next one down and a national shield above the stripes. First Lieutenants wore three evenly spaced stripes, Second Lieutenants two and Third Lieutenants one all under the shield. Chief Engineers wore three stripes, first assistants two and second assistants one, all without the shield (6).

The next available information comes from the 1891 uniform regulations. The system was the same as in 1864 but the stripes were only 1/4 inch wide. Black stripes, without the shield, were worn on the blue service coat and overcoat and white braid may have been worn the white service coat. Enlisted men holding the rates of Quartermaster, Coxswain and Oiler wore three 3/16 inch wide white stripes on the cuffs of their jumpers, Seamen, Firemen and Coal Passers wore two and Boys one (7). It should be noted that enlisted men in the navy began wearing stripes in 1866, therefore enlisted men in the cutter service may have worn them long before 1891.

New cuff stripes were prescribed for officers in 1900. Captains were prescribed two thick stripes, probably 1/2 inch, with two thin stripes, probably 1/4 inch, between them, First Lieutenants wore a thick stripe under two thin stripes, Second Lieutenants wore one thick stripe under one thin stripe and Third Lieutenants wore one thick stripe. A national shield continued to be worn above the stripes. Presumably engineers wore the stripes of their equivalent rank without the shield, and Constructors probably did wear the shield (8). Shields were worn above the stripes of the blue service coats in 1900, and it is possible that the stripes were now gold (9).

In 1905 the stripes were changed again to reflect the relative rank of revenue officers with army and navy officers. Captains now wore the two 1/2 inch stripes with one 1/4 inch stripe between of a navy Lieutenant Commander. First Lieutenants now wore the two 1/2 inch stripes of a navy Lieutenant. Second Lieutenants now wore the one 1/2 inch stripe under one 1/4 inch stripe of a navy Lieutenant (Junior Grade) and Third Lieutenants wore the one 1/2 inch stripe of an Ensign (10). Line officers wore the shield above the stripes and engineers, who now held the ranks of captain or lieutenant of engineers, did not, Constructors probably did.

The 1908 uniform regulations prescribed stripes for new ranks, The Captains Commandant wore the four 1/2 inch stripes of a navy Captain and Senior Captains and the Engineer in Chief wore the three 1/2 inch stripes of a navy Commander. On their blue coats, warrant officers were ordered to wear a 2 inch wide black stripe. Petty officers rated as Signal Quartermasters, First Oilers, Assistant Masters at Arms, Quartermasters, Coxswains, Second Oilers and Water Tenders, along with Seamen and Firemen wore three stripes on the jumper cuff, Buglers, Ordinary Seamen and Coal Heavers two and Boys one. Vertical stripes joined the ends of the stripes if there was more than one (11).

The 1908 revenue cutter service uniform regulations did not prescribe a 2 inch wide white stripe on the warrant officers white coat, but the 1916 coast guard uniform regulations did along with a green stripe on the green coats worn by Keepers (12).

By 1918 District Superintendents were wearing light green cloth between the stripes or as piping when there was only one and Constructors wore brown (13). It is not clear when this began.

If the coast guard followed the navy's pattern, when the commandant became a Commodore in 1918, he would have worn one 2 inch gold stripe under the shield.

When the coast guard's officer ranks were made the same as the navy's in 1920, the other stripes would have become, three 1/2 inch for Commanders, two with a 1/4 inch between them for Lieutenant Commanders, two 1/2 stripes for Lieutenants, one under one 1/4 inch stripe for Lieutenants Junior Grade and one alone for Ensigns. Four 1/2 inch stripes would have been worn by Captains when the rank was added in 1923.

In the 1920s warrant officers began to wear gold cuff stripes. There is a photograph (14) that shows what appears to be a 1/4 inch wide unbroken gold stripe with an american shield over it and a specialty mark, the bursting bomb of a gunner in this case, over the shield. Chief warrant officers were authorized in 1926 and the stripes may, or may not, have changed at that point. Whenever the changed happened it is reflected in the 1930 uniform regulations. Chief warrant officers wore a 1/2 inch gold stripe with 1/2 inch blue breaks every 2 inches, and warrant officers wore the same in a 1/4 inch stripe. An american shield was worn above the stripes and the specialty mark above the shield (15).

Since the enlisted ratings were made the same as the navy in 1920, the cuff strips would have reflected the navy's grades. Petty officers and those in the Seaman First Class grade wore three stripes, those in the Seaman Second Class grade wore two stripes and those in the Seaman Third Class grade wore one stripe.

Black stripes were worn on the aviation green and khaki uniforms under the 1930 uniform regulations (16). The green coat had carried shoulder boards in the 1920s and it is not clear when the black stripes began. It is also not clear how the broken stripes of warrant officers were handled. The navy used solid stripes until 1944 or at least there is some evidence they did) when green breaks were added. The black stripes were replaced by shoulder boards on the khaki coat in 1941 (17). How long the green stripes lasted is not clear.

The commandant would have begun wearing one 2 inch stripe under one 1/2 inch stripe when he became a Rear Admiral in 1923. This would have continued to one 2 inch stripe under two 1/2 inch stripes for a Vice Admiral in 1942 and one 2 inch stripe under three 1/2 inch stripes for a full Admiral in 1945.

Female uniforms were authorized during World War II. If the coast guard followed the navy's pattern, and there is some photographic evidence that they did (18), officers wore cuff stripes of reserve blue on blue uniforms until they were changed to gold in 1951. Stripes on white coats were dark blue from 1942 to 1948, white from 1948 to 1960 (19) and gold from 1960 to sometime between 1985 (20) and 1997 (21), when they were replaced with shoulder boards.

The black stripes that had been worn on the overcoat since at least 1891 were probably removed in 1947.

The navy replaced enlisted cuff stripes with group rate marks in 1948 and the coast guard probably followed suit (22).

The stripes for warrant officers were changed in 1954 to reflect four ranks instead of two. W-4s wore a 1/2 inch stripe with one blue break, W-3 had two breaks, two inches apart and W-2s three breaks, two inches apart. W-1s wore a 1/4 inch stripe with three breaks (23).

Petty Officer's Devices and Rating Badges

Under the 1862 uniform regulations, petty officers were distinguished by blue jackets instead of the standard enlisted jumper (1).

The next information we have come from the 1891 uniform regulations. The ratings of Boatswain, Gunner, Carpenter and Master at Arms wore a double breasted sack coat instead of the jumper with a gold specialty mark on the right upper sleeve. The ratings of Quartermaster, Coxswain and Oiler did wear the jumper with a white specialty mark on the blue dress jumper and in blue on the white working jumper (2).

A navy petty officer's eagle with it's wings pointing up was added above the specialty mark under the 1900 regulations (3).

Under the 1908 uniform regulations the "jacketed" ratings of Master at Arms, Electrician, Electrician First Class, Ship's Writer and Wheelman were allowed both a blue and white coat. On the blue coat three gold chevrons were worn point down with arc over the top chevron with the eagle embroidered in gold resting on the arc and the specialty mark embroidered in silver under the arc. On the white coat the entire badge was rendered in dark blue. The ratings of Signal Quartermaster and First Oiler wore three white chevrons outlined in scarlet piping under the eagle and specialty mark that were white on blue clothing and blue on white clothing. Assistant Masters at Arms. Quartermasters, Coxswains, Second Oilers and Watertenders wore only two chevrons under the white/blue eagle and specialty mark. Buglers, who were not petty officers, wore a bugle in red on blue and blue on white (4). This is the basic design of rating badges worn by navy petty officers since 1894, but the colors were unique to the cutter service.

As far as is known the rating badges remained the same until the cutter service became the coast guard in 1915. The 1916 uniform regulations prescribe scarlet chevrons with white eagles and specialty marks on blue uniforms and all blue on white uniforms and the olive drab uniforms worn at lifesaving stations. Petty officers with 12 years good conduct were allowed to wear gold chevrons with a silver eagle and specialty mark on blue uniforms (5). The three chevrons and one arc were now worn by Masters at Arms, Number one Surfmen, Electricians, Electricians First Class, Yeomen, Ship's Writers, Wheelmen, Machinists First Class and Carpenters First Class. Three chevrons were worn by Painters First Class, Plumbers First Class, Signal Quartermasters, Oilers First Class Blacksmiths and

Sailmakers. Two Chevrons were worn by Assistant Masters at Arms, Quartermasters, Electricians Second Class, Oilers Second Class, Carpenters Second Class, Painters Second Class, Plumbers Second Class, Coxswains and Watertenders. One Chevrons was worn by Electricians Third Class and Baymen. Buglers continued to wear the red/blue bugle (6).

When the coast guard's ratings were made identical to the navy's in 1920, the chevrons were applied to the navy's pay grades. The three chevrons and one arc was worn by Chief Petty Officers, the three chevrons by Petty Officers First Class, the two chevrons by Petty Officers Second Class and the one chevron by Petty Officers Third Class. The rating badges were worn on the right sleeve by ratings in the seaman branch and on the left arm by other ratings (7).

In 1941 the eagles for ratings of the seaman branch had their heads reversed to face right, making all eagles face the wearers front (8).

The use of rating badges by the coast guard on the green and khaki aviation uniforms of the 1920s and 1930s and the khaki uniforms thereafter is far from clear. The 1930 uniform regulations calls for rating badges to be "to be those prescribed by the Regulations" (9). That tells us nothing about what colors were to be used. The coast guard may have followed the navy practice, but even that is not clear until 1944 when all blue badges were ordered to be worn on all but blue uniforms. This included the gray uniforms adopted during the war. The navy changed the eagle and specialty mark on the khaki coat to silver in 1949, and the coast guard did follow suit (9a).

1948 saw the end of rating badges on the right sleeve. From then on all ratings wore the badge on the left sleeve with the eagle facing forward (10).

When the rates of Senior Chief Petty Officer and Master Chief Petty Officer were added in 1958, stars, the same color as the eagle, were added above the badge, one for senior chiefs and two for master chiefs (11).

The uniform change of the 1970s eliminated enlisted white uniforms and the need for all blue rating badges. Chiefs were allowed a white mess jacket with a gold/ silver rating badge. The dates are not certain but the new uniforms appear to have eliminated the gold chevrons for good conduct. Chiefs now wore gold chevrons and arc with a silver eagle, stars and specialty mark and other petty officers scarlet chevrons and a white eagle and specialty mark (12).

Group Rate Marks

The navy created what became group rate marks in 1944 when a method was developed to show the rate of non rated women who didn't wear jumpers with cuff stripes. The solution was two or three hash marks on the upper sleeve to represent the two or three cuff stripes, no mark represented one stripe (1). The coast guard also used these mark, and may have used red stripes for female Firemen (2).

The navy adopted the hash mark stripes in 1948 as the insignia for the lower three pay grades replacing cuff stripes and branch marks (3), and the coast guard probably adopted them at the same time.

The navy's system was three white/ blue stripes for Seamen, Hospitalmen, Dentalmen and Stewardsmen, three red stripes for Firemen, three light blue stripes for Constructionmen and three green stripes for Airmen. Hospitalmen wore a caduceus over the stripes, Dentalmen wore a caduceus and letter D and Stewardsmen a crescent. Seamen Apprentices, Hospitalmen Apprentices, Dentalmen Apprentices, Stewardsmen Apprentices, Firemen Apprentices, Constructionmen Apprentices and Airman Apprentices wore the same colors and badges with two stripes and Seaman Recruits, Hospitalmen Recruits, Dentalmen Recruits, Strewardsmen Recruits, Firemen Recruits, Constructionmen Recruits and Airman Recruits the same with one stripe. A list of rates and ratings for the coast guard (4) creates some confusion as to which of these rates were used by the coast guard and when, but the system was probably the same.

The stewardsman rates were eliminated in the 1970s and the hospital and dental rates in 1982 (5). It is not clear how long the coast guard has used the airman rates, they may have not been used until 1975.

Watch Marks and Branch Marks

The navy began using watch marks in 1866 to show what side of a ship that a man was assigned to. In 1886 they became a strip of cloth tape around the shoulder seam of the jumper of non petty officers to show not only what side of the ship they belonged on, but also helping to show their rate with firemen wearing red tape instead of white/blue tape.

As far as is known, the cutter service began wearing similar watch marks in 1908. The 1908 uniform regulations describe them as "To be worn on the overshirt and undress jumper by all enlisted men except petty officers. To consist of a strip of braid 3/8 inch wide, white on overshirts and blue on undress jumpers, placed on the shoulder seam of the sleeve and extending entirely around the arm. For firemen and coal heavers the braid to be red on both blue and white clothes and of the same width and disposition as above. Men of the starboard watch will wear the mark on the right sleeve; those of the port watch on the left sleeve." (1).

The navy changed watch marks to branch marks in 1912 and the coast guard's 1916 uniform regulations refer to them that way. They were no longer used to show what side of the ship a man was assigned to. All branch marks were worn on the right side with the engine room force wearing red and all other non petty officers wearing white/blue, except Buglers and Mess Boys who did not wear branch marks at all (2).

It is not clear if the coast guard ever adopted the navy's system of the branch mark on the right for the seaman branch and the left for other branches. However they did adopt the navy's system for what side petty officers rating badges were worn on in 1920 (3), therefore they probably did adopt the navy's branch mark system as well.

The coast guard probably followed the navy in replacing enlisted cuff stripe and branch marks with group rate marks in 1948.

Chapter 3.
Coast Guard Ranks and Rates

Admiral

The title "admiral" comes from the Arabic Amir-al-Bahr or leader of the sea. The Romans used the term Sarraccenorum Admirati which led to the Latin Admiralius and was then corrupted to the Anglo Admyrall (1). For clarity Admirals are sometimes referred to as "full" Admirals.

Neither the revenue cutter service or the coast guard were large enough to require a full Admiral until the commandant, Russell Waesche, was given the rank under a law of March 21, 1945 (2). The law stated that it would expire six month after the end of the World War II.

Waesche would have worn similar insignia as navy Admirals one two inch stripe under three 1/2 inch stripes under an american shield on the cuffs, four silver stars in a diamond on the outer end on the shoulder boards and four silver stars as a badge of rank (3).

Waesche retired on December 31, 1945 (4), but was allowed to regain his rank under a law of March 23, 1946 (5) that rewarded senior officers from the war It stated. Waesche died on October 17, 1946.

Waesche's replacement was Joseph Farley who became a full Admiral upon taking the office of Commandant on January 1, 1946 under both the 1945 and 1946 laws (6).

Laws laying out the post war structure of the coast guard were passed on July 23, 1947 (7) and August 4, 1949 (8). The 1947 law listed Rear Admiral as the guard's highest rank and the 1949 specified that the commandant be a Vice Admiral. Neither law had any immediate effect until Farley retired on January 1, 1950 (9), and his successor Merlin O'Neill took office as a Vice Admiral. O'Neill was allowed to retire as a full Admiral in 1954 under a 1925 law that moved long serving officers up one grade on retirement (10).

The Career Compensation Act of October 12, 1949 (11) placed the rank of Admiral in pay grade O-8 which it shared with Vice Admiral and Rear Admiral (Upper Half). This lasted until May 20, 1958 when a new law (12) created pay grade O-10 for full Admirals.

O'Neill's successor, Alfred Richmond, remained a Vice Admiral until May 14, 1960 when a new law (13) permanently made the commandant a full Admiral.

An illustration in the 2009 uniform regulations shows that the insignia for an Admiral continues to be one two inch stripe under three 1/2 inch stripes under an american shield on the cuffs, four silver stars in a diamond on the outer end on the shoulder boards and four silver stars as a badge of rank (14).

Airman

The navy created the rate of Airman from the rate of Seaman First Class in 1948 (1) in grade five, which became grade E-3 in 1949 (2). It is not clear if the coast guard started to use the rate at the same time. A list of all the coast guard's rates and ratings compiled in 1993 (3) shows, but not clearly, that Airmen began in 1975.

Whenever they began, Airmen wear a group rate mark of three green hash marks (4).

Airman Apprentice

The navy created the rate of Airman Apprentice from the rate of Seaman Second Class in 1948 (1) in grade six, which became grade E-2 in 1949 (2). It is not clear if the coast guard started to use the rate at the same time. A list of all the coast guard's rates and ratings compiled in 1993 (3) shows, but not clearly, that Airman Apprentices began in 1975.

Whenever they began, Airman Apprentices wear a group rate mark of two green hash marks (4).

Airman Recruit

The navy created the rate of Airman Recruit in 1948 (1) in grade seven, which became grade E-1 in 1949 (2). It is not clear if the coast guard started to use the rate at the same time. A list of all the coast guard's rates and ratings compiled in 1993 (3) shows, but not clearly, that Airmen Recruit began in 1975.

They would have worn a group rate mark of one green hash mark.

It is also unclear when the coast guard abolished the rate of Airman Recruit. It still existed under the 1993 rate and rating list (4), but is gone by the 1997 uniform regulations (5), that only shows the white mark of a Seaman Recruit.

Apprentice Seaman

When the rates and ratings of the coast guard were made the same as the navy's by law on May 18, 1920 (1), the rate of Seaman Apprentice was created in the Seaman Third Class pay grade (2).

They wore one stripe on the cuff of the jumpers and a white/blue watch mark or branch mark (3).

The Seaman Third Class or Nonrated man third class pay grade officially became grade seven on June 10, 1922 (4).

Apprentice Seamen became Seamen Recruit in 1948 (5).

Area Command Master Chief Petty Officer

The 2009 uniform regulations include a rating badge for Command Master Chief of an area (1).

The coast guard divides the country into Atlantic and Pacific areas along the western boarders of the Dakotas, Wyoming, Colorado and New Mexico, each area is then divided into districts, five in the Atlantic Area and four in the Pacific area (2). A Master Chief Petty Officer serves as the senior enlisted advisor for each area, making two in all.

They are distinguished by a standard master chief's rating badge, three gold chevrons and one arc with a silver eagle and two silver stars above it. The specialty mark is replaced with a gold american shield (3).

Assistant Engineer

The rank of Assistant Engineer was created on March 3, 1845 (1).

They were ordered to wear uniforms "same as Third Lieutenants, omitting the epaulet and strap, and with the addition of the Treasury arms embroidered in silver on each side of the collar." (2).

The uniforms were changed in 1862 to three buttons on the cuff and a gold paddle wheel in the shoulder straps for a "First" Assistant Engineer and the same with no paddle wheel for a "Second" Assistant Engineer (3). This is strange because the rank was not split into first and second assistant engineer until February 4, 1863 (4). It is possible that "first" and "second" were in use before they were legally recognized, or it is equally possible that the date of the uniform change is wrong.

Baker Second Class

The rate of Baker Second Class was created when the coast guard's rates were made the same as the navy's on May 18, 1920. The rate was placed in the Seaman Second Class pay grade (other bakers were first class petty officers) (1).

They wore two stripes on the cuff of the jumpers and probably no branch mark (2).

It is not clear how long the rate of Baker Second Class lasted. The navy made it a petty officers rating in 1921 (3), but there is no record of a baker's rating in the coast guard.

Boatswain

Boatswain, pronounced bow-sun, comes for the saxon swein meaning boy or servant of a boat (1). Boatswains are placed in charge of a ships deck operations.

Boatswains were known to exist in the revenue cutter service as early as 1799 (2), but their status is not clear. In the navy Boatswains were warrant officers but there was no law that created warrant officers in the cutter service. On the other hand a list of officers from 1832 (3) does list men holding the rank of "Warrant Officer" and some of them may have been Boatswains.

The first known uniforms for warrant officers were prescribed in 1836. They were described as "Blue cloth coat or jacket, with nine revenue buttons on the lapels, three under the pocket flap, and on each cuff: white or blue pantaloons, according to season (4).

An estimate of the payroll costs of the cutter service from 1843 (5) does not list warrant officers, only petty officers. As a result, Boatswain may have become a petty officer's rating.

Boatswain is listed as a petty officer's rating in the 1891 uniform regulations, distinguished by gold crossed anchors on the upper right sleeve (6).

Beginning with an apportions law of June 30, 1906 (7), funds were allocated to pay "warrant and petty officers" instead of just the term "petty officers", that had been used in earlier laws. This is probably the point that Boatswains became warrant officers, or warrant officers again if the had been prior to 1843.

The 1908 uniform regulations confirm the status as warrant officers and prescribe the crossed anchors as a badge of rank on the collar (8).

On May 18, 1920, the warrant ranks Master's Mate and Keeper were combined into Boatswain (9).

Warrant officers were prescribed 1/4 inch wide gold stripes on cuffs and shoulder boards in 1920 (10). There is some photographic evidence (11), by no means conclusive, that the stripes were not originally broken by blue breaks. It is possible that this changed in 1926 when chief warrant officers were authorized. The 1930 uniform regulations do prescribe broken stripes described as "Warrant officer. One 1/4 inch stripe, the gold lace to be woven at intervals of 2 inches with dark blue silk thread in widths of one half inch.". The stripes on shoulder boards had a single blue break in the center of the stripe. The crossed anchors were worn above and american shield worn above the stripes. The anchors were also worn on aviation garrison caps (12).

In 1941 the gold anchors became a badge of rank worn on khaki shirt collars (13).

The Career Compensation Act of October 12, 1949 (14) placed Boatswains in pay grade W-1.

A standard, warrant officers badge of rank was introduced, probably in 1952 at the same time as the navy (15), consisting of a gold bar with a 1/16 inch blue break across the middle (16).

Boatswain became Warrant Officer 1, with the Warrant Officer Act of 1954 (17).

Boy, Boy First Class and Boy Second Class.

The rate of Boy existed from the beginning of revenue cutters on August 4, 1790 (1), until the coast guard's rates and ratings were made the same as the navy's on May 18, 1920, when they were renamed Mess Attendants (2).

The navy used Boy as an entry level rate for young sailors, but the change to Mess Attendants may indicate that, at least by the end, the coast guard was using them as wait staff in officer's messes.

When the change occurred, two classes of Boy were converted into two classes of Mess Attendants. It is not clear when or how boys were split into classes, but it was before 1908 (3).

As far as is known, the cutter service did not prescribe enlisted uniforms until 1862 when Boys were ordered to wear the standard jumper and bell bottoms with no other insignia (4).

The next known uniforms come from the 1891 uniform regulations. Boys were prescribed one stripe on the cuff (5).

Bugler

The rate of bugler first appears in the laws appropriating funds for the revenue cutter service on June 4, 1897 (1). Their status is not clear, and it is possible that Bugler was originally a petty officer's rating, not a non rated rate.

The 1900 uniform regulations prescribe a white/blue bugle under a petty officer's eagle (2), which would seam to indicate that they were petty officers.

By 1908 they were clearly non rated men, ranking between Firemen and Ordinary Seamen (2a).

Both the cutter service's 1908 uniform regulations (3) and the coast guard's 1916 uniform regulations (4) prescribe two cuff stripes on the jumpers along with a red on blue or blue on white bugle on the upper sleeve. The 1908 regulations call for a white/blue watch mark (5), but by the 1916 regulations, they were called branch marks and buglers did not wear them (6).

When the coast guard's rates were made the same as the navy's on May 18, 1920, Buglers were placed in the Seaman Second Class pay grade (7), which became grade six on June 10, 1922.

From there on the picture becomes unclear. The navy divided Buglers into first and second class in 1920 (8), placing them in what became grades five and six. They remained there until being abolished in 1948 (9). However the coast guard's 1930 uniform regulations shows a specialty mark for buglers to be worn on a petty officer's rating badge (10), so Bugler may have become a petty officer's rating at some point in the 1920s.

Cabin Steward

On March 25, 1895 the regulations of the cutter service were amended to state "Messmen shall take precedence as follows: Cabin steward, wardroom steward, ship's cook" (1). Stewards and cooks had been listed in appropriations laws since they started enumerating ranks and rates in 1872 (2), and these may be the "messmen" referred to in 1895.

The 1891 uniform regulations had prescribed for "stewards and cooks" a single breasted blue coat, closed with five black buttons and a blue visored cap (3). The 1908 regulations reduced the buttons to four (4).

As of 1908, Cabin Stewards were considered non rated men ranking between Coal Heaver and Wardroom Steward (5).

The change to the cutter service's rating structure on May 18, 1920 placed them in a special Messmen branch (6).

The Navy converted it's Cabin Stewards to Officer's Stewards First Class in 1923 (7), and coast guard may have followed suit. The 1930 uniform regulations refer to "Officer's Stewards and Officer's Cooks" (8).

Cadet

When the School of Instruction of the Revenue Cutter Service, which would later become the Coast Guard Academy, was established in 1876 (1), it's students were given the title of Cadet (2).

Unlike navy midshipmen, the cadets were never part of the cutter service or the coast guard's regular organization.

As of 1908 Cadets ranked as line officers below Third Lieutenants (3).

The uniforms and insignia for Cadets were prescribed by the academy and did not appear in the regular uniform regulations. The 1930 regulations do contain a paragraph stating "The duly authorized and approved uniforms for cadets at the United States Coast Guard Academy shall be designated in terms used in these regulations, in order that when cadets are serving with other forces and a uniform for any occasion is designated it will apply also to cadets uniforms for the occasion." (4).

Cadet Cook

The rate of Cadet Cook appears in the general order that changed the coast guard's rates and ratings to conform the navy on May 18, 1920 (1). The order changes the title to Wardroom Steward.

It is not clear when the rate of Cadet Cook began.

They more than likely wore the single breasted coat and visored cap of other cooks and steward.

Cadet Engineer

On June 23, 1906 a new law stated "That hereafter appointments into the grade of second assistant engineer in the Revenue-Cutter Service shall be as at present, except that, before being commissioned, the candidate who has successfully passed the required examinations shall serve a probationary terns of not less than six months as a cadet engineer to determine his fitness for a commission in said Service," (1).

Cadet Engineers ranked after Second Assistant Engineers (2).

The rank does not appear in uniform regulations, which may, or may not, mean that they wore uniforms similar to other cadets.

The rank of Cadet Engineer was abolished on July 2, 1926 (3).

Captain

The title Captain comes from the Latin caput meaning head, this led to the term capitaneus or head man (1). In the middle ages captain was an army rank of an officer commanding companies of soldiers. It came to navies when those companies were placed on merchant ships in time of war. Captains were in charge of fighting while the ships

Master was in charge of sailing (2). As permanent navies were created, the captain became the man in overall charge of a ship.

When revenue cutters were first authorized in law on August 4, 1790 (3), their commanding officers held the rank of Master not Captain. It is not clear when this was changed. The next law when the cutters are mentioned on March 2, 1799 (4) used the term "captain or master", and a pay table from the same year uses the title Captain (5). Lists of officers from the War of 1812 (6) list Captains, so the title was in use by then.

Revenue officers are known to have worn epaulets as early as 1819 (7), and may have worn them since 1790. It would make sense that Captains wore an epaulet on each shoulder, but there is no proof of this until the first known uniform regulations in 1830.

The 1830 regulations describe the uniform for Captains as "Blue dress coats, rolling collar, nine buttons on each lapel, four on each cuff, four on each pocket flap and four on skirts. All seams of coat to be piped with yellow cord. Two plain gold epaulets. Trousers blue to be worn outside of boots. Vest blue or white with four buttons on each pocket flap. Hat, pattern known as "Stove pipe", ornamented on the left side with a black cockade with brass buttons in center." (8).

In 1833 the four buttons on the cuff were replaced with one inch wide strip of gold lace (9). This was short lived as both the gray uniforms of 1834 and the blue uniforms of 1836 had the four buttons under a strip of black braid. The gold epaulets remained (10).

Shoulder straps, consisting of a strip of gold lace on each shoulder, were introduced in 1838 (11).

A treasury shied under an anchor was added to the epaulet frogs in 1844 (12).

In 1853 shoulder straps became a gold rectangle with a blue center worn on both shoulders (13). Captains wore a gold treasury shield on an anchor in the center with a star above and below and two gold bars at each end of the strap (14).

New uniforms were authorized in 1862 (15). Those for a Captain had two stripes of 1/2 inch gold lace on the cuffs (putting an end to the four buttons), gold crossed anchors in the center of the shoulder straps and the epaulets were one again plain (16).

A law of February 4, 1863 (17) made Captains in the revenue cutter service equal to lieutenants commanding in the navy. The concept of "lieutenants commanding" in the navy had been replaced with the rank of Lieutenant Commander on July 16, 1862 (18).

New uniform regulations in 1864 added the gold oak leaf of a navy Lieutenant Commander at each end of the shoulder strap and changed the cuff stripes to four, all under an american shield. The stripes were 1/4 inch apart except for the top two that were 1/2 inch apart (19).

The gold oak leaf as a badge of rank were placed at either end of the frog of the epaulet, with an anchor between, and on the collar in 1871 between an anchor and the letter U.S.R.M.. The collar insignia was meant to replace shoulder straps but were unpopular and shoulder straps returned in 1873 (20), this time with a treasury shield and an anchor in the center (21).

The oak leafs, accompanied by a treasury shield, returned to the collars of service coats in 1878 (22).

The 1891 uniform regulations prescribe 1/4 inch cuff stripes, instead of the 1/2 inch stripes prescribed in 1864. The spacing was the same as was the american shield. A gold anchor with a silver american shield was worn as a corps device in the center of epaulet frogs and shoulder straps, and on the blue service coat collar. The gold oak leaf remained the badge of rank (23).

New cuff stripes were authorized in 1900. Captains were prescribed two thick stripes, probably 1/2 inch, with two thin stripes, probably 1/4 inch (24).

The cuff stripes were made the same as a navy Lieutenant Commander in 1905, two 1/2 inch stripes with one 1/4 inch stripe between them (25).

The 1908 uniform regulations continue the stripes and gold oak leaf and corps device on the collar. The leaf and device is also worn on shoulder knots, which had replaced epaulets, and on shoulder boards (26).

By 1917 the shoulder boards carried the stripes from the cuff instead of the leaf and corps device (27).

On June 5, 1920 the officer's rank structure of the coast guard was made the same as the navy's, and all Captains became Lieutenant Commanders (28).

A new rank of Captain, equal to a navy Captain, was created on January 13, 1923 (29).

Navy Captains were identified by four 1/2 inch stripes on the cuffs and shoulder boards and a silver eagle as a badge of rank (30), and more than likely coast guard Captains were as well. This is confirmed by the 1930 uniform regulations (31).

The Career Compensation Act of October 12, 1949 (32) placed the rank of Captain in pay grade O-6.

An illustration in the 2009 uniform regulations shows that the insignia for a Captain continues to be four 1/2 inch stripes under an american shield on the cuffs and on the shoulder boards and a silver eagle as a badge of rank (33).

Captain Commandant

On November 1, 1843 new regulations for the revenue cutter service set up the "Revenue Marine Bureau" as a shore establishment for the service to answer to. The regulations stated "Until other provisions shall be made, a captain in the Revenue Service will be detailed to take charge of the Bureau" (1). The job went to Captain Alexander Fraser, who served until 1848 when he was replaced by Captain Richard Evans (2).

The revenue marine bureau was abolished in 1849 and the service answered to the Commissioner of Customs until the bureau was revived in 1869, with a civilian head N. Broughton Devereax who held the job until 1871. His replacements were Sumner Kimball in 1871, Ezra Clark in 1878 and Peter Bonnett in 1885. Bonnett's replacement was a commissioned revenue captain named Leonard Sheapard in 1889, and Sheapard is considered the first commandant (3).

The Treasury Department was reorganized by a law of July 31, 1894 that created a Division of Revenue Cutter Service. The law stated "That the Secretary of the Treasury shall detail a captain of the Revenue Cutter Service who shall be chief of the division of the Revenue Cutter Service" (4). Sheapard was given this position and remained in charge of the cutter service until he died of pneumonia on March 1, 1895 (5), and was replaced by Captain Charles Shoemaker on March 19th (6). Shoemaker retired on March 27, 1905 and was replaced by Captain Worth Ross (7).

The rank of Captain Commandant was created on April 16, 1908 for the chief of the division of revenue cutter service (8). The rank would be equal to a navy Captain or an army Colonel. Ross was duly promoted and Sheapard was made a Captain Commandant on the retired list.

Under the 1908 uniform regulations, Ross was ordered to cuff stripes of "Four stripes of gold lace, 1/2 inch wide, spaced 1/4 inch apart, lower stripe to be placed 2 inches above the edge of the cuff.", under an american shield. On the collar of his blue service coat, shoulder knots and shoulder boards he wore "A silver embroidered spread eagle, 2 inches between the tips of the wings, having in the right talon an olive branch and in the left a bundle of arrows; an escutcheon on the breast as represented in the "Arms of the United States;" and a gold-embroidered foul anchor 11/4 inches long, with a 5/8 inch shield embroidered in silver on the shank and perpendicular to the crown of the anchor." (9).

Ross retired on April 30, 1911 and was replaced by Ellswoth Betholf on June 19th (10).

A law of July 1, 1918 (11) temporally raised the rank of the Captain Commandant to Commodore for the duration of World War I.

There is a photograph of Betholf (12) wearing a star (that would have been the badge of rank for a navy Commodore if the rank had existed in the navy) on his collar. He more than likely wore the one two inch cuff stripe as well.

It appears that Betholf retained his rank until his retirement on June 13, 1919 (13), and his successor, William Reynolds, also held the title of "Captain Commandant with rank of Commodore" (14).

The position, and rank, of Captain Commandant was abolished on January 13, 1923. The law stated "That the title of captain commandant in the Coast Guard is hereby changed to commandant. Hereafter the commandant shall be selected from the active list of line officers not below the grade of commander and shall have, while serving as commandant, the rank, pay, and allowances of a rear admiral (lower half) of the Navy:" (15).

Captain (Engineering)

The rank of Captain (Engineering) was created on January 13, 1923 (1).

It is not clear what uniforms were worn before 1930. As of 1918 engineering officers did not wear the shield above the stripes on the cuffs and shoulder boards (2). Under the 1930 uniform regulations they wore the same uniforms as other Captains, four 1/2 inch stripes on the cuffs and shoulder boards and a silver eagle as a badge of rank, including the shield (3).

It is also not clear when the rank of Captain (Engineering) was abolished. The rank is shown in the 1941 register (4) but not the 1944 register (5).

Captain of Engineers

The title of the cutter service's Engineer in Chief was changed to Captain of Engineers on June 4, 1897 (1).

Under the 1891 uniform regulations, the Captain of Engineers would have worn the uniform of a Captain with a silver four bladed propellor replacing the corps device and no shield above the stripes (2).

On February 26, 1906, the title was changed back to Engineer in Chief (3).

The rank returned on April 16, 1908 (4) and was equal to other Captains in the cutter service who were in turn equal to Lieutenant Commanders in the navy.

Under the 1908 uniform regulations, Captains of Engineers wore the two 1/2 inch and one 1/4 inch stripes and gold oak leaf of a Captain with no shield over the stripes and a corps device of a gold anchor and silver crossed oak branches (5).

Captains of Engineers became Lieutenant Commanders (Engineering) on June 5, 1920 (6).

Carpenter

Carpenters were known to exist in the revenue cutter service as early as 1799 (2), but their status is not clear. In the navy Carpenters were warrant officers (there was a petty officer's rating for a time) but there was no law that created warrant officers in the cutter service. On the other hand a list of officers from 1832 (3) does list men holding the rank of "Warrant Officer" and some of them may have been Carpenters.

The first known uniforms for warrant officers were prescribed in 1836. They were described as "Blue cloth coat or jacket, with nine revenue buttons on the lapels, three under the pocket flap, and on each cuff: white or blue pantaloons, according to season (4).

An estimate of the payroll costs of the cutter service from 1843 (5) does not list warrant officers, only petty officers. As a result, Carpenter may have become a petty officer's rating.

Carpenter is listed as a petty officer's rating in the 1891 uniform regulations, distinguished by a gold chevron and anchor on the upper right sleeve (6). The chevron was probably meant to represent a carpenter's square.

Beginning with an apportions law of June 30, 1906 (7), funds were allocated to pay "warrant and petty officers" instead of just the term "petty officers", that had been used in earlier laws. This is probably the point that Carpenters became warrant officers, or warrant officers again if the had been prior to 1843.

The 1908 uniform regulations confirm the status as warrant officers and prescribe the chevron as a badge of rank on the collar (8).

Warrant officers were prescribed 1/4 inch wide gold stripes on cuffs and shoulder boards in 1920 (9). There is some photographic evidence (10), by no means conclusive, that the stripes were not originally broken by blue breaks. It is possible that this changed in 1926 when chief warrant officers were authorized. The 1930 uniform regulations do prescribe broken stripes described as "Warrant officer. One 1/4 inch stripe, the gold lace to be woven at intervals of 2 inches with dark blue silk thread in widths of one half inch.". The stripes on shoulder boards had a single blue break in the center of the stripe. The chevron was worn above and american shield worn above the stripes. The chevron was also worn on aviation garrison caps (11).

In 1941 the gold chevron became a badge of rank worn on khaki shirt collars (12).

The Career Compensation Act of October 12, 1949 (13) placed Carpenters in pay grade W-1.

A standard, warrant officers badge of rank was introduced, probably in 1952 at the same time as the navy (14), consisting of a gold bar with a 1/16 inch blue break across the middle (15).

Carpenter became Warrant Officer 1, with the Warrant Officer Act of 1954 (16).

It should be noted that there was also a petty officer's rating of Carpenter in the coast guard from 1915 to 1920 (17) when it became the rating of Carpenter's Mate (18).

Chief Boatswain

Chief warrant officers were authorized in the coast guard by a law of July 1, 1926 (1), and the rank of Chief Boatswain was born. The law refers to acting appointments becoming permanent, so there must have been acting Chief Boatswains prior to 1926, but there is no listings for chief warrant officers in the Coast Guard Register until 1927 (2).

Under the 1930 uniform regulations, Chief Boatswains were distinguished by a 1/2 inch wide gold cuff stripe with 1/2 inch blue breaks every two inches under a gold american shield that was in turn under gold crossed anchors. Shoulder boards were the same with only one break in the stripe. The crossed anchors, apparently in gold, were also worn on aviation garrison caps (3).

The crossed anchors, in silver this time, became the a pin on badge of rank in 1941 (4).

The Career Compensation Act of October 12, 1949 (5) spread Chief Boatswains across pay grades W-2, W-3 and W-4.

A standard, chief warrant officers badge of rank was introduced, probably in 1952 at the same time as the navy (6), consisting of a gold bar with a 1/8 inch blue break across the middle (7).

Chief Boatswains became Chief Warrant Officer 2, Chief Warrant Officer 3 and Chief Warrant Officer 4, with the Warrant Officer Act of 1954 (8).

Chief Carpenter

Chief warrant officers were authorized in the coast guard by a law of July 1, 1926 (1), and the rank of Chief Carpenter was born. The law refers to acting appointments becoming permanent, so there must have been acting Chief Carpenters prior to 1926, but there is no listings for chief warrant officers in the Coast Guard Register until 1927 (2).

Under the 1930 uniform regulations, Chief Carpenters were distinguished by a 1/2 inch wide gold cuff stripe with 1/2 inch blue breaks every two inches under a gold american shield that was in turn under gold a chevron representing a carpenter's square. Shoulder boards were the same with only one break in the stripe. The chevron, apparently in gold, were also worn on aviation garrison caps (3).

The chevron, in silver this time, became the a pin on badge of rank in 1941 (4).

The Career Compensation Act of October 12, 1949 (5) spread Chief Carpenters across pay grades W-2, W-3 and W-4.

A standard, chief warrant officers badge of rank was introduced, probably in 1952 at the same time as the navy (6), consisting of a gold bar with a 1/8 inch blue break across the middle (7).

Chief Carpenters became Chief Warrant Officer 2, Chief Warrant Officer 3 and Chief Warrant Officer 4, with the Warrant Officer Act of 1954 (8).

Chief Electrician

Chief warrant officers were authorized in the coast guard by a law of July 1, 1926 (1), but no Chief Electricians were appointed until October 9, 1935 when Charles Geiss, Harry Rowalnd and Conrad Bilz took office (2).

Under the 1930 uniform regulations, Chief Electricians were distinguished by a 1/2 inch wide gold cuff stripe with 1/2 inch blue breaks every two inches under a gold american shield that was in turn under gold hemisphere of a globe. Shoulder boards were the same with only one break in the stripe. The globe, apparently in gold, were also worn on aviation garrison caps (3).

The globe, in silver this time, became the a pin on badge of rank in 1941 (4).

The Career Compensation Act of October 12, 1949 (5) spread Chief Electricians across pay grades W-2, W-3 and W-4.

A standard, chief warrant officers badge of rank was introduced, probably in 1952 at the same time as the navy (6), consisting of a gold bar with a 1/8 inch blue break across the middle (7).

Chief Electricians became Chief Warrant Officer 2, Chief Warrant Officer 3 and Chief Warrant Officer 4, with the Warrant Officer Act of 1954 (8).

Chief Engineer

Chief Engineers were added to the revenue cutter service by a law of March 3, 1845 (1). The first five Chief Engineers were W.W. Luke, P.H. Bonham, James Wright, Charles French and Thomas Farron (2).

They were ordered to wear uniforms "same as First Lieutenants, omitting the epaulet and strap, and with the addition of the Treasury arms embroidered in gold on each side of the collar." (2).

In 1862 Chief engineers were given shoulder straps with a paddle wheel superimposed on an anchor in the center and a single strip of 1/2 inch gold lace on the cuffs (4).

A law of February 4, 1863 gave Chief Engineers the relative rank of First Lieutenants (5).

The uniforms were changed in 1864 to allow Chief Engineers to wear the three cuff stripes of a First Lieutenant and add two gold bars to the end of the shoulder straps (6).

In 1871, the shoulder straps were replaced with collar insignia consisting of the letters U.S.R.M. arched over a propellor, all over two bars (7). It is not clear if engineering officers were allowed epaulets in 1871. If they were, they probably wore the propellor in the center of the frog and a set of bars on either side.

The collar insignia was replaced with shoulder straps in 1873. This time the propellor was worn in the center between the to bars (8). Collar insignia, of the bars in front of the propellor, would return in 1878 (9).

The 1891 uniform regulations prescribe three cuff stripes that were only 1/4 inch wide, shoulder straps with a silver propellor with a gold boss in the center and two gold bars at each end and epaulets with same devices in the frog (10).

The cuff stripes were changed in 1900. First Lieutenant's, and therefore presumably Chief Engineers, wore a thick stripe, probably 1/2 inch, under two thin stripes, probably 1/4 inch (11).

A law of April 12, 1902 (12) gave Chief Engineers of the revenue service equal rank to Captains in the army and Lieutenants in the navy. Cuff stripes were changed to reflect this in 1905 when Chief Engineers were give the two 1/2 inch stripes of a navy Lieutenant (13).

Chief Engineers became First Lieutenants of Engineers on April 16, 1908 (14).

Chief Gunner

Chief warrant officers were authorized in the coast guard by a law of July 1, 1926 (1), and the rank of Chief Gunner was born. The law refers to acting appointments becoming permanent, so there must have been acting Chief Gunners prior to 1926, but there is no listings for chief warrant officers in the Coast Guard Register until 1927 (2).

Under the 1930 uniform regulations, Chief Gunners were distinguished by a 1/2 inch wide gold cuff stripe with 1/2 inch blue breaks every two inches under a gold american shield that was in turn under gold bursting bomb. Shoulder boards were the same with only one break in the stripe. The bursting bomb, apparently in gold, were also worn on aviation garrison caps (3).

The bursting bomb, in silver this time, became the a pin on badge of rank in 1941 (4).

The Career Compensation Act of October 12, 1949 (5) spread Chief Gunners across pay grades W-2, W-3 and W-4.

A standard, chief warrant officers badge of rank was introduced, probably in 1952 at the same time as the navy (6), consisting of a gold bar with a 1/8 inch blue break across the middle (7).

Chief Gunners became Chief Warrant Officer 2, Chief Warrant Officer 3 and Chief Warrant Officer 4, with the Warrant Officer Act of 1954 (8).

Chief Machinist

Chief warrant officers were authorized in the coast guard by a law of July 1, 1926 (1), and the rank of Chief Machinist was born. The law refers to acting appointments becoming permanent, so there must have been acting Chief Machinists prior to 1926, but there is no listings for chief warrant officers in the Coast Guard Register until 1927 (2).

Under the 1930 uniform regulations, Chief Machinists were distinguished by a 1/2 inch wide gold cuff stripe with 1/2 inch blue breaks every two inches under a gold american shield that was in turn under gold propellor. Shoulder boards were the same with only one break in the stripe. The propellor, apparently in gold, were also worn on aviation garrison caps (3).

The propellor, in silver this time, became the a pin on badge of rank in 1941 (4).

The Career Compensation Act of October 12, 1949 (5) spread Chief Machinists across pay grades W-2, W-3 and W-4.

A standard, chief warrant officers badge of rank was introduced, probably in 1952 at the same time as the navy (6), consisting of a gold bar with a 1/8 inch blue break across the middle (7).

Chief Machinists became Chief Warrant Officer 2, Chief Warrant Officer 3 and Chief Warrant Officer 4, with the Warrant Officer Act of 1954 (8).

Chief Oiler

The 1906 register lists 12 men with the warrant rank of Chief Oiler (1). The existence of warrant officers in the cutter service in this era is not clear. They were not mentioned in law for decades until a law of May 26, 1906 (2) concerning the punishment of service personnel. The law appropriating funds to pay for the cutter service on March 3, 1905 (3) does not mention warrant officers but the next law on June 30, 1906 (4) does.

The 1907 register lists the same men, among others, as Machinists (5).

There is no information on uniforms or insignia for Chief Oilers. It is possible that they wore the uniform prescribed for Machinists in the 1908 uniform regulations.

Chief Pay Clerk

Chief warrant officers were authorized in the coast guard by a law of July 1, 1926 (1), and the rank of Chief Pay Clerk was born. The law refers to acting appointments becoming permanent, so there must have been acting Chief Pay Clerks prior to 1926, but there is no listings for chief warrant officers in the Coast Guard Register until 1927 (2).

Under the 1930 uniform regulations, Chief Pay Clerks were distinguished by a 1/2 inch wide gold cuff stripe with 1/2 inch blue breaks every two inches under a gold american shield that was in turn under gold sprig of three oak leaves. Shoulder boards were the same with only one break in the stripe. The sprig of three oak leaves, apparently in gold, were also worn on aviation garrison caps (3).

The sprig of three oak leaves, in silver this time, became the a pin on badge of rank in 1941 (4).

The Career Compensation Act of October 12, 1949 (5) spread Chief Pay Clerks across pay grades W-2, W-3 and W-4.

A standard, chief warrant officers badge of rank was introduced, probably in 1952 at the same time as the navy (6), consisting of a gold bar with a 1/8 inch blue break across the middle (7).

Chief Pay Clerks became Chief Warrant Officer 2, Chief Warrant Officer 3 and Chief Warrant Officer 4, with the Warrant Officer Act of 1954 (8).

Chief Petty Officer

The rate of Chief Petty Officer was created in the coast guard when it's rates and ratings were made the same as the navy's by law on May 18, 1920 (1).

Acting warrant officers were made into Chief Petty Officers with Acting Keepers and acting Boatswains being given the rating of Chief Boatswain's Mate, Acting Gunners the rating of Chief Gunner's Mate, Acting Machinists the rating of Chief Machinist's Mate and Acting Carpenters the rating of Chief Carpenter's Mate. Petty officers who had held the rating of Master at Arms for more than three years became Chief Commissary Stewards. Electricians First Class with more than three years in the rating became Chief Electricians. The same system was applied to Yeomen and Ship's Writers over three years service becoming Chief Yeomen, Wheelmen over three years service becoming Chief Boatswain's Mates, Signal Quartermasters over three years service becoming Chief Quartermasters and rated Carpenter's First Class becoming Chief Carpenter's Mates. Machinists First Class with three years service as a Machinist First Class or as an Oiler first or second class became Chief Machinist's Mates. Also created were the ratings of Chief Watertender, Chief Storekeeper and Chief Pharmacist's Mate (2). The ratings would expand from there.

The rating badge assigned to Chief Petty Officers was a continuation of one worn by some, but not all, first class ratings. Three point down chevrons under one arc with an eagle with it's wings up resting on the arc and a specialty mark in the angle of the chevrons. On blue coats, the chevrons and arc were scarlet and the eagle and specialty mark were white, and an all blue badge was worn on white coats (3). Chiefs with more 12 years good conduct could wear the chevrons and arc in gold on the blue coat, and if the navy's pattern was followed the eagle and specialty mark were silver.

The Chief Petty Officer's pay grade became grade one on June 10, 1922 (4).

By the 1930 uniform regulations the eagle and mark were silver even with scarlet chevrons (5).

The rating badges used by chiefs on the green and khaki aviation uniforms of the 1920s and 1930s and the khaki uniforms thereafter is far from clear. The 1930 uniform regulations calls for rating badges to be "to be those prescribed by the Regulations" (6). That tells us nothing about what colors were to be used. The coast guard may have followed the navy practice, but even that is not clear until 1944 when all blue badges were ordered to be worn on all but blue uniforms. This included the gray uniforms adopted during the war. The navy changed the eagle and specialty mark on the khaki coat to silver in 1949, and the coast guard did follow suit (7).

The Career Compensation Act of October 12, 1949 made grade one into grade E-7 (8).

A badge of rank was created in 1959 consisting of a gold folded anchor and a silver shield (9).

The uniform change of the 1970s eliminated white uniforms and the need for all blue rating badges. Chiefs were allowed a white mess jacket with a gold/ silver rating badge. The dates are not certain but the new uniforms appear to have eliminated the gold chevrons for good conduct. Chiefs now wore gold chevrons and arc with a silver eagle, stars and specialty mark and other petty officers scarlet chevrons and a white eagle and specialty mark (10).

The 2009 uniform regulations describe the badge of rank for Chief Petty Officers as "The chief petty officer collar insignia will consist of a 15/16 inch gold metal fouled anchor with a silver shield superimposed on the shank." (11). The rating badge for all grades is described as "The rating badge indicates the wearer's rate/pay grade. It consists of a perched eagle with the wings extended upward and the head to eagle's right. Chevron(s) and star(s) indicate the wearer's rate/pay grade. The colors of the chevrons are scarlet for E-4 through E-6 and gold E-7 through E-9, and MCPOCG. The background is the same color as the jacket. Chevrons and stars worn on the Dinner Dress White Jacket will be with a white background and dark blue chevrons and stripes." (12) and the three chevrons and one arc are shown in illustration (13).

Chief Pharmacist

Chief warrant officers were authorized in the coast guard by a law of July 1, 1926 (1), but no Chief Pharmacist were appointed until July 20, 1936 when Theodore Le Blanc took office (2).

Under the 1930 uniform regulations, Chief Pharmacists were distinguished by a 1/2 inch wide gold cuff stripe with 1/2 inch blue breaks every two inches under a gold american shield that was in turn under gold caduceus. Shoulder boards were the same with only one break in the stripe. The caduceus, apparently in gold, was also worn on aviation garrison caps (3).

The caduceus, in silver this time, became the a pin on badge of rank in 1941 (4).

The Career Compensation Act of October 12, 1949 (5) spread Chief Pharmacist across pay grades W-2, W-3 and W-4.

A standard, chief warrant officers badge of rank was introduced, probably in 1952 at the same time as the navy (6), consisting of a gold bar with a 1/8 inch blue break across the middle (7).

Chief Pharmacist became Chief Warrant Officer 2, Chief Warrant Officer 3 and Chief Warrant Officer 4, with the Warrant Officer Act of 1954 (8).

Chief Photographer

The warrant grade of Chief Photographer was created in the navy by a law of July 28, 1942 (1). Apparently the rank was created in the coast guard at the same time (2).

Navy Chief Photographers wore gold lace on the cuffs that was 1/2 inch wide with 1/2 inch long blue breaks every 2 inches. The device of a Photographer, an old fashioned camera with the bellows extend, was worn above the stripes. Shoulder boards showed the 1/2 inch lace with a single 1/2 inch break, under the device. The camera device, in silver, was also used as a badge of rank (3), the coast guard used the same insignia (4).

The Career Compensation Act of October 12, 1949 (5) spread Chief Photographers across pay grades W-2, W-3 and W-4.

A standard, chief warrant officers badge of rank was introduced, probably in 1952 at the same time as the navy (6), consisting of a gold bar with a 1/8 inch blue break across the middle (7).

Chief Photographer became Chief Warrant Officer 2, Chief Warrant Officer 3 and Chief Warrant Officer 4, with the Warrant Officer Act of 1954 (8).

Chief Radio Electrician

Chief warrant officers were authorized in the coast guard by a law of July 1, 1926 (1), but no Chief Radio Electricians were appointed until October 1, 1928 when Walter Reynolds and William O'Steen took office (2).

Under the 1930 uniform regulations, Chief Radio Electricians were distinguished by a 1/2 inch wide gold cuff stripe with 1/2 inch blue breaks every two inches under a gold american shield that was in turn under four lightning bolts. Shoulder boards were the same with only one break in the stripe. The bolts, apparently in gold, were also worn on aviation garrison caps (3).

The bolts, in silver this time, became the a pin on badge of rank in 1941 (4).

The Career Compensation Act of October 12, 1949 (5) spread Chief Radio Electricians across pay grades W-2, W-3 and W-4.

A standard, chief warrant officers badge of rank was introduced, probably in 1952 at the same time as the navy (6), consisting of a gold bar with a 1/8 inch blue break across the middle (7).

Chief Radio Electricians became Chief Warrant Officer 2, Chief Warrant Officer 3 and Chief Warrant Officer 4, with the Warrant Officer Act of 1954 (8).

Chief Ship's Clerk

The warrant grade of Chief Ship's Clerk was created in the navy by a law of July 28, 1942 (1). Apparently the rank was created in the coast guard at the same time (2).

Navy Chief Ship's Clerks wore gold lace on the cuffs that was 1/2 inch wide with 1/2 inch long blue breaks every 2 inches. The device of a Ship's Clerks, crossed quill pens, was worn above the stripes. Shoulder boards showed the 1/2 inch lace with a single 1/2 inch break, under the device. The pens device, in silver, was also used as a badge of rank (3), the coast guard used the same insignia (4).

The Career Compensation Act of October 12, 1949 (5) spread Chief Pharmacist across pay grades W-2, W-3 and W-4.

A standard, chief warrant officers badge of rank was introduced, probably in 1952 at the same time as the navy (6), consisting of a gold bar with a 1/8 inch blue break across the middle (7).

Chief Ship's Clerks became Chief Warrant Officer 2, Chief Warrant Officer 3 and Chief Warrant Officer 4, with the Warrant Officer Act of 1954 (8).

Chief Warrant Officer 2

Chief Warrant Officer 2 was created by the "Warrant Officer Act of 1954" (1) in pay grade W-2, from the various chief warrant grades.

New insignia was prescribed in 1954. The cuff stripes were to be 1/2 inch wide with three 1/2 inch blue breaks, two inches apart, under an american shield, under a specialty device. On the shoulder boards, the 1/2 inch stripe had breaks 1/2 inch apart (which resulted in three blue portions and two gold portions) under an american shield, under the specialty device. The pin on badge of rank conformed to the unified system shared with other services, a gold bar with a blue square in the center and a blue rectangle at each end (2).

These insignias are still in use (3).

Chief Warrant Officer 3

Chief Warrant Officer 3 was created by the "Warrant Officer Act of 1954" (1) in pay grade W-3, from the various chief warrant grades.

New insignia was prescribed in 1954. The cuff stripes were to be 1/2 inch wide with two 1/2 inch blue breaks, two inches apart, under an american shield, under a specialty device. On the shoulder boards, the 1/2 inch stripe had breaks 1/2 inch apart (which resulted in three gold portions and two blue portions) under an american shield, under the specialty device. The pin on badge of rank conformed to the unified system shared with other services, a silver bar with two blue rectangles, showing a square of silver in the middle (2).

These insignias are still in use (3).

Chief Warrant Officer 4

Chief Warrant Officer 4 was created by the "Warrant Officer Act of 1954" (1) in pay grade W-4, from the various chief warrant grades.

New insignia was prescribed in 1954. The cuff stripes were to be 1/2 inch wide with one 1/2 inch blue break, under an american shield, under a specialty device. On the shoulder boards, the 1/2 inch stripe one break under an american shield, under the specialty device. The pin on badge of rank conformed to the unified system shared with other services, a silver bar with a blue square in the center and a blue rectangle at each end (2).

These insignias are still in use (3).

Coal Heaver

The rate of Coal Passer became Coal Heaver in the appropriations law of March 3, 1899 (1).

Under the 1891 uniform regulations, Coal Passers had worn two cuff stripes (2), and Coal Heavers continued to wear them along with a red branch mark under the 1908 regulations (3).

When the coast guard's rates and ratings were made the same as the navy's on May 18, 1920, Coal Heavers became Firemen Third Class (4).

Coal Passer

Coal Passers were probably added to the revenue cutter service when engineering officers were added in 1845 (1).

As far as is known, the cutter service did not prescribe enlisted uniforms until 1862 when Coal Passers were ordered to wear the standard jumper and bell bottoms with no other insignia (2).

The next known uniforms come from the 1891 uniform regulations. Coal Passers were prescribed two stripes on the cuff (3).

The rate of Coal Passer became Coal Heaver in the appropriations law of March 3, 1899 (4).

Command Master Chief Petty Officer

It is unclear when the coast guard began appointing Command Master Chief Petty Officers as the senior enlisted advisor to large commands, but the do apear in the 1985 uniform regulations (1)

They are distinguished by a standard master chief's rating badge, three gold chevrons and one arc with a silver eagle and two silver stars above it. The specialty mark is replaced with a silver american shield (2).

The History of American Ranks and Rank Insignia

Commander

The rank of Commander originated in the British Royal Navy as Master and Commander. It was used for officers commanding ships that were small enough that the commanding officer also did duty as the Sailing Master, hence "master <u>and</u> commander". The Royal Navy shortened the title of Commander in 1794 (1).

In the United States Coast Guard the rank of Senior Captain became Commander, it's navy equivalent, on June 5, 1920 (2).

The Senior Captain's insignia, three 1/2 inch stripes under an american shield on the cuffs and shoulder boards and a silver oak leaf as a badge of rank was continued (3).

The Career Compensation Act of October 12, 1949 (4) placed the rank of Commander in pay grade O-5.

An illustration in the 2009 uniform regulations shows that the insignia for a Commander continues to be three 1/2 inch stripes under an american shield on the cuffs and on the shoulder boards and a silver oak leaf as a badge of rank (5).

Commander (Engineering)

The rank of Commander (Engineering) was created on on January 13, 1923 (1).

It is not clear what uniforms were worn before 1930. As of 1918 engineering officers did not wear the shield above the stripes on the cuffs and shoulder boards (2). Under the 1930 uniform regulations they wore the same uniforms as other Commanders, three 1/2 inch stripes on the cuffs and shoulder boards and a silver oak leaf as a badge of rank, including the shield (3).

It is also not clear when the rank of Commander (Engineering) was abolished. The rank is shown in the 1941 register (4) but not the 1944 register (5).

Commodore

The title Commodore comes from the Dutch rank of comendador (1). The navy used it as a title for senior officers until it became an official rank in 1862 (2). Neither the revenue service or the coast guard were big enough for this to come up until World War I.

A law of July 1, 1918 stated "That the President be, and he is hereby, authorized during the sent war to promote temporarily, with the advice and consent o the Senate, the captain commandant of the Coast Guard to the rank of commodore in the Navy and brigadier general in the Army," (3). The Captain Commandant, Ellsworth P. Bertholf, was duly promoted.

There is a photograph of Betholf (4) wearing a star (that would have been the badge of rank for a navy Commodore if the rank had existed in the navy) on his collar. He more than likely wore the one two inch cuff stripe as well.

It appears that Betholf retained his rank until his retirement on June 13, 1919 (5), and that his successor, William Reynolds, also held the title of "Captain Commandant with rank of Commodore" (6), until the rank of the commandant was raised to Rear Admiral on January 13, 1923 (7).

Congress reestablished the rank of Commodore in the navy on April 9, 1943 and the law contains the sentence "Personnel of the Coast Guard in relationship to the Coast Guard in the same manner and to the same extent as they apply to personnel of the Navy in relationship to the Navy." (8).

The Coast Guard Register dated June 30, 1944 shows four commodores, Philip Roach, Gordon Finlay, Wilfred Derby and Karl Ross (9).

The insignia of coast guard Commodores remained one two inch stripe under an american shield on the cuffs and one silver star on the shoulder boards and as a badge of rank (10).

The coast guard's post World War Ii rank structure was laid out in a law of July 23, 1947 (11). The law replaced the rank of Commodore with the rank of Rear Admiral (lower half).

The navy revived the rank as Commodore Admiral in 1980 (12) and changed it to just Commodore in 1981 (13), but the coast guard's equivalent rank in the O-7 pay grade remained Rear Admiral (lower half) until October 30, 1984 with the title was changed to Commodore in both services (14).

The insignia of one two inch stripe under an american shield on the cuffs and one silver star on the shoulder boards and as a badge of rank was revived (15).

The title was changed back to Rear Admiral (lower half) on November 8, 1985 (16).

Constructor

On July 1, 1898, a new law added "one constructor in and for the Revenue-Cutter Service, who shall have the relative rank and pay of a first lieutenant" (1). The job was given to James Lee on July 12th (2).

On June 23, 1906 a new law stated "That a chief engineer of the Revenue-Cutter Service, to be selected for his special ability in naval construction from the present list of chief engineers by the Secretary of the Treasury, may be commissioned a constructor for engineering duty in said Service with the rank, pay, and emoluments now provided by' law for a chief engineer:" (3). John Walton was transferred from an engineering officer to a Constructor (4).

Lee resigned on December 31, 1906 (5), and was replaced by William Besselievre (6).

The first information on uniforms comes from the 1908 uniform regulations. Walton and Besselievre were to wear the uniform of a First Lieutenant with a branch of oak leafs replacing the shield on the anchor of the corps device (7). The shield was probably not worn above the stripes (7a)

The records are not complete but it is known that Besselievre died on June 20, 1913 (8) at age 48, and Frederick Hunnewell became a Constructor on September 2nd (9).

By 1918, Constructors were wearing brown cloth between the stripes on their cuffs and shoulder boards (10).

A law of July 1, 1918 (11) allowed Walton and Hunnewell to be promoted to relative Captain, which became the rank of Lieutenant Commander in 1920.

A law of January 12, 1923 raised the prestige of Constructors even more by stating "That a constructor, after ten years commissioned service in the Revenue-Cutter Service and Coast Guard, shall have the rank, pay, and allowances of a lieutenant commander, and after twenty years' commissioned service the rank, pay, and allowances of a commander." (12). This law made Walton a relative Commander and Hunnewell remained a relative Lieutenant Commander.

The number of Constructors in the coast guard was increased to five on July 3, 1926 (13). Rutherford Lank was appointed on August 15, 1927 and Dale Simonson on October 10th (14). The last slot was not filled until March 3, 1928 when Edward Kent was appointed (15).

Walton retired on April 1, 1933 (16) and was replaced by Charles Brush (17).

The rank of Constructor was abolished on August 5, 1939 (18) and Hunnewell, Lank, Simonson, Kent and Brush became line officers at their equivalent rank.

Cook

Cooks were probably on revenue cutters from the beginning, the crew had to eat. The first evidence of a rate of Cook comes from a 1799 pay table (1). It is not clear if Cook was a non rated rate, a petty officer's rating or a warrant rank.

The status of Cooks became clearer in 1843 when an estimate of the services' payroll costs lists Cooks separate, and after, petty officers, making them non rated (2).

The 1862 uniform regulations prescribe standard enlisted, jumper style, uniforms for Cooks (3).

By the 1891 regulations, Stewards and Cooks were to wear a sack coat and cap. The coat was described as "To be of dark navy blue cloth, single-breasted sack pattern, rolling collar, lined with blue flannel or black Italian cloth; five medium size black navy buttons on front. A pocket in the left breast and one in each front near the bottom; front and back of skirt to descend to top of inseam of trousers. Coat to be buttoned when worn.". The cap was to be the same as jacketed petty officers which was described as "Dark navy-blue cloth; band, lustrous black mohair: visor, black patent leather, bound with same, green underneath chin strap, black patent leather 1/2 inch wide fastened at the side with two small gilt navy buttons and provided with one gilt and one leather slide. Two small eyelet ventilating holes, in each side of the quarters." (4).

The 1908 uniform regulations are basically the same but the coat had only four buttons, black buttons were worn on the cap and a white version of the same uniform worn in the summer (5).

When the coast guard's rates and ratings were made the same as the navy's on Mary 18, 1920, Cooks serving on vessels were made Ship's Cooks Second Class who were petty officers and those not serving on vessels were made Ship's Cooks Third Class in the Seaman First Class pay grade (6).

District Commander

District Superintendents became District Commanders on July 2, 1926 (1).

The 1927 Coast Guard Register shows four District Commanders holding the relative rank of Lieutenant Commander, Gus Lofberg, James Phillips, Simon Sands and Chester Lippincott, and ten holding the relative rank of Lieutenant, Frank Lincoln, John Kelly, Martin Rasmussen, Ralph Crowley, Howard Wilcox, James Price, Oswald Littlefield, Eugene Osborn, Christopher J. Sullivan and William Wolf (2).

Under the 1930 uniform regulations, District Commanders wore the uniform of their relative ranks with light green cloth between the stripes on the cuffs and shoulder boards (3).

Loftberg retired on July 31, 1929 (3) and Crowley died on March 6, 1931 (4).

By the 1932 register, Phillips, Sands, Lippincott, Lincoln, Kelly and Rasmussen were relative Lieutenant Commanders and two new relative Lieutenants had been appointed, Ward Bennett and Sigval Johnson (5). Wilcox was a relative Lieutenant Commander by 1933 (6). Kelly died on November 11, 1933 (7) and Phillips died on October 3, 1934 (8). Wilcox retired on July 1, 1934 (9). By the 1935 register, Littlefield was a relative Lieutenant Commander and new relative Lieutenants Irwin Steel, Charles walker and Martinus Jensen had been appointed (10). Osborn was a Lieutenant Commander by 1934 (11) and Sullivan and Wolf by 1937 (12). Lippincott retired on August 1, 1936 and Price on July 1, 1937 (13). A new relative Lieutenant named Frank Allison was appointed on

June 19, 1937 (14) and another, Anthony Glaza on August 6th (15). Sands retired on June 1, 1939 (16). By the 1939 register all of the District Commanders except Walker and Glaza were relative Lieutenant Commanders (17).

The rank of District Commander was abolished on August 5, 1939 (18) and all officers became line officers at their equivalent rank.

District Superintendent

The life saving service had been organized into 13 districts, each lead by a Superintendent. When the life saving service was merged with the revenue cutter service to form the coast guard on January 28, 1915 (1), the 13 District Superintendents became commissioned officers. The law had made all superintendents into officers, but it appears that the General Superintendent Sumner Kimball and the Assistant General Superintendent Oliver Maxam, remained civilians (2).

The superintendent's rank would be District Superintendent but they would hold relative rank with line officers according to seniority. There would be one relative Captain, Edwin Chapman, three relative First Lieutenants, Herbert Knowles, George Bowley and William Tunnell, Four relative Second Lieutenants, John Cole, Otto Wellander, Gus Loftberg and James Phillips, and five relative Third Lieutenants, Edgar Chadwick, Simon Sands, Chester Lippincott, Peter Jensen and John Richardson (3).

District Superintendents wore the uniform of their relative rank with no shied above the stripes on the cuffs and shoulder boards. Light green cloth was worn between the stripes and a lifesaver replaced the shield on the collar anchor (4).

Wellander died on July 29, 1919 (5). Richardson retired on August 20, 1919 (6), Knowles on March 26, 1920 and Chapman on July 21st (7).

When the line officer's ranks were changed on June 5, 1920, the relative ranks of District Superintendents changed as well. Captain was now Lieutenant Commander, First Lieutenant was now Lieutenant, Second Lieutenant was now Lieutenant (Junior Grade) and Third Lieutenant was now Ensign.

The 1921 register shows Bowley as a relative Lieutenant Commander, Tunnell, Cole and Loftberg a relative Lieutenants, Phillips, Chadwick Sands and Jensen as relative Lieutenants (Junior Grade) and Lippincott was a relative Ensign joined by four new appointments. Frank Lincoln and John Kelly on March 11, 1920, Martin Rassmusen on August 17, 1920 and Ralph Crowley on August 28th (8).

Chadwick died on April 5, 1922 (9), and a new relative Ensign named Howard Wilcox was appointed on August 29th (10). By 1923 Lippincott was a Lieutenant (Junior Grade). Bowley retired on August 13, 1923 (11), making Tunnell a relative Lieutenant Commander, Phillips a relative Lieutenant and making room for a new relative Ensign named James Price, appointed on November 19th (12). Jensen retired on June 26, 1924 (13) and was replaced by relative Ensign Oswald Littlefield (14). Tunnell retired on March 24, 1925 (15) making Cole a relative Lieutenant Commander, Sands a Relative Lieutenant and Eugene Osborn a relative Ensign appointed on August 6th (16).

District Superintendents became District Commanders on July 2, 1926 (17).

Electrician

The warrant rank of Electrician were created in the navy on March 4, 1925 (1), and the coast guard followed suit (2). Previously Gunners had been assigned to electrical duties. The petty officers rating of Electrician had been changed to Electrician's Mate in 1920 (3).

Under the 1930 uniform regulations, Electricians were distinguished by a 1/4 inch wide gold cuff stripe with 1/2 inch blue breaks every two inches under a gold american shield that was in turn under a gold hemisphere of a globe.

Shoulder boards were the same with only one break in the stripe. The globe was also worn on aviation garrison caps (4).

A gold globe was used as the Electrician's pin on badge of rank starting in 1941 (5).

The Career Compensation Act of October 12, 1949 (6) placed Electricians in pay grade W-1.

A standard, warrant officers badge of rank was introduced, probably in 1952 at the same time as the navy (7), consisting of a gold bar with a 1/16 inch blue break across the middle (8).

Electricians became Warrant Officer 1, with the Warrant Officer Act of 1954 (9).

Engineer in Chief

The position, but not the rank, of Engineer in Chief was created on July 31, 1894 with a law stating "That the Secretary of the Treasury shall detail a captain of the Revenue Cutter Service who shall be chief of the division of Revenue Cutter Service, and a chief engineer, who shall be engineer in chief of said Service, but no additional pay or emoluments shall be allowed on account of such detail" (1).

The title was changed to Captain of Engineers on June 4, 1897 (3).

On February 26, 1906 the title of the Captain of Engineers was changed back with a law stating "the President may select and appoint, by and with the advice and consent of the Senate, a chief engineer of said service, who has served not less than three years in that grade, as Engineer-in-Chief of the Revenue-Cutter Service, for a period of four years, and no longer, unless reappointed or sooner retired by reason of age or disability; and provided further, That the Engineer-in-Chief thus appointed shall thereafter receive the rank, pay, and allowances, while holding said appointment, that are now or may hereafter be prescribed for a Captain of the Revenue-Cutter Service," (4).

The 1908 uniform regulations prescribe for the Engineer in Chief, the uniform of a Captain, three stripes on the cuffs and a silver oak leaf as a badge of rank, with no shield above the stripes and crossed oak branches replacing the shield on the corps device (5).

A law of July 1, 1918 allowed the Engineer in Chief to temporarily hold rank equal to a navy Captain until the end of World War I (6).

The 1921 Coast Guard Register shows that the rank of Engineer in Chief survived the overhaul of the guard's rank structure in 1920 and held the relative rank of Commander (7). The relative rank was raised to Captain on January 13, 1923 (8) and Rear Admiral (Lower Half) on May 24, 1939 (9).

Under the 1930 uniform regulations, engineering officers wore the uniform of their relative rank with no special distinction (10).

It is also not clear when engineering ranks were abolished. The ranks are shown in the 1941 register (11) but not the 1944 register (12).

Ensign

Historically, an Ensign is the lowest ranking officer in an infantry regiment. It became a rank of the U.S. Navy on July 16, 1862, ranking below Master (1). The rank hadn't been used by the army since 1814 (2) and there is no information as to why it was suddenly being used in the navy.

In the coast guard the rank of Third Lieutenant became the rank of Ensign on June 5, 1920 (3).

As of 1918 Third Lieutenants were wearing one 1/2 inch stripe under and american shield on the cuffs and shoulder boards and no badge of rank (4). A gold bar had become the badge of rank by the 1930 uniform regulations (5). The navy had added the bar in 1922 (6), but it is not clear if the coast guard added the bar at the same time.

The Career Compensation Act of October 12, 1949 (7) placed the rank of Ensign in pay grade O-1.

An illustration in the 2009 uniform regulations shows that the insignia for an Ensign continues to be one 1/2 inch stripe under an american shield on the cuffs and on the shoulder boards and a gold bar as a badge of rank (8).

Ensign (Engineering)

Third Lieutenants (Engineering) became Ensigns (Engineering) on June 5, 1920 (1).

Under the 1930 uniform regulations they wore the uniform of an Ensign with no special distinction (2).

It is also not clear when engineering ranks were abolished. The ranks are shown in the 1941 register (3) but not the 1944 register (4).

Fireman

Fireman is the non rated title for engineering sailors. It is not clear when the rate was added to the cutter service. It was may have been when engineering officers were added in 1845 (1).

Under the 1862 uniform regulations, Firemen wore the standard enlisted jumper style uniform with no insignia (2).

The next information we have come from the 1891 uniform regulations that call for a two stripes on the cuff (3). The navy had begun wearing such stripes in 1866 and the cutter service may have worn them long before 1891.

The 1908 uniform regulations call for a red watch mark (4).

On October 10, 1917 an order was issued to clarify the equivalency of the rates and ratings of the navy and coast guard. Firemen were made equivalent to navy Firemen First Class (5).

Firemen became Firemen First Class when the guard's rates and ratings were made the same as the navy's on May 18, 1920 (6).

Fireman First Class was changed back to Fireman in 1948 (7).

It continued the Fireman First Class position in pay grade five. Grade five became grade E-3 with The Career Compensation Act of October 12, 1949 (8).

Firemen are distinguished by a group rate mark of three red hash marks (9), and presumably have been since 1948.

Fireman Apprentice

Fireman Second Class became Fireman Apprentice in 1948 (1).

It continued the Fireman Second Class position in pay grade six. Grade Six became grade E-2 with The Career Compensation Act of October 12, 1949 (2).

Firemen Apprentice are distinguished by a group rate mark of two red hash marks (3), and presumably have been since 1948.

Fireman First Class

Firemen became Firemen First Class when the coast guard's rates and ratings were made the same as the navy's on May 18, 1920 (1). It was placed in the Seaman First Class pay grade (2), that became grade five on June 22, 1922 (3).

As a grade five rate, Firemen First Class were entitled to three stripes on the cuff and as engineering men they wore a red branch mark on the left sleeve (4).

Women were rated as Firemen during World War II and were given hash marks on the upper sleeve as insignia (5). Firemen First Class probably wore three stripes and they may have been red.

The rate of Fireman First Class was changed back to Fireman in 1948 (6).

Fireman Recruit

The history, or even the existence, of the rate of Fireman Recruit in the coast guard is not clear.

The navy created the rate in 1948 (1) in grade seven that became grade E-1 under The Career Compensation Act of October 12, 1949 (2), and the coast guard may have created the rate at the same time. A list of coast guard rates and ratings compiled in 1993 does show some striker ratings (a rating earned by a non petty officer) such as Controlman Fireman Recruit beginning in 1948 (3), but only lists Fireman and Fireman Apprentice as rates in their own right.

Following the navy's pattern, a Fireman Recruit wore one red hash mark as a group rate mark.

If the rate existed, it is gone by the 1997 uniform regulations (4), that only shows the white mark of a Seaman Recruit.

Fireman Second Class

The rate of Firemen Second Class when the coast guard's rates and ratings were made the same as the navy's on May 18, 1920 (1). It was placed in the Seaman Second Class pay grade (2), that became grade five on June 22, 1922 (3).

As a grade five rate, Firemen First Class were entitled to two stripes on the cuff and as engineering men they wore a red branch mark on the left sleeve (4).

Women were rated as Firemen during World War II and were given hash marks on the upper sleeve as insignia (5). Firemen Second Class probably wore two stripes and they may have been red.

The rate of Fireman First Class became Fireman Apprentice in 1948 (6).

Fireman Third Class

Coal Heavers became Firemen Third Class when the coast guard's rates and ratings were made the same as the navy's on May 18, 1920 (1). It was placed in the Seaman Third Class pay grade (2), that became grade seven on June 22, 1922 (3).

As a grade seven rate, Firemen First Class were entitled to one stripe on the cuff and as engineering men they wore a red branch mark on the left sleeve (4).

The rate of Fireman Third Class was abolished in 1948 (6).

First Assistant Engineer

In 1862 uniforms were prescribed for First Assistant Engineers three buttons on the cuff and a gold paddle wheel in the center of the shoulder straps (1). However, as far as the law goes, the rank of Assistant Engineer was not split into First Assistant and Second Assistant until February 4, 1863 (2). The law gave First Assistant Engineers the relative rank of Second Lieutenant.

In 1864 First Assistant Engineers were given two 1/4 inch gold stripes on the cuff and added a gold bar at each end of the shoulder strap (3).

The gold bar as a badge of rank was placed on the collar in 1871 under a four bladed propellor and the letter U.S.R.M.. The collar insignia was meant to replace shoulder straps but were unpopular and shoulder straps returned in 1873 (4), this time with the propellor in the center (5). It is not clear if engineering officers wore epaulets. If they did the bars were probably worn at either side of the frog with the propellor in the middle.

The bar, accompanied by the propellor, returned to the collars of service coats in 1878 (6).

New cuff stripes were authorized in 1900. Second Lieutenants, and therefore First Assistant Engineers, were prescribed one thick stripe, probably 1/2 inch, under one thin stripe, probably 1/4 inch (7).

First Assistant Engineers became Second Lieutenants of Engineers on April 16, 1908 (8).

First Lieutenant

The term lieutenant comes from the French for "placeholder" (1). It can be thought of a someone who hold a place or is a tenant instead of or in lieu of. A tenant in lieu of is a lieutenant.

When revenue cutters were first authorized in law on August 4, 1790 (3), their second ranking officers held the rank of First Mate. It is not clear when this was changed. The next law when the cutters are mentioned on March 2, 1799 (4) used the term "first lieutenant or, mate,", but a pay table from the same year uses the title First Mate (5). Lists of officers from the War of 1812 (6) list First Mates, so the title was not in use then. The date certain for the use of the title of First Lieutenant is July 2, 1836 when it is used in a law setting the pay of officers (7).

Revenue officers are known to have worn epaulets as early as 1819 (8), and may have worn them since 1790. It would make sense that First Lieutenants or Mates wore an epaulet on the right shoulder, but there is no proof of this until the first known uniform regulations in 1830.

The 1830 regulations prescribe three buttons on the cuff and a gold epaulet on the right shoulder (9).

In 1833 the three buttons on the cuff were replaced with one 1/2 inch wide strip of gold lace (10). This was short lived as both the gray uniforms of 1834 and the blue uniforms of 1836 had the three buttons under a strip of black braid. The gold epaulet remained (11).

Shoulder straps, consisting of a strip of gold lace on the right shoulder, were introduced in 1838 (12).

A treasury shied under an anchor was added to the epaulet frogs in 1844 (13).

In 1853 Epaulets, and therefore shoulder straps, were ordered to be worn on both shoulders, and shoulder straps became a gold rectangle with a blue center (14). First Lieutenants wore a gold treasury shield on an anchor in the center with a star above and below and one gold bar at each end of the strap (15).

New uniforms were authorized in 1862 (16). Those for a First Lieutenant had one stripe of 1/2 inch gold lace on the cuffs (putting an end to the three buttons), a gold anchor and treasury shield the center of the shoulder straps with two gold bars at each end and the epaulets were one again plain (17).

A law of February 4, 1863 (18) made First Lieutenants in the revenue cutter service equal to lieutenants in the navy.

New uniform regulations in 1864 continued the two gold bars, which were also the badge of rank of a navy Lieutenant, at each end of the shoulder strap and changed the cuff stripes to three, all under an american shield (19).

The two gold bars as a badge of rank were placed at either end of the frog of the epaulet, with an anchor between, and on the collar in 1871 between an anchor and the letter U.S.R.M.. The collar insignia was meant to replace shoulder straps but were unpopular and shoulder straps returned in 1873 (20), this time with a treasury shield and an anchor in the center (21).

The bars, accompanied by a treasury shield, returned to the collars of service coats in 1878 (22).

The 1891 uniform regulations prescribe 1/4 inch cuff stripes, instead of the 1/2 inch stripes prescribed in 1864. A gold anchor with a silver american shield was worn as a corps device in the center of epaulet frogs and shoulder straps, and on the blue service coat collar. The two gold bars remained the badge of rank (23).

New cuff stripes were authorized in 1900. First Lieutenants were prescribed one thick stripe, probably 1/2 inch, with two thin stripes, probably 1/4 inch (24).

The cuff stripes were made the same as a navy Lieutenant in 1905, two 1/2 inch stripes (25).

The 1908 uniform regulations continue the stripes and gold bars and corps device on the collar. The bars and device is also worn on shoulder knots, which had replaced epaulets, and on shoulder boards (26).

By 1917 the shoulder boards carried the stripes from the cuff instead of the bars and corps device (27).

On June 5, 1920 the officer's rank structure of the coast guard was made the same as the navy's, and all First Lieutenants became just Lieutenants (28).

First Lieutenant of Engineers

The rank of Chief Engineer became the rank of First Lieutenant of Engineers on April 16, 1908 (1).

Under the 1908 uniform regulations First Lieutenants of Engineers wore two 1/2 inch cuff stripes, with no shield, two gold bars as a badge of rank on shoulder knots, shoulder boards and collars joined by a corps device of an anchor and crossed oak branches (2).

By 1917 the two stripes, instead of the bars and corps device, were worn on the shoulder boards (3).

First Lieutenants of Engineers became Lieutenants (Engineering) on June 5, 1920 (4).

First Mate

First Mate was the original number 2 rank after Master when revenue cutters were authorized on August 4, 1790 (1). It is not clear how long this lasted. The next law when the cutters are mentioned on March 2, 1799 (2) used the term "first lieutenant or, mate,", but a pay table from the same year uses the title First Mate (3). Lists of officers from the War of 1812 (4) list First Mates, so the title was not in use then. The date certain for the end of the title of First Mate is July 2, 1836 when a law setting the pay of officers lists First Lieutenants (5).

It is possible that First Mates wore a gold epaulet on the right shoulder, but there is no proof.

Gunner

Gunners were known to exist in the revenue cutter service as early as 1799 (1), but their status is not clear. In the navy Gunners were warrant officers but there was no law that created warrant officers in the cutter service. On the other hand a list of officers from 1832 (2) does list men holding the rank of "Warrant Officer" and some of them may have been Gunners.

The first known uniforms for warrant officers were prescribed in 1836. They were described as "Blue cloth coat or jacket, with nine revenue buttons on the lapels, three under the pocket flap, and on each cuff: white or blue pantaloons, according to season (3).

An estimate of the payroll costs of the cutter service from 1843 (4) does not list warrant officers, only petty officers. As a result, Gunner may have become a petty officer's rating.

Gunner is listed as a petty officer's rating in the 1891 uniform regulations, distinguished by gold crossed cannons and a cannon ball on the upper right sleeve (5).

Beginning with an apportions law of June 30, 1906 (6), funds were allocated to pay "warrant and petty officers" instead of just the term "petty officers", that had been used in earlier laws. This is probably the point that Gunners became warrant officers, or warrant officers again if the had been prior to 1843.

The 1908 uniform regulations confirm the status as warrant officers and prescribe a bursting bomb as a badge of rank on the collar (7).

Warrant officers were prescribed 1/4 inch wide gold stripes on cuffs and shoulder boards in 1920 (8). There is some photographic evidence (9), by no means conclusive, that the stripes were not originally broken by blue breaks. It is possible that this changed in 1926 when chief warrant officers were authorized. The 1930 uniform regulations do prescribe broken stripes described as "Warrant officer. One 1/4 inch stripe, the gold lace to be woven at intervals of 2 inches with dark blue silk thread in widths of one half inch.". The stripes on shoulder boards had a single blue break in the center of the stripe. The bursting bomb was worn above and american shield worn above the stripes. The bomb were also worn on aviation garrison caps (10).

In 1941 the gold bomb became a badge of rank worn on khaki shirt collars (11).

The Career Compensation Act of October 12, 1949 (12) placed Gunners in pay grade W-1.

A standard, warrant officers badge of rank was introduced, probably in 1952 at the same time as the navy (13), consisting of a gold bar with a 1/16 inch blue break across the middle (14).

Gunner became Warrant Officer 1, with the Warrant Officer Act of 1954 (15).

Hospital Apprentice (First Class and Second Class?)

The 1930 uniform regulations prescribe insignia for Hospital Apprentices of a red cross on the upper sleeve (1).

The rate does not appear in the general order of May 18, 1920 that made the coast guard's rates and ratings, mostly, the same as the navy's (2). Nor does it appear in a list of coast guard and revenue cutter service rates and ratings compiled in 1993 (3). However it must have existed at one time.

In the navy there were two classes of Hospital Apprentice, a first class in grade five and a second class in grade six. They also wore the red cross along with no branch mark and two (for second class) or three (for first class) cuff stripes (4). It is possible that the coast guard used the same system.

In September of 1944, female Hospital Apprentices in the navy were allowed to wear two or three white/blue hash marks on the upper left sleeve, with the red cross directly above (5). Female Hospital Apprentices in the coast guard are known to have worn the cross and may have worn the hash marks (6).

The rates of Hospitalman, Hospitalman Apprentice and Hospitalman Recruit were created in 1948 (7), and more than likely replaced Hospital Apprentices.

Hospitalman

The rate of Hospitalman was created in 1948 (1), probably from Hospital Apprentices First Class.

It was placed in pay grade five (2). Grade five became grade E-3 with The Career Compensation Act of October 12, 1949 (3).

In the navy it was given a group rate mark of three white/blue hash marks under a caduceus (3), and the coast guard may have worn the same insignia.

The rate of Hospitalman was abolished in 1982 (4).

Hospitalman Apprentice

The rate of Hospitalman Apprentice was created in 1948 (1), probably from Hospital Apprentices Second Class.

It was placed in pay grade six (2). Grade five became grade E-2 with The Career Compensation Act of October 12, 1949 (3).

In the navy it was given a group rate mark of two white/blue hash marks under a caduceus (3), and the coast guard may have worn the same insignia.

The rate of Hospitalman Apprentice was abolished in 1982 (4).

Hospitalman Recruit

The rate of Hospitalman Recruit was created in 1948 (1).

It was placed in pay grade seven (2). Grade five became grade E-1 with The Career Compensation Act of October 12, 1949 (3).

In the navy it was given a group rate mark of one white/blue hash mark under a caduceus (3), and the coast guard may have worn the same insignia, and it is possible that the caduceus was worn alone by the late 1970s.

The rate of Hospitalman Recruit was abolished in 1982 (4).

Keeper

The rank of Keeper came to the coast guard from the life saving service. A keeper was the man in charge of a life saving station. When the revenue cutter service and the life saving service were combined to form the coast guard on January 28, 1915, Keeper was made a warrant rank (1).

The 1899 uniform regulations for the life saving service prescribed a uniform of a dark blue coat, trousers and visored cap. The coat was described as "Coat--To be of dark indigo-blue kersey or flannel, sack pattern, double-breasted, rolling collar; five large regulation gilt buttons on each side, the top buttons placed close to the collar, the lower ones about 6 inches from the bottom, and the others regularly spaced between. The bottom of the coat should not extend below the second joint of the thumb when the arms hang naturally by the side. There will be two inside breast pockets, and two outside pockets, without flaps, at the hips. Cuffs to be plain, with two small regulation gilt buttons on outside seam. All buttons to be attached with rings." The trousers were plain and the cap carried a badge described as "On the front of the band there will be worn an ornament embroidered in gold, consisting of a life buoy (inside diameter 3/4 inch, outside diameter 1 1/4 inches), crossed and interlocked with an oar and a boat hook, each 2 inches long. Above the device there will be embroidered, also in gold, the letters "U. S." and below it "L. S. S."" (2).

Under the 1916 coast guard uniform regulations, warrant officers were prescribed standing collar blue or white coats with black (on the blue coat) or white (on the white coat) braid 1 1/4 inches wide outlining the edges, covering the collar and worn 2 1/2 inches from the edge of the coat. Keepers were allowed, in addition to the blue and white coats, an olive drab coat with olive drab braid. The coat was worn with matching trousers and visored caps. Black braid was worn around the band of all three colors of cap. Insignia of crossed oars on a life saver was worn in gold on the collars of the blue and white coat and bronze on the olive drab coat. Crossed anchors were worn on the cap in gold on blue and white and bronze on olive drab (3).

The rank of Keeper was merged with the rank of Boatswain on May 18, 1920 (4).

Landsman

A Landsman is someone who is not an experienced sailor, hence "landsman" not "seaman".

Landsman became a rate in the coast guard when it's rates and ratings were made the same as the navy's on May 18, 1920 (1). It was placed in the Seaman Third Class pay grade in both the Artificer Branch and the Special Branch (2).

The rate's pay grade would have entitled it to one stripe on the cuff and a white/blue branch mark (3).

The navy abolished the rate of Landsman in 1921 (4), and the coast guard probably did as well.

Lieutenant

The term lieutenant comes from the French for "placeholder" (1). It can be thought of a someone who hold a place or is a tenant instead of or in lieu of. A tenant in lieu of is a lieutenant.

The rank of First Lieutenant became just Lieutenant, it's navy equivalent, on June 5, 1920 (2).

The First Lieutenant's insignia, two 1/2 inch stripes under an american shield on the cuffs and shoulder boards and two silver bars as a badge of rank was continued (3).

The Career Compensation Act of October 12, 1949 (4) placed the rank of Lieutenant in pay grade O-3.

An illustration in the 2009 uniform regulations shows that the insignia for a Lieutenant continues to be two 1/2 inch stripes under an american shield on the cuffs and on the shoulder boards and two silver bars as a badge of rank (5).

Lieutenant (Engineering)

First Lieutenants (Engineering) became Lieutenants (Engineering) on June 5, 1920 (1).

Under the 1930 uniform regulations they wore the uniform of a Lieutenant with no special distinction (2).

It is also not clear when engineering ranks were abolished. The ranks are shown in the 1941 register (3) but not the 1944 register (4).

Lieutenant (Junior Grade)

The term lieutenant comes from the French for "placeholder" (1). It can be thought of a someone who hold a place or is a tenant instead of or in lieu of. A tenant in lieu of is a lieutenant.

The rank of Second Lieutenant became Lieutenant (Junior Grade), it's navy equivalent, on June 5, 1920 (2).

The Second Lieutenant's insignia, one 1/2 inch stripes, under on 1/4 inch stripe, under an american shield on the cuffs and shoulder boards and a silver bar as a badge of rank was continued (3).

The Career Compensation Act of October 12, 1949 (4) placed the rank of Lieutenant (Junior Grade) in pay grade O-2.

An illustration in the 2009 uniform regulations shows that the insignia for a Lieutenant (Junior Grade) continues to be one 1/2 inch stripes, under on 1/4 inch stripe, under an american shield on the cuffs and shoulder boards and a silver bar as a badge of rank (5).

Lieutenant (Junior Grade) (Engineering)

Second Lieutenants (Engineering) became Lieutenants (Junior Grade) (Engineering) on June 5, 1920 (1).

Under the 1930 uniform regulations they wore the uniform of a Lieutenant (Junior Grade) with no special distinction (2).

It is also not clear when engineering ranks were abolished. The ranks are shown in the 1941 register (3) but not the 1944 register (4).

Lieutenant Commander

The original rank of Captain became the rank of Lieutenant Commander, it's navy equivalent, on June 5, 1920 (1).

The Captain's insignia, two 1/2 inch stripes with a 1/4 inch stripe between them, under an american shield on the cuffs and shoulder boards and a gold oak leaf as a badge of rank was continued (2).

The Career Compensation Act of October 12, 1949 (3) placed the rank of Lieutenant Commander in pay grade O-4.

An illustration in the 2009 uniform regulations shows that the insignia for a Lieutenant Commander continues to be two 1/2 inch stripes with a 1/4 inch stripe between them, under an american shield on the cuffs and shoulder boards and a gold oak leaf as a badge of rank (4).

Lieutenant Commander (Engineering)

Captains of Engineers became Lieutenant Commanders (Engineering) on June 5, 1920 (1).

Under the 1930 uniform regulations they wore the uniform of a Lieutenant Commander with no special distinction (2).

It is also not clear when engineering ranks were abolished. The ranks are shown in the 1941 register (3) but not the 1944 register (4).

Machinist

Men who where listed as Chief Oilers in the 1906 register (1) are listed as Machinists in the 1907 Register (2). Both were listed as warrant ranks.

The 1908 uniform regulations prescribe a three bladed propellor as a badge of rank on the collar (3).

Warrant officers were prescribed 1/4 inch wide gold stripes on cuffs and shoulder boards in 1920 (4). There is some photographic evidence (5), by no means conclusive, that the stripes were not originally broken by blue breaks. It is possible that this changed in 1926 when chief warrant officers were authorized. The 1930 uniform regulations do prescribe broken stripes described as "Warrant officer. One 1/4 inch stripe, the gold lace to be woven at intervals of 2 inches with dark blue silk thread in widths of one half inch.". The stripes on shoulder boards had a single blue break in the center of the stripe. The propellor was worn above and american shield worn above the stripes. The propellor were also worn on aviation garrison caps (6).

In 1941 the gold propellor became a badge of rank worn on khaki shirt collars (7).

The Career Compensation Act of October 12, 1949 (8) placed Gunners in pay grade W-1.

A standard, warrant officers badge of rank was introduced, probably in 1952 at the same time as the navy (9), consisting of a gold bar with a 1/16 inch blue break across the middle (10).

Machinist became Warrant Officer 1, with the Warrant Officer Act of 1954 (11).

Marine

Pay tables for the crews of revenue cutters form 1799 list cutters with 14 guns carrying 14 Marines and cutters with 10 guns carrying eight Marines (1).

Did this mean that revenue cutters were carrying Marines, as in sea soldiers? Probably not. The tables were probably attempting to list Mariners, The term used for common sailors in the laws that set up the cutter service (2)(3).

Mariner

The law of August 4, 1790 (1) that created revenue cutters, and another law on March 2, 1799 (2) reefer to the enlisted sailors as Mariners. This was more than likely a term used for common sailors.

The term Seaman was used on an estimate for the service's payroll expenses in 1843 (3), meaning that the term Mariner was no longer in use by that point

Master

Mater was the original title of commanders of revenue cutters when they were authorized on August 4, 1790 (1). It is not clear when this was changed. The next law when the cutters are mentioned on March 2, 1799 (2) used the term "captain or master", and a pay table from the same year uses the title Captain (3). Lists of officers from the War of 1812 (4) list Captains, so the title was in use by then

It is possible that Masters wore a gold epaulet on each shoulder, but there is no proof.

Master Chief Petty Officer

When the E-9 pay grade was created on May 20, 1958 (1), the rate of Master Chief Petty Officer was created to fill it (2).

The rating badge was a standard Chief Petty Officers badge, three chevrons and one arc under an eagle with a specialty mark under the arc, with two stars above the eagle (3).

In 1959 all three grades of chiefs were given a pin on badge of rank. A smaller version of the gold fouled anchor and silver american shield that had been used as a cap device. Two silver stars were added above the anchor stock for Master Chiefs in 1961 (4).

The 2009 uniform regulations describe the badge of rank for all three grades of Chief Petty Officer as "The chief petty officer collar insignia will consist of a 15/16 inch gold metal fouled anchor with a silver shield superimposed on the shank. One, two, or three stars are attached to the stock to designate senior and master chief petty officers and the Master Chief Petty Officer of the Coast Guard, respectively." (5). The rating badge for all grades is described as "The rating badge indicates the wearer's rate/pay grade. It consists of a perched eagle with the wings extended upward and the head to eagle's right. Chevron(s) and star(s) indicate the wearer's rate/pay grade. The colors of the chevrons are scarlet for E-4 through E-6 and gold E-7 through E-9, and MCPOCG. The background is the same color as the jacket. Chevrons and stars worn on the Dinner Dress White Jacket will be with a white background and dark blue chevrons and stripes." (6) and the three chevrons and one arc, along with the stars, are shown in illustration (7).

Master Chief Petty Officer of the Coast Guard

A position for a senior enlisted advisor to the Commandant of the Coast Guard was created in 1969, and was given the rate of Master Chief Petty Officer of the Coast Guard (1).

The first Master Chief Petty Officer of the Coast Guard was Charles Calhoun who took office on August 1, 1969 (2).

A black and white photograph of Calhoun shaking hands with President Nixon shows him wearing a chief petty officer's rating badge, three gold point down chevrons under one arc with a silver eagle sitting on the arc, with three stars above the eagle and the specialty mark of a Boatswain's mate, crossed anchors, between the arc and chevrons. A later color photo shows the specialty mark having been replaced by an american shield. In the second photo, the stars and the shield appear to be silver, but this may just be the quality of the color film of the time (3).

A photograph of Calhoun's successor, Philip Smith who took office on August 1, 1973, shows the shield and star in gold and a badge of rank on the collar of a gold anchor and silver shield under three silver stars (4).

Smith was replaced by Hollis Stephen's on August 1, 1977 (5), and he was replaced by Carl Constantine on August 1,1981 (6). Next up was Allen Thiele on May 1, 1986 (7), then came R. Jay Lloyd on June 29, 1990 (8). Rick Trent became Master Chief Petty Officer of the Coast Guard on July 1, 1994 (9), followed by Vincent Patton on May 31, 1998 (10). Charles Bowen filled in on an interim basis from July to October 2002 when Franklin Welch took office (11). Bowen was given the position permanently in 2006 (12) and was replaced by Michael Leavitt on May 21, 2010 (13). At this writing in the spring of 2012, Leavitt is still in office.

The 2009 uniform regulations describe the badge of rank for all three grades of Chief Petty Officer as "The chief petty officer collar insignia will consist of a 15/16 inch gold metal fouled anchor with a silver shield superimposed on the shank. One, two, or three stars are attached to the stock to designate senior and master chief petty officers and the Master Chief Petty Officer of the Coast Guard, respectively." (14). The rating badge for all grades is described as "The rating badge indicates the wearer's rate/pay grade. It consists of a perched eagle with the wings extended upward and the head to eagle's right. Chevron(s) and star(s) indicate the wearer's rate/pay grade. The colors of the chevrons are scarlet for E-4 through E-6 and gold E-7 through E-9, and MCPOCG. The background is the same color as the jacket. Chevrons and stars worn on the Dinner Dress White Jacket will be with a white background and dark blue chevrons and stripes." (15) and the three chevrons, one arc and two stars are shown in illustration (16).

Master's Mate

The July 1907 register lists seven men with the warrant rank of Master's Mate, all appointed on May 7, 1907. Three of the men are named Bradley, a John and two James. The others were named E.N. Thacher, Robert Hudson, John Patricio and James Dunn (1).

The existence of warrant officers in the cutter service in this era is not clear. They were not mentioned in law for decades until a law of May 26, 1906 (2) concerning the punishment of service personnel. The law appropriating funds to pay for the cutter service on March 3, 1905 (3) does not mention warrant officers but the next law on June 30, 1906 (4) does.

The 1908 uniform regulations prescribe "Two foul anchors, embroidered in gold crossed on centers of shanks, placed upon the crossing of the two anchors, a shield embroidered in silver." (5) as a badge of rank.

The rank of Master's Mate was combined with the rank of Boatswain on May 18, 1920 (6).

Mess Attendant First Class

Boy First Class became Mess Attendant First Class with the alignment of rates and ratings with those of the navy on May 18, 1920 (1).

If the coast guard followed the navy's practice, Mess Attendants of all classes wore one stripe on the cuff and no branch mark (2), with a white/blue crescent added to the upper left sleeve in 1921 (3).

The navy moved Mess Attendant's First Class to grade five in 1922 (4), and the coast guard may have as well. This would have given them three stripes on the cuff.

The coast guard's 1930 uniform regulation confirms the crescent and the lack of a branch mark (5).

The navy changed the title to Steward's Mate First Class in 1943 (6), and the coast guard may have as well. If they did not, Mess Attendants First Class became Stewardsmen in 1948 (7).

Mess Attendant Second Class

Boy First Class became Mess Attendant Second Class with the alignment of rates and ratings with those of the navy on May 18, 1920 (1).

If the coast guard followed the navy's practice, Mess Attendants of all classes wore one stripe on the cuff and no branch mark (2), with a white/blue crescent added to the upper left sleeve in 1921 (3).

The navy moved Mess Attendant's Second Class to grade six in 1922 (4), and the coast guard may have as well. This would have given them two stripes on the cuff.

The coast guard's 1930 uniform regulation confirms the crescent and the lack of a branch mark (5).

The navy changed the title to Steward's Mate Second Class in 1943 (6), and the coast guard may have as well. If they did not, Mess Attendants Second Class became Stewardsmen Apprentice in 1948 (7).

Mess Attendant Third Class

The rate of Mess Attendant Third Class was created with the alignment of rates and ratings with those of the navy on May 18, 1920 (1).

If the coast guard followed the navy's practice, Mess Attendants of all classes wore one stripe on the cuff and no branch mark (2), with a white/blue crescent added to the upper left sleeve in 1921 (3).

The navy moved Mess Attendant's Third Class to grade seven in 1922 (4), and the coast guard may have as well. If this is true they would have continued to wear one stripe.

The coast guard's 1930 uniform regulation confirms the crescent and the lack of a branch mark (5).

The navy changed the title to Steward's Mate Third Class in 1943 (6), and the coast guard may have as well. If they did not, Mess Attendants Third Class became Stewardsmen Recruit in 1948 (7).

(Officer's) Chief Cook

It is not clear if the rate of Officer's Chief Cook ever existed in the coast guard.

The navy created the rate in 1942, in grade one (1). They wore a white/blue crescent over our horizontal bars as insignia (2) until 1944 when they were given a Chief Petty Officer's rating badge with the crescent as a specialty mark (3). At that time navy changed the title to Chief Cook. It was combined with Chief Steward in 1948 into the rate of Steward (4).

It is possible all of this was duplicated in the coast guard.

(Officer's) Chief Steward

It is not clear if the rate of Officer's Chief Steward ever existed in the coast guard.

The navy created the rate in 1942, in grade one (1). They wore a white/blue crescent over our horizontal bars as insignia (2) until 1944 when they were given a Chief Petty Officer's rating badge with the crescent as a specialty mark (3). At that time navy changed the title to Chief Steward. It was combined with Chief Cook in 1948 into the rate of Steward (4).

It is possible all of this was duplicated in the coast guard.

(Officer's) Cook First Class

Insignia for Officer's Cooks First Class, a crescent over three horizontal bars, appears in the 1930 uniform regulations (1).

The navy had created the rate in 1924, in grade two (2), and the coast guard may have created the rate at the same time.

The insignia was changed to a standard rating badge for a First Class Petty Officer with the crescent as the specialty mark in 1944 (3).

In the navy, the title was changed to Cook First Class in 1944 (4) and combined with the rate of Steward First Class into the rate of Steward, still not a petty officer's rating (5) in 1948 (6). It is possible that this happened in the coast guard as well, or it is possible that a petty officer's rating of Steward was created in the coast guard in 1944 (7).

(Officer's) Cook Second Class

Insignia for Officer's Cooks Second Class, a crescent over two horizontal bars, appears in the 1930 uniform regulations (1).

The navy had created the rate in 1924, in grade three (2), and the coast guard may have created the rate at the same time.

The insignia was changed to a standard rating badge for a Second Class Petty Officer with the crescent as the specialty mark in 1944 (3).

In the navy, the title was changed to Cook Second Class in 1944 (4) and combined with the rate of Steward Second Class into the rate of Steward, still not a petty officer's rating (5) in 1948 (6). It is possible that this happened in the coast guard as well, or it is possible that a petty officer's rating of Steward was created in the coast guard in 1944 (7).

(Officer's) Cook Third Class

Insignia for Officer's Cooks Third Class, a crescent over one horizontal bar, appears in the 1930 uniform regulations (1).

The navy had created the rate in 1924, in grade four (2), and the coast guard may have created the rate at the same time.

The insignia was changed to a standard rating badge for a Third Class Petty Officer with the crescent as the specialty mark in 1944 (3).

In the navy, the title was changed to Cook Third Class in 1944 (4) and combined with the rate of Steward Third Class into the rate of Steward, still not a petty officer's rating (5) in 1948 (6). It is possible that this happened in the coast guard as well, or it is possible that a petty officer's rating of Steward was created in the coast guard in 1944 (7).

(Officer's) Steward First Class

Insignia for Officer's Steward First Class, a crescent over three horizontal bars, appears in the 1930 uniform regulations (1).

The navy had created the rate in 1924, in grade two (2), and the coast guard may have created the rate at the same time.

The insignia was changed to a standard rating badge for a First Class Petty Officer with the crescent as the specialty mark in 1944 (3).

In the navy, the title was changed to Steward First Class in 1944 (4) and combined with the rate of Cook First Class into the rate of Steward, still not a petty officer's rating (5) in 1948 (6). It is possible that this happened in the coast guard as well, or it is possible that a petty officer's rating of Steward was created in the coast guard in 1944 (7).

(Officer's) Steward Second Class

Insignia for Officer's Steward Second Class, a crescent over two horizontal bars, appears in the 1930 uniform regulations (1).

The navy had created the rate in 1924, in grade three (2), and the coast guard may have created the rate at the same time.

The insignia was changed to a standard rating badge for a Second Class Petty Officer with the crescent as the specialty mark in 1944 (3).

In the navy, the title was changed to Steward Second Class in 1944 (4) and combined with the rate of Cook Second Class into the rate of Steward, still not a petty officer's rating (5) in 1948 (6). It is possible that this happened in the coast guard as well, or it is possible that a petty officer's rating of Steward was created in the coast guard in 1944 (7).

(Officer's) Steward Third Class

Insignia for Officer's Steward Third Class, a crescent over one horizontal bar, appears in the 1930 uniform regulations (1).

The navy had created the rate in 1924, in grade four (2), and the coast guard may have created the rate at the same time.

The insignia was changed to a standard rating badge for a Third Class Petty Officer with the crescent as the specialty mark in 1944 (3).

In the navy, the title was changed to Steward Third Class in 1944 (4) and combined with the rate of Cook Third Class into the rate of Steward, still not a petty officer's rating (5) in 1948 (6). It is possible that this happened in the coast guard as well, or it is possible that a petty officer's rating of Steward was created in the coast guard in 1944 (7).

Ordinary Seaman

An Ordinary Seaman is just that, an ordinary seaman. Not a trainee like a Boy or lacking naval skills like a Landsman, but below a Seaman. It was the midlevel rank among the non rated. Ordinary Seamen had existed in the navy from the beginning, but he first evidence of the rate in the cutter service comes from a book on the organization of the federal government published in 1908 (1).

The rate does not appear in the 1891 uniform regulations (2), but does in the 1908 regulations, where it was to wear two cuff stripes and a white/blue watch mark (3).

Ordinary Seamen became Seaman Second Class on May 18, 1920 (4).

Pay Clerk and Acting Pay Clerk

When a law of May 18, 1920 stated "the grades and ratings of warrant officers, chief petty officers, petty officers and other enlisted persons in the Coast Guard shall be the same as in the Navy..." (1), the warrant ranks of Pay Clerk and Acting Pay Clerk were born.

The 1921 Coast Guard Register lists 15 Acting Pay Clerks all with a date of rank of December 21, 1920 (2). By the 1923 register most of the same names are listed as Pay Clerks and a group of new Acting Pay Clerks had been appointed on October 2, 1922 (3). The Acting Pay Clerks were down to one, William Montague, in the 1925 register (4) and gone by the 1926 register (5).

Pay Clerks, as warrant officers, were prescribed 1/4 inch wide gold stripes on cuffs and shoulder boards under an american shield, under a sprig of three oak leafs (6). There is some photographic evidence (7), by no means conclusive, that the stripes were not originally broken by blue breaks. It is possible that this changed in 1926 when chief warrant officers were authorized. The 1930 uniform regulations do prescribe broken stripes described as "Warrant officer. One 1/4 inch stripe, the gold lace to be woven at intervals of 2 inches with dark blue silk thread in widths of one half inch.". The stripes on shoulder boards had a single blue break in the center of the stripe. The leafs were also worn on aviation garrison caps (8).

In 1941 the gold leafs became a badge of rank worn on khaki shirt collars (9).

The Career Compensation Act of October 12, 1949 (10) placed Pay Clerks in pay grade W-1.

A standard, warrant officers badge of rank was introduced, probably in 1952 at the same time as the navy (11), consisting of a gold bar with a 1/16 inch blue break across the middle (12).

Pay Clerk became Warrant Officer 1, with the Warrant Officer Act of 1954 (13).

Petty Officer (Before 1906?)

Petty Officers are the noncommissioned officers of the navy. The term derives from the French petite meaning small. In medieval English villages the assistants to senior officials became known as petite or petty officials. Sailors took this concept to sea with them calling the assistants to officers and warrant officers "Petty Officers" (1). A Petty Officer is a specialist in a particular job, this is known as a "rating".

The early history of petty officers on revenue cutters is not clear. A law of March 2, 1799 refers to "noncommissioned officers" (2), this may have meant petty officer. Pay tables from 1799 list Boatswains, Gunners, Carpenters and Cooks, but were they petty officers or warrant officers? There is no clear answer.

Petty officers are listed in an estimate of the payroll expense for 1843 (3), so they did exist by then (there were 45 of them).

Under the 1862 uniform regulations, petty officers were ordered to wear "Blue cloth jacket, with nine revenue buttons on each lappel, three under each pocket flap, and three on each cuff; white or blue pantaloons (according to season)." (4).

By the time of the 1891 uniform regulations, only some ratings, Boatswain, Gunner, Carpenter and Master At Arms, were wearing coats, others, Quartermaster, Coxswain and Oiler, were wearing regular jumper style uniforms. Rating was shown by specialty marks that were to be worn as "All petty officers shall wear on the outer garment (excepting the overcoat) a rating badge as per pattern. For the Boatswain, Gunner, Carpenter, and Master at Arms, the badges shall be embroidered in gold on dark navy blue cloth; and for Quartermasters, Coxswains, and Oilers, the badges shall be worked in white silk on blue clothing and in blue silk on white clothing. The badge shall be worn on the outer side of the right sleeve, half way between the shoulder and elbow...". Quartermasters, Coxswains, and Oilers were also to wear three stripes on the cuff of the jumper (5).

An eagle was placed over the rating badge in under the 1900 uniform regulations (6).

It is not clear exactly when the revenue cutter service divided petty officers into classes. It may have been under a reorganization in 1906. A book on the organization of the federal government published in 1908, before the service was reorganized again on April 16th, lists petty officers in two classes (7), so the change had happened by then.

Petty Officer First Class

Petty officers had been divided into two classes by 1908, but it is not clear exactly when it happened.

As of early 1908 the first class contained the ratings of Master at Arms, Electrician, Ship's Writer and Signal Quartermaster (1).

By the time of the 1908 uniform regulations, the first class ratings were Master at Arms, Wheelman, Ship's Writer, Electrician, Signal Quartermaster and First Oiler. Masters at Arms, Wheelmen, Ship's Writers and Electricians wore a coat and cap uniform with a rating badge with an eagle on an arc over three point down chevrons and a specialty mark in the angle of the top chevron. The badge was gold with the specialty mark in silver on blue coats and all blue on white coats. Signal Quartermasters and First Oilers wore jumper style uniforms with three stripes on the cuff and rating badges of three white chevrons, outlined in red, under a white/blue eagle and specialty mark (2).

When the life saving service and the revenue cutter service merged to form the coast guard on January 28, 1915 (3), the Number One Surfman, the senior man on a life saving boat, was made a First Class Petty Officer

By the time of the 1916 uniform regulations for the newly formed coast guard, the three chevrons and one arc on a coat and cap style uniform were worn by the ratings of Master at Arms, Number One Surfman, Electrician, Electrician First Class, Yeoman, Ship's Writer, Wheelman, Machinist First Class, and Carpenter First Class. Three chevrons were worn on a jumper style uniform by Painters First Class, Plumbers First Class, Signal Quartermasters, Oilers First Class Blacksmiths and Sailmakers. The chevrons, and arc if authorized, of all first class petty officers were red on blue uniforms and blue on white uniforms and blue on the olive drab uniforms worn by Number One Surfmen. The eagle and specialty mark were white on blue and blue on white and olive drab. Those with 12 continuous years of good conduct could wear gold chevrons (and arc) with silver eagles and marks on blue uniforms (4).

When the coast guard's rates and ratings were made the same as the navy's on May 18, 1920, the coast and cap uniforms and the rating badges with an arc were moved up to the new rate of Chief Petty Officer. Three chevrons under the eagle was now the only badge for a Petty Officer First Class. The rating badges were worn on the right sleeve by ratings in the seaman branch and on the left arm by other ratings (5).

In 1941 the eagles for ratings of the seaman branch had their heads reversed to face right, making all eagles face the wearers front (6).

1948 saw the end of rating badges on the right sleeve. From then on all ratings wore the badge on the left sleeve with the eagle facing forward (7).

The navy prescribed badges of rank for Petty Officers First Class in 1969 of a silver eagle with the three silver chevrons. It is probable that the coast guard wore these badges as well, but not certain. Eventually, probably with the uniform changes in the 1970s, a badge of three gold chevrons under a silver shield came into use (8).

The use of gold chevrons on the blue uniforms sleeves of petty officers with 12 years good conduct also ended sometime in the 1970s.

The 2009 uniform regulations describe the badges of rank for petty officers as "The petty officer collar insignia consists of one, two, or three metal, gold chevrons indicating third class, second class, and first class respectively; mounted under a silver Coast Guard shield." (9). Rating badges for all grades are described as "The rating badge indicates the wearer's rate/pay grade. It consists of a perched eagle with the wings extended upward and the head to eagle's right. Chevron(s) and star(s) indicate the wearer's rate/pay grade. The colors of the chevrons are scarlet for E-4 through E-6 and gold E-7 through E-9, and MCPOCG. The background is the same color as the jacket. Chevrons and stars worn on the Dinner Dress White Jacket will be with a white background and dark blue chevrons and stripes." (10) and the three chevrons are shown in illustration (11).

Petty Officer Second Class

Petty officers had been divided into two classes by 1908, but it is not clear exactly when it happened.

As of early 1908 the second class contained the ratings of Assistant Master at Arms, Quartermaster, First and Second Oiler, Coxswain and Water tender (1).

By the time of the 1908 uniform regulations, the second class ratings were Assistant Master at Arms, Quartermaster, Coxswain, Second Oiler and Watertender. They wore jumper style uniforms with three stripes on the cuff and rating badges of two white chevrons, outlined in red, under a white/blue eagle and specialty mark (2).

By the time of the 1916 uniform regulations the various second class ratings wore chevrons of red on blue uniforms and blue on white uniforms. The eagle and specialty mark were white on blue and blue on white and olive drab. Those with 12 continuous years of good conduct could wear gold chevrons with silver eagles and marks on blue uniforms (3).

As of 1920 the rating badges were worn on the right sleeve by ratings in the seaman branch and on the left arm by other ratings (4).

In 1941 the eagles for ratings of the seaman branch had their heads reversed to face right, making all eagles face the wearers front (5).

1948 saw the end of rating badges on the right sleeve. From then on all ratings wore the badge on the left sleeve with the eagle facing forward (6).

The navy prescribed badges of rank for Petty Officers Second Class in 1969 of a silver eagle with the two silver chevrons. It is probable that the coast guard wore these badges as well, but not certain. Eventually, probably with the uniform changes in the 1970s, a badge of two gold chevrons under a silver shield came into use (7).

The use of gold chevrons on the blue uniforms sleeves of petty officers with 12 years good conduct also ended sometime in the 1970s.

The 2009 uniform regulations describe the badges of rank for petty officers as "The petty officer collar insignia consists of one, two, or three metal, gold chevrons indicating third class, second class, and first class respectively; mounted under a silver Coast Guard shield." (8). Rating badges for all grades are described as "The rating badge indicates the wearer's rate/pay grade. It consists of a perched eagle with the wings extended upward and the head to eagle's right. Chevron(s) and star(s) indicate the wearer's rate/pay grade. The colors of the chevrons are scarlet for E-4 through E-6 and gold E-7 through E-9, and MCPOCG. The background is the same color as the jacket. Chevrons and stars worn on the Dinner Dress White Jacket will be with a white background and dark blue chevrons and stripes." (9) and the two chevrons are shown in illustration (10).

Petty Officer Third Class

It appears there was no rate of Petty Officer Third Class in the revenue cutter service. It is probable that the rate was created along with the coast guard in 1915.

The 1916 uniform regulations prescribe a rating badge of one chevron under an eagle and specialty mark. The chevrons of red on blue uniforms and blue on white uniforms. The eagle and specialty mark were white on blue and blue on white and olive drab. Those with 12 continuous years of good conduct could wear gold chevrons with silver eagles and marks on blue uniforms (1).

As of 1920 the rating badges were worn on the right sleeve by ratings in the seaman branch and on the left arm by other ratings (2).

In 1941 the eagles for ratings of the seaman branch had their heads reversed to face right, making all eagles face the wearers front (3).

1948 saw the end of rating badges on the right sleeve. From then on all ratings wore the badge on the left sleeve with the eagle facing forward (4).

The navy prescribed badges of rank for Petty Officers Third Class in 1969 of a silver eagle over a silver chevron. It is probable that the coast guard wore these badges as well, but not certain. Eventually, probably with the uniform changes in the 1970s, a badge of one gold chevron under a silver shield came into use (5).

The use of gold chevrons on the blue uniforms sleeves of petty officers with 12 years good conduct also ended sometime in the 1970s.

The 2009 uniform regulations describe the badges of rank for petty officers as "The petty officer collar insignia consists of one, two, or three metal, gold chevrons indicating third class, second class, and first class respectively; mounted under a silver Coast Guard shield." (6). Rating badges for all grades are described as "The rating badge indicates the wearer's rate/pay grade. It consists of a perched eagle with the wings extended upward and the head to eagle's right. Chevron(s) and star(s) indicate the wearer's rate/pay grade. The colors of the chevrons are scarlet for E-4 through E-6 and gold E-7 through E-9, and MCPOCG. The background is the same color as the jacket. Chevrons and stars worn on the Dinner Dress White Jacket will be with a white background and dark blue chevrons and stripes." (7) and the one chevron are shown in illustration (8).

Pharmacist

The legal authority for the warrant rank of Pharmacist came on May 18, 1920 (1), but there were no Pharmacists appointed until December 26, 1934. The original appointments went to Theodore Le Blanc, Max Lanke, Robert Wechter and David Higgins (2).

The 1930 uniform regulations prescribe broken stripes described as "Warrant officer. One 1/4 inch stripe, the gold lace to be woven at intervals of 2 inches with dark blue silk thread in widths of one half inch.". The stripes on shoulder boards had a single blue break in the center of the stripe (3). An american shield was worn over the stripes and a caduceus was worn over that by (4). The caduceus were also worn on aviation garrison caps (8).

In 1941 the gold caduceus became a badge of rank worn on khaki shirt collars (5).

The Career Compensation Act of October 12, 1949 (6) placed Pharmacists in pay grade W-1.

A standard, warrant officers badge of rank was introduced, probably in 1952 at the same time as the navy (7), consisting of a gold bar with a 1/16 inch blue break across the middle (8).

Pharmacist became Warrant Officer 1, with the Warrant Officer Act of 1954 (9).

Photographer

The warrant grade of Photographer was created in the navy by a law of July 28, 1942 (1). Apparently the rank was created in the coast guard at the same time (2).

Navy Photographers wore gold lace on the cuffs that was 1/4 inch wide with 1/2 inch long blue breaks every 2 inches. The device of a Photographer, an old fashioned camera with the bellows extend, was worn above the stripes. Shoulder boards showed the 1/4 inch lace with a single 1/2 inch break, under the device. The camera device, in gold, was also used as a badge of rank (3), the coast guard used the same insignia (4).

The Career Compensation Act of October 12, 1949 (5) placed Photographer in pay grade W-1.

A standard, warrant officers badge of rank was introduced, probably in 1952 at the same time as the navy (6), consisting of a gold bar with a 1/16 inch blue break across the middle (7).

Photographer became Warrant Officer 1 with the Warrant Officer Act of 1954 (8).

Radio Electrician

The warrant rank of Radio Electrician were created in the navy on March 4, 1925 (1), and the coast guard followed suit (2). Previously Gunners had been assigned to electrical duties.

Under the 1930 uniform regulations, Radio Electricians were distinguished by a 1/4 inch wide gold cuff stripe with 1/2 inch blue breaks every two inches under a gold american shield that was in turn under a device of four lightning bolts. Shoulder boards were the same with only one break in the stripe. The bolts was also worn on aviation garrison caps (3).

The gold bolts was used as the Radio Electrician's pin on badge of rank starting in 1941 (4).

The Career Compensation Act of October 12, 1949 (5) placed Radio Electricians in pay grade W-1.

A standard, warrant officers badge of rank was introduced, probably in 1952 at the same time as the navy (6), consisting of a gold bar with a 1/16 inch blue break across the middle (7).

Radio Electricians became Warrant Officer 1, with the Warrant Officer Act of 1954 (8).

Rear Admiral, Rear Admiral (Upper Half) and Rear Admiral (Lower Half)

The title of Rear Admiral originated in the Sixteenth or Seventeenth Century. English fleets were organized into three lines with the admiral commanding the middle line, his deputy or vice admiral commanding the front line and the lowest ranking admiral commanding the rear line. As a result the most junior rank of admiral became Rear Admiral (1).

In 1899 the navy abolished the rank of Commodore and divided it's Rear Admirals into two grades, Rear Admiral (Upper Half), and Rear Admiral (Lower Half).

The cutter service, or later the coast guard, were not large enough to require an admiral until January 13, 1923 when a law stated "That the title of captain commandant in the Coast Guard is hereby changed to commandant. Hereafter the commandant shall be selected from the active list of line officers not below the grade of commander and shall have, while serving as commandant, the rank, pay, and allowances of a rear admiral (lower half) of the Navy" (2). With that the commandant, William Reynolds, became the coast guard's first Rear Admiral (Lower Half) (3).

Reynolds retired on January 11, 1924 (4), and was replaced by Frederick Billard (5).

The 1930 uniform regulations (6), along with photographs of both Reynolds (7) and Billard (8) show cuff stripes of one two inch stripe under one 1/2 inch stripe under an american shield. The 1930 regulations describe the shoulder boards as "To be from 5 to 5 1/2 inches long, 2 1/4 inches wide, the outer end squared, and the inner end terminating in a symmetrical triangular peak, extending 1 inch beyond the parallel sides. To be made of dark blue cloth, lined with black silk, worked over one thickness of thickening material that will not curl when wet. At the center of the peak a small Coast Guard gilt button, snap fastening, is to be placed for the purpose of attaching the mark to the coat by fastening the under strap to the body of the shoulder mark. For officers of the rank of rear admiral and commodore, the top of the shoulder mark shall be covered with 2 inch gold lace, showing a margin of 1/8 inch of blue cloth. Devices shall be worked over the lace as follows: Rear Admiral. - A silver foul anchor, 1 5/8 inches long over all, width from tip to tip 1 inch, stock 15/16 inch long; mounted with the crown pointing outboard on the middle line of the shoulder mark, one half inch clear between the anchor and the button; two silver five pointed stars, each of a size to be inscribed in a circle three fourths inch in diameter, mounted with one ray pointed inward and with the centers of the stars set on the center line of the shoulder mark, 1 1/4 inches apart, from center to center of stars, the outer star three fourths inch from end of shoulder mark.". It should be noted that there is no shield on the anchor. Two silver stars were used as a badge of rank.

Billard died on May 17, 1932 (9) and was replaced by Harry Hamlet on June 14th (10). Apparently Hamelt was paid as Rear Admiral (Upper Half). The next commandant was Russell Waesche who took office on June 14, 1936 (11).

There are no laws reorganizing calling for it, but the 1944 register shows Waseche had been promoted to Vice Admiral on March 10, 1942 and other officers serving in the ranks of Rear Admiral and Commodore (12). The existence of the rank of Commodore probably means that the rank of Rear Admiral was not divided in half.

By the time of World War II, exactly when is not clear, a shield had been added to the anchor on admiral's shoulder boards (13).

The coast guard's post war commissioned rank structure was set by a law of July 23, 1947 (14), which included both the ranks of Rear Admiral (Upper Half) and Rear Admiral (Lower Half). If the navy's practice was followed, both ranks wore the same insignia, one two inch stripe under one 1/2 inch stripe on the cuff and two silver stars on the shoulder board and as a badge of rank.

The Career Compensation Act of October 12, 1949 (15) placed the rank of Rear Admiral (Upper Half) in pay grade O-8 and Rear Admiral (Lower Half) in pay grade O-7.

On October 30, 1984 the wording of the law governing officer's rank titles was changed "by striking "Rear admiral (Navy) and Rear admiral (upper half) (Coast Guard)" and inserting in lieu thereof "Rear admiral"; and"... "by striking "Commodore (Navy) and Rear admiral (lower half) (Coast Guard)" and inserting in lieu there of "Commodore" ." (16). The O-8 rank was now simply Rear Admiral and the O-7 rank was Commodore.

The new system lasted 374 days. On November 8, 1985 the wording was changed again by a law stating "Section 5501 of title 10, United States Code, is amended by striking out "Commodore" in clause (4) and inserting in lieu thereof "Rear admiral (lower half)" . " (17). The title Rear Admiral (Upper Half) is still used for clarity, but the legal title of the O-8 rank is just Rear Admiral.

In subsequent regulations (18) Rear Admirals (Lower Half) continued to use the insignia of Commodores, one two inch cuff stripe and one star on the shoulder boards and as a badge of rank. Presumably this was a continuation of what was worn before 1985.

An illustration in the 2009 uniform regulations shows that the insignia for a Rear Admiral (Upper Half) continues to be one two inch stripe under one 1/2 inch stripe under an american shield on the cuffs, two silver stars, one above the other, on the outer end on the shoulder boards and two silver stars as a badge of rank. The insignia for a Rear Admiral (Lower Half) is shown as one two inch stripe under an american shield on the cuffs, one silver star on the outer end on the shoulder boards and one silver star as a badge of rank (19).

Sailmaker

The 1921 coast guard register includes a Sailmaker named Henry Tall (1). It is not clear when Tall was warranted as a Sailmaker. His date of appointment is shown as February 3, 1911, but Tall, or any other Sailmakers, are not listed in other registers (2). It is possible that Tall was rated as a petty officer in 1911.

Tall retired on August 21, 1921 (3).

Tall would have worn same the uniform as other warrant officers with a gold diamond as a badge of rank.

Seaman (or Able Seaman)

Seaman is the basic title of a non rated sailor. The 1790 (1) and 1799 (2) laws for revenue cutters refer to common sailors as Mariners, but a 1799 pay table refers to Able Seaman (3). The "Able" was probably used to differentiate form Ordinary Seamen. From then on, Seaman was the basic non rated rate used.

The first known uniforms come from 1836 when they are described as "Blue cloth jacket, nine revenue buttons on lapels, white frock collar and facings of blue with a star worked on each side of collar, and two on each side of breast, white or blue trousers, according to the season with blue belt." (4).

The 1862 uniform regulations prescribe "White frock with collar and facings of blue, or blue frock (according to season); white of blue trousers; blue mustering cap or sennet hat."(5).

The 1891 regulations call for two stripes on the cuff (6). The navy had used cuff stripes since 1866, so the stripes may have been worn before 1891.

By the 1908 regulations the cuff stripes had been upped to three and a white/blue watch mark had been added (7).

When the coast guard's rates and ratings were changed to match the those of the navy on May 18, 1920, the rate of Seaman was placed in the Seaman First Class pay grade (8).

The navy changed Seamen to Seamen First Class in 1921 (10), and the coast guard may have as well. On the other hand a list of coast guard rates and ratings shows the rate of Seaman First Class begin created in 1934 (11).

Whenever it was created the rate of Seaman First Class was changed back to Seaman in 1948 (12).

It continued the Seaman First Class position in pay grade five. Grade five became grade E-3 with The Career Compensation Act of October 12, 1949 (13).

Seaman are distinguished by a group rate mark of three white/blue hash marks (14), and presumably have been since 1948.

Seaman Apprentice

Seaman Second Class became Seaman Apprentice in 1948 (1).

It continued the Seaman Second Class position in pay grade six. Grade Six became grade E-2 with The Career Compensation Act of October 12, 1949 (2).

Seaman Apprentice are distinguished by a group rate mark of two white/blue hash marks (3), and presumably have been since 1948.

Seaman First Class

The navy changed Seamen to Seamen First Class in 1921 (1), and the coast guard may have as well. On the other hand a list of coast guard rates and ratings shows the rate of Seaman First Class begin created in 1934 (2).

In 1921 the rate of Seaman First Class was in the Seaman First Class pay grade (3), which became grade five on June 10, 1922 (4), where it would have been in 1934.

As a grade five rate, Seaman First Class were entitled to three stripes on the cuff with a white/blue branch mark on the right sleeve (5).

Women were rated as Seaman during World War II and were given hash marks on the upper sleeve as insignia (6). Seaman First Class probably wore three stripes in white/blue.

The rate of Seaman First Class was changed back to Seaman in 1948 (7).

Seaman Recruit

Apprentice Seamen became Seamen Recruit in 1948 (1).

It continued the Apprentice Seaman position in pay grade seven. Grade Seven became grade E-1 with The Career Compensation Act of October 12, 1949 (2).

Seaman Recruits are distinguished by a group rate mark of one white/blue hash mark (3), and presumably have been since 1948.

Seaman Second Class

Ordinary Seaman became Seaman Second Class when the coast guard's rates and ratings were made the same as the navy's on May 18, 1920 (1). It was placed in the Seaman Second Class pay grade (2), that became grade five on June 22, 1922 (3).

As a grade five rate, Seaman First Class were entitled to two stripes on the cuff with a white/blue branch mark on the right sleeve (4).

Women were rated as Firemen during World War II and were given hash marks on the upper sleeve as insignia (5). Seaman Second Class probably wore two stripes in white/blue.

The rate of Seaman First Class became Seaman Apprentice in 1948 (6).

Second Assistant Engineer

In 1862 uniforms were prescribed for Second Assistant Engineers three buttons on the cuff and empty shoulder straps (1). However, as far as the law goes, the rank of Assistant Engineer was not split into First Assistant and Second Assistant until February 4, 1863 (2). The law gave Second Assistant Engineers the relative rank of Third Lieutenant.

In 1864 Second Assistant Engineers were given one 1/4 inch gold stripe on the cuff and added a gold bar at each end of the shoulder strap (3).

A four bladed propellor and the letter U.S.R.M. were placed on the collar in 1871 The collar insignia was meant to replace shoulder straps but were unpopular and shoulder straps returned in 1873 (4), this time with the propellor in the center (5). It is not clear if engineering officers wore epaulets. If they did the propellor would have been worn alone in the frog.

The propellor, returned to the collars of service coats in 1878 (6).

New cuff stripes were authorized in 1900. Third Lieutenants, and therefore Second Assistant Engineers, were prescribed one thick stripe, probably 1/2 inch (7).

Second Assistant Engineers became Third Lieutenants of Engineers on April 16, 1908 (8).

Second Lieutenant

The History of American Ranks and Rank Insignia

The term lieutenant comes from the French for "placeholder" (1). It can be thought of a someone who hold a place or is a tenant instead of or in lieu of. A tenant in lieu of is a lieutenant.

When revenue cutters were first authorized in law on August 4, 1790 (3), their third ranking officers held the rank of Second Mate. It is not clear when this was changed. The next law when the cutters are mentioned on March 2, 1799 (4) used the term "second lieutenant or, mate,", but a pay table from the same year uses the title Second Mate (5). Lists of officers from the War of 1812 (6) list Second Mates, so the title was not in use then. The date certain for the use of the title of Second Lieutenant is July 2, 1836 when it is used in a law setting the pay of officers (7).

Revenue officers are known to have worn epaulets as early as 1819 (8), and may have worn them since 1790. It would make sense that Second Lieutenants or Mates wore an epaulet on the left shoulder, but there is no proof of this until the first known uniform regulations in 1830.

The 1830 regulations prescribe a gold epaulet on the left shoulder and "omitting one button on the cuff". The problem is the way the regulations are written, it is not clear what "omitting one button on the cuff" means. Captain's uniforms are described in detail with four buttons then First Lieutenant's uniforms are described as the same "omitting one button on the cuff" and with an epaulet on the right. Then Second Lieutenants uniforms are described as the same "omitting one button on the cuff" and the epaulet on the left. Does this mean one less than a Captain, meaning three, or does it mean one less than a First Lieutenant meaning two (9)?

In 1833 the buttons on the cuff, however many there were, were replaced with two 1/2 inch wide strips of gold lace (10). This was short lived as both the gray uniforms of 1834 and the blue uniforms of 1836 had the three, yes three, buttons under a strip of black braid. The gold epaulet remained (11).

Shoulder straps, consisting of a strip of gold lace on the left shoulder, were introduced in 1838 (12).

A treasury shied under an anchor was added to the epaulet frogs in 1844 (13).

In 1853 Epaulets, and therefore shoulder straps, were ordered to be worn on both shoulders, and shoulder straps became a gold rectangle with a blue center (14). Second Lieutenants wore a gold treasury shield on an anchor in the center and one gold bar at each end of the strap (15).

New uniforms were authorized in 1862 (16). Those for a Second Lieutenant had one stripe of 1/2 inch gold lace on the cuffs (putting an end to the three buttons), a gold anchor and treasury shield the center of the shoulder straps with one gold bar at each end and the epaulets were one again plain (17).

A law of February 4, 1863 (18) made Second Lieutenants in the revenue cutter service equal to Masters in the navy.

New uniform regulations in 1864 continued the one gold bar, which were also the badge of rank of a navy Master, at each end of the shoulder strap and changed the cuff stripes to two, under an american shield (19).

The one gold bar as a badge of rank were placed at either end of the frog of the epaulet, with an anchor between, and on the collar in 1871 between an anchor and the letter U.S.R.M.. The collar insignia was meant to replace shoulder straps but were unpopular and shoulder straps returned in 1873 (20), this time with a treasury shield and an anchor in the center (21).

The bar, accompanied by a treasury shield, returned to the collars of service coats in 1878 (22).

The 1891 uniform regulations prescribe 1/4 inch cuff stripes, instead of the 1/2 inch stripes prescribed in 1864. A gold anchor with a silver american shield was worn as a corps device in the center of epaulet frogs and shoulder straps, and on the blue service coat collar. The gold bar remained the badge of rank (23).

New cuff stripes were authorized in 1900. Second Lieutenants were prescribed one thick stripe, probably 1/2 inch, with one thin stripe, probably 1/4 inch (24).

The cuff stripes were made the same as a navy Lieutenant (Junior Grade), as Masters were now called, in 1905, one 1/2 inch stripe under one 1/4 inch stripe (25).

The 1908 uniform regulations continue the stripes and gold bar and corps device on the collar. The bar and device is also worn on shoulder knots, which had replaced epaulets, and on shoulder boards (26).

By 1917 the shoulder boards carried the stripes from the cuff instead of the bars and corps device (27).

On June 5, 1920 the officer's rank structure of the coast guard was made the same as the navy's, and all Second Lieutenants became Lieutenants (Junior Grade) (28).

Second Lieutenant of Engineers

The rank of First Assistant Engineer became the rank of Second Lieutenant of Engineers on April 16, 1908 (1).

Under the 1908 uniform regulations Second Lieutenants of Engineers wore one 1/2 inch stripes under one 1/4 inch stripe with no shield on the cuffs, one gold bar as a badge of rank on shoulder knots, shoulder boards and collars joined by a corps device of an anchor and crossed oak branches (2).

By 1917 the stripes, instead of the bars and corps device, were worn on the shoulder boards (3).

Second Lieutenants of Engineers became Lieutenants (Junior Grade) (Engineering) on June 5, 1920 (4).

Second Mate

Second Mate was the original number 3 rank after First Mate when revenue cutters were authorized on August 4, 1790 (1). It is not clear how long this lasted. The next law when the cutters are mentioned on March 2, 1799 (2) used the term "second lieutenant or, mate,", but a pay table from the same year uses the title Second Mate (3). Lists of officers from the War of 1812 (4) list Second Mates, so the title was not in use then. The date certain for the end of the title of Second Mate is July 2, 1836 when a law setting the pay of officers lists Second Lieutenants (5).

It is possible that First Mates wore a gold epaulet on the left shoulder, but there is no proof.

Senior Captain

The rank of Senior Captain was created on April 16, 1908, and was equal to a navy Commander (1).

The 1908 uniform regulations prescribe three 1/2 inch cuff stripes under an american shield and a silver oak leaf as a badge of rank on shoulder boards, shoulder knots and collars (2).

By 1917 the shoulder boards carried the stripes from the cuff instead of the bars and corps device (3).

On June 5, 1920 the officer's rank structure of the coast guard was made the same as the navy's, and all Senior Captains became Commanders (4).

Senior Chief Petty Officer
When the E-8 pay grade was created on May 20, 1958 (1), the rate of Senior Chief Petty Officer was created to fill it (2).

The rating badge was a standard Chief Petty Officers badge, three chevrons and one arc under an eagle with a specialty mark under the arc, with a star above the eagle (3).

In 1959 all three grades of chiefs were given a pin on badge of rank. A smaller version of the gold fouled anchor and silver american shield that had been used as a cap device. The silver star was added above the anchor stock for Senior Chiefs in 1961 (4).

The 2009 uniform regulations describe the badge of rank for all three grades of Chief Petty Officer as "The chief petty officer collar insignia will consist of a 15/16 inch gold metal fouled anchor with a silver shield superimposed on the shank. One, two, or three stars are attached to the stock to designate senior and master chief petty officers and the Master Chief Petty Officer of the Coast Guard, respectively." (5). The rating badge for all grades is described as "The rating badge indicates the wearer's rate/pay grade. It consists of a perched eagle with the wings extended upward and the head to eagle's right. Chevron(s) and star(s) indicate the wearer's rate/pay grade. The colors of the chevrons are scarlet for E-4 through E-6 and gold E-7 through E-9, and MCPOCG. The background is the same color as the jacket. Chevrons and stars worn on the Dinner Dress White Jacket will be with a white background and dark blue chevrons and stripes." (6) and the three chevrons and one arc, along with the star, are shown in illustration (7).

Ship's Clerk

The warrant grade of Ship's Clerk was created in the navy by a law of July 28, 1942 (1). Apparently the rank was created in the coast guard at the same time (2).

Navy Ship's Clerks wore gold lace on the cuffs that was 1/4 inch wide with 1/2 inch long blue breaks every 2 inches. The device of a Ship's Clerk, crossed quill pens, was worn above the stripes. Shoulder boards showed the 1/4 inch lace with a single 1/2 inch break, under the device. The quills device, in gold, was also used as a badge of rank (3), the coast guard used the same insignia (4).

The Career Compensation Act of October 12, 1949 (5) placed Ship's Clerk in pay grade W-1.

A standard, warrant officers badge of rank was introduced, probably in 1952 at the same time as the navy (6), consisting of a gold bar with a 1/16 inch blue break across the middle (7).

Ship's Clerk became Warrant Officer 1 with the Warrant Officer Act of 1954 (8).

Ship's Cook Fourth Class

When the coast guard's rates and ratings were made the same as the navy's on May 18, 1920, the rate of Ship's Cook Fourth Class was created in the Seaman Second Class pay grade (1).

The pay grade would have entitled them to two cuff stripes.

It is not clear what happened for there. The navy made all Ship's Cooks into petty officers in 1921 (2), and the coast guard may have done the same.

Ship's Cook Third Class

When the coast guard's rates and ratings were made the same as the navy's on May 18, 1920, the rate of Ship's Cook Third Class was created in the Seaman First Class pay grade (1). Ship's Cooks first and second class were petty officers.

The pay grade would have entitled them to three cuff stripes.

It is not clear what happened for there. The navy made all Ship's Cooks into petty officers in 1921 (2), and the coast guard may have done the same.

Steerage Cook

The rate of Steerage Cook appears in the general order that changed the coast guard's rates and ratings to conform the navy on May 18, 1920 (1). The order changes the title to Warrant Officer's Steward.

It is not clear when the rate of Steerage Cook began.

They more than likely wore the single breasted coat and visored cap of other cooks and steward.

Steward (Chief, First Class, Second Class and Third Class)

In the navy the four grades of stewards and cooks were combined into four grades of Steward in 1948 (1). They were not recognized as petty officers (2) until 1949 but did wear the same rating badges (3).

It is possible that this happened in the coast guard as well, or it is possible that a petty officer's rating of Steward was created in 1944 (4).

Steward's Mate (First Class, Second Class and Third Class)

It is not clear if the coast guard used the various rates of Steward's Mate or not.

The navy changed Mess Attendants into Steward's Mates in 1943 (1). First class was in grade five, second class in grade six and third class in grade seven. They wore from one, for third class, to three, for first class, stripes on the cuff of the jumper (3), a white/blue crescent on the left upper sleeve (4) and no branch mark (5). This may have been the same in the coast guard, but it is not clear.

If the rates were used, Steward's Mates First Class became Stewardsmen, Steward's Mates Second Class became Stewardsmen Apprentice and Steward's Mates Third Class became Stewardsmen Recruit in 1948 (6).

Stewardsman

The rate of Stewardman was created in 1948 (1) either from Mess Attendant First Class or Steward's Mate First Class.

It continued to be in pay grade five. Grade five became grade E-3 with The Career Compensation Act of October 12, 1949 (2).

In the navy they wore a group rate mark of three white/blue hash marks under a crescent (3), and they probably did in the coast guard as well.

According to a list of rates and ratings compiled in 1993, the rate of Stewardsman was abolished in the 1970s (4).

Stewardsman Apprentice

The rate of Stewardman Apprentice was created in 1948 (1) either from Mess Attendant Second Class or Steward's Mate Second Class.

It continued to be in pay grade six. Grade six became grade E-2 with The Career Compensation Act of October 12, 1949 (2).

In the navy they wore a group rate mark of two white/blue hash marks under a crescent (3), and they probably did in the coast guard as well.

According to a list of rates and ratings compiled in 1993, the rate of Stewardsman Apprentice was abolished in the 1970s (4).

Stewardsman Recruit

The rate of Stewardman Recruit was created in 1948 (1) either from Mess Attendant Third Class or Steward's Mate Third Class.

It continued to be in pay grade seven. Grade seven became grade E-1 with The Career Compensation Act of October 12, 1949 (2).

In the navy they wore a group rate mark of one white/blue hash mark under a crescent (3), and they probably did in the coast guard as well.

According to a list of rates and ratings compiled in 1993, the rate of Stewardsman Recruit was abolished in the 1970s (4).

Surfman

Surfman was the title used by boat crews in the life savings service. Surfmen were numbered by seniority. The Number One Surfman was the senior man in the boat and the numbers went down from there (1).

The 1899 uniform regulations for the life saving service prescribed a uniform of a dark blue coat, trousers and visored cap. The coat was described as "1. Coat--To be of dark indigo-blue kersey or flannel, single-breasted, straight front sack, rolling collar, and lapels to close to within 4 inches of neck, with four medium-sized plain black buttons, the front and back of coat to descend to top of inseam of trousers. From the point where the collar and shoulder seams meet a plait 2 inches wide, descending through the center of each forepart, and also in the back through the center of each half back, to bottom of coat. A belt of same material as garment, 2-1/2 inches wide and double-stitched on the edges, confined at the waist line by passing through and under the four plaits, the loose ends being closed by two small black buttons. One inside breast and two outside hand pockets. Upon the right sleeve of the coat, midway between the shoulder and the elbow, will be placed the emblem of the Life-Saving Service (the life-buoy, oar, and boat hook), and in a corresponding position upon the left sleeve the number of the surfman will appear. The emblem and the number will be of white silk or linen, embroidered upon a square of dark-blue cloth. The buoy of the emblem will have an outer diameter of 2-1/4 inches. The number will be 2-1/4 inches in height. In placing these devices upon the sleeves the stitches will be placed through the edges of the cloth; not "overhanded.". Trousers were plain and the cap was described as "Cap--to be of dark-blue cloth, the same as for keepers, except that the ornament and chin strap will be omitted, and around lower part of crown there will be a black silk ribbon 1-1/2 inches wide, with" U. S. LIFE-SAVING SERVICE" printed thereon in gold block letters 7/8 inch in height." (2).

When the life saving service was merged with the revenue cutter service to form the coast guard on January 28, 1915, Number One Surfmen were made into First Class Petty Officers and the other Surfmen became non rated (3).

Surfmen wore different uniforms than other enlisted men. There was a plain blue, standing collar, seven button coat worn with a blue visored cap with "U.S. Coast Guard" in gold on the band. There was also an olive drab version with patch pockets on the coat and a blue band with gold lettering on the olive cap (4).

The law of May 18, 1920 (5) that made the coast guard's rates and ratings the navy's contained an exemption for Surfmen, and the rate continued.

By the 1930 uniform regulations, Surfmen were wearing blue or white point lapel coats with a device on the collar consisting of a life saver and crossed oars. A blue or white cap was worn with the same insignia (5).

It is not clear when the rate of Surfman ended. The term is now used as a qualification for those qualified as coxswains on rescue boats (6).

Surgeon

On March 3, 1905, Congress passed this law:
"Be it enacted by the Senate and House of Representatives of the United States of America in Congress assembled,. That the President of the United States be, and is hereby, authorized to appoint S . J . Call surgeon in the United States Revenue-Cutter Service, with rank, pay, and allowance of first lieutenant in said Service, including longevity pay under provisions of existing law." (1).

Call had been employed as a civilian doctor by the cutter service and had provided medical services on an expedition to rescue the crews of trapped whaling ships in the winter of 1897-98. He was given the commission as a reward (2).

Call retired in September of 1908 (3).

He probably wore the uniform of a First Lieutenant, possibly without the shield above the stripes. The navy's medical insignia of a gold oak leaf with a silver acorn may also have been worn.

Third Lieutenant

The term lieutenant comes from the French for "placeholder" (1). It can be thought of a someone who hold a place or is a tenant instead of or in lieu of. A tenant in lieu of is a lieutenant.

When revenue cutters were first authorized in law on August 4, 1790 (3), their junior ranking officers held the rank of Third Mate. It is not clear when this was changed. The next law when the cutters are mentioned on March 2, 1799 (4) used the term "third lieutenant or, mate,", but a pay table from the same year uses the title Third Mate (5). Lists of officers from the War of 1812 (6) list Third Mates, so the title was not in use then. The date certain for the use of the title of Third Lieutenant is July 2, 1836 when it is used in a law setting the pay of officers (7).

Revenue officers are known to have worn epaulets as early as 1819 (8), and may have worn them since 1790. It would make sense that Third Lieutenants or Mates wore officer's uniforms without epaulets, but there is no proof of this until the first known uniform regulations in 1830.

The 1830 regulations prescribe a gold epaulet on the left shoulder and "omitting one button on the cuff". The problem is the way the regulations are written, it is not clear what "omitting one button on the cuff" means. Captain's uniforms are described in detail with four buttons then First Lieutenant's uniforms are described as the same "omitting one button on the cuff" and with an epaulet on the right. Then Second Lieutenants uniforms are described as the same "omitting one button on the cuff" and the epaulet on the left, followed by Third Lieutenants "omitting one button on the cuff" and no epaulet. Does this mean one less than a Captain, meaning three, or does it mean one less than a Second Lieutenant meaning one, if Second Lieutenants were wearing one less that First Lieutenants (9)?

In 1833 the buttons on the cuff, however many there were, were replaced with three 1/4 inch wide strips of gold lace (10). This was short lived as both the gray uniforms of 1834 and the blue uniforms of 1836 had the three, yes three, buttons under a strip of black braid (11).

In 1853 Epaulets, and therefore shoulder straps, were ordered to be worn on both shoulders, and shoulder straps became a gold rectangle with a blue center (12). Third Lieutenants wore a gold treasury shield on an anchor in the center (13).

New uniforms were authorized in 1862 (14). Those for a Third Lieutenant had one stripe of 1/2 inch gold lace on the cuffs (putting an end to the three buttons), a gold anchor and treasury shield the center of the shoulder straps and the epaulets were one again plain (15).

A law of February 4, 1863 (16) made Third Lieutenants in the revenue cutter service equal to Passed Midshipmen in the navy. However the navy had replaced the rank of Passed Midshipmen with the rank of Ensign on July 1, 1862 (17).

New uniform regulations in 1864 placed an anchor with three stars on it in the center of the shoulder straps and added an american shield above the cuff stripe (18).

In 1871 an anchor was placed in the center of the epaulet frog and on the collar under the letters U.S.R.M.. The collar insignia was meant to replace shoulder straps but were unpopular and shoulder straps returned in 1873 (19), this time with a treasury shield and an anchor in the center (20).

The treasury shield, returned to the collars of service coats in 1878 (21).

The 1891 uniform regulations prescribe 1/4 inch cuff stripes, instead of the 1/2 inch stripes prescribed in 1864. A gold anchor with a silver american shield was worn as a corps device in the center of epaulet frogs and shoulder straps, and on the blue service coat collar (22).

New cuff stripes were authorized in 1900. Third Lieutenants were prescribed one thick stripe, probably 1/2 inch (23).

The cuff stripes were made the same as a navy Ensigns in 1905, one 1/2 inch stripe under (24).

The 1908 uniform regulations continue the stripes and corps device on the collar. The device is also worn on shoulder knots, which had replaced epaulets, and on shoulder boards (25).

By 1917 the shoulder boards carried the stripes from the cuff instead of the bars and corps device (26).

On June 5, 1920 the officer's rank structure of the coast guard was made the same as the navy's, and all Third Lieutenants became Ensigns (27).

Third Lieutenant of Engineers

The rank of Second Assistant Engineer became the rank of Third Lieutenant of Engineers on April 16, 1908 (1).

Under the 1908 uniform regulations Third Lieutenants of Engineers wore one 1/2 inch stripe with no shield on the cuffs and a corps device of an anchor and crossed oak branches on the collar, shoulder boards and shoulder knots (2).

By 1917 the stripes, instead of the bars and corps device, were worn on the shoulder boards (3).

Third Lieutenants of Engineers became Ensigns (Engineering) on June 5, 1920 (4).

Vice Admiral

According to the 1944 Coast Guard Register, the commandant, Russell Waseche was promoted to Vice Admiral on March 10, 1942 (1).

Waesche would have worn similar insignia as navy Vice Admirals one two inch stripe under two 1/2 inch stripes under an american shield on the cuffs, three silver stars in a triangle on the outer end on the shoulder boards and three silver stars as a badge of rank (2).

The commandant, and therefore Waseche, was made a full Admiral on March 21, 1945 (3).

The rank of Vice Admiral became a permanent part of the coast guard on August 4, 1949 (4).

The Career Compensation Act of October 12, 1949 (5) placed the rank of Vice Admiral in pay grade O-8 which it shared with Admiral and Rear Admiral (Upper Half). This lasted until May 20, 1958 when a new law (6) created pay grade O-9 for full Vice Admirals.

An illustration in the 2009 uniform regulations shows that the insignia for a Vice Admiral continues to be one two inch stripe under two 1/2 inch stripes under an american shield on the cuffs, three silver stars in a triangle on the outer end on the shoulder boards and three silver stars as a badge of rank (7).

Wardroom Steward

On March 25, 1895 the regulations of the cutter service were amended to state "Messmen shall take precedence as follows: Cabin steward, wardroom steward, ship's cook" (1). Stewards and cooks had been listed in appropriations laws since they started enumerating ranks and rates in 1872 (2), and these may be the "messmen" referred to in 1895.

The 1891 uniform regulations had prescribed for "stewards and cooks" a single breasted blue coat, closed with five black buttons and a blue visored cap (3). The 1908 regulations reduced the buttons to four (4).

As of 1908, Wardroom Stewards were considered non rated men ranking between Cabin Steward and Cook (5).

The change to the cutter service's rating structure on May 18, 1920 placed them in a special Messmen branch (6).

The Navy converted it's Wardroom Stewards to Officer's Stewards Second Class in 1923 (7), and coast guard may have followed suit. The 1930 uniform regulations refer to "Officer's Stewards and Officer's Cooks" (8).

Warrant Officer 1

Warrant Officer 1 was created by the "Warrant Officer Act of 1954" (1) in pay grade W-1, from the various warrant grades.

New insignia was prescribed in 1954. The cuff stripes were to be 1/4 inch wide with three 1/2 inch blue breaks, two inches apart, under an american shied, under the specialty device. On the shoulder boards, the 1/4 inch stripe had breaks 1/2 inch apart (which resulted in three blue portions and two gold portions), under an american shield, under the specialty device. The pin on badge of rank conformed to the unified system shared with other services, a gold bar with two blue rectangles, showing a square of gold in the middle (2).

In the navy, the creation of the rates of Master Chief and Senior Chief Petty Officer in 1958, made Warrant Officer 1 redundant. A chief who was made a warrant officer would take a pay cut. As a result the rank was eliminated in 1975 (3). It appears that the coast guard followed the same path.

Warrant Officer's Steward

Steerage Cooks became Warrant Officer's Stewards on May 18, 1920 (1).

They may have worn the coat and cap style uniform of prescribed for stewards and cooks (2)

The Navy converted it's Warrant Officers Stewards to Officer's Stewards Second Class in 1923 (3), and coast guard may have followed suit. The 1930 uniform regulations refer to "Officer's Stewards and Officer's Cooks" (4).

Part 6.
The Public Health Service

Chapter 1.
PHS Organization

The Commissioned Corps of the Public Health Service is one of the seven uniformed services of the United States, and one of two that is not part of the armed forces (1). It began in 1798 as a fund for hospitals to serve merchant seaman (2), became a service to run those hospitals in 1870 (3), with it's medical officers being made commissioned officers in 1889 (4).

The Marine Hospital Fund

On July 16, 1798 (1), Congress created a fund to provide health care to merchant seamen. Twenty cents a month was deducted from each sailors pay and this, along with private donations, funded hospitals in various ports. The hospitals were usually privately owed and operated (2). By the end of the Civil War there was a great dissatisfaction with the operation of the hospitals, and the poor organization had lead to epidemics along with charges of corruption and misuse of funds (3).

On June 29, 1870 (4), Congress placed the hospitals under the control of a Supervising Surgeon, and created the Marine Hospital Service.

The Marine Hospital Service

The Marine Hospital Fund was converted to the Marine Hospital Service on June 29, 1870 (1), and a new Supervising Surgeon, John Woodworth, was appointed on March 29, 1871 (2).

Woodworth had been Medical Director of the Army of the Tennessee during the Civil War, and imposed a military structure on the hospital service, placing the doctors in uniform and having them answer to him, not the individual hospitals (3).

An outbreak of yellow fever in Caribbean countries in 1878 brought a wave of refugees and fear that the epidemic would spread to the United States (4). In response, Congress passed the Quarantine Act on April 29th (5) that tasked the hospital service with overseeing the quarantine of ships with possible infection.

A law of January 4, 1889, made the medical officers of the marine hospital service into commissioned officers (6).

The services' role was expanded in 1891 to include examination of new immigrants (7). The new duties lead to a new name in 1902.

The Public Health and Marine Hospital Service

The Marine Hospital Service became the Public Health and Marine Hospital service on July 1, 1902 (1), and would keep that name until 1912.

The Public Health Service

The "marine hosptial" part of the name was dropped on August 14, 1912 (1), and the name became simply The United States Public Health Service.

Rank Structure

The law that made medical officers of the hospital service into commissioned officers stated "That original appointments in the service shall only be made to the rank of assistant surgeon; and no officer shall be promoted to the rank of passed assistant surgeon until after four years' service and a second examination as aforesaid; and no passed assistant surgeon shall be promoted to be surgeon until after due examination" (1). These three ranks, along with the Supervising Surgeon General were the ranks of the service. The "general" had first been mentioned as part of the Supervising Surgeon's title in 1875 (2).

The service did have, or at least acted as if it had, other ranks, such as Acting Assistant, Interne, Surgeon, Hospital Steward and Hospital Attendant. Regulations treated these as ranks (3) and they wore uniforms and rank insignia. However there was no law that made them anything other that civilian federal employees.

The 1897 hospital service regulations give officers of the service relative rank with officers of the revenue cutter service. Surgeons were relative Captains, Passed Assistant Surgeons were relative First Lieutenants and Assistant Surgeons were relative Second Lieutenants (4). There is no legal basis for this. The navy had granted relative rank to staff officers during the Civil War, but in 1869 the Attorney General ruled that relative rank could only be given by Congress, and Congress had never passed a law granting relative rank to hospital service officers.

The 1902 law that lengthened the name of the service to public health and marine hospital service, shortened the title of the Supervising Surgeon General to just Surgeon General and added the rank of Assistant Surgeon General (6).

When the name was changed again in 1912 the rank of Senior Surgeon was added (7). The same law set pay rates along with yearly increases for each rank, the same system used by the armed forces.

Both the question of Congress granting relative rank and the question of the other than commissioned titles being ranks or the titles of civilian employees were answered courtesy of a navy doctor, Lieutenant Commander Edgar Woods. Woods had been an Interne in the public health service from October 4, 1904 to August 15, 1905, then joined the navy on October 19th. Woods believed his time in the public health service should count when figuring his yearly pay increases. On July 18, 1924 the Comptroller General of the United States issued a decision stating that the services' noncommissioned ranks were civilian federal employees and Woods was not entitled to extra pay. The decision also states that when congress made the pay system the same as the armed forces, this "apparently" recognized the relative rank of PHS officers (8).

Congress passed a compensative law on April 9, 1930. It allowed commissions to be given to "medical, dental, sanitary engineer, and pharmacist officers" instead of just medical officers. It also stated "The President is authorized to prescribe appropriate titles for commissioned officers of the Public Health Service other than medical officers, corresponding to the grades of medical officers.". The law also created the rank of Medical Director and placed all PHS officers on the same footing as army officers (9). As far as can be deduced, the new officers replaced the word Surgeon with Dental Surgeon (10), Sanitary Engineer (11) or Pharmacist (12).

The October 1930 Public Health Service Register shows officers with the ranks of Senior Dental Surgeon, Dental Surgeon, Passed Assistant Dental Surgeon, Assistant Dental Surgeon, Senior Sanitary Engineer, Sanitary Engineer, Passed Assistant Sanitary Engineer, Assistant Sanitary Engineer and Assistant Pharmacist (13).

In 1943, Sanitarians were added to the PHS ranks (14).

Insignia charts from World War II show Chaplains and Internes wearing officer's insignia (15), but the 1943 register does not list them (16). Despite their insignia, their were not commissioned officers.

On July 1, 1944, a law (17) was passed that is still the basis for PHS ranks. The Surgeon General was now joined by a Deputy Surgeon General. The Surgeon General had relative rank equal the army Surgeon General (he was a Major General), and the Deputy and Assistant Surgeons General were made relative Brigadier Generals. The other ranks were divided into six grades, the Director grade was equal to an army Colonel, the Senior grade was equal to a Lieutenant Colonel, the Full grade was equal to a Major, the Senior Assistant grade was equal to a Captain, the

Assistant Grade was equal to a First Lieutenant and the Junior Assistant grade was equal to a Second Lieutenant. The ranks of medical officers were still laid out by the law and the President was still allowed to prescribe ranks for other officers. Commissions were allowed in the categories of "medicine, surgery, dentistry, hygiene, sanitary engineering, pharmacy, nursing, or related scientific specialties in the field of public health". The law retained the ranks of Medical Director (in the Director grade), Senior Surgeon, (in the Senior grade),Surgeon (in the Full grade) and Assistant Surgeon (in the Assistant grade). Passed Assistant Surgeon became Senior Assistant Surgeons (in the Senior Assistant grade) and a new rank of Junior Assistant Surgeon was created (in the Junior Assistant grade). The law also expanded the categories of non medical officer, and a law of February 28, 1948 (18) placed the creation of new categories under the authority of the Surgeon General.

The 1946 register shows ranks of Surgeon General, Medical Director (strangely no Deputy Surgeon General or Assistant Surgeons General), Senior Surgeon, Surgeon, Senior Assistant Surgeon, Assistant Surgeon, (strangely no Junior Assistant Surgeons), Dental Director, Senior Dental Surgeon, Dental Surgeon, Senior Assistant Dental Surgeon, Assistant Dental Surgeon (again no Junior Assistants), Sanitary Engineer Director, Senior Sanitary Engineer, Sanitary Engineer, Senior Assistant Sanitary Engineer, Pharmacist, Scientist Director, Senior Scientist, Scientist, Senior Assistant Scientist, Nurse Officer, Senior Assistant Nurse Officer, Assistant Nurse Officer, Junior Assistant Nurse Officer, Senior Assistant Dietitian, Assistant Dietitian, Junior Assistant Dietitian and one Junior Assistant Physical Therapist (19).

The Career Compensation Act of October 12, 1949 (20) placed the grades under the military's standard pay grade system. As commissioned officer ranks each grade began with an "O" followed by a number. The Junior Assistant grade was in grade O-1, Assistants in O-2, Senior Assistants in O-3, the Full grade in O-4, Seniors in O-5, Directors in O-6, Some Assistant Surgeons General in O-7 and the rest, along with the Deputy Surgeon General and the Surgeon General were in grade O-8. This system was unchanged when new tables were included in laws of May 20, 1958 (21) and September 7, 1962 (22).

In 1968 control of the health service passed from the Surgeon General to the Assistant Secretary of Health and Scientific Affairs, a civilian political appointee (23). The title was shortened to Assistant Secretary for Health in 1972 (24).

In 1977 Julius Richmond was appointed as both Assistant Secretary for Health and Surgeon General. He served as a commissioned officer in both offices until 1981 (25).

On September 29, 1979 a new law moved the Surgeon General up the O-9 grade and added warrant officer grades W-1, W-2, W-3 and W-4 to the health service (26). As of this writing 33 years later, no warrant officers have ever been appointed.

The Assistant Secretary for Health was placed in the O-10 pay grade on November 3, 1990, if a member of the commissioned corps (27). An appointed civilian remains a civilian.

Information on how the rank title system worked comes from The Commissioned Corps Supervisor's Guide published in 1995 (28). As of 1995 the categories were Dental, Nurse, Engineer, Scientist Sanitarians, Veterinary, Pharmacy, Dietetics, Therapy and Health Services. Dental officers use Dental Surgeon instead of Surgeon. Other non medical officers in the Director grade add the word Director after the category, such as Nurse Director or Scientist Director. Other grades add the word Officer after the category along with the modification of the grade. Examples of titles in the Senior grade would be Senior Dietetics Officer or Senior Engineer Officer. The Full grade uses the titles with no modification, such as Surgeon for medical officer or Veterinary Officer for an example of the others. The Senior Assistant, Assistant and Junior Assistant Grades add those modifiers to the front of the title. The guide also states that it is proper to refer to most of the grades by their navy equivalent, Ensign for Junior Assistant, Lieutenant (Junior Grade) for Assistant, Lieutenant for Senior Assistant, Lieutenant Commander for Full, Commander for Senior, Captain for Director and Rear Admiral for Assistant Surgeon General was exemptible but not preferable. The Surgeon General, Deputy Surgeon General and Assistant Secretary for Health are referred to by those titles only.

Chapter 2.
PHS Rank Insignia

There is nowhere near enough information available to construct a full history of rank distinctions used by the Marine Hospital/Public Health and Marine Hospital/Public Health Service. All we can do is piece together what information we have.

It is known that uniforms were worn as early as 1870 (1), but it is not clear exactly what they looked like.

The 1896 uniform regulations call for epaulets for the Surgeon General, in full dress with other officers wearing shoulder knots, all ranks wore cuff stripes. On the dress uniform, cuff stripes were worn with the Surgeon General wearing shoulder knots and other officers shoulder straps. A blue fatigue uniform carried cuff stripes in gold for the Surgeon General and black for other and badges of rank on the collar, and a white version, probably, showed rank by white cuff stripes. There was also an overcoat with rank shown by elaborate knots of black cord on the cuff (2).

The 1904 uniform regulations prescribe full dress, evening dress, dress, fatigue, white and khaki uniforms. The full dress and dress uniforms had rank shown by gold cuff stripes and shoulder knots, with the Surgeon General substituting epaulets in full dress. The evening dress coat carried the same cuff stripes and basic shoulder knots with a badge of rank worn by the Surgeon General only (2). The fatigue uniform showed rank by shoulder straps and black cuff stripes. The white coat was the same as the fatigue coat, but in white with white braid. The khaki coat showed rank by badges of rank on the shoulder loops "in yellow metal". The overcoat continued to show the black cords on the cuff (3).

The 1914 uniform regulations call for a full dress uniform with a frock coat that showed rank by gold cuff stripes, with maroon cloth, and epaulets for the Surgeon General or maroon and gold shoulder loops for other officers, a dress sack coat with blue and maroon shoulder loops and olive drab, khaki and white uniforms with badges of rank pinned to plain shoulder loops. A white dinner jacket also carried badges of rank on the shoulder loops and a blue evening jacket was decorated the same as the frock coat. Overcoats carried black cuff stripes (4).

By the time of the 1937 regulations, the uniforms of the health service had become the same a those of the navy. Rank was shown by gold cuff stripes and by shoulder boards (5).

Information on PHS insignia from World War II (6), shows badges of rank being used in addition to the cuff stripes and shoulder boards, and the insignia has been the same as the navy's ever since.

Epaulets

The term epaulet comes from epaulet, the French for shoulder (1). It is often used in the modern world for any shoulder decoration, but here it refers to a specific type of decoration. An epaulet in this context is a strap on the shoulder with fringe at the end called bullion. Above the bullion is a stiffening called a crescent. The area inside the crescent is called the frog and the area from the top of the crescent to the button by the collar is called the strap.

The Surgeon General, and only the Surgeon General was wearing epaulets on his full dress uniform by 1896. They were gold with 3/8 inch wide by 3 inch long bullion, with a silver badge of rank of a silver star in the frog and a gold corps device of an anchor crossed with a caduceus on the strap (2). The same epaulets were being worn in 1904 (3) and 1914 (4).

Shoulder Straps

Shoulder straps are included in the 1896 (1) and 1904 uniform regulations (2), but were gone by 1914 (3).

They were described as being a rectangle of 1/4 inch gold bullion four inches long and 1 3/8 inches wide, edged with twisted gold wire and with a dark blue center. The Surgeon General wore a silver star (gold in 1896) in the center of the strap and Assistant Surgeons General wore a silver eagle (in 1904). Surgeons who had been in the service for more than 20 years wore a silver oak leaf at each end and other Surgeons wore gold leafs. Passed Assistant Surgeons wore two gold bars at each end of the strap and Assistant Surgeons one gold bar.

Shoulder Knots

Shoulder knots are also included in the 1896 (1) and 1904 uniform regulations (2), and were also gone by 1914 (3).

The knots were worn with the dress uniform and the full dress uniform, except the Surgeon General used epaulets in full dress. They were made from two gold cords twisted together and outlined with gold wire and formed into a figure 8 with large third loop forming a large pad over the shoulder, all on a blue cloth background. A button was placed in the top loop of the figure 8. Badges of rank were worn on the pad, a silver (gold in 1896) star in the center for the Surgeon General, a silver eagle for Assistant Surgeons General (by 1904), a silver oak leaf on each side of the pad for Surgeons who had been in the service for more that 20 years (not prescribed for knots in 1896 but are in 1904), gold leafs for other Surgeon, two gold bars on either side for Passed Assistant Surgeons and one gold bar on each side for Assistant Surgeons. A gold corps device of an anchor crossed with a caduceus was worn in the lower loop of the Figure 8 by the Surgeon General and Assistant Surgeons General and in the center of the pad by other officers.

A simple knot of four gold cords was worn on the 1904 evening dress coat with the Surgeon General adding a silver star (4).

Maroon Shoulder Loops

The 1914 uniform regulations prescribe a unique form of insignia.

Shoulder loops of maroon cloth were worn on full dress frock coats, dress sack coats and evening coats. The loops were three inches wide where they were set into the shoulder seam and narrowed to 1 3/4 inches at a point 1/2 inch from the other end. From that point on they taper to a point and are buttoned down. On the full dress and evening coats 3/4 inch gold lace ran up the sides meeting at the point. Badges of rank were embroidered 1 1/4 inches from the shoulder seam consisting of a silver star for the Surgeon General on his evening coat only, he wore epaulets in full dress, a silver eagle for Assistant Surgeons General, a silver oak leaf for Senior Surgeons, a gold oak leaf for Surgeons, two gold bars for Passed Assistant Surgeons and one for Assistant Surgeons. Halfway between the badge of rank and the button, an anchor crossed with a caduceus corps device was worn. The dress coat loops replaced the gold lace with dark blue cloth and eliminated the corps device (1).

Shoulder Boards

Shoulder boards were created by the navy in 1899 as a rank distinction that could be easily removed to allow the coat to be cleaned. They consisted of a rectangle of stiffened, dark blue cloth with one pointed end containing a button.

Shoulder boards were not part of the 1914 PHS uniform regulations (1). They are in the 1937 regulations but the available version of the regulations does not describe them very well (2).

The 1937 regulations infer that the shoulder boards, called shoulder marks at the time, followed the navy's pattern of duplicating the cuff stripes for all but admirals, or in this case the Surgeon General. It that is the case Assistant Surgeon Generals and Medical Directors wore four 1/2 inch gold stripes, Senior Surgeons three 1/2 inch stripes, Surgeons two 1/2 inch stripes with one 1/4 inch stripe between them, Passed Assistant Surgeons two 1/2 inch stripes and Assistant Surgeons one 1/2 inch stripe under one 1/4 inch stripe. All ranks wore the anchor crossed with a caduceus corps device above the stripes. The boards for the Surgeon General are not clear. If navy, and future PHS, patterns were followed, he wore a two inch wide gold stripe running long ways down the board with the corps device near the button at the pointed end and silver stars at the other. How many stars is complicated by the prescribing the three stripes of a Vice Admiral on the cuffs, meaning there may have been three stars on the boards, but two is also possible. It is also possible that maroon cloth was worn between the stripes (3).

A chart from World War II shows the Surgeon General with two stars and no maroon cloth (4).

The only changes since then have been the addition of more stars as the senior ranks have changed and the use of one 1/2 inch stripe by the Junior Assistant grade. The 1944 act made the Deputy Surgeon General and Assistant Surgeons General into relative Brigadier Generals which would have given them one star on their boards, however the navy's practice of the rank of Rear Admiral being equal to both Brigadier and Major Generals while still wearing two stars may have lead the PHS ranks to wear two as well. The Surgeon General would have begun wearing three stars in 1979 and the Assistant Secretary for Health four in 1990.

The navy's strange use of the O-7 pay grade did eventually effect the health service. A note in the 1993 uniform regulations states that Assistant Surgeons General in the O-7 pay grade who were appointed before September 30, 1987 could continue to wear the insignia of the O-8 pay grade (5).

Shoulder Marks

Shoulder marks, or soft shoulder marks as PHS regulations now call them refers to a scaled down version of the shoulder boards that are applied to an open ended tube of cloth that can be slipped over a cloth shoulder loop of a shirt or sweater.

The navy began wearing them in 1979 (1), and the health service may have as well. They are presribed, as "soft shoulder boards" in the 1993 uniform regulations (2) and are still around in the 2009 regulations, where they are described as "Soft Shoulder Marks (SSM). SSM are designed to fit over the straps of epauletted shirts and the optional wear sweater. The arrangement of the Corps device and rank stripes is the same as for the HSBs, but the SSM is made to 3/4 scale of the men's HSB" (meaing hard shoulder boards) "for both male and female. There is no gilt button on the SSM. The Corps device on the SSM is 7/8 inch in width and height." (3).

Badges of Rank

Badges of rank is the term we shall use for the stars, eagles, leafs and bars used by officers to show rank.

The badges were used on the Surgeon General's epaulets, shoulder knots, shoulder straps and the 1914 maroon shoulder loops, but they were also used by themselves.

The 1896 uniform regulations prescribe badges on the collar of the blue fatigue coat. The Surgeon General wore a gold star, Surgeons, regardless of time of service, wore a gold oak leaf, Passed Assistant Surgeons wore two gold bars and Assistant Surgeons one gold bar. All ranks wore the anchor and caduceus corps device behind the badges (1).

Under the 1904 uniform regulations the badges of rank were a silver star for the Surgeon General, A silver eagle for Assistant Surgeons General, a silver oak leaf for Surgeons who had been in the service for more that 20 years, a gold oak leaf for other Surgeons, two gold bars for Passed Assistant Surgeons and one gold bar for Assistant Surgeons (2). The description of the khaki coat states "All commissioned officers to wear the insignia of their grade in yellow metal, on shoulder straps, about one-third distant from the shoulder seam to the collar." (3). Since some of the badges were silver the yellow metal seams strange, but that is what is said. The badges were no longer worn on the collar of the blue coat.

By the 1914 regulations the badges were worn alone on the shoulder loops of white, khaki and olive drab coats, with the silver oak leaf now belonging to the rank of Senior Surgeon (4).

The badges are not used alone under the 1937 uniform regulations (5), but by World War II they were, with the Surgeon General using two stars and Assistant Surgeons General and Medical Directors sharing the eagle. The bars had become silver by then as well (6).

Under the 1944 act the badges would have been applied to the grades by giving the Surgeon General two silver stars as before, The Deputy Surgeon General and Assistant Surgeons General might have worn one star but may have worn two because of the navy's strange use of that equivalent grade, the Director grade wore the silver eagle, the Senior grade the silver oak leaf, the Full grade the gold oak leaf, the Senior Assistant grade the two now silver bars, the Assistant grade one silver bar and the Junior Assistant grade one gold bar.

The Surgeon General was given three stars in 1979 and the Assistant Secretary for Health four in 1990.

The navy's strange use of the O-7 pay grade did eventually effect the health service. A note in the 1993 uniform regulations states that Assistant Surgeons General in the O-7 pay grade who were appointed before September 30, 1987 could continue to wear the insignia of the O-8 pay grade (7).

Overcoat Cuff knots

The 1896 and 1904 uniform regulation prescribe unique insignia on the cuffs of overcoats.

For the Surgeon General it was a band of 1 1/2 inch black braid and a band of 1/2 inch braid with a black star between them. This was similar to the insignia on the overcoats of army generals (1).

Other officers wore what was referred to as a cinquefoil, which means a design with five sides (2). In this case it refers to a five loop knot, two on each side and one on top, made from black cord. Assistant Surgeons General had a knot made up of five cords, Surgeons who had been in the service over 20 years a knot of four cords, other Surgeons three cords, Passed Assistant Surgeons two cords and Assistant Surgeons one cord (3).

By the 1914 regulations, rank was shown on overcoats by black stripes (4).

Cuff Stripes

Photographs of Supervising Surgeon General John Hamilton, who served form 1879 to 1891 and Surgeon General Walter Wyman, who served from 1891 to 1911, show what appears to be five stripes on the cuff, with the top stripe spaced above the others (1). This is similar to the cuff stripe system used by the revenue cutter service, and since the health service considered it's officers to have relative rank with officers of the cutter service, they may have used the same cuff stripes from the very early days. This is confirmed by the 1896 uniform regulations that describe the cuff stripes of the Surgeon General as "Five bands of one-fourth inch gold-wire lace around each sleeve; lower band two inches from lower edge of cuff; first four bands one-fourth inch apart; upper band one-half inch above fourth band." Surgeons wore the same "omitting two bands" unless they had been in the service over 20 years, then they added one back. Passed Assistant Surgeons wore the same as Surgeons "omitting one band", leaving two. Assistant Surgeons omitted another band leaving one (2). The stripes were black on the blue fatigue coat for all but the Surgeon General who wore gold. On the white coat white stripes were probably worn but the regulations are not clear (3).

The 1904 uniform regulations prescribe one two inch stripe under one 1/2 inch stripe for the Surgeon General, Assistant Surgeons General wore three 1/2 inch stripes, alternating with two 1/2 inch stripes, Surgeons who had been in the service over 20 years wore a 1/4 inch stripe over a 1/2 inch stripe over another 1/4 inch stripe over another 1/2 inch stripe, other Surgeons wore two 1/2 inch stripes with a 1/4 inch stripe between, Passed Assistant

Surgeons wore two 1/2 inch stripes and Assistant Surgeons wore one one 1/2 inch stripes under one 1/4 inch stripe. The stripes were gold on full dress, evening and dress coats, black on fatigue coats and white on white coats (4).

By the time of the 1914 regulations Assistant Surgeons General were wearing four 1/2 inch stripes and Senior Surgeons three. The space between the gold stripes were now filled by maroon cloth on the full dress and evening coats and black stripes without maroon cloth were worn on the overcoat (5).

The 1937 uniform regulations show the anchor and caduceus corps device was worn above the stripes. They also prescribe two 1/2 inch stripes above one two inch stripe for the Surgeon General (6).

A World War II rank chart shows the Surgeon General back down to one 1/2 inch stripe and no maroon cloth (7). All the ranks were now wearing the stripes of their navy equivalent.

The navy removed the stripes from the overcoat in 1947 (8), and the health service may have as well

PHS officers still wear the stripes of their navy equivalent, with the corps device above them. If the holder of the office is a member of the commissioned corps, the Assistant Secretary for Health wears the one two inch stripe under three 1/2 stripes of a navy Admiral. The Surgeon General wore one two inch stripe of a navy Rear Admiral (Upper Half) under one 1/2 inch stripe until his rank was raised to the O-9 pay grade in 1979, at which time the rank would wear the one two inch stripe under two 1/2 inch stripes of a navy Vice Admiral. The Deputy Surgeon General wore either the one two inch stripe of a navy Commodore or the one two inch under one 1/2 inch stripe of a navy Rear Admiral (Lower Half) until 1949 when the rank was placed in the O-8 pay grade confirming the one two inch under one 1/2 inch stripe of a navy Rear Admiral (Upper Half). Assistant Surgeons General were in the same grade, with the same stripe possibilities as the Deputy Surgeon General until 1949 when some were placed in the O-7 pay grade and others in the O-8 pay grade. They probably wore the one two inch under one 1/2 inch stripe of a navy Rear Admiral (Upper Half) and Rear Admiral (Lower Half). A note in the 1993 uniform regulations states that Assistant Surgeons General in the O-7 pay grade who were appointed before September 30, 1987 could continue to wear the insignia of the O-8 pay grade (9). After that those in the O-7 pay grade wore one two inch stripe. The Director grade wears the four 1/2 inch stripes of a navy Captain, the Senior grade the three 1/2 inch stripes of a navy Commander, the Full grade wears the two 1/2 inch stripes with one 1/4 inch stripe between them of a navy Lieutenant Commander, the Senior Assistant grade wears the two 1/2 inch stripes of a navy Lieutenant, the Assistant grade wears the one 1/2 inch stripe under one 1/4 inch stripe of a navy Lieutenant (Junior Grade) and the Junior Assistant grade wears the one 1/2 inch stripe of a navy Ensign.

Chapter 3.
PHS Ranks

Assistant (Lieutenant (Junior Grade))

The Assistant grade was created by the Public Health Service Act of July 1, 1944 (1). The law made it equal to an army First Lieutenant and therefore a navy Lieutenant (Junior Grade). It is a continuation of the rank of Assistant Surgeon and equivalent non medical titles.

Assistant Surgeons had worn the insignia of a navy Lieutenant (Junior Grade), one 1/2 inch under one 1/4 inch stripes, under the PHS corps device, on the cuffs and shoulder boards and a silver bar as a badge of rank (2).

The Career Compensation Act of October 12, 1949 (3) placed the Assistant grade in pay grade O-2.

By 1995 the titles used in the Assistant grade were Assistant Surgeon, still the title for medical officers by law, Assistant Dental Surgeon, Assistant Nurse Officer, Assistant Engineer Officer, Assistant Scientist Officer, Assistant Sanitarian, Assistant Veterinary Officer, Assistant Pharmacy Officer, Assistant Dietetics Officer, Assistant Therapy Officer and Assistant Health Services Officer, or simply Lieutenant (Junior Grade) was acceptable (4).

In later years there seams to have been more emphasis on the navy title than the various PHS titles (5).

The 2009 uniform regulations prescribes the insignia for the Assistant grade by describing cuff stripes for all ranks as "Rank Lace Stripes. Stripes are gold lace in 1/4 inch, 1/2 inch or 2 inch widths. The stripes are sewn onto each sleeve so as to be parallel with the cuff and completely encircle the sleeve. The lower edge of the bottom stripe is 2 inches from the edge of the cuff and there is a 1/4 inch space between stripes. The officer shall wear the stripe or combinations of stripes which correspond to the officer's pay grade/rank."(6), with one 1/2 inch stripe under one 1/4 inch stripe shown in illustration (7). Shoulder boards for all ranks are described as "Officers Below Flag Grade. The surface of the shoulder board is covered with blue (black in appearance) cloth. Gold lace stripes indicate rank and are of the same width, spacing and arrangement as specified for sleeve insignia in Section 6-2. However, the first stripe is positioned 1/4 inch (1/2 inch for the Junior Assistant/Ensign, O-1) from the squared end of the board. The Corps device is positioned 1/4 inch above the uppermost stripe." (8), with one 1/2 inch stripe under one 1/4 inch stripe shown in illustration (9). Badges of rank are described as "Assistant Grade (LIEUTENANT JUNIOR GRADE/LTJG) (O-2). Single silver bars centered front to back on the strap, with the long dimension of the bar parallel with the outboard shoulder seam." (10).

Assistant Dental Surgeon

Dental officers were granted commissions under a law of April 9, 1930 (1), creating the rank of Assistant Dental Surgeon.

By 1937 they were wearing the insignia of a navy Lieutenant (Junior Grade), one 1/2 inch under one 1/4 inch stripe, under the PHS corps device, on the cuffs and shoulder boards and a silver bar as a badge of rank (2).

Assistant Dental Surgeons became part of the Assistant grade on July 1, 1944 (3), but the title has continued (4).

Assistant Pharmacist

Pharmacist had existed in the health service a civilian employees. The title had been changed from Hospital Steward in 1902 (1).

They were granted commissions under a law of April 9, 1930 (2), creating the rank of Assistant Pharmacist.

By 1937 they were wearing the insignia of a navy Lieutenant (Junior Grade), one 1/2 inch under one 1/4 inch stripes, under the PHS corps device, on the cuffs and shoulder boards and a silver bar as a badge of rank (3).

Assistant Pharmacists became part of the Assistant grade on July 1, 1944 (4).

As of 1995 the title in use was Assistant Pharmacy Officer (5).

Assistant Sanitary Engineer

Sanitary Engineers were granted commissions under a law of April 9, 1930 (1), creating the rank of Assistant Sanitary Engineer.

By 1937 they were wearing the insignia of a navy Lieutenant (Junior Grade), one 1/2 inch under one 1/4 inch stripes, under the PHS corps device, on the cuffs and shoulder boards and a silver bar as a badge of rank (2).

Assistant Sanitary Engineer became part of the Assistant grade on July 1, 1944 (3).

Assistant Secretary for Health

The office of Assistant Secretary for Health began in 1967 as the Assistant Secretary for Health and Scientific Affairs in the Department of Health Education and Welfare. The title was shortened when the department became the Department of Health and Human Service in 1979 (1). With the creation of the office, the Assistant Secretary, a civilian political appointee, became the head of the public health service, with the Surgeon General now only leading the commissioned corp.

In 1977 Julius Richmond was nominated to be Assistant Secretary. He accepted the position on the condition that he would also hold the office of Surgeon General (2), making him a commissioned officer in the health service.

As Surgeon General he wore the insignia of a navy Vice Admiral (3), one two inch stripe under two 1/2 inch stripes under the anchor and caduceus corps device on the cuff, three silver stars in a triangle under the anchor and caduceus corps device on the shoulder boards and three silver stars as a badge of rank.

Richmond left office at the end of the presidency of Jimmy Carter in 1981, and the new administration appointed a civilian, Edward Brandt (4).

On November 3, 1990, Congress added Assistant Secretary for Health to the list of commissioned ranks (5), placing it in the O-10 pay grade equal to a navy Admiral.

The Assistant Secretary at the time was James Mason and he had served as acting, but only acting, Surgeon General until an appointment could be made. Antonia Novello was made Surgeon General on March 9, 1990 (6), long before November 3rd. It is therefore doubtful that Mason can be counted as a commissioned officer with the relative rank of Admiral.

In 1998 President Clinton appointed David Sachter to fill both the office of Assistant Secretary for Health and Surgeon General (7), and under the 1990 law Sachter held a commission in the O-10 pay grade. Satcher left office at the end of Clinton administration in 2001.

In 2006 John Agwunobi was named Assistant Secretary for Health by President Bush (8) and given a commission in the health service at the same time. Aguwinobi resigned in 2007 and was replaced by Joxel Garcia, who was also given a commission (9).

Neither Agwunobi or Garcia were officially the Surgeon General, but that office was filled by acting appointments during their terms (10).

Garcia left office at the end of the Bush administration and President Obama's choice for the office was Howard Koh, who was not made a commissioned officer (11). At this writing in the spring of 2012, Koh is still in office.

The 2009 uniform regulations prescribes the insignia for the Assistant Secretary for Health by describing cuff stripes for all ranks as "Rank Lace Stripes. Stripes are gold lace in 1/4 inch, 1/2 inch or 2 inch widths. The stripes are sewn onto each sleeve so as to be parallel with the cuff and completely encircle the sleeve. The lower edge of the bottom stripe is 2 inches from the edge of the cuff and there is a 1/4 inch space between stripes. The officer shall wear the stripe or combinations of stripes which correspond to the officer's pay grade/rank."(12), with one two inch stripe under three 1/2 inch stripes shown in illustration (13). Shoulder boards for all flag ranks are described as "Flag Officers. The shoulder board is covered with a gold lace leaving a 1/8 inch cloth margin along each side. The Corps device is embroidered with the head of the staff of the caduceus positioned 11/4 inches from the pointed end of the board. Rank shall be indicated by the use of 1 (O-7), 2 (O-8), 3 (O-9), or 4 (O-10), silver colored, embroidered, 5-pointed stars, arranged as shown in the Appendix B." (14), and Appendix B shows four stars in a diamond (15). Badges of rank are described as "Flag Officers. 4 (O-10) Admiral, 3 (O-9) Vice Admiral, 2 (O-8) Rear Admiral Upper Half, 5-pointed, silver stars arranged in a straight line along a thin silver connecting bar, with 1 ray of each star pointing along the connecting bar." (16), with four stars shown in illustration (17).

Assistant Surgeon

Assistant Surgeon was one of the original ranks created when marine hospital service officers were granted commissions on January 4, 1889 (1).

The 1896 uniform regulations prescribe one 1/4 inch cuff stripe (2), a gold bar as a badge of rank on shoulder knots, shoulder straps (3) and collars and a cinquefoil knot of one cord on the cuff of the overcoat (4).

Regulations, but not laws, of 1897 made marine hospital service Assistant Surgeons equal to Second Lieutenants of the revenue cutter service (5), however relative rank can only be given in law, so this was not official.

The 1904 uniform regulations prescribe cuff stripes of one 1/2 inch under one 1/4 inch (6), and continued the gold bar as a badge of rank on shoulder knots and shoulder straps, but not the collar (7) and the cinquefoil knot of one cord on the cuff of the overcoat (8).

The 1914 uniform regulations continued the gold bar, now on maroon shoulder loops and kept the cuff stripes the same (9).

By the 1937 regulations the one 1/2 inch stripe under one 1/4 inch stripe were worn on shoulder boards and the anchor and caduceus corps device was worn above the stripes on both the shoulder and cuff (10).

Badges of rank were not generally used under the 1937 regulations but had returned by World War II, however the bar was now silver (11).

Assistant Surgeons became part of the Assistant grade on July 1, 1944 (12), but by law, the title has continued (13).

Assistant Surgeon General

The rank of Assistant Surgeon General was added to the public health and marine hospital service on July 1, 1902 (1).

The 1904 uniform regulations prescribe four 1/2 inch cuff stripes (2), a silver eagle as a badge of rank on shoulder knots and shoulder straps (3) and a cinquefoil knot of five cords on the cuff of the overcoat (4).

The 1914 uniform regulations continued the silver eagle, now on maroon shoulder loops and kept the cuff stripes the same (5).

By the 1937 regulations the four 1/2 inch stripes were worn on shoulder boards and the anchor and caduceus corps device was worn above the stripes on both the shoulder and cuff (6).

Badges of rank were not generally used under the 1937 regulations but had returned by World War II (7).

The Public Health Service Act of July 1, 1944 (8) made Assistant Surgeons General equal to an army Brigadier General. This creates a problem in determining what insignia they wore. The equivalency was with the army, but the insignia came from the navy and the navy had no rank equal to a Brigadier General from 1899 to 1943, and even then appointments to the rank of Commodore were only temporary. It is therefore possible that Assistant Surgeons General wore the one two inch stripe under one 1/2 inch stripe on the cuffs and two silver stars on shoulder boards and as a badge of rank of a navy Rear Admiral. It is also possible they wore the one two inch stripe and one star of a navy Commodore.

The Career Compensation Act of October 12, 1949 (9) placed some Assistant Surgeons General in the O-8 pay grade, equal to an army Major General, and placed the rest in the O-7 pay grade, equal to a Brigadier General. What insignia did they wear? Probably the two stripes and two stars of a navy Rear Admiral. A note in the 1993 uniform regulations states that Assistant Surgeons General in the O-7 pay grade who were appointed before September 30, 1987 could continue to wear the insignia of the O-8 pay grade (10). This implies that they were previously wearing O-8 insignia.

One two inch stripe under one 1/2 inch stripe on the cuffs and two silver stars on shoulder boards and as a badge of rank was worn by Assistant Surgeons General appointed after September 30, 1987 (11).

The 2009 uniform regulations prescribes the insignia for the Assistant Surgeon General by describing cuff stripes for all ranks as "Rank Lace Stripes. Stripes are gold lace in 1/4 inch, 1/2 inch or 2 inch widths. The stripes are sewn onto each sleeve so as to be parallel with the cuff and completely encircle the sleeve. The lower edge of the bottom stripe is 2 inches from the edge of the cuff and there is a 1/4 inch space between stripes. The officer shall wear the stripe or combinations of stripes which correspond to the officer's pay grade/rank."(12), with one two inch stripe under one 1/2 inch stripes for O-8 and one two inch stripe for O-7 shown in illustration (13). Shoulder boards for all flag ranks are described as "Flag Officers. The shoulder board is covered with a gold lace leaving a 1/8 inch cloth margin along each side. The Corps device is embroidered with the head of the staff of the caduceus positioned 11/4 inches from the pointed end of the board. Rank shall be indicated by the use of 1 (O-7), 2 (O-8), 3 (O-9), or 4 (O-10), silver colored, embroidered, 5-pointed stars, arranged as shown in the Appendix B." (14), and Appendix B shows two stars, one above the other for O-8 and one star for O-7 (15). Badges of rank are described as "Flag Officers. 4 (O-10) Admiral, 3 (O-9) Vice Admiral, 2 (O-8) Rear Admiral Upper Half, 5-pointed, silver stars arranged in a straight line along a thin silver connecting bar, with 1 ray of each star pointing along the connecting bar." (16), with two stars for O-8 and one for O-7 shown in illustration (17).

Dental Surgeon

Dental officers were granted commissions under a law of April 9, 1930 (1), creating the rank of Dental Surgeon.

By 1937 they were wearing the insignia of a navy Lieutenant Commander, two 1/2 inch with one 1/4 inch stripe between them, under the PHS corps device, on the cuffs and shoulder boards and a gold oak leaf as a badge of rank (2).

Dental Surgeons became part of the Full grade on July 1, 1944 (3), but the title has continued (4).

Deputy Surgeon General

The Deputy Surgeon General was authorized by the Public Health Service Act of July 1, 1944 (1).

The 1944 law made the position equal to an army Brigadier General. This creates a problem in determining what insignia they wore. The equivalency was with the army, but the insignia came from the navy and the navy had no rank equal to a Brigadier General from 1899 to 1943, and even then appointments to the rank of Commodore were only temporary. It is therefore possible that the Deputy Surgeon General wore the one two inch stripe under one 1/2 inch stripe on the cuffs and two silver stars on shoulder boards and as a badge of rank of a navy Rear Admiral. It is also possible he wore the one two inch stripe and one star of a navy Commodore.

The Career Compensation Act of October 12, 1949 solved the insignia problem by placing the Deputy Surgeon General in the O-8 grade, equal to an army Major General or navy Rear Admiral.

The 2009 uniform regulations prescribes the insignia for the Deputy Surgeon General by describing cuff stripes for all ranks as "Rank Lace Stripes. Stripes are gold lace in 1/4 inch, 1/2 inch or 2 inch widths. The stripes are sewn onto each sleeve so as to be parallel with the cuff and completely encircle the sleeve. The lower edge of the bottom stripe is 2 inches from the edge of the cuff and there is a 1/4 inch space between stripes. The officer shall wear the stripe or combinations of stripes which correspond to the officer's pay grade/rank."(2), with one two inch stripe under one 1/2 inch stripes shown in illustration (3). Shoulder boards for all flag ranks are described as "Flag Officers. The shoulder board is covered with a gold lace leaving a 1/8 inch cloth margin along each side. The Corps device is embroidered with the head of the staff of the caduceus positioned 11/4 inches from the pointed end of the board. Rank shall be indicated by the use of 1 (O-7), 2 (O-8), 3 (O-9), or 4 (O-10), silver colored, embroidered, 5-pointed stars, arranged as shown in the Appendix B." (4), and Appendix B shows two stars, one above the other (5). Badges of rank are described as "Flag Officers. 4 (O-10) Admiral, 3 (O-9) Vice Admiral, 2 (O-8) Rear Admiral Upper Half, 5-pointed, silver stars arranged in a straight line along a thin silver connecting bar, with 1 ray of each star pointing along the connecting bar." (6), with two stars shown in illustration (7).

Director (Captain)

The Director grade was created by the Public Health Service Act of July 1, 1944 (1). The law made it equal to an army Colonel and therefore a navy Captain. It is a continuation of the rank of Medical Director and equivalent non medical titles.

Medical Directors had worn the insignia of a navy Captain, four 1/2 inch stripes, under the PHS corps device, on the cuffs and shoulder boards and a silver eagle as a badge of rank (2).

The Career Compensation Act of October 12, 1949 (3) placed the Director grade in pay grade O-6.

By 1995 the titles used in the Director grade were Medical Director, still the title for medical officers by law, Dental Director, Nurse Director, Engineer Director, Scientist Director, Sanitarian Director, Veterinary Director, Pharmacy Director, Dietetics Officer, Therapy Officer and Health Services Officer, or simply Captain was acceptable (4).

In later years there seams to have been more emphasis on the navy title than the various PHS titles (5).

The 2009 uniform regulations prescribes the insignia for the Assistant grade by describing cuff stripes for all ranks as "Rank Lace Stripes. Stripes are gold lace in 1/4 inch, 1/2 inch or 2 inch widths. The stripes are sewn onto each sleeve so as to be parallel with the cuff and completely encircle the sleeve. The lower edge of the bottom stripe is 2 inches from the edge of the cuff and there is a 1/4 inch space between stripes. The officer shall wear the stripe or combinations of stripes which correspond to the officer's pay grade/rank."(6), with four 1/2 inch stripes shown in illustration (7). Shoulder boards for all ranks are described as "Officers Below Flag Grade. The surface of the shoulder board is covered with blue (black in appearance) cloth. Gold lace stripes indicate rank and are of the same width, spacing and arrangement as specified for sleeve insignia in Section 6-2. However, the first stripe is positioned 1/4 inch (1/2 inch for the Junior Assistant/Ensign, O-1) from the squared end of the board. The Corps device is positioned 1/4 inch above the uppermost stripe." (8), with four 1/2 inch stripes shown in illustration (9). Badges of rank are described as "Director Grade (CAPTAIN/CAPT) (O-6). Left and right silver eagles, with the talons of one foot grasping an olive branch and the other talons grasping a bundle of arrows. Each eagle is worn with the top of the head pointing towards the collar and eagle's beak and the olive branches pointing forward." (10).

Full (Lieutenant Commander)

The Full grade was created by the Public Health Service Act of July 1, 1944 (1). The law made it equal to an army Major and therefore a navy Lieutenant Commander. It is a continuation of the rank of Surgeon and equivalent non medical titles. The "full" is a reference to titles having no modifiers.

Surgeons had worn the insignia of a navy Lieutenant Commander, two 1/2 inch stripes with one 1/4 inch stripes between them, under the PHS corps device, on the cuffs and shoulder boards and a gold oak leaf as a badge of rank (2).

The Career Compensation Act of October 12, 1949 (3) placed the Full grade in pay grade O-4.

By 1995 the titles used in the Assistant grade were Surgeon, still the title for medical officers by law, Dental Surgeon, Nurse Officer, Engineer Officer, Scientist Officer, Sanitarian, Veterinary Officer, Pharmacy Officer, Dietetics Officer, Therapy Officer and Health Services Officer, or simply Lieutenant Commander was acceptable (4).

In later years there seams to have been more emphasis on the navy title than the various PHS titles (5).

The 2009 uniform regulations prescribes the insignia for the Assistant grade by describing cuff stripes for all ranks as "Rank Lace Stripes. Stripes are gold lace in 1/4 inch, 1/2 inch or 2 inch widths. The stripes are sewn onto each sleeve so as to be parallel with the cuff and completely encircle the sleeve. The lower edge of the bottom stripe is 2 inches from the edge of the cuff and there is a 1/4 inch space between stripes. The officer shall wear the stripe or combinations of stripes which correspond to the officer's pay grade/rank."(6), with two 1/2 inch stripes with one 1/4 inch stripes between them shown in illustration (7). Shoulder boards for all ranks are described as "Officers Below Flag Grade. The surface of the shoulder board is covered with blue (black in appearance) cloth. Gold lace stripes indicate rank and are of the same width, spacing and arrangement as specified for sleeve insignia in Section 6-2. However, the first stripe is positioned 1/4 inch (1/2 inch for the Junior Assistant/Ensign, O-1) from the squared end of the board. The Corps device is positioned 1/4 inch above the uppermost stripe." (8), two 1/2 inch stripes with one 1/4 inch stripes between them shown in illustration (9). Badges of rank are described as "Full Grade (LIEUTENANT COMMANDER/LCDR) (O-4). Gold oak leaves, smooth finished, raised and veined; worn with the stem of the oak leaf pointing outboard and the center lobe of the leaf pointing inboard." (10).

Junior Assistant (Ensign)

The Junior Assistant grade was created by the Public Health Service Act of July 1, 1944 (1). The law made it equal to an army Second Lieutenant and therefore a navy Ensign.

Navy Ensigns wore one 1/2 inch stripe, under the PHS corps device, on the cuffs and shoulder boards and a gold bar as a badge of rank (2).

The Career Compensation Act of October 12, 1949 (3) placed the Assistant grade in pay grade O-1.

By 1995 the titles used in the Junior Assistant grade were Junior Assistant Surgeon, the title for medical officers by law, Junior Assistant Dental Surgeon, Junior Assistant Nurse Officer, Junior Assistant Engineer Officer, Junior Assistant Scientist Officer, Junior Assistant Sanitarian, Junior Assistant Veterinary Officer, Junior Assistant Pharmacy Officer, Junior Assistant Dietetics Officer, Junior Assistant Therapy Officer and Junior Assistant Health Services Officer, or simply Ensign was acceptable (4).

In later years there seams to have been more emphasis on the navy title than the various PHS titles (5).

The 2009 uniform regulations prescribes the insignia for the Assistant grade by describing cuff stripes for all ranks as "Rank Lace Stripes. Stripes are gold lace in 1/4 inch, 1/2 inch or 2 inch widths. The stripes are sewn onto each sleeve so as to be parallel with the cuff and completely encircle the sleeve. The lower edge of the bottom stripe is 2 inches from the edge of the cuff and there is a 1/4 inch space between stripes. The officer shall wear the stripe or combinations of stripes which correspond to the officer's pay grade/rank."(6), with one 1/2 inch stripe shown in illustration (7). Shoulder boards for all ranks are described as "Officers Below Flag Grade. The surface of the shoulder board is covered with blue (black in appearance) cloth. Gold lace stripes indicate rank and are of the same width, spacing and arrangement as specified for sleeve insignia in Section 6-2. However, the first stripe is positioned 1/4 inch (1/2 inch for the Junior Assistant/Ensign, O-1) from the squared end of the board. The Corps device is positioned 1/4 inch above the uppermost stripe." (8), with one 1/2 inch stripe shown in illustration (9). Badges of rank are described as "Junior Assistant Grade (ENSIGN/ENS) (O-1). Single gold bars centered front to back on the strap, with the long dimension of the bar parallel with the outboard shoulder seam." (10).

Medical Director

The rank of Medical Director was created by a law of April 9, 1930 (1).

By 1937 they were wearing the insignia of a navy Captain, four 1/2 inch stripes, under the PHS corps device, on the cuffs and shoulder boards and a silver eagle as a badge of rank (2).

Medical Directors became part of the Director grade on July 1, 1944 (3), but the title has continued (4).

Passed Assistant Dental Surgeon

Dental officers were granted commissions under a law of April 9, 1930 (1), creating the rank of Passed Assistant Dental Surgeon.

By 1937 they were wearing the insignia of a navy Lieutenant, two 1/2 inch stripes, under the PHS corps device, on the cuffs and shoulder boards and a two silver bars as a badge of rank (2).

Passed Assistant Dental Surgeons became part of the Senior Assistant grade on July 1, 1944 (3), and the title used became Senior Assistant Dental Surgeon (4).

Passed Assistant Pharmacist

Pharmacists were granted commissions under a law of April 9, 1930 (1). Pharmacist had existed in the health service a civilian employees. The title had been changed from Hospital Steward in 1902 (2). The 1930 register lists 10 commissioned officers with the rank of Assistant Pharmacist (3) and no officers in higher ranks. It wasn't until December 1, 1933 that the rank of Passed Assistant Pharmacist was given to B.E. Holsendorf (4). By the 1943 register the only Pharmacists listed were three Passed Assistant Pharmacists, Charles Bierman, Raymond Kinsey and Thomas Armstrong (5).

By 1937 they were wearing the insignia of a navy Lieutenant, two 1/2 inch stripes, under the PHS corps device, on the cuffs and shoulder boards and a two silver bars as a badge of rank (6).

Passed Assistant Pharmacists became part of the Senior Assistant grade on July 1, 1944 (3).

Passed Assistant Sanitary Engineer

Sanitary Engineers were granted commissions under a law of April 9, 1930 (1), creating the rank of Passed Assistant Sanitary Engineer.

By 1937 they were wearing the insignia of a navy Lieutenant, two 1/2 inch stripes, under the PHS corps device, on the cuffs and shoulder boards and a two silver bars as a badge of rank (2).

Passed Assistant Sanitary Engineers became part of the Senior Assistant grade on July 1, 1944 (3).

Passed Assistant Surgeon

Passed Assistant Surgeon was one of the original ranks created when marine hospital service officers were granted commissions on January 4, 1889 (1).

The 1896 uniform regulations prescribe two 1/4 inch cuff stripes (2), two gold bars as a badge of rank on shoulder knots, shoulder straps (3) and collars and a cinquefoil knot of two cords on the cuff of the overcoat (4).

Regulations, but not laws, of 1897 made marine hospital service Passed Assistant Surgeons equal to First Lieutenants of the revenue cutter service (5), however relative rank can only be given in law, so this was not official.

The 1904 uniform regulations prescribe two 1/2 inch cuff stripes (6), two gold bars as a badge of rank on shoulder knots and shoulder straps, but not the collar (7) and a cinquefoil knot of two cords on the cuff of the overcoat (8).

The 1914 uniform regulations continued the gold bars, now on maroon shoulder loops and kept the cuff stripes the same (9).

By the 1937 regulations the two 1/2 inch stripes were worn on shoulder boards and the anchor and caduceus corps device was worn above the stripes on both the shoulder and cuff (10).

Badges of rank were not generally used under the 1937 regulations but had returned by World War II, however the bars were now silver (11).

Passed Assistant Surgeons became part of the Senior Assistant grade on July 1, 1944 (12), and the title, by law, became Senior Assistant Surgeon (13).

Sanitarian

Sanitarians were added to the health service in 1943 (1).

It is not clear what ranks they occupied from then until the rank structure was overhauled on July 1, 1944 (2).

Sanitary Engineer

Sanitary Engineers were granted commissions under a law of April 9, 1930 (1), creating the rank of Sanitary Engineer.

By 1937 they were wearing the insignia of a navy Lieutenant Commander, two 1/2 inch with one 1/4 inch stripe between them, under the PHS corps device, on the cuffs and shoulder boards and a gold oak leaf as a badge of rank (2).

Sanitary Engineers became part of the Full grade on July 1, 1944 (3).

Sanitary Engineer Director

Sanitary Engineers were granted commissions under a law of April 9, 1930 (1), but no appointments to Sanitary Engineer Director were made until July 23, 1936 when Joseph Le Prince took office (2).

Under 1937 the various director ranks were wearing the insignia of a navy Captain, four 1/2 inch stripes, under the PHS corps device, on the cuffs and shoulder boards and a silver eagle as a badge of rank (3).

Sanitary Engineers Directors became part of the Director grade on July 1, 1944 (4).

Senior (Commander)

The Senior grade was created by the Public Health Service Act of July 1, 1944 (1). The law made it equal to an army Lieutenant Colonel and therefore a navy Commander. It is a continuation of the rank of Senior Surgeon and equivalent non medical titles.

Senior Surgeons had worn the insignia of a navy Commander, three 1/2 inch stripes, under the PHS corps device, on the cuffs and shoulder boards and a silver oak leaf as a badge of rank (2).

The Career Compensation Act of October 12, 1949 (3) placed the Senior grade in pay grade O-5.

By 1995 the titles used in the Assistant grade were Senior Surgeon, still the title for medical officers by law, Senior Dental Surgeon, Senior Nurse Officer, Senior Engineer Officer, Senior Scientist Officer, Sanitarian, Senior Veterinary Officer, Senior Pharmacy Officer, Senior Dietetics Officer, Senior Therapy Officer and Senior Health Services Officer, or simply Commander was acceptable (4).

In later years there seams to have been more emphasis on the navy title than the various PHS titles (5).

The 2009 uniform regulations prescribes the insignia for the Assistant grade by describing cuff stripes for all ranks as "Rank Lace Stripes. Stripes are gold lace in 1/4 inch, 1/2 inch or 2 inch widths. The stripes are sewn onto each sleeve so as to be parallel with the cuff and completely encircle the sleeve. The lower edge of the bottom stripe is 2 inches from the edge of the cuff and there is a 1/4 inch space between stripes. The officer shall wear the stripe or combinations of stripes which correspond to the officer's pay grade/rank."(6), with three 1/2 inch stripes shown in illustration (7). Shoulder boards for all ranks are described as "Officers Below Flag Grade. The surface of the shoulder board is covered with blue (black in appearance) cloth. Gold lace stripes indicate rank and are of the same width, spacing and arrangement as specified for sleeve insignia in Section 6-2. However, the first stripe is positioned 1/4 inch (1/2 inch for the Junior Assistant/Ensign, O-1) from the squared end of the board. The Corps device is positioned 1/4 inch above the uppermost stripe." (8), three 1/2 inch stripes are shown in illustration (9). Badges of rank are described as "Senior Grade (COMMANDER/CDR) (O-5). Silver oak leaves, smooth finished, raised and veined; worn with the stem of the oak leaf pointing outboard and the center lobe of the leaf pointing inboard." (10).

Senior Assistant (Lieutenant)

The Senior Assistant grade was created by the Public Health Service Act of July 1, 1944 (1). The law made it equal to an army Captain and therefore a navy Lieutenant. It is a continuation of the rank of Passed Assistant Surgeon and equivalent non medical titles.

Senior Assistant Surgeons had worn the insignia of a navy Lieutenant, two 1/2 inch stripes, under the PHS corps device, on the cuffs and shoulder boards and a two silver bars as a badge of rank (2).

The Career Compensation Act of October 12, 1949 (3) placed the Senior Assistant grade in pay grade O-3.

By 1995 the titles used in the Senior Assistant grade were Senior Assistant Surgeon, still the title for medical officers by law, Senior Assistant Dental Surgeon, Senior Assistant Nurse Officer, Senior Assistant Engineer Officer, Senior Assistant Scientist Officer, Sanitarian, Senior Assistant Veterinary Officer, Senior Assistant Pharmacy

Officer, Senior Assistant Dietetics Officer, Senior Assistant Therapy Officer and Senior Assistant Health Services Officer, or simply Lieutenant was acceptable (4).

In later years there seams to have been more emphasis on the navy title than the various PHS titles (5).

The 2009 uniform regulations prescribes the insignia for the Assistant grade by describing cuff stripes for all ranks as "Rank Lace Stripes. Stripes are gold lace in 1/4 inch, 1/2 inch or 2 inch widths. The stripes are sewn onto each sleeve so as to be parallel with the cuff and completely encircle the sleeve. The lower edge of the bottom stripe is 2 inches from the edge of the cuff and there is a 1/4 inch space between stripes. The officer shall wear the stripe or combinations of stripes which correspond to the officer's pay grade/rank."(6), with two 1/2 inch stripes shown in illustration (7). Shoulder boards for all ranks are described as "Officers Below Flag Grade. The surface of the shoulder board is covered with blue (black in appearance) cloth. Gold lace stripes indicate rank and are of the same width, spacing and arrangement as specified for sleeve insignia in Section 6-2. However, the first stripe is positioned 1/4 inch (1/2 inch for the Junior Assistant/Ensign, O-1) from the squared end of the board. The Corps device is positioned 1/4 inch above the uppermost stripe." (8), two 1/2 inch stripes are shown in illustration (9). Badges of rank are described as "Senior Assistant Grade (LIEUTENANT/LT) (O-3). Two silver bars attached near the ends by silver connecting bars. The bars are smooth with no bevel; worn centered front to back on the strap, with the long dimension of the rank bar parallel with the outboard shoulder seam." (10).

Senior Dental Surgeon

Dental officers were granted commissions under a law of April 9, 1930 (1), creating the rank of Senior Dental Surgeon.

By 1937 they were wearing the insignia of a navy Commander, three 1/2 inch stripes, under the PHS corps device, on the cuffs and shoulder boards and a silver oak leaf as a badge of rank (2).

Senior Dental Surgeons became part of the Senior grade on July 1, 1944 (3), but the title has continued (4).

Senior Sanitary Engineer

Sanitary Engineers were granted commissions under a law of April 9, 1930 (1), creating the rank of Senior Sanitary Engineer.

By 1937 they were wearing the insignia of a navy Commander, three 1/2 inch stripes, under the PHS corps device, on the cuffs and shoulder boards and a silver oak leaf as a badge of rank (2).

Senior Sanitary Engineers became part of the Senior grade on July 1, 1944 (3), but the title has continued (4).

Senior Surgeon

The rank of Senior Surgeon was created on August 14, 1912 (1)

It replaced the position, or at least the insignia, of Surgeons who had been in the service for more than 20 years.

Under the 1914 uniform regulations Senior Surgeons wore three 1/2 inch stripe on the cuffs and a silver oak leaf as a badge of rank on the maroon shoulder loops (2).

By the 1937 regulations the three 1/2 inch stripes were worn on shoulder boards and the anchor and caduceus corps device was worn above the stripes on both the shoulder and cuff (3).

Badges of rank were not generally used under the 1937 regulations but had returned by World War II (4).

Senior Surgeons became part of the Assistant grade on July 1, 1944 (5), but by law, the title has continued (6).

Surgeon

Surgeon is the basic rank of a medical officer, and was one of the original ranks created when marine hospital service officers were granted commissions on January 4, 1889 (1).

The 1896 uniform regulations prescribe three 1/4 inch cuff stripes (2), a gold oak leaf as a badge of rank on shoulder knots, shoulder straps (3) and collars and a cinquefoil knot of three cords on the cuff of the overcoat (4). Surgeons who had been in the service over 20 years could wear four stripes and cords on the cuffs.

Regulations, but not laws, of 1897 made marine hospital service Surgeons equal to Captains of the revenue cutter service (5), however relative rank can only be given in law, so this was not official.

The 1904 uniform regulations prescribe cuff stripes of two 1/2 inch alternating with two 1/4 inch stripes starting with a 1/4 inch stripe on top for Surgeons who had been in the service over 20 years and two 1/2 inch stripes with a 1/4 inch stripe between them for other Surgeons (6). For a badge of rank on shoulder knots and shoulder straps those over 20 years service wore a silver oak leaf and those under a gold oak leaf (7). On the overcoat a cinquefoil knot of four cords was worn by those over 20 years service and three for those under (8).

By the time of the 1914 uniform regulations, the insignia of Surgeons over 20 years service was taken by the rank of Senior Surgeon. Surgeons continued to wear two 1/2 inch stripes with one 1/4 inch stripe between them on the cuffs and the gold oak leaf, now on maroon shoulder loops continued to be the badge of rank (9).

By the 1937 regulations the two 1/2 inch stripes with a 1/4 inch stripe between them were worn on shoulder boards and the anchor and caduceus corps device was worn above the stripes on both the shoulder and cuff (10).

Badges of rank were not generally used under the 1937 regulations but had returned by World War II (11).

Surgeons became part of the Full grade on July 1, 1944 (12), but by law, the title has continued (13).

Surgeon General/Supervising Surgeon/ Supervising Surgeon General

On June 29, 1870, a new law placed a single man in charge of the hospitals funded by the marine hospital fund by stating "That the Secretary of the Treasury is hereby authorized to appoint a surgeon to act as supervising surgeon of marine hospital service, whose duty it shall be, under the direction of the Secretary, to supervise all matters connected with the marine-hospital service, and with the disbursement of the fund provided by this act, at a salary not exceeding the rate of two thousand dollars per annum, and his necessary traveling expenses, who shall be required to make monthly reports to the Secretary of the Treasury." (1). The job went to John Woodworth who had been an army surgeon during the civil war.

Woodworth organized the marine hospital service along military lines, placing the medical staffs into uniforms and having them service the hospital service in general instead of the individual hospitals, allowing them to be moved around to better meet the health care needs of the time. Woodworth died in office on March 4, 1879 (2). Woodworth's term of officer predates the creation of the commissioned corps in 1889, but he is considered the first Surgeon General.

The first mention in law of the title Supervising Surgeon General, instead of Supervising Surgeon was on March 3, 1875 (3) stating "That hereafter the salary of the supervising surgeon-general of the United States marine hospital service shall be paid out of the marine hospital fund, at the rate of four thousand dollars per year; and the supervising surgeon-general shall be appointed by the President, with the advice and consent of the Senate."

John Hamilton was appointed on April 3, 1879 to replace Woodworth (4).

The commissioned corps was created on January 4, 1889 (5), making Hamilton a commissioned officer in the Marine Hospital Service.

There is a photograph of Hamilton wearing five cuff stripes with an extra space under the top one (6). This is similar to the stripes worn by officers of the revenue cutter service, but the cutter service had no rank with five stripes.

Hamilton resigned on June 1, 1891 (7), and was replaced by Walter Wyman (8).

The 1896 uniform regulations called for Wyman to wear epaulets of gold with 3/8 inch wide by 3 inch long bullion, with a badge of rank of a star (what color is not mentioned) in the frog and a gold corps device of an anchor crossed with a caduceus on the strap (9), shoulder straps with a gold star in the center, shoulder knots with the gold star in the center of the pad (10), cuff stripes of "Five bands of one-fourth inch gold-wire lace around each sleeve; lower band two inches from lower edge of cuff; first four bands one-fourth inch apart; upper band one-half inch above fourth band."(11). Gold stripes were worn on the blue fatigue coat where other ranks wore black. A cinquefoil knot of five cords on the cuff of the overcoat (12).

Under the 1904 uniform regulations the star became silver, the cuff stripes were one two inch stripe under one 1/2 inch stripe and overcoat cuffs of a band of 1 1/2 inch black braid and a band of 1/2 inch braid with a black star between them (13).

Wyman died in office on November 21, 1911 (14), and was replaced by Rupert Blue on January 13, 1912 (15).

The law of August 14, 1912 that changed the name of the service to Public Health Service, refers to the Surgeon General instead of Supervising Surgeon General (16).

Under the 1914 uniform regulations Blue wore cuff stripes of two inch stripe under one 1/2 inch stripe, a silver star on the maroon shoulder loops and the same epaulets as 1904 (17).

Hugh Cumming replaced Blue on March 3, 1920, serving until he retired on January 31, 1936 (18). His replacement of April 6th was Thomas Parran (19).

The 1937 uniform regulations prescribe for Parran, cuff stripes of one two inch stripe under two 1/2 inch stripes under the corps device, the same as a navy Vice Admiral. Shoulder boards are prescribed but not described. They probably were the same as those for navy admirals with a two wide strip of gold lace running long ways down the board with the anchor and caduceus near the top and stars to denote rank at the other end. How many stars is the problem. The Vice Admiral's stripes may have meant three stars, but it is also possible Parran wore only two (20).

By World War II Parran was wearing only one 1/2 inch stripe over his two inch stripe, shoulder boards with two stars and two stars as a badge of rank (21).

Parran retired on October 1, 1948 (22), and was replaced by Leonard Scheele (23).

The Career Compensation Act of October 12, 1949 (24) placed the Surgeon General in the O-8 pay grade, confirming his World War II insignia.

Scheele resigned in 1956 (25) and was replaced by Leroy Burney on August 8th (26). Burney served until the beginning of the Kennedy administration in 1961. President Kennedy's choice for Surgeon General was Luther Terry (27). Terry retired in 1965 and President Johnson appointed William Stewart to replace him (28).

In 1968 the Assistant Secretary for Health became head of the public health service with the Surgeon General as an advisor (29).

Stewart resigned on August 1, 1969 (30), and was replaced by Jesse Steinfeld on December 18th. Steinfeld resigned on January 30, 1973 (31), and was not replaced.

The country made due without a permanent Surgeon General until President Carter appointed Julius Richmond as Assistant Secretary for Health in 1977. As condition of taking the job as assistant secretary, Richmond insisted he also be made Surgeon General (32). As such Richmond was the first commissioned officer to be Assistant Secretary for Health.

On September 29, 1979 the rank of the Surgeon General up the O-9 grade equal to a Vice Admiral (33). With that rank Richmond was entitled to one two inch stripe under two 1/2 inch stripes under the corps device and three stars on his shoulder boards and as a badge of rank.

Richmond left office at the end of the Carter administration and President Reagan appointed C. Everett Koop to replace him, as Surgeon General only (34). Koop brought the office back in to prominence practically becoming a household name in the 1980s. By 1987 the Surgeon General had regained some authority over the health service (35). Koop resigned on October 1, 1989 (36).

Koop's replacement, Antonia Novello, was appointed by President Bush on March 9, 1990. She was the first woman to hold the office. She left office on June 30, 1993 (37).

President Clinton appointed Joycelyn Elders to be his first Surgeon General. Controversy over the new administration's plans for health care reform delayed her confirmation until September. Once in office she was outspoken on a variety of controversial health care issues, which lead President Clinton to fire her in December of 1994 (38).

No permanent appointment was made until 1998 when David Satcher was made both the Surgeon General and the Assistant Secretary for Health. Satcher left both offices at the end of the Clinton Administration (39).

The next Surgeon General was Richard Carmona who served from August 5, 2002 to July 31, 2006 (40).

Once again there was no permanent appointment. The Assistant Secretary for Health, John Agwunobi, was a commissioned officer, and therefore the senior officer in the health service.

Regina Benjamin was appointed Surgeon General by President Obama in 2009 and at this writing in June of 2012, she is still in office.

The 2009 uniform regulations prescribes the insignia for the Surgeon General by describing cuff stripes for all ranks as "Rank Lace Stripes. Stripes are gold lace in 1/4 inch, 1/2 inch or 2 inch widths. The stripes are sewn onto each sleeve so as to be parallel with the cuff and completely encircle the sleeve. The lower edge of the bottom stripe is 2 inches from the edge of the cuff and there is a 1/4 inch space between stripes. The officer shall wear the stripe or combinations of stripes which correspond to the officer's pay grade/rank."(2), with one two inch stripe under two 1/2 inch stripes shown in illustration (3). Shoulder boards for all flag ranks are described as "Flag Officers. The shoulder board is covered with a gold lace leaving a 1/8 inch cloth margin along each side. The Corps device is embroidered with the head of the staff of the caduceus positioned 11/4 inches from the pointed end of the board. Rank shall be indicated by the use of 1 (O-7), 2 (O-8), 3 (O-9), or 4 (O-10), silver colored, embroidered, 5-pointed stars, arranged as shown in the Appendix B." (4), and Appendix B shows three stars in a triangle (5). Badges of rank are described as "Flag Officers. 4 (O-10) Admiral, 3 (O-9) Vice Admiral, 2 (O-8) Rear Admiral Upper Half, 5-pointed, silver stars arranged in a straight line along a thin silver connecting bar, with 1 ray of each star pointing along the connecting bar." (6), with three stars shown in illustration (7).

Part 7.
NOAA Corps

Chapter 1.
NOAA Organization

America's seventh service, a title they wear proudly, is The National Oceanic and Atmospheric Administration Commissioned Corps or NOAA (pronounced noah) Corps for short. It is a small corps of commissioned officers who operate research vessels and aircraft, among other scientific duties. The corps mission statement is " Provide officers technically competent to assume positions of leadership and command in the National Oceanic and Atmospheric Administration (NOAA) and Department of Commerce (DOC) programs and in the Armed Forces during times of war or national emergency. Discipline and flexibility are inherent in the Corps personnel system. Officers are trained for positions of leadership and command in the operation of ships and aircraft; in the conduct of field projects on land, at and under the sea, and in the air; in the management of NOAA observational and support facilities; as members or leaders of research efforts; and in the management of various organizational elements throughout NOAA. " (1). It began a the coast survey in 1807, became the Coast and Geodetic Survey in 1878, The Commissioned Corps of the Environmental Science Service Administration in 1965 and finally the NOAA Corps in 1970 (2).

Coast Survey

On February 10, 1807 a law was passed calling for a survey of the country's extensive coast line (1).

Congress repealed most of the 1807 law on April 14, 1818 (2), believing the work was going to slow and costing too much (3). The 1818 law left the survey in the hands of the army and navy, who did nothing. It was cheaper but not productive.

The survey was revived on July 10, 1832 (4) using a combination of civilian, army and navy personnel. The navy was given control of the survey form 1834 to 1836 when it reverted back to the Treasury Department (5).

When the Civil War broke out in 1861, the military removed it's personnel from the survey, having better things for them to do. As for the civilian survey employees, they spent the war supporting both the army and the navy with maps and charts (6). This lead them to be exposed to being executed as spies if captured on the battlefield because they were not military personnel. However this problem was not addressed until a later war.

In 1871 the survey was expanded to the land as well as the coast line (7).

Coast and Geodetic Survey

With new duties came a new name. An Appropriations law of June 19, 1878 (1) refers to the survey as the coast and geodetic survey. Geodesy is the science of measuring position of things on the earth (2).

The problem of civilians in a war zone returned in World War I. This lead to the survey's field officers, known as Assistants, and their aides to be given commissions on May 22, 1917 (3), thus creating the commissioned corps (3).

Environmental Science Services Administration

In 1965 the coast and geodetic survey was combined with the weather bureau, under the Department of Commerce, to from the Environmental Science Services Administration (1). The survey's commissioned officers became the commissioned corps of the Environmental Science Services Administration, or ESSA corp.

National Oceanic and Atmospheric Administration

After a further reorganization of federal scientific agencies in 1970, the environmental science services administration became national oceanic and atmospheric administration or NOAA (1), and the ESSA corps became the NOAA corps.

Rank Structure

Prior to the granting of commissions, the field staff of the survey consisted of Assistants and Aids. A law appropriating funds for salaries of the survey from July 1, 1916 laid out how this was organized by stating "Salaries: Superintendent, $6,000; assistants, to be employed in the field or office, as the superintendent may direct, one of whom may be designated by the Secretary of Commerce to act as assistant superintendent- two at $4,000 each, one $3,200, five at $3,000 each, five at $2,500 each, eight at $2,400 each (including one at $2,280 now paid from appropriation "offshore soundings"), nine at $2,200 each (including one at $2,100 now paid from appropriation "offshore soundings"), eight at $2,000 each, nine at $1,800 each (including one now paid from appropriation "offshore soundings"), nine at $1,600 each (including one now paid from appropriation "offshore soundings"), nine at $1,400 each (including one at $1,320 now paid from appropriation "offshore soundings"), ten at $1,200 each; aids-ten at $1,100 each, nineteen at $1,000 each; in all, $184,900." (1). It is interesting to note the different pay rates of various assistants and the different budgets their salaries came from.

The Assistants and Aids were made commissioned officers on May 22, 1917. The law stated "That the President is authorized to appoint by and with the advice and consent of the Senate the field officers of the Coast and Geodetic Survey, who are now officially designated assistants and aids, as follows: Officers now designated assistants and receiving a salary of $2,000 or more per annum shall be appointed hydrographic and geodetic engineers; officers now designated assistants and receiving a salary of $1,200 or greater but less than $2,000 per annum shall be appointed junior hydrographic and geodetic engineers; officers now designated aids shall be appointed aids:". The law went on to give relative rank to the officers based on their rate of pay by stating "When serving with the Army or Navy the relative rank shall be as follows:
Hydrographic and geodetic engineers receiving $4,000 or more shall rank with and after colonels in the Army and captains in the Navy.
Hydrographic and geodetic engineers receiving $3,000 or more but less than $4,000 shall rank with and after lieutenant colonels in the Army and commanders in the Navy.
Hydrographic and geodetic engineers receiving $2,500 or more but less than $3,000 shall rank with and after majors in the Amy and lieutenant commanders in the Navy.
Hydrographic and geodetic engineers' receiving $2,000 or more but less than $2,500 shall rank with and after captains in the Army and lieutenants in the Navy.
Junior hydrographic and geodetic engineers shall rank with and after first lieutenants in the Army and lieutenants (junior grade) in the Navy.
Aids shall rank with and after second lieutenants in the Army and ensigns in the Navy." (2).

The new titles, Hydrographic and Geodetic Engineer, Junior Hydrographic and Geodetic Engineer and Aid, were reflected in the next appropriations law on June 12th (3), and on an insignia chart in the Military and Naval Recognition book by Joel Bunkley published in 1917 (4). The chart also shows insignia for surgeons, chief engineers, watch officers and deck officers on survey vessels but the law is clear on whom the commissions were given to, making these other ranks civilian federal employes despite their insignia. This is made completely clear during World War II, when the survey's regulations stated that "civil service officers" could apply for reserve commissions in the navy and the crews of the survey's ships could apply for ratings in the naval reserve (5).

On May 18, 1920 a new law gave survey officers the same pay as their equivalent officers in other services (6). Did this change their titles? The law says nothing but the next appropriations law, from June 5th, is worded "Pay, commissioned officers: For pay and allowances prescribed by law for commissioned officers on sea duty and other duty, holding relative rank with officers of the Navy, including one director with rank of captain, two hydrographic and geodetic engineers with relative rank of captain, seven Hydrographic and geodetic engineers with relative rank of commander, nine hydrographic and geodetic engineers with relative rank of lieutenant commander, thirty-eight hydrographic and geodetic engineers with relative rank of lieutenant, fifty-five Junior hydrographic and geodetic engineers with relative rank of lieutenant (junior grade), twenty-nine aids with relative rank of ensign, and including officers retired in accordance with existing law, $510,797:" (7). Uniform regulations dated June 18, 1920 use the naval equivalent titles with no mention of relative rank (8). The navy had stopped using relative rank title in 1918, with staff officers still legally holding ranks such as Surgeon of Paymaster but were always referred to by their relative line rank. It is possible this custom extended to the survey as well. The final appropriations law to use this wording was on June 28, 1941 (9).

On March 18, 1936, congress gave the survey's director the "rank, pay, and allowances of a Chief of Bureau of the Navy Department." (10). Navy bureau chiefs were Rear Admirals.

A law of January 19, 1942 stated "That the total number of commissioned officers on the active list of the Coast and Geodetic Survey shall be distributed in rank relative with officers of the Navy in the proportion of five in the grade of captain to eight in the grade of commander, to eighty-seven in the grades of lieutenant commander, lieutenant, lieutenant (junior grade) and ensign, inclusive: Provided, That the number of officers in the grade of lieutenant commander shall-not exceed 35 per centum of the total authorized number of commissioned officers on the active list." (11). The words "hydrographic and geodetic engineer" are noticeably absent and even "relative" only used once. The director is not mentioned by remained a Rear Admiral (12).

On June 3, 1948, Congress passed the Coast and Geodetic Survey Commissioned Officers' Act of 1948. The first paragraph stated "Of the total authorized number of commissioned officers on the active list of the Coast and Geodetic Survey, there are authorized numbers in permanent grade, in relative rank with officers of the Navy, in the proportion of eight in the grade of captain, to fourteen in the grade of commander, to nineteen in the grade of lieutenant commander, to twenty-three in the grade of lieutenant, to eighteen in the grade of lieutenant (junior grade), to eighteen in the grade of ensign." (13).

The Career Compensation Act of October 12, 1949 (14) placed the ranks of all the uniformed services into pay grades. The survey was in a column with the navy and the coast guard, the ranks being identical. The grades used by the survey were all officer grades, and therefore began with and "O". The O-1 grade was for Ensigns, the O-2 grade for Lieutenants (Junior Grade), O-3 was for Lieutenants, O-4 was for Lieutenant Commanders, O-5 was for Commanders, O-6 was for Captains, O-7 was for Rear Admirals (Lower Half) and O-8 was for Rear Admirals (Upper Half).

The 1965 reorganization plan that changed the survey into the ESSA corps, allowed for a Deputy Administrator who, if chosen from the commissioned corps, held the rank of Vice Admiral in the O-9 grade, and kept the ESSA corps director as a Rear Admiral (Upper Half) (15). The 1970 plan that made ESSA into NOAA allowed for an Associate, instead of Deputy, Administrator as a Vice Admiral and also stated "The President may appoint in the Administration, by and with the advice and consent of the Senate, two commissioned officers to serve at any one time as the designated heads of two principal constituent organizational entities of the Administration, or the President may designate one such officer as the head of such an organizational entity and the other as the head of the commissioned corps of the Administration. Any such designation shall create a vacancy on the active list and the officer while serving under this subsection shall have the rank, pay, and allowances of a rear admiral (upper half)." (16). In practice there was only one Vice Admiral, who served from 1965 to 1967 (17).

The subject of admirals in the NOAA corps was modified on October 19, 1984 when a new law stated "The Secretary may designate positions in the Administration as being positions of importance and responsibility for which it is appropriate that commissioned officers of the Administration, if serving in those positions, serve in the grade of vice admiral, rear admiral, or commodore as designated by the Secretary for each position, and may assign officers to those positions. An officer assigned to any position under this section has the grade designated for that position if appointed to that grade by the President, by and with the advice and consent of the Senate. "(b) The number of officers serving on active duty under appointments under this section may not exceed-
"(1) one in the grade of vice admiral;
"(2) three in the grade of rear admiral; and
"(3) three in the grade of commodore. (18).

The rank of Commodore was changed to Rear Admiral (Lower Half) on November 8, 1985 (19).

Chapter 2.
NOAA Rank Insignia

While not a lot of information is available on the history of insignia of the coast and geodetic survey or it's successor organizations, the story is not hard to trace because not much has changed in rank insignia since 1917.

The earliest information available on the survey's insignia comes from the Military and Naval Recognition book by Joel Bunkley published in 1917 (1). It shows badges of rank on shoulder loops of white coats and cuff stripes on the cuffs of other uniforms.

The 1920 uniform regulations prescribe a standing collar blue coat, a design the navy had abandoned in 1919, with badges of rank on the collar and cuff stripes and standing collar white and khaki coats with shoulder boards. The shoulder boards were also worn on overcoats (2).

By World War II the survey was wearing the same uniforms as the navy with rank still shown by cuff stripes, shoulder boards and badges of rank (3).

There is no reason to go any further. The standard navy system of showing rank in World War II is still in use.

Shoulder Boards

The navy began wearing shoulder boards in 1899 as a way of displaying rank that was easy to remove to allow the coat to be cleaned. They consisted of a rectangle of stiffened blue cloth with a point at one end and a button near the point.

The survey, apparently did not wear them in 1917 (1), but did by 1920 (2). For Captains four stripes of 1/2 inch gold lace, 1/4 inch apart, starting 1/4 inch from the end were worn with the survey's corps device of a silver disc with a gold triangle in the center 1/4 inch above the top stripe. Commanders wore three stripes, Lieutenant Commanders wore two 1/2 inch stripes with one 1/4 inch stripes between them and Lieutenants two 1/2 inch stripes. The stripes, one 1/2 inch under one 1/4 inch, for Lieutenants (Junior Grade) began 3/4 inch from the end of the board and Ensigns wore one 1/2 inch stripe 3/4 inch form the end.

When admirals were added they wore a two inch wide strip of gold lace running long ways down the middle of the board with a silver anchor with the corps device superimposed near the pointed end and silver stars at the other end to show rank. Initially the Rear Admiral wore two stars one above the other (3). When the rank of Vice Admiral existed three stars were worn in a triangle and when the O-7 grade was used after 1984 a single star was worn alone (4).

It is possible that the survey followed the navy into gray uniforms during World War II. If they did, gray cloth shoulder boards with rounded ends with all stripes and devices in black, may have been worn.

At some point the corps device was changed from a silver disc and gold triangle to gold disc and a gold triangle outlined in silver.

Shoulder Marks

What we will call shoulder marks are referred in regulations as soft shoulder boards. This refers to a scaled down version of the shoulder boards that are applied to an open ended tube of cloth that can be slipped over a cloth shoulder loop of a shirt or sweater.

They are described as "Soft Shoulder Boards shall be made of navy-blue gabardine or similar material, sewn in a loop to fit over the shoulder straps. They shall be 4-3/16 inches long, squared at both the inner and outer ends, tapering from 2-1/4 inches wide at the outer end to 1- 7/8 inches wide at the inner end" (1).

The navy began wearing them in 1979 (2), and the NOAA corps probably began around the same time.

Badges of Rank

Badges of rank is the term we shall use for the stars, eagles, leafs and bars used by officers to show rank on shirt collars, caps and shoulder loops.

In 1917 survey officers wore badges of rank on the shoulder loops of white uniforms. Hydrographic and Geodetic Engineers equal to Captains wore a silver eagle, those equal to Commanders wore a silver oak leaf, those equal to Lieutenant Commanders wore a gold oak leaf and those equal to Lieutenants wore two bars, probably in silver, Junior Hydrographic and Geodetic Engineers wore one bar and Aides wore no insignia. All ranks wore the corps device of a silver disc with a gold triangle in the center in the middle of the loop (1).

The 1920 uniform regulations prescribe the same devices, with the bars were definitely in silver, for the collar of the blue coat with a corps device on a silver anchor behind them (2).

By World War II Ensigns were wearing one gold bar and Rear Admirals two silver stars (3).

The Vice Admiral would have worn three silver stars and a Commodore or Rear Admiral (Lower Half) wears one (4).

Cuff Stripes

Gold cuff stripes were worn on blue coats right from the beginning in 1917 (1), and have continued ever since.

The only changes have been the addition of ranks and the change of the corps device from a silver disc and gold triangle to gold disc and a gold triangle outlined in silver. It is not clear when this change in the device was made.

The 2004 uniform regulations describe the stripes as:

"Sleeve Insignia consist of stripes of gold lace in widths of 2-inch, 1/2-inch, or 1/4-inch indicating an officer's grade. Stripes encircle the sleeve with the lower edge of the first stripe 2 inches from the edge of the sleeve. Multiple stripes are separated by 1/4-inch intervals. Sleeve insignia are worn as indicated below:
(1) Vice Admiral - One 2-inch stripe with two 1/2-inch stripes above it.
(2) Rear Admiral - One 2-inch stripe with one 1/2-inch stripe above it.
(3) Rear Admiral (Lower Half) - One 2-inch stripe.
(4) Captain - Four 1/2-inch stripes.
(5) Commander - Three 1/2-inch stripes.
(6) Lieutenant Commander - Two 1/2-inch stripes with one 1/4-inch stripe in between.
(7) Lieutenant - Two 1/2-inch stripes.
(8) Lieutenant (junior grade) - One 1/2-inch stripe with one 1/4-inch stripe above it.
(9) Ensign - One 1/2-inch stripe." (2)."

Chapter 3.
NOAA Ranks

Aid

Aids were the junior members of the survey's field officers prior to 1917. When commissions were granted on May 22, 1917, Aids were to rank "with and after second lieutenants in the Army and ensigns in the Navy." (1).

In 1917 they wore one 1/2 inch stripe under a corps device on the cuff and no badge of rank (2).

On May 18, 1920 the officers of the survey were given the same pay as officers in other services (3). This probably ended the use of the title Aid and replaced it with Ensign. Appropriations laws from June 5, 1920 (4) to June 28, 1941(5) use the term "aids with relative rank of ensign", while the uniform regulations from June 18, 1920 simply reefers to Ensigns (6). Finally on January 19, 1942 a law distributing the officer's of the survey in their ranks uses only the term Ensign never mentioning Aids (7).

Captain

On May 22, 1917 Assistants who were paid more that $4000.00 per year were given commissions as Hydrographic and Geodetic Engineers ranking "with and after colonels in the Army and captains in the Navy." (1).

On May 18, 1920 the officers of the survey were given the same pay as officers in other services (2). This is probably when the use of the title Hydrographic and Geodetic Engineer ended and the use of the title Captain began. Appropriations laws from June 5, 1920 (3) to June 28, 1941(4) use the term "hydrographic and geodetic engineers with relative rank of captain", while the uniform regulations from June 18, 1920 simply reefers to Captains (5). Finally on January 19, 1942 a law distributing the officer's of the survey in their ranks uses only the term Captain never mentioning Hydrographic and Geodetic Engineer (6). From 1929 to 1937 the Director of the Coast and Geodetic Survey was also a relative Captain.

The 1920 uniform regulations prescribe four 1/2 inch gold stripes, under the corps device, on the cuff and shoulder boards and a silver eagle as a badge of rank (7).

The Career Compensation Act of October 12, 1949 placed Captains in the O-6 pay grade (8).

The 2004 uniform regulations show that the insignia for Captains is the same as it was in 1920. Describing cuff stripes as "Captain - Four 1/2-inch stripes", shoulder boards in general are described as "For officers below flag grade the outside face of the hard shoulder board shall be covered with navy-blue cloth lined with black silk, rayon, or similar cloth. Grade shall be designated by stripes of gold lace of the same width and number and with the same spacing as specified in 12602A for stripes on the sleeves of the coat, except that the outer edge of the first stripe shall be 1/4- inch (1/2-inch for ensigns) from the squared end of the shoulder board. A Corps device 15/16-inch in diameter, embroidered in gold, shall be affixed 1/4 inch above the innermost stripe.", and a Captain's badge or rank are described as "Captain - A silver-colored spread eagle, worn with the top of eagle's head toward the collar, and head and olive branch pointing to the front (rights and lefts)." (9).

Commander

On May 22, 1917 Assistants who were paid between $3000.00 and $4000.00 per year were given commissions as Hydrographic and Geodetic Engineers ranking "with and after lieutenant colonels in the Army and commanders in the Navy." (1).

On May 18, 1920 the officers of the survey were given the same pay as officers in other services (2). This is probably when the use of the title Hydrographic and Geodetic Engineer ended and the use of the title Commander began. Appropriations laws from June 5, 1920 (3) to June 28, 1941(4) use the term "hydrographic and geodetic engineers with relative rank of Commander", while the uniform regulations from June 18, 1920 simply reefers to Commanders (5). Finally on January 19, 1942 a law distributing the officer's of the survey in their ranks uses only the term Commander never mentioning Hydrographic and Geodetic Engineer (6).

The 1920 uniform regulations prescribe three 1/2 inch gold stripes, under the corps device, on the cuff and shoulder boards and a silver oak leaf as a badge of rank (7).

The Career Compensation Act of October 12, 1949 placed Commanders in the O-5 pay grade (8).

The 2004 uniform regulations show that the insignia for Commanders is the same as it was in 1920. Describing cuff stripes as "Commander - Three 1/2-inch stripes", shoulder boards in general are described as "For officers below flag grade the outside face of the hard shoulder board shall be covered with navy-blue cloth lined with black silk, rayon, or similar cloth. Grade shall be designated by stripes of gold lace of the same width and number and with the same spacing as specified in 12602A for stripes on the sleeves of the coat, except that the outer edge of the first stripe shall be 1/4- inch (1/2-inch for ensigns) from the squared end of the shoulder board. A Corps device 15/16-inch in diameter, embroidered in gold, shall be affixed 1/4 inch above the innermost stripe.", and a Commander's badge or rank are described as "Commander - A silver-colored oak leaf, plain, raised, and veined, worn with the tip of leaf toward the collar." (9).

Commodore

The rank of Commodore was placed in the O-7 pay grade, alongside the rank of Rear Admiral (Lower Half), on December 12, 1980 (1). It is not clear if the NOAA corps used the rank at the time, but it was on the list, as was full Admiral which has never been used.

On October 19, 1984 a law allowed the Secretary of Commerce to create "positions of importance and responsibility" in the corps (2). This allowed managerial positions to be created as needed. The law allowed up to three Commodores in such positions. The same law contains a curious provision allowing officer who had held the rank of Rear Admiral (Lower Half) before the law took effect would hold the rank of Commodore but retain the title and insignia of a Rear Admiral. This would seem to imply that the rank of Commodore had not been in use before 1984.

From the 1984 law we can infer that Commodores who had been paid in the O-7 grade before October 18, 1984 (the day before the law was passed) called themselves Rear Admirals and wore one two inch stripe under one 1/2 inch stripe under the corps device on the cuffs and two silver stars on the shoulder boards and as a badge of rank. Officer's appointed after October 18, 1984 called themselves Commodores and wore one two inch stripe under the corps device on the cuffs and one silver star on the shoulder boards and as a badge of rank. As complicated as this sounds we must remember that this only applied to a maximum of three people.

The rank of Commodore was changed back to Rear Admiral (Lower Half) on November 8, 1985 (3).

Ensign

On May 22, 1917 Aids were given commissions ranking "with and after second lieutenants in the Army and ensigns in the Navy." (1).

On May 18, 1920 the officers of the survey were given the same pay as officers in other services (2). This is probably when the use of the title Aid ended and the use of the title Ensign began. Appropriations laws from June 5, 1920 (3) to June 28, 1941(4) use the term "aids with relative rank of ensign", while the uniform regulations from

June 18, 1920 simply reefers to Ensigns (5). Finally on January 19, 1942 a law distributing the officer's of the survey in their ranks uses only the term Ensign never mentioning Aids at all (6).

The 1920 uniform regulations prescribe one 1/2 inch gold stripe, under the corps device, on the cuff and shoulder boards and no badge of rank (7).

By World War II a gold bar was being used as a badge of rank (8)

The Career Compensation Act of October 12, 1949 placed Ensigns in the O-1 pay grade (9).

The 2004 uniform regulations show that the insignia for Ensigns is the same as it was in 1920, except for the gold bar added later. Describing cuff stripes as "Ensign - One 1/2-inch stripe", shoulder boards in general are described as "For officers below flag grade the outside face of the hard shoulder board shall be covered with navy-blue cloth lined with black silk, rayon, or similar cloth. Grade shall be designated by stripes of gold lace of the same width and number and with the same spacing as specified in 12602A for stripes on the sleeves of the coat, except that the outer edge of the first stripe shall be 1/4- inch (1/2-inch for ensigns) from the squared end of the shoulder board. A Corps device 15/16-inch in diameter, embroidered in gold, shall be affixed 1/4 inch above the innermost stripe.", and an Ensign's badge or rank are described as "Ensign - A gold-colored bar worn on the shoulder strap in the same manner as prescribed for lieutenant (junior grade)." (10).

Hydrographic and Geodetic Engineer

The rank of Hydrographic and Geodetic Engineer was created on May 22, 1917 from the coast and geodetic survey personnel known as Assistants who had been paid over $2000.00 per year. Assistants who had made more than $4000.00 per year were made Hydrographic and Geodetic Engineers and ranked with army Colonels and Navy Captains.
Those who had made between $3000.00 and $4000.00 per year ranked with army Lieutenant Colonels and Navy Commanders. Those who had made between $2500.00 and $3000.00 per year ranked with army Majors and Navy Lieutenant Commanders, and those making between $2000.00 and $2500.00 ranked with army Captains and navy Lieutenants (1).

All Hydrographic and Geodetic Engineers wore the insignia of their equivalent grade, consisting of cuff stripes and badges of rank. The highest grade wore four 1/2 inch stripes and a silver eagle, the next three 1/2 inch stripes and a silver oak leaf, the next two 1/2 inch stripes with one 1/4 inch stripe between them and a gold oak leaf and the lowest grade wore two 1/2 inch stripes and two bars, probably in silver. The corps device of a silver disc with a gold triangle in the center was worn above the stripes and in the center of shoulder loops above the badge of rank (2).

On May 18, 1920 the officers of the survey were given the same pay as officers in other services (3). This probably ended the use of the title Hydrographic and Geodetic Engineer and replaced it with equivalent navy titles. Appropriations laws from June 5, 1920 (4) to June 28, 1941(5) use the term "hydrographic and geodetic engineers with relative rank of...", while the uniform regulations from June 18, 1920 simply uses the navy titles (6). Finally on January 19, 1942 a law distributing the officer's of the survey in their ranks uses only the navy titles, never mentioning Hydrographic and Geodetic Engineers (7).

Junior Hydrographic and Geodetic Engineer

The rank of Junior Hydrographic and Geodetic Engineer was created on May 22, 1917 from the coast and geodetic survey personnel known as Assistants who had been paid less than $2000.00 per year. They ranked with army First Lieutenants and navy Lieutenants (Junior Grade) (1).

Junior Hydrographic and Geodetic Engineers wore one 1/2 inch stripe under one 1/4 inch stripe and a bar, probably in silver. The corps device of a silver disc with a gold triangle in the center was worn above the stripes and in the center of shoulder loops above the badge of rank (2).

On May 18, 1920 the officers of the survey were given the same pay as officers in other services (3). This probably ended the use of the title Junior Hydrographic and Geodetic Engineer and replaced it with Lieutenant (Junior Grade). Appropriations laws from June 5, 1920 (4) to June 28, 1941(5) use the term "Junior hydrographic and geodetic engineers with relative rank of lieutenant junior grade)", while the uniform regulations from June 18, 1920 simply uses Lieutenant (Junior Grade) (6). Finally on January 19, 1942 a law distributing the officer's of the survey in their ranks uses only Lieutenant (Junior Grade) never mentioning Junior Hydrographic and Geodetic Engineers (7).

Lieutenant

On May 22, 1917 Assistants who were paid between $2000.00 and $2500.00 per year were given commissions as Hydrographic and Geodetic Engineers ranking "with and after captains in the Army and lieutenants in the Navy." (1).

On May 18, 1920 the officers of the survey were given the same pay as officers in other services (2). This is probably when the use of the title Hydrographic and Geodetic Engineer ended and the use of the title Lieutenant began. Appropriations laws from June 5, 1920 (3) to June 28, 1941(4) use the term "hydrographic and geodetic engineers with relative rank of Lieutenant", while the uniform regulations from June 18, 1920 simply reefers to Lieutenants (5). Finally on January 19, 1942 a law distributing the officer's of the survey in their ranks uses only the term Lieutenant never mentioning Hydrographic and Geodetic Engineer (6).

The 1920 uniform regulations prescribe two 1/2 inch gold stripes, under the corps device, on the cuff and shoulder boards and two silver bars as a badge of rank (7).

The Career Compensation Act of October 12, 1949 placed Lieutenants in the O-3 pay grade (8).

The 2004 uniform regulations show that the insignia for Lieutenants is the same as it was in 1920. Describing cuff stripes as "Lieutenant - Two 1/2-inch stripes", shoulder boards in general are described as "For officers below flag grade the outside face of the hard shoulder board shall be covered with navy-blue cloth lined with black silk, rayon, or similar cloth. Grade shall be designated by stripes of gold lace of the same width and number and with the same spacing as specified in 12602A for stripes on the sleeves of the coat, except that the outer edge of the first stripe shall be 1/4- inch (1/2-inch for ensigns) from the squared end of the shoulder board. A Corps device 15/16-inch in diameter, embroidered in gold, shall be affixed 1/4 inch above the innermost stripe.", and a Lieutenant's badge or rank are described as "Lieutenant - Two silver-colored bars, attached at the ends, placed on the long center line of each shoulder strap with the longer dimension of the bars in a fore and aft line." (9).

Lieutenant (Junior Grade)

On May 22, 1917 Assistants who were paid less than $2000.00 per year were given commissions as Junior Hydrographic and Geodetic Engineers ranking "with and after first lieutenants in the Army and lieutenants (junior grade) in the Navy." (1).

On May 18, 1920 the officers of the survey were given the same pay as officers in other services (2). This is probably when the use of the title Junior Hydrographic and Geodetic Engineer ended and the use of the title Lieutenant (Junior Grade) began. Appropriations laws from June 5, 1920 (3) to June 28, 1941(4) use the term "Junior hydrographic and geodetic engineers with relative rank of lieutenant (junior grade)", while the uniform regulations from June 18, 1920 simply reefers to Lieutenants (Junior Grade) (5). Finally on January 19, 1942 a law distributing the officer's of the survey in their ranks uses only the term Lieutenant (Junior Grade) never mentioning Junior Hydrographic and Geodetic Engineers (6).

The 1920 uniform regulations prescribe one 1/2 inch gold stripes under one 1/2 inch stripe, under the corps device, on the cuff and shoulder boards and one silver bar as a badge of rank (7).

The Career Compensation Act of October 12, 1949 placed Lieutenants in the O-2 pay grade (8).

The 2004 uniform regulations show that the insignia for Lieutenants is the same as it was in 1920. Describing cuff stripes as "Lieutenant (junior grade) - One 1/2-inch stripe with one 1/4-inch stripe above it.", shoulder boards in general are described as "For officers below flag grade the outside face of the hard shoulder board shall be covered with navy-blue cloth lined with black silk, rayon, or similar cloth. Grade shall be designated by stripes of gold lace of the same width and number and with the same spacing as specified in 12602A for stripes on the sleeves of the coat, except that the outer edge of the first stripe shall be 1/4- inch (1/2-inch for ensigns) from the squared end of the shoulder board. A Corps device 15/16-inch in diameter, embroidered in gold, shall be affixed 1/4 inch above the innermost stripe.", and a J.G's badge or rank are described as "Lieutenant (junior grade) - One silver-colored bar placed on the long center line of each shoulder strap with the longer dimension of the bar in a fore and aft line" (9).

Lieutenant Commander

On May 22, 1917 Assistants who were paid between $2500.00 and $3000.00 per year were given commissions as Hydrographic and Geodetic Engineers ranking "with and after majors in the Amy and lieutenant commanders in the Navy." (1).

On May 18, 1920 the officers of the survey were given the same pay as officers in other services (2). This is probably when the use of the title Hydrographic and Geodetic Engineer ended and the use of the title Lieutenant Commander began. Appropriations laws from June 5, 1920 (3) to June 28, 1941(4) use the term "hydrographic and geodetic engineers with relative rank of Lieutenant Commander", while the uniform regulations from June 18, 1920 simply reefers to Lieutenant Commanders (5). Finally on January 19, 1942 a law distributing the officer's of the survey in their ranks uses only the term Lieutenant Commander never mentioning Hydrographic and Geodetic Engineer (6).

The 1920 uniform regulations prescribe two 1/2 inch gold stripes with one 1/4 inch stripe between them, under the corps device, on the cuff and shoulder boards and a gold oak leaf as a badge of rank (7).

The Career Compensation Act of October 12, 1949 placed Commanders in the O-4 pay grade (8).

The 2004 uniform regulations show that the insignia for Commanders is the same as it was in 1920. Describing cuff stripes as "Lieutenant Commander - Two 1/2-inch stripes with one 1/4-inch stripe in between.", shoulder boards in general are described as "For officers below flag grade the outside face of the hard shoulder board shall be covered with navy-blue cloth lined with black silk, rayon, or similar cloth. Grade shall be designated by stripes of gold lace of the same width and number and with the same spacing as specified in 12602A for stripes on the sleeves of the coat, except that the outer edge of the first stripe shall be 1/4- inch (1/2-inch for ensigns) from the squared end of the shoulder board. A Corps device 15/16-inch in diameter, embroidered in gold, shall be affixed 1/4 inch above the innermost stripe.", and a Lieutenant Commander's badge or rank are described as "Lieutenant Commander - A gold-colored oak leaf of the same design as that prescribed for commander, worn in the same manner." (9).

Rear Admiral

When it was a civilian organization, the head of the coast and geodetic survey was known as the Superintendent. When the commissioned corps was created in 1917, he was not given a commission. This changed on June 4, 1920 when a new law sated "That the Superintendent of the Coast and Geodetic Survey shall have the relative rank, pay, and allowances of a captain in the Navy, and that hereafter he shall be appointed by the President, by and with the advice and consent of the Senate, from the list of commissioned officers of the Coast and Geodetic Survey not below the rank of commander or a term of four years, and may be reappointed for further periods of four years each." (1). The next day congress changed the title from Superintendent to Director (2).

It does not appear that the Superintendent/Director in 1920, E. Lester Jones was given a commission in the survey. He had taken a leave of absence during World War I to serve in the army and had come out as a Colonel, and that may have been enough title for him. Jones died on April 9, 1929 (3).

Jones' successor, Raymond Patton, became the first Director with the rank of Captain on April 29, 1920 (4).

On March 18, 1936, congress gave the director the "rank, pay, and allowances of a Chief of Bureau of the Navy Department." (5). This created the rank of Rear Admiral in the coast and geodetic survey.

Rear Admirals wore one two inch stripe under one 1/2 inch stripe on the cuffs, gold covered shoulder boards with a silver anchor and corps device at one end and two silver stars at the other and two silver stars as a badge of rank (6).

The navy had divided the rank of Rear Admiral in half in 1899, eliminating the rank of Commodore (7). The Career Compensation Act of October 12, 1949 (8) placed the upper half of the rank in the O-8 grade and the lower half in the O-7 grade. How this applied to the survey is not clear.

On October 19, 1984 a law allowed the Secretary of Commerce to create "positions of importance and responsibility" in the corps (9). This allowed managerial positions to be created as needed. The same law contains a curious provision allowing officer who had held the rank of Rear Admiral (Lower Half) before the law took effect would hold the rank of Commodore but retain the title and insignia of a Rear Admiral.

From the 1984 law we can infer that Commodores who had been paid in the O-7 grade before October 18, 1984 (the day before the law was passed) called themselves Rear Admirals and wore one two inch stripe under one 1/2 inch stripe under the corps device on the cuffs and two silver stars on the shoulder boards and as a badge of rank. Officer's appointed after October 18, 1984 called themselves Commodores and wore one two inch stripe under the corps device on the cuffs and one silver star on the shoulder boards and as a badge of rank. This was made simpler on November 8, 1985 when the rank of Commodore was changed back to Rear Admiral (Lower Half) (10).

The 2004 uniform regulations describe the insignia for a Rear Admiral, the "upper half" is not used, as cuff stripes of "Rear Admiral - One 2-inch stripe with one 1/2-inch stripe above it.", Shoulder boards of "Rear Admiral - Two five-pointed stars embroidered in silver, each of a size to be inscribed in a circle 3/4-inch in diameter, placed on the centerline of the board, with the centers of the stars 13/16-inch apart, and the center of the outer star 3/4-inch from the squared end of the board. A ray of each star shall point toward the other.", and badges of rank of "Rear Admiral - Two silver-colored, five-pointed, pyramidically shaped stars, worn in the same manner as prescribed for vice admiral.". For a Rear Admiral (Lower Half) the cuff stripes are described as "Rear Admiral (Lower Half) - One 2-inch stripe.", Shoulder boards as "Rear Admiral (Lower Half) - One five-pointed star located on the center line of the shoulder board and centered between the crown of the anchor and the squared end of the shoulder board, with one ray pointing toward the pointed end of the shoulder board." and badges of rank as "Rear Admiral (Lower Half) - One silver-colored, five-pointed, pyramidically shaped star, one ray of which shall point toward the collar." (11).

Vice Admiral

When the Survey became the ESSA corps in 1965, a Position of Deputy Administrator was created. If chosen from the commissioned corps, the Deputy Administrator held the rank of Vice Admiral in the O-9 grade (1). When the ESSA corps became the NOAA corps in 1970 the position was changed to Associate Administrator (2).

On October 19, 1984 a law allowed the Secretary of Commerce to create "positions of importance and responsibility" in the corps (3). This allowed managerial positions to be created as needed, and one Vice Admiral was authorized.

As far as is known, the only Vice Admiral ever appointed was H. Arnold Karo who served as Deputy Administrator from 1865 to 1867 (4).

Despite it's lack of use, the rank is included in the 2004 uniform regulations. The prescribed insignia is cuff stripes described as "Vice Admiral - One 2-inch stripe with two 1/2-inch stripes above it.", Shoulder boards described as "Vice Admiral - Three five-pointed stars placed to form an isosceles triangle with a 1-1/8 inch base and altitude. Inner star shall have a ray pointing toward the squared end of the shoulder board. Centers of the outermost stars shall be 3/4-inch from the squared end of the shoulder board and have a ray of each pointing toward the other." and badges of rank described as "Vice Admiral - Three silver-colored, five-pointed pyramidically shaped stars, worn lengthwise on the strap so that the single ray of each star points toward the collar." (5).

The History of American Ranks and Rank Insignia

Introduction

Uniformed Services
1. United States Statutes at Large, Vol. 6p. 804.

Types of Rank
1.
http://www.defense.gov/specials/insignias/officers.html, November 2010.
2.
http://www.navy.mil/navydata/navy_legacy_hr.asp?id=260, February 2011.

Pay Grades
1. U.S. Navy Regulation Circular, No. 41, January 8, 1885.
2. http://www.history.navy.mil/faqs/faq46-3.htm,April 2011.
3. United States Statutes at Large, Vol. 39, p. 166.
4. United States Statutes at Large, Vol. 41, p. 761
5. United States Statutes at Large, Vol. 42, p. 630.
6. Journals of the Continental Congress, Vol. 6, p. 954.
7. United States Statutes at Large, Vol. 12, p. 585.
8. United States Statutes at Large, Vol. 63, p. 804.
9. United States Statutes at Large, Vol. 72, p. 123.
10. United States Statutes at Large, Vol. 105, p. 1491.

Part 1. Army
Chapter 1. Army Organization
The Continental Army
1. Journal of the Continental Congress, Vol. 2 p. 89
2. http://en.wikipedia.org/wiki/Continental_Army, November 2010
3. Journal of the Continental Congress, Vol. 25 p. 703
4. FRANCIS B. HEITMAN.,HISTORICAL REGISTER AND DICTIONARY OF THE UNITED STATES ARMY, Vol. 1, Washington: GPO, 1903. p. 19
5. Powell, William H., List of Officers of the Army of the United States form 1779 to 1900, New York: L.R. Hamersly & CO, 1900, p. 31-34
6. Journal of the Continental Congress, Vol. 27 p. 524
7. Heitman, F.B., Historical Register Officers of the Continental Army during the War of Revolution, Washington: 1893,
8. ibid

The "Federal Army"
1. Journal of the Continental Congress, Vol. 27 p. 531

Subdivisions of ranks
1.
http://www.defense.gov/specials/insignias/officers.html, November 2010

Brevet ranks
1. http://en.wikipedia.org/wiki/Brevet_(military), November 2010

Medical Ranks
1. United States Statutes at Large, Vol. 35, p. 67
2. United States Statutes at Large, Vol. 4, p. 714

Law
1. United States Statutes at Large, Vol. 2, p. 133
2. Journal of the Continental Congress, Vol. 2 p. 89
3. FRANCIS B. HEITMAN.,HISTORICAL REGISTER AND DICTIONARY OF THE UNITED STATES ARMY, Vol. 2, Washington: GPO, 1903, p. 569
4. United States Statutes at Large, Vol. 39, p. 166
5. Regulations for the Army of the United States, May 1, 1861, p. A
6. Regulations for the Army of the United States, 1913 Corrected to April 15, 1917, p. 12-13
7. United States Statutes at Large, Vol. 41, p. 761

The enlisted grade reorganization of 1920
1. Emerson, William K., Chevrons, Washington: Smithsonian Institution Press, 1983, p. 251
2. ibid p. 193.
3. ibid p. 196

Pay Grades
1. United States Statutes at Large, Vol. 63, p. 807
2. United States Statutes at Large, Vol. 68, p. 157
3.
http://www.tioh.hqda.pentagon.mil/UniformedServices/Insignia_Rank/enlisted_history.aspx, September 2010
4. United States Statutes at Large, Vol. 72, p. 123
5. Emerson, William K., Chevrons, Washington: Smithsonian Institution Press, 1983, p. 197.
6. ibid. p. 198
7. United States Statutes at Large, Vol. 105, p. 1491

The Army Register, Historical Register and Tables of Organization
1. Journal of the Senate of the United States of America, Volume 6, p. 38.

Chapter 2. Army Rank Insignia

1. http://memory.loc.gov/cgi-bin/query/r?ammem/mgw:@field(DOCID+@lit(gw030237)), December 2010
2. http://memory.loc.gov/cgi-bin/query/r?ammem/mgw:@field(DOCID+@lit(gw030251)), December 2010
3. http://memory.loc.gov/cgi-bin/query/r?ammem/mgw:@field(DOCID+@lit(gw030254)), December 2010
4. Peterson, Harold L. , The Book of the Continental Soldier, Harrisburg: Stackpole, 1968., p. 244
5. Steffen, Randy, The Horse Soldier 1776-1943, Vol. 1., Norman: University of Oklahoma Press, 1977, p. 44
6. Emerson, William K., Chevrons, Washington: Smithsonian Institution Press, 1983, p. 40
7. ibid
8. ibid, p. 41
9. ibid, p. 42
10. Emerson, William K., Encyclopedia of United States Army Insignia and Uniforms, Norman: University of Oklahoma Press, 1996, p. 124
11. Steffen, Randy, The Horse Soldier 1776-1943, Vol. 1., Norman: University of Oklahoma Press, 1977, p. 94
12. Emerson, William K., Encyclopedia of United States Army Insignia and Uniforms, Norman: University of Oklahoma Press, 1996, p. 436-438
13. Lanham Howard G., Straps, Westminster, MD: Johnson Graphics, 1998, p. 10
14. Steffen, Randy, The Horse Soldier 1776-1943, Vol. 1., Norman: University of Oklahoma Press, 1977, p. 91
15. Lanham Howard G., Straps, Westminster, MD: Johnson Graphics, 1998, p. 12
16. Steffen, Randy, The Horse Soldier 1776-1943, Vol. 1., Norman: University of Oklahoma Press, 1977, p. 113
17. Emerson, William K., Chevrons, Washington: Smithsonian Institution Press, 1983, p. 44
18. Steffen, Randy, The Horse Soldier 1776-1943, Vol. 2., Norman: University of Oklahoma Press, 1977, p. 10-11
19.
http://www.qmfound.com/changes_in_the_army_uniform_1895.htm, December 2010
20. General Order 286, November 22, 1864
21. Steffen, Randy, The Horse Soldier 1776-1943, Vol. 2., Norman: University of Oklahoma Press, 1977, p. 97
22. ibid. p. 96
23. ibid. p. 111
24. ibid. p. 112, Steffen maintains thru illustrations that it was a badge of rank in a circle.
25. Emerson, William K., Chevrons, Washington: Smithsonian Institution Press, 1983, p. 66.
26. Emerson, William K., Encyclopedia of United States Army Insignia and Uniforms, Norman: University of Oklahoma Press, 1996, p. 495.
27. ibid. p. 486.
28. ibid. p. 598.
29. Steffen, Randy, The Horse Soldier 1776-1943, Vol. 3., Norman: University of Oklahoma Press, 1977, p. 95-138
30. Emerson, William K., Chevrons, Washington: Smithsonian Institution Press, 1983, p. 113.
31. ibid. p. 115
32. Emerson, William K., Encyclopedia of United States Army Insignia and Uniforms, Norman: University of Oklahoma Press, 1996, p. 574.
33. Steffen, Randy, The Horse Soldier 1776-1943, Vol. 3., Norman: University of Oklahoma Press, 1977, p. 155
34. Steffen, Randy, The Horse Soldier 1776-1943, Vol. 4., Norman: University of Oklahoma Press, 1977, p. 15
35. Emerson, William K., Encyclopedia of United States Army Insignia and Uniforms, Norman: University of Oklahoma Press, 1996, p. 539.
36. Steffen, Randy, The Horse Soldier 1776-1943, Vol. 4., Norman: University of Oklahoma Press, 1977, p. 20
37. ibid. p. 66
38. ibid. p. 20
39. ibid. p. 66
40. Emerson, William K., Encyclopedia of United States Army Insignia and Uniforms, Norman: University of Oklahoma Press, 1996, p. 474.
41. Steffen, Randy, The Horse Soldier 1776-1943, Vol. 4., Norman: University of Oklahoma Press, 1977, p. 63
42. ibid p. 77-92
43. Emerson, William K., Encyclopedia of United States Army Insignia and Uniforms, Norman: University of Oklahoma Press, 1996, p. 490
44. ibid. p. 541.
45. ibid. p. 563
46. ibid. p. 573
47. ibid. p. 592
48. ibid. p. 465
49. Emerson, William K., Chevrons, Washington: Smithsonian Institution Press, 1983, p. 202
50. Emerson, William K., Encyclopedia of United States Army Insignia and Uniforms, Norman: University of Oklahoma Press, 1996, p. 591
51. ibid. p. 574
52. Emerson, William K., Chevrons, Washington: Smithsonian Institution Press, 1983, p. 203
53. Emerson, William K., Encyclopedia of United States Army Insignia and Uniforms, Norman: University of Oklahoma Press, 1996, p. 591
54. Ar 670-1, February 3, 2005, p. 148.
55.
http://en.wikipedia.org/wiki/Extended_Cold_whether_Clothing_System, December 2010
56 . loops mentioned in AR 670-1, July 2002, p. 38, but not in the May 2000 version.
57. http://en.wikipedia.org/wiki/Army_Combat_Uniform, December 2010

Epaulets
1. Oliver, Raymond, Why is a Kernal called a Colonel?, Tuscon: Fireship press, 1983, p. 17
2. Peterson, Harold L. , The Book of the Continental Soldier, Harrisburg: Stackpole, 1968, p. 242
3. ibid p. 243-244
4. Kochan, James and Rickman, David, The United States Army 1781-1811, Oxford: Osprey, 2001, p. 34
5. Lanham Howard G., Straps, Westminster, MD: Johnson Graphics, 1998, p. 7
6. Steffen, Randy, The Horse Soldier 1776-1943, Vol. 1., Norman: University of Oklahoma Press, 1977, p. 94
7. Emerson, William K., Encyclopedia of United States Army Insignia and Uniforms, Norman: University of Oklahoma Press, 1996, p. 178
8. ibid. p. 274
9. Steffen, Randy, The Horse Soldier 1776-1943, Vol. 1., Norman: University of Oklahoma Press, 1977, p. 94
10. Emerson, William K., Encyclopedia of United States Army Insignia and Uniforms, Norman: University of Oklahoma Press, 1996, p. 438
11. Steffen, Randy, The Horse Soldier 1776-1943, Vol. 1., Norman: University of Oklahoma Press, 1977, p. 91
12. Emerson, William K., Encyclopedia of United States Army Insignia and Uniforms, Norman: University of Oklahoma Press, 1996, p. 209
13. ibid. p. 210
14. ibid. p. 178
15. ibid. p. 274
16. Steffen, Randy, The Horse Soldier 1776-1943, Vol. 2., Norman: University of Oklahoma Press, 1977, p. 10
17. ibid p. 6-7
18. ibid p. 41
19. Steffen, Randy, The Horse Soldier 1776-1943, Vol. 2., Norman: University of Oklahoma Press, 1977, p. 111
20. Emerson, William K., Encyclopedia of United States Army Insignia and Uniforms, Norman: University of Oklahoma Press, 1996, p. 275
21. ibid. p. 561
22. ibid. p. 309
23. Specifications for the uniform of the Army, Washington:GPO, 1913 p. 15
24. Emerson, William K., Encyclopedia of United States Army Insignia and Uniforms, Norman: University of Oklahoma Press, 1996, p. 560
25. ibid p. 563
26. ibid

Button Color
1. http://memory.loc.gov/mss/mgw/mgwtext/0426.tif, January 2011
2. Steffen, Randy, The Horse Soldier 1776-1943, Vol. 1., Norman: University of Oklahoma Press, 1977, p. 7
3. ibid. p. 38

4. ibid p. 44-45
5. ibid p. 90-91
6. Emerson, William K., Chevrons, Washington: Smithsonian Institution Press, 1983, p. 40
7. Lanham Howard G., Straps, Westminster, MD: Johnson Graphics, 1998, p. 10
8. Steffen, Randy, The Horse Soldier 1776-1943, Vol. 2., Norman: University of Oklahoma Press, 1977, p. 6-14

The 1813 General Staff Uniform
The Army Register of the United States, December 1, 1813, p. 85-86

Shoulder Straps
1. Lanham Howard G., Straps, Westminster, MD: Johnson Graphics, 1998, p. 7
2. ibid. p. 10
3. ibid.
4. WILLIAM A. GORDON.,A COMPILATION OF REGISTERS OF THE ARMY OF THE UNTIED STATES, Washington: James C. Dunn, 1837. p. 515-529
5. Lanham Howard G., Straps, Westminster, MD: Johnson Graphics, 1998, p. 9
6. FRANCIS B. HEITMAN.,HISTORICAL REGISTER AND DICTIONARY OF THE UNITED STATES ARMY, Vol. 1, Washington: GPO, 1903, p. 622
7. Lanham Howard G., Straps, Westminster, MD: Johnson Graphics, 1998, p. 11
8. United States Statutes at Large, Vol. 4, p. 713
9. Lanham Howard G., Straps, Westminster, MD: Johnson Graphics, 1998, p. 17
10. ibid. p. 12
11. Steffen, Randy, The Horse Soldier 1776-1943, Vol. 1., Norman: University of Oklahoma Press, 1977, p. 113.
12. Steffen, Randy, The Horse Soldier 1776-1943, Vol. 2., Norman: University of Oklahoma Press, 1977, p. 10-11.
13. ibid. p. 111
14. Lanham Howard G., Straps, Westminster, MD: Johnson Graphics, 1998, p. 105-106.
15. ibid p. 107
16. ibid
17. ibid. p. 109-110
18. Steffen, Randy, The Horse Soldier 1776-1943, Vol. 4., Norman: University of Oklahoma Press, 1977, p. 92.
19. Emerson, William K., Encyclopedia of United States Army Insignia and Uniforms, Norman: University of Oklahoma Press, 1996, p. 563
20. Lanham Howard G., Straps, Westminster, MD: Johnson Graphics, 1998, p. 119
21. ibid. p. 123
22. ibid. p. 39
23. Emerson, William K., Encyclopedia of United States Army Insignia and Uniforms, Norman: University of Oklahoma Press, 1996, p. 265-266

Badges of rank
1. Peterson, Harold L. , The Book of the Continental Soldier, Harrisburg: Stackpole, 1968. p. 241-242
2. Steffen, Randy, The Horse Soldier 1776-1943, Vol. 1., Norman: University of Oklahoma Press, 1977, p. 94.
3. ibid. p. 104
4. Emerson, William K., Encyclopedia of United States Army Insignia and Uniforms, Norman: University of Oklahoma Press, 1996, p. 266-267
5. ibid. p. 387
6. ibid. p. 391
7. AR-600-35, Change 1, September 4, 1942, page 6
8. Steffen, Randy, The Horse Soldier 1776-1943, Vol. 2., Norman: University of Oklahoma Press, 1977, p. 10.
9. ibid. p. 111
10. Lanham Howard G., Straps, Westminster, MD: Johnson Graphics, 1998, p. 53
11. Steffen, Randy, The Horse Soldier 1776-1943, Vol. 2., Norman: University of Oklahoma Press, 1977, p. 147.
12. Foster, Frank c., The Decorations, Medals, Ribbions, Badges and Insignia of the United States Army World War II to Present, Fountain Inn: MOA press, 2001, p. 16
13. Steffen, Randy, The Horse Soldier 1776-1943, Vol. 3., Norman: University of Oklahoma Press, 1977, p. 68.
14. Emerson, William K., Encyclopedia of United States Army Insignia and Uniforms, Norman: University of Oklahoma Press, 1996, p. 498
15. Steffen, Randy, The Horse Soldier 1776-1943, Vol. 3., Norman: University of Oklahoma Press, 1977, p. 68.
16. ibid. p. 73
17. Emerson, William K., Encyclopedia of United States Army Insignia and Uniforms, Norman: University of Oklahoma Press, 1996, p. 486
18. Steffen, Randy, The Horse Soldier 1776-1943, Vol. 3., Norman: University of Oklahoma Press, 1977, p. 100.
20. Specifications for the uniform of the united states army,GPO, 1912 p. 29.
21. ibid. p. 27
22. Emerson, William K., Encyclopedia of United States Army Insignia and Uniforms, Norman: University of Oklahoma Press, 1996, p. 490
23. Regulations for the uniform of the united states army, GPO, 1917 p. 36.
24. Emerson, William K., Encyclopedia of United States Army Insignia and Uniforms, Norman: University of Oklahoma Press, 1996, p. 490
25. ibid. p. 540-541
26. ibid. p. 490
27. ibid. p. 473
28. ibid. p. 490
29. ibid. p. 541.
30. ibid. p. 387
31. AR-600-35, Change 1, September 4, 1942, page 6
32. ibid. p. 2
33. Foster, Frank c., The Decorations, Medals, Ribbions, Badges and Insignia of the United States Army World War II to Present, Fountain Inn: MOA press, 2001, p. 19
34. http://www.tioh.hqda.pentagon.mil/UniformedServices/Insignia_Rank/warrant_officers.aspx, January 2011
35. AR-670-1, February 2005, p 193-194
36. Ar-670-1, September 1992, p. 126
37. Emerson, William K., Encyclopedia of United States Army Insignia and Uniforms, Norman: University of Oklahoma Press, 1996, p. 489
38. http://en.wikipedia.org/wiki/Army_Combat_Uniform, January 2011

Chevrons
1. Oliver, Raymond, Why is a Kernal called a Colonel?, Tuscon: Fireship press, 1983, p. 1
2. Emerson, William K., Chevrons, Washington: Smithsonian Institution Press, 1983, p. 40
3. ibid.
4. ibid p. 41
5. ibid p. 53
6. ibid
7. United States Statutes at Large, Vol. 3, p. 615
8. Emerson, William K., Chevrons, Washington: Smithsonian Institution Press, 1983, p. 42
9. ibid. p. 55
10. Steffen, Randy, The Horse Soldier 1776-1943, Vol. 1., Norman: University of Oklahoma Press, 1977, p. 91.
11. Emerson, William K., Chevrons, Washington: Smithsonian Institution Press, 1983, p. 42
12. http://www.ushist.com/mexican-war_uniforms_us_mw_f.shtml, January 2011
13. Emerson, William K., Chevrons, Washington: Smithsonian Institution Press, 1983, p. 53
14. ibid
15. http://www.aztecclub.com/uniforms/uni-table1.htm, January 2011
16. Steffen, Randy, The Horse Soldier 1776-1943, Vol. 2., Norman: University of Oklahoma Press, 1977, p. 11.
17. Emerson, William K., Chevrons, Washington: Smithsonian Institution Press, 1983, p. 46
18. ibid. p. 254-260
19. ibid. p. 70
20. Steffen, Randy, The Horse Soldier 1776-1943, Vol. 3., Norman: University of Oklahoma Press, 1977, p. 12.
21. Emerson, William K., Chevrons, Washington: Smithsonian Institution Press, 1983, p. 63
22. ibid p. 70
23. ibid. p. 63
24. Emerson, William K., Encyclopedia of United States Army Insignia and Uniforms, Norman: University of Oklahoma Press, 1996, p. 486
25. Emerson, William K., Chevrons, Washington: Smithsonian Institution Press, 1983, p. 63
26. ibid
27. ibid. p. 112
28. Official Army Register, July 1, 1902, p. 498-504
29. Emerson, William K., Chevrons, Washington: Smithsonian Institution Press, 1983, p. 114.
30. ibid. p. 115.
31. Emerson, William K., Encyclopedia of United States Army Insignia and Uniforms, Norman: University of Oklahoma Press, 1996, p. 567-568
32. ibid .p. 496
33. Emerson, William K., Chevrons, Washington: Smithsonian Institution Press, 1983, p. 115.
34. ibid
35. ibid p. 116
36. ibid p. 117
37. ibid p. 118
38. ibid
39. Fisher, Ernest, Guardians of the Republic, New York: Ballentine, 1994, p. 211
40. Official Army Register, December 1, 1915, p. 670-673
41. Emerson, William K., Chevrons, Washington: Smithsonian Institution Press, 1983, p. 119-120.
42. ibid. p. 214
43. Emerson, William K., Encyclopedia of United States Army Insignia and Uniforms, Norman: University of Oklahoma Press, 1996, p. 509
41. Emerson, William K., Chevrons, Washington: Smithsonian Institution Press, 1983, p. 188.
45. Steffen, Randy, The Horse Soldier 1776-1943, Vol. 4., Norman: University of Oklahoma Press, 1977, p. 66.
46. Emerson, William K., Chevrons, Washington: Smithsonian Institution Press, 1983, p. 188.
47. Emerson, William K., Encyclopedia of United States Army Insignia and Uniforms, Norman: University of Oklahoma Press, 1996, p. 564-565
48. ibid. p.565
49. Emerson, William K., Chevrons, Washington: Smithsonian Institution Press, 1983, p. 205.
50. ibid. p. 190
51. ibid.
52. ibid. p. 205
53. ibid. p. 214
54. ibid. p. 198
55. ibid. p. 202
56. ibid. p. 206
57. Emerson, William K., Encyclopedia of United States Army Insignia and Uniforms, Norman: University of Oklahoma Press, 1996, p. 481
58. ibid. p. 574
59. Ar-670-1, September 1992, summary of changes
60. Ar-670-1, Interin Change No. 106, July 28, 1980
61. Emerson, William K., Chevrons, Washington: Smithsonian Institution Press, 1983, p. 203
62. http://www.tioh.hqda.pentagon.mil/UniformedServices/Insignia_Rank/enlisted_history.aspx, January 2011
63. Alaract 202/2008, August 20, 2008

Facing and Piping color
1. Steffen, Randy, The Horse Soldier 1776-1943, Vol. 1., Norman: University of Oklahoma Press, 1977, p. 6-14.
2. Zlatich, Marko and Younghusband, Bill., General Washinton's Army: (2) 1779-1783 , , London: Reed International Books Ltd., 1995, p. 7.
3. ibid.
4. ibid. p. 5
5. ibid. p. 8
6. Kochan, James and Rickman, David, The United States Army 1812-1815, Oxford: Osprey, 2000, p. 14
7. Emerson, William K., Encyclopedia of United States Army Insignia and Uniforms, Norman: University of Oklahoma Press, 1996, p. 306-307
8. Steffen, Randy, The Horse Soldier 1776-1943, Vol. 1., Norman: University of Oklahoma Press, 1977, p. 6-14.
9. Emerson, William K., Encyclopedia of United States Army Insignia and Uniforms, Norman: University of Oklahoma Press, 1996, p. 527
10. ibid. p. 457
11. Steffen, Randy, The Horse Soldier 1776-1943, Vol.3., Norman: University of Oklahoma Press, 1977, p. 106.
12. "Color Changes in Rules for Officers Caps," Stars and Stripes, September 13, 1918, p.1
13. Emerson, William K., Encyclopedia of United States Army Insignia and Uniforms, Norman: University of Oklahoma Press, 1996, p. 541
13a. http://www.tioh.hqda.pentagon.mil/UniformedServices/Branches/acquisition.aspx, February 2011
14. United States Statutes at Large, Vol. 64, p. 269
15. Lanham Howard G., Straps, Westminster, MD: Johnson Graphics, 1998, p. 159
16. United States Statutes at Large, Vol. 2, p. 819
17. United States Statutes at Large, Vol. 33, p. 262
18. United States Statutes at Large, Vol. 34, p. 1158
18a. Emerson, William K., Encyclopedia of United States Army Insignia and Uniforms, Norman: University of Oklahoma Press, 1996, p. 239
19. Lanham Howard G., Straps, Westminster, MD: Johnson Graphics, 1998, p. 159
20. United States Statutes at Large, Vol. 44, p. 780

21. United States Statutes at Large, Vol. 61, p. 503
22. Lanham Howard G., Straps, Westminster, MD: Johnson Graphics, 1998, p. 159
23. http://en.wikipedia.org/wiki/United_States_Army_Air_Forces, February, 2011
24. United States Statutes at Large, Vol. 41, p. 759
25. United States Statutes at Large, Vol. 44, p. 780
26. Emerson, William K., Encyclopedia of United States Army Insignia and Uniforms, Norman: University of Oklahoma Press, 1996, p. 540
27. Lanham Howard G., Straps, Westminster, MD: Johnson Graphics, 1998, p. 159
28. United States Statutes at Large, Vol. 64, p. 273
29. Foster, Frank c., The Decorations, Medals, Ribbions, Badges and Insignia of the United States Army World War II to Present, Fountain Inn: MOA press, 2001, p. 26
30. Emerson, William K., Encyclopedia of United States Army Insignia and Uniforms, Norman: University of Oklahoma Press, 1996, p. 368
31. United States Statutes at Large, Vol. 64, p. 273
32. Lanham Howard G., Straps, Westminster, MD: Johnson Graphics, 1998, p. 159
33. Emerson, William K., Encyclopedia of United States Army Insignia and Uniforms, Norman: University of Oklahoma Press, 1996, p. 381
34. Lanham Howard G., Straps, Westminster, MD: Johnson Graphics, 1998, p. 160
35. Emerson, William K., Encyclopedia of United States Army Insignia and Uniforms, Norman: University of Oklahoma Press, 1996, p. 416
36. Foster, Frank c., The Decorations, Medals, Ribbions, Badges and Insignia of the United States Army World War II to Present, Fountain Inn: MOA press, 2001, p. 31
37. United States Statutes at Large, Vol. 1, p. 119
38. United States Statutes at Large, Vol. 1, p. 366
39. United States Statutes at Large, Vol. 1, p. 552
40. United States Statutes at Large, Vol. 2, p. 132
41. United States Statutes at Large, Vol. 2, p. 481
42. United States Statutes at Large, Vol. 2, p. 671
43. United States Statutes at Large, Vol. 3, p. 113
44. United States Statutes at Large, Vol. 3, p. 615
45. United States Statutes at Large, Vol. 31, p. 749
46. United States Statutes at Large, Vol. 34, p. 861
47. United States Statutes at Large, Vol. 64, p. 273
48. Foster, Frank c., The Decorations, Medals, Ribbions, Badges and Insignia of the United States Army World War II to Present, Fountain Inn: MOA press, 2001, p. 25
49. Emerson, William K., Encyclopedia of United States Army Insignia and Uniforms, Norman: University of Oklahoma Press, 1996, p. 436-437
50. United States Statutes at Large, Vol. 32, p. 831
51. Lanham Howard G., Straps, Westminster, MD: Johnson Graphics, 1998, p. 106
52. Foster, Frank c., The Decorations, Medals, Ribbions, Badges and Insignia of the United States Army World War II to Present, Fountain Inn: MOA press, 2001, p. 27
53. Lanham Howard G., Straps, Westminster, MD: Johnson Graphics, 1998, p. 159
54. Foster, Frank c., The Decorations, Medals, Ribbions, Badges and Insignia of the United States Army World War II to Present, Fountain Inn: MOA press, 2001, p. 41
55. United States Statutes at Large, Vol. 32, p. 712
56. United States Statutes at Large, Vol. 53, p. 1433
57. Lanham Howard G., Straps, Westminster, MD: Johnson Graphics, 1998, p. 159
58. United States Statutes at Large, Vol. 13, p. 144
59. United States Statutes at Large, Vol. 23, p. 113
60. United States Statutes at Large, Vol. 10, p. 639
61. United States Statutes at Large, Vol. 64, p. 273
62. Emerson, William K., Chevrons, Washington: Smithsonian Institution Press, 1983, p. 47.
63. Emerson, William K., Encyclopedia of United States Army Insignia and Uniforms, Norman: University of Oklahoma Press, 1996, p. 265
64. Lanham Howard G., Straps, Westminster, MD: Johnson Graphics, 1998, p. 89
65. United States Statutes at Large, Vol. 60, p. 861
66. Lanham Howard G., Straps, Westminster, MD: Johnson Graphics, 1998, p. 159
67. Emerson, William K., Encyclopedia of United States Army Insignia and Uniforms, Norman: University of Oklahoma Press, 1996, p. 375
68. United States Statutes at Large, Vol. 41, p. 760
69. Lanham Howard G., Straps, Westminster, MD: Johnson Graphics, 1998, p. 159
70. Emerson, William K., Encyclopedia of United States Army Insignia and Uniforms, Norman: University of Oklahoma Press, 1996, p. 417
71. Lanham Howard G., Straps, Westminster, MD: Johnson Graphics, 1998, p. 159
72. Emerson, William K., Encyclopedia of United States Army Insignia and Uniforms, Norman: University of Oklahoma Press, 1996, p. 207
73. United States Statutes at Large, Vol. 1, p. 366
74. United States Statutes at Large, Vol. 2, p. 132
75. United States Statutes at Large, Vol. 2, p. 206
76. United States Statutes at Large, Vol. 3, p. 615
77. United States Statutes at Large, Vol. 9, p. 12
78. Kochan, James and Rickman, David, The United States Army 1812-1815, Oxford: Osprey, 2000, p. 37
79. Steffen, Randy, The Horse Soldier 1776-1943, Vol.2., Norman: University of Oklahoma Press, 1977, p. 6-7.
80. ibid p. 108
81. Lanham Howard G., Straps, Westminster, MD: Johnson Graphics, 1998, p. 159
82. Emerson, William K., Encyclopedia of United States Army Insignia and Uniforms, Norman: University of Oklahoma Press, 1996, p. 380
83. Ibid. p. 540
84. Official Army Register, January 1883, p. 10
85. Official Army Register, January 1884, p. 10
86. United States Statutes at Large, Vol. 23, p. 113
87. Lanham Howard G., Straps, Westminster, MD: Johnson Graphics, 1998, p. 159
88. United States Statutes at Large, Vol. 5, p. 256
89. United States Statutes at Large, Vol. 12, p. 317
90. United States Statutes at Large, Vol. 12, p. 743
91. Emerson, William K., Encyclopedia of United States Army Insignia and Uniforms, Norman: University of Oklahoma Press, 1996, p. 208-209
92. http://www.history.army.mil/reference/1839U.htm, July 2010
93. Steffen, Randy, The Horse Soldier 1776-1943, Vol.2., Norman: University of Oklahoma Press, 1977, p. 8.
94. United States Statutes at Large, Vol. 41, p. 775
95. Emerson, William K., Encyclopedia of United States Army Insignia and Uniforms, Norman: University of Oklahoma Press, 1996, p. 542 and 534
96. United States Statutes at Large, Vol. 1, p. 241
97. United States Statutes at Large, Vol. 2, p. 86
98. United States Statutes at Large, Vol. 2, p. 481
99. United States Statutes at Large, Vol. 3, p. 224
100. United States Statutes at Large, Vol. 12, p. 289
101. Zlatich, Marko and Younghusband, Bill., General Washinton's Army: (2) 1779-1783 , , London: Reed International Books Ltd., 1995, p. 4.
102. ibid p. 8
103. Kochan, James and Rickman, David, The United States Army 1781-1811, Oxford: Osprey, 2001, p. 19
104. ibid. plate F
105. Steffen, Randy, The Horse Soldier 1776-1943, Vol.1., Norman: University of Oklahoma Press, 1977, p. 44.
106. ibid p. 90-91
107. Steffen, Randy, The Horse Soldier 1776-1943, Vol.2., Norman: University of Oklahoma Press, 1977, p. 6.
108. United States Statutes at Large, Vol. 64, p. 269
109. Lanham Howard G., Straps, Westminster, MD: Johnson Graphics, 1998, p. 159
110. United States Statutes at Large, Vol. 41, p. 766
111. Foster, Frank c., The Decorations, Medals, Ribbions, Badges and Insignia of the United States Army World War II to Present, Fountain Inn: MOA press, 2001, p. 34
112. Emerson, William K., Encyclopedia of United States Army Insignia and Uniforms, Norman: University of Oklahoma Press, 1996, p. 375
113. United States Statutes at Large, Vol. 14, p. 333
114. Emerson, William K., Encyclopedia of United States Army Insignia and Uniforms, Norman: University of Oklahoma Press, 1996, p. 288
115. Steffen, Randy, The Horse Soldier 1776-1943, Vol.3., Norman: University of Oklahoma Press, 1977, p. 55.
116. ibid. p. 135
117. Steffen, Randy, The Horse Soldier 1776-1943, Vol.2., Norman: University of Oklahoma Press, 1977, p. 6-7.
118. Emerson, William K., Chevrons, Washington: Smithsonian Institution Press, 1983, p. 66
119. ibid.
120. http://www.qmfound.com/chevrons_dress_cavalry_infantry_1907.jpg, February 2011, the infantry chevrons are white
121. Specifications for the uniform of the Army, Washington:GPO, 1913 p. 15
122. United States Statutes at Large, Vol. 2, p. 819
123. Emerson, William K., Encyclopedia of United States Army Insignia and Uniforms, Norman: University of Oklahoma Press, 1996, p. 307
124. ibid. p. 271
125. "Color Changes in Rules for Officers Caps," Stars and Stripes, September 13, 1918, p.1
126. Lanham Howard G., Straps, Westminster, MD: Johnson Graphics, 1998, p. 111
126a. Foster, Frank c., The Decorations, Medals, Ribbions, Badges and Insignia of the United States Army World War II to Present, Fountain Inn: MOA press, 2001, p. 32
127. Emerson, William K., Encyclopedia of United States Army Insignia and Uniforms, Norman: University of Oklahoma Press, 1996, p. 380
128. ibid. p. 534
110. United States Statutes at Large, Vol. 41, p. 129
130. Lanham Howard G., Straps, Westminster, MD: Johnson Graphics, 1998, p. 159
131. United States Statutes at Large, Vol. 23, p. 113
132. United States Statutes at Large, Vol. 41, p. 129
133. "Color Changes in Rules for Officers Caps," Stars and Stripes, September 13, 1918, p.1
134. Lanham Howard G., Straps, Westminster, MD: Johnson Graphics, 1998, p. 111
135. http://www.army.mil/-news/2008/01/09/6943-logistics-officers-don-new-branch-insignia/, February 2011
136. http://www.tioh.hqda.pentagon.mil/UniformedServices/Branches/logistics.aspx, February 2011
137. United States Statutes at Large, Vol. 2, p. 816
138. United States Statutes at Large, Vol. 11, p. 51
139. United States Statutes at Large, Vol. 24, p. 435
140. Emerson, William K., Encyclopedia of United States Army Insignia and Uniforms, Norman: University of Oklahoma Press, 1996, p. 177
141. Steffen, Randy, The Horse Soldier 1776-1943, Vol.2., Norman: University of Oklahoma Press, 1977, p. 8-9.
142. Katcher, Philip, The Civil War Source Book, New York: Facts on File, 1992, p. 175
143. Steffen, Randy, The Horse Soldier 1776-1943, Vol.2., Norman: University of Oklahoma Press, 1977, p. 108-109.
118. Emerson, William K., Chevrons, Washington: Smithsonian Institution Press, 1983, p. 70
144. Steffen, Randy, The Horse Soldier 1776-1943, Vol.3., Norman: University of Oklahoma Press, 1977, p. 106.
145. ibid. p. 113
134. Lanham Howard G., Straps, Westminster, MD: Johnson Graphics, 1998, p. corrigendum to page 107.
148. Foster, Frank c., The Decorations, Medals, Ribbions, Badges and Insignia of the United States Army World War II to Present, Fountain Inn: MOA press, 2001, p. 32
149. Emerson, William K., Encyclopedia of United States Army Insignia and Uniforms, Norman: University of Oklahoma Press, 1996, p. 380
150. Foster, Frank c., The Decorations, Medals, Ribbions, Badges and Insignia of the United States Army World War II to Present, Fountain Inn: MOA press, 2001, p. 31
151. Emerson, William K., Encyclopedia of United States Army Insignia and Uniforms, Norman: University of Oklahoma Press, 1996, p. 396
152. Foster, Frank c., The Decorations, Medals, Ribbions, Badges and Insignia of the United States Army World War II to Present, Fountain Inn: MOA press, 2001, p. 30
153. United States Statutes at Large, Vol. 33, p. 262
154. United States Statutes at Large, Vol. 34, p. 1158
155. United States Statutes at Large, Vol. 39, p. 203
156. United States Statutes at Large, Vol. 48, p. 159
157. Lanham Howard G., Straps, Westminster, MD: Johnson Graphics, 1998, p. 160
157a. Emerson, William K., Encyclopedia of United States Army Insignia and Uniforms, Norman: University of Oklahoma Press, 1996, p. 383
157b. ibid. p.540
158. United States Statutes at Large, Vol. 9, p. 13
159. United States Statutes at Large, Vol. 12, p. 289
160. Steffen, Randy, The Horse Soldier 1776-1943, Vol.1., Norman: University of Oklahoma Press, 1977, p. 119.
161. Steffen, Randy, The Horse Soldier 1776-1943, Vol.2., Norman: University of Oklahoma Press, 1977, p. 6.

162. United States Statutes at Large, Vol. 48, p. 159
163. Lanham Howard G., Straps, Westminster, MD: Johnson Graphics, 1998, p. 160
164. United States Statutes at Large, Vol. 64, p. 269
165. Lanham Howard G., Straps, Westminster, MD: Johnson Graphics, 1998, p. 160
166. United States Statutes at Large, Vol. 2, p. 732
167. United States Statutes at Large, Vol. 3, p. 615
168. United States Statutes at Large, Vol. 4, p. 504
169. United States Statutes at Large, Vol. 64, p. 269
170. http://www.history.army.mil/reference/1839U.htm, July 2010
171. Steffen, Randy, The Horse Soldier 1776-1943, Vol.2., Norman: University of Oklahoma Press, 1977, p. 6.
172. Foster, Frank c., The Decorations, Medals, Ribbions, Badges and Insignia of the United States Army World War II to Present, Fountain Inn: MOA press, 2001, p. 31
173. United States Statutes at Large, Vol. 2, p. 784
174. United States Statutes at Large, Vol. 37, p. 591
175. Lanham Howard G., Straps, Westminster, MD: Johnson Graphics, 1998, p. 160
176. Steffen, Randy, The Horse Soldier 1776-1943, Vol.2., Norman: University of Oklahoma Press, 1977, p. 6.
177. Emerson, William K., Encyclopedia of United States Army Insignia and Uniforms, Norman: University of Oklahoma Press, 1996, p. 540
178. http://www.tioh.hqda.pentagon.mil/UniformedServices/Branches/psych_ops.aspx, February 2011
179. Foster, Frank c., The Decorations, Medals, Ribbions, Badges and Insignia of the United States Army World War II to Present, Fountain Inn: MOA press, 2001, p. 37
180. United States Statutes at Large, Vol. 3, p. 297
181. United States Statutes at Large, Vol. 5, p. 512
182. United States Statutes at Large, Vol. 37, p. 591
183. Lanham Howard G., Straps, Westminster, MD: Johnson Graphics, 1998, p. 160
184. ibid. p. 109
185. Specifications for the uniform of the Army, Washington:GPO, 1913 p. 13
186. United States Statutes at Large, Vol. 2, p. 696
187. United States Statutes at Large, Vol. 23, p. 109
188. United States Statutes at Large, Vol. 37, p. 591
189. Emerson, William K., Encyclopedia of United States Army Insignia and Uniforms, Norman: University of Oklahoma Press, 1996, p. 254
190. Steffen, Randy, The Horse Soldier 1776-1943, Vol.2., Norman: University of Oklahoma Press, 1977, p. 6.
191. Emerson, William K., Chevrons, Washington: Smithsonian Institution Press, 1983, p. 70
192. United States Statutes at Large, Vol. 2, p. 670
193. United States Statutes at Large, Vol. 3, p. 224
194. United States Statutes at Large, Vol. 4, p. 533
195. United States Statutes at Large, Vol. 4, p. 652
196. United States Statutes at Large, Vol. 27, p. 27
197. United States Statutes at Large, Vol. 33, p. 262
198. United States Statutes at Large, Vol. 9, p. 124
199. United States Statutes at Large, Vol. 9, p. 247
200. United States Statutes at Large, Vol. 1, p. 752
201. United States Statutes at Large, Vol. 1, p. 86
201. United States Statutes at Large, Vol. 2, p. 481
203. United States Statutes at Large, Vol. 3, p. 615
204. United States Statutes at Large, Vol. 5, p. 512
205. United States Statutes at Large, Vol. 5, p. 654
206. United States Statutes at Large, Vol. 3, p. 47
207. United States Statutes at Large, Vol. 3, p. 219
208. United States Statutes at Large, Vol. 35, p. 733
209. Emerson, William K., Chevrons, Washington: Smithsonian Institution Press, 1983, p. 124
210. United States Statutes at Large, Vol. 41, p. 775
211. United States Statutes at Large, Vol. 12, p. 744
212. United States Statutes at Large, Vol. 14, p. 332
213. United States Statutes at Large, Vol. 20, p. 206
214. Katcher, Philip, The Civil War Source Book, New York: Facts on File, 1992, p. 170
215. Emerson, William K., Chevrons, Washington: Smithsonian Institution Press, 1983, p. 48
216. Steffen, Randy, The Horse Soldier 1776-1943, Vol.2., Norman: University of Oklahoma Press, 1977, p. 113.
216. Emerson, William K., Chevrons, Washington: Smithsonian Institution Press, 1983, p. 70
218. Steffen, Randy, The Horse Soldier 1776-1943, Vol.3., Norman: University of Oklahoma Press, 1977, p. 106&113.
219. Foster, Frank c., The Decorations, Medals, Ribbions, Badges and Insignia of the United States Army World War II to Present, Fountain Inn: MOA press, 2001, p. 28
220. ibid. p. 40
221. United States Statutes at Large, Vol. 3, p. 426
222. United States Statutes at Large, Vol. 17, p. 485
223. United States Statutes at Large, Vol. 37, p. 591
224. Emerson, William K., Encyclopedia of United States Army Insignia and Uniforms, Norman: University of Oklahoma Press, 1996, p. 307
225. Steffen, Randy, The Horse Soldier 1776-1943, Vol.2., Norman: University of Oklahoma Press, 1977, p. 8.
225. Emerson, William K., Chevrons, Washington: Smithsonian Institution Press, 1983, p. 70
227. Emerson, William K., Encyclopedia of United States Army Insignia and Uniforms, Norman: University of Oklahoma Press, 1996, p. 542
228. ibid. p. 367
229. ibid p. 540
230. Foster, Frank c., The Decorations, Medals, Ribbions, Badges and Insignia of the United States Army World War II to Present, Fountain Inn: MOA press, 2001, p. 37
231. ibid p. 41
232. United States Statutes at Large, Vol. 26, p. 167
233. Emerson, William K., Chevrons, Washington: Smithsonian Institution Press, 1983, p. 67
234. ibid. p. 125
235. Steffen, Randy, The Horse Soldier 1776-1943, Vol.3., Norman: University of Oklahoma Press, 1977, p. 109.
236. Lanham Howard G., Straps, Westminster, MD: Johnson Graphics, 1998, p. 160
237. Ar 210-26, December 9, 2009, p. 7
238. Steffen, Randy, The Horse Soldier 1776-1943, Vol.4., Norman: University of Oklahoma Press, 1977, p. 84.
239. ALARACT 42/2004
240. United States Statutes at Large, Vol. 37, p. 371
241. United States Statutes at Large, Vol. 92, p. 1627
242. Foster, Frank c., The Decorations, Medals, Ribbions, Badges and Insignia of the United States Army World War II to Present, Fountain Inn: MOA press, 2001, p. 42

Cuff Insignia

1. Emerson, William K., Encyclopedia of United States Army Insignia and Uniforms, Norman: University of Oklahoma Press, 1996, p. 436
2. ibid. p. 437
3. ibid. p. 307
4. ibid. p. 208
5. Steffen, Randy, The Horse Soldier 1776-1943, Vol.1., Norman: University of Oklahoma Press, 1977, p. 91.
6. Emerson, William K., Encyclopedia of United States Army Insignia and Uniforms, Norman: University of Oklahoma Press, 1996, p. 435
7. ibid. p. 208
8. ibid. p. 178
9. ibid. p. 275
10. http://www.history.army.mil/reference/1839U.htm, July 2010
11. Langellier, John p., Army Blue, The Uniform of Uncle Sams Regulars ,Atglen, PA: Schiffer Publishing Ltd., 1998, p. 279
12. ibid. p. 27
13. ibid. p. 280
14. ibid. p. 307
15. General Order 102, November 25, 1861
16. General Order 286, November 22, 1864
17. Steffen, Randy, The Horse Soldier 1776-1943, Vol.2., Norman: University of Oklahoma Press, 1977, p. 91.
18. ibid. p. 112
19. Emerson, William K., Encyclopedia of United States Army Insignia and Uniforms, Norman: University of Oklahoma Press, 1996, p. 473
20. Steffen, Randy, The Horse Soldier 1776-1943, Vol.3., Norman: University of Oklahoma Press, 1977, p. 97.
21. Emerson, William K., Encyclopedia of United States Army Insignia and Uniforms, Norman: University of Oklahoma Press, 1996, p. 473-474
22. ibid. p. 574
23. Steffen, Randy, The Horse Soldier 1776-1943, Vol.4., Norman: University of Oklahoma Press, 1977, p. 7.
24. Emerson, William K., Encyclopedia of United States Army Insignia and Uniforms, Norman: University of Oklahoma Press, 1996, p. 473
25. http://www.tioh.hqda.pentagon.mil/UniformedServices/Insignia_Rank/warrant_officers.aspx, February 2011
23. Steffen, Randy, The Horse Soldier 1776-1943, Vol.4., Norman: University of Oklahoma Press, 1977, p. 20.
27. Emerson, William K., Encyclopedia of United States Army Insignia and Uniforms, Norman: University of Oklahoma Press, 1996, p. 391
28. ibid. p. 390
29. ibid.p. 474
30. Steffen, Randy, The Horse Soldier 1776-1943, Vol.4., Norman: University of Oklahoma Press, 1977, p. 66.
31. ibid.p. 77-92
32. Emerson, William K., Encyclopedia of United States Army Insignia and Uniforms, Norman: University of Oklahoma Press, 1996, p. 575-576
33. Stanton, Shelby ., U.S. Army Uniforms of the Cold War 1948-1973, Mechanicsburg: Stackpole, 1994, p. 215
34. Emerson, William K., Encyclopedia of United States Army Insignia and Uniforms, Norman: University of Oklahoma Press, 1996, p. 576
35. AR-670-1, July 1, 2002, p. 137
36. Emerson, William K., Encyclopedia of United States Army Insignia and Uniforms, Norman: University of Oklahoma Press, 1996, p. 591

Shoulder Knots

1. http://www.qmfound.com/changes_in_the_army_uniform_1895.htm, December 2010
2..http://howardlanham.tripod.com/link23r.htm, February 2011
3. Steffen, Randy, The Horse Soldier 1776-1943, Vol.2., Norman: University of Oklahoma Press, 1977, p. 125.
4. Emerson, William K., Encyclopedia of United States Army Insignia and Uniforms, Norman: University of Oklahoma Press, 1996, p. 165
5. ibid. p.167
6. ibid. p.179
7. ibid. p. 210
8. ibid. p. 245
9. ibid. p. 239
10. ibid. p. 280
11. ibid. p. 167
12. General Order 67, June 25, 1873
13. Steffen, Randy, The Horse Soldier 1776-1943, Vol.3., Norman: University of Oklahoma Press, 1977, p. 104.
14. ibid. p. 155
15. Emerson, William K., Encyclopedia of United States Army Insignia and Uniforms, Norman: University of Oklahoma Press, 1996, p. 10
16. ibid. p. 563

Shoulder Boards

1. Emerson, William K., Encyclopedia of United States Army Insignia and Uniforms, Norman: University of Oklahoma Press, 1996, p. 563
2. ibid. p. 593
3. AR 670-1, February 3, 2005, p. 148
4. ibid.p. 207

Shoulder Marks

1. AR 670-1, Interim Change no. 106, July 28, 1980, p. 2
2. Emerson, William K., Chevrons, Washington: Smithsonian Institution Press, 1983, p. 203
15. Emerson, William K., Encyclopedia of United States Army Insignia and Uniforms, Norman: University of Oklahoma Press, 1996, p. 12.Chapter 3.Army Ranks

Acting Hospital Steward

1. United States Statutes at Large, Vol. 25, p. 435
2. Emerson, William K., Chevrons, Washington: Smithsonian Institution Press, 1983, p. 90
3. ibid., p. 72
4. Emerson, William K., Encyclopedia of United States Army Insignia and Uniforms, Norman: University of Oklahoma Press, 1996, p. 200
5. Emerson, William K., Chevrons, Washington: Smithsonian Institution Press, 1983, p. 92
6. ibid., p.156
7. United States Statutes at Large, Vol. 32, p. 930

Apothecary

1.
http://history.amedd.army.mil/booksdocs/rev/MedMen/MedMenAppB.html, June 2010

Apothecary General
1.
http://history.amedd.army.mil/booksdocs/rev/MedMen/MedMenAppB.html, June 2010
2. United States Statutes at Large, Vol. 1, p. 721
3. United States Statutes at Large, Vol. 2, p. 820
4. Emerson, William K., Encyclopedia of United States Army Insignia and Uniforms, Norman: University of Oklahoma Press, 1996, p. 306
5. FRANCIS B. HEITMAN.,HISTORICAL REGISTER AND DICTIONARY OF THE UNITED STATES ARMY, Vol. 1, Washington: GPO, 1903.

Armorer
1. http://www.historycarper.com/resources/tca/chap6.htm: may 2010

Artificer
1. United States Statutes at Large, Vol. 39, p. 166
2. Emerson, William K., Chevrons, Washington: Smithsonian Institution Press, 1983, p. 105

Assistant Apothecary (General)
1.
http://history.amedd.army.mil/booksdocs/rev/MedMen/MedMenAppB.html, June 2010
2. United States Statutes at Large, Vol. 3, p. 115
3. FRANCIS B. HEITMAN.,HISTORICAL REGISTER AND DICTIONARY OF THE UNITED STATES ARMY, Vol. 1, Washington: GPO, 1903.

Assistant Band Leader
1. United States Statutes at Large, Vol. 39, p. 166
2. Emerson, William K., Chevrons, Washington: Smithsonian Institution Press, 1983, p. 145-147
3. ibid. p 251

Assistant Commissary (of Issues) (Purchases)
1. United States Statutes at Large, Vol. 2, p. 816
2. WILLIAM A. GORDON.,A COMPILATION OF REGISTERS OF THE ARMY OF THE UNTIED STATES, Washington: James C. Dunn, 1837. p. 8
3. Ibid. p. 77
4. FRANCIS B. HEITMAN.,HISTORICAL REGISTER AND DICTIONARY OF THE UNITED STATES ARMY, Vol. 1, Washington: GPO, 1903. p- 287 and 916
5.United States Statutes at Large, Vol. 3, p. 297
6. WILLIAM A. GORDON.,A COMPILATION OF REGISTERS OF THE ARMY OF THE UNTIED STATES, Washington: James C. Dunn, 1837. p. 124
7. United States Statutes at Large, Vol. 3, p. 615
8. FRANCIS B. HEITMAN.,HISTORICAL REGISTER AND DICTIONARY OF THE UNITED STATES ARMY, Vol. 1, Washington: GPO, 1903.
9. Emerson, William K., Encyclopedia of United States Army Insignia and Uniforms, Norman: University of Oklahoma Press, 1996, p. 306

Assistant Deputy Apothecary
1. Heitman, F.B., Historical Register Officers of the Continental Army during the War of Revolution, Washington: 1893, p. 116

Assistant Deputy Director of Hospitals
1.
http://history.amedd.army.mil/booksdocs/rev/MedMen/MedMenAppB.html, June 2010

Assistant Deputy Paymaster General
1. United States Statutes at Large, Vol. 2, p. 784
2. Raphael Thian, Legilative history of the Army of the United States, Washington: GPO, 1901, p. 463

Assistant Director of Hospitals
1.
http://history.amedd.army.mil/booksdocs/rev/MedMen/MedMenAppB.html, June 2010

Assistant District Paymaster
1. United States Statutes at Large, Vol. 3, p. 128
2. FRANCIS B. HEITMAN.,HISTORICAL REGISTER AND DICTIONARY OF THE UNITED STATES ARMY, Vol. 1, Washington: GPO, 1903.

Assistant Engineer
1. United States Statutes at Large, Vol. 39, p. 166
2. Emerson, William K., Chevrons, Washington: Smithsonian Institution Press, 1983, p. 162
3. ibid. p 251

Assistant Medical Purveyor
1. United States Statutes at Large, Vol. 14, p. 332
2. FRANCIS B. HEITMAN.,HISTORICAL REGISTER AND DICTIONARY OF THE UNITED STATES ARMY, Vol. 1, Washington: GPO, 1903.
3. United States Statutes at Large, Vol. 27, p. 276
4. Emerson, William K., Encyclopedia of United States Army Insignia and Uniforms, Norman: University of Oklahoma Press, 1996, p. 179
5. ibid.

Assistant Purveyor
1.
http://history.amedd.army.mil/booksdocs/rev/MedMen/MedMenAppB.html, June 2010

Assistant Steward, Mine Planter Service
1. United States Statutes at Large, Vol. 40, p. 882
2. Emerson, William K., Chevrons, Washington: Smithsonian Institution Press, 1983, p. 228
3. ibid. p. 253

Assistant Surgeon
1.
http://history.amedd.army.mil/booksdocs/medicaldepartment/partthree.html, June 2010
2. United States Statutes at Large, Vol. 3, p. 615
3. United States Statutes at Large, Vol. 4, p. 550
4. WILLIAM A. GORDON.,A COMPILATION OF REGISTERS OF THE ARMY OF THE UNTIED STATES, Washington: James C. Dunn, 1837. p. 516
4. United States Statutes at Large, Vol. 4, p. 714
5. United States Statutes at Large, Vol. 9, p. 17
6. United States Statutes at Large, Vol. 14, p. 332
7. United States Statutes at Large, Vol. 31, p. 752
8. United States Statutes at Large, Vol. 35, p. 67
9. Emerson, William K., Encyclopedia of United States Army Insignia and Uniforms, Norman: University of Oklahoma Press, 1996, p. 177
10. ibid.
11. ibid . p 179

Assistant Surgeon General
1. United States Statutes at Large, Vol. 3, p. 426
2. FRANCIS B. HEITMAN.,HISTORICAL REGISTER AND DICTIONARY OF THE UNITED STATES ARMY, Vol. 1, Washington: GPO, 1903.
3. United States Statutes at Large, Vol. 3, p. 615
3. Emerson, William K., Encyclopedia of United States Army Insignia and Uniforms, Norman: University of Oklahoma Press, 1996, p. 306
4. United States Statutes at Large, Vol. 12, p. 378
5. FRANCIS B. HEITMAN.,HISTORICAL REGISTER AND DICTIONARY OF THE UNITED STATES ARMY, Vol. 1, Washington: GPO, 1903.
6. United States Statutes at Large, Vol. 27, p. 276
7. United States Statutes at Large, Vol. 35, p. 67
8. Emerson, William K., Encyclopedia of United States Army Insignia and Uniforms, Norman: University of Oklahoma Press, 1996, p. 179
9. ibid. p 498

Aviator
1. United States Statutes at Large, Vol. 39, p. 175
2. Specifications for the uniform of the united states army, GPO, 1917p. 47

Band Corporal
1. United States Statutes at Large, Vol. 39, p. 178-9
2. Emerson, William K., Chevrons, Washington: Smithsonian Institution Press, 1983, p. 171
3. ibid. p 148
4. ibid. p 252

Band Leader
1. United States Statutes at Large, Vol. 39, p. 178-9
2. Emerson, William K., Chevrons, Washington: Smithsonian Institution Press, 1983, p. 146
3. ibid. p 147
4. ibid. p 148
5. United States Statutes at Large, Vol. 41, p. 761

Band Sergant
1. United States Statutes at Large, Vol. 39, p. 178-9
2. Emerson, William K., Chevrons, Washington: Smithsonian Institution Press, 1983, p. 171
3. ibid. p 148
4. ibid. p 252

Battalion Commissary Sergeant
1. United States Statutes at Large, Vol. 12, p. 279
2. United States Statutes at Large, Vol.12, p. 599
3. United States Statutes at Large, Vol. 14, p. 332

Battalion Hospital Steward
1. United States Statutes at Large, Vol. 12, p. 279
2. United States Statutes at Large, Vol. 12, p. 599
3. United States Statutes at Large, Vol. 14, p. 332

Battalion Quartermaster Sergeant
1. United States Statutes at Large, Vol. 12, p. 279
2. United States Statutes at Large, Vol. 12, p. 599
3. United States Statutes at Large, Vol. 14, p. 332
4. United States Statutes at Large, Vol. 34, p. 863
5. United States Statutes at Large, Vol. 39, p. 173
6. Emerson, William K., Chevrons, Washington: Smithsonian Institution Press, 1983, p. 87

Battalion Saddler Sergeant
1. United States Statutes at Large, Vol. 12, p. 279
2. United States Statutes at Large, Vol. 12, p. 599

Battalion Sergeant Major
1. United States Statutes at Large, Vol. 12, p. 279
2. United States Statutes at Large, Vol. 14, p. 332
3. United States Statutes at Large, Vol. 12, p. 599
4. United States Statutes at Large, Vol. 14, p. 335
5. Emerson, William K., Chevrons, Washington: Smithsonian Institution Press, 1983, p. 85
6. United States Statutes at Large, Vol. 30, p. 364
6a. United States Statutes at Large, Vol. 30, p. 978
7. Emerson, William K., Chevrons, Washington: Smithsonian Institution Press, 1983, p. 87
8. United States Statutes at Large, Vol. 34, p. 863
9. Emerson, William K., Chevrons, Washington: Smithsonian Institution Press, 1983, p. 171

Battalion Supply Sergeant
1. United States Statutes at Large, Vol. 39, p. 173
2. Emerson, William K., Chevrons, Washington: Smithsonian Institution Press, 1983, p. 166
3. ibid p171

Battalion Veterinary Sergeant
1. United States Statutes at Large, Vol. 12, p. 279
2. United States Statutes at Large, Vol. 12, p. 599

Battery Quartermaster Sergeant
1. United States Statutes at Large, Vol. 30, p. 363
2. Emerson, William K., Chevrons, Washington: Smithsonian Institution Press, 1983, p. 88
3. United States Statutes at Large, Vol. 39, p. 180

Battery Supply Sergeant
1. United States Statutes at Large, Vol. 39, p. 180
2. Emerson, William K., Chevrons, Washington: Smithsonian Institution Press, 1983, p. 167
3. ibid.
4. ibid.
5. ibid. p-172

Blacksmith
1. United States Statutes at Large, Vol. 1, p. 750
2. United States Statutes at Large, Vol. 2, p. 86
3. FRANCIS B. HEITMAN.,HISTORICAL REGISTER AND DICTIONARY OF THE UNITED STATES ARMY, Vol. 2, Washington: GPO, 1903., p 568
4. United States Statutes at Large, Vol. 2, p. 482
5. United States Statutes at Large, Vol. 2, p. 764
6. United States Statutes at Large, Vol. 3, p. 224

Boatswain
1. United States Statutes at Large, Vol. 3, p. 47
2. United States Statutes at Large, Vol. 3, p. 219
3. http://www.military-historians.org/company/plates/images/US.htm#z, June 2010

Bombardier
1. Journal of the Continental Congress, Vol. 2 p. 223
2. Journal of the Continental Congress, Vol. 16 p. 118
3. Journal of the Continental Congress, Vol. 28 p. 248

4. Steffen, Randy, The Horse Soldier 1776-1943, Vol. 1., Norman: University of Oklahoma Press, 1977, p. 7

Brigadier General
1. http://memory.loc.gov/cgi-bin/query/r?ammem/mgw:@field(DOCID+@lit(gw030237))#N0371-281, June 2010
2. http://memory.loc.gov/cgi-bin/query/r?ammem/mgw:@field(DOCID+@lit(gw190033)), June 2010
3. FRANCIS B. HEITMAN.,HISTORICAL REGISTER AND DICTIONARY OF THE UNITED STATES ARMY, Vol. 1, Washington: GPO, 1903.,
4. Journal of the Continental Congress, Vol. 33 p. 437-438
5. United States Statutes at Large, Vol. 1, p. 221
6. United States Statutes at Large, Vol. 1, p. 246
7. United States Statutes at Large, Vol. 1, p. 604
8. FRANCIS B. HEITMAN.,HISTORICAL REGISTER AND DICTIONARY OF THE UNITED STATES ARMY, Vol. 1, Washington: GPO, 1903.,
9. United States Statutes at Large, Vol. 2, p. 133
10. United States Statutes at Large, Vol. 2, p. 482
11. United States Statutes at Large, Vol. 3, p. 225
12. United States Statutes at Large, Vol. 3, p. 297
13. United States Statutes at Large, Vol. 3, p. 496
14. United States Statutes at Large, Vol. 3, p. 615
15. FRANCIS B. HEITMAN.,HISTORICAL REGISTER AND DICTIONARY OF THE UNITED STATES ARMY, Vol. 1, Washington: GPO, 1903.,
16. Emerson, William K., Encyclopedia of United States Army Insignia and Uniforms, Norman: University of Oklahoma Press, 1996, p. 439
17. ibid. p. 124
18. Lanham Howard G., Straps, Westminster, MD: Johnson Graphics, 1998, p. 7
18a. ibid p. 9
19. ibid. p. 10
20. ibid. p. 12
21. ibid. p. 11
22. ibid. p. 10
23. ibid p. 17
24. FRANCIS B. HEITMAN.,HISTORICAL REGISTER AND DICTIONARY OF THE UNITED STATES ARMY, Vol. 1, Washington: GPO, 1903.,
25. United States Statutes at Large, Vol. 9, p. 17
26. FRANCIS B. HEITMAN.,HISTORICAL REGISTER AND DICTIONARY OF THE UNITED STATES ARMY, Vol. 1, Washington: GPO, 1903.,
27. United States Statutes at Large, Vol. 9, p. 20
28. United States Statutes at Large, Vol. 9, p. 184
29. FRANCIS B. HEITMAN.,HISTORICAL REGISTER AND DICTIONARY OF THE UNITED STATES ARMY, Vol. 1, Washington: GPO, 1903.,
30. United States Statutes at Large, Vol. 9, p. 247
31. Steffen, Randy, The Horse Soldier 1776-1943, Vol. 2., Norman: University of Oklahoma Press, 1977, p. 6
30. United States Statutes at Large, Vol. 10, p. 639
32. FRANCIS B. HEITMAN.,HISTORICAL REGISTER AND DICTIONARY OF THE UNITED STATES ARMY, Vol. 1, Washington: GPO, 1903.,
33. Lanham Howard G., Straps, Westminster, MD: Johnson Graphics, 1998, p. 39
34. United States Statutes at Large, Vol. 14, p. 332
35. Emerson, William K., Encyclopedia of United States Army Insignia and Uniforms, Norman: University of Oklahoma Press, 1996
36. Steffen, Randy, The Horse Soldier 1776-1943, Vol. 3., Norman: University of Oklahoma Press, 1977, p. 69
37. Emerson, William K., Encyclopedia of United States Army Insignia and Uniforms, Norman: University of Oklahoma Press, 1996, p. 486
37a. ibid. p. 74
38. ibid. p. 96
39. Specifications for the Uniform of the United States Army, Washington: gpo, 1913, p.15
40. Emerson, William K., Encyclopedia of United States Army Insignia and Uniforms, Norman: University of Oklahoma Press, 1996, p. 474
41. Specifications for the Uniform of the United States Army, Washington: gpo, 1913, p. 24
42. Emerson, William K., Encyclopedia of United States Army Insignia and Uniforms, Norman: University of Oklahoma Press, 1996, p. 574
43. ibid. p. 561
44. ibid. p. 563
45. ibid.
45a. ibid p. 475
46. ibid.
47. ibid. p. 573
48. United States Statutes at Large, Vol. 63, p. 802
49. Emerson, William K., Encyclopedia of United States Army Insignia and Uniforms, Norman: University of Oklahoma Press, 1996, p. 465

Bugler
1. United States Statutes at Large, Vol. 3, p. 114
2. FRANCIS B. HEITMAN.,HISTORICAL REGISTER AND DICTIONARY OF THE UNITED STATES ARMY, Vol. 2, Washington: GPO, 1903., p. 577
3. United States Statutes at Large, Vol. 3, p. 225
4. United States Statutes at Large, Vol. 4, p. 652
5. Steffen, Randy, The Horse Soldier 1776-1943, Vol. 1., Norman: University of Oklahoma Press, 1977, p. 91
6. United States Statutes at Large, Vol. 5, p. 512
7. United States Statutes at Large, Vol. 5, p. 654
8. United States Statutes at Large, Vol. 9, p. 13
9. Steffen, Randy, The Horse Soldier 1776-1943, Vol. 2., Norman: University of Oklahoma Press, 1977, p. 7
10. ibid. p. 19
11. United States Statutes at Large, Vol. 10, p. 639
12. Steffen, Randy, The Horse Soldier 1776-1943, Vol. 2., Norman: University of Oklahoma Press, 1977, p. 34
13. United States Statutes at Large, Vol. 12, p. 289
14. United States Statutes at Large, Vol. 12, p. 787
15. United States Statutes at Large, Vol. 13, p. 144
16. United States Statutes at Large, Vol. 39, p. 166
17. Emerson, William K., Chevrons, Washington: Smithsonian Institution Press, 1983, p. 147
18. ibid. p. 251

Bugler First Class
1. United States Statutes at Large, Vol. 40, p. 893
2. Emerson, William K., Chevrons, Washington: Smithsonian Institution Press, 1983, p. 147
18. ibid. p. 251

Captain
1. Oliver, Raymond, Why is a Kernal called a Colonel?, Tuscon: Fireship press, 1983, p. 29
2. http://memory.loc.gov/cgi-bin/query/r?ammem/mgw:@field(DOCID+@lit(gw030251)), June 2010
3. http://memory.loc.gov/cgi-bin/query/r?ammem/mgw:@field(DOCID+@lit(gw050405)), June 2010
4. Peterson, Harold L. , The Book of the Continental Soldier, Harrisburg: Stackpole, 1968.
5. http://memory.loc.gov/cgi-bin/query/r?ammem/mgw:@field(DOCID+@lit(gw190033)), June 2010
6. United States Statutes at Large, Vol. 1, p. 241
7. United States Statutes at Large, Vol. 2, p. 132
8. United States Statutes at Large, Vol. 2, p. 481
9. Steffen, Randy, The Horse Soldier 1776-1943, Vol. 1., Norman: University of Oklahoma Press, 1977, p. 44
10. ibid. p. 80
11. United States Statutes at Large, Vol.3, p. 224
12. Emerson, William K., Chevrons, Washington: Smithsonian Institution Press, 1983, p. 40
13. FRANCIS B. HEITMAN.,HISTORICAL REGISTER AND DICTIONARY OF THE UNITED STATES ARMY, Vol. 2, Washington: GPO, 1903., p. 580
14. Emerson, William K., Chevrons, Washington: Smithsonian Institution Press, 1983, p. 42
15. Emerson, William K., Encyclopedia of United States Army Insignia and Uniforms, Norman: University of Oklahoma Press, 1996, p. 439
16. ibid. p. 124
17. Lanham Howard G., Straps, Westminster, MD: Johnson Graphics, 1998, p. 7
18. Steffen, Randy, The Horse Soldier 1776-1943, Vol. 1., Norman: University of Oklahoma Press, 1977, p. 94
19. Lanham Howard G., Straps, Westminster, MD: Johnson Graphics, 1998, p. 13
20. Steffen, Randy, The Horse Soldier 1776-1943, Vol. 2., Norman: University of Oklahoma Press, 1977, p. 10-11
21. ibid. p. 111
22. Steffen, Randy, The Horse Soldier 1776-1943, Vol. 3., Norman: University of Oklahoma Press, 1977, p. 96
23. Emerson, William K., Encyclopedia of United States Army Insignia and Uniforms, Norman: University of Oklahoma Press, 1996, p. 486
24. Emerson, William K., Encyclopedia of United States Army Insignia and Uniforms, Norman: University of Oklahoma Press, 1996, p. 490
25. Specifications for the uniform of the Army, Washington:GPO, 1913 p. 24
26. Steffen, Randy, The Horse Soldier 1776-1943, Vol. 4., Norman: University of Oklahoma Press, 1977, p. 92
27. Lanham Howard G., Straps, Westminster, MD: Johnson Graphics, 1998, p. 113
28. Steffen, Randy, The Horse Soldier 1776-1943, Vol. 4., Norman: University of Oklahoma Press, 1977, p. 98
29. United States Statutes at Large, Vol. 63, p. 802
30. Emerson, William K., Encyclopedia of United States Army Insignia and Uniforms, Norman: University of Oklahoma Press, 1996, p. 465
31. AR-670-1, February 2005, p 191

Captain Lieutenant
1. Journal of the Continental Congress, vol11, p. 539
2. Peterson, Harold L. , The Book of the Continental Soldier, Harrisburg: Stackpole, 1968. p. 241

Chaplain
1. Journal of the Continental Congress, Vol 27. , p. 531
2. United States Statutes at Large, Vol. 1, p. 222
3. FRANCIS B. HEITMAN.,HISTORICAL REGISTER AND DICTIONARY OF THE UNITED STATES ARMY, Vol. 1, Washington: GPO, 1903
4. United States Statutes at Large, Vol. 1, p. 604
5. Senate Executive Journal -April 24, 1800.
6. United States Statutes at Large, Vol. 2, p. 481
7. FRANCIS B. HEITMAN.,HISTORICAL REGISTER AND DICTIONARY OF THE UNITED STATES ARMY, Vol. 2, Washington: GPO, 1903. p. 570
8. United States Statutes at Large, Vol. 2, p. 674
9.. FRANCIS B. HEITMAN.,HISTORICAL REGISTER AND DICTIONARY OF THE UNITED STATES ARMY, Vol. 2, Washington: GPO, 1903. p. 572
10. United States Statutes at Large, Vol. 2, p. 796
11.. FRANCIS B. HEITMAN.,HISTORICAL REGISTER AND DICTIONARY OF THE UNITED STATES ARMY, Vol. 2, Washington: GPO, 1903. p. 574
12. United States Statutes at Large, Vol. 3, p. 297
13. United States Statutes at Large, Vol. 3, p. 426
14. FRANCIS B. HEITMAN.,HISTORICAL REGISTER AND DICTIONARY OF THE UNITED STATES ARMY, Vol. 1, Washington: GPO, 1903
15. United States Statutes at Large, Vol. 4, p. 259
16. United States Statutes at Large, Vol. 4, p. 308
17. United States Statutes at Large, Vol. 9, p. 124
18. FRANCIS B. HEITMAN.,HISTORICAL REGISTER AND DICTIONARY OF THE UNITED STATES ARMY, Vol. 1, Washington: GPO, 1903 p. 654
19. United States Statutes at Large, Vol. 9, p. 350
20. United States Statutes at Large, Vol. 12, p. 270
21. United States Statutes at Large, Vol. 12, p. 404
22. Emerson, William K., Encyclopedia of United States Army Insignia and Uniforms, Norman: University of Oklahoma Press, 1996, p. 265
23. ibid.
24. Lanham Howard G., Straps, Westminster, MD: Johnson Graphics, 1998, p. 77
25. United States Statutes at Large, Vol. 14, p. 837
26. Lanham Howard G., Straps, Westminster, MD: Johnson Graphics, 1998, p. 89
27. Emerson, William K., Encyclopedia of United States Army Insignia and Uniforms, Norman: University of Oklahoma Press, 1996, p. 266
28. Steffen, Randy, The Horse Soldier 1776-1943, Vol. 2., Norman: University of Oklahoma Press, 1977, p. 140
29. http://www.grandarmyofthefrontier.org/uniforms/usa1898.htm, July 2010
30. Emerson, William K., Encyclopedia of United States Army Insignia and Uniforms, Norman: University of Oklahoma Press, 1996, p. 267
31. United States Statutes at Large, Vol. 33, p. 226
32. Emerson, William K., Encyclopedia of United States Army Insignia and Uniforms, Norman: University of Oklahoma Press, 1996, p. 267
33. ibid. p 269
34. ibid. p 268
35. United States Statutes at Large, Vol. 41, p. 769
36. Emerson, William K., Encyclopedia of United States Army Insignia and Uniforms, Norman: University of Oklahoma Press, 1996, p. 269
37. ar-670-1 interem change 106, July 1980
38. Emerson, William K., Encyclopedia of United States Army Insignia and Uniforms, Norman: University of Oklahoma Press, 1996, p. 269

39. ALARACT MSG DTG 2022002, April 2005

Chauffeur
1. United States Statutes at Large, Vol. 40, p. 244
2. Emerson, William K., Chevrons, Washington: Smithsonian Institution Press, 1983, p. 175
3. Official Army Register, January 1, 1920 p. 1107
4. Emerson, William K., Chevrons, Washington: Smithsonian Institution Press, 1983, p. 253

Chauffeur First Class
1. United States Statutes at Large, Vol. 40, p. 244
2. Emerson, William K., Chevrons, Washington: Smithsonian Institution Press, 1983, p. 175
3. Official Army Register, January 1, 1920 p. 1107
4. Emerson, William K., Chevrons, Washington: Smithsonian Institution Press, 1983, p. 253

Chief Bugler
1. United States Statutes at Large, Vol. 4, p. 652
2. United States Statutes at Large, Vol. 12, p. 599
3. Steffen, Randy, The Horse Soldier 1776-1943, Vol. 1., Norman: University of Oklahoma Press, 1977, p. 91
4. Steffen, Randy, The Horse Soldier 1776-1943, Vol. 2., Norman: University of Oklahoma Press, 1977, p. 7
5. ibid. p. 19

Chief Hospital Physician
1. Journal of the Continental Congrees, Vol. 18, p. 878
2. Heitman, F.B., Historical Register Officers of the Continental Army during the War of Revolution, Washington: 1893, p. 138
3. Journal of the Continental Congrees, Vol. 22, p. 5

Chief Mechanic
1. United States Statutes at Large, Vol. 34, p. 862
2. Emerson, William K., Chevrons, Washington: Smithsonian Institution Press, 1983, p. 252
3. ibid. p- 173-174

Chief Medical Purveyor
1. United States Statutes at Large, Vol. 14, p. 334.
2. FRANCIS B. HEITMAN.,HISTORICAL REGISTER AND DICTIONARY OF THE UNITED STATES ARMY, Vol. 1, Washington: GPO, 1903
3. Emerson, William K., Encyclopedia of United States Army Insignia and Uniforms, Norman: University of Oklahoma Press, 1996, p. 179
4. United States Statutes at Large, Vol. 18, p. 244.
5. FRANCIS B. HEITMAN.,HISTORICAL REGISTER AND DICTIONARY OF THE UNITED STATES ARMY, Vol. 1, Washington: GPO, 1903
6. United States Statutes at Large, Vol. 27, p. 276.

Chief Musician
1. United States Statutes at Large, Vol. 1, p. 759.
2. United States Statutes at Large, Vol. 4, p. 652.
3. WILLIAM A. GORDON.,A COMPILATION OF REGISTERS OF THE ARMY OF THE UNTIED STATES, Washington: James C. Dunn, 1837. p. 539
4. ibid. p. 597.
5. United States Statutes at Large, Vol. 15, p. 318.
6. Emerson, William K., Chevrons, Washington: Smithsonian Institution Press, 1983, p. 89
7. United States Statutes at Large, Vol. 39, p. 178-9

Chief Physician
Heitman, F.B., Historical Register Officers of the Continental Army during the War of Revolution, Washington: 1893,

Chief Physician and Hospital Surgeon
1. Heitman, F.B., Historical Register Officers of the Continental Army during the War of Revolution, Washington: 1893,

Chief Physician and Surgeon of the Army
1. Heitman, F.B., Historical Register Officers of the Continental Army during the War of Revolution, Washington: 1893,

Chief Trumpeter
1. United States Statutes at Large, Vol. 12, p. 599
2. Emerson, William K., Encyclopedia of United States Army Insignia and Uniforms, Norman: University of Oklahoma Press, 1996, p. 14
3. Emerson, William K., Chevrons, Washington: Smithsonian Institution Press, 1983, p. 89
4. United States Statutes at Large, Vol. 39, p. 178-9

Chief Warrant Officer
1. United States Statutes at Large, Vol. 55, p. 651
2. AR-600-35, Change 1, September 4, 1942, page 6
3. Lanham Howard G., Straps, Westminster, MD: Johnson Graphics, 1998, p. 119
4. Emerson, William K., Encyclopedia of United States Army Insignia and Uniforms, Norman: University of Oklahoma Press, 1996, p. 574
5. United States Statutes at Large, Vol. 63, p. 802
6. http://penfed.org/usawoa/woheritage/Hist_of_Army_WO.htm, July 2010
7. Emerson, William K., Encyclopedia of United States Army Insignia and Uniforms, Norman: University of Oklahoma Press, 1996, p. 391
8. United States Statutes at Large, Vol. 68, p. 157

Chief Warrant Officer 2
1. United States Statutes at Large, Vol. 68, p. 157
2. Foster, Frank c., The Decorations, Medals, Ribbions, Badges and Insignia of the United States Army World War II to Present, Fountain Inn: MOA press, 2001, p. 19
3. Emerson, William K., Encyclopedia of United States Army Insignia and Uniforms, Norman: University of Oklahoma Press, 1996, p. 465
4. http://forum.uniforminsignia.org/viewtopic.php?t=6150&sid=24a746a5563b9933501504205b082425, July 2010
5. AR-670-1, February 2005, p 193

Chief Warrant Officer 3
1. United States Statutes at Large, Vol. 68, p. 157
2. Foster, Frank c., The Decorations, Medals, Ribbions, Badges and Insignia of the United States Army World War II to Present, Fountain Inn: MOA press, 2001, p. 19
3. Emerson, William K., Encyclopedia of United States Army Insignia and Uniforms, Norman: University of Oklahoma Press, 1996, p. 465
4. http://forum.uniforminsignia.org/viewtopic.php?t=6150&sid=24a746a5563b9933501504205b082425, July 2010
5. AR-670-1, February 2005, p 193

Chief Warrant Officer 4
1. United States Statutes at Large, Vol. 68, p. 157
2. Foster, Frank c., The Decorations, Medals, Ribbions, Badges and Insignia of the United States Army World War II to Present, Fountain Inn: MOA press, 2001, p. 19
3. Emerson, William K., Encyclopedia of United States Army Insignia and Uniforms, Norman: University of Oklahoma Press, 1996, p. 465
4. http://forum.uniforminsignia.org/viewtopic.php?t=6150&sid=24a746a5563b9933501504205b082425, July 2010
5. AR-670-1, February 2005, p 193

Chief Warrant Officer 5
1. Foster, Frank c., The Decorations, Medals, Ribbions, Badges and Insignia of the United States Army World War II to Present, Fountain Inn: MOA press, 2001, p. 19
2. United States Statutes at Large, Vol. 105, p. 1491
3. Foster, Frank c., The Decorations, Medals, Ribbions, Badges and Insignia of the United States Army World War II to Present, Fountain Inn: MOA press, 2001, p. 19
5. AR-670-1, July 2002, p 195
6. ALARACT 042/2004, March 2004
7. AR-670-1, February 2005, p 192
8. Emerson, William K., Encyclopedia of United States Army Insignia and Uniforms, Norman: University of Oklahoma Press, 1996, p. 390
9. Steffen, Randy, The Horse Soldier 1776-1943, Vol. 4., Norman: University of Oklahoma Press, 1977, p. 77

Clothier General
1. Thian, Raphael, Legislative History of the General Staff of the Army of the United States, Washington: GPO, 1901, p. 238

Colonel
1. Oliver, Raymond, Why is a Kernal called a Colonel?, Tuscon: Fireship press, 1983, p. 39
2. Peterson, Harold L. , The Book of the Continental Soldier, Harrisburg: Stackpole, 1968. p 242
3. United States Statutes at Large, Vol. 2, p. 132

4a. Steffen, Randy, The Horse Soldier 1776-1943, Vol. 1., Norman: University of Oklahoma Press, 1977, p. 44
5. Emerson, William K., Chevrons, Washington: Smithsonian Institution Press, 1983, p. 40
6. Emerson, William K., Encyclopedia of United States Army Insignia and Uniforms, Norman: University of Oklahoma Press, 1996, p. 124
7. Lanham Howard G., Straps, Westminster, MD: Johnson Graphics, 1998, p. 7
8. Steffen, Randy, The Horse Soldier 1776-1943, Vol. 1., Norman: University of Oklahoma Press, 1977, p. 94
9. http://www.history.army.mil/reference/1839U.htm, July 2010
10. Steffen, Randy, The Horse Soldier 1776-1943, Vol. 2., Norman: University of Oklahoma Press, 1977, p. 6
11. ibid. p. 111
12. Emerson, William K., Encyclopedia of United States Army Insignia and Uniforms, Norman: University of Oklahoma Press, 1996, p. 165
13. ibid. p. 271
14. ibid. p. 250
15. ibid. p. 254
16. ibid. p. 263
17. ibid. p. 274
18. ibid. p. 239
19. ibid. p. 245
20. ibid. p. 498
21. Steffen, Randy, The Horse Soldier 1776-1943, Vol. 3., Norman: University of Oklahoma Press, 1977, p. 76
22. ibid. p. 97
23. ibid. p 100
24. http://www.tioh.hqda.pentagon.mil/UniformedServices/Insignia_Rank/insignia_colonel.aspx, July 2010
25. United States Statutes at Large, Vol. 63, p. 802
26. AR-670-1, February 2005, p 190

Color Sergeant
1. http://www.spiritus-temporis.com/colour-sergeant/, July 2010
2. Emerson, William K., Chevrons, Washington: Smithsonian Institution Press, 1983, p. 97
3. U.S. Army Uniforms and Equipment, 1889, forward by Jerome Greene: bison, 1986, p. 335
4. United States Statutes at Large, Vol. 31, p. 748
5. Emerson, William K., Chevrons, Washington: Smithsonian Institution Press, 1983, p. 97
6. ibid. p. 251

Command Sergeant Major

1. Fisher, Ernest, Guardians of the Republic, New York: Ballentine, 1994, p. 316
2. Emerson, William K., Chevrons, Washington: Smithsonian Institution Press, 1983, p. 202
3. Emerson, William K., Encyclopedia of United States Army Insignia and Uniforms, Norman: University of Oklahoma Press, 1996, p. 401
4. AR-670-1, February 2005, p 195

Commissary General of Issues
1. Journal of the Continental Congress, volume 8, p. 434
2. Heitman, F.B., Historical Register Officers of the Continental Army during the War of Revolution, Washington: 1893, p. 333
3. Journal of the Continental Congress, volume 20, p. 734

Commissary General of Purchases
1. Journal of the Continental Congress, volume 8, p. 434
2. Heitman, F.B., Historical Register Officers of the Continental Army during the War of Revolution, Washington: 1893,
3. Journal of the Continental Congress, volume 20, p. 734
4. United States Statutes at Large, Vol. 2, p. 697
5. United States Statutes at Large, Vol. 2, p. 816
6. FRANCIS B. HEITMAN.,HISTORICAL REGISTER AND DICTIONARY OF THE UNITED STATES ARMY, Vol. 1, Washington: GPO, 1903
7. United States Statutes at Large, Vol. 5, p. 513
8. United States Statutes at Large, Vol. 3, p. 616
9. United States Statutes at Large, Vol. 5, p. 513
10. Emerson, William K., Encyclopedia of United States Army Insignia and Uniforms, Norman: University of Oklahoma Press, 1996, p. 306-07

Commissary of Hides
1. Journal of the Continental Congress, volume 8, p. 487
2. Journal of the Continental Congress, volume 8, p. 489
3. Journal of the Continental Congress, volume 8, p. 607
4. Journal of the Continental Congress, volume 13, p. 478
5. Journal of the Continental Congress, volume 20, p. 695

Commissary of Military Stores
1. Heitman, F.B., Historical Register Officers of the Continental Army during the War of Revolution, Washington: 1893,

Commissary Sergeant
1. United States Statutes at Large, Vol. 17, p. 485
2. Emerson, William K., Chevrons, Washington: Smithsonian Institution Press, 1983, p. 98
3. United States Statutes at Large, Vol. 30, p. 977
4. Emerson, William K., Chevrons, Washington: Smithsonian Institution Press, 1983, p. 98

Commissary Sergeant (Regimental)
1. United States Statutes at Large, Vol. 12, p. 269
2. United States Statutes at Large, Vol. 12, p. 280
3. United States Statutes at Large, Vol. 14, p. 332
4. Emerson, William K., Chevrons, Washington: Smithsonian Institution Press, 1983, p. 50.
5. United States Statutes at Large, Vol. 16, p. 318
6. United States Statutes at Large, Vol. 30, p. 977
7. Emerson, William K., Chevrons, Washington: Smithsonian Institution Press, 1983, p. 87 and 165.
8. United States Statutes at Large, Vol. 39, p. 166

Company Commissary Sergeant
1. United States Statutes at Large, Vol. 12, p. 599
2. United States Statutes at Large, Vol. 14, p. 332

Company Quartermaster Sergeant
1. United States Statutes at Large, Vol. 12, p. 280
2. Katcher, Philip, The Civil War Source Book, New York: Facts on File, 1992, p. 145
3. Emerson, William K., Chevrons, Washington: Smithsonian Institution Press, 1983, p. 50
4. United States Statutes at Large, Vol. 13, p. 333
5. Emerson, William K., Chevrons, Washington: Smithsonian Institution Press, 1983, p. 88
6. United States Statutes at Large, Vol. 30, p. 366
7. Emerson, William K., Chevrons, Washington: Smithsonian Institution Press, 1983, p. 88
8. United States Statutes at Large, Vol. 31, p. 750
9. United States Statutes at Large, Vol. 39, p. 180

Company Supply Sergeant
1. United States Statutes at Large, Vol. 39, p. 180
2. Emerson, William K., Chevrons, Washington: Smithsonian Institution Press, 1983, p. 167
3. ibid.
4. ibid.
5. ibid. p-172

Cook
1. United States Statutes at Large, Vol. 30, p. 721
2. Emerson, William K., Chevrons, Washington: Smithsonian Institution Press, 1983, p. 103
3. United States Statutes at Large, Vol. 31, p. 750
4. United States Statutes at Large, Vol. 35, p. 109
5. United States Statutes at Large, Vol. 37, p. 593
6. United States Statutes at Large, Vol. 40, p. 882
7. Emerson, William K., Chevrons, Washington: Smithsonian Institution Press, 1983, p. 252

Cornet
1. http://www.xenograg.com/101/excerpts/origins-of-european-army-ranks, July 2010
2. Peterson, Harold L. , The Book of the Continental Soldier, Harrisburg: Stackpole, 1968, p. 242
3. United States Statutes at Large, Vol. 1, p. 241
4. FRANCIS B. HEITMAN.,HISTORICAL REGISTER AND DICTIONARY OF THE UNITED STATES ARMY, Vol. 1, Washington: GPO, 1903
5. United States Statutes at Large, Vol. 1, p. 750
6. FRANCIS B. HEITMAN.,HISTORICAL REGISTER AND DICTIONARY OF THE UNITED STATES ARMY, Vol. 1, Washington: GPO, 1903
7. United States Statutes at Large, Vol. 2, p. 85
6. FRANCIS B. HEITMAN.,HISTORICAL REGISTER AND DICTIONARY OF THE UNITED STATES ARMY, Vol. 2, Washington: GPO, 1903, p. 568
8. Senate Exectuive Journal, vol 1, p. 342
9. FRANCIS B. HEITMAN.,HISTORICAL REGISTER AND DICTIONARY OF THE UNITED STATES ARMY, Vol. 1, Washington: GPO, 1903
10. United States Statutes at Large, Vol. 2, p. 132
11. United States Statutes at Large, Vol. 2, p. 482
12. Steffen, Randy, The Horse Soldier 1776-1943, Vol. 1., Norman: University of Oklahoma Press, 1977, p. 46
13. United States Statutes at Large, Vol. 3, p. 224

Corporal
1. Oliver, Raymond, Why is a Kernal called a Colonel?, Tuscon: Fireship press, 1983, p. 7
2. Peterson, Harold L. , The Book of the Continental Soldier, Harrisburg: Stackpole, 1968, p. 242
3. Emerson, William K., Chevrons, Washington: Smithsonian Institution Press, 1983, p. 41
4. ibid. p. 42
5. Emerson, William K., Encyclopedia of United States Army Insignia and Uniforms, Norman: University of Oklahoma Press, 1996, p. 438
6. United States Statutes at Large, Vol. 4, p. 652
7. Steffen, Randy, The Horse Soldier 1776-1943, Vol. 1., Norman: University of Oklahoma Press, 1977, p. 91
8. Emerson, William K., Chevrons, Washington: Smithsonian Institution Press, 1983, p. 42
9. ibid. p. 252
10. United States Statutes at Large, Vol. 63, p. 802
11. AR-670-1, February 2005, p 198

Corporal Bugler
1. United States Statutes at Large, Vol. 40, p. 893
2. Emerson, William K., Chevrons, Washington: Smithsonian Institution Press, 1983, p. 252
3. ibid. p. 147

Deck hand, Mine Planter Service
1. United States Statutes at Large, Vol. 40, p. 882
2. Emerson, William K., Chevrons, Washington: Smithsonian Institution Press, 1983, p. 228
3. ibid. p. 253

Deputy Commissary General of Issues
1. Journal of the Continental Congress, volume 8, p. 434
2. Journal of the Continental Congress, volume 20, p. 734
3. Heitman, F.B., Historical Register Officers of the Continental Army during the War of Revolution, Washington: 1893,

Deputy Commissary General of Military Stores
1. Heitman, F.B., Historical Register Officers of the Continental Army during the War of Revolution, Washington: 1893,

Deputy Commissary (of Purchases)
1. United States Statutes at Large, Vol. 2, p. 697
2. FRANCIS B. HEITMAN.,HISTORICAL REGISTER AND DICTIONARY OF THE UNITED STATES ARMY, Vol. 1, Washington: GPO, 1903
3. United States Statutes at Large, Vol. 3, p. 298
4. United States Statutes at Large, Vol. 3, p. 615
5. Emerson, William K., Encyclopedia of United States Army Insignia and Uniforms, Norman: University of Oklahoma Press, 1996, p. 306

Deputy Commissary General of Purchases
1. Journal of the Continental Congress, volume 8, p. 434
2. Journal of the Continental Congress, volume 20, p. 734
3. Heitman, F.B., Historical Register Officers of the Continental Army during the War of Revolution, Washington: 1893,

Deputy Director General of Hospitals
1. Journal of the Continental Congress, volume 7, p. 232
2. Heitman, F.B., Historical Register Officers of the Continental Army during the War of Revolution, Washington: 1893,
3. Journal of the Continental Congress, volume 18, p. 878

Deputy Paymaster General
1. Heitman, F.B., Historical Register Officers of the Continental Army during the War of Revolution, Washington: 1893,
2. United States Statutes at Large, Vol. 2, p.784
3. FRANCIS B. HEITMAN.,HISTORICAL REGISTER AND DICTIONARY OF THE UNITED STATES ARMY, Vol. 1, Washington: GPO, 1903. p. 626
4. Thian, Raphael, Legislative History of the General Staff of the Army of the United States, Washington: GPO, 1901, p. 463
5. WILLIAM A. GORDON.,A COMPILATION OF REGISTERS OF THE ARMY OF THE UNTIED STATES, Washington: James C. Dunn, 1837. p. 55
6. United States Statutes at Large, Vol. 3, p. 297

Deputy Surgeon General
1. United States Statutes at Large, Vol. 27, p. 276
2. Emerson, William K., Encyclopedia of United States Army Insignia and Uniforms, Norman: University of Oklahoma Press, 1996, p. 179
7. Steffen, Randy, The Horse Soldier 1776-1943, Vol. 3., Norman: University of Oklahoma Press, 1977, p. 107
1. United States Statutes at Large, Vol. 35, p. 67

Director General (and Chief Physician)
1. Journal of the Continental Congress, volume 2, p. 209
2. Heitman, F.B., Historical Register Officers of the Continental Army during the War of Revolution, Washington: 1893,
3. http://history.amedd.army.mil/booksdocs/rev/gillett1/ch2.html, July 2010
4. http://en.wikipedia.org/wiki/Benjamin_Church, July 2010
5. Heitman, F.B., Historical Register Officers of the Continental Army during the War of Revolution, Washington: 1893,
6. http://history.amedd.army.mil/booksdocs/rev/gillett1/ch2.html, July 2010
7. ibid.
8. Journal of the Continental Congress, volume 7, p. 231
9. Heitman, F.B., Historical Register Officers of the Continental Army during the War of Revolution, Washington: 1893,
10. ibid.

District Paymaster
1. United States Statutes at Large, Vol. 2, p. 735
2. Powell, William H., List of Officers of the Army of the United States form 1779 to 1900, New York: L.R. Hamersly & CO, 1900, p. 73
3. United States Statutes at Large, Vol. 3, p. 113
4. FRANCIS B. HEITMAN.,HISTORICAL REGISTER AND DICTIONARY OF THE UNITED STATES ARMY, Vol. 1, Washington: GPO, 1903. p. 436
5. ibid. p. 305
6. ibid. p. 155
7. ibid. p. 1034
8. ibid. p. 789
9. ibid. p. 1030
10. ibid. p. 601
11. ibid. p. 781
12. ibid. p. 880
13. United States Statutes at Large, Vol. 3, p. 225
14. FRANCIS B. HEITMAN.,HISTORICAL REGISTER AND DICTIONARY OF THE UNITED STATES ARMY, Vol. 1, Washington: GPO, 1903.
15. United States Statutes at Large, Vol. 3, p. 297

Dragoon
1. United States Statutes at Large, Vol. 1, p. 241
2. United States Statutes at Large, Vol. 1, p. 483
3. http://en.wikipedia.org/wiki/Private_(rank), July 2010

Driver
1. United States Statutes at Large, Vol. 2, p. 735
2. United States Statutes at Large, Vol. 3, p. 113

Drum Major
1. Journal of the Continental Congress, volume 5, p. 563
2. United States Statutes at Large, Vol. 1, p. 280
3. United States Statutes at Large, Vol. 14, p. 332
4. United States Statutes at Large, Vol. 30, p. 977
5. Emerson, William K., Chevrons, Washington: Smithsonian Institution Press, 1983, p. 98
6. United States Statutes at Large, Vol. 31, p. 750
7. United States Statutes at Large, Vol. 39, p. 166
8. Emerson, William K., Chevrons, Washington: Smithsonian Institution Press, 1983, p. 149

Electrician Sergeant
1. Emerson, William K., Chevrons, Washington: Smithsonian Institution Press, 1983, p. 105
2. United States Statutes at Large, Vol. 30, p. 978

3. Emerson, William K., Chevrons, Washington: Smithsonian Institution Press, 1983, p. 106
4. United States Statutes at Large, Vol. 34, p. 862

Electrician Sergeant First Class
1. United States Statutes at Large, Vol. 34, p. 862
2. Emerson, William K., Chevrons, Washington: Smithsonian Institution Press, 1983, p. 167
3. ibid. p. 160
4. ibid. p. 161
5. ibid. p. 251

Electrician Sergeant Second Class
1. United States Statutes at Large, Vol. 34, p. 862
2. Emerson, William K., Chevrons, Washington: Smithsonian Institution Press, 1983, p. 160
3. ibid.
4. ibid. p. 167.
5. ibid. p. 251

Engineer
1. United States Statutes at Large, Vol. 34, p. 862
2. Emerson, William K., Chevrons, Washington: Smithsonian Institution Press, 1983, p. 162
3. ibid.
4. ibid. p. 251

Enlisted Men of (for) Ordnance
1. United States Statutes at Large, Vol. 2, p. 732
2. United States Statutes at Large, Vol. 3, p. 115
3. United States Statutes at Large, Vol. 3, p. 204
4. United States Statutes at Large, Vol. 3, p. 615
5. WILLIAM A. GORDON.,A COMPILATION OF REGISTERS OF THE ARMY OF THE UNTIED STATES, Washington: James C. Dunn, 1837. p. 208
6. Emerson, William K., Encyclopedia of United States Army Insignia and Uniforms, Norman: University of Oklahoma Press, 1996, p. 244
7. United States Statutes at Large, Vol. 4, p. 504
8. http://www.history.army.mil/reference/1839U.htm, August 2010
9. Steffen, Randy, The Horse Soldier 1776-1943, Vol. 2., Norman: University of Oklahoma Press, 1977, p. 9
10. United States Statutes at Large, Vol. 12, p. 508
11. http://www.tioh.hqda.pentagon.mil/UniformedServices/Insignia_Rank/enlisted_history.aspx, August 2010

Ensign
1. http://www.xenograg.com/101/excerpts/origins-of-european-army-ranks, July 2010
2. Peterson, Harold L. , The Book of the Continental Soldier, Harrisburg: Stackpole, 1968, p. 242
3. Journal of the Continental Congress, Vol. 27, p. 531
4. United States Statutes at Large, Vol. 1, p. 750
5. United States Statutes at Large, Vol. 2, p. 132
6. United States Statutes at Large, Vol. 3, p. 224
7. Kochan, James and Rickman, David, The United States Army 1781-1811, Oxford: Osprey, 2001, plate c1
8. ibid. plate f2

Farrier
1. Peterson, Harold L. , The Book of the Continental Soldier, Harrisburg: Stackpole, 1968, p. 244
2. United States Statutes at Large, Vol. 1, p. 241
3. United States Statutes at Large, Vol. 2, p. 133
4. United States Statutes at Large, Vol. 2, p. 481
5. United States Statutes at Large, Vol. 3, p. 224
6. United States Statutes at Large, Vol. 36, p. 245
7. Emerson, William K., Chevrons, Washington: Smithsonian Institution Press, 1983, p. 171
8. United States Statutes at Large, Vol. 39, p. 172
9. Emerson, William K., Chevrons, Washington: Smithsonian Institution Press, 1983, p. 171
10. Official Army Register, January 1, 1920, p 1108
11. Emerson, William K., Chevrons, Washington: Smithsonian Institution Press, 1983, p. 252

Farrier and Blacksmith
1. United States Statutes at Large, Vol. 7, p. 652
2. United States Statutes at Large, Vol. 36, p. 245
3. Emerson, William K., Chevrons, Washington: Smithsonian Institution Press, 1983, p. 105
4. ibid. p. 171

Field Clerk
1. United States Statutes at Large, Vol. 39, p. 625
2. United States Statutes at Large, Vol. 5, p. 257
3. United States Statutes at Large, Vol. 37, p. 592
3a. United States Statutes at Large, Vol. 39, p. 170.
4. United States Statutes at Large, Vol. 24, p. 167
5. United States Statutes at Large, Vol. 28, p. 236
6. Emerson, William K., Encyclopedia of United States Army Insignia and Uniforms, Norman: University of Oklahoma Press, 1996, p. 387
7. ibid.
8. ibid
9. United States Statutes at Large, Vol. 41, p. 761
10. Emerson, William K., Encyclopedia of United States Army Insignia and Uniforms, Norman: University of Oklahoma Press, 1996, p. 387
11. United States Statutes at Large, Vol. 44, p. 328

Fife Major
1. Journal of the Continental Congress, volume 5, p. 563

Fireman
1. United States Statutes at Large, Vol. 34, p. 862
2. Emerson, William K., Chevrons, Washington: Smithsonian Institution Press, 1983, p. 162
3. ibid. p. 163
4. United States Statutes at Large, Vol. 40, p. 882
5. Emerson, William K., Chevrons, Washington: Smithsonian Institution Press, 1983, p. 228
6. ibid. p. 252

First Lieutenant
1. Oliver, Raymond, Why is a Kernal called a Colonel?, Tuscon: Fireship press, 1983, p. 25
2. http://www.xenograg.com/101/excerpts/origins-of-european-army-ranks, August 2010
3. Journal of the Continental Congress, volume 27, p. 531
4. United States Statutes at Large, Vol. 1, p. 759
5. Peterson, Harold L. , The Book of the Continental Soldier, Harrisburg: Stackpole, 1968, p. 242
6. Steffen, Randy, The Horse Soldier 1776-1943, Vol. 1., Norman: University of Oklahoma Press, 1977, p. 46
7. Emerson, William K., Chevrons, Washington: Smithsonian Institution Press, 1983, p. 40
8. ibid. p. 41
9. ibid. p. 42
10. Steffen, Randy, The Horse Soldier 1776-1943, Vol. 1., Norman: University of Oklahoma Press, 1977, p. 94
11. Lanham Howard G., Straps, Westminster, MD: Johnson Graphics, 1998, p. 13
12. Steffen, Randy, The Horse Soldier 1776-1943, Vol. 2., Norman: University of Oklahoma Press, 1977, p. 10-11
13. ibid. p. 111
14. Steffen, Randy, The Horse Soldier 1776-1943, Vol. 3., Norman: University of Oklahoma Press, 1977, p. 96
15. Emerson, William K., Encyclopedia of United States Army Insignia and Uniforms, Norman: University of Oklahoma Press, 1996, p. 486
16. Steffen, Randy, The Horse Soldier 1776-1943, Vol. 4., Norman: University of Oklahoma Press, 1977, p. 92
17. ibid. p. 98
18. United States Statutes at Large, Vol. 63, p. 802
19. Emerson, William K., Encyclopedia of United States Army Insignia and Uniforms, Norman: University of Oklahoma Press, 1996, p. 465
20. AR-670-1, February 2005, p 192

First Sergeant
1. Fisher, Ernest, Guardians of the Republic, New York: Ballentine, 1994, p. 35
2. ibid. p. 32
3. Urwin, Gregory, The United States Infantry an Illustrated History, London: Blanford, 1988, p. 55
4. Steffen, Randy, The Horse Soldier 1776-1943, Vol. 1., Norman: University of Oklahoma Press, 1977, p. 91
5. United States Statutes at Large, Vol. 5, p. 258
6. FRANCIS B. HEITMAN.,HISTORICAL REGISTER AND DICTIONARY OF THE UNITED STATES ARMY, Vol. 2, Washington: GPO, 1903. p. 588
7. Emerson, William K., Chevrons, Washington: Smithsonian Institution Press, 1983, p. 43
8. United States Statutes at Large, Vol. 12, p. 269 est
9. Emerson, William K., Chevrons, Washington: Smithsonian Institution Press, 1983, Color Plate I
10. ibid. p. 100
11. Official Army Register, January 1872, p. 214b
12. United States Statutes at Large, Vol. 30, p. 364
13. Emerson, William K., Chevrons, Washington: Smithsonian Institution Press, 1983, P. 251
14. ibid p. 193
15. Foster, Frank c., The Decorations, Medals, Ribbions, Badges and Insignia of the United States Army World War II to Present, Fountain Inn: MOA press, 2001, p. 21
16. United States Statutes at Large, Vol. 63, p. 802
17. United States Statutes at Large, Vol. 72, p. 122
18. AR-670-1, February 2005, p 196

Flight Officer
1. United States Statutes at Large, Vol. 56, p. 649
2. AR-600-35, change 2, page 2
3. United States Statutes at Large, Vol. 61, p. 504

Garrison Surgeon
1. United States Statutes at Large, Vol. 2, p. 133
2. FRANCIS B. HEITMAN.,HISTORICAL REGISTER AND DICTIONARY OF THE UNITED STATES ARMY, Vol. 1, Washington: GPO, 1903. p. 283 and 357
3. Powell, William H., List of Officers of the Army of the United States form 1779 to 1900, New York: L.R. Hamersly & CO, 1900, p. 41
4. FRANCIS B. HEITMAN.,HISTORICAL REGISTER AND DICTIONARY OF THE UNITED STATES ARMY, Vol. 1, Washington: GPO, 1903. p. 622 and 911
5. Powell, William H., List of Officers of the Army of the United States form 1779 to 1900, New York: L.R. Hamersly & CO, 1900, p. 52
6. ibid. p. 71
7. ibid p. 107
8. FRANCIS B. HEITMAN.,HISTORICAL REGISTER AND DICTIONARY OF THE UNITED STATES ARMY, Vol. 1, Washington: GPO, 1903. p. 941
9. United States Statutes at Large, Vol. 3, p. 224
10. WILLIAM A. GORDON.,A COMPILATION OF REGISTERS OF THE ARMY OF THE UNTIED STATES, Washington: James C. Dunn, 1837. p. 60
11. United States Statutes at Large, Vol. 3, p. 297
12. Emerson, William K., Encyclopedia of United States Army Insignia and Uniforms, Norman: University of Oklahoma Press, 1996, p. 306

Garrison Surgeon's Mate
1. FRANCIS B. HEITMAN.,HISTORICAL REGISTER AND DICTIONARY OF THE UNITED STATES ARMY, Vol. 2, Washington: GPO, 1903. p. 562
2. United States Statutes at Large, Vol. 1, p. 222
3. United States Statutes at Large, Vol. 1, p. 430
4. United States Statutes at Large, Vol. 2, p. 133
5. United States Statutes at Large, Vol. 3, p. 297
6. Emerson, William K., Encyclopedia of United States Army Insignia and Uniforms, Norman: University of Oklahoma Press, 1996, p. 306

General
1. Oliver, Raymond, Why is a Kernal called a Colonel?, Tuscon: Fireship press, 1983, p. 49
2. United States Statutes at Large, Vol. 40, p. 410
3. Official Army Register,January 1, 1920, p. 910
4. Specifications for the uniform of the united states army,GPO, 1917p. 28
5. The National Geographic Magazine , October 1917, p. 414
6. United States Statutes at Large, Vol. 41, p. 283
7. Official Army Register,January 1, 1921, p. 6
8. United States Statutes at Large, Vol. 45, p. 1255
9. http://en.wikipedia.org/wiki/List_of_United_States_Army_four-star_generals, august 2010
10. Official Army Register,January 1, 1944, p. 1
11. http://en.wikipedia.org/wiki/Military_career_of_Dwight_D._Eisenhower, august 2010
12. http://en.wikipedia.org/wiki/List_of_United_States_Army_four-star_generals, august 2010
13. ibid
14. Official Army Register,January 1, 1946, p. 1099
15. ibid, p. 770
16. Official Army Register,January 1, 1947, p. 1257
17. ibid. p. 709
18. ibid, p. 330
19. ibid, p. 1502
20. Official Army Register,January 1, 1946, p. 24
21. Official Army Register,January 1, 1951, p. 72
22. Official Army Register,January 1, 1947, p. 1617
23. ibid, p. 1483
24. Official Army Register,January 1, 1948, volume 2, p. 2481
25. Official Army Register,January 1, 1950, p. 742
26. ibid, p. 695

27. Official Army Register,January 1, 1955, volume 1, p. 935
28. ibid. p. 958
29. United States Statutes at Large, Vol. 61, p. 885
30. United States Statutes at Large, Vol. 63, p. 807
31. United States Statutes at Large, Vol. 72, p. 124
32. Emerson, William K., Encyclopedia of United States Army Insignia and Uniforms, Norman: University of Oklahoma Press, 1996, p. 465
33. AR-670-1, February 2005, p 187

General and Commander in Chief
1. Journals of the Continental Congress, Volume 2, p 96
2. Peterson, Harold L. , The Book of the Continental Soldier, Harrisburg: Stackpole, 1968, p. 242
3. ibid p. 243
4. FRANCIS B. HEITMAN.,HISTORICAL REGISTER AND DICTIONARY OF THE UNITED STATES ARMY, Vol. 1, Washington: GPO, 1903. p. 19
5. Letter from Washington to Congress, January 22, 1777 (http://memory.loc.gov/cgi-bin/query/r?ammem/mgw:@field(DOCID+@lit(gw070057))), August 2010
6. http://xenophongroup.com/patriot/washington/rank.htm, August 2010
7. FRANCIS B. HEITMAN.,HISTORICAL REGISTER AND DICTIONARY OF THE UNITED STATES ARMY, Vol. 1, Washington: GPO, 1903. p. 19

General of the Armies of the United States
1. United States Statutes at Large, Vol. 1, p. 752
2. FRANCIS B. HEITMAN.,HISTORICAL REGISTER AND DICTIONARY OF THE UNITED STATES ARMY, Vol. 1, Washington: GPO, 1903. p. 1007
3. United States Statutes at Large, Vol. 14, p. 223
4. United States Statutes at Large, Vol. 41, p. 283
5. Official Army Register,January 1, 1921, p. 5
6. http://en.wikipedia.org/wiki/File:GEN_Pershing_as_Chief_Of_Staff.jpg, august 2010
7. Official Army Register,January 1, 1924, p. 772
8. United States Statutes at Large, Vol. 58, p. 803
9. http://www.eisenhowermemorial.org/stories/Ike-fifth-star.htm, august 2010
10. United States Statutes at Large, Vol. 90, p. 2078

General of the Army
1. http://www.eisenhowermemorial.org/stories/Ike-fifth-star.htm, august 2010
2. ibid.
3. United States Statutes at Large, Vol. 38, p. 802
4. Official Army Register, January 1, 1945, p. 1
5. http://www.eisenhowermemorial.org/stories/Ike-fifth-star.htm, august 2010
6. http://en.wikipedia.org/wiki/General_of_the_Army_(United_States), aurugst 2010
7. Official Army Register, January 1, 1947, p. 1277
8. Official Army Register, January 1, 1948, p. 740
9. United States Statutes at Large, Vol. 62, p. 1069
10. http://en.wikipedia.org/wiki/George_C._Marshall, august 2010
11. Official Army Register, January 1, 1951, p. 429
12. United States Statutes at Large, Vol. 64, p. 853
13. http://en.wikipedia.org/wiki/George_C._Marshall, august 2010
14. Official Army Register, January 1, 1951, p. 72
15. Official Army Register, January 1, 1953, p. 837
16. United States Statutes at Large, Vol. 75, p. 5
17. http://en.wikipedia.org/wiki/Dwight_D._Eisenhower, august 2010
18. http://en.wikipedia.org/wiki/Douglas_MacArthur, august 2010
19. http://en.wikipedia.org/wiki/Omar_Bradley, august 2010
20. Lanham Howard G., Straps, Westminster, MD: Johnson Graphics, 1998, p. 120
21. ibid. p. 122
22. AR-670-1, February 15, 1979, p- 6-2

General of the Army of the United States
1. United States Statutes at Large, Vol. 14, p. 223
2. http://www.history.army.mil/faq/faq-5star.htm, August 2010
3. FRANCIS B. HEITMAN.,HISTORICAL REGISTER AND DICTIONARY OF THE UNITED STATES ARMY, Vol. 1, Washington: GPO, 1903. p. 19
4. Steffen, Randy, The Horse Soldier 1776-1943, Vol. 2., Norman: University of Oklahoma Press, 1977, p. 111
5. ibid. p. 113
6. United States Statutes at Large, Vol. 16, p. 316
7. FRANCIS B. HEITMAN.,HISTORICAL REGISTER AND DICTIONARY OF THE UNITED STATES ARMY, Vol. 1, Washington: GPO, 1903. p. 19
8. United States Statutes at Large, Vol. 25, p. 165
9. United States Statutes at Large, Vol. 14, p. 333

Gunner
1. Peterson, Harold L. , The Book of the Continental Soldier, Harrisburg: Stackpole, 1968, p. 224
2. United States Statutes at Large, Vol. 3, p. 47

Horseshoer
1. United States Statutes at Large, Vol. 36, p. 245
2. Emerson, William K., Chevrons, Washington: Smithsonian Institution Press, 1983, p. 172
3. United States Statutes at Large, Vol. 39, p. 166
4. Emerson, William K., Chevrons, Washington: Smithsonian Institution Press, 1983, p. 252

Hospital Chaplain
1. United States Statutes at Large, Vol. 12, p. 404
2. Emerson, William K., Encyclopedia of United States Army Insignia and Uniforms, Norman: University of Oklahoma Press, 1996, p. 265
3. United States Statutes at Large, Vol. 13, p. 46

Hospital Physician and Surgeon
1. Journal of the Continental Congress, volume 18, page 878.

Hospital Sergeant
1. United States Statutes at Large, Vol. 39, p. 172
2. Emerson, William K., Chevrons, Washington: Smithsonian Institution Press, 1983, p. 156-157
3. ibid. p. 251

Hospital Steward
1. United States Statutes at Large, Vol. 1, p. 721
2. United States Statutes at Large, Vol. 11, p. 51
3. Emerson, William K., Chevrons, Washington: Smithsonian Institution Press, 1983, p. 46
4. ibid.
5. Steffen, Randy, The Horse Soldier 1776-1943, Vol. 2., Norman: University of Oklahoma Press, 1977, p. 109
6. Emerson, William K., Chevrons, Washington: Smithsonian Institution Press, 1983, p. 90
7. ibid.
8. ibid. p. 92
9. ibid.
10. ibid. p. 156
11. United States Statutes at Large, Vol. 32, p. 930

Hospital Steward (Regimental)
1. United States Statutes at Large, Vol. 12, p. 269
2. United States Statutes at Large, Vol. 12, p. 280
3. Emerson, William K., Chevrons, Washington: Smithsonian Institution Press, 1983, p. 45.
3. United States Statutes at Large, Vol. 14, p. 332
4. Emerson, William K., Chevrons, Washington: Smithsonian Institution Press, 1983, p. 51.
5. United States Statutes at Large, Vol. 16, p. 318

Hospital Surgeon
1. Heitman, F.B., Historical Register Officers of the Continental Army during the War of Revolution, Washington: 1893,
2. United States Statutes at Large, Vol. 1, p. 721
3. United States Statutes at Large, Vol. 2, p. 481
4. FRANCIS B. HEITMAN.,HISTORICAL REGISTER AND DICTIONARY OF THE UNITED STATES ARMY, Vol. 1, Washington: GPO, 1903. p. 353
5. United States Statutes at Large, Vol. 2, p. 671
6. FRANCIS B. HEITMAN.,HISTORICAL REGISTER AND DICTIONARY OF THE UNITED STATES ARMY, Vol. 1, Washington: GPO, 1903., Key/Kerr on p. 593
7. United States Statutes at Large, Vol. 3, p. 224
8. WILLIAM A. GORDON.,A COMPILATION OF REGISTERS OF THE ARMY OF THE UNTIED STATES, Washington: James C. Dunn, 1837. p. 61
9. FRANCIS B. HEITMAN.,HISTORICAL REGISTER AND DICTIONARY OF THE UNITED STATES ARMY, Vol. 1, Washington: GPO, 1903., p. 404
10. WILLIAM A. GORDON.,A COMPILATION OF REGISTERS OF THE ARMY OF THE UNTIED STATES, Washington: James C. Dunn, 1837. p. 76
11. United States Statutes at Large, Vol. 3, p. 426
12. WILLIAM A. GORDON.,A COMPILATION OF REGISTERS OF THE ARMY OF THE UNTIED STATES, Washington: James C. Dunn, 1837. p. 134
13. Emerson, William K., Encyclopedia of United States Army Insignia and Uniforms, Norman: University of Oklahoma Press, 1996, p. 306

Hospital Surgeon's Mate
1. United States Statutes at Large, Vol. 1, p. 721
2. United States Statutes at Large, Vol. 2, p. 481
3. FRANCIS B. HEITMAN.,HISTORICAL REGISTER AND DICTIONARY OF THE UNITED STATES ARMY, Vol. 1, Washington: GPO, 1903., p. 955
4. United States Statutes at Large, Vol. 2, p. 671
5. United States Statutes at Large, Vol. 3, p. 224
6. United States Statutes at Large, Vol. 3, p. 297
7. United States Statutes at Large, Vol. 3, p. 426
8. WILLIAM A. GORDON.,A COMPILATION OF REGISTERS OF THE ARMY OF THE UNTIED STATES, Washington: James C. Dunn, 1837. p. 134
9. Emerson, William K., Encyclopedia of United States Army Insignia and Uniforms, Norman: University of Oklahoma Press, 1996, p. 306

Indian Scouts
1. United States Statutes at Large, Vol. 14, p. 333
2. Official Army Register for 1868, p. 140A
3. United States Statutes at Large, Vol. 19, p. 97
4. Official Army Register for January 1881, p. 281
5. Official Army Register for January 1885, p. 376-77

Judge Advocate
1. Heitman, F.B., Historical Register Officers of the Continental Army during the War of Revolution, Washington: 1893, p. 405
2. ibid. p. 258
3. Raphael Thian, Legilative history of the Army of the United States, Washington: GPO, 1901, p. 127
4. United States Statutes at Large, Vol. 1, p. 507
5. FRANCIS B. HEITMAN.,HISTORICAL REGISTER AND DICTIONARY OF THE UNITED STATES ARMY, Vol. 1, Washington: GPO, 1903. p. 895
6. United States Statutes at Large, Vol. 2, p. 132
7. United States Statutes at Large, Vol. 2, p. 671
8. FRANCIS B. HEITMAN.,HISTORICAL REGISTER AND DICTIONARY OF THE UNITED STATES ARMY, Vol. 1, Washington: GPO, 1903.
9. United States Statutes at Large, Vol. 3, p. 297
10. FRANCIS B. HEITMAN.,HISTORICAL REGISTER AND DICTIONARY OF THE UNITED STATES ARMY, Vol. 1, Washington: GPO, 1903.
11. United States Statutes at Large, Vol. 3, p. 426
12 United States Statutes at Large, Vol. 3, p. 615
13. Emerson, William K., Encyclopedia of United States Army Insignia and Uniforms, Norman: University of Oklahoma Press, 1996, p. 250

Lance Acting Hospital Steward
1. Emerson, William K., Chevrons, Washington: Smithsonian Institution Press, 1983, p. 92
2. ibid.
3. ibid. p. 157
4. ibid

Lance Corporal
1. Emerson, William K., Chevrons, Washington: Smithsonian Institution Press, 1983, p. 103
2. ibid
3. ibid p. 95
4. ibid p. 157
5. ibid
6. United States Statutes at Large, Vol. 39, p. 166
7. Emerson, William K., Chevrons, Washington: Smithsonian Institution Press, 1983, p. 171.

Leader of the Band
1. United States Statutes at Large, Vol. 12, p. 280
2. United States Statutes at Large, Vol. 12, p. 594
3. Official Army Register for 1863, p. 110A
4. United States Statutes at Large, Vol. 14, p. 332

Lieutenant
1. Oliver, Raymond, Why is a Kernal called a Colonel?, Tuscon: Fireship press, 1983, p. 25

2. http://www.xenograg.com/101/excerpts/origins-of-european-army-ranks, August 2010
3. Peterson, Harold L. , The Book of the Continental Soldier, Harrisburg: Stackpole, 1968, p. 242
4. United States Statutes at Large, Vol. 1, p. 750

Lieutenant Colonel
1. http://www.xenograg.com/101/excerpts/origins-of-european-army-ranks, august 2010
2. Peterson, Harold L. , The Book of the Continental Soldier, Harrisburg: Stackpole, 1968. p 242
3. Journal of the Continental Congress, Vol. 33 p. 437-438
4. FRANCIS B. HEITMAN.,HISTORICAL REGISTER AND DICTIONARY OF THE UNITED STATES ARMY, Vol. 1, Washington: GPO, 1903., p. 501
5. United States Statutes at Large, Vol. 1, p. 222
6. FRANCIS B. HEITMAN.,HISTORICAL REGISTER AND DICTIONARY OF THE UNITED STATES ARMY, Vol. 1, Washington: GPO, 1903., p. 1037
7. FRANCIS B. HEITMAN.,HISTORICAL REGISTER AND DICTIONARY OF THE UNITED STATES ARMY, Vol. 2, Washington: GPO, 1903., p. 562
8. FRANCIS B. HEITMAN.,HISTORICAL REGISTER AND DICTIONARY OF THE UNITED STATES ARMY, Vol. 1, Washington: GPO, 1903., p. 140-141
9. United States Statutes at Large, Vol. 1, p. 366
10. FRANCIS B. HEITMAN.,HISTORICAL REGISTER AND DICTIONARY OF THE UNITED STATES ARMY, Vol. 1, Washington: GPO, 1903., p. 50
11. United States Statutes at Large, Vol. 2, p. 132
12. Steffen, Randy, The Horse Soldier 1776-1943, Vol. 1., Norman: University of Oklahoma Press, 1977, p. 44
13. Emerson, William K., Chevrons, Washington: Smithsonian Institution Press, 1983, p. 40
14. Emerson, William K., Encyclopedia of United States Army Insignia and Uniforms, Norman: University of Oklahoma Press, 1996, p. 124
15. Lanham Howard G., Straps, Westminster, MD: Johnson Graphics, 1998, p. 7
16. Steffen, Randy, The Horse Soldier 1776-1943, Vol. 1., Norman: University of Oklahoma Press, 1977, p. 94
17. http://www.history.army.mil/reference/1839U.htm, august 2010
18. Steffen, Randy, The Horse Soldier 1776-1943, Vol. 2., Norman: University of Oklahoma Press, 1977, p. 6
19. Emerson, William K., Encyclopedia of United States Army Insignia and Uniforms, Norman: University of Oklahoma Press, 1996, p. 165
20. United States Statutes at Large, Vol. 63, p. 802
21. AR-670-1, February 2005, p 190

Lieutenant General
1. http://www.xenograg.com/101/excerpts/origins-of-european-army-ranks, august 2010
2. Letter from Washington to Congress, January 22, 1777 (http://memory.loc.gov/cgi-bin/query/r?ammem/mgw:@field(DOCID+@lit(gw070057))), August 2010
3. http://xenophongroup.com/patriot/washington/rank.htm, August 2010
4. United States Statutes at Large, Vol. 1, p. 558
5. United States Statutes at Large, Vol. 1, p. 752
6. FRANCIS B. HEITMAN.,HISTORICAL REGISTER AND DICTIONARY OF THE UNITED STATES ARMY, Vol. 1, Washington: GPO, 1903. p. 1007
7. Senate Execuitve Journal, Vol. 9, p. 420
8. Steffen, Randy, The Horse Soldier 1776-1943, Vol. 2., Norman: University of Oklahoma Press, 1977, p. 10
9. http://en.wikipedia.org/wiki/Alexander_Macomb_(American_general)
10. FRANCIS B. HEITMAN.,HISTORICAL REGISTER AND DICTIONARY OF THE UNITED STATES ARMY, Vol. 1, Washington: GPO, 1903. p. 19
11. United States Statutes at Large, Vol. 13, p. 11
12. United States Statutes at Large, Vol. 14, p. 333
13. FRANCIS B. HEITMAN.,HISTORICAL REGISTER AND DICTIONARY OF THE UNITED STATES ARMY, Vol. 1, Washington: GPO, 1903. p. 19
14. Steffen, Randy, The Horse Soldier 1776-1943, Vol. 2., Norman: University of Oklahoma Press, 1977, p. 10-11
15. United States Statutes at Large, Vol. 16, p. 318
16. United States Statutes at Large, Vol. 25, p. 165
17. FRANCIS B. HEITMAN.,HISTORICAL REGISTER AND DICTIONARY OF THE UNITED STATES ARMY, Vol. 1, Washington: GPO, 1903. p. 19
18. United States Statutes at Large, Vol. 28, p. 938
19. FRANCIS B. HEITMAN.,HISTORICAL REGISTER AND DICTIONARY OF THE UNITED STATES ARMY, Vol. 1, Washington: GPO, 1903. p. 19
20. United States Statutes at Large, Vol. 31, p. 655
21. United States Statutes at Large, Vol. 31, p. 748
22. http://en.wikipedia.org/wiki/List_of_lieutenant_generals_in_the_United_States_Army_before_1960, august 2010
23. United States Statutes at Large, Vol. 32, p. 830
24. http://en.wikipedia.org/wiki/List_of_lieutenant_generals_in_the_United_States_Army_before_1960, august 2010
25. ibid
26. http://www.arlingtoncemetery.net/amacart.htm, august 2010
27. United States Statutes at Large, Vol. 34, p. 1160
28. Steffen, Randy, The Horse Soldier 1776-1943, Vol. 3., Norman: University of Oklahoma Press, 1977, p. 97 and 107
29. Emerson, William K., Encyclopedia of United States Army Insignia and Uniforms, Norman: University of Oklahoma Press, 1996, p. 473
40. United States Statutes at Large, Vol. 34, p. 410
31. http://en.wikipedia.org/wiki/List_of_lieutenant_generals_in_the_United_States_Army_before_1960, august 2010
32. United States Statutes at Large, Vol. 53, p. 1214
33. United States Statutes at Large, Vol. 63, p. 807
34. United States Statutes at Large, Vol. 72, p. 124
35. Emerson, William K., Encyclopedia of United States Army Insignia and Uniforms, Norman: University of Oklahoma Press, 1996, p. 465
36. AR-670-1, February 2005, p 188

Major
1. http://www.xenograg.com/101/excerpts/origins-of-european-army-ranks, august 2010
2. Oliver, Raymond, Why is a Kernal called a Colonel?, Tuscon: Fireship press, 1983, p. 32
3. Peterson, Harold L. , The Book of the Continental Soldier, Harrisburg: Stackpole, 1968. p 242
4. FRANCIS B. HEITMAN.,HISTORICAL REGISTER AND DICTIONARY OF THE UNITED STATES ARMY, Vol. 1, Washington: GPO, 1903., p. 17
5. Steffen, Randy, The Horse Soldier 1776-1943, Vol. 1., Norman: University of Oklahoma Press, 1977, p. 44
6. Emerson, William K., Chevrons, Washington: Smithsonian Institution Press, 1983, p. 40
7. Emerson, William K., Encyclopedia of United States Army Insignia and Uniforms, Norman: University of Oklahoma Press, 1996, p. 124
8. Lanham Howard G., Straps, Westminster, MD: Johnson Graphics, 1998, p. 7
9. Steffen, Randy, The Horse Soldier 1776-1943, Vol. 1., Norman: University of Oklahoma Press, 1977, p. 94
10. Lanham Howard G., Straps, Westminster, MD: Johnson Graphics, 1998, p. 13
11. Steffen, Randy, The Horse Soldier 1776-1943, Vol. 2., Norman: University of Oklahoma Press, 1977, p. 6
12. ibid. p. 111
13. Emerson, William K., Encyclopedia of United States Army Insignia and Uniforms, Norman: University of Oklahoma Press, 1996, p. 165
14. United States Statutes at Large, Vol. 63, p. 802
15. AR-670-1, February 2005, p 190

Major General
1. http://www.xenograg.com/101/excerpts/origins-of-european-army-ranks, august 2010
2. Peterson, Harold L. , The Book of the Continental Soldier, Harrisburg: Stackpole, 1968. p 241-242
3. ibid
4. FRANCIS B. HEITMAN.,HISTORICAL REGISTER AND DICTIONARY OF THE UNITED STATES ARMY, Vol. 1, Washington: GPO, 1903., p. 19
5. United States Statutes at Large, Vol. 1, p. 222
6. FRANCIS B. HEITMAN.,HISTORICAL REGISTER AND DICTIONARY OF THE UNITED STATES ARMY, Vol. 1, Washington: GPO, 1903., p. 19
7. ibid, p. 1010
8. United States Statutes at Large, Vol. 1, p. 507
9. United States Statutes at Large, Vol. 1, p. 559
10. FRANCIS B. HEITMAN.,HISTORICAL REGISTER AND DICTIONARY OF THE UNITED STATES ARMY, Vol. 1, Washington: GPO, 1903., p. 19
11. United States Statutes at Large, Vol. 1, p. 604
12. FRANCIS B. HEITMAN.,HISTORICAL REGISTER AND DICTIONARY OF THE UNITED STATES ARMY, Vol. 1, Washington: GPO, 1903., p. 19
13. http://en.wikipedia.org/wiki/List_of_major_generals_in_the_United_States_Regular_Army_before_July_1,_1920, august 2010
14. Senate Executive Journal, Vol. 1, p. 292
15. United States Statutes at Large, Vol. 1, p. 752
16. http://www.history.army.mil/books/r&h/R&H-QM.htm, September 2010
17. FRANCIS B. HEITMAN.,HISTORICAL REGISTER AND DICTIONARY OF THE UNITED STATES ARMY, Vol. 1, Washington: GPO, 1903., p. 1036
18. ibid p. 40 (footnote at the bottom of the list of quartermaster generals)
19. United States Statutes at Large, Vol. 2, p. 86
20. United States Statutes at Large, Vol. 2, p. 134
21. FRANCIS B. HEITMAN.,HISTORICAL REGISTER AND DICTIONARY OF THE UNITED STATES ARMY, Vol. 1, Washington: GPO, 1903., p. 40
22. United States Statutes at Large, Vol. 2, p. 671
23. FRANCIS B. HEITMAN.,HISTORICAL REGISTER AND DICTIONARY OF THE UNITED STATES ARMY, Vol. 1, Washington: GPO, 1903., p. 363
24. ibid. p. 793
25. United States Statutes at Large, Vol. 2, p. 801
26. FRANCIS B. HEITMAN.,HISTORICAL REGISTER AND DICTIONARY OF THE UNITED STATES ARMY, Vol. 1, Washington: GPO, 1903., p. 19
27. ibid. p. 496
28. ibid. p. 506
29. ibid. p. 566
30. United States Statutes at Large, Vol. 3, p. 225
31. United States Statutes at Large, Vol. 3, p. 615
32. FRANCIS B. HEITMAN.,HISTORICAL REGISTER AND DICTIONARY OF THE UNITED STATES ARMY, Vol. 1, Washington: GPO, 1903., p. 19
33. ibid. p. 252
34. ibid. p. 680
35. http://en.wikipedia.org/wiki/Alexander_Macomb_(American_general)
36. Lanham Howard G., Straps, Westminster, MD: Johnson Graphics, 1998, p. 11
37. http://www.history.army.mil/reference/1839U.htm
38. FRANCIS B. HEITMAN.,HISTORICAL REGISTER AND DICTIONARY OF THE UNITED STATES ARMY, Vol. 1, Washington: GPO, 1903., p. 20
39. United States Statutes at Large, Vol. 9, p. 17
40. FRANCIS B. HEITMAN.,HISTORICAL REGISTER AND DICTIONARY OF THE UNITED STATES ARMY, Vol. 1, Washington: GPO, 1903., p. 20
41. United States Statutes at Large, Vol. 9, p. 20
42. FRANCIS B. HEITMAN.,HISTORICAL REGISTER AND DICTIONARY OF THE UNITED STATES ARMY, Vol. 1, Washington: GPO, 1903., p. 20
43. United States Statutes at Large, Vol. 9, p. 184
44. FRANCIS B. HEITMAN.,HISTORICAL REGISTER AND DICTIONARY OF THE UNITED STATES ARMY, Vol. 1, Washington: GPO, 1903., p. 20
45. United States Statutes at Large, Vol. 9, p. 247
46. FRANCIS B. HEITMAN.,HISTORICAL REGISTER AND DICTIONARY OF THE UNITED STATES ARMY, Vol. 1, Washington: GPO, 1903., p. 949
47. ibid. p. 270
48. ibid. p. 775
49. ibid. p. 792
50. ibid. p. 812
51. FRANCIS B. HEITMAN.,HISTORICAL REGISTER AND DICTIONARY OF THE UNITED STATES ARMY, Vol. 1, Washington: GPO, 1903.,
52. Steffen, Randy, The Horse Soldier 1776-1943, Vol. 2., Norman: University of Oklahoma Press, 1977, p. 10-11
51. FRANCIS B. HEITMAN.,HISTORICAL REGISTER AND DICTIONARY OF THE UNITED STATES ARMY, Vol. 1, Washington: GPO, 1903., p. 17
54. Steffen, Randy, The Horse Soldier 1776-1943, Vol. 3., Norman: University of Oklahoma Press, 1977, p. 54
55. ibid. p. 95-108
56. United States Statutes at Large, Vol. 63, p. 807
57. United States Statutes at Large, Vol. 72, p. 124
58. Emerson, William K., Encyclopedia of United States Army Insignia and Uniforms, Norman: University of Oklahoma Press, 1996, p. 465
59. AR-670-1, February 2005, p 188

Master Chemical Sergeant

1. Emerson, William K., Chevrons, Washington: Smithsonian Institution Press, 1983, p. 167

Master Electrician
1. United States Statutes at Large, Vol. 32, p. 930
2. Emerson, William K., Chevrons, Washington: Smithsonian Institution Press, 1983, p. 167
3. ibid. p. 161
4. ibid.
5. ibid . p. 251
6. United States Statutes at Large, Vol. 37, p. 593
7. Emerson, William K., Chevrons, Washington: Smithsonian Institution Press, 1983, p. 152
8. United States Statutes at Large, Vol. 39, p. 168

Master Engineer Junior Grade
1. United States Statutes at Large, Vol. 39, p. 173
2. Emerson, William K., Chevrons, Washington: Smithsonian Institution Press, 1983, p. 158
3. ibid. p. 181
4. ibid. p. 182
5. ibid. p. 251

Master Engineer Senior Grade
1. United States Statutes at Large, Vol. 39, p. 173
2. Emerson, William K., Chevrons, Washington: Smithsonian Institution Press, 1983, p. 158
3. ibid. p. 181
4. ibid. p. 182
5. ibid. p. 251

Master Gunner
1. United States Statutes at Large, Vol. 34, p. 862
2. Emerson, William K., Chevrons, Washington: Smithsonian Institution Press, 1983, p. 161
3. ibid
4. ibid p. 251

Master Hospital Sergeant
1. United States Statutes at Large, Vol. 39, p. 172
2. Emerson, William K., Chevrons, Washington: Smithsonian Institution Press, 1983, p. 157
3. ibid. p. 251

Master of the Sword
1. United States Statutes at Large, Vol. 2, p. 764
2. United States Statutes at Large, Vol. 3, p. 224

Master Sergeant
1. Emerson, William K., Chevrons, Washington: Smithsonian Institution Press, 1983, p. 251
2. ibid. p. 196
3. United States Statutes at Large, Vol. 63, p. 802
4. United States Statutes at Large, Vol. 72, p. 122
5. AR-670-1, February 2005, p 197

Master Signal Electrician
1. United States Statutes at Large, Vol. 33, p. 261
2. Emerson, William K., Chevrons, Washington: Smithsonian Institution Press, 1983, p. 167
3. ibid. p. 155
4. ibid. p. 179
5. ibid. p. 251

Master Specialist
1. http://www.tioh.hqda.pentagon.mil/UniformedServices/Insignia_Rank/enlisted_history.aspx, September 2010
2. Emerson, William K., Chevrons, Washington: Smithsonian Institution Press, 1983, p. 200

Master Wagoner
1. United States Statutes at Large, Vol. 12, p. 287
2. Official Army Register, January 1880, p. 274-77

Master Warrant Officer
1. http://penfed.org/usawoa/woheritage/Hist_of_Army_WO.htm, September 2010
2. Ar-670-1, September 1992, p. 126
3. http://penfed.org/usawoa/woheritage/Hist_Army_CW5_Insignia.htm, September 2010
4. ibid.

Mechanic
1. United States Statutes at Large, Vol. 30, p. 978
2. Emerson, William K., Chevrons, Washington: Smithsonian Institution Press, 1983, p. 105
3. United States Statutes at Large, Vol. 31, p. 748
4. United States Statutes at Large, Vol. 34, p. 862
5. United States Statutes at Large, Vol. 39, p. 166
6. Emerson, William K., Chevrons, Washington: Smithsonian Institution Press, 1983, p. 253

Medical Cadet
1. United States Statutes at Large, Vol. 12, p. 288
2. Katcher, Philip, The Civil War Source Book, New York: Facts on File, 1992, p. 175

Medical Inspector
1. United States Statutes at Large, Vol. 12, p. 379
2. FRANCIS B. HEITMAN.,HISTORICAL REGISTER AND DICTIONARY OF THE UNITED STATES ARMY, Vol. 1, Washington: GPO, 1903.
3. United States Statutes at Large, Vol. 12, p. 683
4. FRANCIS B. HEITMAN.,HISTORICAL REGISTER AND DICTIONARY OF THE UNITED STATES ARMY, Vol. 1, Washington: GPO, 1903.
5. ibid.

Medical Inspector General
1. United States Statutes at Large, Vol. 12, p. 379
2. FRANCIS B. HEITMAN.,HISTORICAL REGISTER AND DICTIONARY OF THE UNITED STATES ARMY, Vol. 1, Washington: GPO, 1903.

Medical Storekeeper
1. United States Statutes at Large, Vol. 12, p. 403
2. FRANCIS B. HEITMAN.,HISTORICAL REGISTER AND DICTIONARY OF THE UNITED STATES ARMY, Vol. 1, Washington: GPO, 1903.
3. Emerson, William K., Encyclopedia of United States Army Insignia and Uniforms, Norman: University of Oklahoma Press, 1996, p. 308
4. United States Statutes at Large, Vol. 14, p. 332-337
5. Emerson, William K., Encyclopedia of United States Army Insignia and Uniforms, Norman: University of Oklahoma Press, 1996, p. 308
6. Acker, James, Regulations and notes of the uniform of the army of the united states, 1872, war dept, p. 6
7. United States Statutes at Large, Vol. 19, p. 61
8. FRANCIS B. HEITMAN.,HISTORICAL REGISTER AND DICTIONARY OF THE UNITED STATES ARMY, Vol. 1, Washington: GPO, 1903.

Mess Sergeant
1. United States Statutes at Large, Vol. 39, p. 173
2. Emerson, William K., Chevrons, Washington: Smithsonian Institution Press, 1983, p. 175
3. ibid p. 252

Military Agent
1. United States Statutes at Large, Vol. 2, p. 132.
2. FRANCIS B. HEITMAN.,HISTORICAL REGISTER AND DICTIONARY OF THE UNITED STATES ARMY, Vol. 1, Washington: GPO, 1903
3. United States Statutes at Large, Vol. 2, p. 696.

Military Storekeeper
1. United States Statutes at Large, Vol. 2, p. 816.
1a. United States Statutes at Large, Vol. 2, p. 563
1b. FRANCIS B. HEITMAN.,HISTORICAL REGISTER AND DICTIONARY OF THE UNITED STATES ARMY, Vol. 1, Washington: GPO, 1903, p. 292
2. United States Statutes at Large, Vol. 5, p. 512.
2a. United States Statutes at Large, Vol. 5, p. 259.
3. Emerson, William K., Encyclopedia of United States Army Insignia and Uniforms, Norman: University of Oklahoma Press, 1996, p. 306
4. www.history.army.mil/reference/1839U.htm, September 2010
5. Steffen, Randy, The Horse Soldier 1776-1943, Vol. 2., Norman: University of Oklahoma Press, 1977, p. 14
6. Acker, James, Regulations and notes of the uniform of the army of the united states, 1872, war dept, p. 6
7. United States Statutes at Large, Vol. 14, p. 332-337
8. United States Statutes at Large, Vol. 18, p. 339.
9. Official Army Register, 1875, p. 17-18
10. FRANCIS B. HEITMAN.,HISTORICAL REGISTER AND DICTIONARY OF THE UNITED STATES ARMY, Vol. 1, Washington: GPO, 1903, p. 802
11. ibid p. 160
12. ibid. p. 841
13. ibid. p. 553
14. ibid. p. 632
15. ibid. p. 980
16. ibid. p. 693
17. Ibid. p. 636
18. ibid. p. 194
19. United States Statutes at Large, Vol. 30, p. 571
20. FRANCIS B. HEITMAN.,HISTORICAL REGISTER AND DICTIONARY OF THE UNITED STATES ARMY, Vol. 1, Washington: GPO, 1903, p. 638
21. United States Statutes at Large, Vol. 39, p. 626
22. United States Statutes at Large, Vol. 41, p. 760
23. Official Army Register, January 1, 1927, p. 829

Motor Sergeant
1. Emerson, William K., Chevrons, Washington: Smithsonian Institution Press, 1983, p. 174

Musician
1. Steffen, Randy, The Horse Soldier 1776-1943, Vol. 1., Norman: University of Oklahoma Press, 1977, p. 6
2. Kochan, James and Rickman, David, The United States Army 1781-1811, Oxford: Osprey, 2001, p. 39
3. Kochan, James and Rickman, David, The United States Army 1812-1815, Oxford: Osprey, 2001, p. 14
4. ibid. p. 17-18
5. ibid. p. 38
6. Emerson, William K., Encyclopedia of United States Army Insignia and Uniforms, Norman: University of Oklahoma Press, 1996, p. 438
7. Steffen, Randy, The Horse Soldier 1776-1943, Vol. 2., Norman: University of Oklahoma Press, 1977, p. 7
8. ibid. p. 19
9. ibid. p. 109
10. Emerson, William K., Encyclopedia of United States Army Insignia and Uniforms, Norman: University of Oklahoma Press, 1996, p. 225
11. ibid. p. 229
12. United States Statutes at Large, Vol. 39, p. 173

Musician First Class
1. United States Statutes at Large, Vol. 39, p. 173
2. Emerson, William K., Chevrons, Washington: Smithsonian Institution Press, 1983, p. 149
3. ibid p. 252

Musician Second Class
1. United States Statutes at Large, Vol. 39, p. 173
2. Emerson, William K., Chevrons, Washington: Smithsonian Institution Press, 1983, p. 149
3. ibid p. 252

Musician Third Class
1. United States Statutes at Large, Vol. 39, p. 173
2. Emerson, William K., Chevrons, Washington: Smithsonian Institution Press, 1983, p. 149
3. ibid p. 252

Oiler
1. United States Statutes at Large, Vol. 39, p. 882
2. Emerson, William K., Chevrons, Washington: Smithsonian Institution Press, 1983, p. 228
3. ibid. p. 162
4. ibid. p. 252

Ordnance Sergeant
1. United States Statutes at Large, Vol. 4, p. 504
2. Fisher, Ernest, Guardians of the Republic, New York: Ballentine, 1994, p. 71
3. www.history.army.mil/reference/1839U.htm, September 2010
4. Steffen, Randy, The Horse Soldier 1776-1943, Vol. 2., Norman: University of Oklahoma Press, 1977, p. 11
5. Emerson, William K., Chevrons, Washington: Smithsonian Institution Press, 1983, p. 96
6. ibid
7. ibid. p. 153
8. ibid. p. 154
9. ibid
10. ibid. p. 251

Ordnance Storekeeper
1. United States Statutes at Large, Vol. 14, p. 332
2. FRANCIS B. HEITMAN.,HISTORICAL REGISTER AND DICTIONARY OF THE UNITED STATES ARMY, Vol. 1, Washington: GPO, 1903,
3. Acker, James, Regulations and notes of the uniform of the army of the united states, 1872, war dept, p. 6
4. FRANCIS B. HEITMAN.,HISTORICAL REGISTER AND DICTIONARY OF THE UNITED STATES ARMY, Vol. 1, Washington: GPO, 1903,
5. United States Statutes at Large, Vol. 22, p. 52

6. FRANCIS B. HEITMAN.,HISTORICAL REGISTER AND DICTIONARY OF THE UNITED STATES ARMY, Vol. 1, Washington: GPO, 1903,
7. United States Statutes at Large, Vol. 32, p. 511

Paymaster
1. Journal of the Continental Congress, Vol. 11, p. 539
2. United States Statutes at Large, Vol. 2, p. 132
3. United States Statutes at Large, Vol. 3, p. 225
4. United States Statutes at Large, Vol. 3, p. 297
5. WILLIAM A. GORDON.,A COMPILATION OF REGISTERS OF THE ARMY OF THE UNTIED STATES, Washington: James C. Dunn, 1837. p. 121-133
6. FRANCIS B. HEITMAN.,HISTORICAL REGISTER AND DICTIONARY OF THE UNITED STATES ARMY, Vol. 1, Washington: GPO, 1903, p. 794
7. ibid. p. 814
8. ibid. p. 250
9. ibid. p. 489
10. ibid. p. 759
11. ibid. p. 895
12. WILLIAM A. GORDON.,A COMPILATION OF REGISTERS OF THE ARMY OF THE UNTIED STATES, Washington: James C. Dunn, 1837. p. 176
13. FRANCIS B. HEITMAN.,HISTORICAL REGISTER AND DICTIONARY OF THE UNITED STATES ARMY, Vol. 1, Washington: GPO, 1903, p. 1063
14. ibid. p. 606
15. ibid. p. 794
16. ibid. p. 696
17. WILLIAM A. GORDON.,A COMPILATION OF REGISTERS OF THE ARMY OF THE UNTIED STATES, Washington: James C. Dunn, 1837. p. 189
18. ibid p. 191
19. FRANCIS B. HEITMAN.,HISTORICAL REGISTER AND DICTIONARY OF THE UNITED STATES ARMY, Vol. 1, Washington: GPO, 1903, p. 489
20. ibid. p. 217
21. United States Statutes at Large, Vol. 3, p. 615
22. WILLIAM A. GORDON.,A COMPILATION OF REGISTERS OF THE ARMY OF THE UNTIED STATES, Washington: James C. Dunn, 1837. p. 200
23. United States Statutes at Large, Vol. 5, p. 117
24. United States Statutes at Large, Vol. 5, p. 256
25. United States Statutes at Large, Vol. 9, p. 184
26. Emerson, William K., Encyclopedia of United States Army Insignia and Uniforms, Norman: University of Oklahoma Press, 1996, p. 274
27. ibid. (Col. Emerson's reference is to General Regulations of the Army 1825, Article 65, Par. 44)
28. Emerson, William K., Encyclopedia of United States Army Insignia and Uniforms, Norman: University of Oklahoma Press, 1996, p. 274
29. ibid.

Paymaster General/ Paymaster of the Army
1. Journal of the Continental Congress, Vol. 2, p. 94
2. Heitman, F.B., Historical Register Officers of the Continental Army during the War of Revolution, Washington: 1893, p. 418
3. Journal of the Continental Congress, Vol. 2, p. 529
4. Heitman, F.B., Historical Register Officers of the Continental Army during the War of Revolution, Washington: 1893, p. 316
5. ibid p. 328
6. Journal of the Continental Congress, Vol. 32, p. 129
7. United States Statutes at Large, Vol. 1, p. 279
8. FRANCIS B. HEITMAN.,HISTORICAL REGISTER AND DICTIONARY OF THE UNITED STATES ARMY, Vol. 1, Washington: GPO, 1903, p. 938
9. United States Statutes at Large, Vol. 1, p. 483
10. United States Statutes at Large, Vol. 1, p. 507
11. United States Statutes at Large, Vol. 1, p. 558
12. United States Statutes at Large, Vol. 1, p. 749
13. United States Statutes at Large, Vol. 2, p. 132
14. FRANCIS B. HEITMAN.,HISTORICAL REGISTER AND DICTIONARY OF THE UNITED STATES ARMY, Vol. 1, Washington: GPO, 1903, p. 938
15. ibid. p. 242
16. United States Statutes at Large, Vol. 3, p. 297
14. FRANCIS B. HEITMAN.,HISTORICAL REGISTER AND DICTIONARY OF THE UNITED STATES ARMY, Vol. 1, Washington: GPO, 1903, p. 242
18. ibid p. 968
19. ibid p. 768
20. ibid p. 968
21. United States Statutes at Large, Vol. 3, p. 128
22. United States Statutes at Large, Vol. 3, p. 615
23. United States Statutes at Large, Vol. 5, p. 256
24. United States Statutes at Large, Vol. 9, p. 184
25. Emerson, William K., Encyclopedia of United States Army Insignia and Uniforms, Norman: University of Oklahoma Press, 1996, p. 274
26. ibid.
27. ibid.
28. ibid.
29. ibid.

Physician and Surgeon General
1. Journal of the Continental Congress, Vol. 7, p. 235
2. Journal of the Continental Congress, Vol. 7, p. 254
3. Heitman, F.B., Historical Register Officers of the Continental Army during the War of Revolution, Washington: 1893,
4. United States Statutes at Large, Vol. 2, p. 820
5. FRANCIS B. HEITMAN.,HISTORICAL REGISTER AND DICTIONARY OF THE UNITED STATES ARMY, Vol. 1, Washington: GPO, 1903, p. 962
6. Emerson, William K., Encyclopedia of United States Army Insignia and Uniforms, Norman: University of Oklahoma Press, 1996, p. 306

Physician General
1. United States Statutes at Large, Vol. 1, p. 558
2. Senate Executive Journal, Vol. 1, p. 292
3. FRANCIS B. HEITMAN.,HISTORICAL REGISTER AND DICTIONARY OF THE UNITED STATES ARMY, Vol. 1, Washington: GPO, 1903, p. 334
4. ibid.

Physician General of Hospitals
1. Journal of the Continental Congress, Vol. 7, p. 235
2. Heitman, F.B., Historical Register Officers of the Continental Army during the War of Revolution, Washington: 1893,
3. ibid.

Pioneer
1. http://www.civilwarhome.com/terms.htm, September 2010
2. Emerson, William K., Chevrons, Washington: Smithsonian Institution Press, 1983, p. 46
3. ibid. p. 106

Platoon Sergeant
1. Fisher, Ernest, Guardians of the Republic, New York: Ballentine, 1994, p. 309
2. Emerson, William K., Chevrons, Washington: Smithsonian Institution Press, 1983, p. 201
3. ar-670-1, January 1, 1979, p. 26-14
4. http://www.tioh.hqda.pentagon.mil/UniformedServices/Insignia_Rank/enlisted_history.aspx, September 2010
5. ibid.
6. ar-670-1, September 1, 1992, p. 105

Post Chaplain
1. United States Statutes at Large, Vol. 14, p. 333
2. Emerson, William K., Encyclopedia of United States Army Insignia and Uniforms, Norman: University of Oklahoma Press, 1996, p. 265
3. Lanham Howard G., Straps, Westminster, MD: Johnson Graphics, 1998, p. 89
4. Emerson, William K., Encyclopedia of United States Army Insignia and Uniforms, Norman: University of Oklahoma Press, 1996, p. 266
5. Steffen, Randy, The Horse Soldier 1776-1943, Vol. 2., Norman: University of Oklahoma Press, 1977, p. 140
6. http://www.grandarmyofthefrontier.org/uniforms/usa1898.htm, July 2010
7. United States Statutes at Large, Vol. 31, p. 750

Post Commissary Sergeant
1. United States Statutes at Large, Vol. 17, p. 485
2. Emerson, William K., Chevrons, Washington: Smithsonian Institution Press, 1983, p. 98
3. ibid p. 98 & 150
4. United States Statutes at Large, Vol. 37, p. 592

Post Quartermaster Sergeant
1. United States Statutes at Large, Vol. 23, p. 109
2. Emerson, William K., Chevrons, Washington: Smithsonian Institution Press, 1983, p. 98.
3. U.S. Army Uniforms and Equipment, 1889, forward by Jerome Greene: bison, 1986, p. 171.
4. Emerson, William K., Chevrons, Washington: Smithsonian Institution Press, 1983, p. 151.
5. United States Statutes at Large, Vol. 37, p. 592

Post Surgeon
1. United States Statutes at Large, Vol. 3, p. 297
2. FRANCIS B. HEITMAN.,HISTORICAL REGISTER AND DICTIONARY OF THE UNITED STATES ARMY, Vol. 1, Washington: GPO, 1903, p. 941
3. http://history.amedd.army.mil/booksdocs/medicaldepartment/partthree.html, June 2010
4. Emerson, William K., Encyclopedia of United States Army Insignia and Uniforms, Norman: University of Oklahoma Press, 1996, p. 306

1. United States Statutes at Large, Vol. 2, p. 482
2. United States Statutes at Large, Vol. 39, p. 166
3. Emerson, William K., Chevrons, Washington: Smithsonian Institution Press, 1983, p. 147.
4. Emerson, William K., Chevrons, Washington: Smithsonian Institution Press, 1983, p. 41.
5. Emerson, William K., Encyclopedia of United States Army Insignia and Uniforms, Norman: University of Oklahoma Press, 1996, p. 437
6. Steffen, Randy, The Horse Soldier 1776-1943, Vol. 2., Norman: University of Oklahoma Press, 1977, p. 7
7. ibid. p. 19.
4. Emerson, William K., Chevrons, Washington: Smithsonian Institution Press, 1983, p. 90.

Principal Teamster
1. United States Statutes at Large, Vol. 9, p. 185
2. United States Statutes at Large, Vol. 9, p. 306

Private
1. Oliver, Raymond, Why is a Kernal called a Colonel?, Tuscon: Fireship press, 1983, p. 5.
2. ibid
3. Emerson, William K., Encyclopedia of United States Army Insignia and Uniforms, Norman: University of Oklahoma Press, 1996, p. 438
4. Emerson, William K., Chevrons, Washington: Smithsonian Institution Press, 1983, p. 48.
5. ibid. p. 157

6. ibid. p. 252.
7. United States Statutes at Large, Vol. 63, p. 802
8. Fisher, Ernest, Guardians of the Republic, New York: Ballentine, 1994, p. 287
9. Emerson, William K., Chevrons, Washington: Smithsonian Institution Press, 1983, p. 197-198.
10. AR-670-1, February 2005, p 198-199

Private First Class
1. United States Statutes at Large, Vol. 9, p. 12
2. United States Statutes at Large, Vol. 12, p. 318
3. United States Statutes at Large, Vol. 12, p. 743
4. United States Statutes at Large, Vol. 12, p. 508
5. United States Statutes at Large, Vol. 12, p. 753
6. Official Army Register, 1866, p. 150c
7. United States Statutes at Large, Vol. 14, p. 332
8. Steffen, Randy, The Horse Soldier 1776-1943, Vol. 2., Norman: University of Oklahoma Press, 1977, p. 113
9. United States Statutes at Large, Vol. 20, p. 219
10. Official Army Register, 1885, p. 377
11. Official Army Register, 1889, p. 377
12. United States Statutes at Large, Vol. 26, p. 654
13. United States Statutes at Large, Vol. 30, p. 365
14. United States Statutes at Large, Vol. 30, p. 977
15. Emerson, William K., Chevrons, Washington: Smithsonian Institution Press, 1983, p. 96.
16. ibid. p. 159
17. ibid. p. 153
18. http://www.qmfound.com/chevrons_dress_engineer_signal_1907.jpg, September 2010
19. Steffen, Randy, The Horse Soldier 1776-1943, Vol. 3., Norman: University of Oklahoma Press, 1977, p. 116
21. Emerson, William K., Chevrons, Washington: Smithsonian Institution Press, 1983, p. 156.
22. Specifications for the uniform of the united states army,GPO, 1913, p. 30
23. United States Statutes at Large, Vol. 32, p. 930
24. Emerson, William K., Chevrons, Washington: Smithsonian Institution Press, 1983, p. 157.
25. United States Statutes at Large, Vol. 37, p. 591

26. Emerson, William K., Chevrons, Washington: Smithsonian Institution Press, 1983, p. 152.
27. United States Statutes at Large, Vol. 39, p. 166
28. Emerson, William K., Chevrons, Washington: Smithsonian Institution Press, 1983, p. 175-176.
29. ibid.
30. ibid. p. 177
31. ibid. p. 252
32. ibid. p. 193
33. United States Statutes at Large, Vol. 63, p. 802
34. Fisher, Ernest, Guardians of the Republic, New York: Ballentine, 1994, p. 287
35. Emerson, William K., Chevrons, Washington: Smithsonian Institution Press, 1983, p. 197-198.
36. ibid. p. 198
37. AR-670-1, February 2005, p 198

Private of the Hospital Corps.
1. United States Statutes at Large, Vol. 24, p. 435
2. Emerson, William K., Chevrons, Washington: Smithsonian Institution Press, 1983, p. 92.
3. ibid. p. 157
4. United States Statutes at Large, Vol. 32, p. 930

Private Second Class
1. United States Statutes at Large, Vol. 9, p. 12
2. United States Statutes at Large, Vol. 39, p. 166
3. United States Statutes at Large, Vol. 12, p. 318
4. United States Statutes at Large, Vol. 12, p. 743
5. United States Statutes at Large, Vol. 12, p. 508
6. Official Army Register, January 1, 1920, p. 1108
7. United States Statutes at Large, Vol. 12, p. 753
8. Steffen, Randy, The Horse Soldier 1776-1943, Vol. 2., Norman: University of Oklahoma Press, 1977, p. 113
9. United States Statutes at Large, Vol. 20, p. 219
10. Official Army Register, 1885, p. 377
11. Official Army Register, 1889, p. 377
12. United States Statutes at Large, Vol. 26, p. 654
13. United States Statutes at Large, Vol. 30, p. 365
14. United States Statutes at Large, Vol. 30, p. 977
15. United States Statutes at Large, Vol. 32, p. 507

Purveyor
1. United States Statutes at Large, Vol. 1, p. 721

Quarter Gunner
1. United States Statutes at Large, Vol. 3, p. 47
2. United States Statutes at Large, Vol. 3, p. 219
3. http://www.military-historians.org/company/plates/images/US.htm#z, June 2010

Quartermaster (General)
1. United States Statutes at Large, Vol. 1, p. 222
2. FRANCIS B. HEITMAN.,HISTORICAL REGISTER AND DICTIONARY OF THE UNITED STATES ARMY, Vol. 1, Washington: GPO, 1903, p. 533
3. Senate Executive Journal, Volume 1, p. 120
4. United States Statutes at Large, Vol. 1, p. 430
5. FRANCIS B. HEITMAN.,HISTORICAL REGISTER AND DICTIONARY OF THE UNITED STATES ARMY, Vol. 1, Washington: GPO, 1903, p. 757
6. United States Statutes at Large, Vol. 1, p. 483
7. FRANCIS B. HEITMAN.,HISTORICAL REGISTER AND DICTIONARY OF THE UNITED STATES ARMY, Vol. 1, Washington: GPO, 1903, p. 1036
8. United States Statutes at Large, Vol. 1, p. 558
9. United States Statutes at Large, Vol. 1, p. 749
10. FRANCIS B. HEITMAN.,HISTORICAL REGISTER AND DICTIONARY OF THE UNITED STATES ARMY, Vol. 1, Washington: GPO, 1903, p. 1036
11. United States Statutes at Large, Vol. 2, p. 132
12. FRANCIS B. HEITMAN.,HISTORICAL REGISTER AND DICTIONARY OF THE UNITED STATES ARMY, Vol. 1, Washington: GPO, 1903, p. 1036

Quartermaster Sergeant (Regimental)
1. Journal of the Continental Congress, volume 5, p. 563
2. United States Statutes at Large, Vol. 1, p. 242
3. United States Statutes at Large, Vol. 2, p. 133
4. United States Statutes at Large, Vol. 2, p. 482
5. Emerson, William K., Chevrons, Washington: Smithsonian Institution Press, 1983, p. 41.
5a. Ibid p. 42.
6. Emerson, William K., Encyclopedia of United States Army Insignia and Uniforms, Norman: University of Oklahoma Press, 1996, p. 438
7. http://www.history.army.mil/reference/1839U.htm, July 2010
8. Emerson, William K., Encyclopedia of United States Army Insignia and Uniforms, Norman: University of Oklahoma Press, 1996, p. 438
9. Steffen, Randy, The Horse Soldier 1776-1943, Vol. 1., Norman: University of Oklahoma Press, 1977, p. 91.
10. Emerson, William K., Chevrons, Washington: Smithsonian Institution Press, 1983, p. 44.
11. Emerson, William K., Chevrons, Washington: Smithsonian Institution Press, 1983, p. 165.
12. United States Statutes at Large, Vol. 39, p. 166

Quartermaster Sergeant (Quartermaster Corps)
1. United States Statutes at Large, Vol. 37, p. 592
2. Emerson, William K., Chevrons, Washington: Smithsonian Institution Press, 1983, p. 151.
3. ibid.
4. ibid. p. 152
5. ibid. p. 182
6. ibid. p. 252

Quartermaster Sergeant Senior Grade
1. United States Statutes at Large, Vol. 39, p. 170
2. Emerson, William K., Chevrons, Washington: Smithsonian Institution Press, 1983, p. 152.
3. ibid p. 180
4. ibid p. 182
5. ibid. p. 251

Radio Sergeant
1. United States Statutes at Large, Vol. 39, p. 180
2. Emerson, William K., Chevrons, Washington: Smithsonian Institution Press, 1983, p. 159.
3. ibid. p. 167.
4. ibid
5. ibid. p 251

Regimental Supply Sergeant
1. United States Statutes at Large, Vol. 39, p. 166
2. Emerson, William K., Chevrons, Washington: Smithsonian Institution Press, 1983, p. 165.
3. ibid p. 251

Riding Master

1. Journal of the Continental Congress, volume 7, p. 178
2. Journal of the Continental Congress, volume 11, p. 540
3. United States Statutes at Large, Vol. 2, p. 482
4. United States Statutes at Large, Vol. 2, p. 764

Saddler
1. Journal of the Continental Congress, volume 7, p. 178
2. Peterson, Harold L. , The Book of the Continental Soldier, Harrisburg: Stackpole, 1968., p. 244
3. United States Statutes at Large, Vol. 1, p. 241
4. United States Statutes at Large, Vol. 2, p. 132
5. United States Statutes at Large, Vol. 2, p. 482
6. United States Statutes at Large, Vol. 3, p. 224
7. United States Statutes at Large, Vol. 12, p. 280
8. Emerson, William K., Chevrons, Washington: Smithsonian Institution Press, 1983, p. 105.
9. ibid. p. 174.
10. United States Statutes at Large, Vol. 36, p. 166
11. Emerson, William K., Chevrons, Washington: Smithsonian Institution Press, 1983, p. 253.

Saddler Sergeant
1. United States Statutes at Large, Vol. 12, p. 280
2. Emerson, William K., Chevrons, Washington: Smithsonian Institution Press, 1983, p. 99.
3. United States Statutes at Large, Vol. 30, p. 977

Second Lieutenant
1. Oliver, Raymond, Why is a Kernal called a Colonel?, Tuscon: Fireship press, 1983, p. 25
2. http://www.xenograg.com/101/excerpts/origins-of-european-army-ranks, August 2010
3. Journal of the Continental Congress, volume 27, p. 531
4. United States Statutes at Large, Vol. 1, p. 759
5. United States Statutes at Large, Vol. 2, p. 132
6. Peterson, Harold L. , The Book of the Continental Soldier, Harrisburg: Stackpole, 1968, p. 242
7. Steffen, Randy, The Horse Soldier 1776-1943, Vol. 1., Norman: University of Oklahoma Press, 1977, p. 46
8. Emerson, William K., Chevrons, Washington: Smithsonian Institution Press, 1983, p. 40
9. ibid. p. 41
10. ibid. p. 42
11. Steffen, Randy, The Horse Soldier 1776-1943, Vol. 1., Norman: University of Oklahoma Press, 1977, p. 94
12. Lanham Howard G., Straps, Westminster, MD: Johnson Graphics, 1998, p. 13
13. Steffen, Randy, The Horse Soldier 1776-1943, Vol. 2., Norman: University of Oklahoma Press, 1977, p. 10-11
14. ibid. p. 111
15. Steffen, Randy, The Horse Soldier 1776-1943, Vol. 3., Norman: University of Oklahoma Press, 1977, p. 68
16. ibid. p. 95-108
17. ibid. p. 157
18. Steffen, Randy, The Horse Soldier 1776-1943, Vol. 4., Norman: University of Oklahoma Press, 1977, p. 16
19. Emerson, William K., Encyclopedia of United States Army Insignia and Uniforms, Norman: University of Oklahoma Press, 1996, p. 473.
20. Lanham Howard G., Straps, Westminster, MD: Johnson Graphics, 1998, p. 113
21. Steffen, Randy, The Horse Soldier 1776-1943, Vol. 4., Norman: University of Oklahoma Press, 1977, p. 98.
22. United States Statutes at Large, Vol. 63, p. 802
23. Emerson, William K., Encyclopedia of United States Army Insignia and Uniforms, Norman: University of Oklahoma Press, 1996, p. 465
24. AR-670-1, February 2005, p 192

Senior Enlisted Advisor to the Chairman
1. http://en.wikipedia.org/wiki/Senior_Enlisted_Advisor_to_the_Chairman, October 2010
2. United States Statutes at Large, Vol. 119, p. 3325
3. Memorandum for Joint Staff 1235-05.
4. http://en.wikipedia.org/wiki/Senior_Enlisted_Advisor_to_the_Chairman, October 2010
5. ibid.
6. http://www.jcs.mil/biography.aspx?ID=137, October 2011

Senior Musician
1. United States Statutes at Large, Vol. 1, p. 120
2. United States Statutes at Large, Vol. 1, p. 483
3. United States Statutes at Large, Vol. 1, p. 750
4. United States Statutes at Large, Vol. 2, p. 671

Sergeant
1. Oliver, Raymond, Why is a Kernal called a Colonel?, Tuscon: Fireship press, 1983, p. 9.
2. Peterson, Harold L. , The Book of the Continental Soldier, Harrisburg: Stackpole, 1968, p. 242
3. Emerson, William K., Chevrons, Washington: Smithsonian Institution Press, 1983, p. 41
4. ibid. p. 42.
5. Emerson, William K., Encyclopedia of United States Army Insignia and Uniforms, Norman: University of Oklahoma Press, 1996, p. 438.
6. Emerson, William K., Chevrons, Washington: Smithsonian Institution Press, 1983, p. 42.
7. ibid. p. 44.
8. ibid. p. 252
9. Emerson, William K., Chevrons, Washington: Smithsonian Institution Press, 1983, p. 196.
10. United States Statutes at Large, Vol. 63, p. 802
11. Emerson, William K., Chevrons, Washington: Smithsonian Institution Press, 1983, p. 196.
12. AR-670-1, February 2005, p 198

Sergeant Bugler
1. United States Statutes at Large, Vol. 40, p. 893
2. Emerson, William K., Chevrons, Washington: Smithsonian Institution Press, 1983, p. 252
3. ibid. p. 147

Sergeant First Class
1. United States Statutes at Large, Vol. 26, p. 654
2. Emerson, William K., Chevrons, Washington: Smithsonian Institution Press, 1983, p. 94.
3. United States Statutes at Large, Vol. 32, p. 930
4. Emerson, William K., Chevrons, Washington: Smithsonian Institution Press, 1983, p. 156.
5. United States Statutes at Large, Vol. 37, p. 593
6. Emerson, William K., Chevrons, Washington: Smithsonian Institution Press, 1983, p. 151.
7. United States Statutes at Large, Vol. 39, p. 173
8. Emerson, William K., Chevrons, Washington: Smithsonian Institution Press, 1983, p. 158.

9. ibid. p. 154
10. Official Army Register, December 1, 1918, p. 1138-1139
11. Official Army Register, January 1, 1920, p. 1106-1107
12. Emerson, William K., Chevrons, Washington: Smithsonian Institution Press, 1983, p. 177.
13. ibid p. 251.
14. United States Statutes at Large, Vol. 63, p. 802
15. Fisher, Ernest, Guardians of the Republic, New York: Ballentine, 1994, p. 288
16. Emerson, William K., Chevrons, Washington: Smithsonian Institution Press, 1983, p. 195.
17. AR-670-1, February 2005, p 197

Sergeant Major
1. http://www.xenograg.com/101/excerpts/origins-of-european-army-ranks, October 2010
2. http://memory.loc.gov/cgi-bin/query/r?ammem/mgw:@field(DOCID+@lit(gw010376)), October 2010.
3. Journal of the Continental Congress, volume 5, p. 563
4. http://www.nwta.com/couriers/4-96/sergeant.html, October 2010
5. United States Statutes at Large, Vol. 1, p. 242
6. United States Statutes at Large, Vol. 1, p. 483
7. Emerson, William K., Chevrons, Washington: Smithsonian Institution Press, 1983, p. 41.
8. ibid. p. 42.
9. ibid.
10. Emerson, William K., Encyclopedia of United States Army Insignia and Uniforms, Norman: University of Oklahoma Press, 1996, p. 438.
11. Steffen, Randy, The Horse Soldier 1776-1943, Vol. 1., Norman: University of Oklahoma Press, 1977, p. 91.
12. Emerson, William K., Chevrons, Washington: Smithsonian Institution Press, 1983, p. 44.
13. United States Statutes at Large, Vol. 30, p. 978
14. United States Statutes at Large, Vol. 31, p. 748
15. Emerson, William K., Chevrons, Washington: Smithsonian Institution Press, 1983, p. 251.
16. United States Statutes at Large, Vol. 72, p. 123
17. Emerson, William K., Chevrons, Washington: Smithsonian Institution Press, 1983, p. 197.
18. ibid. p. 201.
19. AR-670-1, February 2005, p 196

Sergeant Major, Junior Grade
1. United States Statutes at Large, Vol. 31, p. 748
2. Emerson, William K., Chevrons, Washington: Smithsonian Institution Press, 1983, p. 87.
3. United States Statutes at Large, Vol. 34, p. 861
4. United States Statutes at Large, Vol. 39, p. 180
5. Official Army Register, 1909, p. 582-583
6. ibid. p. 574-575
7. Emerson, William K., Chevrons, Washington: Smithsonian Institution Press, 1983, p. 251.

Sergeant Major of the Army
1. http://www.army.mil/leaders/sma/Former/sma_bio1.html, October 2010
2. Emerson, William K., Chevrons, Washington: Smithsonian Institution Press, 1983, p. 199.
3. p. 201.
4. http://www.army.mil/leaders/sma/Former/, October 2010
5. http://www.tioh.hqda.pentagon.mil/UniformedServices/Insignia_Rank/enlisted_history.aspx, October 2010
6. http://www.army.mil/leaders/sma/Former/, October 2010
7. http://www.tioh.hqda.pentagon.mil/UniformedServices/Insignia_Rank/enlisted_history.aspx, October 2010
8. http://www.army.mil/leaders/sma/Former/, October 2010
9. AR-670-1, February 2005, p 195

Sergeant Major, Senior Grade
1. United States Statutes at Large, Vol. 31, p. 748
2. Emerson, William K., Chevrons, Washington: Smithsonian Institution Press, 1983, p. 87.
3. United States Statutes at Large, Vol. 34, p. 861
4. United States Statutes at Large, Vol. 39, p. 180
5. Official Army Register, 1909, p. 582-583
6. ibid. p. 574-575
7. Emerson, William K., Chevrons, Washington: Smithsonian Institution Press, 1983, p. 251.

Specialist Grades 1920-1942
1. United States Statutes at Large, Vol. 41, p. 761
2. Official Army Register, 1921, p. 1406-1407
3. Emerson, William K., Chevrons, Washington: Smithsonian Institution Press, 1983, p. 252-253.
4. United States Statutes at Large, Vol. 56, p. 363
5. Fisher, Ernest, Guardians of the Republic, New York: Ballentine, 1994, p. 252.

Specialist
1. http://www.tioh.hqda.pentagon.mil/UniformedServices/Insignia_Rank/enlisted_history.aspx, October 2010.
2. http://en.wikipedia.org/wiki/Specialist_(rank), October 2010
3. AR-670-1, February 2005, p 199

Specialist 4
1. http://www.tioh.hqda.pentagon.mil/UniformedServices/Insignia_Rank/enlisted_history.aspx, October 2010.
2. Emerson, William K., Chevrons, Washington: Smithsonian Institution Press, 1983, p. 198
3. ibid p. 200.
4. http://www.tioh.hqda.pentagon.mil/UniformedServices/Insignia_Rank/enlisted_history.aspx, October 2010.

Specialist 5
1. http://www.tioh.hqda.pentagon.mil/UniformedServices/Insignia_Rank/enlisted_history.aspx, October 2010.
2. Emerson, William K., Chevrons, Washington: Smithsonian Institution Press, 1983, p. 198
3. ibid p. 200.
4. http://www.tioh.hqda.pentagon.mil/UniformedServices/Insignia_Rank/enlisted_history.aspx, October 2010.

Specialist 6
1. http://www.tioh.hqda.pentagon.mil/UniformedServices/Insignia_Rank/enlisted_history.aspx, October 2010.
2. Emerson, William K., Chevrons, Washington: Smithsonian Institution Press, 1983, p. 198
3. ibid p. 200.
4. http://www.tioh.hqda.pentagon.mil/UniformedServices/Insignia_Rank/enlisted_history.aspx, October 2010.

Specialist 7
1. http://www.tioh.hqda.pentagon.mil/UniformedServices/Insignia_Rank/enlisted_history.aspx, October 2010.
2. Emerson, William K., Chevrons, Washington: Smithsonian Institution Press, 1983, p. 198
3. ibid p. 200.
4. htt://www.tioh.hqda.pentagon.mil/UniformedServices/Insignia_Rank/enlisted_history.aspx, October 2010.

Specialist 8
1. Emerson, William K., Chevrons, Washington: Smithsonian Institution Press, 1983, p. 198.
2. http://www.tioh.hqda.pentagon.mil/UniformedServices/Insignia_Rank/enlisted_history.aspx, October 2010.
3. Emerson, William K., Chevrons, Washington: Smithsonian Institution Press, 1983, p. 198.

Specialist 9
1. Emerson, William K., Chevrons, Washington: Smithsonian Institution Press, 1983, p. 198.
2. http://www.tioh.hqda.pentagon.mil/UniformedServices/Insignia_Rank/enlisted_history.aspx, October 2010.
3. Emerson, William K., Chevrons, Washington: Smithsonian Institution Press, 1983, p. 198.

Specialist First Class
1. http://www.tioh.hqda.pentagon.mil/UniformedServices/Insignia_Rank/enlisted_history.aspx, September 2010
2. Emerson, William K., Chevrons, Washington: Smithsonian Institution Press, 1983, p. 200

Specialist Second Class
1. http://www.tioh.hqda.pentagon.mil/UniformedServices/Insignia_Rank/enlisted_history.aspx, September 2010
2. Emerson, William K., Chevrons, Washington: Smithsonian Institution Press, 1983, p. 200

Specialist Third Class
1. http://www.tioh.hqda.pentagon.mil/UniformedServices/Insignia_Rank/enlisted_history.aspx, September 2010
2. Emerson, William K., Chevrons, Washington: Smithsonian Institution Press, 1983, p. 200

Squadron Sergeant Major
1. United States Statutes at Large, Vol. 30, p. 977
2. Emerson, William K., Chevrons, Washington: Smithsonian Institution Press, 1983, p. 87.
3. ibid. p. 251

Squadron Supply Sergeant
1. Emerson, William K., Chevrons, Washington: Smithsonian Institution Press, 1983, p. 166.
2. ibid. p. 251.

Stable Sergeant
1. United States Statutes at Large, Vol. 30, p. 978
2. Emerson, William K., Chevrons, Washington: Smithsonian Institution Press, 1983, p. 100.
3. United States Statutes at Large, Vol. 39, p. 166
2. Emerson, William K., Chevrons, Washington: Smithsonian Institution Press, 1983, p. 168.
4. ibid p. 252.

Staff Sergeant
1. Emerson, William K., Chevrons, Washington: Smithsonian Institution Press, 1983, p. 252.
2. ibid. p. 193
3. ibid. p. 194
4. United States Statutes at Large, Vol. 72, p. 123
6. Emerson, William K., Chevrons, Washington: Smithsonian Institution Press, 1983, p. 195.
6. AR-670-1, February 2005, p 199

Staff Sergeant Major
1. Emerson, William K., Chevrons, Washington: Smithsonian Institution Press, 1983, p. 197.
2. ibid.
3. ibid. p. 196

Steward, Mine Planter Service
1. United States Statutes at Large, Vol. 40, p. 882
2. Emerson, William K., Chevrons, Washington: Smithsonian Institution Press, 1983, p. 228
3. ibid. p. 253

Supply Sergeant
1. United States Statutes at Large, Vol. 39, p. 166
2. Emerson, William K., Chevrons, Washington: Smithsonian Institution Press, 1983, p. 167.
3. Specifications for the uniform of the united states army, GPO, 1917p. 36.
4. Emerson, William K., Chevrons, Washington: Smithsonian Institution Press, 1983, p. 167.
5. ibid. p. 252.

Surgeon
1. Journal of the Continental Congress, volume 18, page 878.
2. http://history.amedd.army.mil/booksdocs/rev/gillett1/ch2.html, October 2010
3. Heitman, F.B., Historical Register Officers of the Continental Army during the War of Revolution, Washington: 1893, p. 212
4. Powell, William H., List of Officers of the Army of the United States form 1779 to 1900, New York: L.R. Hamersly & CO, 1900, p. 35
5. Journal of the Continental Congress, volume 27, page 531.
6. FRANCIS B. HEITMAN.,HISTORICAL REGISTER AND DICTIONARY OF THE UNITED STATES ARMY, Vol. 1, Washington: GPO, 1903, p. 160
7. United States Statutes at Large, Vol. 1, p. 222
8. Heitman, F.B., Historical Register Officers of the Continental Army during the War of Revolution, Washington: 1893, p. 401
9. United States Statutes at Large, Vol. 1, p. 241

10.
http://history.amedd.army.mil/booksdocs/rev/gillett1/ch6.html, October 2010
11. FRANCIS B. HEITMAN.,HISTORICAL REGISTER AND DICTIONARY OF THE UNITED STATES ARMY, Vol. 1, Washington: GPO, 1903
12. United States Statutes at Large, Vol. 1, p. 366
13. Senate Executive Journal, Vol. 1, P. 159.
11. FRANCIS B. HEITMAN.,HISTORICAL REGISTER AND DICTIONARY OF THE UNITED STATES ARMY, Vol. 1, Washington: GPO, 1903, p. 139
15. United States Statutes at Large, Vol. 1, p. 483
16. FRANCIS B. HEITMAN.,HISTORICAL REGISTER AND DICTIONARY OF THE UNITED STATES ARMY, Vol. 1, Washington: GPO, 1903
17. United States Statutes at Large, Vol. 1, p. 552
18. Senate Executive Journal, Vol. 1, P. 277.
19. FRANCIS B. HEITMAN.,HISTORICAL REGISTER AND DICTIONARY OF THE UNITED STATES ARMY, Vol. 1, Washington: GPO, 1903
20. Senate Executive Journal, Vol. 2, P. 133.
21. FRANCIS B. HEITMAN.,HISTORICAL REGISTER AND DICTIONARY OF THE UNITED STATES ARMY, Vol. 1, Washington: GPO, 1903
22. United States Statutes at Large, Vol. 2, p. 481
23. FRANCIS B. HEITMAN.,HISTORICAL REGISTER AND DICTIONARY OF THE UNITED STATES ARMY, Vol. 1, Washington: GPO, 1903
24. Emerson, William K., Encyclopedia of United States Army Insignia and Uniforms, Norman: University of Oklahoma Press, 1996, p. 306
25. United States Statutes at Large, Vol. 3, p. 224
26. United States Statutes at Large, Vol. 3, p. 113
27. WILLIAM A. GORDON.,A COMPILATION OF REGISTERS OF THE ARMY OF THE UNTIED STATES, Washington: James C. Dunn, 1837, p. 57-58
28. FRANCIS B. HEITMAN.,HISTORICAL REGISTER AND DICTIONARY OF THE UNITED STATES ARMY, Vol. 1, Washington: GPO, 1903
29. ibid p. 388
30. WILLIAM A. GORDON.,A COMPILATION OF REGISTERS OF THE ARMY OF THE UNTIED STATES, Washington: James C. Dunn, 1837. p. 187
31. FRANCIS B. HEITMAN.,HISTORICAL REGISTER AND DICTIONARY OF THE UNITED STATES ARMY, Vol. 1, Washington: GPO, 1903
32. ibid. p. 741
33. ibid. p. 955
34. ibid. p. 1033
35. ibid. p. 702
36. ibid. p. 443
37. WILLIAM A. GORDON.,A COMPILATION OF REGISTERS OF THE ARMY OF THE UNTIED STATES, Washington: James C. Dunn, 1837. p. 146
38. ibid. p. 160
39. ibid. p. 176
40. ibid. p. 194
41. United States Statutes at Large, Vol. 3, p. 616
42. WILLIAM A. GORDON.,A COMPILATION OF REGISTERS OF THE ARMY OF THE UNTIED STATES, Washington: James C. Dunn, 1837. p. 200
43. FRANCIS B. HEITMAN.,HISTORICAL REGISTER AND DICTIONARY OF THE UNITED STATES ARMY, Vol. 1, Washington: GPO, 1903, p. 683
44. ibid. p. 809
45. ibid. p. 853
46. Emerson, William K., Encyclopedia of United States Army Insignia and Uniforms, Norman: University of Oklahoma Press, 1996, p. 177
47. United States Statutes at Large, Vol. 4, p. 714
48. Emerson, William K., Encyclopedia of United States Army Insignia and Uniforms, Norman: University of Oklahoma Press, 1996, p. 178
49. United States Statutes at Large, Vol. 9, p. 125
50. FRANCIS B. HEITMAN.,HISTORICAL REGISTER AND DICTIONARY OF THE UNITED STATES ARMY, Vol. 1, Washington: GPO, 1903
51. Steffen, Randy, The Horse Soldier 1776-1943, Vol. 2., Norman: University of Oklahoma Press, 1977, p. 10.
52. Emerson, William K., Encyclopedia of United States Army Insignia and Uniforms, Norman: University of Oklahoma Press, 1996, p. 179
53. United States Statutes at Large, Vol. 19, p. 61
54. Emerson, William K., Encyclopedia of United States Army Insignia and Uniforms, Norman: University of Oklahoma Press, 1996, p. 179
55. United States Statutes at Large, Vol. 27, p. 276
56. Emerson, William K., Encyclopedia of United States Army Insignia and Uniforms, Norman: University of Oklahoma Press, 1996, p. 179
57. Steffen, Randy, The Horse Soldier 1776-1943, Vol. 3., Norman: University of Oklahoma Press, 1977, p. 68.
58. ibid p. 95.
59. United States Statutes at Large, Vol. 35, p. 67

Surgeon General
1. United States Statutes at Large, Vol. 3, p. 426
2. FRANCIS B. HEITMAN.,HISTORICAL REGISTER AND DICTIONARY OF THE UNITED STATES ARMY, Vol. 1, Washington: GPO, 1903, p. 644
3. Emerson, William K., Encyclopedia of United States Army Insignia and Uniforms, Norman: University of Oklahoma Press, 1996, p. 306
4. ibid. p. 177
2. FRANCIS B. HEITMAN.,HISTORICAL REGISTER AND DICTIONARY OF THE UNITED STATES ARMY, Vol. 1, Washington: GPO, 1903, p. 644
6. ibid. p. 619
7. Emerson, William K., Encyclopedia of United States Army Insignia and Uniforms, Norman: University of Oklahoma Press, 1996, p. 178
8. FRANCIS B. HEITMAN.,HISTORICAL REGISTER AND DICTIONARY OF THE UNITED STATES ARMY, Vol. 1, Washington: GPO, 1903, p. 619
9. ibid. p. 420
10. United States Statutes at Large, Vol. 12, p. 379
11. FRANCIS B. HEITMAN.,HISTORICAL REGISTER AND DICTIONARY OF THE UNITED STATES ARMY, Vol. 1, Washington: GPO, 1903, p. 496\
12.
http://history.amedd.army.mil/surgeongenerals/W_Hammond.html, October 2010
13. FRANCIS B. HEITMAN.,HISTORICAL REGISTER AND DICTIONARY OF THE UNITED STATES ARMY, Vol. 1, Washington: GPO, 1903, p. 192
14. ibid. p. 335.
15. ibid. p. 735
16. ibid. p. 722
17. ibid. p. 200
18. ibid. p. 937
19. ibid. p. 921
20. Emerson, William K., Encyclopedia of United States Army Insignia and Uniforms, Norman: University of Oklahoma Press, 1996, p. 179
21.
http://www.grandarmyofthefrontier.org/uniforms/usa1898.htm, October 2010
22. FRANCIS B. HEITMAN.,HISTORICAL REGISTER AND DICTIONARY OF THE UNITED STATES ARMY, Vol. 1, Washington: GPO, 1903, p. 921
23. ibid. p. 430
24. ibid p. 760
25. United States Statutes at Large, Vol. 35, p. 67

Surgeon's Mate
1. Journal of the Continental Congress, Vol. 2, p. 210
2. Heitman, F.B., Historical Register Officers of the Continental Army during the War of Revolution, Washington: 1893, p. 130
3. United States Statutes at Large, Vol. 1, p. 483
4. United States Statutes at Large, Vol. 2, p. 133
5. United States Statutes at Large, Vol. 3, p. 615
6. Emerson, William K., Encyclopedia of United States Army Insignia and Uniforms, Norman: University of Oklahoma Press, 1996, p. 306

Teacher of Drawing
1. United States Statutes at Large, Vol. 2, p. 206
2. United States Statutes at Large, Vol. 2, p. 720

Teacher of Music
1. United States Statutes at Large, Vol. 2, p. 133
2. United States Statutes at Large, Vol. 2, p. 206
3. United States Statutes at Large, Vol. 2, p. 482
4. United States Statutes at Large, Vol. 2, p. 720
5. United States Statutes at Large, Vol. 3, p. 615

Teacher of The French Language
1. United States Statutes at Large, Vol. 2, p. 206
2. United States Statutes at Large, Vol. 2, p. 720

Teamster
1. http://en.wikipedia.org/wiki/Teamster, October 2010
2. United States Statutes at Large, Vol. 9, p. 185
3. United States Statutes at Large, Vol. 9, p. 306

Technical Sergeant
1. Emerson, William K., Chevrons, Washington: Smithsonian Institution Press, 1983, p. 251.
2. ibid. p. 193
3. Ibid. p. 194

Technician Grade 3
1. United States Statutes at Large, Vol. 56, p. 363
2. Fisher, Ernest, Guardians of the Republic, New York: Ballentine, 1994, p. 252
3. Ar 600-35, Change 1, p. 6
4.
http://www.tioh.hqda.pentagon.mil/UniformedServices/Insignia_Rank/enlisted_history.aspx, October 2010

Technician Grade 4
1. United States Statutes at Large, Vol. 56, p. 363
2. Fisher, Ernest, Guardians of the Republic, New York: Ballentine, 1994, p. 252
3. Ar 600-35, Change 1, p. 6
4.
http://www.tioh.hqda.pentagon.mil/UniformedServices/Insignia_Rank/enlisted_history.aspx, October 2010

Technician Grade 5
1. United States Statutes at Large, Vol. 56, p. 363
2. Fisher, Ernest, Guardians of the Republic, New York: Ballentine, 1994, p. 252
3. Ar 600-35, Change 1, p. 6
4.
http://www.tioh.hqda.pentagon.mil/UniformedServices/Insignia_Rank/enlisted_history.aspx, October 2010

Third Lieutenant
1. United States Statutes at Large, Vol. 2, p. 791
2. United States Statutes at Large, Vol. 3, p. 47
3. United States Statutes at Large, Vol. 3, p. 74
4. United States Statutes at Large, Vol. 3, p. 203
5. United States Statutes at Large, Vol. 3, p. 224
6. WILLIAM A. GORDON.,A COMPILATION OF REGISTERS OF THE ARMY OF THE UNTIED STATES, Washington: James C. Dunn, 1837. p. 55
7. United States Statutes at Large, Vol. 3, p. 299
8. United States Statutes at Large, Vol. 3, p. 615
9. WILLIAM A. GORDON.,A COMPILATION OF REGISTERS OF THE ARMY OF THE UNTIED STATES, Washington: James C. Dunn, 1837. p. 186
10. FRANCIS B. HEITMAN.,HISTORICAL REGISTER AND DICTIONARY OF THE UNITED STATES ARMY, Vol. 1, Washington: GPO, 1903,
11. United States Statutes at Large, Vol. 4, p. 533
12. United States Statutes at Large, Vol. 4, p. 652

Troop Quartermaster Sergeant
1. United States Statutes at Large, Vol. 30, p. 365
2. Emerson, William K., Chevrons, Washington: Smithsonian Institution Press, 1983, p. 88
3. United States Statutes at Large, Vol. 39, p. 180

Trumpeter
1. Journal of the Continental Congress, Vol. 2, p. 90
2. United States Statutes at Large, Vol. 1, p. 241
3. United States Statutes at Large, Vol. 1, p. 750
4. United States Statutes at Large, Vol. 2, p. 671
5. United States Statutes at Large, Vol. 3, p. 114
6. United States Statutes at Large, Vol. 3, p. 224
7. United States Statutes at Large, Vol. 12, p. 787
8. United States Statutes at Large, Vol. 39, p. 178
9. Steffen, Randy, The Horse Soldier 1776-1943, Vol. 1., Norman: University of Oklahoma Press, 1977, p. 6
10. Steffen, Randy, The Horse Soldier 1776-1943, Vol. 2., Norman: University of Oklahoma Press, 1977, p. 19
11. ibid. p. 109

Veterinary Surgeon
1. United States Statutes at Large, Vol. 12, p. 787
2. Official Army Register, 1872, p. 214a
3. Emerson, William K., Encyclopedia of United States Army Insignia and Uniforms, Norman: University of Oklahoma Press, 1996, p. 185.
4. Steffen, Randy, The Horse Soldier 1776-1943, Vol. 3., Norman: University of Oklahoma Press, 1977, p. 109
5. United States Statutes at Large, Vol. 39, p. 176

Wagoner
1. United States Statutes at Large, Vol. 12, p. 269

2. Emerson, William K., Chevrons, Washington: Smithsonian Institution Press, 1983, p. 253.
3. ibid. p. 174

Warrant Officer
1. United States Statutes at Large, Vol. 40, p. 881
3. Emerson, William K., Encyclopedia of United States Army Insignia and Uniforms, Norman: University of Oklahoma Press, 1996, p. 81.
3. United States Statutes at Large, Vol. 41, p. 761
4. http://www.tioh.hqda.pentagon.mil/UniformedServices/Insignia_Rank/warrant_officers.aspx, October 2010
5. Emerson, William K., Encyclopedia of United States Army Insignia and Uniforms, Norman: University of Oklahoma Press, 1996, p. 391.
5a. Steffen, Randy, The Horse Soldier 1776-1943, Vol. 4., Norman: University of Oklahoma Press, 1977, p. 89 & 91
6. United States Statutes at Large, Vol. 54, p. 1177.
7. United States Statutes at Large, Vol. 55, p. 651.

Warrant Officer 1
1. United States Statutes at Large, Vol. 68, p. 157
2. Foster, Frank c., The Decorations, Medals, Ribbions, Badges and Insignia of the United States Army World War II to Present, Fountain Inn: MOA press, 2001, p. 19
3. Emerson, William K., Encyclopedia of United States Army Insignia and Uniforms, Norman: University of Oklahoma Press, 1996, p. 465
4. http://forum.uniforminsignia.org/viewtopic.php?t=6150&sid=24a746a5563b9933501504205b082425, July 2010
5. AR-670-1, February 2005, p 194

Warrant Officer Junior Grade
1. United States Statutes at Large, Vol. 55, p. 651
2. Emerson, William K., Encyclopedia of United States Army Insignia and Uniforms, Norman: University of Oklahoma Press, 1996, p. 391
3. AR-600-35, Change 1, September 4, 1942, page 6
4. Lanham Howard G., Straps, Westminster, MD: Johnson Graphics, 1998, p. 119
5. Emerson, William K., Encyclopedia of United States Army Insignia and Uniforms, Norman: University of Oklahoma Press, 1996, p. 574
6. United States Statutes at Large, Vol. 63, p. 802
7. http://penfed.org/usawoa/woheritage/Hist_of_Army_WO.htm, July 2010
8. Emerson, William K., Encyclopedia of United States Army Insignia and Uniforms, Norman: University of Oklahoma Press, 1996, p. 391
9. United States Statutes at Large, Vol. 68, p. 157

Part 2. Navy
Chapter 1. Navy Organization

The Continental Navy

1. Journals of the Continental Congress, Vol. 3, p. 293
2. Journals of the Continental Congress, Vol. 28, p. 422

The "Federal Navy"
1. United States Statutes at Large, Vol. 1, p. 350.
2. Senate Executive Journal, vol 1. p. 202
3. United States Statutes at Large, Vol. 1, p. 453.
4. United States Statutes at Large, Vol. 1, p. 523.
5. United States Statutes at Large, Vol. 1, p. 608.

Subdivisions of ranks
1. http://mysite.verizon.net/vzeohzt4/Seaflags/personal/fo.html, February 2011
2. http://www.defense.gov/specials/insignias/officers.html, November 2010
3. http://en.wikipedia.org/wiki/Restricted_Line_Officer, February 2011
4. http://www.navy.mil/navydata/navy_legacy_hr.asp?id=268, February 2011
5. http://www.navy.mil/navydata/navy_legacy_hr.asp?id=260, February 2011

Ratings
1. http://bluejacket.com/usn_ratings.html, February 2011
2. http://www.history.navy.mil/faqs/faq78-3.html, February 2011

Civil or Staff Ranks, Assimilated Ranks and Relative Ranks
1. Journals of the Continental Congress, Vol. 3, p. 384
2. United States Statutes at Large, Vol. 1, p. 350.
3. United States Statutes at Large, Vol. 2, p. 699.
4. United States Statutes at Large, Vol. 4, p. 755.
5. General Regulations for the Navy and Marine Corps of the United States, 1841, p. 2.
6. Tily, James C., The Uniforms of the United States Navy, Cranbury: Thomas Yoseloff, 1964, p. 45-46.
6. United States Statutes at Large, Vol. 5, p. 577.
7. General Order, August 31, 1846.
8. General Order, May 27, 1847.
9. United States Statutes at Large, Vol. 10, p. 587
10. General Order, January 13, 1859.
11. United States Statutes at Large, Vol. 11, p. 407.
12. United States Statutes at Large, Vol. 12, p. 583.
13. Tily, James C., The Uniforms of the United States Navy, Cranbury: Thomas Yoseloff, 1964, p. 51.
14. United States Statutes at Large, Vol. 16, p. 586-587.
15. United States Statutes at Large, Vol. 17, p. 192.
16. General Order No. 263, February 24, 1881.
17. United States Statutes at Large, Vol. 30, p. 1006.
18. Tily, James C., The Uniforms of the United States Navy, Cranbury: Thomas Yoseloff, 1964, p. 163.
19. United States Statutes at Large, Vol. 61, p. 872.

Pay Grades
1. U.S. Navy Regulation Circular, No. 41, January 8, 1885.
2. United States Statutes at Large, Vol. 41, p. 602.
3. United States Statutes at Large, Vol. 41, p. 836.
4. Bureau of Navigation Circular Letter No. 9-21, March 24, 1921.
5. Bureau of Navigation Circular Letter No. 16-21, May 2, 1921.
6. United States Statutes at Large, Vol. 42, p. 630.
7. United States Statutes at Large, Vol. 63, p. 807
8. United States Statutes at Large, Vol. 68, p. 157
9. United States Statutes at Large, Vol. 72, p. 123
10. United States Statutes at Large, Vol. 105, p. 1491
11. NAVADMIN 337/02, October 2, 2002
12. Chapter 2. Navy Rank and Rate Insignia

1. http://www.history.navy.mil/faqs/faq59-3.htm, April 2011.
2. General Order, Navy Department, May 1, 1830.
3. http://www.history.navy.mil/faqs/faq59-26.htm, September 2011.
4. Tily, James C., The Uniforms of the United States Navy, Cranbury: Thomas Yoseloff, 1964, p. 86.
5. ibid. p. 99.
6. http://www.history.navy.mil/faqs/faq59-28.htm, March 2011.
7. Tily, James C., The Uniforms of the United States Navy, Cranbury: Thomas Yoseloff, 1964, p. 111-113.
8. ibid. p. 115.
9. ibid. p. 119.
10. http://www.history.navy.mil/faqs/faq59-8.htm, September, 2011.
11. Tily, James C., The Uniforms of the United States Navy, Cranbury: Thomas Yoseloff, 1964, p. 134-135.
12. ibid. 188-189.
13. Stacy, John A., United States Navy Rating Badges and Marks 1833 to 2008, Mathews N.C.: ASMIC Pubs, 2008, p. 3-5.
14. General Order No. 90, March 11, 1869
15. Navy Regulation Circular, October 3, 1871.
16. Tily, James C., The Uniforms of the United States Navy, Cranbury: Thomas Yoseloff, 1964, p. 200.
17. ibid. p. 201.
18. ibid. p. 202.
19. ibid. p. 204-205.
20. ibid. p. 205.
21. Regulations Governing the Uniform of Officers of the United States Navy, 1883, p. 10.
22. ibid. p. 6.
23. ibid. p. 7.
24. Stacy, John A., United States Navy Rating Badges and Marks 1833 to 2008, Mathews N.C.: ASMIC Pubs, 2008, p. 7 & 9.
25. Tily, James C., The Uniforms of the United States Navy, Cranbury: Thomas Yoseloff, 1964, p. 217-218.
26. Stacy, John A., United States Navy Rating Badges and Marks 1833 to 2008, Mathews N.C.: ASMIC Pubs, 2008, p. 11.
27. ibid, p. 222.
28. uniform regulations governing the insignia and uniforms of commissioned officers, warrant officers, and enlistedmen of the United States Navy, January 21, 1905.
29. Stacy, John A., United States Navy Rating Badges and Marks 1833 to 2008, Mathews N.C.: ASMIC Pubs, 2008, p. 14.
30. Uniform Regulations United States Navy, revised January 25, 1913.
31. Tily, James C., The Uniforms of the United States Navy, Cranbury: Thomas Yoseloff, 1964, p. 234.
32. ibid. p. 238-240.
33. General Order No. 328, October 10, 1917.
34. Tily, James C., The Uniforms of the United States Navy, Cranbury: Thomas Yoseloff, 1964, p. 243.
35. ibid. p. 244.
36. The American hatter, "The Passing of the Cocked Hat", August 1919, p. 92.
37. General Order No. 44, April 25, 1921.
38. Tily, James C., The Uniforms of the United States Navy, Cranbury: Thomas Yoseloff, 1964, p. 245-246.
39. Uniform Regulations United States Navy, September 20, 1922, p. 16.
40. Tily, James C., The Uniforms of the United States Navy, Cranbury: Thomas Yoseloff, 1964, p. 249.
41. ibid.
42. Bureau of Navigation Bulletin ,Number 291, April 26, 1941, p. 28.
43. Tily, James C., The Uniforms of the United States Navy, Cranbury: Thomas Yoseloff, 1964, p. 269.
44. Henry, Mark, The US Navy in Worrld War II, Oxford: Osprey, 2002, p. 50-52.
45. ibid. p. 53.
46. U.S. Navy Uniform Regulations, May 31, 1941, p. 24.
47. Henry, Mark, The US Navy in Worrld War II, Oxford: Osprey, 2002, p. 31-42.
48. Tily, James C., The Uniforms of the United States Navy, Cranbury: Thomas Yoseloff, 1964, p. 260.
49. ibid p. 264.
50. All Hands, "WAVES Get Slacks, White Uniforms", March 1943, p. 20.
51. All Hands, "Navy's New Slate-Gray Uniform...", June 1943, p. 31.
52. All Hands, "Distinguishing Marks and Seaman Stripes Approved...", November 1944, p. 71.
53. All Hands, "Current and Future Changes in Uniform Regs Listed", May 1947, p. 56.
54. Stacy, John A., United States Navy Rating Badges and Marks 1833 to 2008, Mathews N.C.: ASMIC Pubs, 2008, p. 33.
55. Tily, James C., The Uniforms of the United States Navy, Cranbury: Thomas Yoseloff, 1964, p. 270.
56. Stacy, John A., United States Navy Rating Badges and Marks 1833 to 2008, Mathews N.C.: ASMIC Pubs, 2008, p. 31.
57. All Hands, "CPO Collar Devices", November 1959, p. 26.
58. All Hands, "The Word, Changes to Uniform Regulations", August 1960, p. 42.
59. All Hands, "Bulletin Board", June 1969, p. 50.
60. All Hands, "New Officer, CPO Uniforms...", June 1979, p. 2.
61. NAVADMIN 011/99.
62. NAVADMIN 190/08.
63. http://en.wikipedia.org/wiki/Uniforms_of_the_United_States_Navy, September 2011.

Epaulets
1. Oliver, Raymond, Why is a Kernal called a Colonel?, Tuscon: Fireship press, 1983, p. 17.
2. http://www.history.navy.mil/faqs/faq59-3.htm, April 2011.
3. http://www.history.navy.mil/faqs/faq59-25.htm, April 2011.
4. http://www.history.navy.mil/faqs/faq59-4.htm, April 2011.
5. General Order, Navy Department, May 10, 1820.
6. General Order, Navy Department, May 1, 1830.
7. http://www.history.navy.mil/faqs/faq59-27.htm, March 2011.
8. Tily, James C., The Uniforms of the United States Navy, Cranbury: Thomas Yoseloff, 1964, p. 97.
9. ibid. p. 99.
10. http://www.history.navy.mil/faqs/faq59-28.htm, March 2011.
11. Tily, James C., The Uniforms of the United States Navy, Cranbury: Thomas Yoseloff, 1964, p. 110.

12. ibid. p. 113.
13. ibid.p. 119.
14. http://www.history.navy.mil/faqs/faq59-8.htm, September, 2011.
15. http://www.history.navy.mil/library/online/uniform_insignia.htm, March 2011.
16. General Order No. 90, March 11, 1869.
17. Navy Department Circular, October 3, 1871.
18. Regulations for the Goverment of the Navy of the United States, August 7, 1876, p. 193.
19. Regulations Governing the Uniform of Officers of the United States Navy, 1883, p. 10.
20. ibid.
21. Tily, James C., The Uniforms of the United States Navy, Cranbury: Thomas Yoseloff, 1964, p. 222.
22. Uniform Regulations United States Navy, revised January 25, 1913, p. 42-43.
23. Tily, James C., The Uniforms of the United States Navy, Cranbury: Thomas Yoseloff, 1964, p. 238.
24. The American hatter, "The Passing of the Cocked Hat", August 1919, p. 92.
25. General Order No. 44, April 25, 1921.
26. Uniform Regulations United States Navy, September 20, 1922, p. 10-11.
27. Tily, James C., The Uniforms of the United States Navy, Cranbury: Thomas Yoseloff, 1964, p. 269.

Shoulder Straps
1. General Order, Navy Department, May 1, 1830.
2. http://www.history.navy.mil/faqs/faq59-27.htm, March 2011.
3. Tily, James C., The Uniforms of the United States Navy, Cranbury: Thomas Yoseloff, 1964, p. 97.
4. ibid. p. 99-100. (Captain Tily states that the acorns and bars were silver, but the 1852 uniform regulations call for gold).
5. http://www.history.navy.mil/faqs/faq59-28.htm, March 2011.
6. Tily, James C., The Uniforms of the United States Navy, Cranbury: Thomas Yoseloff, 1964, p. 110.
7. ibid. p. 113 (Captain Tily uses an illustration added the a copy of the 1852 regulations as a reference and admits there is no text to support it).
8. ibid. p. 119.
9. http://www.history.navy.mil/faqs/faq59-8.htm, September, 2011.
10. U.S. Navy Regulation Circular, January 14, 1865.
11. http://www.history.navy.mil/library/online/uniform_insignia.htm, March 2011.
12. ibid.
13. General Order No. 90, March 11, 1869.
14. Navy Department Circular, October 3, 1871.
15. Tily, James C., The Uniforms of the United States Navy, Cranbury: Thomas Yoseloff, 1964, p. 205.
16. Regulations for the Goverment of the Navy of the United States, August 7, 1876, p. 193.
17. Regulations Governing the Uniform of Officers of the United States Navy, 1883, p. 10.
18. Tily, James C., The Uniforms of the United States Navy, Cranbury: Thomas Yoseloff, 1964, p. 205.
19. Regulations Governing the Uniform of Officers of the United States Navy, 1883, p. 10.
20. Tily, James C., The Uniforms of the United States Navy, Cranbury: Thomas Yoseloff, 1964, p. 222.
21. ibid. p. 224.
10. uniform regulations governing the insignia and uniforms of commissioned officers, warrant officers, and enlistedmen of the United States Navy, January 21, 1905, p 31- 32.

Shoulder Knots
1. General Order No. 90, March 11, 1869.
2. Regulations for the Goverment of the Navy of the United States, August 7, 1876, p. 193.
3. http://www.usmilitariaforum.com/forums/lofiversion/index.php/t95381.html, September 2011.
4. Tily, James C., The Uniforms of the United States Navy, Cranbury: Thomas Yoseloff, 1964, p. 198.
5. Navy Department Circular, October 3, 1871.
11. Regulations Governing the Uniform of Officers of the United States Navy, 1883, p. 10.

Shoulder Boards
1. Tily, James C., The Uniforms of the United States Navy, Cranbury: Thomas Yoseloff, 1964, p. 222.
2. uniform regulations governing the insignia and uniforms of commissioned officers, warrant officers, and enlistedmen of the United States Navy, January 21, 1905, p. 31.
3. ibid, plate XIV.
4. Tily, James C., The Uniforms of the United States Navy, Cranbury: Thomas Yoseloff, 1964, p. 224.
5. http://www.history.navy.mil/library/online/uniform_insignia.htm, March 2011.
6. Uniform Regulations United States Navy, revised January 25, 1913, p. 36-39.
7. Tily, James C., The Uniforms of the United States Navy, Cranbury: Thomas Yoseloff, 1964, p. 234.
8. Uniform Regulations United States Navy, revised January 15, 1917, p. 29 & 42.
9. Tily, James C., The Uniforms of the United States Navy, Cranbury: Thomas Yoseloff, 1964, p. 239-241.
10. ibid. p. 243.
11. ibid. p. 243-244.
12. http://www.history.navy.mil/library/online/uniform_insignia.htm, March 2011, the fact that the stripes were unbroken courtesy of Justin Broderick.
21. Uniform Regulations United States Navy, September 20, 1922, p. 17-18.
22. Bureau of Navigation Bulletin ,Number 291, April 26, 1941, p. 28.
23. Tily, James C., The Uniforms of the United States Navy, Cranbury: Thomas Yoseloff, 1956, p. 260.
24. All Hands, "Navy's New Slate-Gray Uniform...", June 1943, p. 31.
25. http://www.usmilitariaforum.com/forums/lofiversion/index.php/t33036.html, September 2011.
26. Tily, James C., The Uniforms of the United States Navy, Cranbury: Thomas Yoseloff, 1964, p. 259.
27. All Hands, "Option of Shoulder Marks, Buttons Revoked OnGray Uniforms", Aprl 1944, p. 65.
28. All Hands, ""NNC" Eliminated from Insignia of Navy Nurse Corps", August 1944, p. 71.
29. All Hands, "Insignia Approved for Fleet Admiral", February 1945, p. 73.
30. All Hands, "Gold Shoulder Marks, Gilt Buttons May Now Be Worn With Grays", April 1946, p. 69.
31. Tily, James C., The Uniforms of the United States Navy, Cranbury: Thomas Yoseloff, 1964, p. 259.
32. ibid. p. 270.
33. U.S. Navy Uniform Regulations, June 5, 1947, p. 3-10, collar insignia is prescribed on tropical white shirt collars.
34. All Hands, "Report on Taiwan Tour for the Navyman Taking His Family", July 1956, p. 55. "shoulder marks" are listed as part of the tropical uniform.
35. All Hands, "New Insignia and Markings go into effect on 1 November For Four Warrant Ranks", October 1954, p. 45.
36. NAVPERS 15665F, July 18, 1985, p. 9-13.
37. United States Navy Uniform Regulations, April 2010, Para. 4103 2d.

Shoulder Marks
1. United States Navy Uniform Regulations, July 2011, para. 4103.
2. All Hands, "New Officer, CPO Uniforms...", June 1979, p. 2.
3. All Hands, "New Uniforms for Women Okayed", August 1979, p. 3.
4. NAVPERS 15665F, July 18, 1985, p. 9-13.
5. NAVADMIN 011/99, June 30, 1999.

Badges of Rank
1. http://www.history.navy.mil/faqs/faq59-25.htm, April 2011.
2. General Order, Navy Department, May 10, 1820.
3. General Order, Navy Department, May 1, 1830.
4. http://www.history.navy.mil/faqs/faq59-27.htm, March 2011.
5. Tily, James C., The Uniforms of the United States Navy, Cranbury: Thomas Yoseloff, 1964, p. 97.
6. ibid. p. 100.
7. ibid. p. 99.
8. http://www.history.navy.mil/faqs/faq59-28.htm, March 2011.
9. Tily, James C., The Uniforms of the United States Navy, Cranbury: Thomas Yoseloff, 1964, p. 113. (Captain Tily uses an illustration added the a copy of the 1852 regulations as a reference and admits there is no text to support it).
10. ibid.p. 117.
11. http://www.history.navy.mil/faqs/faq59-8.htm, September, 2011.
12. Navy Department Circular, January 15, 1865.
13. Tily, James C., The Uniforms of the United States Navy, Cranbury: Thomas Yoseloff, 1964, p. 134.
14. ibid. p .189.
15. General Order No. 90, March 11, 1869.
16. Regulations for the Goverment of the Navy of the United States, August 7, 1876, p. 191.
17. http://www.usmilitariaforum.com/forums/lofiversion/index.php/t95381.html, September 2011.
18. Tily, James C., The Uniforms of the United States Navy, Cranbury: Thomas Yoseloff, 1964, p. 198.
19. ibid. p. 204-205.
20. Regulations for the Goverment of the Navy of the United States, August 7, 1876, p. 191.
21. Regulations Governing the Uniform of Officers of the United States Navy, 1883, p. 10.
22. ibid. p. 10-11.
23. http://www.history.navy.mil/library/online/uniform_insignia.htm, March 2011
24. Tily, James C., The Uniforms of the United States Navy, Cranbury: Thomas Yoseloff, 1964, p. 222-233.
25. http://www.history.navy.mil/library/online/uniform_insignia.htm, March 2011.
26. Uniform Regulations United States Navy, revised January 25, 1913, p. 45.
27. ibid. plate 14.
28. Tily, James C., The Uniforms of the United States Navy, Cranbury: Thomas Yoseloff, 1964, p. 234.
29. ibid. p. 238.
30. ibid. p. 244.
31. General Order No. 44, April 25, 1921.
32. Uniform Regulations United States Navy, September 20, 1922, p. 10-11.
33. Tily, James C., The Uniforms of the United States Navy, Cranbury: Thomas Yoseloff, 1964, p. 249.
34. U.S. Navy Uniform Regulations, May 31, 1941, p. 37-38.
35. ibid. p. 14.
36. http://www.history.navy.mil/library/online/uniform_insignia.htm, March 2011.
37. All Hands, "Warrant Officers' Collar Devices", October 1952, p. 24.
38. All Hands, "New Insignia and Markings go into effect on 1 November For Four Warrant Ranks", October 1954, p. 45.
39. All Hands, "CPO Collar Devices", November 1959, p. 26.
40. All Hands, "Top Chiefs Will Now Wear Stars on Their Collars", January 1961, p. 54.
41. All Hands, "Bulletin Board", June 1969, p. 50.
42. U.S. Navy Uniform Regulations, 1975 p. 5-48.
43. United States Navy Uniform Regulations, April 2010, Para. 4227.b

Cuff Stripes (and buttons)
1. http://bluejacket.com/sea-service_uniform_a.htm, April 2011.
2. http://www.history.navy.mil/faqs/faq59-3.htm, April 2011
3. http://www.history.navy.mil/faqs/faq59-25.htm, April 2011.
4. http://www.history.navy.mil/faqs/faq59-4.htm, April 2011.
5. General Order, Navy Department, May 10, 1820.
6. General Order, Navy Department, May 1, 1830.
7. Tily, James C., The Uniforms of the United States Navy, Cranbury: Thomas Yoseloff, 1964, p. 83 & 86.
8. http://www.history.navy.mil/faqs/faq59-27.htm, March 2011.
9. Tily, James C., The Uniforms of the United States Navy, Cranbury: Thomas Yoseloff, 1964, p. 100.
10. http://www.history.navy.mil/faqs/faq59-28.htm, March 2011.
11. Tily, James C., The Uniforms of the United States Navy, Cranbury: Thomas Yoseloff, 1964, p. 111.
12. ibid. p. 113.
13. ibid p. 114.
14. ibid. p. 117-118.
15. ibid. p. 121-126 (Captain Tily admits he couldn't find a copy of the order but includes multiple secondary sources to prove the date.)

16. http://www.history.navy.mil/faqs/faq59-8.htm, September, 2011.
17. Tily, James C., The Uniforms of the United States Navy, Cranbury: Thomas Yoseloff, 1964, p. 131.
18. ibid.
19. ibid. p. 189.
20. Stacy, John A., United States Navy Rating Badges and Marks 1833 to 2008, Mathews N.C.: ASMIC Pubs, 2008, p. 5.
21. General Order No. 90, March 11, 1869.
22. General Order No. 126, May 27, 1869.
23. Stacy, John A., United States Navy Rating Badges and Marks 1833 to 2008, Mathews N.C.: ASMIC Pubs, 2008, p. 6.
24. Regulations for the Goverment of the Navy of the United States, August 7, 1876, p. 197.
25. Tily, James C., The Uniforms of the United States Navy, Cranbury: Thomas Yoseloff, 1964, p. 222.
26. ibid. p. 201.
27. ibid.
28. ibid. p. 202-203.
29. ibid.p. 204.
30. Regulations Governing the Uniform of Officers of the United States Navy, 1883, p. 7.
31. Tily, James C., The Uniforms of the United States Navy, Cranbury: Thomas Yoseloff, 1964, p. 205.
32. Regulations Governing the Uniform of Officers of the United States Navy, 1883, p. 8.
33. ibid.p. 6.
34. regulations governing the uniform of commissioned officers, warrant officers, and enlisted men of the United States Navy, 1886, p. 25.
35. Tily, James C., The Uniforms of the United States Navy, Cranbury: Thomas Yoseloff, 1964, p. 217.
36. http://grandarmyofthefrontier.org/uniforms/usn1897.htm, June 2011.
37. Tily, James C., The Uniforms of the United States Navy, Cranbury: Thomas Yoseloff, 1964, p. 221.
38. ibid.p. 222.
39. uniform regulations governing the insignia and uniforms of commissioned officers, warrant officers, and enlistedmen of the United States Navy, January 21, 1905, p. 42.
40. Uniform Regulations United States Navy, revised January 25, 1913, p. 32.
41. Tily, James C., The Uniforms of the United States Navy, Cranbury: Thomas Yoseloff, 1964, p. 241.
42. ibid. p. 243.
43. http://www.history.navy.mil/library/online/uniform_insignia.htm, March 2011. the fact that the stripes were unbroken courtesy of Justin Broderick.
44. Uniform Regulations United States Navy, September 20, 1922, p. 16.
45. Tily, James C., The Uniforms of the United States Navy, Cranbury: Thomas Yoseloff, 1964, p. 249.
46. https://picasaweb.google.com/Booker1942/1943TheNavalOfficersUniformPlan#5537445144858829890, March 2011.
47 Bureau of Navigation Bulletin No. 291, April 26, 1941, p. 28.
48. Tily, James C., The Uniforms of the United States Navy, Cranbury: Thomas Yoseloff, 1964, p. 260.
49. ibid.
50. All Hands, "WAVES Get Slacks, White Uniforms", March 1943, p. 20.
51. All Hands, "Women Staff Officers to Wear Corps Devices", September 1943, p. 77.
52. All Hands, "Green Unifroms Mandatory...", June 1944, p. 71.
53. All Hands, ""NNC" Eliminated from Insignia of Navy Nurse Corps", August 1944, p. 71.
54. All Hands, "W-V(s) Officers to Wear Stars on Their Uniforms", October 1944, p. 68.
55. All Hands, "Insignia Approved for Fleet Admiral", February 1945, p. 73.
56. All Hands, "Current and Future Changes in Uniform Regs Listed", May 1947, p. 56.
57. Stacy, John A., United States Navy Rating Badges and Marks 1833 to 2008, Mathews N.C.: ASMIC Pubs, 2008, p. 33.
58. Tily, James C., The Uniforms of the United States Navy, Cranbury: Thomas Yoseloff, 1964, p. 270.
59, All Hands, "Women Officers Will Wear Gold Stripes and Insignia", June 1950, p. 43.
60. All Hands, "New Insignia and Markings go into effect on 1 November For Four Warrant Ranks", October 1954, p. 45.
61. All Hands, "The Word, Changes to Uniform Regulations", August 1960, p. 42.
62. United States Navy Uniform Regulations, April 2010, Para. 4101 2b.
63. http://en.wikipedia.org/wiki/Uniforms_of_the_United_States_Navy, September 2011.

Petty Officer's Device
1. http://www.history.navy.mil/faqs/faq59-26.htm, September 2011.
2. http://www.history.navy.mil/faqs/faq59-27.htm, March 2011.
3. http://www.history.navy.mil/faqs/faq59-28.htm, March 2011.
4. http://www.history.navy.mil/faqs/faq59-8.htm, September 2011.
5. http://www.history.navy.mil/faqs/faq78-3.htm, October 2011.
6. Stacy, John A., United States Navy Rating Badges and Marks 1833 to 2008, Mathews N.C.: ASMIC Pubs, 2008, p. 3.
7. ibid. p. 7.

Rating Badges
1. regulations governing the uniform of commissioned officers, warrant officers, and enlisted men of the United States Navy, 1886, p. 24.
2. U.S. Navy Regulation Circular, No. 41, January 8, 1885.
3. regulations governing the uniform of commissioned officers, warrant officers, and enlisted men of the United States Navy, 1886, p. 23-24 & plates xvi, xiv 7 xvii.
4. opinion of Justin Broderick.
5. Stacy, John A., United States Navy Rating Badges and Marks 1833 to 2008, Mathews N.C.: ASMIC Pubs, 2008, p. 9.
6. ibid. p. 9-11.
7. Uniform Regulations United States Navy, revised January 25, 1913, p. 63-64.
8. Stacy, John A., United States Navy Rating Badges and Marks 1833 to 2008, Mathews N.C.: ASMIC Pubs, 2008, p. 18.
9. ibid. p. 19.
10. U.S. Navy Uniform Regulations, May 31, 1941, plate 35.
11. https://picasaweb.google.com/Booker1942/1943TheNavalOfficersUniformPlan#5537445372679463554, April 2011
12. https://picasaweb.google.com/Booker1942/1943TheNavalOfficersUniformPlan#5537445660794743042, April 2011
13. Stacy, John A., United States Navy Ratring Badges and Marks 1833 to 2008, Mathews N.C.: ASMIC Pubs, 2008, p. 27.
14. ibid. p. 21.
15. ibid. p. 30.
16. ibid. p. 31.
17. All Hands, "Rating Badges on Khaki Shirts", October 1950, p. 30.
18. All Hands, October 1951, cover.
19. All Hands, "CPO Rating Badge", July 1952, p. 9.
20. Stacy, John A., United States Navy Rating Badges and Marks 1833 to 2008, Mathews N.C.: ASMIC Pubs, 2008, p. 31.
21. All Hands, "The Word: Insignia for E-8, E-9", August 1958, p. 46.
22. http://www.quarterdeck.org/WindsOfChange/012-29%20MCPON%20Black.htm, May 2011.
23. All Hands, "From the desk of the Master Chief Petty Officer of the Navy: MCPOC", July 1971, p. 56.
24. All Hands, "One Uniform For All", June 1971, p. 4.
25. Stacy, John A., United States Navy Ratring Badges and Marks 1833 to 2008, Mathews N.C.: ASMIC Pubs, 2008, p. 38.
26. Stacy, John A., United States Navy Rating Badges and Marks 1833 to 2008, Mathews N.C.: ASMIC Pubs, 2008, p. 38.
40. NAVADMIN 020/10, January 10, 2010.

Group Rate Marks
1. All Hands, "Distinguishing Marks" and Seaman Stripes Approved For Non-Rated Waves", November 1944, p. 71.
2. All Hands, "Designs, Wearing of Insignia", March 1948, p. 31.
3. All Hands, "Changes Made in Rating Structure,...", August 1948, p. 53.
4. Stacy, John A., United States Navy Ratring Badges and Marks 1833 to 2008, Mathews N.C.: ASMIC Pubs, 2008, p. 40.

Watch Marks and Branch Marks
1. Stacy, John A., United States Navy Rating Badges and Marks 1833 to 2008, Mathews N.C.: ASMIC Pubs, 2008, p. 5.
2. regulations governing the uniform of commissioned officers, warrant officers, and enlisted men of the United States Navy, 1886, p. 25.
3. uniform regulations governing the insignia and uniforms of commissioned officers, warrant officers, and enlistedmen of the United States Navy, January 21, 1905, p. 50.
4. Stacy, John A., United States Navy Rating Badges and Marks 1833 to 2008, Mathews N.C.: ASMIC Pubs, 2008, p. 14.
5. All Hands, "Designs, Wearing of Insignia", March 1948, p. 31.

Distinguishing Marks
1. Stacy, John A., United States Navy Rating Badges and Marks 1833 to 2008, Mathews N.C.: ASMIC Pubs, 2008, p. 99.
2. ibid.p. 64.
3. Uniform Regulations United States Navy, revised January 25, 1913, p. 64.
4. Stacy, John A., United States Navy Rating Badges and Marks 1833 to 2008, Mathews N.C.: ASMIC Pubs, 2008, p. 99.
5. ibid.p. 59.
6. ibid.p. 57.
7. ibid. p. 33.

Chapter 3. Navy Ranks and Rates

Able Seaman
1. http://en.wikipedia.org/wiki/Able_Seaman_(rank), February 2011
2. http://www.history.navy.mil/faqs/faq78-3.html, February 2011
3. Journals of the Continental Congress, Vol. 3, p. 384
4. United States Statutes at Large, Vol. 1, p. 350.
5. United States Statutes at Large, Vol. 1, p. 523.
6. United States Statutes at Large, Vol. 2, p. 390.
7. United States Statutes at Large, Vol. 2, p. 443.
8. United States Statutes at Large, Vol. 2, p. 514.
9. United States Statutes at Large, Vol. 2, p. 789.
10. United States Statutes at Large, Vol. 3, p. 763.
11. United States Statutes at Large, Vol. 5, p. 699.
12. United States Statutes at Large, Vol. 12, p. 315.
13. Register of the Commissioned and Warrant officers of the Navy of the United States, 1842. p. iv.
14. Register of the Commissioned and Warrant officers of the Navy of the United States, 1854. p. 7.
15. Register of the Commissioned and Warrant officers of the Navy of the United States, 1860. p. 9.

Admiral
1. Mack, William P. and Connell, Royal W., Naval Ceremonies, Customs, and Traditions, 5th edition, Annapolis:Naval Institute Press, 1980, p. 226.
2. United States Statutes at Large, Vol. 14, p. 222.
3. Hamersly,, Thomas H.,'General Navy Register for One Hundred Years, Baltimore:Willam K. Boyle, 1882, p. 244
4. Tily, James C., The Uniforms of the United States Navy, Cranbury: Thomas Yoseloff, 1964, p. 189.
5. ibid .p. 196
6. Hamersly,, Thomas H.,'General Navy Register for One Hundred Years, Baltimore:Willam K. Boyle, 1882, p. 244
7. ibid. p. 575
8. Tily, James C., The Uniforms of the United States Navy, Cranbury: Thomas Yoseloff, 1964, p. 222.
9. United States Statutes at Large, Vol. 17, p. 418.
10. Tily, James C., The Uniforms of the United States Navy, Cranbury: Thomas Yoseloff, 1964, p. 204.
11. Regulations Governing the Uniform of Officers of the United States Navy, 1883, p. 6
12. http://www.history.navy.mil/books/callahan/reg-usn-p.htm, March 2011
13. United States Statutes at Large, Vol. 38, p. 941.
14. United States Statutes at Large, Vol. 39, p. 556.
15. Uniform Regulations United States Navy, revised January 15, 1917, p. 28
16. ibid. p. 36
17. ibid. p. 32

18. ibid. p. 39
19. ibid. p. 42
20. Tily, James C., The Uniforms of the United States Navy, Cranbury: Thomas Yoseloff, 1964, p. 244.
21. Uniform Regulations United States Navy, September 20, 1922, p. 17
22. Tily, James C., The Uniforms of the United States Navy, Cranbury: Thomas Yoseloff, 1964, p. 249.
22a Bureau of Navigation Bulletin No. 291, April 26, 1941, p. 28
23. All Hands, "Current and Future Canges in Uniform Regs Listed", May 1947, p. 56
23a. United States Statutes at Large, Vol. 63, p. 807
23b. United States Statutes at Large, Vol. 72, p. 124
24. United States Navy Uniform Regulations, April 2010, Para. 4101
25. United States Navy Uniform Regulations, April 2010, Para. 4103.2a
26. United States Navy Uniform Regulations, April 2010, Para. 4103.4

Admiral of the Navy
1. United States Statutes at Large, Vol. 30, p. 995.
2. Callahan, Edward, List of Officers of the Navy of the United States and the Marine Corps from 1775 to 1900, New York: L. R. Hamerlsy & CO., 1901, p. 160
3. http://www.history.navy.mil/bios/dewey_george.htm, March 2011
4. Register for the Commissioned and Warrant Officers of the Navy of the United States and of the Marine Corps, January 1, 1900, p. 6
5. Register for the Commissioned and Warrant Officers of the Navy of the United States and of the Marine Corps, January 1, 1902, p.4
6. Register for the Commissioned and Warrant Officers of the Navy of the United States and of the Marine Corps, January 1, 1903, p. 6. A 1904 register has proved unavailable.
7. United States Statutes at Large, Vol. 15, p. 346.
8. United States Statutes at Large, Vol. 39, p. 558.
9. Tily, James C., The Uniforms of the United States Navy, Cranbury: Thomas Yoseloff, 1964, p. 222.
10. uniform regulations governing the insignia and uniforms of commissioned officers, warrant officers, and enlistedmen of the United States Navy, January 21, 1905, p. 24, 31 & 32
11. Uniform Regulations United States Navy, revised January 25, 1913, p. 45
12. Tily, James C., The Uniforms of the United States Navy, Cranbury: Thomas Yoseloff, 1964, p. 234.
13. http://www.history.navy.mil/bios/dewey_george.htm, March 2011

Airman
1. All Hands, "Here's a Complete List of Rating Changes...", March 1948, p. 57
2. United States Statutes at Large, Vol. 63, p. 802
3. Stacy, John A., United States Navy Rating Badges and Marks 1833 to 2008, Mathews N.C.: ASMIC Pubs, 2008, p. 33.
4. United States Navy Uniform Regulations, April 2010, Para. 4227.b

Airman Apprentice
1. All Hands, "Here's a Complete List of Rating Changes...", March 1948, p. 57
2. United States Statutes at Large, Vol. 63, p. 802
3. Stacy, John A., United States Navy Ratring Badges and Marks 1833 to 2008, Mathews N.C.: ASMIC Pubs, 2008, p. 33.
4. United States Navy Uniform Regulations, April 2010, Para. 4227.b

Airman Recruit
1. All Hands, "Changes Made in Rating Structure,...", August 1948, p. 53.
2. United States Statutes at Large, Vol. 63, p. 802
3. All Hands, "Uniform Changes Published...", December 1948, p. 48
4. Stacy, John A., United States Navy Ratring Badges and Marks 1833 to 2008, Mathews N.C.: ASMIC Pubs, 2008, p. 40.

Apprentice (First, Second and Third Class)
1. All Hands, "The Story Behind Your Rating Badge", August 1958, p. 31
2. http://www.history.navy.mil/faqs/faq78-3.html, February 2011
3. ibid.
4. http://www.history.navy.mil/faqs/faq78-1.htm#anchor93132, March 2011
5. Register for the Commissioned and Warrant Officers of the Navy of the United States and of the Marine Corps, January 1, 1886, p. 6
6. Register for the Commissioned and Warrant Officers of the Navy of the United States and of the Marine Corps, January 1, 1890, p. 170
7. Register for the Commissioned and Warrant Officers of the Navy of the United States and of the Marine Corps, January 1, 1899, p. 161
8. regulations governing the uniform of commissioned officers, warrant officers, and enlisted men of the United States Navy, 1886, p. 25
9. http://www.quarterdeck.org/uniforms/1897/21-37%20Enlisted%201897.htm
10. Stacy, John A., United States Navy Ratring Badges and Marks 1833 to 2008, Mathews N.C.: ASMIC Pubs, 2008, p. 105.
11. http://www.history.navy.mil/faqs/faq78-1.htm#anchor93132, March 2011

Apprentice Seaman
1. http://www.history.navy.mil/faqs/faq78-3.html, February 2011
2. uniform regulations governing the insignia and uniforms of commissioned officers, warrant officers, and enlisted men of the United States Navy, January 21, 1905, p. 42.
3. ibid. p. 50
4. Stacy, John A., United States Navy Ratring Badges and Marks 1833 to 2008, Mathews N.C.: ASMIC Pubs, 2008, p. 14.
5. United States Statutes at Large, Vol. 42, p. 630.
6. http://www.history.navy.mil/faqs/faq78-3.html, February 2011

Aerographer
1. United States Statutes at Large, Vol. 56, p. 724.
2. Stacy, John A., United States Navy Ratring Badges and Marks 1833 to 2008, Mathews N.C.: ASMIC Pubs, 2008, p. 53.
3. All Hands, "Ranks and Rates...", May 1943, p. 29-35
4. All Hands, "Green Unifroms Mandatory...", June 1944, p. 71
5. https://picasaweb.google.com/Booker1942/1943TheNavalOfficersUniformPlan#5537445144858829890, March 2011
6. United States Statutes at Large, Vol. 63, p. 807
7. http://www.history.navy.mil/library/online/uniform_insignia.htm, March 2011
8. All Hands, "Warrant Officers' Collar Devices", October 1952, p. 24
9. United States Statutes at Large, Vol. 68, p. 157

Assistant Civil Engineer
1. United States Statutes at Large, Vol. 32, p. 1197
2. uniform regulations governing the insignia and uniforms of commissioned officers, warrant officers, and enlistedmen of the United States Navy, January 21, 1905, p. 22
3. Tily, James C., The Uniforms of the United States Navy, Cranbury: Thomas Yoseloff, 1964, p. 206.
4. ibid p. 225
5. United States Statutes at Large, Vol. 39, p. 577
6. All Hands, "175th Anniversary The Navy Supply Corps", March 1970, p. 41
7. Tily, James C., The Uniforms of the United States Navy, Cranbury: Thomas Yoseloff, 1964, p. 243-244.
8. United States Statutes at Large, Vol. 61, p. 872

Assistant Dental Surgeon
1. United States Statutes at Large, Vol. 37, p. 344
2. Uniform Regulations, United States Navy, January 25, 1913, p. 32
3. ibid . p. 35
4. ibid. p. 44
5. All Hands, "175th Anniversary The Navy Supply Corps", March 1970, p. 41
6. Tily, James C., The Uniforms of the United States Navy, Cranbury: Thomas Yoseloff, 1964, p. 243-244.
7. United States Statutes at Large, Vol. 61, p. 872

Assistant Engineer
1. United States Statutes at Large, Vol. 18, p. 17
2. United States Statutes at Large, Vol. 16, p. 586
3. Regulations for the Goverment of the Navy of the United States, August 7, 1876, p. 189-195
4. ibid.
5. Tily, James C., The Uniforms of the United States Navy, Cranbury: Thomas Yoseloff, 1964, p. 198-199.
6. ibid. p. 204
7. ibid. p. 205
8. ibid.
9. United States Statutes at Large, Vol. 22, p. 472
10. Regulations Governing the Uniform of Officers of the United States Navy, 1883.
11. Tily, James C., The Uniforms of the United States Navy, Cranbury: Thomas Yoseloff, 1964, p. 219-220.
12. United States Statutes at Large, Vol. 30, p. 1005

Assistant Naval Constructor
1. Tily, James C., The Uniforms of the United States Navy, Cranbury: Thomas Yoseloff, 1964, p. 51.
2. Callahan, Edward, List of Officers of the Navy of the United States and the Marine Corps from 1775 to 1900, New York: L. R. Hamerlsy & CO., 1901, p. 150
3. http://www.history.navy.mil/faqs/faq59-8.htm, March 2011
4. Tily, James C., The Uniforms of the United States Navy, Cranbury: Thomas Yoseloff, 1964, p. 134.
5. Callahan, Edward, List of Officers of the Navy of the United States and the Marine Corps from 1775 to 1900, New York: L. R. Hamerlsy & CO., 1901, p. 574
6. Tily, James C., The Uniforms of the United States Navy, Cranbury: Thomas Yoseloff, 1964, p. 189.
7. Callahan, Edward, List of Officers of the Navy of the United States and the Marine Corps from 1775 to 1900, New York: L. R. Hamerlsy & CO., 1901.
8. United States Statutes at Large, Vol. 14, p. 223
9. Callahan, Edward, List of Officers of the Navy of the United States and the Marine Corps from 1775 to 1900, New York: L. R. Hamerlsy & CO., 1901, p. 574
10. General Order 120, April 1, 1869, with letter attached.
11. United States Statutes at Large, Vol. 16, p. 536
12. Tily, James C., The Uniforms of the United States Navy, Cranbury: Thomas Yoseloff, 1964, p. 201.
13. United States Statutes at Large, Vol. 30, p. 1005
14. United States Statutes at Large, Vol. 39, p. 577
15. All Hands, "175th Anniversary The Navy Supply Corps", March 1970, p. 41
16. United States Statutes at Large, Vol. 54, p. 527

Assistant Paymaster
1. United States Statutes at Large, Vol. 12, p. 258
2. Tily, James C., The Uniforms of the United States Navy, Cranbury: Thomas Yoseloff, 1964, p. 114.
3. ibid. p. 120
4. ibid. p. 51
5. ibid. p. 123-124
6. http://www.history.navy.mil/faqs/faq59-8i.htm, March 2011
7. General Order 120, April 1, 1869, with letter attached.
8. Tily, James C., The Uniforms of the United States Navy, Cranbury: Thomas Yoseloff, 1964, p. 198-199. with regulation quote courtesy of Justin Broderick.
9. United States Statutes at Large, Vol. 16, p. 536
10. United States Statutes at Large, Vol. 30, p. 1006
11. http://www.history.navy.mil/library/online/uniform_insignia.htm, March 2011
12. All Hands, "175th Anniversary The Navy Supply Corps", March 1970, p. 41
13. Tily, James C., The Uniforms of the United States Navy, Cranbury: Thomas Yoseloff, 1964, p. 243-244.
14. United States Statutes at Large, Vol. 61, p. 872

Assistant Surgeon
1. United States Statutes at Large, Vol. 4, p. 313
2. American State Papers, Senate, 20th Congress, 1st Session Naval Affairs: Volume 3, p 101.
3. American State Papers, Senate, 20th Congress, 2nd Session Naval Affairs: Volume 3, p 253.
4. http://www.history.navy.mil/faqs/faq59-4.htm, March 2011 (regulations of 1814)
5. Tily, James C., The Uniforms of the United States Navy, Cranbury: Thomas Yoseloff, 1964, p. 72. (stating most uniforms same as 1814).
6. General Order, Navy Department, May 1, 1830
7. Tily, James C., The Uniforms of the United States Navy, Cranbury: Thomas Yoseloff, 1964, p. 83 & 86.
8. http://www.history.navy.mil/faqs/faq59-27.htm, March 2011

9. Tily, James C., The Uniforms of the United States Navy, Cranbury: Thomas Yoseloff, 1964, p. 45.
10. General Order, Navy Department, August 31, 1846
11. United States Statutes at Large, Vol. 10, p. 587
12. Tily, James C., The Uniforms of the United States Navy, Cranbury: Thomas Yoseloff, 1964, p. 99-100.
13. http://www.history.navy.mil/faqs/faq59-28.htm, March 2011
14. Tily, James C., The Uniforms of the United States Navy, Cranbury: Thomas Yoseloff, 1964, p. 109-110.
15. ibid. p. 117-120.
16. ibid. p. 51.
17. http://www.history.navy.mil/faqs/faq59-8i.htm, March 2011
18. General Order 120, April 1, 1869, with letter attached.
19. Tily, James C., The Uniforms of the United States Navy, Cranbury: Thomas Yoseloff, 1964, p. 198-199. with regulation quote courtesy of Justin Broderick.
20. United States Statutes at Large, Vol. 16, p. 536
21. Tily, James C., The Uniforms of the United States Navy, Cranbury: Thomas Yoseloff, 1964, p. 207.
22. United States Statutes at Large, Vol. 30, p. 1006
23. United States Statutes at Large, Vol. 37, p. 344
24. Tily, James C., The Uniforms of the United States Navy, Cranbury: Thomas Yoseloff, 1964, p. 233.
25. All Hands, "175th Anniversary The Navy Supply Corps", March 1970, p. 41
26. Tily, James C., The Uniforms of the United States Navy, Cranbury: Thomas Yoseloff, 1964, p. 243-244.
27. United States Statutes at Large, Vol. 61, p. 872

Attendant
1. http://www.history.navy.mil/faqs/faq78-3.html, March 2011
2. U.S. Navy Regulation Circular, No. 41, January 8, 1885
3. Regulations for the Uniform of the Commissioned Officers, Warrant Officers, and Enlisted Men of the Navy of the United States, 1886, p. 16
4. http://www.history.navy.mil/faqs/faq78-3.html, March 2011

Baker First Class
1. http://www.history.navy.mil/faqs/faq78-3.html, March 2011
2. Stacy, John A., United States Navy Rating Badges and Marks 1833 to 2008, Mathews N.C.: ASMIC Pubs, 2008, p. 13.
3. uniform regulations governing the insignia and uniforms of commissioned officers, warrant officers, and enlistedmen of the United States Navy, January 21, 1905, p. 50.
4. Stacy, John A., United States Navy Rating Badges and Marks 1833 to 2008, Mathews N.C.: ASMIC Pubs, 2008, p. 14.
5. ibid. p. 74

Baker Second Class
1. http://www.history.navy.mil/faqs/faq78-3.html, March 2011
2. Stacy, John A., United States Navy Rating Badges and Marks 1833 to 2008, Mathews N.C.: ASMIC Pubs, 2008, p. 13.
3. uniform regulations governing the insignia and uniforms of commissioned officers, warrant officers, and enlistedmen of the United States Navy, January 21, 1905, p. 50.
4. Stacy, John A., United States Navy Rating Badges and Marks 1833 to 2008, Mathews N.C.: ASMIC Pubs, 2008, p. 14.
5. ibid. p. 74
6. ibid.

Barber
1. http://www.history.navy.mil/faqs/faq78-3.html, March 2011
2. U.S. Navy Regulation Circular, No. 41, January 8, 1885
3. regulations governing the uniform of commissioned officers, warrant officers, and enlisted men of the United States Navy, 1886, p. 25

Bayman
1. U.S. Navy Regulation Circular, No. 41, January 8, 1885

2. regulations governing the uniform of commissioned officers, warrant officers, and enlisted men of the United States Navy, 1886, p. 25
3. Register for the Commissioned and Warrant Officers of the Navy of the United States and of the Marine Corps, January 1, 1890, p. 170
4. Stacy, John A., United States Navy Rating Badges and Marks 1833 to 2008, Mathews N.C.: ASMIC Pubs, 2008, p. 118.
5. http://www.history.navy.mil/faqs/faq78-3.html, March 2011

Boatswain
1. Mack, William P. and Connell, Royal W., Naval Ceremonies, Customs, and Traditions, 5th edition, Annapolis:Naval Institute Press, 1980, p. 233.
2. Journals of the Continental Congress, Vol. 3, p. 384
3. United States Statutes at Large, Vol. 1, p. 350.
4. United States Statutes at Large, Vol. 1, p. 524.
5. http://www.history.navy.mil/faqs/faq59-4.htm, March 2011
6. General Order, Navy Department, May 1, 1830
7. http://www.history.navy.mil/faqs/faq59-27.htm, March 2011
8. Tily, James C., The Uniforms of the United States Navy, Cranbury: Thomas Yoseloff, 1964, p. 101.
9. http://www.history.navy.mil/faqs/faq59-28.htm, March 2011
10. Tily, James C., The Uniforms of the United States Navy, Cranbury: Thomas Yoseloff, 1964, p. 110.
11. ibid. appendix c, chart shows no buttons on cuff after 1862.
12. http://www.history.navy.mil/faqs/faq59-8.htm
13. General Order No. 90, March 11, 1869
14. Regulations for the Goverment of the Navy of the United States, August 7, 1876, p. 191.
15. Tily, James C., The Uniforms of the United States Navy, Cranbury: Thomas Yoseloff, 1964, p. 204.
16. Regulations Governing the Uniform of Officers of the United States Navy, 1883, p. 11-12.
17. http://www.history.navy.mil/library/online/uniform_insignia.htm, March 2011
18. ibid.
19. Uniform Regulations United States Navy, September 20, 1922, p. 16-18
20. https://picasaweb.google.com/Booker1942/1943TheNavalOfficersUniformPlan#5537445144858829890, March 2011
21. Bureau of Navigation Bulletin ,Number 291, April 26, 1941, p. 28.
22. All Hands, "Green Unifroms Mandatory...", June 1944, p. 71
23. United States Statutes at Large, Vol. 63, p. 807
24. http://www.history.navy.mil/library/online/uniform_insignia.htm, March 2011
25. All Hands, "Warrant Officers' Collar Devices", October 1952, p. 24
26. United States Statutes at Large, Vol. 68, p. 157

Boy, Boy First Class, Boy Second Class and Boy Third Class
1. Journals of the Continental Congress, Vol. 9, p. 1067
2. Journals of the Continental Congress, Vol. 3, p. 384
3. United States Statutes at Large, Vol. 1, p. 350.
4. United States Statutes at Large, Vol. 1, p. 524
5. United States Statutes at Large, Vol. 2, p. 390
6. United States Statutes at Large, Vol. 2, p. 789
7. United States Statutes at Large, Vol. 3, p. 763
8. United States Statutes at Large, Vol. 5, p. 153
9. Report of the Secretary of the Navy, December 3, 1836
10. http://navalapprentice.white-navy.com/563.shtml
11. New York Times, "THE NAVAL APPRENTICE SYSTEM.; Trip of the Sabine to New-London Sketch of the Rise and Progress of the Apprentice System", August 2, 1865.
12. http://www.history.navy.mil/faqs/faq78-3.html, March 2011
13. ibid.
14. Tily, James C., The Uniforms of the United States Navy, Cranbury: Thomas Yoseloff, 1964, p. 193.
15. ibid. p. 200
16. regulations governing the uniform of commissioned officers, warrant officers, and enlisted men of the United States Navy, 1886, p. 25
17. http://www.history.navy.mil/faqs/faq78-3.html, March 2011

Bugler
1. U.S. Navy Regulation Circular, No. 41, January 8, 1885
2. regulations governing the uniform of commissioned officers, warrant officers, and enlisted men of the United States Navy, 1886, p. 25
3. Register for the Commissioned and Warrant Officers of the Navy of the United States and of the Marine Corps, January 1, 1890, p. 170
4. Register for the Commissioned and Warrant Officers of the Navy of the United States and of the Marine Corps, January 1, 1895, p. 176
5. Stacy, John A., United States Navy Rating Badges and Marks 1833 to 2008, Mathews N.C.: ASMIC Pubs, 2008, p. 13.
6. ibid. p. 58.
7. http://www.history.navy.mil/faqs/faq78-3.html, March 2011

Bugler First Class
1. http://www.history.navy.mil/faqs/faq78-3.html, March 2011
2. Uniform Regulations United States Navy, revised January 25, 1913, p. 54
3. ibid. p. 66.
4. ibid. p. 65.
5. All Hands, "Here's a complete list of rating changes...", March 1948, p. 54

Bugler Second Class
1. http://www.history.navy.mil/faqs/faq78-3.html, March 2011
2. Uniform Regulations United States Navy, revised January 25, 1913, p. 54
3. ibid. p. 66.
4. ibid. p. 65.
5. All Hands, "Here's a complete list of rating changes...", March 1948, p. 54

Cabin Cook
1. http://www.history.navy.mil/faqs/faq78-3.html, March 2011
2. Regulations for the government of the Navy of the United States, 1841, p. 164 (lists petty officer's rates that could be entered directly at enlistment, including Officer's cooks.)
3. Regulations for the government of the Navy of the United States, 1865, p. 6-7
4. U.S. Navy Regulation Circular, No. 41, January 8, 1885
5. regulations governing the uniform of commissioned officers, warrant officers, and enlisted men of the United States Navy, 1886, p. 16
6. http://www.quarterdeck.org/uniforms/1897/21-37%20Enlisted%201897.htm, March 2011
7. uniform regulations governing the insignia and uniforms of commissioned officers, warrant officers, and enlistedmen of the United States Navy, January 21, 1905, p. 40
8. Stacy, John A., United States Navy Rating Badges and Marks 1833 to 2008, Mathews N.C.: ASMIC Pubs, 2008, p. 74.
9. Uniform Regulations, United States Navy, September 20, 1922, p. 56.
10. Register of the Commissioned And Warrant Officers of the Navy of the United States..., 1923, p. 307.
11. http://www.history.navy.mil/faqs/faq78-3.html, March 2011

Cabin Steward
1. http://www.history.navy.mil/faqs/faq78-3.html, March 2011
2. Regulations for the government of the Navy of the United States, 1841, p. 164 (lists petty officer's rates that could be entered directly at enlistment, including Officer's Stewards.)
3. Regulations for the government of the Navy of the United States, 1865, p. 6-7
4. http://www.history.navy.mil/faqs/faq59-8n.htm, March 2011
5. U.S. Navy Regulation Circular, No. 41, January 8, 1885
6. regulations governing the uniform of commissioned officers, warrant officers, and enlisted men of the United States Navy, 1886, p. 16
7, http://www.quarterdeck.org/uniforms/1897/21-37%20Enlisted%201897.htm, March 2011

8. uniform regulations governing the insignia and uniforms of commissioned officers, warrant officers, and enlistedmen of the United States Navy, January 21, 1905, p. 40
9. Stacy, John A., United States Navy Rating Badges and Marks 1833 to 2008, Mathews N.C.: ASMIC Pubs, 2008, p. 74.
10. Uniform Regulations, United States Navy, September 20, 1922, p. 56.
11. Register of the Commissioned And Warrant Officers of the Navy of the United States..., 1923, p. 307.
12. http://www.history.navy.mil/faqs/faq78-3.html, March 2011

Cadet Engineer
1. United States Statutes at Large, Vol. 13, p. 393.
2. United States Statutes at Large, Vol. 22, p. 285.

Cadet Midshipman

Captain
1. Oliver, Raymond, Why is a Kernal called a Colonel?, Tuscon: Fireship press, 1983, p. 29
2. ibid. p. 41.
3. Journals of the Continental Congress, Vol. 3, p. 384
4. http://www.history.navy.mil/books/callahan/contnav.htm, April 2011
5. Journals of the Continental Congress, Vol. 6, p. 954
6. http://bluejacket.com/sea-service_uniform_a.htm, April 2011
7. United States Statutes at Large, Vol. 1, p. 350.
8. Senate Executive Journal, vol 1, p. 161
9. Toll, Ian W., Six Frigates, New York: W.W. Norton & Company, 2006, p. 57
10. McKee, Christopher., A Gentlemanly and Honorable Profession, Annapolis: Naval Institute Press, 1991, p. 45
11. Callahan, Edward, List of Officers of the Navy of the United States and the Marine Corps from 1775 to 1900, New York: L. R. Hamerlsy & CO., 1901, p. 11.
12. http://en.wikipedia.org/wiki/Original_six_frigates_of_the_United_States_Navy, April 2011.
13. http://www.history.navy.mil/faqs/faq59-3.htm, April 2011
14. Toll, Ian W., Six Frigates, New York: W.W. Norton & Company, 2006, p. 128-131.
15. http://www.history.navy.mil/faqs/faq59-25.htm, April 2011
16. http://www.history.navy.mil/faqs/faq59-4.htm, April 2011
17. Tily, James C., The Uniforms of the United States Navy, Cranbury: Thomas Yoseloff, 1964, p. 72.
18. http://www.ibiblio.org/pha/USN/1820/NavyReg1820.html, April 2011
19. General Order, Navy Department, May 1, 1830
20. http://www.history.navy.mil/faqs/faq59-27.htm, April 2011
21. Tily, James C., The Uniforms of the United States Navy, Cranbury: Thomas Yoseloff, 1964, p. 97.
22. http://www.history.navy.mil/faqs/faq59-28.htm, April 2011
23. Tily, James C., The Uniforms of the United States Navy, Cranbury: Thomas Yoseloff, 1964, p. 117-119.
24. ibid. p. 123-124
25. http://www.history.navy.mil/faqs/faq59-8c.htm, April 2011
26. http://www.history.navy.mil/faqs/faq59-8a.htm, April 2011
27. http://www.history.navy.mil/faqs/faq59-8e.htm, April 2011
28. http://www.history.navy.mil/faqs/faq59-8b.htm, April 2011
29. Tily, James C., The Uniforms of the United States Navy, Cranbury: Thomas Yoseloff, 1964, p. 133-134.
30. http://www.history.navy.mil/library/online/uniform_insignia.htm, April 2011
31. General Order, No. 90, Navy Department, March 11, 1869
32. General Order, No. 126, Navy Department, May 27, 1869
33. Tily, James C., The Uniforms of the United States Navy, Cranbury: Thomas Yoseloff, 1964, p. 204.
34. Regulations Governing the Uniform of Officers of the United States Navy, 1883, p. 11-12
34a. Tily, James C., The Uniforms of the United States Navy, Cranbury: Thomas Yoseloff, 1964, p. 219-220.
35. ibid. p 222.
36. uniform regulations governing the insignia and uniforms of commissioned officers, warrant officers, and enlistedmen of the United States Navy, January 21, 1905, p. 31
37. Uniform Regulations United States Navy, revised January 25, 1913, p. 37
38. Tily, James C., The Uniforms of the United States Navy, Cranbury: Thomas Yoseloff, 1964, p. 234.
39. Uniform Regulations United States Navy, revised January 25, 1913, p. 43
40. Tily, James C., The Uniforms of the United States Navy, Cranbury: Thomas Yoseloff, 1964, p. 238.
41. ibid. , p. 243-244.
42. Uniform Regulations United States Navy, September 20, 1922, p. 19
43. Tily, James C., The Uniforms of the United States Navy, Cranbury: Thomas Yoseloff, 1964, p. 247-248.
44. ibid p. 271.
45. United States Statutes at Large, Vol. 63, p. 807
46. United States Navy Uniform Regulations, April 2010, Para. 4101
47. United States Navy Uniform Regulations, April 2010, Para. 4103.2a
48. United States Navy Uniform Regulations, April 2010, Para. 4103.4

Captain Commanding a Squadron
1. http://en.wikipedia.org/wiki/Esek_Hopkins, April 2011
2. http://www.history.navy.mil/faqs/faq59-25.htm, April 2011
3. Tily, James C., The Uniforms of the United States Navy, Cranbury: Thomas Yoseloff, 1964, p. 72.
4. General Order, Navy Department, May 1, 1830
5. http://www.history.navy.mil/faqs/faq59-27.htm, April 2011
6. http://www.history.navy.mil/faqs/faq59-28.htm, April 2011
7. United States Statutes at Large, Vol. 11, p. 154

Carpenter
1. http://www.history.navy.mil/faqs/faq78-3.html, April 2011
2. Journals of the Continental Congress, Vol. 3, p. 384
3. United States Statutes at Large, Vol. 1, p. 350.
4. United States Statutes at Large, Vol. 1, p. 524.
5. http://www.history.navy.mil/faqs/faq59-4.htm, March 2011
6. General Order, Navy Department, May 1, 1830
7. http://www.history.navy.mil/faqs/faq59-27.htm, March 2011
8. Tily, James C., The Uniforms of the United States Navy, Cranbury: Thomas Yoseloff, 1964, p. 101.
9. http://www.history.navy.mil/faqs/faq59-28.htm, March 2011
10. Tily, James C., The Uniforms of the United States Navy, Cranbury: Thomas Yoseloff, 1964, p. 110.
11. ibid. appendix c, chart shows no buttons on cuff after 1862.
12. http://www.history.navy.mil/faqs/faq59-8.htm
13. General Order No. 90, March 11, 1869
14. Regulations for the Goverment of the Navy of the United States, August 7, 1876, p. 191.
15. Tily, James C., The Uniforms of the United States Navy, Cranbury: Thomas Yoseloff, 1964, p. 204.
16. Regulations Governing the Uniform of Officers of the United States Navy, 1883, p. 11-12.
17. http://www.history.navy.mil/library/online/uniform_insignia.htm, March 2011
18. ibid.
19. Uniform Regulations United States Navy, September 20, 1922, p. 16-18
20. https://picasaweb.google.com/Booker1942/1943TheNavalOfficersUniformPlan#5537445144858829890, March 2011
21. Bureau of Navigation Bulletin ,Number 291, April 26, 1941, p. 28.
22. All Hands, "Green Unifroms Mandatory...", June 1944, p. 71
22a. United States Statutes at Large, Vol. 63, p. 807
23. http://www.history.navy.mil/library/online/uniform_insignia.htm, March 2011
24. All Hands, "Warrant Officers' Collar Devices", October 1952, p. 24
25. United States Statutes at Large, Vol. 68, p. 157
26. http://www.history.navy.mil/faqs/faq78-3.html, April 2011
27. regulations governing the uniform of commissioned officers, warrant officers, and enlisted men of the United States Navy, 1886, p. 25
28. http://www.history.navy.mil/faqs/faq78-3.html, April 2011

Carpenter and Caulker
1. http://www.history.navy.mil/faqs/faq78-3.html, April 2011.
2. U.S. Navy Regulation Circular, No. 41, January 8, 1885

Caulker
1. http://www.history.navy.mil/faqs/faq78-3.html, April 2011
2. regulations governing the uniform of commissioned officers, warrant officers, and enlisted men of the United States Navy, 1886, p. 25
3. http://www.history.navy.mil/faqs/faq78-3.html, April 2011

Chaplain
1. McKee, Christopher., A Gentlemanly and Honorable Profession, Annapolis: Naval Institute Press, 1991, p. 31.
2. Journals of the Continental Congress, Vol. 3, p. 384
3. Journals of the Continental Congress, Vol. 6, p. 954
4. United States Statutes at Large, Vol. 1, p. 350.
5. United States Statutes at Large, Vol. 1, p. 524.
6. Callahan, Edward, List of Officers of the Navy of the United States and the Marine Corps from 1775 to 1900, New York: L. R. Hamerlsy & CO., 1901.
6. General Order, Navy Department, May 1, 1830
7. http://www.history.navy.mil/faqs/faq59-27.htm, April 2011
8. http://www.history.navy.mil/faqs/faq59-28.htm, April 2011
9. Tily, James C., The Uniforms of the United States Navy, Cranbury: Thomas Yoseloff, 1964, p. 110.
10. ibid. p. 51
11. http://www.history.navy.mil/faqs/faq59-8.htm, April 2011
12. General Order 120, April 1, 1869, with letter attached.
13. Tily, James C., The Uniforms of the United States Navy, Cranbury: Thomas Yoseloff, 1964, p. 200.
14. United States Statutes at Large, Vol. 16, p. 536.
15. Regulations for the Goverment of the Navy of the United States, August 7, 1876, p. 189.
16. ibid. p. 193
17. ibid. p. 192
18. Regulations Governing the Uniform of Officers of the United States Navy, 1883, p. 15.
19. regulations governing the uniform of commissioned officers, warrant officers, and enlisted men of the United States Navy, 1886, p. 15.
20. http://www.grandarmyofthefrontier.org/uniforms/usn1897.htm, April 2011
21. Tily, James C., The Uniforms of the United States Navy, Cranbury: Thomas Yoseloff, 1964, p. 221.
22. ibid. Captain Tily refers to "service coats", other officers wore shoulder straps on the white coat, but those for chaplains must have been plain.
23. Tily, James C., The Uniforms of the United States Navy, Cranbury: Thomas Yoseloff, 1964, p. 221.
24. uniform regulations governing the insignia and uniforms of commissioned officers, warrant officers, and enlistedmen of the United States Navy, January 21, 1905, p. 24, 22 & 32
25. United States Statutes at Large, Vol. 30, p. 1006
26. Tily, James C., The Uniforms of the United States Navy, Cranbury: Thomas Yoseloff, 1964, p. 224.
27. United States Statutes at Large, Vol. 24, p. 554
28. Tily, James C., The Uniforms of the United States Navy, Cranbury: Thomas Yoseloff, 1964, p. 225.
29. Uniform Regulations United States Navy, revised January 25, 1913, p. 33-34.
30. Tily, James C., The Uniforms of the United States Navy, Cranbury: Thomas Yoseloff, 1964, p. 243.
31. Uniform Regulations United States Navy, September 20, 1922, p. 2
32. ibid. p. 16
33. Tily, James C., The Uniforms of the United States Navy, Cranbury: Thomas Yoseloff, 1964, p. 259.
34. U.S. Navy Uniform Regulations, May 31, 1941, p. 9
35. United States Statutes at Large, Vol. 61, p. 93.

36. http://www.paklinks.com/gs/religion-and-scripture/72204-first-muslim-chaplain-in-us-navy.html, April 2011
37. United States Navy Uniform Regulations, April 2010, Para. 4102
38. http://www.navy.mil/search/display.asp?story_id=14398, April 2011
39. United States Navy Uniform Regulations, April 2010, Para. 4102

Chief Areographer
1. United States Statutes at Large, Vol. 56, p. 724.
2. All Hands, "Ranks and Rates...", May 1943, p. 29-35
3. All Hands, "Green Unifroms Mandatory...", June 1944, p. 71
4. https://picasaweb.google.com/Booker1942/1943TheNavalOfficersUniformPlan#5537445144858829890, March 2011
5. United States Statutes at Large, Vol. 63, p. 807
6. http://www.history.navy.mil/library/online/uniform_insignia.htm, March 2011
7. All Hands, "Warrant Officers' Collar Devices", October 1952, p. 24
8. United States Statutes at Large, Vol. 68, p. 157

Chief Boatswain
1. United States Statutes at Large, Vol. 30, p. 1007
2. Tily, James C., The Uniforms of the United States Navy, Cranbury: Thomas Yoseloff, 1964, p. 222-223.
3. uniform regulations governing the insignia and uniforms of commissioned officers, warrant officers, and enlistedmen of the United States Navy, January 21, 1905, p. 32.
4. ibid. p. 31
5. http://www.history.navy.mil/library/online/uniform_insignia.htm, March 2011
6. Uniform Regulations United States Navy, revised January 25, 1913, p. 34
7. ibid. p. 37
8. Tily, James C., The Uniforms of the United States Navy, Cranbury: Thomas Yoseloff, 1964, p. 234.
9. http://www.history.navy.mil/library/online/uniform_insignia.htm, March 2011
10. Uniform Regulations United States Navy, September 20, 1922, p. 16-18
11. https://picasaweb.google.com/Booker1942/1943TheNavalOfficersUniformPlan#5537445144858829890, March 2011
12. Bureau of Navigation Bulletin ,Number 291, April 26, 1941, p. 28.
13. All Hands, "Green Unifroms Mandatory...", June 1944, p. 71
14. United States Statutes at Large, Vol. 63, p. 807
15. http://www.history.navy.mil/library/online/uniform_insignia.htm, March 2011
16. All Hands, "Warrant Officers' Collar Devices", October 1952, p. 24
17. United States Statutes at Large, Vol. 68, p. 157

Chief Carpenter
1. United States Statutes at Large, Vol. 30, p. 1007
2. Tily, James C., The Uniforms of the United States Navy, Cranbury: Thomas Yoseloff, 1964, p. 222-223.
3. uniform regulations governing the insignia and uniforms of commissioned officers, warrant officers, and enlistedmen of the United States Navy, January 21, 1905, p. 32.
4. ibid. p. 31
5. http://www.history.navy.mil/library/online/uniform_insignia.htm, March 2011
6. Uniform Regulations United States Navy, revised January 25, 1913, p. 34
7. ibid. p. 37
8. Tily, James C., The Uniforms of the United States Navy, Cranbury: Thomas Yoseloff, 1964, p. 234.
9. http://www.history.navy.mil/library/online/uniform_insignia.htm, March 2011
10. Uniform Regulations United States Navy, September 20, 1922, p. 16-18
11. https://picasaweb.google.com/Booker1942/1943TheNavalOfficersUniformPlan#5537445144858829890, March 2011
12. Bureau of Navigation Bulletin ,Number 291, April 26, 1941, p. 28.
13. All Hands, "Green Unifroms Mandatory...", June 1944, p. 71
14. United States Statutes at Large, Vol. 63, p. 807
15. http://www.history.navy.mil/library/online/uniform_insignia.htm, March 2011
16. All Hands, "Warrant Officers' Collar Devices", October 1952, p. 24
17. United States Statutes at Large, Vol. 68, p. 157

Chief Constructor
1. United States Statutes at Large, Vol. 16, p. 537
2. Regulations for the Goverment of the Navy of the United States, August 7, 1876, p. 192-193.
3. Callahan, Edward, List of Officers of the Navy of the United States and the Marine Corps from 1775 to 1900, New York: L. R. Hamerlsy & CO., 1901, p. 244.
4. ibid. p. 177.
5. ibid.
6. Register of the Commissioned, Warrant, And Volunteer Officers of the Navy of the United States..., July 1, 1882, p. 43.
7. Register of the Commissioned And Warrant Officers of the Navy of the United States..., January 1, 1895, p. 58.
8. United States Statutes at Large, Vol. 30, p. 1006
9. Register of the Commissioned And Warrant Officers of the Navy of the United States..., January 1, 1902, p. 62.
10. Register of the Commissioned And Warrant Officers of the Navy of the United States..., January 1, 1904, p. 164.
11. ibid p. 72.
12. Register of the Commissioned And Warrant Officers of the Navy of the United States..., January 1, 1911, p. 92.
13. Register of the Commissioned And Warrant Officers of the Navy of the United States..., January 1, 1915, p. 110.
14. All Hands, "175th Anniversary The Navy Supply Corps", March 1970, p. 41
15. United States Statutes at Large, Vol. 54, p. 527

Chief Electrician
1. United States Statutes at Large, Vol. 43, p. 1274.
2. http://www.history.navy.mil/library/online/uniform_insignia.htm, March 2011
3. https://picasaweb.google.com/Booker1942/1943TheNavalOfficersUniformPlan#5537445144858829890, March 2011
4. Bureau of Navigation Bulletin ,Number 291, April 26, 1941, p. 28.
5. All Hands, "Green Unifroms Mandatory...", June 1944, p. 71
6. United States Statutes at Large, Vol. 63, p. 807
7. http://www.history.navy.mil/library/online/uniform_insignia.htm, March 2011
8. All Hands, "Warrant Officers' Collar Devices", October 1952, p. 24
9. United States Statutes at Large, Vol. 68, p. 157

Chief Engineer
1. Callahan, Edward, List of Officers of the Navy of the United States and the Marine Corps from 1775 to 1900, New York: L. R. Hamerlsy & CO., 1901, p. 252
2. Tily, James C., The Uniforms of the United States Navy, Cranbury: Thomas Yoseloff, 1964, p. 86.
3. Callahan, Edward, List of Officers of the Navy of the United States and the Marine Corps from 1775 to 1900, New York: L. R. Hamerlsy & CO., 1901.
4. United States Statutes at Large, Vol. 5, p. 577
2. Tily, James C., The Uniforms of the United States Navy, Cranbury: Thomas Yoseloff, 1964, p. 97.
6. Callahan, Edward, List of Officers of the Navy of the United States and the Marine Corps from 1775 to 1900, New York: L. R. Hamerlsy & CO., 1901, p. 592.
7. http://www.history.navy.mil/books/callahan/index.htm, April 2011.
8. http://www.history.navy.mil/faqs/faq59-28.htm, April 2011
9. Callahan, Edward, List of Officers of the Navy of the United States and the Marine Corps from 1775 to 1900, New York: L. R. Hamerlsy & CO., 1901.
10. United States Statutes at Large, Vol. 11, p. 407.
11. Tily, James C., The Uniforms of the United States Navy, Cranbury: Thomas Yoseloff, 1964, p. 113. (Captain Tily uses an illustration added the a copy of the 1852 regulations as a reference and admits there is no text to support it).
12. Ibid. p. 119.
13. ibid. p. 51.
14. http://www.history.navy.mil/faqs/faq59-8.htm, April 2011
15. Tily, James C., The Uniforms of the United States Navy, Cranbury: Thomas Yoseloff, 1964, p. 189.
16. General Order 90, March 11, 1869.
17. General Order 120, April 1, 1869, with letter attached.
18. United States Statutes at Large, Vol. 16, p. 536
19. Register of the Commissioned And Warrant Officers of the Navy of the United States..., January 1, 1871, p. 59.
20. United States Statutes at Large, Vol. 30, p. 1006

Chief Gunner
1. United States Statutes at Large, Vol. 30, p. 1007
2. Tily, James C., The Uniforms of the United States Navy, Cranbury: Thomas Yoseloff, 1964, p. 222-223.
3. uniform regulations governing the insignia and uniforms of commissioned officers, warrant officers, and enlistedmen of the United States Navy, January 21, 1905, p. 32.
4. ibid. p. 31
5. http://www.history.navy.mil/library/online/uniform_insignia.htm, March 2011
6. Uniform Regulations United States Navy, revised January 25, 1913, p. 34
7. ibid. p. 37
8. Tily, James C., The Uniforms of the United States Navy, Cranbury: Thomas Yoseloff, 1964, p. 234.
9. http://www.history.navy.mil/library/online/uniform_insignia.htm, March 2011
10. Uniform Regulations United States Navy, September 20, 1922, p. 16-18
11. https://picasaweb.google.com/Booker1942/1943TheNavalOfficersUniformPlan#5537445144858829890, March 2011
12. Bureau of Navigation Bulletin ,Number 291, April 26, 1941, p. 28.
13. All Hands, "Green Unifroms Mandatory...", June 1944, p. 71
14. United States Statutes at Large, Vol. 63, p. 807
15. http://www.history.navy.mil/library/online/uniform_insignia.htm, March 2011
16. All Hands, "Warrant Officers' Collar Devices", October 1952, p. 24
17. United States Statutes at Large, Vol. 68, p. 157

Chief Machinist
1. United States Statutes at Large, Vol. 35, p. 771
2. http://www.history.navy.mil/library/online/uniform_insignia.htm, March 2011
3. Uniform Regulations United States Navy, revised January 25, 1913, p. 34
4. ibid. p. 37
5. Tily, James C., The Uniforms of the United States Navy, Cranbury: Thomas Yoseloff, 1964, p. 234.
6. http://www.history.navy.mil/library/online/uniform_insignia.htm, March 2011
7. Uniform Regulations United States Navy, September 20, 1922, p. 16-18
8. https://picasaweb.google.com/Booker1942/1943TheNavalOfficersUniformPlan#5537445144858829890, March 2011
9. Bureau of Navigation Bulletin ,Number 291, April 26, 1941, p. 28.
10. All Hands, "Green Unifroms Mandatory...", June 1944, p. 71
11. United States Statutes at Large, Vol. 63, p. 807
12. http://www.history.navy.mil/library/online/uniform_insignia.htm, March 2011
13. All Hands, "Warrant Officers' Collar Devices", October 1952, p. 24
14. United States Statutes at Large, Vol. 68, p. 157

Chief of Bureau of Construction and Repair
1. United States Statutes at Large, Vol. 5, p. 579
2. United States Statutes at Large, Vol. 12, p. 510
3. Callahan, Edward, List of Officers of the Navy of the United States and the Marine Corps from 1775 to 1900, New York: L. R. Hamerlsy & CO., 1901, p. 5.
4. Tily, James C., The Uniforms of the United States Navy, Cranbury: Thomas Yoseloff, 1964, p. 51-52.
5. http://www.history.navy.mil/faqs/faq59-8.htm, April 2011
6. United States Statutes at Large, Vol. 14, p. 223
7. General Order 120, April 1, 1869, with letter attached.
8. Callahan, Edward, List of Officers of the Navy of the United States and the Marine Corps from 1775 to 1900, New York: L. R. Hamerlsy & CO., 1901, p. 5.
9. United States Statutes at Large, Vol. 16, p. 537

Chief of Bureau of Medicine and Surgery
1. United States Statutes at Large, Vol. 5, p. 579
2. Callahan, Edward, List of Officers of the Navy of the United States and the Marine Corps from 1775 to 1900, New York: L. R. Hamerlsy & CO., 1901, p. 5.
3. General Order, Navy Department, August 31, 1846
4. United States Statutes at Large, Vol. 10, p. 587
5. Tily, James C., The Uniforms of the United States Navy, Cranbury: Thomas Yoseloff, 1964, p. 99.
6. http://www.history.navy.mil/faqs/faq59-28.htm, April 2011
7. Tily, James C., The Uniforms of the United States Navy, Cranbury: Thomas Yoseloff, 1964, p. 110.
8. Callahan, Edward, List of Officers of the Navy of the United States and the Marine Corps from 1775 to 1900, New York: L. R. Hamerlsy & CO., 1901, p. 5.
9. Tily, James C., The Uniforms of the United States Navy, Cranbury: Thomas Yoseloff, 1964, p. 51-52.
10. http://www.history.navy.mil/faqs/faq59-8.htm, April 2011
11. Callahan, Edward, List of Officers of the Navy of the United States and the Marine Corps from 1775 to 1900, New York: L. R. Hamerlsy & CO., 1901, p. 5.
12. General Order 90, March 11, 1869.
13. General Order 120, April 1, 1869, with letter attached.
14. Callahan, Edward, List of Officers of the Navy of the United States and the Marine Corps from 1775 to 1900, New York: L. R. Hamerlsy & CO., 1901, p. 5.
15. United States Statutes at Large, Vol. 16, p. 537.

Chief of Bureau of Provisions and Clothing
1. United States Statutes at Large, Vol. 5, p. 579
2. Callahan, Edward, List of Officers of the Navy of the United States and the Marine Corps from 1775 to 1900, New York: L. R. Hamerlsy & CO., 1901, p. 5.
3. Tily, James C., The Uniforms of the United States Navy, Cranbury: Thomas Yoseloff, 1964, p. 99.
4. ibid. p. 110.
5. Callahan, Edward, List of Officers of the Navy of the United States and the Marine Corps from 1775 to 1900, New York: L. R. Hamerlsy & CO., 1901, p. 5.
6. United States Statutes at Large, Vol. 12, p. 83
7. Tily, James C., The Uniforms of the United States Navy, Cranbury: Thomas Yoseloff, 1964, p. 51-52.
8. http://www.history.navy.mil/faqs/faq59-8.htm, April 2011
9. General Order 90, March 11, 1869.
10. General Order 120, April 1, 1869, with letter attached.
11. Callahan, Edward, List of Officers of the Navy of the United States and the Marine Corps from 1775 to 1900, New York: L. R. Hamerlsy & CO., 1901, p. 5.
12. United States Statutes at Large, Vol. 16, p. 537

Chief of Bureau of Steam Engineering
1. United States Statutes at Large, Vol. 12, p. 510
2. Callahan, Edward, List of Officers of the Navy of the United States and the Marine Corps from 1775 to 1900, New York: L. R. Hamerlsy & CO., 1901, p. 5.
3. Register of the Commissioned And Warrant Officers of the Navy of the United States..., January 1, 1864, p. 5.
4. Register of the Commissioned And Warrant Officers of the Navy of the United States..., January 1, 1865, p. 5.
5. http://www.history.navy.mil/faqs/faq59-28.htm, April 2011
6. Tily, James C., The Uniforms of the United States Navy, Cranbury: Thomas Yoseloff, 1964, p. 114.
7. ibid. p. 51-52.
8. http://www.history.navy.mil/faqs/faq59-8.htm, April 2011
9. General Order 90, March 11, 1869.
10. General Order 120, April 1, 1869, with letter attached.
11. Callahan, Edward, List of Officers of the Navy of the United States and the Marine Corps from 1775 to 1900, New York: L. R. Hamerlsy & CO., 1901, p. 5.
12. United States Statutes at Large, Vol. 16, p. 537

Chief Pay Clerk
1. United States Statutes at Large, Vol. 38, p. 942
2. http://www.history.navy.mil/library/online/uniform_insignia.htm, March 2011
3. http://www.history.navy.mil/library/online/uniform_insignia.htm, March 2011
4. Uniform Regulations United States Navy, September 20, 1922, p. 16-18
5. https://picasaweb.google.com/Booker1942/1943TheNavalOfficersUniformPlan#5537445144858829890, March 2011
6. Bureau of Navigation Bulletin ,Number 291, April 26, 1941, p. 28.
7. All Hands, "Green Unifroms Mandatory...", June 1944, p. 71
8. United States Statutes at Large, Vol. 63, p. 807
9. http://www.history.navy.mil/library/online/uniform_insignia.htm, March 2011
10. All Hands, "Warrant Officers' Collar Devices", October 1952, p. 24
11. United States Statutes at Large, Vol. 68, p. 157

Chief Petty Officer
1. http://www.history.navy.mil/faqs/faq46-3.htm,April 2011
2. McKee, Christopher., A Gentlemanly and Honorable Profession, Annapolis: Naval Institute Press, 1991, p. 31-32
3. Tily, James C., The Uniforms of the United States Navy, Cranbury: Thomas Yoseloff, 1964, p. 114-115.
4. http://www.history.navy.mil/faqs/faq46-3.htm,April 2011
5. Tily, James C., The Uniforms of the United States Navy, Cranbury: Thomas Yoseloff, 1964, p. 202.
6. Register of the Commissioned And Warrant Officers of the Navy of the United States..., January 1, 1865, p. 6.
7. http://www.history.navy.mil/faqs/faq46-3.htm
8. U.S. Navy Regulation Circular, No. 41, January 8, 1885
9. Stacy, John A., United States Navy Ratring Badges and Marks 1833 to 2008, Mathews N.C.: ASMIC Pubs, 2008, p. 7.
10. U.S. Navy Regulaiton Circular No. 1, March 13, 1893.
11. http://www.history.navy.mil/faqs/faq46-3.htm,April 2011
12. regulations governing the uniform of commissioned officers, warrant officers, and enlisted men of the United States Navy, 1886, p. 20.
13. Stacy, John A., United States Navy Ratring Badges and Marks 1833 to 2008, Mathews N.C.: ASMIC Pubs, 2008, p. 9.
14. ibid. p. 7.
15. ibid. p. 10.
16. Tily, James C., The Uniforms of the United States Navy, Cranbury: Thomas Yoseloff, 1964, p. 220.
17. Uniform Regulations United States Navy, revised January 25, 1913, p. 63.
18. Stacy, John A., United States Navy Ratring Badges and Marks 1833 to 2008, Mathews N.C.: ASMIC Pubs, 2008, p. 18.
19. United States Statutes at Large, Vol. 42, p. 630
20. U.S. Navy Uniform Regulations, May 31, 1941, plate 35.
21. https://picasaweb.google.com/Booker1942/1943TheNavalOfficersUniformPlan#5537445372679463554, April 2011
22. https://picasaweb.google.com/Booker1942/1943TheNavalOfficersUniformPlan#5537445660794743042, April 2011
23. Stacy, John A., United States Navy Ratring Badges and Marks 1833 to 2008, Mathews N.C.: ASMIC Pubs, 2008, p. 27.
24. All Hands, "CPOs, Cooks, Stewards To Wear Officer-Style...", September 1945, p. 75.
25. regulations governing the uniform of commissioned officers, warrant officers, and enlisted men of the United States Navy, 1886, p. 20
26. uniform regulations governing the insignia and uniforms of commissioned officers, warrant officers, and enlistedmen of the United States Navy, January 21, 1905, p. 40.
27. Stacy, John A., United States Navy Ratring Badges and Marks 1833 to 2008, Mathews N.C.: ASMIC Pubs, 2008, p. 30.
28. ibid. p. 31.
29. United States Statutes at Large, Vol. 63, p. 807
30. All Hands, "Rating Badges on Khaki Shirts", October 1950, p. 30.
31. All Hands, October 1951, cover.
32. All Hands, "CPO Rating Badge", July 1952, p. 9.
33. All Hands, "CPO Collar Devices", November 1959, p. 26.
34. All Hands, "Uniform Changes Provide for New Style White Jacket for CPOs Beginning in 1971", July 1970, p. 45.
35. All Hands, "One Uniform For All", June 1971, p. 4.
36. Stacy, John A., United States Navy Ratring Badges and Marks 1833 to 2008, Mathews N.C.: ASMIC Pubs, 2008, p. 38.
37. All Hands, "New Officer, CPO Uniform...", June 1979, p. 2.
38. NAVADMIN 011/99, June 30, 1999
39. http://en.wikipedia.org/wiki/Uniforms_of_the_United_States_Navy#Obsolete_uniforms, April 2011
40. NAVADMIN 020/10, January 10, 2010

Chief Pharmacist
1. United States Statutes at Large, Vol. 37, p. 807
2. Uniform Regulations United States Navy, revised January 25, 1913, p. 34
3. ibid. p. 37
4. Tily, James C., The Uniforms of the United States Navy, Cranbury: Thomas Yoseloff, 1964, p. 234.
5. http://www.history.navy.mil/library/online/uniform_insignia.htm, March 2011
6. Uniform Regulations United States Navy, September 20, 1922, p. 16-18
7. https://picasaweb.google.com/Booker1942/1943TheNavalOfficersUniformPlan#5537445144858829890, March 2011
8. Bureau of Navigation Bulletin ,Number 291, April 26, 1941, p. 28.
9. All Hands, "Green Unifroms Mandatory...", June 1944, p. 71
10. Tily, James C., The Uniforms of the United States Navy, Cranbury: Thomas Yoseloff, 1964, p. 249.
11. United States Statutes at Large, Vol. 61, p. 738

Chief Photographer
1. United States Statutes at Large, Vol. 56, p. 724.
2. All Hands, "Ranks and Rates...", May 1943, p. 29-35
3. All Hands, "Green Unifroms Mandatory...", June 1944, p. 71
4. https://picasaweb.google.com/Booker1942/1943TheNavalOfficersUniformPlan#5537445144858829890, March 2011
5. United States Statutes at Large, Vol. 63, p. 807
6. http://www.history.navy.mil/library/online/uniform_insignia.htm, March 2011
7. All Hands, "Warrant Officers' Collar Devices", October 1952, p. 24
8. United States Statutes at Large, Vol. 68, p. 157

Chief Radio Electrician
1. United States Statutes at Large, Vol. 43, p. 1274.
2. http://www.history.navy.mil/library/online/uniform_insignia.htm, March 2011
3. https://picasaweb.google.com/Booker1942/1943TheNavalOfficersUniformPlan#5537445144858829890, March 2011
4. Bureau of Navigation Bulletin ,Number 291, April 26, 1941, p. 28.
5. All Hands, "Green Unifroms Mandatory...", June 1944, p. 71
6. United States Statutes at Large, Vol. 63, p. 807
7. http://www.history.navy.mil/library/online/uniform_insignia.htm, March 2011

8. All Hands, "Warrant Officers' Collar Devices", October 1952, p. 24
9. United States Statutes at Large, Vol. 68, p. 157

Chief Sail-Maker
1. United States Statutes at Large, Vol. 30, p. 1007
2. http://www.history.navy.mil/library/online/uniform_insignia.htm, April 2011
3. Register of the Commissioned And Warrant Officers of the Navy of the United States..., January 1, 1900, p. 79.
4. Tily, James C., The Uniforms of the United States Navy, Cranbury: Thomas Yoseloff, 1964, p. 222-223.
5. uniform regulations governing the insignia and uniforms of commissioned officers, warrant officers, and enlistedmen of the United States Navy, January 21, 1905, p. 32.
6. ibid. p. 31
7. http://www.history.navy.mil/library/online/uniform_insignia.htm, March 2011
8. Uniform Regulations United States Navy, revised January 25, 1913, p. 34
9. Register of the Commissioned And Warrant Officers of the Navy of the United States..., January 1, 1919, p. 88.
10. Register of the Commissioned And Warrant Officers of the Navy of the United States..., January 1, 1922, p. 358.

Chief Ship's Clerk
1. United States Statutes at Large, Vol. 56, p. 724.
2. All Hands, "Ranks and Rates...", May 1943, p. 29-35
3. All Hands, "Green Unifroms Mandatory...", June 1944, p. 71
4. https://picasaweb.google.com/Booker1942/1943TheNavalOfficersUniformPlan#5537445144858829890, March 2011
5. United States Statutes at Large, Vol. 63, p. 807
6. http://www.history.navy.mil/library/online/uniform_insignia.htm, March 2011
7. All Hands, "Warrant Officers' Collar Devices", October 1952, p. 24
8. United States Statutes at Large, Vol. 68, p. 157

Chief Steward
1. All Hands, "Here's a Complete List of Rating Changes...", March 1948, p. 57
2. All Hands, "Wants Clarification", July 1946, p. 39
3. All Hands, "Stewards Have Acquired New Uniforms", January 1950, p. 51.

Chief Torpedoman
1. United States Statutes at Large, Vol. 56, p. 724.
2. All Hands, "Ranks and Rates...", May 1943, p. 29-35
3. All Hands, "Green Unifroms Mandatory...", June 1944, p. 71
4. https://picasaweb.google.com/Booker1942/1943TheNavalOfficersUniformPlan#5537445144858829890, March 2011
5. United States Statutes at Large, Vol. 63, p. 807
6. http://www.history.navy.mil/library/online/uniform_insignia.htm, March 2011
7. All Hands, "Warrant Officers' Collar Devices", October 1952, p. 24
8. United States Statutes at Large, Vol. 68, p. 157

Chief Warrant Officer 2
1. United States Statutes at Large, Vol. 68, p. 157
2. All Hands, "New Insignia and Markings go into effect on 1 November For Four Warrant Ranks", October 1954, p. 45
3. United States Navy Uniform Regulations, April 2010, Para. 41012b, 4103 2d and 4103 8e.

Chief Warrant Officer 3
1. United States Statutes at Large, Vol. 68, p. 157
2. All Hands, "New Insignia and Markings go into effect on 1 November For Four Warrant Ranks", October 1954, p. 45
3. United States Navy Uniform Regulations, April 2010, Para. 41012b, 4103 2d and 4103 8e.

Chief Warrant Officer 4
1. United States Statutes at Large, Vol. 68, p. 157
2. All Hands, "New Insignia and Markings go into effect on 1 November For Four Warrant Ranks", October 1954, p. 45
3. United States Navy Uniform Regulations, April 2010, Para. 41012b, 4103 2d and 4103 8e.

Chief Warrant Officer 5
1. United States Statutes at Large, Vol. 105, p. 1491
2. NAVADMIN 337/02, October 2, 2002
3. United States Navy Uniform Regulations, April 2010, Para. 41012b, 4103 2d and 4103 8e.

Chief Warrant Officer, Hospital Corps.
1. http://www.history.navy.mil/library/online/uniform_insignia.htm, April 2011
2. United States Statutes at Large, Vol. 61, p. 738
3. http://www.history.navy.mil/library/online/uniform_insignia.htm, April 2011
4. United States Statutes at Large, Vol. 63, p. 807
5. http://www.history.navy.mil/library/online/uniform_insignia.htm, March 2011
6. All Hands, "Warrant Officers' Collar Devices", October 1952, p. 24
7. United States Statutes at Large, Vol. 68, p. 157

Civil Engineer
1. United States Statutes at Large, Vol. 14, p. 490
2. Register of the Commissioned And Warrant Officers of the Navy of the United States..., July 1, 1868, p. 36.
3. Callahan, Edward, List of Officers of the Navy of the United States and the Marine Corps from 1775 to 1900, New York: L. R. Hamerlsy & CO., 1901.
4. Register of the Commissioned And Warrant Officers of the Navy of the United States..., January 1, 1871, p. 70.
5. United States Statutes at Large, Vol. 16, p. 536
6. Callahan, Edward, List of Officers of the Navy of the United States and the Marine Corps from 1775 to 1900, New York: L. R. Hamerlsy & CO., 1901.
7. General Order No. 263, February 24, 1881
8. Register of the Commissioned And Warrant Officers of the Navy of the United States..., July 1, 1882, p. 44.
9. Tily, James C., The Uniforms of the United States Navy, Cranbury: Thomas Yoseloff, 1964, p. 205.
10. Regulations Governing the Uniform of Officers of the United States Navy, 1883, p. 10
11. Register of the Commissioned And Warrant Officers of the Navy of the United States..., January 1, 1899, p. 56.
12. United States Statutes at Large, Vol. 30, p. 1006
13. Tily, James C., The Uniforms of the United States Navy, Cranbury: Thomas Yoseloff, 1964, p. 225.
14. All Hands, "175th Anniversary The Navy Supply Corps", March 1970, p. 41
15. United States Statutes at Large, Vol. 61, p. 872

Clerk

1. General Order, Navy Department, May 1, 1830.
2. United States Statutes at Large, Vol. 1, p. 350.
3. United States Statutes at Large, Vol. 1, p. 523.
4. General Order, Navy Department, May 1, 1830.
5. http://en.wikipedia.org/wiki/Frock_coat, April 2011
6. Emerson, William K., Encyclopedia of United States Army Insignia and Uniforms, Norman: University of Oklahoma Press, 1996, p. 439.
7. http://www.history.navy.mil/faqs/faq78-3.html, March 2011
8. United States Statutes at Large, Vol. 4, p. 755
9. General Regulations for the Navy and Marine Corps of the United States, 1841, p. 2.
10. Tily, James C., The Uniforms of the United States Navy, Cranbury: Thomas Yoseloff, 1964, p. 45.
11. http://www.history.navy.mil/faqs/faq59-27.htm, April 2011
12. United States Statutes at Large, Vol. 5, p. 536.
13. http://www.history.navy.mil/faqs/faq59-28.htm, April 2011
14. Tily, James C., The Uniforms of the United States Navy, Cranbury: Thomas Yoseloff, 1964, p. 51.
15. http://www.history.navy.mil/faqs/faq59-8.htm, April 2011
16. http://www.history.navy.mil/library/online/uniform_insignia.htm, March 2011
17. United States Statutes at Large, Vol. 20, p. 50.
18. Regulations Governing the Uniform of Officers of the United States Navy, 1883, p. 11
19. United States Statutes at Large, Vol. 35, p. 755.
20. United States Statutes at Large, Vol. 38, p. 942.

Coal Heaver
1. United States Statutes at Large, Vol. 5, p. 577.
2. Stacy, John A., United States Navy Ratring Badges and Marks 1833 to 2008, Mathews N.C.: ASMIC Pubs, 2008, p. 5.
3. ibid. p. 6
4. U.S. Navy Regulation Circular, No. 41, January 8, 1885
5. regulations governing the uniform of commissioned officers, warrant officers, and enlisted men of the United States Navy, 1886, p. 25.
6. http://www.history.navy.mil/faqs/faq78-3.html, March 2011.

Coal Passer
1. http://www.history.navy.mil/faqs/faq78-3.html, March 2011.
2. U.S. Navy Regulation Circular No. 1, March 13, 1893.
3. Stacy, John A., United States Navy Ratring Badges and Marks 1833 to 2008, Mathews N.C.: ASMIC Pubs, 2008, p. 14.
4. http://www.history.navy.mil/faqs/faq78-3.html, March 2011

Command Master Chief Petty Officer
1. http://www.quarterdeck.org/WindsOfChange/046-62.MCPON%20Robert%20Walker.htm, April 2011
2. Stacy, John A., United States Navy Ratring Badges and Marks 1833 to 2008, Mathews N.C.: ASMIC Pubs, 2008, p. 35.

Commander
1. http://en.wikipedia.org/wiki/Commander, May 2011.
2. Oliver, Raymond, Why is a Kernal called a Colonel?, Tuscon: Fireship press, 1983, p. 37.
3. United States Statutes at Large, Vol. 5, p. 163.
4. General Order, Navy Department, May 1, 1830
5. http://www.history.navy.mil/faqs/faq59-27.htm, April 2011
6. Tily, James C., The Uniforms of the United States Navy, Cranbury: Thomas Yoseloff, 1964, p. 97.
7. ibid. p. 100.
8. http://www.history.navy.mil/faqs/faq59-28.htm, April 2011
9. Tily, James C., The Uniforms of the United States Navy, Cranbury: Thomas Yoseloff, 1964, p. 117-119.
10. ibid. p. 123-124
11. http://www.history.navy.mil/faqs/faq59-8c.htm, April 2011
12. http://www.history.navy.mil/faqs/faq59-8a.htm, April 2011
13. http://www.history.navy.mil/faqs/faq59-8e.htm, April 2011
14. http://www.history.navy.mil/faqs/faq59-8b.htm, April 2011
15. Tily, James C., The Uniforms of the United States Navy, Cranbury: Thomas Yoseloff, 1964, p. 133-134.
16. http://www.history.navy.mil/library/online/uniform_insignia.htm, April 2011
17. General Order, No. 90, Navy Department, March 11, 1869
18. General Order, No. 126, Navy Department, May 27, 1869
19. Tily, James C., The Uniforms of the United States Navy, Cranbury: Thomas Yoseloff, 1964, p. 204.
20. Regulations Governing the Uniform of Officers of the United States Navy, 1883, p. 11-12
21. Tily, James C., The Uniforms of the United States Navy, Cranbury: Thomas Yoseloff, 1964, p. 222.
22. uniform regulations governing the insignia and uniforms of commissioned officers, warrant officers, and enlistedmen of the United States Navy, January 21, 1905, p. 31
23. Uniform Regulations United States Navy, revised January 25, 1913, p. 37
24. Tily, James C., The Uniforms of the United States Navy, Cranbury: Thomas Yoseloff, 1964, p. 234.
25. Uniform Regulations United States Navy, revised January 25, 1913, p. 43
26. Tily, James C., The Uniforms of the United States Navy, Cranbury: Thomas Yoseloff, 1964, p. 238.
27. ibid. , p. 243-244.
28. Uniform Regulations United States Navy, September 20, 1922, p. 19

29. Tily, James C., The Uniforms of the United States Navy, Cranbury: Thomas Yoseloff, 1964, p. 247-248.
30. ibid p. 271.
31. United States Statutes at Large, Vol. 63, p. 807
32. United States Navy Uniform Regulations, April 2010, Para. 4101
33. United States Navy Uniform Regulations, April 2010, Para. 4103.2a
34. UnitedStates Navy Uniform Regulations, April 2010, Para. 4103.4

Commodore
1. Oliver, Raymond, Why is a Kernal called a Colonel?, Tuscon: Fireship press, 1983, p. 43
2. United States Statutes at Large, Vol. 12, p. 583
3. Tily, James C., The Uniforms of the United States Navy, Cranbury: Thomas Yoseloff, 1964, p. 119.
4. ibid. p. 123-124
5. http://www.history.navy.mil/faqs/faq59-8.htm, April 2011
6. Tily, James C., The Uniforms of the United States Navy, Cranbury: Thomas Yoseloff, 1964, p. 133-134.
7. http://www.history.navy.mil/library/online/uniform_insignia.htm, April 2011
8. Tily, James C., The Uniforms of the United States Navy, Cranbury: Thomas Yoseloff, 1964, p. 204.
9. Regulations Governing the Uniform of Officers of the United States Navy, 1883, p. 11-12
10. United States Statutes at Large, Vol. 30, p. 1004
11. http://users.sisna.com/justinb/cop.html, December 1999
12. Rodgers v. US, 185 U.S. 83, 1902
13. United States Statutes at Large, Vol. 57, p. 59
14. All Hands, "Rank of Commodore Asked by Navy", April 1943, p. 24.
15. All Hands, "Rank and Rates", May 1943, p. 32.
16 Oliver, Raymond, Why is a Kernal called a Colonel?, Tuscon: Fireship press, 1983, p. 44.
17. United States Statutes at Large, Vol. 94, p. 2887.
18. United States Statutes at Large, Vol. 95, p. 1105.
19. United States Statutes at Large, Vol. 99, p. 628.
20. Crocker,Lawrence, Army Officer's Guide 41st Edition, Harrisburg: Stackpole, 1981, p. 316.

Commodore Admiral
1. United States Statutes at Large, Vol. 94, p. 2887.
2. United States Statutes at Large, Vol. 95, p. 1105.
3. Crocker,Lawrence, Army Officer's Guide 41st Edition, Harrisburg: Stackpole, 1981, p. 316.

Constructionman
1. All Hands, "Here's a Complete List of Rating Changes...", March 1948, p. 57
2. All Hands, "Changes Made in Rating Structure,...", August 1948, p. 53.
3. United States Statutes at Large, Vol. 63, p. 802
4. Stacy, John A., United States Navy Rating Badges and Marks 1833 to 2008, Mathews N.C.: ASMIC Pubs, 2008, p. 33.
5. United States Navy Uniform Regulations, April 2010, Para. 4227.b

Constructionman Apprentice
1. All Hands, "Here's a Complete List of Rating Changes...", March 1948, p. 57
2. All Hands, "Changes Made in Rating Structure,...", August 1948, p. 53.
3. United States Statutes at Large, Vol. 63, p. 802
4. Stacy, John A., United States Navy Rating Badges and Marks 1833 to 2008, Mathews N.C.: ASMIC Pubs, 2008, p. 33.
5. United States Navy Uniform Regulations, April 2010, Para. 4227.b

Constructionman Recruit
1. All Hands, "Changes Made in Rating Structure,...", August 1948, p. 53.
2. United States Statutes at Large, Vol. 63, p. 802
3. All Hands, "Uniform Changes Published...", December 1948, p. 48
4. Stacy, John A., United States Navy Ratring Badges and Marks 1833 to 2008, Mathews N.C.: ASMIC Pubs, 2008, p. 40.

Cook to Commander in Chief
1. http://www.history.navy.mil/faqs/faq78-3.html, March 2011
2. Regulations for the government of the Navy of the United States, 1841, p. 164 (lists petty officer's rates that could be entered directly at enlistment, including Officer's cooks.)
3. Regulations for the government of the Navy of the United States, 1865, p. 6-7
4. U.S. Navy Regulation Circular, No. 41, January 8, 1885
5. regulations governing the uniform of commissioned officers, warrant officers, and enlisted men of the United States Navy, 1886, p. 16
6. http://www.quarterdeck.org/uniforms/1897/21-37%20Enlisted%201897.htm, March 2011
7. uniform regulations governing the insignia and uniforms of commissioned officers, warrant officers, and enlistedmen of the United States Navy, January 21, 1905, p. 40
8. Stacy, John A., United States Navy Rating Badges and Marks 1833 to 2008, Mathews N.C.: ASMIC Pubs, 2008, p. 74.
9. http://www.history.navy.mil/faqs/faq78-3.html, March 2011

Cook to Navy yard Commandant
1. http://www.history.navy.mil/faqs/faq78-3.html, March 2011
2. U.S. Navy Regulation Circular, No. 41, January 8, 1885
3. regulations governing the uniform of commissioned officers, warrant officers, and enlisted men of the United States Navy, 1886, p. 16
4. http://www.quarterdeck.org/uniforms/1897/21-37%20Enlisted%201897.htm, March 2011
5. uniform regulations governing the insignia and uniforms of commissioned officers, warrant officers, and enlistedmen of the United States Navy, January 21, 1905, p. 40
6. Stacy, John A., United States Navy Rating Badges and Marks 1833 to 2008, Mathews N.C.: ASMIC Pubs, 2008, p. 74.
7. http://www.history.navy.mil/faqs/faq78-3.html, March 2011

Dental Surgeon
1. United States Statutes at Large, Vol. 37, p. 903
2. Register of the Commissioned And Warrant Officers of the Navy of the United States..., January 1, 1915, p. 94.
3. ibid
4. Register of the Commissioned And Warrant Officers of the Navy of the United States..., January 1, 1919, p. 240.
5. Uniform Regulations United States Navy, revised January 25, 1913, p. 32.
6. ibid. p. 44.

Dentalman
1. All Hands, "Here's a Complete List of Rating Changes...", March 1948, p. 57
2. United States Statutes at Large, Vol. 63, p. 802
3. Stacy, John A., United States Navy Rating Badges and Marks 1833 to 2008, Mathews N.C.: ASMIC Pubs, 2008, p. 33.
4. United States Navy Uniform Regulations, April 2010, Para. 4227.b
5. http://www.navy.mil/navydata/navy_legacy_hr.asp?id=262, May 2011
6. http://www.navy.mil/navydata/navy_legacy_hr.asp?id=261, May 2011
7. United States Navy Uniform Regulations, April 2011, Art. 4226-21.

Dentalman Apprentice
1. All Hands, "Here's a Complete List of Rating Changes...", March 1948, p. 57
2. United States Statutes at Large, Vol. 63, p. 802
3. Stacy, John A., United States Navy Rating Badges and Marks 1833 to 2008, Mathews N.C.: ASMIC Pubs, 2008, p. 33.
4. United States Navy Uniform Regulations, April 2010, Para. 4227.b
5. http://www.navy.mil/navydata/navy_legacy_hr.asp?id=262, May 2011
6. http://www.navy.mil/navydata/navy_legacy_hr.asp?id=261, May 2011
7. United States Navy Uniform Regulations, April 2011, Art. 4226-21.

Dentalman Recruit
1. All Hands, "Changes Made in Rating Structure,...", August 1948, p. 53.
2. United States Statutes at Large, Vol. 63, p. 802
3. All Hands, "Uniform Changes Published...", December 1948, p. 48
4. Stacy, John A., United States Navy Ratring Badges and Marks 1833 to 2008, Mathews N.C.: ASMIC Pubs, 2008, p. 40.
5. http://www.navy.mil/navydata/navy_legacy_hr.asp?id=261, May 2011
6. United States Navy Uniform Regulations, April 2011, Art. 4226-21.

Electrician
1. United States Statutes at Large, Vol. 43, p. 1274.
2. Stacy, John A., United States Navy Ratring Badges and Marks 1833 to 2008, Mathews N.C.: ASMIC Pubs, 2008, p. 61.
3. http://www.history.navy.mil/library/online/uniform_insignia.htm, March 2011
4. https://picasaweb.google.com/Booker1942/1943TheNavalOfficersUniformPlan#5537445144858829890, March 2011
5. Bureau of Navigation Bulletin ,Number 291, April 26, 1941, p. 28.
6. All Hands, "Green Unifroms Mandatory...", June 1944, p. 71
7. Stacy, John A., United States Navy Ratring Badges and Marks 1833 to 2008, Mathews N.C.: ASMIC Pubs, 2008, p. 61.
8. United States Statutes at Large, Vol. 63, p. 807
9. http://www.history.navy.mil/library/online/uniform_insignia.htm, March 2011
10. All Hands, "Warrant Officers' Collar Devices", October 1952, p. 24
11. United States Statutes at Large, Vol. 68, p. 157

Engineer-in-Chief
1. United States Statutes at Large, Vol. 5, p. 577
2. Bennett, Frank Marion, The steam navy of the United States, Pittsburgh: Warrem & CO., 1896, p. 39-41
3. Callahan, Edward, List of Officers of the Navy of the United States and the Marine Corps from 1775 to 1900, New York: L. R. Hamerlsy & CO., 1901, p. 542.
4. Bennett, Frank Marion, The steam navy of the United States, Pittsburgh: Warrem & CO., 1896, p. 117
5. Callahan, Edward, List of Officers of the Navy of the United States and the Marine Corps from 1775 to 1900, New York: L. R. Hamerlsy & CO., 1901, p.. p. 353.
6. ibid. p. 26.
7. ibid. p. 291.
8. United States Statutes at Large, Vol. 12, p. 510
9. Register of the Commissioned And Warrant Officers of the Navy of the United States..., January 1, 1864, p. 5.
10. Register of the Commissioned And Warrant Officers of the Navy of the United States..., January 1, 1865, p. 5.
11. United States Statutes at Large, Vol. 16, p. 537.
12. Callahan, Edward, List of Officers of the Navy of the United States and the Marine Corps from 1775 to 1900, New York: L. R. Hamerlsy & CO., 1901, p. 314.
13. Regulations for the Goverment of the Navy of the United States, August 7, 1876, p. 192-193.
14. Callahan, Edward, List of Officers of the Navy of the United States and the Marine Corps from 1775 to 1900, New York: L. R. Hamerlsy & CO., 1901, p. 601.
15. ibid. p. 496.
16. ibid. p. 4
17. United States Statutes at Large, Vol. 30, p. 10

Ensign

1. United States Statutes at Large, Vol. 12, p. 583
2. United States Statutes at Large, Vol. 3, p. 224
3. Tily, James C., The Uniforms of the United States Navy, Cranbury: Thomas Yoseloff, 1964, p. 119.
4. ibid. p. 121.

5. http://www.history.navy.mil/faqs/faq59-8.htm, April 2011
6. Tily, James C., The Uniforms of the United States Navy, Cranbury: Thomas Yoseloff, 1964, p. 134.
7. ibid. p. 189.
8. General Order No. 90, March 11, 1869
9. General Order No. 123, April 27, 1869
10. Tily, James C., The Uniforms of the United States Navy, Cranbury: Thomas Yoseloff, 1964, p. 198.
11. ibid. p. 204.
12. ibid. p. 205.
13. Regulations Governing the Uniform of Officers of the United States Navy, 1883, p. 10.
14. Tily, James C., The Uniforms of the United States Navy, Cranbury: Thomas Yoseloff, 1964, p. 222.
15. Uniform Regulations United States Navy, revised January 25, 1913, p. 37.
16. Tily, James C., The Uniforms of the United States Navy, Cranbury: Thomas Yoseloff, 1964, p. 238.
17. ibid. , p. 243-244.
18. Uniform Regulations United States Navy, September 20, 1922, p. 19
19. Tily, James C., The Uniforms of the United States Navy, Cranbury: Thomas Yoseloff, 1964, p. 247-248.
20. ibid p. 271.
21. United States Statutes at Large, Vol. 63, p. 807
22. United States Navy Uniform Regulations, April 2010, Para. 4101
23. United States Navy Uniform Regulations, April 2010, Para. 4103.2a
24. UnitedStates Navy Uniform Regulations, April 2010, Para. 4103.4

Ensign Junior Grade
1. United States Statutes at Large, Vol. 22, p. 472.
2. United States Statutes at Large, Vol. 16, p. 334.
3. United States Statutes at Large, Vol. 22, p. 285.
4. Regulations Governing the Uniform of Officers of the United States Navy, 1883, p. 8.
5. Ibid. p. 10.
6. United States Statutes at Large, Vol. 23, p. 60.

Fireman
1. United States Statutes at Large, Vol. 5, p. 577.
2. http://www.history.navy.mil/faqs/faq78-3.html, March 2011, First apperas in two classes in 1849 pay table.
3. All Hands, "Here's a Complete List of Rating Changes...", March 1948, p. 50
4. United States Statutes at Large, Vol. 63, p. 802
5. Stacy, John A., United States Navy Rating Badges and Marks 1833 to 2008, Mathews N.C.: ASMIC Pubs, 2008, p. 33.
6. United States Navy Uniform Regulations, April 2010, Para. 4227.b

Fireman Apprentice
1. All Hands, "Here's a Complete List of Rating Changes...", March 1948, p. 50
2. United States Statutes at Large, Vol. 63, p. 802
3. Stacy, John A., United States Navy Rating Badges and Marks 1833 to 2008, Mathews N.C.: ASMIC Pubs, 2008, p. 33.
4. United States Navy Uniform Regulations, April 2010, Para. 4227.b

Fireman First Class
1. http://www.history.navy.mil/faqs/faq78-3.html, March 2011, First apperas in two classes in 1849 pay table.
2. Tily, James C., The Uniforms of the United States Navy, Cranbury: Thomas Yoseloff, 1964, p. 192-193.
3. U.S. Navy Regulation Circular, No. 41, January 8, 1885
4. regulations governing the uniform of commissioned officers, warrant officers, and enlisted men of the United States Navy, 1886, p. 25.
5. Stacy, John A., United States Navy Ratring Badges and Marks 1833 to 2008, Mathews N.C.: ASMIC Pubs, 2008, p. 14.
6. United States Statutes at Large, Vol. 42, p. 630.
7. Register of the Commissioned And Warrant Officers of the Navy of the United States..., January 1, 1924, p. 398.
8. BuPers Circular letter 205-43
9. All Hands, "Here's a Complete List of Rating Changes...", March 1948, p. 50

Fireman Recruit
1. All Hands, "Changes Made in Rating Structure,...", August 1948, p. 53.
2. United States Statutes at Large, Vol. 63, p. 802
3. All Hands, "Uniform Changes Published...", December 1948, p. 48
4. Stacy, John A., United States Navy Ratring Badges and Marks 1833 to 2008, Mathews N.C.: ASMIC Pubs, 2008, p. 40.

Fireman Second Class
1. http://www.history.navy.mil/faqs/faq78-3.html, March 2011, First apperas in two classes in 1849 pay table.
2. Tily, James C., The Uniforms of the United States Navy, Cranbury: Thomas Yoseloff, 1964, p. 192-193.
3. U.S. Navy Regulation Circular, No. 41, January 8, 1885
4. regulations governing the uniform of commissioned officers, warrant officers, and enlisted men of the United States Navy, 1886, p. 25.
5. Stacy, John A., United States Navy Ratring Badges and Marks 1833 to 2008, Mathews N.C.: ASMIC Pubs, 2008, p. 14.
6. United States Statutes at Large, Vol. 42, p. 630.
7. Register of the Commissioned And Warrant Officers of the Navy of the United States..., January 1, 1924, p. 398.
8. BuPers Circular letter 205-43
9. All Hands, "Here's a Complete List of Rating Changes...", March 1948, p. 50

Fireman Third Class
1. http://www.history.navy.mil/faqs/faq78-3.html, March 2011
2. Register of the Commissioned And Warrant Officers of the Navy of the United States..., January 1, 1919, p. 1011.
3. United States Statutes at Large, Vol. 42, p. 630.
4. Register of the Commissioned And Warrant Officers of the Navy of the United States..., January 1, 1924, p. 398.
5. BuPers Circular letter 205-43
9. http://www.history.navy.mil/faqs/faq78-3.html, March 2011

First Assistant Engineer
1. Bennett, Frank Marion, The steam navy of the United States, Pittsburgh: Warrem & CO., 1896, p. 25.
2. Tily, James C., The Uniforms of the United States Navy, Cranbury: Thomas Yoseloff, 1964, p. 86-89.
3. United States Statutes at Large, Vol. 5, p. 577
4. Tily, James C., The Uniforms of the United States Navy, Cranbury: Thomas Yoseloff, 1964, p. 97.
5. http://www.history.navy.mil/faqs/faq59-28.htm, April 2011
6. Tily, James C., The Uniforms of the United States Navy, Cranbury: Thomas Yoseloff, 1964, p. 110.
7. ibid. p. 48.
10. United States Statutes at Large, Vol. 11, p. 407.
9. Tily, James C., The Uniforms of the United States Navy, Cranbury: Thomas Yoseloff, 1964, p. 113.
10. Ibid. p. 119.
11. ibid. p. 51.
12. http://www.history.navy.mil/faqs/faq59-8.htm, April 2011
13. Tily, James C., The Uniforms of the United States Navy, Cranbury: Thomas Yoseloff, 1964, p. 189.
14. General Order 90, March 11, 1869.
13. Tily, James C., The Uniforms of the United States Navy, Cranbury: Thomas Yoseloff, 1964, p. 199.
16. General Order 120, April 1, 1869, with letter attached.
17. United States Statutes at Large, Vol. 16, p. 536
18. Navy Regulation Circular, October 3, 1871
19. United States Statutes at Large, Vol. 18, p. 17

Flag Officer
1. United States Statutes at Large, Vol. 11, p. 154
2. Navy Register for the United States for the year 1858, p. 18.
3. http://www.history.navy.mil/faqs/faq59-28.htm, April 2011
4. United States Statutes at Large, Vol. 12, p. 583

Fleet Admiral
1. United States Statutes at Large, Vol. 38, p. 802
2. http://www.eisenhowermemorial.org/stories/Ike-fifth-star.htm, May 2011
3. http://en.wikipedia.org/wiki/Fleet_Admiral_(United_States), May 2011
5. All Hands, "Insignia Approved for Fleet Admiral", February 1945, p. 73
6. http://www.history.navy.mil/faqs/faq36-1.htm, May 2011
7. http://www.history.navy.mil/faqs/faq36-5.htm, May 2011
8. http://www.history.navy.mil/faqs/faq36-3.htm, May 2011
9. http://www.history.navy.mil/faqs/faq36-2.htm, May 2011
10. http://www.history.navy.mil/faqs/faq36-5.htm, May 2011
11. http://www.history.navy.mil/faqs/faq36-4.htm, May 2011
12. http://www.public.navy.mil/bupers-npc/support/uniforms/uniformregulations/chapter4/Pages/4101.aspx, May 2011

Fleet Engineer
1. Tily, James C., The Uniforms of the United States Navy, Cranbury: Thomas Yoseloff, 1964, p. 51.
2. http://www.history.navy.mil/faqs/faq59-8.htm, April 2011
3. Circular, September 29, 1866.
4. General Order, No. 228, August 1, 1877.

Fleet/Force Master Chief Petty Officer
1. http://www.quarterdeck.org/WindsOfChange/046-62.MCPON%20Robert%20Walker.htm, April 2011
2. Stacy, John A., United States Navy Ratring Badges and Marks 1833 to 2008, Mathews N.C.: ASMIC Pubs, 2008, p. 35.

Fleet Paymaster
1. Tily, James C., The Uniforms of the United States Navy, Cranbury: Thomas Yoseloff, 1964, p. 51.
2. http://www.history.navy.mil/faqs/faq59-8.htm, April 2011
3. Circular, September 29, 1866.
4. General Order, No. 228, August 1, 1877.

Fle1. United States Statutes at Large, Vol. 12, p. 23
2. Tily, James C., The Uniforms of the United States Navy, Cranbury: Thomas Yoseloff, 1964, p. 51.
3. http://www.history.navy.mil/faqs/faq59-8.htm, April 2011
3. Circular, September 29, 1866.
4. General Order, No. 228, August 1, 1877.

Gunner
1. Journals of the Continental Congress, Vol. 3, p. 384
2. United States Statutes at Large, Vol. 1, p. 350.
3. United States Statutes at Large, Vol. 1, p. 524.
4. http://www.history.navy.mil/faqs/faq59-4.htm, March 2011
5. General Order, Navy Department, May 1, 1830
6. http://www.history.navy.mil/faqs/faq59-27.htm, March 2011
7. Tily, James C., The Uniforms of the United States Navy, Cranbury: Thomas Yoseloff, 1964, p. 101.
8. http://www.history.navy.mil/faqs/faq59-28.htm, March 2011
9. Tily, James C., The Uniforms of the United States Navy, Cranbury: Thomas Yoseloff, 1964, p. 110.
10. ibid. appendix c, chart shows no buttons on cuff after 1862.
11. http://www.history.navy.mil/faqs/faq59-8.htm
12. General Order No. 90, March 11, 1869
13. Regulations for the Goverment of the Navy of the United States, August 7, 1876, p. 191.
14. Tily, James C., The Uniforms of the United States Navy, Cranbury: Thomas Yoseloff, 1964, p. 204.
15. Regulations Governing the Uniform of Officers of the United States Navy, 1883, p. 11-12.
16. http://www.history.navy.mil/library/online/uniform_insignia.htm, March 2011
17. ibid.
18. Uniform Regulations United States Navy, September 20, 1922, p. 16-18
19. https://picasaweb.google.com/Booker1942/1943TheNavalOfficersUniformPlan#5537445144858829890, March 2011
20. Bureau of Navigation Bulletin ,Number 291, April 26, 1941, p. 28.
21. All Hands, "Green Unifroms Mandatory...", June 1944, p. 71
22. United States Statutes at Large, Vol. 63, p. 807

23. http://www.history.navy.mil/library/online/uniform_insignia.htm, March 2011
24. All Hands, "Warrant Officers' Collar Devices", October 1952, p. 24
25. United States Statutes at Large, Vol. 68, p. 157

Hospital Apprentice First Class
1. United States Statutes at Large, Vol. 30, p. 474
2. Stacy, John A., United States Navy Ratring Badges and Marks 1833 to 2008, Mathews N.C.: ASMIC Pubs, 2008, p. 64.
3. United States Statutes at Large, Vol. 39, p. 572
4. United States Statutes at Large, Vol. 42, p. 630.
5. Uniform Regulations United States Navy, September 20, 1922, p. 26-27.
6. Stacy, John A., United States Navy Ratring Badges and Marks 1833 to 2008, Mathews N.C.: ASMIC Pubs, 2008, p. 22.
7. All Hands, "Here's a Complete List of Rating Changes...", March 1948, p. 50

Hospital Apprentice Second Class
1. United States Statutes at Large, Vol. 30, p. 474
2. Stacy, John A., United States Navy Ratring Badges and Marks 1833 to 2008, Mathews N.C.: ASMIC Pubs, 2008, p. 11.
3. ibid. p. 14.
4. United States Statutes at Large, Vol. 39, p. 572
5. United States Statutes at Large, Vol. 42, p. 630.
6. Uniform Regulations United States Navy, September 20, 1922, p. 26-27.
7. Stacy, John A., United States Navy Ratring Badges and Marks 1833 to 2008, Mathews N.C.: ASMIC Pubs, 2008, p. 22.
8. All Hands, "Here's a Complete List of Rating Changes...", March 1948, p. 50.

Hospital Surgeon
1. http://www.history.navy.mil/faqs/faq59-4.htm, April 2011
2. General Order, Navy Department, May 10, 1820
3. http://www.history.navy.mil/faqs/faq59-4.htm, April 2011
4. General Order, Navy Department, May 10, 1820
5. General Order, Navy Department, May 1, 1830

Hospitalman
1. All Hands, "Here's a Complete List of Rating Changes...", March 1948, p. 57
2. United States Statutes at Large, Vol. 63, p. 802
3. Stacy, John A., United States Navy Rating Badges and Marks 1833 to 2008, Mathews N.C.: ASMIC Pubs, 2008, p. 33.
4. United States Navy Uniform Regulations, April 2010, Para. 4227.b

Hospitalman Apprentice
1. All Hands, "Here's a Complete List of Rating Changes...", March 1948, p. 57
2. United States Statutes at Large, Vol. 63, p. 802
3. Stacy, John A., United States Navy Rating Badges and Marks 1833 to 2008, Mathews N.C.: ASMIC Pubs, 2008, p. 33.
4. United States Navy Uniform Regulations, April 2010, Para. 4227.b

Hospitalman Recruit
1. All Hands, "Changes Made in Rating Structure,...", August 1948, p. 53.
2. United States Statutes at Large, Vol. 63, p. 802
3. All Hands, "Uniform Changes Published...", December 1948, p. 48
4. Stacy, John A., United States Navy Ratring Badges and Marks 1833 to 2008, Mathews N.C.: ASMIC Pubs, 2008, p. 40.

Jack of the Dust
1. http://bluejacket.com/sea-service_tradition.htm#J, May 2011
2. http://www.history.navy.mil/faqs/faq78-3.html, March 2011
3. U.S. Navy Regulation Circular, No. 41, January 8, 1885
4. regulations governing the uniform of commissioned officers, warrant officers, and enlisted men of the United States Navy, 1886, p. 25
5. http://www.history.navy.mil/faqs/faq78-3.html, March 2011

Lamplighter
1. http://www.history.navy.mil/faqs/faq78-3.html, March 2011
2. U.S. Navy Regulation Circular, No. 41, January 8, 1885
3. regulations governing the uniform of commissioned officers, warrant officers, and enlisted men of the United States Navy, 1886, p. 25
4. http://www.history.navy.mil/faqs/faq78-3.html, March 2011

Landsman
1. http://en.wikipedia.org/wiki/Landman_(rank), May 2011
2. Journals of the Continental Congress, Vol. 3, p. 384
3. Journals of the Continental Congress, Vol. 6, p. 954
4. Journals of the Continental Congress, Vol. 20, p. 633
5. Journals of the Continental Congress, Vol. 26, p. 161
6. United States Statutes at Large, Vol. 1, p. 524
7. United States Statutes at Large, Vol. 1, p. 576
8. American State Papers, 20th Congress, 2nd Session Naval Affairs: Volume 3, p. 220
9. http://www.history.navy.mil/faqs/faq78-3.html, March 2011
10. Stacy, John A., United States Navy Ratring Badges and Marks 1833 to 2008, Mathews N.C.: ASMIC Pubs, 2008, p. 5.
11. Tily, James C., The Uniforms of the United States Navy, Cranbury: Thomas Yoseloff, 1964, p. 200.
12. U.S. Navy Regulation Circular, No. 41, January 8, 1885
13. regulations governing the uniform of commissioned officers, warrant officers, and enlisted men of the United States Navy, 1886, p. 25.
14. Register of the Commissioned And Warrant Officers of the Navy of the United States..., January 1, 1905, p. 224.
15. uniform regulations governing the insignia and uniforms of commissioned officers, warrant officers, and enlistedmen of the United States Navy, January 21, 1905, p. 50
16. Stacy, John A., United States Navy Ratring Badges and Marks 1833 to 2008, Mathews N.C.: ASMIC Pubs, 2008, p. 14.
17. Uniform Regulations United States Navy, revised January 25, 1913, p. 66
18. http://www.history.navy.mil/faqs/faq78-3.html, March 2011

Lieutenant
1. Oliver, Raymond, Why is a Kernal called a Colonel?, Tuscon: Fireship press, 1983, p. 25.
2. Mack, William P. and Connell, Royal W., Naval Ceremonies, Customs, and Traditions, 5th edition, Annapolis:Naval Institute Press, 1980, p. 263.
3. Journals of the Continental Congress, Vol. 3, p. 384
4. Journals of the Continental Congress, Vol. 6, p. 954
5. http://bluejacket.com/sea-service_uniform_a.htm, April 2011
6. United States Statutes at Large, Vol. 1, p. 350.
7. United States Statutes at Large, Vol. 1, p. 523.
8. http://www.history.navy.mil/faqs/faq59-3.htm, April 2011
9. http://www.history.navy.mil/faqs/faq59-25.htm, April 2011
10. http://www.history.navy.mil/faqs/faq59-4.htm, April 2011
11. General Order, Navy Department, May 10, 1820
12. General Order, Navy Department, May 1, 1830
13. http://www.history.navy.mil/faqs/faq59-27.htm, April 2011
14. Tily, James C., The Uniforms of the United States Navy, Cranbury: Thomas Yoseloff, 1964, p. 97.
15. http://www.history.navy.mil/faqs/faq59-28.htm, April 2011
16. Tily, James C., The Uniforms of the United States Navy, Cranbury: Thomas Yoseloff, 1964, p. 119.
17. ibid. p. 121.
18. http://www.history.navy.mil/faqs/faq59-8.htm, April 2011
19. Tily, James C., The Uniforms of the United States Navy, Cranbury: Thomas Yoseloff, 1964, p. 131.
20. ibid. p. 189.
21. General Order, No. 90, Navy Department, March 11, 1869
22. Uniform Circular, Navy Department, November 7, 1874
23. Tily, James C., The Uniforms of the United States Navy, Cranbury: Thomas Yoseloff, 1964, p. 204.
24. Regulations Governing the Uniform of Officers of the United States Navy, 1883, p. 10-12.
25. ibid. p. 6
26. Tily, James C., The Uniforms of the United States Navy, Cranbury: Thomas Yoseloff, 1964, p. 219-220.
27. ibid. p. 222
28. uniform regulations governing the insignia and uniforms of commissioned officers, warrant officers, and enlistedmen of the United States Navy, January 21, 1905, p. 31
29. Uniform Regulations United States Navy, revised January 25, 1913, p. 37
30. Tily, James C., The Uniforms of the United States Navy, Cranbury: Thomas Yoseloff, 1964, p. 234.
31. Uniform Regulations United States Navy, revised January 25, 1913, p. 43
32. Tily, James C., The Uniforms of the United States Navy, Cranbury: Thomas Yoseloff, 1964, p. 238.
33. ibid. , p. 243-244.
34. Uniform Regulations United States Navy, September 20, 1922, p. 19
35. Tily, James C., The Uniforms of the United States Navy, Cranbury: Thomas Yoseloff, 1964, p. 247-248.
36. ibid p. 271.
37. United States Statutes at Large, Vol. 63, p. 807
38. United States Navy Uniform Regulations, April 2010, Para. 4101
39. United States Navy Uniform Regulations, April 2010, Para. 4103.2a
40. United States Navy Uniform Regulations, April 2010, Para. 4103.4

Lieutenant Commander
1. United States Statutes at Large, Vol. 12, p. 583
2. Oliver, Raymond, Why is a Kernal called a Colonel?, Tuscon: Fireship press, 1983, p. 35
3. Tily, James C., The Uniforms of the United States Navy, Cranbury: Thomas Yoseloff, 1964, p. 117-119.
4. ibid. p. 123-124
5. http://www.history.navy.mil/faqs/faq59-8c.htm, April 2011
6. http://www.history.navy.mil/faqs/faq59-8a.htm, April 2011
7. http://www.history.navy.mil/faqs/faq59-8e.htm, April 2011
8. http://www.history.navy.mil/faqs/faq59-8b.htm, April 2011
9. Tily, James C., The Uniforms of the United States Navy, Cranbury: Thomas Yoseloff, 1964, p. 133-134.
10. http://www.history.navy.mil/library/online/uniform_insignia.htm, April 2011
11. General Order, No. 90, Navy Department, March 11, 1869
12. Uniform Circular, Navy Department, November 7, 1874
13. Tily, James C., The 19. Uniforms of the United States Navy, Cranbury: Thomas Yoseloff, 1964, p. 204.
14. Regulations Governing the Uniform of Officers of the United States Navy, 1883, p. 11-12
15. Tily, James C., The Uniforms of the United States Navy, Cranbury: Thomas Yoseloff, 1964, p. 222.
16. uniform regulations governing the insignia and uniforms of commissioned officers, warrant officers, and enlistedmen of the United States Navy, January 21, 1905, p. 31
17. Uniform Regulations United States Navy, revised January 25, 1913, p. 37
18. Tily, James C., The Uniforms of the United States Navy, Cranbury: Thomas Yoseloff, 1964, p. 234.
19. Uniform Regulations United States Navy, revised January 25, 1913, p. 43
20. Tily, James C., The Uniforms of the United States Navy, Cranbury: Thomas Yoseloff, 1964, p. 238.
21. ibid. , p. 243-244.
22. Uniform Regulations United States Navy, September 20, 1922, p. 19
23. Tily, James C., The Uniforms of the United States Navy, Cranbury: Thomas Yoseloff, 1964, p. 247-248.
24. ibid p. 271.
25. United States Statutes at Large, Vol. 63, p. 807
26. United States Navy Uniform Regulations, April 2010, Para. 4101
27. United States Navy Uniform Regulations, April 2010, Para. 4103.2a

28. UnitedStates Navy Uniform Regulations, April 2010, Para. 4103.4

Lieutenant Junior Grade
1. United States Statutes at Large, Vol. 22, p. 472.
2. Regulations Governing the Uniform of Officers of the United States Navy, 1883, p. 8 & 10.
3. Tily, James C., The Uniforms of the United States Navy, Cranbury: Thomas Yoseloff, 1964, p. 222.
4. uniform regulations governing the insignia and uniforms of commissioned officers, warrant officers, and enlistedmen of the United States Navy, January 21, 1905, p. 31
5. Uniform Regulations United States Navy, revised January 25, 1913, p. 37
6. Tily, James C., The Uniforms of the United States Navy, Cranbury: Thomas Yoseloff, 1964, p. 234.
7. Uniform Regulations United States Navy, revised January 25, 1913, p. 43
8. Tily, James C., The Uniforms of the United States Navy, Cranbury: Thomas Yoseloff, 1964, p. 238.
9. ibid. , p. 243-244.
10. Uniform Regulations United States Navy, September 20, 1922, p. 19
11. Tily, James C., The Uniforms of the United States Navy, Cranbury: Thomas Yoseloff, 1964, p. 247-248.
12. ibid p. 271.
13. United States Statutes at Large, Vol. 63, p. 807
14. United States Navy Uniform Regulations, April 2010, Para. 4101
15. United States Navy Uniform Regulations, April 2010, Para. 4103.2a
16. United States Navy Uniform Regulations, April 2010, Para. 4103.4

Machinist
1. United States Statutes at Large, Vol. 35, p. 771
2. http://www.history.navy.mil/library/online/uniform_insignia.htm, March 2011
3. Uniform Regulations United States Navy, revised January 25, 1913, p. 34
4. ibid. p. 37
5. Tily, James C., The Uniforms of the United States Navy, Cranbury: Thomas Yoseloff, 1964, p. 234.
6. http://www.history.navy.mil/library/online/uniform_insignia.htm, March 2011
7. Uniform Regulations United States Navy, September 20, 1922, p. 16-18
8. https://picasaweb.google.com/Booker1942/1943TheNavalOfficersUniformPlan#5537445144858829890, March 2011
9. Bureau of Navigation Bulletin ,Number 291, April 26, 1941, p. 28.
10. All Hands, "Green Unifroms Mandatory...", June 1944, p. 71
11. United States Statutes at Large, Vol. 63, p. 807
12. http://www.history.navy.mil/library/online/uniform_insignia.htm, March 2011
13. All Hands, "Warrant Officers' Collar Devices", October 1952, p. 24
14. United States Statutes at Large, Vol. 68, p. 157
15. http://www.history.navy.mil/faqs/faq78-3.html, March 2011

Master
0. http://users.sisna.com/justinb/msp.html, December 1999.
1. United States Statutes at Large, Vol. 5, p. 163
2. General Order, Navy Department, May 1, 1830
3. http://www.history.navy.mil/faqs/faq59-27.htm, April 2011
4. United States Statutes at Large, Vol. 9, p. 97
5. Register of the Commissioned And Warrant Officers of the Navy of the United States..., 1846, p. 59.
6. Register of the Commissioned And Warrant Officers of the Navy of the United States..., 1847, p. 86.
7. ibid. p. 108-109.
8. ibid. p. 58.
9. Register of the Commissioned And Warrant Officers of the Navy of the United States..., 1846, p. 42-43.
10. Register of the Commissioned And Warrant Officers of the Navy of the United States..., 1842, p. 33.
11. Tily, James C., The Uniforms of the United States Navy, Cranbury: Thomas Yoseloff, 1964, p. 34.
12. http://www.history.navy.mil/faqs/faq59-28.htm, April 2011
13. United States Statutes at Large, Vol. 10, p. 617
14. Register of the Commissioned And Warrant Officers of the Navy of the United States..., 1855, p. 76.
15. Register of the Commissioned And Warrant Officers of the Navy of the United States..., 1856, p. 98.
16. Tily, James C., The Uniforms of the United States Navy, Cranbury: Thomas Yoseloff, 1964, p. 119.
17. ibid. p. 121.
18. http://www.history.navy.mil/faqs/faq59-8.htm, April 2011
19. Tily, James C., The Uniforms of the United States Navy, Cranbury: Thomas Yoseloff, 1964, p. 134.
20. ibid. p. 189.
21. General Order No. 90, March 11, 1869
22. General Order No. 123, April 27, 1869
23. Tily, James C., The Uniforms of the United States Navy, Cranbury: Thomas Yoseloff, 1964, p. 198.
24. Navy Department Circular, October 3, 1871
25. Tily, James C., The Uniforms of the United States Navy, Cranbury: Thomas Yoseloff, 1964, p. 204.
26. ibid. p. 205
27. United States Statutes at Large, Vol. 22, p. 472.

Master Chief Petty Officer
1. United States Statutes at Large, Vol. 72, p. 123
2. All Hands, "The Word: New Pay Grades", June 1958, p. 43
3. All Hands, "The Word: Insignia for E-8, E-9", August 1958, p. 46
4. All Hands, "CPO Collar Devices", November 1959, p. 26.
5. All Hands, "Top Chiefs Will Now Wear Stars on Their Collars", January 1961, p. 54.
6. Stacy, John A., United States Navy Ratring Badges and Marks 1833 to 2008, Mathews N.C.: ASMIC Pubs, 2008, p. 38.
7. All Hands, "New Officer, CPO Uniform...", June 1979, p. 2.
8. NAVADMIN 011/99, June 30, 1999
9. http://en.wikipedia.org/wiki/Uniforms_of_the_United_States_Navy#Obsolete_uniforms, April 2011
10. NAVADMIN 020/10, January 10, 2010

Master Chief Petty Officer of the Command
1. All Hands, "From the desk of the Master Chief Petty Officer of the Navy: MCPOC", July 1971, p. 56
2. Stacy, John A., United States Navy Ratring Badges and Marks 1833 to 2008, Mathews N.C.: ASMIC Pubs, 2008, p. 35.
3. navpers 15665B, 1975, para. 5401c.

Master Chief Petty Officer of the Fleet/Force
1. All Hands, "PAC Fleet Selects Top Chief", April 1971, p. 42
2. Stacy, John A., United States Navy Ratring Badges and Marks 1833 to 2008, Mathews N.C.: ASMIC Pubs, 2008, p. 35.
3. http://www.quarterdeck.org/WindsOfChange/046-62.MCPON%20Robert%20Walker.htm, April 2011

Master Chief Petty Officer of the Navy
1. All Hands, "Bulletin Board: Prestige of the Petty Officer", December 1966, p. 50
2. http://www.quarterdeck.org/WindsOfChange/002%20Acknowledgments-11.htm#The%20Pulsetakers, May 2011
3. http://www.history.navy.mil/faqs/faq46-8.htm, May 2011
4. http://www.quarterdeck.org/WindsOfChange/012-29%20MCPON%20Black.htm, May 2011
5. http://www.history.navy.mil/faqs/faq46-8.htm, May 2011
6. Stacy, John A., United States Navy Ratring Badges and Marks 1833 to 2008, Mathews N.C.: ASMIC Pubs, 2008, p. 35.
7. All Hands, "From the desk of the Master Chief Petty Officer of the Navy: MCPOC", July 1971, p. 56
8. Stacy, John A., United States Navy Ratring Badges and Marks 1833 to 2008, Mathews N.C.: ASMIC Pubs, 2008, p. 35.
9. http://www.history.navy.mil/faqs/faq46-8.htm, May 2011

Master Commandant
1. http://en.wikipedia.org/wiki/Commander, May 2011.
2. Oliver, Raymond, Why is a Kernal called a Colonel?, Tuscon: Fireship press, 1983, p. 37.
3. United States Statutes at Large, Vol. 1, p. 618
4. Callahan, Edward, List of Officers of the Navy of the United States and the Marine Corps from 1775 to 1900, New York: L. R. Hamerlsy & CO., 1901.
5. Senate Executive Journal, December 13, 1799
6. Senate Executive Journal, Volume 1, p. 334.
7. Senate Executive Journal, Volume 1, p. 358.
8. Callahan, Edward, List of Officers of the Navy of the United States and the Marine Corps from 1775 to 1900, New York: L. R. Hamerlsy & CO., 1901.
9. United States Statutes at Large, Vol. 2, p. 110
10. Callahan, Edward, List of Officers of the Navy of the United States and the Marine Corps from 1775 to 1900, New York: L. R. Hamerlsy & CO., 1901.
11. Senate Executive Journal, Volume 1, p. 472.
12. United States Statutes at Large, Vol. 2, p. 390
13. http://www.history.navy.mil/faqs/faq59-4.htm, April 2011
14. General Order, Navy Department, May 10, 1820
15. General Order, Navy Department, May 1, 1830
16. United States Statutes at Large, Vol. 5, p. 163

Master's Mate
0. Journals of the Continental Congress, Vol. 3, p. 384
1. United States Statutes at Large, Vol. 1, p. 350.
2. United States Statutes at Large, Vol. 1, p. 523.
3. United States Statutes at Large, Vol. 2, p. 789.
4. Callahan, Edward, List of Officers of the Navy of the United States and the Marine Corps from 1775 to 1900, New York: L. R. Hamerlsy & CO., 1901, p. 576
5. Callahan, Edward, List of Officers of the Navy of the United States and the Marine Corps from 1775 to 1900, New York: L. R. Hamerlsy & CO., 1901, p. 315.
6. United States Statutes at Large, Vol. 4, p. 756.
7. http://www.history.navy.mil/faqs/faq78-3.html, March 2011
8. General Regulations for the Navy and Marine Corps of the United States, 1841, p. 1
9. ibid. p. 14
10. Callahan, Edward, List of Officers of the Navy of the United States and the Marine Corps from 1775 to 1900, New York: L. R. Hamerlsy & CO., 1901.
11. United States Statutes at Large, Vol. 12, p. 273.
12. Tily, James C., The Uniforms of the United States Navy, Cranbury: Thomas Yoseloff, 1964, p. 114-115.
13. ibid. p. 120.
14. ibid. p. 121.
15. http://www.history.navy.mil/faqs/faq59-8b.htm, June 2011
16. United States Statutes at Large, Vol. 13, p. 539.

Mate
1. United States Statutes at Large, Vol. 13, p. 539.
2. http://www.history.navy.mil/faqs/faq59-8b.htm, June 2011
3. Regulations for the Goverment of the Navy of the United States, August 7, 1876, p. 191.
4. http://www.history.navy.mil/library/online/uniform_insignia.htm, March 2011
5. Tily, James C., The Uniforms of the United States Navy, Cranbury: Thomas Yoseloff, 1964, p. 204-205.
6. Regulations Governing the Uniform of Officers of the United States Navy, 1883, p. 11.
7. United States Statutes at Large , Vol. 13, p. 539.
8. Register of the Commissioned And Warrant Officers of the Navy of the United States..., January 1, 1898, p. 61.
9. ibid. p. 134
10. Register of the Commissioned And Warrant Officers of the Navy of the United States..., January 1, 1910, p. 269.
11. Register of the Commissioned And Warrant Officers of the Navy of the United States..., January 1, 1907, p. 106. shows 39 Mates.
12. Register of the Commissioned And Warrant Officers of the Navy of the United States..., January 1, 1908, p. 110. has no Mates.
13. http://www.history.navy.mil/library/online/uniform_insignia.htm, March 2011.
14. Uniform Regulations United States Navy, revised January 25, 1913, p. 37
15. Tily, James C., The Uniforms of the United States Navy, Cranbury: Thomas Yoseloff, 1964, p. 234.
16.

http://www.history.navy.mil/library/online/uniform_insignia.htm, March 2011
17. United States Statutes at Large, Vol. 42, p. 630.
18. Uniform Regulations United States Navy, September 20, 1922, p. 17.
19. U.S. Navy Uniform Regulations, May 31, 1941, p. 14.
20. Register of the Commissioned And Warrant Officers of the Navy of the United States..., July 1, 1943, p. 584.

Medical Director
1. United States Statutes at Large, Vol. 16, p. 535.
2. Regulations for the Goverment of the Navy of the United States, August 7, 1876, p. 192-193.
3. Regulations Governing the Uniform of Officers of the United States Navy, 1883, p. 9-10.
4. United States Statutes at Large, Vol. 30, p. 1006.
5. Register of the Commissioned And Warrant Officers of the Navy of the United States..., Janary 1, 1917, p. 80.
6. All Hands, "175th Anniversary The Navy Supply Corps", March 1970, p. 41
7. Tily, James C., The Uniforms of the United States Navy, Cranbury: Thomas Yoseloff, 1964, p. 243-244.
8. United States Statutes at Large, Vol. 61, p. 872.

Medical Inspector
1. United States Statutes at Large, Vol. 16, p. 535.
2. Regulations for the Goverment of the Navy of the United States, August 7, 1876, p. 192-193.
3. Regulations Governing the Uniform of Officers of the United States Navy, 1883, p. 9-10.
4. United States Statutes at Large, Vol. 30, p. 1006.
5. All Hands, "175th Anniversary The Navy Supply Corps", March 1970, p. 41
6. Tily, James C., The Uniforms of the United States Navy, Cranbury: Thomas Yoseloff, 1964, p. 243-244.
7. United States Statutes at Large, Vol. 61, p. 872.

Mess Attendant
1. http://www.history.navy.mil/faqs/faq78-3.html, March 2011
2. Regulations for the Uniform of the Commissioned Officers, Warrant Officers, and Enlisted Men of the Navy of the United States, 1886, p. 16
3. http://www.quarterdeck.org/uniforms/1897/21-37%20Enlisted%201897.htm, June 2011.
4. http://www.history.navy.mil/faqs/faq78-3.html, March 2011

Mess Attendant First Class
1. http://www.history.navy.mil/faqs/faq78-3.html, March 2011
2. uniform regulations governing the insignia and uniforms of commissioned officers, warrant officers, and enlistedmen of the United States Navy, January 21, 1905, p. 42.
3. ibid. p 50.
4. Stacy, John A., United States Navy Ratring Badges and Marks 1833 to 2008, Mathews N.C.: ASMIC Pubs, 2008, p. 74. all other messmen rates began to wear the crescent at this time and the 1922 regulations p. 27 specifies them for Mess Attendants.
5. Register of the Commissioned And Warrant Officers of the Navy of the United States..., January 1, 1923, p. 307.
6. http://www.history.navy.mil/faqs/faq78-3.html, March 2011

Mess Attendant Second Class
1. http://www.history.navy.mil/faqs/faq78-3.html, March 2011
2. uniform regulations governing the insignia and uniforms of commissioned officers, warrant officers, and enlistedmen of the United States Navy, January 21, 1905, p. 42.
3. ibid. p 50.
4. Stacy, John A., United States Navy Ratring Badges and Marks 1833 to 2008, Mathews N.C.: ASMIC Pubs, 2008, p. 74. all other messmen rates began to wear the crescent at this time and the 1922 regulations p. 27 specifies them for Mess Attendants.
5. Register of the Commissioned And Warrant Officers of the Navy of the United States..., January 1, 1923, p. 307.
6. http://www.history.navy.mil/faqs/faq78-3.html, March 2011

Mess Attendant Third Class
1. http://www.history.navy.mil/faqs/faq78-3.html, March 2011
2. uniform regulations governing the insignia and uniforms of commissioned officers, warrant officers, and enlistedmen of the United States Navy, January 21, 1905, p. 42.
3. ibid. p 50.
4. Stacy, John A., United States Navy Ratring Badges and Marks 1833 to 2008, Mathews N.C.: ASMIC Pubs, 2008, p. 74. all other messmen rates began to wear the crescent at this time and the 1922 regulations p. 27 specifies them for Mess Attendants.
5. Register of the Commissioned And Warrant Officers of the Navy of the United States..., January 1, 1923, p. 307.
6. http://www.history.navy.mil/faqs/faq78-3.html, March 2011

Mess Management Specialist
1. United States Navy Uniform Regulations, 1975, p. 5-44.

Midshipman
1. http://en.wikipedia.org/wiki/Midshipman, June 2011
2. http://www.hmsrichmond.org/avast/customs.htm, June 2011
3. http://www.tpub.com/content/administration/12966/css/12966_380.htm, June 2011
4. Journals of the Continental Congress, Vol. 3, p. 384
5. http://bluejacket.com/sea-service_uniform_a.htm, June 2011
6. United States Statutes at Large, Vol. 1, p. 350.
7. United States Statutes at Large, Vol. 1, p. 523.
8. http://www.history.navy.mil/faqs/faq59-3.htm, June 2011
9. http://www.history.navy.mil/faqs/faq59-25.htm, June 2011
10. http://www.history.navy.mil/faqs/faq59-4.htm, June 2011
11. General Order, Navy Department, May 10, 1820
12. General Order, Navy Department, May 1, 1830
13. http://www.history.navy.mil/faqs/faq59-27.htm, June 2011
14. http://www.usna.edu/VirtualTour/150years/, June 2011
15. Register of the Commissioned And Warrant Officers of the Navy of the United States..., 1852, p. 87.
16. http://www.history.navy.mil/faqs/faq59-28.htm, April 2011
17. United States Statutes at Large, Vol. 12, p. 583.
18. Tily, James C., The Uniforms of the United States Navy, Cranbury: Thomas Yoseloff, 1964, p. 117.
19. Register of the Commissioned And Warrant Officers of the Navy of the United States..., January 1, 1863, p. 40.
20. Benjamin, Park ., The United States naval academy, New York: G.P. Putman's Sons, 1900, p. 257.
21. United States Statutes at Large, Vol. 13, p. 539.
22. Tily, James C., The Uniforms of the United States Navy, Cranbury: Thomas Yoseloff, 1964, p. 121.
23. United States Statutes at Large, Vol. 13, p. 393.
24. Tily, James C., The Uniforms of the United States Navy, Cranbury: Thomas Yoseloff, 1964, p. 134. jacket mentioned for academy midshipmen in general order 90. March 11, 1869.
25. Benjamin, Park ., The United States naval academy, New York: G.P. Putman's Sons, 1900, p. 282.
26. General Order, No. 90, March 11, 1869.
27. Tily, James C., The Uniforms of the United States Navy, Cranbury: Thomas Yoseloff, 1964, p. 198.
28. United States Statutes at Large, Vol. 16, p. 334.
29. Regulations for the Goverment of the Navy of the United States, August 7, 1876, p. 189-195.
30. The 1866 and 1869 regulations have proved unavailable.
31. United States Statutes at Large, Vol. 22, p. 285.
32. United States Statutes at Large, Vol. 22, p. 472.
32. United States Statutes at Large, Vol. 32, p. 686.

Musician First Class
1. http://www.history.navy.mil/faqs/faq78-3.html, March 2011
2. Stacy, John A., United States Navy Ratring Badges and Marks 1833 to 2008, Mathews N.C.: ASMIC Pubs, 2008, p. 69.
3. U.S. Navy Regulation Circular, No. 41, January 8, 1885.
4. regulations governing the uniform of commissioned officers, warrant officers, and enlisted men of the United States Navy, 1886, p. 25.
5. Stacy, John A., United States Navy Ratring Badges and Marks 1833 to 2008, Mathews N.C.: ASMIC Pubs, 2008, p. 69.
6. ibid. p. 14.
7. Register of the Commissioned And Warrant Officers of the Navy of the United States..., 1924, p. 329.

Musician Second Class
1. http://www.history.navy.mil/faqs/faq78-3.html, March 2011
2. Stacy, John A., United States Navy Ratring Badges and Marks 1833 to 2008, Mathews N.C.: ASMIC Pubs, 2008, p. 69.
3. U.S. Navy Regulation Circular, No. 41, January 8, 1885.
4. regulations governing the uniform of commissioned officers, warrant officers, and enlisted men of the United States Navy, 1886, p. 25.
5. Stacy, John A., United States Navy Ratring Badges and Marks 1833 to 2008, Mathews N.C.: ASMIC Pubs, 2008, p. 69.
6. ibid. p. 14.
7. Register of the Commissioned And Warrant Officers of the Navy of the United States..., 1924, p. 329.

Naval Cadet
1. United States Statutes at Large, Vol. 22, p. 285.
2. Regulations Governing the Uniform of Officers of the United States Navy, 1883, p. 9&10.
3. Tily, James C., The Uniforms of the United States Navy, Cranbury: Thomas Yoseloff, 1964, p. 198.
4. Regulations Governing the Uniform of Officers of the United States Navy, 1883, p. 8.
5. ibid. p. 12.
6. http://grandarmyofthefrontier.org/uniforms/usn1897.htm, June 2011
7. United States Statutes at Large, Vol. 32, p. 686.

Naval Constructor
1. http://en.wikipedia.org/wiki/Original_six_frigates_of_the_United_States_Navy, June 2011.
2. Callahan, Edward, List of Officers of the Navy of the United States and the Marine Corps from 1775 to 1900, New York: L. R. Hamerlsy & CO., 1901.
3. Tily, James C., The Uniforms of the United States Navy, Cranbury: Thomas Yoseloff, 1964, p. 51.
4. Register of the Commissioned And Warrant Officers of the Navy of the United States..., January 1, 1864, p. 108.
5. http://www.history.navy.mil/faqs/faq59-8.htm, June 2011.
6. United States Statutes at Large, Vol. 14, p. 223
7. General Order 120, April 1, 1869, with letter attached.
8. United States Statutes at Large, Vol. 16, p. 536
9. Tily, James C., The Uniforms of the United States Navy, Cranbury: Thomas Yoseloff, 1964, p. 201.
10. United States Statutes at Large, Vol. 30, p. 1005
11. United States Statutes at Large, Vol. 39, p. 577
12. All Hands, "175th Anniversary The Navy Supply Corps", March 1970, p. 41
13. United States Statutes at Large, Vol. 54, p. 527

(Officers') Chief Cook
1. Stacy, John A., United States Navy Ratring Badges and Marks 1833 to 2008, Mathews N.C.: ASMIC Pubs, 2008, p. 111.
2. ibid.
3. http://www.history.navy.mil/library/online/uniform_regs.htm, June 2011.
4. All Hands, "Changes Made in Rating Structure,...", August 1948, p. 57.
5. All Hands, "Wants Clarification", July 1946, p. 39

Officer's Chief Steward
1. Stacy, John A., United States Navy Ratring Badges and Marks 1833 to 2008, Mathews N.C.: ASMIC Pubs, 2008, p. 111.
2. ibid.
3. http://www.history.navy.mil/library/online/uniform_regs.htm, June 2011.
4. All Hands, "Changes Made in Rating Structure,...", August 1948, p. 57.
5. All Hands, "Wants Clarification", July 1946, p. 39

Officers' Cook
1. http://www.history.navy.mil/faqs/faq78-3.html, March 2011

(Officer's) Cook First Class
1. Stacy, John A., United States Navy Rating Badges and Marks 1833 to 2008, Mathews N.C.: ASMIC Pubs, 2008, p. 111.
2. ibid.
3. http://www.history.navy.mil/library/online/uniform_regs.htm, June 2011.
4. All Hands, "Changes Made in Rating Structure,...", August 1948, p. 57.
5. All Hands, "Wants Clarification", July 1946, p. 39

(Officers') Cook Second Class
1. Stacy, John A., United States Navy Rating Badges and Marks 1833 to 2008, Mathews N.C.: ASMIC Pubs, 2008, p. 111.
2. ibid.
3. http://www.history.navy.mil/library/online/uniform_regs.htm, June 2011.
4. All Hands, "Changes Made in Rating Structure,...", August 1948, p. 57.
5. All Hands, "Wants Clarification", July 1946, p. 39

(Officers') Cook Third Class
1. Stacy, John A., United States Navy Rating Badges and Marks 1833 to 2008, Mathews N.C.: ASMIC Pubs, 2008, p. 111.
2. ibid.
3. http://www.history.navy.mil/library/online/uniform_regs.htm, June 2011.
4. All Hands, "Changes Made in Rating Structure,...", August 1948, p. 57.
5. All Hands, "Wants Clarification", July 1946, p. 39

(Officers') Steward First Class
1. Stacy, John A., United States Navy Rating Badges and Marks 1833 to 2008, Mathews N.C.: ASMIC Pubs, 2008, p. 111.
2. ibid.
3. http://www.history.navy.mil/library/online/uniform_regs.htm, June 2011.
4. All Hands, "Changes Made in Rating Structure,...", August 1948, p. 57.
5. All Hands, "Wants Clarification", July 1946, p. 39.

(Officers') Steward Second Class
1. Stacy, John A., United States Navy Rating Badges and Marks 1833 to 2008, Mathews N.C.: ASMIC Pubs, 2008, p. 111.
2. ibid.
3. http://www.history.navy.mil/library/online/uniform_regs.htm, June 2011.
4. All Hands, "Changes Made in Rating Structure,...", August 1948, p. 57.
5. All Hands, "Wants Clarification", July 1946, p. 39.

(Officers') Steward Third Class
1. Stacy, John A., United States Navy Rating Badges and Marks 1833 to 2008, Mathews N.C.: ASMIC Pubs, 2008, p. 111.
2. ibid.
3. http://www.history.navy.mil/library/online/uniform_regs.htm, June 2011.
4. All Hands, "Changes Made in Rating Structure,...", August 1948, p. 57.
5. All Hands, "Wants Clarification", July 1946, p. 39

Ordinary Seaman
1. United States Statutes at Large, Vol. 1, p. 350.
2. United States Statutes at Large, Vol. 1, p. 523.
3. Tily, James C., The Uniforms of the United States Navy, Cranbury: Thomas Yoseloff, 1964, p. 193.
4. ibid. p. 200.
5. U.S. Navy Regulation Circular, No. 41, January 8, 1885
6. regulations governing the uniform of commissioned officers, warrant officers, and enlisted men of the United States Navy, 1886, p. 25.
7. Stacy, John A., United States Navy Ratring Badges and Marks 1833 to 2008, Mathews N.C.: ASMIC Pubs, 2008, p. 14.
8. http://www.history.navy.mil/faqs/faq78-3.html, March 2011

Ordinary Seaman Second Class
1. http://www.history.navy.mil/faqs/faq78-3.html, March 2011

Passed Assistant Dental Surgeon
1. United States Statutes at Large, Vol. 40, p. 708.
2. All Hands, "175th Anniversary The Navy Supply Corps", March 1970, p. 41.
3. Uniform Regulations United States Navy, September 20, 1922, p. 17.
4. United States Statutes at Large, Vol. 61, p. 872

Passed Assistant Engineer
1. United States Statutes at Large, Vol. 18, p. 17.
2. Regulations for the Goverment of the Navy of the United States, August 7, 1876, p. 192-193.
3. United States Statutes at Large, Vol. 30, p. 1006

Passed Assistant Paymaster
1. United States Statutes at Large, Vol. 14, p. 43.
2. Register of the Commissioned And Warrant Officers of the Navy of the United States..., January 1, 1867, p. 56.
3. Tily, James C., The Uniforms of the United States Navy, Cranbury: Thomas Yoseloff, 1964, p. 189.
4. General Order 120, April 1, 1869, with letter attached.
5. Register of the Commissioned And Warrant Officers of the Navy of the United States..., January 1, 1870, p. 52.
6. General Order No. 90, March 11, 1869.
7. United States Statutes at Large, Vol. 16, p. 536.
8. United States Statutes at Large, Vol. 30, p. 1006.
9. http://www.history.navy.mil/library/online/uniform_insignia.htm, March 2011
10. All Hands, "175th Anniversary The Navy Supply Corps", March 1970, p. 41
11. United States Statutes at Large, Vol. 61, p. 872

Passed Assistant Surgeon
1. United States Statutes at Large, Vol. 4, p. 755.
2. http://www.history.navy.mil/faqs/faq59-27.htm, April 2011.
3. Tily, James C., The Uniforms of the United States Navy, Cranbury: Thomas Yoseloff, 1964, p. 45.
4. General Order, August 31, 1846.
4a. United States Statutes at Large, Vol. 10, p. 587
5. Tily, James C., The Uniforms of the United States Navy, Cranbury: Thomas Yoseloff, 1964, p. 99.
6. http://www.history.navy.mil/faqs/faq59-28.htm, March 2011
7. Tily, James C., The Uniforms of the United States Navy, Cranbury: Thomas Yoseloff, 1964, p. 109-110.
8. ibid. p. 117-120.
9. ibid. p. 51
10. http://www.history.navy.mil/faqs/faq59-8i.htm, March 2011.
11. Tily, James C., The Uniforms of the United States Navy, Cranbury: Thomas Yoseloff, 1964, p. 189.
12. General Order 120, April 1, 1869, with letter attached.
13. Tily, James C., The Uniforms of the United States Navy, Cranbury: Thomas Yoseloff, 1964, p. 198-199. with regulation quote courtesy of Justin Broderick.
14. United States Statutes at Large, Vol. 16, p. 536
15. Tily, James C., The Uniforms of the United States Navy, Cranbury: Thomas Yoseloff, 1964, p. 207.
16. United States Statutes at Large, Vol. 30, p. 1006
17. United States Statutes at Large, Vol. 37, p. 344
18. Tily, James C., The Uniforms of the United States Navy, Cranbury: Thomas Yoseloff, 1964, p. 233.
19. All Hands, "175th Anniversary The Navy Supply Corps", March 1970, p. 41
20. Tily, James C., The Uniforms of the United States Navy, Cranbury: Thomas Yoseloff, 1964, p. 243-244.
21. United States Statutes at Large, Vol. 61, p. 872

Passed Midshipman
1. http://www.ibiblio.org/pha/USN/1829/NavReg1829.html, June 2011.
2. United States Statutes at Large, Vol. 4, p. 311-312.
3. United States Statutes at Large, Vol. 4, p. 304.
4. United States Statutes at Large, Vol. 4, p. 313.
5. United States Statutes at Large, Vol. 4, p. 756.
6. General Order, Navy Department, May 1, 1830
7. http://www.history.navy.mil/faqs/faq59-27.htm, April 2011.
8. http://www.history.navy.mil/faqs/faq59-28.htm, April 2011.
9. United States Statutes at Large, Vol. 10, p. 617.
10. Register of the Commissioned And Warrant Officers of the Navy of the United States..., 1857, p. 56.
11. United States Statutes at Large, Vol. 12, p. 583.

Pay Clerk
1. United States Statutes at Large, Vol. 38, p. 942
2. http://www.history.navy.mil/library/online/uniform_insignia.htm, March 2011
3. http://www.history.navy.mil/library/online/uniform_insignia.htm, March 2011
4. Uniform Regulations United States Navy, September 20, 1922, p. 16-18
5. https://picasaweb.google.com/Booker1942/1943TheNavalOfficersUniformPlan#5537445144858829890, March 2011
6. Bureau of Navigation Bulletin ,Number 291, April 26, 1941, p. 28.
7. All Hands, "Green Unifroms Mandatory...", June 1944, p. 71
8. United States Statutes at Large, Vol. 63, p. 807
9. http://www.history.navy.mil/library/online/uniform_insignia.htm, March 2011
10. All Hands, "Warrant Officers' Collar Devices", October 1952, p. 24
11. United States Statutes at Large, Vol. 68, p. 157

Pay Director
1. United States Statutes at Large, Vol. 16, p. 526.
2. United States Statutes at Large, Vol. 30, p. 1006
3. All Hands, "175th Anniversary The Navy Supply Corps", March 1970, p. 41.
4. United States Statutes at Large, Vol. 61, p. 872

Pay Inspector
1. United States Statutes at Large, Vol. 16, p. 526.
2. United States Statutes at Large, Vol. 30, p. 1006
3. All Hands, "175th Anniversary The Navy Supply Corps", March 1970, p. 41.
4. United States Statutes at Large, Vol. 61, p. 872

Paymaster General
1. United States Statutes at Large, Vol. 16, p. 537
2. Regulations for the Goverment of the Navy of the United States, August 7, 1876, p. 189-195.
3. Callahan, Edward, List of Officers of the Navy of the United States and the Marine Corps from 1775 to 1900, New York: L. R. Hamerlsy & CO., 1901, p. 174.
4. ibid. p. 71.
5. ibid. p. 571.
6. ibid. p. 5.
7. United States Statutes at Large, Vol. 30, p. 1006.
8. Callahan, Edward, List of Officers of the Navy of the United States and the Marine Corps from 1775 to 1900, New York: L. R. Hamerlsy & CO., 1901, p. 5
9. Register of the Commissioned And Warrant Officers of the Navy of the United States..., January 1, 1904, p. 164.
10. ibid p. 60.
11. Register of the Commissioned And Warrant Officers of the Navy of the United States..., January 1, 1906, p. 168.
12. Register of the Commissioned And Warrant Officers of the Navy of the United States..., January 1, 1907, p. 64.
13. Register of the Commissioned And Warrant Officers of the Navy of the United States..., January 1, 1911, p. 204.
14. ibid. p. 78.
15. All Hands, "175th Anniversary The Navy Supply Corps", March 1970, p. 41
16. United States Statutes at Large, Vol. 61, p. 872

Paymaster
1. United States Statutes at Large, Vol. 12, p. 83
2. Register of the Commissioned And Warrant Officers of the Navy of the United States..., August 31, 1861, p. 26.
3. Tily, James C., The Uniforms of the United States Navy, Cranbury: Thomas Yoseloff, 1964, p. 108.

4. ibid.
5. ibid. p. 119.
6. ibid. p. 51.
7. http://www.history.navy.mil/faqs/faq59-8.htm, June 2011.
8. General Order 120, April 1, 1869, with letter attached.
9. General Order No. 90, March 11, 1869.
10. United States Statutes at Large, Vol. 16, p. 536.
11. uniform regulations governing the insignia and uniforms of commissioned officers, warrant officers, and enlistedmen of the United States Navy, January 21, 1905, plate xv.
12. United States Statutes at Large, Vol. 30, p. 1006.
13. All Hands, "175th Anniversary The Navy Supply Corps", March 1970, p. 41
14. United States Statutes at Large, Vol. 61, p. 872

Petty Officer (before 1885)
1. Oliver, Raymond, Why is a Kernal called a Colonel?, Tuscon: Fireship press, 1983, p. 11.
2. http://www.history.navy.mil/faqs/faq78-3.html, March 2011.
3. Journals of the Continental Congress, Vol. 3, p. 384.
4. Journals of the Continental Congress, Vol. 6, p. 954.
5. United States Statutes at Large, Vol. 1, p. 350.
6. United States Statutes at Large, Vol. 1, p. 523.
7. Stacy, John A., United States Navy Ratring Badges and Marks 1833 to 2008, Mathews N.C.: ASMIC Pubs, 2008, p. 2.
8. http://www.history.navy.mil/faqs/faq59-27.htm, April 2011.
9. http://www.history.navy.mil/faqs/faq59-28.htm, April 2011
10. Tily, James C., The Uniforms of the United States Navy, Cranbury: Thomas Yoseloff, 1964, p. 115.
11. ibid. p. 120.
12. http://www.history.navy.mil/faqs/faq46-1.htm, June 2011
13. http://www.history.navy.mil/faqs/faq59-8.htm, April 2011
14. Stacy, John A., United States Navy Ratring Badges and Marks 1833 to 2008, Mathews N.C.: ASMIC Pubs, 2008, p. 3.
15. Tily, James C., The Uniforms of the United States Navy, Cranbury: Thomas Yoseloff, 1964, p. 193.
16. Stacy, John A., United States Navy Ratring Badges and Marks 1833 to 2008, Mathews N.C.: ASMIC Pubs, 2008, p. 4.
17. Tily, James C., The Uniforms of the United States Navy, Cranbury: Thomas Yoseloff, 1964, p. 193.
18. ibid. p. 100.
19. Stacy, John A., United States Navy Ratring Badges and Marks 1833 to 2008, Mathews N.C.: ASMIC Pubs, 2008, p. 6.
20. Tily, James C., The Uniforms of the United States Navy, Cranbury: Thomas Yoseloff, 1964, p. 202.
21. U.S. Navy Regulation Circular, No. 41, January 8, 1885

Petty Officer First Class
1. U.S. Navy Regulation Circular, No. 41, January 8, 1885.
2. regulations governing the uniform of commissioned officers, warrant officers, and enlisted men of the United States Navy, 1886, p. 20.
3. ibid. p. 24.
4. Stacy, John A., United States Navy Ratring Badges and Marks 1833 to 2008, Mathews N.C.: ASMIC Pubs, 2008, p. 9.
5. Tily, James C., The Uniforms of the United States Navy, Cranbury: Thomas Yoseloff, 1964, p. 217.
6. http://www.history.navy.mil/faqs/faq46-1.htm, June 2011.
7. Stacy, John A., United States Navy Ratring Badges and Marks 1833 to 2008, Mathews N.C.: ASMIC Pubs, 2008, p. 9.
8. United States Statutes at Large, Vol. 42, p. 630
9. United States Statutes at Large, Vol. 63, p. 807
10. All Hands, "Bulletin Board", June 1969, p. 50.

Petty Officer Second Class
1. U.S. Navy Regulation Circular, No. 41, January 8, 1885.
2. regulations governing the uniform of commissioned officers, warrant officers, and enlisted men of the United States Navy, 1886, p. 24.
3. Stacy, John A., United States Navy Ratring Badges and Marks 1833 to 2008, Mathews N.C.: ASMIC Pubs, 2008, p. 9.
4. United States Statutes at Large, Vol. 42, p. 630
5. United States Statutes at Large, Vol. 63, p. 807
6. All Hands, "Bulletin Board", June 1969, p. 50.

Petty Officer Third Class
1. U.S. Navy Regulation Circular, No. 41, January 8, 1885.
2. regulations governing the uniform of commissioned officers, warrant officers, and enlisted men of the United States Navy, 1886, p. 24.
3. Stacy, John A., United States Navy Ratring Badges and Marks 1833 to 2008, Mathews N.C.: ASMIC Pubs, 2008, p. 9.
4. United States Statutes at Large, Vol. 42, p. 630
5. United States Statutes at Large, Vol. 63, p. 807
6. All Hands, "Bulletin Board", June 1969, p. 50.

Pharmacist
1. United States Statutes at Large, Vol. 30, p. 474
2. http://www.history.navy.mil/library/online/uniform_insignia.htm, March 2011
3. Uniform Regulations United States Navy, revised January 25, 1913, p. 34
4. ibid. p. 37
5. Tily, James C., The Uniforms of the United States Navy, Cranbury: Thomas Yoseloff, 1964, p. 234.
6. http://www.history.navy.mil/library/online/uniform_insignia.htm, March 2011
7. Uniform Regulations United States Navy, September 20, 1922, p. 16-18
8. https://picasaweb.google.com/Booker1942/1943TheNavalOfficersUniformPlan#5537445144858829890, March 2011
9. Bureau of Navigation Bulletin ,Number 291, April 26, 1941, p. 28.
10. All Hands, "Green Unifroms Mandatory...", June 1944, p. 71
11. Tily, James C., The Uniforms of the United States Navy, Cranbury: Thomas Yoseloff, 1964, p. 249.
12. United States Statutes at Large, Vol. 61, p. 738

Photographer
1. United States Statutes at Large, Vol. 56, p. 724.
2. All Hands, "Ranks and Rates...", May 1943, p. 29-35
3. All Hands, "Green Unifroms Mandatory...", June 1944, p. 71
4. https://picasaweb.google.com/Booker1942/1943TheNavalOfficersUniformPlan#5537445144858829890, March 2011
5. United States Statutes at Large, Vol. 63, p. 807
6. http://www.history.navy.mil/library/online/uniform_insignia.htm, March 2011
7. All Hands, "Warrant Officers' Collar Devices", October 1952, p. 24
8. United States Statutes at Large, Vol. 68, p. 157

Professor of Mathematics
1. United States Statutes at Large, Vol. 4, p. 756.
2. http://www.history.navy.mil/faqs/faq59-27.htm, April 2011.
3. General Order, Navy Department, May 1, 1830.
4. United States Statutes at Large, Vol. 5, p. 576.
5. United States Statutes at Large, Vol. 9, p. 272.
6. http://www.history.navy.mil/faqs/faq59-28.htm, April 2011.
7. Tily, James C., The Uniforms of the United States Navy, Cranbury: Thomas Yoseloff, 1964, p. 51.
8. http://www.history.navy.mil/faqs/faq59-8.htm, April 2011.
9. General Order 120, April 1, 1869, with letter attached.
10. Tily, James C., The Uniforms of the United States Navy, Cranbury: Thomas Yoseloff, 1964, p. 199.
11. United States Statutes at Large, Vol. 17, p. 192.
12. Tily, James C., The Uniforms of the United States Navy, Cranbury: Thomas Yoseloff, 1964, p. 201.
13. United States Statutes at Large, Vol. 30, p. 1006.
14. United States Statutes at Large, Vol. 39, p. 577.
15. All Hands, "175th Anniversary The Navy Supply Corps", March 1970, p. 41.
16. Register of the Commissioned And Warrant Officers of the Navy of the United States..., 1936, p. 482.

Purser
1. McKee, Christopher., A Gentlemanly and Honorable Profession, Annapolis: Naval Institute Press, 1991, p. 350-351.
2. Journals of the Continental Congress, Vol. 3, p. 384.
3. Journals of the Continental Congress, Vol. 6, p. 954.
4. Journals of the Continental Congress, Vol. 3, p. 379.
5. United States Statutes at Large, Vol. 1, p. 350.
6. United States Statutes at Large, Vol. 1, p. 524.
7. http://www.history.navy.mil/faqs/faq59-3.htm, June 2011.
8. http://www.history.navy.mil/faqs/faq59-25.htm, June 2011.
9. McKee, Christopher., A Gentlemanly and Honorable Profession, Annapolis: Naval Institute Press, 1991, p. 357.
10. United States Statutes at Large, Vol. 2, p. 699.
11. http://www.history.navy.mil/faqs/faq59-4.htm, June 2011.
12. General Order, Navy Department, May 10, 1820.
13. General Order, Navy Department, May 1, 1830.
14. http://www.history.navy.mil/faqs/faq59-27.htm, April 2011.
15. Tily, James C., The Uniforms of the United States Navy, Cranbury: Thomas Yoseloff, 1964, p. 47.
16. United States Statutes at Large, Vol. 10, p. 587.
17. Tily, James C., The Uniforms of the United States Navy, Cranbury: Thomas Yoseloff, 1964, p. 99-100.
18. http://www.history.navy.mil/faqs/faq59-28.htm, April 2011.
19. Tily, James C., The Uniforms of the United States Navy, Cranbury: Thomas Yoseloff, 1964, p. 108-110.
20. ibid. p. 111.
21. United States Statutes at Large, Vol. 12, p. 83.

Radio Electrician
1. United States Statutes at Large, Vol. 43, p. 1274.
2. http://www.history.navy.mil/library/online/uniform_insignia.htm, March 2011
3. https://picasaweb.google.com/Booker1942/1943TheNavalOfficersUniformPlan#5537445144858829890, March 2011
4. Bureau of Navigation Bulletin ,Number 291, April 26, 1941, p. 28.
5. All Hands, "Green Unifroms Mandatory...", June 1944, p. 71
6. United States Statutes at Large, Vol. 63, p. 807
7. http://www.history.navy.mil/library/online/uniform_insignia.htm, March 2011
8. All Hands, "Warrant Officers' Collar Devices", October 1952, p. 24
9. United States Statutes at Large, Vol. 68, p. 157

Rear Admiral/ Rear Admiral (upper half)
1. Oliver, Raymond, Why is a Kernal called a Colonel?, Tuscon: Fireship press, 1983, p. 45-46.
2. United States Statutes at Large, Vol. 12, p. 583.
3. Tily, James C., The Uniforms of the United States Navy, Cranbury: Thomas Yoseloff, 1964, p. 118-119.
4. ibid. p. 123-124
5. http://www.history.navy.mil/faqs/faq59-8.htm, April 2011.
6. Navy Department Circular, January 15, 1865.
7. Tily, James C., The Uniforms of the United States Navy, Cranbury: Thomas Yoseloff, 1964, p. 789.
8. General Order, No. 90, Navy Department, March 11, 1869.
9. Tily, James C., The Uniforms of the United States Navy, Cranbury: Thomas Yoseloff, 1964, p. 201-202.
10. ibid. p. 204.
11. Regulations Governing the Uniform of Officers of the United States Navy, 1883, p. 12.
12. Tily, James C., The Uniforms of the United States Navy, Cranbury: Thomas Yoseloff, 1964, p. 222.
13. uniform regulations governing the insignia and uniforms of commissioned officers, warrant officers, and enlistedmen of the United States Navy, January 21, 1905, p. 31
14. Uniform Regulations United States Navy, revised January 25, 1913, p. 37
15. Tily, James C., The Uniforms of the United States Navy, Cranbury: Thomas Yoseloff, 1964, p. 234.
16. Uniform Regulations United States Navy, revised January 25, 1913, p. 43
17. Tily, James C., The Uniforms of the United States Navy, Cranbury: Thomas Yoseloff,

1964, p. 238.
18. United States Statutes at Large, Vol. 40, p. 411.
19. http://en.wikipedia.org/wiki/Commodore_Admiral, July 2011
20. Tily, James C., The Uniforms of the United States Navy, Cranbury: Thomas Yoseloff, 1964, p. 243-244.
21. Uniform Regulations United States Navy, September 20, 1922, p. 19
22. Tily, James C., The Uniforms of the United States Navy, Cranbury: Thomas Yoseloff, 1964, p. 247-248.
23. United States Statutes at Large, Vol. 63, p. 802.
24. United States Statutes at Large, Vol. 70a, p. 33.
25. United States Statutes at Large, Vol. 94, p. 2912.
26. United States Navy Uniform Regulations, April 2010, Para. 4101
27. United States Navy Uniform Regulations, April 2010, Para. 4103.2a
28. United States Navy Uniform Regulations, April 2010, Para. 4103.4

Rear Admiral (lower half)
1. United States Statutes at Large, Vol. 30, p. 1006.
2. http://en.wikipedia.org/wiki/Commodore_Admiral, July 2011.
3. United States Statutes at Large, Vol. 40, p. 411.
4. United States Statutes at Large, Vol. 94, p. 2912.
5. http://en.wikipedia.org/wiki/Commodore_Admiral, July 2011.
6. United States Statutes at Large, Vol. 95, p. 1105.
7. United States Statutes at Large, Vol. 99, p. 628.
8. United States Navy Uniform Regulations, April 2010, Para. 4101
9. United States Navy Uniform Regulations, April 2010, Para. 4103.2a
10. United States Navy Uniform Regulations, April 2010, Para. 4103.4

Sailing Master
1. http://users.sisna.com/justinb/msp.html, December 1999.
2. United States Statutes at Large, Vol. 1, p. 350.
3. United States Statutes at Large, Vol. 1, p. 524.
4. McKee, Christopher., A Gentlemanly and Honorable Profession, Annapolis: Naval Institute Press, 1991, p. 31.
5. http://www.history.navy.mil/faqs/faq59-3.htm, April 2011.
6. http://www.history.navy.mil/faqs/faq59-25.htm, April 2011.
7. McKee, Christopher., A Gentlemanly and Honorable Profession, Annapolis: Naval Institute Press, 1991, p. 311-319.
8. http://www.history.navy.mil/faqs/faq59-4.htm, April 2011.
9. General Order, Navy Department, May 10, 1820.
10. General Order, Navy Department, May 1, 1830.
11. United States Statutes at Large, Vol. 5, p. 163

Sailmaker
1. Journals of the Continental Congress, Vol. 3, p. 384
2. United States Statutes at Large, Vol. 1, p. 350.
3. United States Statutes at Large, Vol. 1, p. 524.
4. http://www.history.navy.mil/faqs/faq59-4.htm, March 2011
5. General Order, Navy Department, May 1, 1830
6. http://www.history.navy.mil/faqs/faq59-27.htm, March 2011
7. Tily, James C., The Uniforms of the United States Navy, Cranbury: Thomas Yoseloff, 1964, p. 101.
8. http://www.history.navy.mil/faqs/faq59-28.htm, March 2011
9. Tily, James C., The Uniforms of the United States Navy, Cranbury: Thomas Yoseloff, 1964, p. 110.
10. ibid. appendix c, chart shows no buttons on cuff after 1862.
11. http://www.history.navy.mil/faqs/faq59-8.htm
12. General Order No. 90, March 11, 1869
13. Regulations for the Goverment of the Navy of the United States, August 7, 1876, p. 191.
14. Tily, James C., The Uniforms of the United States Navy, Cranbury: Thomas Yoseloff, 1964, p. 204.
15. Regulations Governing the Uniform of Officers of the United States Navy, 1883, p. 11-12.
16. Register of the Commissioned And Warrant Officers of the Navy of the United States..., January 1, 1900, p. 79.
17. United States Statutes at Large, Vol. 30, p. 1007

Schoolmaster
1. http://www.history.navy.mil/faqs/faq78-3.html, March 2011.
2. McKee, Christopher., A Gentlemanly and Honorable Profession, Annapolis: Naval Institute Press, 1991, p. 31.
3. http://www.ibiblio.org/pha/USN/1834/NavReg1834.html, July 2011.
4. United States Statutes at Large, Vol. 4, p. 756.
5. McKee, Christopher., A Gentlemanly and Honorable Profession, Annapolis: Naval Institute Press, 1991, p. 33.
6. General Order, Navy Department, May 1, 1830.
7. http://www.history.navy.mil/faqs/faq78-3.html, March 2011.

Seaman
1. Journals of the Continental Congress, Vol. 3, p. 384.
2. Journals of the Continental Congress, Vol. 6, p. 954.
3. United States Statutes at Large, Vol. 1, p. 350.
4. United States Statutes at Large, Vol. 1, p. 523.
5. Stacy, John A., United States Navy Ratring Badges and Marks 1833 to 2008, Mathews N.C.: ASMIC Pubs, 2008, p. 5.
6. Tily, James C., The Uniforms of the United States Navy, Cranbury: Thomas Yoseloff, 1964, p. 200.
7. U.S. Navy Regulation Circular, No. 41, January 8, 1885.
8. regulations governing the uniform of commissioned officers, warrant officers, and enlisted men of the United States Navy, 1886, p. 25.
9. Stacy, John A., United States Navy Ratring Badges and Marks 1833 to 2008, Mathews N.C.: ASMIC Pubs, 2008, p. 14.
10. http://www.history.navy.mil/faqs/faq78-3.html, March 2011.
11. All Hands, "Here's a Complete List of Rating Changes...", March 1948, p. 57
12. United States Statutes at Large, Vol. 63, p. 802
13. Stacy, John A., United States Navy Rating Badges and Marks 1833 to 2008, Mathews N.C.: ASMIC Pubs, 2008, p. 33.
14. United States Navy Uniform Regulations, April 2010, Para. 4227.b

Seaman Apprentice
1. All Hands, "Here's a Complete List of Rating Changes...", March 1948, p. 50
2. United States Statutes at Large, Vol. 63, p. 802
3. Stacy, John A., United States Navy Rating Badges and Marks 1833 to 2008, Mathews N.C.: ASMIC Pubs, 2008, p. 33.
4. United States Navy Uniform Regulations, April 2010, Para. 4227.b

Seaman First Class
1. http://www.history.navy.mil/faqs/faq78-3.html, March 2011.
2. Register of the Commissioned And Warrant Officers of the Navy of the United States..., January 1, 1922, p. 316.
3. United States Statutes at Large, Vol. 42, p. 630.
4. Uniform Regulations United States Navy, September 20, 1922, p. 26-27.
5. All Hands, "Distinguishing Marks" and Seaman Stripes Approved For Non-Rated Waves", November 1944, p. 71.
6. All Hands, "Here's a Complete List of Rating Changes...", March 1948, p. 57.

Seaman Gunner
1. http://www.history.navy.mil/faqs/faq78-3.html, March 2011.
2. Register of the Commissioned And Warrant Officers of the Navy of the United States..., January 1, 1871, p. 5.
3. Regulations for the Goverment of the Navy of the United States, August 7, 1876, p. 8.
4. ibid. p. 196.
5. General Order 272, June 28, 1881.
6. U.S. Navy Regulation Circular, No. 41, January 8, 1885.
7. General Order 341, January 1, 1886.
8. regulations governing the uniform of commissioned officers, warrant officers, and enlisted men of the United States Navy, 1886, p. 25.
9. Stacy, John A., United States Navy Ratring Badges and Marks 1833 to 2008, Mathews N.C.: ASMIC Pubs, 2008, p. 113.
10. http://www.history.navy.mil/faqs/faq78-3.html, March 2011

Seaman Recruit
1. All Hands, "Here's a Complete List of Rating Changes...", March 1948, p. 50
2. United States Statutes at Large, Vol. 63, p. 802
3. All Hands, "Uniform Changes Published...", December 1948, p. 48
4. Stacy, John A., United States Navy Ratring Badges and Marks 1833 to 2008, Mathews N.C.: ASMIC Pubs, 2008, p. 40.

Seaman Second Class
1. http://www.history.navy.mil/faqs/faq78-3.html, March 2011.
2. Register of the Commissioned And Warrant Officers of the Navy of the United States..., January 1, 1922, p. 316.
3. United States Statutes at Large, Vol. 42, p. 630.
4. Uniform Regulations United States Navy, September 20, 1922, p. 26-27.
5. All Hands, "Distinguishing Marks" and Seaman Stripes Approved For Non-Rated Waves", November 1944, p. 71.
6. All Hands, "Here's a Complete List of Rating Changes...", March 1948, p. 57.

Second Assistant Engineer
1. Bennett, Frank Marion, The steam navy of the United States, Pittsburgh: Warrem & CO., 1896, p. 25.
2. Tily, James C., The Uniforms of the United States Navy, Cranbury: Thomas Yoseloff, 1964, p. 86-89.
3. United States Statutes at Large, Vol. 5, p. 577
4. Tily, James C., The Uniforms of the United States Navy, Cranbury: Thomas Yoseloff, 1964, p. 97.
5. http://www.history.navy.mil/faqs/faq59-28.htm, April 2011
6. Tily, James C., The Uniforms of the United States Navy, Cranbury: Thomas Yoseloff, 1964, p. 110.
7. ibid. p. 48.
8. United States Statutes at Large, Vol. 11, p. 407.
9. Tily, James C., The Uniforms of the United States Navy, Cranbury: Thomas Yoseloff, 1964, p. 113.
10. Ibid. p. 119.
11. ibid. p. 51.
12. http://www.history.navy.mil/faqs/faq59-8.htm, April 2011
13. Tily, James C., The Uniforms of the United States Navy, Cranbury: Thomas Yoseloff, 1964, p. 189.
14. General Order 90, March 11, 1869.
13. Tily, James C., The Uniforms of the United States Navy, Cranbury: Thomas Yoseloff, 1964, p. 199.
16. General Order 120, April 1, 1869, with letter attached.
17. United States Statutes at Large, Vol. 16, p. 536
18. Navy Regulation Circular, October 3, 1871
19. United States Statutes at Large, Vol. 18, p. 17

Second Master
1. United States Statutes at Large, Vol. 4, p. 756.
2. General Regulations for the Navy and Marine Corps of the United States, 1841, p. 2.
3. http://www.history.navy.mil/faqs/faq59-27.htm, April 2011.
4. Callahan, Edward, List of Officers of the Navy of the United States and the Marine Corps from 1775 to 1900, New York: L. R. Hamerlsy & CO., 1901, p. 414.
5. ibid. p. 192 (listed as Second Mate but listed as a Second Master on page 86 of the 1850 Navy Register).
6. ibid. p. 394.

Secretary
1. United States Statutes at Large, Vol. 4, p. 756.
2. General Regulations for the Navy and Marine Corps of the United States, 1841, p. 2.
3. http://www.history.navy.mil/faqs/faq59-27.htm, April 2011.
4. http://www.history.navy.mil/faqs/faq59-28.htm, April 2011.
5. Tily, James C., The Uniforms of the United States Navy, Cranbury: Thomas Yoseloff, 1964, p. 52.
6. United States Statutes at Large, Vol. 14, p. 48.
7. United States Statutes at Large, Vol. 14, p. 222.
8. General Order 120, April 1, 1869, with letter attached.
9. United States Statutes at Large, Vol. 16, p. 332.
10. Regulations for the Goverment of the Navy of the United States, August 7, 1876, p. 193.
11. Register of the Commissioned And Warrant Officers of the Navy of the United States..., January 1, 1870, p. 66.

12. Register of the Commissioned And Warrant Officers of the Navy of the United States..., January 1, 1871, p. 68.
13. Register of the Commissioned And Warrant Officers of the Navy of the United States..., January 1, 1872, p. 70.
14. Register of the Commissioned And Warrant Officers of the Navy of the United States..., January 1, 1879, p. 75.
15. United States Statutes at Large, Vol. 20, p. 50.
16. Register of the Commissioned And Warrant Officers of the Navy of the United States..., July 1, 1887, p. 60.
17. Register of the Commissioned And Warrant Officers of the Navy of the United States..., January 1, 1890, p. 60.
18. Register of the Commissioned And Warrant Officers of the Navy of the United States..., January 1, 1891, p. 60.
19. Register of the Commissioned And Warrant Officers of the Navy of the United States..., January 1, 1892, p. 60. Where Secrataries were they are no longer.
20. Regulations Governing the Uniform of Officers of the United States Navy, 1883, p. 11.
21. regulations governing the uniform of commissioned officers, warrant officers, and enlisted men of the United States Navy, 1886, p. 11.
22. Register of the Commissioned And Warrant Officers of the Navy of the United States..., January 1, 1900, p. 60.
23. uniform regulations governing the insignia and uniforms of commissioned officers, warrant officers, and enlistedmen of the United States Navy, January 21, 1905, p. 31.
24. Register of the Commissioned And Warrant Officers of the Navy of the United States..., January 1, 1908, p. 80.
25. Register of the Commissioned And Warrant Officers of the Navy of the United States..., January 1, 1918, p. 193.

Senior Flag Officer
1. United States Statutes at Large, Vol. 11, p. 442.
2. Register of the Commissioned And Warrant Officers of the Navy of the United States..., 1860, p. 18.
3. Callahan, Edward, List of Officers of the Navy of the United States and the Marine Corps from 1775 to 1900, New York: L. R. Hamerlsy & CO., 1901, p. 521.

Senior Chief Petty Officer
1. United States Statutes at Large, Vol. 72, p. 123
2. All Hands, "The Word: New Pay Grades", June 1958, p. 43
3. All Hands, "The Word: Insignia for E-8, E-9", August 1958, p. 46
4. All Hands, "CPO Collar Devices", November 1959, p. 26.
5. All Hands, "Top Chiefs Will Now Wear Stars on Their Collars", January 1961, p. 54.
6. Stacy, John A., United States Navy Ratring Badges and Marks 1833 to 2008, Mathews N.C.: ASMIC Pubs, 2008, p. 38.
7. All Hands, "New Officer, CPO Uniform...", June 1979, p. 2.
8. NAVADMIN 011/99, June 30, 1999
9. http://en.wikipedia.org/wiki/Uniforms_of_the_United_States_Navy#Obsolete_uniforms, April 2011
10. NAVADMIN 020/10, January 10, 2010

Ships's Barber
1. http://www.history.navy.mil/faqs/faq78-3.html, March 2011.
2. U.S. Navy Regulation Circular, No. 41, January 8, 1885.

Ship's Clerk
1. United States Statutes at Large, Vol. 56, p. 724.
2. All Hands, "Ranks and Rates...", May 1943, p. 29-35
3. All Hands, "Green Unifroms Mandatory...", June 1944, p. 71
4. https://picasaweb.google.com/Booker1942/1943TheNavalOfficersUniformPlan#5537445144858829890, March 2011
5. United States Statutes at Large, Vol. 63, p. 807
6. http://www.history.navy.mil/library/online/uniform_insignia.htm, March 2011
7. All Hands, "Warrant Officers' Collar Devices", October 1952, p. 24
8. United States Statutes at Large, Vol. 68, p. 157

Ship's Cook (First, Second, Third and Fourth Class)
1. Register of the Commissioned And Warrant Officers of the Navy of the United States..., January 1, 1891, p. 172.
2. General Order 409, February 25, 1893.
3. Register of the Commissioned And Warrant Officers of the Navy of the United States..., January 1, 1895, p. 176.
4. http://grandarmyofthefrontier.org/uniforms/usn1897.htm, June 2011
5. Register of the Commissioned And Warrant Officers of the Navy of the United States..., January 1, 1895, p. 224.
10. uniform regulations governing the insignia and uniforms of commissioned officers, warrant officers, and enlistedmen of the United States Navy, January 21, 1905, p. 42.
11. ibid. p. 50.
12. Stacy, John A., United States Navy Ratring Badges and Marks 1833 to 2008, Mathews N.C.: ASMIC Pubs, 2008, p. 74.
13. ibid. p. 14.
14. Register of the Commissioned And Warrant Officers of the Navy of the United States..., January 1, 1910, p. 271.
15. Uniform Regulations United States Navy, revised January 25, 1913, p. 65.
16. ibid.p. 54.
17. Bureau of Navigation Circular Letter No. 9-21, March 24, 1921.

Ship's Lamplighter
1. http://www.history.navy.mil/faqs/faq78-3.html, March 2011.
2. U.S. Navy Regulation Circular, No. 41, January 8, 1885

Ship's Tailor
1. http://www.history.navy.mil/faqs/faq78-3.html, March 2011.
2. U.S. Navy Regulation Circular, No. 41, January 8, 1885.

Shipwright
1. http://www.history.navy.mil/faqs/faq78-3.html, March 2011
2. Register of the Commissioned And Warrant Officers of the Navy of the United States..., January 1, 1895, p. 176.
3. http://grandarmyofthefrontier.org/uniforms/usn1897.htm, June 2011
4. Register of the Commissioned And Warrant Officers of the Navy of the United States..., January 1, 1905, p. 224.
5. Stacy, John A., United States Navy Ratring Badges and Marks 1833 to 2008, Mathews N.C.: ASMIC Pubs, 2008, p. 59.
6. ibid.p. 14.
7. Bureau of Navigation Circular Letter No. 9-21, March 24, 1921.

Steerage Cook
1. http://www.history.navy.mil/faqs/faq78-3.html, March 2011
2. Regulations for the government of the Navy of the United States, 1841, p. 164 (lists petty officer's rates that could be entered directly at enlistment, including Officer's Stewards.)
3. Regulations for the government of the Navy of the United States, 1865, p. 6-7
4. U.S. Navy Regulation Circular, No. 41, January 8, 1885
5. regulations governing the uniform of commissioned officers, warrant officers, and enlisted men of the United States Navy, 1886, p. 16
6. http://www.quarterdeck.org/uniforms/1897/21-37%20Enlisted%201897.htm, March 2011
7. uniform regulations governing the insignia and uniforms of commissioned officers, warrant officers, and enlistedmen of the United States Navy, January 21, 1905, p. 40
8. Stacy, John A., United States Navy Rating Badges and Marks 1833 to 2008, Mathews N.C.: ASMIC Pubs, 2008, p. 74.
9. Uniform Regulations, United States Navy, September 20, 1922, p. 56.
10. Register of the Commissioned And Warrant Officers of the Navy of the United States..., 1923, p. 307.
11. http://www.history.navy.mil/faqs/faq78-3.html, March 2011

Steerage Steward
1. http://www.history.navy.mil/faqs/faq78-3.html, March 2011
2. Regulations for the government of the Navy of the United States, 1841, p. 164 (lists petty officer's rates that could be entered directly at enlistment, including Officer's Stewards.)
3. Regulations for the government of the Navy of the United States, 1865, p. 6-7
4. http://www.history.navy.mil/faqs/faq59-8n.htm, March 2011
5. U.S. Navy Regulation Circular, No. 41, January 8, 1885
6. regulations governing the uniform of commissioned officers, warrant officers, and enlisted men of the United States Navy, 1886, p. 16
7. http://www.quarterdeck.org/uniforms/1897/21-37%20Enlisted%201897.htm, March 2011
8. uniform regulations governing the insignia and uniforms of commissioned officers, warrant officers, and enlistedmen of the United States Navy, January 21, 1905, p. 40
9. Stacy, John A., United States Navy Rating Badges and Marks 1833 to 2008, Mathews N.C.: ASMIC Pubs, 2008, p. 74.
10. Uniform Regulations, United States Navy, September 20, 1922, p. 56.
11. Register of the Commissioned And Warrant Officers of the Navy of the United States..., 1923, p. 307.
12. http://www.history.navy.mil/faqs/faq78-3.html, March 2011

Steward First Class
1. All Hands, "Here's a Complete List of Rating Changes...", March 1948, p. 57
2. All Hands, "Wants Clarification", July 1946, p. 39
3. All Hands, "Stewards Have Acquired New Uniforms", January 1950, p. 51.

Steward Second Class
1. All Hands, "Here's a Complete List of Rating Changes...", March 1948, p. 57
2. All Hands, "Wants Clarification", July 1946, p. 39
3. All Hands, "Stewards Have Acquired New Uniforms", January 1950, p. 51.

Steward Third Class
1. All Hands, "Here's a Complete List of Rating Changes...", March 1948, p. 57
2. All Hands, "Wants Clarification", July 1946, p. 39
3. All Hands, "Stewards Have Acquired New Uniforms", January 1950, p. 51.

Steward to Commander in Chief
1. http://www.history.navy.mil/faqs/faq78-3.html, March 2011
2. Regulations for the government of the Navy of the United States, 1841, p. 164 (lists petty officer's rates that could be entered directly at enlistment, including Officer's stewards.)
3. Regulations for the government of the Navy of the United States, 1865, p. 6-7
4. U.S. Navy Regulation Circular, No. 41, January 8, 1885.
5. Regulations for the Goverment of the Navy of the United States, August 7, 1876, p. 197.
6. regulations governing the uniform of commissioned officers, warrant officers, and enlisted men of the United States Navy, 1886, p. 16
7. http://www.quarterdeck.org/uniforms/1897/21-37%20Enlisted%201897.htm, March 2011
8. uniform regulations governing the insignia and uniforms of commissioned officers, warrant officers, and enlistedmen of the United States Navy, January 21, 1905, p. 40
9. Stacy, John A., United States Navy Rating Badges and Marks 1833 to 2008, Mathews N.C.: ASMIC Pubs, 2008, p. 74.
10. http://www.history.navy.mil/faqs/faq78-3.html, March 2011.

Steward to Navy yard Commandant
1. http://www.history.navy.mil/faqs/faq78-3.html, March 2011
2. U.S. Navy Regulation Circular, No. 41, January 8, 1885

3. regulations governing the uniform of commissioned officers, warrant officers, and enlisted men of the United States Navy, 1886, p. 16
4. http://www.quarterdeck.org/uniforms/1897/21-37%20Enlisted%201897.htm, March 2011
5. uniform regulations governing the insignia and uniforms of commissioned officers, warrant officers, and enlistedmen of the United States Navy, January 21, 1905, p. 40
6. Stacy, John A., United States Navy Rating Badges and Marks 1833 to 2008, Mathews N.C.: ASMIC Pubs, 2008, p. 74.
7. http://www.history.navy.mil/faqs/faq78-3.html, March 2011

Steward's Mate First Class
1. http://www.history.navy.mil/faqs/faq78-3.html, March 2011.
2. uniform regulations governing the insignia and uniforms of commissioned officers, warrant officers, and enlistedmen of the United States Navy, 1944, p. 749.
3. U.S. Navy Uniform Regulations, May 31, 1941, p. 28.
4. ibid plate 68.
5. ibid. p. 27.
1. All Hands, "Here's a Complete List of Rating Changes...", March 1948, p. 57.

Steward's Mate Second Class
1. http://www.history.navy.mil/faqs/faq78-3.html, March 2011.
2. uniform regulations governing the insignia and uniforms of commissioned officers, warrant officers, and enlistedmen of the United States Navy, 1944, p. 749.
3. U.S. Navy Uniform Regulations, May 31, 1941, p. 28.
4. ibid plate 68.
5. ibid. p. 27.
1. All Hands, "Here's a Complete List of Rating Changes...", March 1948, p. 57.

Steward's Mate Third Class
1. http://www.history.navy.mil/faqs/faq78-3.html, March 2011.
2. uniform regulations governing the insignia and uniforms of commissioned officers, warrant officers, and enlistedmen of the United States Navy, 1944, p. 749.
3. U.S. Navy Uniform Regulations, May 31, 1941, p. 28.
4. ibid plate 68.
5. ibid. p. 27.
1. All Hands, "Here's a Complete List of Rating Changes...", March 1948, p. 57.

Stewardsman
1. All Hands, "Here's a Complete List of Rating Changes...", March 1948, p. 50
2. United States Statutes at Large, Vol. 63, p. 802
3. Stacy, John A., United States Navy Rating Badges and Marks 1833 to 2008, Mathews N.C.: ASMIC Pubs, 2008, p. 33.
4. ibid. p. 60.
5. United States Navy Uniform Regulations, 1975, p. 5-44.

Stewardsman Apprentice
1. All Hands, "Here's a Complete List of Rating Changes...", March 1948, p. 50
2. United States Statutes at Large, Vol. 63, p. 802
3. Stacy, John A., United States Navy Rating Badges and Marks 1833 to 2008, Mathews N.C.: ASMIC Pubs, 2008, p. 33.
4. ibid. p. 60.
5. United States Navy Uniform Regulations, 1975, p. 5-44.

Stewardsman Recruit
1. All Hands, "Here's a Complete List of Rating Changes...", March 1948, p. 50
2. United States Statutes at Large, Vol. 63, p. 802
3. Stacy, John A., United States Navy Rating Badges and Marks 1833 to 2008, Mathews N.C.: ASMIC Pubs, 2008, p. 33.
4. ibid. p. 60.
5. United States Navy Uniform Regulations, 1975, p. 5-44.

Surgeon
1. Journals of the Continental Congress, Vol. 3, p. 384
2. United States Statutes at Large, Vol. 1, p. 350.
3. United States Statutes at Large, Vol. 1, p. 523.
4. All Hands, "175th Anniversary The Navy Supply Corps", March 1970, p. 41
5. United States Statutes at Large, Vol. 61, p. 872.
6. http://www.history.navy.mil/faqs/faq59-3.htm, April 2011.
7. http://www.history.navy.mil/faqs/faq59-25.htm, April 2011.
8. http://www.history.navy.mil/faqs/faq59-4.htm, April 2011.
9. General Order, Navy Department, May 10, 1820.
10. General Order, Navy Department, May 1, 1830.
11. Stacy, John A., United States Navy Ratring Badges and Marks 1833 to 2008, Mathews N.C.: ASMIC Pubs, 2008, p. 83-86.
12. ibid. p. 86.
13. http://www.history.navy.mil/faqs/faq59-27.htm, April 2011.
14. General Regulations for the Navy and Marine Corps of the United States, 1841, p. 2.
15. General Order, Navy Department, August 31, 1846.
16. United States Statutes at Large, Vol. 10, p. 587.
17. Stacy, John A., United States Navy Ratring Badges and Marks 1833 to 2008, Mathews N.C.: ASMIC Pubs, 2008, p. 99.
18. http://www.history.navy.mil/faqs/faq59-28.htm, April 2011.
19. Tily, James C., The Uniforms of the United States Navy, Cranbury: Thomas Yoseloff, 1964, p. 108-110.
20. ibid. p. 111.
21. ibid. p. 118.
22. ibid p. 51.
23. http://www.history.navy.mil/faqs/faq59-8.htm, April 2011.
24. General Order 120, April 1, 1869, with letter attached.
25. General Order No. 90, March 11, 1869.
26. United States Statutes at Large, Vol. 16, p. 536.
27. Regulations Governing the Uniform of Officers of the United States Navy, 1883, p. 9.
28. ibid. p. 10.
29. United States Statutes at Large, Vol. 37, p. 344
30. Tily, James C., The Uniforms of the United States Navy, Cranbury: Thomas Yoseloff, 1964, p. 233.
31. ibid.p. 243-244.

Surgeon General
1. United States Statutes at Large, Vol. 16, p. 537.
2. Regulations for the Goverment of the Navy of the United States, August 7, 1876, p. 192-193.
3. Callahan, Edward, List of Officers of the Navy of the United States and the Marine Corps from 1775 to 1900, New York: L. R. Hamerlsy & CO., 1901, p. 601.
4. ibid. p.199.
5. ibid. p. 5.
6. Regulations Governing the Uniform of Officers of the United States Navy, 1883, p. 9.
7. ibid. p. 10.
8. Callahan, Edward, List of Officers of the Navy of the United States and the Marine Corps from 1775 to 1900, New York: L. R. Hamerlsy & CO., 1901, p. 5.
9. United States Statutes at Large, Vol. 30, p. 1006.

Surgeon of the Fleet
1. United States Statutes at Large, Vol. 4, p. 313.
2. Tily, James C., The Uniforms of the United States Navy, Cranbury: Thomas Yoseloff, 1964, p. 99.
3. ibid. p. 110
4. United States Statutes at Large, Vol. 12, p. 23

Surgeon's Mate
1. Journals of the Continental Congress, Vol. 3, p. 384.
2. United States Statutes at Large, Vol. 1, p. 523.
3. United States Statutes at Large, Vol. 1, p. 608.
4. http://www.history.navy.mil/faqs/faq59-3.htm, April 2011.
5. http://www.history.navy.mil/faqs/faq59-25.htm, April 2011.
6. http://www.history.navy.mil/faqs/faq59-4.htm, April 2011.
7. General Order, Navy Department, May 10, 1820
8. United States Statutes at Large, Vol. 4, p. 313
9. American State Papers, Senate, 20th Congress, 1st Session Naval Affairs: Volume 3, p 101.
10. American State Papers, Senate, 20th Congress, 2nd Session Naval Affairs: Volume 3, p 253.

Tailor
1. http://www.history.navy.mil/faqs/faq78-3.html, March 2011.
2. U.S. Navy Regulation Circular, No. 41, January 8, 1885.
3. http://www.history.navy.mil/faqs/faq78-3.html, March 2011.

Third Assistant Engineer
1. Bennett, Frank Marion, The steam navy of the United States, Pittsburgh: Warrem & CO., 1896, p. 25.
2. Tily, James C., The Uniforms of the United States Navy, Cranbury: Thomas Yoseloff, 1964, p. 86-89.
3. United States Statutes at Large, Vol. 5, p. 577
4. Tily, James C., The Uniforms of the United States Navy, Cranbury: Thomas Yoseloff, 1964, p. 97.
5. http://www.history.navy.mil/faqs/faq59-28.htm, April 2011
6. Tily, James C., The Uniforms of the United States Navy, Cranbury: Thomas Yoseloff, 1964, p. 48.
7. United States Statutes at Large, Vol. 11, p. 407.
8. Tily, James C., The Uniforms of the United States Navy, Cranbury: Thomas Yoseloff, 1964, p. 113.
9. Ibid. p. 119.
10. ibid. p. 51.
11. http://www.history.navy.mil/faqs/faq59-8.htm, April 2011
12. Tily, James C., The Uniforms of the United States Navy, Cranbury: Thomas Yoseloff, 1964, p. 189.
13. General Order 90, March 11, 1869.
14. General Order 120, April 1, 1869, with letter attached.
15. United States Statutes at Large, Vol. 16, p. 536

Torpedoman
1. United States Statutes at Large, Vol. 56, p. 724.
2. All Hands, "Ranks and Rates...", May 1943, p. 29-35
3. All Hands, "Green Uniforms Mandatory...", June 1944, p. 71
4. https://picasaweb.google.com/Booker1942/1943TheNavalOfficersUniformPlan#5537445144858829890, March 2011
5. United States Statutes at Large, Vol. 63, p. 807
6. http://www.history.navy.mil/library/online/uniform_insignia.htm, March 2011
7. All Hands, "Warrant Officers' Collar Devices", October 1952, p. 24
8. United States Statutes at Large, Vol. 68, p. 157

Vice Admiral
1. United States Statutes at Large, Vol. 13, p. 420.
2. Callahan, Edward, List of Officers of the Navy of the United States and the Marine Corps from 1775 to 1900, New York: L. R. Hamerlsy & CO., 1901, p. 189.
3. Navy Department Circular, January 15, 1865.
4. Callahan, Edward, List of Officers of the Navy of the United States and the Marine Corps from 1775 to 1900, New York: L. R. Hamerlsy & CO., 1901, p. 441.
5. Tily, James C., The Uniforms of the United States Navy, Cranbury: Thomas Yoseloff, 1964, p. 189.
6. Regulations for the Goverment of the Navy of the United States, August 7, 1876, p. 190.
7. General Order No. 90, March 11, 1869.
8. Callahan, Edward, List of Officers of the Navy of the United States and the Marine Corps from 1775 to 1900, New York: L. R. Hamerlsy & CO., 1901, p. 475.
9. United States Statutes at Large, Vol. 17, p. 418.
10. Tily, James C., The Uniforms of the United States Navy, Cranbury: Thomas Yoseloff, 1964, p. 204.
11. Regulations Governing the Uniform of Officers of the United States Navy, 1883, p. 6
12. Callahan, Edward, List of Officers of the Navy of the United States and the Marine Corps from 1775 to 1900, New York: L. R. Hamerlsy & CO., 1901, p. 475
13. United States Statutes at Large, Vol. 38, p. 942.
14. United States Statutes at Large, Vol. 39, p. 556.
15. Uniform Regulations United States Navy, revised January 25, 1913, p. 31.
16. ibid. p. 34
17. ibid. p. 39
18. ibid. p. 43
18a. ibid. p. 45.
19. ibid. p. 42
20. Tily, James C., The Uniforms of the United States Navy, Cranbury: Thomas Yoseloff, 1964, p. 244.
21. Uniform Regulations United States Navy, September 20, 1922, p. 17

22. Tily, James C., The Uniforms of the United States Navy, Cranbury: Thomas Yoseloff, 1964, p. 249.
22a Bureau of Navigation Bulletin No. 291, April 26, 1941, p. 28
23. All Hands, "Current and Future Canges in Uniform Regs Listed", May 1947, p. 56
23a. United States Statutes at Large, Vol. 63, p. 807
23b. United States Statutes at Large, Vol. 72, p. 124
24. United States Navy Uniform Regulations, April 2010, Para. 4101
25. United States Navy Uniform Regulations, April 2010, Para. 4103.2a
26. United States Navy Uniform Regulations, April 2010, Para. 4103.4

Wardroom Cook
1. http://www.history.navy.mil/faqs/faq78-3.html, March 2011
2. Regulations for the government of the Navy of the United States, 1841, p. 164 (lists petty officer's rates that could be entered directly at enlistment, including Officer's Stewards.)
3. Regulations for the government of the Navy of the United States, 1865, p. 6-7
4. U.S. Navy Regulation Circular, No. 41, January 8, 1885
5. regulations governing the uniform of commissioned officers, warrant officers, and enlisted men of the United States Navy, 1886, p. 16
6. http://www.quarterdeck.org/uniforms/1897/21-37%20Enlisted%201897.htm, March 2011
7. uniform regulations governing the insignia and uniforms of commissioned officers, warrant officers, and enlistedmen of the United States Navy, January 21, 1905, p. 40
8. Stacy, John A., United States Navy Rating Badges and Marks 1833 to 2008, Mathews N.C.: ASMIC Pubs, 2008, p. 74.
9. Uniform Regulations, United States Navy, September 20, 1922, p. 56.
10. Register of the Commissioned And Warrant Officers of the Navy of the United States..., 1923, p. 307.
11. http://www.history.navy.mil/faqs/faq78-3.html, March 2011

Wardroom Steward
1. http://www.history.navy.mil/faqs/faq78-3.html, March 2011
2. Regulations for the government of the Navy of the United States, 1841, p. 164 (lists petty officer's rates that could be entered directly at enlistment, including Officer's Stewards.)
3. Regulations for the government of the Navy of the United States, 1865, p. 6-7
4. http://www.history.navy.mil/faqs/faq59-8n.htm, March 2011
5. U.S. Navy Regulation Circular, No. 41, January 8, 1885
6. regulations governing the uniform of commissioned officers, warrant officers, and enlisted men of the United States Navy, 1886, p. 16
7. http://www.quarterdeck.org/uniforms/1897/21-37%20Enlisted%201897.htm, March 2011
8. uniform regulations governing the insignia and uniforms of commissioned officers, warrant officers, and enlistedmen of the United States Navy, January 21, 1905, p. 40
9. Stacy, John A., United States Navy Rating Badges and Marks 1833 to 2008, Mathews N.C.: ASMIC Pubs, 2008, p. 74.
10. Uniform Regulations, United States Navy, September 20, 1922, p. 56.
11. Register of the Commissioned And Warrant Officers of the Navy of the United States..., 1923, p. 307.
12. http://www.history.navy.mil/faqs/faq78-3.html, March 2011

Warrant Machinist
1. United States Statutes at Large, Vol. 30, p. 369.
2. http://www.history.navy.mil/library/online/uniform_insignia.htm, March 2011.
3. United States Statutes at Large, Vol. 30, p. 1007.
4. http://www.history.navy.mil/library/online/uniform_insignia.htm, March 2011.
5. United States Statutes at Large, Vol. 35, p. 771.

Warrant Officer 1
1. United States Statutes at Large, Vol. 68, p. 157
2. All Hands, "New Insignia and Markings go into effect on 1 November For Four Warrant Ranks", October 1954, p. 45.
3. http://en.wikipedia.org/wiki/Warrant_Officer_(United_States), September 2011.

Warrant Officer's Cook
1. http://www.history.navy.mil/faqs/faq78-3.html, March 2011
2. Regulations for the government of the Navy of the United States, 1841, p. 164 (lists petty officer's rates that could be entered directly at enlistment, including Officer's Stewards.)
3. Regulations for the government of the Navy of the United States, 1865, p. 6-7
4. U.S. Navy Regulation Circular, No. 41, January 8, 1885
5. regulations governing the uniform of commissioned officers, warrant officers, and enlisted men of the United States Navy, 1886, p. 16
6. http://www.quarterdeck.org/uniforms/1897/21-37%20Enlisted%201897.htm, March 2011
7. uniform regulations governing the insignia and uniforms of commissioned officers, warrant officers, and enlistedmen of the United States Navy, January 21, 1905, p. 40
8. Stacy, John A., United States Navy Rating Badges and Marks 1833 to 2008, Mathews N.C.: ASMIC Pubs, 2008, p. 74.
9. Uniform Regulations, United States Navy, September 20, 1922, p. 56.
10. Register of the Commissioned And Warrant Officers of the Navy of the United States..., 1923, p. 307.
11. http://www.history.navy.mil/faqs/faq78-3.html, March 2011

Warrant Officer's Steward
1. http://www.history.navy.mil/faqs/faq78-3.html, March 2011
2. Regulations for the government of the Navy of the United States, 1841, p. 164 (lists petty officer's rates that could be entered directly at enlistment, including Officer's Stewards.)
3. Regulations for the government of the Navy of the United States, 1865, p. 6-7
4. http://www.history.navy.mil/faqs/faq59-8n.htm, March 2011
5. U.S. Navy Regulation Circular, No. 41, January 8, 1885
6. regulations governing the uniform of commissioned officers, warrant officers, and enlisted men of the United States Navy, 1886, p. 16
7. http://www.quarterdeck.org/uniforms/1897/21-37%20Enlisted%201897.htm, March 2011
8. uniform regulations governing the insignia and uniforms of commissioned officers, warrant officers, and enlistedmen of the United States Navy, January 21, 1905, p. 40
9. Stacy, John A., United States Navy Rating Badges and Marks 1833 to 2008, Mathews N.C.: ASMIC Pubs, 2008, p. 74.
10. Uniform Regulations, United States Navy, September 20, 1922, p. 56.
11. Register of the Commissioned And Warrant Officers of the Navy of the United States..., 1923, p. 307.
12. http://www.history.navy.mil/faqs/faq78-3.html, March 2011

Warrant Officer, Hospital Corps.
1. http://www.history.navy.mil/library/online/uniform_insignia.htm, April 2011
2. United States Statutes at Large, Vol. 61, p. 738
3. http://www.history.navy.mil/library/online/uniform_insignia.htm, April 2011
4. United States Statutes at Large, Vol. 63, p. 807
5. http://www.history.navy.mil/library/online/uniform_insignia.htm, March 2011
6. All Hands, "Warrant Officers' Collar Devices", October 1952, p. 24
7. United States Statutes at Large, Vol. 68, p. 157

Part 3. Marine Corps

Chapter 1. Marine Corps Organization

The Continental Marines/The United States Marine Corps
1. http://en.wikipedia.org/wiki/History_of_the_United_States_Marine_Corps, October 2011.
2. Journals of the Continental Congress, Vol. 3, p. 348.
3. Chenoweth, Avery H., Semper Fi The Definitive Illustrated history of the U.S. Marines, New York: Main Street, 2005, p. 45.
5. United States Statutes at Large, Vol. 1, p. 523.
6. United States Statutes at Large, Vol. 1, p. 608.
7. United States Statutes at Large, Vol. 1, p. 594.

Subdivisions of Rank
1. http://www.defense.gov/specials/insignias/officers.html, November 2010

Marine Staff Ranks
1. United States Statutes at Large, Vol. 1, p. 595.
2. United States Statutes at Large, Vol. 3, p. 124.
3. United States Statutes at Large, Vol. 3, p. 377.
4. United States Statutes at Large, Vol. 4, p. 712.
5. United States Statutes at Large, Vol. 9, p. 155.
6. Register of the Commissioned And Warrant Officers of the Navy of the United States..., 1848, p. 104.
7. United States Statutes at Large, Vol. 12, p. 275.
8. United States Statutes at Large, Vol. 30, p. 1009.
9. United States Statutes at Large, Vol. 32, p. 1198.
10. Register of the Commissioned And Warrant Officers of the Navy of the United States..., January 1, 1904, p. 148.
11. United States Statutes at Large, Vol. 35, p. 155.
12. United States Statutes at Large, Vol. 39, p. 610.
13. Register of the Commissioned And Warrant Officers of the Navy of the United States..., January 1, 1916, p. 218-220.
19. Register of the Commissioned And Warrant Officers of the Navy of the United States..., 1939, p. 571.

Pay Grades
1. U.S. Navy Regulation Circular, No. 41, January 8, 1885.
2. United States Statutes at Large, Vol. 42, p. 629.
3. Register of the Commissioned And Warrant Officers of the Navy of the United States..., 1922, p. 323.
4. Uniform Regulations United States Marine Corps, July 13, 1937, p. 33-34.
5. Nalty, Bernard C., Unted States Marine Corps Ranks and Grades 1775-1969, Washington: Headquarters U.S. Marine Corps, 1970, p. 27.
6. ibid. p. 36-37.
7. ibid. p. 37-39.
8. United States Statutes at Large, Vol. 63, p. 807.
9. Nalty, Bernard C., Unted States Marine Corps Ranks and Grades 1775-1969, Washington: Headquarters U.S. Marine Corps, 1970, p. 39.
10. United States Statutes at Large, Vol. 68, p. 157.
11. United States Statutes at Large, Vol. 72, p. 123.
12. Thompson, James G, Decorations, Medals, Ribbons, Badges and Insignia of the Unted States Marine Corps World War II to Present, Fountain Inn: MOA Press, 1998, p. 23.
13. Nalty, Bernard C., Unted States Marine Corps Ranks and Grades 1775-1969, Washington: Headquarters U.S. Marine Corps, 1970, p. 40.
14. United States Statutes at Large, Vol. 105, p. 1491.Chapter 2. Marine Corps Rank Insignia
1. http://bluejacket.com/sea-service_uniform_a.htm, April 2011.
2. Rankin, Robert, Uniforms of the Marines, New York: Putnam, 1970, p. 22.
3. http://www.history.navy.mil/faqs/faq59-3.htm, April 2011.
4. Rankin, Robert, Uniforms of the Marines, New York: Putnam, 1970, p. 28.
5. ibid. p. 31-32.
6. ibid. p. 34.
7. ibid. p. 41-42.
8. Rankin, Robert, Uniforms of the Sea Servce, Annapolis: Naval Institute, 1962, p. 139.
9. http://www.history.navy.mil/faqs/faq59-28.htm, March 2011.
10. Lanham Howard G., Straps, Westminster, MD: Johnson Graphics, 1998, p. 139.
11. Rankin, Robert, Uniforms of the Marines, New York: Putnam, 1970, p. 43.

12. http://www.history.navy.mil/faqs/faq59-28.htm, March 2011.
13. http://members.cox.net/malachi.thorne/Uniform%20Regulations/M1859%20Regs.pdf, October 2011.
14. http://members.cox.net/malachi.thorne/Uniform%20Regulations/M1875%20Regs.pdf, October 2011.
15. Rankin, Robert, Uniforms of the Marines, New York: Putnam, 1970, p. 65.
16. ibid. p. 66.
17. http://members.cox.net/malachi.thorne/Uniform%20Regulations/M1892%20Regs.pdf, Octobr 2011.
18. General Order No. 427, July 18, 1894.
19. Special Order No. 50, July 25, 1896.
20. http://members.cox.net/malachi.thorne/Uniform%20Regulations/M1900%20Regs.pdf, Octobr 2011.
21. Regulations Governing the Uniform and Equipments of Officers and Enlisted Men of the United States Marine Corps, March 16, 1904, p. 19-22.
22. ibid. p. 10.
23. ibid. p. 18.
24. ibid. p. 16.
25. ibid. p. 20
26. Rankin, Robert, Uniforms of the Sea Servce, Annapolis: Naval Institute, 1962, p. 176.
27. Uniform Regulations United States Marine Corps, November 29, 1912, p. 28.
28. ibid. p. 40.
29. ibid. p. 77-78.
30. ibid. p. 65.
31. Henry, Mark R., US Marine Corps in World War I, Oxford: Osprey, 1999, p. 17-18.
32. Uniform Regulations United States Marine Corps, 1922, p. 2.
33. ibid. p. 11-18.
34. ibid. p. 89-90.
35. ibid. p. 90-93.
36. ibid. p. 97.
37. ibid. p. 98.
38. ibid. p. 20-22.
39. ibid. p. 45.
40. Uniform Regulations United States Marine Corps, 1929, p. 15.
41. Uniform Regulations United States Marine Corps, July 13, 1937, p. 110-111.
42. Rankin, Robert, Uniforms of the Marines, New York: Putnam, 1970, p. 102.
43. http://www.angelfire.com/ca4/gunnyg/enlrank.html, November 2011.
44. ALMAR 028/02, May 2, 2002.

Epaulets
1. Oliver, Raymond, Why is a Kernal called a Colonel?, Tuscon: Fireship press, 1983, p. 17.
2. http://bluejacket.com/sea-service_uniform_a.htm, April 2011.
3. http://www.history.navy.mil/faqs/faq59-3.htm, April 2011.
4. Rankin, Robert, Uniforms of the Marines, New York: Putnam, 1970, p. 28.
5. ibid. p. 31.
6. http://www.angelfire.com/ca4/gunnyg/enlrank.html, November 2011.
7. Rankin, Robert, Uniforms of the Marines, New York: Putnam, 1970, p. 34.
8. ibid. p. 42.
9. ibid. p. 43.
10. http://www.history.navy.mil/faqs/faq59-28.htm, March 2011.
11. http://members.cox.net/malachi.thorne/Uniform%20Regulations/M1859%20Regs.pdf, October 2011.
12. Rankin, Robert, Uniforms of the Marines, New York: Putnam, 1970, p. 56.
13. http://members.cox.net/malachi.thorne/Uniform%20Regulations/M1875%20Regs.pdf, October 2011.
14. Rankin, Robert, Uniforms of the Marines, New York: Putnam, 1970, p. 62.
15. ibid. p. 68.
16. Regulations Governing the Uniform and Equipments of Officers and Enlisted Men of the United States Marine Corps, March 16, 1904, p. 27.
17. Uniform Regulations United States Marine Corps, November 29, 1912, p. 50.
18. Uniform Regulations United States Marine Corps, 1922, p. 11.
19. Uniform Regulations United States Marine Corps, July 13, 1937, p. 79-80.

Shoulder Straps
1. Lanham Howard G., Straps, Westminster, MD: Johnson Graphics, 1998, p. 139.
2. http://www.history.navy.mil/faqs/faq59-28.htm, March 2011.
3. Lanham Howard G., Straps, Westminster, MD: Johnson Graphics, 1998, p. 139.
4. ibid.

Shoulder Knots
1. http://www.angelfire.com/ca4/gunnyg/enlrank.html, November 2011.
2. http://members.cox.net/malachi.thorne/Uniform%20Regulations/M1859%20Regs.pdf, October 2011.
3. http://gallery.pictopia.com/usni/gallery/94252/photo/8565793/?o=14, December 2011.
4. http://members.cox.net/malachi.thorne/Uniform%20Regulations/M1875%20Regs.pdf, October 2011.
5. Kenneth L. Smith-Christmas, Marine Corps Museum Cataloging and Identification Guide for 20th Century Uniforms.
6. http://members.cox.net/malachi.thorne/Uniform%20Regulations/M1892%20Regs.pdf, Octobr 2011.
7. Rankin, Robert, Uniforms of the Marines, New York: Putnam, 1970, p. 68.
8. http://members.cox.net/malachi.thorne/Uniform%20Regulations/M1900%20Regs.pdf, Octobr 2011.
9. Regulations Governing the Uniform and Equipments of Officers and Enlisted Men of the United States Marine Corps, March 16, 1904, p. 38.
10. Uniform Regulations United States Marine Corps, November 29, 1912, p. 50.
11. Uniform Regulations United States Marine Corps, 1922, p. 93.
12. Uniform Regulations United States Marine Corps, 1929, p. 15.
13. Uniform Regulations United States Marine Corps, July 13, 1937, p. 110.
14. Kenneth L. Smith-Christmas, Marine Corps Museum Cataloging and Identification Guide for 20th Century Uniforms.

Badges of rank
1. Lanham Howard G., Straps, Westminster, MD: Johnson Graphics, 1998, p. 139.
2. http://www.history.navy.mil/faqs/faq59-28.htm, March 2011.
3. http://members.cox.net/malachi.thorne/Uniform%20Regulations/M1859%20Regs.pdf, October 2011.
4. http://members.cox.net/malachi.thorne/Uniform%20Regulations/M1875%20Regs.pdf, October 2011.
5. http://members.cox.net/malachi.thorne/Uniform%20Regulations/M1892%20Regs.pdf, Octobr 2011.
6. http://members.cox.net/malachi.thorne/Uniform%20Regulations/M1900%20Regs.pdf, Octobr 2011.
7. Regulations Governing the Uniform and Equipments of Officers and Enlisted Men of the United States Marine Corps, March 16, 1904, p. 19-22.
8. ibid. p. 10.
9. ibid. p. 18.
10. Uniform Regulations United States Marine Corps, November 29, 1912, p. 28.
11. ibid. p. 40.
12. Uniform Regulations United States Marine Corps, November 29, 1912 with changes to May 12, 1917, p. 24 & 60.
14. Henry, Mark R., US Marine Corps in World War I, Oxford: Osprey, 1999, p. 18.
15. Uniform Regulations United States Marine Corps, 1922, p. 39-40.
16. Uniform Regulations United States Marine Corps, 1929, p. 109.
17. Uniform Regulations United States Marine Corps, July 13, 1937, p. 82.
18. All Hands, "Insignia of the United States Armed Forces", December 1954, p. 32-33, Chart shows the new insignia. However it also shows the insignia for army warrant officers, officially adopted in 1956.
19. Thompson, James G, Decorations, Medals, Ribbons, Badges and Insignia of the Unted States Marine Corps World War II to Present, Fountain Inn: MOA Press, 1998, p. 21.
20. http://www.tecom.usmc.mil/HD/Chronologies/Yearly/1992.htm, November 2011.
22. ALMAR 028/02, May 2, 2002.

Cuff Decoration
1. Rankin, Robert, Uniforms of the Marines, New York: Putnam, 1970, p. 40.
2. ibid. p. 43.
3. http://www.history.navy.mil/faqs/faq59-28.htm, March 2011.
4. http://members.cox.net/malachi.thorne/Uniform%20Regulations/M1859%20Regs.pdf, October 2011.
5. ibid.
6. http://members.cox.net/malachi.thorne/Uniform%20Regulations/M1875%20Regs.pdf, October 2011.
7. Rankin, Robert, Uniforms of the Marines, New York: Putnam, 1970, plate, viii.
8. http://en.wikipedia.org/wiki/Charles_Grymes_McCawley, November 2011.
9. http://members.cox.net/malachi.thorne/Uniform%20Regulations/M1892%20Regs.pdf, Octobr 2011.
10. Rankin, Robert, Uniforms of the Marines, New York: Putnam, 1970, p. 66.
11. General Order No. 427, July 18, 1894.
12. http://members.cox.net/malachi.thorne/Uniform%20Regulations/M1900%20Regs.pdf, Octobr 2011.
13. http://en.wikipedia.org/wiki/File:Charles_Heywood.jpg, November 2011.
14. Regulations Governing the Uniform and Equipments of Officers and Enlisted Men of the United States Marine Corps, March 16, 1904, p. 14-15.
15. ibid. p. 19.
16. Rankin, Robert, Uniforms of the Sea Servce, Annapolis: Naval Institute, 1962, p. 176.
17. http://en.wikipedia.org/wiki/File:George_F._Elliott.jpg, November 2011.
18. Uniform Regulations United States Marine Corps, November 29, 1912, plate 26.
19. ibid. plate 27. & p. 36.
20. Uniform Regulations United States Marine Corps, November 29, 1912, p. 39-40.
21. ibid.p. 36.
22. Uniform Regulations United States Marine Corps, November 29, 1912 with changes to May 12, 1917, p. 58.
23. ibid.p. 24 & 60.
24. ibid. plate 27.
25. Uniform Regulations United States Marine Corps, 1922, p. 90-93.
26. Uniform Regulations United States Marine Corps, 1929, p. 98.
27. Uniform Regulations United States Marine Corps, July 13, 1937, p. 74.
28. Kenneth L. Smith-Christmas, Marine Corps Museum Cataloging and Identification Guide for 20th Century Uniforms.

Chevrons

1. Oliver, Raymond, Why is a Kernal called a Colonel?, Tuscon: Fireship press, 1983, p. 1
2. Rankin, Robert, Uniforms of the Marines, New York: Putnam, 1970, p. 34.
3. ibid.
4. http://www.angelfire.com/ca4/gunnyg/enlrank.html, November 2011.
5. Rankin, Robert, Uniforms of the Sea Servce, Annapolis: Naval Institute, 1962, p. 139.
6. http://www.history.navy.mil/faqs/faq59-28.htm, March 2011.
7. http://members.cox.net/malachi.thorne/Uniform%20Regulations/M1859%20Regs.pdf, October 2011.
8. Special Order No. 50, July 25, 1896.

9. http://www.angelfire.com/ca/dickg/oldgunny.html, November 2011.
10. http://members.cox.net/malachi.thorne/Uniform%20Regulations/M1900%20Regs.pdf, Octobr 2011.
11. http://www.angelfire.com/ca/dickg/oldgunny.html, November 2011.
12. ibid.
13. Rankin, Robert, Uniforms of the Sea Servce, Annapolis: Naval Institute, 1962, p. 176.
14. Uniform Regulations United States Marine Corps, November 29, 1912, p. 77-78.
15. Henry, Mark R., US Marine Corps in World War I, Oxford: Osprey, 1999, p. 17.
16. Uniform Regulations United States Marine Corps, 1922, p. VIII.
17. http://www.angelfire.com/ca4/gunnyg/enlrank.html, November 2011.
18. Uniform Regulations United States Marine Corps, 1922, p. 45 & 103-104.
19. Uniform Regulations United States Marine Corps, 1929, p. 62-63 & 126-127.
20. Nalty, Bernard C., Unted States Marine Corps Ranks and Grades 1775-1969, Washington: Headquarters U.S. Marine Corps, 1970, p. 27.
21. Uniform Regulations United States Marine Corps, July 13, 1937, p. 34.
22. http://www.usmilitariaforum.com/forums/index.php?showtopic=3463&hl=usmc+chevron, December 2011
23. Thompson, James G, Decorations, Medals, Ribbons, Badges and Insignia of the Unted States Marine Corps World War II to Present, Fountain Inn: MOA Press, 1998, p. 22.
24. http://www.angelfire.com/ca4/gunnyg/enlrank.html, November 2011.
25. Thompson, James G, Decorations, Medals, Ribbons, Badges and Insignia of the Unted States Marine Corps World War II to Present, Fountain Inn: MOA Press, 1998, p. 22.
26. http://www.tecom.usmc.mil/HD/Chronologies/Yearly/1992.htm, December 2011.

Chapter 3.Marine Corps Ranks

Adjutant and Inspector with rank of Colonel
1. United States Statutes at Large, Vol. 30, p. 1009.
2. http://members.cox.net/malachi.thorne/Uniform%20Regulations/M1892%20Regs.pdf, October 2011.
3. General Order No. 427, July 18, 1894.
4. Register of the Commissioned And Warrant Officers of the Navy of the United States..., January 1, 1905, p. 173.
5. http://members.cox.net/malachi.thorne/Uniform%20Regulations/M1900%20Regs.pdf, October 2011.
6. Regulations Governing the Uniform and Equipments of Officers and Enlisted Men of the United States Marine Corps, March 16, 1904, p. 15.
7. ibid. p. 14
8. http://en.wikipedia.org/wiki/George_F._Elliott, October 2011.
9. Uniform Regulations United States Marine Corps, November 29, 1912, plate 29.
10. ibid. p. 60.
11. ibid. p. 50.
12. United States Statutes at Large, Vol. 39, p. 610.

Adjutant and Inspector with rank of Major
1. United States Statutes at Large, Vol. 9, p. 155.
2. United States Statutes at Large, Vol. 3, p. 377.
3. Register of the Commissioned And Warrant Officers of the Navy of the United States..., 1821, p. 29, lists Samuel Miller as Adjutant and Inspector but the 1822 register "http://www.ibiblio.org/pha/USN/1822/NavReg1822.html", October 2011, show the position filled by Howle.
4. http://www.history.navy.mil/faqs/faq59-28.htm, March 2011.
5. Callahan, Edward, List of Officers of the Navy of the United States and the Marine Corps from 1775 to 1900, New York: L. R. Hamerlsy & CO., 1901, p. 689.
6. Senate Executive Journal, vol 10, p. 288.
7. http://www.grandarmyofthefrontier.org/uniforms/usmc1859.htm, October 2011.
8. Callahan, Edward, List of Officers of the Navy of the United States and the Marine Corps from 1775 to 1900, New York: L. R. Hamerlsy & CO., 1901, p. 700.
9. ibid. p. 694.
10. http://members.cox.net/malachi.thorne/Uniform%20Regulations/M1875%20Regs.pdf, October 2011.
11. Rankin, Robert, Uniforms of the Marines, New York: Putnam, 1970, p. 65.
12. Callahan, Edward, List of Officers of the Navy of the United States and the Marine Corps from 1775 to 1900, New York: L. R. Hamerlsy & CO., 1901, p. 694.
13. ibid. p. 695.
14. General Order No. 427, July 18, 1894.
15. United States Statutes at Large, Vol. 30, p. 1009.

Assistant Adjutant and Inspector with rank of Lieutenant Colonel
1. United States Statutes at Large, Vol. 32, p. 1198.
2. Register of the Commissioned And Warrant Officers of the Navy of the United States..., January 1, 1904, p. 148.
3. http://members.cox.net/malachi.thorne/Uniform%20Regulations/M1900%20Regs.pdf, October 2011.
4. Regulations Governing the Uniform and Equipments of Officers and Enlisted Men of the United States Marine Corps, March 16, 1904, p. 15.
5. ibid. p. 19-20.
6. Register of the Commissioned And Warrant Officers of the Navy of the United States..., January 1, 1905, p. 154.
7. United States Statutes at Large, Vol. 35, p. 155.
8. Register of the Commissioned And Warrant Officers of the Navy of the United States..., January 1, 1910, p. 180.
9. Uniform Regulations United States Marine Corps, November 29, 1912, p. 60.
10. ibid. p. 50.
11. United States Statutes at Large, Vol. 39, p. 610.

Assistant Adjutant and Inspector with rank of Major
1. United States Statutes at Large, Vol. 30, p. 1009.
2. Register of the Commissioned And Warrant Officers of the Navy of the United States..., January 1, 1900, p. 126.
3. General Order No. 427, July 18, 1894.
4. http://members.cox.net/malachi.thorne/Uniform%20Regulations/M1900%20Regs.pdf, October 2011.
5. United States Statutes at Large, Vol. 32, p. 1198.
6. Register of the Commissioned And Warrant Officers of the Navy of the United States..., January 1, 1904, p. 148.
7. Regulations Governing the Uniform and Equipments of Officers and Enlisted Men of the United States Marine Corps, March 16, 1904, p. 15.
8. ibid. p. 19-20.
9. United States Statutes at Large, Vol. 35, p. 155.
10. Register of the Commissioned And Warrant Officers of the Navy of the United States..., January 1, 1910, p. 180.
11. Uniform Regulations United States Marine Corps, November 29, 1912, p. 60.
12. ibid. p. 50.
13. United States Statutes at Large, Vol. 39, p. 610.

Assistant Baker
1. Nalty, Bernard C., United States Marine Corps Ranks and Grades 1775-1969, Washington: Headquarters U.S. Marine Corps, 1970, p. 30.
2. Uniform Regulations United States Marine Corps, July 13, 1937, p. 34.
3. Nalty, Bernard C., United States Marine Corps Ranks and Grades 1775-1969, Washington: Headquarters U.S. Marine Corps, 1970, p. 31.

Assistant Cook
1. Nalty, Bernard C., United States Marine Corps Ranks and Grades 1775-1969, Washington: Headquarters U.S. Marine Corps, 1970, p. 29.
2. ibid. p. 27.
3. Uniform Regulations United States Marine Corps, July 13, 1937, p. 34.
1. Nalty, Bernard C., United States Marine Corps Ranks and Grades 1775-1969, Washington: Headquarters U.S. Marine Corps, 1970, p. 31.

Assistant Cook (Baker)
1. Nalty, Bernard C., United States Marine Corps Ranks and Grades 1775-1969, Washington: Headquarters U.S. Marine Corps, 1970, p. 30.
2. Uniform Regulations United States Marine Corps, July 13, 1937, p. 34.
3. Nalty, Bernard C., United States Marine Corps Ranks and Grades 1775-1969, Washington: Headquarters U.S. Marine Corps, 1970, p. 30-31.
4. ibid.
5. Uniform Regulations United States Marine Corps, July 13, 1937, p. 34.
6. Nalty, Bernard C., United States Marine Corps Ranks and Grades 1775-1969, Washington: Headquarters U.S. Marine Corps, 1970, p. 39.

Assistant Cook (Commissary)
1. Nalty, Bernard C., United States Marine Corps Ranks and Grades 1775-1969, Washington: Headquarters U.S. Marine Corps, 1970, p. 31.
2. Uniform Regulations United States Marine Corps, July 13, 1937, p. 34.
3. Nalty, Bernard C., United States Marine Corps Ranks and Grades 1775-1969, Washington: Headquarters U.S. Marine Corps, 1970, p. 39.

Assistant Paymaster with rank of Captain
1. United States Statutes at Large, Vol. 32, p. 1198.
2. Register of the Commissioned And Warrant Officers of the Navy of the United States..., January 1, 1904, p. 148.
3. http://members.cox.net/malachi.thorne/Uniform%20Regulations/M1900%20Regs.pdf, October 2011.
4. United States Statutes at Large, Vol. 35, p. 155.
5. Register of the Commissioned And Warrant Officers of the Navy of the United States..., January 1, 1909, p. 176.
6. Register of the Commissioned And Warrant Officers of the Navy of the United States..., January 1, 1910, p. 182.
7. Uniform Regulations United States Marine Corps, November 29, 1912, p. 60.
8. ibid. p. 50.
9. United States Statutes at Large, Vol. 39, p. 610.

Assistant Paymaster with rank of Lieutenant Colonel
1. United States Statutes at Large, Vol. 32, p. 1198.
2. Register of the Commissioned And Warrant Officers of the Navy of the United States..., January 1, 1904, p. 148.
3. http://members.cox.net/malachi.thorne/Uniform%20Regulations/M1900%20Regs.pdf, October 2011.
4. Regulations Governing the Uniform and Equipments of Officers and Enlisted Men of the United States Marine Corps, March 16, 1904, p. 15.
5. Register of the Commissioned And Warrant Officers of the Navy of the United States..., January 1, 1910, p. 182.
6. Uniform Regulations United States Marine Corps, November 29, 1912, p. 60.
7. ibid. p. 50.
8. United States Statutes at Large, Vol. 39, p. 610.

Assistant Paymaster with rank of Major
1. United States Statutes at Large, Vol. 30, p. 1009.
2. Register of the Commissioned And Warrant Officers of the Navy of the United States..., January 1, 1900, p. 126.
3. General Order No. 427, July 18, 1894.
4. http://members.cox.net/malachi.thorne/Uniform%20Regulations/M1900%20Regs.pdf, October 2011.
5. Register of the Commissioned And Warrant Officers of the Navy of the United States..., January 1, 1904, p. 148.
6. Regulations Governing the Uniform and Equipments of Officers and Enlisted Men of the United States Marine Corps, March 16, 1904, p. 15.
7. ibid. p. 19-20.
8. United States Statutes at Large, Vol. 35, p. 155.
9. Register of the Commissioned And Warrant Officers of the Navy of the United States..., January 1, 1909, p. 176.
10. Register of the Commissioned And Warrant Officers of the Navy of the United States..., January 1, 1910, p. 182.

11. Uniform Regulations United States Marine Corps, November 29, 1912, p. 60.
12. ibid. p. 50.
13. United States Statutes at Large, Vol. 39, p. 610.

Assistant Quartermaster with rank of Captain
1. United States Statutes at Large, Vol. 9, p. 155.
2. United States Statutes at Large, Vol. 4, p. 712.
3. Senate Executive Journal, vol 5, p. 91.
4. http://www.history.navy.mil/faqs/faq59-28.htm, March 2011.
5. Senate Executive Journal, vol 10, p. 16.
6. Senate Executive Journal, vol 10, p. 288.
7. http://www.grandarmyofthefrontier.org/uniforms/usmc1859.htm, October 2011.
8. United States Statutes at Large, Vol. 12, p. 275.
9. Callahan, Edward, List of Officers of the Navy of the United States and the Marine Corps from 1775 to 1900, New York: L. R. Hamerlsy & CO., 1901, p. 701.
10. ibid. p. 691.
11. http://members.cox.net/malachi.thorne/Uniform%20Regulations/M1875%20Regs.pdf, October 2011.
12. Rankin, Robert, Uniforms of the Marines, New York: Putnam, 1970, p. 65.
13. Callahan, Edward, List of Officers of the Navy of the United States and the Marine Corps from 1775 to 1900, New York: L. R. Hamerlsy & CO., 1901, p. 691.
14. ibid. p. 697.
15. ibid. p. 691.
16. ibid. p. 683.
17. General Order No. 427, July 18, 1894.
18. Callahan, Edward, List of Officers of the Navy of the United States and the Marine Corps from 1775 to 1900, New York: L. R. Hamerlsy & CO., 1901, p. 697.
19. ibid. p. 684.
20. ibid.
21. ibid. p. 695.
22. ibid. p. 683.
23. ibid. p. 692.
24. United States Statutes at Large, Vol. 30, p. 1009.
25. Callahan, Edward, List of Officers of the Navy of the United States and the Marine Corps from 1775 to 1900, New York: L. R. Hamerlsy & CO., 1901, p. 695.
26. ibid. p. 692.
27. Register of the Commissioned And Warrant Officers of the Navy of the United States..., January 1, 1900, p. 126.
28. http://members.cox.net/malachi.thorne/Uniform%20Regulations/M1900%20Regs.pdf, October 2011.
29. Register of the Commissioned And Warrant Officers of the Navy of the United States..., January 1, 1902, p. 145.
30. ibid. p. 130.
31. United States Statutes at Large, Vol. 32, p. 1198.
32. Register of the Commissioned And Warrant Officers of the Navy of the United States..., January 1, 1905, p. 154.
33. Register of the Commissioned And Warrant Officers of the Navy of the United States..., January 1, 1904, p. 126.
34. United States Statutes at Large, Vol. 35, p. 155.
35. Register of the Commissioned And Warrant Officers of the Navy of the United States..., January 1, 1910, p. 180.
36. ibid.
37. Register of the Commissioned And Warrant Officers of the Navy of the United States..., January 1, 1912, p. 192.
38. Uniform Regulations United States Marine Corps, November 29, 1912, p. 60.
39. ibid. p. 50.
40. Register of the Commissioned And Warrant Officers of the Navy of the United States..., January 1, 1915, p. 216.
41. United States Statutes at Large, Vol. 39, p. 610.

Assistant Quartermaster with rank of Lieutenant Colonel
1. United States Statutes at Large, Vol. 32, p. 1198.
2. Register of the Commissioned And Warrant Officers of the Navy of the United States..., January 1, 1904, p. 148.
3. http://members.cox.net/malachi.thorne/Uniform%20Regulations/M1900%20Regs.pdf, October 2011.
4. Regulations Governing the Uniform and Equipments of Officers and Enlisted Men of the United States Marine Corps, March 16, 1904, p. 15.
5. United States Statutes at Large, Vol. 35, p. 155.
6. Register of the Commissioned And Warrant Officers of the Navy of the United States..., January 1, 1910, p. 180.
7. Register of the Commissioned And Warrant Officers of the Navy of the United States..., January 1, 1912, p. 204.
8. ibid. p. 190.
9. Uniform Regulations United States Marine Corps, November 29, 1912, p. 60.
10. ibid. p. 50.
11. Register of the Commissioned And Warrant Officers of the Navy of the United States..., January 1, 1914, p. 200.
12. United States Statutes at Large, Vol. 39, p. 610.

Assistant Quartermaster with rank of Major
1. United States Statutes at Large, Vol. 30, p. 1009.
2. Register of the Commissioned And Warrant Officers of the Navy of the United States..., January 1, 1900, p. 126.
3. General Order No. 427, July 18, 1894.
4. http://members.cox.net/malachi.thorne/Uniform%20Regulations/M1900%20Regs.pdf, October 2011.
5. Register of the Commissioned And Warrant Officers of the Navy of the United States..., January 1, 1904, p. 148.
6. Regulations Governing the Uniform and Equipments of Officers and Enlisted Men of the United States Marine Corps, March 16, 1904, p. 15.
7. ibid. p. 19-20.
8. United States Statutes at Large, Vol. 35, p. 155.
9. Register of the Commissioned And Warrant Officers of the Navy of the United States..., January 1, 1909, p. 174.
10. Register of the Commissioned And Warrant Officers of the Navy of the United States..., January 1, 1912, p. 190.
11. Uniform Regulations United States Marine Corps, November 29, 1912, p. 60.
12. ibid. p. 50.
10. Register of the Commissioned And Warrant Officers of the Navy of the United States..., January 1, 1916, p. 218.
14. United States Statutes at Large, Vol. 39, p. 610.

Brigadier General
1. Callahan, Edward, List of Officers of the Navy of the United States and the Marine Corps from 1775 to 1900, New York: L. R. Hamerlsy & CO., 1901, p. 679.
2. Nalty, Bernard C., United States Marine Corps Ranks and Grades 1775-1969, Washington: Headquarters U.S. Marine Corps, 1970, p. 4.
3. http://members.cox.net/malachi.thorne/Uniform%20Regulations/M1859%20Regs.pdf, October 2011.
4. United States Statutes at Large, Vol. 12, p. 275.
5. United States Statutes at Large, Vol. 14, p. 517.
6. Callahan, Edward, List of Officers of the Navy of the United States and the Marine Corps from 1775 to 1900, New York: L. R. Hamerlsy & CO., 1901, p. 679.
7. http://members.cox.net/malachi.thorne/Uniform%20Regulations/M1859%20Regs.pdf, October 2011.
8. United States Statutes at Large, Vol. 18, p. 58.
9. http://members.cox.net/malachi.thorne/Uniform%20Regulations/M1875%20Regs.pdf, October 2011.
10. Callahan, Edward, List of Officers of the Navy of the United States and the Marine Corps from 1775 to 1900, New York: L. R. Hamerlsy & CO., 1901, p. 679.
11. United States Statutes at Large, Vol. 30, p. 1008.
12. http://members.cox.net/malachi.thorne/Uniform%20Regulations/M1900%20Regs.pdf, October 2011.
13. United States Statutes at Large, Vol. 32, p. 686.
14. Register of the Commissioned And Warrant Officers of the Navy of the United States..., January 1, 1904, p. 165.
15. ibid. p. 148.
16. Regulations Governing the Uniform and Equipments of Officers and Enlisted Men of the United States Marine Corps, March 16, 1904, p. 14, 17, 18, 27 & 28.
17. United States Statutes at Large, Vol. 35, p. 155.
18. United States Statutes at Large, Vol. 39, p. 611.
19. Uniform Regulations United States Marine Corps, November 29, 1912 with changes to May 12, 1917, p. 58.
20. ibid. plate 26-A.
21. Uniform Regulations United States Marine Corps, 1922, p. 91.
22. Kenneth L. Smith-Christmas, Marine Corps Museum Cataloging and Identification Guide for 20th Century Uniforms.
23. United States Statutes at Large, Vol. 63, p. 802.
24. MARINE CORPS UNIFORM REGULATIONS, 2003, p. 4-24.

Captain
1. Oliver, Raymond, Why is a Kernal called a Colonel?, Tucson: Fireship press, 1983, p. 29.
2. Journals of the Continental Congress, Vol. 3, p. 348.
3. Journals of the Continental Congress, Vol. 3, p. 384.
4. http://www.history.navy.mil/books/callahan/contmc.htm, October 2011.
5. http://bluejacket.com/sea-service_uniform_a.htm, April 2011
6. United States Statutes at Large, Vol. 1, p. 350.
7. United States Statutes at Large, Vol. 1, p. 453.
8. Callahan, Edward, List of Officers of the Navy of the United States and the Marine Corps from 1775 to 1900, New York: L. R. Hamerlsy & CO., 1901.
9. Rankin, Robert, Uniforms of the Marines, New York: Putnam, 1970, p. 31.
10. Callahan, Edward, List of Officers of the Navy of the United States and the Marine Corps from 1775 to 1900, New York: L. R. Hamerlsy & CO., 1901.
11. Senate Executive Journal, vol 2, p. 95.
12. Callahan, Edward, List of Officers of the Navy of the United States and the Marine Corps from 1775 to 1900, New York: L. R. Hamerlsy & CO., 1901.
13. Senate Executive Journal, vol 2, p. 119.
14. Callahan, Edward, List of Officers of the Navy of the United States and the Marine Corps from 1775 to 1900, New York: L. R. Hamerlsy & CO., 1901.
15. United States Statutes at Large, Vol. 3, p. 124.
16. United States Statutes at Large, Vol. 3, p. 377.
17. Rankin, Robert, Uniforms of the Marines, New York: Putnam, 1970, p. 34.
18. ibid. p. 41-42.
19. Lanham Howard G., Straps, Westminster, MD: Johnson Graphics, 1998, p. 139.
20. http://www.history.navy.mil/faqs/faq59-28.htm, March 2011.
20a. ibid.
21. http://members.cox.net/malachi.thorne/Uniform%20Regulations/M1859%20Regs.pdf, October 2011.
22. http://members.cox.net/malachi.thorne/Uniform%20Regulations/M1875%20Regs.pdf, October 2011.
23. Kenneth L. Smith-Christmas, Marine Corps Museum Cataloging and Identification Guide for 20th Century Uniforms.
24. United States Statutes at Large, Vol. 63, p. 802
25. MARINE CORPS UNIFORM REGULATIONS, 2003, p. 4-24.

Chief Baker
1. Nalty, Bernard C., United States Marine Corps Ranks and Grades 1775-1969, Washington: Headquarters U.S. Marine Corps, 1970, p. 30.
2. Uniform Regulations United States Marine Corps, July 13, 1937, p. 34.
3. Nalty, Bernard C., United States Marine Corps Ranks and Grades 1775-1969, Washington: Headquarters U.S. Marine Corps, 1970, p. 31

Chief Cook
1. Nalty, Bernard C., United States Marine Corps Ranks and Grades 1775-1969, Washington: Headquarters U.S. Marine Corps, 1970, p. 29.
2. ibid. p. 27.
3. Uniform Regulations United States Marine Corps, July 13, 1937, p. 34.
1. Nalty, Bernard C., United States Marine Corps Ranks and Grades 1775-1969, Washington: Headquarters U.S. Marine Corps, 1970, p. 31.

Chief Cook (baker)
1. Nalty, Bernard C., United States Marine Corps Ranks and Grades 1775-1969, Washington: Headquarters U.S. Marine Corps, 1970, p. 30.

2. Uniform Regulations United States Marine Corps, July 13, 1937, p. 34.
3. Nalty, Bernard C., United States Marine Corps Ranks and Grades 1775-1969, Washington: Headquarters U.S. Marine Corps, 1970, p. 30-31.
4. ibid.
5. Uniform Regulations United States Marine Corps, July 13, 1937, p. 34.
6. Nalty, Bernard C., United States Marine Corps Ranks and Grades 1775-1969, Washington: Headquarters U.S. Marine Corps, 1970, p. 39.

Chief Cook (Commissary)
1. Nalty, Bernard C., United States Marine Corps Ranks and Grades 1775-1969, Washington: Headquarters U.S. Marine Corps, 1970, p. 31.
2. Uniform Regulations United States Marine Corps, July 13, 1937, p. 34.
3. Nalty, Bernard C., United States Marine Corps Ranks and Grades 1775-1969, Washington: Headquarters U.S. Marine Corps, 1970, p. 39.

Chief Marine Gunner
1. United States Statutes at Large, Vol. 44, p. 725.
2. Uniform Regulations United States Marine Corps, 1929, p. 109.
3. United States Statutes at Large, Vol. 57, p. 574.
4. http://1stbn4thmarines.com/other-things-interest/warrant_officer_history.htm, October 2011.

Chief Paymaster Clerk
1. United States Statutes at Large, Vol. 44, p. 725.
2. Uniform Regulations United States Marine Corps, 1929, p. 109.
3. United States Statutes at Large, Vol. 57, p. 574.

Chief Quartermaster Clerk
1. United States Statutes at Large, Vol. 44, p. 725.
2. Uniform Regulations United States Marine Corps, 1929, p. 109.
3. United States Statutes at Large, Vol. 57, p. 574.

Chief Warrant Officer 2
1. United States Statutes at Large, Vol. 68, p. 157.
2. All Hands, "Insignia of the United States Armed Forces", December 1954, p. 32-33, Chart shows the new insignia. However it also shows the insignia for army warrant officers, officially adopted in 1956.
3. MARINE CORPS UNIFORM REGULATIONS, 2003, p. 4-25.

Chief Warrant Officer 3
1. United States Statutes at Large, Vol. 68, p. 157.
2. All Hands, "Insignia of the United States Armed Forces", December 1954, p. 32-33, Chart shows the new insignia. However it also shows the insignia for army warrant officers, officially adopted in 1956.
3. MARINE CORPS UNIFORM REGULATIONS, 2003, p. 4-25.

Chief Warrant Officer 4
1. United States Statutes at Large, Vol. 68, p. 157.
2. All Hands, "Insignia of the United States Armed Forces", December 1954, p. 32-33, Chart shows the new insignia. However it also shows the insignia for army warrant officers, officially adopted in 1956.
3. MARINE CORPS UNIFORM REGULATIONS, 2003, p. 4-25.

Chief Warrant Officer 5
1. United States Statutes at Large, Vol. 105, p. 1491
2. http://www.tecom.usmc.mil/HD/Chronologies/Yearly/1992.htm, November 2011.
3. MARINE CORPS UNIFORM REGULATIONS, 2003, p. 4-25.

Colonel
1. Oliver, Raymond, Why is a Kernal called a Colonel?, Tucson: Fireship press, 1983, p. 39.
2. United States Statutes at Large, Vol. 4, p. 713.
3. Rankin, Robert, Uniforms of the Marines, New York: Putnam, 1970, p. 41-42.
4. http://www.history.navy.mil/faqs/faq59-28.htm, March 2011, shows the bullion sizes as of 1840.
4a. Lanham Howard G., Straps, Westminster, MD: Johnson Graphics, 1998, p. 139.
5. Callahan, Edward, List of Officers of the Navy of the United States and the Marine Corps from 1775 to 1900, New York: L. R. Hamerlsy & CO., 1901, p. 679.
6. http://members.cox.net/malachi.thorne/Uniform%20Regulations/M1859%20Regs.pdf, October 2011.
7. United States Statutes at Large, Vol. 12, p. 275.
8. Callahan, Edward, List of Officers of the Navy of the United States and the Marine Corps from 1775 to 1900, New York: L. R. Hamerlsy & CO., 1901, p. 685.
9. ibid. p. 679.
10. Senate Executive Journal, vol 13, p. 577.
11. United States Statutes at Large, Vol. 14, p. 517.
12. Senate Executive Journal, vol 18, p. 48.
13. http://members.cox.net/malachi.thorne/Uniform%20Regulations/M1875%20Regs.pdf, October 2011.
14. United States Statutes at Large, Vol. 18, p. 58.
15. Callahan, Edward, List of Officers of the Navy of the United States and the Marine Corps from 1775 to 1900, New York: L. R. Hamerlsy & CO., 1901, p. 679.
16. http://en.wikipedia.org/wiki/Charles_Grymes_McCawley, November, 2011.
17. Callahan, Edward, List of Officers of the Navy of the United States and the Marine Corps from 1775 to 1900, New York: L. R. Hamerlsy & CO., 1901.
18. http://members.cox.net/malachi.thorne/Uniform%20Regulations/M1892%20Regs.pdf, October 2011.
19. General Order No. 427, July 18, 1894.
20. http://www.spanamwar.com/1stmarinehuntington.html, November 2011
21. United States Statutes at Large, Vol. 30, p. 1009.
22. Register of the Commissioned And Warrant Officers of the Navy of the United States..., 1900, p. 126.
23. Register of the Commissioned And Warrant Officers of the Navy of the United States..., 1901, p. 140.
24. ibid. p. 127.
25. ibid. p. 141.
26. ibid. p. 141 and 127.
27. Register of the Commissioned And Warrant Officers of the Navy of the United States..., 1904, p. 165.
28. ibid. p. 151
29. United States Statutes at Large, Vol. 32, p. 1198.
30. Register of the Commissioned And Warrant Officers of the Navy of the United States..., 1904, p. 151.
31. Regulations Governing the Uniform and Equipments of Officers and Enlisted Men of the United States Marine Corps, March 16, 1904, p. 15.
32. Register of the Commissioned And Warrant Officers of the Navy of the United States..., 1905, p. 173.
33. ibid. p. 157.
34. ibid. p. 173.
35. ibid. p. 157.
36. Register of the Commissioned And Warrant Officers of the Navy of the United States..., 1906, p. 168.
37. ibid. p. 153.
38. ibid. p. 168.
39. ibid. p. 153.
40. ibid. p. 168.
41. ibid. p. 153.
42. Register of the Commissioned And Warrant Officers of the Navy of the United States..., 1907, p. 178.
43. ibid. p. 163.
44. ibid.
45. United States Statutes at Large, Vol. 35, p. 155.
46. Uniform Regulations United States Marine Corps, November 29, 1912, plate 29.
47. http://en.wikipedia.org/wiki/George_F._Elliott, November 2011.
48. Kenneth L. Smith-Christmas, Marine Corps Museum Cataloging and Identification Guide for 20th Century Uniforms.
49. United States Statutes at Large, Vol. 63, p. 802.
50. MARINE CORPS UNIFORM REGULATIONS, 2003, p. 4-24.

Commissioned Warrant Officer
1. United States Statutes at Large, Vol. 57, p. 574.
2. All Hands, "Insignia of the United States Armed Forces", November 1950, p. 32-33.
3. All Hands, "Warrant Officers' Collar Devices", October 1952, p. 24.
4. United States Statutes at Large, Vol. 63, p. 807.
5. United States Statutes at Large, Vol. 68, p. 157.

Cook First Class
1. Nalty, Bernard C., United States Marine Corps Ranks and Grades 1775-1969, Washington: Headquarters U.S. Marine Corps, 1970, p. 31.
2. Uniform Regulations United States Marine Corps, July 13, 1937, p. 34.
3. Nalty, Bernard C., United States Marine Corps Ranks and Grades 1775-1969, Washington: Headquarters U.S. Marine Corps, 1970, p. 35.

Cook Second Class
1. Nalty, Bernard C., United States Marine Corps Ranks and Grades 1775-1969, Washington: Headquarters U.S. Marine Corps, 1970, p. 31.
2. Uniform Regulations United States Marine Corps, July 13, 1937, p. 34.
3. Nalty, Bernard C., United States Marine Corps Ranks and Grades 1775-1969, Washington: Headquarters U.S. Marine Corps, 1970, p. 35.

Cook Third Class
1. Nalty, Bernard C., United States Marine Corps Ranks and Grades 1775-1969, Washington: Headquarters U.S. Marine Corps, 1970, p. 31.
2. Uniform Regulations United States Marine Corps, July 13, 1937, p. 34.
3. Nalty, Bernard C., United States Marine Corps Ranks and Grades 1775-1969, Washington: Headquarters U.S. Marine Corps, 1970, p. 35.

Corporal
1. Oliver, Raymond, Why is a Kernal called a Colonel?, Tucson: Fireship press, 1983, p. 7.
2. Journals of the Continental Congress, Vol. 3, p. 384.
3. United States Statutes at Large, Vol. 1, p. 350.
4. United States Statutes at Large, Vol. 1, p. 453.
5. United States Statutes at Large, Vol. 1, p. 595.
6. http://www.angelfire.com/ca4/gunnyg/enlrank.html, November 2011.
7. Rankin, Robert, Uniforms of the Sea Service, Annapolis: Naval Institute, 1962, p. 139.
8. http://www.angelfire.com/ca4/gunnyg/enlrank.html, November 2011.
9. Rankin, Robert, Uniforms of the Sea Service, Annapolis: Naval Institute, 1962, p. 139.
10. http://www.history.navy.mil/faqs/faq59-28.htm, March 2011.
11. http://members.cox.net/malachi.thorne/Uniform%20Regulations/M1859%20Regs.pdf, October 2011.
12. United States Statutes at Large, Vol. 42, p. 629.
13. Nalty, Bernard C., United States Marine Corps Ranks and Grades 1775-1969, Washington: Headquarters U.S. Marine Corps, 1970, p. 25.
14. United States Statutes at Large, Vol. 63, p. 807.
15. Nalty, Bernard C., United States Marine Corps Ranks and Grades 1775-1969, Washington: Headquarters U.S. Marine Corps, 1970, p. 41.
16. Thompson, James G, Decorations, Medals, Ribbons, Badges and Insignia of the United States Marine Corps World War II to Present, Fountain Inn: MOA Press, 1998, p. 23.
17. MARINE CORPS UNIFORM REGULATIONS, 2003, p. 4-16.

Drum Corporal
1. Nalty, Bernard C., United States Marine Corps Ranks and Grades 1775-1969, Washington: Headquarters U.S. Marine Corps, 1970, p. 28.
2. ibid. p. 27.
3. Uniform Regulations United States Marine Corps, July 13, 1937, p. 34.
4. Nalty, Bernard C., United States Marine Corps Ranks and Grades 1775-1969, Washington: Headquarters U.S. Marine Corps, 1970, p. 29.

Drum Major
1. United States Statutes at Large, Vol. 1, p. 595.
2. Nalty, Bernard C., United States Marine Corps Ranks and Grades 1775-1969, Washington: Headquarters U.S. Marine Corps, 1970, p. 17.
3. United States Statutes at Large, Vol. 3, p. 377.
4. United States Statutes at Large, Vol. 4, p. 647.
5. Rankin, Robert, Uniforms of the Sea Service, Annapolis: Naval Institute, 1962, p. 134.
6. http://www.history.navy.mil/faqs/faq59-28.htm, March 2011.
7. http://members.cox.net/malachi.thorne/Uniform%20Regulations/M1859%20Regs.pdf, October 2011.

8. Nalty, Bernard C., United States Marine Corps Ranks and Grades 1775-1969, Washington: Headquarters U.S. Marine Corps, 1970, p. 17.
9.
http://www.marineband.usmc.mil/learning_tools/our_history/directors_history.htm, November 2011.
10.
http://www.marineband.usmc.mil/learning_tools/our_history/drum_majors_history.htm, November 2011.
11. Uniform Regulations United States Marine Corps, November 29, 1912, plate 46.
12. ibid. p. 88.
13. United States Statutes at Large, Vol. 42, p. 629.
14. Uniform Regulations United States Marine Corps, 1922, p. 45.
15. Register of the Commissioned And Warrant Officers of the Navy of the United States..., 1922, p. 323.
16. Nalty, Bernard C., United States Marine Corps Ranks and Grades 1775-1969, Washington: Headquarters U.S. Marine Corps, 1970, p. 27.
17. Uniform Regulations United States Marine Corps, July 13, 1937, p. 34.
18.
http://www.marineband.usmc.mil/learning_tools/our_history/drum_majors_history.htm, November 2011.

Drum Sergeant
1. Nalty, Bernard C., United States Marine Corps Ranks and Grades 1775-1969, Washington: Headquarters U.S. Marine Corps, 1970, p. 28.
2. ibid. p. 27.
3. Uniform Regulations United States Marine Corps, July 13, 1937, p. 34.
4. Nalty, Bernard C., United States Marine Corps Ranks and Grades 1775-1969, Washington: Headquarters U.S. Marine Corps, 1970, p. 29.

Drummer
1. Journals of the Continental Congress, Vol. 3, p. 384.
2. Journals of the Continental Congress, Vol. 6, p. 954.
3. United States Statutes at Large, Vol. 1, p. 350.
4. United States Statutes at Large, Vol. 1, p. 524.
5. United States Statutes at Large, Vol. 1, p. 595.
6. Rankin, Robert, Uniforms of the Marines, New York: Putnam, 1970, p. 42.
7. Regulations Governing the Uniform and Equipments of Officers and Enlisted Men of the United States Marine Corps, March 16, 1904, p. 39.
8. http://www.angelfire.com/ca4/gunnyg/enlrank.html, November 2011.
9. Uniform Regulations United States Marine Corps, July 13, 1937, p. 34.
10. Nalty, Bernard C., United States Marine Corps Ranks and Grades 1775-1969, Washington: Headquarters U.S. Marine Corps, 1970, p. 29.

Drummer First Class
. Nalty, Bernard C., United States Marine Corps Ranks and Grades 1775-1969, Washington: Headquarters U.S. Marine Corps, 1970, p. 28.
2. ibid. p.27.
3. Uniform Regulations United States Marine Corps, July 13, 1937, p. 34.
4. Nalty, Bernard C., United States Marine Corps Ranks and Grades 1775-1969, Washington: Headquarters U.S. Marine Corps, 1970, p. 29.

Field Baker
1. Nalty, Bernard C., United States Marine Corps Ranks and Grades 1775-1969, Washington: Headquarters U.S. Marine Corps, 1970, p. 30.
2. Uniform Regulations United States Marine Corps, July 13, 1937, p. 34.
3. Nalty, Bernard C., United States Marine Corps Ranks and Grades 1775-1969, Washington: Headquarters U.S. Marine Corps, 1970, p. 31.

Field Cook
1. Nalty, Bernard C., United States Marine Corps Ranks and Grades 1775-1969, Washington: Headquarters U.S. Marine Corps, 1970, p. 29.
2. ibid. p. 27.
3. Uniform Regulations United States Marine Corps, July 13, 1937, p. 34.
1. Nalty, Bernard C., United States Marine Corps Ranks and Grades 1775-1969, Washington: Headquarters U.S. Marine Corps, 1970, p. 31.

Field Cook (baker)
1. Nalty, Bernard C., United States Marine Corps Ranks and Grades 1775-1969, Washington: Headquarters U.S. Marine Corps, 1970, p. 30.
2. Uniform Regulations United States Marine Corps, July 13, 1937, p. 34.
3. Nalty, Bernard C., United States Marine Corps Ranks and Grades 1775-1969, Washington: Headquarters U.S. Marine Corps, 1970, p. 30-31.
4. ibid.
5. Uniform Regulations United States Marine Corps, July 13, 1937, p. 34.
6. Nalty, Bernard C., United States Marine Corps Ranks and Grades 1775-1969, Washington: Headquarters U.S. Marine Corps, 1970, p. 39.

Field Cook (Commissary)
1. Nalty, Bernard C., United States Marine Corps Ranks and Grades 1775-1969, Washington: Headquarters U.S. Marine Corps, 1970, p. 31.
2. Uniform Regulations United States Marine Corps, July 13, 1937, p. 34.
3. Nalty, Bernard C., United States Marine Corps Ranks and Grades 1775-1969, Washington: Headquarters U.S. Marine Corps, 1970, p. 39.
Field Music
1. Nalty, Bernard C., United States Marine Corps Ranks and Grades 1775-1969, Washington: Headquarters U.S. Marine Corps, 1970, p. 29.
2. ibid. p. 39.

Field Music Corporal
1. Nalty, Bernard C., United States Marine Corps Ranks and Grades 1775-1969, Washington: Headquarters U.S. Marine Corps, 1970, p. 29.
2. Uniform Regulations United States Marine Corps, July 13, 1937, p. 34.
3. Nalty, Bernard C., United States Marine Corps Ranks and Grades 1775-1969, Washington: Headquarters U.S. Marine Corps, 1970, p. 39.

Field Music First Class
1. Nalty, Bernard C., United States Marine Corps Ranks and Grades 1775-1969, Washington: Headquarters U.S. Marine Corps, 1970, p. 29.
2. Uniform Regulations United States Marine Corps, July 13, 1937, p. 34.
3. Nalty, Bernard C., United States Marine Corps Ranks and Grades 1775-1969, Washington: Headquarters U.S. Marine Corps, 1970, p. 39.

Field Music Sergeant
1. Nalty, Bernard C., United States Marine Corps Ranks and Grades 1775-1969, Washington: Headquarters U.S. Marine Corps, 1970, p. 29.
2. Uniform Regulations United States Marine Corps, July 13, 1937, p. 34.
3. Nalty, Bernard C., United States Marine Corps Ranks and Grades 1775-1969, Washington: Headquarters U.S. Marine Corps, 1970, p. 39.

Fifer
1. Journals of the Continental Congress, Vol. 3, p. 384.
2. Journals of the Continental Congress, Vol. 6, p. 954.
3. United States Statutes at Large, Vol. 1, p. 350.
4. United States Statutes at Large, Vol. 1, p. 524.
5. United States Statutes at Large, Vol. 1, p. 595.
6. Rankin, Robert, Uniforms of the Marines, New York: Putnam, 1970, p. 42.
7. Regulations Governing the Uniform and Equipments of Officers and Enlisted Men of the United States Marine Corps, March 16, 1904, p. 39.
8. Nalty, Bernard C., United States Marine Corps Ranks and Grades 1775-1969, Washington: Headquarters U.S. Marine Corps, 1970, p. 21.
9. United States Statutes at Large, Vol. 30, p. 1009.

Fife Major
1. United States Statutes at Large, Vol. 1, p. 595.
2. Nalty, Bernard C., United States Marine Corps Ranks and Grades 1775-1969, Washington: Headquarters U.S. Marine Corps, 1970, p. 17.
3. United States Statutes at Large, Vol. 3, p. 377.
4. United States Statutes at Large, Vol. 4, p. 713.
5. Rankin, Robert, Uniforms of the Sea Service, Annapolis: Naval Institute, 1962, p. 134.
6. http://www.history.navy.mil/faqs/faq59-28.htm, March 2011.
7.
http://members.cox.net/malachi.thorne/Uniform%20Regulations/M1859%20Regs.pdf, October 2011.
8. United States Statutes at Large, Vol. 12, p. 275.
9.
http://www.marineband.usmc.mil/learning_tools/our_history/directors_history.htm, November 2011.

First Lieutenant
1. Journals of the Continental Congress, Vol. 3, p. 348.
2. Journals of the Continental Congress, Vol. 3, p. 384.
3. United States Statutes at Large, Vol. 1, p. 350.
4. United States Statutes at Large, Vol. 1, p. 524.
5. United States Statutes at Large, Vol. 1, p. 595.
5a. Journals of the Continental Congress, Vol. 5, p. 478.
6. http://www.history.navy.mil/faqs/faq59-3.htm, April 2011.
7. Rankin, Robert, Uniforms of the Marines, New York: Putnam, 1970, p. 31.
8. ibid. p. 34.
9.
http://www.ibiblio.org/pha/USN/1821/NavyReg1821.html, September 2011.
10.
http://www.ibiblio.org/pha/USN/1822/NavReg1822.html, September 2011.
11.
http://www.ibiblio.org/pha/USN/1823/NavReg1823.html, September 2011.
12.
http://www.ibiblio.org/pha/USN/1824/NavReg1824.html, September 2011.
13. Rankin, Robert, Uniforms of the Marines, New York: Putnam, 1970, p. 41-42.
14. Lanham Howard G., Straps, Westminster, MD: Johnson Graphics, 1998, p. 139.
14a. http://www.history.navy.mil/faqs/faq59-28.htm, March 2011
15.
http://members.cox.net/malachi.thorne/Uniform%20Regulations/M1859%20Regs.pdf, October 2011.
16.
http://members.cox.net/malachi.thorne/Uniform%20Regulations/M1875%20Regs.pdf, October 2011.
17. Kenneth L. Smith-Christmas, Marine Corps Museum Cataloging and Identification Guide for 20th Century Uniforms.
18. United States Statutes at Large, Vol. 63, p. 802
19. MARINE CORPS UNIFORM REGULATIONS, 2003, p. 4-24.

First Sergeant
1. United States Statutes at Large, Vol. 4, p. 647.
2. Rankin, Robert, Uniforms of the Sea Service, Annapolis: Naval Institute, 1962, p. 134.
3.
http://members.cox.net/malachi.thorne/Uniform%20Regulations/M1859%20Regs.pdf, October 2011.
4. Nalty, Bernard C., United States Marine Corps Ranks and Grades 1775-1969, Washington: Headquarters U.S. Marine Corps, 1970, p. 25.
5. ibid. p. 27.
6. Uniform Regulations United States Marine Corps, July 13, 1937, p. 34.
7. Nalty, Bernard C., United States Marine Corps Ranks and Grades 1775-1969, Washington: Headquarters U.S. Marine Corps, 1970, p. 31.
8. Grosvenor, Gilbert H., Insignia and decorations of the U.S. armed forces, National Geographic Society, 1945, plate XXI.
9. ibid. p. 742 end section.
10. Nalty, Bernard C., United States Marine Corps Ranks and Grades 1775-1969, Washington: Headquarters U.S. Marine Corps, 1970, p. 37.
11. ibid. p. 39.
12. All Hands, "Quiz Aweigh", November 1955, p. 9.
13. Nalty, Bernard C., United States Marine Corps Ranks and Grades 1775-1969, Washington: Headquarters U.S. Marine Corps, 1970, p. 41.
14. MARINE CORPS UNIFORM REGULATIONS, 2003, p. 4-16.

First Sergeant (Aviation)
1. Nalty, Bernard C., United States Marine Corps Ranks and Grades 1775-1969, Washington: Headquarters U.S. Marine Corps, 1970, p. 36.
2. ibid. p. 37
3. Grosvenor, Gilbert H., Insignia and decorations of the U.S. armed forces, National Geographic Society, 1945, p. 742 end section.

General
1. Oliver, Raymond, Why is a Kernal called a Colonel?, Tucson: Fireship press, 1983, p. 49.
2. United States Statutes at Large, Vol. 59, p. 36.
3. Thompson, James G, Decorations, Medals, Ribbons, Badges and Insignia of the United States Marine Corps World War II to Present, Fountain Inn: MOA Press, 1998, p. 20.
4. http://en.wikipedia.org/wiki/Roy_Geiger, November 2011.
5. http://en.wikipedia.org/wiki/List_of_United_States_Marine_Corps_four-star_generals, November 2011.
6. United States Statutes at Large, Vol. 63, p. 807.
7. United States Statutes at Large, Vol. 72, p. 124.
8. United States Statutes at Large, Vol. 86, p. 8.
9. http://en.wikipedia.org/wiki/Peter_Pace, November 2011.
10. MARINE CORPS UNIFORM REGULATIONS, 2003, p. 4-20.

Gunnery Sergeant
1. United States Statutes at Large, Vol. 30, p. 370.
2. United States Statutes at Large, Vol. 30, p. 1009.
3. http://www.angelfire.com/ca/dickg/oldgunny.html, November 2011.
4. Nalty, Bernard C., United States Marine Corps Ranks and Grades 1775-1969, Washington: Headquarters U.S. Marine Corps, 1970, p. 25.
5. http://www.angelfire.com/ca/dickg/rank1929.gif, November 2011.
6. Uniform Regulations United States Marine Corps, July 13, 1937, p. 34.
7. Nalty, Bernard C., United States Marine Corps Ranks and Grades 1775-1969, Washington: Headquarters U.S. Marine Corps, 1970, p. 39.
8. ibid. p. 40-41.
9. Thompson, James G, Decorations, Medals, Ribbons, Badges and Insignia of the United States Marine Corps World War II to Present, Fountain Inn: MOA Press, 1998, p. 23.
10. MARINE CORPS UNIFORM REGULATIONS, 2003, p. 4-16.

Lance Corporal
1. Nalty, Bernard C., United States Marine Corps Ranks and Grades 1775-1969, Washington: Headquarters U.S. Marine Corps, 1970, p. 24.
2. Uniform Regulations United States Marine Corps, November 29, 1912, p. 80.
3. Uniform Regulations United States Marine Corps, 1929, p. 127.
4. Thompson, James G, Decorations, Medals, Ribbons, Badges and Insignia of the United States Marine Corps World War II to Present, Fountain Inn: MOA Press, 1998, p. 23.

Leader of the Band/ Principal Musician/ Chief Musician
1. United States Statutes at Large, Vol. 1, p. 595.
2. United States Statutes at Large, Vol. 12, p. 275.
3. United States Statutes at Large, Vol. 20, p. 55.
4. http://www.marineband.usmc.mil/learning_tools/our_history/directors_history.htm, November 2011.
5. http://members.cox.net/malachi.thorne/Uniform%20Regulations/M1859%20Regs.pdf, October 2011.
6. http://www.marineband.usmc.mil/learning_tools/our_history/directors_history.htm, November 2011.
7. Rankin, Robert, Uniforms of the Marines, New York: Putnam, 1970, p. 68.
8. http://www.cwu.edu/president/series/sousa.html, November 2011.
9. United States Statutes at Large, Vol. 30, p. 1009.
10. http://members.cox.net/malachi.thorne/Uniform%20Regulations/M1900%20Regs.pdf, October 2011.
11. Regulations Governing the Uniform and Equipments of Officers and Enlisted Men of the United States Marine Corps, March 16, 1904, p. 49.
12. United States Statutes at Large, Vol. 39, p. 612.
13. Uniform Regulations United States Marine Corps, November 29, 1912 with changes to May 12, 1917, p. 86-94.
14. United States Statutes at Large, Vol. 49, p. 331.
15. Uniform Regulations United States Marine Corps, July 13, 1937, p. 37.
16. http://www.marineband.usmc.mil/learning_tools/our_history/directors_history.htm, November 2011.
17. http://www.whha.org/whha_exhibits/marine_band/06_marine-band.html, November 2011.
18. http://www.marineband.usmc.mil/learning_tools/our_history/directors_history.htm, November 2011.
19. United States Statutes at Large, Vol. 63, p. 833.
20. http://www.marineband.usmc.mil/learning_tools/our_history/directors_history.htm, November 2011.
21. United States Statutes at Large, Vol. 70, p. 628.

Lieutenant
1. Oliver, Raymond, Why is a Kernal called a Colonel?, Tucson: Fireship press, 1983, p. 25.
2. Journals of the Continental Congress, Vol. 3, p. 348.
3. Journals of the Continental Congress, Vol. 3, p. 384.
4. United States Statutes at Large, Vol. 1, p. 350.
5. United States Statutes at Large, Vol. 1, p. 524.
6. United States Statutes at Large, Vol. 1, p. 595.
7. http://bluejacket.com/sea-service_uniform_a.htm, April 2011.
8. http://www.history.navy.mil/faqs/faq59-3.htm, April 2011

Lieutenant Colonel
0. http://www.xenograg.com/101/excerpts/origins-of-european-army-ranks, august 2010
1. United States Statutes at Large, Vol. 2, p. 39.
2. Rankin, Robert, Uniforms of the Marines, New York: Putnam, 1970, p. 31.
3. Callahan, Edward, List of Officers of the Navy of the United States and the Marine Corps from 1775 to 1900, New York: L. R. Hamerlsy & CO., 1901, p. 679.
4. http://en.wikipedia.org/wiki/Anthony_Gale, November 2011
5. Callahan, Edward, List of Officers of the Navy of the United States and the Marine Corps from 1775 to 1900, New York: L. R. Hamerlsy & CO., 1901, p. 679.
5a. Rankin, Robert, Uniforms of the Marines, New York: Putnam, 1970, p. 41-42.
6. United States Statutes at Large, Vol. 4, p. 713.
7. Callahan, Edward, List of Officers of the Navy of the United States and the Marine Corps from 1775 to 1900, New York: L. R. Hamerlsy & CO., 1901, p. 700.
8. Lanham Howard G., Straps, Westminster, MD: Johnson Graphics, 1998, p. 139.
9. http://www.history.navy.mil/faqs/faq59-28.htm, March 2011
10. Callahan, Edward, List of Officers of the Navy of the United States and the Marine Corps from 1775 to 1900, New York: L. R. Hamerlsy & CO., 1901, p. 700.
11. ibid. p. 693.
12. Senate Executive Journal, Vol. 10, p. 29.
13. Callahan, Edward, List of Officers of the Navy of the United States and the Marine Corps from 1775 to 1900, New York: L. R. Hamerlsy & CO., 1901, p. 679.
14. ibid. p. 691.
15. http://members.cox.net/malachi.thorne/Uniform%20Regulations/M1859%20Regs.pdf, October 2011.
16. Senate Executive Journal, Vol. 12, p. 168.
17. United States Statutes at Large, Vol. 12, p. 275.
18. Senate Executive Journal, Vol. 12, p. 168.
19. Callahan, Edward, List of Officers of the Navy of the United States and the Marine Corps from 1775 to 1900, New York: L. R. Hamerlsy & CO., 1901, p. 691.
20. ibid. p. 696.
21. ibid. p. 690.
22. ibid. p. 689.
23. Senate Executive Journal, Vol. 18, p. 206.
24. http://members.cox.net/malachi.thorne/Uniform%20Regulations/M1875%20Regs.pdf, October 2011
25. Callahan, Edward, List of Officers of the Navy of the United States and the Marine Corps from 1775 to 1900, New York: L. R. Hamerlsy & CO., 1901, p. 685.
26. ibid. p. 682.
27. ibid. p. 688.
28. ibid. p. 679.
29. ibid. p. 683.
30. ibid. p. 689.
31. ibid. p. 686.
32. ibid. p. 699.
33. ibid. p. 688.
34. General Order No. 427, July 18, 1894.
35. Callahan, Edward, List of Officers of the Navy of the United States and the Marine Corps from 1775 to 1900, New York: L. R. Hamerlsy & CO., 1901, p. 689.
36. ibid. p. 295.
37. ibid. p. 692.
38. United States Statutes at Large, Vol. 30, p. 1009.
39. Register of the Commissioned And Warrant Officers of the Navy of the United States..., January 1, 1900, p. 198.
40. Regulations Governing the Uniform and Equipments of Officers and Enlisted Men of the United States Marine Corps, March 16, 1904, p. 15.
41. United States Statutes at Large, Vol. 63, p. 802.
42. MARINE CORPS UNIFORM REGULATIONS, 2003, p. 4-24.

Lieutenant General
1. United States Statutes at Large, Vol. 56, p. 10.
2. Nalty, Bernard C., United States Marine Corps Ranks and Grades 1775-1969, Washington: Headquarters U.S. Marine Corps, 1970, p. 56.
3. Thompson, James G, Decorations, Medals, Ribbons, Badges and Insignia of the United States Marine Corps World War II to Present, Fountain Inn: MOA Press, 1998, p. 20.
4. http://en.wikipedia.org/wiki/1st_Marine_Amphibious_Corps, November 2011.
5. Nalty, Bernard C., United States Marine Corps Ranks and Grades 1775-1969, Washington: Headquarters U.S. Marine Corps, 1970, p. 8.
6. United States Statutes at Large, Vol. 63, p. 807.
7. United States Statutes at Large, Vol. 72, p. 124.
8. MARINE CORPS UNIFORM REGULATIONS, 2003, p. 4-24.

Major
1. Journals of the Continental Congress, Vol. 5, p. 478.
2. http://bluejacket.com/sea-service_uniform_a.htm, April 2011
3. United States Statutes at Large, Vol. 1, p. 594.
4. Callahan, Edward, List of Officers of the Navy of the United States and the Marine Corps from 1775 to 1900, New York: L. R. Hamerlsy & CO., 1901, p. 679.
5. United States Statutes at Large, Vol. 2, p. 39.
6. United States Statutes at Large, Vol. 2, p. 544.
7. Nalty, Bernard C., United States Marine Corps Ranks and Grades 1775-1969, Washington: Headquarters U.S. Marine Corps, 1970, p. 2.
8. Callahan, Edward, List of Officers of the Navy of the United States and the Marine Corps from 1775 to 1900, New York: L. R. Hamerlsy & CO., 1901, p. 682.
9. Rankin, Robert, Uniforms of the Marines, New York: Putnam, 1970, p. 31.
10. United States Statutes at Large, Vol. 3, p. 124.
11. Callahan, Edward, List of Officers of the Navy of the United States and the Marine Corps from 1775 to 1900, New York: L. R. Hamerlsy & CO., 1901, p. 687.
12. http://en.wikipedia.org/wiki/Daniel_Carmick, November 2011.
13. United States Statutes at Large, Vol. 3, p. 377.
14. http://www.history.navy.mil/danfs/c3/carmick.htm, November 2011.
15. Callahan, Edward, List of Officers of the Navy of the United States and the Marine Corps from 1775 to 1900, New York: L. R. Hamerlsy & CO., 1901, p. 687.
16. United States Statutes at Large, Vol. 4, p. 713.
17. Senate Executive Journal, Vol. 4, p. 452.
18. Lanham Howard G., Straps, Westminster, MD: Johnson Graphics, 1998, p. 139.
19. Callahan, Edward, List of Officers of the Navy of the United States and the Marine Corps from 1775 to 1900, New York: L. R. Hamerlsy & CO., 1901, p. 682.
20. ibid. p. 699.
21. ibid. p. 679.
22. ibid. p. 690.
23. ibid. p. 685.
24. ibid.
25. ibid.
26. ibid. p. 691.
27. ibid.
28. http://members.cox.net/malachi.thorne/Uniform%20Regulations/M1859%20Regs.pdf, October 2011.
29. http://www.tfoenander.com/usmc.html, November 2011.

30. Callahan, Edward, List of Officers of the Navy of the United States and the Marine Corps from 1775 to 1900, New York: L. R. Hamerlsy & CO., 1901, p. 696.
31. Senate Executive Journal, Vol. 12, p. 168.
32. Callahan, Edward, List of Officers of the Navy of the United States and the Marine Corps from 1775 to 1900, New York: L. R. Hamerlsy & CO., 1901, p. 700.
33. ibid. p. 684.
34. ibid. p. 679.
35. ibid. p. 686.
36. Register of the Commissioned And Warrant Officers of the Navy of the United States..., January 1, 1865, p. 107.
37. Callahan, Edward, List of Officers of the Navy of the United States and the Marine Corps from 1775 to 1900, New York: L. R. Hamerlsy & CO., 1901, p. 683.
38. ibid. p. 690.
39. http://members.cox.net/malachi.thorne/Uniform%20Regulations/M1875%20Regs.pdf, October 2011.
40. Kenneth L. Smith-Christmas, Marine Corps Museum Cataloging and Identification Guide for 20th Century Uniforms.
41. Callahan, Edward, List of Officers of the Navy of the United States and the Marine Corps from 1775 to 1900, New York: L. R. Hamerlsy & CO., 1901, p. 687.
42. ibid. p. 690.
43. ibid. p. 685.
44. Register of the Commissioned And Warrant Officers of the Navy of the United States..., January 1, 1877, p. 133.
45. Register of the Commissioned And Warrant Officers of the Navy of the United States..., January 1, 1879, p. 136.
46. Callahan, Edward, List of Officers of the Navy of the United States and the Marine Corps from 1775 to 1900, New York: L. R. Hamerlsy & CO., 1901, p. 682.
47. ibid. p. 683.
48. ibid. p. 689.
49. ibid. p. 686.
50. ibid. p. 699.
51. ibid. p. 688.
52. ibid. p. 689.
53. ibid. p. 681.
54. ibid. p. 695.
55. ibid. p. 682.
56. ibid. p. 692.
57. General Order No. 427, July 18, 1894.
58. Callahan, Edward, List of Officers of the Navy of the United States and the Marine Corps from 1775 to 1900, New York: L. R. Hamerlsy & CO., 1901, p. 701.
59. ibid. p. 683.
60. United States Statutes at Large, Vol. 30, p. 1008.
61. Regulations Governing the Uniform and Equipments of Officers and Enlisted Men of the United States Marine Corps, March 16, 1904, 5.
62. United States Statutes at Large, Vol. 63, p. 802.
63. MARINE CORPS UNIFORM REGULATIONS, 2003, p. 4-24

Major General
0. http://www.xenograg.com/101/excerpts/origins-of-european-army-ranks, August 2010.
1. United States Statutes at Large, Vol. 32, p. 685.
2. http://en.wikipedia.org/wiki/File:Charles_Heywood.jpg, November 2011.
3. http://members.cox.net/malachi.thorne/Uniform%20Regulations/M1900%20Regs.pdf, October 2011.
3. Register of the Commissioned And Warrant Officers of the Navy of the United States..., January 1, 1904, p. 158.
4. United States Statutes at Large, Vol. 35, p. 155.
5. http://en.wikipedia.org/wiki/File:George_F._Elliott.jpg, November 2011.
6. Register of the Commissioned And Warrant Officers of the Navy of the United States..., January 1, 1911, p. 198.
7. Register of the Commissioned And Warrant Officers of the Navy of the United States..., January 1, 1912, p. 191.
8. Uniform Regulations United States Marine Corps, November 29, 1912, plate 26.
9. ibid. plate 27. & p. 36.
10. ibid. p. plate 24. & p. 157.
11. ibid. p. 49.
12. ibid. p. 50.
13. Nalty, Bernard C., United States Marine Corps Ranks and Grades 1775-1969, Washington: Headquarters U.S. Marine Corps, 1970, p. 56.
14. Uniform Regulations United States Marine Corps, November 29, 1912 with changes to May 12, 1917, plate 27.
15. United States Statutes at Large, Vol. 40, p. 715.
16. Register of the Commissioned And Warrant Officers of the Navy of the United States..., January 1, 1919, p. 792.
17. Register of the Commissioned And Warrant Officers of the Navy of the United States..., January 1, 1921, p. 324.
18. Nalty, Bernard C., United States Marine Corps Ranks and Grades 1775-1969, Washington: Headquarters U.S. Marine Corps, 1970, p. 56.
19. Register of the Commissioned And Warrant Officers of the Navy of the United States..., January 1, 1921, p. 292.
20. Register of the Commissioned And Warrant Officers of the Navy of the United States..., January 1, 1922, p. 274.
21. http://en.wikipedia.org/wiki/George_Barnett, November 2011.
22. Register of the Commissioned And Warrant Officers of the Navy of the United States..., January 1, 1924, p. 406.
23. Register of the Commissioned And Warrant Officers of the Navy of the United States..., January 1, 1925, p. 446.
24. ibid. p. 400.
25. Register of the Commissioned And Warrant Officers of the Navy of the United States..., 1930, p. 483.
26. ibid. p. 432.
27. http://en.wikipedia.org/wiki/Wendell_Cushing_Neville, November 2011.
28. http://en.wikipedia.org/wiki/Smedley_Butler, November 2011.
29. Register of the Commissioned And Warrant Officers of the Navy of the United States..., 1930, p. 470.
30. http://en.wikipedia.org/wiki/Logan_Feland, November 2011.
31. Register of the Commissioned And Warrant Officers of the Navy of the United States..., 1934, p. 480.
32. Register of the Commissioned And Warrant Officers of the Navy of the United States..., 1935, p. 554 & 556.
33. Register of the Commissioned And Warrant Officers of the Navy of the United States..., 1935, p. 510.
34. Register of the Commissioned And Warrant Officers of the Navy of the United States..., 1936, p. 524.
35. http://en.wikipedia.org/wiki/John_H._Russell,_Jr., November 2011.
36. Register of the Commissioned And Warrant Officers of the Navy of the United States..., 1942, p. 834.
37. ibid. p. 734.
38. United States Statutes at Large, Vol. 63, p. 807.
39. United States Statutes at Large, Vol. 72, p. 124.
40. MARINE CORPS UNIFORM REGULATIONS, 2003, p. 4-24

Marine Gunner
1. United States Statutes at Large, Vol. 39, p. 611.
2. Uniform Regulations United States Marine Corps, November 29, 1912 with changes to May 12, 1917, p. 24 & 60.
3. ibid. p. 33.
4. Uniform Regulations United States Marine Corps, 1922, p. 97.
5. ibid. p. 40.
6. United States Statutes at Large, Vol. 57, p. 574.
7. http://1stbn4thmarines.com/other-things-interest/warrant_officer_history.htm, October 2011.

Master Cook
1. Nalty, Bernard C., United States Marine Corps Ranks and Grades 1775-1969, Washington: Headquarters U.S. Marine Corps, 1970, p. 31.
2. Uniform Regulations United States Marine Corps, July 13, 1937, p. 34.
3. Nalty, Bernard C., United States Marine Corps Ranks and Grades 1775-1969, Washington: Headquarters U.S. Marine Corps, 1970, p. 37.

Master Gunnery Sergeant
1. Nalty, Bernard C., United States Marine Corps Ranks and Grades 1775-1969, Washington: Headquarters U.S. Marine Corps, 1970, p. 29.
2. ibid. p. 27.
3. Uniform Regulations United States Marine Corps, July 13, 1937, p. 34.
4. Nalty, Bernard C., United States Marine Corps Ranks and Grades 1775-1969, Washington: Headquarters U.S. Marine Corps, 1970, p. 37.
5. ibid. p. 41.
6. Thompson, James G, Decorations, Medals, Ribbons, Badges and Insignia of the United States Marine Corps World War II to Present, Fountain Inn: MOA Press, 1998, p. 23.
7. MARINE CORPS UNIFORM REGULATIONS, 2003, p. 4-16.

Master Sergeant
1. Nalty, Bernard C., United States Marine Corps Ranks and Grades 1775-1969, Washington: Headquarters U.S. Marine Corps, 1970, p. 37.
2. Thompson, James G, Decorations, Medals, Ribbons, Badges and Insignia of the United States Marine Corps World War II to Present, Fountain Inn: MOA Press, 1998, p. 23.
3. United States Statutes at Large, Vol. 63, p. 807.
4. Nalty, Bernard C., United States Marine Corps Ranks and Grades 1775-1969, Washington: Headquarters U.S. Marine Corps, 1970, p. 41.
5. Thompson, James G, Decorations, Medals, Ribbons, Badges and Insignia of the United States Marine Corps World War II to Present, Fountain Inn: MOA Press, 1998, p. 23.
6. MARINE CORPS UNIFORM REGULATIONS, 2003, p. 4-16.

Master Steward
1. Nalty, Bernard C., United States Marine Corps Ranks and Grades 1775-1969, Washington: Headquarters U.S. Marine Corps, 1970, p. 31.
2. Uniform Regulations United States Marine Corps, July 13, 1937, p. 33.
3. Nalty, Bernard C., United States Marine Corps Ranks and Grades 1775-1969, Washington: Headquarters U.S. Marine Corps, 1970, p. 37.

Master Technical Sergeant
1. Nalty, Bernard C., United States Marine Corps Ranks and Grades 1775-1969, Washington: Headquarters U.S. Marine Corps, 1970, p. 26.
2. ibid. p. 27.
3. ibid. p. 37.

Master Technical Sergeant (Baker)
1. Nalty, Bernard C., United States Marine Corps Ranks and Grades 1775-1969, Washington: Headquarters U.S. Marine Corps, 1970, p. 30.
2. Uniform Regulations United States Marine Corps, July 13, 1937, p. 33.
3. Nalty, Bernard C., United States Marine Corps Ranks and Grades 1775-1969, Washington: Headquarters U.S. Marine Corps, 1970, p. 37.

Master Technical Sergeant (Clerical) line
1. Nalty, Bernard C., United States Marine Corps Ranks and Grades 1775-1969, Washington: Headquarters U.S. Marine Corps, 1970, p. 31.
2. Thompson, James G, Decorations, Medals, Ribbons, Badges and Insignia of the United States Marine Corps World War II to Present, Fountain Inn: MOA Press, 1998, p. 23.
3. Nalty, Bernard C., United States Marine Corps Ranks and Grades 1775-1969, Washington: Headquarters U.S. Marine Corps, 1970, p. 37.

Master Technical Sergeant (Clerical) (RW)
1. Nalty, Bernard C., United States Marine Corps Ranks and Grades 1775-1969, Washington: Headquarters U.S. Marine Corps, 1970, p. 31.
2. Thompson, James G, Decorations, Medals, Ribbons, Badges and Insignia of the United States Marine Corps World War II to Present, Fountain Inn: MOA Press, 1998, p. 23.
3. Nalty, Bernard C., United States Marine Corps Ranks and Grades 1775-1969, Washington: Headquarters U.S. Marine Corps, 1970, p. 37.

Master Technical Sergeant (Clerical) (SplW)

1. Nalty, Bernard C., United States Marine Corps Ranks and Grades 1775-1969, Washington: Headquarters U.S. Marine Corps, 1970, p. 31.
2. Thompson, James G, Decorations, Medals, Ribbons, Badges and Insignia of the United States Marine Corps World War II to Present, Fountain Inn: MOA Press, 1998, p. 23.
3. Nalty, Bernard C., United States Marine Corps Ranks and Grades 1775-1969, Washington: Headquarters U.S. Marine Corps, 1970, p. 37.

Master Technical Sergeant (Commissary)
1. Nalty, Bernard C., United States Marine Corps Ranks and Grades 1775-1969, Washington: Headquarters U.S. Marine Corps, 1970, p. 31.
2. Uniform Regulations United States Marine Corps, July 13, 1937, p. 33.
3. Nalty, Bernard C., United States Marine Corps Ranks and Grades 1775-1969, Washington: Headquarters U.S. Marine Corps, 1970, p. 37.

Master Technical Sergeant (Mess)
1. Nalty, Bernard C., United States Marine Corps Ranks and Grades 1775-1969, Washington: Headquarters U.S. Marine Corps, 1970, p. 29.
2. ibid. p. 26.
3. Uniform Regulations United States Marine Corps, July 13, 1937, p. 33.
4. Nalty, Bernard C., United States Marine Corps Ranks and Grades 1775-1969, Washington: Headquarters U.S. Marine Corps, 1970, p. 31.

Mess Corporal
1. Nalty, Bernard C., United States Marine Corps Ranks and Grades 1775-1969, Washington: Headquarters U.S. Marine Corps, 1970, p. 29.
2. ibid. p. 27.
3. Uniform Regulations United States Marine Corps, July 13, 1937, p. 34.
1. Nalty, Bernard C., United States Marine Corps Ranks and Grades 1775-1969, Washington: Headquarters U.S. Marine Corps, 1970, p. 31.

Mess Sergeant
1. Nalty, Bernard C., United States Marine Corps Ranks and Grades 1775-1969, Washington: Headquarters U.S. Marine Corps, 1970, p. 29.
2. ibid. p. 27.
3. Uniform Regulations United States Marine Corps, July 13, 1937, p. 34.
1. Nalty, Bernard C., United States Marine Corps Ranks and Grades 1775-1969, Washington: Headquarters U.S. Marine Corps, 1970, p. 31.

Musician, Marine Band (Principal, First Class, Second Class and Third Class)
1. United States Statutes at Large, Vol. 12, p. 275.
2. Register of the Commissioned And Warrant Officers of the Navy of the United States..., January 1, 1879, p. 129.
3. United States Statutes at Large, Vol. 30, p. 1009.
4. United States Statutes at Large, Vol. 39, p. 612.
5. United States Statutes at Large, Vol. 60, p. 342.
6. United States Statutes at Large, Vol. 63, p. 833.
7. http://members.cox.net/malachi.thorne/Uniform%20Regulations/M1859%20Regs.pdf, October 2011.
8. http://members.cox.net/malachi.thorne/Uniform%20Regulations/M1900%20Regs.pdf, October 2011.
9. Uniform Regulations United States Marine Corps, November 29, 1912 with changes to May 12, 1917, p. 94.
10. Nalty, Bernard C., United States Marine Corps Ranks and Grades 1775-1969, Washington: Headquarters U.S. Marine Corps, 1970, p. 26.

Orderly Sergeant
1. United States Statutes at Large, Vol. 4, p. 647.
2. Rankin, Robert, Uniforms of the Sea Service, Annapolis: Naval Institute, 1962, p. 134.
3. Nalty, Bernard C., United States Marine Corps Ranks and Grades 1775-1969, Washington: Headquarters U.S. Marine Corps, 1970, p. 25.

Pay Clerk or Paymaster's Clerk
1. United States Statutes at Large, Vol. 31, p. 704.
2. United States Statutes at Large, Vol. 36, p. 625.
3. United States Statutes at Large, Vol. 36, p. 1284.
4. Register of the Commissioned And Warrant Officers of the Navy of the United States..., January 1, 1912, p. 208.
5. United States Statutes at Large, Vol. 40, p. 86.
6. United States Statutes at Large, Vol. 40, p. 735.
7. Register of the Commissioned And Warrant Officers of the Navy of the United States..., January 1, 1918, p. 458.
9. Register of the Commissioned And Warrant Officers of the Navy of the United States..., January 1, 1919, p. 862.
10. Uniform Regulations United States Marine Corps, 1922, p. 40.
11. United States Statutes at Large, Vol. 44, p. 725.
12. United States Statutes at Large, Vol. 57, p. 574.

Paymaster Sergeant
1. Nalty, Bernard C., United States Marine Corps Ranks and Grades 1775-1969, Washington: Headquarters U.S. Marine Corps, 1970, p. 26.
2. ibid. p. 27.
3. Uniform Regulations United States Marine Corps, July 13, 1937, p. 33.
4. Nalty, Bernard C., United States Marine Corps Ranks and Grades 1775-1969, Washington: Headquarters U.S. Marine Corps, 1970, p. 37.

Paymaster with rank of Colonel
1. United States Statutes at Large, Vol. 30, p. 1009.
2. http://members.cox.net/malachi.thorne/Uniform%20Regulations/M1892%20Regs.pdf, October 2011.
3. General Order No. 427, July 18, 1894.
4. http://members.cox.net/malachi.thorne/Uniform%20Regulations/M1900%20Regs.pdf, October 2011.
5. Regulations Governing the Uniform and Equipments of Officers and Enlisted Men of the United States Marine Corps, March 16, 1904, p. 15.
6. ibid. p. 14
7. http://en.wikipedia.org/wiki/George_F._Elliott, October 2011.
8. Uniform Regulations United States Marine Corps, November 29, 1912, plate 29.
9. Register of the Commissioned And Warrant Officers of the Navy of the United States..., January 1, 1910, p. 182 & 200.
10. ibid. p. 60.
11. ibid. p. 50.
12. United States Statutes at Large, Vol. 39, p. 610.

Paymaster with rank of Major
1. United States Statutes at Large, Vol. 9, p. 155.
2. Senate Executive Journal, vol 7, p. 271.
3. http://www.history.navy.mil/faqs/faq59-28.htm, March 2011.
4. Callahan, Edward, List of Officers of the Navy of the United States and the Marine Corps from 1775 to 1900, New York: L. R. Hamerlsy & CO., 1901, p. 700.
5. Senate Executive Journal, vol 8, p. 338.
6. http://www.grandarmyofthefrontier.org/uniforms/usmc1859.htm, October 2011.
7. Callahan, Edward, List of Officers of the Navy of the United States and the Marine Corps from 1775 to 1900, New York: L. R. Hamerlsy & CO., 1901, p. 696.
8. Senate Executive Journal, vol 13, p. 6.
9. http://members.cox.net/malachi.thorne/Uniform%20Regulations/M1875%20Regs.pdf, October 2011.
10. Callahan, Edward, List of Officers of the Navy of the United States and the Marine Corps from 1775 to 1900, New York: L. R. Hamerlsy & CO., 1901, p. 683.
11. ibid. p. 687.
12. Rankin, Robert, Uniforms of the Marines, New York: Putnam, 1970, p. 65.
13. General Order No. 427, July 18, 1894.
14. United States Statutes at Large, Vol. 30, p. 1009.

Platoon Sergeant
1. Nalty, Bernard C., United States Marine Corps Ranks and Grades 1775-1969, Washington: Headquarters U.S. Marine Corps, 1970, p. 29.
2. ibid. p. 27.
3. Uniform Regulations United States Marine Corps, July 13, 1937, p. 34.
4. Nalty, Bernard C., United States Marine Corps Ranks and Grades 1775-1969, Washington: Headquarters U.S. Marine Corps, 1970, p. 37.

Private First Class
1. United States Statutes at Large, Vol. 40, p. 714.
2. Henry, Mark R., US Marine Corps in World War I, Oxford: Osprey, 1999, p. 17.
3. United States Statutes at Large, Vol. 42, p. 629.
4. Nalty, Bernard C., United States Marine Corps Ranks and Grades 1775-1969, Washington: Headquarters U.S. Marine Corps, 1970, p. 25.
5. Uniform Regulations United States Marine Corps, 1922, p. 45.
6. Uniform Regulations United States Marine Corps, 1929, p. 63.
7. Uniform Regulations United States Marine Corps, July 13, 1937, p. 34.
8. United States Statutes at Large, Vol. 63, p. 807.
9. MARINE CORPS UNIFORM REGULATIONS, 2003, p. 4-16.

Quartermaster Clerk
1. United States Statutes at Large, Vol. 39, p. 611.
2. Uniform Regulations United States Marine Corps, November 29, 1912 with changes to May 12, 1917, p. 24 & 60.
3. ibid. p. 33.
4. Uniform Regulations United States Marine Corps, 1922, p. 40.
5. ibid. p. 97.
6. Uniform Regulations United States Marine Corps, July 13, 1937, p. 82.
7. United States Statutes at Large, Vol. 57, p. 574

Quartermaster Sergeant
1. United States Statutes at Large, Vol. 1, p. 595.
2. Nalty, Bernard C., United States Marine Corps Ranks and Grades 1775-1969, Washington: Headquarters U.S. Marine Corps, 1970, p. 17.
3. United States Statutes at Large, Vol. 3, p. 377.
4. United States Statutes at Large, Vol. 4, p. 647.
5. Rankin, Robert, Uniforms of the Sea Service, Annapolis: Naval Institute, 1962, p. 134.
6. Rankin, Robert, Uniforms of the Marines, New York: Putnam, 1970, p. 45.
7. Rankin, Robert, Uniforms of the Sea Service, Annapolis: Naval Institute, 1962, p. 139.
8. ibid.
9. http://www.history.navy.mil/faqs/faq59-28.htm, March 2011.
10. http://members.cox.net/malachi.thorne/Uniform%20Regulations/M1859%20Regs.pdf, October 2011.
11. United States Statutes at Large, Vol. 30, p. 1009.
12. United States Statutes at Large, Vol. 42, p. 629.
13. Nalty, Bernard C., United States Marine Corps Ranks and Grades 1775-1969, Washington: Headquarters U.S. Marine Corps, 1970, p. 25.
14. http://www.angelfire.com/ca4/gunnyg/enlrank.html, November 2011.
15. Uniform Regulations United States Marine Corps, July 13, 1937, p. 33.
16. Nalty, Bernard C., United States Marine Corps Ranks and Grades 1775-1969, Washington: Headquarters U.S. Marine Corps, 1970, p. 37.

Quartermaster Sergeant, Adjutant and Inspector's Dept.
1. Uniform Regulations United States Marine Corps, 1929, p. 126.
2. http://www.angelfire.com/ca4/gunnyg/enlrank.html, November 2011.
3. Uniform Regulations United States Marine Corps, July 13, 1937, p. 33.
4. United States Statutes at Large, Vol. 57, p. 84.

Quartermaster Sergeant, Paymaster's Dept.
1. United States Statutes at Large, Vol. 32, p. 155.
2. http://www.angelfire.com/ca4/gunnyg/enlrank.html, November 2011.
3. Nalty, Bernard C., United States Marine Corps Ranks and Grades 1775-1969, Washington: Headquarters U.S. Marine Corps, 1970, p. 26.

Quartermaster with rank of Colonel
1. United States Statutes at Large, Vol. 30, p. 1009.
2. http://members.cox.net/malachi.thorne/Uniform%20Regulations/M1892%20Regs.pdf, October 2011.
3. General Order No. 427, July 18, 1894.
4.

http://members.cox.net/malachi.thorne/Uniform%20Regulations/M1900%20Regs.pdf, October 2011.
5. Regulations Governing the Uniform and Equipments of Officers and Enlisted Men of the United States Marine Corps, March 16, 1904, p. 15.
6. ibid. p. 14
7. http://en.wikipedia.org/wiki/George_F._Elliott, October 2011.
8. Uniform Regulations United States Marine Corps, November 29, 1912, plate 29.
9. ibid. p. 60.
10. ibid. p. 50.
11. Register of the Commissioned And Warrant Officers of the Navy of the United States..., January 1, 1913, p. 224.
12. Register of the Commissioned And Warrant Officers of the Navy of the United States..., January 1, 1916, p. 218.
13. United States Statutes at Large, Vol. 39, p. 610.

Quartermaster with rank of Major
1. United States Statutes at Large, Vol. 9, p. 155.
2. Senate Executive Journal, vol 5, p. 91.
3. http://www.history.navy.mil/faqs/faq59-28.htm, March 2011.
4. Callahan, Edward, List of Officers of the Navy of the United States and the Marine Corps from 1775 to 1900, New York: L. R. Hamerlsy & CO., 1901, p. 693.
5. Senate Executive Journal, vol 10, p. 16.
6. Senate Executive Journal, vol 10, p. 288.
7. http://www.grandarmyofthefrontier.org/uniforms/usmc1859.htm, October 2011.
8. Callahan, Edward, List of Officers of the Navy of the United States and the Marine Corps from 1775 to 1900, New York: L. R. Hamerlsy & CO., 1901, p. 698.
9. Senate Executive Journal, vol 11, p. 232.
10. http://members.cox.net/malachi.thorne/Uniform%20Regulations/M1875%20Regs.pdf, October 2011.
11. Rankin, Robert, Uniforms of the Marines, New York: Putnam, 1970, p. 65.
12. General Order No. 427, July 18, 1894.
13. Callahan, Edward, List of Officers of the Navy of the United States and the Marine Corps from 1775 to 1900, New York: L. R. Hamerlsy & CO., 1901, p. 697.
14. ibid. p. 691.
15. ibid. p. 684
16. United States Statutes at Large, Vol. 30, p. 1009.

Second Leader of the Band
1. http://www.marineband.usmc.mil/learning_tools/our_history/assistant_directors/petrola.htm, December 2011.
2. United States Statutes at Large, Vol. 30, p. 1009.
3. http://www.marineband.usmc.mil/learning_tools/our_history/assistant_directors_history.htm, December 2011.
4. http://members.cox.net/malachi.thorne/Uniform%20Regulations/M1900%20Regs.pdf, October 2011.
5. Regulations Governing the Uniform and Equipments of Officers and Enlisted Men of the United States Marine Corps, March 16, 1904, p. 53.
6. Uniform Regulations United States Marine Corps, November 29, 1912, p. 77.
7. http://www.marineband.usmc.mil/learning_tools/our_history/assistant_directors_history.htm, December 2011.
8. Uniform Regulations United States Marine Corps, 1922, p. viii.
9. http://www.marineband.usmc.mil/learning_tools/our_history/assistant_directors_history.htm, December 2011.
10. http://www.marineband.usmc.mil/learning_tools/our_history/assistant_directors/weber.htm, December 2011 (picture shows weber in an officer's uniform).
11. Rosignoli, Guido, Badges and Insignia of World War II AirForce-Naval-Marine, London: Peerage, 1976, p. 340.
12. United States Statutes at Large, Vol. 60, p. 343.
13. United States Statutes at Large, Vol. 63, p. 833.
14. http://www.marineband.usmc.mil/learning_tools/our_history/assistant_directors_history.htm, December 2011.
15. United States Statutes at Large, Vol. 70, p. 628.

Second Lieutenant
1. Journals of the Continental Congress, Vol. 4, p. 478.
2. Journals of the Continental Congress, Vol. 3, p. 384.
3. United States Statutes at Large, Vol. 1, p. 595.
4. Rankin, Robert, Uniforms of the Marines, New York: Putnam, 1970, p. 31.
5. ibid. p. 34.
6. ibid. p. 41-42.
7. Lanham Howard G., Straps, Westminster, MD: Johnson Graphics, 1998, p. 139.
7a. http://www.history.navy.mil/faqs/faq59-28.htm, March 2011
8. http://members.cox.net/malachi.thorne/Uniform%20Regulations/M1859%20Regs.pdf, October 2011.
9. http://members.cox.net/malachi.thorne/Uniform%20Regulations/M1875%20Regs.pdf, October 2011.
10. Kenneth L. Smith-Christmas, Marine Corps Museum Cataloging and Identification Guide for 20th Century Uniforms.
11. Henry, Mark R., US Marine Corps in World War I, Oxford: Osprey, 1999, p. 18.
12. United States Statutes at Large, Vol. 63, p. 802
13. MARINE CORPS UNIFORM REGULATIONS, 2003, p. 4-24.

Senior Enlisted Advisor to the Chairman
1. http://en.wikipedia.org/wiki/Senior_Enlisted_Advisor_to_the_Chairman, October 2010.
2. http://www.jcs.mil/biography.aspx?ID=137, October 2011.
3. United States Statutes at Large, Vol. 119, p. 3325
4. http://www.jcs.mil/biography.aspx?ID=137, December 2011.

Sergeant
1. Oliver, Raymond, Why is a Kernal called a Colonel?, Tucson: Fireship press, 1983, p. 9.
2. Journals of the Continental Congress, Vol. 3, p. 384.
3. United States Statutes at Large, Vol. 1, p. 350.
4. United States Statutes at Large, Vol. 1, p. 524.
5. United States Statutes at Large, Vol. 1, p. 595.
6. http://www.angelfire.com/ca4/gunnyg/enlrank.html, November 2011.
7. United States Statutes at Large, Vol. 1, p. 595.
8. United States Statutes at Large, Vol. 1, p. 729.
9. United States Statutes at Large, Vol. 3, p. 124.
10. United States Statutes at Large, Vol. 3, p. 377.
11. United States Statutes at Large, Vol. 4, p. 712.
12. United States Statutes at Large, Vol. 4, p. 647.
13. Rankin, Robert, Uniforms of the Marines, New York: Putnam, 1970, p. 42.
13a. Rankin, Robert, Uniforms of the Sea Service, Annapolis: Naval Institute, 1962, p. 139.
13b. http://www.history.navy.mil/faqs/faq59-28.htm, March 2011.
14. http://www.history.navy.mil/faqs/faq59-28.htm, March 2011.
15. http://members.cox.net/malachi.thorne/Uniform%20Regulations/M1859%20Regs.pdf, October 2011.
16. Thompson, James G, Decorations, Medals, Ribbons, Badges and Insignia of the United States Marine Corps World War II to Present, Fountain Inn: MOA Press, 1998, p. 23.
17. United States Statutes at Large, Vol. 42, p. 629.
18. Nalty, Bernard C., United States Marine Corps Ranks and Grades 1775-1969, Washington: Headquarters U.S. Marine Corps, 1970, p. 25.
19. United States Statutes at Large, Vol. 63, p. 807.
20. Nalty, Bernard C., United States Marine Corps Ranks and Grades 1775-1969, Washington: Headquarters U.S. Marine Corps, 1970, p. 41.
21. MARINE CORPS UNIFORM REGULATIONS, 2003, p. 4-16.

Sergeant Major
1. United States Statutes at Large, Vol. 1, p. 595.
2. Nalty, Bernard C., United States Marine Corps Ranks and Grades 1775-1969, Washington: Headquarters U.S. Marine Corps, 1970, p. 17.
3. United States Statutes at Large, Vol. 3, p. 377.
4. United States Statutes at Large, Vol. 4, p. 647.
5. Rankin, Robert, Uniforms of the Sea Service, Annapolis: Naval Institute, 1962, p. 134.
6. Rankin, Robert, Uniforms of the Marines, New York: Putnam, 1970, p. 45.
7. Rankin, Robert, Uniforms of the Sea Service, Annapolis: Naval Institute, 1962, p. 139.
8. ibid.
9. http://www.history.navy.mil/faqs/faq59-28.htm, March 2011.
10. http://members.cox.net/malachi.thorne/Uniform%20Regulations/M1859%20Regs.pdf, October 2011.
11. United States Statutes at Large, Vol. 30, p. 1007.
12. United States Statutes at Large, Vol. 42, p. 629.
13. Nalty, Bernard C., United States Marine Corps Ranks and Grades 1775-1969, Washington: Headquarters U.S. Marine Corps, 1970, p. 25.
14. ibid. p. 37.
15. ibid. p. 39.
16. All Hands, "Quiz Aweigh", November 1955, p. 9.
17. Nalty, Bernard C., United States Marine Corps Ranks and Grades 1775-1969, Washington: Headquarters U.S. Marine Corps, 1970, p. 41.
18. Thompson, James G, Decorations, Medals, Ribbons, Badges and Insignia of the United States Marine Corps World War II to Present, Fountain Inn: MOA Press, 1998, p. 23.
19. MARINE CORPS UNIFORM REGULATIONS, 2003, p. 4-16.

Sergeant Major (Aviation)
1. Nalty, Bernard C., United States Marine Corps Ranks and Grades 1775-1969, Washington: Headquarters U.S. Marine Corps, 1970, p. 36.
2. ibid. p. 37
3. Grosvenor, Gilbert H., Insignia and decorations of the U.S. armed forces, National Geographic Society, 1945, p. 742 end section.

Sergeant Major of the Marine Corps
1. http://www.marines.mil/unit/hqmc/smmc/Pages/history.aspx, December 2011.
2. Nalty, Bernard C., United States Marine Corps Ranks and Grades 1775-1969, Washington: Headquarters U.S. Marine Corps, 1970, p. 43.
3. http://www.marines.mil/unit/hqmc/smmc/Pages/prior.aspx, December, 2011.
4. Nalty, Bernard C., United States Marine Corps Ranks and Grades 1775-1969, Washington: Headquarters U.S. Marine Corps, 1970, p. 44.
5. MARINE CORPS UNIFORM REGULATIONS, 2003, p. 4-16.

Staff Sergeant
1. United States Statutes at Large, Vol. 42, p. 629.
2. Nalty, Bernard C., United States Marine Corps Ranks and Grades 1775-1969, Washington: Headquarters U.S. Marine Corps, 1970, p. 25.
3. ibid. p. 26.
4. ibid. p. 27.
5. ibid. p. 28.
6. ibid. p. 39.
7. Thompson, James G, Decorations, Medals, Ribbons, Badges and Insignia of the United States Marine Corps World War II to Present, Fountain Inn: MOA Press, 1998, p. 23.
8. United States Statutes at Large, Vol. 42, p. 629.
9. Nalty, Bernard C., United States Marine Corps Ranks and Grades 1775-1969, Washington: Headquarters U.S. Marine Corps, 1970, p. 41.
10. Thompson, James G, Decorations, Medals, Ribbons, Badges and Insignia of the United States Marine Corps World War II to Present, Fountain Inn: MOA Press, 1998, p. 23.
11. MARINE CORPS UNIFORM REGULATIONS, 2003, p. 4-16.

Staff Sergeant (Clerical)
1. Nalty, Bernard C., United States Marine Corps Ranks and Grades 1775-1969, Washington: Headquarters U.S. Marine Corps, 1970, p. 28.
2. ibid. p. 27.
3. Uniform Regulations United States Marine Corps, July 13, 1937, p. 33. (an arc is shown on the 1936 chart).
1. Nalty, Bernard C., United States Marine Corps Ranks and Grades 1775-1969, Washington: Headquarters U.S. Marine Corps, 1970, p. 39.

Staff Sergeant (Mechanical)
1. Nalty, Bernard C., United States Marine Corps Ranks and Grades 1775-1969, Washington: Headquarters U.S. Marine Corps, 1970, p. 28.
2. ibid. p. 27.
3. Uniform Regulations United States Marine Corps, July 13, 1937, p. 33. (an arc is shown on the 1936 chart).
1. Nalty, Bernard C., United States Marine Corps Ranks and Grades 1775-1969, Washington: Headquarters U.S. Marine Corps, 1970, p. 39.

Staff Sergeant (Baker)
1. Nalty, Bernard C., United States Marine Corps Ranks and Grades 1775-1969, Washington: Headquarters U.S. Marine Corps, 1970, p. 30.
2. Uniform Regulations United States Marine Corps, July 13, 1937, p. 33.
3. Nalty, Bernard C., United States Marine Corps Ranks and Grades 1775-1969, Washington: Headquarters U.S. Marine Corps, 1970, p. 30-31.
4. ibid. p. 31.

Staff Sergeant (Commissary)
1. Nalty, Bernard C., United States Marine Corps Ranks and Grades 1775-1969, Washington: Headquarters U.S. Marine Corps, 1970, p. 31.
2. Uniform Regulations United States Marine Corps, July 13, 1937, p. 33.
3. Nalty, Bernard C., United States Marine Corps Ranks and Grades 1775-1969, Washington: Headquarters U.S. Marine Corps, 1970, p. 39.

Staff Sergeant (Mess)
1. Nalty, Bernard C., United States Marine Corps Ranks and Grades 1775-1969, Washington: Headquarters U.S. Marine Corps, 1970, p. 29.
2. ibid. p. 27.
3. Uniform Regulations United States Marine Corps, July 13, 1937, p. 33.
4. Nalty, Bernard C., United States Marine Corps Ranks and Grades 1775-1969, Washington: Headquarters U.S. Marine Corps, 1970, p. 31.

Steward First Class
1. Nalty, Bernard C., United States Marine Corps Ranks and Grades 1775-1969, Washington: Headquarters U.S. Marine Corps, 1970, p. 31.
2. Uniform Regulations United States Marine Corps, July 13, 1937, p. 34.
3. Nalty, Bernard C., United States Marine Corps Ranks and Grades 1775-1969, Washington: Headquarters U.S. Marine Corps, 1970, p. 35.

Steward Second Class
1. Nalty, Bernard C., United States Marine Corps Ranks and Grades 1775-1969, Washington: Headquarters U.S. Marine Corps, 1970, p. 31.
2. Uniform Regulations United States Marine Corps, July 13, 1937, p. 34.
3. Nalty, Bernard C., United States Marine Corps Ranks and Grades 1775-1969, Washington: Headquarters U.S. Marine Corps, 1970, p. 35.

Steward Third Class
1. Nalty, Bernard C., United States Marine Corps Ranks and Grades 1775-1969, Washington: Headquarters U.S. Marine Corps, 1970, p. 31.
2. Uniform Regulations United States Marine Corps, July 13, 1937, p. 34.
3. Nalty, Bernard C., United States Marine Corps Ranks and Grades 1775-1969, Washington: Headquarters U.S. Marine Corps, 1970, p. 35.

Supply Sergeant
1. Nalty, Bernard C., United States Marine Corps Ranks and Grades 1775-1969, Washington: Headquarters U.S. Marine Corps, 1970, p. 26.
2. http://www.angelfire.com/ca4/gunnyg/enlrank.html, November 2011.
3. Uniform Regulations United States Marine Corps, July 13, 1937, p. 33.
4. ibid. p. 39.

Technical Sergeant
1. Nalty, Bernard C., United States Marine Corps Ranks and Grades 1775-1969, Washington: Headquarters U.S. Marine Corps, 1970, p. 26.
2. ibid. p. 27.
3. ibid. p. 37.
4. Thompson, James G, Decorations, Medals, Ribbons, Badges and Insignia of the United States Marine Corps World War II to Present, Fountain Inn: MOA Press, 1998, p. 23.
5. United States Statutes at Large, Vol. 63, p. 807.
6. Nalty, Bernard C., United States Marine Corps Ranks and Grades 1775-1969, Washington: Headquarters U.S. Marine Corps, 1970, p. 41.

Technical Sergeant (Baker)
1. Nalty, Bernard C., United States Marine Corps Ranks and Grades 1775-1969, Washington: Headquarters U.S. Marine Corps, 1970, p. 30.
2. Uniform Regulations United States Marine Corps, July 13, 1937, p. 33.
3. Nalty, Bernard C., United States Marine Corps Ranks and Grades 1775-1969, Washington: Headquarters U.S. Marine Corps, 1970, p. 37.

Technical Sergeant (Clerical) line
1. Nalty, Bernard C., United States Marine Corps Ranks and Grades 1775-1969, Washington: Headquarters U.S. Marine Corps, 1970, p. 31.
2. Thompson, James G, Decorations, Medals, Ribbons, Badges and Insignia of the United States Marine Corps World War II to Present, Fountain Inn: MOA Press, 1998, p. 23.
3. Nalty, Bernard C., United States Marine Corps Ranks and Grades 1775-1969, Washington: Headquarters U.S. Marine Corps, 1970, p. 37.

Technical Sergeant (Clerical) (RW)
1. Nalty, Bernard C., United States Marine Corps Ranks and Grades 1775-1969, Washington: Headquarters U.S. Marine Corps, 1970, p. 31.
2. Thompson, James G, Decorations, Medals, Ribbons, Badges and Insignia of the United States Marine Corps World War II to Present, Fountain Inn: MOA Press, 1998, p. 23.
3. Nalty, Bernard C., United States Marine Corps Ranks and Grades 1775-1969, Washington: Headquarters U.S. Marine Corps, 1970, p. 37.

Technical Sergeant (Clerical) (SplW)
1. Nalty, Bernard C., United States Marine Corps Ranks and Grades 1775-1969, Washington: Headquarters U.S. Marine Corps, 1970, p. 31.
2. Thompson, James G, Decorations, Medals, Ribbons, Badges and Insignia of the United States Marine Corps World War II to Present, Fountain Inn: MOA Press, 1998, p. 23.
3. Nalty, Bernard C., United States Marine Corps Ranks and Grades 1775-1969, Washington: Headquarters U.S. Marine Corps, 1970, p. 37.

Technical Sergeant (Commissary)
1. Nalty, Bernard C., United States Marine Corps Ranks and Grades 1775-1969, Washington: Headquarters U.S. Marine Corps, 1970, p. 31.
2. Uniform Regulations United States Marine Corps, July 13, 1937, p. 33.
3. Nalty, Bernard C., United States Marine Corps Ranks and Grades 1775-1969, Washington: Headquarters U.S. Marine Corps, 1970, p. 37.

Technical Sergeant (Mess)
1. Nalty, Bernard C., United States Marine Corps Ranks and Grades 1775-1969, Washington: Headquarters U.S. Marine Corps, 1970, p. 29.
2. ibid. p. 26.
3. Uniform Regulations United States Marine Corps, July 13, 1937, p. 33.
4. Nalty, Bernard C., United States Marine Corps Ranks and Grades 1775-1969, Washington: Headquarters U.S. Marine Corps, 1970, p. 31.

Trumpet Corporal
1. Nalty, Bernard C., United States Marine Corps Ranks and Grades 1775-1969, Washington: Headquarters U.S. Marine Corps, 1970, p. 28.
2. ibid. p. 27.
3. Uniform Regulations United States Marine Corps, July 13, 1937, p. 34.
4. Nalty, Bernard C., United States Marine Corps Ranks and Grades 1775-1969, Washington: Headquarters U.S. Marine Corps, 1970, p. 29.

Trumpet Sergeant
1. Nalty, Bernard C., United States Marine Corps Ranks and Grades 1775-1969, Washington: Headquarters U.S. Marine Corps, 1970, p. 28.
2. ibid. p. 27.
3. Uniform Regulations United States Marine Corps, July 13, 1937, p. 34.
4. Nalty, Bernard C., United States Marine Corps Ranks and Grades 1775-1969, Washington: Headquarters U.S. Marine Corps, 1970, p. 29.

Trumpeter
1. Nalty, Bernard C., United States Marine Corps Ranks and Grades 1775-1969, Washington: Headquarters U.S. Marine Corps, 1970, p. 21.
2. United States Statutes at Large, Vol. 30, p. 1009.
3. http://members.cox.net/malachi.thorne/Uniform%20Regulations/M1900%20Regs.pdf, October 2011
4. http://www.angelfire.com/ca4/gunnyg/enlrank.html, November 2011.
5. Uniform Regulations United States Marine Corps, July 13, 1937, p. 34.
6. Nalty, Bernard C., United States Marine Corps Ranks and Grades 1775-1969, Washington: Headquarters U.S. Marine Corps, 1970, p. 29.

Trumpeter First Class
1. Nalty, Bernard C., United States Marine Corps Ranks and Grades 1775-1969, Washington: Headquarters U.S. Marine Corps, 1970, p. 28.
2. ibid. p.27.
3. Uniform Regulations United States Marine Corps, July 13, 1937, p. 34.
4. Nalty, Bernard C., United States Marine Corps Ranks and Grades 1775-1969, Washington: Headquarters U.S. Marine Corps, 1970, p. 29.

Warrant Officer
1. United States Statutes at Large, Vol. 57, p. 574.
2. All Hands, "Insignia of the United States Armed Forces", November 1950, p. 32-33.
3. All Hands, "Warrant Officers' Collar Devices", October 1952, p. 24.
4. United States Statutes at Large, Vol. 63, p. 807.
5. United States Statutes at Large, Vol. 68, p. 157.

Warrant Officer 1
1. United States Statutes at Large, Vol. 68, p. 157.
2. All Hands, "Insignia of the United States Armed Forces", December 1954, p. 32-33, Chart shows the new insignia. However it also shows the insignia for army warrant officers, officially adopted in 1956.
3. MARINE CORPS UNIFORM REGULATIONS, 2003, p. 4-25.

Part 4. Air Force
Chapter 1 Air Force Organization
1. Daso, Dik Alan, U.S. Air Force A Complete History, Washington: Hugh Lauter Levin Assic, 2006, p. 14.
2. http://en.wikipedia.org/wiki/Union_Army_Balloon_Corps, December 2011/
3. http://en.wikipedia.org/wiki/Aeronautical_Division,_U.S._Signal_Corps, December, 2011.
4. Daso, Dik Alan, U.S. Air Force A Complete History, Washington: Hugh Lauter Levin Assic, 2006, p. 24.
5. ibid.p. 25.
6. United States Statutes at Large, Vol. 38, p. 514.
7. http://en.wikipedia.org/wiki/Division_of_Military_Aeronautics,_Secretary_of_War, December 2011.
8. United States Statutes at Large, Vol. 40, p. 556.
9. Daso, Dik Alan, U.S. Air Force A Complete History, Washington: Hugh Lauter Levin Assic, 2006, p. 74.
10. United States Statutes at Large, Vol. 41, p. 108.
11. United States Statutes at Large, Vol. 41, p. 759.
12. United States Statutes at Large, Vol. 44, p. 780.
13. http://en.wikipedia.org/wiki/United_States_Army_Air_Forces, December 2011.
14. United States Statutes at Large, Vol. 61, p. 503.

Transfer of rank from the Army
1. United States Statutes at Large, Vol. 61, p. 504.

Pay Grades

1. Air Force Magazine, "First Shirts", January 2008.
2. United States Statutes at Large, Vol. 63, p. 807.
3. Aldebol, Anthony, Army Air force and United States Air Force Decorations, Medals, Ribbons, Badges and Insignia Fountain Inn: MOA Press, 1997, p. 56-57.
4. United States Statutes at Large, Vol. 68, p. 157.
5. United States Statutes at Large, Vol. 72, p. 123.
6. Air Force Magazine, "The In-Betweeners", November 1991.
7. http://en.wikipedia.org/wiki/Basic_Airman, January 2012.
8. Spink, Barry L ., A CHRONOLOGY OF THE ENLISTED RANK CHEVRON OF THE UNITED STATES AIR FORCE, Air Force Historical Research Agency, February 19, 1992.
9. http://en.wikipedia.org/wiki/Chief_Master_Sergeant#Command_Chief_Master_Sergeant, January 2012.

Chapter 2. Air Force Rank Insignia
1. The Air Officer's Guide, 5th edition, military service publishing, 1951, p. 222.
2. ibid. p. 248-251.
3. http://usafflagranks.com/usaf_formal_evening_dress_uniform.html, January 2012.
4. http://usafflagranks.com/usaf_mess_dress_uniform.html, January 2012.
5. http://usafflagranks.com/usaf_informal_dress_uniform.html, January 2012.
6. Spink, Barry L ., A CHRONOLOGY OF THE ENLISTED RANK CHEVRON OF THE UNITED STATES AIR FORCE, Air Force Historical Research Agency, February 19, 1992.
7. http://usafflagranks.com/usaf_formal_evening_dress_uniform.html, January 2012.
8. afr 35-10, September 15, 1983, p. 171.
9. Airman, "New Uniform Unveiled", December 1991, p. 46.
10. http://en.wikipedia.org/wiki/Merrill_A._McPeak, January 2012.
11. http://usafflagranks.com/usaf_service_dress_coat_uniform.html, January 2012.
12. http://usafflagranks.com/usaf_informal_dress_uniform.html, January 2012.
13. http://www.af.mil/news/story.asp?storyID=123023950, January 2012.

Badges of Rank
1. All Hands, "Insignia of the United States Armed Forces", November 1950.
2. The Air Officer's Guide, 5th edition, military service publishing, 1951, p. 249-251.
3. Aldebol, Anthony, Army Air force and United States Air Force Decorations, Medals, Ribbons, Badges and Insignia Fountain Inn: MOA Press, 1997, p. 59.
4. The Air Officer's Guide, 20th edition, military service publishing, 1969, p.72.
5. http://www.usmilitariaforum.com/forums/index.php?showtopic=5846&hl=usaf%20fatigue%20uniform&st=40< January 2012.
6. afr 35-10, September 15, 1983, p. 29.

Shoulder Broads
1. http://usafflagranks.com/usaf_mess_dress_uniform.html, January 2012.
2. http://usafflagranks.com/usaf_informal_dress_uniform.html, January 2012.
3. afr 35-10, September 15, 1983, p. 31-33.
4. http://usafflagranks.com/usaf_informal_dress_uniform.html, January 2012.
5. http://usafflagranks.com/usaf_mess_dress_uniform.html, January 2012.
6. afi-36-2903, July 18, 2011, P. 179.

Cuff Decoration and Cuff Stripes
1. http://usafflagranks.com/usaf_formal_evening_dress_uniform.html, January 2011.
2. The Air Officer's Guide, 5th edition, military service publishing, 1951, p. 222.
3. http://usafflagranks.com/usaf_formal_evening_dress_uniform.html, January 2011.
4. ibid.
5. ibid.
6. afr 35-10, September 15, 1983, p. 50.
3. Aldebol, Anthony, Army Air force and United States Air Force Decorations, Medals, Ribbons, Badges and Insignia Fountain Inn: MOA Press, 1997, p. 60-61.

Shoulder Marks
1. Spink, Barry L ., A CHRONOLOGY OF THE ENLISTED RANK CHEVRON OF THE UNITED STATES AIR FORCE, Air Force Historical Research Agency, February 19, 1992.
2. afr 35-10, September 15, 1983, p. 23-24.
3. ibid.p. 169 & 171.
4. Aldebol, Anthony, Army Air force and United States Air Force Decorations, Medals, Ribbons, Badges and Insignia Fountain Inn: MOA Press, 1997, p. 61.
5. Airman, "Air Force Grades and Insignia", September 1995, p. 41.
6. afi-36-2903, July 18, 2011, P. 179.

Chevrons
1. Oliver, Raymond, Why is a Kernal called a Colonel?, Tucson: Fireship press, 1983, p. 1.
2. Aldebol, Anthony, Army Air force and United States Air Force Decorations, Medals, Ribbons, Badges and Insignia Fountain Inn: MOA Press, 1997, p. 56-57.
3. Spink, Barry L ., A CHRONOLOGY OF THE ENLISTED RANK CHEVRON OF THE UNITED STATES AIR FORCE, Air Force Historical Research Agency, February 19, 1992.
4. Aldebol, Anthony, Army Air force and United States Air Force Decorations, Medals, Ribbons, Badges and Insignia, Fountain Inn: MOA Press, 1997, p. 56-57.
5. http://en.wikipedia.org/wiki/Military_aircraft_insignia, January 2012.
6. http://www.midway42.org/roundels.html, January 2012.
7. Smith, Richard, Shoulder Sleeve Insignia of the U.S. Armed Forces 1941-1945 , 1981, p. 158.
8. Spink, Barry L ., A CHRONOLOGY OF THE ENLISTED RANK CHEVRON OF THE UNITED STATES AIR FORCE, Air Force Historical Research Agency, February 19, 1992.
9. ibid.
10. ibid.
11. ibid.
12. ibid.
13. afr 35-10, September 15, 1983, p. 29.
14. Spink, Barry L ., A CHRONOLOGY OF THE ENLISTED RANK CHEVRON OF THE UNITED STATES AIR FORCE, Air Force Historical Research Agency, February 19, 1992.
15. http://www.af.mil/art/mediagallery.asp?galleryID=5192, January 2012.
16. Airman, "The Distinctive New Uniform", March 1993, p. 43.
17. http://www.absoluteastronomy.com/topics/Airman_Battle_Uniform, January 2012.Chapter 3 Air Force Ranks

Airman
1. Spink, Barry L ., A CHRONOLOGY OF THE ENLISTED RANK CHEVRON OF THE UNITED STATES AIR FORCE, Air Force Historical Research Agency, February 19, 1992.
2. ibid.
3. ibid.
4. afi-36-2903, July 18, 2011, P. 172.

Airman First Class
1. Spink, Barry L ., A CHRONOLOGY OF THE ENLISTED RANK CHEVRON OF THE UNITED STATES AIR FORCE, Air Force Historical Research Agency, February 19, 1992.
2. ibid.
3. ibid.
4. ibid.
5. afi-36-2903, July 18, 2011, P. 172.

Airman Second Class
1. Spink, Barry L ., A CHRONOLOGY OF THE ENLISTED RANK CHEVRON OF THE UNITED STATES AIR FORCE, Air Force Historical Research Agency, February 19, 1992.
2. ibid.
3. ibid.

Airman Third Class
1. Spink, Barry L ., A CHRONOLOGY OF THE ENLISTED RANK CHEVRON OF THE UNITED STATES AIR FORCE, Air Force Historical Research Agency, February 19, 1992.
2. ibid.
3. ibid.

Brigadier General
1. United States Statutes at Large, Vol. 63, p. 802.
2. afi-36-2903, July 18, 2011, P. 172.

Captain
1. Oliver, Raymond, Why is a Kernal called a Colonel?, Tucson: Fireship press, 1983, p. 29.
2. United States Statutes at Large, Vol. 63, p. 802.

Chief Master Sergeant
1. United States Statutes at Large, Vol. 72, p. 123.
2. Spink, Barry L ., A CHRONOLOGY OF THE ENLISTED RANK CHEVRON OF THE UNITED STATES AIR FORCE, Air Force Historical Research Agency, February 19, 1992.
3. Aldebol, Anthony, Army Air force and United States Air Force Decorations, Medals, Ribbons, Badges and Insignia Fountain Inn: MOA Press, 1997, p. 56-57.
4. ibid.
5. afi-36-2903, July 18, 2011, P. 172.

Chief Master Sergeant of the Air Force
1. http://www.nationalmuseum.af.mil/factsheets/factsheet.asp?id=9090, January 2012.
2. http://en.wikipedia.org/wiki/Chief_Master_Sergeant_of_the_Air_Force, January 2012.
3. Spink, Barry L ., A CHRONOLOGY OF THE ENLISTED RANK CHEVRON OF THE UNITED STATES AIR FORCE, Air Force Historical Research Agency, February 19, 1992.
4. http://en.wikipedia.org/wiki/Chief_Master_Sergeant_of_the_Air_Force, January 2012.
5. Aldebol, Anthony, Army Air force and United States Air Force Decorations, Medals, Ribbons, Badges and Insignia Fountain Inn: MOA Press, 1997, p. 56-57.
6. http://en.wikipedia.org/wiki/Chief_Master_Sergeant_of_the_Air_Force, January 2012.
7. ibid.
8. ibid.
9. afi-36-2903, July 18, 2011, P. 172.

Chief Warrant Officer
1. AR-600-35, Change 1, September 4, 1942, page 6
2. United States Statutes at Large, Vol. 63, p. 802.
3. http://penfed.org/usawoa/woheritage/Hist_of_Army_WO.htm, July 2010.
4. United States Statutes at Large, Vol. 68, p. 157.

Chief Warrant Officer 2
1. United States Statutes at Large, Vol. 68, p. 157.
2. Aldebol, Anthony, Army Air force and United States Air Force Decorations, Medals, Ribbons, Badges and Insignia Fountain Inn: MOA Press, 1997, p. 59.
3. Air Force Magazine, "The In-Betweeners", November 1991.

Chief Warrant Officer 3
1. United States Statutes at Large, Vol. 68, p. 157.
2. Aldebol, Anthony, Army Air force and United States Air Force Decorations, Medals, Ribbons, Badges and Insignia Fountain Inn: MOA Press, 1997, p. 59.
3. Air Force Magazine, "The In-Betweeners", November 1991.

Chief Warrant Officer 4
1. United States Statutes at Large, Vol. 68, p. 157.

2. Aldebol, Anthony, Army Air force and United States Air Force Decorations, Medals, Ribbons, Badges and Insignia Fountain Inn: MOA Press, 1997, p. 59.
3. Air Force Magazine, "The In-Betweeners", November 1991.
4. http://en.wikipedia.org/wiki/Warrant_Officer_(United_States)#Air_Force, January 2012.

Colonel
1. Oliver, Raymond, Why is a Kernal called a Colonel?, Tucson: Fireship press, 1983, p. 29.
2. United States Statutes at Large, Vol. 63, p. 802.

Command Chief Master Sergeant
1. http://en.wikipedia.org/wiki/Chief_Master_Sergeant#Command_Chief_Master_Sergeant, January 2012.
2. afi-36-2903, July 18, 2011, P. 172.

Corporal
1. Oliver, Raymond, Why is a Kernal called a Colonel?, Tucson: Fireship press, 1983, p. 7.
2. Aldebol, Anthony, Army Air force and United States Air Force Decorations, Medals, Ribbons, Badges and Insignia Fountain Inn: MOA Press, 1997, p. 56-57.
3. United States Statutes at Large, Vol. 63, p. 802.
4. Spink, Barry L ., A CHRONOLOGY OF THE ENLISTED RANK CHEVRON OF THE UNITED STATES AIR FORCE, Air Force Historical Research Agency, February 19, 1992.

First Lieutenant
1. Oliver, Raymond, Why is a Kernal called a Colonel?, Tucson: Fireship press, 1983, p. 25
2. http://www.xenograg.com/101/excerpts/origins-of-european-army-ranks, August 2010.
3. United States Statutes at Large, Vol. 63, p. 802.
4. afi-36-2903, July 18, 2011, P. 172.

First Sergeant
1. Air Force Magazine, "First Shirts", January 2008.
2. Spink, Barry L ., A CHRONOLOGY OF THE ENLISTED RANK CHEVRON OF THE UNITED STATES AIR FORCE, Air Force Historical Research Agency, February 19, 1992.
3. Aldebol, Anthony, Army Air force and United States Air Force Decorations, Medals, Ribbons, Badges and Insignia Fountain Inn: MOA Press, 1997, p. 56-57.
4. Spink, Barry L ., A CHRONOLOGY OF THE ENLISTED RANK CHEVRON OF THE UNITED STATES AIR FORCE, Air Force Historical Research Agency, February 19, 1992.

General
1. Oliver, Raymond, Why is a Kernal called a Colonel?, Tucson: Fireship press, 1983, p. 49.
2. United States Statutes at Large, Vol. 63, p. 802.
3. United States Statutes at Large, Vol. 72, p. 124.
4. afi-36-2903, July 18, 2011, P. 172.

General of the Air Force
1. United States Statutes at Large, Vol. 63, p. 65.
2. Official Army Register, January 1, 1945, p. 1.
3. Official Army Register, January 1, 1947, p. 1277.
4. United States Statutes at Large, Vol. 62, p. 1069.
5. http://en.wikipedia.org/wiki/General_of_the_Air_Force, January 2012.

General of the Army
1. United States Statutes at Large, Vol. 38, p. 802
2. Official Army Register, January 1, 1945, p. 1.
3. Official Army Register, January 1, 1947, p. 1277.
4. United States Statutes at Large, Vol. 62, p. 1069.
5. United States Statutes at Large, Vol. 63, p. 65.

Lieutenant Colonel
1. http://www.xenograg.com/101/excerpts/origins-of-european-army-ranks, august 2010.
2. United States Statutes at Large, Vol. 63, p. 802.
3. afi-36-2903, July 18, 2011, P. 172.

Lieutenant General
1. http://www.xenograg.com/101/excerpts/origins-of-european-army-ranks, august 2010.
2. United States Statutes at Large, Vol. 63, p. 802.
3. United States Statutes at Large, Vol. 72, p. 124.
4. afi-36-2903, July 18, 2011, P. 172.

Major
1. http://www.xenograg.com/101/excerpts/origins-of-european-army-ranks, august 2010.
2 . Oliver, Raymond, Why is a Kernal called a Colonel?, Tucson: Fireship press, 1983, p. 32,
2. United States Statutes at Large, Vol. 63, p. 802.
3. afi-36-2903, July 18, 2011, P. 172.

Major General
1. http://www.xenograg.com/101/excerpts/origins-of-european-army-ranks, august 2010.
2. United States Statutes at Large, Vol. 63, p. 802.
3. United States Statutes at Large, Vol. 72, p. 124.
4. afi-36-2903, July 18, 2011, P. 172.

Master Sergeant
1. Spink, Barry L ., A CHRONOLOGY OF THE ENLISTED RANK CHEVRON OF THE UNITED STATES AIR FORCE, Air Force Historical Research Agency, February 19, 1992.
2. United States Statutes at Large, Vol. 63, p. 802.
3. Aldebol, Anthony, Army Air force and United States Air Force Decorations, Medals, Ribbons, Badges and Insignia Fountain Inn: MOA Press, 1997, p. 56-57.
4. afi-36-2903, July 18, 2011, P. 172.

Private
1. Aldebol, Anthony, Army Air force and United States Air Force Decorations, Medals, Ribbons, Badges and Insignia Fountain Inn: MOA Press, 1997, p. 56-57.
2. United States Statutes at Large, Vol. 63, p. 802.
3. Spink, Barry L ., A CHRONOLOGY OF THE ENLISTED RANK CHEVRON OF THE UNITED STATES AIR FORCE, Air Force Historical Research Agency, February 19, 1992.

Private First Class
1. Aldebol, Anthony, Army Air force and United States Air Force Decorations, Medals, Ribbons, Badges and Insignia Fountain Inn: MOA Press, 1997, p. 56-57.
2. United States Statutes at Large, Vol. 63, p. 802.
3. Spink, Barry L ., A CHRONOLOGY OF THE ENLISTED RANK CHEVRON OF THE UNITED STATES AIR FORCE, Air Force Historical Research Agency, February 19, 1992.

Second Lieutenant
1. Oliver, Raymond, Why is a Kernal called a Colonel?, Tucson: Fireship press, 1983, p. 25
2. http://www.xenograg.com/101/excerpts/origins-of-european-army-ranks, August 2010.
3. United States Statutes at Large, Vol. 63, p. 802.
4. afi-36-2903, July 18, 2011, P. 172.

Senior Airman
1. Spink, Barry L ., A CHRONOLOGY OF THE ENLISTED RANK CHEVRON OF THE UNITED STATES AIR FORCE, Air Force Historical Research Agency, February 19, 1992.
2. Aldebol, Anthony, Army Air force and United States Air Force Decorations, Medals, Ribbons, Badges and Insignia Fountain Inn: MOA Press, 1997, p. 56-57.
3. Spink, Barry L ., A CHRONOLOGY OF THE ENLISTED RANK CHEVRON OF THE UNITED STATES AIR FORCE, Air Force Historical Research Agency, February 19, 1992.
4. afi-36-2903, July 18, 2011, P. 172.

Senior Master Sergeant
1. United States Statutes at Large, Vol. 72, p. 123.
2. Spink, Barry L ., A CHRONOLOGY OF THE ENLISTED RANK CHEVRON OF THE UNITED STATES AIR FORCE, Air Force Historical Research Agency, February 19, 1992.
3. Aldebol, Anthony, Army Air force and United States Air Force Decorations, Medals, Ribbons, Badges and Insignia Fountain Inn: MOA Press, 1997, p. 56-57.
4. ibid.
5. afi-36-2903, July 18, 2011, P. 172.

Sergeant
1. Oliver, Raymond, Why is a Kernal called a Colonel?, Tucson: Fireship press, 1983, p. 9.
2. Aldebol, Anthony, Army Air force and United States Air Force Decorations, Medals, Ribbons, Badges and Insignia Fountain Inn: MOA Press, 1997, p. 56-57.
3. United States Statutes at Large, Vol. 63, p. 802.
4. Spink, Barry L ., A CHRONOLOGY OF THE ENLISTED RANK CHEVRON OF THE UNITED STATES AIR FORCE, Air Force Historical Research Agency, February 19, 1992.
5. Aldebol, Anthony, Army Air force and United States Air Force Decorations, Medals, Ribbons, Badges and Insignia Fountain Inn: MOA Press, 1997, p. 57.
6. http://forums.myarmedforces.com/topic/531/Last_airforce_buck_sergeant, January 2012.

Staff Sergeant
1. Spink, Barry L ., A CHRONOLOGY OF THE ENLISTED RANK CHEVRON OF THE UNITED STATES AIR FORCE, Air Force Historical Research Agency, February 19, 1992.
2. United States Statutes at Large, Vol. 63, p. 802.
3. afi-36-2903, July 18, 2011, P. 172.

Technical Sergeant
1. Spink, Barry L ., A CHRONOLOGY OF THE ENLISTED RANK CHEVRON OF THE UNITED STATES AIR FORCE, Air Force Historical Research Agency, February 19, 1992.
2. United States Statutes at Large, Vol. 63, p. 802.
3. afi-36-2903, July 18, 2011, P. 172.

Warrant Officer 1
1. United States Statutes at Large, Vol. 68, p. 157.
3. Aldebol, Anthony, Army Air force and United States Air Force Decorations, Medals, Ribbons, Badges and Insignia Fountain Inn: MOA Press, 1997, p. 59.
3. Air Force Magazine, "The In-Betweeners", November 1991.

Warrant Officer Junior Grade
1. AR-600-35, Change 1, September 4, 1942, page 6
2. United States Statutes at Large, Vol. 63, p. 802.
3. http://penfed.org/usawoa/woheritage/Hist_of_Army_WO.htm, July 2010.
4. United States Statutes at Large, Vol. 68, p. 157.

Part 5.Coast Guard
Chapter 1 Coast Guard Organization
1. United States Statutes at Large, Vol. 38, p. 800.
2. United States Statutes at Large, Vol. 53, p. 1215 &1432.
3. Executive Order 9083, February 28, 1942.
4. http://www.uscg.mil/history/faqs/when.asp, January 2012.

The Reveune Cutter Service
1. United States Statutes at Large, Vol. 1, p. 145.
2. United States Statutes at Large, Vol. 1, p. 699.

The Life Saving Service
1. United States Statutes at Large, Vol. 9, p. 381.
2. http://www.uscg.mil/tcyorktown/ops/nmlbs/Surf/surf2.asp, January 2012.
3. http://www.uscg.mil/tcyorktown/ops/nmlbs/Surf/surf3.asp, Januray 2012.
4. United States Statutes at Large, Vol. 20, p. 163.

The Lighthouse Service
1. United States Statutes at Large, Vol. 1, p. 53.
2. http://en.wikipedia.org/wiki/United_States_Lighthouse_Board, January 2012.
3. United States Statutes at Large, Vol. 10, p. 119.
4. United States Statutes at Large, Vol. 36, p. 537.

Bureau of Marine Inspection and Navigation
1. United States Statutes at Large, Vol. 5, p. 304.
2. United States Statutes at Large, Vol. 10, p. 74.
3. United States Statutes at Large, Vol. 16, p. 458.
4. United States Statutes at Large, Vol. 32, p. 826.
5. United States Statutes at Large, Vol. 37, p. 415.

6. United States Statutes at Large, Vol. 49, p. 1380.

Types of Rank
1.
http://www.defense.gov/specials/insignias/officers.html, November 2010

Rank Structure
1. United States Statutes at Large, Vol. 38, p. 801.
2. United States Statutes at Large, Vol. 53, p. 1215.
3. United States Statutes at Large, Vol. 1, p. 175.
4. United States Statutes at Large, Vol. 1, p. 709.
5. Davis Smith, Horatio, Early History of the United States Revenue Marine Service , Naval Historical Foundation, 1932, p. 18-19.
6. ibid. p. 25.
7. ibid. p. 38.
8. United States Statutes at Large, Vol. 5, p. 65.
9. Davis Smith, Horatio, Early History of the United States Revenue Marine Service , Naval Historical Foundation, 1932, p. 62.
10. United States Statutes at Large, Vol. 5, p. 794.
11. United States Statutes at Large, Vol. 12, p. 275.
12. Davis Smith, Horatio, Early History of the United States Revenue Marine Service , Naval Historical Foundation, 1932, p. 62.
13. United States Statutes at Large, Vol. 12, p. 640.
14. United States Statutes at Large, Vol. 12, p. 583.
15. United States Statutes at Large, Vol. 17, p. 347.
16. United States Statutes at Large, Vol. 18, p. 107.
17. United States Statutes at Large, Vol. 28, p. 172.
18. United States Statutes at Large, Vol. 29, p. 149.
19. United States Statutes at Large, Vol. 30, p. 17.
20. United States Statutes at Large, Vol. 30, p. 604.
21. United States Statutes at Large, Vol. 30, p. 1081.
22. United States Statutes at Large, Vol. 32, p. 100.
23. United States Statutes at Large, Vol. 33, p. 1036.
24. United States Statutes at Large, Vol. 32, p. 1046.
25. United States Statutes at Large, Vol. 33, p. 460.
26. United States Statutes at Large, Vol. 33, p. 1163.
27. United States Statutes at Large, Vol. 34, p. 702.
28. United States Statutes at Large, Vol. 34, p. 30.
28a. United States Statutes at Large, Vol. 34, p. 452.
29. United States Statutes at Large, Vol. 34, p. 200.
30. Regulations Governing the Uniform of Officers and Enlisted Men of the United States Revenue Marine, 1891.
31. United States Statutes at Large, Vol. 34, p. 702.
31a. Gauss, Henry C., The American Goverment, Organization and Officials, NewYork: Hamerlsy, 1908, p. 404-406.
32. United States Statutes at Large, Vol. 35, p. 62.
33. United States Statutes at Large, Vol. 36, p. 711.
34. United States Statutes at Large, Vol. 37, p. 420.
35. United States Statutes at Large, Vol. 38, p. 620.
36. United States Statutes at Large, Vol. 38, p. 801.
37. United States Statutes at Large, Vol. 20, p. 163.
38. Regiser of the Officers, Vessels, and Stations of the United States Coast Guard, August 1, 1915, p. 38.
38a. ibid. p. 41-50.
39. United States Statutes at Large, Vol. 40, p. 732.
40. Regiser of the Commissioned and Warrant Officers and Sadets, and Ships, and Stations of the United States Coast Guard, January 1, 1921, p. 6 & 28.
41. United States Statutes at Large, Vol. 41, p. 603.
42. Lewis, Dana., U. S. COAST GUARD ENLISTED RATINGS RATING SPECIALTY MARKS & DISTINGUISHING MARKS 1915 ~ 2011, p. 17-22.
43. United States Statutes at Large, Vol. 41, p. 879.
44. United States Statutes at Large, Vol. 42, p. 630.
45. United States Statutes at Large, Vol. 42, p. 1130.
46. United States Statutes at Large, Vol. 44, p. 815.
47. Regiser of the Officers, Vessels, and Stations of the United States Coast Guard, 1927, p. 42.
48. United States Statutes at Large, Vol. 53, p. 1217.
49. United States Statutes at Large, Vol. 53, p. 1218.
50. United States Coast Guard list of Commissioned and Warrant Officers on Active Duty in Order of Presedence and Temporary Menbers of the Reserve, June 30, 1944, p. 1.
51. United States Statutes at Large, Vol. 57, p. 60.
52. United States Statutes at Large, Vol. 59, p. 37.
53. United States Statutes at Large, Vol. 60, p. 60.
54. United States Statutes at Large, Vol. 61, p. 409.
54a. www.uscg.mil/history/uscghist/USCGRates.pdf, March 2012.
55. United States Statutes at Large, Vol. 63, p. 497.
56. United States Statutes at Large, Vol. 63, p. 802.
57. United States Statutes at Large, Vol. 68, p. 157.
58. United States Statutes at Large, Vol. 72, p. 123.
59. History of the Chief Warrant & Warrant Officers Association, USCG, 1994, P. 19.
61. United States Statutes at Large, Vol. 98, p. 2873.
62. United States Statutes at Large, Vol. 99, p. 628.Chapter 2.

Coast Guard Rank and Rate Insignia
1. Davis Smith, Horatio, Early History of the United States Revenue Marine Service , Naval Historical Foundation, 1932, p. 36.
2. ibid.p. 39.
3. Canney, Donald, Uniforms of the U.S. Coast Guard, Revenue Service, Lighthouse Service and Life Saving Service, 1997.
4. ibid.
5. Davis Smith, Horatio, Early History of the United States Revenue Marine Service , Naval Historical Foundation, 1932, p. 39-40.
6. ibid. p. 40.
7. ibid. p. 41.
8. ibid. p. 69.
9. Canney, Donald, Uniforms of the U.S. Coast Guard, Revenue Service, Lighthouse Service and Life Saving Service, 1997.
10. Katcher, Philip, The Civil War Source Book, New York: Facts on File, 1992, p. 197-198.
11. Canney, Donald, Uniforms of the U.S. Coast Guard, Revenue Service, Lighthouse Service and Life Saving Service, 1997.
12. ibid.
12a. Regulations Governing the Uniform of Officers and Enlisted Men of the United States Revenue Marine, 1891.
13. Lewis, Dana., U. S. COAST GUARD ENLISTED RATINGS RATING SPECIALTY MARKS & DISTINGUISHING MARKS 1915 ~ 2011, p. 3.
14. U.S. REVENUE CUTTER SERVICE UNIFORM REGULATIONS OFFICERS, WARRANT OFFICERS AND ENLISTED MEN, 1908.
15. The National Geographic Magazine, "Insignia of the Uniformed Forces of the United States", October 1917, p. 418.
16. Williams, Dion., Uniforms & Insignia of the U.S. Coast Guard 1918, p. 3.
17. Canney, Donald, Uniforms of the U.S. Coast Guard, Revenue Service, Lighthouse Service and Life Saving Service, 1997.
18. REGULATIONS GOVERNING THE UNIFORMS FOR COMMISSIONED AND WARRANT OFFICERS AND ENLISTED MEN OF THE UNITED STATES COAST GUARD, July 24, 1930.
19. REGULATIONS GOVERNING THE UNIFORMS FOR COMMISSIONED AND WARRANT OFFICERS AND ENLISTED MEN OF THE UNITED STATES COAST GUARD, Amendment No. 7, June 18, 1941.
20. Canney, Donald, Uniforms of the U.S. Coast Guard, Revenue Service, Lighthouse Service and Life Saving Service, 1997.
25. The Coast Guard Reservist , "Uniform Notes", July 1970, p. 4.
22.
http://www.uscg.mil/history/uscghist/USCG_Uniform_Photos_SPARS.asp, February 2012.
22a. Lewis, Dana., U. S. COAST GUARD ENLISTED RATINGS RATING SPECIALTY MARKS & DISTINGUISHING MARKS 1915 ~ 2011, p. 34.
23. Canney, Donald, Uniforms of the U.S. Coast Guard, Revenue Service, Lighthouse Service and Life Saving Service, 1997.
24. Lewis, Dana., U. S. COAST GUARD ENLISTED RATINGS RATING SPECIALTY MARKS & DISTINGUISHING MARKS 1915 ~ 2011, p. 38.
25. The Coast Guard Reservist , "SPAR Uniform Notes", May 1961, p. 2.
26. The Coast Guard Reservist , "New Coast Guard Blue is the Prescribed Uniform", August 1975, p. 3-4.

Epaulets

1. Oliver, Raymond, Why is a Kernal called a Colonel?, Tuscon: Fireship press, 1983, p. 17.
2. Davis Smith, Horatio, Early History of the United States Revenue Marine Service , Naval Historical Foundation, 1932, p. 36.
3. ibid.p. 39.
4. Canney, Donald, Uniforms of the U.S. Coast Guard, Revenue Service, Lighthouse Service and Life Saving Service, 1997.
5.
http://www.uscg.mil/history/gifs/RCS_1800_Accoutrements.jpg, February 2012.
6. Canney, Donald, Uniforms of the U.S. Coast Guard, Revenue Service, Lighthouse Service and Life Saving Service, 1997.
7. ibid.
8. ibid.
9. Regulations Governing the Uniform of Officers and Enlisted Men of the United States Revenue Marine, 1891.
10. U.S. REVENUE CUTTER SERVICE UNIFORM REGULATIONS OFFICERS, WARRANT OFFICERS AND ENLISTED MEN, 1908.
11. Williams, Dion., Uniforms & Insignia of the U.S. Coast Guard 1918, p. 3.
12. REGULATIONS GOVERNING THE UNIFORMS FOR COMMISSIONED AND WARRANT OFFICERS AND ENLISTED MEN OF THE UNITED STATES COAST GUARD, July 24, 1930.

Shoulder Straps
1. Davis Smith, Horatio, Early History of the United States Revenue Marine Service , Naval Historical Foundation, 1932, p. 41.
2. Canney, Donald, Uniforms of the U.S. Coast Guard, Revenue Service, Lighthouse Service and Life Saving Service, 1997.
3.
http://www.usmilitariaforum.com/forums/index.php?showtopic=30608, February 2012.
4. Canney, Donald, Uniforms of the U.S. Coast Guard, Revenue Service, Lighthouse Service and Life Saving Service, 1997.
5.
http://www.usmilitariaforum.com/forums/index.php?showtopic=30608, February 2012.
6. Canney, Donald, Uniforms of the U.S. Coast Guard, Revenue Service, Lighthouse Service and Life Saving Service, 1997.
7.
http://www.usmilitariaforum.com/forums/index.php?showtopic=30608, February 2012.
8. Canney, Donald, Uniforms of the U.S. Coast Guard, Revenue Service, Lighthouse Service and Life Saving Service, 1997.
9.
http://www.usmilitariaforum.com/forums/index.php?showtopic=30608, February 2012.
10. Regulations Governing the Uniform of Officers and Enlisted Men of the United States Revenue Marine, 1891.

Shoulder Knots

1. U.S. REVENUE CUTTER SERVICE UNIFORM REGULATIONS OFFICERS, WARRANT OFFICERS AND ENLISTED MEN, 1908.
2. Williams, Dion., Uniforms & Insignia of the U.S. Coast Guard 1918.

Shoulder Boards
1. U.S. REVENUE CUTTER SERVICE UNIFORM REGULATIONS OFFICERS, WARRANT OFFICERS AND ENLISTED MEN, 1908.
2. ibid.
3. The National Geographic Magazine, "Insignia of the Uniformed Forces of the United States", October 1917, p. 418.
4. REGULATIONS GOVERNING THE UNIFORMS FOR COMMISSIONED AND WARRANT OFFICERS AND ENLISTED MEN OF THE UNITED STATES COAST GUARD, July 24, 1930.
5. http://noelcoleman.blogspot.com/2012/02/my-first-wikipedia-contribution-admiral.html, February 2012.
5a. Canney, Donald, Uniforms of the U.S. Coast Guard, Revenue Service, Lighthouse Service and Life Saving Service, 1997.
6. Lewis, Dana., U. S. COAST GUARD ENLISTED RATINGS RATING SPECIALTY MARKS & DISTINGUISHING MARKS 1915 ~ 2011, p. 42.
6a.
http://www.uscg.mil/history/gifs/1920s_Warrant_Full_Dress.jpg, March 2012.
7. REGULATIONS GOVERNING THE UNIFORMS FOR COMMISSIONED AND WARRANT OFFICERS AND ENLISTED MEN OF THE UNITED STATES COAST GUARD, Amendment No. 7, June 18, 1941.
8. Canney, Donald, Uniforms of the U.S. Coast Guard, Revenue Service, Lighthouse Service and Life Saving Service, 1997.
9. http://noelcoleman.blogspot.com/2012/02/my-first-wikipedia-contribution-admiral.html, February 2012.

10. Canney, Donald, Uniforms of the U.S. Coast Guard, Revenue Service, Lighthouse Service and Life Saving Service, 1997.
11. The Coast Guard Reservist, "Uniform Changes are Announced", January 1956, p. 1.
12. ibid.
13. COMDTINST M1020.6F, Febraury 2009, para. 3.D.1.

Shoulder Marks
1. The Coast Guard Reservist, "Your Uniform Matters", September-October 1991, p. 19.
2. COMDTINST M1020.6F, July 2003, para. 3.D.1a.

Badges of Rank
1. Canney, Donald, Uniforms of the U.S. Coast Guard, Revenue Service, Lighthouse Service and Life Saving Service, 1997.
2. Schuyler Hartly and Graham Illustrated Catalog of Civil War Military Goods, New York: Dover, 1985.
3. http://www.usmilitariaforum.com/forums/index.php?showtopic=30608, February 2012.
4. ibid.
5. Canney, Donald, Uniforms of the U.S. Coast Guard, Revenue Service, Lighthouse Service and Life Saving Service, 1997.
6. http://www.usmilitariaforum.com/forums/index.php?showtopic=30608, February 2012.
7. Canney, Donald, Uniforms of the U.S. Coast Guard, Revenue Service, Lighthouse Service and Life Saving Service, 1997.
8://www.uscg.mil/history/gifs/RCS_1871_Insignia.jpg, March 2012, the illustration show one bar worn by "Assistant Engineers".
9. Canney, Donald, Uniforms of the U.S. Coast Guard, Revenue Service, Lighthouse Service and Life Saving Service, 1997.
9. ibid.
10. ibid
11. http://www.usmilitariaforum.com/forums/index.php?showtopic=30608, March 2011.
12. Regulations Governing the Uniform of Officers and Enlisted Men of the United States Revenue Marine, 1891.
13. U.S. REVENUE CUTTER SERVICE UNIFORM REGULATIONS OFFICERS, WARRANT OFFICERS AND ENLISTED MEN, 1908.
14. Williams, Dion., Uniforms & Insignia of the U.S. Coast Guard 1918.
15. http://en.wikipedia.org/wiki/File:Bertholf_portrait_3.jpg, March 2012.
16. Canney, Donald, Uniforms of the U.S. Coast Guard, Revenue Service, Lighthouse Service and Life Saving Service, 1997.
17. REGULATIONS GOVERNING THE UNIFORMS FOR COMMISSIONED AND WARRANT OFFICERS AND ENLISTED MEN OF THE UNITED STATES COAST GUARD, July 24, 1930.
18. REGULATIONS GOVERNING THE UNIFORMS FOR COMMISSIONED AND WARRANT OFFICERS AND ENLISTED MEN OF THE UNITED STATES COAST GUARD, Amendment No. 7, June 18, 1941.
19. Lewis, Dana., U. S. COAST GUARD ENLISTED RATINGS RATING SPECIALTY MARKS & DISTINGUISHING MARKS 1915 ~ 2011, p. 44.
20. ibid.p. 43.
21. ibid.
22. ibid.p. 38.
23. COMDTINST M1020.6a, Febraury 2009, para. 2-C-4, c (13-15).

Cuff Stripes (and buttons)
1. Davis Smith, Horatio, Early History of the United States Revenue Marine Service , Naval Historical Foundation, 1932, p. 39.
2. Canney, Donald, Uniforms of the U.S. Coast Guard, Revenue Service, Lighthouse Service and Life Saving Service, 1997.
3. Davis Smith, Horatio, Early History of the United States Revenue Marine Service , Naval Historical Foundation, 1932, p. 40-41.
4. ibid. p. 69.
5. Katcher, Philip, The Civil War Source Book, New York: Facts on File, 1992, p. 198.
6. ibid.
7. Regulations Governing the Uniform of Officers and Enlisted Men of the United States Revenue Marine, 1891.
8. http://www.uscg.mil/history/gifs/1900_Reg_Rank_Sleeve.jpg, March 2012.
9. http://www.uscg.mil/history/gifs/1900_Reg_Service_Dress.jpg, March 2012.
10. Canney, Donald, Uniforms of the U.S. Coast Guard, Revenue Service, Lighthouse Service and Life Saving Service, 1997.
11. U.S. REVENUE CUTTER SERVICE UNIFORM REGULATIONS OFFICERS, WARRANT OFFICERS AND ENLISTED MEN, 1908.
12. REGULATIONS GOVERNING THE UNIFORMS FOR WARRANT OFFICERS AND ENLISTED PERSONS OF THE UNITED STATES COAST GUARD, February 18, 1916, p. 11-12.
13. Williams, Dion., Uniforms & Insignia of the U.S. Coast Guard 1918.
14. http://www.uscg.mil/history/gifs/1920s_Warrant_Full_Dress.jpg, March 2012.
15. REGULATIONS GOVERNING THE UNIFORMS FOR COMMISSIONED AND WARRANT OFFICERS AND ENLISTED MEN OF THE UNITED STATES COAST GUARD, July 24, 1930.
16. ibid.
17. REGULATIONS GOVERNING THE UNIFORMS FOR COMMISSIONED AND WARRANT OFFICERS AND ENLISTED MEN OF THE UNITED STATES COAST GUARD, Amendment No. 7, June 18, 1941.
18. http://www.uscg.mil/history/uscghist/USCG_Uniform_Photos_SPARS.asp, February 2012.
19. The Coast Guard Reservist, "SPAR Uniform Notes", May 1961, p. 2.
20. COMDTINST M1020.6A, July 23, 1985, para. 3.C.3.
21. COMDTINST M1020.6D, May 27, 1997, para. 4.H.
22. Lewis, Dana., U. S. COAST GUARD ENLISTED RATINGS RATING SPECIALTY MARKS & DISTINGUISHING MARKS 1915 ~ 2011, p. 31.
23. ibid. p. 43.

Petty Officer's Devices and Rating Badges
1. Schuyler Hartly and Graham Illustrated Catalog of Civil War Military Goods, New York: Dover, 1985.
2. Regulations Governing the Uniform of Officers and Enlisted Men of the United States Revenue Marine, 1891.
3. Lewis, Dana., U. S. COAST GUARD ENLISTED RATINGS RATING SPECIALTY MARKS & DISTINGUISHING MARKS 1915 ~ 2011, p. 3.
4. U.S. REVENUE CUTTER SERVICE UNIFORM REGULATIONS OFFICERS, WARRANT OFFICERS AND ENLISTED MEN, 1908.
5. REGULATIONS GOVERNING THE UNIFORMS FOR WARRANT OFFICERS AND ENLISTED PERSONS OF THE UNITED STATES COAST GUARD, February 18, 1916, p. 15-16.
6. Lewis, Dana., U. S. COAST GUARD ENLISTED RATINGS RATING SPECIALTY MARKS & DISTINGUISHING MARKS 1915 ~ 2011, p. 12-13.
7. ibid. p. 27.
8. ibid. p. 30.
9. REGULATIONS GOVERNING THE UNIFORMS FOR COMMISSIONED AND WARRANT OFFICERS AND ENLISTED MEN OF THE UNITED STATES COAST GUARD, July 24, 1930.
9a. http://www.uscg.mil/history/gifs/1960s_Khakis.jpg, March 2012.
10. Lewis, Dana., U. S. COAST GUARD ENLISTED RATINGS RATING SPECIALTY MARKS & DISTINGUISHING MARKS 1915 ~ 2011, p. 32.
11. ibid.
12. COMDTINST M1020.6A, July 23, 1985, para. 2-C-2 table 2-2.

Group Rate Marks
1. All Hands, "Distinguishing Marks" and Seaman Stripes Approved For Non-Rated Waves", November 1944, p. 71.
2. Lewis, Dana., U. S. COAST GUARD ENLISTED RATINGS RATING SPECIALTY MARKS & DISTINGUISHING MARKS 1915 ~ 2011, p. 34.
3. All Hands, "Designs, Wearing of Insignia", March 1948, p. 31.
4. www.uscg.mil/history/uscghist/USCGRates.pdf, March 2012.
5. ibid.

Watch Marks and Branch Marks
1. U.S. REVENUE CUTTER SERVICE UNIFORM REGULATIONS OFFICERS, WARRANT OFFICERS AND ENLISTED MEN, 1908.
2. REGULATIONS GOVERNING THE UNIFORMS FOR WARRANT OFFICERS AND ENLISTED PERSONS OF THE UNITED STATES COAST GUARD, February 18, 1916, p. 17.
3. Lewis, Dana., U. S. COAST GUARD ENLISTED RATINGS RATING SPECIALTY MARKS & DISTINGUISHING MARKS 1915 ~ 2011, p. 12.
4. Chapter 3. Coast Guard Ranks and Rates

Admiral
1. Mack, William P. and Connell, Royal W., Naval Ceremonies, Customs, and Traditions, 5th edition, Annapolis:Naval Institute Press, 1980, p. 226.
2. United States Statutes at Large, Vol. 59, p. 37.
3. Rosignoli, Guido, Badges and Insignia of World War II AIr Force-Naval-Marine, London:Peerage, 1976, p. 332-333.
4. http://en.wikipedia.org/wiki/Russell_R._Waesche, March 2012.
5. United States Statutes at Large, Vol. 60, p. 60.
6. http://en.wikipedia.org/wiki/Commandant_of_the_coast_guard, March 2012.
7. United States Statutes at Large, Vol. 61, p. 409.
8. United States Statutes at Large, Vol. 63, p. 497.
9. http://www.uscg.mil/history/people/JFFarleyBio.asp, March 2012.
10. United States Statutes at Large, Vol. 63, p. 807.
11. United States Statutes at Large, Vol. 72, p. 124.
12. http://en.wikipedia.org/wiki/List_of_United_States_Coast_Guard_four-star_admirals, March 2012.
13. United States Statutes at Large, Vol. 74, p. 144.
14. COMDTINST M1020.6F, February 18, 2009, p. 3-46.

Airman
1. All Hands, "Here's a Complete List of Rating Changes...", March 1948, p. 57.
2. United States Statutes at Large, Vol. 63, p. 802.
3. www.uscg.mil/history/uscghist/USCGRates.pdf, March 2012.
4. COMDTINST M1020.6F, February 18, 2009, p. 3-56.

Airman Apprentice
1. All Hands, "Here's a Complete List of Rating Changes...", March 1948, p. 57.
2. United States Statutes at Large, Vol. 63, p. 802.
3. www.uscg.mil/history/uscghist/USCGRates.pdf, March 2012.
4. COMDTINST M1020.6F, February 18, 2009, p. 3-56.

Airman Recruit
1. All Hands, "Here's a Complete List of Rating Changes...", March 1948, p. 57.
2. United States Statutes at Large, Vol. 63, p. 802.
3. www.uscg.mil/history/uscghist/USCGRates.pdf, March 2012.
4. ibid.
4. COMDTINST M1020.6D, May 27, 1997, p. 2D-3.

Apprentice Seaman
1. United States Statutes at Large, Vol. 41, p. 603.
2. Lewis, Dana., U. S. COAST GUARD ENLISTED RATINGS RATING SPECIALTY MARKS & DISTINGUISHING MARKS 1915 ~ 2011, p. 17-22.
3. REGULATIONS GOVERNING THE UNIFORMS FOR COMMISSIONED AND WARRANT OFFICERS AND ENLISTED MEN OF THE UNITED STATES COAST GUARD, July 24, 1930.
4. United States Statutes at Large, Vol. 42, p. 630.
5. www.uscg.mil/history/uscghist/USCGRates.pdf, March 2012.

Area Command Master Chief Petty Officer
1. COMDTINST M1020.6F, February 18, 2009, p. 3-57.
2. http://www.uscg.mil/top/units/, March 2012.
3. COMDTINST M1020.6F, February 18, 2009, p. 3-57.

Assistant Engineer
1. United States Statutes at Large, Vol. 5, p. 794.
2. Davis Smith, Horatio, Early History of the United

States Revenue Marine Service , Naval Historical Foundation, 1932, p. 69.
3. Katcher, Philip, The Civil War Source Book, New York: Facts on File, 1992, p. 197-198.
4. United States Statutes at Large, Vol. 12, p. 640.

Baker Second Class

1. Lewis, Dana., U. S. COAST GUARD ENLISTED RATINGS RATING SPECIALTY MARKS & DISTINGUISHING MARKS 1915 ~ 2011, p. 17-22.
2. REGULATIONS GOVERNING THE UNIFORMS FOR COMMISSIONED AND WARRANT OFFICERS AND ENLISTED MEN OF THE UNITED STATES COAST GUARD, July 24, 1930.
3. Stacy, John A., United States Navy Rating Badges and Marks 1833 to 2008, Mathews N.C.: ASMIC Pubs, 2008, p. 74.

Boatswain
1. Mack, William P. and Connell, Royal W., Naval Ceremonies, Customs, and Traditions, 5th edition, Annapolis:Naval Institute Press, 1980, p. 233.
2. Davis Smith, Horatio, Early History of the United States Revenue Marine Service , Naval Historical Foundation, 1932, p. 18-19.
3. ibid. p. 38.
4. ibid. p. 41.
5. ibid. p. 62.
6. Regulations Governing the Uniform of Officers and Enlisted Men of the United States Revenue Marine, 1891.
7. United States Statutes at Large, Vol. 34, p. 708.
8. U.S. REVENUE CUTTER SERVICE UNIFORM REGULATIONS OFFICERS, WARRANT OFFICERS AND ENLISTED MEN, 1908.
9. United States Statutes at Large, Vol. 41, p. 603.
10. Lewis, Dana., U. S. COAST GUARD ENLISTED RATINGS RATING SPECIALTY MARKS & DISTINGUISHING MARKS 1915 ~ 2011, p. 19.
11. http://www.uscg.mil/history/gifs/1920s_Warrant_Full_Dress.jpg, March 2012.
12. REGULATIONS GOVERNING THE UNIFORMS FOR COMMISSIONED AND WARRANT OFFICERS AND ENLISTED MEN OF THE UNITED STATES COAST GUARD, July 24, 1930.
13. REGULATIONS GOVERNING THE UNIFORMS FOR COMMISSIONED AND WARRANT OFFICERS AND ENLISTED MEN OF THE UNITED STATES COAST GUARD, Amendment No. 7, June 18, 1941.
14. United States Statutes at Large, Vol. 63, p. 807.
15. http://www.history.navy.mil/library/online/uniform_insignia.htm, March 2011.
16. Lewis, Dana., U. S. COAST GUARD ENLISTED RATINGS RATING SPECIALTY MARKS & DISTINGUISHING MARKS 1915 ~ 2011, p. 43.
17. United States Statutes at Large, Vol. 68, p. 157

Boy, Boy First Class and Boy Second Class.
1. United States Statutes at Large, Vol. 1, p. 175.
2. Lewis, Dana., U. S. COAST GUARD ENLISTED RATINGS RATING SPECIALTY MARKS & DISTINGUISHING MARKS 1915 ~ 2011, p. 17-22.
3. Gauss, Henry C., The American Goverment, Organization and Officials, NewYork: Hamerlsy, 1908, p. 406.
4. Schuyler Hartly and Graham Illustrated Catalog of Civil War Military Goods, New York: Dover, 1985.
5. Regulations Governing the Uniform of Officers and Enlisted Men of the United States Revenue Marine, 1891.

Bugler
1. United States Statutes at Large, Vol. 30, p. 17.
2. Lewis, Dana., U. S. COAST GUARD ENLISTED RATINGS RATING SPECIALTY MARKS & DISTINGUISHING MARKS 1915 ~ 2011, p. 3.
2a. Gauss, Henry C., The American Goverment, Organization and Officials, NewYork: Hamerlsy, 1908, p. 406.

3. U.S. REVENUE CUTTER SERVICE UNIFORM REGULATIONS OFFICERS, WARRANT OFFICERS AND ENLISTED MEN, 1908.
4. REGULATIONS GOVERNING THE UNIFORMS FOR WARRANT OFFICERS AND ENLISTED PERSONS OF THE UNITED STATES COAST GUARD, February 18, 1916, p. 18.
5. U.S. REVENUE CUTTER SERVICE UNIFORM REGULATIONS OFFICERS, WARRANT OFFICERS AND ENLISTED MEN, 1908.
6. REGULATIONS GOVERNING THE UNIFORMS FOR WARRANT OFFICERS AND ENLISTED PERSONS OF THE UNITED STATES COAST GUARD, February 18, 1916, p. 17.
7. General Order 43, May 18, 1920. (overlooked by Dana Lewis).
8. http://www.history.navy.mil/faqs/faq78-3.html, March 2011.
9. All Hands, "Here's a complete list of rating changes...", March 1948, p. 54.
10. REGULATIONS GOVERNING THE UNIFORMS FOR COMMISSIONED AND WARRANT OFFICERS AND ENLISTED MEN OF THE UNITED STATES COAST GUARD, July 24, 1930.

Cabin Steward
1. Amendment of Revenue Cutter Service Regulations, 1894, Treasury Department, March 25, 1895.
2. United States Statutes at Large, Vol. 17, p. 247.
3. Regulations Governing the Uniform of Officers and Enlisted Men of the United States Revenue Marine, 1891.
4. U.S. REVENUE CUTTER SERVICE UNIFORM REGULATIONS OFFICERS,
5. Gauss, Henry C., The American Goverment, Organization and Officials, NewYork: Hamerlsy, 1908, p. 406.
6. Lewis, Dana., U. S. COAST GUARD ENLISTED RATINGS RATING SPECIALTY MARKS & DISTINGUISHING MARKS 1915 ~ 2011, p. 19.
7. http://www.history.navy.mil/faqs/faq78-3.html, March 2011.
8. REGULATIONS GOVERNING THE UNIFORMS FOR COMMISSIONED AND WARRANT OFFICERS AND ENLISTED MEN OF THE UNITED STATES COAST GUARD, July 24, 1930.

Cadet
1. http://en.wikipedia.org/wiki/Coast_Guard_Academy, March 2012.
2. United States Statutes at Large, Vol. 19, p. 345.
3. Gauss, Henry C., The American Goverment, Organization and Officials, NewYork: Hamerlsy, 1908, p. 405.
4. REGULATIONS GOVERNING THE UNIFORMS FOR COMMISSIONED AND WARRANT OFFICERS AND ENLISTED MEN OF THE UNITED STATES COAST GUARD, July 24, 1930.

Cadet Cook
1. Lewis, Dana., U. S. COAST GUARD ENLISTED RATINGS RATING SPECIALTY MARKS & DISTINGUISHING MARKS 1915 ~ 2011, p.21.

Cadet Engineer
1. United States Statutes at Large, Vol. 34, p. 452.
2. Gauss, Henry C., The American Goverment, Organization and Officials, NewYork: Hamerlsy, 1908, p. 405.
3. United States Statutes at Large, Vol. 44, p. 817.

Captain
1. Oliver, Raymond, Why is a Kernal called a Colonel?, Tuscon: Fireship press, 1983, p. 29
2. ibid. p. 41.
3. United States Statutes at Large, Vol. 1, p. 175.
4. United States Statutes at Large, Vol. 1, p. 709.
5. Davis Smith, Horatio, Early History of the United States Revenue Marine Service , Naval Historical Foundation, 1932, p. 18-19.
6. ibid. p. 25.
7. ibid. p. 36.
8. ibid. p. 39.
9. Canney, Donald, Uniforms of the U.S. Coast Guard, Revenue Service, Lighthouse Service and Life Saving Service, 1997.
10. Davis Smith, Horatio, Early History of the United States Revenue Marine Service , Naval Historical Foundation, 1932, p. 40.
11. ibid. p. 41.
12. Canney, Donald, Uniforms of the U.S. Coast Guard, Revenue Service, Lighthouse Service and Life Saving Service, 1997.
13. ibid
14. http://www.usmilitariaforum.com/forums/index.php?showtopic=30608, February 2012.
15. Katcher, Philip, The Civil War Source Book, New York: Facts on File, 1992, p. 197-198.
16. Schuyler Hartly and Graham Illustrated Catalog of Civil War Military Goods, New York: Dover, 1985.
17. United States Statutes at Large, Vol. 12, p. 640.
18. United States Statutes at Large, Vol. 12, p. 583.
19. Canney, Donald, Uniforms of the U.S. Coast Guard, Revenue Service, Lighthouse Service and Life Saving Service, 1997.
20. ibid.
21. http://www.usmilitariaforum.com/forums/index.php?showtopic=30608, February 2012.
22. ibid.
23. Regulations Governing the Uniform of Officers and Enlisted Men of the United States Revenue Marine, 1891.
24. http://www.uscg.mil/history/gifs/1900_Reg_Rank_Sleeve.jpg, March 2012.
25. Canney, Donald, Uniforms of the U.S. Coast Guard, Revenue Service, Lighthouse Service and Life Saving Service, 1997.
26. U.S. REVENUE CUTTER SERVICE UNIFORM REGULATIONS OFFICERS, WARRANT OFFICERS AND ENLISTED MEN, 1908.
27. The National Geographic Magazine, "Insignia of the Uniformed Forces of the United States", October 1917, p. 418.
28. United States Statutes at Large, Vol. 41, p. 879.
29. United States Statutes at Large, Vol. 42, p. 1130.
30. Uniform Regulations United States Navy, September 20, 1922.
31. REGULATIONS GOVERNING THE UNIFORMS FOR COMMISSIONED AND WARRANT OFFICERS AND ENLISTED MEN OF THE UNITED STATES COAST GUARD, July 24, 1930.
32. United States Statutes at Large, Vol. 63, p. 807
33. COMDTINST M1020.6F, February 18, 2009, p. 3-46.

Captain Commandant
1. Davis Smith, Horatio, Early History of the United States Revenue Marine Service , Naval Historical Foundation, 1932, p. 54.
2. http://www.uscg.mil/history/FAQS/comm.asp, March 2012.
3. ibid.
4. United States Statutes at Large, Vol. 28, p. 172.
5. http://www.uscg.mil/history/people/LGShepardBio.asp, March 2012.
6. http://www.uscg.mil/history/people/CFShoemakerBio.asp , March 2012.
7. http://www.uscg.mil/history/people/WGRossBio.asp, March 2012.
8. United States Statutes at Large, Vol. 35, p. 61.
9. U.S. REVENUE CUTTER SERVICE UNIFORM REGULATIONS OFFICERS, WARRANT OFFICERS AND ENLISTED MEN, 1908.
10. http://www.uscg.mil/history/people/EPBertholfBio.asp, March 2012.
11. United States Statutes at Large, Vol. 40, p. 732.
12. http://www.uscg.mil/history/gifs/bertholf_portrait_3.jpg, March 2012.
13. http://www.uscg.mil/history/people/EPBertholfBio.asp, March 2012.
14. Register of the Commissioned and Warrant Officers and Cadets, and Ships, and Stations of the United States Coast Guard, January 1, 1921, p. 6 & 28.
15. United States Statutes at Large, Vol. 42, p. 1130.

Captain (Engineering)
1. United States Statutes at Large, Vol. 42, p. 1130.
2. Williams, Dion., Uniforms & Insignia of the U.S. Coast Guard 1918.
3. REGULATIONS GOVERNING THE UNIFORMS FOR COMMISSIONED AND WARRANT OFFICERS AND ENLISTED MEN OF THE UNITED STATES COAST GUARD, July 24, 1930.
4. Register of the Officers and Vessels of the Revenue Cutter Service of the United States, July 1, 1941, p. 52.
5. United States Coast Guard list of Commissioned and Warrant Officers on Active Duty in Order of Presedence and Temporary Menbers of the Reserve, June 30, 1944.

Captain of Engineers
1. United States Statutes at Large, Vol. 30, p. 17.
2. Regulations Governing the Uniform of Officers and Enlisted Men of the United States Revenue Marine, 1891.
3. United States Statutes at Large, Vol. 34, p. 30.
4. United States Statutes at Large, Vol. 35, p. 62.
5. U.S. REVENUE CUTTER SERVICE UNIFORM REGULATIONS OFFICERS, WARRANT OFFICERS AND ENLISTED MEN, 1908.
6. United States Statutes at Large, Vol. 41, p. 879.

Carpenter
1. Mack, William P. and Connell, Royal W., Naval Ceremonies, Customs, and Traditions, 5th edition, Annapolis:Naval Institute Press, 1980, p. 233.
2. Davis Smith, Horatio, Early History of the United States Revenue Marine Service , Naval Historical Foundation, 1932, p. 18-19.
3. ibid. p. 38.
4. ibid. p. 41.
5. ibid. p. 62.
6. Regulations Governing the Uniform of Officers and Enlisted Men of the United States Revenue Marine, 1891.
7. United States Statutes at Large, Vol. 34, p. 708.
8. U.S. REVENUE CUTTER SERVICE UNIFORM REGULATIONS OFFICERS, WARRANT OFFICERS AND ENLISTED MEN, 1908.
9. Lewis, Dana., U. S. COAST GUARD ENLISTED RATINGS RATING SPECIALTY MARKS & DISTINGUISHING MARKS 1915 ~ 2011, p. 19.
10. http://www.uscg.mil/history/gifs/1920s_Warrant_Full_Dress.jpg, March 2012.
11. REGULATIONS GOVERNING THE UNIFORMS FOR COMMISSIONED AND WARRANT OFFICERS AND ENLISTED MEN OF THE UNITED STATES COAST GUARD, July 24, 1930.
12. REGULATIONS GOVERNING THE UNIFORMS FOR COMMISSIONED AND WARRANT OFFICERS AND ENLISTED MEN OF THE UNITED STATES COAST GUARD, Amendment No. 7, June 18, 1941.
13. United States Statutes at Large, Vol. 63, p. 807.
14. http://www.history.navy.mil/library/online/uniform_insignia.htm, March 2011.
15. Lewis, Dana., U. S. COAST GUARD ENLISTED RATINGS RATING SPECIALTY MARKS & DISTINGUISHING MARKS 1915 ~ 2011, p. 43.
16. United States Statutes at Large, Vol. 68, p. 157.
17. Lewis, Dana., U. S. COAST GUARD ENLISTED RATINGS RATING SPECIALTY MARKS & DISTINGUISHING MARKS 1915 ~ 2011, p. 12.
18. ibid. p. 16.

Chief Boatswain
1. United States Statutes at Large, Vol. 44, p. 817.
2. Register of the Officers, Vessels, and Stations of the United States Coast Guard, 1927, p. 42.
3. REGULATIONS GOVERNING THE UNIFORMS FOR COMMISSIONED AND WARRANT OFFICERS AND ENLISTED MEN OF THE UNITED STATES COAST GUARD, July 24, 1930.
4. REGULATIONS GOVERNING THE UNIFORMS FOR COMMISSIONED AND WARRANT OFFICERS AND ENLISTED MEN OF THE UNITED STATES COAST GUARD, Amendment No. 7, June 18, 1941.
5. United States Statutes at Large, Vol. 63, p. 807.
6. http://www.history.navy.mil/library/online/uniform_insignia.htm, March 2011.
7. Lewis, Dana., U. S. COAST GUARD ENLISTED RATINGS RATING SPECIALTY MARKS & DISTINGUISHING MARKS 1915 ~ 2011, p. 43.
8. United States Statutes at Large, Vol. 68, p. 157.

Chief Carpenter

Chief warran1. United States Statutes at Large, Vol. 44, p. 817.
2. Register of the Officers, Vessels, and Stations of the United States Coast Guard, 1927, p. 42.
3. REGULATIONS GOVERNING THE UNIFORMS FOR COMMISSIONED AND WARRANT OFFICERS AND ENLISTED MEN OF THE UNITED STATES COAST GUARD, July 24, 1930.
4. REGULATIONS GOVERNING THE UNIFORMS FOR COMMISSIONED AND WARRANT OFFICERS AND ENLISTED MEN OF THE UNITED STATES COAST GUARD, Amendment No. 7, June 18, 1941.
5. United States Statutes at Large, Vol. 63, p. 807.
6. http://www.history.navy.mil/library/online/uniform_insignia.htm, March 2011.
7. Lewis, Dana., U. S. COAST GUARD ENLISTED RATINGS RATING SPECIALTY MARKS & DISTINGUISHING MARKS 1915 ~ 2011, p. 43.
8. United States Statutes at Large, Vol. 68, p. 157.

Chief Electrician
1. United States Statutes at Large, Vol. 44, p. 817.
2. Register of the Officers, Vessels, and Stations of the United States Coast Guard, July 1, 1936, p. 57.
3. REGULATIONS GOVERNING THE UNIFORMS FOR COMMISSIONED AND WARRANT OFFICERS AND ENLISTED MEN OF THE UNITED STATES COAST GUARD, July 24, 1930.
4. REGULATIONS GOVERNING THE UNIFORMS FOR COMMISSIONED AND WARRANT OFFICERS AND ENLISTED MEN OF THE UNITED STATES COAST GUARD, Amendment No. 7, June 18, 1941.
5. United States Statutes at Large, Vol. 63, p. 807.
6. http://www.history.navy.mil/library/online/uniform_insignia.htm, March 2011.
7. Lewis, Dana., U. S. COAST GUARD ENLISTED RATINGS RATING SPECIALTY MARKS & DISTINGUISHING MARKS 1915 ~ 2011, p. 43.
8. United States Statutes at Large, Vol. 68, p. 157.

Chief Engineer
1. United States Statutes at Large, Vol. 5, p. 794.
2. Davis Smith, Horatio, Early History of the United States Revenue Marine Service , Naval Historical Foundation, 1932, p. 68.
3. ibid. p. 69.
4. Katcher, Philip, The Civil War Source Book, New York: Facts on File, 1992, p. 197-198.
5. United States Statutes at Large, Vol. 12, p. 640.
6. Canney, Donald, Uniforms of the U.S. Coast Guard, Revenue Service, Lighthouse Service and Life Saving Service, 1997.
7. http://www.usmilitariaforum.com/forums/index.php?showtopic=30608, April 2012.
8. ibid.
9. Canney, Donald, Uniforms of the U.S. Coast Guard, Revenue Service, Lighthouse Service and Life Saving Service, 1997.
10. Regulations Governing the Uniform of Officers and Enlisted Men of the United States Revenue Marine, 1891.
11. http://www.uscg.mil/history/gifs/1900_Reg_Service_Dress.jpg, March 2012.
12. United States Statutes at Large, Vol. 32, p. 100.
13. Canney, Donald, Uniforms of the U.S. Coast Guard, Revenue Service, Lighthouse Service and Life Saving Service, 1997.
14. United States Statutes at Large, Vol. 35, p. 62.

Chief Gunner
1. United States Statutes at Large, Vol. 44, p. 817.
2. Register of the Officers, Vessels, and Stations of the United States Coast Guard, 1927, p. 42.
3. REGULATIONS GOVERNING THE UNIFORMS FOR COMMISSIONED AND WARRANT OFFICERS AND ENLISTED MEN OF THE UNITED STATES COAST GUARD, July 24, 1930.
4. REGULATIONS GOVERNING THE UNIFORMS FOR COMMISSIONED AND WARRANT OFFICERS AND ENLISTED MEN OF THE UNITED STATES COAST GUARD, Amendment No. 7, June 18, 1941.
5. United States Statutes at Large, Vol. 63, p. 807.
6. http://www.history.navy.mil/library/online/uniform_insignia.htm, March 2011.
7. Lewis, Dana., U. S. COAST GUARD ENLISTED RATINGS RATING SPECIALTY MARKS & DISTINGUISHING MARKS 1915 ~ 2011, p. 43.
8. United States Statutes at Large, Vol. 68, p. 157.

Chief Machinist
1. United States Statutes at Large, Vol. 44, p. 817.
2. Register of the Officers, Vessels, and Stations of the United States Coast Guard, 1927, p. 42.
3. REGULATIONS GOVERNING THE UNIFORMS FOR COMMISSIONED AND WARRANT OFFICERS AND ENLISTED MEN OF THE UNITED STATES COAST GUARD, July 24, 1930.
4. REGULATIONS GOVERNING THE UNIFORMS FOR COMMISSIONED AND WARRANT OFFICERS AND ENLISTED MEN OF THE UNITED STATES COAST GUARD, Amendment No. 7, June 18, 1941.
5. United States Statutes at Large, Vol. 63, p. 807.
6. http://www.history.navy.mil/library/online/uniform_insignia.htm, March 2011.
7. Lewis, Dana., U. S. COAST GUARD ENLISTED RATINGS RATING SPECIALTY MARKS & DISTINGUISHING MARKS 1915 ~ 2011, p. 43.
8. United States Statutes at Large, Vol. 68, p. 157.

Chief Oiler
1. Register of the Officers and Vessels of the Revenue Cutter Service of the United States, July 1, 1906, p. 39.
2. United States Statutes at Large, Vol. 34, p. 200.
3. United States Statutes at Large, Vol. 33, p. 1163.
4. United States Statutes at Large, Vol. 34, p. 702.
5. Register of the Officers and Vessels of the Revenue Cutter Service of the United States, July 1, 1907, p. 39.

Chief Pay Clerk
1. United States Statutes at Large, Vol. 44, p. 817.
2. Register of the Officers, Vessels, and Stations of the United States Coast Guard, 1927, p. 42.
3. REGULATIONS GOVERNING THE UNIFORMS FOR COMMISSIONED AND WARRANT OFFICERS AND ENLISTED MEN OF THE UNITED STATES COAST GUARD, July 24, 1930.
4. REGULATIONS GOVERNING THE UNIFORMS FOR COMMISSIONED AND WARRANT OFFICERS AND ENLISTED MEN OF THE UNITED STATES COAST GUARD, Amendment No. 7, June 18, 1941.
5. United States Statutes at Large, Vol. 63, p. 807.
6. http://www.history.navy.mil/library/online/uniform_insignia.htm, March 2011.
7. Lewis, Dana., U. S. COAST GUARD ENLISTED RATINGS RATING SPECIALTY MARKS & DISTINGUISHING MARKS 1915 ~ 2011, p. 43.
8. United States Statutes at Large, Vol. 68, p. 157.

Chief Petty Officer
1. United States Statutes at Large, Vol. 41, p. 603.
2. Lewis, Dana., U. S. COAST GUARD ENLISTED RATINGS RATING SPECIALTY MARKS & DISTINGUISHING MARKS 1915 ~ 2011, p. 17-19.
3. ibid. p. 11-12.
4. United States Statutes at Large, Vol. 42, p. 630.
5. REGULATIONS GOVERNING THE UNIFORMS FOR COMMISSIONED AND WARRANT OFFICERS AND ENLISTED MEN OF THE UNITED STATES COAST GUARD, July 24, 1930.
6. ibid.
7. http://www.uscg.mil/history/gifs/1960s_Khakis.jpg, March 2012.
8. United States Statutes at Large, Vol. 63, p. 807.
9. Lewis, Dana., U. S. COAST GUARD ENLISTED RATINGS RATING SPECIALTY MARKS & DISTINGUISHING MARKS 1915 ~ 2011, p. 38.
10. COMDTINST M1020.6A, July 23, 1985, para. 2-C-2 table 2-2.
11. COMDTINST M1020.6F, February 18, 2009, p. 3-53.
12. ibid. p. 3-56.
13. ibid. p. 3-57.

Chief Pharmacist
1. United States Statutes at Large, Vol. 44, p. 817.
2. Register of the Officers, Vessels, and Stations of the United States Coast Guard, July 1, 1937, p. 51.
3. REGULATIONS GOVERNING THE UNIFORMS FOR COMMISSIONED AND WARRANT OFFICERS AND ENLISTED MEN OF THE UNITED STATES COAST GUARD, July 24, 1930.
4. REGULATIONS GOVERNING THE UNIFORMS FOR COMMISSIONED AND WARRANT OFFICERS AND ENLISTED MEN OF THE UNITED STATES COAST GUARD, Amendment No. 7, June 18, 1941.
5. United States Statutes at Large, Vol. 63, p. 807.
6. http://www.history.navy.mil/library/online/uniform_insignia.htm, March 2011.
7. Lewis, Dana., U. S. COAST GUARD ENLISTED RATINGS RATING SPECIALTY MARKS & DISTINGUISHING MARKS 1915 ~ 2011, p. 43.
8. United States Statutes at Large, Vol. 68, p. 157.

Chief Photographer
1. United States Statutes at Large, Vol. 56, p. 724.
2. Lewis, Dana., U. S. COAST GUARD ENLISTED RATINGS RATING SPECIALTY MARKS & DISTINGUISHING MARKS 1915 ~ 2011, p. 44.
3. All Hands, "Ranks and Rates...", May 1943, p. 29-35.
4. Lewis, Dana., U. S. COAST GUARD ENLISTED RATINGS RATING SPECIALTY MARKS & DISTINGUISHING MARKS 1915 ~ 2011, p. 44.
5. United States Statutes at Large, Vol. 63, p. 807.
6. http://www.history.navy.mil/library/online/uniform_insignia.htm, March 2011.
7. Lewis, Dana., U. S. COAST GUARD ENLISTED RATINGS RATING SPECIALTY MARKS & DISTINGUISHING MARKS 1915 ~ 2011, p. 43.
8. United States Statutes at Large, Vol. 68, p. 157.

Chief Radio Electrician
1. United States Statutes at Large, Vol. 44, p. 817.
2. Register of the Officers, Vessels, and Stations of the United States Coast Guard, January 1, 1938, p. 41
3. REGULATIONS GOVERNING THE UNIFORMS FOR COMMISSIONED AND WARRANT OFFICERS AND ENLISTED MEN OF THE UNITED STATES COAST GUARD, July 24, 1930.
4. REGULATIONS GOVERNING THE UNIFORMS FOR COMMISSIONED AND WARRANT OFFICERS AND ENLISTED MEN OF THE UNITED STATES COAST GUARD, Amendment No. 7, June 18, 1941.
5. United States Statutes at Large, Vol. 63, p. 807.
6. http://www.history.navy.mil/library/online/uniform_insignia.htm, March 2011.
7. Lewis, Dana., U. S. COAST GUARD ENLISTED RATINGS RATING SPECIALTY MARKS & DISTINGUISHING MARKS 1915 ~ 2011, p. 43.
8. United States Statutes at Large, Vol. 68, p. 157.

Chief Ship's Clerk
1. United States Statutes at Large, Vol. 56, p. 724.
2. Lewis, Dana., U. S. COAST GUARD ENLISTED RATINGS RATING SPECIALTY MARKS & DISTINGUISHING MARKS 1915 ~ 2011, p. 44.
3. All Hands, "Ranks and Rates...", May 1943, p. 29-35.
4. Lewis, Dana., U. S. COAST GUARD ENLISTED RATINGS RATING SPECIALTY MARKS & DISTINGUISHING MARKS 1915 ~ 2011, p. 44.
5. United States Statutes at Large, Vol. 63, p. 807.
6. http://www.history.navy.mil/library/online/uniform_insignia.htm, March 2011.
7. Lewis, Dana., U. S. COAST GUARD ENLISTED RATINGS RATING SPECIALTY MARKS & DISTINGUISHING MARKS 1915 ~ 2011, p. 43.
8. United States Statutes at Large, Vol. 68, p. 157.

Chief Warrant Officer 2
1. United States Statutes at Large, Vol. 68, p. 157
2. Lewis, Dana., U. S. COAST GUARD ENLISTED RATINGS RATING SPECIALTY MARKS & DISTINGUISHING MARKS 1915 ~ 2011, p. 43.
3. COMDTINST M1020.6F, February 18, 2009, p. 3-46.

Chief Warrant Officer 3
1. United States Statutes at Large, Vol. 68, p. 157
2. Lewis, Dana., U. S. COAST GUARD ENLISTED RATINGS RATING SPECIALTY MARKS & DISTINGUISHING MARKS 1915 ~ 2011, p. 43.
3. COMDTINST M1020.6F, February 18, 2009, p. 3-46.

Chief Warrant Officer 4
1. United States Statutes at Large, Vol. 68, p. 157.
2. Lewis, Dana., U. S. COAST GUARD ENLISTED RATINGS RATING SPECIALTY MARKS & DISTINGUISHING MARKS 1915 ~ 2011, p. 43.
3. COMDTINST M1020.6F, February 18, 2009, p. 3-46.

Coal Heaver
1. United States Statutes at Large, Vol. 30, p. 1081.
2. Regulations Governing the Uniform of Officers and Enlisted Men of the United States Revenue Marine, 1891.
3. U.S. REVENUE CUTTER SERVICE UNIFORM REGULATIONS OFFICERS, WARRANT OFFICERS AND ENLISTED MEN, 1908.
4. Lewis, Dana., U. S. COAST GUARD ENLISTED RATINGS RATING SPECIALTY MARKS & DISTINGUISHING MARKS 1915 ~ 2011, p. 21.

Coal Passer
1. United States Statutes at Large, Vol. 5, p. 794.
2. Schuyler Hartly and Graham Illustrated Catalog of Civil War Military Goods, New York: Dover, 1985.
3. Regulations Governing the Uniform of Officers and Enlisted Men of the United States Revenue Marine, 1891.
4. United States Statutes at Large, Vol. 30, p. 1081.

Command Master Chief Petty Officer
1. COMDTINST M1020.6A, July 23, 1985, p. 2-C page 6.
2. COMDTINST M1020.6F, February 18, 2009, p. 3-57.

Commander
1. Oliver, Raymond, Why is a Kernal called a Colonel?, Tuscon: Fireship press, 1983, p. 37.
2. United States Statutes at Large, Vol. 41, p. 879.
3. REGULATIONS GOVERNING THE UNIFORMS FOR COMMISSIONED AND WARRANT OFFICERS AND ENLISTED MEN OF THE UNITED STATES COAST GUARD, July 24, 1930.
4. United States Statutes at Large, Vol. 63, p. 807.
5. COMDTINST M1020.6F, February 18, 2009, p. 3-46.

Commander (Engineering)
1. United States Statutes at Large, Vol. 42, p. 1130.
2. Williams, Dion., Uniforms & Insignia of the U.S. Coast Guard 1918.
3. REGULATIONS GOVERNING THE UNIFORMS FOR COMMISSIONED AND WARRANT OFFICERS AND ENLISTED MEN OF THE UNITED STATES COAST GUARD, July 24, 1930.
4. Register of the Officers and Vessels of the Revenue Cutter Service of the United States, July 1, 1941, p. 54.
5. United States Coast Guard list of Commissined and Warrant Officers on Active Duty in Order of Presedence and Temporary Menbers of the Reserve, June 30, 1944.

Commodore
1. Oliver, Raymond, Why is a Kernal called a Colonel?, Tuscon: Fireship press, 1983, p. 43.
2. United States Statutes at Large, Vol. 12, p. 583.
3. United States Statutes at Large, Vol. 40, p. 732.
4. http://www.uscg.mil/history/gifs/bertholf_portrait_3.jpg, March 2012.
5. http://www.uscg.mil/history/people/EPBertholfBio.asp, March 2012.
6. Register of the Commissioned and Warrant Officers and Cadets, and Ships, and Stations of the United States Coast Guard, January 1, 1921, p. 6 & 28.
7. United States Statutes at Large, Vol. 42, p. 1130.
8. United States Statutes at Large, Vol. 57, p. 59.
9. List of regular and reserve commissioned and warrant officers on active duty in order of precedence, and temporary members of the reserve, June 30, 1944, p. 1.
10. Rosignoli, Guido, Badges and Inisnigia of World War II AIr Force-Naval-Marine, London: Peerage, 1976, 1983, p. 330-332.
11. United States Statutes at Large, Vol. 61, p. 409.
12. United States Statutes at Large, Vol. 94, p. 2887.
13. United States Statutes at Large, Vol. 95, p. 1105.
14. United States Statutes at Large, Vol. 98, p. 2873.
15. COMDTINST M1020.6A, July 23, 1985, p. 2-c 4, 2-c 13 and 2-c 15.
16. United States Statutes at Large, Vol. 99, p. 628.

Constructor
1. United States Statutes at Large, Vol. 30, p. 604.
2. Register of the Officers and Vessels of the Revenue Cutter Service of the United States, July 1, 1906, p. 32.
3. United States Statutes at Large, Vol. 34, p. 453.
4. Register of the Officers and Vessels of the Revenue Cutter Service of the United States, July 1, 1906, p. 39.
5. Register of the Officers and Vessels of the Revenue Cutter Service of the United States, July 1, 1907, p. 61.
6. ibid. p. 32.
7. U.S. REVENUE CUTTER SERVICE UNIFORM REGULATIONS OFFICERS, WARRANT OFFICERS AND ENLISTED MEN, 1908.
7a. The National Geographic Magazine, "Insignia of the Uniformed Forces of the United States", October 1917, p. 418.
8. http://wc.rootsweb.ancestry.com/cgi-bin/igm.cgi?op=GET&db=yarnall1&id=I07661, April 2012
9. Register of the Officers and Vessels of the Revenue Cutter Service of the United States, August 15, 1915, p. 36.
16. Williams, Dion., Uniforms & Insignia of the U.S. Coast Guard 1918.
11. United States Statutes at Large, Vol. 40, p. 732.
12. United States Statutes at Large, Vol. 42, p. 1131.
13. United States Statutes at Large, Vol. 44, p. 817.
14. Register of the Officers and Vessels of the Coast Guard of the United States, January 1, 1928, p. 38.
15. Register of the Officers and Vessels of the Coast Guard of the United States, January 1, 1929, p. 38.
16. Register of the Officers and Vessels of the Coast Guard of the United States, January 1, 1934, p. 74.
17. Register of the Officers and Vessels of the Coast Guard of the United States, July 1, 1936, p. 53.
18. United States Statutes at Large, Vol. 53, p. 1218.

Cook
1. Davis Smith, Horatio, Early History of the United States Revenue Marine Service , Naval Historical Foundation, 1932, p. 18-19.
2. ibid. p. 62.
3. Schuyler Hartly and Graham Illustrated Catalog of Civil War Military Goods, New York: Dover, 1985.
4. Regulations Governing the Uniform of Officers and Enlisted Men of the United States Revenue Marine, 1891.
5. U.S. REVENUE CUTTER SERVICE UNIFORM REGULATIONS OFFICERS, WARRANT OFFICERS AND ENLISTED MEN, 1908.
6. Lewis, Dana., U. S. COAST GUARD ENLISTED RATINGS RATING SPECIALTY MARKS & DISTINGUISHING MARKS 1915 ~ 2011, p. 21.

District Commander
1. United States Statutes at Large, Vol. 44, p. 815.
2. Register of the Officers and Vessels of the Coast Guard of the United States, March 15, 1927, p. 38.
3. Register of the Officers and Vessels of the Coast Guard of the United States, January 1, 1930, p. 71.
4. Register of the Officers and Vessels of the Coast Guard of the United States, January 1, 1932, p. 72.
5. ibid.p. 41.
6. Register of the Officers and Vessels of the Coast Guard of the United States, February 1, 1933, p. 45.
7. Register of the Officers and Vessels of the Coast Guard of the United States, January 1, 1935, p. 78.
8. Register of the Officers and Vessels of the Coast Guard of the United States, July 1, 1934, p. 75.
9. Register of the Officers and Vessels of the Coast Guard of the United States, January 1, 1935, p. 78.
10. Register of the Officers and Vessels of the Coast Guard of the United States, July 1, 1935, p. 47.
11. Register of the Officers and Vessels of the Coast Guard of the United States, July 1, 1936, p. 53.
12. Register of the Officers and Vessels of the Coast Guard of the United States, July 1, 1937, p. 46.
13. ibid. p. 79.
14. ibid. p. 46.
15. Register of the Officers and Vessels of the Coast Guard of the United States, July 1, 1938, p. 50.
16. Register of the Officers and Vessels of the Coast Guard of the United States, July 1, 1939, p. 79.
17. ibid. p. 48.
18. United States Statutes at Large, Vol. 53, p. 1218.

District Superintendent
1. United States Statutes at Large, Vol. 38, p. 800.
2. Register of the Officers and Vessels of the Coast Guard of the United States, August 1, 1915, p. 3.
3. ibid. p. 37.
4. The National Geographic Magazine, "Insignia of the Uniformed Forces of the United States", October 1917, p. 418.
5. http://www.histopolis.com/Grave/Detail.aspx?GraveID=809566332, April 2012.
6. Register of the Officers and Vessels of the Coast Guard of the United States, August 1, 1921, p. 61.
7. ibid. p. 66.
8. ibid. p. 42.
9. Register of the Officers and Vessels of the Coast Guard of the United States, January 1, 1923, p. 68.
10. ibid. p. 40.
11. Register of the Officers and Vessels of the Coast Guard of the United States, January 1, 1924, p. 55.
12. ibid. p. 36.
13. Register of the Officers and Vessels of the Coast Guard of the United States, January 1, 1926, p. 77.

14. Register of the Officers and Vessels of the Coast Guard of the United States, January 1, 1925, p. 40.
15. Register of the Officers and Vessels of the Coast Guard of the United States, January 1, 1926, p. 77.
16. ibid. p. 40.
17. United States Statutes at Large, Vol. 44, p. 815.

Electrician
1. United States Statutes at Large, Vol. 43, p. 1274.
2. Register of the Officers and Vessels of the Coast Guard of the United States, January 1, 1926, p. 50.
3. Lewis, Dana., U. S. COAST GUARD ENLISTED RATINGS RATING SPECIALTY MARKS & DISTINGUISHING MARKS 1915 ~ 2011, p. 28.
4. REGULATIONS GOVERNING THE UNIFORMS FOR COMMISSIONED AND WARRANT OFFICERS AND ENLISTED MEN OF THE UNITED STATES COAST GUARD, July 24, 1930.
5. REGULATIONS GOVERNING THE UNIFORMS FOR COMMISSIONED AND WARRANT OFFICERS AND ENLISTED MEN OF THE UNITED STATES COAST GUARD, Amendment No. 7, June 18, 1941.
6. United States Statutes at Large, Vol. 63, p. 807
7. http://www.history.navy.mil/library/online/uniform_insignia.htm, March 2011.
8. Lewis, Dana., U. S. COAST GUARD ENLISTED RATINGS RATING SPECIALTY MARKS & DISTINGUISHING MARKS 1915 ~ 2011, p. 43.
9. United States Statutes at Large, Vol. 68, p. 157

Engineer in Chief
1. United States Statutes at Large, Vol. 28, p. 172.
3. United States Statutes at Large, Vol. 30, p. 17.
4. United States Statutes at Large, Vol. 34, p. 30.
5. U.S. REVENUE CUTTER SERVICE UNIFORM REGULATIONS OFFICERS, WARRANT OFFICERS AND ENLISTED MEN, 1908.
6. United States Statutes at Large, Vol. 40, p. 732.
7. Regiser of the Commissioned and Warrant Officers and Cadets, and Ships, and Stations of the United States Coast Guard, January 1, 1921, p. 28.
8. United States Statutes at Large, Vol. 42, p. 1130.
9. United States Statutes at Large, Vol. 53, p. 757.
10. REGULATIONS GOVERNING THE UNIFORMS FOR COMMISSIONED AND WARRANT OFFICERS AND ENLISTED MEN OF THE UNITED STATES COAST GUARD, July 24, 1930, (the word "engineer" no mentioned).
11. Register of the Officers and Vessels of the Revenue Cutter Service of the United States, July 1, 1941, p. 54.
12. United States Coast Guard list of Commissined and Warrant Officers on Active Duty in Order of Presedence and Temporary Menbers of the Reserve, June 30, 1944.

Ensign
1. United States Statutes at Large, Vol. 12, p. 583.
2. United States Statutes at Large, Vol. 3, p. 224.
3. United States Statutes at Large, Vol. 41, p. 879.
4. Williams, Dion., Uniforms & Insignia of the U.S. Coast Guard 1918.
5. REGULATIONS GOVERNING THE UNIFORMS FOR COMMISSIONED AND WARRANT OFFICERS AND ENLISTED MEN OF THE UNITED STATES COAST GUARD, July 24, 1930.
6. Uniform Regulations United States Navy, September 20, 1922, p. 19.
7. United States Statutes at Large, Vol. 63, p. 807.
8. COMDTINST M1020.6F, February 18, 2009, p. 3-46.

Ensign (Engineering)
1. United States Statutes at Large, Vol. 41, p. 879.
2. REGULATIONS GOVERNING THE UNIFORMS FOR COMMISSIONED AND WARRANT OFFICERS AND ENLISTED MEN OF THE UNITED STATES COAST GUARD, July 24, 1930.
3. Register of the Officers and Vessels of the Revenue Cutter Service of the United 4, July 1, 1941, p. 54.
12. United States Coast Guard list of Commissined and Warrant Officers on Active Duty in Order of Presedence and Temporary Menbers of the Reserve, June 30, 1944.

Fireman
1. United States Statutes at Large, Vol. 5, p. 794.
2. Schuyler Hartly and Graham Illustrated Catalog of Civil War Military Goods, New York: Dover, 1985.
3. Regulations Governing the Uniform of Officers and Enlisted Men of the United States Revenue Marine, 1891.
4. U.S. REVENUE CUTTER SERVICE UNIFORM REGULATIONS OFFICERS, WARRANT OFFICERS AND ENLISTED MEN, 1908.
5. Lewis, Dana., U. S. COAST GUARD ENLISTED RATINGS RATING SPECIALTY MARKS & DISTINGUISHING MARKS 1915 ~ 2011, p. 16.
6. ibid. p. 19.
7. www.uscg.mil/history/uscghist/USCGRates.pdf, March 2012.
8. United States Statutes at Large, Vol. 63, p. 802.
9. COMDTINST M1020.6F, February 18, 2009, p. 3-56.

Fireman Apprentice
1. www.uscg.mil/history/uscghist/USCGRates.pdf, March 2012.
2. United States Statutes at Large, Vol. 63, p. 802.
3. COMDTINST M1020.6F, February 18, 2009, p. 3-56.

Fireman First Class
1. United States Statutes at Large, Vol. 41, p. 603.
2. Lewis, Dana., U. S. COAST GUARD ENLISTED RATINGS RATING SPECIALTY MARKS & DISTINGUISHING MARKS 1915 ~ 2011, p. 19.
3. United States Statutes at Large, Vol. 42, p. 630.
4. REGULATIONS GOVERNING THE UNIFORMS FOR COMMISSIONED AND WARRANT OFFICERS AND ENLISTED MEN OF THE UNITED STATES COAST GUARD, July 24, 1930.
5. Lewis, Dana., U. S. COAST GUARD ENLISTED RATINGS RATING SPECIALTY MARKS & DISTINGUISHING MARKS 1915 ~ 2011, p. 34.
6. www.uscg.mil/history/uscghist/USCGRates.pdf, March 2012.

Fireman Recruit
1. All Hands, "Changes Made in Rating Structure,...", August 1948, p. 53.
2. United States Statutes at Large, Vol. 63, p. 802
3. www.uscg.mil/history/uscghist/USCGRates.pdf, March 2012.
4. COMDTINST M1020.6D, May 27, 1997, p. 2D-3.

Fireman Second Class
1. United States Statutes at Large, Vol. 41, p. 603.
2. Lewis, Dana., U. S. COAST GUARD ENLISTED RATINGS RATING SPECIALTY MARKS & DISTINGUISHING MARKS 1915 ~ 2011, p. 19.
3. United States Statutes at Large, Vol. 42, p. 630.
4. REGULATIONS GOVERNING THE UNIFORMS FOR COMMISSIONED AND WARRANT OFFICERS AND ENLISTED MEN OF THE UNITED STATES COAST GUARD, July 24, 1930.
5. Lewis, Dana., U. S. COAST GUARD ENLISTED RATINGS RATING SPECIALTY MARKS & DISTINGUISHING MARKS 1915 ~ 2011, p. 34.
6. www.uscg.mil/history/uscghist/USCGRates.pdf, March 2012.

Fireman Third Class
1. United States Statutes at Large, Vol. 41, p. 603.
2. Lewis, Dana., U. S. COAST GUARD ENLISTED RATINGS RATING SPECIALTY MARKS & DISTINGUISHING MARKS 1915 ~ 2011, p. 19.
3. United States Statutes at Large, Vol. 42, p. 630.
4. REGULATIONS GOVERNING THE UNIFORMS FOR COMMISSIONED AND WARRANT OFFICERS AND ENLISTED MEN OF THE UNITED STATES COAST GUARD, July 24, 1930.
5. Lewis, Dana., U. S. COAST GUARD ENLISTED RATINGS RATING SPECIALTY MARKS & DISTINGUISHING MARKS 1915 ~ 2011, p. 34.
6. www.uscg.mil/history/uscghist/USCGRates.pdf, March 2012.

First Assistant Engineer
1. Katcher, Philip, The Civil War Source Book, New York: Facts on File, 1992, p. 197-198.
2. United States Statutes at Large, Vol. 12, p. 583.
3. Canney, Donald, Uniforms of the U.S. Coast Guard, Revenue Service, Lighthouse Service and Life Saving Service, 1997.
4. ibid.
5. http://www.usmilitariaforum.com/forums/index.php?showtopic=30608, February 2012.
6. ibid.
7. http://www.uscg.mil/history/gifs/1900_Reg_Rank_Sleeve.jpg, March 2012.

8. United States Statutes at Large, Vol. 35, p. 62.

First Lieutenant
1. Oliver, Raymond, Why is a Kernal called a Colonel?, Tuscon: Fireship press, 1983, p. 25.
2. ibid. p. 41.
3. United States Statutes at Large, Vol. 1, p. 175.
4. United States Statutes at Large, Vol. 1, p. 709.
5. Davis Smith, Horatio, Early History of the United States Revenue Marine Service , Naval Historical Foundation, 1932, p. 18-19.
6. ibid. p. 25.
7. United States Statutes at Large, Vol. 5, p. 65.
8. Davis Smith, Horatio, Early History of the United States Revenue Marine Service , Naval Historical Foundation, 1932, p. 36.
9. ibid. p. 39.
10. Canney, Donald, Uniforms of the U.S. Coast Guard, Revenue Service, Lighthouse Service and Life Saving Service, 1997.
11. Davis Smith, Horatio, Early History of the United States Revenue Marine Service , Naval Historical Foundation, 1932, p. 40.
12. ibid. p. 41.
13. Canney, Donald, Uniforms of the U.S. Coast Guard, Revenue Service, Lighthouse Service and Life Saving Service, 1997.
14. ibid
15. http://www.usmilitariaforum.com/forums/index.php?showtopic=30608, February 2012.
16. Katcher, Philip, The Civil War Source Book, New York: Facts on File, 1992, p. 197-198.
17. Schuyler Hartly and Graham Illustrated Catalog of Civil War Military Goods, New York: Dover, 1985.
18. United States Statutes at Large, Vol. 12, p. 640.
19. Katcher, Philip, The Civil War Source Book, New York: Facts on File, 1992, p. 197-198.
20. ibid.
21. http://www.usmilitariaforum.com/forums/index.php?showtopic=30608, February 2012.
22. ibid.
23 Regulations Governing the Uniform of Officers and Enlisted Men of the United States Revenue Marine, 1891.
24. http://www.uscg.mil/history/gifs/1900_Reg_Rank_Sleeve.jpg, March 2012.
25. Canney, Donald, Uniforms of the U.S. Coast Guard, Revenue Service, Lighthouse Service and Life Saving Service, 1997.
26. U.S. REVENUE CUTTER SERVICE UNIFORM REGULATIONS OFFICERS, WARRANT OFFICERS AND ENLISTED MEN, 1908.
27. The National Geographic Magazine, "Insignia of the Uniformed Forces of the United States", October 1917, p. 418.
28. United States Statutes at Large, Vol. 41, p. 879.

First Lieutenant of Engineers
1. United States Statutes at Large, Vol. 35, p. 62.
2. U.S. REVENUE CUTTER SERVICE UNIFORM REGULATIONS OFFICERS, WARRANT OFFICERS AND ENLISTED MEN, 1908.
3. The National Geographic Magazine, "Insignia of the Uniformed Forces of the United States", October 1917, p. 418.
4. United States Statutes at Large, Vol. 41, p. 879.

First Mate
1. United States Statutes at Large, Vol. 1, p. 175.
2. United States Statutes at Large, Vol. 1, p. 709.
3. Davis Smith, Horatio, Early History of the United States Revenue Marine Service , Naval Historical Foundation, 1932, p. 18-19.
4. ibid. p. 25.
5. United States Statutes at Large, Vol. 5, p. 65.

Gunner
1. Davis Smith, Horatio, Early History of the United States Revenue Marine Service , Naval Historical Foundation, 1932, p. 18-19.
2. ibid. p. 38.
3. ibid. p. 41.
4. ibid. p. 62.
5. Regulations Governing the Uniform of Officers and Enlisted Men of the United States Revenue Marine, 1891.
6. United States Statutes at Large, Vol. 34, p. 708.

7. U.S. REVENUE CUTTER SERVICE UNIFORM REGULATIONS OFFICERS, WARRANT OFFICERS AND ENLISTED MEN, 1908.
8. Lewis, Dana., U. S. COAST GUARD ENLISTED RATINGS RATING SPECIALTY MARKS & DISTINGUISHING MARKS 1915 ~ 2011, p. 19.
9. http://www.uscg.mil/history/gifs/1920s_Warrant_Full_Dress.jpg, March 2012.
10. REGULATIONS GOVERNING THE UNIFORMS FOR COMMISSIONED AND WARRANT OFFICERS AND ENLISTED MEN OF THE UNITED STATES COAST GUARD, July 24, 1930.
11. REGULATIONS GOVERNING THE UNIFORMS FOR COMMISSIONED AND WARRANT OFFICERS AND ENLISTED MEN OF THE UNITED STATES COAST GUARD, Amendment No. 7, June 18, 1941.
12. United States Statutes at Large, Vol. 63, p. 807.
13. http://www.history.navy.mil/library/online/uniform_insignia.htm, March 2011.
14. Lewis, Dana., U. S. COAST GUARD ENLISTED RATINGS RATING SPECIALTY MARKS & DISTINGUISHING MARKS 1915 ~ 2011, p. 43.
15. United States Statutes at Large, Vol. 68, p. 157

Hospital Apprentice (First Class and Second Class?)
1. REGULATIONS GOVERNING THE UNIFORMS FOR COMMISSIONED AND WARRANT OFFICERS AND ENLISTED MEN OF THE UNITED STATES COAST GUARD, July 24, 1930.
2. General Order 43, May 18, 1920.
3. www.uscg.mil/history/uscghist/USCGRates.pdf, March 2012.
4. Uniform Regulations United States Navy, September 20, 1922, p. 26-27.
5. Stacy, John A., United States Navy Ratring Badges and Marks 1833 to 2008, Mathews N.C.: ASMIC Pubs, 2008, p. 22.
6. Lewis, Dana., U. S. COAST GUARD ENLISTED RATINGS RATING SPECIALTY MARKS & DISTINGUISHING MARKS 1915 ~ 2011, p. 34.
7. www.uscg.mil/history/uscghist/USCGRates.pdf, March 2012.

Hospitalman
1. www.uscg.mil/history/uscghist/USCGRates.pdf, March 2012.
2. ibid.
3. United States Statutes at Large, Vol. 63, p. 802.
4. www.uscg.mil/history/uscghist/USCGRates.pdf, March 2012.

Hospitalman Apprentice
1. www.uscg.mil/history/uscghist/USCGRates.pdf, March 2012.
2. ibid.
3. United States Statutes at Large, Vol. 63, p. 802.
4. www.uscg.mil/history/uscghist/USCGRates.pdf, March 2012.

Hospitalman Recruit
1. www.uscg.mil/history/uscghist/USCGRates.pdf, March 2012.
2. ibid.
3. United States Statutes at Large, Vol. 63, p. 802.
4. www.uscg.mil/history/uscghist/USCGRates.pdf, March 2012.

Keeper
1. United States Statutes at Large, Vol. 38, p. 800.
2. Regulations for the Government of the Life-Saving Service of the United States, 1899 , Washington , D.C.: Government Printing Office, 1899.
3. REGULATIONS GOVERNING THE UNIFORMS FOR WARRANT OFFICERS AND ENLISTED PERSONS OF THE UNITED STATES COAST GUARD, February 18, 1916, p. 3-6.
4. Lewis, Dana., U. S. COAST GUARD ENLISTED RATINGS RATING SPECIALTY MARKS & DISTINGUISHING MARKS 1915 ~ 2011, p. 19.

Landsman
1. United States Statutes at Large, Vol. 41, p. 603.
2. Lewis, Dana., U. S. COAST GUARD ENLISTED RATINGS RATING SPECIALTY MARKS & DISTINGUISHING MARKS 1915 ~ 2011, p. 19.

3. Williams, Dion., Uniforms & Insignia of the U.S. Coast Guard 1918.
4. http://www.history.navy.mil/faqs/faq78-3.htm, October 2011.

Lieutenant
1. Oliver, Raymond, Why is a Kernal called a Colonel?, Tuscon: Fireship press, 1983, p. 25.
2. United States Statutes at Large, Vol. 41, p. 879.
3. REGULATIONS GOVERNING THE UNIFORMS FOR COMMISSIONED AND WARRANT OFFICERS AND ENLISTED MEN OF THE UNITED STATES COAST GUARD, July 24, 1930.
4. United States Statutes at Large, Vol. 63, p. 807.
5. COMDTINST M1020.6F, February 18, 2009, p. 3-46.

Lieutenant (Engineering)
1. United States Statutes at Large, Vol. 41, p. 879.
2. REGULATIONS GOVERNING THE UNIFORMS FOR COMMISSIONED AND WARRANT OFFICERS AND ENLISTED MEN OF THE UNITED STATES COAST GUARD, July 24, 1930.
3. Register of the Officers and Vessels of the Revenue Cutter Service of the United 4, July 1, 1941, p. 54.
12. United States Coast Guard list of Commissined and Warrant Officers on Active Duty in Order of Presedence and Temporary Menbers of the Reserve, June 30, 1944.

Lieutenant (Junior Grade)
1. Oliver, Raymond, Why is a Kernal called a Colonel?, Tuscon: Fireship press, 1983, p. 25.
2. United States Statutes at Large, Vol. 41, p. 879.
3. REGULATIONS GOVERNING THE UNIFORMS FOR COMMISSIONED AND WARRANT OFFICERS AND ENLISTED MEN OF THE UNITED STATES COAST GUARD, July 24, 1930.
4. United States Statutes at Large, Vol. 63, p. 807.
5. COMDTINST M1020.6F, February 18, 2009, p. 3-46.

Lieutenant (Junior Grade) (Engineering)
1. United States Statutes at Large, Vol. 41, p. 879.
2. REGULATIONS GOVERNING THE UNIFORMS FOR COMMISSIONED AND WARRANT OFFICERS AND ENLISTED MEN OF THE UNITED STATES COAST GUARD, July 24, 1930.
3. Register of the Officers and Vessels of the Revenue Cutter Service of the United 4, July 1, 1941, p. 54.
12. United States Coast Guard list of Commissined and Warrant Officers on Active Duty in Order of Presedence and Temporary Menbers of the Reserve, June 30, 1944.

Lieutenant Commander
1. United States Statutes at Large, Vol. 41, p. 879.
2. REGULATIONS GOVERNING THE UNIFORMS FOR COMMISSIONED AND WARRANT OFFICERS AND ENLISTED MEN OF THE UNITED STATES COAST GUARD, July 24, 1930.
3. United States Statutes at Large, Vol. 63, p. 807.
4. COMDTINST M1020.6F, February 18, 2009, p. 3-46.

Lieutenant Commander (Engineering)
1. United States Statutes at Large, Vol. 41, p. 879.
2. REGULATIONS GOVERNING THE UNIFORMS FOR COMMISSIONED AND WARRANT OFFICERS AND ENLISTED MEN OF THE UNITED STATES COAST GUARD, July 24, 1930.
3. Register of the Officers and Vessels of the Revenue Cutter Service of the United 4, July 1, 1941, p. 54.
12. United States Coast Guard list of Commissined and Warrant Officers on Active Duty in Order of Presedence and Temporary Menbers of the Reserve, June 30, 1944.

Machinist
1. Register of the Officers and Vessels of the Revenue Cutter Service of the United States, July 1, 1906, p. 39.
2. Register of the Officers and Vessels of the Revenue Cutter Service of the United States, July 1, 1907, p. 39.
3. U.S. REVENUE CUTTER SERVICE UNIFORM REGULATIONS OFFICERS, WARRANT OFFICERS AND ENLISTED MEN, 1908.
4. Lewis, Dana., U. S. COAST GUARD ENLISTED RATINGS RATING SPECIALTY MARKS & DISTINGUISHING MARKS 1915 ~ 2011, p. 19.
5. http://www.uscg.mil/history/gifs/1920s_Warrant_Full_Dress.jpg, March 2012.
6. REGULATIONS GOVERNING THE UNIFORMS FOR COMMISSIONED AND WARRANT OFFICERS AND ENLISTED MEN OF THE UNITED STATES COAST GUARD, July 24, 1930.
7. REGULATIONS GOVERNING THE UNIFORMS FOR COMMISSIONED AND WARRANT OFFICERS AND ENLISTED MEN OF THE UNITED STATES COAST GUARD, Amendment No. 7, June 18, 1941.
8. United States Statutes at Large, Vol. 63, p. 807.
9. http://www.history.navy.mil/library/online/uniform_insignia.htm, March 2011.
10. Lewis, Dana., U. S. COAST GUARD ENLISTED RATINGS RATING SPECIALTY MARKS & DISTINGUISHING MARKS 1915 ~ 2011, p. 43.
11. United States Statutes at Large, Vol. 68, p. 157

Marine
1. Davis Smith, Horatio, Early History of the United States Revenue Marine Service , Naval Historical Foundation, 1932, p. 18-19.
2. United States Statutes at Large, Vol. 1, p. 175.
3. United States Statutes at Large, Vol. 1, p. 709.

Mariner
1. United States Statutes at Large, Vol. 1, p. 175.
2. United States Statutes at Large, Vol. 1, p. 709.
3. Davis Smith, Horatio, Early History of the United States Revenue Marine Service , Naval Historical Foundation, 1932, p. 62.

Master
1. United States Statutes at Large, Vol. 1, p. 175.
2. United States Statutes at Large, Vol. 1, p. 709.
3. Davis Smith, Horatio, Early History of the United States Revenue Marine Service , Naval Historical Foundation, 1932, p. 18-19.
4. ibid. p. 25.

Master Chief Petty Officer
1. United States Statutes at Large, Vol. 72, p. 123
2. Lewis, Dana., U. S. COAST GUARD ENLISTED RATINGS RATING SPECIALTY MARKS & DISTINGUISHING MARKS 1915 ~ 2011, p. 32.
3. ibid.
4. ibid.
5. COMDTINST M1020.6F, February 18, 2009, p. 3-53.
6. ibid. p. 3-56.
7. ibid. p. 3-57.

Master Chief Petty Officer of the Coast Guard
1. The Coast Guard Reservist , "Master Chief Petty Officer of the Coast Guard", November 1969, p. 2.
2. http://www.uscg.mil/history/people/Charles_Calhoun.asp, May 2012.
3. ibid.
4. http://www.uscg.mil/history/people/Phillip_Smith.asp, May 2012.
5. http://www.uscg.mil/history/people/Hollis_Stephens.asp, May 2012.
6. http://www.uscg.mil/history/people/Carl_Constantine.asp, May 2012.
7. http://www.uscg.mil/history/people/Allen_Thiele.asp, May 2012.
8. http://www.uscg.mil/history/people/Jay_Lloyd.asp, May 2012.
9. http://www.uscg.mil/history/people/Rick_Trent.asp, May 2012.
10. http://www.uscg.mil/history/people/vincent_patton.asp, May 2012.
11. http://www.uscg.mil/history/people/mcpocg_welch.asp, May 2012.
12. http://www.uscg.mil/history/people/mcpocg_Bowen.asp, May 2012.
13. http://en.wikipedia.org/wiki/Michael_P._Leavitt, May 2012.
14. COMDTINST M1020.6F, February 18, 2009, p. 3-53.
15. ibid. p. 3-56.
16. ibid. p. 3-57.

Master's Mate
1. Register of the Officers and Vessels of the Revenue Cutter Service of the United States, July 1, 1907, p. 36.

2. United States Statutes at Large, Vol. 34, p. 200.
3. United States Statutes at Large, Vol. 33, p. 1163.
4. United States Statutes at Large, Vol. 34, p. 702.
5. U.S. REVENUE CUTTER SERVICE UNIFORM REGULATIONS OFFICERS, WARRANT OFFICERS AND ENLISTED MEN, 1908.
6. Lewis, Dana., U. S. COAST GUARD ENLISTED RATINGS RATING SPECIALTY MARKS & DISTINGUISHING MARKS 1915 ~ 2011, p. 19.

Mess Attendant First Class
1. Lewis, Dana., U. S. COAST GUARD ENLISTED RATINGS RATING SPECIALTY MARKS & DISTINGUISHING MARKS 1915 ~ 2011, p. 21.
2. uniform regulations governing the insignia and uniforms of commissioned officers, warrant officers, and enlistedmen of the United States Navy, January 21, 1905, p. 42.
3. Stacy, John A., United States Navy Ratring Badges and Marks 1833 to 2008, Mathews N.C.: ASMIC Pubs, 2008, p. 74. all other messmen rates began to wear the crescent at this time and the 1922 regulations p. 27 specifies them for Mess Attendants.
4. Register of the Commissioned And Warrant Officers of the Navy of the United States..., January 1, 1923, p. 307.
5. REGULATIONS GOVERNING THE UNIFORMS FOR COMMISSIONED AND WARRANT OFFICERS AND ENLISTED MEN OF THE UNITED STATES COAST GUARD, July 24, 1930.
6. http://www.history.navy.mil/faqs/faq78-3.html, March 2011.
7. www.uscg.mil/history/uscghist/USCGRates.pdf, March 2012.

Mess Attendant Second Class
1. Lewis, Dana., U. S. COAST GUARD ENLISTED RATINGS RATING SPECIALTY MARKS & DISTINGUISHING MARKS 1915 ~ 2011, p. 21.
2. uniform regulations governing the insignia and uniforms of commissioned officers, warrant officers, and enlistedmen of the United States Navy, January 21, 1905, p. 42.
3. Stacy, John A., United States Navy Ratring Badges and Marks 1833 to 2008, Mathews N.C.: ASMIC Pubs, 2008, p. 74. all other messmen rates began to wear the crescent at this time and the 1922 regulations p. 27 specifies them for Mess Attendants.
4. Register of the Commissioned And Warrant Officers of the Navy of the United States..., January 1, 1923, p. 307.
5. REGULATIONS GOVERNING THE UNIFORMS FOR COMMISSIONED AND WARRANT OFFICERS AND ENLISTED MEN OF THE UNITED STATES COAST GUARD, July 24, 1930.
6. http://www.history.navy.mil/faqs/faq78-3.html, March 2011.
7. www.uscg.mil/history/uscghist/USCGRates.pdf, March 2012.

Mess Attendant Third Class
1. Lewis, Dana., U. S. COAST GUARD ENLISTED RATINGS RATING SPECIALTY MARKS & DISTINGUISHING MARKS 1915 ~ 2011, p. 21.
2. uniform regulations governing the insignia and uniforms of commissioned officers, warrant officers, and enlistedmen of the United States Navy, January 21, 1905, p. 42.
3. Stacy, John A., United States Navy Ratring Badges and Marks 1833 to 2008, Mathews N.C.: ASMIC Pubs, 2008, p. 74. all other messmen rates began to wear the crescent at this time and the 1922 regulations p. 27 specifies them for Mess Attendants.
4. Register of the Commissioned And Warrant Officers of the Navy of the United States..., January 1, 1923, p. 307.
5. REGULATIONS GOVERNING THE UNIFORMS FOR COMMISSIONED AND WARRANT OFFICERS AND ENLISTED MEN OF THE UNITED STATES COAST GUARD, July 24, 1930.
6. http://www.history.navy.mil/faqs/faq78-3.html, March 2011.
7. www.uscg.mil/history/uscghist/USCGRates.pdf, March 2012.

(Officer's) Chief Cook
1. Stacy, John A., United States Navy Rating Badges and Marks 1833 to 2008, Mathews N.C.: ASMIC Pubs, 2008, p. 111.
2. ibid.
3. http://www.history.navy.mil/library/online/uniform_regs.htm, June 2011.
4. All Hands, "Changes Made in Rating Structure,...", August 1948, p. 57.

(Officer's) Chief Steward
1. Stacy, John A., United States Navy Rating Badges and Marks 1833 to 2008, Mathews N.C.: ASMIC Pubs, 2008, p. 111.
2. ibid.
3. http://www.history.navy.mil/library/online/uniform_regs.htm, June 2011.
4. All Hands, "Changes Made in Rating Structure,...", August 1948, p. 57.

(Officer's) Cook First Class
1. REGULATIONS GOVERNING THE UNIFORMS FOR COMMISSIONED AND WARRANT OFFICERS AND ENLISTED MEN OF THE UNITED STATES COAST GUARD, July 24, 1930.
2. Stacy, John A., United States Navy Rating Badges and Marks 1833 to 2008, Mathews N.C.: ASMIC Pubs, 2008, p. 111.
3. Lewis, Dana., U. S. COAST GUARD ENLISTED RATINGS RATING SPECIALTY MARKS & DISTINGUISHING MARKS 1915 ~ 2011, p. 31.
4. http://www.history.navy.mil/library/online/uniform_regs.htm, June 2011.
5. All Hands, "Wants Clarification", July 1946, p. 39
6. All Hands, "Changes Made in Rating Structure,...", August 1948, p. 57.
7. Lewis, Dana., U. S. COAST GUARD ENLISTED RATINGS RATING SPECIALTY MARKS & DISTINGUISHING MARKS 1915 ~ 2011, p. 31.

(Officer's) Cook Second Class
1. REGULATIONS GOVERNING THE UNIFORMS FOR COMMISSIONED AND WARRANT OFFICERS AND ENLISTED MEN OF THE UNITED STATES COAST GUARD, July 24, 1930.
2. Stacy, John A., United States Navy Rating Badges and Marks 1833 to 2008, Mathews N.C.: ASMIC Pubs, 2008, p. 111.
3. Lewis, Dana., U. S. COAST GUARD ENLISTED RATINGS RATING SPECIALTY MARKS & DISTINGUISHING MARKS 1915 ~ 2011, p. 31.
4. http://www.history.navy.mil/library/online/uniform_regs.htm, June 2011.
5. All Hands, "Wants Clarification", July 1946, p. 39
6. All Hands, "Changes Made in Rating Structure,...", August 1948, p. 57.
7. Lewis, Dana., U. S. COAST GUARD ENLISTED RATINGS RATING SPECIALTY MARKS & DISTINGUISHING MARKS 1915 ~ 2011, p. 31.

(Officer's) Cook Third Class
1. REGULATIONS GOVERNING THE UNIFORMS FOR COMMISSIONED AND WARRANT OFFICERS AND ENLISTED MEN OF THE UNITED STATES COAST GUARD, July 24, 1930.
2. Stacy, John A., United States Navy Rating Badges and Marks 1833 to 2008, Mathews N.C.: ASMIC Pubs, 2008, p. 111.
3. Lewis, Dana., U. S. COAST GUARD ENLISTED RATINGS RATING SPECIALTY MARKS & DISTINGUISHING MARKS 1915 ~ 2011, p. 31.
4. http://www.history.navy.mil/library/online/uniform_regs.htm, June 2011.
5. All Hands, "Wants Clarification", July 1946, p. 39
6. All Hands, "Changes Made in Rating Structure,...", August 1948, p. 57.
7. Lewis, Dana., U. S. COAST GUARD ENLISTED RATINGS RATING SPECIALTY MARKS & DISTINGUISHING MARKS 1915 ~ 2011, p. 31.

(Officer's) Steward First Class
1. REGULATIONS GOVERNING THE UNIFORMS FOR COMMISSIONED AND WARRANT OFFICERS AND ENLISTED MEN OF THE UNITED STATES COAST GUARD, July 24, 1930.
2. Stacy, John A., United States Navy Rating Badges and Marks 1833 to 2008, Mathews N.C.: ASMIC Pubs, 2008, p. 111.
3. Lewis, Dana., U. S. COAST GUARD ENLISTED RATINGS RATING SPECIALTY MARKS & DISTINGUISHING MARKS 1915 ~ 2011, p. 31.
4. http://www.history.navy.mil/library/online/uniform_regs.htm, June 2011.
5. All Hands, "Wants Clarification", July 1946, p. 39
6. All Hands, "Changes Made in Rating Structure,...", August 1948, p. 57.
7. Lewis, Dana., U. S. COAST GUARD ENLISTED RATINGS RATING SPECIALTY MARKS & DISTINGUISHING MARKS 1915 ~ 2011, p. 31.

(Officer's) Steward Second Class
1. REGULATIONS GOVERNING THE UNIFORMS FOR COMMISSIONED AND WARRANT OFFICERS AND ENLISTED MEN OF THE UNITED STATES COAST GUARD, July 24, 1930.
2. Stacy, John A., United States Navy Rating Badges and Marks 1833 to 2008, Mathews N.C.: ASMIC Pubs, 2008, p. 111.
3. Lewis, Dana., U. S. COAST GUARD ENLISTED RATINGS RATING SPECIALTY MARKS & DISTINGUISHING MARKS 1915 ~ 2011, p. 31.
4. http://www.history.navy.mil/library/online/uniform_regs.htm, June 2011.
5. All Hands, "Wants Clarification", July 1946, p. 39
6. All Hands, "Changes Made in Rating Structure,...", August 1948, p. 57.
7. Lewis, Dana., U. S. COAST GUARD ENLISTED RATINGS RATING SPECIALTY MARKS & DISTINGUISHING MARKS 1915 ~ 2011, p. 31.

(Officer's) Steward Third Class
1. REGULATIONS GOVERNING THE UNIFORMS FOR COMMISSIONED AND WARRANT OFFICERS AND ENLISTED MEN OF THE UNITED STATES COAST GUARD, July 24, 1930.
2. Stacy, John A., United States Navy Rating Badges and Marks 1833 to 2008, Mathews N.C.: ASMIC Pubs, 2008, p. 111.
3. Lewis, Dana., U. S. COAST GUARD ENLISTED RATINGS RATING SPECIALTY MARKS & DISTINGUISHING MARKS 1915 ~ 2011, p. 31.
4. http://www.history.navy.mil/library/online/uniform_regs.htm, June 2011.
5. All Hands, "Wants Clarification", July 1946, p. 39
6. All Hands, "Changes Made in Rating Structure,...", August 1948, p. 57.
7. Lewis, Dana., U. S. COAST GUARD ENLISTED RATINGS RATING SPECIALTY MARKS & DISTINGUISHING MARKS 1915 ~ 2011, p. 31.

Ordinary Seaman
1. Gauss, Henry C., The American Goverment, Organization and Officials, NewYork: Hamerlsy, 1908, p. 404-406.
2. Regulations Governing the Uniform of Officers and Enlisted Men of the United States Revenue Marine, 1891.
3. U.S. REVENUE CUTTER SERVICE UNIFORM REGULATIONS OFFICERS, WARRANT OFFICERS AND ENLISTED MEN, 1908.
4. Lewis, Dana., U. S. COAST GUARD ENLISTED RATINGS RATING SPECIALTY MARKS & DISTINGUISHING MARKS 1915 ~ 2011, p. 21.

Pay Clerk and Acting Pay Clerk
1. United States Statutes at Large, Vol. 41, p. 603.
2. Register of the Commissioned and Warrant Officers and Cadets, and Ships, and Stations of the United States Coast Guard, January 1, 1921, p. 56.
3. Register of the Commissioned and Warrant Officers and Cadets, and Ships, and Stations of the United States Coast Guard, January 1, 1923, p. 55.
4. Register of the Commissioned and Warrant Officers and Cadets, and Ships, and Stations of the United States Coast Guard, January 1, 1925, p. 52.
5. Register of the Commissioned and Warrant Officers and Cadets, and Ships, and Stations of the United States Coast Guard, January 1, 1926, p. 50.
6. Lewis, Dana., U. S. COAST GUARD ENLISTED RATINGS RATING SPECIALTY MARKS & DISTINGUISHING MARKS 1915 ~ 2011, p. 19.

7. http://www.uscg.mil/history/gifs/1920s_Warrant_Full_Dress.jpg, March 2012.
8. REGULATIONS GOVERNING THE UNIFORMS FOR COMMISSIONED AND WARRANT OFFICERS AND ENLISTED MEN OF THE UNITED STATES COAST GUARD, July 24, 1930.
9. REGULATIONS GOVERNING THE UNIFORMS FOR COMMISSIONED AND WARRANT OFFICERS AND ENLISTED MEN OF THE UNITED STATES COAST GUARD, Amendment No. 7, June 18, 1941.
10. United States Statutes at Large, Vol. 63, p. 807.
11. http://www.history.navy.mil/library/online/uniform_insignia.htm, March 2011.
12. Lewis, Dana., U. S. COAST GUARD ENLISTED RATINGS RATING SPECIALTY MARKS & DISTINGUISHING MARKS 1915 ~ 2011, p. 43.
13. United States Statutes at Large, Vol. 68, p. 157

Petty Officer (Before 1906?)
1. Oliver, Raymond, Why is a Kernal called a Colonel?, Tuscon: Fireship press, 1983, p. 11.
2. United States Statutes at Large, Vol. 1, p. 709.
3. Davis Smith, Horatio, Early History of the United States Revenue Marine Service , Naval Historical Foundation, 1932, p. 62.
4. Schuyler Hartly and Graham Illustrated Catalog of Civil War Military Goods, New York: Dover, 1985.
5. Regulations Governing the Uniform of Officers and Enlisted Men of the United States Revenue Marine, 1891.
6. Lewis, Dana., U. S. COAST GUARD ENLISTED RATINGS RATING SPECIALTY MARKS & DISTINGUISHING MARKS 1915 ~ 2011, p. 3.
7. Gauss, Henry C., The American Goverment, Organization and Officials, NewYork: Hamerlsy, 1908, p. 404-406.

Petty Officer First Class
1. Gauss, Henry C., The American Goverment, Organization and Officials, NewYork: Hamerlsy, 1908, p. 404-406.
2. U.S. REVENUE CUTTER SERVICE UNIFORM REGULATIONS OFFICERS, WARRANT OFFICERS AND ENLISTED MEN, 1908.
3. United States Statutes at Large, Vol. 38, p. 800.
4. REGULATIONS GOVERNING THE UNIFORMS FOR WARRANT OFFICERS AND ENLISTED PERSONS OF THE UNITED STATES COAST GUARD, February 18, 1916, p. 15-16.
5. Lewis, Dana., U. S. COAST GUARD ENLISTED RATINGS RATING SPECIALTY MARKS & DISTINGUISHING MARKS 1915 ~ 2011, p. 27.
6. ibid. p. 30.
7. ibid. p. 42.
8. COMDTINST M1020.6a, Febraury 2009, para. 2-C-4, c (13-15).
9. ibid. p. 3-53.
10. ibid. p. 3-56.
11. ibid. p. 3-57.

Petty Officer Second Class
1. Gauss, Henry C., The American Goverment, Organization and Officials, NewYork: Hamerlsy, 1908, p. 404-406.
2. U.S. REVENUE CUTTER SERVICE UNIFORM REGULATIONS OFFICERS, WARRANT OFFICERS AND ENLISTED MEN, 1908.
3. REGULATIONS GOVERNING THE UNIFORMS FOR WARRANT OFFICERS AND ENLISTED PERSONS OF THE UNITED STATES COAST GUARD, February 18, 1916, p. 15-16.
4. Lewis, Dana., U. S. COAST GUARD ENLISTED RATINGS RATING SPECIALTY MARKS & DISTINGUISHING MARKS 1915 ~ 2011, p. 27.
5. ibid. p. 30.
6. ibid. p. 42.
7. COMDTINST M1020.6a, Febraury 2009, para. 2-C-4, c (13-15).
8. ibid. p. 3-53.
9. ibid. p. 3-56.
10. ibid. p. 3-57.

Petty Officer Third Class
1. REGULATIONS GOVERNING THE UNIFORMS FOR WARRANT OFFICERS AND ENLISTED PERSONS OF THE UNITED STATES COAST GUARD, February 18, 1916, p. 15-16.
2. Lewis, Dana., U. S. COAST GUARD ENLISTED RATINGS RATING SPECIALTY MARKS & DISTINGUISHING MARKS 1915 ~ 2011, p. 27.
3. ibid. p. 30.
4. ibid. p. 42.
5. COMDTINST M1020.6a, Febraury 2009, para. 2-C-4, c (13-15).
6. ibid. p. 3-53.
7. ibid. p. 3-56.
8. ibid. p. 3-57.

Pharmacist
1. United States Statutes at Large, Vol. 41, p. 603.
2. Register of the Commissioned and Warrant Officers and Cadets, and Ships, and Stations of the United States Coast Guard, January 1, 1935, p. 59.
3. REGULATIONS GOVERNING THE UNIFORMS FOR COMMISSIONED AND WARRANT OFFICERS AND ENLISTED MEN OF THE UNITED STATES COAST GUARD, July 24, 1930.
4. Lewis, Dana., U. S. COAST GUARD ENLISTED RATINGS RATING SPECIALTY MARKS & DISTINGUISHING MARKS 1915 ~ 2011, p. 44.
5. REGULATIONS GOVERNING THE UNIFORMS FOR COMMISSIONED AND WARRANT OFFICERS AND ENLISTED MEN OF THE UNITED STATES COAST GUARD, Amendment No. 7, June 18, 1941.
6. United States Statutes at Large, Vol. 63, p. 807.
7. http://www.history.navy.mil/library/online/uniform_insignia.htm, March 2011.
8. Lewis, Dana., U. S. COAST GUARD ENLISTED RATINGS RATING SPECIALTY MARKS & DISTINGUISHING MARKS 1915 ~ 2011, p. 43.
9. United States Statutes at Large, Vol. 68, p. 157

Photographer
1. United States Statutes at Large, Vol. 56, p. 724.
2. Lewis, Dana., U. S. COAST GUARD ENLISTED RATINGS RATING SPECIALTY MARKS & DISTINGUISHING MARKS 1915 ~ 2011, p. 44.
3. All Hands, "Ranks and Rates...", May 1943, p. 29-35.
4. Lewis, Dana., U. S. COAST GUARD ENLISTED RATINGS RATING SPECIALTY MARKS & DISTINGUISHING MARKS 1915 ~ 2011, p. 44.
5. United States Statutes at Large, Vol. 63, p. 807.
6. http://www.history.navy.mil/library/online/uniform_insignia.htm, March 2011.
7. Lewis, Dana., U. S. COAST GUARD ENLISTED RATINGS RATING SPECIALTY MARKS & DISTINGUISHING MARKS 1915 ~ 2011, p. 43.
8. United States Statutes at Large, Vol. 68, p. 157.

Radio Electrician
1. United States Statutes at Large, Vol. 43, p. 1274.
2. Register of the Officers and Vessels of the Coast Guard of the United States, January 1, 1926, p. 50.
3. REGULATIONS GOVERNING THE UNIFORMS FOR COMMISSIONED AND WARRANT OFFICERS AND ENLISTED MEN OF THE UNITED STATES COAST GUARD, July 24, 1930.
4. REGULATIONS GOVERNING THE UNIFORMS FOR COMMISSIONED AND WARRANT OFFICERS AND ENLISTED MEN OF THE UNITED STATES COAST GUARD, Amendment No. 7, June 18, 1941.
5. United States Statutes at Large, Vol. 63, p. 807
6. http://www.history.navy.mil/library/online/uniform_insignia.htm, March 2011.
7. Lewis, Dana., U. S. COAST GUARD ENLISTED RATINGS RATING SPECIALTY MARKS & DISTINGUISHING MARKS 1915 ~ 2011, p. 43.
8. United States Statutes at Large, Vol. 68, p. 157

Rear Admiral, Rear Admiral (Upper Half) and Rear Admiral (Lower Half)
1. Oliver, Raymond, Why is a Kernal called a Colonel?, Tuscon: Fireship press, 1983, p. 45-46.
2. United States Statutes at Large, Vol. 42, p. 1130.
3. http://www.uscg.mil/history/people/WFReynoldsBio.asp, May 2012.
4. ibid.
5. http://www.uscg.mil/history/people/FCBillardBio.asp, May 2012.
6. REGULATIONS GOVERNING THE UNIFORMS FOR COMMISSIONED AND WARRANT OFFICERS AND ENLISTED MEN OF THE UNITED STATES COAST GUARD, July 24, 1930.
7. http://www.uscg.mil/history/people/WFReynoldsBio.asp, May 2012.
8. http://www.uscg.mil/history/people/FCBillardBio.asp, May 2012.
9. ibid.
10. http://www.uscg.mil/history/people/HGHamletBio.asp, May 2012.
11. http://www.uscg.mil/history/people/RRWaescheSRBio.asp, May 2012.
12. United States Coast Guard list of Commissined and Warrant Officers on Active Duty in Order of Presedence and Temporary Menbers of the Reserve, June 30, 1944, p. 1.
13. http://noelcoleman.blogspot.com/2012/02/my-first-wikipedia-contribution-admiral.html, February 2012.
14. United States Statutes at Large, Vol. 61, p. 409.
15. United States Statutes at Large, Vol. 63, p. 802.
16. United States Statutes at Large, Vol. 98, p. 2873.
17. United States Statutes at Large, Vol. 99, p. 628.
18. COMDTINST M1020.6D, May 27, 1997, p. 2-3 (3),(7), & (9).
19. COMDTINST M1020.6F, February 18, 2009, p. 3-46.

Sailmaker
1. Register of the Commissioned and Warrant Officers and Cadets, and Ships, and Stations of the United States Coast Guard, January 1, 1921, p. 55.
2. Register of the officers, vessels and stations of the United States Coast Guard, January 1, 1918, P. 88 (the 1919 and 1920 registers proved unavailable).
3. Register of the Commissioned and Warrant Officers and Cadets, and Ships, and Stations of the United States Coast Guard, January 1, 1922, p. 61.
13. Lewis, Dana., U. S. COAST GUARD ENLISTED RATINGS RATING SPECIALTY MARKS & DISTINGUISHING MARKS 1915 ~ 2011, p. 43-44.

Seaman (or Able Seaman)
1. United States Statutes at Large, Vol. 1, p. 175.
2. United States Statutes at Large, Vol. 1, p. 709.
3. Davis Smith, Horatio, Early History of the United States Revenue Marine Service , Naval Historical Foundation, 1932, p. 18-19.
4. ibid.p. 41.
5. Schuyler Hartly and Graham Illustrated Catalog of Civil War Military Goods, New York: Dover, 1985.
6. Regulations Governing the Uniform of Officers and Enlisted Men of the United States Revenue Marine, 1891.
7. U.S. REVENUE CUTTER SERVICE UNIFORM REGULATIONS OFFICERS, WARRANT OFFICERS AND ENLISTED MEN, 1908.
8. Lewis, Dana., U. S. COAST GUARD ENLISTED RATINGS RATING SPECIALTY MARKS & DISTINGUISHING MARKS 1915 ~ 2011, p. 19.
10. http://www.history.navy.mil/faqs/faq78-3.html, March 2011.
11. www.uscg.mil/history/uscghist/USCGRates.pdf, March 2012.
12. ibid.
13. United States Statutes at Large, Vol. 63, p. 802.
14. COMDTINST M1020.6F, February 18, 2009, p. 3-56.

Seaman Apprentice
1. www.uscg.mil/history/uscghist/USCGRates.pdf, March 2012.
2. United States Statutes at Large, Vol. 63, p. 802.
3. COMDTINST M1020.6F, February 18, 2009, p. 3-56.

Seaman First Class
1. http://www.history.navy.mil/faqs/faq78-3.html, March 2011.
2. www.uscg.mil/history/uscghist/USCGRates.pdf, March 2012.
3. Lewis, Dana., U. S. COAST GUARD ENLISTED RATINGS RATING SPECIALTY MARKS & DISTINGUISHING MARKS 1915 ~ 2011, p. 19.
4. United States Statutes at Large, Vol. 42, p. 630.
5. REGULATIONS GOVERNING THE UNIFORMS FOR COMMISSIONED AND WARRANT OFFICERS AND ENLISTED MEN OF THE UNITED STATES COAST GUARD, July 24, 1930.
6. Lewis, Dana., U. S. COAST GUARD ENLISTED RATINGS RATING SPECIALTY MARKS & DISTINGUISHING MARKS 1915 ~ 2011, p. 34.

7. www.uscg.mil/history/uscghist/USCGRates.pdf, March 2012.

Seaman Recruit
1. www.uscg.mil/history/uscghist/USCGRates.pdf, March 2012.
2. United States Statutes at Large, Vol. 63, p. 802.
3. COMDTINST M1020.6F, February 18, 2009, p. 3-56.

Seaman Second Class
1. United States Statutes at Large, Vol. 41, p. 603.
2. Lewis, Dana., U. S. COAST GUARD ENLISTED RATINGS RATING SPECIALTY MARKS & DISTINGUISHING MARKS 1915 ~ 2011, p. 19.
3. United States Statutes at Large, Vol. 42, p. 630.
4. REGULATIONS GOVERNING THE UNIFORMS FOR COMMISSIONED AND WARRANT OFFICERS AND ENLISTED MEN OF THE UNITED STATES COAST GUARD, July 24, 1930.
5. Lewis, Dana., U. S. COAST GUARD ENLISTED RATINGS RATING SPECIALTY MARKS & DISTINGUISHING MARKS 1915 ~ 2011, p. 34.
6. www.uscg.mil/history/uscghist/USCGRates.pdf, March 2012.

Second Assistant Engineer
1. Katcher, Philip, The Civil War Source Book, New York: Facts on File, 1992, p. 197-198.
2. United States Statutes at Large, Vol. 12, p. 583.
3. Canney, Donald, Uniforms of the U.S. Coast Guard, Revenue Service, Lighthouse Service and Life Saving Service, 1997.
4. ibid.
5. http://www.usmilitariaforum.com/forums/index.php?showtopic=30608, February 2012.
6. ibid.
7. http://www.uscg.mil/history/gifs/1900_Reg_Rank_Sleeve.jpg, March 2012.
8. United States Statutes at Large, Vol. 35, p. 62.

Second Lieutenant
1. Oliver, Raymond, Why is a Kernal called a Colonel?, Tuscon: Fireship press, 1983, p. 25.
2. ibid. p. 41.
3. United States Statutes at Large, Vol. 1, p. 175.
4. United States Statutes at Large, Vol. 1, p. 709.
5. Davis Smith, Horatio, Early History of the United States Revenue Marine Service , Naval Historical Foundation, 1932, p. 18-19.
6. ibid. p. 25.
7. United States Statutes at Large, Vol. 5, p. 65.
8. Davis Smith, Horatio, Early History of the United States Revenue Marine Service , Naval Historical Foundation, 1932, p. 36.
9. ibid. p. 39.
10. Canney, Donald, Uniforms of the U.S. Coast Guard, Revenue Service, Lighthouse Service and Life Saving Service, 1997.
11. Davis Smith, Horatio, Early History of the United States Revenue Marine Service , Naval Historical Foundation, 1932, p. 40.
12. ibid. p. 41.
13. Canney, Donald, Uniforms of the U.S. Coast Guard, Revenue Service, Lighthouse Service and Life Saving Service, 1997.
14. ibid
15. http://www.usmilitariaforum.com/forums/index.php?showtopic=30608, February 2012.
16. Katcher, Philip, The Civil War Source Book, New York: Facts on File, 1992, p. 197-198.
17. Schuyler Hartly and Graham Illustrated Catalog of Civil War Military Goods, New York: Dover, 1985.
18. United States Statutes at Large, Vol. 12, p. 640.
19. Katcher, Philip, The Civil War Source Book, New York: Facts on File, 1992, p. 197-198.
20. ibid.
21. http://www.usmilitariaforum.com/forums/index.php?showtopic=30608, February 2012.
22. ibid.
23 Regulations Governing the Uniform of Officers and Enlisted Men of the United States Revenue Marine, 1891.
24. http://www.uscg.mil/history/gifs/1900_Reg_Rank_Sleeve.jpg, March 2012.
25. Canney, Donald, Uniforms of the U.S. Coast Guard, Revenue Service, Lighthouse Service and Life Saving Service, 1997.
26. U.S. REVENUE CUTTER SERVICE UNIFORM REGULATIONS OFFICERS, WARRANT OFFICERS AND ENLISTED MEN, 1908.
27. The National Geographic Magazine, "Insignia of the Uniformed Forces of the United States", October 1917, p. 418.
28. United States Statutes at Large, Vol. 41, p. 879.

Second Lieutenant of Engineers
1. United States Statutes at Large, Vol. 35, p. 62.
2. U.S. REVENUE CUTTER SERVICE UNIFORM REGULATIONS OFFICERS, WARRANT OFFICERS AND ENLISTED MEN, 1908.
3. The National Geographic Magazine, "Insignia of the Uniformed Forces of the United States", October 1917, p. 418.
4. United States Statutes at Large, Vol. 41, p. 879.

Second Mate
1. United States Statutes at Large, Vol. 1, p. 175.
2. United States Statutes at Large, Vol. 1, p. 709.
3. Davis Smith, Horatio, Early History of the United States Revenue Marine Service , Naval Historical Foundation, 1932, p. 18-19.
4. ibid. p. 25.
5. United States Statutes at Large, Vol. 5, p. 65.

Senior Captain
1. United States Statutes at Large, Vol. 35, p. 62.
2. U.S. REVENUE CUTTER SERVICE UNIFORM REGULATIONS OFFICERS, WARRANT OFFICERS AND ENLISTED MEN, 1908.
3. The National Geographic Magazine, "Insignia of the Uniformed Forces of the United States", October 1917, p. 418.
4. United States Statutes at Large, Vol. 41, p. 879.

Senior Chief Petty Officer
1. United States Statutes at Large, Vol. 72, p. 123
2. Lewis, Dana., U. S. COAST GUARD ENLISTED RATINGS RATING SPECIALTY MARKS & DISTINGUISHING MARKS 1915 ~ 2011, p. 32.
3. ibid.
4. ibid.
5. COMDTINST M1020.6F, February 18, 2009, p. 3-53.
6. ibid. p. 3-56.
7. ibid. p. 3-57.

Ship's Clerk
1. United States Statutes at Large, Vol. 56, p. 724.
2. Lewis, Dana., U. S. COAST GUARD ENLISTED RATINGS RATING SPECIALTY MARKS & DISTINGUISHING MARKS 1915 ~ 2011, p. 44.
3. All Hands, "Ranks and Rates...", May 1943, p. 29-35.
4. Lewis, Dana., U. S. COAST GUARD ENLISTED RATINGS RATING SPECIALTY MARKS & DISTINGUISHING MARKS 1915 ~ 2011, p. 44.
5. United States Statutes at Large, Vol. 63, p. 807.
6. http://www.history.navy.mil/library/online/uniform_insignia.htm, March 2011.
7. Lewis, Dana., U. S. COAST GUARD ENLISTED RATINGS RATING SPECIALTY MARKS & DISTINGUISHING MARKS 1915 ~ 2011, p. 43.
8. United States Statutes at Large, Vol. 68, p. 157.

Ship's Cook Fourth Class
1. Lewis, Dana., U. S. COAST GUARD ENLISTED RATINGS RATING SPECIALTY MARKS & DISTINGUISHING MARKS 1915 ~ 2011, p. 19.
2. Bureau of Navigation Circular Letter No. 9-21, March 24, 1921.

Ship's Cook Third Class
1. Lewis, Dana., U. S. COAST GUARD ENLISTED RATINGS RATING SPECIALTY MARKS & DISTINGUISHING MARKS 1915 ~ 2011, p. 19.
2. Bureau of Navigation Circular Letter No. 9-21, March 24, 1921.

Steerage Cook
1. Lewis, Dana., U. S. COAST GUARD ENLISTED RATINGS RATING SPECIALTY MARKS & DISTINGUISHING MARKS 1915 ~ 2011, p.21.

Steward (Chief, First Class, Second Class and Third Class)
1. All Hands, "Here's a Complete List of Rating Changes...", March 1948, p. 57
2. All Hands, "Wants Clarification", July 1946, p. 39
3. All Hands, "Stewards Have Acquired New Uniforms", January 1950, p. 51.
4. Lewis, Dana., U. S. COAST GUARD ENLISTED RATINGS RATING SPECIALTY MARKS & DISTINGUISHING MARKS 1915 ~ 2011, p. 31.

Steward's Mate (First Class, Second Class and Third Class)
1. http://www.history.navy.mil/faqs/faq78-3.html, March 2011.
2. uniform regulations governing the insignia and uniforms of commissioned officers, warrant officers, and enlistedmen of the United States Navy, 1944, p. 749.
3. U.S. Navy Uniform Regulations, May 31, 1941, p. 28.
4. ibid plate 68.
5. ibid. p. 27.
6. www.uscg.mil/history/uscghist/USCGRates.pdf, March 2012.

Stewardsman
1. www.uscg.mil/history/uscghist/USCGRates.pdf, March 2012.
2. United States Statutes at Large, Vol. 63, p. 802.
3. Stacy, John A., United States Navy Rating Badges and Marks 1833 to 2008, Mathews N.C.: ASMIC Pubs, 2008, p. 33.
4. www.uscg.mil/history/uscghist/USCGRates.pdf, March 2012.

Stewardsman Apprentice
1. www.uscg.mil/history/uscghist/USCGRates.pdf, March 2012.
2. United States Statutes at Large, Vol. 63, p. 802.
3. Stacy, John A., United States Navy Rating Badges and Marks 1833 to 2008, Mathews N.C.: ASMIC Pubs, 2008, p. 33.
4. www.uscg.mil/history/uscghist/USCGRates.pdf, March 2012.

Stewardsman Recruit
1. www.uscg.mil/history/uscghist/USCGRates.pdf, March 2012.
2. United States Statutes at Large, Vol. 63, p. 802.
3. Stacy, John A., United States Navy Rating Badges and Marks 1833 to 2008, Mathews N.C.: ASMIC Pubs, 2008, p. 33.
4. www.uscg.mil/history/uscghist/USCGRates.pdf, March 2012.

Surfman
1. United States Statutes at Large, Vol. 20, p. 163.
2. Regulations for the Government of the Life-Saving Service of the United States, 1899 , Washington , D.C.: Government Printing Office, 1899.
3. United States Statutes at Large, Vol. 38, p. 801.
4. REGULATIONS GOVERNING THE UNIFORMS FOR WARRANT OFFICERS AND ENLISTED PERSONS OF THE UNITED STATES COAST GUARD, February 18, 1916, p. 12-14.
4. United States Statutes at Large, Vol. 41, p. 603.
5. REGULATIONS GOVERNING THE UNIFORMS FOR COMMISSIONED AND WARRANT OFFICERS AND ENLISTED MEN OF THE UNITED STATES COAST GUARD, July 24, 1930.
6. http://www.uscg.mil/d5/staBarnegat/surfman.asp, May 2012.

Surgeon
1. United States Statutes at Large, Vol. 33, p. 1036.
2. http://explorenorth.com/library/yafeatures/bl-DrCall.htm, May 2012.
3. ibid.

Third Lieutenant
1. Oliver, Raymond, Why is a Kernal called a Colonel?, Tuscon: Fireship press, 1983, p. 25.
2. ibid. p. 41.
3. United States Statutes at Large, Vol. 1, p. 175.
4. United States Statutes at Large, Vol. 1, p. 709.

5. Davis Smith, Horatio, Early History of the United States Revenue Marine Service , Naval Historical Foundation, 1932, p. 18-19.
6. ibid. p. 25.
7. United States Statutes at Large, Vol. 5, p. 65.
8. Davis Smith, Horatio, Early History of the United States Revenue Marine Service , Naval Historical Foundation, 1932, p. 36.
9. ibid. p. 39.
10. Canney, Donald, Uniforms of the U.S. Coast Guard, Revenue Service, Lighthouse Service and Life Saving Service, 1997.
11. Davis Smith, Horatio, Early History of the United States Revenue Marine Service , Naval Historical Foundation, 1932, p. 40.
12. Canney, Donald, Uniforms of the U.S. Coast Guard, Revenue Service, Lighthouse Service and Life Saving Service, 1997.
13. http://www.usmilitariaforum.com/forums/index.php?showtopic=30608, February 2012.
14. Katcher, Philip, The Civil War Source Book, New York: Facts on File, 1992, p. 197-198.
15. Schuyler Hartly and Graham Illustrated Catalog of Civil War Military Goods, New York: Dover, 1985.
16. United States Statutes at Large, Vol. 12, p. 640.
17. United States Statutes at Large, Vol. 12, p. 583.
18. Katcher, Philip, The Civil War Source Book, New York: Facts on File, 1992, p. 197-198.
19. ibid.
20. http://www.usmilitariaforum.com/forums/index.php?showtopic=30608, February 2012.
21. ibid.
22 Regulations Governing the Uniform of Officers and Enlisted Men of the United States Revenue Marine, 1891.
23. http://www.uscg.mil/history/gifs/1900_Reg_Rank_Sleeve.jpg, March 2012.
24. Canney, Donald, Uniforms of the U.S. Coast Guard, Revenue Service, Lighthouse Service and Life Saving Service, 1997.
25. U.S. REVENUE CUTTER SERVICE UNIFORM REGULATIONS OFFICERS, WARRANT OFFICERS AND ENLISTED MEN, 1908.
26. The National Geographic Magazine, "Insignia of the Uniformed Forces of the United States", October 1917, p. 418.
27. United States Statutes at Large, Vol. 41, p. 879.

Third Lieutenant of Engineers
1. United States Statutes at Large, Vol. 35, p. 62.
2. U.S. REVENUE CUTTER SERVICE UNIFORM REGULATIONS OFFICERS, WARRANT OFFICERS AND ENLISTED MEN, 1908.
3. The National Geographic Magazine, "Insignia of the Uniformed Forces of the United States", October 1917, p. 418.
4. United States Statutes at Large, Vol. 41, p. 879.

Vice Admiral
1. United States Coast Guard list of Commissined and Warrant Officers on Active Duty in Order of Presedence and Temporary Menbers of the Reserve, June 30, 1944, p. 1.
2. Rosignoli, Guido, Badges and Insignia of World War II AIr Force-Naval-Marine, London:Peerage, 1976, p. 332-333.
3. United States Statutes at Large, Vol. 59, p. 37.
4. United States Statutes at Large, Vol. 63, p. 497.
5. United States Statutes at Large, Vol. 63, p. 807
6. United States Statutes at Large, Vol. 72, p. 124
7. COMDTINST M1020.6F, February 18, 2009, p. 3-46.

Wardroom Steward
1. Amendment of Revenue Cutter Service Regulations, 1894, Treasury Department, March 25, 1895.
2. United States Statutes at Large, Vol. 17, p. 247.
3. Regulations Governing the Uniform of Officers and Enlisted Men of the United States Revenue Marine, 1891.
4. U.S. REVENUE CUTTER SERVICE UNIFORM REGULATIONS OFFICERS, 5. Gauss, Henry C., The American Goverment, Organization and Officials, NewYork: Hamerlsy, 1908, p. 406.
6. Lewis, Dana., U. S. COAST GUARD ENLISTED RATINGS RATING SPECIALTY MARKS & DISTINGUISHING MARKS 1915 ~ 2011, p. 19.
7. http://www.history.navy.mil/faqs/faq78-3.html, March 2011.
8. REGULATIONS GOVERNING THE UNIFORMS FOR COMMISSIONED AND WARRANT OFFICERS AND ENLISTED MEN OF THE UNITED STATES COAST GUARD, July 24, 1930.

Warrant Officer 1
1. United States Statutes at Large, Vol. 68, p. 157
2. All Hands, "New Insignia and Markings go into effect on 1 November For Four Warrant Ranks", October 1954, p. 45.
3. http://en.wikipedia.org/wiki/Warrant_Officer_(United_States), September 2011.

Warrant Officer's Steward
1. Lewis, Dana., U. S. COAST GUARD ENLISTED RATINGS RATING SPECIALTY MARKS & DISTINGUISHING MARKS 1915 ~ 2011, p. 21.
2. REGULATIONS GOVERNING THE UNIFORMS FOR WARRANT OFFICERS AND ENLISTED PERSONS OF THE UNITED STATES COAST GUARD, February 18, 1916, p. 19-10.
3. http://www.history.navy.mil/faqs/faq78-3.html, March 2011.
4. REGULATIONS GOVERNING THE UNIFORMS FOR COMMISSIONED AND WARRANT OFFICERS AND ENLISTED MEN OF THE UNITED STATES COAST GUARD, July 24, 1930.

Part 6.The Public Health Service
Chapter 1. PHS Organization

1. United States Statutes at Large, Vol. 80, p. 408.
2. United States Statutes at Large, Vol. 1, p. 605.
3. United States Statutes at Large, Vol. 16, p. 169.
4. United States Statutes at Large, Vol. 25, p. 639.

The Marine Hospital Fund
1. United States Statutes at Large, Vol. 80, p. 408.
2. http://www.nlm.nih.gov/exhibition/nih_origins/independent.html, May 2012.
3. Strandber, John E., The Call of Duty, San Jose CA.: Bender Publisheing, 1994, p.305-306.
4. United States Statutes at Large, Vol. 16, p. 169.

The Marine Hospital Service
1. United States Statutes at Large, Vol. 16, p. 169.
2. http://www.surgeongeneral.gov/about/previous/biowoodworth.html, May 2012.
3. Strandber, John E., The Call of Duty, San Jose CA.: Bender Publisheing, 1994, p.305-306.
4. http://www.milestonedocuments.com/documents/view/national-quarantine-act. May 2012.
5. United States Statutes at Large, Vol. 20, p. 39.
6. United States Statutes at Large, Vol. 26, p. 639.
7. United States Statutes at Large, Vol. 26, p. 1085.

The Public Health and Marine Hospital Service
1. United States Statutes at Large, Vol. 32, p. 712.

The Public Health Service
1. United States Statutes at Large, Vol. 37, p. 309.

Rank Structure
1. United States Statutes at Large, Vol. 26, p. 639.
2. United States Statutes at Large, Vol. 18, p. 377.
3. Revised Regulations For The Government of the United States Marine-Hospital Service , November 29, 1897, p 5.
4. ibid.
5. U.S. Navy General Order 120, April 1, 1869, with letter attached.
6. United States Statutes at Large, Vol. 32, p. 712.
7. United States Statutes at Large, Vol. 37, p. 309.
8. Decisions of the Comptroller General of the United States, Vol. 4, p. 73-76.
9. United States Statutes at Large, Vol. 46, p. 150.
10. Awards and Decorations Presented to Officers of the US Public Health Service During the World WarII era, 2009, lists various rank.
11. ibid.
12. http://dcp.psc.gov/ccbulletin/articles/PharmacyAnniversaryCelebration.htm, May 2012.
13. Official List of Commissioned and Other Officers of the United States Public Health Service, October 1, 1930.
14. www.phscof.org/events/.../dellapenna_tuesday_eho_915_dellapenna.pdf, May 2012.
15. Grosvenor, Gilbert , Insignia and decorations of the U.S. armed forces, National Geographic Society, 1945, plate II after page 720.
16. Official List of Commissioned Officers of the United States Public Health Service, January 1, 1943.
17. United States Statutes at Large, Vol. 58, p. 684.
18. United States Statutes at Large, Vol. 62, p. 42.
19. Official List of Commissioned Officers of the United States Public Health Service, January 1, 1946.
20. United States Statutes at Large, Vol. 63, p. 807.
21. United States Statutes at Large, Vol. 72, p. 124
22. United States Statutes at Large, Vol. 76, p. 453.
23. http://www.surgeongeneral.gov/about/previous/biostewart.html, May 2012.
24. http://en.wikipedia.org/wiki/Assistant_Secretary_for_Health, May 2012.
25. http://www.surgeongeneral.gov/about/previous/biorichmond.html, May 2012.
26. United States Statutes at Large, Vol. 93, p. 584-586.
27. United States Statutes at Large, Vol. 104, p. 1289.
28. The Commissioned Corps Supervisor's Guide, 1995, p 7-8.
29. Chapter 2 PHS Rank Insignia
1. Strandber, John E., The Call of Duty, San Jose CA.: Bender Publisheing, 1994, p.305-306.
2. Regulations Governing The Uniforms of Officers and Employees of The Marine-Hospital Service of the United States, 1896, p. 5-9.
3. Regulations Governing The Uniforms of Officers and Employees of The Public Health and Marine-Hospital Service of the United States, 1904, p. 5-11.
4. Regulations governing the uniforms of officers and employees of the United States Public health service, 1914, p. 18-19.
5. http://www.usmilitariaforum.com/forums/index.php?showtopic=21815&hl=public+health+service, May 2012.
6. Grosvenor, Gilbert , Insignia and decorations of the U.S. armed forces, National Geographic Society, 1945, plate II after page 720.

Epaulets
1. Oliver, Raymond, Why is a Kernal called a Colonel?, Tuscon: Fireship press, 1983, p. 17.
2. Regulations Governing The Uniforms of Officers and Employees of The Marine-Hospital Service of the United States, 1896, p. 11.
3. Regulations Governing The Uniforms of Officers and Employees of The Public Health and Marine-Hospital Service of the United States, 1904, p. 14.
4. Regulations governing the uniforms of officers and employees of the United States Public health service, 1914, p. 20.

Shoulder Straps
1. Regulations Governing The Uniforms of Officers and Employees of The Marine-Hospital Service of the United States, 1896, p. 12.
2. Regulations Governing The Uniforms of Officers and Employees of The Public Health and Marine-Hospital Service of the United States, 1904, p. 15.
3. Regulations governing the uniforms of officers and employees of the United States Public health service, 1914.

Shoulder Knots
1. Regulations Governing The Uniforms of Officers and Employees of The Marine-Hospital Service of the United States, 1896, p. 11-12.
2. Regulations Governing The Uniforms of Officers and Employees of The Public Health and Marine-Hospital Service of the United States, 1904, p. 14.
3. Regulations governing the uniforms of officers and employees of the United States Public health service, 1914.
4. Regulations Governing The Uniforms of Officers and Employees of The Public Health and Marine-Hospital Service of the United States, 1904, p. 6-7.

Maroon Shoulder Loops
1. Regulations governing the uniforms of officers and employees of the United States Public health service, 1914, p. 18-21.

Shoulder Boards
1. Regulations governing the uniforms of officers and employees of the United States Public health service, 1914.
2. http://www.usmilitariaforum.com/forums/index.php?showtopic=21815&hl=public+health+service, May 2012.
3. ibid.
4. Grosvenor, Gilbert , Insignia and decorations of the U.S. armed forces, National Geographic Society, 1945, plate II after page 720.
5. CCPM Pamphlet NO. 61, September 1993, p. 107.

Shoulder Marks
1. All Hands, "New Officer, CPO Uniforms...", June 1979, p. 2.
2. CCPM Pamphlet NO. 61, September 1993, p. 107.
3. CC26.3.6, March 1, 2009, p. 3.

Badges of Rank
1. Regulations Governing The Uniforms of Officers and Employees of The Marine-Hospital Service of the United States, 1896, p. 12-13.
2. Regulations Governing The Uniforms of Officers and Employees of The Public Health and Marine-Hospital Service of the United States, 1904, p. 15.
3. ibid. p. 10.
4. Regulations governing the uniforms of officers and employees of the United States Public health service, 1914, p. 21.
5. http://www.usmilitariaforum.com/forums/index.php?showtopic=21815&hl=public+health+service, May 2012.
6. Grosvenor, Gilbert , Insignia and decorations of the U.S. armed forces, National Geographic Society, 1945, plate II after page 720.
7. CCPM Pamphlet NO. 61, September 1993, p. 107.

Overcoat Cuff knots
1. Regulations Governing The Uniforms of Officers and Employees of The Public Health and Marine-Hospital Service of the United States, 1904, p. 11.
2. http://www.thefreedictionary.com/cinquefoil, May 2012.
3. Regulations Governing The Uniforms of Officers and Employees of The Public Health and Marine-Hospital Service of the United States, 1904, p. 11.
4. Regulations governing the uniforms of officers and employees of the United States Public health service, 1914, p. 22.

Cuff Stripes
1. http://www.surgeongeneral.gov/about/previous/index.html, May 2012.
2. Regulations Governing The Uniforms of Officers and Employees of The Marine-Hospital Service of the United States, 1896, p. 13.
3. ibid. p. 8.
4. Regulations Governing The Uniforms of Officers and Employees of The Public Health and Marine-Hospital Service of the United States, 1904, p. 15.
5. Regulations governing the uniforms of officers and employees of the United States Public health service, 1914, p. 21-22.
6. http://www.usmilitariaforum.com/forums/index.php?showtopic=21815&hl=public+health+service, May 2012.
7. Grosvenor, Gilbert , Insignia and decorations of the U.S. armed forces, National Geographic Society, 1945, plate II after page 720.
8. All Hands, "Current and Future Changes in Uniform Regs Listed", May 1947, p. 56.
9. CCPM Pamphlet NO. 61, September 1993, p. 107.Chapter 3. PHS Ranks

Assistant (Lieutenant (Junior Grade))
1. United States Statutes at Large, Vol. 58, p. 684.
2. Grosvenor, Gilbert , Insignia and decorations of the U.S. armed forces, National Geographic Society, 1945, plate II after page 720.
3. United States Statutes at Large, Vol. 63, p. 807.
4. The Commissioned Corps Supervisor's Guide, 1995, p 7-8.
5. http://www.usphs.gov/docs/pdfs/uniform/Uniformed%20Service%20Rank%20Chart.pdf, May 2012.
6. CC26.3.6, March 1, 2009, p. 2.
7. ibid. p. 9.
8. ibid. p. 2-3.
9. ibid. p. 10-11.
10. ibid. p. 3.

Assistant Dental Surgeon
1. United States Statutes at Large, Vol. 46, p. 150.
2. http://www.usmilitariaforum.com/forums/index.php?showtopic=21815&hl=public+health+service, May 2012.
3. United States Statutes at Large, Vol. 58, p. 684.
4. The Commissioned Corps Supervisor's Guide, 1995, p 7-8.

Assistant Pharmacist
1. Proceedings of the American Pharmaceutical Association at the ..., Volume 50. p. 203.
2. United States Statutes at Large, Vol. 46, p. 150.
3. http://www.usmilitariaforum.com/forums/index.php?showtopic=21815&hl=public+health+service, May 2012.
4. United States Statutes at Large, Vol. 58, p. 684.
5. The Commissioned Corps Supervisor's Guide, 1995, p 7-8.

Assistant Sanitary Engineer
1. United States Statutes at Large, Vol. 46, p. 150.
2. http://www.usmilitariaforum.com/forums/index.php?showtopic=21815&hl=public+health+service, May 2012.
3. United States Statutes at Large, Vol. 58, p. 684.

Assistant Secretary for Health
1. http://en.wikipedia.org/wiki/Assistant_Secretary_for_Health, May 2012.
2. http://www.surgeongeneral.gov/about/previous/biorichmond.html, May 2012.
3. http://en.wikipedia.org/wiki/File:Julius_Richmond,_Surgeon_General_official_photo.jpg, May 2012.
4. http://en.wikipedia.org/wiki/Assistant_Secretary_for_Health, May 2012.
5. United States Statutes at Large, Vol. 104, p. 1289.
6. http://www.surgeongeneral.gov/about/previous/bionovello.html, May 2012.
7. http://www.surgeongeneral.gov/about/previous/biosatcher.html, May 2012.
8. http://en.wikipedia.org/wiki/John_O._Agwunobi, May 2012.
9. http://en.wikipedia.org/wiki/Joxel_Garc%C3%ADa, may 2012.
10. http://en.wikipedia.org/wiki/United_States_Surgeon_General, May 2012.
11. http://en.wikipedia.org/wiki/Howard_Koh, May 2012.
12. CC26.3.6, March 1, 2009, p. 2.
13. ibid. p. 9.
14. ibid. p. 2-3.
15. ibid. p. 10-11.
16. ibid. p. 3.
17. ibid. p. 12.

Assistant Surgeon
1. United States Statutes at Large, Vol. 26, p. 639.
2. Regulations Governing The Uniforms of Officers and Employees of The Marine-Hospital Service of the United States, 1896, p. 13.
3. ibid. p. 12
4. ibid. p. 9.
5. Revised Regulations For The Government of the United States Marine-Hospital Service , November 29, 1897, p 5.
6. Regulations Governing The Uniforms of Officers and Employees of The Public Health and Marine-Hospital Service of the United States, 1904, p. 16.
7. ibid. p. 15.
8. ibid. p. 11.
9. Regulations governing the uniforms of officers and employees of the United States Public health service, 1914, p. 21-22.
10. http://www.usmilitariaforum.com/forums/index.php?showtopic=21815&hl=public+health+service, May 2012.
11. Grosvenor, Gilbert , Insignia and decorations of the U.S. armed forces, National Geographic Society, 1945, plate II after page 720.
12. United States Statutes at Large, Vol. 58, p. 684.
13. The Commissioned Corps Supervisor's Guide, 1995, p 7-8.

Assistant Surgeon General
1. United States Statutes at Large, Vol. 32, p. 712.
2. Regulations Governing The Uniforms of Officers and Employees of The Public Health and Marine-Hospital Service of the United States, 1904, p. 16.
3. ibid. p. 15.
4. ibid. p. 11.
5. Regulations governing the uniforms of officers and employees of the United States Public health service, 1914, p. 21-22.
6. http://www.usmilitariaforum.com/forums/index.php?showtopic=21815&hl=public+health+service, May 2012.
7. Grosvenor, Gilbert , Insignia and decorations of the U.S. armed forces, National Geographic Society, 1945, plate II after page 720.
8. United States Statutes at Large, Vol. 58, p. 684.
9. United States Statutes at Large, Vol. 63, p. 807.
10. CCPM Pamphlet NO. 61, September 1993, p. 107.
11. ibid.
12. CC26.3.6, March 1, 2009, p. 2.
13. ibid. p. 9.
14. ibid. p. 2-3.
15. ibid. p. 10-11.
16. ibid. p. 3.
17. ibid. p. 12.

Dental Surgeon
1. United States Statutes at Large, Vol. 46, p. 150.
2. http://www.usmilitariaforum.com/forums/index.php?showtopic=21815&hl=public+health+service, May 2012.
3. United States Statutes at Large, Vol. 58, p. 684.
4. The Commissioned Corps Supervisor's Guide, 1995, p 7-8.

Deputy Surgeon General
1. United States Statutes at Large, Vol. 58, p. 684.
2. CC26.3.6, March 1, 2009, p. 2.
3. ibid. p. 9.
4. ibid. p. 2-3.
5. ibid. p. 10-11.
6. ibid. p. 3.
7. ibid. p. 12.

Director (Captain)
1. United States Statutes at Large, Vol. 58, p. 684.
2. Grosvenor, Gilbert , Insignia and decorations of the U.S. armed forces, National Geographic Society, 1945, plate II after page 720.
3. United States Statutes at Large, Vol. 63, p. 807.
4. The Commissioned Corps Supervisor's Guide, 1995, p 7-8.
5. http://www.usphs.gov/docs/pdfs/uniform/Uniformed%20Service%20Rank%20Chart.pdf, May 2012.
6. CC26.3.6, March 1, 2009, p. 2.
7. ibid. p. 9.
8. ibid. p. 2-3.
9. ibid. p. 10-11.
10. ibid. p. 3.

Full (Lieutenant Commander)
1. United States Statutes at Large, Vol. 58, p. 684.
2. Grosvenor, Gilbert , Insignia and decorations of the U.S. armed forces, National Geographic Society, 1945, plate II after page 720.
3. United States Statutes at Large, Vol. 63, p. 807.
4. The Commissioned Corps Supervisor's Guide, 1995, p 7-8.
5. http://www.usphs.gov/docs/pdfs/uniform/Uniformed%20Service%20Rank%20Chart.pdf, May 2012.
6. CC26.3.6, March 1, 2009, p. 2.
7. ibid. p. 9.

8. ibid. p. 2-3.
9. ibid. p. 10-11.
10. ibid. p. 3.

Junior Assistant (Ensign)
1. United States Statutes at Large, Vol. 58, p. 684.
2. Grosvenor, Gilbert , Insignia and decorations of the U.S. armed forces, National Geographic Society, 1945, plate XIV.
3. United States Statutes at Large, Vol. 63, p. 807.
4. The Commissioned Corps Supervisor's Guide, 1995, p 7-8.
5. http://www.usphs.gov/docs/pdfs/uniform/Uniformed%20Service%20Rank%20Chart.pdf, May 2012.
6. CC26.3.6, March 1, 2009, p. 2.
7. ibid. p. 9.
8. ibid. p. 2-3.
9. ibid. p. 10-11.
10. ibid. p. 3.

Medical Director

1. United States Statutes at Large, Vol. 46, p. 150.
2. http://www.usmilitariaforum.com/forums/index.php?showtopic=21815&hl=public+health+service, May 2012.
3. United States Statutes at Large, Vol. 58, p. 684.
4. The Commissioned Corps Supervisor's Guide, 1995, p 7-8.

Passed Assistant Dental Surgeon
1. United States Statutes at Large, Vol. 46, p. 150.
2. http://www.usmilitariaforum.com/forums/index.php?showtopic=21815&hl=public+health+service, May 2012.
3. United States Statutes at Large, Vol. 58, p. 684.
4. The Commissioned Corps Supervisor's Guide, 1995, p 7-8.

Passed Assistant Pharmacist
1. United States Statutes at Large, Vol. 46, p. 150.
2. Proceedings of the American Pharmaceutical Association at the ..., Volume 50. p. 203.
3. Official List of Commissioned and Other Officers of the United States Public Health Service, October 1, 1930, p. 13.
4. Official List of Commissioned and Other Officers of the United States Public Health Service, January 1, 1934, p. 13.
5. Official List of Commissioned and Other Officers of the United States Public Health Service, January 1, 1943, p. 22.
6. http://www.usmilitariaforum.com/forums/index.php?showtopic=21815&hl=public+health+service, May 2012.

Passed Assistant Sanitary Engineer
1. United States Statutes at Large, Vol. 46, p. 150.
2. http://www.usmilitariaforum.com/forums/index.php?showtopic=21815&hl=public+health+service, May 2012.
3. United States Statutes at Large, Vol. 58, p. 684.

Passed Assistant Surgeon
1. United States Statutes at Large, Vol. 26, p. 639.
2. Regulations Governing The Uniforms of Officers and Employees of The Marine-Hospital Service of the United States, 1896, p. 13.
3. ibid. p. 12
4. ibid. p. 9.
5. Revised Regulations For The Government of the United States Marine-Hospital Service , November 29, 1897, p 5.
6. Regulations Governing The Uniforms of Officers and Employees of The Public Health and Marine-Hospital Service of the United States, 1904, p. 16.
7. ibid. p. 15.
8. ibid. p. 11.
9. Regulations governing the uniforms of officers and employees of the United States Public health service, 1914, p. 21-22.
10. http://www.usmilitariaforum.com/forums/index.php?showtopic=21815&hl=public+health+service, May 2012.
11. Grosvenor, Gilbert , Insignia and decorations of the U.S. armed forces, National Geographic Society, 1945, plate II after page 720.
12. United States Statutes at Large, Vol. 58, p. 684.
13. The Commissioned Corps Supervisor's Guide, 1995, p 7-8.

Sanitarian
1. www.phscof.org/events/.../dellapenna_tuesday_eho_915_dellapenna.pdf, May 2012.
2. United States Statutes at Large, Vol. 58, p. 684.

Sanitary Engineer
1. United States Statutes at Large, Vol. 46, p. 150.
2. http://www.usmilitariaforum.com/forums/index.php?showtopic=21815&hl=public+health+service, May 2012.
3. United States Statutes at Large, Vol. 58, p. 684.

Sanitary Engineer Director
1. United States Statutes at Large, Vol. 46, p. 150.
2. Official List of Commissioned and Other Officers of the United States Public Health Service, October 1, 1937, p. 15.
3. http://www.usmilitariaforum.com/forums/index.php?showtopic=21815&hl=public+health+service, May 2012.
4. United States Statutes at Large, Vol. 58, p. 684.

Senior (Commander)
1. United States Statutes at Large, Vol. 58, p. 684.
2. Grosvenor, Gilbert , Insignia and decorations of the U.S. armed forces, National Geographic Society, 1945, plate II after page 720.
3. United States Statutes at Large, Vol. 63, p. 807.
4. The Commissioned Corps Supervisor's Guide, 1995, p 7-8.
5. http://www.usphs.gov/docs/pdfs/uniform/Uniformed%20Service%20Rank%20Chart.pdf, May 2012.
6. CC26.3.6, March 1, 2009, p. 2.
7. ibid. p. 9.
8. ibid. p. 2-3.
9. ibid. p. 10-11.
10. ibid. p. 3

Senior Assistant (Lieutenant)
1. United States Statutes at Large, Vol. 58, p. 684.
2. Grosvenor, Gilbert , Insignia and decorations of the U.S. armed forces, National Geographic Society, 1945, plate II after page 720.
3. United States Statutes at Large, Vol. 63, p. 807.
4. The Commissioned Corps Supervisor's Guide, 1995, p 7-8.
5. http://www.usphs.gov/docs/pdfs/uniform/Uniformed%20Service%20Rank%20Chart.pdf, May 2012.
6. CC26.3.6, March 1, 2009, p. 2.
7. ibid. p. 9.
8. ibid. p. 2-3.
9. ibid. p. 10-11.
10. ibid. p. 3

Senior Dental Surgeon
1. United States Statutes at Large, Vol. 46, p. 150.
2. http://www.usmilitariaforum.com/forums/index.php?showtopic=21815&hl=public+health+service, May 2012.
3. United States Statutes at Large, Vol. 58, p. 684.
4. The Commissioned Corps Supervisor's Guide, 1995, p 7-8.

Senior Sanitary Engineer
1. United States Statutes at Large, Vol. 46, p. 150.
2. http://www.usmilitariaforum.com/forums/index.php?showtopic=21815&hl=public+health+service, May 2012.
3. United States Statutes at Large, Vol. 58, p. 684.
4. The Commissioned Corps Supervisor's Guide, 1995, p 7-8.

Senior Surgeon
1. United States Statutes at Large, Vol. 37, p. 309.
2. Regulations governing the uniforms of officers and employees of the United States Public health service, 1914, p. 21-22.
3. http://www.usmilitariaforum.com/forums/index.php?showtopic=21815&hl=public+health+service, May 2012.
4. Grosvenor, Gilbert , Insignia and decorations of the U.S. armed forces, National Geographic Society, 1945, plate II after page 720.
5. United States Statutes at Large, Vol. 58, p. 684.
6. The Commissioned Corps Supervisor's Guide, 1995, p 7-8.

Surgeon
1. United States Statutes at Large, Vol. 26, p. 639.
2. Regulations Governing The Uniforms of Officers and Employees of The Marine-Hospital Service of the United States, 1896, p. 13.
3. ibid. p. 12
4. ibid. p. 9.
5. Revised Regulations For The Government of the United States Marine-Hospital Service , November 29, 1897, p 5.
6. Regulations Governing The Uniforms of Officers and Employees of The Public Health and Marine-Hospital Service of the United States, 1904, p. 16.
7. ibid. p. 15.
8. ibid. p. 11.
9. Regulations governing the uniforms of officers and employees of the United States Public health service, 1914, p. 21-22.
10. http://www.usmilitariaforum.com/forums/index.php?showtopic=21815&hl=public+health+service, May 2012.
11. Grosvenor, Gilbert , Insignia and decorations of the U.S. armed forces, National Geographic Society, 1945, plate II after page 720.
12. United States Statutes at Large, Vol. 58, p. 684.
13. The Commissioned Corps Supervisor's Guide, 1995, p 7-8.

Surgeon General/Supervising Surgeon/ Supervising Surgeon General
1. United States Statutes at Large, Vol. 16, p. 169.
2. http://www.surgeongeneral.gov/about/previous/biowoodworth.html, June 2012.
3. United States Statutes at Large, Vol. 18, p. 377.
4. http://www.surgeongeneral.gov/about/previous/biohamilton.html, June 2012.
5. United States Statutes at Large, Vol. 26, p. 639.
6. http://www.surgeongeneral.gov/about/previous/index.html, June 2012.
7. http://www.surgeongeneral.gov/about/previous/biohamilton.html, June 2012.
8. http://www.surgeongeneral.gov/about/previous/biowyman.html, June 2012.
9. Regulations Governing The Uniforms of Officers and Employees of The Marine-Hospital Service of the United States, 1896, p. 11.
10. ibid. p. 12.
11. ibid. p. 13.
12. ibid. p. 8.
13. Regulations Governing The Uniforms of Officers and Employees of The Public Health and Marine-Hospital Service of the United States, 1904, p. 14 & 11.
14. http://www.surgeongeneral.gov/about/previous/biowyman.html, June 2012.
15. http://www.surgeongeneral.gov/about/previous/bioblue.html, June 2012.
16. United States Statutes at Large, Vol. 37, p. 309.
17. Regulations governing the uniforms of officers and employees of the United States Public health service, 1914, p. 21-22.
18. http://www.surgeongeneral.gov/about/previous/biocumming.html, June 2012.
19. http://www.surgeongeneral.gov/about/previous/bioparran.html, June 2012.
20. http://www.usmilitariaforum.com/forums/index.php?showtopic=21815&hl=public+health+service, May 2012.
21. Grosvenor, Gilbert , Insignia and decorations of the U.S. armed forces, National Geographic Society, 1945, plate II after page 720.
22. http://www.surgeongeneral.gov/about/previous/bioparran.html, June 2012.

23. http://www.surgeongeneral.gov/about/previous/bioscheele.html, June 2012.
24. United States Statutes at Large, Vol. 63, p. 807.
25. http://www.surgeongeneral.gov/about/previous/bioscheele.html, June 2012.
26. http://www.surgeongeneral.gov/about/previous/bioburney.html, June 2012.
27. http://www.surgeongeneral.gov/about/previous/bioterry.html, June 2012.
28. http://www.surgeongeneral.gov/about/previous/biostewart.ht, June 2012.
29. http://www.surgeongeneral.gov/about/history/index.html, June 2012.
30. http://www.surgeongeneral.gov/about/previous/biostewart.ht, June 2012.
31. http://www.surgeongeneral.gov/about/previous/biosteinfeld.html, June 2012.
32. http://www.surgeongeneral.gov/about/previous/biorichmond.html, June 2012.
33. United States Statutes at Large, Vol. 93, p. 584-586.
34. http://www.surgeongeneral.gov/about/previous/biokoop.html, June 2012.
35. http://www.surgeongeneral.gov/about/history/index.html, June 2012.
36. http://www.surgeongeneral.gov/about/previous/biokoop.html, June 2012.
37. http://www.surgeongeneral.gov/about/previous/bionovello.html, June 2012.
38. http://en.wikipedia.org/wiki/Joycelyn_Elders, June 2012.
39. http://www.surgeongeneral.gov/about/previous/biosatcher.html, June 2012.
40. http://www.surgeongeneral.gov/about/previous/biocarmona.html, June 2012.

Part 7. NOAA Corps
Chapter 1. NOAA Organization
1. http://www.noaacorps.noaa.gov/about/about.html#mission, June 2012.
2. http://en.wikipedia.org/wiki/U.S._Coast_and_Geodetic_Survey, June 2012.

Coast Survey
1. United States Statutes at Large, Vol. 2, p. 413.
2. United States Statutes at Large, Vol. 3, p. 425.
3. http://www.lib.noaa.gov/noaainfo/heritage/coastsurveyvol1/HASSLER1.html#SURPRISE, June 2012.
4. United States Statutes at Large, Vol. 4, p. 570.
5. http://en.wikipedia.org/wiki/U.S._Coast_and_Geodetic_Survey, June 2012.
6. http://www.history.noaa.gov/legacy/corps.html, June 2012.
7. http://www.history.noaa.gov/legacy/corps.html, June 2012.

Coast and Geodetic Survey
1. United States Statutes at Large, Vol. 20, p. 215.
2. http://www.thefreedictionary.com/geodesy, June 2012.
3. United States Statutes at Large, Vol. 41, p. 88.

Environmental Science Services Administration
1. http://www.history.noaa.gov/legacy/act5.html, June 2012.

National Oceanic and Atmospheric Administration
1. http://www.history.noaa.gov/legacy/corps.html, June 2012.

Rank Structure
1. United States Statutes at Large, Vol. 39, p. 319.
2. United States Statutes at Large, Vol. 40, p. 88.
3. United States Statutes at Large, Vol. 40, p. 163.
4. Bunkley, Joel W., Military and naval recognition book:, New York: D. Van Nostrand, 1917, p. 123.
5. WORLD WAR II HISTORY OF THE DEPARTMENT OF COMMERCE, PART 5 US COAST AND GEODETIC SURVEY, GPO, 1951.
6. United States Statutes at Large, Vol. 41, p. 603.
7. United States Statutes at Large, Vol. 41, p. 929.
8. Uniform Regulations for the Field Corps of the United States Coast and Geodetic Survey, June 18, 1920, p. 8.
9. United States Statutes at Large, Vol. 55, p. 283.
10. United States Statutes at Large, Vol. 49, p. 1164.
11. United States Statutes at Large, Vol. 56, p. 6.
12. Grosvenor, Gilbert , Insignia and decorations of the U.S. armed forces, National Geographic Society, 1945, plate III after page 720.
13. United States Statutes at Large, Vol. 62, p. 297.
14. United States Statutes at Large, Vol. 63, p. 807.
15. http://www.lib.noaa.gov/noaainfo/heritage/ReorganizationPlan2.html, June 2012.
16. http://www.lib.noaa.gov/noaainfo/heritage/ReorganizationPlan4.html, June 2012.
17. http://www.history.noaa.gov/cgsbios/biok1.html, June 2012.
18. United States Statutes at Large, Vol. 98, p. 2308.
19. United States Statutes at Large, Vol. 99, p. 628.

Chapter 2. NOAA Rank Insignia
1. Bunkley, Joel W., Military and naval recognition book:, New York: D. Van Nostrand, 1917, p. 123-124.
2. Uniform Regulations for the Field Corps of the United States Coast and Geodetic Survey, June 18, 1920, p. 7-9.
3. Grosvenor, Gilbert , Insignia and decorations of the U.S. armed forces, National Geographic Society, 1945, p. 730-731.

Shoulder Boards
1. Bunkley, Joel W., Military and naval recognition book:, New York: D. Van Nostrand, 1917, p. 123-124.
2. Uniform Regulations for the Field Corps of the United States Coast and Geodetic Survey, June 18, 1920, p. 9.
3. Grosvenor, Gilbert , Insignia and decorations of the U.S. armed forces, National Geographic Society, 1945, plate III after page 720.

Shoulder Marks
1. NOAA Corps Directives, April 26, 2004, Chapter 12, p. 8.
2. All Hands, "New Officer, CPO Uniforms...", June 1979, p. 2.

Badges of Rank
1. Bunkley, Joel W., Military and naval recognition book:, New York: D. Van Nostrand, 1917, p. 123-124.
2. Uniform Regulations for the Field Corps of the United States Coast and Geodetic Survey, June 18, 1920, p. 7-8.
3. Grosvenor, Gilbert , Insignia and decorations of the U.S. armed forces, National Geographic Society, 1945, plate III after page 720.
4. NOAA Corps Directives, April 26, 2004, Chapter 12, p. 10.

Cuff Stripes
1. Bunkley, Joel W., Military and naval recognition book:, New York: D. Van Nostrand, 1917, p. 123-124.
2. NOAA Corps Directives, April 26, 2004, Chapter 12, p. 5-6.

Chapter 3. NOAA Ranks

Aid
1. United States Statutes at Large, Vol. 40, p. 88.
2. Bunkley, Joel W., Military and naval recognition book:, New York: D. Van Nostrand, 1917, p. 123.
3. United States Statutes at Large, Vol. 41, p. 603.
4. United States Statutes at Large, Vol. 41, p. 929.
5. United States Statutes at Large, Vol. 55, p. 283.
6. Uniform Regulations for the Field Corps of the United States Coast and Geodetic Survey, June 18, 1920, p. 8.
7. United States Statutes at Large, Vol. 56, p. 6.

Captain
1. United States Statutes at Large, Vol. 40, p. 88.
2. United States Statutes at Large, Vol. 41, p. 603.
3. United States Statutes at Large, Vol. 41, p. 929.
4. United States Statutes at Large, Vol. 55, p. 283.
5. Uniform Regulations for the Field Corps of the United States Coast and Geodetic Survey, June 18, 1920, p. 8.
6. United States Statutes at Large, Vol. 56, p. 6.
7. Uniform Regulations for the Field Corps of the United States Coast and Geodetic Survey, June 18, 1920, p. 7-9.
8. United States Statutes at Large, Vol. 63, p. 807.
9. NOAA Corps Directives, April 26, 2004, Chapter 12, p. 6-9.

Commander
1. United States Statutes at Large, Vol. 40, p. 88.
2. United States Statutes at Large, Vol. 41, p. 603.
3. United States Statutes at Large, Vol. 41, p. 929.
4. United States Statutes at Large, Vol. 55, p. 283.
5. Uniform Regulations for the Field Corps of the United States Coast and Geodetic Survey, June 18, 1920, p. 8.
6. United States Statutes at Large, Vol. 56, p. 6.
7. Uniform Regulations for the Field Corps of the United States Coast and Geodetic Survey, June 18, 1920, p. 7-9.
8. United States Statutes at Large, Vol. 63, p. 807.
9. NOAA Corps Directives, April 26, 2004, Chapter 12, p. 6-9.

Commodore
1. United States Statutes at Large, Vol. 94, p. 2919.
2. United States Statutes at Large, Vol. 98, p. 2308.
3. United States Statutes at Large, Vol. 99, p. 628.

Ensign
1. United States Statutes at Large, Vol. 40, p. 88.
2. United States Statutes at Large, Vol. 41, p. 603.
3. United States Statutes at Large, Vol. 41, p. 929.
4. United States Statutes at Large, Vol. 55, p. 283.
5. Uniform Regulations for the Field Corps of the United States Coast and Geodetic Survey, June 18, 1920, p. 8.
6. United States Statutes at Large, Vol. 56, p. 6.
7. Uniform Regulations for the Field Corps of the United States Coast and Geodetic Survey, June 18, 1920, p. 7-9.
8. Grosvenor, Gilbert , Insignia and decorations of the U.S. armed forces, National Geographic Society, 1945, plate III after page 720.
9. United States Statutes at Large, Vol. 63, p. 807.
10. NOAA Corps Directives, April 26, 2004, Chapter 12, p. 6-9.

Hydrographic and Geodetic Engineer
1. United States Statutes at Large, Vol. 40, p. 88.
2. Bunkley, Joel W., Military and naval recognition book:, New York: D. Van Nostrand, 1917, p. 123-124.
3. United States Statutes at Large, Vol. 41, p. 603.
4. United States Statutes at Large, Vol. 41, p. 929.
5. United States Statutes at Large, Vol. 55, p. 283.
6. Uniform Regulations for the Field Corps of the United States Coast and Geodetic Survey, June 18, 1920, p. 8.
7. United States Statutes at Large, Vol. 56, p. 6.

Junior Hydrographic and Geodetic Engineer
1. United States Statutes at Large, Vol. 40, p. 88.
2. Bunkley, Joel W., Military and naval recognition book:, New York: D. Van Nostrand, 1917, p. 123-124.
3. United States Statutes at Large, Vol. 41, p. 603.
4. United States Statutes at Large, Vol. 41, p. 929.
5. United States Statutes at Large, Vol. 55, p. 283.
6. Uniform Regulations for the Field Corps of the United States Coast and Geodetic Survey, June 18, 1920, p. 8.
7. United States Statutes at Large, Vol. 56, p. 6.

Lieutenant
1. United States Statutes at Large, Vol. 40, p. 88.
2. United States Statutes at Large, Vol. 41, p. 603.
3. United States Statutes at Large, Vol. 41, p. 929.
4. United States Statutes at Large, Vol. 55, p. 283.
5. Uniform Regulations for the Field Corps of the United States Coast and Geodetic Survey, June 18, 1920, p. 8.
6. United States Statutes at Large, Vol. 56, p. 6.
7. Uniform Regulations for the Field Corps of the United States Coast and Geodetic Survey, June 18, 1920, p. 7-9.
8. United States Statutes at Large, Vol. 63, p. 807.
9. NOAA Corps Directives, April 26, 2004, Chapter 12, p. 6-9.

Lieutenant (Junior Grade)
1. United States Statutes at Large, Vol. 40, p. 88.
2. United States Statutes at Large, Vol. 41, p. 603.
3. United States Statutes at Large, Vol. 41, p. 929.

4. United States Statutes at Large, Vol. 55, p. 283.
5. Uniform Regulations for the Field Corps of the United States Coast and Geodetic Survey, June 18, 1920, p. 8.
6. United States Statutes at Large, Vol. 56, p. 6.
7. Uniform Regulations for the Field Corps of the United States Coast and Geodetic Survey, June 18, 1920, p. 7-9.
8. United States Statutes at Large, Vol. 63, p. 807.
9. NOAA Corps Directives, April 26, 2004, Chapter 12, p. 6-9.

Lieutenant Commander
1. United States Statutes at Large, Vol. 40, p. 88.
2. United States Statutes at Large, Vol. 41, p. 603.
3. United States Statutes at Large, Vol. 41, p. 929.
4. United States Statutes at Large, Vol. 55, p. 283.
5. Uniform Regulations for the Field Corps of the United States Coast and Geodetic Survey, June 18, 1920, p. 8.
6. United States Statutes at Large, Vol. 56, p. 6.
7. Uniform Regulations for the Field Corps of the United States Coast and Geodetic Survey, June 18, 1920, p. 7-9.
8. United States Statutes at Large, Vol. 63, p. 807.
9. NOAA Corps Directives, April 26, 2004, Chapter 12, p. 6-9.

Rear Admiral
1. United States Statutes at Large, Vol. 41, p. 825.
2. United States Statutes at Large, Vol. 41, p. 929.
3. http://www.history.noaa.gov/cgsbios/bioj7.html, June 2012.
4. http://www.history.noaa.gov/cgsbios/biop5.html, June 2012.
5. United States Statutes at Large, Vol. 49, p. 1164.
6. Grosvenor, Gilbert , Insignia and decorations of the U.S. armed forces, National Geographic Society, 1945, plate III after page 720.
7. United States Statutes at Large, Vol. 30, p. 1004.
8. United States Statutes at Large, Vol. 63, p. 807.
9. United States Statutes at Large, Vol. 98, p. 2308.
10. United States Statutes at Large, Vol. 99, p. 628.
11. NOAA Corps Directives, April 26, 2004, Chapter 12, p. 6-9.

Vice Admiral
1. http://www.lib.noaa.gov/noaainfo/heritage/ReorganizationPlan2.html, June 2012.
2. http://www.lib.noaa.gov/noaainfo/heritage/ReorganizationPlan4.html, June 2012.
3. United States Statutes at Large, Vol. 98, p. 2308.
4. http://en.wikipedia.org/wiki/National_Oceanic_and_Atmospheric_Administration_Commissioned_Corps, June 2012.
5. NOAA Corps Directives, April 26, 2004, Chapter 12, p. 6-9.

Manufactured by Amazon.ca
Acheson, AB